FEDERAL INCOME TAXATION
OF CORPORATIONS

FEDERAL INCOME TAXATION OF CORPORATIONS

RICHARD L. DOERNBERG
K. H. Gyr Professor of Law
Emory University

HOWARD E. ABRAMS
Professor of Law
Emory University

BORIS I. BITTKER
Sterling Professor of Law, Emeritus
Yale University

LAWRENCE M. STONE
Former Professor of Law
University of California at Berkeley
Member, California Bar

LITTLE, BROWN AND COMPANY
Boston   New York   Toronto   London

Library of Congress Catalog Card No. 94-75307

ISBN 0-316-18838-7

Second Edition

MV-NY

Published simultaneously in Canada
by Little, Brown & Company (Canada) Limited

PRINTED IN THE UNITED STATES OF AMERICA

To Nancy, Alison, and Sarah

RLD

To my parents, Leonard and Diana. And to Jan

HEA

SUMMARY OF CONTENTS

IV

MISCELLANEOUS CORPORATE TAX TOPICS 581

CONTENTS

3

Corporate Operation   81

II

CORPORATE DISTRIBUTIONS:
NONLIQUIDATING AND LIQUIDATING   117

4

Distributions of Cash and Property   119

5

Redemptions and Partial Liquidations   185

6

Distributions of Stock 279

III

ACQUISITION OF A CORPORATE BUSINESS: TAXABLE AND TAX FREE

9

Taxable Acquisitions

10

Acquisitive Reorganizations

PREFACE

This book traces its ancestry back to Professor Bittker's one-volume Federal Income Taxation casebook, published in 1955. Over the years, virtually every section of the Internal Revenue Code has been amended, almost always in the direction of greater complexity. Professor Bittker's original work has split three-for-one, with separate volumes on individual, estate and gift, and corporate taxation. This book is the second edition of the volume on corporate taxation.

Ironically, increasing complexity in the corporate tax area mandates a more straightforward treatment of teaching materials than ever before. It is no longer possible (and certainly not desirable) in an introductory corporate taxation course to devour the sea of minutiae that now comprises subchapter C. Instead it is our hope that through a thoughtful and orderly presentation of the themes that permeate the corporate tax provisions, readers will develop the sophistication and expertise necessary to confront new challenges that are the practice of law.

Part I of the book focuses on the tax consequences of the formation and operation of a corporation. After a brief introduction to some of the policy and economic issues in Chapter 1, Chapter 2 discusses the tax consequences involved in the formation of a corporation. Once a corporation is formed, Chapter 3 considers the tax consequences of a corporation's day-to-day operations, including decisions concerning a corporation's capital structure.

Part II is devoted to corporate distributions. Chapters 4 through 6 discuss nonliquidating distributions by a corporation, including distributions of cash and other property, stock redemptions, and distributions of a corporation's own stock. Chapter 7 analyzes the tax consequences of a corporation's liquidating distributions. Chapter 8 discusses the corporate double tax inherent in the treatment of a corporation's distributions and how it can be alleviated through various integration alternatives.

Part III considers corporate acquisitions and other rearrangements —

both taxable and tax free. Chapter 9 addresses the tax considerations involved in a taxable acquisition of another corporation or another corporation's assets. Chapters 10 through 12 consider various tax-free organizations. Chapter 10 discusses the tax consequences of an acquisitive corporate reorganization. Chapter 11 deals with tax-free divisive reorganizations. One-party reorganizations (e.g., recapitalizations) are the subject of Chapter 12. Chapter 13 analyzes certain tax attributes of combined corporations, including net operating losses, and surveys the tax aspects of affiliated corporations.

Part IV covers areas of corporate tax that do not fit neatly in the preceding parts. The consignment of these areas to Part IV certainly does not signify their lack of importance. Chapter 14 describes a panoply of penalty provisions that involve corporations, including the accumulated earnings tax, the personal holding company tax, and the collapsible corporation provisions. Chapter 15 covers a variety of issues involving the corporation as a separate entity, including the definition of a corporation for tax purposes, the rise of limited liability companies, the use of dummy corporations, and assignment of income problems involving corporations. Finally, Chapter 16 features the special rules attending S corporations found in subchapter S.

The materials selected for the book are deliberately noncomprehensive. We have tried to choose illustrative cases that not only describe typical commercial transactions but also emphasize major themes that run through subchapter C and related provisions. It is our belief the book can be covered in a three- or four-hour corporate tax course, but it can easily be adapted to a two-hour course as well.

Corporate taxation is a difficult subject even under the best of circumstances. We have tried not to "hide the ball." Our approach is to make liberal use of examples and to simplify some of the intricacies. We have no doubt that, notwithstanding our approach, students will be left with plenty to ponder. We have tried to clear away some of the underbrush so that students can contemplate the beauty of the forest. In addition to the cases and note materials, the book features problems in almost every chapter. They can be used to lead students through the fundamentals of the corporate tax provisions and can form a centerpiece for discussion of the cases and notes. While the problems are found at the end of each chapter, they have been drafted and ordered to be used with daily assignments.

Students should not hesitate to consult additional references when interested: sophistication often brings with it hidden symmetries and simplicities. Bittker and Eustice's Federal Income Taxation of Corporations and Shareholders (6th ed. 1994) with supplementation is a student's ready companion, offering lucid and more detailed explanations of all areas of corporate taxation.

Students of taxation must possess an eye-hand coordination not required of other students. Not only must they read and study the casebook, but at the same time they must consume the Internal Revenue Code and corresponding regulations. The ability to read two or more things at the same time is a residual benefit one receives from the study of taxation. The book refers to the Code incessantly; rather than reproduce its splendor, the authors rely on students to study the Code as they study the book.

A few ministerial comments are in order at this point. First, the book makes ample use of cross-references. Corporate tax provisions do not operate in a vacuum. As students learn more and more pieces of the subchapter C puzzle, the pieces will begin to interrelate and form a pattern. Second, the cases have been heavily edited to feature the salient points. We have endeavored to indicate the omissions, but readers should be aware that citations and footnotes in the cases have often been omitted or abridged. Third, we have tried to incorporate some of the themes developed in the individual tax course. Assignment of income, the value of deferral, the interplay of the original issue discount with the installment sales rules, and the concept of recapture are often invoked in the context of corporate transactions. Fourth, while we hope the book has a certain timeless quality to it, we would be remiss if we did not note that it is current through the end of 1993. Fifth, we express our gratitude to Mr. Fred T. Witt of the Arizona and Texas bars for his insights into the complex issues surrounding cancellation of indebtedness generally as well as his great help in the section on bankruptcy reorganizations more particularly. Finally, we would like to thank the American Law Institute for permission to reprint an excerpt from the Reporter's Study of Corporate Tax Integration (Federal Income Tax Project 1993). Copyright © 1993 by the American Law Institute. Reprinted by permission.

Richard L. Doernberg
Howard E. Abrams

May 1994

FEDERAL INCOME TAXATION
OF CORPORATIONS

1

Introduction to the Corporate Income Tax

You may recall that the Supreme Court struck down the 1894 federal individual income tax in Pollack v. Farmers' Loan & Trust Co., 158 U.S. 601 (1895), as a direct tax requiring apportionment pursuant to article I, §9, clause 4, of the Constitution. In Flint v. Stone Tracy Co., 220 U.S. 107 (1911), the Supreme Court upheld a corporate income tax antedating the enactment of the sixteenth amendment as an indirect or "excise" tax imposed on corporations exercising the privilege of engaging in business as a corporation. In *Pollack* the Court also invalidated a corporate income tax too intertwined with the individual income tax to stand on its own. Congress has taxed corporate profit continuously since the 1909 statute upheld in Flint v. Stone Tracy Co. With the enactment of the sixteenth amendment in 1913, the constitutional validity of the federal corporate income tax was made doubly secure.

The 1909 act imposed a tax of 1 percent on corporate net income in excess of $5,000. Some 262,500 corporations filed returns for 1909, paying an aggregate amount of about $21 million. As of 1993, the highest corporate tax rate became 35 percent, see I.R.C. §11(b), and as of 1990 the number of annual corporate returns exceeded 3.7 million.[1] These 3.7 million returns reported income of about $366 billion and produced about $96 billion in revenue. For comparison, in 1990 more than 105 million individual returns were filed, generating more than $375 billion in revenue. Thus, the corporate income tax produces about one-quarter of the revenue generated by the individual income tax. Combined, the corporate

---

1. The Internal Revenue Service publishes in its quarterly Statistics of Income (SOI) bulletins various reports analyzing statistical data distilled from filed tax returns. Unfortunately but understandably, these reports appear several years after the underlying data are generated. The figures in the text were taken from the Summer of 1993 SOI bulletin.

and individual income taxes account for more than half of all federal revenues and represent in excess of 10 percent of the gross national product (GNP).

As you know, this country imposes an income tax on every citizen and resident alien. Dividends received, as well as most other accessions to wealth, form the base of that tax. Together, the corporate and individual income taxes form what is often called a double tax on corporate income. It is called a double tax because under this system the earnings of a corporation are taxed once when earned by the corporation and a second time when distributed to its shareholders as dividends.

For example, suppose corporate earnings are taxed at a flat rate of 30 percent while dividends are taxed to shareholders at a flat rate of 40 percent. The combined tax burden imposed by the corporate double tax is 58 percent, computed as follows. If the corporation earns $100, it must remit $30 in taxes, given the rates assumed in this example. That leaves $70 available for distribution, and if that entire amount is distributed, the shareholder receiving this $70 will in turn owe $28 in taxes. Thus, the shareholder will have only $70 − $28, or $42, to spend, and that means $58 of the $100 in earnings was paid in taxes.

Because a double tax is imposed on corporate earnings while only a single tax is imposed on unincorporated profits, you might suspect that businesses would eschew the corporate form in favor of some less heavily taxed enterprise such as a partnership. There are several nontax reasons why taxpayers might prefer the corporate form even at the cost of higher taxes. Limited liability is one obvious reason for preferring a corporation to a partnership. In addition, the corporation is the most common form of business organization, and using such a familiar form may result in significant economies. Surprisingly, though, use of the corporate form can be tax advantageous, depending on the relative rates of the individual and corporate taxes.

For example, assume that the individual tax is imposed at a 50 percent rate while the corporate tax is imposed at a 10 percent rate. If $100 of corporate earnings are distributed in the year earned, they will be subject to a combined tax of $55, $10 at the corporate level and an additional $45 (50 percent of the remaining $90) at the shareholder level. This of course compares unfavorably with profits earned directly by a shareholder, taxed (under our assumptions) at a flat 50 percent.

But now suppose that the corporation delays for 3 years distributing its after-tax $90 of earnings. The shareholder-level tax remains $45, but because the distribution has been delayed for 3 years, the present value of that tax burden as of the year in which earned is only about $34, assuming a 10 percent annual discount rate.[2] Thus, the total effective tax burden is only about $44 (the $10 corporate-level tax plus the present value of the

---

2. That is, $34 invested for 3 years at 10 percent annual interest will grow to about $45.

shareholder-level tax), which compares favorably with a single, immediate tax of $50. In other words, if the shareholder-level income tax can be deferred and the corporate-level income tax is sufficiently low, the combined burden of the double tax on corporate earnings can be less than the single tax imposed on unincorporated profits. Similarly, if distributed corporate earnings are taxed to the shareholders at a preferential rate as compared with unincorporated profits, the combined burden of the corporate double tax may be less than the burden of the single, individual income tax.

Historically, the highest corporate tax rate was well below that of the highest individual tax rate. Accordingly, taxpayers often structured their transactions to deflect income away from themselves and their family members and to their controlled and family corporations. Between 1986 and 1992, however, the highest corporate individual tax rate exceeded the highest individual income tax rate. During this period, taxpayers shifted their strategy, trying instead to deflect income away from corporations and to individual taxpayers. As a result, some existing businesses were disincorporated, some new businesses were started in unincorporated form, and presumably many transactions were structured to minimize or wholly avoid the corporate income tax.

Starting in 1993, the highest marginal corporate tax rate became 35 percent while the highest individual rate became 39.6 percent.[3] Thus, we are back where we began, with taxpayers once again able to reduce their tax liabilities by sheltering taxable income within the corporate form. To be sure, a second tax may be due if corporate earnings are eventually distributed as dividends, but that second tax often can be postponed almost indefinitely by astute tax planners.

When corporate earnings must be reported by shareholders, they often can be reported as capital gain. Historically, the highest tax rate imposed on capital gains was only 40 percent of that imposed on ordinary income. For example, if the highest marginal tax rate was 70 percent, the highest rate applicable to long-term capital gain was only 28 percent. Now, though, the relative capital gains preference is diminished[4] so that the total burden of an immediate corporate-level tax and a deferred individual tax at capital gain rates may exceed the burden of an immediate shareholder-level tax at ordinary rates. Depending on the amount of deferral and the anticipated capital gain preference, tax planners may see the corporate form as a tax haven or as a tax pitfall. This issue is explored in Chapter 8.

If a corporation could deduct the dividends it pays, the corporate

---

3. While 39.6 percent is the highest nominal tax rate, the effective tax rate on individual income may be significantly higher because personal exemptions as well as itemized deductions are phased out for high-bracket individuals. Thus, the highest marginal rate for individual taxpayers is closer to 46 percent.
4. The highest rate imposed on capital gains of individuals remains at 28 percent, but the highest rate imposed on ordinary income is now much less than 70 percent.

double tax would be eliminated because the shareholder-level taxation would always be accompanied by a corporate-level deduction. While corporations cannot, in general, deduct their dividends, they can like other taxpayers deduct interest paid or accrued. §163. Interest and dividends are to some extent substitutes for each other because each is the price paid by a corporation to its investors for the use of their funds. For example, a corporation using debt to finance a continuing or new project will be entitled to deduct interest payments made to its lenders for the use of their money. On the other hand, if equity is used instead of debt, what would have been deductible interest payments becomes nondeductible dividends. It should come as no surprise that the use of corporate debt is widespread, due in part to the deductibility of payments on debt (interest) versus the nondeductibility of payments on equity (dividends).

For most of the income and deduction provisions with which you are already familiar, a corporation is a taxpayer like any other. Subchapter C addresses those issues peculiar to corporate taxpayers: In particular, it addresses corporate formations, corporate terminations (called *liquidations* in tax parlance), corporate rearrangements (*reorganizations*), and the complex set of problems incidental to corporate distributions made to shareholders as part of a corporation's ongoing operations. Subchapter C is divided into seven parts, the first three of which form the primary concern of this course. Take a moment to examine subchapter C, particularly part I, §§301-318 (distributions by corporations), part II, §§331-346 (corporate liquidations), and part III, §§351-368 (corporate organizations and reorganizations). Examination of these and other provisions of the Code begins in Chapter 2.

I

FORMATION AND OPERATION OF A CORPORATION

2

Corporate Formation

A. INTRODUCTION

1. The §351 Philosophy

Normally, when a taxpayer exchanges property for other property, any gain or loss realized on the exchange must be recognized by the transferor. §1001(c). The propriety of taxation is weakened, though, if the exchange does not significantly alter the nature of the taxpayer's investment. For example, §1031 provides for the nonrecognition of a taxpayer's gain or loss on the exchange property for other property of like kind. Consider *T*, an individual who owns an office building with an adjusted basis of $30,000 and a fair market value of $100,000. If *T* sells the building for $100,000, *T* has realized and must recognize gain of $70,000. If instead *T* exchanges the office building for another office building also worth $100,000, *T*'s realized gain is again $70,000, but none of this gain is currently recognized. §1031(a). Because *T*'s basis in the old building becomes the basis in the new building, the $70,000 unrecognized gain is deferred until disposition of the new building.

Section 1031 reflects the congressional belief that taxation is inappropriate when there is substantial continuity of investment after the exchange. Reconsider the example above, but assume that now *T* exchanges the office building for all the stock of newly created *X* Corp. While §1031 does not apply to this exchange, *T* has hardly altered the substance of the original investment even though the form has changed: *X* Corp. owns the building, and *T* owns *X* Corp.

Since 1921 Congress has provided that this type of property-for-stock exchange should not be a taxable event. At the same time, it has never been the case that all transfers of property to corporations have been tax free. For example, a taxpayer who sells property to a corporation for cash is, and properly should be, subject to the general recognition rule of §1001(a).

Current §351 permits a taxpayer to defer taxation only if the taxpayer-transferor (1) transfers property to a corporation, (2) receives stock of the transferee corporation in exchange, and (along with other transferors of property, if any) (3) is in control of the corporation immediately after the transaction. Through these requirements, §351 seeks to differentiate those exchanges more closely resembling mere changes in the form of investment from those exchanges resembling sales. Note that §351 can apply both to the formation of new corporations and to transfers to existing corporations (sometimes called "midstream" contributions).

Underlying all three requirements is the notion of continuity of investment. While the form of a taxpayer's investment may have changed from unincorporated to incorporated, the nature of the investment remains the same. These considerations apply only to a transfer of property. For example, suppose T and three other transferors form X Corp., with T contributing services while the other transferors contribute property. Although all transferors receive back X Corp. stock, the stock received by T is merely compensation for services rendered. Regardless of the form it takes, compensation will be immediately taxable on receipt. By its own terms, §351 does not apply to the exchange of services for stock and securities. See §351(d)(1). Because such an exchange radically alters the form of a taxpayer's investment from human to corporate capital, immediate taxation seems appropriate. Moreover, the failure of T to qualify under §351 may render the provision inapplicable to the other three transferors (i.e., the transferors of property), whose stock interest in the corporation may be insufficient to satisfy the "control" requirement.

Under the second requirement of §351, the transferors must receive stock of the transferee corporation. Suppose T and three other joint owners of an office building that has appreciated in value transfer the property to X Corp. If T receives cash back while the other transferors receive X Corp. stock, will nonrecognition be appropriate? For T, who is not an X Corp. shareholder, nonrecognition under §351 is not available. There is no continuity; T simply has sold his share of the building. If T were to receive stock, however, nonrecognition seems appropriate since T would continue to enjoy the financial benefits of an interest in the property indirectly through stock ownership. If T receives both stock and cash for his interest in the building, gain will be recognized to the extent of the cash since pro tanto T has terminated (i.e., sold) the investment.

What happens if T receives an interest in the corporation that carries less continuity than stock but more continuity than cash? Historically, a transferor receiving a long-term debt instrument (i.e., a security) from the transferee corporation could qualify for nonrecognition under §351. Now debt instruments, even those of long duration, are not qualifying property under §351.

Even if T transfers property in exchange for corporate stock, the third requirement — sufficient control over the corporate entity — may not be met. Suppose T and the other transferors exchange their interests in the building to General Motors for General Motors stock. The transferors' relationship to the original property is now far more attenuated than if they had incorporated the building into a newly formed, closely held corporation. This transaction would be treated like an all-cash transaction, substantially as if the transferors had sold the building to General Motors and then used the proceeds to purchase General Motors stock. To qualify for nonrecognition, the transferors of property must collectively satisfy §368(c), which requires that the transferors of property own at least 80 percent of the total combined voting power of all classes of stock entitled to vote and at least 80 percent of the total number of shares of all other classes of stock. See pages 52-56 infra.

Somewhere between the transfer of property to a wholly owned corporation and a transfer to General Motors is the transfer by a group of taxpayers, including T, of a variety of assets to X Corp. Suppose T transfers a building, A transfers machinery and equipment, and B transfers a truck, each receiving stock in exchange from X Corp. Now T has a stock interest in more than his original asset. At the same time, T no longer has the sole interest in his transferred property. Is the continuity sufficient in this type of transfer? Nonrecognition under §351 does envision incorporation by multiple transferors of property if together they meet the control requirement. But see discussion of "swap funds" at page 11 infra.

2. *The Statutory Terrain*

When a corporation is formed, we are concerned with tax consequences both to the transferors and the transferee corporation:

Transferors

- §351 and §357 determine whether any gain or loss realized on the exchange is recognized;
- §358 determines the transferor's basis in stock and property received from the corporation; and
- §1223(1) determines the holding period of stock received from the corporation.

Transferee Corporation

- §1032 provides nonrecognition for the corporation issuing stock in exchange for money or other property;
- §362(a) determines the corporation's basis in property received; and
- §1223(2) determines the holding period of the property received.

To illustrate: *B* owns a building with a basis of $30,000 and a fair market value of $75,000. *C* owns undeveloped real estate with a basis of $60,000 and a fair market value of $25,000. Together they form *X* Corp. in exchange for their assets. *B* receives $75,000 of *X* Corp. stock, and *C* receives $25,000 of *X* Corp. stock. Section 351 prevents *B* and *C* from recognizing gain and loss, respectively, on the exchange. One "price" *B* pays for nonrecognition of his gain is the transfer of *B*'s $30,000 basis in the building to the stock received. §358(a). When and if *B* sells his stock, the previously realized but unrecognized $45,000 gain attributable to the building will be taken into account. The "consolation" *C* gets for the nonrecognition of her loss is the transfer of her $60,000 basis to the stock. When and if *C* sells her stock, the $35,000 loss that went unrecognized on the formation of the corporation will be taken into account. On a sale or exchange of their stock, both *B* and *C* must "tack" the holding period of their respective capital or §1231 assets on to the holding period of their stock. Thus, if the total period of time during which *B* held his capital asset and stock is more than one year, the sale of stock will produce long-term capital gain, assuming the stock is a capital asset in the hands of *B*.

X Corp., which exchanges its own stock for assets, receives nonrecognition treatment under §1032. The basis of the assets received carries over from the transferors to *X* Corp., resulting in a $30,000 basis in the building and a $60,000 basis in the undeveloped real estate pursuant to §362(a). Upon a sale or exchange of the assets, *X* Corp. must tack the holding period of the transferors in those assets. §1223(2).

Note that if *B* immediately sells his stock for $75,000, he will recognize a $45,000 gain, and if *X* Corp. sells the building for $75,000, it will also recognize a $45,000 gain. This double gain may seem an unfair product of the corporate income tax. See discussion at page 361 infra. The same double counting can occur with losses as well. A sale by *C* of stock and by *X* Corp. of the undeveloped real estate results in a double loss deduction. Can you think of a way to avoid this double gain or loss? Indeed, if both the stock and the asset basis did not preserve the previously unrealized gain, then indefinite postponement of gain might be possible. If the asset's basis were increased on incorporation, the asset could be converted to cash with no further gain. If the stock basis were increased, however, a shareholder could sell at no gain the stock whose value reflects the property's appreciation.

Suppose a dozen independent businesspeople transfer their separate businesses to a newly organized corporation, each receiving stock equal to the value of the assets given up. Does §351 apply even though the nature of each transferor's investment has changed, or must there be a showing (although no statutory provision explicitly requires it) that the transferors have not drastically altered their economic status? The cases and the rulings do not require any such showing in general, but Congress has focused on this issue in a specific area.

Section 351(e)(1) deals with so-called swap funds. These were investment pools organized by stockbrokers to enable investors holding appreciated securities (ordinarily in a single company or in a few companies) to transfer these undiversified investments to a holding company in exchange for stock in a newly organized company that would obtain a wide range of investments (because the transferors as a group held a variety of securities, even though each individual might not). Note how such an exchange would satisfy the three requirements of §351 set out at page 8 supra. The result was diversification on a tax-free basis, assuming the applicability of §351. After a few favorable rulings, the IRS announced that it would no longer accede to §351 treatment for swap fund exchanges. See Treas. Regs. §1.351-1(c)(1). Congress thereafter enacted §351(e) to settle the question.

With these general principles in mind, we turn to the specific requirements of §351.

B. PROPERTY

James v. Commissioner ⎯⎯⎯⎯⎯⎯⎯⎯⎯⎯⎯⎯⎯⎯⎯⎯⎯⎯⎯⎯⎯
53 T.C. 63 (1969)

SIMPSON, Judge. . . .

The issue for decision is whether the transaction by which Mr. James and Mr. Talbot acquired stock in a corporation was taxable or whether such transaction was tax free under section 351 of the Internal Revenue Code of 1954. The answer to the question thus posed with respect to each person depends on the determination of whether Mr. James received his stock in exchange for a transfer of property or as compensation for services.

FINDINGS OF FACT

For many years, Mr. James was a builder, real estate promoter, and developer with offices in Myrtle Beach, S.C. He has held the office of vice president of the National Association of Home Builders and was chairman of the association's Senior Citizens Housing Committee. During 1963, the

James Construction Co. was licensed by the State of South Carolina to engage in the business of general contracting.

On January 12, 1963, Mr. and Mrs. Talbot entered into an agreement with Mr. James for the promotion and construction of a rental apartment project, consisting of not less than 50 apartments, the project to conform to Federal Housing Administration (FHA) standards. The agreement provided that on completion of the project the parties would form a corporation to take title to the project. The voting stock in such corporation was to be distributed one-half to the Talbots and one-half to Mr. James, and nonvoting stock was to be issued to the parties "as the equity of each party in the corporation shall be," with the proviso that Mr. James should have the right to purchase up to 50 percent of such stock over a period of years. The Talbots agreed to transfer to the corporation the land on which the apartment project was to be built, such land to be the only asset contributed by the Talbots to the venture. Mr. James agreed "to promote the project . . . and . . . [to] be responsible for the planning, architectural work, construction, landscaping, legal fees, and loan processing of the entire project." . . .

After the execution of the January 12 agreement, Mr. James began negotiations to fulfill his part of the contract. He made arrangements with an attorney and an architectural firm to perform the work necessary to meet FHA requirements — development of legal documents, preparation of architectural plans, and the like; and he obtained from United Mortgagee Service Corp. (United Mortgagee), a lender, its agreement to finance the project and a commitment by FHA to insure the financing. Mr. James personally met with the FHA only twice — once in connection with the amount of the commitment and again at the final closing of the loan, after construction of the project was completed in the late summer of 1964. Most of the arrangements necessary to the securing of the loan and the FHA commitment were handled by the attorney, the architectural firm, and United Mortgagee. The attorney's and architect's fees were not paid by Mr. James but were paid out of the proceeds of the construction loan by the corporation subsequently established.

On August 8, 1963, the FHA issued to United Mortgagee a commitment for the insurance of advances in the amount of $850,700 to Chicora Apartments, Inc., for the apartment project sponsored by Mr. James and the Talbots. On August 27, 1963, United Mortgagee sent Mr. James a draft of a proposed agreement to make a first mortgage loan of $850,700 on the Chicora Apartment project in accordance with Mr. James' application for such loan. . . .

On November 5, 1963, Chicora Apartments, Inc. (Chicora), was granted, upon application of Messrs. Talbot and James, a corporate charter, stating its authorized capital stock to consist of 20 no-par common shares. On the same date, the land on which the apartment project was to be constructed was conveyed to Chicora by Mrs. Talbot in consideration for 10 shares of stock. Nine of these shares were issued to Mrs. Talbot, and one share was issued to Mr. Talbot. . . . Also on November 5, 1963, 10 shares of stock were issued to Mr. James. The minutes of a meeting of Chicora's board of directors held on that date state that those 10 shares were issued to Mr. James in consideration of his "transfer" to the corporation of the "following described property":

> 1. FHA Commitment issued pursuant to Title 2, Section 207 of the National Housing Act, whereby the FHA agrees to insure a mortgage loan in the amount of $850,700.00, on a parcel of land in Myrtle Beach, South Carolina. . . .
> 2. Commitment from United Mortgagee Servicing Corp., agreeing to make a mortgage loan on said property in the amount of $850,700.00 and also commitment from said mortgagee to make an interim construction loan in an identical amount.
> 3. Certain contracts and agreement which W. A. James over the past two years have [sic] worked out and developed in connection with the architectural and construction services required for said project.
> 4. The use of the finances and credit of W. A. James during the past two years (and including the construction period) in order to make it possible to proceed with the project.

Thus, as a result of these transactions, Chicora had outstanding all 20 of its authorized shares of stock. . . .

Both Mr. and Mrs. James and Mr. and Mrs. Talbot deemed their receipt of Chicora common stock to be in return for a transfer of property to a controlled corporation under section 351. Accordingly, neither family reported any income from such receipt on their respective income tax returns for 1963. In his statutory notice of deficiency, the respondent determined that Mr. James received such stock, with a value of $22,000, for services rendered and not in exchange for property, and thus received taxable income in that amount. He further determined that the Talbot's [sic] transfer of property to Chicora did not meet the requirements of section 351, with the result that they should have recognized a long-term capital gain of $14,675 — the difference between $7,325, the basis of the land transferred, and $22,000, the value of the stock received.

OPINION

The first, and critical, issue for our determination is whether Mr. James received his Chicora stock in exchange for the transfer of property or as compensation for services. The petitioners argue that he received such stock in consideration of his transfer to Chicora of the FHA and United Mortgagee commitments and that such commitments constituted "property" within the meaning of section 351. . . . The respondent does not appear to challenge the petitioners' implicit assertion that Mr. James was not expected to render future services to the corporation in exchange for the issuance of stock to him. Although the accuracy of this assertion is subject to some question, the state of the record is such that we must decide the issues as the parties have presented them. Thus, the sole question on this issue is whether Mr. James' personal services, which the petitioners freely admit were rendered, resulted in the development of a property right which was transferred to Chicora, within the meaning of section 351. . . .

[The predecessor to §351(d)(1)] was first included in the statute as a part of the 1954 Code, although it is said merely to restate the case law. See Bittker & Eustice, Federal Income Taxation of Corporations and Shareholders 70 (2d ed. 1966). In explaining the [provision], the House Ways and Means Committee stated:

> In accordance with this provision, such stock or securities received by a person who has rendered or will render services to the transferee corporation would be fully taxable as compensation upon receipt. Your committee does not intend, however, to vitiate the remaining portion of the transaction, through application of this provision.

(H. Rept. No. 1337, to accompany H.R. 8300 (Pub. L. 591), 83d Cong., 2d Sess., p. A117 (1954).)

According to the petitioners' argument, Mr. James, as a result of the services performed by him, acquired certain contract rights which constituted property and which he transferred to Chicora. The fact that such rights resulted from the performance of personal services does not, in their view, disqualify them from being treated as property for purposes of section 351. In support of this position, the petitioners refer to situations involving the transfer of patents and secret processes. . . .

It is altogether clear that for purposes of section 351, not every right is to be treated as property. . . . [Section 351(d)(1)] indicates that, whatever may be considered as property for purposes of local law, the performance of services, or the agreement to perform services, is not to be treated as a transfer of property for purposes of section 351. Thus, if in this case we have merely an agreement to perform services in exchange for stock of the corporation to be created, the performance of such services does not constitute the transfer of property within the meaning of section 351.

Although patents and secret processes — the product of services — are treated as property for purposes of section 351, we have carefully analyzed the arrangement in this case and have concluded that Mr. James did not transfer any property essentially like a patent or secret process; he merely performed services for Chicora. In January of 1963, he entered into an agreement to perform services for the corporation to be created. He was to secure the necessary legal and architectural work and to arrange for the financing of the project, and these were the services performed by him. Although he secured the services of the lawyer and the architect, they were paid for by the corporation. He put in motion the wheels that led to the FHA commitment, but it was not a commitment to him — it was a commitment to United Mortgagee to insure a loan to Chicora, a project sponsored by Mr. James. It was stipulated that under the FHA regulations, a commitment would not be issued to an individual, but only to a corporation. Throughout these arrangements, it was contemplated that a corporation would be created and that the commitment would run to the corporation. The petitioners rely heavily on the claim that Mr. James had a right to the commitment, that such right constituted property, and that such right was transferred to the corporation in return for his stock. However, the commitment was not his to transfer; he never acquired ownership of the commitment — he could not and did not undertake to acquire such ownership. The evidence as to the commitment by United Mortgagee to make a loan for the construction of the project is somewhat incomplete, but since all the parties knew that a corporation was to be formed and that the FHA commitment would be made to that corporation, it seems clear that there was no commitment to loan to Mr. James the funds necessary for the construction of the project. Thus, throughout these arrangements, Mr. James never undertook to acquire anything for himself; he was, in accordance with his agreement with the Talbots, making the preliminary arrangements for the construction of the apartment project. The enterprise would be operated, once the initial steps were completed, by a corporation, Chicora, and everything that was done by him was done on behalf of the contemplated corporation. In these circumstances, it seems clear that Mr. James received his share of the stock in the corporation in return for the services performed by him and that he did not transfer any property, within the meaning of section 351, to the corporation. . . .

The facts of this case are substantially similar to those in United States v. Frazell, 335 F.2d 487 (C.A.5, 1964), . . . certiorari denied 380 U.S. 961 (1964). In that case, the taxpayer, a geologist, investigated certain oil and gas properties to be acquired by a joint venture, and he was to receive an interest in the joint venture. However, before any transfer was made to him, a corporation was formed to take over the assets of the joint venture, and part of the stock was transferred to the taxpayer. It was not clear whether the taxpayer acquired an interest in the joint venture which was then exchanged for his share of the stock or whether he acquired the stock directly in exchange for the services performed by him. The court found that, in either event, the taxpayer received compensation for his services. If he received the stock in return for the services performed by him, such stock was taxable as compensation; and he did not transfer any property to the corporation within the meaning of section 351. See also Mailloux v. Commissioner, 320 F.2d 60 (C.A.5, 1963), affirming on this issue a Memorandum Opinion of this Court.

The next question is whether the Talbots are taxable on the gain realized from the exchange of their land for Chicora stock. Section 351(a) applies only if immediately after the transfer those who transferred property in exchange for stock owned at least 80 percent of Chicora's stock. Sec. 368(c). Since Mr. James is not to be treated as a transferor of property, he cannot be included among those in control for purposes of this test. Fahs v. Florida Machine & Foundry Co., 168 F.2d 957 (C.A.5, 1948); . . . Bittker & Eustice, supra. The transferors of property, the Talbots, did not have the required 80-percent control of Chicora immediately after the transfer, and therefore, their gain must be recognized. This result is inconsistent with the apparent meaning of the second sentence from the committee report, but the statutory scheme does not permit any other conclusion.

Decisions will be entered for the respondent.

NOTE

1. *Services.* Services transferred to a corporation do not qualify as property for purposes of §351. §351(d)(1). One reason for this restriction is to prevent conversion of ordinary income from services into capital gains when the worker sells the stock received. Note the inconsistency between the treatment of services that do not qualify as property under §351 and inventory that does qualify even though its sale would produce ordinary income. If a transferor of appreciated inventory receives stock in a §351 transaction, does the sale of stock produce a capital gain? See §341, discussed at page 616 infra, which seeks to curb attempts through the use of collapsible corporations to convert ordinary income to capital gains.

As *James* indicates, the consequences that flow from a transfer of services can be devastating both to the transferor of services as well as to the transferors of property. James, unable to avail himself of the nonrecognition provisions of §351, was forced to treat the stock received as compensation. What effect did James's failure to satisfy §351 have on the Talbots? After all, they did transfer property in receipt for stock. Since *the transferors of property* were not in "control" of Chicora, however, they too failed to satisfy the requirements of §351. In accordance with §1001, they were taxed on the difference between the adjusted basis of the property transferred and the fair market value of the stock received. Given §351's purpose, is this an appropriate outcome? Note that the consequences of a transfer of services may be welcome, rather than devastating, to transferors of property who wish to recognize gain because of the availability of offsetting losses from other transactions and to those who wish to recognize losses on the exchange. See page 56 infra.

Suppose James had transferred property as well as services in exchange for stock. Would he have gain to recognize? Would the Talbots? One who transfers both property and personal services is considered a transferor for purposes of satisfying the 80 percent control group requirement. Gain or loss attributable to the property transferred for stock will not be recognized under §351, and *all* the stock received can be counted toward the 80 percent control test. Treas. Regs. §1.351-1(a)(2) (example 3). What if James had transferred $1 of cash and $21,999 of services in exchange for his $22,000 stock interest? See Treas. Regs. §1.351-1(a)(1)(ii) and Rev. Proc. 77-37, 1977-2 C.B. 568 (for ruling purposes, property transferred must be equal at least to 10 percent of the stock received).

Note that the Talbots and James had some tax counseling before forming the corporation. The Chicora corporate minutes stated that the transfer of stock to James was in exchange for property. What property? The line between services and property is fuzzy at best. In United States v. Frazell, discussed in *James,* the taxpayer-geologist was to locate certain properties for a group of unincorporated investors in return for an interest in the properties. When the taxpayer received stock in a corporation organized to hold the acquired properties, he did not report the fair market value of the stock as income, arguing instead that he had transferred a partnership interest to the corporation. The Fifth Circuit ruled against the taxpayer without having to decide whether the taxpayer transferred a property interest. Either the taxpayer received stock for services, in which case §351 would be inapplicable, or if property (that is, a partnership interest) was transferred, the taxpayer was taxable on the receipt of the partnership interest for services rendered. In the latter case, the transfer of the partnership interest would qualify under §351. For a collection of cases on the property versus services question, see Stafford v. United States, 727 F.2d 1043 (11th Cir. 1984).

2. *Intellectual property. James* and *Frazell* illustrate the tension between services and service-flavored property. Nowhere is the line more blurred than in cases involving industrial "know how," secret processes and formulas, etc. In Rev. Rul. 64-56, 1964-1 C.B. (pt. 1) 133, and Rev. Rul. 71-564, 1971-2 C.B. 179, amplifying it, the Service set forth guidelines for distinguishing between industrial know-how and services. Did the court in *James* adequately address this issue?

Section 351 requires that property be "transferred." What constitutes a transfer? The issue arises most often when intangibles are assigned to corporations. The Service takes the position that there must be a sale or exchange within the meaning of the capital gains provisions of §1222 in order to qualify under §351 or else the transaction will be considered a license resulting in income to the licensor in the amount of the stock or securities received. The Service's requirement means that an exclusive, unqualified right in perpetuity must be given to the transferee. See Rev. Rul. 71-564, 1971-2 C.B. 179; Rev. Rul. 69-156, 1969-1 C.B. 101; Rev. Rul.

64-56, 1964-1 C.B. (pt. 1) 133. In E.I. DuPont de Nemours & Co. v. United States, 471 F.2d 1211 (Ct. Cl. 1973), however, the court held that the sale or exchange requirement of §1221 is not embodied in §351. The court determined that a nonexclusive, royalty-free license in exchange for stock was a sufficient transfer to qualify under §351.

   3.   *Accounts receivable.* Suppose a cash basis transferor has performed services for a third party prior to incorporation in exchange for an account receivable. What treatment is appropriate if the receivable is transferred to a newly formed corporation as part of a §351 transaction? In Hempt Bros., Inc. v. United States, 490 F.2d 1172 (3d Cir. 1974), the court held that accounts receivable constituted property for purposes of §351. Does the assignment of income doctrine render the transferor or the corporation taxable when the receivable is paid? See page 74 infra. Suppose a cash basis taxpayer performs services for the transferee corporation in exchange for an account receivable. If the taxpayer exchanges the receivable for stock, does the receivable constitute property? Is this more or less what happened in *James*?

   4.   *Miscellaneous property interests.* Money constitutes property for purposes of §351. See Rev. Rul. 69-357, 1969-1 C.B. 101. An equitable interest in property constitutes property for purposes of §351. In Roberts Co. v. Commissioner, 5 T.C. 1 (1945), attorneys who had a contingent fee interest in the proceeds from an eventual sale of land were, along with the landowners, considered transferors of property.

   Section 351(d)(2) and (3) excludes debt of the transferee not evidenced by a security as well as accrued interest, which in effect is treated as paid with stock. Presumably, this exclusion from property status will allow the creditor to claim a bad debt deduction under §166 if the debt is only partially satisfied with the transferee's stock, but the creditor must recognize gain to the extent that the fair market value of the stock exceeds the basis in the debt. For the treatment of the debtor corporation, see §108(e)(10).

C.   STOCK

1.   *Boot*

Before considering what constitutes stock, consider why it matters. Section 351(a) mandates nonrecognition on an exchange only if it is *solely* for stock of the transferee corporation. Receipt of stock carries a continuity of investment in the assets transferred. Yet §351(b) tells us that "solely" does not mean solely. If a transfer would be covered by §351(a) but for the fact that nonqualifying property ("boot") is received in addition to stock, §351 protection is still available. The fair market value of the non-qualifying property will, however, be taxable to the extent of any gain realized on the transfer. For example, suppose T transfers an asset with a basis of $10 and fair market value of $50 to X Corp. in exchange for $20 of X Corp. stock and $30 of cash in a transaction that would otherwise qualify under §351. In accordance with §351(b), T would include in income the $30 of boot since it does not exceed the $40 realized gain.

The character — capital gain or ordinary income — of any recognized gain will be determined by looking at the nature of the property transferred. Any taxable gain is treated as ordinary income to the extent the transferred property is subject to depreciation recapture. Note that in the absence of boot, depreciable property transferred in a §351 exchange will not be subject to recapture. §§1245(b)(3) and 1250(d)(3).

It should be noted that when property whose basis exceeds its fair market value (i.e., loss property) is transferred to a corporation, the receipt of boot does not remove the transaction from the reach of §351, thereby permitting a loss to be recognized. §351(b)(2).

In a transaction that otherwise qualifies under §351, the receipt of boot is taxable to a transferor exchanging appreciated property for stock. If a transferor transfers more than one piece of property to a transferee corporation, how is boot allocated?

Rev. Rul. 68-55
1968-1 C.B. 140

In determining the amount of gain recognized under section 351(b) . . . where several assets were transferred to a corporation, each asset must be considered transferred separately in exchange for a portion of each category of consideration received. The fair market value of each category of consideration received is separately allocated to the transferred assets in proportion to the relative fair market values of the transferred assets. Where as a result of such allocation there is a realized loss with respect to any asset, such loss is not recognized under section 351(b)(2) of the Code.

Advice has been requested as to the correct method of determining the amount and character of the gain to be recognized by Corporation X under section 351(b) . . . under the circumstances described below.

Corporation Y was organized by X and A, an individual who owned no stock in X. A transferred $20x$ dollars to Y in exchange for stock of Y having a fair market value of $20x$ dollars and X transferred to Y three separate assets and received in exchange stock of Y having a fair market value of $100x$ dollars plus cash of $10x$ dollars.

In accordance with the facts set forth in the table below if X had sold at fair market value each of the three assets it transferred to *Y*, the result would have been as follows:

	Asset I	*Asset II*	*Asset III*
Character of asset	Capital asset held more than [one year]	Capital asset held not more than [one year]	Section 1245 property.
Fair market value	$22*x*	$33*x*	$55*x*
Adjusted basis	40*x*	20*x*	25*x*
Gain (loss)	($18*x*)	$13*x*	$30*x*
Character of gain or loss	Long-term capital loss.	Short-term capital gain.	Ordinary income.

The facts in the instant case disclose that with respect to the section 1245 property the depreciation subject to recapture exceeds the amount of gain that would be recognized on a sale at fair market value. Therefore, all of such gain would be treated as ordinary income under section 1245(a)(1) of the Code.

Under section 351(a) of the Code, no gain or loss is recognized if property is transferred to a corporation solely in exchange for its stock and immediately after the exchange the transferor is in control of the corporation. If section 351(a) of the Code would apply to an exchange but for the fact that there is received, in addition to the property permitted to be received without recognition of gain, other property or money, then under section 351(b) of the Code gain (if any) to the recipient will be recognized, but in an amount not in excess of the sum of such money and the fair market value of such other property received, and no loss to the recipient will be recognized.

The first question presented is how to determine the amount of gain to be recognized under section 351(b) of the Code. The general rule is that each asset transferred must be considered to have been separately exchanged. See the authorities cited in Revenue Ruling 67-192, C.B. 1967-2, 140, and in Revenue Ruling 68-23, [1968-1 C.B. 144], which hold that there is no netting of gains and losses for purposes of applying sections 367 and 356(c) of the Code. Thus, for purposes of making computations under section 351(b) of the Code, it is not proper to total the bases of the various assets transferred and to subtract this total from the fair market value of the total consideration received in the exchange. Moreover, any treatment other than an asset-by-asset approach would have the effect of allowing losses that are specifically disallowed by section 351(b)(2) of the Code.

The second question presented is how, for purposes of making computations under section 351(b) of the Code, to allocate the cash and stock received to the amount realized as to each asset transferred in the exchange. The asset-by-asset approach for computing the amount of gain realized in the exchange requires that for this purpose the fair market value of each category of consideration received must be separately allocated to the transferred assets in proportion to the relative fair market values of the transferred assets. See section 1.1245-4(c)(1) of the Income Tax Regulations which, for the same reasons, requires that for purposes of computing the amount of gain to which section 1245 of the Code applies each category of consideration received must be allocated to the properties transferred in proportion to their relative fair market values.

Accordingly, the amount and character of the gain recognized in the exchange should be computed as follows:

	Total	*Asset I*	*Asset II*	*Asset III*
Fair market value of asset transferred	$110x$	$22x$	$33x$	$55x$
Percent of total fair market value		20%	30%	50%
Fair market value of Y stock received in exchange	$100x$	$20x$	$30x$	$50x$
Cash received in exchange	$10x$	$2x$	$3x$	$5x$
Amount realized	$110x$	$22x$	$33x$	$55x$
Adjusted basis		$40x$	$20x$	$25x$
Gain (loss) realized		($18x$)	$13x$	$30x$

Under section 351(b)(2) of the Code the loss of $18x$ dollars realized on the exchange of Asset Number I is not recognized. Such loss may not be used to offset the gains realized on the exchanges of the other assets. Under section 351(b)(1) of the Code, the gain of $13x$ dollars realized on the exchange of Asset Number II will be recognized as short-term capital gain in the amount of $3x$ dollars, the amount of cash received. Under sections 351(b)(1) and 1245(b)(3) of the Code, the gain of $30x$ dollars realized on the exchange of Asset Number III will be recognized as ordinary income in the amount of $5x$ dollars, the amount of cash received.

NOTE

Y's basis in the assets received under §362 is equal to A's basis plus any gain recognized to A. Accordingly, for Asset I, Y's basis is $40x$; for Asset II, Y's basis is $23x$ (transferred basis of $20x$ plus $3x$ of recognized gain); for Asset III, Y's basis is $30x$ (transferred basis of $25x$ plus $5x$

gain recognized). Notice that the basis Y takes in the transferred assets preserves the gain (or loss) that went unrecognized by X on the §351 transfer.

Next consider the basis X takes in the stock it receives from Y under §358. Is the basis (and holding period) of the stock received determined in the aggregate (i.e., by looking at the aggregate bases of the property transferred by X and the aggregate gain recognized)? Or does that portion of the stock received by X in exchange for each asset derive its basis (and holding period) from that asset?

Rev. Rul. 85-164
1985-2 C.B. 117

ISSUE

May a transferor determine the bases and holding periods of stock . . . received in a transfer under section 351 of the Internal Revenue Code by designating the specific property to be exchanged for particular stock . . . ?

FACTS

A, an individual, was engaged in a business as a sole proprietor. The assets of the sole proprietorship consisted of trade accounts receivable with an adjusted basis of zero and a fair market value of $60x$ dollars, machinery with an adjusted basis of $5x$ dollars and a fair market value of $10x$ dollars, and real estate (land and building) with an adjusted basis of $25x$ dollars and a fair market value of $30x$ dollars. A had held the real estate and machinery for over one year. Both the real estate and machinery were property described in section 1231 of the Code.

In order to limit personal liability, A transferred all of the assets associated with the sole proprietorship to a new corporation, Y, in exchange for all of Y's stock. . . . A transferred the accounts receivable to Y in exchange for 100 shares of common stock, the fair market value of which was $60x$ dollars. A transferred the machinery and real estate to Y in exchange for [100 shares of preferred stock],* which had a principal amount and a fair market value of $40x$ dollars. The selection of specific items for exchange was made to allocate assets with a high basis and long-term holding period to the [preferred stock].

---

* In the ruling, A receives common stock and securities that under the law then in effect were qualifying property under §351. Because securities are no longer qualifying property under §351, the ruling will apply to allocate basis to any stock received (e.g., common and preferred stock). — EDS.

LAW AND ANALYSIS

Section 351(a) of the Code provides that no gain or loss will be recognized if property is transferred to a corporation by a person solely in exchange for stock . . . in such corporation and immediately after the exchange such person is in control (as defined in section 368(c)) of the corporation.

Section 358(a)(1) of the Code and section 1.358-1 of the Income Tax Regulations provide that in the case of an exchange to which section 351 applies in which only nonrecognition property is received, the basis of all of the stock . . . received in the exchange shall be the same as the basis of all property exchanged therefor. Section 358(b)(1) directs that, under regulations prescribed by the Secretary, the basis determined under subsection (a)(1) shall be allocated among the properties permitted to be received without the recognition of gain or loss.

Section 1.358-2(a) of the regulations prescribes rules for the allocation of basis among nonrecognition property received in corporate reorganization exchanges governed by sections 354, 355, 356. . . . In general, these rules allow limited tracing of the basis of old stock . . . into new only with respect to (i) persons who owned stock . . . of more than one class . . . before the exchange and (ii) corporate recapitalizations under section 368(a)(1)(E). In all other cases, including exchanges under section 351, section 1.358-2(b)(2) provides that the basis of property transferred shall be allocated among all the stock . . . received in proportion to the fair market values of the stock of each class. . . .

Section 1223(1) and section 1.1223-1(a) of the regulations require that, in determining the period for which a taxpayer has held property received in an exchange, there shall be included the period for which he held the property exchanged if (i) in the taxpayer's hands the property received has the same basis in whole or in part as the property exchanged and (ii) for exchanges after March 1, 1954, the property exchanged was at the time of exchange a capital asset as defined in section 1221 or property used in a trade or business as described in section 1231.

Rev. Rul. 62-140, 1962-2 C.B. 181, holds that a share of stock received in exchange for a debenture and a cash payment had a split holding period. The portion of each share received attributable to ownership of the debenture was treated as including the period for which the taxpayer held the debenture and the portion of each share received attributable to the cash payment was treated as held beginning with the date following the date of acquisition.

Rev. Rul. 68-55, 1968-1 C.B. 140, holds that when property is transferred to a corporation under section 351(a) of the Code each asset must be considered transferred separately in exchange for a proportionate share of each of the various categories of the total consideration received.

In the instant case, *A* formed *Y* by transferring all of the business assets of the sole proprietorship to *Y* in exchange solely for all of *Y*'s stock. . . .

Y will continue to carry on the business that A conducted, and A will remain in control of Y. The transfer, therefore, is subject to section 351 of the Code, with the bases and holding periods of the Y stock . . . in the hands of A determined under sections 358 and 1223 of the Code respectively.

A may not determine the bases and holding periods of the Y stock . . . received by designating specific property to be exchanged for particular stock. . . . Under sections 1.358-1 and 1.358-2(b)(2) of the regulations, the aggregate basis of the property transferred is allocated among the stock . . . received in proportion to the fair market values of each class. The holding period of the Y stock . . . received by A is determined by referring to the assets deemed exchanged for each portion of the stock. . . . The aggregate basis of the property transferred was $30x$ dollars. Since the [common and preferred] stock . . . A received had fair market values of $60x$ dollars and $40x$ dollars, respectively, a basis of $18x$ dollars ($60x/100x \times 30x$) is allocated to the Y [common] stock received by A, and a basis of $12x$ dollars ($40x/100x \times 30x$) is allocated to the Y [preferred stock] received. In addition, each share of Y stock . . . received by A has a split holding period and a split basis for purposes of determining long-term or short-term capital gain or loss. That fraction of each share of Y stock . . . attributable to the real estate and machinery ($40x/100x$) is treated as including the period (over one year) for which A held the real estate and machinery and has a basis solely attributable to the real estate and machinery (e.g., the $40x/100x$ of each share of stock attributable to the real estate and machinery will have a basis of $.18x$ dollars ($18x/100$ shares)). The fraction of each share of Y stock . . . attributable to the accounts receivable ($60x/100x$) has a holding period beginning on the day after the exchange and has a zero basis. If part or all of the stock . . . received in the exchange is disposed of at a time when the split holding period is relevant in determining tax liability, the same fractions will be applied to apportion the amount realized among the above components of the stock. . . .

This holding would be unaffected if A were to make a transfer in exchange for stock at separate times, and the transfers were part of a single integrated transaction.

2.   Assumption of Liabilities

If the transferee corporation assumes an indebtedness of the transferor on the exchange, that benefit may be the equivalent of boot. The parallel is particularly pronounced if the transferor mortgages the property immediately before the exchange, keeps the cash thus raised, and then transfers the property for stock plus an assumption of the mortgage. The economic consequences to the transferor are substantially similar to a transfer of the unencumbered property for stock plus cash. In United States v. Hendler,

303 U.S. 564 (1938), the court held that an assumption of the transferor's indebtedness constituted boot under somewhat parallel reorganization sections. The "victory" by the Service threatened the federal coffers since transferee corporations would probably be entitled to a stepped-up basis under §362(a) for gain that should have been recognized by the transferors — even if that gain was unreachable because the statute of limitations had run on the year of the exchange. Consider the mitigation provisions of §§1311-1314. The Treasury hastened to relinquish its victory, culminating in the enactment of §357.

The general rule of §357(a) provides that the assumption of a liability or the acquisition of property subject to a liability by the transferee corporation is not to be treated as money or other property exchanged and does not prevent the exchange from qualifying as a tax-free transaction under §351. Section 357(b) provides an exception, treating the assumption as boot if the principal purpose of the assumption was not a "bona fide business purpose" or was to avoid federal income tax on the exchange. For example, it might cover the case of a mortgage placed on property on the eve of incorporation. See Thompson v. Campbell, 353 F.2d 787 (5th Cir. 1965).

Section 357(c) is another exception to the rule of §357(a). If the liabilities assumed by the transferee corporation exceed the adjusted bases of all the property transferred by the transferor, the excess is treated as gain on the sale or exchange of such property. To the extent of the excess, the taxpayer has cashed in the gain inherent in the property transferred. For example, suppose T transfers property with a basis of $1,000 and a fair market value of $15,000 to X Corp. in a transaction that qualifies under §351. In exchange, T receives $12,000 of X Corp. stock and X Corp. assumes T's $3,000 mortgage obligation. Sections 357(c) and 351 cause T to recognize the $2,000 gain on the transfer of property — the amount by which the assumed indebtedness exceeds the adjusted basis. Section 357(c) applies even when the transferor remains legally responsible for the liabilities assumed by the corporate transferee. See Owen v. Commissioner, 881 F.2d 832 (9th Cir. 1989).

Suppose T transfers to X Corp. equipment with a basis of $30 and a fair market value of $50 and a building with a basis of $10 and a fair market value of $100 in exchange for stock and X's assumption of a $40 liability encumbering the building. Does T experience a $30 gain under §357(c), or can the basis of *all* assets be aggregated to produce $0 gain? See Treas. Regs. §1.357-2(a). The theory seems to be that T has cashed in gain only to the extent that debt relief exceeds the basis of all transferred assets. What if B transfers the equipment and T the building? Can T use the basis of B's asset to avoid §357(c) gain? Compare the language of §357(c) with Rev. Rul. 66-142, 1966-2 C.B. 66 (using a person-by-person approach).

Suppose T conducts a business as a sole proprietor with assets having combined bases of $60,000 and a fair market value of $100,000. The assets are subject to a $75,000 mortgage incurred for business reasons. If *T* transfers the assets to newly formed *X* Corp. in a transaction qualifying under §351, *T* faces a $15,000 recognition of gain under §357(c).

Suppose instead that in addition to the assets, *T* transfers $15,000 of cash to *X* Corp. Under §357(c), *T* would not recognize gain on the §351 transaction because the liabilities do not exceed the "total of adjusted basis of the property transferred." Would it matter whether *T* contributed his own money or money borrowed from a bank? Suppose *T* had borrowed $15,000 from *X* Corp. years ago. What is the result if *T* transfers a promise (i.e., *T*'s own note) to pay $15,000 to *X* Corp. in five years, bearing appropriate interest? This raises the issue of determining whether *T*'s own note is "property" for purposes of §351, and, if so, *T*'s basis in that note.

Lessinger v. Commissioner _____
872 F.2d 519 (2d Cir. 1989)

OAKES, Chief Judge

Taxpayers Sol and Edith Lessinger appeal from that portion of a decision of the United States Tax Court, Charles E. Clapp II, Judge, finding them liable for income taxes of $113,242.55 for the tax year 1977. Lessinger v. Commissioner, 85 T.C. 824 (1985). . . .

The Tax Court found, and the parties seem to agree, that section 351 of the Internal Revenue Code governs the transaction at issue here. Section 351 provides for the nonrecognition of income when a controlling shareholder transfers property to a corporation. The taxpayer here transferred the assets and liabilities of a proprietorship he operated to a corporation he owned for reasons entirely unrelated to tax planning. It is clear that he was oblivious to the ramifications of his actions in terms of his tax liability. Prior to the consolidation, the proprietorship had a negative net worth. Nevertheless, the Tax Court found that the taxpayer had to recognize a gain because he transferred liabilities to the corporation which exceeded his adjusted basis in the assets of the proprietorship. The Tax Court applied section 357(c) of the Code, which is an exception to the general rule of nonrecognition in section 351 transactions. Under section 357(c), gain is recognized to the extent that a transferor-shareholder disposes of liabilities exceeding the total adjusted basis of the assets transferred. I.R.C. §357(c).

The taxpayer attacks the Tax Court's decision from two directions. First, he argues that the Tax Court overstated the amount of liabilities transferred, because, he claims, he did not actually transfer short-term accounts payable to the corporation. His second argument is that the Tax Court understated the amount of assets transferred. The Tax Court decided to ignore a $255,500 accounting entry which, the taxpayer argues, represented his personal debt to the corporation and should be counted as a transferred asset.

Sol Lessinger operated a proprietorship under the name "Universal Screw and Bolt Co." for over twenty-five years prior to 1977. Since 1962 he was also the sole shareholder and chief executive officer of Universal Screw & Bolt Co., Inc. Both businesses were engaged in the wholesale distribution of metal fasteners, and they were conducted from the same location on Ninth Avenue in New York City.

In 1976, the factor that had provided working capital to the proprietorship refused to continue lending funds to it as a noncorporate entity because under New York law one can charge higher interest rates of a corporation. See N.Y. Gen. Oblig. Law §5-521 (McKinney 1978) (corporation prohibited from interposing defense of usury). The taxpayer instructed the individual who was his attorney and accountant to do whatever was necessary to make the proprietorship a corporation. The Universal proprietorship was then consolidated into the Universal corporation in 1977. The Tax Court found that the taxpayer was not informed of the details of the transaction. . . .

The consolidation of the proprietorship into the corporation was conducted in a most casual manner, the transfer transaction being naked in its simplicity. The taxpayer already owned all of the corporation's stock, and no new stock was issued. There were no written agreements documenting the transfer. On January 1, 1977, the proprietorship's bank account was closed, and the corporation took over the proprietorship's operating assets. Only two items of any significance were not transferred: The taxpayer had borrowed funds from Chemical Bank to purchase mutual fund shares, and the shares secured the loan. . . . The taxpayer retained the shares and sold them to pay the loan himself later in January 1977. . . .

On June 1, 1977, journal entries were made to the corporation's books to reflect the consolidation. Various corporate asset accounts were debited (i.e., increased) to show the addition of the proprietorship's assets, and corporate liability accounts were credited (i.e., increased) by the amount of the proprietorship's liabilities. Total proprietorship liabilities exceeded total proprietorship assets by $255,499.37, and that amount was debited to a corporate asset account in an entry entitled "Loan Receivable — SL." A ledger sheet entitled "Sol Lessinger" showed the debit with the description "merger of company" as well as a $3,500 debit for a personal debt the corporation paid for Sol.

When in January 1977 the taxpayer sold his mutual funds, he used the proceeds not only to pay off the partnership's Chemical Bank loan, but also, with the remaining $62,209.35, to pay the corporation part of his $259,000 debt to it. Thus, at the end of 1977, he owed $196,790 to the corporation. In 1981, Marine Midland Bank, a principal creditor of the corporation, requested that the taxpayer execute a promissory note for the debt, and he did so, the note being used as collateral for the bank's loan to the corporation. No interest was ever paid on the debt, however, and the debt had risen to $237,044 by the end of 1982, by which point the corporation was insolvent. The corporation's retained earnings were $29,638 at the beginning of 1977 and $38,671 at the end of 1977, so the taxpayer's debt to the corporation greatly outweighed his equity in it. . . .

DISCUSSION

The first question is whether section 351 applies when no new shares are issued to the shareholder, having in mind the statutory language that a transfer must be made "solely in exchange for stock or securities." See §351(a). . . . We agree . . . with the Tax Court's ultimate conclusion that the exchange requirements of section 351 are met where a sole stockholder transfers property to a wholly-owned corporation even though no stock [is] issued therefor. Issuance of new stock in this situation would be a meaningless gesture. See Jackson v. Commissioner, 708 F.2d 1402, 1405 (9th Cir. 1983). . . .

The taxpayer's principal argument, broadly stated, is that section 357 is inapplicable to him because in neither an accounting nor an economic sense did he realize a gain. He "merely exchanged creditors" from trade creditors to Universal, and his gain, therefore, was a "phantom" which Congress did not intend to tax.

Narrowly stated, the taxpayer's argument takes two different forms, each of which complements the other:

First, the corporation did not take the affirmative action necessary to assume the trade accounts payable of the taxpayer's proprietorship. . . .

Second, even if the corporation did "assume" the taxpayer's trade accounts payable, there was no taxable gain since he contributed "property," that is, the account receivable from him in the approximate amount of $250,000, which, contrary to Alderman v. Commissioner, 55 T.C. 662 (1971), should be deemed to have a basis equal to its face value. . . .

[The court first found that the corporation did assume Lessinger's liabilities.]

Having determined that the proprietorship's accounts payable should be included in the category of liabilities assumed, we must determine whether the taxpayer's purported debt to his corporation would offset those liabilities and prevent a net excess of liabilities over assets. The obligation which the taxpayer owed to his wholly-owned corporation, it must quickly be conceded, was not as well documented as a debt to a third party would be.

A journal entry of the corporation showed $255,499.37 as a loan receivable from the taxpayer, which in turn was posted on a general ledger sheet as a debit to the taxpayer's account. That account was credited with a $62,209.35 adjustment resulting from the sale of the taxpayer's mutual funds and the paydown of the Chemical Bank loan. No credits on account of subsidized rent . . . were made, and the debit balance of $196,790 in the taxpayer's account after the adjustment was never paid down; instead it increased to the sum of $237,044 in 1982. Marine Midland Bank required the open account to be formalized in 1981 in a note which collateralized the bank's loan to the corporation.

The Tax Court refused to count the debt as "property" transferred in the transaction, although its reasoning is not explicit. First, the opinion says that the corporate accounting entry entitled "Loan receivable — [Sol Lessinger]" "merely represents the excess of the liabilities over the adjusted basis," noting that the debt was not at first represented by a promissory note and that Lessinger paid no interest on it. The Tax Court then cites a decision in which it had ignored an entry that the taxpayer had characterized as an "artificial receivable." 85 T.C. at 837 n.8 (citing Christopher v. Commissioner, T.C. Memo 1984-394, 48 Tax Ct. Mem. Dec. (CCH) 663 (1984)). The Tax Court opinion concludes that "even if [Lessinger] had executed a note, it would have a zero basis in the hands of the corporation." Id. at 837 (citing Alderman v. Commissioner, 55 T.C. 662(1971)). The Tax Court thus apparently believed there were two independently sufficient reasons to ignore the debt: first, that it was artificial, and, second, that it would have had a zero basis.

We are unpersuaded by the argument that the obligation was artificial. . . . The Commissioner points out that the receivable lacked a due date, interest, security, or "other accepted features of true debt," but this analysis begs the question we have before us. The Commissioner's argument is not aided by likening this case to Carolina, Clinchfield and Ohio Railway v. Commissioner, 823 F.2d 33 (2d Cir. 1987) (per curiam), where an existing debt was replaced by a new debt payable ten centuries later, the present value of which was two quadrillionths of a cent. We believe that the receivable was an enforceable demand obligation. The decisions that the Commissioner cites for the definition of "true debt" concern the advance of funds to a close corporation by its shareholders. Gilbert v. Commissioner, 248 F.2d 399, 402 (2d Cir. 1957); see also Raymond v. United States, 511 F.2d 185, 190 (6th Cir. 1975). A taxpayer in that setting may seek to mischaracterize a capital contribution as debt in order for the corporation to be able to treat the obligation in a way that would disguise nondeductible dividends as deductible interest payments. In that context, the courts have defined "classic debt" narrowly as "an unqualified obligation to pay a sum certain at a reasonably close fixed maturity date along with a fixed percentage in interest," although the essential factor is a "binding obligation." Gilbert, 248 F.2d at 402.

We believe, however, that a due date, interest, and security are not necessary to characterize Lessinger's obligation to his corporation as debt, and that his obligation was binding. The promissory note he signed in 1981, which the corporation endorsed to Marine Midland as collateral for a loan, is significant because it shows that Marine Midland depended on his personal responsibility. And, in general, it is obvious that the creditors of the corporation continued to do business with it on the strength of the taxpayer's personal credit (whether as evidenced by the liability on the books or by operation of New York law protecting creditors of a partnership that is succeeded by an alter ego corporation, e.g., Reif v. Williams Sportswear, Inc., 9 N.Y.2d 387, 174 N.E.2d 492, 214 N.Y.S.2d 395 (1961); Woodland-Nursing Home Corp. v. Harris, 514 F. Supp. 110 (S.D.N.Y. 1981), aff'd mem., 697 F.2d 302 (2d Cir. 1982)). Lessinger received consideration when he gave his promise to the corporation, and we have no doubt that any court would enforce that promise to protect the corporate creditors if the corporation failed, even in the absence of alter ego liability. We conclude that the taxpayer's obligation to the corporation was real, not artificial.

We now turn to the Tax Court's second reason for ignoring the debt. The Tax Court quoted *Alderman,* supra, which, like our case, involved the incorporation of an accrual basis proprietorship with a negative net worth. In *Alderman,* the Tax Court disregarded the taxpayers' personal promissory note to their corporation

> because the Aldermans incurred no cost in making the note, so its basis to them was zero. The basis to the corporation was the same as in the hands of the transferor, i.e., zero. Consequently, the application of section 357(c) is undisturbed by the creation and transfer of the personal note to the corporation.

55 T.C. at 665; see also Rev. Rul. 68-629, 1968-2 C.B. 154-55 (same). *Alderman* purported to follow the literal language of the Tax Code. Section 357(c) does support the *Alderman* court's reliance on the concept of basis, but the statutory language is not addressed to a transaction such as Lessinger's, where the transferor's obligation has a value to the transferee corporation. The *Alderman* court did not consider the value of the obligation to the transferee. . . .

"Basis," as used in tax law, refers to assets, not liabilities. Section 1012 provides that "the basis of property shall be the cost of such property, except as otherwise provided." Liabilities by definition have no "basis" in tax law generally or in section 1012 terms specifically. . . . The concept of "basis" prevents double taxation of income by identifying amounts that have already been taxed or are exempt from tax. 3 J. Mertens, Law of Federal Income Taxation §21.01, at 11 (1988). The taxpayer could, of course, have no "basis" in his own promise to pay the corporation $255,000, because that item is a liability for him. We would add parenthetically that to this extent *Alderman* was correct in describing the taxpayers' note there. But the corporation should have a basis in its obligation from Lessinger, because it incurred a cost in the transaction involving the transfer of the obligation by taking on the liabilities of the proprietorship that exceeded its assets, and because it would have to recognize income upon

Lessinger's payment of the debt if it had no basis in the obligation. . . . Assets transferred under section 351 are taken by the corporation at the transferor's basis, to which is added any gain recognized in the transfer. §362(a). Consideration of "adjusted basis" in section 357(c) therefore normally does not require determining whether the section refers to the "adjusted basis" in the hands of the transferor-shareholder or the transferee-corporation, because the basis does not change. But here, the "basis" in the hands of the corporation should be the face amount of the taxpayer's obligation. . . . We now hold that in the situation presented here, where the transferor undertakes genuine personal liability to the transferee, "adjusted basis" in section 357(c) refers to the transferee's basis in the obligation, which is its face amount. . . .

Yet the Commissioner says that to reverse the Tax Court would, as *Alderman*, 55 T.C. at 665, suggested, "effectively eliminate section 357(c) from the Internal Revenue Code." Would it? The question of substance is whether the taxpayer in fact realized a gain from the transaction. He certainly did not do so by a cancellation of his indebtedness. If there was any cancellation, it was illusory: While his trade creditors at the time of the incorporation may have been paid off (or their accounts rolled over as a result of sales and payments by the corporation and further advances of credit by the trade creditors), the taxpayer's indebtedness to the corporation itself continued (except to the extent he paid it off). If Lessinger had a "gain" from the incorporation, it did not show up in his personal balance sheet, let alone by way of economic benefit in his pocket.

The purpose of section 357(c) is to provide a limited exception to section 351's nonrecognition treatment that operates, as the Commissioner reminds us here, "where the transferor realized economic benefit which, if not recognized, would otherwise go untaxed." Brief at 27 (quoting Focht v. Commissioner, 68 T.C. 223, 235 (1977)). Section 351 was intended to allow changes in business form without requiring the recognition of income. Bongiovanni v. Commissioner, 470 F.2d 921, 924 (2d Cir. 1972). . . . The transferor-shareholder recognizes income only to the extent that he receives boot in the form of money or other property. §351(b). In 1938, the Supreme Court held that under the predecessor of section 351 . . . , any assumption of liability by the transferee would be considered a payment of money or property to the transferor, causing the transferor to recognize income. United States v. Hendler, 303 U.S. 564 (1938). Congress reacted immediately by enacting . . . the predecessor of section 357(a), which provided that the assumption of a liability should not be considered the payment of property or money and should not provoke the recognition of gain. . . .

Congress did not add section 357(c), which requires the recognition of gain when liabilities exceed assets, until 1954, when a House committee referred to the section as an "additional safeguard [ ] against tax avoidance not found in existing law." H.R. Rep. No. 1337, 83d Cong., 2d Sess. 40, *reprinted in* 1954 U.S. Code Cong. & Admin. News 4017, 4066 ("House Report"). Some provision was necessary to ensure that manipulations of credit and depreciation were not used to realize tax-free gains. *Focht*, 68 T.C. at 235. The House and Senate committees that approved section 357(c) both cited a single example of a transaction that the section was intended to govern: If a taxpayer transfers property with an adjusted basis of $20,000 subject to a $50,000 mortgage, he should recognize $30,000 gain. House Report at A129, *reprinted in* 1954 U.S. Code Cong. & Admin. News at 4267 (describing what was then called §356); S. Rep. No. 1622, 83d Cong., 2d Sess. 270, *reprinted in* 1954 U.S. Code Cong. & Admin. News 4621, 4908. . . . The transferor, who has already benefited by depreciating the property or holding it while its value appreciates, has income because he will never have to pay the mortgage. Forcing the taxpayer in our case to recognize a gain, however, would be contrary to Congress's intent because it would tax a truly phantom gain, because his liability to the corporation, as we have said, was real, continuing, and indirectly, at least, enforceable by the corporation's creditors.

That section 357(c)'s language can be construed to require unjust and economically unfounded results is clear from the continuing debate over other aspects of the section's operation. In Rosen v. Commissioner, 62 T.C. 11 (1974), aff'd mem., 515 F.2d 507 (3d Cir. 1975), for example, the Tax Court held that a transferor had to recognize gain from the assumption of liabilities, even though he remained personally liable and, in fact, paid the obligations himself. The Tax Court commented on section 357(c)'s harshness, noting that it "may even result in the realization of a gain for tax purposes where none in fact exists." Id. at 19. After oral argument, counsel for the Commissioner directed us to a case upholding the constitutionality of section 357(c). The court in that case, however, was not confronted with an exception to its optimistic observation that "it is only when some tax benefit occurs, for example depreciation or further indebtedness on the property which yields tax-free cash not included in cost, that the liabilities will exceed the adjusted basis therein." Wiebusch v. Commissioner, 59 T.C. 777, 781, aff'd per curiam, 487 F.2d 515 (8th Cir. 1973). While we do not rest our decision today on constitutional grounds, we note that *Wiebusch*'s analysis would not apply here.

Section 357(c) was amended in 1978 to solve a problem that had forced the courts to fashion delicate constructions of the section's language in order to conform with legislative intent. A cash basis transferor has no basis in accounts receivable. The Tax Court originally held that such a transferor would have to recognize gain if, after counting her accounts payable as transferred liabilities, liabilities exceeded assets. . . . This analysis meant that the owner of almost any ongoing business transferred liabilities exceeding assets when incorporating. The Tax Court later developed an approach that excluded accounts payable from liabilities, see *Focht*, supra, after this court and the Court of Appeals for the Ninth Circuit announced different interpretations that achieved this result. See *Bongiovanni*, supra; Thatcher v. Commissioner, 533 F.2d 1114 (9th Cir. 1976). Congress added section 357(c)(3) in 1978, and it now excludes from subsection (c)(1) "a liability the payment of which . . . would give rise to a deduction." This history, while not directly relevant to Lessinger,[8] is instructive. In *Bongiovanni*, "a too literal reading of the words of the statute [would have] produce[d] an inequitable result which cannot be allowed to stand," 470 F.2d at 924, and "Congress certainly could not have intended such an inequitable result especially in light of its expressed purposes in enacting Sections 351 and 357(c)," id. at 925. We find those words equally applicable here.

We conclude that our holding will not "effectively eliminate section 357(c)." Lessinger experienced no enrichment and had no unrecognized gains whose recognition was appropriate at the time of the consolidation. Any logic that would tax him would certainly represent a "trap for the unwary." *Bongiovanni*, 470 F.2d at 924 (quoting the Commissioner's characterization of the Tax Court's early treatment of cash basis taxpayers under section 351). Lessinger could have achieved incorporation without taxation under the Commissioner's theory by borrowing $260,000 cash, transferring the cash to the corporation (or paying some of the trade accounts payable personally), and later causing the corporation to buy his promissory note from the lender (or pay it off in consideration of his new promise to pay the corporation). If taxpayers who transfer liabilities exceeding assets to controlled corporations are willing to undertake genuine personal liability for the excess, we see no reason to require recognition of a gain, and we do not believe that Congress intended for any gain to be recognized. . . .

NOTE

1. *Basis in a taxpayer's own note.* The court in *Lessinger* reached the right conclusion that for purposes of §357(c) a taxpayer has a basis in his own note equal to its fair market value. Basis in an asset under U.S. tax law is the amount that can be received tax free on a sale of that asset. If a taxpayer makes a promissory note for $5,000 bearing a market rate of interest, the taxpayer is not taxed on a "sale" of that note by the maker in exchange for $5,000. In effect, a taxpayer must be deemed to have a $5,000 basis in his own note.

Nevertheless, the Second Circuit decision in *Lessinger* is contrary to the result in Alderman v. Commissioner, 55 T.C. 662 (1971), which was

---

8. Section 357(c)(3) is inapplicable because Lessinger's proprietorship was on the accrual basis. None of the liabilities would have produced deductions if paid by the transferor because those expenses had been previously deducted when they were entered in the proprietorship's records. . . .

relied upon by the Tax Court in *Lessinger*. If *Alderman* was correctly decided (i.e., a taxpayer has no basis in his own note), then what basis does the transferee corporation take in the note following §351 transaction? Suppose *T* transfers her own $5,000 note bearing a market rate of interest to *X* Corp. in exchange for $5,000 of *X* Corp. stock in a §351 transaction. If *T* has a basis of $0 in her own note, then under §362, *X* Corp. would take a $0 basis in *T*'s note. What happens when *T* pays off the note? Should *X* Corp. have $5,000 of income? That would be an odd result. If *T* had originally transferred $5,000 in cash to *X* Corp., *X* Corp. would have had no income; there is no reason why a different result should occur if the $5,000 is paid at a later date. *X* Corp. should have no income when *T* pays off the note. To achieve that result, *X* Corp. must have a $5,000 basis in the note. Because *X* Corp.'s basis derives from *T*'s basis under §362, *T* must have a $5,000 basis in her own note.

If Lessinger had borrowed the $255,499.37 from a bank and then contributed the borrowed funds along with his other assets and liabilities, there would have been no liability under §357(c) because the liabilities assumed by the corporation did not exceed the total bases of the assets transferred. After such a transfer, the bank would have been Lessinger's creditor. Should there be a different result if the transferee corporation is Lessinger's creditor?

Note that the result in *Lessinger* is consistent with the result in Crane v. Commissioner, 331 U.S. 1 (1947), that borrowed funds used to acquire property are included in basis. In a sense, Lessinger borrowed funds from the transferee corporation in making the promise to repay the transferee corporation in the future. Whether Lessinger transfers cash or the promise to pay that cash in the future, Lessinger's basis in the asset transferred should be the same. See generally Manning, "The Issuer's Paper: Property or What? Zero Basis and Other Income Tax Mysteries," 39 Tax L. Rev. 159 (1984).

2. *Deductible liabilities.* Prior its amendment in 1978, §357(c) generated considerable litigation regarding the treatment of a cash basis taxpayer who transfers accounts receivable with zero basis (e.g., the right to be paid for goods or services provided to customers on credit) in exchange for stock and the assumption by the corporation of the transferor's accounts payable (e.g., a liability to pay a supplier of raw materials). Since the liability necessarily exceeds the basis of the transferred receivable, assumption of that liability by the corporation triggers the recognition of gain. For example, suppose *T* transfers a receivable with a basis of $0 and a fair market value of $100 for $70 of *X* Corp. stock and the assumption by *X* of *T*'s $30 account payable. We might recharacterize the transaction in the following manner: *X* Corp. borrows $30 from the creditor of the account payable and distributes that $30 along with $70 of stock to *T*, who then uses the $30 to pay off her obligation to the creditor. Viewed in this manner, the transaction would produce income to *T* equal to the $30 boot

received, but *T* would have an offsetting deduction for the payment of an expense deductible under §162(a). Accordingly, when *X* Corp. assumes responsibility for an account payable or any other deductible obligation, the transferor should not be taxed.

Courts reached this conclusion by employing a variety of rationales. In Bongiovanni v. Commissioner, 470 F.2d 921 (2d Cir. 1972), the court held that the term "liability" for purposes of §357(c) does not include accounts payable. In Thatcher v. Commissioner, 533 F.2d 1114 (9th Cir. 1976), the court allowed a constructive deduction against §357(c) income. Finally, in Focht v. Commissioner, 66 T.C. 233 (1977), the court, following *Bongiovanni,* held that an obligation of a cash basis taxpayer should not be treated as a liability under §357(c) to the extent that its payment would have been deductible if made by the transferor. See Rev. Rul. 80-199, 1980-2 C.B. 122 (following *Focht* for transactions occurring prior to 1978).

Section 357(c)(3) now codifies the result reached in *Focht.* Does §357(c)(3) imply that the transferee will be able to deduct the liabilities when paid even though they were incurred by another taxpayer (i.e., the transferor) who received "credit" for the deduction by offsetting §357(c) gain? Apparently it does. Rev. Rul. 80-198, 1980-2 C.B. 113. This is contrary to the usual rule that one cannot get a deduction for paying the expenses of another. It is another manifestation of the double taxation, and sometimes double benefit, created by the corporate income tax. Does the treatment of payables imply that the transferred receivables will be taxable to the corporation and not to the transferor contrary to the assignment of income rules? See Hempt Bros. v. United States, 490 F.2d 1172 (3d Cir. 1974) (assignment of income doctrine not applicable). See also page 71 infra.

In Orr v. Commissioner, 78 T.C. 1059 (1982), a cash basis taxpayer arranged vacation packages for clients as a sole proprietor. When he incorporated, he transferred all the operating assets to the corporation in exchange for stock and the corporation's assumption of his liabilities. The liabilities consisted of refundable customer deposits for tours. He did not transfer the cash deposits. The Service argued that §357(c) required the recognition of gain to the extent that the assumed liabilities exceeded the taxpayer's basis. The taxpayer countered that §357(c) was inapplicable because *Focht,* now codified as §357(c)(3), dictates that the deposits not be considered liabilities for purposes of §357(c). The court sided with the Service, noting that the customer deposits were not included in income when received and would not be deductible when refunded.

In *Lessinger,* the taxpayer transferred accounts payable that arose when the business was conducted as a sole proprietorship. In light of §357(c)(3), why was there any tax issue under §357(c)(1)? Notice that for §357(c)(3) to apply, the liabilities must be deductible when paid. For Lessinger, an accrual basis taxpayer, would the accounts payable be deductible when paid?

3. *Relationship between §357(b) and (c).* If transferred property is sub-

ject both to §357(b) (because of the taxpayer's improper purpose) and to §357(c), does the taxpayer recognize the entire liability as boot under §357(b), or only the excess of basis under §357(c)? See §357(c)(2)(A).

3.   Stock

With the treatment of boot in mind, consider the thorny question of what property constitutes boot and what constitutes stock.

The term "stock" is defined neither in the Code nor in the regulations. Stock unquestionably is qualifying property under §351 whether common or preferred, voting or nonvoting. Stock rights, options, warrants, or other rights to purchase stock at a fixed price are not treated as stock for purposes of §351. Treas. Regs. §1.351-1(a)(1); cf. Helvering v. Southwest Consolidated Corp., 315 U.S. 194 (1942) (warrants issued as part of a reorganization are not voting stock). What are the tax consequences if T transfers property to X Corp. in exchange for some stock and a certificate for additional shares to be issued later, contingent on valuation of T's property? Contingent stock interests have been distinguished from stock rights because no additional payment is required from the transferor. See Carlberg v. United States, 281 F.2d 507, 517-518 (8th Cir. 1960), and Hamrick v. Commissioner, 43 T.C. 21, 32-33 (1964). Is this a distinction without a difference? Why should stock rights and warrants not be treated in the same manner as stock?

Suppose a taxpayer transfers an asset to a preexisting corporation that is wholly owned. The asset is encumbered by a nondeductible liability that exceeds the adjusted basis but is less than the fair market value of the asset. For example, the basis might be $100, the fair market value $500, and the liability $300. The transferor receives no stock in exchange for the asset. Does §351 apply, or is the transfer a contribution to capital? Why does it matter? Consider §357(c), which applies only if §351 applies. In *Lessinger,* the court applied §351 even though no stock was received by the transferor.

4.   Securities

Suppose T transfers property to X Corp. in exchange for an X Corp. debt instrument as part of a transaction that otherwise qualifies under §351. Certainly the debt instrument provides T with more continuity with the property transferred than an outright sale of the property for cash. If the transferee corporation is productive, T is more likely to be paid. Indeed, in some circumstances, a debt instrument may provide more continuity than stock. For financially disabled corporations, for example, debt owner-ship may provide greater ownership rights than stock ownership.

Until 1990, §351 granted nonrecognition upon the receipt of stock or securities (generally long-term debt instruments). The distinction between securities (i.e., qualifying property) and short-term debt (i.e., nonqualify-ing property) proved troublesome. Section 351 now draws a sharper line, providing that only the receipt of stock may qualify a transferor for nonrec-ognition treatment. Even so, it may not always be easy to determine whether a financial instrument constitutes stock or debt. See Bradshaw v. United States, page 57 infra.

Although §351 does not provide nonrecognition to a transferor who receives a debt instrument in exchange for appreciated property, it does not follow that the transferor is immediately taxable on the fair market value of the debt instrument received. See the discussion of installment reporting below.

The distinction between short-term debt and long-term securities is still important in the reorganization area. See page 476 infra.

5. Boot and Installment Reporting

In a §351 transaction, if a transferor exchanges appreciated property for a combination of debt and stock, the debt constitutes boot. If, however, the transferor simply sells the property in exchange for a debt instrument, gain from the sale might be recognized not when the sale takes place but when the debt is paid off in accordance with the installment reporting provisions. §453. Because §351 taxes the receipt of boot only to the extent of the transferor's gain, installment reporting under §453 is also available to a transferor in a §351 transaction. See Prop. Treas. Regs. §1.453-1(f)(3)(ii). For example, suppose T transfers appreciated land with a basis of $120 and a fair market value of $200 to X Corp. in a transaction that qualifies under §351. In exchange T receives $100 of stock and $100 of debt. Although the debt constitutes boot, the transferor normally is taxable on $80 of gain under §351(b) when the debtor pays off the debt rather than when the debt instrument is received. For the allocation of basis between the stock and debt, see page 39 infra.

A transferor is not always entitled to report under the installment method when property is exchanged for debt in a transaction qualifying under §351. For example, §453(g) restricts the use of the installment method if depreciable property is transferred to a corporation by a trans-feror owning more than 50 percent of the stock of the corporation. Also, §453 does not apply to transfers of inventory or property held for sale to customers or to publicly traded debt instruments received by the trans-feror. Even if installment reporting is available, §453(i) requires immediate recognition of any gain subject to depreciation recapture under §§1245 or 1250. Finally, a transferor may elect out of installment reporting (if, for example, the transferor has an expiring loss deduction that will offset the gain).

6.   Transferor's Basis

To restate our exploration to this point: Section 351 can confer nonrecognition of gain or loss on a transferor who exchanges property for stock. A transferor will, however, recognize gain on the exchange to the extent of boot received; the receipt of boot does not result in the recognition of any loss that may be realized in the exchange. Nonrecognition under §351 postpones but does not forgive realized gain. Rather, the basis provisions of §358 preserve the unrecognized gain or loss for a later date. For example, suppose T transfers property to X Corp. with a basis of $30 and a fair market value of $100 in exchange for $100 of X Corp. stock. Section 358 preserves the $70 unrecognized gain by giving T a basis of $30 in the stock received. If T sells the stock for $120, T would recognize a $90 gain, not merely the $20 appreciation in the value of the stock. If the stock is sold for $20, T would recognize a $10 loss, not the $80 loss representing the loss in stock value.

Suppose T receives a mixture of different classes of stock for the property transferred. How does T allocate basis? See §358(b) and Treas. Regs. §1.358-2(b). Not surprisingly, basis is allocated in accordance with the fair market value of the stock received. In the example above, if T receives $50 of common stock and $50 of preferred stock, T will take a basis of $15 in the common stock and $15 in the preferred stock.

Suppose in exchange for the property T receives $20 of X Corp. stock and $80 of boot in the form of cash or other property. Since T will recognize the $70 gain because it is fully covered by the boot, the basis in the stock received should and does reflect that fact. Section 358(a)(1) requires two adjustments to the taxpayer's original $30 basis. It is adjusted up to reflect the $70 gain recognized on the transfer. §358(a)(1)(B). It is adjusted down by $80 because the boot received takes a fair market value basis under §358(a)(2). §358(a)(1)(A). The result is that the taxpayer holds the stock with a fair market value of $20 and a basis of $20, reflecting the fact that the taxpayer's gain was fully recognized. If T sells the stock, the holding period includes the period during which T held the transferred property. §1223(1).

Suppose T transfers property to X Corp. with a basis of $30 and a fair market value of $100 in exchange for $20 of stock and $80 of debt in a transaction that qualifies under §351. As indicated at page 37 supra, T does not recognize gain until the notes are paid. Does this nonrecognition pose basis problems for T under §358(a)(1)(B)(ii)? See Prop. Treas. Regs.

§1.453-1(f)(3)(ii) (treating the gain as recognized solely for purposes of applying §358). The $80 of debt is boot and will be taxed to the extent of T's $70 gain. But that gain can be reported under the installment method when the debt is paid. T's $30 basis is allocated to any stock received in an amount not in excess of the fair market value of the stock (here, $20). Any remaining basis ($10) is allocated to the debt, paving the way for a $70 gain when the $80 debt instrument is paid. Prop. Treas. Regs. §1.453-1(f)(3)(ii).

In the example above, suppose T receives $70 in stock and X Corp. assumes T's $30 mortgage obligation. While the assumption does not create boot under §357(a), it is treated as cash received for purposes of the basis calculation. §358(d)(1). Therefore, T's basis in the $70 stock would be the original $30 basis minus the deemed cash received (debt assumed) of $30. The $0 basis preserves the $70 gain that goes unrecognized under §351.

Suppose instead that the assumed obligation is a deductible account payable in the amount of $50 and that T received back $50 in stock in exchange for the property transferred. Section 357(c)(3) protects T from recognizing gain on the assumption and §358(d)(2) provides that the assumption is not treated as cash for purposes of calculating basis. T, then, would take a basis of $30 in stock. The $20 gain preserved is equivalent to the $70 gain, lurking in T's original property minus the $50 deduction T would have received for satisfaction of the account payable.

7. Treatment of Transferee Corporation

What happens to the transferee corporation when it issues its stock for the property of the transferor? Section 1032 provides that the corporation does not recognize gain or loss on the receipt of property (including cash) in exchange for stock it distributes. (Section 1032 can apply ouside of the §351 context as well.) What happens if the corporation issues stock in exchange for services? See Treas. Regs. §1.1032-1(a). Can the corporation not only avoid recognition of gain but also take a deduction for compensation under §162? See Rev. Rul. 62-217, 1962-2 C.B. 59, modified by Rev. Rul. 74-503, 1974-2 C.B. 117 (deduction appropriate).

When the transferee corporation receives property in exchange for stock in a §351 transaction, §362(a) provides that the transferor's basis for the transferred property carries over to the transferee corporation. If the transferee corporation receives multiple assets, the transferor's basis in each transferred asset carries over to the corporation. See P.A. Birren & Son v. Commissioner, 116 F.2d 718 (7th Cir. 1940).

If the transferor recognized any gain on the §351 exchange, that gain increases the corporation's bases in the assets acquired. Just how the increase is allocated if the corporation receives multiple assets on the transfer is not clear. Arguments can be made for allocation using basis, fair market value, or increase in value above basis as the determining factor when looking at the transferred assets. See B. Bittker and J. Eustice, Federal Income Taxation of Corporations and Shareholders ¶3.11 (6th ed. 1994). Consistency with Rev. Rul. 68-55, page 19 supra, suggests that any gain recognized by a transferor with respect to a particular asset is allocated to that asset in the hands of the transferee corporation under §362.

If the corporation sells an asset received in a §351 transaction, it can tack on the transferor's holding period in accordance with §1223(2). If the transferred asset was subject to recapture that was not recognized on the §351 exchange, the recapture taint follows the property into the corporation (but the transferor's stock is not tainted). See Treas. Regs. §1.1245-2(c)(2).

Section 362(a) provides the transferee with the transferor's basis in the transferred property increased by gain recognized to the transferor on the exchange. If the transferor receives a debt instrument from the corporation in a §351 transaction, gain may not be recognized by the transferor until payment on the note. See discussion of §453 at page 37 supra. Does the transferee corporation increase its basis in the transferred assets by the gain *to be* recognized? Should the transferee increase its basis as gain is recognized by the transferor? Does the language of §362(a) preclude any increase in basis? See Jacobs, Something Simple: A Tax-Free Incorporation, 37 Tax L. Rev. 133, 148-153 (1983), and Prop. Treas. Regs. §1.453-1(f)(3)(ii) (transferee's basis increases as transferor recognizes gain).

Suppose that part of a transaction qualifying under §351 the transferee corporation distributes nonqualifying property (e.g., real property) with a fair market value in excess of its basis. Under §351(f), the transferee corporation must recognize gain on the §351 transfer as if the property had been sold to the shareholders. A transferee corporation may not recognize a loss if the property has a basis that is greater than its fair market value. See the discussion of §311 at page 135 infra.

D. CONTROL

Kamborian v. Commissioner _____
56 T.C. 847 (1971)

. . . FINDINGS OF FACT

1.   International Shoe Machine Corp. (International) was incorporated in Massachusetts in 1938 and at the time of the trial herein was engaged

in the business of manufacturing and leasing shoe machinery and the sale of related supplies. . . .

On September 1, 1965, prior to the transaction here in question, International's capital stock was held as follows:

	Shares of International	
		Class B
	Class A	[nonvoting]
Name	common	common
Jacob Kamborian Revocable Trust	20,324	182,916
Jacob Kamborian, Jr.	4,220	37,980
Lisabeth (Kamborian) Godley	3,620	32,580
Michael Becka	60	540
Elizabeth Kamborian Trust	5,000	45,000
Others	3,916	35,244
Total	37,140	334,260

Jacob S. Kamborian (Jacob) founded International and served as its president at all times relevant herein. Jacob S. Kamborian, Jr., and Lisabeth Kamborian Godley are the children of Jacob and his wife, Elizabeth. Michael Becka (Becka) is not related to the members of the Kamborian family. At the time of the trial herein he had been employed by International or an affiliate since at least 1943 and had served as International's executive vice president and general manager since approximately 1960. . . .

The Elizabeth Kamborian Trust (Elizabeth's trust) was established by Jacob in 1949. At about that time Jacob and Elizabeth experienced domestic difficulties; they separated for a time; and the trust was established on their reconciliation in order to provide financial security for Mrs. Kamborian. . . .

As of September 1, 1965, Becka and Lisabeth K. Godley were the trustees. Jacob had appointed them as successor trustees in 1963 and 1964, respectively. At all times relevant herein, Becka served as the managing trustee; Mrs. Godley did not live in Boston during this period; and periodically Becka informed her of the trust's activities. As of September 1, 1965, the only assets of the trust were 5,000 shares of International's class A common stock and 45,000 shares of its class B common stock.

As of September 1, 1965, International's board of directors consisted of Jacob, Jacob, Jr., Albert Kamborian (Jacob's brother), Becka, Paul Hirsch II, Harold V. Daniels, and Roy S. Flewelling.

Campex Research & Trading Corp. (Campex), a Swiss corporation with its principal place of business in Zug, Switzerland, was a patent holding and licensing company. It held primarily foreign shoe machine patents (i.e., patents not issued by the United States) and granted and administered licenses under them in a number of European countries and in Mexico. On September 1, 1965, and prior to the transaction here in question, the outstanding stock of Campex was held as follows:

Name	Shares of Campex
Jacob Kamborian Revocable Trust	39
Jacob Kamborian, Jr.	4
Lisabeth (Kamborian) Godley	4
Michael Becka	3

On September 1, 1965, the board of directors of International authorized Jacob to enter into an agreement under which (a) the owners of all of the issued and outstanding shares of Campex would exchange their stock for common stock of International and (b) "certain stockholders" of International would purchase for cash additional shares of International's common stock.

As part of the transaction it was contemplated that the Elizabeth Kamborian Trust would purchase additional shares of theretofore unissued International stock for about $5,000, so that the former owners of the Campex stock and the Elizabeth Kamborian Trust, when considered collectively and treated as transferors under section 351(a) . . . would own at least 80 percent of International's stock immediately after the transaction in an attempt to comply with the requirements of section 368(c). . . . If the Elizabeth Kamborian Trust were not taken into account, the International stock held by the former owners of Campex immediately after the transaction amounted to 77.3 percent of each class of outstanding stock of International—an amount that was insufficient to satisfy the requirements of section 368(c). . . .

International acquired Campex stock as part of its program of preparing for a public issue of its stock. On the advice of underwriters and other specialists, it was thought that ownership of foreign patents would enable International to display worldwide activities which would be of value in establishing the price of the public issue. . . . As of September 1, 1965, no date had been set for the offering and at the time of the trial herein the public offering had not yet been made. . . .

As trustee of Elizabeth's trust, Becka borrowed approximately $5,000 at an interest rate of 6 percent in order to finance the trust's purchase of the total of 418 shares of International stock on September 1, 1965. The corpus of the trust consisted exclusively of International stock, and Becka anticipated that the loan would be repaid out of dividends paid on the stock. In deciding to acquire additional International stock, Becka also anticipated that International would make a public offering which might enhance the value of the stock. Prior to the purchase of the International stock on behalf of the trust, Becka discussed his plans with both Jacob and Elizabeth. Jacob, personally and as grantor of the Jacob S. Kamborian

Revocable Trust, held a sufficient number of International shares to control the corporation and thus to determine whether it would issue additional shares. In his discussions with Elizabeth, Becka explained that because the $5,000 loan would have to be repaid out of dividends paid on the International stock held by the trust, her income from the trust would be diminished until the loan was repaid. Elizabeth told Becka to go ahead with the transaction. . . .

On their respective Federal income tax returns for 1965, petitioners reported no gain or loss stemming from the exchange of their Campex stock for International stock. . . .

OPINION

RAUM, Judge.

1. EXCHANGE OF CAMPEX STOCK FOR INTERNATIONAL STOCK

Petitioners contend that the gain they realized on their transfer of Campex stock to International in return for International's common stock qualifies for nonrecognition under section 351(a). . . . That section provides for nonrecognition of gain or loss on the transfer of property to a corporation in exchange for the corporation's stock or securities — if immediately after the exchange the transferor or transferors are "in control" of the corporation. . . .

Immediately after the exchange here in issue the stock of International was held as follows:

	Shares of —		
	Class A (voting common)	*Class B (nonvoting common)*	*Percent of total of each class*
Jacob S. Kamborian Revocable Trust	22,108	198,971	56.01
Jacob S. Kamborian, Jr.	4,403	39,627	11.16
Lisabeth (Kamborian) Godley	3,803	34,227	9.64
Michael Becka	197	1,775	.50
Elizabeth Kamborian Trust	5,042	45,376	12.77
Others	3,916	35,244	9.92
Total	39,469	355,220	

Petitioners contend that the transferors of property for purposes of section 351(a) were the five named stockholders listed above and that their percentage stockholdings after the transfer satisfy the 80-percent control requirement imposed by sections 351(a) and 368(c).

The Commissioner's position is that only the first four stockholders listed above — i.e., the former owners of Campex — may be considered as transferors of property here, that the fifth (the Elizabeth Kamborian Trust) may not be taken into account in this connection, and that since there would thus be a failure to satisfy the control requirement, all gain realized on the exchange must be recognized. In particular, he urges that International stock issued to the Elizabeth Kamborian Trust in return for $5,016 does not qualify as stock issued for property within the meaning of section 351(a) and that consequently the persons making qualified transfers of property to International in return for its stock held only 77.3 percent of its stock after the exchange. The Commissioner relies on regulations section 1.351-1(a)(1)(ii). . . .

The Commissioner contends that since the Elizabeth Kamborian Trust purchased only 42 shares of class A common and 376 shares of class B common, the securities issued were "of relatively small value" in relation to the 5,000 shares of class A common and 45,000 shares of class B common which is already held and that the primary purpose of the transfer was to qualify the exchange of Campex stock by the other stockholders for nonrecognition treatment under section 351(a).

Petitioners attack the Commissioner's position on a variety of grounds. They urge (a) that regulations section 1.351-1(a)(1)(ii) is invalid; (b) that even if valid it is inapplicable to the transaction in issue. . . .

(a) *Validity of the regulation.* Initially we note the well-settled principle that "Treasury regulations must be sustained unless unreasonable and plainly inconsistent with the revenue statutes and that they constitute contemporaneous constructions by those charged with administration of these statutes which should not be overruled except for weighty reasons." Commissioner v. South Texas Lumber Co., 333 U.S. 496, 501. . . .

Petitioners . . . contend that the regulation's reference to "property which is relatively small value in comparison to the value of stock . . . already owned" and its reliance upon the taxpayer's motive find support nowhere in the language of section 351 and that the regulation is for that reason invalid as beyond the scope of the statute. Again, we must disagree. By disqualifying certain token exchanges, the regulation is reasonably designed to exclude from the scope of section 351 transactions which comply with its requirements in form but not in substance. Far from being unreasonable or inconsistent with the statute, the regulation promotes its purpose by helping to ensure substantial compliance with the control requirement before the nonrecognition provisions become operative. In this light the absence of direct support for the regulation in the language of the statute is of minimal significance. . . . We conclude that the regulation is valid.

(b) *Applicability of the regulation.* Petitioners contend that even if it is valid, the regulation is inapplicable to the transaction here in issue. They argue first that even if Elizabeth's trust had not purchased shares of International stock, the control requirement would have been satisfied, that therefore the purchase was not necessary to meet the control requirement, and that consequently the regulation is by its own terms inapplicable. Petitioners reach this conclusion by asserting that the shares held by Becka and Lisabeth Godley as trustees of Elizabeth's trust should be attributed to them as individuals . . . and added to the shares they held personally in nonfiduciary capacities. On the basis of this premise, petitioners conclude that the 80-percent-control requirement would have been satisfied even if Elizabeth's trust had not participated in the September 1, 1965, transaction. . . . Petitioners' argument is ingenious but unacceptable, for it falters on petitioners' premise that the trust's shares may be attributed to the individual trustees. While legal title to the shares may have been in the names of the trustees, they had no beneficial interest in such shares. The distinction is not one of form but of plain economic reality. . . . In these circumstances we think the trustees' interests in the trust's shares were far too remote to justify attributing the shares to them for purposes of section 351. . . .

Petitioners also contend that the primary purpose for the trust's acquisition of International's stock was not to qualify the other stockholders' exchanges under section 351 and that for this reason the regulation is inapplicable. We note at the outset that the regulation does not make it entirely clear whose purpose is to be taken into account. However, both parties have assumed that the purpose of the transferor of property is critical. The language of the regulation (which appears to distinguish between a "transfer" of property and the issuance of stock) supports their assumption, and we shall therefore proceed on this basis. Although Elizabeth's trust was technically the transferor herein, the parties have also assumed that Becka's purpose is critical in this respect — apparently on the ground that as the managing trustee he was primarily responsible for the decision to make the purchase of International stock. We shall proceed on the basis of this assumption as well.

The question of Becka's primary purpose is one of fact, cf. Malat v. Riddell, 383 U.S. 569, and after a review of all the evidence we conclude that his primary purpose was to qualify the other stockholders' exchanges under section 351. We note in particular that at about the time of the transaction, Jacob was ill and Becka was in charge of International's affairs, that in planning the acquisition Becka participated in lengthy discussions with regard to planning the transaction as a tax-free exchange, and that both the vote of International's board of directors and the agreement of September 1, 1965, treated the purchase by Elizabeth's trust and the exchange of Campex stock by the other stockholders as component parts of an integrated transaction avowedly designed to meet the 80-percent-control requirement and thereby qualify for nonrecognition treatment under section 351.

At the trial herein, Becka testified that if the trust had not participated in the transaction, the issue of International stock to the other major stockholders would have diluted the trust's percentage interest in International and that he authorized the purchase of International stock in order to minimize such dilution. In particular he testified that the total percentage stock interest held by the trust and the two Kamborian children exceeded 33⅓ percent and that preservation of that interest protected Mrs. Kamborian against the making of certain corporate decisions (requiring a two-thirds majority) without her consent. . . . We do not give his testimony very much weight, however. The record does not establish whether or why the children were regarded as allies of Mrs. Kamborian rather than as allies of her husband. Moreover, the trust's participation in the transaction left them with an aggregate stock interest of 33.57 percent — only 0.08 of 1 percent more than they would have held if the trust had not purchased any additional shares.

Becka also testified that he authorized the purchase of the stock because it was a "good investment." While he may well have taken this into account in making his decision, the record leaves us convinced that the purchase was made primarily to qualify the exchanges by the other stockholders (one of whom was Becka himself) . . . under section 351. We conclude that section 1.351-1(a)(1)(ii) is applicable. . . .

Decisions will be entered under Rule 50.

Intermountain Lumber Co. v. Commissioner _____
65 T.C. 1025 (1976)

WILES, Judge. . . .

The only issue for decision is whether a certain corporate formation was nontaxable under section 351(a). . . . This depends solely upon whether the primary incorporator had "control" of the requisite percentage of stock immediately after the exchange within the meaning of section 368(c).

FINDINGS OF FACT

From 1948 until March of 1964, Mr. Dee Shook (hereinafter Shook) individually owned a sawmill at Conner, Mont. During that time Mr. Milo Wilson (hereinafter Wilson) had logs processed there into rough lumber for a fee. Shook owned the remaining logs processed at the sawmill, which constituted about half of all the logs processed there.

From 1954 until March of 1964, rough lumber from the sawmill was processed into finished lumber at a separate finishing plant which Shook and Wilson owned as equal shareholders.

In March of 1964, fire damaged the sawmill. Shook and Wilson wanted to replace it with a larger one so that the finishing plant could operate at full capacity. Shook was financially unable, however, to do so. He accordingly induced Wilson to personally coguarantee a $200,000 loan to provide financing. In return, Wilson insisted upon an equal voice in rebuilding the sawmill and upon an opportunity to become an equal shareholder with Shook in the new sawmill.

On May 28, 1964, Shook, Wilson, and two other individuals, all acting as incorporators, executed articles of incorporation for S&W Sawmill, Inc. (hereinafter S&W). . . .

Minutes of the first stockholders meeting on July 7, 1964, stated in part that "Mr. Shook informed the meeting that a separate agreement was being prepared between he and Mr. Wilson providing for the sale of one-half of his stock to Mr. Wilson." Also on that date, 1 share was issued to each of the other two incorporators.

Shook executed a bill of sale for his sawmill equipment and deeded his sawmill site to S&W on July 15 and 16, 1964, respectively. In exchange, Shook received 364 S&W shares on July 15, 1964. Shook and Wilson also received 1 share each as incorporators. The 364 shares and the 4 incorporation shares constituted all outstanding capital stock of S&W on July 15, 1964.

Also on that date, minutes of a special meeting stated in part that "The President, Dee Shook, announced that he and Milo E. Wilson had entered into an agreement whereby Mr. Wilson was to purchase 182 shares of Mr. Shook's stock." That agreement, dated July 15, 1964, and entitled "Agreement for Sale and Purchase of Stock" (hereinafter agreement for sale) provided in part as follows:

[I]t is the intention of all the incorporators that Shook and Wilson are to be the owners of the majority of the stock of said corporation;

AND WHEREAS, it is the desire and plan of both parties hereto that a sufficient number of shares of stock be sold by Shook to Wilson so that eventually the stock ownership would be equal;

AND WHEREAS, the purchase of said shares of stock by Wilson from Shook is to be financed by a series of payments;

IT IS THEREFORE AGREED, that for and in consideration of the covenants to be performed and the payments to be made as hereinafter set forth, the sale and purchase of said stock is to be as follows:

1.   Dee Shook is to sell to Milo E. Wilson 182 shares of stock in S&W SAWMILL, INC. for the agreed price of $500.00 per share.

2.   Wilson is to pay Shook for said stock as follows:

Interest on unpaid balance due is to be paid annually at 3% per annum from August 1, 1964 to July 31, 1968.

Interest on unpaid balance due is to be paid annually at 4% per annum from August 1, 1968, to July 31, 1970.

Interest on unpaid balance due is to be paid annually at 5% per annum from August 1, 1970, until entire balance is paid in full.

In addition to interest $6,000.00 on the principal is due November 1, 1969.

In addition to interest, $15,000.00 on the principal is due annually, beginning Nov. 1, 1970, and continuing until the entire purchase price is paid. The payments may be made in advance at any time and in any amount.

3.   As each principal payment is made the proportionate number of shares of stock are to be transferred on the corporate records and delivered to Wilson.

4.   In the event any payment of principal is not made on the due date, or within 90 days thereafter, Wilson thereby forfeits and loses his right to purchase that proportionate number of shares of stock; PROVIDED HOW-EVER, that nevertheless any subsequent, or later payment of principal may be made according to the above payment schedule, and thereupon Wilson will be entitled to the proportionate number of shares of stock as represented by such payment. Interest payment must always be kept current before any delivery of stock is to be made resulting from a payment of principal.

5.   For the period of one year from the date hereof Wilson is to have the full power to vote all of the stock herein agreed to be sold to him by Shook. Thereafter the voting rights of the stock is (sic) to be determined by the stock ownership records of the corporation.

On July 15, 1964, Shook also executed an irrevocable proxy granting to Wilson voting rights in 182 shares until September 10, 1965. Two other documents also executed on that date related to share ownership between Shook and Wilson. One, entitled "S&W Sawmill, Inc. Stockholders' Restrictive Agreement," provided in part as follows:

[S]uch provisions (against stock transferability) do not apply to the presently existing Agreement for Sale and Purchase of Stock entered into between Dee Shook and Milo E. Wilson, dated the 15th day of July, 1964, and providing for the purchase by Milo E. Wilson of 182 shares of stock in the company.

IT IS THE INTENTION AND PURPOSE of the incorporators that the majority of the ownership of the corporation is to be held by Dee Shook and Milo E. Wilson on an equal share basis when Milo E. Wilson completes the purchase of the stock certificates which are the subject of said purchase agreement. The other, entitled "Option to Buy Stock Forming Part Of Stockholders' Restrictive Agreement," provided in part that "the ownership of shares in S&W Sawmill, Inc., as the same now stands, to-wit: Dee Shook 365 shares, Milo E. Wilson 1 shares (sic) . . . shall continue."

In connection with the agreement for sale, Shook deposited stock certificates representing 182 shares with an escrow agent on July 17, 1964.

On August 19, 1964, S&W borrowed $200,000, in part upon the personal guarantees of Shook, Wilson, and their wives. The loan agreement referred to Shook and Wilson as "the principal officers and stockholders" of S&W. S&W agreed therein to insure the lives of Shook and Wilson for $100,000 each.

On March 19, 1965, Shook and Wilson agreed to purchase additional shares from S&W in an agreement which provided in part as follows:

Witnesseth

THAT WHEREAS, Prior to this date stock in the Corporation had been purchased by the Stockholders and a number of said shares are subject to an escrow agreement at Citizens State Bank, Hamilton, Montana, providing for the purchase by Milo E. Wilson of a certain number of shares of such stock from Dee Shook; that the purpose of said escrow arrangement is to provide for an equal ownership of the stock of said Corporation by Milo E. Wilson and Dee Shook;

THAT WHEREAS, it is the desire of all parties at this time that each of the Stockholders purchase an additional One Hundred Shares of Stock at Five Hundred Dollars ($500.00) per share, and payment for the same having been made to the Corporation;

NOW, THEREFORE, for and in consideration of the mutual benefits to be derived by all parties hereto, IT IS HEREBY AGREED AS FOLLOWS:

That each of the Stockholders are to purchase One Hundred Shares of stock of the Corporation at Five Hundred Dollars ($500.00) per share;

That, as well as with other stock purchases, it is the desire of the Stockholders that stock ownership held by Dee Shook and Milo E. Wilson are to remain equal; that any stock purchased or issued as a result of this agreement is to be regulated accordingly. . . .

Wilson made all payments in 1965 and 1966 specified in the agreement for sale and accordingly claimed interest deductions on his Federal income tax returns for those years.

On July 1, 1967, before principal payments were required by the agreement for sale, petitioner purchased all outstanding S&W stock. In anticipation of this purchase, a letter to petitioner dated May 3, 1967, and signed by Shook and Wilson stated as follows:

To have it in the record, Milo E. Wilson owes Dee Shook $91,000 for 182 shares of S&W Sawmill Inc. stock in escrow at Citizens State Bank Hamilton Montana. On the purchase contract, Intermountain Lumber Co. would pay Dee Shook $91,000.00 more over the 14 yrs. than Milo E. Wilson.

OPINION . . .

In this case, respondent is in the unusual posture of arguing that a transfer to a corporation in return for stock was nontaxable under section 351, and Intermountain is in the equally unusual posture of arguing that the transfer was taxable because section 351 was inapplicable. The explanation is simply that Intermountain purchased all stock of the corporation, S&W, from its incorporators, and that Intermountain and S&W have filed consolidated income tax returns for years in issue. Accordingly, if section 351 was applicable to the incorporators when S&W was formed, S&W and Intermountain must depreciate the assets of S&W on their consolidated returns on the incorporators' basis. Sec. 362(a). If section 351 was inapplicable, and the transfer of assets to S&W was accordingly to be treated as a sale, S&W and Intermountain could base depreciation on those returns on the fair market value of those assets at the time of incorporation, which was higher than the incorporators' cost and which would accordingly provide larger depreciation deductions. . . .

Petitioner thus maintains that the transfer to S&W of all of S&W's property at the time of incorporation by the primary incorporator, one Dee Shook, was a taxable sale. It asserts that section 351 was inapplicable because an agreement for sale required Shook, as part of the incorporation transaction, to sell almost half of the S&W shares outstanding to one Milo Wilson over a period of time, thereby depriving Shook of the requisite percentage of stock necessary for "control" of S&W immediately after the exchange.

Respondent, on the other hand, maintains that the agreement between Shook and Wilson did not deprive Shook of ownership of the shares immediately after the exchange, as the stock purchase agreement merely gave Wilson an option to purchase the shares. Shook accordingly was in "control" of the corporation and the exchange was thus nontaxable under section 351.

Respondent has abandoned on brief his contention that Wilson was a transferor of property and therefore a person to also be counted for purposes of control under section 351. Respondent is correct in doing so, since Wilson did not transfer any property to S&W upon its initial formation in July of 1964. Wilson's agreement to transfer cash for corporate stock in March of 1965 cannot be considered part of the same transaction.

Since Wilson was not a transferor of property and therefore cannot be counted for control under section 351, William A. James, 53 T.C. 63, 69 (1969), we must determine if Shook alone owned the requisite percentage of shares for control. This determination depends upon whether, under all facts and circumstances surrounding the agreement for sale of 182 shares between Shook and Wilson, ownership of those shares was in Shook or Wilson.

A determination of "ownership," as that term is used in section 368(c) and for purposes of control under section 351, depends upon the obligations and freedom of action of the transferee with respect to the stock when he acquired it from the corporation. Such traditional ownership attributes as legal title, voting rights, and possession of stock certificates are not conclusive. If the transferee, as part of the transaction by which the shares were acquired, has irrevocably foregone or relinquished at that time the legal right to determine whether to keep the shares, ownership in such shares is lacking for purposes of section 351. By contrast, if there are no restrictions upon freedom of action at the time he acquired the shares, it is immaterial how soon thereafter the transferee elects to dispose of his stock or whether such disposition is in accord with a preconceived plan not amounting to a binding obligation. Stephens, Inc. v. United States, 464 F.2d 53, 66-67 (8th Cir. 1972), cert. denied 409 U.S. 1118 (1973). . . . After considering the entire record, we have concluded that Shook and Wilson intended to consummate a sale of the S&W stock, that they never doubted that the sale would be completed, that the sale was an integral part of the incorporation transaction, and that they considered themselves to be co-owners of S&W upon execution of the stock purchase agreement in 1964. These conclusions are supported by minutes of the first stockholders meeting on July 7, 1964, at which Shook characterized the agreement for sale as a "sale"; minutes of a special meeting on July 15, 1964, at which Shook stated Wilson was to "purchase" half of Shook's stock; the "Agreement for Sale and Purchase of Stock" itself, dated July 15, 1964, which is drawn as an installment sale and which provides for payment of interest on unpaid principal; Wilson's deduction of interest expenses in connection with the agreement for sale, which would be inconsistent with an option; the S&W loan agreement, in which Shook and Wilson held themselves out as the "principal stockholders" of S&W and in which S&W covenanted to equally insure Shook and Wilson for $100,000; the March 1965 stock purchase agreement with S&W, which indicated that Shook and Wilson "are to remain equal" shareholders in S&W; the letter of May 1967 from Shook and Wilson to Intermountain, which indicated that Wilson owed Shook the principal balance due on the shares as an unpaid obligation; and all surrounding facts and circumstances leading to corporate formation and execution of the above documents. Inconsistent and self-serving testimony of Shook and Wilson regarding their intent and understanding of the documents in evidence is unpersuasive in view of the record as a whole to alter interpretation of the transaction as a sale of stock by Shook to Wilson.

We accordingly cannot accept respondent's contention that the substance varied from the form of this transaction, which was, of course, labeled a "sale." The parties executed an "option" agreement on the same day that the "agreement for sale" was executed, and we have no doubt that they could and indeed did correctly distinguish between a sale and an option.

The agreement for sale's forfeiture clause, which provided that Wilson forfeited the right to purchase a proportionate number of shares for which timely principal payments were not made, did not convert it into an option agreement. Furthermore, the agreement for sale made no provision for forgiving interest payments on the remaining principal due should principal payments not be made on earlier dates; indeed, it specifically provided that "Interest payment must always be kept current before any delivery of stock is to be made resulting from a payment of principal."

We thus believe that Shook, as part of the same transaction by which the shares were acquired (indeed, the agreement for sale was executed before the sawmill was deeded to S&W), had relinquished when he acquired those shares the legal right to determine whether to keep them. Shook was under an obligation, upon receipt of the shares, to transfer the stock as he received Wilson's principal payments. Cf. S. Klein on the Square, Inc., 14 T.C. 786, 790 (1950), aff'd 188 F.2d 127 (2d Cir. 1951), cert. denied 342 U.S. 824 (1951). We note also that the agreement for sale gave Wilson the right to prepay principal and receive all 182 shares at any time in advance. Shook therefore did not own, within the meaning of section 368(c), the requisite percentage of stock immediately after the exchange to control the corporation as required for nontaxable treatment under section 351.

We note also that the basic premise of section 351 is to avoid recognition of gain or loss resulting from transfer of property to a corporation which works a change of form only. . . . Accordingly, if the transferor sells his stock as part of the same transaction, the transaction is taxable because there has been more than a mere change in form. In this case, the transferor agreed to sell and did sell 50 percent of the stock to be received, placed the certificates in the possession of an escrow agent, and granted a binding proxy to the purchaser to vote the stock being sold. Far more than a mere change in form was effected.

We accordingly hold for petitioner. Because of concessions of other issues, decisions will be entered under Rule 155.

NOTE

1. *Definition of "control."* Nonrecognition under §351 is available only if the transferors of property are in control of the transferee immediately after the transfer. Section 368(c) provides two 80 percent tests in determining control: the ownership of at least 80 percent of the total combined voting power of all classes of stock entitled to vote and 80 percent of all other classes of stock. The determination of control is made by looking at the number of shares rather than the value of the corporation's shares. Suppose after a purported §351 transfer, the transferors own 90 percent of the voting stock, 70 percent of the class A nonvoting preferred and 90 percent of the class B nonvoting preferred, for an overall 83 percent interest in the total preferred outstanding. Do they have control? Compare the language of §368(c) with Rev. Rul. 59-259, 1959-2 C.B. 115 (voting stock classes combined in applying 80 percent test, but 80 percent test applies separately to *each* class of nonvoting stock).

Suppose *T* transfers property to *X* Corp. in exchange for stock in a transaction that appears to qualify under §351 because *T* receives back 80 percent of the *X* Corp. stock. As part of a prearranged plan, *X* Corp. then transfers the assets to its subsidiary, Sub Corp., in a §351 transaction that results in *X* Corp.'s owning 80 percent of the stock of Sub Corp.; 20 percent is owned by outside shareholders. The result is that *T* owns 64 percent (80 percent of an 80 percent interest) of Sub Corp., which holds *T*'s original assets. In Rev. Rul. 83-34, 1983-1 C.B. 79, the Service ruled that §351 does apply to a taxpayer in *T*'s position.

2. *Who is in the "control" group?* As *Kamborian* indicates, an exchange can qualify under §351 even though the transferors do not *acquire* control in the exchange itself. Rather, the transferors can include previously owned stock in satisfying the 80 percent requirement. The problem in *Kamborian* was the amount being transferred by the Elizabeth Kamborian Trust relative to its existing holdings. The trust transferred $5,000 for new stock while it owned almost $600,000 in preexisting stock. If the receipt of stock in an amount less than 1 percent of the value of existing stock is not enough for an accommodation transferor, what *is* the magical amount? In Rev. Proc. 77-37, 1977-2 C.B. 568, the Service stated that for advance ruling purposes, property will not be considered "of relatively small value" within the meaning of Treas. Regs. §1.351-1(a)(1)(ii) if it equals at least 10 percent of the value of stock or securities already owned by the transferor, or to be received for services by the transferor. In *Kamborian,* if the Elizabeth Kamborian trust had purchased $60,000 of additional stock, could the transferor group have included all the trust's stock in the 80 percent calculations?

3. *Unbalanced exchanges.* In *Kamborian* the taxpayer also argued that Treas. Regs. §1.351-1(a)(1)(ii) was invalid because it supposedly adopted a "proportionate interest" test repudiated by Congress in 1954. Section 351 dropped the requirement contained in its predecessor, §112(b)(5) of the 1939 Code, that "in the case of an exchange by two or more persons this paragraph shall apply only if the amount of the stock . . . received by each is substantially in proportion to his interest in the property prior to the exchange." This clause gave rise to difficult questions of valuation as well as to conflicting opinions on how the proportion of change was to be calculated and on what constituted a "substantial" change. Moreover, the purpose of the requirement was obscure.

Though abandoning the proportionate interest requirement, the Code points out that an exchange may have the effect of a gift or of the payment of compensation. §351(g)(3) and (g)(4); Treas. Regs. §1.351-1(b). See also Rev. Rul. 76-454, 1976-2 C.B. 102, in which *T* and his wholly owned subsidiary, *X* Corp., formed *Y* Corp. with *T* receiving a disproportionate amount of stock for the property transferred; held, recharacterized to give *T* and *X* each a proportionate number of shares, followed by a taxable dividend by *X* of the "excess" *Y* stock. What would be the result if *X* had received and retained more than its share of the *Y* stock?

4. *Immediately after.* Section 351 requires that the transferors be in control of the corporation "immediately after the exchange." See Treas.

Regs. §1.351-1(a)(1). *Intermountain* typifies much of the litigation over this term. Most of the cases involve situations where the transferors are momentarily in control of the transferee but thereafter dispose of enough shares to bring the transferor group below the 80 percent requirement.

Notice the litigation posture in *Intermountain*. The taxpayer argued that §351 did not apply, while the Service argued that the nonrecognition provision did apply. Why? Why did the Service care who won the case? If §351 was inapplicable, then Shook should have been taxed on the formation of the corporation. (Presumably, he already had paid a tax on the gain associated with his sale of stock to Wilson.) Can't the Service send him a notice of deficiency for the tax on the gain associated with the stock not sold to Wilson? Is there a statute of limitations problem with the original transfer by Shook that doesn't exist when the Service challenges Intermountain's current depreciation deductions? Consider §§1311-1314, particularly §1312(7). Why else might the Service have litigated *Intermountain*? A disparity in tax rates applicable to Intermountain and Shook? Perhaps Shook's gain would have produced a capital gain, while Intermountain's stepped-up basis produces larger depreciation deductions to offset ordinary income? But see §1239.

The court ruled in favor of the taxpayer because of the preconceived plan for Shook to sell stock to Wilson. But why don't Shook and Wilson together satisfy the control test? Suppose Wilson purchased 20 shares from the corporation when it was first incorporated and then purchased the remainder of his half interest from Shook? Would Wilson be considered a transferor? See page 53 supra, discussing accommodation transferors. Suppose Wilson had transferred his personal note to the corporation in exchange for half of the stock when it was first incorporated. See Lessinger v. Commissioner, page 26 supra.

In Rev. Rul. 79-194, 1979-1 C.B. 145, *B* and *C* transfer property to Newco in exchange for 80 percent and 20 percent of the Newco stock, respectively. Pursuant to a prearranged plan, *B* sells 31 percent of the outstanding stock to *C*, leaving *B* with 49 percent and *C* with 51 percent. Under this fact pattern, the Service ruled that *C* would be considered a transferor and that *B* and *C* as a transferor group would satisfy the control requirement of §351(a) and §368(c). Suppose instead that on the original transfer, *B* received 99 percent of the outstanding stock and *C*, 1 percent, both amounts determined in accordance with value of the property transferred. Pursuant to a prearranged plan, *B* sells 50 percent of the outstanding Newco stock to *C*, leaving *B* with 49 percent and *C* with 51 percent. Relying on Treas. Regs. §1.351-1(a)(1)(ii), the Service ruled that *C* would not qualify as a transferor. Because *B* did not own the requisite 80 percent immediately after the exchange, §351 was inapplicable.

The "immediately after" problem arises in the context of the pervasive step transaction doctrine, examined in more detail on page 347 infra.

That doctrine will sometimes be applied to integrate more than one transaction into a single, unified transaction. *T*'s receipt of control in a purported §351 exchange will sometimes be integrated with a postacquisition sale of stock to spoil nonrecognition treatment. The test most often applied to integrate two transactions is the "mutual interdependence" test. (*Query:* Can there be nonmutual interdependence?) One court stated the test: "Were the steps so interdependent that the legal relations created by one transaction would have been fruitless without a completion of the series?" American Bantam Car Co. v. Commissioner, 11 T.C. 397, 405 (1948), aff'd, 177 F.2d 513 (3d Cir. 1949). The Tax Court, while articulating the mutual interdependence test, refused to integrate steps in the absence of a preexisting binding commitment by the transferors to sell the stock received in McDonald's of Zion, Ill., Inc. v. Commissioner, 76 T.C. 972 (1981), rev'd sub nom. McDonald's Restaurants of Ill., Inc. v. Commissioner, 688 F.2d 520 (7th Cir. 1982). See page 424 infra.

In ascertaining whether steps are interdependent, the amount of time between transactions can be important. If the steps are contemporaneous or separated by short time intervals, courts are more likely to integrate the steps. See American Bantam Car v. Commissioner, supra. But compare Commissioner v. Ashland Oil & Refining Co., 99 F.2d 588 (6th Cir. 1938), cert. denied, 306 U.S. 661 (1939) (steps that occurred six years apart integrated), with Henricksen v. Braicks, 137 F.2d 632 (9th Cir. 1943) (transactions one half-hour apart treated as separate).

In a special statutory rule, Congress has determined that fleeting control is insignificant. Section 351(c) specifically allows corporate transferors to distribute the stock received to their shareholders without violating the control requirement. Does this restricted exception suggest that fleeting control is insufficient where the special rule is inapplicable?

Suppose instead of a transfer followed by a sale, there is a transfer followed by a gift. Is the time factor important? Wilgard Realty Co. v. Commissioner, 127 F.2d 514 (2d Cir. 1942), involved a transfer of appreciated property by an individual to a corporation in exchange for all its stock. Immediately after the stock was issued to him, he transferred more than 20 percent of it by gift to members of his family. On a later sale of the transferred property, the corporation claimed a stepped-up basis on the ground that the incorporation failed the control test and therefore that §351 was inapplicable. The court held that §351 was applicable since the transferor was not legally bound to make a gift. In contrast, the court in Florida Machine & Foundry Co. v. Fahs, 168 F.2d 957 (5th Cir. 1948), ruled that §351 did not apply when more than 20 percent of the shares were issued directly to the transferor's son even though the transferor may have been under an obligation to make the gift. See also Mojonnier & Sons v. Commissioner, 12 T.C. 837 (1949). But see Stanton v. United States, 512 F.2d 13 (3d Cir. 1975), and D'Angelo Associates v. Commissioner, 70

T.C. 121 (1978), rejecting a distinction in gift cases based on whether the donee receives stock directly from the transferee or from the transferor.

Until this point the focus has been on an attempted §351 transaction followed by a sale or gift of the stock received. The "immediately after" issue also arises when soon after the exchange, the transferee corporation issues additional stock. In American Bantam Car Co. v. Commissioner, supra, the transferors transferred assets to the corporation in exchange for common stock. The plan also called for a sale of preferred shares to the public through underwriters who were to get more than 20 percent of the common shares if they sold the preferred. Four months later, the underwriters sold the preferred and received the common shares. The court held §351 applicable by ruling that control existed after the exchange and that a later loss of control was not an integral part of the transaction since the exchange itself would have taken place even if the plan for the public sale of the preferred had failed.

The Service has clarified the area somewhat in Rev. Rul. 78-294, 1978-2 C.B. 141, in which two situations were presented. In each a sole proprietor who needed additional capital decided to incorporate and increase capital by a public offering of stock. In the first situation, the incorporator, the corporation, and the underwriter agreed that the underwriter would use its best efforts to sell 50 percent of the stock directly to the public, and, in fact, it did so within two weeks after the offering. The Service ruled that for the control test of §368(c) the public investors who purchased the shares should be treated along with the incorporator as transferors. In the second situation, the corporation's contract for the sale of 50 percent of the shares with the underwriter was a "firm commitment" underwriting, so that if the underwriter was not successful in selling the shares the underwriter was obliged to retain them. The Service ruled that the underwriter and the incorporator were the transferors who together had all the shares, therefore satisfying the control test and §351.

For a good analysis of the problem, see Tillinghast & Paully, The Effect of the Collateral Issuance of Stock or Securities on the Control Requirement of Section 351, 37 Tax L. Rev. 251 (1982).

E. INTERACTION OF §351 WITH OTHER CODE SECTIONS AND LEGAL DOCTRINES

Section 351 does not operate in a vacuum. Other code provisions and legal doctrines may affect the application of the provision. Indeed, there are a variety of situations where a taxpayer envisions more favorable treatment by seeking to avoid §351. In the two cases that follow, the taxpayers tried to avoid the nonrecognition of §351. Why? As you read, try to determine why one taxpayer was successful while the other was not.

Bradshaw v. United States* ⎯⎯⎯⎯⎯⎯⎯⎯⎯⎯⎯⎯⎯⎯⎯⎯⎯⎯
683 F.2d 365 (Ct. Cl. 1982)

OPINION

BENNETT, Judge.
Both parties agree that there are only two questions for decision. The first is whether the transfer of real property to Castlewood, a [wholly owned] corporation, in exchange for installment obligations was a sale of the property to that corporation or, instead, was either a transfer of property to a controlled corporation solely in exchange for stock . . . of that corporation within the meaning of section 351 or a capital contribution to that corporation. [Discussion of second question omitted].

We find that the transfer of real property to Castlewood in exchange for installment obligations was a sale rather than a transfer governed by section 351 or a capital contribution. . . . Accordingly, we hold for the plaintiffs and against the defendant for the reasons hereafter stated.

I

On January 6, 1961, Thomas E. Swift (Thomas) purchased a tract of land, consisting of approximately 200 acres, in Dalton, Whitfield County, Georgia, for $60,000. Two dispositions of property out of this 200 acres were made by Thomas in the summer of 1968. The consolidated cases herein concern one of these dispositions, the transfer of 40.427 acres, subsequently known as Castlewood Subdivision (the subdivision), to Castlewood [Inc.] on July 29, 1968. The conservative fair market value of the subdivision on the date of transfer was $250,000. Thomas' adjusted basis in this portion of the property was $8,538. In exchange for the transfer, Thomas received from Castlewood five promissory notes (the Castlewood notes), each in the principal amount of $50,000 and bearing interest at the rate of 4 percent per annum. The first note matured on January 29, 1971, with each successive note maturing at 1-year intervals. Thomas received no down payment for the transfer, and no security or other collateral was taken for the purchase price. He elected to report his gain from the transaction on the installment method pursuant to section 453(b).

At the time of transfer, various opportunities were available to Thomas to dispose of the subdivision, including sale to third parties. While he had

⎯⎯⎯⎯⎯⎯⎯⎯
* Bradshaw, a party to the consolidated action, is not affected by this part of the court's opinion. — EDS.

not developed property himself, Thomas was highly expert in real estate matters in the Dalton area. Based upon this knowledge, including knowledge of sales of other real estate in the vicinity of the subdivision, Thomas evaluated the prospects for the development of the subdivision to be bright, whether such development was undertaken by himself, by a corporation that he might organize, or by a third party. He considered the alternative opportunities available to him to dispose of the property and decided to develop the property himself through a corporation rather than sell it to a third party.

Consequently, Castlewood was organized and incorporated on July 29, 1968, under the laws of the State of Georgia, to obtain, subdivide, develop and sell lots in the subdivision. On July 29, 1968, Castlewood issued its Certificate No. 1, representing 50 shares of common stock, to Thomas in exchange for the transfer to the corporation of an automobile valued at $4,500. At all times relevant herein, Thomas was the sole shareholder of Castlewood and was responsible for conducting its business affairs. His expertise was available to and utilized by the corporation in its development of the subdivision, enabling it to minimize development costs and thus increase profits. . . .

Castlewood subdivided the subdivision into two tracts. . . . From August 1970 to April 1973, Castlewood sold 16 lots in Tract I and two lots in Tract II for an aggregate sales price of $239,880. It did not advertise the sale of these lots, use realtors, or pay sales commissions. The property sold had an allocated land cost (of the $250,000 purchase price) and development cost of $159,378.39, yielding a net return to the corporation of $80,501.11. Castlewood reported sales of lots on its federal income tax returns for the fiscal years ended July 31, 1971, July 31, 1972, and July 31, 1973. . . .

By statutory notice of deficiency dated September 20, 1976, the Commissioner determined that additional income tax was due from Castlewood for its 1971 and 1972 tax years, for the reason that the transfer of the subdivision to that corporation by Thomas was not a sale, as treated by the corporation on its tax returns, but rather a transfer of property solely in exchange for stock . . . within the meaning of section 351. Thus, he concluded that, pursuant to section 362, Castlewood's predevelopment basis in the property was equal to that of the transferor immediately before the transfer, or $8,538. This, in turn, increased Castlewood's taxable income on sales of lots. Additionally, the Commissioner concluded that no debtor-creditor relationship was established between Castlewood and Thomas, thereby disallowing certain deductions of interest paid . . . on the notes taken for the purchase price of the property. . . .

II

The first question concerns the proper tax treatment of Thomas' transfer of the subdivision to Castlewood in exchange for the five $50,000 promissory notes. If the transfer is treated as a sale, as plaintiff contends, then Castlewood's adjusted basis for its sales of the lots from the subdivision property would include the $250,000 purchase price (a cost basis), it would be allowed deductions of the interest paid on the notes and its taxable income would be generally as shown on its returns for the years in issue. However, if, as defendant claims, the transfer was not a sale but was either a transfer under section 351 or a contribution to the corporation's capital, then Castlewood's adjusted basis in the lots sold would be reduced to Thomas' original basis (a carryover basis) pursuant to section 362, it would be denied deductions of the interest paid on the notes and its taxable income would be generally as shown on the notice of deficiency issued with respect to it. The sale versus capital contribution problem arises from a situation which often confronts taxpayers with holdings in undeveloped real estate. It is not uncommon for a landowner with a large tract of land suitable for development to want to freeze as capital gain the appreciation in the value of the property that has accrued during its ownership. While an outright sale of the property achieves this result, it also deprives the landowner of any participation in the profits to be reaped from its ultimate development. On the other hand, if the landowner develops and sells the property himself, he runs the risk of being treated as a dealer of the property and any gain generated through sales, including the gain associated with the land's appreciation in value while undeveloped, is taxable to him at ordinary income rates. See, e.g., . . . Suburban Realty Co. v. United States, 615 F.2d 171 (5th Cir.), cert. denied, 449 U.S. 920 (1980).

In the face of such a dilemma, taxpayers have devised an apparently viable solution. By selling the real property to a controlled corporation, they can realize their capital gain on the appreciation which has accrued during their ownership and, at the same time, preserve their opportunity to later participate in the developmental profits as shareholders of the development corporation. Moreover, the corporation obtains a cost basis in the real property, thereby reducing the amount of ordinary income to be received from subsequent sales.

Not unexpectedly, the Commissioner has repeatedly challenged the characterization of such a transaction as a sale, instead maintaining that the transfer is, in reality, a capital contribution and that the transferee corporation is only entitled to a carryover basis for the property. See, e.g., Burr Oaks Corp. v. Commissioner, 365 F.2d 24 (7th Cir. 1966), cert. denied, 385 U.S. 1007 (1967); Aqualane Shores, Inc. v. Commissioner, 269 F.2d 116 (5th Cir. 1959). The two principal reasons asserted for denying the desired tax treatment to the corporation have their origin in the dual subparts of section 362(a). While the main thesis is that section 351 governs such a transaction and that the corporation's basis for the property is to be determined pursuant to section 362(a)(1), it is also maintained that, regardless of the applicability of section 351, the transfer to the corporation is, in substance, a contribution to capital and that the adjusted basis for the property is to be determined under section 362(a)(2). . . .

The proper characterization of a transaction, as a "sale" or a "capital contribution," is a question of fact to be decided as of the time of the transfer on the basis of all of the objective evidence. Gooding Amusement Co. v. Commissioner, 236 F.2d 159, 165 (6th Cir. 1956), cert. denied, 352 U.S. 1031 (1957). While the form of the transaction is relevant, we are required to examine all of the pertinent factors in order to determine whether the substance of the transaction complies with its form. Gregory v. Helvering, 293 U.S. 465, 469-70 (1935). The essential nature of the transaction is to be determined from a consideration of all of the surrounding circumstances. Piedmont Corp. v. Commissioner, 388 F.2d 886, 889 (4th Cir. 1968).

In this case, the objective evidence points to a sale. First, and foremost, the price paid for the subdivision reflected its actual fair market value. Since it has been stipulated that the value of the subdivision was $250,000, the very amount for which it was sold to Castlewood, the transfer cannot be considered a "pretextuous device" to divert the earnings and profits of the corporation, otherwise taxable as ordinary income, into sales proceeds taxable as capital gain. Piedmont Corp. v. Commissioner, 388 F.2d 886, 889 (4th Cir. 1968). The sales price did not constitute an inflated value for the property, and, thus, did not represent an attempt to transfer to Thomas any subsequent capital increment in the value of the property, nor any of the gain from its development. In this respect, the transfer was clearly a sale.

Additionally, the various formalities of a sale were strictly observed. The five instruments involved constituted negotiable instruments in the form of "notes" under Georgia law . . . , contained an unqualified obligation to pay the principal amount, with fixed maturity dates ranging from two and one-half to six and one-half years after the date of sale and bore a reasonable rate of interest. The notes were not subordinated to general corporate creditors and contained a means for collection at maturity, which was never utilized as the principal and interest were always paid as due until the Commissioner challenged the tax treatment of those payments. On these bases, the notes contained all of the traditional elements of sales-generated debt.

Even so, defendant asks that upon consideration of the economic substance of the transfer, the transaction be recast as a capital contribution. This is so, we are told, because Congress has dictated that no tax consequences shall attach to a transaction where direct ownership of property is changed into indirect ownership through a proprietary interest in a corporation. Thus, where the circumstances of a purported sale demonstrate that the transferor, in fact, retained a continuing interest in the property transferred, the transaction is more appropriately characterized as a capital contribution.

Defendant calls our attention to an alleged factual pattern to be discerned in those instances where it has been determined that the economic substance of a purported sale was actually a contribution to capital. In such cases, it is claimed, a newly formed, inadequately capitalized corporation received assets which were essential to its purpose, and which required at the outset substantial improvements to convert them into income-producing property. Whereas, in those cases holding that the transaction resulted in a sale, the transfer involved proven, income-producing assets. Defendant submits that the distinction drawn in these cases turns on the nature and degree of risk inherent in the transfer of unproven assets and that in such instances, because of the high degree of risk, the transferor is likely to have retained a continuing interest in the property transferred.

In the present case, defendant maintains, unproven real property was transferred to an untried, undercapitalized business in return for notes, which were to be satisfied from the proceeds expected to be generated through the sale of lots. From this, defendant urges that we conclude that the notes represented a continuing interest in the corporate business, for repayment was totally dependent upon the success of the enterprise.

We cannot quarrel with the policies underlying section 351, nor with its intended scope. However, even accepting defendant's premise that the prior cases can be meaningfully differentiated along the lines suggested, we are unable to agree with the conclusion defendant draws in this case. Rephrasing defendant's position, we are asked to find that the degree of risk herein was of the type normally associated with a capital contribution. Thus stated, the salient inquiry is whether the notes occupied the position of equity, the assets and prospects of the business being unable to assure payment of the debt according to its terms.

Admittedly, the stipulated facts show Castlewood to have been a "thin" corporation. Its initial capitalization consisted entirely of an automobile valued at $4,500. The corporation then issued five notes, each in the face amount of $50,000, in consideration for the subdivision property. While an additional $3,200 was contributed to Castlewood 4 months later, in practical terms it had no funds of its own with which to conduct business. . . . It cannot be refuted that Castlewood had a very high ratio of debt to equity. But the mere fact that a corporation is or is not thinly capitalized does not, per se, control the character of the transaction. See Gyro Eng. Corp. v. United States, 417 F.2d 437, 439 (9th Cir. 1969). . . . As these cases demonstrate, if the corporation is adequately capitalized for its intended purpose, then we are not prevented from treating the notes as valid debt.

The facts reveal that in addition to its formal capitalization, Castlewood anticipated having access to, did have access to, and utilized funds in the form of loans from C&S, the partnership owned by Thomas and his family, which served as Thomas' personal bank account. Castlewood also had access to an important resource in the expertise Thomas brought to the business, which allowed the corporation to minimize its development expenses. See Murphy Logging Co. v. United States, 378 F.2d 222, 224 (9th Cir. 1967). Given these resources, which were certainly adequate to finance the level of development activities undertaken, and the absence of any need to employ advertising or to use realtors, there was little reason for the corporation to maintain a large surplus of liquid capital. Under the circumstances, we cannot say that undercapitalization is fatal to plaintiff's position.

Integrally related to this discussion, as defendant recognizes, is the nature or quality of the risk assumed by the transferor. However, unlike defendant, we do not find the fact that what was sold to Castlewood was unimproved real estate to be necessarily indicative of a high degree of risk. Concomitantly, nor do we view repayment of the Castlewood notes to have been dependent upon the success of the business. Under the stipulated facts of this case, at the time of transfer, because of the character and location of the subdivision, there was a reasonable anticipation that the development of the property would succeed and yield a profit. And, as planned, the subdivision was developed, a cash flow generated and the notes paid, with interest, as due. . . . Moreover, at all times the value of the property was increasing, irrespective of its development, and, if necessary, the corporation could have borrowed the money against the property to pay off the notes. Clearly, it was always within Castlewood's ability to make payment as required. To be sure, as with any new venture, there was some risk of loss; but the evidence manifests that such risk was significantly reduced in this case. From the beginning, there existed a reasonable assurance of repayment of the notes regardless of the success of the business. To us, this is further indicia that the notes were debt, not equity. The facts just do not support the inference that, in holding the Castlewood notes, Thomas was assuming the risk of loss normally associated with equity participation.

We are referred by defendant to, among others, Burr Oaks Corp. v. Commissioner, 365 F.2d 24 (7th Cir. 1966), cert. denied, 385 U.S. 1007 (1967), and Aqualane Shores, Inc. v. Commissioner, 269 F.2d 116 (5th Cir. 1959), two of the leading decisions to hold a purported sale to be a contribution to capital. In *Burr Oaks,* undeveloped land, intended for subdivision, was transferred to a newly formed corporation for more than twice its fair market value. In exchange therefor, the transferors received back 2-year promissory notes. Development costs ran extremely high and sales of lots were, at best, slow. Consequently, the notes were only partially paid at maturity and new notes were given for the unpaid balance. Moreover, some of the property was eventually retransferred to the noteholders at little or no cost. On these facts, the Seventh Circuit had no difficulty affirming the decision of the Tax Court, finding a strong inference that the transfer was an equity contribution where "payment to the transferors [was] dependent on the success of an untried undercapitalized business with uncertain prospects." 365 F.2d at 27. In *Aqualane Shores,* the land transferred to the development corporation was mangrove swamp. Thus, vast improvements were essential to its successful development, which, even then, was highly speculative. With its only source of revenue being the sale of lots, the corporation was forced to borrow substantial amounts of money in order to put the land in marketable condition. No payments on the notes taken back for the land were made for 4 years after maturity. On this basis, payment of the obligations to the transferors was deemed to be dependent upon and at the risk of the success of the venture, and the transfer subject to . . . the predecessor to section 351. 269 F.2d at 119-20.

The evidentiary basis of the present case, as previously set forth, contrasts sharply with these decisions. Unlike either case, the prospects for financial success were bright, such success was realized, and the corporation was always able to meet its obligations as they matured. Moreover, the promise of repayment was never in jeopardy, for the properties' self-liquidating potential guaranteed that repayment of the notes would not be subject to the fortunes of the business. In all major respects, the present case is more analogous to Piedmont Corp. v. Commissioner, 388 F.2d 886 (4th Cir. 1968), than to either *Burr Oaks* or *Aqualane Shores. Piedmont* involved successive transfers of options to purchase real property to a controlled corporation in exchange for unsecured promissory notes. The Fourth Circuit considered *Burr Oaks* and *Aqualane Shores,* but found both to be distinguishable. In reversing the decision of the Tax Court that the transfers were in effect a contribution to capital, the following were held to be determinative: (1) the facts indicated "some degree of certainty to the financial success of the venture"; (2) "a fair purchase price was paid"; (3) the corporation "paid the interest and installments of principal when due, promptly and regularly"; and (4) the corporation "did not retransfer any portion of any option, or any land which it acquired by exercise of an option" to the noteholders. Thereupon, the court concluded that "an evidentiary basis to disregard the purported sales as bona fide sales [was] lacking." 388 F.2d at 890-91.

These same factors appear in this case and, accordingly, we choose to be guided in our deliberations by *Piedmont,* rather than by *Burr Oaks* or *Aqualane Shores.* As supported by the record and confirmed by *Piedmont,* the transfer was in substance, as well as in form, a sale and not a capital contribution.

Defendant's remaining contention is that, notwithstanding a determination that the Castlewood notes were valid debt, the subject transaction falls within the literal provisions of section 351. . . .

We have already given our reasons as to why the Castlewood notes did not constitute a continuing proprietary interest in Castlewood and we will not repeat them here.

[The court's discussion of other issues including whether the notes constituted "securities" under then existing law is omitted.]

C-lec Plastics v. Commissioner _____
76 T.C. 601 (1981)

DRENNEN, Judge. . . .
The only issue for our decision is, for purposes of section 165(a),
. . . to determine petitioner's adjusted basis in certain plastic molds and
rings which were destroyed by fire.

FINDINGS OF FACT . . .

Edward D. Walsh (hereinafter Walsh) was the president and sole shareholder of petitioner at all times relevant herein.
Prior to May 31, 1970, petitioner, through the individual efforts of
Walsh, created certain property which was used or sold to perform a contract with Physics International. The property consisted of 1 pattern mold,
3 master molds, 50 molds, 48 lite rings, and 1 plastic ring. (Hereinafter,
this property will be referred to collectively as the molds.) The cost involved
in creating the molds was deducted on petitioner's income tax return for
its taxable year ended May 31, 1970.
On or about February 29, 1972, petitioner terminated the lease of
its business premises and abandoned the molds along with various other
properties. On or about the same date, Walsh took possession and acquired
ownership of the abandoned molds. Walsh's basis in the molds for Federal
income tax purposes and for purposes of this proceeding was at all times
zero.
As of May 31, 1973, petitioner's bank account was overdrawn and it
was in a cash-poor financial position. As of that date, petitioner's books
and records showed that it owed $53,785.16 to Walsh. . . .
In early 1973, events occurred which indicated that a new market
could emerge for products made with the molds and, thus, it became
advantageous for petitioner to reacquire the molds.
On June 1, 1973, a special meeting of petitioner's board of directors was held. The corporate minutes of that meeting provide in pertinent
part: . . .

> The Corporation in exchange for the molds and rings would issue common
> stock at the rate of $80.00 per share. If this proposal is accepted, Edward
> Walsh will purchase additional common stock to round the issuance to 500
> shares and permit the Corporation to reduce the officers' loan account
> liability by $2,982.23. . . .

On or about June 1, 1973, Walsh reconveyed possession and ownership
of the molds. At the same time, petitioner issued an additional 500 shares
of common stock to Walsh. Additionally, a net reduction of $2,982.23 was

made in the loan account. Walsh did not receive any cash or monetary consideration, nor any note or evidence of indebtedness from petitioner at the time he reconveyed the molds to petitioner; nor did petitioner pay Walsh any interest.

By journal entry in petitioner's books dated December 31, 1973, petitioner's acquisition of the molds was recorded by: (1) A debit of $37,017.77 in the research and development account; (2) a debit of $2,982.23 in the loan account; and (3) a credit of $40,000 in the common stock issued account. . . .

The molds were destroyed by fire on December 1, 1973. . . .

In the statutory notice of deficiency, respondent determined that petitioner had an adjusted basis of zero in the molds and, thus, was not entitled to any casualty loss deduction for the molds.

Walsh did not report any income arising out of his reconveyance of the molds to petitioner on his individual income tax returns for 1973, or any subsequent year.

OPINION

Section 165(a) allows a deduction for any loss sustained during the taxable year which is not compensated for by insurance or otherwise. There is no dispute that the molds were destroyed by fire, that no compensation was received or receivable therefor, and that any loss thereon is properly deductible under section 165(a). The only issue to be decided is the amount of that loss. Section 165(b) provides that the amount of the deductible loss is measured by the taxpayer's adjusted basis in the property as provided for in section 1011. See also sec. 1.165-7(b), Income Tax Regs. Thus, a determination of petitioner's adjusted basis in the molds is required. . . .

Petitioner argues that the general rule of sections 1011 and 1012 applies, resulting in an adjusted basis of $37,017.77 in the molds, because petitioner did not exchange its common stock for the molds but rather purchased the molds in an arm's-length transaction.

Based on the testimony of its only witness, Robert E. Williams (hereinafter Williams), petitioner's accountant, petitioner contends that on or about June 1, 1973, there were two separate transactions which were entered into for separate and different reasons. One transaction involved petitioner's issuance of $40,000 in common stock to Walsh in consideration for a like-amount debit to the loan account. This was done, petitioner contends, to improve its capital structure and preclude any allegation that it was thinly capitalized.

The second transaction was the purchase of the molds for the cash equivalent of a $37,017.77 credit to the loan account, which amount was in fact paid to Walsh by the conclusion of petitioner's taxable year ended May 31, 1976, at which time the loan account was zero. This purchase, petitioner contends, brings into operation the general rule of sections 1011 and 1012.

Petitioner explains the seemingly inconsistent December 31, 1973, journal entry concerning the acquisition of the molds, as an example of the "common practice" in recordkeeping, whereby the two transactions were "compounded" in one book entry and only the "net effect" thereof was shown. Similarly, petitioner explains the seemingly inconsistent corporate minutes of the special board of directors' meeting as the work of an unsophisticated corporate secretary who also only recorded the "net effect" of the two transactions.

In opposition to petitioner's contentions, respondent argues that the corporate minutes and books and records indicate that the only transaction was an exchange of the common stock for the molds and an incidental amount of cash (in the form of a debit to the loan account) and that such a transaction falls within the purview of section 351. Accordingly, since Walsh recognized no gain on the transfer, petitioner took Walsh's zero basis in the molds pursuant to section 362(a).

It has long been a principle of Federal income tax law that a transaction's substance rather than its form controls. See, e.g., Commissioner v. Court Holding Co., 324 U.S. 331 (1945); Minnesota Tea Co. v. Helvering, 302 U.S. 609 (1938); Gregory v. Helvering, 293 U.S. 465 (1935). . . .

Williams testified that Walsh approached him seeking advice as to effecting petitioner's acquisition of the molds from Walsh. Petitioner's cash-poor financial position precluded an outright cash purchase. Given petitioner's then-existing debt to Walsh in the amount of $53,785.16, Williams also considered it inadvisable for petitioner to purchase the molds solely on credit by increasing the amount it owed to Walsh. Williams testified that he accordingly recommended that petitioner issue $40,000 of common stock to Walsh in exchange for a $40,000 reduction in the loan account and that the petitioner then "purchase" the molds for $37,017.77 by increasing the loan account in an equal amount.

The only possible conclusion that can be drawn from Williams' testimony is that the two transactions were not separable but were two steps of an integrated whole. The impetus for both transactions was the need for petitioner to acquire the molds and there is nothing to suggest that one transaction would have been effected without the other. In substance, petitioner acquired the molds, and reduced its loan account in the amount of $2,982.23, and Walsh received an additional $40,000 in common stock. Despite the accountant's explanation of his "compounded" book entries, the book entries reflect precisely the action taken by the board of directors as reflected in the minutes of their meeting on June 1, 1973. Under these circumstances, to view the acquisition of the molds as a purchase for cash would be to ignore the best evidence of what was actually intended and what took place. That the transaction was "arm's length" in the sense that $37,017.77 may have been a reasonable price for the molds does not alter the basic substance of the transaction as an exchange of common stock for the molds. Moreover, it is of no import that petitioner did not intend for the transaction to qualify under section 351; that provision applies regardless of petitioner's intent. . . .

In this case, the evidence shows that both the substance and the form of the transaction support our conclusion that the molds were exchanged solely for petitioner's common stock and that the transaction falls within the purview of section 351. Thus, section 362 would apply and petitioner's adjusted basis in the molds would be the same as Walsh's, increased by any gain recognized by Walsh.

Furthermore, we do not believe it is necessary in resolving the issue presented to determine whether there were two transactions or one. Even if there were two transactions, it is clear that they were integrated components of a single whole, the substance of which was that petitioner acquired the molds and Walsh only received common stock. . . .

In summary, the carryover basis provision of section 362 results in petitioner's having an adjusted basis of zero in the molds, thereby precluding any casualty loss deduction under section 165.

Decision will be entered for the respondent.

NOTE

1. *Section 351 versus sale.* Section 351 by its terms is not an elective provision. Taxpayers, however, sometimes deliberately fail to comply with the formalities of §351 when noncompliance is to their benefit. Notice in *Bradshaw* that the formation of the corporation and the purported sale took place on the same day. In *C-lec Plastics* the issuance of stock and the purported sale also took place on the same day. Why was one taxpayer successful and the other unsuccessful in the quest to avoid §351 and its carryover basis provisions? Are formalities important?

Could the taxpayer in *C-lec Plastics* have argued that the tangible property transferred (i.e., the molds) embodied the transferor's services and must be so treated for §351 purposes? See the discussion of *James* at page 11 supra. If the molds were not considered property for §351 purposes, how would that determination have helped the taxpayer?

In Kolkey v. Commissioner, 27 T.C. 37 (1956), aff'd, 254 F.2d 51 (7th Cir. 1958), the Tax Court established criteria for making the sale/§351 distinction:

Was the capital and credit structure of the new corporation realistic? What was the business purpose, if any, of organizing the new corporation? Were the noteholders the actual promoters and entrepreneurs of the new adventure? Did the noteholders bear the principal risks of loss attendant upon the adventure? Were payments of "principal and interest" on the notes subordinated to dividends and to the claims of creditors? Did the noteholders have substantial control over the business operations; and, if so, was such control reserved to them as an integral part of the plan under which the notes were issued? Was the "price" of the properties, for which the notes were issued disproportionate to the fair market value of such properties? Did the noteholders, when default of the notes occurred, attempt to enforce the obligations?

In the following cases the court ruled that an attempted sale was a §351 transfer, thereby denying a stepped-up basis to the transferee for the reasons indicated: Hayutin v. Commissioner, 508 F.2d 462 (10th Cir. 1974) (undercapitalization, subordinated debt, excessive purchase price); Burr Oaks Corp. v. Commissioner, 365 F.2d 24 (7th Cir. 1966) (undercapitalization, speculative repayment of purported indebtedness); Nye v. Commissioner, 50 T.C. 203 (1968) (no business reason for separating attempted sale from §351 transfer).

Sale characterization was respected in the following: Murphy Logging Co. v. Commissioner, 378 F.2d 222 (9th Cir. 1967) (despite unfavorable capitalization and a tax avoidance purpose); Piedmont v. Commissioner, 388 F.2d 886 (4th Cir. 1968) (notes bore reasonable interest, were not subordinated, and were paid).

Under §1239, any gain recognized by a transferor on the sale or exchange of property between certain related persons constitutes ordinary income if such property is depreciable in the hands of the transferee. For purposes of §1239, a person is deemed related to a corporation if the transferor owns, directly or indirectly, 50 percent or more of the value of the corporation's outstanding stock. Why didn't §1239 foil the taxpayer's attempt in *Bradshaw* to lock in a capital gain on the transfer of the real property to the transferee corporation? Consider whether the property was depreciable in the hands of the transferee corporation. See §§1221(1) and 167(a).

Receipt of a stepped-up basis by the transferee is only one reason to prefer a sale over §351. A transferor of property with an unrealized loss may seek recognition unavailable through §351. Even if a sale transaction is respected, the transferor must navigate §267, which prevents a loss deduction on a sale by an individual to a corporation, where the transferor directly or indirectly owns more than 50 percent in value of the outstanding stock of the enterprise. See also Higgins v. Smith, 308 U.S. 473 (1940), which may support a judicial expansion of §267.

One reason for a transfer like that in *Bradshaw* is that the tax rate at the corporate level may be less than the rate at the individual level. But even if the applicable corporate tax rate is higher than the tax rate that would apply to an individual, will we still observe transactions like that in *Bradshaw*? Tax rates are not the only consideration. The corporate form offers nontax advantages such as limited liability and perhaps easier access to financial markets. The use of a subchapter S corporation might provide use of the corporate form with individual tax rates. See Chapter 16.

From a tax standpoint, when would a sale to a corporation be preferable to a §351 transaction? There are a host of reasons why a sale may be more advantageous, aside from a lower tax rate at the corporate level. First, if the taxpayer has capital losses, those losses can offset only up to $3,000 of ordinary income. §1211(a). By selling appreciated property to a corporation, a taxpayer can generate a capital gain that will be fully absorbed by the capital losses. Even if the capital gain is not fully offset with corporate losses, an individual taxpayer may prefer the preferential capital gains tax rate to the higher ordinary income rates that would apply if the taxpayer developed and sold the property in parcels. See §1201. Another reason for a *Bradshaw*-type transaction might be an expectation of increased ordinary income rates in the future. A taxpayer might want to lock in a capital gain now rather than risk a higher ordinary income tax at a later point. Or a taxpayer might be willing to recognize gain on a sale in order to provide the purchasing corporation with a stepped-up basis under §1012, particularly if the taxpayer can postpone recognition through installment reporting.

2.   *Contributions to capital by shareholders.* In *Bradshaw* the Service argued that the attempted sale was a contribution to capital. Had the Service prevailed, what would the consequences have been? Section 118 shields a corporation from recognition of income for contributions to the corporation's capital. The corporation's basis for the new capital is determined under §362(a) for transfers by shareholders. As explained in the following Note, §362(c) provides a special rule for contributions "not contributed by a shareholder as such."

The shareholder who contributes capital does not recognize gain or loss on the contribution and can increase stock basis by the property contributed. Treas. Regs. §1.118-1. Should the basis increase be measured by the basis or fair market value of the property contributed?

Notice what would happen in *Bradshaw* and similar cases if the notes received by the "seller" are ignored because they are too speculative. Payments of what would otherwise be interest will be reclassified as dividends. What difference would this make to the recipient? How about the payor? What happens when the corporation "retires the debt"? Normally, the recipient would have no income or perhaps a capital gain. §1271(a). Now the recipient faces the possibility of ordinary income treatment on a failed redemption. See §302(d), discussed at page 186 infra.

The same consequences may befall a transferor and transferee on any occasion where debt is reclassified as stock. See discussion of the debt-equity issue at pages 92-116 infra.

3.   *"Contributions" to the capital of a corporation by nonshareholders.* Over the years, there has been confusion over the treatment to be accorded contributions by governmental agencies, community groups, and private persons to business to encourage or assist the business in providing or expanding a service. The cases involve two basic issues for the recipient:

(1) Is the contribution income? (2) Does the use of the contribution give rise to any tax benefits, such as a deduction for current expenses or a depreciation deduction? The payment also creates tax issues for the contributor. If the contributor is a business and it subsidizes a railroad to extend service to a new area, is the grant a current business deduction or a capital expenditure? If a capital item, it would ordinarily be recovered through a series of deductions over time — that is, depreciation deductions — unless it will last indefinitely (like land). In the latter event there would be no deduction until the recipient sells the land. If the grantor is a charity, grants to private businesses to accomplish the aims of the charity, such as the prevention of community deterioration or providing new employment opportunities, might endanger its exemption.

The exclusion from income of nonshareholder contributions to capital derives from Edwards v. Cuba Railroad Co., 268 U.S. 628 (1925), in which the Court held that government subsidies to a railroad to induce the construction of railroad facilities were not taxable income within the meaning of the sixteenth amendment.

Since 1954 the Code has provided in §118 that gross income does not include any "contribution to capital," thus implicitly recognizing that contributions to capital can be received from nonshareholders. The general rule of §362(a) is that the corporation takes as its tax basis for the property given to it the same basis that the transferor had. Section 362(c), however, provides that contributions by nonshareholders take a zero basis.

Prior to the enactment of §362(c), it was possible under the 1939 Code for the recipient of funds from nonshareholders to receive a double tax benefit. First, the amounts received were not recognized as income; second, the taxpayer was allowed to claim depreciation deductions on the contributor's basis. See Detroit Edison Co. v. Commissioner, 318 U.S. 98 (1943), and United States v. Chicago, Burlington & Quincy Railroad, 339 U.S. 583 (1950), permitting the depreciation. Section 362(c) laid to rest the depreciation issue by providing a zero basis for nonshareholder contributions to capital, but the issue still remains of what is a receipt of taxable income versus a nontaxable contribution to capital by a nonshareholder.

The 1954 codification, via §118, intended as an incorporation of existing decisional law relating to contributions to capital of corporations, was designed to deal with those transfers to a corporation that fall in the gray area between genuine gifts, on the one hand, and payments clearly for direct future services, on the other hand. The legislative history speaks of contributions to capital, as in the case where "the contributor expects to derive indirect benefits, the contribution cannot be called a gift; yet the anticipated future benefits may also be so intangible as to not warrant treating the contributions as a payment for future services." S. Rep. No. 1622, to accompany H.R. 8300 (Pub. L. No. 591), 83d Cong., 2d Sess. 18-19 (1954). See also Treas. Regs. §1.118-1.

The inquiry into the transferor's anticipated benefits was made in Federated Department Stores v. Commissioner, 51 T.C. 500 (1968), aff'd, 426 F.2d 417 (6th Cir. 1970), where it was found that the contribution of money and land by a developer to induce a department store to move into a new shopping center provided only indirect and intangible benefits to the developer; therefore, a tax-free contribution of capital was found. Accord, May Department Stores Co. v. Commissioner, 33 T.C.M. (CCH) 1128 (1974), aff'd per curiam, 519 F.2d 1154 (8th Cir. 1975). But when payments have a reasonable connection with services that are the recipient corporation's business to provide, amounts received are treated as taxable income. John B. White, Inc. v. Commissioner, 55 T.C. 729 (1971), aff'd per curiam, 458 F.2d 989 (3d Cir. 1972) (subsidies from Ford Motor Co. to Ford automobile dealer to induce dealer to move showroom to new location were taxable income). The cases are not easily reconcilable. See Teleservice of Wyoming Valley v. Commissioner, 27 T.C. 722 (1957), aff'd, 254 F.2d 105 (3d Cir. 1958) (payments from prospective customers to finance construction costs to corporation operating community television antenna system were taxable income).

Sometimes receipts can be eliminated from income under what has been known as the conduit theory. In Seven Up Co. v. Commissioner, 14 T.C. 965 (1950), a soft-drink manufacturer received funds from bottlers who voluntarily contributed for an advertising campaign. The manufacturer was held to be a mere conduit for the funds, holding them solely as a trustee and required to disburse them for a specific purpose to benefit the bottlers. Therefore, the funds were not income to the manufacturer under §61. Accord, Ford Dealers Advertising Fund v. Commissioner, 55 T.C. 761 (1971), aff'd per curiam, 456 F.2d 255 (5th Cir. 1972). If the history of these cases seems confusing, see the concluding sentence of Judge Tannenwald's opinion in State Farm Road Corp., 65 T.C. 217 (1975), that in this area "a page of logic is worth a volume of history," taking note of Justice Holmes's statement that normally "a page of history is worth a volume of logic," New York Trust Co. v. Eisner, 256 U.S. 345, 349 (1921).

Section 118(b) provides no exclusion for contributions "in aid of construction or any other contribution as a customer or potential customer." The new provision reverses some of the prior cases, including Edwards v. Cuba Railroad Co., supra, which gave birth to §118.

Hempt Bros., Inc. v. United States ————————————
490 F.2d 1172 (3d Cir. 1974)

ALDISERT, Circuit Judge.

[A cash basis partnership transferred its assets to a newly formed corporation in exchange for all the corporation's stock in a transaction qualifying under §351. Among the transferred assets were $662,820 in accounts receivable with a $0 basis. The Service argued that the corporation, whose basis was $0 under §362, should recognize gain when the receivables were paid off. The taxpayer argued that the transferor partnership should have been taxed, a result that was precluded by the applicable statute of limitations.]

I

Taxpayer argues here, as it did in the district court, that because the term "property" as used in Section 351 does not embrace accounts receivable, the Commissioner lacked statutory authority to apply principles associated with Section 351. The district court properly rejected the legal interpretation urged by the taxpayer.

The definition of Section 351 "property" has been extensively treated by the Court of Claims in E. I. DuPont de Nemours and Co. v. United States, 471 F.2d 1211, 1218-19 (Ct. Cl. 1973), describing the transfer of a non-exclusive license to make, use and sell area herbicides under French patents:

> Unless there is some special reason intrinsic to [Section 351] the general word "property" has a broad reach in tax law. . . . For section 351, in particular, courts have advocated a generous definition of "property," . . . and it has been suggested in one capital gains case that nonexclusive licenses can be viewed as property though not as capital assets. . . .

We see no adequate reason for refusing to follow these leads.

We fail to perceive any special reason why a restrictive meaning should be applied to accounts receivable so as to exclude them from the general meaning of "property." Receivables possess the usual capabilities and attributes associated with jurisprudential concepts of property law. They may be identified, valued, and transferred. Moreover, their role in an ongoing business must be viewed in the context of Section 351 application. The presence of accounts receivable is a normal, rather than an exceptional accoutrement of the type of business included by Congress in the transfer to a corporate form. . . .

The taxpayer next makes a strenuous argument that "[the] government is seeking to tax the wrong person." It contends that the assignment of income doctrine as developed by the Supreme Court applies to a Section 351 transfer of accounts receivable so that the transferor, not the transferee-corporation, bears the corresponding tax liability. It argues that the assignment of income doctrine dictates that where the right to receive income is transferred to another person in a transaction not giving rise to tax at the time of transfer, the transferor is taxed on the income when it is collected by the transferee; that the only requirement for its application is a transfer of a right to receive ordinary income; and that since the transferred accounts receivable are a present right to future income, the sole requirement for the application of the doctrine is squarely met. In essence, this is a contention that the nonrecognition provision of Section 351 is in conflict with the assignment of income doctrine and that Section 351 should be subordinated thereto. Taxpayer relies on the seminal case of Lucas v. Earl, 281 U.S. 111 (1930), and its progeny for support of its proposition that the application of the doctrine is mandated whenever one transfers a right to receive ordinary income.

On its part, the government concedes that a taxpayer may sell for value a claim to income otherwise his own and he will be taxable upon the proceeds of the sale. Such was the case in Commissioner v. P. G. Lake, Inc., 356 U.S. 260 (1958), in which the taxpayer-corporation assigned its oil payment right to its president in consideration for his cancellation of a $600,000 loan. Viewing the oil payment right as a right to receive future income, the Court applied the reasoning of the assignment of income doctrine, normally applicable to a gratuitous assignment, and held that the consideration received by the taxpayer-corporation was taxable as ordinary income since it essentially was a substitute for that which would otherwise be received at a future time as ordinary income.

Turning to the facts of this case, we note that here there was the transfer of accounts receivable from the partnership to the corporation pursuant to Section 351. We view these accounts receivable as a present right to receive future income. In consideration of the transfer of this right, the members of the partnership received stock — a valid consideration. The consideration, therefore, was essentially a substitute for that which would otherwise be received at a future time as ordinary income to the cash basis partnership. Consequently, the holding in *Lake* would normally apply, and income would ordinarily be realized, and thereby taxable, by the cash basis partnership-transferor at the time of receipt of the stock.

But the terms and purpose of Section 351 have to be reckoned with. By its explicit terms Section 351 expresses the Congressional intent that transfers of property for stock or securities will not result in recognition. It therefore becomes apparent that this case vividly illustrates how Section 351 sometimes comes into conflict with another provision of the Internal Revenue Code or a judicial doctrine, and requires a determination of which of two conflicting doctrines will control. . . .

While we cannot fault the general principle ''that income be taxed to him who earns it,'' to adopt taxpayer's argument would be to hamper the incorporation of ongoing businesses; additionally it would impose technical constructions which are economically and practically unsound. None of the cases cited by taxpayer, including *Lake* itself, persuades us otherwise. In *Lake* the Court was required to decide whether the proceeds from the assignment of the oil payment right were taxable as ordinary income or as long term capital gains. Observing that the provision for long term capital gains treatment ''has always been narrowly construed so as to protect the revenue against artful devices," 356 U.S. at 265, the Court predicated its holding upon an emphatic distinction between a conversion of a capital investment — "income-producing property" — and an assignment of income per se. "The substance of what was assigned was the right to receive future income. The substance of what was received was the present value of income which the recipient would otherwise obtain in the future." Ibid., at 266. A Section 351 issue was not presented in *Lake*. Therefore the case does not control in weighing the conflict between the general rule of assignment of income and the Congressional purpose of nonrecognition upon the incorporation of an ongoing business.

We are persuaded that, on balance, the teachings of *Lake* must give way in this case to the broad Congressional interest in facilitating the incorporation of ongoing businesses. As desirable as it is to afford symmetry in revenue law, we do not intend to promulgate a hard and fast rule. We believe that the problems posed by the clash of conflicting internal revenue doctrines are more properly determined by the circumstances of each case. Here we are influenced by the fact that the subject of the assignment was accounts receivable for partnership's goods and services sold in the regular course of business, that the change of business form from partnership to corporation had a basic business purpose and was not designed for the purpose of deliberate tax avoidance, and by the conviction that the totality of circumstances here presented fit the mold of the Congressional intent to give nonrecognition to a transfer of a total business from a noncorporate to a corporate form.

But this too must be said. Even though Section 351(a) immunizes the transferor from immediate tax consequences, Section 358 retains for the transferors a potential income tax liability to be realized and recognized upon a subsequent sale or exchange of the stock certificates received. As to the transferee-corporation, the tax basis of the receivables will be governed by Section 362. . . .

NOTE

1. *Assignment of income.* Nonrecognition under §351 can clash with the well-entrenched assignment of income doctrine developed through a series of Supreme Court cases. See, e.g., Lucas v. Earl, 281 U.S. 111 (1930); Helvering v. Horst, 311 U.S. 112 (1940). We have already seen that the transfer by a cash basis transferor of accounts receivable to a corporation will not trigger recognition at the time of the exchange if the standards of §351 are met. See page 26 supra. A decision reached on this point does not necessarily foreclose the recognition of income by the transferor *when the transferee collects*. Nevertheless, in transactions in which the assets of a going business are incorporated, courts have generally declined to invoke the assignment of income doctrine on collection by the transferee.

In contrast to *Hempt Bros., Inc.,* consider Brown v. Commissioner, 115 F.2d 337 (2d Cir. 1940). There, an attorney brought a lawsuit to collect fees for services rendered. A few months before settling the suit, he transferred the claim to a wholly owned corporation whose only asset was the claim and whose only purpose was to facilitate collection. Under these circumstances the court ruled that the transferor was taxable on the collection of the claim by the transferee. See also Weinberg v. Commissioner, 44 T.C. 233 (1965), aff'd per curiam, 386 F.2d 836 (9th Cir. 1967), where the court treated a sale of growing crops by a newly formed corporation as a sale by the shareholder-transferors who had made the transfer shortly before harvest.

In Rev. Rul. 80-198, 1980-2 C.B. 113, the Service approved of the results in both *Hempt* and *Brown,* citing a business purpose for incorporation, or lack thereof, as determinative.

Notice that in the usual assignment of income situation, a taxpayer who assigns away income from the performance of services avoids taxation of that income. However, when the transferors in *Hempt* transfer the receivables to the transferee corporation, the assignment is not complete. Not only is the transferee corporation taxable when the receivables are collected, but the transferors will also be taxed when the transferee corporation distributes the proceeds (or when the transferors sell their stock, the basis of which reflects the $0 basis in a cash basis taxpayer's accounts receivable). Perhaps it is the corporate double tax that underlies the court's willingness to sidestep the application of Lucas v. Earl in a §351 transaction.

2.   *Tax benefit rule.* In Nash v. United States, 398 U.S. 1 (1970), accrual basis transferors exchanged receivables for stock. The Supreme Court held that there had been no "recovery" of a previously deducted bad debt reserve sufficient to trigger recognition by the transferors. In *Nash* the value of the stock received equaled the value of the receivables minus the bad debt reserve. If the value of the stock received exceeds the value of the property exchanged, the *Nash* rationale may not save the transferor from recognition under the tax benefit doctrine. See United States v. Bliss Dairy, 460 U.S. 370 (1983).

3.   *Business purpose.* This ubiquitous doctrine will sometimes be invoked to ignore a purported §351 transfer. For example, in Rev. Rul. 60-331, 1960-2 C.B. 189, the Service disregarded an attempted transfer of stock in one corporation on which a dividend was due to a second corporation to try to qualify for the dividends-received deduction of §243. See also West Coast Marketing Corp. v. Commissioner, 46 T.C. 32 (1966), in which the court disregarded the formation of a corporation solely for the purpose of qualifying the subsequent exchange of stock for nonrecognition under the reorganization provisions when the direct exchange of property would have subjected the transferor to capital gains treatment.

4.   *Clear reflection of income.* In addition to judicially created doctrines, the Service has several statutory weapons in its arsenal. In Palmer v. Com-

missioner, 267 F.2d 434 (9th Cir. 1959), an individual taxpayer in the construction business, who had been reporting income on the completed contract method, transferred the business to a corporation shortly after a large payment was due for work done prior to the transfer. The court upheld the Commissioner's adjustment under §446(b), putting the transferor on the percentage of completion method of accounting, thereby allocating a large part of the income back to the taxpayer. See also Shore v. Commissioner, 631 F.2d 624 (9th Cir. 1980) (incorporation triggered §481 recognition).

In Rooney v. United States, 305 F.2d 681 (9th Cir. 1962), a husband and wife's farming business was incorporated under §351 after the transferors had taken deductions pertaining to the crop transferred. Employing §482, the court held that the deductions for business expenses could be denied to the transferors and allocated to the corporation, to be matched with the subsequently realized income to which the expenses related. For further discussion of §482, see page 658 infra.

5.   *Organizational expenses.* Besides issuing stock, a new corporation must contend with a host of expenditures incident to its formation, such as legal fees for drafting the charter, bylaws, and stock certificates; accounting fees; expenses for the organizational meeting of directors or stockholders; and fees paid to the state of incorporation. Section 248 permits a corporation to elect to amortize such "organizational expenses" over a period of 60 months or more. For a definition of "organizational expenditures," see §248(b) and Treas. Regs. §1.248-1(b)(2). Expenditures incurred in the process of raising capital — such as commissions and printing costs — are excluded from the reach of §248. Why? If the corporation does not elect to amortize under §248, presumably organizational expenses can be deducted in the year the corporation dissolves. See Bryant Heater Co. v. Commissioner, 231 F.2d 938 (6th Cir. 1956).

6.   *Section 351 and redemptions.* For the interplay among §§351, 302, and 304, see page 267 infra.

7.   *Section 351 and reorganizations.* There is an overlap between §351 and the provisions governing reorganizations. For example, suppose *T* wants to transfer appreciated property to *X* Corp. without recognizing gain. *T* is not a shareholder of *X* Corp. A direct attempt at a §351 transfer would leave *T* short of the control requirement. Suppose, though, that *T* and *X* Corp. together form Sub Corp., with *T* contributing the appreciated property and *X* Corp. all its assets. Together the transferors hold 100 percent of the Sub Corp. stock. The final step is that the *X* Corp. shareholders receive Sub Corp. stock in exchange for their *X* Corp. stock. Assume that the *X* Corp. stock has not appreciated so that no gain is recognized by the shareholders on the exchange. Has *T* made an end run around the control requirements of §351? See Rev. Rul. 68-349, 1968-2 C.B. 143 (transaction treated as reorganization; §351 nonrecognition unavailable to *T*).

8.   *Section 351 and passive activity losses.* Suppose *B*, a transferor in a

§351 transaction, transfers rental real estate that has been subject to the passive loss limitations under §469. Does the §351 transfer trigger suspended passive losses, thereby allowing *B* to use those losses to offset nonpassive income (such as portfolio income or income from services)? A taxable disposition of a passive activity triggers the use of any suspended losses against any type of income. §469(g).

The Senate Finance Committee report accompanying the Tax Reform Act of 1986 makes clear that a §351 transfer does not trigger the suspended losses because *B* retains an interest in the property. To the extent there is taxable boot in the §351 transaction, the suspended passive losses can be used to offset that income. The suspended losses will be fully deductible when *B* disposes of her entire interest in the corporation.

F.   PROBLEMS

1.   *A, B, C,* and *D* organize *X* Corp. by transferring the following:

	Transfers to X		Receives from X	
	Basis	FMV	Shares	Cash
A — cash	—	$10,000	10,000	$ 0
B — land/building	$50,000	$80,000	80,000	$ 0
C — inventory	$ 1,000	$10,000	5,000	$5,000
D — machinery	$15,000	$10,000	5,000	$5,000

With regard to *A, B, C, D,* and *X,* determine (1) the amount of realized and recognized gain or loss and (2) the applicable basis and holding period. How does your answer change as a result of the following alternatives (each considered independently)?

a.   Suppose *B* transferred only services worth $80,000.

b.   Suppose *B* transferred services worth $60,000 and property with a basis of $12,000 and a fair market value of $20,000.

c.   Suppose *B* received from *X* Corp. $40,000 of stock and a debt instrument in the amount of $40,000 bearing an appropriate interest rate.

d.   Suppose *B*'s transfer took place a year after the transfers of *A, C,* and *D.*

e.   Suppose *D*'s transfer took place a year after those of *A, B,* and *C.*

f.   Suppose *C*'s transfer took place three years after those of *A, B,* and *D* and that *B* purchased an additional 2,000 shares for $2,000 at that time.

2.   In the following, *A* starts out with a parcel of land held for investment worth $1,000 with an adjusted basis of $300 and ends up with $500

cash and a 50 percent interest in X Corp., a newly formed corporation that obtains the property. B starts out with $500 and ends up with a 50 percent interest in X Corp. Determine the tax consequences to all the parties of the following:

a. A transfers the property to X Corp. for all of X's stock. Shortly thereafter, A sells half of his X stock to B for $500.

b. Prior to incorporation A sells a half interest in the property to B for $500, and then both A and B form X Corp.

c. A and B both form X Corp., with A contributing his property in exchange for $500 cash (borrowed by X) and a 50 percent stock interest and B receiving a 50 percent stock interest for her cash.

d. A borrows $500 from a lender, using his property as security. A then transfers the property (subject to the debt) to X Corp. in exchange for a 50 percent stock interest, while B receives a 50 percent interest in return for her $500 cash.

3. Suppose in 2(c) that A transfers two parcels, one with a basis of $200 and a value of $700 and the other with a basis of $800 and a value of $300. What are the tax consequences?

4. Suppose in 2(c) that X also issued $100 of nonvoting preferred stock to C, X Corp.'s lawyer for organizing the corporation. What are the tax consequences?

5. T, a cash basis taxpayer, transfers real property and IBM stock to X Corp. in exchange for X stock in a transaction that qualifies under §351. Discuss the tax consequences to T and X Corp. in the following.

a. The real property has a basis of $200,000 and a fair market value of $900,000. It is subject to a liability of $500,000, which X will assume. The IBM stock has a basis of $100,000 and a fair market value of $70,000.

b. Suppose in (a) that X takes the property subject to the liability so that T remains liable on the underlying note. Suppose instead that T guarantees X's payment of the liability.

c. Suppose in (a) that T borrows $200,000 from a bank and contributes the cash as part of the §351 transaction.

d. Suppose in (c) that T had borrowed $200,000 from X in an unrelated transaction. The loan bears a market rate of interest and the loan is due in 10 years. T transfers the loan proceeds as part of the §351 transaction.

e. Suppose in (a) that T makes a promissory note to X in the amount of $200,000 bearing a market rate of interest and transfers the note as part of the §351 transaction. The note is due in 10 years.

6. T, a cash basis taxpayer who operates a sole proprietorship, transfers $1,000 in uncollected accounts receivable (with a basis of $0) to X, a wholly owned corporation. In exchange, T receives $700 of X stock and X's assumption of $300 of T's accounts payable.

a. What are the tax consequences to T and X?

b.   Suppose T is an accrual basis taxpayer transferring property with
a basis of $0 and a fair market value of $1,000 in exchange for
$700 of X stock and X's assumption of $300 of T's account payables. What are the tax consequences?

c.   In (a), what are the tax consequences when X collects on the
accounts receivable and pays off the accounts payable?

7. T owns all the stock of X Corp. T transfers to X Corp. a parcel of
real estate with a basis of $100,000 and a fair market value of $500,000. In
exchange T receives an interest-bearing debt instrument due in five years.
Following the transfer, X Corp. developed the property into 10 single-
family dwellings, each of which was sold for $100,000. Ignoring the develop-
ment costs, discuss the tax consequences of these transactions to T and X
Corp.

3

Corporate Operation

A. CORPORATE TAX RATES AND BASE

1. Taxable Entity

For a discussion of when a corporation is treated as a separate taxable entity, see Chapter 15.

2. Tax Rate

Section 11 imposes graduated tax rates ranging from 15 percent to 35 percent on corporate taxpayers. The graduation is steep: Corporations with taxable income of more than $75,000 find themselves in the 34 percent bracket. The 35 percent bracket applies to corporate taxable income over $10 million. The little graduation that exists is eliminated for corporations with taxable income greater than $18,333,333. Those corporations are taxed at a flat 35 percent rate because Congress wanted to restrict the benefits of the lower rates to smaller businesses.

Section 11 implements this congressional policy in a somewhat convoluted manner. First, an additional tax is imposed on taxable income in excess of $100,000. The additional tax is equal to 5 percent of a corporation's income in excess of $100,000 up to a maximum additional tax of $11,750, which occurs at $335,000 of taxable income. The $11,750 figure represents the difference between taxing the first $75,000 of taxable income at a flat 34 percent ($25,500) and taxing it at the graduated rates ($13,750). As a corporation's taxable income increases from $100,000 to $335,000, the benefits of the reduced tax rates on the first $75,000 vanish.

Note also that for taxable income in the range of $100,000 to $335,000, the marginal tax rate on the next dollar earned is not 34 percent but equals 34 percent plus the 5 percent surtax, or 39 percent.

A second provision of the same type phases out the 34 percent bracket for corporate taxpayers with taxable income exceeding $15 million. These taxpayers must pay 3 percent of taxable income in excess of $15 million or $100,000, whichever is less. Accordingly for taxpayers with taxable income between $15,000,000 and $18,333,333, a 38 percent rate applies. For taxpayers with taxable income exceeding $18,333,333, there is a flat 35 percent rate.

Prior to 1986, the top individual rates were higher than the top corporate rates. As a result of the Tax Reform Act of 1986, the top corporate rates were higher than the top individual rates. As a result of the Revenue Reconciliation Act of 1993, the top individual rates are again above the top corporate rates. The current rate structure may create incentives for taxpayers to use the corporate form to shelter income from top individual rates.

While §11(a) contains only slightly graduated tax rates, even that slight graduation is denied to "qualified personal service corporations," which are taxed at a flat 35 percent rate. A corporation is a qualified personal service corporation if it meets a function test and an ownership test. See §448(d). Under the function test, substantially all of the activities of the corporation must involve the performance of services in the fields of health, law, engineering, architecture, accounting, actuarial science, performing arts, or consulting. Under the ownership test, substantially all of the stock (by value) of the corporation must be held directly or indirectly by employees performing the services, by retired employees who performed the services in the past, by their estates, or by persons who hold stock in the corporation by reason of the death of an employee or retired employee within the past two years.

Notice that the denial of graduated rates applies only to "qualified" personal service corporations. Such corporations are "qualified" to be treated more harshly than other corporations. The definition of qualified personal service corporations used in §§11(b) and 448(d) is quite narrow. Indeed §448 prohibits the use of the cash method of accounting by corporations except for the narrow category of qualified professional corporations. Why would Congress use this narrow category to impose higher tax rates? Notice how Congress both giveth and taketh away. Qualified personal service corporations can use the cash method of accounting but cannot have the advantages of graduated rates. Why are qualified personal service corporations subject to a higher rate schedule than manufacturing or sales corporations? What policy reason, if any, justifies this discrimination?

While it is easy to categorize some businesses as qualified personal service corporations, such as incorporated doctors, dentists, lawyers, and accountants, the treatment of other businesses is not so clear. Are incorporated health clubs, nutritionists, and weight control clinics considered in the health field? Treas. Regs. §1.448-1T provides that health services do not include services not directly related to a medical field even if the services purportedly relate to the health of the recipient. Health clubs and spas are specifically excluded from coverage. Similar questions arise with respect to the performing arts. Under the regulation, performing arts services do not include services of managers or promoters or the activities of broadcasters. Athletes are not considered performing artists.

Perhaps the most uncertain area is consulting. According to the regulations, consulting is the giving of advice and counsel; sales and brokerage activities are not consulting. If compensation is contingent on the consummation of a transaction, any services performed in the transaction are not consulting services. For example, financial planners who are paid on the basis of advice are engaged in consulting and are subject to the flat 35 percent rate while financial planners who are paid on the basis of trade orders in securities or commodities are not consulting.

3.   Taxation of Capital Gains and Losses

The Tax Reform Act of 1986 set the rate of taxation on capital gains equal to the rate on ordinary income. In doing so, Congress opted to leave in place the mechanisms for distinguishing capital gains (and losses) from ordinary gains (and losses) in order to "facilitate reinstatement of a capital gains rate differential if there is a future tax rate increase." Conference Report on H.R. 3838, Tax Reform Act of 1986, filed Sept. 18, 1986, at p. I-106. Perhaps more candidly, Congress might have said *when* there is a future rate increase. Already, there is a capital gains/ordinary income differential (28 percent for capital gains, 39.6 percent for ordinary income) for individual taxpayers.

For noncorporate taxpayers, §1(j) currently provides a rate ceiling of 28 percent on capital gains. Section 1201 accomplishes a similar function for corporations by providing an alternative tax for corporations with net capital gains in lieu of the tax imposed by §11 if the §1201 tax is less. This tax is the sum of (1) the §11 tax on the corporation's taxable income minus the net capital gains and (2) 35 percent of the net capital gains. That is, the maximum tax on corporate net capital gains is 35 percent, compared with 28 percent for individual taxpayers.

Section 1201 is triggered if the rate of tax under §11 exceeds 35 percent. Suppose a corporation with $15 million of ordinary income earns a $500,000 capital gain. Does §1201 provide a top rate on the capital gain of 35 percent since the effective rate under §11 is 35 percent plus the 3 percent additional tax on the $500,000 gain?

There are also some differences in the treatment of capital losses for corporations vis-à-vis other taxpayers. A corporation can deduct capital losses only to the extent of capital gains. §1211(a). No ordinary income can be offset by capital losses. Cf. §1211(b) (other taxpayers can offset up to $3,000 of ordinary income with capital losses). Although individuals can carry unused capital losses forward indefinitely, corporations are generally given a three-year carryback period and a five-year carryforward period. The unused loss is carried back to the earliest year and then carried forward chronologically until the balance is used up or the carryforward period expires.

4.   Corporate Tax Base

The §11 tax (or the §1201 tax) is applied to "taxable income." While in most respects a corporation's taxable income is determined in the same manner as an individual's, there are some differences aside from the capital loss carryover provision discussed above. For individual taxpayers, "adjusted gross income" serves as a halfway house in moving from the calculation of gross income to taxable income. An individual's charitable, medical, and casualty loss deductions are all based on adjusted gross income. A corporation does not have an adjusted gross income. Instead, all appropriate corporate deductions are subtracted directly from gross income in arriving at taxable income.

Some deductions that are treated differently by individual and corporate taxpayers include the following:

1. The standard deduction allowed under §63(c) for individuals is not available for corporations, which instead must itemize their deductions;
2. the personal exemption deduction under §151 is not available for corporations;
3. personal deductions authorized under §§211-220 (including items such as medical expenses and alimony) do not apply to corporations, although §162 permits a corporation to deduct expenses incurred for the production of income not in a trade or business that for individuals are deductible under §212;
4. charitable contribution deductions are allowed to corporations up to 10 percent of taxable income under §170(b)(2).

A number of provisions were enacted specifically to apply to corporate taxpayers. For example, Congress has shown concern over corporations' making large compensation payments to corporate officers in the event of a corporate takeover. These "golden parachutes" appear to some as a raid on the corporate treasury by the officers. To others the payments ensure that the officers will do what is best for the corporation in the event of a takeover attempt without worrying about personal consequences (e.g., the loss of a well-paying job).

Through the use of the tax system, Congress has raised the cost of making golden parachute payments. Section 280G denies a deduction for payments of "excessive" compensation to corporate officers triggered by changes in corporate control. Excessive payments are determined by comparing the payments with a designated base period. In addition, §4999 imposes an excise tax on the recipient.

A publicly held corporation cannot deduct compensation paid to a "covered employee" in excess of $1 million if the compensation is "applicable employee remuneration." §162(m). The term "covered employee" refers to any employee who (1) as of the close of the taxable year is the chief executive officer of the corporation, or (2) is one of the corporation's four highest compensated officers (other than the CEO) for the tax year. The term "applicable employee remuneration" refers to a covered employee's aggregate remuneration for services performed. The term does not apply, however, to commission payments or other performance-based compensation if (1) the performance goals are established by a compensation committee of the board of directors that has two or more outside directors; (2) the material terms of the compensation are approved by a majority vote of the shareholders before compensation is paid; and (3) the compensation committee certifies that the performance goals were satisfied. For example, compensation based on increases in stock price, market share, or earnings per share are not counted in determining the $1 million limit if the specified procedural requirements are satisfied. Notice that the limited deduction imposed by §162(m) applies to publicly held corporations, where there is accountability to outside directors and to the shareholders, but does not apply to privately held corporations, where there is more room for manipulation.

With the increase of corporate takeover activity in the 1980s, members of Congress voiced concern that regulation was needed to stem the tide. While many commentators argue that takeovers are one of the free market's means of disciplining inefficient management and deploying corporate assets in the most efficient manner, others decry the dislocations to workers and communities caused by some takeovers and lament the amount of debt (i.e., leverage) used in some acquisitions.

There is no dispute, however, that Congress has looked to the tax laws as a means of regulating the market for corporate control. Section 279, enacted in 1969, disallows a deduction for corporate interest in excess of $5 million per year on specified "corporate acquisition indebtedness," defined to include certain convertible, subordinated debt. The effect of this provision is to make debt-financed takeovers less attractive. See page 398 infra.

More recent provisions have focused on all aspects of corporate acquisitions. Section 162(l) denies a deduction for any amount paid or incurred by a corporation to redeem its own stock. This provision is aimed at "greenmail" payments made by a corporation to a potential corporate "raider" to repurchase the "raider's" stock. Furthermore, §5881 imposes an excise tax of 50 percent on any gain or other income realized by the greenmail recipient. "Greenmail" is defined in §5881 as consideration paid by a corporation in redemption of its stock held for less than two years if the holder threatened a public tender offer. It is not clear that greenmail payments are "bad," but it is clear that the Code discourages such payments. See Macey and McChesney, A Theoretical Analysis of Corporate Greenmail, 95 Yale L.J. 133 (1985).

Section 382, discussed in more detail in Chapter 13, does not attempt to increase the direct cost of corporate acquisitions. Instead, these provisions limit the ability of acquiring corporations to use net operating losses of the acquired corporation to offset future income, thereby decreasing the attraction of some corporate takeovers.

In addition to the deductions discussed above, a corporation is entitled to a variety of tax credits. Perhaps the most significant one is the foreign tax credit. §§27 and 901. A corporation can offset any applicable U.S. federal income tax on income from foreign sources with foreign income taxes paid on that income. Credits are also available for research (§41), targeted jobs expenditures (§51), and rehabilitation and energy expenditures (§§46-48).

The preceding discussion of the corporate tax rate and base is aimed at domestic corporations (corporations incorporated in any state in the United States). Foreign corporations (corporations incorporated abroad) are subject to U.S. taxation on income that is connected in designated ways to the United States. See generally §§881 and 882. For example, a foreign corporation engaged in a trade or business in the United States is taxed in the same manner as a U.S. corporation on income that is "effectively connected" with the conduct of that U.S. trade or business (i.e., trade or business income). §882. The rules governing tax rates and base apply to such business income. A foreign corporation that has investment income from interest, dividends, rents, royalties, and so on is generally taxed at a flat rate of 30 percent (or in some cases, a lower treaty rate) on the gross amount of the payments. §881. No deductions are permitted. A foreign corporation can elect, however, to have rental payments for the use of U.S. real property taxed as business income that can be offset by appropriate deductions rather than being taxed at the flat 30 percent rate. §882(d).

5. Passive Loss Limitations

In an effort to curtail investment solely or primarily for the purpose of securing tax benefits, Congress enacted §469, a provision that limits the deduction of passive activity expenses against other income (i.e., active business income or portfolio income). Any losses suspended as a result of the limitation can be carried forward and treated as deductions in the following year or can be taken when the taxpayer disposes of the entire interest in the passive activity. §469(b) and (g). In general, an activity is passive if it involves the conduct of a trade or business and if the corporation does not "materially participate" in the activity. By definition, rental activity (e.g., ownership of an apartment building) is considered a passive activity regardless of the level of activity. An important exception, however, applies for taxpayers in the real estate business. See discussion below.

Although an exhaustive discussion of the passive loss provisions is beyond the scope of a corporate tax course, the provisions do apply to certain personal service corporations and closely held corporations. Accordingly, a personal service corporation that also rents real estate may not be able to offset any active income from the performance of services with deductions from the real estate rental activity. A personal service corporation is defined as a corporation whose principal activity is the performance of personal services when such services are performed by an employee who owns any stock of the corporation. See §§469(j)(2) and 269A(b)(2).

In the case of a closely held corporation (other than a personal service corporation) the passive loss rules apply in modified form. §469(e)(2). Passive losses may be used to offset active business income but not portfolio income (e.g., interest, dividends, and royalties). A closely held corporation is defined as a corporation that has more than 50 percent in value of its outstanding stock owned by not more than five individuals. §§469(j)(1), 465(a)(1)(B), 542(a)(2).

Material participation for a corporation that is subject to §469 is achieved if one or more shareholders owning in the aggregate more than 50 percent of the outstanding stock of the corporation materially participate. §469(h)(4). Shareholders materially participate if they spend more than 500 hours on the activity or if they meet one of the other tests specified under the regulations. Treas. Regs. §§1.469-1T(g), -5T.

If more than 50 percent of a closely held corporation's gross receipts for the taxable year are derived from real property trades or businesses in which the corporation materially participates, the rental activities are not considered passive. Accordingly, losses can be used to offset nonpassive income. A real property trade or business is any real property development, redevelopment, construction, reconstruction, acquisition, conversion, rental, operation, management, leasing, or brokerage trade or business. §469(c)(7).

If passive losses are suspended, those losses can be taken in full when the taxpayer disposes (in a taxable transaction) of the entire interest in the passive activity. §469(g)(1). The reason for the rule is that prior to the disposition, it is difficult to determine whether there has actually been gain or loss with respect to the activity. For example, allowable deductions may or may not exceed unrealized appreciation. On a taxable disposition, a final accounting can be made for the activity.

Suppose a personal services corporation is also engaged in a rental real estate activity and that the deductions for the rental activity exceed the passive income from that activity by $20,000. Those excess deductions would not be allowed under §469. If the corporation then disposes of the rental real estate in a taxable transaction that produces a $15,000 gain, the suspended losses first apply against that gain. The remaining $5,000 of suspended loss can then reduce any other passive income. Finally any unused suspended losses then reduce any other income or gain. §469(g). Suspended passive losses are not triggered when the passive activity interest is transferred to a related party. §469(g)(1)(B). On an installment sale, suspended losses can be recognized in proportion to the ratio of recognized gain on the sale for the taxable year to the overall gain from the sale of the property. §469(g)(3).

In general, suspended losses are not triggered by a nontaxable transfer such as a like-kind exchange (except to the extent of any gain recognized on the transaction) but instead are triggered on disposition of the received property. If an activity ceases to be passive (for example, the corporation no longer rents the property but uses it as part of its active service trade or business), any suspended losses can offset net income from the formerly passive but now nonpassive activity or income from other passive activities. §469(f).

6. Taxable Year and Accounting Methods

In general, a corporation can choose any taxable year. §441(b). This flexibility has been exploited by taxpayers seeking to defer recognition of income for tax purposes. For example, prior to the enactment of §441(i), a personal service corporation was free to adopt any taxable year on its federal income tax return that conformed with its annual accounting period. A popular strategy was to adopt a January 31 business year. A doctor earning $200,000 a year might take a $10,000 monthly salary from the personal service corporation and take the remaining $80,000 as a January bonus. As a calendar year taxpayer, the doctor could defer the taxes on the bonus to the following year.

Under §441(i) a personal service corporation must adopt a calendar year unless the taxpayer receives approval from the Treasury Secretary for use of a different taxable year. An exception allows the use of a fiscal year if the deferral period is not more than three months (i.e., fiscal years ending in September through December). §444. See also §280H requiring certain minimum distributions. For purposes of these provisions, a personal service corporation is a corporation whose principal activity is the performance of services if those services are substantially performed by owner-employees who together own more than 10 percent (by value) of the corporation's stock. §269A(b)(1) and (b)(2).

Most corporations are prohibited from using the cash method of accounting. §448. In general, the accrual method of reporting more accurately reflects the economic results of a taxpayer's trade or business over a taxable year. Congress has, however, excepted certain entities, including qualified farming businesses, personal service corporations, and entities with average annual gross receipts of $5 million or less for a three-year testing period from the prohibition against the cash basis accounting method. §448(b).

A qualified personal service corporation is one that meets a function test and an ownership test. The function test is met if substantially all of the activities of the corporation are the performance of services in the fields of health, law, engineering, architecture, accounting, actuarial science, performing arts, or consulting. §448(d)(2)(A). Can you think of any policy reason to limit the cash basis method to these enterprises? The ownership test is met if substantially all the value of the outstanding stock of the corporation is owned by employees (present or retired). §448(d)(2)(B).

In some situations a corporation's method of accounting is modified to conform with the accounting method of shareholders. For example, §267(a)(1) prevents the deduction of losses on the sale or exchange of property between a corporation and a shareholder owning 50 percent (or more) in value of the corporation's stock. Section 267(a)(2) requires an accrual basis corporation to deduct compensation, interest, and other deductible payments made to a cash basis owner-employee when such payment is made rather than when the payment accrues. The purpose of this provision is to prevent a mismatching of deduction and income when the liability for payment accrues in one year but actual payment is deferred to a subsequent year.

7. Corporate Alternative Minimum Tax

As you have already discovered, the Code is littered with provisions that provide tax incentives to engage in or abstain from various activities. Although Congress presumably has tailored these provisions to provide the desired level of activity in the aggregate, it also has shown a desire to prevent any particular taxpayer from benefiting too much from an induced tax incentive. If 10 taxpayers engage in a particular tax-favored activity, each may be able to take a deduction because the activity is one that Congress has purposefully encouraged, but if one taxpayer engages in the activity tenfold, there may be limitations on the deduction even though in the aggregate the level of activity may be precisely what Congress intended. Rather than limit the deduction directly, in general Congress has opted for a minimum tax mechanism.

The alternative minimum tax (AMT) under §55 operates mechanically as a tax added on to the regular tax under §11. Conceptually, it is more accurate to think of the AMT as a shadow tax so that a corporation pays whichever is greater, the regular tax or the AMT. As compared with the regular tax under §11, the AMT has a broader tax base and a lower tax rate. In general, the tax base is the corporation's regular taxable income increased by the taxpayer's tax preferences and by certain other adjustments. §55(b)(2). The resulting amount is "alternative minimum taxable income" (AMTI), a term that seeks to identify the corporation's economic income before it behaves in a tax-induced manner. The AMTI is then reduced by an exemption amount and is subject to a 20 percent tax. §55(b)(1)(A). The exemption amount for corporations is $40,000, reduced by 25 percent of the amount by which AMTI exceeds $150,000. §55(d). Therefore, for a corporation with AMTI of $310,000 or more, no exemption is available.

The adjustments that must be made to the taxpayer's taxable income to arrive at AMTI are set out in §§56-58. For example, to the extent that a corporation's depreciation deductions exceed depreciation calculated under an alternative method, the excess will be treated as a tax preference that must be added to taxable income. §56(a)(1). The reason for the adjustment is Congress's concern that depreciation permitted under §168 as an investment incentive exceeds actual economic depreciation. The alternative method for real property is defined as straight line depreciation over a specified life that is longer than the period permitted for figuring depreciation deductions under §168(b) (e.g., 40 years for residential real property under the AMT compared with 27.5 under §168). §§56(a)(1), 168(g).

Note that even though a taxpayer must depreciate real property under a straight-line method for regular tax purposes, there may still be a preference for AMT purposes because the deductions taken over 27.5 (residential) or 39 (nonresidential) years will be greater than straight line depreciation taken over the 40-year useful life required for AMT purposes. Suppose that X Corp. correctly took $100 of depreciation deductions in connection with an apartment building for regular tax purposes. If the AMT method would have produced only $60 of depreciation deductions, then X Corp. must increase taxable income by $40 in calculating AMTI. Depreciation for tangible depreciable property uses the 150 percent declining balance method rather than the 200 percent declining balance method used to calculate regular tax liability.

A significant preference affecting corporations is the adjustment for "adjusted current earnings" (ACE). §56(g). Congress was concerned that corporations such as General Electric Co. and W.R. Grace that reported substantial earnings to their shareholders for financial purposes (either through public reporting requirements or through voluntary disclosure) were able to report little or no earnings for tax purposes because of available deductions or credits (e.g., the foreign tax credit). Presumably, Congress regarded this phenomenon as a threat to taxpayer morale because appearances suggested that profitable corporations were escaping appropriate taxation.

Although adding back specific preferences to taxable income in arriving at AMTI addresses the problem somewhat, Congress has backstopped the process by requiring a corporation to add to its AMTI an amount equal to 75 percent of the excess of the corporation's ACE over its AMTI (computed without this ACE adjustment). "Adjusted current earnings" is defined as AMTI with a variety of adjustments intended to reflect a corporation's economic income available for distribution. §56(g)(4). For example, tax-exempt interest that increases a corporation's wealth is not included in the AMTI calculation but is added back for purposes of calculating the ACE. For a better understanding of the ACE adjustments, see the discussion of earnings and profits at page 129 infra.

Other adjustments that must be made to taxable income in determining AMTI include using the percentage of completion method of accounting rather than the completed contract method, adding accelerated depletion in connection with mineral exploration, and ignoring the deferral of installment reporting in the case of certain property. §56(a).

In attempting to reconstruct an economic tax base for purposes of determining minimum tax liability, an adjustment must be made to net operating losses (NOLs). §56(a)(4). For AMT purposes, NOLs tend to be overstated because they may reflect the tax preferences the AMT is trying to address. Consequently, for purposes of the AMT, net operating loss is determined by adding to taxable income any tax preferences or adjustments. For example, if in year 1 a taxpayer has $20,000 of income and $35,000 of deductions, of which $10,000 is a preference item (such as accelerated depreciation), the AMT net operating loss for the year would be $5,000. §56(d). Thus, in any subsequent (or prior) year to which the loss may be carried, a $5,000 net operating loss deduction is allowed to reduce income subject to the AMT. Assume that in year 2 the taxpayer has $20,000 of AMTI before accounting for the AMT net operating loss. The taxpayer reduces AMTI to $15,000 by the AMT net operating loss deduction. §56(a)(4). The net operating loss deduction for the regular tax is not affected by this computation (that is, the taxpayer has a $15,000 loss carryover from year 1 for use against the regular tax). Moreover, the alternative tax net operating loss deduction cannot exceed 90 percent of AMTI. §56(d)(1)(A). Suppose that for the year in question a taxpayer has $10 million of AMTI and an AMT net operating loss of $11 million. The net operating loss reduces AMTI to $1 million, giving rise to $200,000 of AMT liability. The taxpayer may then carry forward $2 million of AMT net operating loss.

Once AMTI is determined, the tentative minimum tax equals 20 percent of the excess of AMTI over the exemption. §55(b)(1)(A). A taxpayer can in some cases then offset the tax with a specially computed foreign tax credit. §55(b)(1)(B). First, the credit is recomputed to account for any preferences that decreased U.S. source income and thereby increased the foreign tax credit. Second, no more than 90 percent of tentative minimum tax liability can be offset by foreign tax credits. §59(a). Although conceptually the AMT applies if it is higher than the regular tax, under §55(a) the excess of the alternative minimum tax over the regular tax under §11 is added to the regular tax to determine total tax liability.

Section 53 introduces a credit for a prior year's AMT liability. The credit can be taken against a taxpayer's regular tax, not the AMT. The purpose of the credit is to reflect the fact that some of the tax preferences added to taxable income in determining AMTI reflect deferral preferences (such as accelerated depreciation) rather than permanent avoidance (such as percentage depletion). For example, taxpayers paying the AMT as a result of taking accelerated depreciation deductions potentially face a double penalty. First, the AMT must be paid. Then in a later year, the taxpayer loses a part of the deduction that would have been available if no accelerated depreciation had been taken (instead, that part was taken in the earlier year, giving rise to the AMT liability). The result is a higher regular tax in the later year.

The AMT credit is intended to allow the taxpayer in the later year to offset the regular tax liability with a prior year's AMT liability. The AMT credit can be carried forward indefinitely. The credit is allowed only with respect to liability arising as a result of deferral preferences (that is, preferences other than those that result in permanent exclusion of certain income for regular tax purposes). Accordingly, the amount of the AMT liability that can be credited is reduced by the AMT liability that would have arisen if the only applicable preferences were exclusion preferences.

B. CAPITAL STRUCTURE

A corporation can raise capital either by issuing stock (equity) or by issuing a debt instrument in exchange for cash or property. In either case, an investor holds a financial instrument with a claim on corporate assets. The nature of those claims can be very different. A prototypical debt instrument provides that the borrower (i.e., the corporation) will repay the debt after a fixed term. Moreover, while the loan is outstanding, the borrower promises to pay the investor a fixed rate of interest regardless of the corporation's performance. Whether the corporation performs well or poorly, the return to the lender is fixed and, in the prototypical case, subject to little risk.

In contrast, the prototypical common stock instrument is riskier because it entitles the holder to no guarantees. Unlike the prototypical loan, there is no fixed date of repayment. While interest is paid with respect to a debt instrument, stock ownership does not guarantee the receipt of dividends. Under state corporate law, creditors must be paid before any dividend distributions are made to shareholders. In many cases, the payment of dividends depends on the corporation's performance. The value of an investor's stock also depends on the performance of the corporation. If the corporation does well and is expected to do well in the future, typically the fair market value of the outstanding common stock increases. Conversely, if the corporation does poorly, the fair market value of the stock usually declines. At the extremes, prototypical debt has little risk and a limited upside potential; stock has more risk and an unlimited upside potential. Between these extremes is a bewildering assortment of financial instruments bearing various risk levels and expected profit levels.

In deciding whether to issue debt or equity, a corporation must consider both nontax and tax factors. Many financial theorists believe that, taxes aside, the value of a corporation is independent of financial structure. See Modigliani and Miller, The Cost of Capital, Corporation Finance, and the Theory of Investment, Am. Econ. Rev. 261-267 (June 1958). Nevertheless, a corporation with a high ratio of outstanding debt to equity may find difficulty in obtaining additional bank financing and in attracting future investors. Conversely, a corporation with little or no debt may be viewed as underperforming and may be a takeover candidate.

The following excerpt considers the effect of federal taxes on a corporation's financial structure.

Joint Committee on Taxation, Federal Income Tax Aspects of Corporate Financial Structures* _____
101st Cong., 1st Sess. (Jan. 18, 1989)

IV.   POLICY ISSUES

A.   TAX ADVANTAGE OF DEBT VERSUS EQUITY

The total effect of the tax system on the incentives for corporations to use debt or equity depends on the interaction between the tax treatment at the shareholder and corporate levels.

The case of no income taxes. — In a simple world without taxes or additional costs in times of financial distress, economic theory suggests that the value of a corporation, as measured by the total value of the outstanding debt and equity, would be unchanged by the degree of leverage of the firm. This conclusion explicitly recognizes that debt issued by the corporation represents an ownership right to future income of the corporation in a fashion similar to that of equity. In this simple world there would

* Footnotes omitted. — EDS.

be no advantage to debt or to equity and the debt-equity ratio of the firm would not affect the cost of financing investment.

Effect of Corporate Income Tax

Tax Advantages

Taxes greatly complicate this analysis. Since the interest expense on debt is deductible for computing the corporate income tax while the return to equity is not, the tax at the corporate level provides a strong incentive for debt rather than equity finance.

The advantages of debt financing can be illustrated by comparing two corporations with $1,000 of assets that are identical except for financial structure: the first is entirely equity financed; while the second is 50-percent debt financed. Both corporations earn $150 of operating income. The all-equity corporation pays $51 in corporate tax and retains or distributes $99 of after-tax income ($150 less $51). Thus, as shown in Table IV-A, the return on equity is 9.9 percent ($99 divided by $1,000).

The leveraged corporation is financed by $500 of debt and $500 of stock. If the interest rate is 10 percent, then interest expense is $50 (10 percent times $500). Taxable income is $100 after deducting interest expense. The leveraged corporation is liable for $34 in corporate tax (34 percent times $100) and distributes or retains $66 of after-tax income

Table IV-A _____
Effect of Debt Financing on Returns to Equity Investment

Item	All-equity corporation	50-percent debt-financed corporation
Beginning Balance Sheet:		
Total assets	$1,000	$1,000
Debt	0	500
Shareholders' equity	1,000	500
Income Statement:		
Operating income	150	150
Interest expense	0	50
Taxable income	150	100
Income tax	51	34
Income after corporate tax	99	66
Return on Equity[1] (percent)	9.9	13.2

1. Return on equity is computed as income after corporate tax divided by beginning shareholders' equity.

($100 less $34). Consequently, the return on equity is 13.2 percent ($66 divided by $500). Thus, as shown in Table IV-A, increasing the debt ratio from zero to 50 percent increases the rate of return on equity from 9.9 to 13.2 percent.

This arithmetic demonstrates that a leveraged corporation can generate a higher return on equity (net of corporate income tax) than an unleveraged company or, equivalently, that an unleveraged company needs to earn a higher profit before corporate tax to provide investors the same return net of corporate tax as could be obtained with an unleveraged company. More generally, the return on equity rises with increasing debt capitalization so long as the interest rate is less than the pre-tax rate of return on corporate assets. This suggests that the Code creates an incentive to raise the debt-equity ratio to the point where the corporate income tax (or outstanding equity) is eliminated.

Costs of Financial Distress

With higher levels of debt the possibility of financial distress increases, as do expected costs to the firm which occur with such distress. These additional costs include such items as the increase in the costs of debt funds; constraints on credit, expenditure or operating decisions; and the direct costs of being in bankruptcy. These expected costs of financial distress may, at sufficiently high debt-equity ratios, offset the corporate tax advantage to additional debt finance.

Effect of Shareholder Income Tax

The above analysis focuses solely on the effect of interest deductibility at the corporate level. Shareholder-level income taxation may offset to some degree the corporate tax incentive for corporate debt relative to equity.

Shareholder Treatment of Debt and Equity

The conclusion that debt is tax favored relative to equity remains unchanged if interest on corporate debt and returns on equity are taxed at the same effective rate to investors. In this case, the returns to investors on both debt and equity are reduced proportionately by the income tax; the advantage to debt presented by corporate tax deductibility remains. One noteworthy exception exists if the marginal investments on both debt and equity are effectively tax-exempt. Given the previously documented importance of tax-exempt pension funds in the bond and equity markets, this case may be of some importance.

Shareholder-Level Tax Treatment of Equity

In general, returns to shareholders and debtholders are not taxed the same. Although dividends, like interest income, are taxed currently, equity income in other forms may reduce the effective investor-level tax on equity below that on debt. First, the firm may retain earnings and not pay dividends currently. In general, the accumulation of earnings by the firm will cause the value of the firm's shares to rise. Rather than being taxed currently on corporate earnings, a shareholder will be able to defer the taxation on the value of the retained earnings reflected in the price of the stock until the shareholder sells the stock. Thus, even though the tax rates on interest, dividends, and capital gains are the same, the ability to defer the tax on returns from equity reduces the effective rate of individual tax on equity investment below that on income from interest on corporate debt.

Other aspects of capital gain taxation serve to reduce further the individual income tax on equity. Since tax on capital gain is normally triggered after a voluntary recognition event (e.g., the sale of stock), the taxpayer can time the realization of capital gain income when the effective rate of tax is low. The rate of tax could be low if the taxpayer is in a low or zero tax bracket because other income is abnormally low, if other capital losses shelter the capital gain, or if changes in the tax law cause the statutory rate on capital gains to be low. Perhaps most important, the step up in the adjusted tax basis of the stock upon the death of the shareholder may permit the shareholder's heirs to avoid tax completely on capital gains. For all these reasons, the effective rate of tax on undistributed earnings may be already quite low.

Corporations can distribute their earnings to owners of equity in forms that generally result in less tax to shareholders than do dividend distributions. Share repurchases have become an important method of distributing corporate earnings to equity holders. When employed by large publicly traded firms, repurchases of the corporation's own shares permit the shareholders to treat the distribution as a sale of stock (i.e., to obtain capital gain treatment, and recover the basis in the stock without tax). The remaining shareholders may benefit because they have rights to a larger fraction of the firm and may see a corresponding increase in the value of their shares. Thus, less individual tax will generally be imposed on a $100 repurchase of stock than on $100 of dividends. In addition, share repurchases allow shareholders to choose whether to receive corporate distributions by choosing whether to sell or retain shares, so as to minimize tax liability.

Acquisitions of the stock of one corporation for cash or property of another corporation provides a similar method for distributing corporate earnings out of corporate solution with less shareholder tax than through a dividend. The target shareholders generally treat the acquisition as a sale and recover their basis free of tax. For purposes of analyzing the individual tax effect of corporate earnings disbursements, this transaction can be thought of as equivalent to a stock merger of the target with the acquiror followed by the repurchase of the target shareholders' shares by the resulting merged firm. The result is similar to the case of a share repurchase in that cash is distributed to shareholders with less than the full dividend tax, except that two firms are involved instead of one.

Since dividends typically are subject to more tax than other methods for providing returns to shareholders, the puzzle of why firms pay dividends remains. Because dividends are paid at the discretion of the firm, it appears that firms cause their shareholders to pay more tax on equity income than is strictly necessary. Until a better understanding of corporate distribution policy exists, the role of dividend taxation on equity financing decisions remain uncertain.

To summarize, although the current taxation of dividends to investors is clearly significant, there are numerous reasons why the overall individual tax on equity investments may be less than that on interest income from debt. Since the effective shareholder tax on returns from equity may be less than that on debt holdings, the shareholder tax may offset some or all of the advantage to debt at the corporate level.

Interaction of Corporate and Shareholder Taxation

With shareholders in different income tax brackets, high tax rate taxpayers will tend to concentrate their wealth in the form of equity and low tax rate taxpayers will tend to concentrate their wealth in the form of debt. The distribution of wealth among investors with different marginal tax rates affects the demand for investments in the form of debt or equity. The interaction between the demand of investors, and the supply provided by corporations, determines the aggregate amount of corporate debt and equity in the economy.

At some aggregate mix between debt and equity, the difference in the investor-level tax on income from equity and debt may be sufficient to offset completely, at the margin, the apparent advantage of debt at the corporate level. Even if the difference in investor tax treatment of debt and equity is not sufficient to offset completely the corporate tax advantage, the advantage to debt may be less than the corporate-level tax treatment alone would provide.

Implications for Policy

The analysis above suggests that any policy change designed to reduce the tax incentive for debt must consider the interaction of both corporate and shareholder taxes. For example, proposals to change the income tax rates for individuals or corporations will change the incentive for corporate debt. Likewise, proposals to change the tax treatment of tax-exempt entities may alter the aggregate mix and distribution of debt and equity.

In addition, proposals to reduce the bias toward debt over equity, for example, by reducing the total tax on dividends, must confront the somewhat voluntary nature of the dividend tax. Since the payment of dividends by corporations generally is discretionary and other means exist for providing value to shareholders with less tax, corporations can affect the level of shareholder-level tax incurred. Until a better understanding of the determinants of corporate distribution behavior exists, the total impact of policies designed to reduce the bias between debt and equity are uncertain.

This excerpt points out that at the corporate level, the payment of interest generates a deduction while the payment of dividends does not. At the shareholder level, while both interest and dividends received are taxable to the recipients in the same manner, shareholders holding equity can lessen, or in some cases eliminate, shareholder-level tax. The mere appreciation of a shareholder's stock is not a taxable event. By allowing accumulation at the corporate level, shareholders can defer any shareholder-level taxation. When shareholders eventually sell or exchange their stock, any gain is taxed at a capital gains rate, entitled to any capital gains preference that might exist. Moreover, upon the death of a shareholder, any appreciated stock takes a fair market value basis, permitting disposition without any recognition of gain.

Notwithstanding the advantages of equity at the shareholder level, the deductibility of interest payments at the corporate level may create a corporate bias in favor of debt over equity. But whether a financial instrument is treated as debt or equity is an issue that haunts our federal income tax system. Much may ride on the distinction, and yet the distinction is often difficult to make. After all, debt and equity are each paper representations of an interest in corporate assets. Although a debt instrument signifies a contractual relationship for repayment while stock provides residual rights for shareholders once creditors have been paid, the price of each kind of instrument reflects the associated risks. Is there a justification for treating debt differently from equity for tax purposes?

Whatever the theoretical answer to the previous question, the practical answer is that the two types of financial instruments are treated very differently. The characterization often determines (1) the gain to a transferor and the basis to the corporate transferee during the formation of a corporation, see Bradshaw v. United States, page 57 supra; (2) the treatment of the borrower (or issuer) as periodic payments are made to the instrument holder; and (3) the treatment of the instrument holder on surrender of the obligation.

The most significant difference in the treatment of debt and equity involves the second category above. The return on borrowed money (debt) typically is deductible as interest. §163. The return on stock (equity) constitutes a nondeductible dividend payment. To an instrument holder, both interest and dividends are includible as ordinary income. For corporate instrument holders, §243 provides a deduction to the recipient of from 70 to 100 percent, depending on the degree of ownership. See discussion at pages 134-135 infra.

Because interest is deductible by the corporation while dividends are not, there is a tax incentive for a corporation to raise needed capital through the issuance of debt rather than stock. Moreover, certain personal tax advantages will accrue to the organizers or principal owners of the corporation if they become creditors as well as stockholders. If the corporation prospers, it may pay off its debt, and the creditor-stockholders will realize income only to the extent that the payment exceeds the adjusted basis of the debt instruments paid off. The income, if any, will be capital gain. §1271. If the organizers hold only stock, however, amounts distributed to them by the corporation as shareholders (including amounts paid for a pro rata reacquisition of stock) may be taxed as dividends. See the discussion of §302 in Chapter 5. For the use of debt in connection with corporate acquisitions, see page 398 infra.

In light of the advantages that debt can offer to corporate issuers, not surprisingly taxpayers often like to label financial instruments as debt. Notwithstanding the label, the Service will attempt to recharacterize an instrument if it resembles equity more than debt. The following case illustrates a typical situation.

Bauer v. Commissioner
748 F.2d 1365 (9th Cir. 1984)

Before Chambers, Hug, and Boochever, Circuit Judges.

Hug, Circuit Judge.

This case concerns a determination of whether cash payments by two stockholders to their wholly-owned corporation were loans or contributions to capital. The Commissioner of Internal Revenue contended that the payments by the stockholders were contributions to capital and not loans, as the stockholders and the corporation maintained. The documentation between the parties and the books of the corporation reflected the cash payments as loans and the periodic payments by the corporation as principal and interest payments to the stockholders. The corporation deducted the interest payments and the stockholders declared the interest payments as income and treated the principal payments as a return of capital. The Commissioner contended that because the stockholders' cash advances to the corporation were contributions to capital and not loans, the corporation could not deduct the claimed interest and the stockholders were required to treat the payments made to them as taxable dividends. The Commissioner assessed deficiencies accordingly. The stockholders and the corporation contested the assessments in the Tax Court and the cases were consolidated for trial. The Tax Court held for the Commissioner in each instance. On appeal, the sole issue is whether the Tax Court was clearly erroneous in holding that the stockholders' cash advances to the corporation were capital contributions rather than loans. We reverse.

FACTS

The parties entered into a stipulation of facts, which we summarize here.

Philip Bauer and his father-in-law, Phillip Himmelfarb, are officers and sole stockholders of the Federal Meat Company ("Federal"). They formed Federal in 1958 with paid-in capital of $20,000. The initial and only stock issuance was 2,000 shares, of which Bauer owns 25 percent and Himmelfarb 75 percent. Federal is a custom slaughterer in the business of selling dressed meat to chain store buyers, retailers, and wholesalers. It buys live animals and has them custom slaughtered for fixed fees. Federal does not own a packing house, and it leases its premises and delivery equipment.

Since Federal's incorporation, and continuing throughout the years at issue, Bauer and Himmelfarb advanced various amounts of money to Federal. By the end of the calendar year 1958, a total of $102,650 had been advanced by Bauer and Himmelfarb. Numerous advances and repayments then occurred so that as of December 31, 1972, the net balance advanced by Bauer and Himmelfarb totaled $810,068. . . .

The parties treated all of the transactions as loans and repayments. Each advance to Federal was evidenced by a negotiable promissory note that was unsecured and was payable on demand. The notes carried a seven percent interest rate during 1972-1974 and a ten percent interest rate in 1976. The notes were not convertible into stock, nor were they subordinated to any other obligation. For each advance made to Federal, an amount representing "accrued interest payable" was entered in the corporate ledger at the end of each month as an addition to liabilities in the form of "outstanding loans payable-officers." Each year's total of accrued interest was paid within two and one-half months of the close of Federal's fiscal year. On its financial statements, Federal included the outstanding balances as a current liability labeled "loan payable-officers."

On its corporate federal income tax returns for the years at issue, Federal claimed interest expense deductions in the amounts of $79,638, $103,506, and $103,007, for its fiscal years ending April 30 of 1974, 1975, and 1976, respectively, for the amounts paid as interest to Bauer and Himmelfarb. These amounts, in turn, were reported by Bauer and Himmelfarb as interest income in the calendar year in which they were received. The amounts received from Federal characterized as loan principal repayments were not reported as income. These amounts for Bauer were: $65,000 in 1973, $25,000 in 1974, and $35,000 in 1975; for Himmelfarb, the amount was $75,000 in 1975. Bauer and Himmelfarb each received a yearly salary of $70,000 or $80,000. Federal has never paid dividends; the earnings of the corporation from its inception in 1958 were retained and reinvested to meet the continued growth of the corporation. By the end of the fiscal years in issue, the retained earnings were: 1974, $634,107; 1975, $657,973; and 1976, $486,092. (In the 1976 fiscal year, Federal suffered a net loss.)

The Tax Court concluded that the advances by Bauer and Himmelfarb to Federal were capital contributions and disallowed the interest deductions claimed by Federal on the ground that no debtor-creditor relationship was established to support treatment of the payments as interest. In addition, the principal payments made by Federal to Bauer and Himmelfarb were held to be taxable dividends. . . .

ANALYSIS

The determination of whether an advance is debt or equity depends on the distinction between a creditor who seeks a definite obligation that is payable in any event, and a shareholder who seeks to make an investment and to share in the profits and risks of loss in the venture. . . . The outward form of the transaction is not controlling; rather, characterization depends on the taxpayer's actual intent, as evidenced by the circumstances and conditions of the advance. . . .

In 1969, Congress authorized the Secretary of the Treasury to prescribe regulations setting forth the factors to be considered in determining whether an advance is debt or equity. 26 U.S.C. §385. The Secretary did not issue such regulations until 1982. . . .* Here we must still be guided by the case law and by the five factors that Congress suggested, as part of the 1969 statute, might be included in the regulations. This court has identified eleven factors:

> (1) the names given to the certificates evidencing the indebtedness; (2) the presence or absence of a maturity date; (3) the source of the payments; (4) the right to enforce the payment of principal and interest; (5) participation in management; (6) a status equal to or inferior to that of regular corporate creditors; (7) the intent of the parties; (8) "thin" or adequate capitalization; (9) identity of interest between creditor and stockholder; (10) payment of interest only out of "dividend" money; and (11) the ability of the corporation to obtain loans from outside lending institutions.

A. R. Lantz Co., 424 F.2d at 1333. No one factor is controlling or decisive, and the court must look to the particular circumstances of each case. Id. "The object of the inquiry is not to count factors, but to evaluate them." Tyler v. Tomlinson, 414 F.2d 844, 848 (5th Cir. 1969). The burden of

---

* The regulations under §385 were withdrawn in 1984. See page 110 infra. In addition, they were not applicable to the years in controversy. — EDS.

establishing that the advances were loans rather than capital contributions rests with the taxpayer. O. H. Kruse Grain & Milling v. Commissioner, 279 F.2d 123, 125 (9th Cir. 1960).

A. RATIO OF DEBT TO EQUITY

In the present case, the Tax Court gave great weight to the eighth factor: whether Federal was adequately capitalized. The court found that Federal's debt-to-equity ratio was as high as 92 to 1 during the years in question and that Federal was seriously undercapitalized. The Tax Court found this to be a strong indication that the advances were capital contributions rather than loans. The Tax Court apparently based its finding of a debt-to-equity ratio of 92 to 1 on a paragraph of the Stipulation of Facts signed by the parties. That paragraph states:

> The ratio of stockholder debt to corporate stock was approximately 92 to 1 for the fiscal year ending April 30, 1976.

This is accurate insofar as it compares the ending debt owed to the stockholders in 1976 of $1,850,067 to their initial stock purchase in 1958 of $20,000. This is not a true or meaningful debt-to-equity ratio. First, it completely ignores the earnings that had been retained in the corporation as it grew over the 18- year period. The stockholders' equity in a corporation is composed not only of the paid-in-capital, but also of the profits that have been generated and retained in the corporation as "retained earnings." Thus, if the debt-to-equity ratio were considered to be a comparison of stockholder loans to the correct calculation of stockholder equity including retained earnings in the corporation, this "debt-to-equity" ratio would be only 1.5 to 1 in 1974-1975 and 3.6 to 1 in 1976, as hereinafter shown.

The more meaningful debt-to-equity ratio compares the total liabilities to the stockholders' equity. The stockholders' equity would include both the initial paid-in capital and the retained earnings. Basically, the stockholders' equity is the difference between the assets and liabilities of the corporation.

Congress recognized this as the appropriate method of calculating the debt-to-equity ratio in enacting section 385.

> The debt-equity ratio of the issuing corporation for purposes of this test generally is determined by comparing the corporation's total indebtedness with the excess of its money and other assets over that indebtedness.

S. Rep. No. 552, 91st Cong., 1st Sess., *reprinted in* 1969 U.S. Code Cong. & Ad. News 1645, 2027, 2172. The calculation of Federal's debt-to-equity ratio for the years in question would therefore be as follows. In our view, the total debt-to-equity ratio is the appropriate ratio to review in determining whether a corporation is too thinly capitalized;

however, we also show the stockholder debt-to-equity ratio for illustrative purposes. . . .

Total Debt-to-Equity Ratio
1974: $1,410,603 divided by $654,107 = 2.15 to 1
1975: $1,952,944 divided by $677,973 = 2.88 to 1
1976: $3,880,642 divided by $506,092 = 7.66 to 1

Stockholder Debt-to-Equity Ratio
1974: $1,025,067 divided by $654,107 = 1.56 to 1
1975: $1,030,067 divided by $657,973 = 1.56 to 1
1976: $1,850,067 divided by $506,092 = 3.65 to 1

Thus, during the years in question, the total debt-to-equity ratio, as reflected on the books of the corporation, was not 92 to 1, but ranged from a little over 2 to 1 to less than 8 to 1. The stockholder debt-to-equity ratio during those years was a minimum of 1.5 to 1 and a maximum of 3.6 to 1.

The purpose of examining the debt-to-equity ratio in characterizing a stockholder advance is to determine whether a corporation is so thinly capitalized that a business loss would result in an inability to repay the advance; such an advance would be indicative of venture capital rather than a loan. Gilbert v. Commissioner, 248 F.2d 399, 407 (2d Cir. 1957). Essentially, we are concerned with the degree of risk the loan presents to the lender and whether an independent lender, such as a bank, would be willing to make the loan. In addition to the numerical debt-to-equity ratio, other factors in the financial picture would also be important to an independent lender in analyzing the risk. Federal's history was that of a successful company whose increasing cash needs arose from growth, not a lack of profits or business reverses. Federal had virtually no fixed assets; its plant and equipment were leased. The assets were principally current assets which could be quickly turned into cash. At all times during the years in question, Federal's current assets exceeded all liabilities by at least $300,000, which presents a strong financial picture.

Federal's financial structure and these other factors indicate that Federal could readily have obtained a loan from a bank or other financial institution for the purpose for which the stockholders' loans were made, which was to finance inventory and accounts receivable. There is specific evidence in this case that one bank would have been willing to make these loans. In a letter from a vice president of Bank of America that was attached to the Stipulated Facts, the officer noted that it had dealt with Federal and was familiar with Federal's financing during the years in question and the bank was "ready to make bank loans for those amounts of officers' loans and/or more if Federal Meat Co. desired to use bank financing." The bank officer also noted that "in the event Federal wanted to liquidate during this period, Federal would have paid off its creditors, the bank, the officers' loans from conversion of its meat inventory, and accounts receivable within a three to four week cycle most likely without any need of selling the small amount of fixed assets."

Neither the numerical debt-to-equity ratio nor other factors in the analysis of the corporation's financial structure justify a conclusion that the advances should be characterized as venture capital rather than loans.

B. PROPORTIONAL HOLDINGS OF DEBT AND EQUITY

The Tax Court also gave weight to the alleged fact that Bauer and Himmelfarb had loaned Federal amounts that were roughly proportional to their respective capital investments. The court found that during the years in question Himmelfarb had advanced a total of $970,000 to Federal while Bauer had advanced $270,000, a ratio of about 3½ to 1 as compared to the 3 to 1 ratio of their stockholdings. We agree that where a stockholder owns "debt" in the same proportion to which he holds stock in a certain corporation, the characterization as "debt" may be suspect. See *Gilbert*, 248 F.2d at 407. However, the Tax Court clearly miscalculated the amounts of Bauer's and Himmelfarb's advances to Federal.

The Tax Court looked only at the gross amount of Bauer and Himmelfarb's advances during the years in question. It failed to consider either the amount of the loans outstanding at the beginning of the three-year period or the effect of the repayments that Federal made during this period. At the beginning of the three-year period, Federal already owed $805,068 to Himmelfarb, but only $5,000 to Bauer. At the end of the period, the figures had grown to $1,700,068 and $150,000, a ratio of about 11 to 1. Even if the three-year period is considered in isolation — an approach that makes little sense given that the stockholders had been making loans to Federal since 1958 — the net amounts advanced by Himmelfarb and Bauer during that period were $895,000 and $145,000, respectively, a ratio of about 6 to 1. These figures simply will not support a finding that Bauer and Himmelfarb made advances to Federal in proportion to their capital investments.

C. OTHER FACTORS

The Tax Court also found it significant that all of Federal's shareholder debt was evidenced by demand notes with no fixed date of maturity. Although some repayments were made during the years in question, repayments never kept up with advances. We agree that lack of a fixed date of maturity on the debt instruments, together with continual growth of the debt, may suggest that there is no intention to make full repayment. But that one factor is not enough to carry the entire weight of this case. Many other factors favor the petitioners, as the Tax Court conceded: the existence of notes; fixed and reasonable interest rates; actual timely payment of interest; corresponding treatment of the interest as income by Bauer and Himmelfarb; the cash-flow demands of the custom slaughter business; and the lack of subordination of shareholder debt to other corporate debt. Additionally, this court concludes that Federal's ratio of debt to equity was within reasonable bounds and that Bauer and Himmelfarb did not own debt in proportion to their stockholdings.

CONCLUSION

The Tax Court erred in the basis of its calculation of Federal's debt-to-equity ratio. In reviewing the actual debt-to-equity ratio and the current assets in relation to the liabilities, and considering the general strength of the corporate financial picture, there is no reason to justify a conclusion that the loans were in fact "venture capital." Also, the record does not support the Tax Court's finding that Bauer and Himmelfarb made advances to Federal in rough proportion to their stockholdings. The documentation and the accounting procedures followed support the taxpayers' contention that the advances were loans. For these reasons and the other reasons above specified, we hold that the Tax Court's recharacterization of Federal's debt as equity is clearly erroneous, and the decision of the Tax Court is therefore reversed.

Rev. Rul. 90-27
1990-1 C.B. 50

ISSUES

(1) Does the dutch-auction rate preferred stock described below represent an equity interest in the issuing corporation?

(2) If a corporation holding the dutch-auction rate preferred stock described below receives a dividend distribution with respect to the stock, do the terms of the issue cause the distribution to fail to qualify for the dividends received deduction under section 243(a) of the Code?

FACTS

X, a publicly-held domestic corporation, issued 1000 shares of dutch-auction rate preferred stock for $100 million. The stock carries a liquidation preference of $100,000 per share. As a condition of sale, each prospective purchaser was required to execute a purchaser's letter, agreeing to sell shares of the X preferred only through a "dutch-auction" proceeding, to an authorized broker-dealer, or to a purchaser who similarly has executed a purchaser's letter.

The initial dividend rate for the preferred shares was set by X at the time of issue. Under a prearranged schedule (generally every 49 days), the rate is then reset pursuant to a "dutch auction," a process in which orders to purchase or sell the preferred stock are submitted through registered broker-dealers to a designated auction agent. In each auction, existing holders that wish to increase the number of shares held and potential new holders bid to purchase shares offered for sale. The stock is designed to trade at the liquidation preference ($100,000). Therefore, each bid consists of a proposed dividend rate at which the bidder is willing to purchase the offered shares at a price equal to the liquidation preference.

An existing holder may choose to hold its preferred shares at whatever rate is set for the next dividend period. Alternatively, an existing holder may place a bid order to hold its shares provided the applicable rate for the next dividend period is not below the rate specified in the bid. If the applicable rate for the next dividend period is below the specified rate, then the bid is treated as a sell order. Lastly, an existing holder may place an order to sell its shares regardless of the applicable rate. A holder may place differing orders for each of its shares.

The lowest dividend rate bid that enables all the shares offered for sale to be sold to potential purchasers is the rate that applies to all shares for the next dividend period. If all of the current holders of the preferred shares elect to hold their shares without specifying a minimum dividend rate (place hold orders on their shares), the dividend rate for the next period is 59% of the AA Composite Commercial Paper Rate.

If there are insufficient bids to purchase all of the shares offered for sale, the auction "fails" and the dividend rate is then the applicable maximum bid rate for that auction. The maximum bid rates are expressed as a percentage of the AA Composite Commercial Paper Rate. The rate applicable to a particular auction depends on the prevailing rating for the preferred stock as determined by a designated investor service:

Prevailing Rating	Percentage
AA/aa or above	110%
A/a	125%
BBB/baa	150%
BB/ba	200%
Below BB/ba	250%

A broker-dealer may buy and sell shares of X preferred in an auction both on behalf of customers and for its own account. Moreover, a broker-dealer may "make a market," that is, trade shares for its own account with a view toward maintaining an orderly market. There is no express or implied agreement between a broker-dealer or any other party and the issuer or any holder, however, that the broker-dealer or other party will guarantee or otherwise arrange to ensure that any holder of the X preferred stock will be able to sell its shares.

Dividends with respect to the X preferred stock are cumulative and must be declared by the Board of Directors and paid out of legally available funds. Holders have no direct right to compel the payment of dividends, and there is no arrangement ensuring that dividends will be paid. However, although the preferred shares generally have no voting rights, if accrued dividends remain unpaid for a specified period, the holders of the preferred stock obtain the right to vote as a class for seats on the Board of Directors.

With proper notice, X may redeem part or all of the preferred shares at any time at par ($100,000) plus accrued but unpaid dividends. Holders, however, may not compel redemption. In the event of any voluntary or involuntary dissolution, liquidation, or winding up of the affairs of X, the holders of the preferred stock are entitled to be paid before holders of shares ranking junior. The liquidation preference is at par plus any unpaid accrued dividends. The claims of the holders of the preferred are subordinate, however, to the claims of X's creditors.

Corporation Y acquired ten shares of the auction rate preferred stock issued by X.

LAW AND ANALYSIS

DEBT/EQUITY ISSUE

The initial question with respect to dutch-auction rate preferred stock is whether it is equity or debt for federal income tax purposes. This classification depends on the facts and circumstances of each case. No particular fact is conclusive in making such a determination. John Kelley Co. v. Commissioner, 326 U.S. 521 (1946), 1946-1 C.B. 191.

From the perspective of the holders, dutch-auction rate preferred stock is an investment alternative to commercial paper or other short-term debt. In certain critical respects, however, the legal rights embodied in the dutch-auction rate preferred described above are similar to those found in traditional preferred stock and are unlike those usually associated with debt. As a holder of the preferred, Y has no right to receive a sum certain either on demand or on a specified date, and, at liquidation or in bankruptcy, Y's rights are subordinate to the claims of X's creditors. Subject to that limitation, X may redeem the stock, but the holder cannot compel redemption. Moreover, X has not guaranteed or otherwise arranged to ensure that Y can sell its stock in an auction. Y's receipt of dividends is dependent upon dividends being declared by X and paid out of legally available funds.

The terms of the dutch-auction rate preferred stock issued by *X,* including those discussed above, cause the stock to be equity for federal income tax purposes.

HOLDING PERIOD

The remaining question is whether section 246(c) of the Code limits *Y*'s holding period in the *X* preferred and thus precludes the dividends received deduction under section 243(a).

Under section 243(a)(1) of the Code, a corporation generally is allowed a deduction equal to 70 percent of the amount received as dividends from a domestic corporation.

Section 246(c)(1) of the Code excludes from the deduction allowed under section 243 any dividend on a share of stock that is held by the taxpayer for 45 days or less.

Section 246(c)(4) of the Code reduces the holding period of the taxpayer for any period in which (A) the taxpayer has an option to sell, is under a contractual obligation to sell, or has made (and not closed) a short sale of, substantially identical stock or securities, (B) the taxpayer is the grantor of an option to buy substantially identical stock or securities, or (C) under regulations prescribed by the Secretary, a taxpayer has diminished its risk of loss by holding one or more positions with respect to substantially similar or related property.

The dutch-auction mechanism in this case serves the dual function of resetting the dividend rate on the preferred stock and providing a vehicle for the purchase and sale of the shares. Each successful auction resets the dividend rate on the preferred stock to the rate that allows the shares to trade at par. Thus, so long as auctions are successful, the holder of the stock is protected from fluctuations in value of the stock that otherwise would result from changes in interest rates and the credit rating of the issuer. Although this protection insulates the holder from certain market risks, the legislative history of the Tax Reform Act of 1984 expressly states that an instrument providing a similar type of protection (adjustable rate preferred stock that is indexed to the Treasury bill rate) does not offer the risk diminution prescribed by section 246(c)(4)(C) of the Code. See H.R. Conf. Rep. No. 816, 98th Cong., 2d Sess. 817, 818 (1984), 1984-3 (Vol. 2) C.B. 71.

The auctions also provide a vehicle for the purchase and sale of shares. Although a holder of the preferred stock has the expectation of being able to sell its stock in any auction, there is no guarantee that a holder will be able to do so. In other words, the holder does not have an option to sell.

Section 246(c)(4) may apply not only if the holder has a formal option to sell, but also if the holder has rights equivalent to an option to sell. For example, if a broker-dealer had agreed to guarantee the success of each auction, *Y* would have had the equivalent of an option to sell its stock at each auction. Similarly, if X were in such a position that it had no practical alternative but to redeem the stock in the event of a failed auction, the combination of the auction mechanism and the forced redemption would give Y the equivalent of an option to sell its stock. Such facts, however, are not present here.

If an auction fails, the dividend rate for the next dividend period automatically resets to the maximum rate. This rate, which depends upon the rating of the preferred stock and is determined as a percentage of the commercial paper rate, may substantially exceed the rate that would be anticipated in a successful auction. The resulting rate may provide X with an incentive to redeem the stock rather than pay the increased dividends. On the facts presented, however, the maximum rate is not so high that it assures Y that the failure of an auction will be followed by a redemption of the stock. Moreover, the circumstances under which an auction is likely to fail (e.g., unforeseen financial difficulties of X) raise serious doubts as to whether X would be able to redeem the preferred stock even if the reset dividend rate provided it with a significant incentive to do so. Thus, the combination of the auction mechanism and the dividend increase following a failed auction do not give Y rights equivalent to an option to sell.

HOLDINGS

(1) The dutch-auction rate preferred stock described above represents an equity interest in the issuing corporation.

(2) Neither the dutch-auction mechanism, the dividend increase required following a failed auction, nor any other term of the dutch-auction rate preferred stock described above prevents a corporation receiving a dividend distribution with respect to the stock from claiming the dividends received deduction under section 243(a) of the Code.

NOTE

1. *Statutory and regulatory classification of "equity" and "debt."* The House version of the 1954 Code contained definitions designed to indicate precisely what instruments would qualify for the interest deduction and for other tax privileges. But the Senate dropped these definitions, stating "Your committee believes that any attempt to write into the statute precise definitions which will classify for tax purposes the many types of corporate stocks and securities will be frustrated by the numerous characteristics of an interchangeable nature which can be given to these instruments." S. Rep. No. 1622, 83d Cong., 2d Sess. 42 (1954).

Despite this pessimistic conclusion, the Tax Reform Act of 1969 added §385 to the Code authorizing the Treasury to issue regulations to determine whether an interest in a corporation is to be treated "for purposes of this title as stock or indebtedness." The Treasury may take into account, along with other factors, the existence of a written unconditional promise to pay a sum certain and a fixed rate of interest, the subordination or preference over any indebtedness, the debt-equity ratio, the convertibility into stock, and the relationship between holdings of stock and of the interest in question. The Treasury has made three attempts to promulgate suitable regulations. Each attempt has been heavily criticized and ultimately withdrawn.

In some cases, the IRS has been "whipsawed" by inconsistent treatment of financial instruments by the issuer and the holders. For example, the issuer might prefer to treat a financial instrument as debt in order to deduct the interest. A corporate holder of the instrument, however, may prefer to treat periodic distributions as dividends that may not increase taxable income because of the dividends-received deduction in §243. See page 134 infra. Under §385(c)(1), the characterization by the issuer of an instrument as debt or equity is binding on the holders of the instrument. For example, in Rev. Rul. 90-27, supra, if the issuer treated the dutch-auction rate preferred stock as debt, that characterization would be binding on the holder. Section 385(c)(2), however, does permit a holder of an instrument to adopt an inconsistent treatment so long as such treatment is dislocated on the holder's tax return.

2. *Judicial classification of "equity" and "debt."* In *Bauer* the court was concerned with the ratio of debt to equity. For those corporations whose outstanding debt far exceeds equity, debtholders would likely regard themselves as stockholders or potential stockholders because of the risk associated with repayment. Their chances of repayment would rise and fall with the success or failure of the corporation. See, e.g., Dobkin v. Commissioner, 15 T.C. 31 (1950), aff'd per curiam, 192 F.2d 392 (2d Cir. 1951); Burr Oaks Corp. v. Commissioner, 365 F.2d 24 (7th Cir. 1966). For well-capitalized corporations, the risk of default on outstanding debt instruments is lower.

There is no mathematical threshold for determining permissible debt-equity ratios. In Briggs Co. v. Commissioner, 1946 T.C.M. ¶46,109, a ratio of 4 to 1 was found excessive in light of surrounding financial considerations, while in Baker Commodities v. Commissioner, 48 T.C. 374 (1967), a ratio of 700 to 1 was upheld as justified since cash flow and earnings power were sufficient to support repayment. A ratio of debt to equity that does not exceed 3 to 1 is likely to withstand attack. See B. Bittker and J. Eustice, Federal Income Taxation of Corporations and Shareholders ¶4.04 (6th ed. 1994).

In *Bauer* the outcome hinged on how to measure the value of stock for purposes of determining the debt-equity ratio. Who has the stronger point, the Ninth Circuit, which used the fair market value of the outstanding stock (actually book value plus retained earnings), or the Tax Court, which used the book value of the stock?

Thin capitalization is only one sign pointing toward recharacterizing debt as equity. For closely held corporations, when debt is owned in the same proportions as equity, the courts tend to scrutinize the situation closely. In *Bauer* the ratio of stock held by the two shareholders was 3 to 1, while the ratio of new loans to the corporation incurred by the shareholders during the years in question was $3\frac{1}{2}$ to 1. Why did the Ninth Circuit find that the holdings were not roughly proportionate?

Under the withdrawn §385 regulations, proportionality was deemed a key factor. Straight debt with no equity features held disproportionately would be respected as debt; proportionately held debt was subject to much stricter scrutiny. Disproportionality was helpful to the taxpayer in Green Bay Steel v. Commissioner, 53 T.C. 451 (1969). Proportionality alone would not necessarily cause recharacterization. See, e.g., Litton Business Systems v. Commissioner, 61 T.C. 367 (1973), in which a parent corporation's advances to subsidiaries were held valid debt despite an absence of formalities. Interest was charged, the parent expected repayment, outside funding was available, and the subsidiary was not thinly capitalized. Cf. United States v. Uneco, Inc., 532 F.2d 1204 (8th Cir. 1976).

Other factors considered by some courts when characterizing financial instruments include whether repayment in fact took place, whether formalities were observed when the "loan" was made, and whether the proceeds were used for "essential" assets. In *Bauer* the Tax Court found that the loans were made during the formative stages of the corporation for essential operating assets and were therefore equity contributions. Should the timing of the loans be a factor?

3. *Hybrid securities: bifurcation.* When a corporation is unable to issue ordinary evidences of indebtedness, usually because of a fear of damaging its credit position, there have been attempts to get the same tax effect by issuing "hybrid" securities. These instruments often look like preferred stock to creditors, but it is hoped that they will be treated as bonds, debentures, or notes by the IRS. Among the characteristics of such "hybrid" securities are the following: (a) They are often held only by shareholders and in the same proportions as the stock; (b) they may be transferable only with stock; (c) they have long maturities or no maturity dates; (d) the "interest" is geared to corporate income or is discretionary with the directors; (e) payment of the "interest" or "principal" (or both) is subordinated to the claims of general creditors; and (f) they are sometimes issued only to present stockholders and not for new consideration. If too many of these features are found, the instruments will be treated as preferred stock rather than as evidences of indebtedness.

The leading case on the subject is John Kelley Co. v. Commissioner, 326 U.S. 521 (1946). In that case, the nominal debt instruments provided for 8 percent interest, which was noncumulative, and payment was contingent on sufficient corporate earnings. The instruments matured in 20 years and were subordinate to all creditors. In determining that the hybrid instruments constituted debt, the Supreme Court reasoned that the corporation had a lot of outstanding stock and was not thinly capitalized.

In Farley Realty Corp. v. Commissioner, 279 F.2d 701 (2d Cir. 1960), a nonshareholder lent money to a corporation for the acquisition of a building. The obligation provided for a fixed payment of interest and a fixed maturity date. Furthermore, the lender was entitled to 50 percent of any appreciation on the sale of the building even if the sale took place after the maturity date. The court permitted a deduction for the fixed interest but not for the lender's share of the realized appreciation. But see Rev. Rul. 83-51, 1983-1 C.B. 48 (allowing a deduction for shared appreciation paid by a borrower to a lender on a home residence loan (i.e., a noncommercial context) with payment due upon sale of the residence or at the end of the 10-year loan term).

In Helvering v. Richmond, F & P.R.R., 90 F.2d 971 (4th Cir. 1937), the court permitted an interest deduction for guaranteed 7 percent dividend payments on preferred stock when the guaranteed dividends were a first lien on corporate assets ahead of all creditors. Payments in excess of the guaranteed amount were treated as nondeductible dividends.

Notwithstanding these cases, in general courts have resisted bifurcation. See Madison, The Deductibility of "Interest" on Hybrid Securities, 39 Tax Law. 465 (1986). Several recently enacted Code provisions, however, permit or mandate bifurcation. Section 385(a) authorizes regulations permitting the bifurcation of a corporate obligation as part equity and part debt. The legislative history of this provision explains: "[S]uch treatment may be appropriate in circumstances where a debt instrument provides for payments that are dependent to a significant extent (whether in whole or in part) on corporate performance, whether through equity kickers, contingent interest, significant deferral of payment, subordination, or an interest rate sufficiently high to suggest a significant risk of default." H.R. Rep. No. 247, 101st Cong., 1st Sess. 1235-1236 (1989).

Congress has also clamped down on the availability of a corporate interest deduction in connection with certain corporate takeovers by bifurcating certain high-yield discount obligations. See page 408 infra.

Another form of bifurcation is found in §163(j), the "earnings stripping" provision. If an interest expense is deductible but the recipient is not taxable upon receipt, there is a loss to the U.S. tax system as a whole and an incentive to borrow from tax-exempt lenders such as related foreign corporations and certain U.S. pension funds. Congress has addressed the practice of stripping away earnings of a taxable U.S. corporation through an interest payment to a tax-exempt related party by denying an interest deduction under specified circumstances.

Section 163(j) essentially disallows an interest deduction on "excess interest expense" of a payor corporation with a ratio of debt to equity in excess of 1.5 to 1 at the end of the tax year. "Excess interest expense" is defined as the amount by which the corporation's net interest expense exceeds 50 percent of its adjusted taxable income. Any interest deduction disallowed under §163(j) may be carried over to a subsequent year, when it may be deductible if there is no excess interest expense.

On the regulatory front, the Treasury has issued a proposed regulation that bifurcates payments made on certain original issue discount debt instruments that provide for both noncontingent and contingent payments. Prop. Treas. Regs. §1.1275-4(g). In general, the noncontingent payments are deductible but the contingent payments are not.

Can a financial instrument ever be bifurcated over time? That is, can an instrument that is considered equity when it is issued (e.g., because a corporation is thinly capitalized) be considered a debt instrument at a later time (e.g., when the corporation's debt-equity ratio improves)? For the possibility that an instrument may be a chameleon, see Edwards v. Commissioner, 50 T.C. 220 (1968) (notes that constituted bona fide debt in hands of original owners must be treated as equity in hands of purchasers, who had simultaneously purchased the stock of the obligor corporation when it was in a deficit position), rev'd, 415 F.2d 578 (10th Cir. 1969) (purchasers "took the capital financial structure as they found it," including valid debt); Cuyuna Realty Co. v. United States, 382 F.2d 298 (Cl. Ct. 1967) (debtor-creditor relationship changed with passage of time to equity-investor relationship).

4. *Hybrid securities: convertibility.* A debt instrument that is convertible into corporate stock contains both debt and equity features. A holder of the instrument may enjoy a fixed rate of return with relatively little risk, but the holder also has the right to share in future corporate growth by exercising the conversion privilege. As a general rule, a conversion feature by itself does not automatically result in the treatment of a financial instrument as equity. In Rev. Rul. 85-119, 1985-2 C.B. 60, a publicly traded debt instrument contained a conversion feature that was mandated by banking regulations. At maturity, the note was convertible into stock of the issuing corporation equal to the face value of the note. A holder could also elect to receive cash instead of stock. In determining that the note was a debt instrument (and that interest payments were deductible), the ruling highlighted the following factors: The note was publicly traded and not held in proportion to stock ownership; the issuing corporation was not thinly capitalized; the instrument had a fixed maturity date; interest payments were not contingent on earnings; and instrument holders did not participate in corporate governance. The convertibility feature was not controlling because the amount of stock to be received was equal to the face value of the note.

In contrast, Rev. Rul. 83-98, 1983-2 C.B. 40, ruled that a nominal debt instrument was really an equity instrument, in part because the instrument contained a conversion feature. Under the conversion feature, a holder could convert the note to 50 shares of the issuer's stock (worth $1,000 at the time the instrument was issued) or receive $600 when the instrument matured. The issuer also had the right to call the instrument for $600 at any time. These conversion characteristics made it highly likely that holders would convert to stock.

5.   *Preferred stock versus debt.* If common stock and straight debt are the endpoints on the debt-equity spectrum, preferred stock is right in the middle. Typically, preferred stockholders receive fixed payments (like debtholders) and do not share in the growth of the issuing corporations (like debtholders). But preferred shareholders do not receive dividends until creditors have been paid (like common shareholders) and stand in line behind creditors in the event of liquidation (like common shareholders).

In Rev. Rul. 90-27, above, the issue is whether the financial instrument is preferred stock or really a debt instrument (although labeled preferred stock). Typically, an issuer wants the instrument to be characterized as debt because of the deduction. But notice that in contrast to *Bauer,* here the taxpayer (i.e., the shareholder, Corporation Y) wanted the financial instrument to be treated as preferred stock and the distributions to be treated as dividends. A corporation that receives dividends must include them in income but then can deduct a percentage of the dividends received. See §243, discussed at page 134 infra. In contrast, interest received on debt instruments is fully includible.

As the ruling points out, the financial instruments are very much like short-term debt to the holders. The principal amount of the obligation is always $100,000, and the rate of return is adjusted every 49 days in accordance with the market to keep the fair market value of the instrument at $100,000. Nevertheless, the ruling points out that the equity features of the instruments outweigh the debt features. The holders are not entitled to receive a sum certain either on demand or on a specified date, and distributions can be made only in accordance with state law dividend requirements.

The "dutch auction" process is a method of determining the market interest rate. Suppose each of the following purchasers, P, is willing to purchase one share of preferred stock for $100,000 if the dividend rate is equal to or greater than:

P1	10%
P2	12%
P3	9%
P4	8%
P5	18%

Each of the current holders of the stock, S, is willing to sell one share for $100,000 if the dividend rate for the next period is equal to or less than:

S1	10%
S2	11%
S3	13%
S4	8%
S5	sell at any dividend rate
S6	hold regardless of dividend rate

At a dividend rate of 11 percent, the market clears: *P1, P3,* and *P4* will buy; *S2, S3,* and *S5* will sell. The market would not clear at 10 percent because then *S1* would want to sell and could not do so. Similarly, the market does not clear at 12 percent because then *S2* no longer wants to sell and *P2* now wants to buy. Because an 11 percent dividend rate clears the market, that is the dividend rate for the next 49 days.

6. *Retirement, redemption, and worthlessness.* The decision whether to issue debt or equity affects not only the characterization of the payments made on the obligation — whether such payments constitute interest or dividends — but also the treatment of the obligation itself on retirement or redemption. Generally, any gain (or loss) on the retirement of a debt instrument because of postpurchase fluctuation in the market interest rate will produce capital gain or loss. See §1271, but see §1276, which treats gain from prepurchase fluctuation in the market interest rate as ordinary income. Gain (or loss) on the redemption of stock by a corporation may result in ordinary or capital gain (or loss), depending on the successful navigation of the safe harbors of §302, which offer exchange treatment. See Chapter 5.

If retirement or redemption is unavailable because a corporation fails, then worthless stock, bonds, and other evidence of debt that are "securities" under §165(g)(2) ordinarily give rise to long- or short-term capital loss under §165(g)(1). Debt instruments that are not "securities" under §165(g)(2) are nonbusiness bad debts and produce short-term capital losses under §166(d). See, e.g., Litwin v. United States, 983 F.2d 997 (10th Cir. 1993) (bad debt deduction allowed for advances by taxpayer with respect to his closely held business when taxpayer convinced the court that the corporation was formed to allow him to earn a salary).

In light of the attendant restrictions on capital losses imposed by §§1211 and 1212, Congress enacted §1244 in 1958, under which an individual's loss on "§1244 stock" can be deducted from ordinary income with certain limitations. The principal features of §1244 include the following: (1) Section 1244 stock must be issued by a corporation whose capital does not exceed $1 million; (2) only common stock qualifies; (3) the corporation must have been active for a period of time prior to the stock's worthlessness; (4) the stock must be issued to an individual for money or other property; (5) the aggregate amount that can be treated as an ordinary loss for any taxable year may not exceed $50,000 ($100,000 per joint return). See also §165(g)(3), which affords corporations ordinary losses for worthless securities in certain subsidiaries. This ordinary loss treatment strangely does not apply if the corporation sells the securities.

C. PROBLEMS

1.   What is the highest corporate marginal tax rate?
2.   How might a profitable U.S. corporation pay no U.S. taxes?
3.   Suppose X Corp., a construction company engaged in a major project, in year 1 has no regular tax liability under its regular completed contract method of accounting. It does have $100,000 of AMT liability, principally because of §56(a)(3) which mandates the percentage of completion method of accounting for AMT purposes. In year 2, when the project is completed, X Corp.'s regular tax liability is $400,000 (there is no AMT liability in year 2). Why might X Corp. complain about this result? Does the Code offer any relief?
4.   X Corp., with only one class of stock outstanding, issues adjustable rate convertible notes with the following characteristics. The instruments are offered in exchange for either $1,000 or 50 shares of X Corp. stock (trading at $20 per share). The investor will receive annual payments equal to the dividends payable on 50 shares of X Corp. stock plus 2 percent of the $1,000 issue price ($20). The annual payment was guaranteed to be at least $60 and no more than $175 in all years. Stated differently, the investor was guaranteed a return of between 6 percent and 17.5 percent of face value. The notes were convertible at any time by the investor into 50 shares of X Corp. stock. If the investor chooses not to convert, the instrument will be redeemed for $600 at the end of 20 years. X Corp. retains an option to call the note for $600 at any time more than two years after issuance, although the investor can elect to convert if X Corp. exercises its option. X Corp. consults you about the tax treatment of the annual payments made on the instruments. See Rev. Rul. 83-98, 1983-2 C.B. 40.
5.   X Corp., a U.S. corporation, borrows $10 million from Y Corp., its Dutch parent. Pursuant to an income tax treaty between the Netherlands and the United States, Y Corp. is not subject to U.S. taxation on its interest income. The loan has a 10-year term and bears a 10 percent rate, the market rate when the loan was made. Discuss the tax treatment of the interest payments made from X Corp. to Y Corp.

II

CORPORATE DISTRIBUTIONS: NONLIQUIDATING AND LIQUIDATING

4

Distributions of Cash and Property

In Chapter 2 we looked at the formation of a corporation. Once in existence, a corporation reports income and takes deductions in much the same way as individuals. See pages 81-92 supra. At some point, however, the shareholders may want the corporation to distribute some or all of what it has earned or even part of their capital contributions.

Section 61(a)(7) includes "dividends" in a taxpayer's gross income. But what are dividends? Certainly not every distribution by a corporation is a taxable dividend. Suppose T forms X Corp. with $100. At the end of its first year, X Corp. has lost $10 and holds $90 in assets. T, in need of cash, causes X Corp. to distribute $20. Is the distribution a dividend, subjecting T to tax? If not, what is it?

The labyrinth of statutory provisions governing this subject begins with §301(a), referring to distributions of "property," as defined by §317(a). This provision excludes the corporation's own stock from the term "property." Such distributions are governed by §305, discussed in Chapter 6. In Rev. Rul. 90-11, 1990-1 C.B. 10, the Service ruled that the adoption by a corporation of a "poison pill" plan, which provides for the issuance of a separately tradable right to purchase a fractional share of preferred stock for every share of common stock in the event of an unfriendly takeover attempt, is not a distribution of "property" to shareholders even though the adoption of the plan was a dividend under state law.

Returning from §317(a) to §301(a), note that there must be a distribution of property by a corporation to a shareholder *with respect to its stock* in order for §301 to apply. Transfers such as salaries or debt repayment, even if the recipient is a shareholder, are not covered by §301(a) because they are not made "with respect to [the paying corporation's] stock." The amount of a distribution made with respect to a shareholder's stock is

119

computed under §301(b). While the amount of a cash distribution is self-evident, distributions of property create some complexity. Is the amount distributed equal to the fair market value of the property, its basis to the corporation, or some other measure? How do liabilities encumbering the property affect the amount distributed? These issues are addressed at page 138 infra.

Once the "amount" of a distribution is determined, its tax treatment is governed by §301(c), which consists of three tiers: §301(c)(1), (c)(2), and (c)(3). Section 301(c)(1) states that dividends are to be included in gross income, a rule already announced in §61(a)(7). For the definition of "dividend," §301(c)(1) refers us to §316. Section 316(a) informs us that distributions out of certain "earnings and profits" will be treated as dividends. Section 316(a)(1) specifies "accumulated" earnings and profits and §316(a)(2) addresses "current" earnings and profits, but nowhere does the Code provide a definition of earnings and profits. Section 312 instructs us to increase or decrease earnings and profits to take account of various transactions but fails to tell us just what we are adjusting. See discussion at page 129 infra.

Returning to §301(c), distributions that are not dividends are applied to reduce the adjusted basis of the taxpayer's stock. §301(c)(2). If the stock basis is reduced to zero, further distributions will be given sale or exchange treatment, resulting in capital gains if the stock is a capital asset. §301(c)(3)(A).

Section 301 and the related sections summarized above govern the tax treatment of the distributee shareholder. Distributions may also cause tax consequences to the distributing corporation. Is the distributing corporation taxable on a distribution of cash? On a distribution of appreciated property? Can it deduct a loss if the distributed property is worth less than its basis? Section 311 controls the tax consequences to the distributing corporation. Historically, a distributing corporation was generally not taxed on a distribution of appreciated property. §311(a). The Tax Reform Act of 1986, however, radically altered this area by providing that a distributing corporation will recognize gain on the distribution of appreciated property. Moreover, distributions require adjustments to the corporation's earnings and profits account that will affect the tax consequences to the shareholders of *future* distributions. §312.

This quick trip through the distributions maze becomes slightly more bewildering when one realizes that we have encountered only some types of distributions, albeit the ones that are most frequently encountered. See §301(f). Stock distributions are governed by §305. Distributions in redemption or partial liquidation are governed by §302. Liquidations are governed by §§331-338. Distributions in connection with reorganizations are discussed in §§354-368. In Chapter 2 we already considered distributions in connection with the formation of a corporation. §351(b).

This chapter is divided into four parts, each focusing on a different type of distribution: (1) cash distributions; (2) property distributions other than cash; (3) disguised or constructive dividends; and (4) intercorporate dividends. All these subjects require an understanding of the concept of "earnings and profits," which is examined at the outset, in the context of a cash distribution.

A. CASH DISTRIBUTIONS

Rev. Rul. 74-164
1974-1 C.B. 74

Advice has been requested concerning the taxable status of corporate distributions under the circumstances described below.

X corporation and Y corporation each using the calendar year for Federal income tax purposes made distributions of $15,000 to their respective shareholders on July 1, 1971, and made no other distributions to their shareholders during the taxable year. The distributions were taxable as provided by section 301(c) of the Internal Revenue Code of 1954.

SITUATION 1

At the beginning of its taxable year 1971, X corporation had earnings and profits accumulated after February 28, 1913, of $40,000. It had an operating loss for the period January 1, 1971 through June 30, 1971, of $50,000 but had earnings and profits for the entire year 1971 of $5,000.

SITUATION 2

At the beginning of its taxable year 1971, Y corporation had a deficit in earnings and profits accumulated after February 28, 1913, of $60,000. Its net profits for the period January 1, 1971 through June 30, 1971, were $75,000 but its earnings and profits for the entire taxable year 1971 were only $5,000.

SITUATION 3

Assume the same facts as in Situation 1 except that X had a deficit in earnings and profits of $5,000 for the entire taxable year 1971.

SITUATION 4

Assume the same facts as in Situation 1 except that X had a deficit in earnings and profits of $55,000 for the entire taxable year 1971.

Sections 301(a) and 301(c) of the Code provide, in part, that: (1) the portion of a distribution of property made by a corporation to a shareholder with respect to its stock which is a dividend (as defined in section 316), shall be included in the shareholder's gross income; (2) the portion of the distribution which is not a dividend shall be applied against and reduce the adjusted basis of the stock; and (3) the portion which is not a dividend to the extent that it exceeds the adjusted basis of the stock and is not out of increase in value accrued before March 1, 1913, shall be treated as gain from the sale or exchange of property.

Section 316(a) of the Code provides that the term "dividend" means any distribution of property made by a corporation to its shareholders out of its earnings and profits accumulated after February 28, 1913, or out of its earnings and profits of the taxable year computed as of the close of the taxable year without diminution by reason of any distribution made during the year, and without regard to the amount of earnings and profits at the time the distribution was made.

Section 1.316-2(a) of the Income Tax Regulations provides, in part, that in determining the source of a distribution, consideration should be given first, to the earnings and profits of the taxable year; and second, to the earnings and profits accumulated since February 28, 1913, only in the case where, and to the extent that, the distributions made during the taxable year are not regarded as out of the earnings and profits of that year.

Applying the foregoing principles, in Situation 1, the earnings and profits of X corporation for the taxable year 1971 of $5,000 and the earnings and profits accumulated since February 28, 1913, and prior to the taxable year 1971, of $40,000 were applicable to the distribution paid by it on July 1, 1971. Thus, $5,000 of the distribution of $15,000 was paid from the earnings and profits of the taxable year 1971 and the balance of $10,000 was paid from the earnings and profits accumulated since February 28, 1913. Therefore, the entire distribution of $15,000 was a dividend within the meaning of section 316 of the Code.

In Situation 2 the earnings and profits of Y corporation for the taxable year 1971 of $5,000 were applicable to the distribution paid by Y corporation on July 1, 1971. Y corporation had no earnings and profits accumulated after February 28, 1913, available at the time of the distribution. Thus, only $5,000 of the distribution by Y corporation of $15,000 was a dividend within the meaning of section 316 of the Code. The balance of such distribution, $10,000 which was not a dividend, applied against and reduced the adjusted basis of the stock in the hands of the shareholders, and to the extent that it exceeded the adjusted basis of the stock was gain from the sale or exchange of property.

In the case of a deficit in earnings and profits for the taxable year in which distributions are made, the taxable status of distributions is dependent upon the amount of earnings and profits accumulated since February 28, 1913, and available at the dates of distribution. In determining the amount of such earnings and profits, section 1.316-2(b) of the regulations provides, in effect, that the deficit in earnings and profits of the taxable year will be prorated to the dates of distribution.

Applying the foregoing to Situations 3 and 4 the distribution paid by X corporation on July 1, 1971, in each situation was a dividend within the meaning of section 316 of the Code to the extent indicated as follows:

Situation #3

Accumulated Earnings and Profits (E&P) [Jan. 1]	$ 40,000
E&P deficit for entire taxable year ($5,000) Prorate to date of distribution [July 1] (½ of $5,000)	(2,500)
E&P available [July 1]	$ 37,500
Distribution [July 1] ($15,000)	(15,000) taxable as a dividend
E&P deficit from [July 1-Dec. 31]	(2,500)
[Accumulated E&P at end of year]	$ 20,000

Situation #4

Accumulated E&P [Jan. 1]	$ 40,000
E&P deficit for entire taxable year ($55,000) Prorate to date of distribution [July 1] (½ of $55,000)	(27,500)
E&P available [July 1]	$ 12,500
Distribution [July 1] ($15,000)	(12,500) taxable as a dividend
E&P deficit from [July 1-Dec. 31]	(27,500)
Accumulated E&P balance [Dec. 31]	$(27,500)

Divine v. Commissioner
500 F.2d 1041 (2d Cir. 1974)

WATERMAN, Circuit Judge.

I . . .

The outcome of this case depends on our resolution of two legal issues. [The first issue, involving collateral estoppel, is omitted.] Second, when, pursuant to the terms of statutory restricted stock options granted by a corporation to its employees, those employees, in exercising the options, purchased the stock for less than the stock's fair market value, should the corporation's "earnings and profits" under 316 of the Internal Revenue Code ("IRC" or "Code") be reduced by the difference between the fair market value of the stock so purchased and the prices paid by the employees? . . .

Rapid American Corporation (hereinafter "Rapid" or the "Corporation") is a publicly owned corporation. Its common stock during the years 1961 and 1962 was listed on the American Stock Exchange. As of January 31, 1963, Rapid had over 2,000 shareholders who held in the aggregate more than 2,000,000 shares of Rapid's common stock. Appellant Divine was one of those shareholders; his approximate holdings amounted to 37,000 shares in 1961 and rose to 40,000 in 1962.

During the years 1961 and 1962, Rapid made certain cash distributions, totaling some $840,840.53 in 1961, and $1,024,836.93 in 1962, to its shareholders. Appellant's portions of these disbursements were $18,501.40 in 1961 and $20,572.04 in 1962. Rapid advised the shareholders that the distributions did not have to be included by them in their individual personal income tax returns. This advice was predicated on the belief that Rapid's "earnings and profits" were insufficient to render these distributions dividends taxable as ordinary income to the recipients, but, rather, the recipients should consider the payments to be returns of capital and hence non-taxable.

At issue in this case is the manner in which Rapid's "current earnings and profits" and "accumulated earnings and profits" for its taxable years 1961 and 1962 should be computed. Specifically at issue is the correctness of a reduction of earnings and profits to account for purported "compensation expenses" measured by the "loss" Rapid absorbed in making "bargain" sales of its common stock to certain of its employees who possessed restricted stock options to purchase the stock.* Pursuant to the terms of these restricted stock options, during the period from January 1, 1957 to January 31, 1962, Rapid sold 174,395 shares of its common stock to some of its employees. Although these shares had a fair market value of $5,307,206, the corporation received only $1,889,360 from the employees who exercised their options. Rapid thus received $3,417,846 less for its stock than it could have received if the shares had been sold on the open market. In the period from February 1, 1962 to January 31, 1963 corporation employees purchased an additional 12,163 shares pursuant to the terms of options they held. Again, the prices paid by the employees, $155,388 in the aggregate, were substantially below the fair market value of the shares of stock, $363,914. It is argued that these differences of

---

* Pursuant to the restricted stock option at issue, the amount of the "spread" was neither includible by the employees nor deductible by the corporate employer. — EDS.

$3,417,846 and $208,526 represent compensation expense which should reduce corporate earnings and profits. . . .

II

[The collateral estoppel issue is omitted.]

III . . .

In this case the Commissioner claims that the cash distributions made to appellant by Rapid constitute "dividend" income which under §61(a)(7) of the IRC is taxable to appellant as ordinary income. The word "dividend" is a term of art, the definition of which is found in §316 IRC: A "dividend" is "any distribution of property made by a corporation to its shareholders — (1) out of its earnings and profits accumulated after February 28, 1913, or (2) out of its earnings and profits of the [current] taxable year." Much to our chagrin, and that of many of our judicial ancestors, however, the Internal Revenue Code does not define the operative phrase "earnings and profits" or describe the manner in which that elusive quantity should be calculated. Congress could, and certainly should, rectify this deficiency by promulgating guidelines to assist the courts which must control the evolution of the concept. Be that as it may, such legislative guidelines do not now exist, so we must treat the problem as adequately as we can with the resources at our disposal.

Most of the commentators have experienced no difficulty in explaining what "earnings and profits" are not. For example, the term is synonymous with neither "corporate surplus," nor with "taxable income." Notably less successful have been the copious attempts to establish a coherent and workable scheme for determining when particular corporate transactions should reduce or increase a corporation's "earnings and profits." One of the most traditional approaches explains:

> Earnings and profits, on the other hand, are not defined by act; but they have a settled and well defined meaning in accounting. Generally speaking, they are computed by deducting from gross receipts the expense of producing them. Thus, under the ordinary method of accounting, in computing earnings and profits there will be deducted, not only the items shown above, but others which are not, under the statute, deductible in computing taxable net income. In this classification may be listed such items as extraordinary expenses, charitable contributions, taxes paid the Federal Government, and taxes assessed against local benefits tending to increase the value of the property. Again, many items, such as interest upon the obligations of a state or political subdivision, tax-free Federal securities, and dividends from other corpora-

tions, must necessarily be considered in computing earnings and profits, though forming no part of taxable net income.

R. M. Weyerhaeuser, 33 B.T.A. 594, 597 (1935). . . . We propose . . . to determine whether . . . the option spread "loss" suffered by a corporation upon an employee's exercise of a stock option is an "expense of producing gross receipts," resulting in a reduction of "earnings and profits." . . .

Compensation paid to and received by the employees of a business are, of course, business "expenses of producing gross receipts" and therefore reduce earnings and profits. We must therefore ascertain whether the "bargain spread" existing when an employee exercises a stock option is a "compensation expense." Compensation of employees for past, present and future services represents one of the most fundamental and necessary expenses of operating a business. Payment may be made in myriad modes; it need not always be by way of cash disbursement. For instance, an employee may be paid in stock. In lieu of such an immediate transfer of stock to an employee the employee may instead be granted an option to purchase the employer corporation's stock at a fixed price per share from the company at some future date. Employees find the stock option to be a particularly attractive compensation device; in a rising market it gives the employee the opportunity to make a "bargain purchase." The question of whether the "bargain or option spread" (i.e., the difference between the option price and the fair market value of the stock at the time of the exercise of the option) existing at the time the option is exercised is compensatory in nature has been well settled for nearly twenty years. In Commissioner of Internal Revenue v. LoBue, 351 U.S. 243 (1956), the Supreme Court, noting that "it seems impossible to say that (the bargain transfer) was not compensation," id. at 247, commented upon this point:

> When assets are transferred by an employer to an employee to secure better services they are plainly compensation. It makes no difference that the compensation is paid in stock rather than in money.

Id. at 246-247.

When compensation is paid in its conventional form, cash, the magnitude of the expense (and, consequently, the reduction in earnings and profits) is easily visualized because there is an actual outflow of liquid corporate assets. When a bargain sale of stock to employees is made, however, both the existence and the extent of the corporate efflux are not as readily discernible. The same conceptual problems are presented when a corporation incurs an economic detriment when compensating employees by making awards of bonus stock to employees for the receipt of which the employees pay nothing into the corporate treasury. Yet the Service has twice ruled that the transfer of an employer's corporate stock to an employee as compensation produces for the transferor corporation a business expense deduction measured by the fair market value of the transferred stock, irrespective of whether that value exceeds the corporation's cost basis, if any, in the stock. Inasmuch as this deduction is allowed under §162, . . . these rulings appear to recognize that grants of bonus stock are expenses and have caused or should be considered as causing actual depletion of the corporate assets. Furthermore, these rulings demonstrate that the Service itself chooses to regard the *fair market value,* and not the cost basis, as one of the indices to be used in gauging the extent of the corporate expense incurred in compensating an employee by means of a direct award of stock. But the economic impact upon the corporation of the transfer of stock to employees pursuant to the exercise of employee stock options is in all important respects indistinguishable from the transfer of bonus corporation stock to employees. The only distinguishing feature of the option arrangement is that the employee pays something rather than nothing, but, it remains that in both instances, "at the end of these transactions, [the corporate] employer [is] worth . . . less to its stockholders." Commissioner of Internal Revenue v. LoBue, supra at 245. Accordingly, we would expect that the "bargain spread" would be considered to constitute a cognizable expense which would necessarily reduce earnings and profits. . . .

As a concluding comment, we reiterate our belief that the holding which we reach today is one which comports with economic reality and with the mechanics of operating a business. As the Seventh Circuit noted in Luckman v. Commissioner, [418 F.2d 381 (7th Cir. 1969)], if, instead of stock options, the corporation's employees had received cash there obviously would have been a cognizable corporate "expense." These stock options so granted were presumably the product of careful and deliberate negotiations between the corporation and the employees involved, and were apparently considered by the employees to be an acceptable, indeed, probably a superior, alternative to cash. In turn, the corporation undoubtedly expected to profit, and probably did profit, in precisely the same way it would have profited if it had awarded cash to those key employees, for, of course, this supplemental compensation to employees would normally cause the recipients to produce increased earnings and profits for the corporation.

In approaching a proper resolution of the tax issue here it is inequitable and unreasonable not to weigh the tangible corporate detriment resulting from the corporation's lost opportunity to sell the optioned stock to the public at its Fair Market Value, a detriment incurred in the hope that the grant of the options would result in producing added revenues. Moreover, in measuring the extent of the compensation, and the corresponding expense, by the amount of the excess of the Fair Market Value over the option price, realistic account is taken of the relationship between the employer and the employee. A company's revenues and profitability have a strong influence on the value of its stock and thus on the potential compensation accruing to the employee by virtue of the spread existing when the option he holds is exercised. Yet, typically, the employees who hold options are capable of increasing corporate revenues through their intensified labor and, insofar as such employees can affect corporate profitability, these same employees can indirectly influence the magnitude of their own compensation. Thus, the "bargain spread" does, in the form of increased employee compensation to the employees holding options, accurately reflect the economic detriment which the corporation has incurred in order, hopefully, to produce more revenue just like any other "development expense."

FRIENDLY, Circuit Judge (concurring and dissenting).
[Concurrence on collateral estoppel issue is omitted.]
The question in this case reduces to whether the "opportunity cost" incurred by Rapid in issuing the stock to the employees at less than its current market value rather than selling it to others is cognizable for purposes of reducing earnings and profits. There can be no claim that Rapid incurred out-of-pocket costs such as to reduce the earnings and profits available for distribution to shareholders. . . .

With all deference, I think the question can only be answered in the negative. Apart from the absence of evidence that Rapid could have sold the optioned stock at the market prices on the respective days of issuance, or would have done so, precisely the same sort of "cost" is incurred on the exercise of a warrant at a price below current market value, where no one suggests that this spread can be deducted from earnings and profits. The fact that here the options were issued to provide "incentive" to employees is not sufficient to support a different result. Selling stock at less than current market value does not impair the corporation's ability to make distributions without invading capital or paid-in surplus, which is what "earnings and profits" are mainly about. The effect of the exercise of an option, whether issued to an employee or to an outsider, at a "bargain spread" is to decrease the market price and, in some but not all instances, the book value of the shares of other stockholders. It has no adverse effect on the corporate accounts.

The petitioner's principal reliance is on two revenue rulings that, despite the general provision of §1032(a) prohibiting recognition of gain or loss on a corporation's receipt of money or property in exchange for stock (including treasury stock), a corporation may deduct as a business expense under §162 the fair market value of stock issued as compensation, whether the stock be treasury or theretofore unissued stock, Rev. Rul. 62-217, 1962-2 Cum. Bull. 59; Rev. Rul. 69-75, 1969-1 Cum. Bull. 52, with the presumable consequence that the same amount may be deducted from earnings and profits. Not only were these payments clearly compensation and nothing more, but the rulings can be rationalized on the basis that since the employee was subject to tax on the fair market value of the stock issued, allowing the deduction to the corporation was necessary to avoid unfairness. . . . By contrast, in the case of restricted stock options such as that before us, the employee escapes regular income taxation both when the option is issued and when it is exercised. There is therefore no reason to disregard the general principle of allowing no deduction, either from income or from earnings and profits, for mere loss of "opportunity costs." In substance [the restricted stock option] represented a trade-off. In return for the eagerly sought privilege of tax-free receipt and exercise of stock options by executives, the corporation would forego any deduction under §162 for the excess of the market value of the stock, when issued, over the option price. . . . There can be no fair doubt that the Congress that expressly ruled out use of the "bargain spread" to employees as a deduction would also have forbidden its use to reduce earnings and profits if it had ever considered the problem whether the "bargain spread" should enable the corporation to make a later distribution to stockholders as out of capital rather than from earnings and profits in the unusual case where this possibility might exist. . . .

I would affirm the judgment of the Tax Court.

NOTE

1. *"Earnings and profits."* It is a curious fact that the Code, ordinarily so prodigal in its use of words, does not define the term "earnings and profits" even though it is not a term that has a clear independent meaning outside of the Code. The term is partly explained by Treas. Regs. §1.312-6, and the effect of a number of transactions on earnings and profits is prescribed by the Code. See §§312 and 381(c)(2). The concept of earnings and profits is not the same as earned surplus for state law or financial reporting purposes. For example, a distribution of common stock by a corporation decreases earned surplus but has no effect on earnings and profits. Otherwise, nontaxable stock dividends under Eisner v. Macomber, 252 U.S. 189 (1920), would clear away the corporation's earnings and profits account, allowing it to make nontaxable subsequent distributions of cash and property.

Similarly, the term "dividend" as defined for income tax purposes by §316(a) may not correspond with the term "dividend" under state law, with the result that a distribution may be a dividend under §316(a) although it impairs capital under state law. Conversely, it is possible for a distribution to constitute a dividend under state law without qualifying as a dividend under §316(a). In the former instance, the dividend will ordinarily be taxable to the stockholder under the "claim of right" doctrine, notwithstanding a potential liability to creditors under state law. See United States v. Lesoine, 203 F.2d 123 (9th Cir. 1953), holding that the claim of right doctrine requires that dividends be taxed in year of receipt even if the distribution may have been illegal under state law.

The determination of the earnings and profits account is often no simple feat, especially when the account must be traced through a series of corporate reorganizations or similar transactions. It may be necessary to go back many years to decide how a transaction should have been taxed under a now-interred income tax provision because of its effect on earnings and profits. See, e.g., Union Pacific Railroad v. United States, 524 F.2d 1343 (Cl. Ct. 1975), claiming that an accounting error affected earnings and profits between 1900 and 1907.

If a corporation is initially organized for cash, the reason for gearing the taxability of its distributions to its record of earnings and profits is clear enough. Until the corporation has engaged in profitable operations, any distribution to its original stockholders is a return of their investment rather than income. Once the corporation has realized profits, its distributions may pro tanto be fairly regarded as income to the stockholders.

The equity and logic of §§316 and 301(c) may be less clear if we assume that after a period of corporate profits, the stock changes hands, and that before additional earnings arise (the next day, if you will), there is a distribution to the new stockholder. Should the distribution be treated as a return of capital? Sections 316 and 301(c) are inescapable: To the extent of earnings and profits, the surprised shareholder has realized income. This "miracle of income without gain" — the phrase is from Powell, Income from Corporate Dividends, 35 Harv. L. Rev. 363 (1922) — long ago was attested and explained by the Supreme Court in United States v. Phellis, 257 U.S. 156, 171-172 (1921):

> Where, as in this case, the dividend constitutes a distribution of profits accumulated during an extended period and bears a large proportion to the par value of the stock, if an investor happened to buy stock shortly before the dividend, paying a price enhanced by an estimate of the capital plus the surplus of the company, and after distribution of the surplus, with corresponding reduction in the intrinsic and market value of the shares, he was called upon to pay a tax upon the dividend received, it might look in his case like a tax upon his capital. But it is only apparently so. In buying at a price that reflected the accumulated profits, he of course acquired as a part of the valuable rights purchased the prospect of a dividend from the accumulation — bought "dividend on," as the phrase goes — and necessarily took subject to the burden of the income tax proper to be assessed against him by reason of the dividend if and when made. He simply stepped into the shoes, in this as in other respects, of the stockholder whose shares he acquired, and presumably the prospect of a dividend influenced the price paid, and was discounted by the prospect of an income tax to be paid thereon.

2. *Source of distributions.* If a corporation has earnings and profits in a taxable year, any distribution in that year subject to §301 will be taxable

pro tanto even though the corporation has a deficit from prior years equal to or exceeding the current year's profits. §316(a)(2). See Situation 2 of Rev. Rul. 74-164 at page 121 supra. This provision has a curious ancestry. It was enacted in 1936 as a relief measure when the undistributed profits tax was in effect. That tax was imposed on the undistributed part of corporate income, computed by deducting "dividends" from total income. Unless a deficit corporation could treat distributions out of current earnings as "dividends" for this purpose, it would be unable to avoid the undistributed profits tax no matter how large its distributions to stockholders. To enable such corporations to obtain a credit for "dividends" paid out of current earnings, §316(a) was enacted. Apparently, no thought was given to the effect of the new subsection apart from the undistributed profits tax. Nor was §316(a)(2) repealed when the short-lived undistributed profits tax was repealed.

Treas. Regs. §1.316-2 sets forth hierarchical rules for classifying distributions. Distributions are first deemed to come out of the corporation's current earnings and profits account. If the account is exhausted, accumulated earnings and profits are tapped. If there is a deficit in the current earnings and profits account, distributions are deemed to be out of accumulated earnings and profits decreased by the current deficit prorated to the date of distribution unless the actual current deficit as of the transaction date can be ascertained. Rev. Rul. 74-164, above, illustrates these source rules. Note, though, that in Situation 3 of the ruling the current deficit in the earnings and profits account is prorated even though the actual current deficit as of July 1, the distribution date, is known. Doesn't this treatment in the ruling conflict with Treas. Regs. §1.316-2? See also Rev. Rul. 69-440, 1969-2 C.B. 46, discussing priorities among distributions.

If there is more than one distribution during a taxable year, the current earnings and profits are prorated among the distributions for purposes of determining whether a distribution is a dividend. Accumulated earnings and profits, however, are allocated to distributions chronologically on a first come, first served basis. Treas. Regs. §1.316-2(b), (c).

As earnings and profits are distributed, the corporation decreases its earnings and profits account in accordance with §312(a). Note that a corporation cannot create an earnings and profits deficit through distributions. See §312(a) and Estate of Uris v. Commissioner, 605 F.2d 1258 (2d Cir. 1979). How then can there be a deficit in the earnings and profits account?

3. *Relationship of earnings and profits to taxable income.* A determination of earnings and profits most often starts with an analysis of taxable income. To convert taxable income into earnings and profits, three types of adjustments are necessary. First, some items excludible from taxable income are included in earnings and profits. They are included because they represent an accretion to the corporation that can be distributed without impairing the corporation's original capital. The items include proceeds from life

insurance contracts under §101(a), interest on certain government obligations under §103, and amounts received through accident or health insurance for personal injuries to or sickness of insured employees under
§104(a). See Treas. Regs. §1.312-6(b).

Section 312(n) contains some upwards adjustments to earnings and
profits to ensure that earnings and profits conform more closely to economic income. For example, if a corporation sells property at a gain on
the installment method, the entire gain goes into earnings and profits
immediately even though there is deferred recognition of some or all
of the gain. Similarly, a corporation that reports income and expenses
attributable to a long-term contract on the completed contract method
must use the percentage-of-completion method for earnings and profits
purposes. Corporations using "last in, first out" (LIFO) accounting for
inventory must adjust earnings and profits by the LIFO recapture amount.

Second, some items that are deductible in computing taxable income
may not be deducted in computing earnings and profits. Often, these are
"artificial" deductions in that no cash outlay is required that would deplete
the earnings available for distribution. These items include the dividends-
received deduction under §243 (which allows qualifying corporations to
deduct from 70 percent to 100 percent of the amount of intercorporate
dividends received) and the excess of accelerated over straight line depreciation using recovery periods specified in §312(k). In addition, net operating losses under §172 and capital loss carrybacks under §1212 do not
reduce earnings and profits since they represent a carryback or carryover of
losses that reduced earnings and profits in the year in which they occurred.

Several provisions require a slower rate of deduction for earnings
and profits purposes than for the purpose of computing gain or loss. For
example, intangible drilling costs and mineral and development costs to
the extent deductible must be capitalized for earnings and profits purposes. §312(n)(2). Similar rules are provided for expenses amortizable
under §§173, 177, and 248, see §312(n)(3), and for construction period
carrying charges. §312(n)(1).

Third, some items that cannot be deducted in determining taxable
income are deducted in computing earnings and profits because they represent a real drain on earnings available for distribution to shareholders.
Included in this category are dividend distributions in prior years (but
see §312(a)); federal income taxes;[1] excess charitable contributions (not
deductible because of the 10 percent limitation of §170(b)); nondeductible expenses under §265; unreasonable compensation; and deductions
disallowed on public policy grounds under §162(c), (e), (f), or (g). See
Rev. Rul. 77-442, 1977-2 C.B. 264.

---

1. Treas. Regs. §1.312-6(a) provides that the method of accounting used to compute
earnings and profits should be the same as that used for determining taxable income. Accordingly, a cash basis taxpayer cannot accrue a tax liability; for a cash basis taxpayer, earnings
and profits are reduced only when taxes are paid, Webb v. Commissioner, 67 T.C. 293 (1977),
aff'd per curiam, 572 F.2d 135 (5th Cir. 1978).

In *Divine* the court faced an issue involving the third category — whether an item not deductible in computing taxable income (the difference between the cost of the stock and the fair market value of the stock) is deductible in computing earnings and profits.[2] The Tax Court tried its view twice and was reversed both times — once by the Seventh Circuit in Luckman v. Commissioner, 418 F.2d 381 (7th Cir. 1969), and once by the Second Circuit in *Divine,* although the Tax Court did convince Judge Friendly. Who is right, the majority or Judge Friendly? It is true that the purchase of stock by Divine did not deplete the cash or other property available for distribution to shareholders. The same is true, however, if an employee is compensated with stock, a transaction that unquestionably reduces taxable income and therefore earnings and profits. See Rev. Rul. 62-217, 1962-2 C.B. 59. If Divine had been compensated in cash for the "spread" between the option price and fair market value and had then reinvested the cash plus his own cash in the corporation by purchasing some of its stock, would doubts still exist about the transaction's effect on earnings and profits?

While *Divine* involves the effect on earnings and profits of a nondeductible item, in Bangor & Aroostook Railroad v. Commissioner, 193 F.2d 827 (1st Cir. 1951), the court confronted a discharge of indebtedness that went unrecognized — and hence was excluded from gross income — because of the taxpayer's election under the predecessors of §§108 and 1017. Since a reduction in basis accompanied the nonrecognition, the court ruled that there should be no increase in earnings and profits until the assets with the reduced basis were sold. See §312(f), relied on by the court, and §312(*l*)(1), which codified this result.

4.   *The future of earnings and profits.* You may not need much convincing at this point that the concept of earnings and profits adds complexity to the Code. Moreover, if the purpose of the concept is to ensure that shareholders will not be taxed on the return of their capital, curious results abound for a stock purchaser receiving a distribution shortly after purchase and before the accumulation of any additional earnings. See page 130 supra. If there are accumulated earnings and profits, the distribution will be a dividend even though there have been no subsequent earnings following purchase. Finally, there is room for manipulation. For example, the impact of current earnings and profits where the corporation has an accumulated earnings and profits deficit sometimes can be avoided by postponing the distribution until the following year. If the corporation has no earnings in that year and still has an accumulated earnings and profits deficit, the distribution will be received tax free since it will fall under neither §316(a)(1) nor §316(a)(2). If a corporation can deplete its earnings and profits account, it may be able to borrow against appreciated

---

2. *Divine* serves as a nice reminder of the *Golsen* rule — that the Tax Court by its own rules is not bound to follow a court of appeals decision unless appellate jurisdiction is in that circuit. See Golsen v. Commissioner, 54 T.C. 742, 757 (1970), aff'd without discussion of this issue, 445 F.2d 985 (10th Cir. 1971).

property to make tax-free distributions to shareholders and then use the property's earnings to repay the loan.

This combination of complexity, failure of purpose, and potential abuse has led some commentators, as well as some members of Congress, to consider a repeal of the earnings and profits concept, with relief for obvious distributions of capital. See Blum, The Earnings and Profits Limitation on Dividend Income: A Reappraisal, 53 Taxes 68 (1975); Colby, Blackburn, and Trier, Elimination of "Earnings and Profits" from the Internal Revenue Code, 39 Tax Law. 285 (1986). See also Staff of Senate Comm. on Finance, 99th Cong., 1st Sess., The Reform and Simplification of the Income Taxation of Corporations (1985).

5. *Relief from taxation of dividends.* Earnings and profits serve as the benchmark for measuring dividend income, thereby producing the "double tax" — taxation to the corporation earning income and taxation to shareholders on dividend distributions. See discussion of the double tax in Chapter 8. The 1954 Code granted some relief from the double taxation of corporate earnings by providing a small exclusion and credit for individual shareholders. The Tax Reform Act of 1986 eliminated this modest exclusion.

By contrast to this very limited remedy for double taxation of *individual* shareholders, for many years the Code has made special allowances for dividends received by *corporate* shareholders to mitigate the multiple taxation of corporate earnings. This relief provision can be illustrated by considering the tax results that would prevail in its absence. If, for example, individual A owns all the stock in P Corp., which owns all the stock in Q Corp., earnings of Q Corp. might be subject to a triple tax by the time the earnings reach A. Q Corp. would be taxed when it earns income; P Corp. and then A face taxation on the dividend. Since 1935, however, §243 has provided for a deduction by a corporation that is a shareholder in another corporation. Although §243 is a "deduction" provision, it provides, in effect, an exclusion for the shareholder-corporation (i.e., the corporation can deduct some portion of the dividend that has been received).

Currently, §243 permits a shareholder-corporation to deduct 70 percent of the dividend received from a distributing corporation. This provision at current rates makes the effective maximum tax rate on dividends received by a corporation 10.5 percent — that is, the highest corporate rate of 35 percent imposed on 30 percent of dividends received. If the recipient corporation owns 20 percent or more (by vote and value) of the stock of the distributing corporation, the deduction is increased to 80 percent. Notice that dividends paid on "portfolio stock" (i.e., when the receiving corporation owns less than 20 perent) are subject to a higher rate of tax on dividends.

The lowest rate on intercorporate dividends is available with respect to distributions from affiliated corporations. An affiliated group of corporations can eliminate intragroup dividends from gross income entirely by electing to file consolidated returns under the relevant Code provisions. §§1501 et seq. Moreover, §243(a)(3) permits a 100 percent deduction for certain dividends for electing members of an affiliated group, as defined in §1504(a), who are willing to abide by certain restrictions. See §243(b)(3).

For a discussion of problems raised by the dividends-received deduction, see pages 178-181 infra.

B.   PROPERTY DISTRIBUTIONS

1.   The Effect of a Distribution of Property on the Distributing Corporation's Income

The United States employs a classic double tax system. When a corporation earns income from operations, there is a corporate-level tax. When those earnings are distributed to the shareholders as dividends, there is a shareholder-level tax under §301. Similarly, if the corporation sells appreciated property and distributes the sales proceeds, there will typically be a corporate-level tax on the sale and a dividend on the distribution of the sales proceeds. Note that the gain recognized by the corporation on the sale increases the corporation's earnings and profits, making it more likely that the distribution will be taxed as a dividend.

Suppose instead that the corporation distributes the appreciated property to its shareholders, who then sell the property. We know that the shareholders will have dividends equal to the fair market value of the property distributed if the corporation has sufficient earnings and profits. §301(b). If there are insufficient earnings and profits, the shareholders may escape dividend treatment, instead reducing their bases in the distributing corporation's stock. §301(c)(2). In any case, the distributed property will have a basis in the hands of the shareholders equal to its fair market value. §301(d). If the property is then sold, the shareholders will recognize no additional gain. To summarize, the shareholders will recognize, at most, one level of taxation (dividend treatment), and if there are insufficient earnings and profits, the shareholders may have no income as a result of the distribution and sale.

Contrast this treatment with the corresponding tax results when the corporation sells the property and then distributes the proceeds, resulting in both a corporate-level and shareholder-level tax. To prevent the form of the transaction from dictating the tax consequences, it is necessary that there be a corporate-level tax if the appreciated property is distributed and then sold, just as there is if the property is sold and the proceeds distributed. This conclusion is not an endorsement of the system of double taxation. Rather, it takes the double taxation feature as a given, emphasizing the need for consistency. For a consideration of the double tax system, see Chapter 8.

The seminal case considering the tax consequences to a corporation distributing appreciated property is General Utilities & Operating Co. v. Helvering, 296 U.S. 200 (1935). In that case, General Utilities corporation located a purchaser for Islands Edison common stock that it owned. The stock had a value of approximately $1 million and an adjusted basis of $20,000. If General Utilities had completed the sale, there would have been a corporate-level tax followed by a shareholder-level tax if the sales proceeds were distributed to the shareholders as dividends.

To minimize these potential tax consequences, General Utilities distributed the Islands Edison stock to its shareholders with an understanding that they would sell the distributed stock to the purchaser. Four days after the distribution, the shareholders sold the Islands Edison stock to the purchaser on the same terms as negotiated by General Utilities. No gain was reported on the sale because the shareholders took a fair market value basis in the distributed stock. §301(d).

The Service claimed that the distribution by General Utilities was a taxable event at the corporate level because it used appreciated property to discharge the indebtedness it created by declaring a dividend. Before the Board of Tax Appeals, the government relied on the theory that the corporation had (1) by declaring a dividend of $1 million, created a debt of $1 million, and then (2) satisfied the indebtedness by distributing the securities. Before the court of appeals, the government added a second argument — that a sale of the property that occurred immediately after the distribution should be attributed to the corporation, although made in form by the shareholders. (This rationale, commonly known as the *Court Holding Co.* doctrine, has often been accepted if the corporation negotiates the sale and then makes a last-minute effort to avoid recognizing gain by distributing the property to its shareholders before the sale. See page 337 infra.) On this point the court of appeals agreed with the Treasury. In its Supreme Court brief, the Treasury added a third argument — that a corporation must recognize taxable income on a distribution of appreciated property to its stockholders since the transfer is a "sale or other disposition" under §1001.

The Supreme Court agrees with the Board of Tax Appeals that the distributed assets were not used to discharge a corporate debt. As to the second point, the Court held that it should have been raised at the trial level and could not be belatedly argued in the appellate court; the government's third argument was not mentioned. Although the commentators could not agree on whether the theory of realization-by-distribution was rejected on the merits by implication or passed over because it was advanced too late in the proceeding, the former explanation of its fate became popular with the courts, and the *General Utilities* doctrine was born.

From the beginning there were exceptions to the *General Utilities* doctrine. For example, in Commissioner v. First State Bank of Stratford, 168 F.2d 1004 (5th Cir. 1948), a distributing corporation was taxed on a distribution of debt instruments (not its own) to its shareholders when the distributing corporation had taken bad debt deductions with respect to the notes, although payments on the notes were made to the shareholders. Using assignment of income principles, the court taxed the distributing corporation on the collection of the notes.

In 1954 Congress enacted the "general rule" of §311(a), which codified the *General Utilities* rule that no gain or loss shall be recognized to a corporation on a distribution of property with respect to its stock. In recommending the enactment of §311, however, the Senate Finance Committee Report stated: "[Y]our committee does not intend to change existing law with respect to attribution of income of shareholders to their corporation as exemplified for example in the case of Commr. v. First State Bank of Stratford."

Following the enactment of §311(a), courts began to chip away at *General Utilities*. For example, in First Wisconsin Bankshares Corp. v. United States, 369 F. Supp. 1034 (E.D. Wis. 1973), the taxpayer donated to a charity certain notes that had been previously determined worthless by the national banking examiner and had been deducted as bad debts. Relying heavily on *Stratford Bank,* the court found first that the charitable deduction claimed by the taypayer constituted a recovery that offset the prior bad debt deduction and, second, that when the charitable donee received repayment of the notes, the taxpayer realized income under the anticipatory assignment of income principle to the extent that the portion of the note repayments constituted interest. Contra, Continental Illinois National Bank & Trust Co. v. Commissioner, 69 T.C. 357 (1977), in which the court held that no tax benefit was recovered when the taxpayer wrote off a bad debt for which it received virtually worthless stock from the debtors' trustee in bankruptcy. When the common stock increased in value it was donated to charity, and a charitable deduction for its fair market value was claimed. The court viewed the receipt of stock and later donation as two separate transactions and refused to treat the appreciation as a further recovery of the bad debt.

In Bush Brothers & Co. v. Commissioner, 668 F.2d 252 (6th Cir. 1982), the corporation, a food processor, purported to distribute contracts to buy beans at a specified price to its shareholders, who then sold the contracts. The court of appeals attributed the sale to the corporation in light of its extensive involvement in the transactions. At the trial court level, the Tax Court reached the same result because of an improper tax avoidance motive. The approach taken by the Tax Court majority draws strength from United States v. Lynch, 192 F.2d 718 (9th Cir. 1952). There, a corporation in the fruit business distributed a dividend of 22,000 boxes of apples to its shareholders. The fruit remained in the corporation's warehouse and was sold by the corporation two months later on behalf of the shareholders.

The Ninth Circuit attributed the sale to the corporation, not so much because of corporate involvement but because of an improper tax reduction motive. The court relied on Commissioner v. Transport Trading & Terminal Corp., 176 F.2d 570 (2d Cir. 1949), in which the Second Circuit determined that a distribution of appreciated securities from a subsidiary corporation to its parent, followed by a sale, produced a tax at the subsidiary level. The holding was broad, indicating that a tax-motivated distribution in the face of an anticipated shareholder sale would result in a tax to the distributing corporation. Accord, ABCD Lands, Inc. v. Commissioner, 41 T.C. 840 (1964).

Congress also began to chip away at the codification of *General Utilities* under §311(a). By 1984 the exceptions to §311(a) all but swallowed up the nonrecognition rule for appreciated property. The Tax Reform Act of 1986 overturned most of the remaining vestiges of *General Utilities*. Section 311(b) now provides that if a corporation distributes property (other than the distributing corporation's own obligation) in which the fair market value exceeds the distributing corporation's adjusted basis, the distributing corporation will recognize gain as if it had sold the property to the shareholder at fair market value.

Note that the appreciation recognized by the distributing corporation is not limited to post-incorporation appreciation. For example, suppose B forms X Corp. in a §351 transaction by exchanging property including one item with a basis of $100 and a fair market value of $500 for all the X Corp. stock. Before X Corp. earns any income, it distributes that item to B. Under §311(b), X Corp. must recognize the $400 of appreciation. The gain will be ordinary or capital, depending on the nature of the asset. The holding period may be long or short term, but recall that X Corp. tacks on B's holding period under §1223(2). Moreover, X Corp.'s earnings and profits account will increase from $0 to $400 (minus taxes paid by X Corp.) because X Corp.'s taxable income reflects the §311(b) gain. The increase in earnings and profits will cause B to recognize a dividend of about $400 under §301(c)(1). This phenomenon will doubtless precipitate some careful planning as indicated below.

If a corporation distributes property subject to a liability, the fair market value of the property distributed for purposes of §311(b)(1)(B) is not less than the amount of the liability. See §§311(b)(2) and 336(b). For example, suppose X Corp. distributes property with a basis of $700 and a fair market value of $400 to B, a shareholder. The property is subject to a liability of $900. Under §311(b), X Corp. must recognize gain as if the property had been sold to B. Had there been a sale, X Corp. would have recognized a $200 gain under Tufts v. Commissioner, 461 U.S. 300 (1983).

A true repeal of the *General Utilities* doctrine would allow a distributing corporation to deduct a loss on the distribution of property with an adjusted basis that exceeds its fair market value. Suppose X Corp. held property with a basis of $700 and a fair market value of $200. If X Corp. sells the property, it will recognize a $500 loss. The distribution of the proceeds to the shareholders will be taxable to the shareholders under §301(c)(1) if there are sufficient earnings and profits after reducing taxable income by the amount of the loss. If, however, X Corp. distributes the property to its shareholders, §311(b) provides no loss deduction. Moreover, there is no decrease in X Corp.'s earnings and profits as a result of distributing the loss property. The shareholders will have a $200 dividend if there are sufficient earnings and profits. Finally, the shareholders will take the property with a basis of $200, its fair market value under §301(d). Notice that by mandating a fair market value basis, the Code forever eliminates the loss deduction.

Why does §311(b) disallow recognition of losses to the distributing corporation? Perhaps Congress was concerned that shareholders would have it in their power to cause their corporations to distribute "loss property" while not distributing "gain property." In this way corporations could exploit the realization doctrine by recognizing losses but not unrealized gains. If this was the concern, there are several responses. A corporation always has the power to exploit the realization doctrine by selling loss rather than gain property. Indeed, the limitation on capital loss deductions in §§1211 and 1212 is a response to that problem.

But it could be argued that the capital gains limitation is not sufficient when the loss property is transferred to a related party. Congress has addressed that problem as well by enacting §267, which prohibits the deduction of losses with respect to exchanges between related parties. A corporation is considered related to any shareholder who owns, directly or indirectly, more than 50 percent in value of the corporation's stock. For a discussion of the attribution rules, see page 196 infra. A sale of loss property to a 25 percent shareholder, for example, will produce a deductible loss. Why didn't Congress treat all nonliquidating distributions as if the corporation had sold the property to the shareholders and allow §267 to determine the deductibility of losses?

A side effect of not using §267 in connection with distributions of loss property is the basis consequence to the shareholders. Under §267 a purchaser takes a basis equal to cost — generally fair market value. But if the purchaser sells the property at a gain, the loss that went unrecognized to the seller is available to the purchaser to offset the gain. §267(d). There is no equivalent provision in §311.

Suppose X Corp. distributes two pieces of property to B, its shareholder. One has a basis of $200 and a fair market value of $900; the other has a basis of $900 and a fair market value of $200. Has X Corp. made a distribution of appreciated property? Suppose X Corp., a partner in the XY partnership, wants to distribute the appreciated partnership interest to its shareholders. To decrease the amount of gain it has to recognize under §311(b), X transfers loss property to the partnership. The effect of the transfer is to increase the corporation's basis in the partnership interest by the basis of the contributed property under §722 in a manner comparable to §358 in a §351 transaction, while the fair market value of the partnership interest increases by the fair market value of the contributed property. The overall effect, if successful, would be to use the loss property to decrease gain that would otherwise be recognized on the distribution. Section 311(b)(3) allows the Service to promulgate regulations that disregard the contribution of the loss property in determining the basis and fair market value of the distributed partnership interest.

Given the treatment to a distributing corporation of both gain and loss property, what strategies would you expect taxpayers to pursue? Suppose X Corp., with sufficient earnings and profits, wants to get a piece of property with a basis of $200 and a fair market value of $900 into the hands of B, its shareholder. A distribution will trigger gain at both the corporate and shareholder level. Suppose instead that X Corp. sells the property to B, who pays with a note bearing appropriate interest and payable in 10 years. If the transaction is respected, X Corp. will recognize no immediate gain on the sale because of installment reporting. §453. But consider the application of both §§267 and 1239. B, the purchaser, will have no gain on the acquisition of the property and will take a cost basis under §1012 of $900.

Later, if the shareholder defaults on the note, presumably the shareholder will recognize $900 of income as a discharge of indebtedness. §61(a)(12). The distributing corporation should be allowed to take a bad debt deduction under §166 for the $200 basis of the note. Consider first that this treatment is less onerous in absolute income terms than dividend characterization in the year of the property's distribution because there is no corporate-level income (indeed there is a corporate-level loss) in the year of default. Moreover, B has had the benefit of deferral on the $900 of income that would be recognized at the shareholder level. Undoubtedly the Service may try to recharacterize the transaction as a distribution of the appreciated property followed years later by B's contribution to capital when the note is paid.

If X Corp. wants to distribute property to B with a basis of $900 and a fair market value of $200, a similar strategy may be employed. X Corp. could declare a cash dividend and then satisfy the dividend with a distribution of the loss property. See, e.g., Kenan v. Commissioner, 114 F.2d 217 (2d Cir. 1940) (satisfaction of a cash legacy with appreciated stock treated as a sale or disposition). Indeed, this technique is precisely what the Service accused the taxpayer of doing at the trial court in *General Utilities*. The Service presumably would argue that there never was an intention to pay a cash dividend and that the distribution of property cannot generate a loss under §311(b). Again consider the application of §267.

Suppose X Corp. had decided to distribute property with a basis of $900 and fair market value of $200 to shareholder B, who would then sell it to P. Immediately prior to the transaction, X Corp. decides to make the sale itself to P and to distribute the proceeds to B. This fact pattern is the converse of that presented in *General Utilities, Bush Brothers,* and some of the other cases discussed at pages 137-138 supra. There, the distributing corporations made distributions before the sale took place. Here, the corporation sold the property and distributed the proceeds. One can expect that in appropriate circumstances the Service will reverse the argument that it relied on in these cases, claiming that actually the corporation distributed the property before the sale transpired. Such a recharacterization would deny the loss deduction to the distributing corporation. §311(b).

2. The Effect of a Distribution of Property on the Distributing Corporation's Earnings and Profits

Although we have looked at what goes into earnings and profits in general, we need to consider the effect of a distribution on the earnings and profits account. Until the repeal of the *General Utilities* doctrine, distributing corporations did not normally recognize gain on the distribution of appreciated property. Consequently, §312(a)(3) required earnings and profits to be decreased only by the adjusted basis of any property distributed because the appreciation never was taken into income by the corporation. With the repeal of the *General Utilities* doctrine, a corporation that appreciated property must include the appreciation as income. The increase in taxable income results in an increase in earnings and profits. Therefore, it is appropriate to decrease the earnings and profits account after the distribution by the fair market value of the property distributed. Section 312(b)(2) accomplishes that result by substituting fair market value for adjusted basis in §312(a)(3) when appreciated property is distributed.

You may ask why Congress did not simply amend §312(a)(3) to read "fair market value" instead of "adjusted basis." The answer lies in the treatment of loss property. Because a distributing corporation does not take a loss into account for tax purposes when distributing property with a basis that exceeds its fair market value, it would be inappropriate to decrease earnings and profits only by the fair market value of the property distributed. Accordingly, §312(a)(3) allows the distributing corporation to decrease earnings and profits by the higher adjusted basis.

Section 312(b)(1) does not work smoothly with §311(b). Because §311(b) now requires a distributing corporation to recognize gain on the distribution of appreciated property, that gain will go into taxable income and then into earnings and profits (because computation of taxable income is the first step in computing earnings and profits) for purposes of evaluating the tax consequences to the distributees. Read literally, §312(b)(1) would require the appreciation to increase earnings and profits again. But such a reading cannot be justified.

To illustrate the workings of §312(b), suppose *X* Corp., with no earnings and profits, distributes property with a basis of $0 and a fair market value of $400 to its shareholders. *X* Corp. will have $400 of taxable income on the distribution under §311(b). For purposes of evaluating the tax consequences to the shareholders, *X* Corp.'s earnings and profits will increase by the $400 gain recognized. Therefore, the shareholders will have dividend treatment under §301(c)(1). Following the distribution, *X* Corp.'s earnings and profits will be reduced from $400 to $0 under §312(b)(2) and (a)(3) because *X* Corp.'s earnings were fully distributed. Notice that §312(b)(1) increases earnings and profits, then the tax consequences to the shareholders are evaluated, then the earnings and profits account is decreased by the fair market value of the property distributed.

Finally, consider the effect of §312(a) on distributions of a specific type of property — a corporation's own note. For example, suppose *X* Corp., with $100,000 of accumulated earnings and profits, distributes its own notes with a $100,000 principal amount maturing in 10 years and bearing no interest. Assume further that the notes have a present value of $20,000. *X* is not permitted to reduce its earnings and profits by the $100,000 principal amount in order to pave the way for future cash distributions. Instead, §312(a)(2) now mandates a reduction by the $20,000 issue price. Each year, the corporation can reduce its taxable income and its earnings and profits by a portion of the original issue discount. §163(e).

3. The Effect of a Distribution of Property on Shareholders

For both corporate and noncorporate distributees, §301(b)(1) specifies that the fair market value of property is the amount distributed for purposes of determining what constitutes a dividend under §§301(c) and 316. If a corporation distributes an asset to *T* with a basis of $40 and a fair market value of $100, subject to a $70 mortgage, what is the amount distributed? See §301(b)(2). The basis of property received by noncorporate distributees is determined under §301(d). What is *T*'s basis in the asset received? Why isn't it reduced by the mortgage?

C. DISGUISED OR CONSTRUCTIVE DIVIDENDS

Dividend treatment is often an unattractive tax outcome for individual shareholders and their controlled corporations. Not only is the dividend taxable to the recipient as ordinary income, but the distributing corporation does not get a deduction. Moreover, high-bracket shareholders who wish to transfer corporate funds to low-bracket relatives pay the income tax on the dividend and perhaps a gift tax on the transfer to the relative.

To avoid such unpleasantries, taxpayers often try to avoid dividend treatment while still pulling money out of corporate solution. Such attempts by taxpayers generally fall into two categories: (1) a distribution disguised as a deductible item to the distributing corporation even though it is taxable to the recipient, and (2) a distribution disguised as a nontaxable receipt for the recipient even though the corporation gets no deduction. Either category may be preferable to dividend characterization, which offers no deduction to the corporation and requires inclusion by the recipient. In a third category, which combines the first two, the corporation tries to deduct an expenditure while the shareholder excludes it.

The most common illustration of the first category is the excessive compensation situation. If successful, characterizing a corporate payment as salary generates a corporate deduction, even if the payment happens to be made to shareholders, since the payment is not a distribution "with respect to [the corporation's] stock" within the meaning of §301(a). (The same is true for interest and rental payments.) Section 162(a)(1) limits the compensation deduction to a "reasonable" allowance. In determining what is reasonable, courts generally have looked at a variety of factors, including the role of the recipient in the company, the comparative compensation of similarly situated employees of other companies, the character and condition of the company, the power of the recipient to control compensation levels, and internal consistency by the company (e.g., bonuses that are not part of a consistent program or that track the percentage of stock ownership may be suspect). For a discussion of these and other factors, see Elliots, Inc. v. Commissioner, 716 F.2d 1241 (9th Cir. 1983) (mere absence of dividend payments not conclusive as to whether compensation was "reasonable"). For a more detailed discussion of the case law, see page 166 infra.

Corporate loans offer a common version of the second category. Loans produce no corporate deduction, but there is no shareholder inclusion. Predictably, the use of these and other techniques is limited only by the bounds of a taxpayer's imagination. Predictably too, the Service will scrutinize transactions between shareholders and their closely held corporations to determine if the payment constitutes a "disguised" or "constructive" dividend.

The third category is illustrated by a corporation's payment of a shareholder's legal expenses in contesting a divorce that also threatened control of the business. See Dolese v. United States, 605 F.2d 1146 (10th Cir. 1979).

The cases and notes that follow offer a sampling of the litigation in the area of constructive dividends. The recharacterization of a payment as a disguised dividend is by its nature a finding of fact, and examples abound in a wide variety of transactions. The first case deals with a typical attempted characterization of a corporate payment as a loan. The second case involves a more subtle constructive dividend. The third case, a transfer between related corporations, serves notice that dividend consequences may ensue under circumstances not readily apparent to those unfamiliar with the niceties of our tax system. The final case considers the relationship between constructive dividends and earnings and profits.

Jaques v. Commissioner
935 F.2d 104 (6th Cir. 1991)

OPINION

MARTIN, JR., Circuit Judge. Leonard C. and Sybil J. Jaques appeal the decision of the United States Tax Court finding that certain withdrawals made by Leonard Jaques from his wholly-owned professional corporation were taxable dividends under §316 of the Internal Revenue Code rather than non-taxable loans. This determination resulted in deficiencies in their income tax for the taxable years 1983, 1984, and 1985, in the amounts of $24,255, $120,384, and $301,970, respectively. . . . For the following reasons, we affirm the decision of the tax court.

Leonard C. Jaques is an attorney specializing in the practice of plaintiffs' class action law. In 1971, Jaques formed a professional corporation, Leonard C. Jaques, P.C. From the time of incorporation, Jaques has always been the sole shareholder of the corporation. Jaques' basis in the stock of the corporation was $20,000. Prior to the years at issue, the corporation had established a defined pension plan. Beginning in 1977 and continuing throughout the years in issue, Jaques began making withdrawals from the corporation. Jaques used the amounts withdrawn from the corporation during the years at issue to pay day-to-day personal living expenses. . . .

These withdrawals were reflected as "Accounts Receivable-Officer" by bookkeeping entries made on the books and records of the corporation. Jaques did not execute notes for these withdrawals nor was there a maturity date set for repayment. There was no collateral pledged as security for the repayment of the amounts withdrawn by Jaques. . . .

Withdrawals were also made by the corporation from its pension plan. These withdrawals were reflected in executed promissory notes carrying an interest rate of 15 percent. During the years at issue, the corporation made monthly interest payments to the pension plan. The amount of these loans for the years 1983, 1984, and 1985 were $14,750.00, $56,818.77, and $165,502.05, respectively.

During each of the years in issue, the corporation paid Jaques a salary of $150,000.24. During 1984 and 1985, the corporation also reported on its W-2 Forms $37,093 and $131,416, respectively, as other compensation paid to Jaques for imputed interest on the withdrawals.

Jaques' personal financial statement prepared as of December 17, 1987, noted that "Leonard C. Jaques owes his law firm $2,645,000.00, but since the professional corporation stock is wholly owned by Leonard C. Jaques, the 'loan' is a wash." Jaques' personal financial statement prepared as of November 30, 1988, reflected loans payable to the corporation in the amount of $3,042,000. In the note to the financial statement, petitioner disclosed that "The $3,042,000.00 represents monies I have borrowed over the years from the P.C. to be repaid whenever convenience may focus."

This case ilustrates the tension which arises when individual professional practitioners are permitted to create separate corporate identities. For the better part of the history of our country, lawyers were prohibited from utilizing such incorporation. See, e.g., In re N.H. Bar Ass'n, 110 N.H. 356, 266 A.2d 853 (1970); In re Florida Bar, 133 So. 2d 554 (Fla. 1961). Currently, every state and the District of Columbia have statutes permitting such a procedure. See Phillips, McNider, & Riley, Origins of Tax Law: The History of the Professional Service Corporation, 40 Wash. & Lee L. Rev. 433, 439 (1983). The taxpayer in this case, a lawyer by trade, like many accountants, physicians, architects, and other professionals, found it to be financially beneficial to incorporate his legal practice as a professional corporation. See Cooper, The Taming of the Shrewd: Identifying and Controlling Income Tax Avoidance, 85 Colum. L. Rev. 657, 665 n.24 (1985). There is Leonard Jaques the private citizen and Leonard Jaques the professional corporation. In the eyes of the federal tax law, these are two separate taxable entities; in reality, they are a single individual. Not surprisingly, problems frequently arise when the two entities engage in transactions which have federal tax implications.

In the typical business context, business persons engage in business transactions with one another at arms-length. Therefore, it is usually safe to assume that a particular transaction is entered into because each party concludes that it is in his own self-interest to do so. This assumption breaks down, however, when the parties engaging in the transaction are in reality the same individual; the self-interest test usually employed to judge a contemplated transaction ceases to be applied by each party to the transaction. In this case, Leonard Jaques the professional corporation "loaned" Leonard Jaques the private citizen large amounts of money. Because in reality these transactions resulted in nothing more than Jaques lending himself his own money, it is very difficult to characterize the relationship between Jaques and his corporation as one of debtor and creditor. The potential for tax evasion is clear. A sole shareholder of a professional corporation could withdraw large sums from the corporation without incurring any tax liability simply by characterizing the withdrawals as loans, repayment of which could be postponed indefinitely.

The tax court determined that the amounts withdrawn by Jaques were not intended to be loans, but were taxable distributions under [§316]. The court found that Jaques failed to prove that the withdrawals were intended to be loans because he did not offer any "objective manifestations of contemporaneous intent to repay" other than his "own unsupported testimony." Other factors which the tax court relied upon in reaching its conclusion were: (1) the withdrawals were not represented by interest-

bearing notes; (2) Jaques did not periodically repay the principal or interest; (3) the withdrawals were unsecured and were not subject to a fixed
repayment schedule; (4) the withdrawals were in proportion to his holdings as the sole shareholder; and (5) the corporation had substantial current earnings but did not pay any dividends during this period.

Jaques argues that the tax court erred in finding that the withdrawals
in question were constructive dividends and not loans. We may not disturb
the tax court's findings of fact unless they are clearly erroneous. Commissioner v. Duberstein, 363 U.S. 278, 4 L. Ed. 2d 1218 (1960); see also Rose
v. Commissioner, 868 F.2d 851, 853 (6th Cir. 1989) (citing cases). There
is some dispute as to whether the loan versus dividend question is one of
fact or law. See, e.g., Busch v. Commissioner, 728 F.2d 945 (7th Cir. 1984)
(whether shareholder's withdrawals from corporation constituted loans or
dividends is purely a question of fact); Dolese v. United States, 605 F.2d
1146 (10th Cir. 1979) (question of debt or dividend normally a question
of fact, but when there is no dispute in the evidence, whether the facts
add up to debt or equity is a question of law); Alterman Foods, Inc. v.
United States, 505 F.2d 873 (5th Cir. 1974) (whether operative facts add
up to dividend or loan is a question of law). This court has held on a
number of occasions that whether a payment is a loan or a dividend is a
factual question. Dietrick v. Commissioner, 881 F.2d 336 (6th Cir.); Estate
of DeNiro v. Commissioner, 746 F.2d 327 (6th Cir. 1984); Wilkof v. Commissioner, 636 F.2d 1139 (6th Cir. 1981) (per curiam); Berthold v. Commissioner, 404 F.2d 119 (6th Cir. 1968). Thus, we review the tax court's
determination that the withdrawals made by Jaques were constructive dividends and not loans only for clear error.

Whether the withdrawals made by Jaques from his professional corporation are treated for tax purposes as loans or dividends turns on the
intention of the parties at the time the withdrawals were made. Dietrick,
881 F.2d at 340; Livernois Trust v. Commissioner, 433 F.2d 879 (6th Cir.
1970); Berthold, 404 F.2d at 122. To determine whether the taypayer intended to repay the withdrawals, courts have looked to a number of objective factors. See Alterman, 505 F.2d at 876 n.6 (listing factors). The
taxpayer's testimony that he intended to repay is one factor which is considered, but such self-serving testimony "can appropriately be viewed with
some diffidence unless supported by other facts which bring the transaction much closer to a normal arms-length loan." Berthold, 404 F.2d at 122;
Tyler v. Tomilson, 414 F.2d 844, 850 (5th Cir. 1969) ("We therefore look
not to mere labels or to the self-serving declarations of the parties, but to
more reliable criteria of the circumstances surrounding the transaction.").

Jaques argues that the tax court erroneously relied upon the fact that
his corporation did not pay any dividends during the time in issue to
support its finding that the withdrawals were not loans. Jaques argues that
throughout this period his corporation was prohibited under Michigan
law from declaring a dividend. The applicable statute states, "dividends

may be declared or paid and other distributions may be made out of surplus only." Mich. Comp. Laws §450.1351(2). The "surplus" referred to in §450.1351 can be either earned surplus or capital surplus. Earned surplus is defined as "the portion of the surplus of a corporation that represents the accumulated net earnings, gains and profits, after deduction of all losses, that has not been distributed to shareholders as dividends or transferred to stated capital or capital surplus. . . ." Mich. Comp. Laws §450.1107(1). Jaques argues that because the corporation had negative retained earnings during 1983 and 1984, it was unable legally to declare a dividend under Michigan law.

This argument, even if technically correct, does not address the critical issue, namely whether the amounts withdrawn by Jaques from his corporation were dividends for the purposes of the federal tax law. Under §316 of the Tax Code, the term "dividend" is defined as a distribution made out of either earnings and profits of the taxable year or earnings and profits accumulated after February 28, 1913. Thus, Jaques' argument would be persuasive if his corporation lacked sufficient earnings and profits for his withdrawals to be considered dividends under the Code. The phrase, "earnings and profits" is not specifically defined by the Code, however, some courts have defined the phrase as, "the amount of gross receipts minus the cost of producing them." 1 J. Mertens, Law of Federal Income Tax, §38C.01; Divine v. Commissioner, 500 F.2d 1041, 1050-1051 (2d Cir. 1974). Additionally, the calculation of earnings and profits bears no exact relation to either taxable income or to earnings as determined by normal accounting practice. 1 J. Mertens at §38C.01; see also Estate of Uris, 605 F.2d 1258, 1265 (2d Cir. 1979). Jaques has not argued that his corporation lacked sufficient earnings and profits for his withdrawals to be considered dividends under the Code. Presumably his corporation had sufficient earnings and profits to cover his withdrawals and have them properly classified as dividends. The fact that Jaques might have been prohibited under Michigan law from formally declaring a dividend does not preclude a finding that his withdrawals were dividends under §316.

Jaques next argues the tax court erred in holding that without a written loan agreement the advances he received from his corporation were presumptively dividends. However, the tax court's decision did not presume the advances were dividends and not loans merely because of the absence of a written loan agreement. The tax court simply cited the absence of a written loan agreement as one factor which helped illuminate the true intent of the parties. This was entirely proper. *Berthold,* 404 F.2d at 122.

To support his argument, Jaques cites Faitoute v. Commissioner, 38 B.T.A. 32 (1938). In that case, the tax court held that a sole stockholder's withdrawal of money from his corporation was a loan even though there was no written loan agreement, no security interest given, and no interest charged. The court held that the absence of these arrangements did not make the loan a dividend "if the money advanced was in good faith loaned by the corporation to the petitioner. . . ." Id at 35. Jaques argues that *Faitoute* stands for the proposition that such factors as no written loan agreement, no repayment agreement, and no charged interest are irrelevant as a matter of law in determining the taxpayer's intent when repayments are made on the loans. *Faitoute*, however, seems to hold that the absence of these arrangements is not dispositive of the issue; it does not make them irrelevant.

Jaques next argues that the tax court erred in not according adequate consideration to his partial repayment of the loan proceeds in determining whether his withdrawals were legitimate loans. Jaques did repay approximately $48,000 of the $1,220,000 withdrawn during the years at issue. This repayment was addressed by the tax court and found to be "small" and "sporadic." The case which Jaques relies upon to support this argument, Ravano v. Commissioner, T.C. Memo 1967-170, 26 T.C.M. (CCH) 793 (1967), considered total repayment within a reasonable time as more indicative of the true arrangement than the absence of notes evidencing the corporation's indebtedness or maturity date for the repayment. Id. at 800-801. There is no total repayment within a reasonable time in this case.

Finally, Jaques argues that the tax court's findings that he had no obligation to ever repay the corporation the withdrawals is erroneous because he was in fact borrowing from the pension plan and only using the corporation as a conduit. Jaques was the trustee of his corporation's pension plan and as such, he bore a nondelegable fiduciary duty to ensure that these loan proceeds were repaid. If not, he would be personally liable to repay the entire sum under the Employment Retirement Income Security Act, 29 U.S.C. §1109(a). This argument, however, would only be applicable to $237,070.82 of the near $1,220,000, that was withdrawn over this period. This left nearly one million dollars to be repaid "whenever convenience may focus."

Jaques claims throughout his brief that the reason these loans were necessary was that his corporation was experiencing financial difficulty because he received unfavorable results in three major cases. This, he claims, destroyed the corporation's working capital and required Jaques to take a substantial salary reduction. Because of this situation, Jaques claims that the corporation had to borrow funds from its pension plan. The following exchange took place between Jaques and counsel when he testified in the tax court:

Q: What was the need for borrowing from the pension funds?
A: To just to keep going.
Q: In other words, working capital?
A: Working capital, yes.
Q: Would it also be a source of funds for borrowings by you from the corporation?

A: Yes.

Q: Is the corporation expecting to enforce the collection of your borrowing from it?

A: Yes.

Q: Why would they want to enforce it?

A: Well, to stay within the mandates of the law you must enforce it. It had to be enforced with regard to the pension problem. Yes, it had to be. There's no question about it.

During the years in issue the corporation borrowed a total of $237,070.82 from the pension fund. There is "no question" that as to this amount, the law requires repayment and will hold Jaques personally liable. However, during the relevant period Jaques "borrowed" a total of $1,219,767.00 from his professional service corporation. Subtracting these two figures yields $982,696.18 which came directly from the current earnings of his corporation. There is some question whether requirement of repayment of this amount would be enforced by the corporation. Furthermore, the fact that his corporation had sufficient cash available to extend these large loans to Jaques belies his argument that his corporation was experiencing financial difficulty.

There is no doubt that a withdrawal by a controlling stockholder from his corporation can be considered a loan for federal income tax purposes. See Alterman Foods, Inc. v. United States, 222 Ct. Cl. 218, 611 F.2d 866, 869 (1979). Something more is required, however, than the mere representations of the parties that the withdrawals were considered to be loans. There must be at least some evidence of the corporate formalities which usually accompany such transactions. Otherwise, a sole owner of a corporation could have his personal expenses paid by the corporation as a loan and postpone repayment indefinitely, thus escaping the double taxation which is normally incident to the corporate form. Because cases of this type are unique on their facts, we do not attempt to establish the line between those withdrawals that will be considered loans and those that will not. We simply note that the present case exceeds that line. We have little difficulty with the facts before us in affirming the decision of the tax court.

Baumer v. United States
580 F.2d 863 (5th Cir. 1978)

Before WISDOM, GOLDBERG, and RUBIN, Circuit Judges.

GOLDBERG, Circuit Judge.

This appeal presents a novel variation of the recurrent problem of determining the tax consequences of transactions between closely held corporations and their shareholders. Here a corporation granted an option to purchase a one-half interest in a parcel of real estate to the son of the corporation's sole shareholder for nominal consideration. In the proceedings below, the district court held that the grant of this option resulted in a constructive dividend from the corporation to the father, measured by the ascertainable value of the option. . . .

I. THE TRANSACTION

[The following fact statement appears in a later disposition of *Baumer* at 685 F.2d 1319-1320:

> On January 30, 1966, the Seven Eighty-Eight Greenwood Avenue Corporation (Corporation) contracted to purchase a parcel of residential property for $175,000. Erwin G. Baumer (Father) was the sole shareholder of Corporation. When Erwin H. Baumer (Son) learned of this transaction, he asked for an interest in the property and, in May, 1966, was given an option to purchase a one-half interest in the property. The term during which the option was exercisable was one year from its effective date and the exercise price was $88,000 plus five and one-half percent interest calculated from the effective date. In August, 1966, Corporation entered into a contract for the purchase of an adjacent piece of property for $25,000. Son was granted an amended option in January, 1967, which encompassed both properties. The exercise price for the new option was $100,000. The stated consideration for both options was $10, which Son did not recall having paid. Also in January, 1967, Corporation granted Pope & Carter Company, Inc. an option to purchase the properties for $500,000. In early December, 1968, Son exercised his option, giving a note to Corporation for $114,501.23, the entire option price [plus interest]. On December 27, 1968, Pope & Carter exercised its option. The sale by Son and Corporation to an assignee of Pope & Carter was closed on July 1, 1969. Son received $252,700 for his one-half interest in the properties.
>
> The Commissioner determined that upon Son's exercise of his option in 1968, Father received a constructive dividend taxable to Father based on the difference between the exercise price of the option and the fair market value of the property. The Commissioner also determined that Son's gain on the sale of his one-half interest should be imputed to Corporation. The District Court ruled that imputation was not warranted.
>
> The District Court determined that the option and its amendment were distributions of corporate property resulting in a constructive dividend to Father. The court assumed, without deciding, that the constructive dividend occurred when Son was granted the option in 1966 and at the time of its amendment in 1967, years not in issue in the proceedings. The District Court, however, found that the option had no ascertainable value at the time of its grant or its amendment. Therefore, under the open transaction doctrine of Burnet v. Logan 283 U.S. 404 (1931), the District Court ruled that tax liability attached at the time the option was exercised in 1968. The court's valuation of the option was based on the consideration paid by Pope & Carter for [exercising] its option.]

II. IMPUTING SON'S INCOME TO CORPORATION

We first examine the government's contention that the sale by Corporation to Son of a one-half interest in the property immediately prior to the exercise of the Pope & Carter option was a sham transaction designed to shift half of Corporation's gain on that impending sale to Son. The government maintains that under the doctrine of Commissioner v. Court Holding Co., 324 U.S. 331 (1945), the district court should have taxed the Corporation on the entire gain from the sale to Pope & Carter. . . .

In the instant case, the district court concluded that the government's *Court Holding* theory was "inapplicable to the factual situation presented in this case," finding that the distribution of the option to Son occurred before a sale of the property was even contemplated, that Son was personally involved to a substantial extent in the development activity which led to the increased value of the Piedmont-Old Ivy properties, and that Son negotiated with Pope & Carter in his own behalf with respect to his interest in the properties. . . . Our review of the record convinces us that there is ample evidence to support the court's factual determinations. We therefore affirm the court's judgment that this transaction was not stricken by *Court Holding*'s selling virus.

In so holding we are not unaware of certain doubts raised by the government concerning the economic reality of the transactions between Corporation and Son. The government correctly notes that the corporation bore all the risks with respect to the zoning action, which was necessary to make the purchase a profitable venture. Son did not actually exercise his option and acquire title to the property until favorable zoning was obtained and the sale to Pope & Carter became a virtual certainty. Furthermore, Corporation actively participated in the negotiations with Pope & Carter which led to the sale of the Piedmont-Old Ivy properties. Son never expended a single cent on the transaction, either in acquiring the option or in exercising it. Indeed, the note Son gave Corporation as payment for the properties was modified shortly after its execution to allow a pass through to Corporation of Pope & Carter's payments to Son. The government further argues that, as a matter of law, the options granted by Corporation to Son were merely continuing offers to sell which did not transfer a present property interest to Son. Were this the case, no property interest would have been transferred from Corporation to Son until after the agreement with Pope & Carter was negotiated and virtually consummated by Corporation. To the extent Son participated in the negotiations before the sale from Father to Son, his activities would have been on behalf of Corporation since Son would have had no interest of his own. In such circumstances, a finding that the sale of Son's interest to Pope & Carter's assignee was made by Son, rather than by Corporation, would be difficult, if not impossible, to support. . . .

Nonetheless, there is other evidence in the record which supports the district court's findings and conclusions. . . . It is absurd to suggest that income may be imputed to the Corporation simply because it negotiated with third parties concerning this disposition *of its own interest* in the property. Instead, the crucial question becomes whether the Corporation "actively participated" in the sale of Son's share of the property. . . .

The court found that at the time the option was granted, Father and Son intended to use the property themselves "for a motel." This finding, supported by evidence in the record, indicates that no sale of the property was contemplated when Son received the property interest reflected by the option. This, in turn, supports the conclusion that the option was not merely a subterfuge designed to conceal Corporation's subsequent sale of the entire property, but instead was intended to pass an interest to Son which Son, and not Corporation, later disposed of in the sale to Pope & Carter.

The court's determination that Son, rather than Corporation, negotiated with respect to Son's interest in the property is further supported by evidence that Son was personally involved to a substantial extent in the development activity which led to the increased value of the properties. The district court found that these efforts were attributable to Son's belief that he had an interest in the property. The fact that Son had previously treated the option as constituting a personal property interest and had relied on this personal interest in developing the Piedmont-Old Ivy tracts strongly suggests that when Son later participated in the negotiations with Pope & Carter, he also did so in his own behalf. The prior treatment of a transaction by the parties is a relevant consideration, which in this case, supports the finding that Son, and not Corporation, negotiated with Pope & Carter with respect to Son's interest in the property.

In sum, we are not persuaded that the transactions at issue must necessarily be characterized as a sham, as less than bona fide, or as, "in substance," a sale by Corporation. . . . Accordingly, we affirm the court's decision not to impute income from that sale to Corporation under the *Court Holding* rationale.

III.   THE OPTION: ARM'S-LENGTH TRANSACTION OR CONSTRUCTIVE DIVIDEND?

Our conclusion that income from the sale of Son's interest in the Piedmont-Old Ivy property is not imputable to Corporation under *Court Holding* requires us to examine the government's alternative theory that the ascertainable value of property conferred by Corporation on Son without adequate consideration is taxable to Father as a constructive dividend. The district court substantially agreed with this theory and held that Father received a constructive dividend when Corporation granted the option to Son in 1966 and amended it in 1967. However, finding that the value of the option was not ascertainable in 1966 or 1967, the court deferred recognition of the dividend and liability for the tax until Son exercised his option in 1968. The court then valued the option with reference to the consideration paid by Pope & Carter for monthly extensions of its option.

Our review of the court's holding involves several distinct inquiries. In subsection III(A) we discuss why, as a general matter, the district court was correct in refusing to assume at once that a transaction between a corporation and the sole shareholder's son was an arm's-length transaction. We then consider in subsection III(B) whether constructive dividend treatment was warranted in this case. Finally, in subsection III(C) we examine the district court's valuation of the constructive dividend. . . .

A. JUDICIAL SCRUTINY OF TRANSACTIONS BETWEEN CLOSELY HELD CORPORATIONS AND THEIR SHAREHOLDERS: A GENERAL DISCUSSION

We begin by considering taxpayers' contention that the option to Son was granted by Corporation at a fair price in an arm's-length transaction. According to taxpayers, no tax consequences should attach either to the grant or to the exercise of the option. In taxpayers' view, Son's option should be treated no differently than the option granted to Pope & Carter. We conclude that this argument is untenable. In order to elucidate our views on the oft-perplexing problem of the conferral of benefits on a controlling shareholder by a closely held corporation, we begin with first principles.

Distributions of "property" made by a corporation to a shareholder with respect to its stock are dividends to the extent of the corporation's current and accumulated earnings and profits, . . . and must be included by the shareholder in gross income. [§§301(a), 301(c)(1), and 316].

In accordance with [the] broad definition of property, dividends may be "in cash or in kind, and may also result when the corporation makes a 'bargain sale' of its property to the shareholder at less than fair market value. When there is a 'bargain sale,' the shareholder receives a dividend in the amount of the difference between the fair market value and the price paid for the corporate property. . . ." Green v. United States, 460 F.2d 412, 419 (5th Cir. 1972). As the Supreme Court has recognized, "a sale, if for substantially less than the value of the property sold, may be as effective a means of distributing profits among stockholders as the formal declaration of a dividend." Palmer v. Commissioner, 302 U.S. 63 (1937). No such formal declaration is required for a shareholder to be charged with a constructive dividend. Crosby v. United States, 496 F.2d 1384 (5th Cir. 1974).

Two other guiding principles require mention at this stage. It is clear that the intent of the parties does not govern the characterization of a distribution. Instead, courts have looked to the economic *effect* of the trans-action at issue in determining the existence of a dividend. It is also well settled that a dividend does not escape taxation "simply because it fails to pass through the hands of the particular taxpayer when . . . the divi-dend is diverted at the behest of the shareholder into the hands of others." Green v. United States, supra, 460 F.2d at 419, quoting Sammons v. United States, 433 F.2d 728, 730 (5th Cir. 1970), cert. denied, 402 U.S. 945 (1971). . . .

These expansive principles governing the treatment of constructive dividends reflect an awareness by Congress and the courts of the ingenious methods which have been devised by owners of closely held corporations trying to escape taxes at the corporate or shareholder level. . . . As a consequence, courts have generally examined dealings between a closely held corporation and its shareholders or relatives of shareholders with a jaundiced eye and microscopic vision. Such transactions are simply not entitled to the presumption that they are conducted at arm's length. In-deed, they call for special scrutiny. We suggest that the metaphor of a corporation and its sole shareholder walking arm-in-arm is more descrip-tive of reality than the vision of the corporation and shareholder holding each other apart at arm's length. . . .

B. THE GRANT OF THE OPTION AS A CONSTRUCTIVE DIVIDEND

Our inquiry is in two parts. First, we must focus on whether, in fact, the grant of the option conferred a benefit on Son by distributing valuable rights without consideration. If we determine that the option conferred such a benefit, we must then examine whether the resulting corporate distribution constituted a constructive dividend to Father. . . .

1. The Option: Valuable Rights or Fair Bargain?

Our initial task of valuing the option to determine whether the corpo-ration distributed valuable rights to Son is greatly complicated by the unset-tled state of the law in this area. Neither the Code nor the applicable case law provides clear guidance. Taxpayers maintain that under the Supreme Court's decision in Palmer v. Commissioner, 302 U.S. 63 (1937), there is no dividend if the exercise price of the option represents the fair market value of the underlying property at the time the option is issued, even if the value of the underlying property has appreciated greatly by the time the option is exercised. Taxpayers argue that the $100,000 exercise price of the option on the combined properties was a reasonable valuation of the fair market value of those properties at the time the option was granted to Son. Thus, according to taxpayers, no valuable rights constituting a dividend were distributed by Corporation.

The government responds first that taxpayer's argument rests on an erroneous reading of *Palmer,* and, second, that the 1954 Code has modified this aspect of the *Palmer* decision in any event. We agree with the government that the position contended for by taxpayers is justified neither by good sense nor by the applicable case law.

The Supreme Court's decision in *Palmer* has been a controversial one. In that case, a corporation distributed options, exercisable for 15 days, to its shareholders, entitling those shareholders to purchase from the corporation portfolio shares in a second corporation. On the date distribution of the option was authorized, the exercise price of the options equaled the market value of the portfolio shares. By the time the options were issued, eight days later, the market value of the portfolio shares had increased considerably.

The Court held first that under the Revenue Act of 1928, a shareholder who is granted an option to purchase portfolio shares is not subject to income tax on the receipt of the option, even though the option itself is valuable. "The mere issue of rights to subscribe and their receipt by stockholders, is not a dividend. No distribution of corporate assets or diminution of the net worth of the corporation results in any practical sense." 58 S. Ct. at 70. The Court then considered whether the shareholders would be taxable upon exercise of their option rights when a spread developed between the option price and the market value of the shares. The Court held that the exercise of these rights does not result in a dividend if the circumstances demonstrate "that distribution of corporate assets, effected by the sale, was not intended to be a means of distributing earnings, and that the price when fixed represented the fair market value of the property to be distributed." Id. at 71. Such a distribution "is not converted into a dividend by the mere circumstance that later, at the time of their delivery to the stockholders, [the assets] have a higher value." Id.

We recognize that this language appears to support taxpayers' contention that because the exercise price of Son's option equaled the fair market value of the property when the option was granted . . . , no dividend should result from either the grant or exercise of the option. The continuing vitality of this aspect of the *Palmer* decision under the 1954 Code, however, is far from self-evident. . . .

The 1954 Code . . . specifies the method for determining the value of a distribution. Under section 301(b)(1)(A), the amount of the distribution is measured by the *fair market value* of the property received. Thus, in the case at bar the amount of the distribution should be measured by the *fair market value* of the option, rather than by the spread between the exercise price and the value of the underlying property at the time of grant. . . . While that spread in some cases may approximate the fair market value of the option, here the duration of the option period and the likelihood of obtaining favorable rezoning must also be considered in determining the option's fair market value. . . . Thus the determination of whether the grant of the option conferred a benefit on Son is governed by the value of the option, rather than by the spread between the exercise price and the value of the underlying property.

Applying this standard, we are in complete agreement with the district court's finding that the rights granted under the option were of great value to Son. The option entitled Son to reap the benefits of the comtemplated rezoning without incurring any of the risks associated with the real estate venture. He paid no consideration for his rights. If, during the two and one half year option period the properties appreciated in value, Son would realize a gain. If the value of the property decreased or remained the same, Son would be no worse off. Son was truly in a "heads I win, tails I don't lose" position. This "option privilege" represented valuable property to Son. . . .

Any doubts that Corporation distributed valuable rights to Son when it granted the option are dispelled by comparing Son's option with that received by Pope & Carter. Pope & Carter agreed to pay substantial amounts to keep its option open and, in addition, obligated itself to devote reasonable time and effort to obtaining favorable rezoning. In return it received the right to acquire the property for $500,000, a price far in excess of the fair market value of the property at the time the option was granted. Son's option, on the other hand, remained in effect for a longer period, imposed no obligations on Son, and allowed him to purchase a one-half interest in the property for only $100,000 plus $5\frac{1}{2}$ percent interest. Even if we ignore the fact that the amendment to Son's option, which extended the exercise period for an additional two years without increasing the exercise price, was granted a mere thirteen days before the grant of the Pope & Carter option . . . , it is apparent that in granting the option, Corporation conferred a benefit on Son by distributing valuable rights.

2.   The Corporate Distribution: A Constructive Dividend?

Having concluded that Corporation distributed valuable rights to Son, we can easily dispose of taxpayers' contention that the grant of the option should not result in a constructive dividend to Father. . . .

Taxpayers maintain that the option was granted because of Corporation's interest in obtaining the benefit of Son's services. The evidence, however, more than adequately supports the conclusion that the grant of the option primarily served the personal interests of Father in his shareholder capacity. Indeed, taxpayers admit that the option was granted to satisfy the moral obligation of Father to compensate Son for taking advantage of a business opportunity Father had personally discouraged Son from pursuing. . . .

Since we hold that there is no clear error in the findings of the district court, we affirm the district court's conclusion that Father received a constructive dividend from the grant by Corporation to Son of the option on the Piedmont-Old Ivy property.

C. VALUING THE DIVIDEND

The final issue presented by this appeal is whether the district court properly valued Father's constructive dividend. In particular, questions have been raised concerning the district court's use of the consideration paid by Pope & Carter in valuing Son's option. To resolve this issue, we must first examine whether the dividend occurred upon the grant of the option or upon its exercise by Son. If we determine that *grant* of the option constituted a dividend, we must then consider both the district court's finding that the option had no ascertainable value at the time of grant and the Court's subsequent valuation of the option at the time of exercise in 1968. If, on the other hand, the dividend arose only upon Son's *exercise* of the option, we need only consider the proper valuation of the option at that time.

[The court ruled that the taxable event was the grant of the option but that since valuation was impossible at that time, the "open transaction" doctrine was appropriate. See Burnet v. Logan, 283 U.S. 404 (1931). However, the court rejected the district court's reliance on the value of the Pope & Carter option as evidence of the value of Son's option, since the options were different in duration, price and required activity by the optionee.]

Thus in the instant case the option should be valued by subtracting the exercise price of approximately $100,000 from the fair market value of the underlying property when the option was exercised on December 6, 1968. . . . We therefore remand the case to the district court for a redetermination of the value of the constructive dividend taxable to Father.

IV. CONCLUSION

The concepts of imputed income and constructive dividend have been developed to prevent taxpayers from clothing their activities in tax-repellant garb. Both doctrines require courts to look behind the superficial or formal nature of a transaction. Application of these concepts in complicated tax cases involves the difficult task of characterizing elusive transactions. . . .

Here the district court found that Son, rather than Corporation, negotiated and consummated the sale of Son's interest in the Piedmont-Old Ivy property to Pope & Carter and therefore concluded that income from this sale should not be imputed to Corporation. The court also found that valuable rights were distributed by Corporation to Son without business purposes because of Father's position as the controlling shareholder of

Corporation and therefore concluded that Father received a constructive dividend from Corporation. These factual determinations are supported by the record, and the court's ultimate conclusions rest on a correct application of the controlling law. These determinations are therefore affirmed. The court, however, failed to apply the proper standard for determining the value of Son's option at the time of exercise and therefore improperly computed the amount of Father's constructive dividend. Accordingly, this portion of the case must be remanded for further proceedings consistent with this opinion. The judgment of the district court is affirmed in part, reversed in part, and remanded in part.

Gilbert v. Commissioner _____
74 T.C. 60 (1980)

TANNENWALD, Judge.

Respondent determined a deficiency in petitioners' income tax for the year 1975 in the amount of $7,483. The issue for decision is whether a transfer of $20,000 by Jetrol, Inc., to G & H Realty Corp. constituted a constructive dividend to petitioner Gilbert L. Gilbert, the common shareholder of each corporation.

FINDINGS OF FACT . . .

During the years 1974 and 1975, Gilbert was the president and sole shareholder of Jetrol, Inc. (Jetrol), a manufacturing company. He was also, during the first part of 1975, a 50-percent shareholder of G & H Realty Corp. His brother, Henry Gilbert (Henry), was the other 50-percent shareholder. G & H Realty Corp. (Realty) owned the building at 27 Lois Street, Rochester, N.Y., in which Jetrol conducted its business as a tenant. Jet Rochester, Inc., another manufacturing company, occupied the balance of the premises. Henry was the sole shareholder of Jet Rochester, Inc., until February 1975, at which time he sold all his stock to two former employees unrelated to Gilbert.

During 1975, Henry and Gilbert decided to redeem Henry's stock in Realty because Henry wanted to retire. Henry had no legal restrictions as to whom he could sell his stock nor was there ever a contractual relationship between Gilbert and Henry obligating Gilbert to purchase the stock. The parties have stipulated that Realty did not have sufficient funds to redeem the stock.

Realty attempted to borrow $20,000 from Central Trust Co. (the bank) in Rochester, N.Y., but the bank was unwilling to loan the funds to Realty. The bank might have considered refinancing the mortgage on Realty's property, but that would have involved an appraisal, a higher interest rate, and related problems which would have delayed the redemption, and

Henry was in a hurry. The bank was willing to loan, and did loan, $20,000 to Jetrol on April 9, 1975, with Gilbert personally guaranteeing the loan.

On April 17, 1975, Jetrol transferred the same $20,000 to Realty, which forthwith used the money to redeem all of its stock owned by Henry. The check from Jetrol to Realty had the words "Loan to G & H Realty" typed on its face. The $20,000 was recorded on the books of account of Jetrol as a loan receivable and on the books of Realty as a loan payable. No note or other indicia of indebtedness was executed by Realty. No rate of interest was stated on the "loan" between Jetrol and Realty to Jetrol. The $20,000 was carried on the books of account of the two corporations until Realty furnished the $20,000 to Jetrol in 1977. . . .

Jetrol's business was growing in 1975 and subsequently. It needed room to expand its facilities, preferably at 27 Lois Street. Jet Rochester operated in the building on annual leases with Realty, effective February 1, 1975, and February 1, 1976. In December 1976, Gilbert sent Jet Rochester a letter stating that he would not renew the lease in 1977 because Jetrol needed the space. Jet Rochester vacated the building around April 1977, at which time Jetrol began to occupy the entire building.

Later in 1977, Gilbert contracted to sell all of the capital stock of Jetrol to the Pantasote Co. (Pantasote). As part of the purchase agreement, Gilbert guaranteed payment of the obligations owed by Realty to Jetrol. Pantasote would not close the sale until the Realty "loan" was off the books. On August 12, 1977, Gilbert borrowed money from the bank and "loaned" it to Realty. Realty used the money to repay Jetrol, without interest, on August 15, 1977. Thereafter, Jetrol repaid its bank loan. Following the sale of Jetrol to Pantasote, Gilbert repaid his note at the bank.

As of December 31, 1975, Jetrol had accumulated earnings and profits of $127,310.

OPINION

It is well established that transfer between related corporations can result in constructive dividends to their common shareholder if they were made primarily for his benefit and if he received a direct or tangible benefit therefrom. Schwartz v. Commissioner, 69 T.C. 877, 884 (1978); Rapid Electric Co. v. Commissioner, 61 T.C. 232, 239 (1973). However, if the transfer represents a bona fide loan or, even though not a loan, if the benefit to the shareholder is indirect or derivative in nature, there is no constructive dividend. Joseph Lupowitz Sons, Inc. v. Commissioner, 497 F.2d 862, 868 (3d Cir. 1974). . . . The issues of existence of a loan or the nature of the benefit to the shareholder are issues of fact and turn upon the circumstances of the particular case. See Schwartz v. Commissioner, supra at 884. The burden of proof is on the petitioners. Welch v. Helvering, 290 U.S. 111 (1933); Rule 142(a), Tax Court Rules of Practice and Procedure.

Petitioners argue that the transfer at issue constituted a bona fide loan, thereby negating respondent's determination of a dividend. The critical question in resolving this issue is whether there was a genuine intention to create a debt, which, in turn, depends upon weighing such objective factors as reasonable expectation of repayment and the economic reality of the claimed debtor-creditor relationship. Litton Business Systems, Inc. v. Commissioner, 61 T.C. 367, 377 (1973).

Petitioners rely on Gilbert's testimony that a loan was intended. They further point to the facts that the transfer was consistently treated as a loan on the books of account and balance sheets of both corporations and that the check issued by Jetrol to Realty included a notation that it was a loan. More importantly, they contend that the subsequent repayment of the amount transferred demonstrates that it was a valid debt of Realty. Finally, they claim that since Pantasote treated the transfer as a debt (after examining Jetrol's books), so should we. Respondent replies that, since there was no note, no stated interest nor interest paid, no security given, no repayment schedule nor a fixed repayment date, it was not a bona fide debt.

We agree with respondent that, on the facts revealed by the record . . . , no real indebtedness was created. The factors that petitioners argue establish an intent to repay are not convincing. "Such allegedly objective economic indicia of debt such as consistent bookkeeping and consistent financial reporting on balance sheets are in our opinion little more than additional declarations of intent, without any accompanying objective economic indicia of debt." Alterman Foods, Inc. v. United States, 505 F.2d 873, 879 (5th Cir. 1974). See also Dean v. Commissioner, 57 T.C. 32, 44 (1971). These declarations of intent must be viewed with some diffidence unless supported by objective factors demonstrating economic reality.

The fact that the advance was repaid, at Pantasote's insistence, prior to the closing of the sale of Gilbert's stock in Jetrol, is also not determinative of the parties' intent at the time the initial transfer was made. The lapse of some 2½ years between the transfer and the sale diminishes any inference which might be drawn from repayment. The repayment demand may merely have been a negotiating tactic which affected Pantasote's net purchase price by extinguishing Jetrol's very real debt to the bank. Moreover, the manner in which repayment occurred, with Gilbert effectively taking Jetrol's place by borrowing the money to enable funds to be applied for the repayment of Jetrol's debt to the bank, tends to indicate that Realty was never really expected to repay Jetrol.

It is true that, in other contexts, we have minimized the importance of some of the factors relied on by respondent. For example, it is clear that a valid debt may exist even where no formal debt instrument exists. Joseph Lupowitz Sons, Inc. v. Commissioner, supra. In fact, the existence of a debt instrument in this context would be of little weight without the accompaniment of other factors. Litton Business Systems, Inc. v. Commissioner, 61 T.C. at 378. Similarly, the absence of interest on such a debt is not determinative. Joseph Lupowitz Sons, Inc. v. Commissioner, supra. We think the absence of interest significant in the instant case, however, because Jetrol borrowed the same money at interest and we see no business purpose for it to have subsidized Realty by "loaning" the same funds without requiring the payment of at least an equivalent rate of interest. Moreover, Realty did not have funds of its own to accomplish the redemption, and the record is devoid of any evidence of the likelihood that it would have funds available to repay at a later date funds "borrowed" for this purpose. Finally, although the other factors relied upon by respondent have not been considered significant in other cases where different fact situations existed, we are not disposed to treat them so lightly here. In short, petitioners have failed to convince us that at the time Realty received the money from Jetrol it intended to repay it. Thus, they have not carried their burden of proving the transfer gave rise to a bona fide debt.

We now turn to the question whether, since no valid indebtedness was created, Gilbert realized a constructive dividend from the transfer. It is clear that neither the finding of an indebtedness nor the mere existence of common ownership is per se determinative that the common shareholder realized a dividend. See Joseph Lupowitz Sons, Inc. v. Commissioner, 497 F.2d 868; Rushing v. Commissioner, 52 T.C. at 893-894. The test is usually the existence of a direct versus indirect benefit (see Rapid Electric Co. v. Commissioner, 61 T.C. at 239) which in turn usually depends upon the existence of a business purpose on the part of the corporate transferor. See and compare Kuper v. Commissioner, 533 F.2d 152 (5th Cir. 1976), revg. 61 T.C. 624 (1974). Petitioners' argument that it was in Jetrol's interest to consolidate ownership of its landlord in friendly hands (due to planned expansion) does not withstand scrutiny. There is no evidence that the relationship between Gilbert and his brother, Henry, was unfriendly or that Jetrol would have encountered any difficulties if Henry had remained as a 50-percent shareholder of Realty. Moreover, we note that Gilbert testified that it would only have cost Jetrol $10,000 to $12,000 to move, including the costs of reinstallation. To have obligated itself for $20,000 (as it is claimed Realty did) to save such expense seems, to put it mildly, a lack of economic sense. Thus, any business purpose which may have been involved is simply too tenuous to be recognized. See Sammons v. Commissioner, 472 F.2d 449, 452 (5th Cir. 1972). . . .

But the absence of business purpose is not necessarily determinative that a constructive dividend occurred. Such a purpose merely refutes, or relegates to the status of incidental or indirect, any benefit to the common shareholder of the two corporations. Obviously, the primary purpose of the transfer in question herein was to redeem Henry's Realty stock, thus making Gilbert the sole shareholder of Realty. Since the funds with which such redemption was made represented fresh funds to Realty, they clearly enhanced the value of Gilbert's Realty stock (even though they were paid out) if not offset by an equivalent liability, and such enhancement could be considered a constructive dividend. Since we have found that no valid indebtedness from Realty to Jetrol was created, there was no such offsetting liability at the corporate level.

Gilbert, however, personally guaranteed the loan of Jetrol and thus had a contingent liability to the bank. Under the circumstances of this case, we think that this potential offset should not be taken into account. According to Gilbert, the bank was unwilling to make the loan to Realty unless the mortgage was refinanced. There is nothing in the record to indicate that the possibility of an unsecured loan to Realty with a personal guaranty by Gilbert would have been acceptable. On the other hand, the bank was willing to make the loan to Jetrol, albeit with the requirement of a personal guaranty by Gilbert. Gilbert testified that Jetrol was an expanding and fast growing business, and the balance sheets of Jetrol, as well as its subsequent acquisition of additional space, confirm this evaluation. From the foregoing, we infer that the bank looked to the primary obligor (Jetrol) for repayment and that Gilbert's guaranty was in effect simply a means of protecting the bank if its expectations were not capable of being realized. The fact that Gilbert personally borrowed the funds utilized to repay the bank at the time of the Pantasote transaction, some $2\frac{1}{2}$ years later, has little significance. . . . The reasons for handling the repayment in the manner set forth in our findings of fact are not revealed in the record. Based upon the foregoing, we are of the opinion that Gilbert's contingent liability as a guarantor, as of February 1975, lacked sufficient substance to warrant taking it into account determining whether Gilbert received a constructive dividend from Jetrol at that time; at the very least, petitioners have not carried their burden of proving otherwise. . . .

In sum, the benefits to Gilbert in 1975 were straightforward. He was able to obtain sole ownership of Realty without reducing the value of his interest in Realty's assets . . . and without investing additional personal funds which would have been subordinated to Realty's mortgage debt. Moreover, he was able to use Jetrol's borrowing power to obtain control of Realty. See Rapid Electric Co. v. Commissioner, 61 T.C. at 239. Realty was unable to accomplish the redemption itself. It is Gilbert's use of Jetrol's earnings and profits for a primarily personal and noncorporate motive of Jetrol that is critical and causes such use to be a constructive dividend to him.

Decision will be entered for the respondent.

Truesdell v. Commissioner
89 T.C. 1280 (1987)

NIMS, Judge.

. . . Respondent takes the position that the entire amounts diverted by petitioner from Asphalt Patch and Jim T. Enterprises during the taxable years 1977 and 1978 are includable in petitioner's income. Petitioner argues that he did not divert any corporate funds to his own use. However, petitioner also maintains that if this Court finds that he did divert corporate funds to his own use, the diverted funds constitute constructive dividends to petitioner, and therefore, the amounts includable in his income are limited to the earnings and profits of the corporations during the years in issue.

[The court found that petitioner did divert corporate funds to his own use.]

Petitioner's most cogent argument, however, is that the funds he diverted constitute constructive dividends to him, and therefore, are taxable as income to him only to the extent of the earnings and profits of the corporations. Under sections 301(c) and 316(a), dividends are taxable to the shareholders as ordinary income to the extent of the earnings and profits of the corporation, and any amount received by the shareholder in excess of earnings and profits is considered as a nontaxable return of capital to the extent of the shareholder's basis in his stock. Any amount received in excess of both the earnings and profits of the corporation and the shareholder's basis in his stock is treated as gain from the sale or exchange of property.

Dividends may be formally declared or they may be constructive. The fact that no dividends are formally declared does not foreclose the finding of a dividend-in-fact. Noble v. Commissioner, 368 F.2d 439, 442 (9th Cir. 1966), affg. T.C. Memo. 1965-84. The crucial concept in a finding that there is a constructive dividend is that the corporation has conferred a benefit on the shareholder in order to distribute available earnings and profits without expectation of repayment. Noble v. Commissioner, 368 F.2d at 443. We find that the diverted funds in this case constitute constructive dividends to petitioner.

. . . Petitioner failed to introduce any evidence that the earnings and profits of either corporation for any of the years in issue were less than the amounts determined by respondent. Accordingly, we find that the earnings and profits of Asphalt Patch were $23,540 and $4,594 in the taxable years 1978 and 1979, respectively, and that the earnings and profits of Jim T. Enterprises were $16,127.69 in the taxable year 1979. . . .

Respondent has failed to prove that the earnings and profits of the corporations were sufficient to permit the full amount of the funds diverted by petitioner during the taxable years 1977 and 1978 to be taxed as ordinary income under a constructive dividend theory. . . . Respondent maintains, nevertheless, that it is unnecessary to characterize the diverted funds as constructive dividends and that therefore the full amount diverted is taxable to petitioner as ordinary income.

Respondent does not attempt to describe the diverted funds as additional salary, illicit bonuses, commissions or anything more than dividends. Instead, respondent argues that any diversions from a corporation by its sole shareholder are taxable to the shareholder as ordinary income.

Respondent relies on Leaf v. Commissioner, 33 T.C. 1093 (1960), affd. per curiam 295 F.2d 503 (6th Cir. 1961), in which we held that the taxpayer, who unlawfully had diverted funds from his insolvent corporation with the intention of defrauding creditors, was liable for taxes on the full amount of the diverted funds regardless of the lack of earnings and profits of the corporation. In *Leaf* we based our holding on . . . the predecessor of section 61(a), which defines gross income as "all income from whatever source derived," and on the following language in Rutkin v. United States, 343 U.S. 130, 137 (1952):

> An unlawful gain, as well as a lawful one, constitutes taxable income when its recipient has such control over it that, as a practical matter, he derives readily realizable economic value from it. . . . That occurs when cash, as here, is delivered by its owner to the taxpayer in a manner which allows the recipient freedom to dispose of it at will, even though it may have been obtained by fraud and his freedom to use it may be assailable by someone with a better title to it.
>
> Such gains are taxable in the yearly period during which they are realized. . . .

Leaf and *Rutkin* are distinguishable from the instant case. *Leaf* and *Rutkin* both involved an unlawful receipt of funds by the taxpayer. The taxpayer in *Rutkin* had extorted funds from another individual, and the issue was whether extorted money was taxable to the extortionist. . . .

In *Leaf* corporate funds that should have been available to creditors were fraudulently transferred to the taxpayer in contemplation of bankruptcy. We need not and do not express an opinion on the need to apply a constructive dividend analysis in a situation where the shareholder utilized the corporation to steal from, embezzle from, or otherwise defraud other stockholders or third parties dealing with the corporation or shareholder. The taxpayer in *Leaf* had argued that the diverted funds were loans and therefore not taxable as income to him. We refused to adopt the taxpayer's characterization in the absence of any evidence of an intention to make repayment at the time of the taking.

The issue in *Leaf* was whether the taxpayer's obligation to repay the diverted funds and his actual restitution of some of those funds in a later year precluded his liability for tax on their receipt. We held that the taxpayer had such control over the funds that they represented taxable income to him for the year in which they were taken. Although the taxpayer in *Leaf* was the sole shareholder of the corporation, he did not argue that the diverted funds constituted constructive dividends, and therefore, this issue was not before the Court. . . .

In this case petitioner's diversions of income from Asphalt Patch and Jim T. Enterprises were not per se unlawful. The diverted funds were not, at least on their face, stolen, embezzled or diverted in fraud of creditors.

There has been no suggestion that the diversions were improper as a matter of corporate law. They are most appropriately described as distributions made by the corporations to their sole shareholder. DiZenzo v. Commissioner, 348 F.2d 122 (2d Cir. 1965), revg. T.C. Memo. 1964-121; Simon v. Commissioner, 248 F.2d 869 (8th Cir. 1957), revg. a Memorandum Opinion of this Court. . . .

Respondent also relies on Davis v. United States, 226 F.2d 331 (6th Cir. 1955), and Weir v. Commissioner, 283 F.2d 675, 684 (6th Cir. 1960), revg. a Memorandum Opinion of this Court, in which the Sixth Circuit held that it is not necessary to classify a sole shareholder's diversions of corporate income as constructive dividends. The Sixth Circuit reasoned in both cases that the taxpayer's dominion and control over the diverted funds warranted taxation of the diverted funds as ordinary income.

We respectfully disagree with the analysis of the Sixth Circuit. As a general proposition, where a taxpayer has dominion and control over diverted funds, they are includable in his gross income under section 61(a), Commissioner v. Glenshaw Glass Co., 348 U.S. 426, 431 (1955), unless some other modifying Code section applies. The latter is the situation here since Congress has provided that funds (or other property) distributed by a corporation to its shareholders over which the shareholders have dominion and control are to be taxed under the provisions of section 301(c).

We believe that the Eighth Circuit more aptly described the manner in which such diversions should be treated for tax purposes:

> The corporate distribution here was made with the knowledge of the stockholders and was acquiesced in by them. The corporation is liable for a substantial tax upon the diverted income it failed to report. Further tax will be collected from taxpayers under the constructive dividend theory. Fraudulent tax dealings should not be encouraged. Criminal penalties are provided for tax evasion, and fraud and delinquency penalties are assessed upon taxes due when the circumstances warrant. The Government should be allowed to collect all tax and penalties authorized by law, but it is not our function to expand tax liability to fields not covered by statute. We find nothing in the Tax Court's opinion to indicate that the diverted sums represented salary or any other recognized ordinary income. We believe that the only way that the diverted income already taxed to the corporation can be taxed to the individual taxpayers is by the treatment of such diversions as dividends and corporate distributions. . . .

[Simon v. Commissioner, 248 F.2d 869, 876-877 (8th Cir. 1957).]

. . . In concluding our discussion of the constructive dividend issue, we would emphasize that in a case such as this diverted amounts taxed to a shareholder as constructive dividends also remain fully taxable to the corporation to which attributable. The record indicates that the corporation in question did not report the diverted funds. But respondent's agents became well aware of the existence of Asphalt Patch and Jim T. Enterprises, and the fact that taxable income had been diverted from them, during the examination of petitioner's tax affairs. We know of nothing which would have prevented a parallel examination of the corporate tax affairs and a determination of the correct taxable income reportable by the corporations.

For the foregoing reasons, we hold that the amounts diverted by petitioner from his corporations constitute constructive dividends and are taxable to him under the provisions of section 301(c). . . .

Reviewed by the Court.

Sterrett, Chabot, Parker, Whitaker, Korner, Shields, Hamblen, Cohen, Clapp, Swift, Jacobs, Gerber, Wright, Parr, Williams, Wells, Ruwe, and Whalen, JJ., agree with this opinion.

NOTE

1. *Shareholders' loans that may not be bona fide.* In *Jaques,* what were the key factors that led to dividend recharacterization? If Jaques' corporation is prohibited by state law from distributing a dividend, how can the Service recharacterize the loan as a dividend? In *Jaques,* the Tax Court found a dividend for federal tax purposes even though under state law no dividend distribution was permitted. Conversely, in Rev. Rul. 90-11, 1990-1 C.B. 10, the Service ruled that the adoption of a "poison pill" plan did not constitute a dividend for federal tax purposes even though the adoption of a plan was a dividend under state law.

In *Jaques,* would it have mattered if the taxpayer had argued that any withdrawal determined not to be a loan for federal tax purposes should be treated as compensation?

In Alterman Foods v. United States, 611 F.2d 866 (Cl. Ct. 1979), a corporate parent was saddled with dividend treatment on "advances" from its subsidiaries. Under the then applicable version of §243, the taxpayer was taxable on 15 percent of the constructive dividends. Among the factors relied on by the court were the paucity of historical dividends despite strong earnings and profits; the lack of a specified interest rate, promissory note, limit on the advances, or collateral; and a pattern of "advances" with no repayment from 57 subsidiaries. Compare Tollefsen v. Commissioner, 431 F.2d 511 (2d Cir. 1970), in which advances by a subsidiary to the controlling shareholder of the parent were treated as a dividend by the parent to the shareholder and not as a bona fide loan, with Gilbert v. Commissioner, 552 F.2d 478 (2d Cir. 1977), in which a bona fide loan was found because of clear intent to repay and because the prompt assignment of assets given were sufficient to secure the amounts owed.

2. *Shareholders' loans with below-market interest rates.* Suppose a corpora-

tion makes a bona fide loan to its shareholder but charges no interest.[3] In
Dean v. Commisisoner, 35 T.C. 1083 (1961), the court found no income
to the borrower since any imputed income would be offset with an interest
deduction. The widely followed *Dean* rule has been thoroughly discussed
for its impact on borrowers and lenders. See Joyce and Del Cotto, Interest-
Free Loans: The Odyssey of a Misnomer, 35 Tax L. Rev. 459 (1980).

Section 7872 substantially altered the *Dean* rule. When the loan is a
demand loan, the shareholder-borrower is deemed to have received a dividend of imputed interest, which in turn is repaid to the corporation-lender.
For the borrower, there may be a wash if the interest is deductible. But
see §265. Also consider §163(h), which denies a deduction in many instances for interest incurred for personal rather than business or investment purposes. For the lender, the dividend is not deductible, but the
deemed interest received must be included in income each year the loan
is outstanding.

If the loan is a term loan, the shareholder-borrower will be deemed
to have received the difference between the loan principal and the present
value of the payments due under the loan as a dividend. In accordance with
the original issue discount rules of §§1271-1273, the borrower is entitled to
deduct the imputed interest over the term of the loan. The mirror image
governs the corporation-lender. It is deemed to have made a dividend
payment in the first year and to receive taxable interest payments over the
life of the loan.

3. *Bargain sale or purchase between corporation and shareholder.* The bargain purchase in *Baumer* was the purchase for $10 (which may never have
been paid) for an option worth more than $10. How much more?

Suppose someone offers to sell you an option to buy property that
has a fair market value of $100. The option has an exercise price of $70
and has a duration of five minutes. Chances are you will pay up to $30 for
the option. Suppose, instead, the exercise price is $100. You would proba-
bly pay nothing for this option since it will cost you $100 if you choose to
exercise it. In Palmer v. Commissioner, 302 U.S. 63, 71 (1937), the Supreme Court broadly stated: "The mere issue of rights to subscribe and
their receipt by stockholders, is not a dividend." The court also ruled that
the later exercise of the option when the property had appreciated in
value was not a dividend. In *Palmer* there was no spread between exercise
price and fair market value of the property at the time the option was
issued. Moreover, the option period was only 15 days. *Palmer* was limited
to its facts by Commissioner v. Gordon, 391 U.S. 83, 90 n.4 (1968), in
which the Court stated: "It has not . . . been authoritively settled whether
an issue of rights to purchase at less than fair market value itself constitutes

---

3. The fact that there is no interest may count against "loan" characterization, but it is
not conclusive. Thus, a "no-interest loan" is not a self-contradictory phenomenon.

a dividend, or the dividend occurs on the actual purchase." In Redding v. Commissioner, 630 F.2d 1169, 1182 (7th Cir. 1980), the court ruled that *Palmer* had been overruled by the enactment in 1954 of the "corporate distribution provisions as a whole" in circumstances in which there was a spread when the option was granted.

Suppose instead that there is no spread between the exercise price and the fair market value of the property, but the duration of the option is two years — the *Baumer* situation. Now is the option worth something? Suppose you pay $20 for the option. If the property decreases in value, you will not exercise the option and will not recoup your $20. If the property increases in value — say, to $200 — you will pay the $100 exercise price, ending up with an $80 profit. The longer the option period, the more valuable the option is. Is anything left of *Palmer* after *Redding* and *Baumer*?

In *Baumer* why wasn't the option taxable to the shareholder when issued rather than when exercised? On remand the district court did conclude that the option should be taxed in the year of receipt. This conclusion meant victory for the taxpayer since that year was not before the court. 518 F. Supp. 813 (N.D. Ga. 1981). The taxpayer's celebration was short-lived as the court of appeals again reversed, holding the law of the case dictated the use of the open transaction method. The district court was directed to find a dividend in the amount by which the fair market value at the time of exercise exceeded the exercise price. 685 F.2d 1318 (11th Cir. 1982). This reversal by the Eleventh Circuit is limited to the law of the case and does not suggest that in future cases the dividend consequences won't be determined in the year in which the option is granted if valuation is possible. See generally Jassy, Dividend Treatment of Distributions of Options to Acquire Assets of the Distributing Corporation, 34 Tax L. Rev. 607 (1979).

If *Baumer* had been decided under current law, would the distributing corporation have been taxed on the distribution of the option? See §311(b). If the distributing corporation should be taxed, when should it be taxed? How and when should the earnings and profits account be adjusted? In light of §311(b), would the Service need to rely on the *Court Holding Co.* doctrine?

Note that in *Baumer* the father was taxed even though the option was granted to the son. In Green v. United States, 460 F.2d 412 (5th Cir. 1972), a bargain element in a sale to the children of a shareholder-officer was held taxable to him even though he was a minority shareholder because he exerted substantial influence over the transaction.

Honigman v. Commissioner, 466 F.2d 412 (5th Cir. 1972), serves as a reminder that shareholders dealing with closely held corporations tread on dangerous ground. There, the shareholder was taxed on the difference between the actual purchase price and the court-determined fair market value on the corporation's distribution of a deteriorating hotel. At trial evidence was introduced that there was no other buyer, the purchasing shareholder was not in control of the corporation and there was a valid business reason for the sale.

The flip side of the bargain purchase is the inflated sale to a controlled corporation. In Pizzarelli v. Commissioner, 40 T.C.M. 156 (1980), the shareholder was taxed on a dividend when he purchased property for $20,000 in 1969 and sold it in 1970 to the corporation for $70,000 with no apparent reason for the sudden appreciation.

4. *Transfers between commonly controlled corporations.* Suppose *A* owns all the stock of *X* Corp. and *Y* Corp. If *X* Corp. makes a purported loan to *Y* Corp. in circumstances suggesting that the funds are not to be repaid, how should the transaction be treated? Since *X* Corp. owns no stock of *Y* Corp., the transfer does not seem to be a distribution by *X* Corp. "with respect to its stock" to *Y* Corp. When transfers between commonly controlled corporations are recharacterized, there is a deemed distribution to the shareholder from one corporation followed by a deemed contribution of the property or cash by the shareholder to the other corporation. The analysis in *Gilbert* is typical of these cases. Often the court will first determine whether there was a bona fide intercorporate loan. If not, did the intercorporate contribution to capital have a business purpose, or did it promote the taxpayer's personal goals?

Compare Sammons v. Commissioner, 472 F.2d 449 (5th Cir. 1972) (a transfer by a parent corporation of funds to its nearly insolvent subsidiary so that the subsidiary could pay off the debt owed to the parent's controlling shareholder was a dividend to the shareholder since the purpose was to benefit the shareholder rather than the transferor), with Rapid Electric Co. v. Commissioner, 61 T.C. 232 (1974) (the extension of credit between two commonly owned corporations was held not a dividend to the sole shareholder because the transfer was beneficial for the transferor corporation's purposes).

In Stinnett's Pontiac Service v. Commissioner, 730 F.2d 634 (11th Cir. 1984), the court found that a purported intercorporate loan from an automobile dealership to a Bahamian corporation constituted a constructive dividend to the common shareholder. The loan was unsecured and subordinated and had no terms of repayment. Furthermore the court could discern no corporate purpose behind the loan. See also Sparks Nugget, Inc. v. Commissioner, 458 F.2d 631 (9th Cir. 1972) (excessive rent paid between commonly controlled corporations taxable to controlling shareholder).

5. *Unreasonable salaries or fees.* The allowance for a reasonable salary deduction under §162 has been interpreted by the IRS and the courts to disallow, by inference, a deduction for any portion of salaries deemed excessive. Such excessive salaries may be reclassified as dividends if, as is often the case, the employee is also a shareholder and there are sufficient earnings and profits. What happens if there are insufficient earnings and

profits? See Note 8 infra. In Charles McCandless Tile Service v. United States, 422 F.2d 1336 (Cl. Ct. 1970), the Court of Claims found that even reasonable salaries could be reclassified as dividends if the distributing corporation was profitable and had not made dividend distributions. In Laure v. Commissioner, 70 T.C. 1087 (1978), the Tax Court rejected the *McCandless* reasoning and upheld a large salary deduction even in the absence of dividends for an 18-year period. See also Rev. Rul. 79-8, 1979-1 C.B. 92 (insubstantial dividends alone do not cause denial of §162 deduction); Elliots, Inc. v. Commissioner, 716 F.2d 1241 (9th Cir. 1983) (*McCandless* rejected).

Shareholders sometimes contractually commit themselves to repay amounts deemed excessive by the IRS. Their hope is that if the salary is held to be a dividend, the repayment of such amounts to the corporation will be a business expense deduction covered by §162. In Oswald v. Commissioner, 49 T.C. 645 (1976), under a corporate by-law a shareholder-officer was so obligated and was permitted a deduction. But in Pahl v. Commissioner, 67 T.C. 286 (1976), there was no *Oswald* contract provision requiring repayment; the excess salary was deemed a disguised dividend, and the repayment was labeled a capital contribution increasing basis.

Sometimes corporations try to use fee payments, rather than salaries, in lieu of dividends to distribute earnings in a manner that provides a §162 deduction. In Tulia Feedlot v. United States, 513 F.2d 800 (5th Cir. 1975), a corporation paid its directors a fee for guaranteeing a corporate loan; the guarantees were made by the director-shareholders in proportion to their stock ownership. The Court held this to be a constructive dividend, nondeductible by the corporation because no evidence was presented to show guarantors' fees were customary in the trade or that the fees were reasonable in amount. See also Olton Feed Yard v. United States, 592 F.2d 272 (5th Cir. 1979) (same result). In a later year and in a different jurisdiction, however, the same company prevailed when the fees were shown to be customary and were paid in proportion to the guarantees rather than the amount of stock owned. Tulia Feedlot v. United States, 52 A.F.T.R.2d 5702 (Cl. Ct. 1983).

6. *Corporate payment of expenses incurred to benefit the stockholder rather than the corporation.* Sometimes a controlling shareholder will cause a corporation to pay his personal expenses in the hope that the corporation can deduct what the shareholder cannot. In these situations, the courts look to see if the payment benefits "primarily" the corporation or the taxpayer. In American Properties v. Commissioner, 262 F.2d 150 (9th Cir. 1958), it was held that the expenses of designing, constructing, and racing speed boats, paid by a one-person corporation, were not deductible under §162(a) by the corporation and constituted disguised dividends to the sole shareholder, who "had an insatiable desire for speed." In Magnon v. Commissioner, 73 T.C. 980 (1980), the sole shareholder received a constructive dividend when the corporation performed electrical contracting services on the shareholder's personal property.

In Dolese v. United States, 605 F.2d 1146 (10th Cir. 1979), payments by a corporation for legal fees and expenses in connection with a divorce of its sole shareholder were deemed constructive dividends. Those payments incurred to fight divorce proceedings that interrupted corporate business were, however, treated as a deductible expense by the corporation with no dividend treatment to the shareholder. But see Jack's Maintenance Contractors v. Commissioner, 703 F.2d 154 (5th Cir. 1983) (dividend to shareholder where corporation incurred legal expenses in defending shareholder against criminal tax evasion charges; benefit to shareholder far outweighed benefit to corporation).

When a court finds a constructive dividend, what is the measure of inclusion? See Ireland v. United States, 621 F.2d 731 (5th Cir. 1980) (amount of dividend from personal use of company plane based on private charter fare, not cost of operation).

7. *Excessive compensation paid to the relatives of shareholders.* Section 162(a)(2) allows a corporation to deduct "a reasonable allowance for salaries or other compensation for personal services actually rendered." Suppose X Corp. is a family-owned corporation whose shareholders are Mom and Pop. Suppose X Corp. compensates Son and Daughter as though they were full-time employees when in fact they perform only minor services for the corporation during vacations. Why might the family choose to distribute corporate earnings in this fashion? How should the payments be treated? In this and similar cases, the transaction will be recharacterized as a dividend payment to Mom or Pop or both, followed by a gift from the shareholder(s) to Son and Daughter. See, e.g., Duffey v. Lethert, 316 F.2d 473 (D. Minn. 1963) (corporate "compensation" to sister of shareholder treated as dividend to shareholder when sister performed only occasional services). Note that in addition to possible dividend treatment, shareholders may have gift tax treatment on the deemed gift.

Should the corporation or shareholders that participate in the diversion of corporate assets to nonworking employees be subject to civil or criminal fraud penalties? Does it matter if the corporation is wholly owned by the shareholders causing the diversion or whether there are outside shareholders?

8. *Constructive dividends and earnings and profits.* Suppose a taxpayer diverts corporate funds for personal use. Normally, there would be dividend consequences to the shareholder. But what is the result if the corporation has no current or accumulated earnings and profits? How does the court in *Truesdell* distinguish a nontaxable diversion from an unlawful diversion that is taxable regardless of the earnings and profits account? See, e.g., Leaf v. Commissioner, 33 T.C. 1093 (1960), aff'd per curiam, 295 F.2d 503 (6th Cir. 1961).

In Di Zenzo v. Commissioner, 348 F.2d 122 (2d Cir. 1965), the court ruled that the taxpayer (the sole shareholder) had no dividend and no §61 income in the absence of earnings and profits. See also Simon v. Commissioner, 248 F.2d 869 (8th Cir. 1957). For a holding to the contrary, see United States v. Miller, 545 F.2d 1204 (9th Cir 1976), in which the existence of earnings and profits was held not necessary in criminal fraud proceedings against taxpayer (not the sole shareholder) diverting corporate monies to himself. Can the cases be distinguished on the basis of whether funds were unlawfully diverted from another person, either another shareholder or a creditor? When a sole shareholder diverts funds from a corporation with no earnings and profits, who is the victim so long as no obligation to a creditor is breached? How is the shareholder enriched?

In Hagaman v. Commissioner, 958 F.2d 684 (6th Cir. 1992), the court affirmed the tax court's determination that a corporation should reduce its accumulated earnings and profits by the amount of constructive dividends deemed paid to the shareholders. The constructive dividends consisted of the fraudulent diversion of vending-machine receipts and rental payments.

D. INTERCORPORATE DIVIDENDS

Litton Industries, Inc. v. Commissioner _____
89 T.C. 1086 (1987)

CLAPP, Judge: Respondent determined a deficiency in petitioner's Federal corporate income tax for the year ended July 29, 1973 in the amount of $11,583,054. After concessions, the issue for decision is whether Litton Industries received a $30,000,000 dividend from Stouffer Corporation, its wholly owned subsidiary, or whether that sum represented proceeds from the sale of Stouffer stock to Nestle Corporation.

FINDINGS OF FACT

. . . On October 4, 1967, petitioner acquired all the outstanding stock of Stouffer Corporation (Stouffer), a corporation whose common stock was listed and traded on the New York stock exchange. Stouffer manufactured and sold frozen prepared food and operated hotels and food management services and restaurants. . . .

In early 1972, Charles B. Thornton (Thornton), the chairman of Litton's board of directors, Joseph Imirie, president of Stouffer, and James Biggar, an executive of Stouffer, discussed project "T.I.B.," i.e., the sale of Stouffer. In July 1972, Litton's board of directors discussed the mechanics and problems of selling Stouffer. As of August 1, 1972 Stouffer's accumulated earnings and profits exceeded $30,000,000. On August 23, 1972, Stouffer declared a $30,000,000 dividend which it paid to Litton in the form of a $30,000,000 negotiable promissory note, and at that time, Thornton believed that Litton would have no difficulty in receiving an adequate offer for Stouffer. Two weeks later, on September 7, 1972, petitioner announced publicly its interest in disposing of Stouffer. Subsequent to said announcement, Litton received inquiries from a number of interested sources, including TWA, Green Giant, investment banking houses, and business brokers about the possible purchase of all or part of the Stouffer business.

Beginning in mid-September 1972, Litton and several underwriters discussed the feasibility of a public offering of Stouffer Stock. In early September 1972, Litton negotiated with Lehman Brothers for a public offering of Stouffer stock, but Lehman Brothers decided not to participate in the offering. During October 1972, Litton, Stouffer and Merrill Lynch, a brokerage firm that thought Stouffer had an excellent outlook, prepared a public offering of Stouffer stock. During November 1972, petitioner, Stouffer, and Hornblower and Weeks prepared a partial public offering of Stouffer stock. Merrill Lynch had a policy of not effecting partial distributions of corporate subsidiaries and thus did not participate in the negotiations with Hornblower and Weeks. In mid-December 1972, Litton decided that a complete public offering was preferable and abandoned the idea of a partial public offering. The S-1 Registration Statement, which Stouffer filed with the Securities and Exchange Commission, stated that $30,000,000 of the proceeds would be used to pay the promissory note which Litton received as a dividend.

On March 1, 1973, Nestle Alimentana S.A. Corporation (Nestle), a Swiss corporation, offered to buy all of Stouffer's stock for $105,000,000. On March 5, 1973, Nestle paid Litton $74,962,518 in cash for all the outstanding stock of Stouffer and $30,000,000 in cash for the promissory note. Because Litton sold Stouffer to Nestle, the underwriters stopped work on the scheduled public offering.

OPINION

The issue for decision is whether the $30,000,000 dividend declared by Stouffer on August 23, 1972, and paid to its parent, Litton, by means of a negotiable promissory note was truly a dividend for tax purposes or whether it should be considered part of the proceeds received by Litton from the sale of all of Stouffer's stock on March 1, 1973. If, as petitioner contends, the $30,000,000 constitutes a dividend, petitioner may deduct 85 percent of that amount as a dividend received credit pursuant to section 243(a), as that section read during the year at issue. However, if the $30,000,000 represents part of the selling price of the Stouffer stock, as contended by respondent, the entire amount will be added to the proceeds of the sale and taxed to Litton as additional capital gain. Respondent's approach, of course produces the larger amount of tax dollars.

The instant case is substantially governed by Waterman Steamship Corp. v. Commissioner, 50 T.C. 650 (1968), revd. 430 F.2d 1185 (5th Cir. 1970), cert. denied 401 U.S. 939 (1971). Respondent urges us to follow the opinion of the Fifth Circuit, which in substance adopted the position of Judge Tannenwald's dissent (concurred in by three other judges) from our Court-reviewed opinion. If we hold for respondent, we must overrule our majority opinion in *Waterman Steamship*. Petitioner contends that the reasoning of the Fifth Circuit in *Waterman Steamship* should not apply since the facts here are more favorable to petitioner. Additionally, petitioner points out that several business purposes were served by the distribution here which provide additional support for recognition of the distribution as a dividend. For the reasons set forth below, we conclude that the $30,000,000 distribution constituted a dividend which should be recognized as such for tax purposes. We believe that the facts in the instant case lead even more strongly than did the facts in *Waterman Steamship* to the conclusion that the $30,000,000 was a dividend. Accordingly, we hold that the Stouffer distribution to Litton was a dividend within the meaning of section 243(a).

In many respects, the facts of this case and those of *Waterman Steamship* are parallel. The principal difference, and the one which we find to be most significant, is the timing of the dividend action. In *Waterman Steamship,* the taxpayer corporation received an offer to purchase the stock of two of its wholly-owned subsidiary corporations, Pan-Atlantic and Gulf Florida, for $3,500,000 cash. The board of directors of Waterman Steamship rejected that offer but countered with an offer to sell the two subsidiaries for $700,000 after the subsidiaries declared and arranged for payments of dividends to Waterman Steamship amounting in the aggregate to $2,800,000. Negotiations between the parties ensued, and the agreements which resulted therefrom included, in specific detail, provisions for the declaration of a dividend by Pan-Atlantic to Waterman Steamship prior to the signing of the sales agreement and the closing of that transaction. Furthermore, the agreements called for the purchaser to loan or otherwise advance funds to Pan-Atlantic promptly in order to pay off the promissory note by which the dividend had been paid. Once the agreement was reached, the entire transaction was carried out by a series of meetings commencing at 12 noon on January 21, 1955, and ending at 1:30 P.M. the same day. At the first meeting the board of directors of Pan-Atlantic met and declared a dividend in the form of a promissory note in the amount of $2,799,820. The dividend was paid by execution and delivery of the promissory note. At 12:30 P.M., the board of directors of the purchaser's nominee corporation ("Securities") met and authorized the purchase and financing of Pan-Atlantic and Gulf Florida. At 1 P.M., the directors of Waterman authorized the sale of all outstanding stock of Pan-Atlantic and Gulf Florida to Securities. Immediately following that meeting, the sales agreement was executed by the parties. The agreement provided that the purchaser guaranteed prompt payment of the liabilities of Pan-Atlantic and Gulf Florida including payment of any notes given by either corporation as a dividend.

Finally at 1:30 P.M., the new board of directors of Pan-Atlantic authorized the borrowing of sufficient funds from the purchaser personally and from his nominee corporation to pay off the promissory note to Waterman Steamship, which was done forthwith. As the Fifth Circuit pointed out, "By the end of the day and within a ninety minute period, the financial cycle had been completed. Waterman had $3,500,000, hopefully tax-free, all of which came from Securities and McLean, the buyers of the stock." 430 F.2d at 1190. This Court concluded that the distribution from Pan-Atlantic to Waterman was a dividend. The Fifth Circuit reversed, concluding that the dividend and sale were one transaction. 430 F.2d at 1192.

The timing in the instant case was markedly different. The dividend was declared by Stouffer on August 23, 1972, at which time the promissory note in payment of the dividend was issued to Litton. There had been some general preliminary discussions about the sale of Stouffer, and it was expected that Stouffer would be a very marketable company which would sell quickly. However, at the time the dividend was declared, no formal action had been taken to initiate the sale of Stouffer. It was not until 2 weeks later that Litton publicly announced that Stouffer was for sale. There ensued over the next 6 months many discussions with various corporations, investment banking houses, business brokers, and underwriters regarding Litton's disposition of Stouffer through sale of all or part of the business to a particular buyer, or through full or partial public offerings of the Stouffer stock. All of this culminated on March 1, 1973, over 6 months after the dividend was declared, with the purchase by Nestle of all of Stouffer's stock. Nestle also purchased the outstanding promissory note for $30,000,000 in cash.

In the instant case, the declaration of the dividend and the sale of the stock were substantially separated in time in contrast to *Waterman Steamship* where the different transactions occurred essentially simultaneously. In *Waterman Steamship*, it seems quite clear that no dividend would have been declared if all of the remaining steps in the transaction had not been lined up in order on the closing table and did not in fact take place. Here, however, Stouffer declared the dividend, issued the promissory note and definitely committed itself to the dividend before even making a public announcement that Stouffer was for sale. Respondent argues that the only way petitioner could ever receive the dividend was by raising revenue through a sale of Stouffer. Therefore, respondent asserts the two events (the declaration of the dividend and then the sale of the company) were inextricably tied together and should be treated as one transaction for tax purposes. In our view, respondent ignores the fact that Stouffer could have raised sufficient revenue for the dividend from other avenues, such as a partial public offering or borrowing. Admittedly, there had been discussions at Litton about the sale of Stouffer which was considered to be a very saleable company. However, there are many slips between the cup and the lip, and it does not take much of a stretch of the imagination to picture a variety of circumstances under which Stouffer might have been taken off the market and no sale consummated. Under these circumstances it is unlikely that respondent would have considered the dividend to be a nullity. On the contrary, it would seem quite clear that petitioner would be charged with a dividend on which it would have to pay a substantial tax. Petitioner committed itself to the dividend and, thereby, accepted the consequences regardless of the outcome of the proposed sale of Stouffer stock. See Crellin v. Commissioner, 17 T.C. 781, 785 (1951), affd. 203 F.2d 812 (9th Cir. 1953), cert. denied 346 U.S. 873 (1953).

Since the facts here are distinguishable in important respects and are so much stronger in petitioner's favor, we do not consider it necessary to consider further the opinion of the Fifth Circuit in *Waterman Steamship*.

The term "dividend" is defined in section 316(a) as a distribution by a corporation to its shareholders out of earnings and profits. The parties have stipulated that Stouffer had earnings and profits exceeding $30,000,000 at the time the dividend was declared. This Court has recognized that a dividend may be paid by a note. T. R. Miller Mill Co. v. Commissioner, 37 B.T.A. 43, 49 (1938), affd. 102 F.2d 599 (5th Cir. 1939). Based on these criteria, the $30,000,000 distribution by Stouffer would clearly constitute a dividend if the sale of Stouffer had not occurred. We are not persuaded that the subsequent sale of Stouffer to Nestle changes that result merely because it was more advantageous to Litton from a tax perspective.

It is well established that a taxpayer is entitled to structure his affairs and transactions in order to minimize his taxes. This proposition does not give a taxpayer carte blanche to set up a transaction in any form which will avoid tax consequences regardless of whether the transaction has substance. Gregory v. Helvering, 293 U.S. 465 (1935). A variety of factors present here preclude a finding of sham or subterfuge. Although the record in this case clearly shows that Litton intended at the time the dividend was declared to sell Stouffer, no formal action had been taken and no announcement had been made. There was no definite purchaser waiting in the wings with the terms and conditions of sale already agreed upon. At that time, Litton had not even decided upon the form of sale of Stouffer. Nothing in the record here suggests that there was any prearranged sale agreement, formal or informal, at the time the dividend was declared.

Petitioner further supports its argument that the transaction was not a sham by pointing out Litton's legitimate business purposes in declaring the dividend. Although the code and case law do not require a dividend to have a business purpose, it is a factor to be considered in determining whether the overall transaction was a sham. TSN Liquidating Corp. v. United States, 624 F.2d 1328 (5th Cir. 1980). Petitioner argues that the distribution allowed Litton to maximize the gross after-tax amount it could receive from its investment in Stouffer. From the viewpoint of a private purchaser of Stouffer, it is difficult to see how the declaration of a dividend would improve the value of the stock since creating a liability in the form of a promissory note for $30,000,000 would reduce the value of Stouffer by approximately that amount. However, since Litton was considering disposing of all or part of Stouffer through a public or private offering, the payment of a dividend by a promissory note prior to any sale had two advantages. First, Litton hoped to avoid materially diminishing the market value of the Stouffer stock. At that time, one of the factors considered in valuing a stock, and in determining the market value of a stock was the "multiple of earnings" criterion. Payment of the dividend by issuance of a promissory note would not substantially alter Stouffer's earnings. Since many investors were relatively unsophisticated, Litton may have been quite right that it could increase its investment in Stouffer by at least some portion of the $30,000,000 dividend. Second, by declaring a dividend and paying it by a promissory note prior to an anticipated public offering, Litton could avoid sharing the earnings with future additional shareholders while not diminishing to the full extent of the pro rata dividend, the amount received for the stock. Whether Litton could have come out ahead after Stouffer paid the promissory note is at this point merely speculation about a public offering which never occurred. The point, however, is that Litton hoped to achieve some business purpose and not just tax benefits in structuring the transaction as it did.

Under these facts, where the dividend was declared 6 months prior to the sale of Stouffer, where the sale was not prearranged, and since Stouffer had earnings and profits exceeding $30,000,000 at the time the dividend was declared, we cannot conclude that the distribution was merely a device designed to give the appearance of a dividend to a part of the sales proceeds. In this case the form and substance of the transaction coincide; it was not a transaction entered into solely for tax reasons, and it should be recognized as structured by petitioner.

On this record, we hold that for Federal tax purposes Stouffer declared a dividend to petitioner on August 23, 1972, and, subsequently, petitioner sold all of its stock in Stouffer to Nestle for $75,000,000.

Decision will be entered under Rule 155.

NOTE

1. *Impact of dividends-received deduction on corporate shareholders.* In the discussion of disguised dividends at page 142 supra, the taxpayer was trying to disguise a dividend as some other type of transaction. Sometimes the tables are turned, and the taxpayer tries to hide some other transaction as a dividend. In Waterman Steamship Corp. v. Commissioner, 430 F.2d

1185 (5th Cir. 1970), the taxpayer found a purchaser willing to pay $3.5 million for the stock of its subsidiary. The taxpayer, with a basis of $700,000 in the subsidiary's stock, was not thrilled with the prospect of a $2.8 million capital gain. Consequently, the transaction was restructured to have the subsidiary distribute a $2.8 million note as a dividend to taxpayer, followed by a sale of the subsidiary's stock to the purchaser for $700,000. The purchaser was to provide funds to the subsidiary in order to discharge the note. Because of the consolidated return provisions, the dividend, if respected, would have been tax free. See page 570 infra for a discussion of consolidated return provisions.

What were the anticipated tax consequences on the sale and later payment on the note? The Service argued successfully that the purported dividend should be ignored and that the purchaser should be deemed to have paid the full $3.5 million purchase price. Accord, Basic, Inc. v. United States, 549 F.2d 740 (Cl. Ct. 1977). But see TSN Liquidating Co. v. United States, 624 F.2d 1328 (5th Cir. 1980), in which the court refused to recharacterize a dividend of unwanted assets by a subsidiary to its parent even though the purchaser of the subsidiary's stock reinfused the subsidiary with cash following the purchase. Accord, Dynamics Corp. of America v. United States, 449 F.2d 402 (Cl. Ct. 1971) (distribution and sale were unconnected events).

In *Litton Industries,* how did the court distinguish *Waterman Steamship?* Is the distinction convincing if the reason Litton declared the dividend was to decrease its tax liability on its intended sale of stock? What were the so-called business reasons that justified dividend treatment in the court's view?

2. *Debt-financed portfolio stock.* The availability of the dividends-received deduction under §243 presents some tax arbitrage possibilities. For example, a shareholder-corporation could finance an investment in stock with borrowed funds, thereby enabling it to receive tax-favored dividend income while deducting the interest on the indebtedness. Suppose that stock of Blue Chip Corp. regularly pays dividends of $8 per year on its common stock selling for $100 per share, an 8 percent return. If Investment Corp. can borrow funds at 10 percent interest, should it borrow money to purchase stock of Blue Chip? Suppose Investment Corp. is in the 34 percent bracket and borrows $100 to buy one share of Blue Chip stock. The after-tax cost of borrowing $100 at 10 percent is $6.60 because of the interest deduction. The after-tax return on the $8 dividend is $7.18, assuming a 70 percent dividends-received deduction, thereby resulting in an $.82 tax on the $2.40 that enters taxable income. The pretax losing proposition becomes a $.58 post-tax winner (i.e., $7.18 minus $6.60). Do we want a tax system that encourages purchases that would not be made in the absence of taxes?

In principle, Congress's response to the problem resembles §265, which prohibits an interest deduction for debt incurred to purchase tax-exempt securities. The primary mechanism employed by §246A (primary rather than exclusive because of the Treasury's power under §246A(f)), however, does not limit the interest deduction. Instead, the provision reduces the dividends-received deduction otherwise available under §§243-246 by a percentage related to the amount of debt used to purchase the stock. Thus, if a taxpayer purchases stock with some cash and some debt such that the "average indebtedness percentage" is 50 percent, then the §243 deduction in the example above will be 35 percent rather than 70 percent. See §246A(a) and (d). Section 246A applies to "portfolio stock" only. Stock will not be considered portfolio stock if the corporate shareholder owns a sufficient interest in the subsidiary (e.g., 50 percent of the voting power or value). §246A(c)(2). Presumably, a substantial ownership interest in the subsidiary suggests that the parent is interested in more than the subsidiary's dividends: The corporations are likely to be part of a multicorporate structure. The enforcement difficulties that plague §265 are likely to dog §246A. In particular, it will be very difficult to ascertain "portfolio indebtedness," indebtedness directly attributable to investment in portfolio stock. §246A(d)(3). In general, portfolio indebtedness refers to debt incurred to finance the stock purchase or to debt incurred after the stock purchase if secured by the stock.

3. *Dividend-related losses.* Even if the purchase of stock is not financed with debt, tax arbitrage opportunities may still be present. For example, suppose X Corp. purchases 100 shares of Y Corp. stock for $10,000 immediately before the dividend "record date." Y distributes a $1,000 dividend, which, after a 70 percent dividends-received deduction, results in $300 of taxable income to X and after-tax income of $898 (i.e., $1,000 minus $102 tax liability). X then sells the stock for $9,000 (i.e., the value of the stock reflects the dividend paid), reporting a $1,000 capital loss. In sum, X, which started with $10,000, ends up with $10,238 (i.e., $898 from the dividend, $9,000 from the stock sale, and $340 in taxes saved as a result of the $1,000 capital loss deduction).

Under §246(c), no dividends-received deduction is available unless the stock is held for more than 45 days (90 days for certain preferred stock). This holding period is tolled if the shareholder-corporation diminishes its risk of loss in specified ways. §246(c)(4). See Rev. Rul. 90-27, page 105 supra, and Progressive Corp. v. United States, 970 F.2d 188 (6th Cir. 1992) (purchase of stock and sale of a call option tolled the holding period). If the dividend to be received is extraordinarily large relative to the price of the stock, a shareholder-corporation may be able to satisfy the holding period of §246(c) with a minimal risk of loss. Accordingly, Congress enacted §1059, mandating a basis reduction for corporate shareholders in their stock on the receipt of "extraordinary dividends," as defined in §1059(c), if the stock on which the dividends are paid is sold before it has been held for two years.

For example, suppose X Corp. purchases the stock of Y Corp. for

$10,000 on January 1, receives an "extraordinary dividend" of $2,000 on February 1, and sells the stock on March 1 for $8,000, the January 1 value reduced by the amount of the dividend. X Corp. includes only $600 of the dividend in taxable income ($1,400 deducted under §243), and in the absence of §1059 would claim a $2,000 loss on the sale of the stock. See, e.g., Silco, Inc. v. United States, 779 F.2d 282 (5th Cir. 1986). Under §1059, X Corp. must reduce its stock basis by the $1,400 deducted under §243. On the sale, X Corp. will recognize a loss of $600 ($8,000 realized less basis of $8,600). This matches the gain reported on the dividend, an appropriate result since X Corp. ends up with $10,000, the amount with which it started.

Section 1059(c) defines an "extraordinary dividend" as a dividend that equals or exceeds 10 percent of the taxpayer's adjusted basis in the underlying stock. Under §1059(c)(4), a taxpayer can use the fair market value of the stock on the day before the ex-dividend day if the value can be established to the satisfaction of the Secretary. For example, if a taxpayer has a stock basis of $100 and the fair market value of the stock is $900, a $50 dividend exceeds 10 percent of the adjusted basis, but the alternative fair market value test would save the taxpayer from basis reduction under §1059. Dividends paid within an 85-day period are aggregated for purposes of the 10 percent test.

For distributions on preferred stock, a dividend is extraordinary if it exceeds 5 percent of the underlying stock's adjusted basis (or fair market value). An exception for certain preferred stock, however, pays fixed dividends not exceeding 15 percent of the lesser of adjusted basis or liquidation preference. §1059(e)(3).

4. *Dividends-received deduction and earnings and profits.* Cases like *Litton Industries* and *Waterman Steamship* illustrate that shareholders that are corporations may prefer dividend treatment for distributions while individual shareholders may try to avoid dividend treatment. As part of this tax schizophrenia, the earnings and profits concept has been broadened so that distributions to individual shareholders are more likely to be treated as dividends. For example, §312(n), discussed on page 132 supra, requires that certain items that are deferred for purposes of computing taxable income (e.g., installment sale gains) be taken into account for purposes of computing earnings and profits. Any increase in earnings and profits resulting from such an adjustment means that a distribution to a shareholder that is a corporation is more likely to be treated as a dividend.

To illustrate the perceived abuse, suppose that in *Litton Industries,* Stouffer had no earnings and profits. If Stouffer had sold an asset on the installment method, thereby deferring any gain, the immediate increase in earnings and profits would permit the distribution of a dividend to Litton, thereby decreasing the capital gain that Litton would have to recognize on the sale of the Stouffer stock to Nestle.

Section 301(e) prevents this result by providing that adjustments to earnings and profits mandated by §312(k) and (n) are not made for purposes of determining the taxable income (and adjusted basis) of any "20 percent corporate shareholder." This term refers to any corporation, entitled to a dividends-received deduction with respect to a distribution, that owns, directly or indirectly, stock possessing at least 20 perent of the total combined voting power or value (excluding nonvoting preferred stock) of the distributing corporation. The effect of §301(e) is that a distribution that might have been a dividend generating a dividends-received deduction now will reduce the shareholder's basis in the distributing corporation's stock. In the example above, if the distribution to Litton was not a dividend but was treated as a return of basis under §301(c)(2), Litton would recognize the same gain on a sale to Nestle that would have been recognized had the distribution not taken place. That is, Nestle would pay less because of the distribution but Litton's basis would be decreased by precisely the amount of the distribution.

E. PROBLEMS

1. Determine the tax consequences in the following situations:
a. On July 1, 1993, X Corp., a calendar year taxpayer, made distributions of $20,000 to A, its sole shareholder, whose stock had a $5,000 basis. No other distributions were made in 1993. As of December 31, 1992, X Corp. had no earnings and profits. In 1993 X Corp. had earnings and profits of $15,000 as of July 1 but only $5,000 for the entire year.
b. Suppose in (a) that X Corp. had an accumulated earnings and profits deficit of $15,000 as of December 31, 1992.
c. Suppose in (a) that X Corp. had accumulated earnings and profits of $15,000 as of December 31, 1992, and that in 1993 X Corp. had a $15,000 earnings and profits deficit on July 1 but a $5,000 earnings and profits account for the entire year.
d. Suppose in (c) that X Corp. had $15,000 of current earnings and profits as of July 1, 1993, but a deficit of $20,000 for the entire year. $15, ~20,00$
2. X Corp. is an accrual basis taxpayer. Compute its current earnings and profits from the following information. Assume that X Corp. is taxed at a flat 30 percent rate.

Gross income from business	$27,000
Dividend income	20,000
Interest on municipal bonds	9,000
Long-term capital gain	5,000
Contribution to capital	2,000
	$63,000

Wages, rent, office supplies	$15,000
Fines and kickbacks	7,000
Depreciation (excess over §168(g)(2) amount = $4,000)	6,000
Interest incurred to purchase municipal bonds	2,000
Dividends-received deduction	14,000
Capital losses	6,000
	$50,000
"Net"	$13,000

3. Discuss the tax consequences in the following, ignoring the quantitative effect of any corporate-level taxes on earnings and profits:

    a. *X* Corp., a cash basis taxpayer with no earnings and profits, makes a distribution of property that has a basis of $3,000 and that *X* Corp. values at $3,000. The recipient is *B*, a shareholder whose basis in the *X* Corp. stock is $5,000. If the Service determines the property has a value of $7,000, what are the tax consequences?

    b. Suppose in (a) that the property has a fair market value of $7,000 but is subject to a mortgage of $8,000.

    c. Suppose in (a) that *X* Corp. transfers the property to *B* in exchange for *B*'s $7,000 note.

    d. Suppose in (a) that *X* Corp. has earnings and profits of $4,000 and that the property *X* Corp. distributes has a basis of $7,000 and a fair market value of $3,000. What happens if the property increases in value after the distribution and then *B* sells the property for $7,000?

    e. Suppose in (d) that *X* Corp. distributes the loss property and another piece of property with a basis of $3,000 and a fair market value of $7,000.

    f. Suppose in (d) that *X* Corp. declares a $3,000 cash dividend and then distributes the loss property in satisfaction of the dividend.

    g. Suppose in (d) that *P*, an unrelated purchaser, wants to buy the property. *X* Corp. prepares to declare a dividend of the loss property so that *B* can execute the sale, but at the last moment, *X* Corp. decides to sell directly to *P* and to distribute the proceeds.

4. *T* is a shareholder of *X* Corp., a "start up" company producing computer software. In its early years, *X* Corp. has experienced large research and development expenses. *X* Corp. makes an interest-free loan of $100,000 to *A*, its sole shareholder, payable on demand by *X* Corp. Discuss the tax consequences to both *X* Corp. and *T*.

5. *X* Corp., with a $5,000 earnings and profits deficit in year 1, issues to *B*, a shareholder, an option to buy a parcel of real estate at a price of $1,000, the property's fair market value and basis. The option has a three-year duration. In year 3, *B* exercises the option. At the time of exercise, the real estate had a fair market value of $3,000. *X* Corp. has no accumu-

lated earnings and profits at the end of year 2 and no current earnings and profits in year 3. Discuss the tax consequences.

6.   *A* owns all the stock in *X* Corp. and *Y* Corp. Each corporation runs a restaurant. *X* Corp. makes a $100,000 loan to *Y* Corp. Discuss the tax consequences.

7.   *X* Corp. rents land from *A,* its sole shareholder, at an annual rental of $2,400, the fair rental value. The lease has a 10-year duration, and there are no renewal options. In year 5, *X* Corp. constructs a building on the property at a cost to *X* Corp. of $50,000. The building has a 20-year useful life, and the lease provides that all improvements made by the lessee revert to the lessor at the termination of the lease. At the end of the lease term, *A* enters into another lease with *X* Corp. at an annual rental of $3,600, the fair rental value for land and building. Is there a constructive dividend? When? Consider the applicability of §§109 and 1019. See Safeway Steel Scaffolds Co. v. United States, 590 F.2d 1360 (5th Cir. 1979).

8.   *X* Corp. has owned all the stock of *Y* Corp. since its formation. The stock has a basis of $2 million and a fair market value of $5 million. *P* Corp. wants to purchase the stock of *Y* Corp. for $5 million. Prior to the sale, *Y* Corp. distributes a note to *X* Corp. in the amount of $3 million payable in one year. The note bears a market rate of interest. In light of *Y* Corp.'s debt obligation, *P* Corp. pays $2 million to *X* Corp. for the *Y* Corp. stock. Within a year of *P* Corp.'s purchase, *Y* Corp. pays *X* Corp. $3 million on the note.

5

Redemptions and Partial Liquidations

A. TREATMENT OF SHAREHOLDERS

Corporate profit can become shareholder cash in a variety of ways. One possibility is for the corporation to distribute some of its profits to its shareholders as a dividend. Assuming the corporation has adequate earnings and profits, the shareholders must include the full amount of the distribution in gross income. §301.

Alternatively, a shareholder can sell some or all of her shares without waiting for a distribution. Here, too, the shareholder will turn some of her corporate investment into cash. But note that the tax consequences of a dividend distribution — no recovery of basis and ordinary income rather than capital gain — are the opposite of the tax consequences of a sale of stock — the shareholder receives an amount equal to her basis tax free and reports any excess as capital gain. These differences result from the conflicting congressional desires to tax distributed corporate profits as ordinary income while treating corporate shares as capital assets.

How should a shareholder be taxed if she sells some or all of her shares *to the corporation?* On one hand, funds will come out of corporate solution just as if there had been a dividend declaration; in this respect, a sale of stock to the issuing corporation (a "redemption") differs from a sale of the stock to a third party. On the other hand, the shareholder's percentage ownership of the corporation may decrease as a result of the transaction; if so, the transaction can be likened to a sale of stock to a third party. Note, though, that if stock is redeemed pro rata from all the shareholders, their proportionate interests in the corporation remain unchanged — as is the case when ordinary dividends are paid. Congress

185

has in §302 sought to distinguish redemptions resembling sales from those resembling dividends.

Before turning to §302, note the definition of a "redemption" in §317(b). A redemption in this context is the distribution of property by a corporation *in exchange for* its own stock. Certain redemptions are taxed to the selling shareholder under §302(a) as sales of stock, allowing the shareholder to be taxed under §§1001 et seq. Other redemptions are taxed to the selling shareholder under §302(d) as distributions subject to the rules of §301, yielding dividend income if the corporation has sufficient earnings and profits. If the property distributed to the selling shareholder includes noncash property, the corporation may recognize taxable gain as on any nonliquidating distribution.

Consider the case of X Corp., having 10,000 shares of common stock outstanding, owned half by P and half by Q. Suppose X Corp. has a fair market value of $100,000, and that P's 5,000 shares are redeemed for $50,000 in cash. Assuming that X Corp. has at least $50,000 of accumulated earnings and profits, how should P be taxed? Since P no longer has any interest in the corporation, the effect of the redemption on P is the same as if he had sold his stock to Q. A redemption resulting in a complete termination of the shareholder's interest in the corporation is a compelling case for sale or exchange treatment, and Congress has recognized this in §302(b)(3). Note, though, that Q becomes the sole shareholder of the corporation without having paid out any additional personal funds; in effect, the corporation's payment to P has transformed Q from a 50 percent to a 100 percent owner (albeit in a company only half its former size). We will return (at pages 221-228, 301-302 infra) to the possible tax consequences to Q of this change in status.

At the opposite end of the spectrum is a redemption of part of the stock of a sole shareholder. Suppose Q, after the redemption of P's stock, has X Corp. redeem half of his stock for $25,000. Has Q's interest in X Corp. been changed? While the number of shares that Q owns decreases from 5,000 to 2,500, his percentage ownership remains at 100. Under state law, the fact that Q surrendered half of his shares would cause some of the distribution to be charged to the corporation's capital or paid-in surplus account — if no shares had been surrendered, presumably the charge would be only to the corporation's earned surplus account. Should Q's taxation turn on this distinction? In §302(b) (excluding the partial liquidation provision of §302(b)(4), discussed at pages 215-219 infra), Congress has elected to focus on the effect of a redemption on the recipient shareholder rather than on the distributing corporation. Accordingly, the redemption of Q's stock will be taxed as a distribution subject to the rules of §301, and, if X Corp. has at least $25,000 in earnings and profits, Q will have a dividend in the entire amount.

Between these two extremes lies a morass; the courts have struggled with an endless variety of factual patterns, in each case attempting to distinguish redemptions taxable as exchanges from redemptions taxable as distributions. Particularly troublesome have been cases in which the shareholder whose stock is redeemed is related to the remaining shareholders. For example, what are the consequences if *P* and *Q* in the example above are husband and wife, mother and daughter, or brother and sister? As you read the following cases, keep in mind this distinction (between redemptions more closely resembling the sale of stock to a third party from those resembling receipt of a nonliquidating distribution from the corporation) that §302 and the courts are trying to draw. If you come away with the sense that no line can be found, reconsider whether nonliquidating corporate distributions should be taxed so much more harshly than sales of corporate shares.

As you study §302, keep in mind that even if capital gains are taxed at the same rate as ordinary income, exchange treatment under §302(a) is more favorable than distribution treatment under §301. Exchange treatment allows the shareholders to offset the amount of the distribution by the basis of the stock surrendered, while (generally) no such offset is permitted against distributions taxable under §301.

1. Complete Terminations under §302(b)(3)

Seda v. Commissioner
82 T.C. 484 (1984)

OPINION

FAY, Judge. . . .

On October 15, 1957, petitioners [Mr. and Mrs. Seda] organized B & B Supply Company (herein the company), and, within two years after incorporation, they had acquired all of the company's stock. Mr. Seda was the company's president and chairman of the board and owned 22,910 shares of the company's stock. Mrs. Seda was a director, vice-president, and secretary and owned 1,010 shares of the company's stock.

The company was engaged in the business of selling garage doors as a wholesaler in Colorado and Wyoming. It purchased most of the garage doors from Frantz Manufacturing Co. (herein Frantz Co.). In addition to working for the company from approximately 1952 until April 1981, Mr. Seda also worked as a manufacturer's representative for Frantz Co., earning a three percent commission on all garage door sales he made to the company on behalf of Frantz Co.

Because of their declining health, in 1979 petitioners decided to terminate their ownership of the company. Their son James L. Seda (James) had worked for the company since 1973 and was ready to assume ownership and control of the company. On June 30, 1979, petitioners entered into a redemption agreement wherein the company redeemed all of petitioners' stock for $299,000 ($12.50 per share). Pursuant to the redemption agreement, the company also issued 1,000 shares of stock to James for $1,000. Thus, James was the sole shareholder of the company after the redemption. Petitioners resigned from their positions as officers and directors of the company on June 30, 1979.

Prior to signing the redemption agreement, petitioners hired an accountant to advise them with respect to the tax consequences of the redemption. The accountant advised them that in order to achieve long-term capital gain treatment they would have to terminate their relationship with the company completely. Because of James' insistence, however, Mr. Seda continued to work for the company after the redemption, and he continued to receive a salary of $1,000 per month. Neither petitioners nor James believed such employment would prevent petitioners from achieving long-term capital gain treatment in connection with the redemption of their stock. In June 1981, immediately after learning that his employment relationship could result in the gain from the redemption of his stock being taxed as ordinary income, Mr. Seda terminated his employment relationship with the company. Mrs. Seda never served as an employee, officer, or director of the company after the redemption.

The company has never paid a dividend, and its retained earnings as of June 30, 1978 were $202,455. . . .

The first issue is whether the redemption of all petitioners' stock in the company is taxable as a dividend distribution under section 301 or as long-term capital gain under section 302(a). Section 302(a) provides that a distribution of property to a shareholder by a corporation in redemption of stock will be treated as a sale or exchange of such stock if the redemption falls within one of four categories enumerated in section 302(b). If the redemption fails to so qualify, it is treated as a dividend distribution to the extent of the corporation's earnings and profits. See secs. 301 and 302(a).

Section 302(b)(3) provides that a shareholder is entitled to sale or exchange treatment if all his stock in the corporation is redeemed. For purposes of determining whether there has been a complete termination within the meaning of section 302(b)(3), the constructive stock ownership rules of section 318(a) will apply unless the requirements set out in section 302(c)(2)(A) are satisfied. Sec. 302(c)(1). Respondent contends that petitioners failed to effect a complete termination within the meaning of section 302(b)(3) because James' interest in the company after the redemption is attributable to petitioners pursuant to section 318(a)(1).

Petitioners counter that James' interest is not attributable to them because they satisfied the requirements of section 302(c)(2)(A).

Section 302(c)(2)(A) provides in relevant part as follows:

> (A)   In the case of a distribution described in subsection (b)(3), section 318(a)(1) shall not apply if —
>> (i)   immediately after the distribution the distributee has no interest in the corporation (*including an interest as officer, director, or employee*), other than an interest as a creditor,
>> (ii)   the distributee does not acquire any such interest (other than stock acquired by bequest or inheritance) within 10 years from the date of such distribution, and
>> (iii)   the distributee, at such time and in such manner as the Secretary by regulations prescribes, files an agreement to notify the Secretary of any acquisition described in clause (ii) and to retain such records as may be necessary for the application of this paragraph.

(Emphasis added.)

Focusing on the parenthetical language in section 302(c)(2)(A)(i), respondent's first argument is that petitioners are not entitled to the relief provided by section 302(c)(2)(A) because Mr. Seda remained an employee of the company after the redemption. Petitioners argue, however, that section 302(c)(2)(A)(i) does not prohibit all employment relationships. Thus, they contend that Mr. Seda's employment after the redemption was not the retention of a prohibited interest in the company. For the following reasons, we agree with respondent.

Congress' purpose in enacting section 302(c)(2) was to ensure that the family attribution rules would not prevent a bona fide severance of a shareholder's interest in a corporation from resulting in capital gains treatment. H. Rept. No. 1337, 83d Cong. 2d Sess., p. 36 (1954); S. Rept. No. 1622, 83d Cong., 2d Sess., p. 45 (1954). This Court has previously stated that it is reasonable to infer from the legislative history that in enacting section 302(c)(2)(A) Congress was primarily concerned with a situation where a redeeming shareholder retained a financial stake in the corporation or continued to control the corporation and benefit by its operations after making only a nominal transfer of his stock. Estate of Lennard v. Commissioner, 61 T.C. 554, 561 (1974).

Although section 302(c)(2)(A)(i) may not prohibit the retention of all employment relationships, it is clear that the level of employment engaged in by Mr. Seda herein is prohibited. After the redemption, Mr. Seda continued to work for the company for almost two years and received a salary of $1,000 per month. By receiving that salary Mr. Seda did retain a financial stake in the company. Moreover, petitioners have failed to show that Mr. Seda ceased to be involved in the management of the company after the redemption. The fact that petitioners did not know that Mr.

Seda's continued employment would prevent them from achieving long-term capital gain treatment is unfortunate, but not controlling. Thus, we find that petitioners failed to satisfy section 302(c)(2)(A)(i).

Accordingly, James' interest in the company is attributable to petitioners and, therefore, petitioners failed to effect a complete redemption of all of their stock within the meaning of section 302(b)(3). Thus, the proceeds from the redemption are taxable under section 302(d) as a dividend distribution to the extent of the company's earnings and profits. . . .

Reviewed by the Court.

Simpson, Wiles, Wilbur, Chabot, Korner, Shields, Cohen and Swift, JJ., agree with the majority opinion.

WHITAKER, J., concurring.

While I concur in the result reached, the majority fails to apply the per se rule which, in my opinion, is mandated by the statute. Section 302(c)(1) and (2)(A)(i) prescribes that the family attribution rules may not be waived if after a redemption the former shareholder performs any services for, or receives any remuneration from, the redeeming corporation as an officer, director or employee. The parenthetical language of section 302(c)(2)(A)(i) — "(including an interest as officer, director, or employee)" — is neither ambiguous nor equivocal; it contains no qualification such as that suggested by the majority. Nothing in the statutory language or legislative history suggests that an "interest as officer, director, or employee" must be substantial to be prohibited. Rather, it contains a flat rule.

While Congress did not address directly the issue of whether a per se rule was to be applied in interpreting the parenthetical language of section 302(c)(2)(A)(i), it is clear that section 302(c) was intended to bring an element of certainty to an area that had become a confusing morass under prior law. Congress recognized that it was necessary to replace the difficult detailed factual inquiries that had become commonplace. With regard to corporate redemptions, the House Report states:

> . . . Redemptions of stock. — Under present law it is not clear when a stock redemption results in capital gain or ordinary income. . . .
>
> Your committee's bill sets forth definite conditions under which stock may be redeemed at capital-gain rates. . . .
>
> . . . At the present time a possible opportunity for tax avoidance results where redemptions are effected in the case of family-owned corporations. To prevent tax avoidance, but at the same time to provide definitive rules for the guidance of taxpayers, your committee has provided precise standards whereby under specific circumstances, a shareholder may be considered as owning stock held by members of his immediate family (or by partnerships, corporations, or trusts which he controls).

[H. Rept. 1337, 83d Cong., 2d Sess. 35-36 (1954).]

Section 302(c) thus was enacted as something of a "safe haven." Facts and circumstances must be considered in the application of some of the section 302(b) and (c) rules, such as the determination under section 302(b)(1) as to dividend equivalency, but we should not judicially modify the mechanical rules where they can be applied mechanically. Contrary to the majority's view, Congress did intend to "prohibit the retention of all employment relationships." In the context of Lewis v. Commissioner, 47 T.C. 129 (1966), I do agree with Judge Simpson that "Congress did not intend us to hold that an officer or director who performs no duties, receives no compensation, and exercises no influence has retained an interest in the corporation." 47 T.C. at 137 (Simpson, J., concurring). The principle of substance over form prevents us from applying the per se rule where no duties are performed and no compensation received by reason of status as an officer, director or employee. But where, as here, the facts are otherwise, the congressional attempt to achieve certainty should be allowed to operate. . . .

Dawson, Sterrett, Goffe, Nims, Parker, Hamblen, and Clapp, JJ., agree with this concurring opinion.

NOTE

1. *Constructive ownership of stock under §302(b)(3).* Although all the stock owned by Mr. Seda was redeemed, he failed to qualify under §302(b)(3) for exchange treatment on the redemption.[1] The complete termination provision of §302(b)(3) was inapplicable in this case solely because Mr. Seda's son owned stock in the corporation after the redemption and this stock was attributed to Mr. Seda under §302(c)(1). Because of §302(c)(1), the constructive attribution rules of §318 generally apply to determinations of stock ownership under §302. The constructive attribution rules of §318 are discussed further at pages 196-198 infra.

One distinctive feature of the complete termination of interest provision in §302(b)(3) is the ability of the redeemed shareholder to waive application of the family attribution rules of §318(a)(1). See §302(c)(2). For such a waiver to be effective, however, the taxpayer must not retain, and agree not to acquire for 10 years, any interest in the corporation other than as a creditor. If a taxpayer whose stock is redeemed fails to make the election provided by §302(c)(2), then the attribution rules will apply in full in determining whether the redemption qualifies under §302(b)(3). In *Seda*, the taxpayers filed a §302(c) election, but the retention of an interest in the corporation by Mr. Seda eviscerated the election's effect.

As part of electing out of the family attribution rules, a taxpayer must

---

1. The opinion does not consider why Mrs. Seda failed to qualify under §302(b)(3). Is Mr. Seda's employment imputed to his wife?

file an agreement under §302(c)(2)(A)(iii) that extends the statute of limitations with respect to his redemption. This agreement allows the Commissioner to reopen the redemption year and collect a deficiency if the taxpayer acquires a tainted interest in the corporation within 10 years.

Under §302(c)(2)(B), a taxpayer may not waive the family attribution rules if any of the redeemed stock was acquired within 10 years from a related person, "related" being defined by reference to §318(a). In addition, a taxpayer may not waive the family attribution rules if he transferred any stock within 10 years to such a related person. These two limitations do not apply, however, if the transfer of stock "did not have as one of its principal purposes the avoidance of Federal income tax."

Suppose X Corp. has 100 shares outstanding, all of which are owned by H. If H gives 10 shares to W, his wife, and then W's ten shares are immediately redeemed, §302(c)(2)(B)(i) operates to prevent W from avoiding application of the family attribution rules. Thus, W will be deemed to own 100 percent of X Corp.'s shares both before and after the redemption, and the redemption will be subject to the distribution rules of §301.

Suppose instead that H gives W all but 10 shares and then has his stock completely redeemed. Now H will seek to waive application of the family attribution rules, but §302(c)(2)(B)(ii) prevents him from doing so. H will thus be deemed to own 100 percent of the X Corp. stock both before and after the redemption and so will be taxed under the distribution rules of §301. Note, however, that §302(c)(2)(B) applies only to transfers that have "the avoidance of Federal income tax" as one of their principal purposes. In Rev. Rul. 77-293, 1977-2 C.B. 91, the Service ruled that a transfer of appreciated stock to the taxpayer's son was not subject to §302(c)(2)(B) when made "solely for the purpose of enabling [the taxpayer] to retire while leaving the business to [his son]." See also Rev. Rul. 85-19, 1985-1 C.B. 94, in which the father gifted stock to his son and subsequently reacquired some of the gifted stock by purchase. The son's remaining stock was redeemed by the corporation, and he filed an election under §302(c)(2)(A)(iii) to waive the family attribution rules. The Service ruled that the waiver was valid because the resale of stock by the son to his father merely returned the stock to its original owner and was not undertaken to avoid tax.

2. *Retention or reacquisition of a tainted interest.* As *Seda* illustrates, a taxpayer desiring to waive the family attribution rules pursuant to §302(c)(2) must not retain (or acquire within 10 years) an interest in the corporation "other than an interest as a creditor." The concurring opinion of Judge Whitaker emphasizes that Congress seemingly drew a bright line in §302(c)(2)(A)(i) by specifically providing that an interest as an "officer, director, or employee" is proscribed. The majority opinion does not specifically embrace that reading of the statute. Judge Whitaker agrees that a nominal directorship entailing no duties and without compensation, the situation litigated in *Lewis,* is not a prohibited interest under

§302(c)(2)(A)(i), and the majority in *Seda* condemn the minimal activity engaged in by the taxpayer in that case. What fact pattern might fall between *Lewis* and *Seda* to justify Judge Whitaker's concerns?

In Lynch v. Commissioner, 83 T.C. 597 (1984), the father was the sole shareholder of *X* Corp. He transferred some of the stock to his son, and thereafter *X* Corp. redeemed all the father's remaining stock. The father continued, as an independent contractor, to render services to *X* Corp. under a consulting agreement. The father sought capital gain treatment on the redemption via §302(b)(3) and a waiver of the family attribution rules. Held, exchange treatment allowed because (1) an independent contractor is not an "employee" within the meaning of §302(c)(2)(A)(i), and (2) the father's transfer to his son did not have as one of its principal purposes the avoidance of federal income tax. What would the Tax Court's opinion in *Lynch* leave of *Seda* (other than a trap for the ill advised)? The court of appeals reversed the Tax Court in *Lynch,* saying that Congress sought certainty in this area of the law by enacting §302(c)(2)(A). 801 F.2d 1176 (9th Cir. 1986). Compare Cerone v. Commissioner, 87 T.C. 1 (1986), in which the Tax Court rejected a bright-line reading of §302(c)(2)(A), saying instead that a taxpayer who continues to perform services for his corporation after a redemption will fail §302(c)(2)(A) only if the taxpayer has a significant financial stake in, or continues to control, the corporation.

How should "creditor" status be defined in the context of §302(c)(2)(A)(i)? Under Treas. Regs. §1.302-4(d), a permissible creditor must have rights neither broader in scope than is necessary for the enforcement of her claim nor subordinate to the claims of general creditors. See Dunn v. Commissioner, 615 F.2d 578 (2d Cir. 1980). See also Lynch v. Commissioner, supra, in which a note was held not to run afoul of Treas. Regs. §1.302-4(d) even though the noteholder agreed, subsequent to the redemption, to subordinate his note to a new debt acquired by the corporation. Would a retiring shareholder be beyond the bounds of §302(c)(2)(A)(i) if he received a note of the corporation secured by corporate stock? What if the retiring shareholder could vote the stock upon default of the note?

In Rev. Rul. 77-467, 1977-2 C.B. 92, the Service ruled that a taxpayer could waive the family attribution rules under §302(c)(2) despite retaining his interest as lessor of the corporation's office building pursuant to a 10-year lease entered into five years before the taxpayer's redemption. The taxpayer's status was not a prohibited interest within the meaning of §302(c)(2)(A)(i) because "[t]he payments under the lease will not be dependent on [the corporation's] future earnings and will not be subordinate to the claims of [the corporation's] general creditors." Was Mr. Seda's salary as an employee any more dependent on future corporate earnings than the lease payments in Rev. Rul. 77-467? Remaining an employee of the corporation after the redemption plainly fails the congressionally delineated test of §302(c)(2)(A)(i). Does this suggest that the reasoning in Rev. Rul. 77-467 is flawed?

Can the family attribution rules be waived if the exiting shareholder retains the right to a lifetime pension from the corporation? If the pension is unfunded, the payments are unrelated to the corporation's future earnings, and the rights of the exiting shareholder are unsubordinated to the claims of general creditors of the corporation, the answer is yes. Rev. Rul. 84-135, 1984-2 C.B. 80.

In a series of rulings, the Service has held that retention of the legal right to vote shares violates a §302(c)(2)(A) waiver even if the taxpayer has no equitable interest in the stock. See Rev. Rul. 81-233, 1981-2 C.B. 83 (custodian of stock under Uniform Gift to Minors Act); Rev. Rul. 71-426, 1971-2 C.B. 173 (retention of interest as trustee of voting trust). But see Rev. Rul. 79-334, 1979-2 C.B. 127 (appointment by will as trustee of trust holding stock not a forbidden "interest"); Rev. Rul. 72-380, 1972-2 C.B. 201 (executor of estate holding stock not a forbidden "interest").

3. *Corporate shareholders and §302.* When a corporate shareholder's stock is redeemed, the taxpayer and the Service often switch sides; the corporation usually prefers dividend treatment because of the generous dividends-received deduction pursuant to §243, and the Service prefers capital gains treatment. To avoid §302(b)(3), a corporate shareholder might arrange to have its stock redeemed in a series of redemptions, arguing that only the final redemption in the series should be taxable as a complete termination. In Bleily & Collishaw v. Commissioner, 72 T.C. 751 (1979), however, the Commissioner successfully argued that a series of redemptions should be combined and taxed as a single, complete termination of the corporate shareholder's interest. See also Rev. Rul. 77-226, 1977-2 C.B. 90, in which the Service found that a corporate shareholder had transacted a §302(b)(3) redemption by combining various steps in a complicated transaction. Can a noncorporate taxpayer "step" a series of redemptions together to qualify for exchange treatment under §302(b)(3)? See Benjamin v. Commissioner, 592 F.2d 1259 (5th Cir. 1979), in which the court refused to treat a partial redemption as part of a complete redemption since (1) there was no time frame in which the "plan for total redemption" was to be completed, and (2) the shareholder had wide discretion as to when the redemption would be completed.

2.   Substantially Disproportionate Redemptions under §302(b)(2)

A less compelling case for exchange treatment than a complete redemption is a disproportionate redemption in which a shareholder's relative equity interest in the corporation is reduced significantly, though not to zero. Under §302(b)(2), a disproportionate redemption will qualify for exchange treatment under §302(a) if it satisfies the following three-part test: (1) The redeemed shareholder must own less than 50 percent of the total combined voting power of the corporation immediately after the redemption; (2) the shareholder's voting power after the redemption must be less than 80 percent of his former voting power; and (3) the shareholder's percentage ownership of all common stock (nonvoting as well as voting) must also be less than 80 percent of his former percentage ownership.

Consider the following example. Assume E Corp. has 300 shares of common stock outstanding, owned 70 percent (210 shares) by P and 30 percent (90 shares) by Q. If E Corp. redeems 20 shares of Q's stock, will the redemption qualify under §302(b)(2)? The following table sets forth the relevant data.

	Total Shares Outstanding	Q's Shares	Q's Percentage
Preredemption	300	90	30
Postredemption	280	70	25

Here, more than 20 percent of Q's stock has been redeemed (20 of 90 shares), and Q's percentage of ownership drops from 30 to 25. To qualify for sale or exchange treatment under §302(b)(2), Q's ownership would have had to fall below 24 percent (since 80 percent of her prior 30 percent is 24 percent). Accordingly, Q does not meet the safe harbor test of §302(b)(2). This example displays the often-overlooked fact that a redemption will not qualify under §302(b)(2) if only 20 percent of a shareholder's stock is redeemed: Because a redemption reduces the total number of shares outstanding as well as the number of shares held by the redeemed shareholder, the percentage of a taxpayer's shares that must be redeemed to qualify under §302(b)(2) always exceeds 20 percent and turns on the redeemed shareholder's preredemption percentage ownership of the corporation.

Now consider a more abstract example. X Corp. has 200 shares of voting stock outstanding, owned half by K and half by L. What is the least number of shares that K must have redeemed if he is to qualify under §302(b)(2)? Before the redemption, K owns 100 of the 200 shares outstanding, or 50 percent. After the redemption, K must own less than 0.80 times 50 percent, or less than 40 percent. If K has x shares redeemed, then his postredemption percentage of ownership will be $(100 - x)/(200 - x) \times 100$ percent. To satisfy §302(b)(2), then, K must choose an x such that $(100 - x)/(200 - x) < .4$, and the smallest x satisfying this condition is 33.34. Accordingly, K must have at least 33.34 of his shares redeemed (and not merely a fraction more than 20 shares!) to qualify under §302(b)(3).[2]

Note the requirement imposed by the concluding paragraph of

---

2. If T is the total number of shares outstanding just prior to the redemption, and if N is the number of those shares held by the shareholder, then the number of shares needed to be redeemed to meet the 80 percent test under §302(b)(2) is any amount above $NT/(5T - 4N)$.

§302(b)(2)(C): Not only must the 80 percent test be satisfied as to all voting stock, but it also must be satisfied with respect to the shareholder's common stock taken alone. The Service has ruled that this test will not disqualify a corporation redeeming voting preferred stock of a shareholder who owns (actually and constructively) no common stock before the redemption. Rev. Rul. 81-41, 1981-1 C.B. 121. In addition, the Service has ruled that if multiple classes of common stock are outstanding, the test of §302(b)(2)(C) is applied to a shareholder's aggregate ownership of common stock rather than on a class-by-class basis. If the test were applied class by class, no redemption could qualify as substantially disproportionate unless shares of each class of stock were redeemed. Rev. Rul 87-88, 1987-2 C.B. 81.

Suppose a corporation is equally owned by two shareholders. While a pro rata redemption of the two shareholders' stock will fail to qualify for exchange treatment under §302(a), can they obtain capital gain treatment if the corporation redeems a substantial portion of one shareholder's stock in one redemption and then redeems an equal portion of the other shareholder's stock in a second transaction? Under §302(b)(2)(D), a redemption that is part of a series of redemptions will not qualify under §302(b)(2) unless the series in total is "substantially disproportionate." Treas. Regs. §1.302-1(a)(3).

Suppose individual A, the controlling shareholder of X Corp., knows that X Corp. will in one month repurchase all the shares of individual B, a minority shareholder. How should A be taxed on a redemption that, viewed in isolation, satisfies the tests of §302(b)(2) but that would fail those tests had the distribution to A come after the complete termination of B? For the Service's position that the distributions to A and to B must be treated as a single transaction, see Rev. Rul. 85-14, 1985-4 C.B. 92.

NOTE

1. *Constructive ownership of stock under §302.* By virtue of §302(c)(1), the constructive attribution rules of §318(a) apply to determinations under §302. The explicit reference in §302(c)(1) to §318(a) is important, for §318 does not apply except when "expressly made applicable." §318(a).

The constructive ownership rules of §318 consist of three main parts: attribution between family members, §318(a)(1); attribution *from* entities to their beneficial owners, §318(a)(2); and attribution *to* entities from their beneficial owners, §318(a)(3). In addition, holders of stock options are treated as owners of the optioned stock even though they have not yet exercised (and may never exercise) the option. §318(a)(4). Finally, §318(a)(5)(A) permits two or more attribution rules of §318 to be applied in sequence, resulting in a chain of links.

The mechanics of §318 can best be gleaned from a number of examples. Assume *X* Corp. has 100 shares of common stock outstanding, owned 25 by *E*, 25 by *F*, 25 by the *T* trust, and 25 by the *P* partnership. While *E*, *F*, *T*, and *P* each actually own 25 percent of *X* Corp., their constructive (or deemed) ownership will depend on the relationships among them. For example, suppose *E* is a 60 percent partner in the *P* partnership. Now, *E* will have a total constructive ownership of 40 shares, 25 actually owned and 60 percent of the 25 shares owned by *P*. §318(a)(2)(A). *P*, however, will be deemed to own 50 shares, for all of *E*'s shares will be imputed to *P* under §318(a)(3)(A).

If *E* is also a beneficiary of the *T* trust, the matter becomes more complicated. Suppose *E*'s actuarially determined interest in the *T* trust is 80 percent of the trust's value. Then *E*'s total constructive ownership jumps by 20 shares to 60, for he must add 80 percent of the trust's holdings to his own under §318(a)(2)(B)(i). Further, *P*'s constructive ownership also increases by 20 shares, for under §318(a)(5)(A), *E*'s constructive ownership can be imputed to a related party such as *P*, as is actual ownership.

Now assume *F* has the other 40 percent interest in the *P* partnership. *P*'s total constructive ownership will increase by 25 shares under §318(a)(3)(A). *F*'s total constructive ownership will increase to 35 shares, 25 actually owned and 10 constructively owned through attribution of 40 percent of *P*'s *actual* ownership. Why is *F* not deemed to own 40 percent of *P*'s actually *and constructively* owned shares? Under §318(a)(5)(C), stock attributed *into* an entity under §318(a)(3) cannot then be reattributed *out of* the entity under §318(a)(2). A similar rule limits reattribution through family members so that, for example, there is no attribution between siblings via the chain: child 1 to parent to child 2. See §318(a)(5)(B). Note also that attribution to and from corporations is limited to its 50 percent shareholders. §318(a)(2)(C), (a)(3)(C).

Recall §302(c)(2), which allows a taxpayer to waive application of the family attribution rules to qualify under the complete termination safe harbor of §302(b)(3). Note that this waiver applies only to the attribution rules in §318(a)(1) — the *family* attribution rules — and that it applies only to determinations under §302(b)(3). In Rickey v. United States, 592 F.2d 1251 (5th Cir. 1979), it was held that an estate could waive the entity attribution rules of §318(a)(3) for purposes of §302(b)(3). In the legislative reports discussing §228 of the Tax Equity and Fiscal Responsibility Act of 1982, Congress indicated that the holding of *Rickey* was specifically disapproved.

Entities as well as individuals can waive the family attribution rules to qualify under §302(b)(3). See §302(c)(2)(C). Such a waiver might be appropriate when a trust completely terminates its interest in a corporation but the parent of a trust beneficiary continues to be a shareholder of the corporation. Note that the restrictions of §302(c)(2)(A) — a 10-year prohibition from acquiring a tainted interest in the corporation and the filing of an extension of the statute of limitations — are imposed on the entity and on all persons related to the entity (related by virtue of the family attribution rules of §318(a)(3)). See §302(c)(2)(C).

2. *The case of the disappearing basis.* When a taxpayer receives an ordinary dividend, the basis of her shares is unaffected by the receipt, and gain or loss on a subsequent disposition of the shares, computed under §1001(a), will be the difference between the amount realized and the basis of the shares. A redemption of some or all of the taxpayer's shares that fails to qualify for exchange treatment under §302(a) similarly leaves the taxpayer's stock basis unaffected, but she no longer has the redeemed shares for a later sale or other disposition. What happens to her basis in the redeemed shares? If it is lost, a §302(d) distribution is not the equivalent of an ordinary dividend; it is worse than one. See Treas. Regs. §1.302-2(c), stating that when a redemption of stock is treated as dividend, "proper adjustment of the basis *of the remaining stock* will be made with respect to the stock redeemed" (emphasis added), and note examples 1 to 3. Note that the shareholder may not own any shares after the redemption, as was true in *Seda.* What is the "proper adjustment" in *Seda?* See Levin v. Commissioner, 385 F.2d 521 (2d Cir. 1967) (transfer of basis to related shareholder).

3.   Redemptions Not Essentially Equivalent to a Dividend

United States v. Davis _____
397 U.S. 301 (1970)

Justice MARSHALL delivered the opinion of the Court.

In 1945, taxpayer and E. B. Bradley organized a corporation. In exchange for property transferred to the new company, Bradley received 500 shares of common stock, and taxpayer and his wife similarly each received 250 such shares. Shortly thereafter, taxpayer made an additional contribution to the corporation, purchasing 1,000 shares of preferred stock at a par value of $25 per share.

The purpose of this latter transaction was to increase the company's working capital and thereby to qualify for a loan previously negotiated through the Reconstruction Finance Corporation. It was understood that the corporation would redeem the preferred stock when the RFC loan had been repaid. Although in the interim taxpayer bought Bradley's 500 shares and divided them between his son and daughter, the total capitalization of the company remained the same until 1963. That year, after the loan was fully repaid and in accordance with the original understanding, the company redeemed taxpayer's preferred stock. . . .

[T]axpayer considered the redemption as a sale of his preferred stock to the company — a capital gains transaction under §302 of the Internal Revenue Code of 1954 resulting in no tax since taxpayer's basis in the stock equaled the amount he received for it. . . . According to the Commissioner, the redemption of taxpayer's stock was essentially equivalent to a dividend and was thus taxable as ordinary income under §§301 and 316 of the Code. Taxpayer paid the resulting deficiency and brought this suit for a refund. The District Court ruled in his favor. . . .

The Court of Appeals held that the $25,000 received by taxpayer was "not essentially equivalent to a dividend" within the meaning of that phrase in §302(b)(1) of the Code because the redemption was the final step in a course of action that had a legitimate business (as opposed to a tax avoidance) purpose. . . . We reverse.

The Internal Revenue Code of 1954 provides generally in §§301 and 316 for the tax treatment of distributions by a corporation to its shareholders; under those provisions, a distribution is includible in a taxpayer's gross income as a dividend out of earnings and profits to the extent such earnings exist. There are exceptions to the application of these general provisions, however, and among them are those found in §302 involving certain distributions for redeemed stock. . . .

Under subsection (a) of §302, a distribution is treated as "payment in exchange for the stock," thus qualifying for capital gains rather than ordinary income treatment, if the conditions contained in any one of the four paragraphs of subsection (b) are met. In addition to paragraph (1)'s "not essentially equivalent to a dividend" test, capital gains treatment is available where (2) the taxpayer's voting strength is substantially diminished, (3) his interest in the company is completely terminated. . . . Paragraph (4) is not involved here, and taxpayer admits that paragraphs (2) and (3) do not apply. Moreover, taxpayer agrees that for the purposes of §§302(b)(2) and (3) the attribution rules of §318(a) apply and he is considered to own the 750 outstanding shares of common stock held by his wife and children in addition to the 250 shares in his own name.

Taxpayer, however, argues that the attribution rules do not apply in considering whether a distribution is essentially equivalent to a dividend under §302(b)(1). According to taxpayer, he should thus be considered to own only 25 percent of the corporation's common stock, and the distribution would then qualify under §302(b)(1) since it was not pro rata or proportionate to his stock interest, the fundamental test of dividend equivalency. See Treas. Reg. §1.302-2(b). However, the plain language of the statute compels rejection of the argument. In subsection (c) of §302, the attribution rules are made specifically applicable "in determining the ownership of stock for purposes of this section." Applying this language, both courts below held that §318(a) applies to all of §302, including §302(b)(1) — a view in accord with the decisions of the other courts of appeals, a long-standing treasury regulation, and the opinion of the leading commentators.

Against this weight of authority, taxpayer argues that the result under paragraph (1) should be different because there is no explicit reference to stock ownership as there is in paragraphs (2) and (3). Neither that fact, however, nor the purpose and history of §302(b)(1) support taxpayer's argument. . . .

Indeed, it was necessary that the attribution rules apply to §302(b)(1) unless they were to be effectively eliminated from consideration with regard to §§302(b)(2) and (3) also. For if a transaction failed to qualify under one of those sections solely because of the attribution rules, it would according to taxpayer's argument nonetheless qualify under §302(b)(1). We cannot agree that Congress intended so to nullify its explicit directive. We conclude, therefore, that the attribution rules of §318(a) do apply; and, for the purposes of deciding whether a distribution is "not essentially equivalent to a dividend" under §302(b)(1), taxpayer must be deemed the owner of all 1,000 shares of the company's common stock.

II

After application of the stock ownership attribution rules, this case viewed most simply involves a sole stockholder who causes part of his shares to be redeemed by the corporation. We conclude that such a redemption is always "essentially equivalent to a dividend" within the meaning of that phrase in §302(b)(1) and therefore do not reach the Government's alternative argument that in any event the distribution should not on the facts of this case qualify for capital gains treatment.[8]

The predecessor of §302(b)(1) came into the tax law as §201(d) of the Revenue Act of 1921. . . . Enacted in response to this Court's decision that pro rata stock dividends do not constitute taxable income, Eisner v. Macomber, 252 U.S. 189 (1920), the provision had the obvious purpose of preventing a corporation from avoiding dividend tax treatment by distributing earnings to its shareholders in two transactions — a pro rata stock dividend followed by a pro rata redemption — that would have the same economic consequences as a simple dividend. Congress, however, soon recognized that even without a prior stock dividend essentially the same result could be effected whereby any corporation, "especially one which has only a few stockholders, might be able to make a distribution to its stockholders which would have the same effect as a taxable dividend." H.R. Rep. No. 1, 69th Cong., 1st Sess., 5. In order to cover this situation, the law was amended to apply "(whether or not such stock was issued as a stock dividend)" whenever a distribution in redemption of stock was made "at such time and in such manner" that it was essentially equivalent to a taxable dividend. Revenue Act of 1926, §201(g), 44 Stat. 11. . . .

---

8. Of course, this just means that a distribution in redemption to a sole shareholder will be treated under the general provisions of §301, and it will only be taxed as a dividend under §316 to the extent that there are earnings and profits.

Unfortunately, however, the policies encompassed within the general language of §115(g)(1) and its predecessors were not clear, and there resulted much confusion in the tax law. . . .

By the time of the general revision resulting in the Internal Revenue Code of 1954, the draftsmen were faced with what has aptly been described as "the morass created by the decisions." Balenger v. United States, 301 F.2d 192, 196 (C.A.4 1962). In an effort to eliminate "the considerable confusion which exists in this area" and thereby to facilitate tax planning, H.R. Rep. No. 1337, 83d Cong., 2d Sess., 35, the authors of the new Code sought to provide objective tests to govern the tax consequences of stock redemptions. Thus, the tax bill passed by the House of Representatives contained no "essentially equivalent" language. Rather, it provided for "safe harbors" where capital gains treatment would be accorded to corporate redemptions that met the conditions now found in §§302(b)(2) and (3) of the Code.

It was in the Senate Finance Committee's consideration of the tax bill that §302(b)(1) was added, and Congress thereby provided that capital gains treatment should be available "if the redemption is not essentially equivalent to a dividend." . . . However . . . we find from the history of the 1954 revisions and the purpose of §302(b)(1) that Congress intended more than merely to re-enact the prior law.

In explaining the reason for adding the "essentially equivalent" test, the Senate Committee stated that the House provisions "appeared unnecessarily restrictive, particularly, in the case of redemptions of preferred stock which might be called by the corporation without the shareholder having any control over when the redemption may take place." S. Rep. No. 1622, 83d Cong., 2d Sess., 44. This explanation gives no indication that the purpose behind the redemption should affect the result. . . .

The intended scope of §302(b)(1) as revealed by this legislative history is certainly not free from doubt. However, we agree with the Government that by making the sole inquiry relevant for the future the narrow one whether the redemption could be characterized as a sale, Congress was apparently rejecting past court decisions that had also considered factors indicating the presence or absence of a tax-avoidance motive.[11] At least that is the implication of the example given. Congress clearly mandated

---

11. This rejection is confirmed by the Committee's acceptance of the House treatment of distributions involving corporate contractions — a factor present in many of the earlier "business purpose" redemptions. In describing its action, the Committee stated as follows:

> Your committee, as did the House bill, separates into their significant elements the kind of transactions now incoherently aggregated in the definition of a partial liquidation. Those distributions which may have capital-gain characteristics *because they are not made pro rata* among the various shareholders would be subjected, at the shareholder level, to the separate tests described in [§§301 to 318]. On the other hand, those distributions characterized by what happens solely at the corporate level by reason of the assets distributed would be included as within the concept of a partial liquidation.

S. Rep. No. 1622, supra, at 49. (Emphasis added.)

that pro rata distributions be treated under the general rules laid down in §§301 and 316 rather than under §302 and nothing suggests that there should be a different result if there were a "business purpose" for the redemption. . . .

Taxpayer strongly argues that to treat the redemption involved here as essentially equivalent to a dividend is to elevate form over substance. Thus, taxpayer argues, had he not bought Bradley's shares or had he made a subordinated loan to the company instead of buying preferred stock, he could have gotten back his $25,000 with favorable tax treatment. However, the difference between form and substance in the tax law is largely problematical, and taxpayer's complaints have little to do with whether a business purpose is relevant under §302(b)(1). It was clearly proper for Congress to treat distributions generally as taxable dividends when made out of earnings and profits and then to prevent avoidance of that result without regard to motivation where the distribution is in exchange for redeemed stock.

We conclude that that is what Congress did when enacting §302(b)(1). If a corporation distributes property as a simple dividend, the effect is to transfer the property from the company to its shareholders without a change in the relative economic interests or rights of the stockholders. Where a redemption has that same effect, it cannot be said to have satisfied the "not essentially equivalent to a dividend" requirement of §302(b)(1). Rather, to qualify for preferred treatment under that section, a redemption must result in a meaningful reduction of the shareholder's proportionate interest in the corporation. Clearly, taxpayer here, who (after application of the attribution rules) was the sole shareholder of the corporation both before and after the redemption, did not qualify under this test. The decision of the Court of Appeals must therefore be reversed and the case remanded to the District Court for dismissal of the complaint.

It is so ordered.

Reversed and remanded.

Mr. Justice Douglas, with whom Mr. Justice Brennan concurs, dissenting. . . .

[R]espondent's contribution of working capital in the amount of $25,000 in exchange for 1,000 shares of preferred stock with a par value of $25 was made in order for the corporation to obtain a loan from the RFC and that the preferred stock was to be redeemed when the loan was repaid. For the reasons stated by the two lower courts, this redemption was not "essentially equivalent to a dividend," for the bona fide business purpose of the redemption belies the payment of a dividend. . . .

When the Court holds it was a dividend, it effectively cancels §302(b)(1) from the Code. This result is not a matter of conjecture, for the Court says that in the case of closely held or one-man corporations a redemption of stock is "always" equivalent to a dividend. I would leave such revision to the Congress.

Henry T. Patterson Trust v. United States _____
729 F.2d 1089 (6th Cir. 1984)

Before Edwards and Krupansky, Circuit Judges, and Peck, Senior Circuit Judge.

KRUPANSKY, Circuit Judge. . . .

Prior to 1969, Henry Patterson, Sr. was the sole shareholder and chief executive officer of Puritan [Laundry and Dry Cleaning Company]. In 1969, he gave forty shares of Puritan stock to each of his children — John, Hank and Ellen. At the time, Ellen was married to Bill Hicks (Hicks), who, along with Hank, was employed by Puritan. Henry Patterson retained 200 shares of Puritan stock.

Bill Hicks was apparently a skilled business manager, while Hank Patterson (Hank) lacked effectiveness. Through the years, a bitter tension between Hicks and Hank developed, resulting in numerous altercations, one of which ended with Hank's hospitalization. At one point, John Patterson (John) participated in the management of the business but, because of the Hank-Hicks rivalry, John resigned and pursued a teaching career.

At trial, there was testimony that Henry Patterson desired that Hicks operate the company after Patterson's retirement. In early 1970, Patterson suffered a broken hip which forced him to remain away from the company. He designated Hicks to act as Puritan's president and general manager in his absence. Patterson's health continued to deteriorate and he died in November 1971.

In June 1971, Hicks presented the Puritan directors with a demand for an increase in salary and a proposal that they place all of the Puritan shares in a voting trust which Hicks would then control. The directors demurred and Hicks resigned. He immediately staged a slowdown of Puritan employees and persuaded the company's most substantial commercial accounts to demand that Puritan rehire him. Within ten days of Hicks' resignation, Puritan was on the verge of collapse. John, who had since returned to the business, contacted Hicks and negotiated a five-year employment contract with him.

Hicks' contract provided an increased salary, a profit sharing arrangement, and a five-year option to acquire eighty shares of Puritan stock. Hicks acquired five of those shares and his option on the remaining seventy-five shares remained open. At the same time, Hank also received a five-year contract.

During the ensuing five years, Puritan performed well but problems between Hank and Hicks became increasingly aggravated; Hank, John, and Ella Patterson, their mother, often were at odds with Hicks and his wife, Ellen.

In the spring of 1976, the Patterson estate was closed. Henry Patterson had placed his 200 shares of Puritan stock in the Henry T. Patterson Trust (Trust) with his widow, Ella, as the beneficiary with the power to appoint the corpus at her death. Following the closing of the estate, the Puritan stock was thus distributed:

Henry T. Patterson Trust	200 shares
Ella Patterson	25 shares
Hank Patterson	40 shares
John Patterson	40 shares
Ellen (Patterson) Hicks	40 shares
Bill Hicks	5 shares
Lester Winkler	6 shares

Hicks devised a two-step plan whereby he and his wife could obtain control of Puritan. First, Puritan would redeem the Trust shares and, following the redemption, Hicks would exercise his option and acquire an additional seventy-five shares. As a result, Hicks and his spouse would own 120 shares and the remaining shareholders would control only 111 shares, thus Hicks would acquire a controlling interest in Puritan.

The Reeves Bank, as Trustee, determined that if it refused to redeem the shares, Hicks would leave the company and eventually the Trust corpus would be worthless. Thus, acting in what it perceived as the best interests of the Trust and the beneficiary, the Reeves Bank determined to accept the proposed redemption.

On April 2, 1976, the directors were presented with the proposal. The Trustee reported that it would be in Ella's best interest to redeem the shares and invest the proceeds. . . .

The Trust reported the transaction as a capital gains sale. Upon review, the Commissioner determined that the amount received by the Trust in the redemption, $190,000.00, was a dividend taxable as ordinary income under §301 of the Internal Revenue Code of 1954. . . .

[A]t issue here is the propriety, as a matter of law, of the district court's determination that the Trust's redemption was not essentially a dividend, as defined by §302(b)(1).

In United States v. Davis, 397 U.S. 301 (1970), the Supreme Court evaluated the intended scope of §302(b)(1). In that case, a sole shareholder caused part of his shares to be redeemed by the corporation; the Court concluded that such a redemption is always equivalent to a dividend and thus subject to ordinary income tax. However, the Court's examination of §302(b)(1)'s history is germane to the analysis of this appeal:

> It was clearly proper for Congress to treat distributions generally as taxable dividends when made out of earnings and profits and then to prevent avoid-

ance of that result without regard to motivation where the distribution is in exchange for redeemed stock.

We conclude that that is what Congress did when enacting §302(b)(1). If a corporation distributes property as a simple dividend, the effect is to transfer the property from the company to its shareholders without a change in the relative economic interests or rights of the stockholders. Where a redemption has that same effect, it cannot be said to have satisfied the "not essentially equivalent to a dividend" requirement of §302(b)(1). Rather, to qualify for preferred treatment under that section, a redemption must result in a meaningful reduction of the shareholder's proportionate interest in the corporation. Clearly, taxpayer here, who (after application of the attribution rules) was the sole shareholder both before and after the redemption, did not qualify under this test.

397 U.S. at 313.

As explicated by the Supreme Court, §302(b)(1) provides that corporate distributions which do not alter the shareholder's "relative economic interests or rights" will be taxed as a dividend, regardless of the form or nomenclature given the transactions. The test is to examine the change in the taxpayer's relationship to the corporation; §302(b)(1) is satisfied, under this test, if the examination establishes a "meaningful reduction" of the taxpayer's relative interests or rights in the company.

Whether a distribution by redemption of stock was "essentially equivalent to a dividend" for the purposes of the 1954 Code is a question of fact. The district court's factual determinations must be upheld on appeal if they are supported by substantial evidence within the record considered as a whole. . . .

To determine if the district court properly discerned a meaningful reduction in the Trust's interest and rights in Puritan, the starting point must be a comparison of the Trust's relative holdings prior to and after the redemption. As in United States v. Davis, supra, this comparison requires application of the attribution statutes.

Briefly stated, the 1954 Code provided that a trust constructively owned its shares plus the shares held by the beneficiary, including those shares which §318 attributed to the beneficiary. §§302(c), 318.

Applying this statute, it is readily apparent that prior to the redemption, the Trust constructively owned 345 shares of the Puritan company, computed from its own shares (200), Ella's holdings (25), and the shares owned by Ella's children (John — 40, Hank — 40, Ellen Hicks — 40). Following the redemption, the Trust's constructive holdings were reduced to 145 shares (25 owned by Ella, 120 held by her children). Only 11 other shares remained actually outstanding (Hicks — 5, Winkler — 6); therefore, the Trust held 345/356 shares, or 97%, before and 145/156 shares, or 93%, immediately after the redemption.

When the district court made this comparison it included the seventy-five option shares held by Hicks. Accordingly, the district court determined that the Trust held 80% of the company before redemption (345/431), and 62.8% after redemption (145/231). Because the Trust no longer controlled the company after the redemption (holding less than two-thirds of the stock), the district court concluded that the "meaningful reduction" test had been satisfied. The district court included the Hicks option in its calculations pursuant to the plain language of the attribution statute, §318(a)(4), which stated (emphasis added): "If *any* person has an option to acquire stock, such stock shall be considered as owned by such person."

On appeal, the Government urges that §318(a)(4) actually applies only to the taxpayer or to individuals whose shares are otherwise attributable to the taxpayer. The Government would therefore greatly narrow the scope of §318(a)(4). Under the Government's view of the statute, the Trust's ownership interest in Puritan was reduced only 4% as a result of the redemption, from 97 to 93%, which, it contends, was not meaningful as a matter of law.

"[I]n determining the scope of a statute, one is to look first at its language." Dickerson v. New Banner Institute, Inc., [460 U.S. 103, 100] (1983). . . . "Absent a clearly expressed legislative intention to the contrary, that language must ordinarily be regarded as conclusive." Consumer Product Safety Comm'n v. GTE Sylvania, Inc., 447 U.S. 102, 108 (1980). Further, "[i]t is axiomatic that where a statute is clear and unambiguous on its face, a court will not look to legislative history to alter the application of the statute except in rare and exceptional circumstances." Pope v. Rollins Protective Services Co., 703 F.2d 197, 206 (5th Cir. 1983). . . . Finally, "Congress is presumed to use words in their ordinary sense unless it expressly indicates the contrary." Davis Bros., Inc. v. Donovan, 700 F.2d 1368, 1370 (11th Cir. 1983). . . .

Nevertheless, the Government invites this court to examine the legislative history of §318(a)(4) and conclude that "any person" actually means only those "parties in the line of attribution." . . . The Government relies on the commentary in the "Detailed Discussion of Bill" portion of the Senate Report relative to §318(a)(3) (currently effective as §318(a)(4)). The commentary describes the operation of the relevant portions of the attributive statute in the following manner:

§318. Constructive Ownership of Stock

This section describes the area in which although in fact transactions related to stock ownership are in connection with a specific individual, ownership of stock is deemed to be in the hands of persons other than the person directly involved. Thus, for the purpose of determining whether a redemption of stock qualifies as a disproportionate redemption . . . consideration is given not only to the stock held by such person but also to stock owned by members of his family. . . .

The area of constructive ownership includes members of the family, persons having interests in . . . trusts, . . . such . . . trusts, . . . and stock held under an option.

In the family area (sec. 318(a)(1)) an individual is deemed to own stock owned by his parents, his children, and his grandchildren. . . . In the case of trusts, . . . the beneficiary or grantor is deemed to own his proportionate interest in the stock owned by the trust or estate and the trust or estate is deemed to own all of the stock owned by its beneficiaries or grantors. In any of the cases *above described* where stock, though not owned, is subject to an option, the holder of such option is deemed to own such stock (sec. 318(a)(3)).

S. Rep. No. 1622, 83d Cong., 2d Sess. 45 (emphasis added).

The Government urges that as a result of the commentary's apparent limitation of the option attribution rule to "the cases above described," "the Senate indicated its intent that §318(a)(3) (now §318(a)(4)) should be limited to parties in the line of attribution." The Internal Revenue Service has consistently followed the reasoning herein argued by the Government, see, e.g., Rev. Rul. 68-601, and the tax court has adopted the Service's view as well. However, only two appeals courts have addressed the issue and they, without analysis, adopted diverse positions.

In Friend v. United States, 345 F.2d 761 (1st Cir. 1965), the First Circuit's dictum indicated that that court believed that "Congress intended that section to apply only where options are held by the person whose shares are being redeemed." 345 F.2d at 764. In Sorem v. C.I.R., 334 F.2d 275, 280 (10th Cir. 1964), the court, again without analysis, applied the plain language of the options attribution provision of §318(a), and rejected the Government's view.

The Government argues that this court should defer to the Service's consistently-applied interpretation of the Code. However, while it is axiomatic that where statutory language remains vague even when illuminated by the legislative history, the construction offered by the agency charged with the enforcement of the statute will often be accorded dispositive weight, it is an equal principle that the agency may not so interpret the statute as to controvert its plain and unambiguous language. Except in "rare and exceptional circumstances," Rubin v. United States, supra, such as where Congress "expressly indicates" its intent that the plain meaning of the statutory language be avoided, Davis Bros., Inc. v. Donovan, supra, unambiguous statutory language "is to be regarded as conclusive." Dickerson v. New Banner Institute, supra.

Instantly, the Government asserts only the commentary of the Senate Report, reprinted above, as support for its construction of "any person" in §318(a)(4). The commentary falls short of a clear indication by Congress that the natural impact of the statutory language under review should be restrained. Accordingly, the district court appropriately included the option shares held by Hicks in determining the Trust's relative holdings prior to and following redemption.

It should be noted that, even if the Hicks shares were excluded, on the instant record the district court would have been entitled to enter the factual finding that the transaction under review was not essentially equivalent to a dividend and was therefore properly claimed as a capital gain. "The question whether a distribution in redemption of stock . . . is not essentially equivalent to a dividend . . . depends upon the facts and circumstances of each case." 26 C.F.R. §1.302-3(b) (1983 Treasury Regulations); United States v. Davis, supra. Obviously, one of the pertinent facts would be the relative holdings of the taxpayer as computed under §318's constructive stock ownership provisions, 26 C.F.R. §1.302(b). United States v. Davis. However, neither statutory enactment nor judicial construction would support the proposition that the resulting comparative calculation would become the exclusive and dispositive fact. In this case, the redemption effected "a change in the relative economic interests or rights" of all the stockholders of the Puritan company. Therefore, despite the fact that — excluding operation of §318(a)(4) — the Trust's relative holdings fell only 4% after redemption, under the unique facts and circumstances of this case, such was a "meaningful reduction" and the distribution was therefore not a dividend.

Accordingly, because substantial evidence supports the district court's factual determination that the transaction was not essentially equivalent to a dividend, the judgment below is affirmed.

NOTE

1. *The chain of attribution in* Patterson Trust. At issue in *Patterson Trust* was the taxation of the distribution in redemption of all of the shares owned by the trust. The trust could not qualify for exchange treatment under the complete termination safe harbor of §302(b)(3) because it constructively owned shares in the corporation after the redemption. Which shares did it constructively own?

Because Ella was a beneficiary of the trust, all her shares were attributed to the trust under §318(a)(3)(B)(i). Note that there is complete attribution from Ella to the trust regardless of her actuarial interest in the trust corpus. If however, Ella had had only a remote contingent interest in the trust corpus, then there would have been *no* attribution under §318(a)(3)(B)(i).

Could the trust have filed an election under §302(c)(2)(C) and thereby have avoided all attribution from Ella? Recall that the §302(c)(2) waiver applies only to the *family* attribution rules of §318(a)(1). Since attribution from Ella to the trust arises under §318(a)(3), a §302(c) waiver would have had no effect on the attribution to the trust of the shares actually owned by Ella.

Not only are the shares actually owned by Ella attributed to the trust, but shares constructively owned by Ella may also be attributed to the trust under §318(a)(5)(A). Thus, the shares actually owned by Ella's children — Hank, John, and Ellen — are attributed to Ella and then to the trust under §318(a)(1)(A)(ii), (a)(3)(B)(ii), and (a)(5)(A). While a §302(c)(2) waiver would avoid the attribution from Hank, John, and Ellen to Ella, that waiver applies only to determinations under §302(b)(3).

Are the shares actually owned by Hicks attributed to the trust? No. There can be attribution from Hicks to his wife, Ellen, see §318(a)(1)(A)(i), but those shares cannot be further attributed from Ellen to her mother because of the antisidewise attribution limitation in §318(a)(5)(B). Similarly, in computing Hicks's constructive ownership, there will be attribution of those shares actually owned by Ellen, see §318(a)(1)(A)(i), but he will not be attributed any shares Ellen only constructively owns (i.e., stock actually owned by family members) because of §318(a)(5)(B).

The number of shares owned by Hicks was relevant in *Patterson Trust* because, for making determinations under §302(b)(2), a shareholder's percentage ownership is a function of the number of shares owned (actually and constructively) by the shareholder relative to the total number of shares outstanding. For computing the total number of shares outstanding, should shares attributed from one shareholder to another be counted twice? Did the court in *Patterson Trust* count any shares twice?

Under §318(a)(4), shares subject to an option are treated as owned by the person having the option. The Service argued in *Patterson Trust* that this provision was intended to ensure that a taxpayer could not qualify for exchange treatment on a redemption while possessing the ability to reacquire a substantial interest in the corporation by exercise of an option. Thus, according to the Service, §318(a)(4) is applicable only in determining the constructive ownership of the taxpayer receiving a distribution in redemption of some of his shares.

The court, however, refused to read §318(a)(4) as limited in this way. Accordingly, the court treated the option given to Hicks as shares constructively owned by him, thereby increasing the total number of shares outstanding. The effect of the court's interpretation of §318(a)(4) was to reduce the trust's pre- and postredemption percentage of ownership of the corporation. Can the test of §302(b)(2) be manipulated through the strategic use of options as part of redemption transactions? See Bloom and Willens, How to Treat Option Shares Held by Third Parties in Planning for a Redemption, 62 J. Taxn. 80 (1985).

Suppose the option in *Patterson Trust* had been exercisable only after a specified period of time. Would §318(a)(4) still apply to the option? In Rev. Rul. 89-64, 1989-1 C.B. 91, the Service ruled that §318(a)(4) continues to apply. This ruling does not address the length of the specified period. If an option was exercisable only after 50 years, should the option fall under §318(a)(4)?

2. *The limited role of §302(b)(1).* As *Davis* indicates, the courts have given §302(b)(1) a narrow scope. In Levin v. Commissioner, 385 F.2d 521 (2d Cir. 1967), the court reviewed the legislative history of §302(b)(1) before concluding that "it was intended to play a modest role in the statutory scheme." The court agreed with the observation that the "major function" of §302(b)(1) was to immunize redemptions of minority holdings of (nonvoting) preferred stock, citing B. Bittker and J. Eustice, Federal Income Taxation of Corporations and Shareholders 291 (2d ed. 1966). But see Rev. Rul. 85-106, 1985-2 C.B. 116, in which the Service ruled that §302(b)(1) is inapplicable to the redemption of six of nine shares of preferred stock held by a trust when the trust owns, with attribution, 18 percent of the corporation's voting common stock both before and after the redemption.

What role should §302(b)(1) play? In Wright v. United States, 482 F.2d 600 (8th Cir. 1973), the court held that a redemption reducing a shareholder's ownership from 85 percent to 61.7 percent was not essentially equivalent to a dividend when state law imposed a two-thirds voting requirement on certain corporate actions. Compare Rev. Rul. 78-401, 1978-2 C.B. 127, in which the Service ruled that a reduction in ownership from 90 percent to 60 percent was essentially equivalent to a dividend when no action requiring a supermajority was contemplated. See also Rev. Rul. 75-502, 1975-2 C.B. 111, in which the Service ruled that a reduction from 57 percent to 50 percent could be meaningful when the remaining 50 percent was held by a single other shareholder.

The Supreme Court wrote in *Davis* that "to qualify for preferred treatment under [§302(b)(1)], a redemption must result in a meaningful reduction of the shareholder's proportionate interest in the corporation." How great must a reduction be to be "meaningful"? In Rev. Rul. 76-385, 1976-2 C.B. 92, the Service ruled that a reduction in proportionate interest from 0.0001118 to 0.0001081 was "meaningful." The Service has also ruled, however, that a reduction in interest from 100 percent to 81 percent is not "meaningful." Rev. Rul. 73-2, 1973-1 C.B. 171. Was the court right in *Patterson Trust* when it said that a reduction of the trust's interest from 97 percent to 93 percent could be "meaningful"? Indeed, the court in *Patterson Trust* simply assumed that a reduction from 80 percent to 60 percent is "meaningful." Is this assumption subject to challenge?

In a pre-*Davis* case, the Second Circuit looked to the effect of a redemption on three aspects of stock ownership: (1) the right to vote, (2) the right to participate in nonliquidating distributions, and (3) the right to share in net assets on liquidation. Himmel v. Commissioner, 338 F.2d 815 (2d Cir. 1964). The Service has ruled that a redemption resulting in a reduction of these rights may satisfy the *Davis* "meaningful reduction" standard. Rev. Rul. 75-502, 1975-2 C.B. 111. A redemption of preferred stock might reduce rights (2) and (3) but not (1), while a redemption of common stock with preferred stock outstanding might reduce (1) yet have little effect on (2) and (3). How should these different aspects of stock ownership be combined? Would it be appropriate to look to the relative change in fair market value of the redeemed shareholder's stock?

3.   *Constructive ownership after* Davis. While the narrow issue before the Supreme Court in *Davis* was whether the attribution rules apply to determinations under §302(b)(1), language in the Court's opinion seems to speak to how those attribution rules should be applied to the whole of §302(b). Would it be proper, after *Davis,* to take into account evidence of a shareholder's estrangement from, or independence of, the persons whose shares would be imputed to him under §302(c)(1)? Compare David Metzger Trust v. Commissioner, 693 F.2d 459 (5th Cir. 1982) (family hostility cannot override attribution rules), aff'g 76 T.C. 42 (1981) (court reviewed), with Haft v. Commissioner, 510 F.2d 43 (1st Cir. 1975) (remand to consider whether family hostility might mitigate attribution rules), and David Metzger Trust v. Commissioner, 76 T.C. 42, 80-84 (1981) (Tannenwald, J., concurring); see also Cerone v. Commissioner, 87 T.C. 1 (1986).

4.   *Redemptions by publicly held corporations.* The development of both the statutory and judicial law of redemptions has focused on closely held corporations, which traditionally were the only corporations, that customarily redeemed their shares. In recent years, however, some publicly held corporations have embarked on large-scale programs of repurchasing their own shares. This practice and its tax implications have been described as follows:

> Thus, suppose that *X* Corporation, with one million shares of common stock outstanding, is a stable, non-growth company which annually generates $1 million of earnings after tax, or $1 per share. Unable to reinvest its earnings at a profitable rate of return, *X* decides to distribute the $1 million to its shareholders. The stock of *X,* which normally sells at 10 times earnings, is currently quoted at $11, i.e., normal value of $10 plus $1 per share available for distribution.
>
> If *X* distributes the $1 million as a dividend, and if the shareholders of *X* pay tax at an average rate of 30 percent, then the net wealth per share of an average shareholder following the distribution will be $10.70, i.e., normal value of *X* stock ($10) plus the after-tax value of the dividend ($0.70). In the alternative, if *X* uses the $1 million to repurchase its own shares at $11 per share, it will be able to retire approximately 90,909 shares at that price. Earnings per share will then rise to about $1.10 on the 909,991 shares that remain outstanding, and, with no change in the multiplier of 10, the value of the stock held by non-selling shareholders will be $11, as compared with an average net wealth per share of $10.70 if a dividend is paid. Shareholders who have chosen to resell their stock will hold $11 in cash for each share sold less any capital gain tax resulting from the sale, with the net proceeds varying from individual to individual depending on original cost.
>
> Without detriment to those who prefer to sell, but provided always that the only tax imposed is a capital gain tax on sellers disposing of appreciated shares, *X* Corporation can benefit non-selling shareholders by applying its

"unwanted" cash assets to the retirement of outstanding stock instead of paying dividends. Aside from tax effects, though possibly bearing some relation thereto, share repurchase has the further advantage of providing an option to shareholders, since those who desire current income can obtain it by selling a portion of their shares, while those who do not can avoid it by retaining all of theirs.

The critical assumptions that underlie the tax results just described are, first, that repurchase produces capital gain (or loss) for shareholders who choose to surrender their shares to the company, and second, that repurchase has no present tax consequences (other than the postponement of gain or loss) for those who do not. The Internal Revenue Service has thus far raised no question about the legitimacy of these results as a matter of law. They are also either ignored or taken for granted by the tax bar, presumably for the reason, mentioned above, that dividend equivalency problems are rarely associated with publicly held corporations.

Chirelstein, Optional Redemptions and Optional Dividends: Taxing the Repurchase of Common Shares, 78 Yale L.J. 739 (1969).

What is the statutory foundation for the first "critical assumption" (that capital gain treatment will be available to the tendering shareholder) identified by Professor Chirelstein in the final paragraph of the extract? Is it necessarily the case that any redemption by a publicly held corporation is "substantially disproportionate" (or at least not essentially equivalent to a dividend)? Should the attribution rules be applicable to the redemption of publicly held stock? See Bacon, Share Redemptions by Publicly Held Companies: A New Look at Dividend Equivalency, 26 Tax L. Rev. 283 (1971). As to the second "critical assumption" (that nontendering shareholders are unaffected by the redemption) identified by Professor Chirelstein, you should suspend your judgment until §305 is examined. In general, though, little attention has been focused on the tax consequences of a redemption to a nontendering shareholder. What alternatives are there? See Doernberg, The Taxation of Reinvested Corporate Earnings, 24 Wm. & Mary L. Rev. 1 (1982).

5. *Redemption of stock versus retirement of bonds.* Section 302 speaks of a redemption of "stock." On the repayment of corporate debt, the creditor has no gain or loss unless she receives more than her basis for the debt instrument. Even if there is a gain, the retirement of corporate bonds and other evidences of indebtedness is ordinarily a capital gain or loss transaction by virtue of §1271(a)(1), and there is no counterpart of §302 in the Code to treat the retirement of such creditor instruments as a distribution of earnings and profits. Once more (recall the discussion of equity and debt in Chapter 3), we find the Code smiling on the issuance of debt instruments instead of stock by the newly organized corporation and the ongoing, closely held corporation. Note the radically different treatment Davis would have received had the monies advanced for the preferred stock instead been contributed for bonds. See the penultimate

paragraph in the *Davis* opinion. But the same criteria that turn ostensible bonds or debentures into stock so as to deny an interest deduction may also require the bonds to be treated as stock under §302.

   6.   *Redemption of §306 stock.* A possible end-run around §§302 and 301 takes the form of a sale of a shareholder's stock to an unrelated third party from whom the stock is later redeemed by the corporation. For example, how should a shareholder be taxed if he sells some of his shares in a closely held corporation to a third party subject to the understanding that the shares will be redeemed immediately? How definite must such an "understanding" be for the Commissioner to attribute the redemption to the selling shareholder? In any event, is the Commissioner likely to be able to discern the presence of a prearranged plan of redemption from the facts disclosed on the parties' tax returns?

   A shareholder who tries this route to avoid §§302 and 301 may well find himself out of the frying pan and into the fire if he uses common stock as the bailout mechanism. What happens if, for example, the third party refuses to accede to the redemption? The tax-avoiding shareholder might end up with a stranger owning (and voting) a significant portion of the stock of his corporation. For this reason, sales of stock subject to prearranged redemptions will most often involve nonvoting preferred stock.

   Section 306, dealing with the redemption or sale of certain classes of stock (primarily preferred stock issued as a stock dividend), is examined at page 303 infra. Consider also in this context the tax advantages of the gift of stock to a charitable organization in anticipation of redemption.

   7.   *Redemptions to pay death taxes.* Section 303, relating to distributions in redemption of stock to pay death taxes as well as funeral and administration expenses, first entered the Code in 1950. The general purpose of §303 is to protect against forced sales of family businesses. Consider, for example, the case of a taxpayer who at death leaves a substantial estate composed predominantly of the stock of a closely held corporation. The decedent's executor will need cash for the payment of administrative expenses, funeral costs, the federal estate tax, and possibly a state inheritance tax. With such an illiquid estate, the executor may have no choice but to cause the corporation to redeem some of the estate's stock to raise the needed funds. Although the estate will have a fair market value adjusted basis in the stock pursuant to §1014, in the absence of §303 the estate might incur a tax liability on the redemption pursuant to §§301 and 302. Application of §303, though, will give exchange treatment to the estate on the redemption, thereby eliminating all tax liability by virtue of the basis step-up at death under §1014.

   While the simple example above describes the situation to which §303 was intended to speak, the benefits of §303 are available without any showing that the estate lacks sufficient liquid assets to cover its expenses. The benefit of §303, however, is available only to an estate in which stock of the redeeming corporation constitutes more than 35 percent of its gross value less the deduction provided by §§2053 and 2054 for taxes, expenses, debts, and losses, although the stock of two or more corporations can qualify under certain circumstances, §303(b)(2)(B). Section 303 can apply to taxpayers other than an estate, although it can only apply to owners of stock actually chargeable for debts, expenses, or taxes of the estate and only to the extent thereof.

In Rev. Rul. 87-132, 1987-2 C.B. 82, the Service adopted an expansive interpretation of the transactions covered by §303. An estate and an unrelated individual each owned 50 percent of the outstanding stock of a corporation. The estate wanted the benefits of §303 without diminishing its voting control over the corporation. Accordingly, the corporation declared a stock dividend of new nonvoting stock and then promptly redeemed two-thirds of the nonvoting stock issued to the estate. The Service ruled that this redemption was protected by §303, emphasizing that "the basis of the stock redeemed [was] determined by reference to the basis of the 'old stock' included in the estate."

Because the benefits of §303 are available only to substantial owners of a corporation, shareholders will sometimes seek to inflate their stock ownership beyond their actual holdings. For example, the taxpayer in Estate of Byrd v. Commissioner, 388 F.2d 223 (5th Cir. 1967), argued that the attribution rules of §318 could be applied to determinations under §303. Because §303 does not explicitly reference §318, however, the court held that application of the attribution rules to §303 determinations would be improper, relying on the first clause of §318(a).

In Rev. Rul. 84-76, 1984-1 C.B. 91, the Service ruled that §303 does not apply to redemptions of stock not actually owned by the decedent but includible in his gross estate under §2035(a) (transfers made within three years of death). The Service did rule, however, that such stock can be used to satisfy the 35 percent test of §303(b)(2)(A), thereby allowing stock actually owned by the decedent to qualify for §303 treatment.

Section 303 historically has played a minor role in the drama of subchapter C. Nonetheless, exchange treatment is important not only because of a preferential rate of tax but also because of the recovery of basis obtained prior to the recognition of any income, however taxed. Because of the fair market value basis rule of §1014 applicable to property passing through the estate of a decedent, exchange treatment of postdeath redemptions will avoid recognition of income altogether.

8. *Constructive redemptions.* Suppose a controlling shareholder sells stock at a gain to employees pursuant to a corporate stock bonus plan. Because the corporation had an obligation to sell stock to the employees under the stock bonus plan, the transaction presumably should be recharacterized as a transfer from the controlling shareholder to the corporation and then from the corporation to the employees. In fact, the Seventh Circuit adopted this approach, recharacterizing the transaction as if the corporation redeemed the controlling shareholder's shares (producing

ordinary income under §§302(d) and 301) followed by an issuance of stock by the corporation to the employees. Schneider v. Commissioner, 855 F.2d 435 (7th Cir. 1988).

4. Partial Liquidations under §302(b)(4)

A corporate redemption of stock, if it is a "partial liquidation" within the meaning of §302(b)(4), will be taxed to the tendering shareholders as a sale or exchange. Until 1982, the definition of a "partial liquidation" was in §346. The Tax Equity and Fiscal Responsibility Act of 1982 (TEFRA) repealed that section and moved the definition to §302(e); while the language of §302(e) is not identical to old §346, the changes are not substantive. Accordingly, the case law that developed under old §346 as well as the Treasury regulations promulgated under that section should be considered fully applicable to §302(b)(4).

The definition of a partial liquidation is in §302(e)(1). While the language of subsection (e)(1)(A) mirrors the "not essentially equivalent to a dividend" language of §302(b)(1), the thrust of §302(e)(1)(A) is very different from that of §302(b)(1). Determinations under §302(b)(1) are made by looking to the effect of the redemption on the tendering shareholder and her interest in the redeeming corporation. Determinations under §302(e)(1)(A), in contrast, are made solely by reference to the effect of (and reasons for) the redemption at the corporate level. Compare this with the Supreme Court's holding in *Davis* that corporate purpose is irrelevant to determinations under §302(b)(1). Note also §302(e)(4), which allows a partial liquidation to qualify for exchange treatment under §302(a) even if made pro rata to the distributing corporation's shareholders.

Subsection (e)(1)(B) adds the dual requirement that a partial liquidation be made "pursuant to a plan" and occur "within the taxable year in which the plan is adopted or within the next succeeding taxable year." Note that the "not essentially equivalent to a dividend" language in §302(e)(1)(A) is unlikely to have much impact because §302(e)(2) sets forth a two-part test which, if passed, is deemed to satisfy §302(e)(1)(A).

Rev. Rul. 60-322

1960-2 C.B. 118

Advice has been requested relative to the tax consequences of a proposed distribution by a corporation of cash, realized from the sale of United States Government bonds and excess inventories, to its stockholders under the circumstances described below.

M corporation has 3,800 shares of common stock, par value of 10*x* dollars per share, of which 200 shares are held in the treasury. The balance sheet indicates accumulated earnings of 1,500x dollars.

The corporation was engaged in the business of buying raw skins and tanning and selling the leather to a certain segment of the leather trade. It showed consistent profits until two years ago when the demand therefor suffered a serious, if not a permanent, decline. In an effort to revitalize the business, the corporation changed over to buying raw skins of another kind and tanning and selling the leather to another segment of the leather trade. However, the situation did not improve with the result that continuing losses were incurred and a large inventory of 5,000x dollars was accumulated.

Early in the year under consideration, M corporation determined that further purchases should be curtailed and inventories liquidated. Pursuant to this policy, the inventory was reduced to 3,000x dollars. In doing so, the corporation had sustained substantial operating losses. However, in view of the depressed state of the market and the grim future prospects, the process of liquidating its inventory is expected to be continued and the operations will be carried on at a modified basis with purchases kept at a minimum. In this manner, it is felt that the operating losses can be minimized and if the business decline continues, then a complete liquidation will eventually be voted by the stockholders. Accordingly, the M corporation proposes to redeem a portion of its stock with cash from the sale of United States Series G bonds and from the proceeds of the inventories being liquidated in the ordinary course of business. . . .

Where a corporation has earnings available, in order for the distribution of assets by it to its shareholders to be treated as a partial liquidation, the distribution must result from a genuine contraction of the business of the corporation. See Joseph W. Imler v. Commissioner, 11 T.C. 836. . . . In the instant case, the earnings and profits of prior years were retained in the corporation and resulted in building up a large inventory and investment of funds in Government bonds.

Under the foregoing set of facts, it is held that neither the sale of investments nor the sale of a large part of the inventory in the ordinary course of business constitutes a genuine contraction of the business of the corporation. Accordingly, the proposed distribution of cash for the portion of the stock of M corporation to be redeemed will not constitute a distribution in partial liquidation within the purview of section [302(b)(4)] of the code. The provisions of section 301 will apply to this distribution and, accordingly, the distribution will be taxed as a dividend to the extent provided in section 316.

NOTE

1. *Corporate contractions.* While §302(e) does not explicitly use the term "corporate contraction," that phrase has been the touchstone of a

"partial liquidation" since before the first statutory treatment of partial liquidations. *Imler,* cited in Rev. Rul. 60-322, is the classic example of a contraction of a business.

> The principal building owned by the company had been damaged by fire in 1941. When the company undertook to repair the building it was found that, because of war conditions, the shortage of building materials, and high costs, it was advisable to abandon 2 damaged floors and reduce the 7-story building to one of 5 stories. The consequence was that the company found its facilities inadequate to carry on the retinning and soldering operations formerly engaged in. Moreover, these operations had proved unprofitable in recent experience because of the war conditions and shortage of necessary materials. For these reasons the company discontinued the retinning and soldering operations. This reduction in operations likewise reduced the amount of capital necessary for carrying on the business activities of the company. This was a bona fide contraction of the business operations and consequent reduction in capital used. The company thus had a real and legitimate purpose for reducing its outstanding capital stock.
>
> The motives of the corporation were all related to the above business purpose and were, therefore, legitimate and properly conceived. If the excess of insurance proceeds be set to one side, the surplus of the company had remained almost constant for 10 years. The company had followed a conservative dividend policy throughout its history and had not paid a dividend since 1934. The original issuance of the stock had occurred many years before and there was no connection between the issuance and the redemption of the same. There was no special circumstance or condition relating to the distribution excepting the fact that the company had in its hands the excess insurance proceeds, which formed the basis of the distribution. We are convinced that, except for the fire and excess insurance proceeds, there would have been no distribution.

11 T.C. 836, 840-841.

See Rev. Rul. 74-296, 1974-1 C.B. 80, distinguishing Rev. Rul. 60-322 and finding a genuine contraction in a change of business from a department store to a discount store. Here the taxpayer discontinued most of its operations and then changed the remaining business. Compare Estate of Chandler v. Commissioner, 22 T.C. 1158 (1954), aff'd, 228 F.2d 909 (6th Cir. 1955), in which a corporation distributed substantial cash in a pro rata partial redemption of its shares shortly after selling its general department store and opening a ladies' ready-to-wear store. Held, no valid partial liquidation because the distributed cash came from surplus rather than a reduction in working capital; the new store required as much working capital as did the prior department store.

In an effort to lend a degree of certainty to the concept of "corporate contraction," Congress as part of the 1954 Code enacted the predecessor of §302(e)(2) and (3). Unlike the "not essentially equivalent to a dividend" test of §302(b)(1) and §302(e)(1)(A), the "termination of a business" test in §302(e)(2) is intended to be objectively determinable. To meet the "termination" requirement, the corporation must distribute the assets, *or the proceeds,* of a business that was actively conducted for the five-year period immediately preceding the distribution, and immediately after the distribution it must continue to be engaged in a second trade or business with a similar five-year history. The concepts used by §302(e), and some of its problems, overlap those of §355. Section 355 concerns the so-called divisive reorganizations in which a corporation distributes to its shareholders the stock of a subsidiary corporation operating a going business while the parent corporation continues to operate another trade or business. See pages 510-512 infra.

Regulations under old §346 specify that an "active trade or business" be defined by reference to §355 and Treas. Regs. §1.355-1. New regulations have been promulgated under §355 defining an active trade or business since §364 was repealed, see Treas. Regs. §1.355-3. The examples in Treas. Regs. §1.355-3(c) are especially helpful in determining what activities rise to the level of an active trade or business.

Note that a qualified trade or business must have been conducted for at least five years prior to the partial liquidation. §302(e)(3)(A). If the distributing corporation did not conduct it for that entire period, some other taxpayer must have done so *and* the distributing corporation must have acquired the business in a tax-free transaction. See §302(e)(3)(B). Suppose *X* Corp. purchases all the stock of *Y* Corp. and then liquidates *Y* Corp. in a tax-free §332 liquidation. Has *X* acquired the business formerly conducted by *Y* in a transaction qualifying as tax free under §302(e)(3)(B)? See Treas. Regs. §1.355-3(b)(4)(i).

2. *Distributions of working capital.* The Service has ruled that on a genuine corporate contraction a distribution in partial liquidation may include not only the net proceeds from a sale of the operating assets but also an amount of capital equal to the working capital attributable to the terminated business activity. Rev. Rul. 60-232, 1960-2 C.B. 115. At the same time, if a corporation reinvests the working capital of a ceased business in its other business, a subsequent distribution of cash will not be related back to the business cessation. Rev. Rul. 67-299, 1967-2 C.B. 138. See also Gordon v. Commissioner, 424 F.2d 378 (2d Cir. 1970), holding that a distribution of less than the entire proceeds received from the sale of an active trade or business cannot qualify as a partial liquidation.

3. *Surrender of shares.* If no shares are surrendered, as is true in an informal pro rata partial liquidation of a closely held corporation, the transaction may nevertheless qualify as a redemption. See Fowler Hosiery v. Commissioner, 301 F.2d 394 (7th Cir. 1962). See also Joint Comm. on Taxn., General Explanation of the Tax Equity and Fiscal Responsibility Act of 1982, at 126 (1982). What portion of the shareholders' basis will be applied against the amount realized? See Rev. Rul. 57-334, 1957-2 C.B. 240. Is a distribution likely to qualify as a redemption described in §302(b)(1)-(3) if no shares are surrendered?

If the recipient of a distribution in partial liquidation is itself a corporation, §302(b)(4)(A) renders §302(a) inapplicable. Why this difference in treatment between individual and corporate shareholders of a distributing corporation? Note that because of the dividends-received deduction of §243 this rule will most often work in favor of corporate shareholders. The discontinuance of a subsidiary's business and distribution of its assets (or the proceeds) to the shareholders of its parent may work a partial liquidation of the *parent* corporation. See Rev. Rul. 75-223, 1975-1 C.B. 109, clarified, Rev. Rul. 77-376, 1977-2 C.B. 107. But see Rev. Rul. 79-184, 1979-1 C.B. 143. Until 1982, exchange treatment for partial liquidations was available to corporate and noncorporate shareholders alike.

Consider, for example, the case of *ABC*, Inc., which operates a business and also owns all the stock of *XYZ*, Inc., which operates a second business. Suppose *XYZ* sells its business and distributes the proceeds to *ABC* in a liquidating distribution, which then distributes those proceeds to its own shareholders, all of whom are individuals. How will the distribution to *ABC* be taxed? How should the distribution to the shareholders of *ABC* be taxed?

4.   *Corporate distributees.* Corporate shareholders cannot qualify for sale or exchange treatment under the partial liquidation provision of §302(b)(4). See §302(b)(4)(A). For the most part, this limitation works in favor of corporate shareholders because of the dividends-received deduction provided by §243. Under §1059(e)(1)(A), however, a corporate shareholder receiving a distribution in redemption of stock that would qualify as a partial liquidation to a noncorporate shareholder must treat the distribution as an extraordinary dividend. Recall that, under §1059(a), a corporation must reduce its basis in stock held for less than two years by any extraordinary dividends received with respect to such stock. Thus, a partial liquidation to a corporate distributee eventually will produce the equivalent of sale or exchange treatment if the corporate distributee does not hold its remaining stock in the distributing corporation for two years. See the discussion of §1059 at page 180 supra.

B.   TREATMENT OF THE CORPORATION

As discussed at pages 135-141 supra, a corporation, as a general rule, recognizes gain but not loss on a nonliquidating distribution of property. §311(b). Since redemptions under §302 are a subclass of the more general term "distributions," the redemption of stock with appreciated property ordinarily will result in recognition of gain to the distributing corporation.

A corporation redeeming some of its shares must consider the earnings and profits implication of the transaction. To the extent that gain is recognized by the distributing corporation (because appreciated property is distributed), earnings and profits will be increased pursuant to §312(b). Also, because the transaction involves a distribution of corporate assets, a decrease to the earnings and profits account also might be in order. How should a redemption affect the distributing corporation's earnings and profits? If the redemption is taxed under §301, then presumably the usual rule of §312(a) ought to apply. But what if the redemption is taxed to the shareholder as an exchange pursuant to §302(a)?

A difficulty arises when the corporation has appreciated assets, for in such cases the amount distributed in redemption may exceed each redeemed share's allocable proportion of capital plus retained earnings, the excess being an allocable proportion of unrealized appreciation not yet reflected in the corporation's books or its earnings and profits account. Should this excess be charged, in whole or in part, to the corporation's earnings and profits account? The proper resolution of this question was hotly contested. See Anderson v. Commissioner, 67 T.C. 522 (1976), aff'd per curiam, 583 F.2d 953 (7th Cir. 1978).

In the Deficit Reduction Act of 1984, Congress settled the matter. See §312(n)(7). To understand the workings of that section, consider the following example taken from the conference report accompanying the 1984 act.

X Corp. has outstanding 1,000 shares of class A common stock and 1,000 shares of class B common stock. Both classes are $10 par stock, and both were issued for $20 per share (for a total of $40,000). The class A stock has a preference as to dividends and on liquidation in a ratio of 2 to 1 over the class B stock, while only the class B stock votes. If X Corp. distributes $140,000 in cash in redemption of all the class A stock at a time when it has $120,000 in current and accumulated earnings and profits and assets with net value of $210,000, (i.e., with $50,000 of unrealized appreciation), how much of the distribution should be charged to X Corp.'s earnings and profits?

The committee report specifically states that $80,000 should be charged to the corporation's earnings and profits, leaving only $60,000 to be applied against the corporation's capital account. The amount reducing the earnings and profits account is two-thirds of the corporation's total earnings and profits, a fraction determined by reference to the redeemed stock's preferential claim on the corporation's assets. The effect of §312(n)(7) is to allocate part of the corporation's earnings and profits account to each outstanding share, taking into account not only the total number of shares outstanding but also the legal priorities of each class of stock.

How should a corporation's earnings and profits be allocated between common stock and stock that is preferred and limited as to dividends and on liquidation (i.e., preferred stock)? According to the conference report,

[N]o earnings and profits generally should be allocable to preferred stock which is not convertible [into common stock] or participating to any significant extent in corporate growth. Therefore, a redemption of such preferred stock should result in a reduction of the capital account only, unless the distribution includes dividend arrearages, which will reduce earnings and profits.

H.R. Rep. No. 861, 98th Cong., 2d Sess. 840, 1984-3 C.B. (vol. 2) 94.

What are the tax consequences if a corporation redeems a share of stock for less than the share's allocable portion of earnings and profits? For example, suppose a corporation has 100 shares of common stock outstanding and earnings and profits of $1,000. How should the redemption of one share for $7 affect the corporation's earnings and profits? Note the "not in excess of" language in §312(n)(7). According to the Senate Report accompanying the Deficit Reduction Act of 1984, "the committee does not intend that earnings and profits be reduced by more than the amount of a redemption." S. Rep. No. 169, 98th Cong., 2d Sess. 202 (1984).

C. REDEMPTIONS RELATED TO OTHER TRANSACTIONS

1. Redemptions in Lieu of Buy-Sell Agreements

Holsey v. Commissioner —————————————————————
258 F.2d 865 (3d Cir. 1958)

Before Maris, Goodrich and McLaughlin, Circuit Judges.

MARIS, Circuit Judge. . . .

J.R. Holsey Sales Company, a New Jersey corporation, was organized on April 28, 1936, as an Oldsmobile dealership. Taxpayer has been president and a director of the company since its organization. Only 20 shares were issued out of the 2,500 shares of no par value stock authorized; these 20 shares were issued to Greenville Auto Sales Company, a Chevrolet dealership, in exchange for all of the latter's right, title, and interest to the Oldsmobile franchise and other assets with respect to the franchise which had been owned and operated by the Greenville Company. The 20 shares issued were assigned a value of $11,000. Taxpayer's father, Charles V. Holsey, in 1936, owned more than two-thirds of the outstanding stock of the Greenville Company, and taxpayer was vice-president and a director of that corporation.

On April 30, 1936, taxpayer acquired from the Greenville Company an option to purchase 50% of the outstanding shares of the Holsey Company for $11,000, and a further option to purchase, within ten years after the exercise of the first option, all the remaining shares for a sum to be agreed upon. The Greenville Company owned all of the outstanding stock of the Holsey Company from its organization in 1936 until November,

1939, when taxpayer exercised his first option and purchased 50% of the outstanding stock of the Holsey Company for $11,000.

On June 28, 1946, the further option in favor of taxpayer was revised. Under the terms of the revised option, taxpayer was granted the right to purchase the remaining outstanding shares of the Holsey Company at any time up to and including June 28, 1951, for $80,000. The revised option was in favor of taxpayer individually and was not assignable by him to anyone other than a corporation in which he owned not less than 50% of the voting stock. On the date of the revision of this option, taxpayer's father owned 76% of the stock of the Greenville Company and taxpayer was a vice-president and director of that corporation. . . .

On January 19, 1951, taxpayer assigned his revised option to the Holsey Company; on the same date the Holsey Company exercised the option and paid the Greenville Company $80,000 for the stock held by it. This transaction resulted in taxpayer becoming the owner of 100% of the outstanding stock of the Holsey Company. In his income tax return for the year 1951, taxpayer gave no effect to this transaction.

The principal officers and only directors of the Holsey Company from April 28, 1936, to December 31, 1951, were taxpayer, his brother, Charles D. Holsey, and their father, Charles V. Holsey. On January 19, 1951, when the revised option was exercised, the earned surplus of the Holsey Company was in excess of $300,000.

The Oldsmobile franchise, under which the Holsey Company operated, was a yearly contract entered into by the Corporation and the manufacturer in reliance upon the personal qualifications and representations of taxpayer as an individual. It was the manufacturer's policy to have its dealers own all of the stock in dealership organizations.

The Commissioner determined that the effect of the transaction of January 19, 1951, wherein the Holsey Company paid $80,000 to the Greenville Company for 50% of the outstanding stock of the Holsey Company, constituted a dividend to taxpayer, the remaining stockholder. The Commissioner therefore asserted a deficiency against taxpayer in the sum of $41,385.34. The Tax Court sustained the Commissioner. 28 T.C. 962.

The question presented for decision in this case is whether the Tax Court erred in holding that the payment by the Holsey Company of $80,000 to the Greenville Company for the purchase from that company of its stock in the Holsey Company was essentially equivalent to the distribution of a taxable dividend to the taxpayer, the remaining stockholder of the Holsey Company. . . .

It will be observed that section [316(a)] defines a dividend as a distribution made by a corporation "to its shareholders." Accordingly unless a distribution which is sought to be taxed to a stockholder as a dividend is made to him or for his benefit it may not be regarded as either a dividend or the legal equivalent of a dividend. Here the distribution was made to the Greenville Company, not to the taxpayer. This the Government, of course, concedes but urges that it was made for the benefit of the taxpayer.

It is true that it has been held that a distribution by a corporation in redemption of stock which the taxpayer stockholder has a contractual obligation to purchase is essentially the equivalent of a dividend to him since it operates to discharge his obligation. But where, as here, the taxpayer was never under any legal obligation to purchase the stock held by the other stockholder, the Greenville Company, having merely an option to purchase which he did not exercise but instead assigned to the Holsey Company, the distribution did not discharge any obligation of his and did not benefit him in any direct sense.

It is, of course, true that the taxpayer was benefited indirectly by the distribution. The value of his own stock was increased, since the redemption was for less than book value, and he became sole stockholder. But these benefits operated only to increase the value of the taxpayer's stock holdings; they could not give rise to taxable income within the meaning of the Sixteenth Amendment until the corporation makes a distribution to the taxpayer or his stock is sold. Eisner v. Macomber, 1920, 252 U.S. 189; Schmitt v. Commissioner of Internal Revenue, 3 Cir., 1954, 208 F.2d 819. In the latter case in a somewhat similar connection this court said (at page 821):

> During these years when Wolverine was buying its own shares it, of course, was subject to income tax as a corporation. Mrs. Green was subject to tax on whatever profit she made by the sale of these shares to the corporation. But what happened to warrant imposing a tax upon Schmitt and Lehren? If one owns a piece of real estate and, because of its favorable location in a city, the land becomes increasingly valuable over a period of years, the owner is not subject to income taxation upon the annual increase in value. In the same way, if a man owns shares in a corporation which gradually become more valuable through the years he is not taxed because of the increase in value even though he is richer at the end of each year than he was at the end of the year before. If he disposes of that which has increased, of course he must pay tax upon his profit. All of this is hornbook law of taxation; nobody denies it.

We think that the principle thus stated is equally applicable here. Indeed the Tax Court itself has so held in essentially similar cases.

The question whether payments made by a corporation in the acquisition and redemption of its stock are essentially equivalent to the distribution of a taxable dividend has been often before the courts and certain criteria have been enunciated. The most significant of these is said to be whether the distribution leaves the proportionate interests of the stockholders unchanged as occurs when a true dividend is paid. Ferro v. Commissioner of Internal Revenue, 3 Cir., 1957, 242 F.2d 838, 841. The application of that criterion to the facts of this case compels the conclusion that in the absence of a direct pecuniary benefit to the taxpayer the Tax Court erred in holding the distribution in question taxable to him. For in his case prior to the distribution the taxpayer and the Greenville Company each had a 50% interest in the Holsey Company whereas after it was over the taxpayer had 100% of the outstanding stock and the Greenville Company none.

The Government urges the lack of a corporate purpose for the distribution and the taxpayer seeks to establish one. But we do not consider this point for, as we have recently held, "It is the effect of the redemption, rather than the purpose which actuated it, which controls the determination of dividend equivalence." Kessner v. Commissioner of Internal Revenue, 3 Cir., 1957, 248 F.2d 943, 944. Nor need we discuss the present position of the Government that the transaction must be treated as a sham and the purchase of the stock as having been made by the taxpayer through his alter ego, the Holsey Company. For the Tax Court made no such finding, doubtless in view of the fact that at the time the taxpayer owned only 50% of the stock and was in a minority on the board of directors. On the contrary that court based its decision on the benefit which the distribution by the corporation to the Greenville Company conferred upon the taxpayer, which it thought gave rise to taxable income in his hands.

For the reasons stated we think that the Tax Court erred in its decision. The decision will accordingly be reversed and the cause remanded for further proceedings not inconsistent with this opinion.

McLAUGHLIN, Circuit Judge (dissenting).

I think that the net effect of the facile operation disclosed in this case amounts to the distribution of a taxable dividend to the taxpayer. I do not think that the *Schmitt* decision controls here. Quite the contrary to the *Schmitt* facts, this taxpayer himself acquired a valuable option to buy the shares and solely on the theory of a gift of the option rights would make the corporation the true purchaser. I agree with the Tax Court that "The assignment of the option contract to J.R. Holsey Sales Co. was clearly for the purpose of having that company pay the $80,000 in exercise of the option that was executed for petitioner's personal benefit. The payment was intended to secure and did secure for petitioner exactly what it was always intended he should get if he made the payment personally, namely, all of the stock in J.R. Holsey Sales Co."

I would affirm the Tax Court decision.

Sullivan v. United States
363 F.2d 724 (8th Cir. 1966)

Before Vogel, Chief Judge, Blackmun, Circuit Judge, and Stephenson, District Judge.

STEPHENSON, District Judge.

[T]he taxpayer Sullivan purchased the assets of an automobile dealership in Blytheville, Arkansas in 1941. He then formed a corporation to operate the dealership. The individual who became resident manager of the dealership, Loy Eich, eventually acquired 120 shares of the 300 shares of stock outstanding — the rest being owned by taxpayer Sullivan. When Eich terminated his management of the dealership in February 1948, Sullivan purchased his 120 shares of stock. Thereafter, in September, 1948, Frank Nelson became the resident manager of the dealership under an arrangement which included an agreement permitting Nelson to acquire up to forty (40) per cent of the stock and further providing for taxpayer's repurchase of said stock upon Nelson's termination of his employment. After acquiring approximately 38% of the corporation's outstanding stock, Nelson announced his intention to depart from his position in 1956 and offered to sell his stock to taxpayer Sullivan. The corporation's Board of Directors then authorized the redemption of Nelson's stock by the corporation.

The ultimate question before the District Court involved a determination of whether the payment by the corporation in redemption of Nelson's stock constituted a taxable distribution to taxpayer Sullivan, the sole remaining stockholder of the corporation. The District Court found that taxpayer Sullivan was unconditionally and primarily obligated to purchase Nelson's stock in 1956 and that said stock was purchased by the Corporation out of profits distributable as a dividend and therefore held that the taxpayer constructively received income equivalent to a dividend in the amount paid by the Corporation for said stock, ($198,334.58). Initially, an interpretation of the memorandum agreement entered into by Sullivan and Nelson at the time the latter assumed his managerial functions is necessary. The agreement contained the following provisions:

> 6. TRANSFER OF SHARES OF STOCK. It is understood and agreed that Sullivan is permitting Nelson to buy stock in said corporation for the purpose of giving him a working interest only, and said Nelson agrees that said shares of stock cannot and will not be mortgaged, hypothecated or transferred by him, his heirs, executor, administrator or trustee to any person other than William J. Sullivan or such person as said Sullivan directs in writing. Any such sale, delivery or transfer to any other person, firm or corporation shall be null and void. Said Sullivan agrees that he will, within thirty (30) days after such shares have been offered for sale to him, accept the offer to sell, provided always that such shares shall be offered for sale at a price to be determined according to this contract.
>
> 7. TERMINATION OF CONTRACT. Said Nelson agrees that if he should terminate his employment or relationship with William J. Sullivan or employment by the said corporation, and if his connection and association with the corporation should cease or be terminated by Sullivan or the majority owners of the stock of the corporation, then said Nelson agrees to sell and transfer and deliver to Sullivan at the then book value all shares of stock owned by him in the Sullivan-Nelson Chevrolet Co. . . . If said contract is terminated by Nelson or Sullivan as herein provided or by the death of Nelson, the value of the stock owned by Nelson shall be fixed and determined as set up in paragraphs four and five of this agreement. If said Nelson should die or become so disabled by injury or sickness as to become incapable

of managing and operating the business, then said Sullivan shall have the immediate and exclusive rights to purchase the stock owned by Nelson or by his heirs, administrators or executors in accordance with the terms of this contract. Title so (sic) said shares of stock shall automatically rest in Sullivan upon Nelson's death and said Sullivan shall be obligated to Nelson's personal representative or representatives for the value thereof as fixed by this agreement.

On the face of the agreement it would appear that Sullivan obligated himself to purchase Nelson's stock when it was offered to him for sale. The petitioner contends, however, that such an interpretation is contrary to the intention of the parties to the agreement and is not in conformity with the circumstances existing at the time the parties entered into the agreement. . . .[5]

At this juncture, the payment by the corporation to Nelson presents two basic questions: (1) Was that payment in actuality a dividend and therefore includable in Sullivan's gross income under §§61(a)(7), 316(a) and 301(c)(1) of the Internal Revenue Code? (2) If the payment is considered as a corporate redemption of stock, was the payment includable in Sullivan's gross income as being essentially equivalent to a dividend within the meaning of §302(b)(1)? This court has recognized that both questions are to be resolved as fact issues. Idol v. Commissioner of Internal Revenue, 319 F.2d 647 (8th Cir. 1963). If a finding is supported by substantial evidence on the record as a whole and is not against or induced by an erroneous view of the law, it will not be disturbed on appeal.

When an individual shareholder receives an economic benefit through a diversion of corporate earnings and profits, such a receipt may be taxed as a constructive dividend. This court set forth a criteria for determining whether a payment constitutes a constructive dividend in Sachs v. Commissioner of Internal Revenue, 277 F.2d 879, 882-883 (8th Cir. 1960):

> The motive, or expressed intent of the corporation is not determinative, and constructive dividends have been found contrary to the expressed intent of the corporation. The courts, as arbiters of the true nature of corporate payments, have consistently used as a standard the measure of receipt of economic benefit as the proper occasion for taxation. (footnote omitted)

This court has also adopted criteria for determining whether a redemption of stock is essentially equivalent to a dividend. See Heman v. Commissioner of Internal Revenue, 283 F.2d 227, 230-231 (8th Cir. 1960);

---

5. The taxpayer makes an alternative argument to the effect that, even if he was unconditionally obligated to purchase Sullivan's stock, subsequent events constituted a modification or novation of that agreement. Even if this contention is accepted, the court is at a loss as to how the taxpayer is aided. The novation or modification itself would be considered as resulting in an economic benefit and possible constructive dividend taxable against Sullivan. The taxpayer would be left in essentially the same position with respect to his possible tax liability.

United States v. Carey, 289 F.2d 531, 537 (8th Cir. 1961). While there is no sole decisive test in this connection, the several guidelines for the determination include "whether there is a bona fide corporate business purpose, whether the action was initiated by the corporation or by the shareholders, whether there was a contraction of the business, and whether there was a substantial change in proportionate stock ownership." Idol v. Commissioner of Internal Revenue, 319 F.2d 647, 651 (8th Cir. 1963). In addition, the Court has observed that the "net effect of the transaction is at least an important consideration in determining dividend equivalency." . . .

The general net effect and the purpose of and circumstances surrounding the transaction involved herein must be carefully scrutinized to ascertain whether Sullivan received a taxable dividend. Prior to the transaction, Sullivan held approximately 62% of the shares outstanding while Nelson owned the remaining shares. As previously discussed, Sullivan was unconditionally obligated to purchase Nelson's stock if it was offered to him for sale. After the transaction was completed, the relevant facts were essentially as follows: (1) Sullivan's personal obligation had been discharged (2) Sullivan owned all of the outstanding shares of stock of the corporation (3) the corporation's assets were decreased by the amount paid to Nelson for his stock (4) Nelson's stock was held by the corporation as treasury stock. It is true that in terms of the financial worth of Sullivan's interest in the corporation, it was the same after the transaction as it was before.[7] The transaction still resulted in an economic benefit to Sullivan, however, because he was relieved of his personal obligation to purchase Nelson's stock. After careful consideration this court concludes that there was no corporate business purpose or other factor which justifies the taxpayer's position that as to him the payment must be considered a stock redemption and not the equivalent of a dividend.[9] On the facts of this case, Sullivan received a taxable dividend as the result of the corporation's purchase of Nelson's stock.

This court is aware that it is often difficult to distinguish true substance from mere form. Tax law places some weight and significance on form and the choice of one alternative rather than another for achieving a desired end is often critical and may be determinative of the tax effect

---

7. Prior to the transfer of Nelson's stock Sullivan owned 186 shares of the 300 shares outstanding. His stock at this time was worth approximately $323,597.00. After the transfer, his 186 shares were the only outstanding stock of the corporation. Due to the corporate purchase of Nelson's stock, however, the value of the taxpayer's shares remained at approximately $323,597.00.

9. The taxpayer has strongly urged that there was a corporate business purpose motivating the purchase of Nelson's stock because of the valuable services received from him as resident manager of the corporation. The services had already been performed, however, when the stock was purchased. Moreover, it was Sullivan, not the corporation, who was obligated to purchase the stock. Under these circumstances, the District Court properly found that the purchase was not induced by a business purpose. The net effect of the transaction further indicates that a dividend was received by the taxpayer.

of a transaction. Judge Becker's opinion comprehensively deals with the evidence and the applicable law of this case. The taxpayer has failed to establish grounds for reversal. The judgment of the District Court is affirmed.

NOTE

1. *Form and substance.* Are the facts of *Sullivan* so different from *Holsey* as to justify such diametric tax results? In each case, shares that the taxpayer might have purchased were in fact bought by the corporation. In *Sullivan,* the taxpayer had an obligation to purchase the shares while in *Holsey* the taxpayer had only an option. These two cases should make clear that buy-sell agreements ought never require one shareholder to purchase the shares of another but instead should only require one shareholder *or the corporation* to purchase the shares. Since the pitfall of *Sullivan* can be avoided so easily, should the courts allow it to exist at all? One experienced jurist remarked in this context that he would "leave for another day [the possibility of creating] an exception to the now concretized standard of form over substance in [this area]." Jacobs v. Commissioner, 41 T.C.M. (CCH) 951 (1981) (Tannenwald, J.).

Suppose the shareholders of X Corp. agree that upon the death of any one shareholder, the remaining shareholders will purchase the decedent's stock from her estate. If the shareholders cancel this agreement and replace it with a provision that the corporation will purchase the shares of any deceased shareholder, will they have successfully overcome the *Sullivan* trap? Apparently so, at least if the novation occurs prior to the death of all shareholders. See Rev. Rul. 69-608, 1969-2 C.B. 42.

2. Redemptions as Part of Bootstrap Acquisitions

Redemptions are sometimes utilized to effect "shoestring" purchases of closely held corporations. For example, suppose *A,* who owns all the stock of a corporation, wishes to sell out to *B,* but *B* cannot finance the entire purchase. The corporation's assets include a substantial amount of cash and marketable securities. *A* sells part of his stock to *B,* and the corporation redeems the rest of *A*'s stock, using its cash and securities to make payment. Note that if part of *A*'s stock had been redeemed while *A* was the sole shareholder, the redemption would have been essentially equivalent to a dividend. Despite this fact, it was held under the 1939 Code's predecessor to §302(b)(1) that a redemption following a sale, as described above, is a sale by *A* of his stock, not a dividend. Zenz v. Quinlivan, 213 F.2d 914 (6th Cir. 1954); Edenfield v. Commissioner, 19 T.C. 13 (1952).

The IRS acquiesced in these cases, although it announced that such transactions "will be closely scrutinized to determine whether the selling stockholder 'ceases to be interested in the affairs of the corporation' immediately after redemption.'' Rev. Rul. 54-458, 1954-2 C.B. 167. See Rev. Rul. 75-447, 1975-2 C.B. 113, concerning *Zenz* and a §302(b)(2) "substantially disproportionate" redemption, ruling that the sequence of redemption and sale is irrelevant. For an analysis of this ruling, see Horwood, Clarified IRS Position Enhances Planning for Stock Redemptions with New Shareholder, 46 J. Taxn. 338 (1977). Do not overlook the fact that a bootstrap acquisition using appreciated corporate property can produce taxable gain to the corporation under §311(d).

What is the result if seller *A* does not wholly sever his relationship with the corporation? For example, he might continue to perform services under a profit-sharing agreement, or he might receive a percentage of the future profits as partial payment for his shares. Would the shareholder in either case have retained a forbidden "interest" in the corporation? Recall *Seda v. Commissioner* and the notes thereafter at pages 191-194 supra. And what about *B*? When the Service announced in Rev. Rul. 54-458, supra, that it would follow the *Zenz* case as to the seller, it went on to say that such redemptions "will . . . be examined to determine whether any payment by the corporation for stock has the effect of a dividend to the stockholders who remain interested in the corporation." Recall the *Holsey* and *Sullivan* cases, above.

When a redemption of stock owned by a corporation is taxed as a dividend, the blow is softened by the 70 percent to 100 percent dividends-received deduction of §243. See pages 134-135 supra. But see Waterman Steamship Corp. v. Commissioner, 430 F.2d 1185 (5th Cir. 1970), discussed at page 178 supra, where an ostensible dividend paid by a subsidiary to its parent, coupled with a sale by the parent of its stock in the subsidiary to a third party, was viewed as an integrated transaction so that the "dividend" was recharacterized as part of the purchase price and not a dividend. As a result of the recharacterization, the parent had additional capital gain (or less capital loss) on the sale of the subsidiary stock.

The following cases illustrate how difficult is it for courts to distinguish redemptions contained within bootstrap acquisitions from distributions occurring close in time to stock sales.

Durkin v. Commissioner ─────────────────────────────
99 T.C. 561 (1992)

COLVIN, Judge: . . .

In Estate of Durkin v. Commissioner, filed June 8, 1992, we decided that the fair market value of culm banks acquired by petitioners on June 26, 1975, was $7.25 million. . . . A culm bank is a refuse pile produced as a byproduct of anthracite coal mining. Culm banks are sometimes reprocessed to produce additional coal. . . .

FINDINGS OF FACT . . .

1. PETITIONERS

James J. Durkin, Sr., and Anna Jean Durkin (petitioners) resided in Dallas, Pennsylvania, when the petition was filed. James J. Durkin, Sr., died on June 30, 1989. James J. Durkin, Jr., and Edward E. Durkin are petitioners' sons. References to the Durkins are to petitioners and their sons.

2. THE ENTITIES

Raymond Colliery Co., Inc. (Raymond Colliery), owned all the stock of Blue Coal Corp. (Blue Coal) and Olyphant Premium Anthracite, Inc. (Olyphant), as of April 1973. Petitioners purchased Blue Coal, Raymond Colliery, Olyphant, and various subsidiaries in November 1973 through a holding company called the Great American Coal Co. (GACC).

James Riddle Hoffa (Hoffa), the former general president of the International Brotherhood of Teamsters, Chauffeurs, Warehousemen and Helpers of America (Teamsters), and James J. Durkin, Sr., sought a $13 million loan from the Teamsters' Central States, Southeast, and Southwest Areas Pension Fund (Central States Pension Fund) and the Mellon Bank to finance the stock purchase. The loan was not made.

Hoffa brought Hyman Green (Green), a wealthy entrepreneur, into the transaction. Green sought a loan from Institutional Investors Trust (IIT), which gave GACC a commitment for a loan of about $8.5 million.

Fifty percent of the stock of GACC was issued to Green and 50 percent was issued to petitioners. Between November 1973 and June 26, 1975, petitioners each owned 25 shares of the stock of GACC constituting 50 percent of the total authorized outstanding shares. Green owned the other 50 shares. Hoffa, Green, and James Durkin, Sr., had an understanding under which GACC stock ownership would be 50 percent for Hoffa, 40 percent for petitioners, and 10 percent for Green. However, the stock was not transferred because of restrictions imposed by IIT. . . .

3. THE JUNE 26, 1975, TRANSACTIONS: PETITIONERS' PURCHASE OF CULM BANKS FROM GACC AND SALE OF GACC STOCK TO GREEN

a. Overview

On June 26, 1975, petitioners purchased the Blue Coal culm banks from GACC and sold their GACC stock to Green. Petitioners also agreed to terminate their employment with Blue Coal. Green negotiated the transactions over a period of several months with James J. Durkin, Jr., who acted on behalf of petitioners. The transactions ended petitioners' ownership of GACC stock and transferred coal properties from GACC to petitioners.

Petitioners (through James J. Durkin, Jr.) and Green both exercised control over the transactions. The parties consulted with attorneys and accountants and attempted various structures before arriving at the final form. Tax effects were considered during the negotiations.

b. Sale of Blue Coal Culm Banks to the Durkins and the Durkins' GACC Stock to Green

Early in 1975, James J. Durkin, Jr., began negotiating with Green to buy the Blue Coal culm banks. Green sought to buy the Durkins' stock in Blue Coal on February 27, 1975, for $1.205 million and to have the Durkins resign their positions as officers and directors of GACC and its subsidiaries. On May 28, 1975, petitioners agreed to purchase certain culm banks' access easements and a breaker site from Blue Coal, Raymond Colliery, and Olyphant for $2.97 million and a 1-dollar-per-ton royalty. Also, on May 28, 1975, petitioners and Millard (acting in his capacity as GACC's executive vice president) signed an agreement that petitioners' culm bank purchase would be conditioned on the fact that, at the time of closing, neither petitioner would own or have an option to purchase any GACC stock. The May 28, 1975, purchase agreement was superseded by a June 26, 1975, agreement (the culm agreement), and modified on January 28, 1976.

In the June 26, 1975, agreement, petitioners purchased the culm banks in issue. The purchase price of the assets sold under the June 26, 1975, agreement was $4.17 million and a 1-dollar-per-ton royalty. The $4.17 million consideration was composed of:

Certified check	$ 254,000
Promissory note	400,000
Cancellation of indebtedness by the Durkins	2,333,920
Assumption of GACC debts by the Durkins	610,000
Promissory note from petitioners, cosigned by their sons	572,080
	4,170,000

. . .

c. Sale of Petitioners' GACC Stock to Green

On June 26, 1975, petitioners entered into an agreement to sell their GACC stock to Green for $205,000, to cancel all indebtedness owed to them from GACC, and to resign as officers, directors, and employees of GACC and its subsidiaries. On June 26, 1975, petitioners resigned as officers of GACC and its subsidiaries. On their 1975 Federal income tax return, petitioners reported that they sold their GACC stock and reported their basis in the GACC stock to be $205,000, thus resulting in no gain or loss on the stock sale. They also reported that they purchased the culm banks, and that the purchase was conditioned on the fact that, at the time of closing, petitioners would own no capital stock or options to buy capital stock in GACC.

In Estate of Durkin v. Commissioner, T.C. Memo. 1992-325, we found that the fair market value of the culm banks was $7.25 million on June 26, 1975.

OPINION

The issue for decision is whether petitioners received a constructive dividend as a result of their bargain purchase of culm banks from GACC on June 26, 1975. Petitioners argue that their June 26, 1975, culm bank purchase and stock sale to Green should be taxed as if it had been structured as a redemption, citing Zenz v. Quinlivan, 213 F.2d 914 (6th Cir. 1954). Respondent argues that in *Zenz* the taxpayer consistently sought to have the transaction taxed based on its form, unlike petitioners here, who disavow the form they chose, and that a taxpayer's ability to disavow the form it has chosen for a transaction is circumscribed, especially in the U.S. Court of Appeals for the Third Circuit, to which this case is appealable. Commissioner v. Danielson, 378 F.2d 771 (3d Cir. 1967), revg. 44 T.C. 549 (1965). We agree with respondent.

1. ESSENTIAL NATURE OF PETITIONERS' CULM BANK PURCHASE AND GACC STOCK SALE TRANSACTION

Petitioners and Green negotiated at arm's length to terminate petitioners' interest in GACC. Petitioners argue that they lacked the ability to control this transaction because of animosity between Mr. Durkin and Green. We disagree. We do not believe that the claimed animosity kept petitioners and Green from jointly controlling these transactions. They distributed GACC's culm banks under terms intended to further their mutual advantage. Petitioners purchased the culm banks for less than fair market value on the same day that Green purchased petitioners' GACC stock for $205,000. Petitioners and Green chose a form for the transactions intended to avoid Federal income taxation of the sale of their GACC stock to Green by separately agreeing to that sale at a price equal to petitioners' basis in the stock, and understating the value of the culm banks.[1]

---

1. For analyses of bootstrap transactions, see generally Bittker & Eustice, Federal Income Taxation of Corporations and Shareholders, par. 9.07 (5th ed. 1987); Jassy, "The Tax Treatment of Bootstrap Stock Acquisitions: The Redemption Route vs. the Dividend Route," 87 Harv. L. Rev. 1459 (1974); Kingson, "The Deep Structure of Taxation: Dividend Distributions," 85 Yale L.J. 861 (1976); Lang, "Dividends Essentially Equivalent to Redemptions: The Taxation of Bootstrap Stock Acquisitions," 41 Tax L. Rev. 309 (1986).

2. STATUTORY BACKGROUND

Sections 301(b)(1) and (c)(1) and 316(a) generally provide that the fair market value of property distributed by a corporation out of earnings and profits for the taxable year to a stockholder is a dividend to the extent it exceeds the amount paid for the property.

The Code provides exceptions to dividend treatment of certain stock redemptions. If a corporation redeems its stock, the redemption is not treated as a dividend if it is not essentially equivalent to a dividend, or if it is in complete termination of a shareholder's interest in a corporation. . . .

Under section 317(b), stock is generally treated as redeemed by a corporation if the corporation acquires its stock from a shareholder in exchange for property.

3. TAX TREATMENT OF TRANSACTIONS STRUCTURED BY TAXPAYERS AS A REDEMPTION

Petitioners assert that their purchase of the culm banks and their sale of GACC stock to Green was in substance one integrated transaction in which they disposed of all of their stock, and which should be taxed as if petitioners had structured it as a redemption. Further, petitioners argue that "the real abuse" of the tax laws in this case is that Green, not petitioners, received a constructive dividend, and that "he, not petitioners, should pay any resultant tax consequences."

Petitioners cite Zenz v. Quinlivan, supra, for the proposition that this transaction should be treated as a redemption of petitioners' interest, which, under section 302(b)(3), is taxable as a sale or exchange of their interest in GACC. In *Zenz,* the sole shareholder sought to sell her stock to a competitor. The buyer purchased part of the stock for cash. Three weeks later the corporation redeemed the taxpayer's remaining stock. The taxpayer, in her tax return, reported the transaction as a complete redemption by the corporation in termination of her interest in the corporation and therefore not a dividend. Zenz v. Quinlivan, supra at 916.

The Commissioner contended that the redemption was essentially equivalent to a dividend. The Commissioner argued that a dividend would have resulted if the redemption had preceded the stock sale, and that the taxpayer should not be allowed to avoid dividend treatment by arranging for the stock sale to precede the redemption. . . .

The instant case is fundamentally different from Zenz v. Quinlivan, supra. The taxpayer in *Zenz* structured the transaction as a redemption that completely terminated her interest, reported it as a redemption of all her stock on her income tax return, and consistently sought to have it treated as a redemption. Zenz v. Quinlivan, supra at 916. In contrast, petitioners did not structure or report the transactions as a redemption. In a redemption, the corporation acquires its stock from a shareholder for property. Sec. 317(b). Instead, petitioners sold their GACC stock to Green for $205,000 (the amount of their basis), and purchased culm banks worth $7,250,000 (as we decided in Estate of Durkin v. Commissioner, T.C. Memo. 1992-325) for $4,170,000. They chose this form after informed negotiations which considered tax effects. Their object was to structure the sale and purchase to be totally free of Federal income tax, including capital gains tax that would result if they had patterned the deal after Zenz v. Quinlivan, supra, by using a redemption. But their plan failed. Their concealed bargain sale was revealed, and respondent determined petitioners received a constructive dividend. As a result, after having first tried to avoid the result in Zenz v. Quinlivan, supra, petitioners now rely on *Zenz*. We disagree that this reliance is justified. The taxpayer in *Zenz* sought to give effect to her treatment of the transaction, while petitioners here seek to disavow their treatment of the transaction. . . .

Petitioners also rely on McDonald v. Commissioner, 52 T.C. 82 (1969), in which we held that the step transaction doctrine was applicable in deciding whether a redemption was essentially equivalent to a dividend under section 302(b)(1). However, that case is no more apt than Zenz v. Quinlivan, supra. The taxpayer in *McDonald* structured a transaction as a redemption and reported it as a redemption on his income tax return. He treated it as a redemption during the litigation of his case. We held that, as in *Zenz*, the transaction may be taxed in the form chosen by the taxpayer. . . .

Section 302(b)(3) provides that a redemption is not treated like a dividend if it is in complete termination of a shareholder's interest in a corporation. Petitioners acknowledge that there was no redemption of GACC stock in the instant case. Accordingly, petitioners fail to meet the terms of section 302(b)(3). The Supreme Court has stated that

> although a court may have reference to . . . [the statutory] purpose when there is a genuine question as to the meaning of one of the requirements Congress has imposed, a court is not free to disregard [statutory] requirements simply because it considers them redundant or unsuited to achieving the general purpose in a particular case. . . . [Commissioner v. Gordon, 391 U.S. 83, 93 (1968).]

Petitioners assert, however, that the sale of their GACC stock to Green and their purchase of the culm banks should be treated as a complete redemption because they are interrelated transactions which resulted in termination of their interest in GACC. They argue that "The redemption was not specifically couched in terms 'redemption' since there was an agreement between Mr. & Mrs. Durkin and Green for the sale of the Durkin stock to Green for $205,000." We disagree with that assessment. Instead, we believe petitioners chose to avoid a redemption to conceal their bargain sale. We have previously rejected a taxpayer's argument that a transaction should be treated like a redemption where no redemption occurred or was contemplated. Reitz v. Commissioner, 61 T.C. 443 (1974), affd. without published opinion 507 F.2d 1279 (5th Cir. 1975) (taxpayer donated all the stock of a corporation to a local Government immediately after corporation declared a dividend for the taxpayer). . . .

4. DISAVOWAL OF FORM BY TAXPAYERS

Petitioners seek to disavow the form of this transaction, and to have it recognized for its substance. The Commissioner may look through the form of a transaction to its substance, Gregory v. Helvering, 293 U.S. 465 (1935), and bind a taxpayer to the form in which the taxpayer has cast a transaction. Commissioner v. National Alfalfa Dehydrating & Milling Co., 417 U.S. 134, 149 (1974). In contrast, "the taxpayer may have less freedom than the Commissioner to ignore the transactional form that he has adopted." Bolger v. Commissioner, 59 T.C. 760, 767 n.4 (1973).[3] . . .

The rule binding taxpayers to the form of their transaction is not an absolute; in several situations taxpayers have been permitted to escape taxation based on their own conscious agreements. In Commissioner v. Danielson, 378 F.2d at 778, the court said:

> In Helvering v. F. & R. Lazarus & Co., . . . the Supreme Court noted that one who must "bear the burden of exhaustion of capital investment" is entitled to a deduction for depreciation regardless of the fact that the taxpayer by agreement designated another as the legal owner. Similarly, in Bartels v. Birmingham, . . . the Supreme Court stated that "in the application of social legislation" such as the Social Security Act, "it is the total situation that controls" liability for employment taxes regardless of the fact that the taxpayer by agreement designated itself as the employer.
>
> In contrast, in the present situation there is no discernible policy which would require that the incidence of taxation fall upon a particular individual. As a result of the circumstances that an amount allocable to a covenant not to compete is amortizable by the buyer and ordinary income to the seller, it generally does not matter what amount is allocated. And where a loss of tax revenues from one taxpayer cannot be retrieved entirely from another because of differentials in tax brackets or other factors the Commissioner may challenge the allocation as not reflecting the substance of the transaction. . . .

In this Court, a taxpayer generally may not disavow contract allocations in covenants not to compete without "strong proof" that the agreed allocation does not reflect reality. . . . We have reached a similar result in a step transaction context. Glacier State Electric Supply Co. v. Commissioner, 80 T.C. 1047, 1054-1058 (1983) (taxpayer not allowed to invoke step transaction doctrine to disavow form of transaction). The strong proof require-

---

3. See generally Smith, "Substance and Form: A Taxpayer's Right to Assert the Priority of Substance," 44 Tax Law. 137 (1990).

ment does not apply to the Commissioner. Empire Mortgage & Investment
Co. v. Commissioner, T.C. Memo. 1971-270, affd. sub nom. Dixie Finance
Co. v. United States, 474 F.2d 501, 505 (5th Cir. 1973).

In the Third Circuit, to which this case is appealable, and in certain
other circuits, taxpayers may disavow an allocation to a covenant not to
compete only with evidence that would allow reformation of the agreement
in an action with the other party to the transaction. . . .

In Commissioner v. Danielson, supra, the taxpayers allocated amounts
to sellers' covenants not to compete. The taxpayers reported the amounts
received as derived from the sale of capital assets. The Commissioner disallowed capital treatment for the amounts allocated to covenants not to
compete. The court said:

> the Commissioner here is attempting to hold a party to his agreement unless
> that party can show in effect that it is not truly the agreement of the parties.
> And to allow the Commissioner alone to pierce formal arrangements does
> not involve any disparity of treatment because taxpayers have it within their
> own control to choose in the first place whatever arrangements they care to
> make. . . .
>
> For these reasons we adopt the following rule of law: a party can challenge
> the tax consequences of his agreement as construed by the Commissioner
> only by adducing proof which in an action between the parties to the agree-
> ment would be admissible to alter that construction or to show its unenforce-
> ability because of mistake, undue influence, fraud, duress, etc. . . . [Com-
> missioner v. Danielson, supra at 775.]

The Third Circuit has also applied the *Danielson* rule to bar a taxpayer
from disavowing the allocation of a sales price to leases. Sullivan v. United
States, 618 F.2d 1001, 1007-1008 (3d Cir. 1980).

Petitioners have not produced evidence that would be admissible in
an action involving Green to alter the construction of their agreement, or
to show its unenforceability because of mistake, fraud, undue influence,
etc., and therefore, under *Danielson,* may not disavow the form of their
culm bank purchase and GACC stock sale. . . .

Under either the *Danielson* rule or the strong proof standard, these
petitioners should not be allowed to disavow the form they chose. First,
petitioners seek to disavow their own tax return treatment for the transaction. Second, their tax reporting and actions do not show "an honest and
consistent respect for the substance of . . . [the] transaction." See Estate
of Weinert v. Commissioner, 294 F.2d at 755. Instead, the prices chosen
by petitioners were an attempt to eliminate petitioners from GACC at a
price and in a form designed to conceal the value of the culm banks. Third,
petitioners are unilaterally attempting to have the transaction treated as
a redemption after it has been challenged. In fact, petitioners first contended that the transaction should be treated as a redemption, and first
relied on Zenz v. Quinlivan, 213 F.2d 914 (6th Cir. 1954), in 1991, 15 years

after the transaction at issue. Fourth, it would unjustly enrich petitioners to permit them to belatedly change the deal made after well-informed negotiations with Green.

A party disavowing the form of a transaction may be unjustly enriched, particularly where the party was acting on tax advice, because the price may be influenced by tax considerations. Danielson v. Commissioner, 378 F.2d at 775. If a party disavows the form of a transaction, the Commissioner may be whipsawed between one party claiming taxation based on the form, and the opposite party claiming taxation based on the substance. Petitioners' argument on brief that the dividend concealed by their transactions is Green's, not theirs, illustrates the risk posed to tax administration if a party might unilaterally disavow the form chosen after a negotiation. . . .

Respondent's challenge to the pricing of petitioners' culm bank purchase does not open the door for petitioners to disavow the form of the transaction. E.g., Juden v. Commissioner, 865 F.2d 960 (8th Cir. 1989) (taxpayer was not permitted to disavow his transaction in a case where the Commissioner successfully challenged the value of property included in the transaction), affg. T.C. Memo. 1987-302. To hold otherwise would at a minimum be an untoward invitation to the kind of mispricing and concealment that petitioners attempted here. It is petitioners, not respondent, that seek to recharacterize their 1975 culm bank purchase and stock sale. Respondent's determination accepts the form chosen by petitioners. Respondent determined that petitioners mispriced the culm banks, but a valuation dispute is not a recharacterization. . . .

Petitioner states that the doctrine enunciated in Zenz v. Quinlivan, 213 F.2d 914 (6th Cir. 1954), derives from the step transaction doctrine. However, this is not an appropriate case to permit the taxpayer to invoke the step transaction doctrine. In Penrod v. Commissioner, 88 T.C. 1415, 1428-1430 (1987), we summarized the step transaction doctrine as follows:

> The step transaction doctrine is in effect another rule of substance over form; it treats a series of formally separate "steps" as a single transaction if such steps are in substance integrated, interdependent, and focused toward a particular result. . . .
>
> There is no universally accepted test as to when and how the step transaction doctrine should be applied to a given set of facts. Courts have applied three alternative tests in deciding whether to invoke the step transaction doctrine in a particular situation.
>
> The narrowest alternative is the "binding commitment" test, under which a series of transactions are collapsed if, at the time the first step is entered into, there was a binding commitment to undertake the later step. . . .
>
> At the other extreme, the most far-reaching alternative is the "end result" test. Under this test, the step transaction doctrine will be invoked if it appears that a series of formally separate steps are really prearranged parts of a single transaction intended from the outset to reach the ultimate result. . . .

The third test is the "interdependence" test, which focuses on whether "the steps are so interdependent that the legal relations created by one transaction would have been fruitless without a completion of the series." . . .

None of these tests is met here. The binding commitment test is not met because there was no binding commitment to redeem petitioner's GACC stock at the time of their bargain purchase and stock sale. The end result test is not met because a redemption was not the end result of the transaction. The interdependency test is not met because a redemption was not done, much less made an interdependent part of the transaction.

Petitioner invokes the step transaction doctrine in an effort to synthesize a redemption of GACC stock. Petitioner takes this position 15 years after the transaction at issue because section 302(b)(3) requires a redemption, and here they avoided use of a redemption. Petitioner is in effect arguing that since capital gains would apply if they had cast it in another form — a redemption — we should grant similar treatment to the form they used. This we cannot do. Glacier State Electric Supply Co. v. Commissioner, 80 T.C. 1047, 1054-1058 (1983). . . .

Decision will be entered under Rule 155.

[Concurring opinion of Chief Judge Hamblen omitted.]

[Opinion of Judge Chabot concurring in result only omitted.]

HALPERN, J., dissenting: Although I fully join in Judge Beghe's dissent, I write separately to emphasize my astonishment at the result reached by the majority and to provide an abbreviated critique for those without the appetite for Judge Beghe's seven-course analysis.

Consider the following example: X Corp. is a successful, closely held corporation, whose outstanding stock consists of 100 shares, each worth $1x$, held equally by A and B, unrelated individuals. A decides that she has had enough of the corporate world and wishes to dispose of her shares and move to Florida. B wants to continue with X Corp. A offers her shares to B, but B has insufficient funds to buy them. There is, however, $40x$ in the X Corp. treasury, and B can obtain $10x$. To accomplish a buyout of A, it is agreed that, sequentially, on the same day, (1) X Corp. will distribute $40x$ to A and (2) B will then purchase A's 50 shares for $10x$. Not being advised by tax counsel, A, B, and X Corp. characterize the distribution of $40x$ from X Corp. to A as a dividend. A's tax preparer, however, is wiser, and treats the whole $50x$ received by A as a payment in exchange for her stock. I am certain that, notwithstanding what the parties called the distribution from X Corp., this Court should treat the transaction as reported by A's tax preparer. See Smith v. Commissioner, 82 T.C. 705 (1984); Roth v. Commissioner, T.C. Memo. 1983-651. I do not think that result would change if, in addition to the facts stated, A, at the same time, purchased an asset from X Corp. at a fair market value price. In essence, that latter case is the case at hand, except that, in the case at hand, the "dividend" was achieved by way of a bargain purchase from the corporation. I fail to see how the tax result for the case at hand can be any different than for the hypotheticals here presented. Accordingly, I believe the majority is wrong.

[Dissenting opinion of Judge Beghe omitted.]

Uniroyal, Inc. v. Commissioner
65 T.C.M. (CCH) 2690 (1993)

CHABOT, Judge: Respondent determined a deficiency in Federal corporate income tax against petitioners[1] for 1982[2] in the amount of $1,320,450.

After a concession by respondent . . . the issue for decision is whether a $16,500,000 cash transfer to Uniroyal by a 50-percent subsidiary is to be taxed to Uniroyal as a dividend or as part of the sale price of Uniroyal's stock in the subsidiary.

FINDINGS OF FACT . . .

Uniroyal was a co-owner of Rubicon Chemicals, Inc. (hereinafter sometimes referred to as Rubicon), a corporation organized in 1963 under Louisiana law. Rubicon's outstanding stock consisted of 2,500,000 class A shares and 2,500,000 class B shares. The class A and class B shares were identical, except with respect to voting rights for Rubicon's directors. Uniroyal owned all of Rubicon's class A shares.

Rubicon's other owner was Imperial Chemical Industries, PLC (hereinafter sometimes referred to as Imperial), which owned all of the class B shares. Imperial is a corporation organized under United Kingdom law.

Imperial also owned all the stock of ICI, a corporation organized under Delaware law. ICI is merely a holding company. Another related company, ICI Americas, Inc. (hereinafter sometimes referred to as ICI Americas), was a wholly owned subsidiary of ICI.

Rubicon manufactured chemicals. Rubicon had two separate lines of business. One line involved the production of diphenylamine (hereinafter sometimes referred to as DPA) and aniline. Aniline and DPA were key raw materials used in Uniroyal's rubber chemical business. Rubicon was the main supplier of these products to Uniroyal. The basic arrangement was that Rubicon leased its aniline and DPA facilities to Uniroyal and Imperial,

---

1. The "consolidated subsidiaries" of petitioner Uniroyal, Inc. (hereinafter sometimes referred to as Uniroyal), are certain related corporations that joined Uniroyal in filing a consolidated Federal income tax return for the year in issue. The dispute in the instant case relates to Uniroyal itself.

2. Uniroyal's 1982 taxable year ended on Jan. 3, 1982.

and manufactured the aniline and DPA for their benefit, for cost
($16,752,000 for 1980, $21,409,000 for 1981) plus a set fee of $600,000
per year. Uniroyal took all of Rubicon's DPA production and about 25-30
percent of Rubicon's aniline production; Imperial or its subsidiaries took
the remainder of Rubicon's aniline production. Rubicon did not sell any
DPA or aniline in the open market.

Rubicon's other chemical products line consisted of two isocyanate
compounds, tolylene diisocyanate (hereinafter sometimes referred to as
TDI) and diphenylmethane diisocyanate (hereinafter sometimes referred
to as MDI). Uniroyal had less of a strategic interest in Rubicon's production
of isocyanates than it had in aniline and DPA. Imperial, however, regarded
MDI and TDI production as an important part of its worldwide business
operations. Isocyanate compounds are used in many consumer and industrial products, including automobile products, construction materials,
appliances, mattresses, and furniture cushions. About 80 percent of Rubicon's isocyanate production was sold in the open market, with the remaining 20 percent being available to its shareholders. Because Rubicon
received only $600,000 profit per year from its aniline and DPA production,
most of Rubicon's total profits came from the sale of isocyanates. The
following table shows Rubicon's income and retained earnings for 1980
and 1981.

	1980	1981
Income before income taxes	$16,167,000	$19,412,000
Net income	9,545,000	10,464,000
Retained earnings	19,733,000	30,197,000

Despite these profits, Rubicon had never paid any dividends to either
shareholder, Uniroyal or Imperial. However, Rubicon paid royalties to
Imperial on the sales of MDI, in the amounts of $1,568,000 for 1980 and
$2,299,000 for 1981.

In 1979 and 1980, worldwide demand for isocyanates was strong. Imperial believed that the demand for isocyanates, particularly for MDI, would
be further stimulated by rising energy prices. Furthermore, at that time
only a handful of companies in the world produced MDI. Thus, in 1979
Imperial began to consider expanding Rubicon's isocyanate business. By
early 1981, Imperial proposed that Rubicon expand its isocyanate production at the immediate cost of about $92 million, to be followed by a second,
similar expansion in 1986.

Uniroyal was not willing to pay half the cost of the proposed expansion
of Rubicon's isocyanate business. During 1980 and 1981, Uniroyal was
emerging from a period of severe financial distress. During this time, Uniroyal placed a high priority on improving its balance sheet. In particular,
Uniroyal sought to repay certain of its outstanding debts and to generate
cash to fund its core businesses. Accordingly, Uniroyal was unwilling to

share the cost of Rubicon's isocyanate expansion both for financial reasons and because Uniroyal was less interested in isocyanates than in aniline and DPA.

Because Uniroyal and Imperial were equal co-owners of Rubicon, no major proposal affecting Rubicon could be carried out without the approval of each shareholder. Thus, consideration of the expansion proposal was at a deadlock. Since Uniroyal's main interest in Rubicon was the production of aniline and DPA, and Imperial was primarily concerned with Rubicon's isocyanate business, a possible solution to the deadlock was to split Rubicon into two separate entities, one to produce DPA and aniline, and the other to produce isocyanates. By early 1981, Uniroyal and Imperial began to discuss the possible transfer of Uniroyal's interests in Rubicon's MDI and TDI facilities.

On June 25, 1981, Imperial's board of directors approved a proposal for ICI Americas to proceed towards acquiring Uniroyal's 50-percent interest in Rubicon for not more than $39 million ($31 million cash plus assumption of $8 million debt).

Imperial's negotiators considered three alternative methods of acquiring Uniroyal's share of the isocyanate business, as follows:

(1) Buy-out of Uniroyal's 50% share of stock in Rubicon. This is essentially the mechanism presented to the [Imperial] Main Board on June 25, 1981.

(2) A Uniroyal proposal . . . based on the concept of full leasing of the Rubicon assets. This would involve the establishment of Rubicon as a leasing company with 100% rights to [Imperial] for isocyanates, 100% rights to Uniroyal for DPA, and aniline rights as currently exist, etc.

(3) A two-company concept formulated during preliminary discussions within [Imperial] which would place the isocyanates and offsites into a 100% [Imperial] company (R2) and leave the residual DPA and aniline assets in a jointly held company (R1) as per the current arrangement.

It was recognized that Uniroyal would want assurances about its DPA and aniline source of supply. This concern caused Uniroyal to balk at Imperial's proposal to buy Uniroyal's Rubicon stock. Negotiators then moved to the third of the above-listed methods. Imperial's negotiators then asked Imperial's board of directors to approve the following proposal: Rubicon would be reorganized into two companies. One company would comprise the MDI and TDI assets and business. The other company would continue to manufacture aniline and DPA under a lease arrangement and would continue to be owned equally by Uniroyal and Imperial. Uniroyal would sell to Imperial Uniroyal's 50-percent interest in Rubicon's isocyanate business for $30 million. This price, which Imperial had considered offering for 50 percent of the entire then-present Rubicon, could properly be offered for 50 percent of the stripped-down Rubicon because of significantly improved projections as to the MDI and TDI markets. . . .

On July 9, 1981, the president of Uniroyal Chemical Co., a division of Uniroyal, sent a memorandum to Uniroyal's board of directors, including the following language:

> Approval is requested to divest the MDI/TDI Assets of the Rubicon joint venture at Geismar, Louisiana. We will sell our interests in all urethane operations, MDI and TDI, to our joint venture partner, [Imperial]. Our share of the assets will be sold and [Imperial] will assume the guarantee of our share of the outstanding debt of Rubicon (approximately $25M in total) for a net price of $31M. Uniroyal will retain its interests at Rubicon to produce Aniline and DPA in support of our rubber chemical and other specialty chemical businesses. . . .
>
> In recognition of the above and after considerable negotiation, [Imperial] has agreed to pay Uniroyal $31M (or some $15M in excess of Dec. 31, 1981 equity value) and will assume the outstanding loan obligation (currently guaranteed by Uniroyal, Inc.) of $12.5M for its 50% share of the assets associated with MDI/TDI.
>
> We respectfully request approval to proceed with this divestment for $31M with the form of the transaction to be finalized.

On July 15, 1981, Uniroyal's board of directors approved the transfer of Uniroyal's share of the isocyanate business to Imperial, at a price and on terms approved by Uniroyal's president and chief executive officer.

Still in July, Uniroyal proposed to Imperial a different method of rearranging their interests in Rubicon. Under this proposal, Rubicon would lease its MDI and TDI plants to ICI Americas, and operate those plants for a fee. . . .

At a meeting of Uniroyal and Imperial negotiators on October 13, 1981, Uniroyal's negotiators indicated that Imperial's two-corporation split-off proposal was not practical and very complex. Imperial's negotiators indicated that Uniroyal's lease approach would not sufficiently protect Imperial's interest in the isocyanate production, and other aspects of Uniroyal's proposal probably would be viewed by respondent as a sale. Imperial's negotiators then proposed a detailed version of a two-corporation spin-off which they said appeared to meet Uniroyal's requirements. The negotiators then discussed the tax consequences of the proposals. Uniroyal's negotiators were basically receptive to Imperial's proposals. The negotiating teams agreed that further consideration was necessary. Among other matters, Imperial's tax manager was to present to Uniroyal's tax manager the following:

> (i)   a detailed explanation of the [Imperial] view of the tax exposure in the lease arrangement;

(ii) the mechanics of the spinoff proposal and a qualitative analysis of its tax position.

On November 20, 1981, Uniroyal's counsel wrote to ICI Americas' counsel as follows:

This will confirm that we will meet on . . . November 24th, . . . to move along some of the detail work which will have to be completed by [Imperial] and Uniroyal now that the "working groups" have agreed to the basic elements of the Rubicon restructuring that are set out below. Obviously my understanding as to such agreement is subject to the final review and approval by management. . . .

My understanding of the conceptual framework of the restructuring is as follows:

The restructuring of Rubicon will be accomplished by the dividend route and the subsequent sale of Uniroyal's stock in Rubicon to [Imperial]. . . .

Rubicon's board will declare and pay a dividend in 1981 (presumably close to December 31st) of all of Rubicon's tax earnings and profits currently estimated to be about $37 million, of which $18.5 million will be paid in cash to Uniroyal and $18.5 million will be paid to [Imperial] in the form of a promissory note. Rubicon will finance the cash dividend as required through the sale of receivables to a third party not affiliated with [Imperial].

Rubicon will also dividend out its stock in R-2 to Uniroyal and [Imperial] the effect of which will be to reduce the tax basis of Rubicon's stock in the hands of Uniroyal and [Imperial] to the extent of the perceived value of the R-2 stock. (The valuation issue will be affected by the fact that the assets of R-2 will be held subject to the Leases and the Operating Agreement, thereby limiting the ability of R-2 to exploit those assets, and by the liabilities assumed by R-2. Presumably the perceived value will be relatively nominal.)

The subsequent sale of Uniroyal's stock in Rubicon to [Imperial] will occur in 1982 for $12.5 million in cash.

The restructuring will not be permitted under Rubicon's Credit Agreement with its banks and Rubicon will have to consider first retiring all bank debt or refinancing such debt in a manner permitting the transaction to proceed.

Currently Uniroyal's tax department does not intend to seek any IRS ruling on the transaction. Uniroyal intends to seek review of Rubicon's 1981 tax return even though prepared and filed after the completion of the restructuring.

As a point of timing and mechanics, I envision that all of the agreements including appropriate amendments to existing agreements will be executed at the time the Rubicon board declares the dividend, thus permitting the parties to fix the price to be paid for Uniroyal's Rubicon stock in a separate stock purchase agreement.

Imperial's tax department prepared a table dated November 27, 1981, showing different acquisition scenarios whereby Imperial would acquire Uniroyal's stock interest in Rubicon's isocyanate assets. Under each of the scenarios, which includes a straight stock purchase, a limited cash dividend ($9.5 million cash to Uniroyal), and a full cash dividend ($18.5 million cash to Uniroyal), the net consideration to be paid by Imperial totals $31 million. . . .

On or about December 28, 1981, Rubicon organized a new corporation called Rubicon, Inc. (hereinafter sometimes referred to as R2), as a wholly owned subsidiary. On December 28, 1981, Rubicon transferred its aniline and DPA assets and liabilities to R2. In return, on December 31, 1981, Rubicon received all 400,000 shares of class A common stock and all 400,000 shares of class B common stock in R2.

As of December 29, 1981, Uniroyal and Imperial entered into an Interim Shareholders Agreement, which includes the following items:

> (1)   As of December 28, 1981, (a) Rubicon is to transfer to R2 its aniline and DPA assets and liabilities and (b) R2 is to transfer to Rubicon 400,000 shares of Class A stock and 400,000 shares of Class B stock.
> (2)   Not later than December 31, 1981, Rubicon is to distribute (a) all of the Class A R2 stock to Uniroyal and all of the Class B R2 stock to Imperial, and (b) $16.5 million "in immediately available funds" each to Uniroyal and Imperial, except that Rubicon's distribution to Imperial is to be in the form of an interest-bearing promissory note.
> (3)   After these transfers, on January 15, 1982, Imperial is to lend $800,000 to R2. This is about equal to the unpaid balance (as of December 27, 1981) of a loan from Uniroyal to Rubicon with respect to Uniroyal's share of responsibility for certain Rubicon assets that relate to MDI and TDI operations. R2 is then to promptly repay that amount to Uniroyal.
> (4)   At a closing on January 15, 1982, Uniroyal is to sell, and Imperial is to buy, Uniroyal's stock in Rubicon, for $13.7 million. Imperial is to assume Uniroyal's obligations and liabilities under a guaranty given pursuant to a June 1, 1978, credit agreement.

The Credit Agreement provides that the two banks will make revolving credit loans in the amounts of $15 million (from Chemical Bank) and $10 million (from Continental Illinois) available to Rubicon. As of December 28, 1981, Rubicon had reached its credit limit of $25 million under the Credit Agreement. Uniroyal and Imperial, as Rubicon's two shareholders, each executed a guaranty with respect to the Credit Agreement. The Credit Agreement contains certain negative covenants restricting capital distributions by Rubicon, among other things. However, on December 22, 1981, Continental Illinois and Chemical Bank notified Rubicon, Imperial, and Uniroyal that the two banks were waiving various sections of the Credit Agreement to permit the corporate restructuring of Rubicon. As of December 28, 1981, Rubicon's board of directors authorized Rubicon to borrow $15 million ($9 million from Chemical Bank and $6 million from Continental Illinois) "to meet current working capital needs." This resolution is reported in the board of directors minutes immediately after the dividend resolutions ($16.5 million and 400,000 shares of R2 stock to each Rubicon shareholder).

A telex dated December 29, 1981, from the London office of Continental Illinois to its Chicago office, states that a $6 million transaction credit to Rubicon for 30 days from December 31, 1981, had been approved. The purpose of the transaction credit was to assist with the corporate restructuring of Rubicon under which Imperial would become the 100-percent owner. The telex contains the following:

> Repayment of the loan will come from funds that [Imperial] is making available today to ICI Americas to payout Uniroyal and to repay this transaction credit (and a similar $9 million credit for Chemical Bank). . . .

As of late December 1981, Rubicon (after having transferred its aniline and DPA assets to R2) could have borrowed at least $20 million from third-party lenders on the strength of its credit alone. This $20 million would be in addition to any preexisting borrowings of Rubicon. Rubicon could then have distributed to its shareholders, without legal or other restrictions, the $20 million, along with the $5 million in cash that Rubicon held at the time.

On December 31, 1981, Rubicon transferred to Uniroyal $16.5 million cash, and to Imperial a $16.5 million 30-day interest-bearing (11 percent per year) promissory note. . . .

On its tax return, Imperial . . . treated the promissory note as a dividend.

On January 29, 1982, Rubicon replaced the December 28, 1981, promissory note to Imperial with a new note for $16.5 million, calling for payments of principal in five equal annual installments of $3.3 million beginning on January 29, 1988, and monthly interest payments on the unpaid principal amount at the rate of 13 percent per year, beginning immediately. The earnings and profits of Rubicon as of the close of its taxable year ended December 26, 1982, were sufficient to cover in full the transfer made to Uniroyal on December 31, 1981.

Also on December 31, 1981, Rubicon transferred to Uniroyal and Imperial all of the stock of R2 in equal amounts. Uniroyal received 400,000 class A shares and Imperial received 400,000 class B shares, respectively, of R2. . . .

A stock sales agreement, dated January 5, 1982, provides that Uniroyal will sell its class A shares in Rubicon to Imperial on January 15, 1982, for $13.7 million. . . . On January 15, 1982, the actual transfer of money and stock occurred as planned, and Imperial became the sole owner of Rubicon. As part of the transaction, Imperial bought certain properties from Rubicon by assuming an $800,000 liability from Rubicon to R2. This $800,000 item, Imperial understood, "was included as part of [the] $31 million purchase price."

By the end of November 1981, there was an agreement between Uniroyal and Imperial that Imperial would pay $31 million for Uniroyal's interest in Rubicon's isocyanate business, but that this obligation would be reduced by the cash transfer that Rubicon would make to Uniroyal.

On December 31, 1981, there was no binding agreement for the sale of Uniroyal's stock in Rubicon, and Uniroyal was the legal and beneficial owner of the stock. After the December 31, 1981, transfers, Rubicon had $16.5 million less cash than before and had also incurred a $16.5 million obligation to Imperial.

The primary purpose of the transactions was to meet Uniroyal's and Imperial's business needs of (1) separating Uniroyal from Rubicon's isocyanate business and (2) continuing Uniroyal's and Imperial's joint ownership of Rubicon's aniline and DPA business. The choice of forms to accomplish this purpose was substantially affected by Uniroyal's view of its tax liabilities under different scenarios.

Opinion

Petitioners contend that the $16.5 million cash transferred by Rubicon to Uniroyal on December 31, 1981, is properly treated as a dividend to Uniroyal, eligible for the 85-percent dividends received deduction under section 243. Petitioners contend that the instant case is controlled by Litton Industries, Inc. v. Commissioner, 89 T.C. 1086 (1987).

Respondent contends that the $16.5 million transfer is in substance part of the proceeds from Uniroyal's sale of its Rubicon stock to Imperial for $31 million, and thus is taxable as a capital gain under section 1201. Respondent invokes "form over substance" and contends that under the step transaction doctrine, the dividend and sale should be treated as a single transaction which was a sale of Uniroyal's Rubicon stock. Respondent contends that the instant case is controlled by Waterman Steamship Corp. v. Commissioner, 430 F.2d 1185 (5th Cir. 1970), revg. 50 T.C. 650 (1968).

Neither side contends that the transactions should be treated in whole or in part as a redemption, with section 302 providing the rule for dividend or capital gain treatment. See, e.g., Estate of Schneider v. Commissioner, 855 F.2d 435 (7th Cir. 1988), affg. 88 T.C. 906 (1987); Zenz v. Quinlivan, 213 F.2d 914 (6th Cir. 1954).

We agree with petitioners that the transfer to Uniroyal is a dividend to Uniroyal.

In general, the "incidence of taxation depends upon the substance of a transaction" rather than its mere form. E.g., Commissioner v. Court Holding Co., 324 U.S. 331, 334 (1945). A taxpayer has the right to minimize taxes as far as the law allows, United States v. Cumberland Pub. Serv. Co., 338 U.S. 451, 455 (1950); . . . however, the taxpayer ordinarily may not, through form alone, achieve tax advantages which substantively are without the intent of the statute. Nevertheless, in the area of stock sales and dividends there are many factual variations, and often slight differences in formal procedure lead to substantial tax differences, even though there are small (if any) economic differences. In this area, it is often difficult to identify the "substance" that is supposed to control over the "form." See, e.g., Monson v. Commissioner, 79 T.C. 827, 844-845 (1982); see also comment by L. Hand, J., in Commissioner v. Sansome, 60 F.2d 931, 933 (2d Cir. 1932), revg. 22 B.T.A. 1171 (1931).

The proper tax treatment of a corporate transfer to a shareholder, closely followed (or, in some cases, preceded) by that shareholder's sale of stock has been the subject of many opinions by this Court and by other courts, not all of them consistent. Additionally, the courts have used a variety of analyses to decide whether a transfer is properly taxable as a dividend or as a part of the sale price. The law in this area is further complicated by the fact that tax treatment may also differ depending on whether the shareholder is an individual or a corporation, or even whether the transferor is a foreign corporation or a domestic corporation. If the shareholder is an individual, then a dividend to the shareholder generally is taxable as ordinary income, whereas if the transfer is characterized as part of the sale price for stock, then the gain may be taxable at a lower effective rate as capital gain, and the amount of gain offset by the stock basis. If the shareholder is a corporation, then a dividend is generally eligible for the section 243 dividends received deduction (or if the corporations file consolidated returns, then the corporation receiving the dividend may eliminate it entirely from income), whereas if the transfer is characterized as part of the sale price, then the gain may be taxable at a greater effective rate as a capital gain. A related issue in this context is whether a transfer which is properly a dividend is a dividend to the seller or a dividend to the buyer. . . .

The form of the transfer here in dispute was that of a dividend to Uniroyal. In the instant case we must enquire further, in order to determine how the transfer is to be taxed. See Litton Industries, Inc. v. Commissioner, 89 T.C. at 1099.

The parties have locked horns on the question of whether the transfer of $16.5 million from Rubicon to Uniroyal may be disregarded as a separate transaction under the step transaction doctrine.

In Esmark, Inc. & Affiliated Cos. v. Commissioner, 90 T.C. 171, 195 (1988), affd. without published opinion 886 F.2d 1318 (7th Cir. 1989), this Court described the step transaction doctrine as follows:

> We recently described the step-transaction doctrine as another rule of substance over form that "treats a series of formally separate 'steps' as a single transaction if such steps are in substance integrated, interdependent, and focused toward a particular result." Penrod v. Commissioner, 88 T.C. 1415, 1428 (1987). . . .
>   . . . The existence of an overall plan does not alone, however, justify

application of the step-transaction doctrine. Whether invoked as a result of the "binding commitment," "interdependence," or "end result" tests, the doctrine combines a series of individually meaningless steps into a single transaction.

In Penrod v. Commissioner, 88 T.C. 1415, 1428 (1987), after explaining the step transaction doctrine as in the quotation from *Esmark,* this Court discussed the different tests which have been applied: The "binding commitment" test, the "end result" test, and the "interdependence" test. Id. at 1428-1430. In Walt Disney Inc. v. Commissioner, 97 T.C. 221, 232 (1991), we stated that "However invoked, the step transaction doctrine combines individually meaningless steps into a single transaction."

The following elements cause us to conclude on balance that the transfer was not a meaningless step in a step transaction situation, and should be taxed as a dividend to Uniroyal.

Firstly, as respondent points out, Imperial faced substantial additional costs (which respondent describes on brief as "an additional $1.2 million dividend tax and a $2.0 million refinancing cost") in order to accommodate Uniroyal's preference for a dividend from Rubicon. Thus the dividend form had real-world consequences to others besides petitioners and the Federal fisc. These real-world consequences were bargained out with Imperial, whose interests in this matter conflicted with Uniroyal's interests. See Henry Schwartz Corp. v. Commissioner, 60 T.C. 728, 738-739 (1973). These real-world consequences of the dividend distribution form weigh in favor of a conclusion that the $16.5 million transfer in the form of a dividend distribution from Rubicon to Uniroyal was real and was not a meaningless step.

Secondly, the matter of Rubicon's financial status, and where the funds for the transfers came from, is more complicated than the question of whether the claimed dividend had real-world nontax consequences. Rubicon had less cash and more debts — aggregating $33 million — after the December 31, 1981, transfers. Rubicon could borrow the necessary funds from the banks on its own credit. Rubicon treated the note to Imperial as a true debt (so respondent's witness testified). However we must factor in two other elements, as follows: (1) The reason for the Uniroyal-Imperial dispute and (2) the fungibility of money. Imperial wanted to expand Rubicon's isocyanate production and had called for an infusion of about $92 million into Rubicon in 1981 and a similar expansion in 1986. Imperial's acquisition of Rubicon's isocyanate capabilities was tied to Imperial's intention to put substantial amounts into Rubicon. If Rubicon was $33 million poorer as a result of the December 31, 1981, transfers, then Imperial would have to put about that much more into Rubicon in order to get Rubicon into the condition that Imperial's planners envisioned for Rubicon. Given the general fungibility of money, one may argue that this differs little from the economics that caused the Court of Appeals to hold in Waterman Steamship Corp. v. Commissioner, supra, that the subsidiary was merely a conduit for the buyer. The Court of Appeals there held that there was no dividend to the seller. On the other hand, in Litton Industries, Inc. v. Commissioner, 89 T.C. 1086 (1987), the dividend was paid by the subsidiary in the form of a promissory note; when the subsidiary's stock was sold, the buyer bought the promissory note at face value. Thus, it could be contended that, in *Litton Industries* also, the funds to pay the dividend came from the buyer. This aspect of the instant case is not an element that inclines us one way or the other as to whether the transfer was a meaningful step.

Thirdly, the parties to the December 31, 1981, transfers committed themselves to the transfers, regardless of the outcome of the proposed sale of Uniroyal's stock in Rubicon. Uniroyal, as a 50-percent shareholder, did not have sole control over Rubicon. Uniroyal could not unilaterally control either the declaration of a dividend by Rubicon, or any subsequent events in the transaction. In fact, although Uniroyal and Imperial were each 50-percent shareholders of Rubicon, and had a common interest in accomplishing the sale of stock, the record reflects arm's-length negotiations for the sale of Uniroyal's Rubicon stock. Thus we conclude that Rubicon's shareholders had committed Rubicon to the transfers before the sale occurred, and that neither Uniroyal nor Imperial could have unilaterally changed that commitment if the sale had not occurred. This weighs in favor of a conclusion that the transfer was not a meaningless step.

Fourthly, we conclude, and we have found, that there was no binding agreement for the sale of Uniroyal's stock at the time Rubicon declared a dividend and made the transfer to Uniroyal. Thus, Uniroyal was the legal and beneficial owner of the stock at the time a dividend was declared and the transfer was made; we have so found.

Respondent contends that the transfer and sale were contemporaneous. Respondent bases this assertion on the fact that the Agreement Respecting Sale of Shares is attached to the Interim Shareholders Agreement. . . . The Interim Shareholders Agreement states that it was "made as of the 29th day of December, 1981." The Agreement Respecting Sale of Shares states that it was made "as of the 5th day of January, 1982," but a signed copy is attached to the Interim Shareholders Agreement. However, respondent's witness James M. Carter, senior counsel for ICI Americas, testified that the transfer preceded the sale of shares by 1 or 2 days. We also conclude, and we have found, that Uniroyal was the beneficial owner of the stock until the agreement to sell the stock was signed. Robert Alvine, president of Uniroyal Development Co., a division of Uniroyal, testified that Uniroyal could have voted its shares between the time that the transfer was declared and the time that the sale took place. Nothing in the record indicates otherwise. . . .

We conclude, on the facts of record in the instant case, that the transfer was not a meaningless transaction, that the transfer had independent significance, and that the step transaction doctrine should not be applied.

Under these circumstances, we are left with the facts that Uniroyal, Imperial, and Rubicon created. We reject the notion that, if there are several ways to accomplish an economic transaction, then the taxpayer should be taxed as though it had selected the way that attracts the greatest tax liability. Compare, e.g., Palmer v. Commissioner, 62 T.C. 684, 693 (1974), affd. 523 F.2d 1308 (8th Cir. 1975), with Estate of Schneider v. Commissioner, 88 T.C. 906, 945 (1987), affd. 855 F.2d 435 (7th Cir. 1988). We conclude that, in the instant case, the form that was used fairly represents the substance of what was done. Because we have concluded that Rubicon paid a dividend when it transferred the $16.5 million cash to Uniroyal, and because we have concluded that Uniroyal was the legal and beneficial owner of Uniroyal's Rubicon stock when the dividend was declared and paid, the $16.5 million cash is a dividend to Uniroyal and not to Imperial.

To the concern that our approach may facilitate taxpayer manipulation and abuse, we make the following responses. Firstly, the Congress has established the general policy that corporate income should be taxed once at the corporate level, and then the remainder (i.e., the income less the corporate income tax) should be taxed again when it is distributed out of corporate solution. The intercorporate dividend exclusion is designed to keep corporate income from being taxed more times, and it has a consequence of delaying the imposition of the second tax. Our holding does not contravene this general policy. Rubicon's income was taxed. What we hold to be a dividend to Uniroyal increases Uniroyal's earnings and profits, setting the stage for the second tax to be imposed on Uniroyal's noncorporate shareholders.

Secondly, the Congress reviews its policy from time to time. The 85-percent exclusion of the year in issue was reduced to 80 percent and is now a 70-percent exclusion, thereby increasing the multiplicity of taxation on corporate income. At the same time, the Congress has expanded the availability of subchapter S pass-through treatment, reducing the multiplicity of taxation on corporate income. For decades, the Congress and the Treasury Department have pondered ways of integrating taxation of corporations and their shareholders, so that corporate income would be taxed only once. . . . Thus, if the Congress wishes to revise its objectives, or change the "ground rules" to reduce abuse, then the Congress has both the power and the will to do so.

Thirdly, it may well be maintained that our analysis is as likely as not to reduce the overall incidence of abuse. The Court of Appeals for the Fifth Circuit noted respondent's apparent "tendency to rely on 'substance' when beneficial to the revenues or to rely on 'form' when more beneficial to the revenues." Casner v. Commissioner, 450 F.2d 379, 398 (5th Cir. 1971), affg. in part and revg. in part T.C. Memo. 1969-98.

Petitioners place much emphasis on Rev. Rul. 75-493, 1975-2 C.B. 108, which involves a presale distribution of cash to an individual shareholder. The ruling states that the distribution will be treated as a dividend to the seller because the distribution was made before there was a binding agreement to sell the stock for a fixed price. Petitioners contend that respondent should be estopped from urging a result different from that in respondent's ruling. First, we note that a revenue ruling merely represents respondent's position with respect to a certain set of facts, and does not constitute substantive authority for a position. See, e.g., Haley Bros. Construction Corp. v. Commissioner, 87 T.C. 498, 516-517 (1986), and cases cited therein. Second, because we have decided in petitioners' favor on the basis of the statutes and judicial decisions, we do not attempt to analyze or decide the effect, if any, of respondent's revenue ruling on the instant case.

We conclude that the transfer to Uniroyal is a dividend, eligible for the dividends received deduction under section 243.

We hold for petitioners. . . .

NOTE

1. *The* Durkin *transaction.* The taxpayers in *Durkin* wished to acquire some of the assets of the GACC corporation and to relinquish their claim to the remaining corporate assets. The assets they desired were certain culm banks worth $7,250,000 but for which the taxpayers paid only $4,170,000. Why would Green, the remaining shareholder, stand for this raid on the corporation's treasury? Because the taxpayers agreed to sell their stock in GACC to Green for $205,000 although it was worth much more, presumably about $3 million more. That is, the taxpayers gave up cash of $4,170,000 and stock worth approximately $3,205,000 for culm banks worth $7,250,000 as well as cash of $205,000.

Although appearing in a somewhat unusual form, what the taxpayers sought to do in this case is common. Suppose taxpayer A is a member of the X partnership, and taxpayer B is a member of the Y partnership. If A and B agree to exchange partnership interests, this exchange is a taxable transaction for both A and B. Assuming A and B deal at arm's length, the value of their partnership interests should be equal. Call this common value F. Taxpayer A must report gain equal to the excess of F over A's adjusted basis in her interest in the X partnership, while B must report gain equal to the excess of F over B's adjusted basis in his interest in the Y partnership.

We know that A and B are exchanging equal value — that is the definition of an arm's length transaction. What we do not know is the dollar amount of that common value. Note that the lower that value, the less gain (or more loss) both A and B will recognize. Accordingly, the

Commissioner cannot and will not rely on the taxpayers' valuation in such circumstances.

In *Durkin,* the situation was complicated by the interposition of GACC. If we untangle the two exchanges, we should treat the taxpayers as paying full value for the corporation's culm banks and then treat Green as paying full value for the taxpayer's GACC stock. This recharacterization of the transaction would produce additional income to GACC (on its sale of the culm banks) and to the Durkins (on the sale of their GACC stock to Green). In addition, because the additional value deemed paid by Green for the Durkins' GACC stock actually came out of corporate solution, it might be appropriate to treat Green as receiving a constructive dividend. Indeed, this is what the taxpayers argued for in *Durkin.*

Why, then, did the taxpayers lose in *Durkin?* The court said that the taxpayers' argument was premised on a rejection of the form they chose for their transaction. According to the court, the Commissioner was seeking not to recharacterize the transaction but only to revalue it. Are you confident that the court was accurate when it held that "a valuation dispute is not a recharacterization"?

2. *Form and substance in bootstrap acquisitions.* In *Uniroyal,* the taxpayer argued that the $16.5 million cash it received immediately prior to the sale of its stock in Rubicon was properly characterized as a dividend. The Commissioner argued that the cash should be treated as part of the sales proceeds received from Imperial, the buyer of Uniroyal's stock in Rubicon. For a corporate shareholder such as Uniroyal, dividend income is favorable because of the 70 percent to 100 percent dividends-received deduction in §243.

There was a third possibility: The cash might have been treated as a distribution in redemption of part of Uniroyal's stock in Rubicon. Because the remainder of Uniroyal's stock would be treated as then sold to Imperial, the redemption would be treated as part of a transaction completely terminating Uniroyal's interest in Rubicon. Accordingly, Uniroyal would be saddled with exchange treatment on the redemption under Zenz v. Quinlivan, 213 F.2d 914 (6th Cir. 1954), cited in *Uniroyal.*

In determining that the taxpayer's characterization of the transaction should be upheld, the court observed that "the Congress has established the general policy that corporate income should be taxed [only] once at the corporate level" and that treating the presale cash distribution as a dividend to Uniroyal would effectuate that general policy. Yet Congress has long provided that a corporation is fully taxable on gains derived from dealings in the stock of other corporations without regard to the triple or greater tax this imposes on corporate earnings. Has the court in *Uniroyal* then misidentified the congressional "general policy" in this area, or has it simply recognized that Congress sometimes fails to implement its concerns in a consistent fashion?

Consider the case of *P* Corp., which owns all the stock of *Q* Corp. with adjusted basis of $1,000. Q in turn owns all the stock of R Corp. with adjusted basis and fair market value of $500. If a third party wished to purchase the business of Q and R for $2,000, P can simply sell the stock of Q for a capital gain of $1,000. If, however, in anticipation of sale Q distributes the R stock to P as a dividend, P will take the stock tax-free because of the dividends-received deduction (in this case assume a full 100 percent deduction under §243(a)(3)) and with a basis of $500 (pursuant to §301(d)). Then, when P sells the Q and R stock for $2,000, its capital gain will be reduced to $500. Should this technique be upheld? See Basic, Inc. v. United States, 549 F.2d 740 (Cl. Ct. 1977) (held, dividend distribution ignored and P's capital gain increased by an amount equal to its claimed basis in tne R stock). But cf. Dynamics Corp. of America v. United States, 449 F.2d 402 (Cl. Ct. 1971), in which a distribution in kind from a subsidiary to a parent was treated as a dividend even though followed by the parent's sale of the property nine months later; the various steps were found to be unconnected events. Would it matter if the fair market value of the R Corp. stock were $900? Consider §311(b).

The American Law Institute's (ALI's) proposals on reform of subchapter C include an elegant solution to the problem posed by *Basic, Inc.* and *Dynamics Corp.* The ALI recommends that a parent corporation's basis in the stock of its subsidiary be continuously set equal to the subsidiary's aggregate net asset basis. See ALI, Federal Income Tax Project: Subchapter C 60-65 (1982). Under this proposal, a parent-subsidiary pair will recognize the same amount of gain on the sale by the parent of the subsidiary stock as would be recognized on the distribution of the subsidiary's assets followed by a sale of those assets by the parent.

3. Redemptions for More or Less Than Stock Value

Under some circumstances a corporation may repurchase its shares for more than those shares are worth. If the excess reflects a difference of opinion over valuation or a simple misjudgment, the entire amount paid should be treated as the cost of the shares and neither deducted nor capitalized. But what happens if the excess is paid because the corporation receives something from the tendering shareholder in addition to the shares? For example, the shareholder might agree not to purchase additional stock in the future (called a "standstill" agreement), or the shareholder, especially if she is an employee as well as a shareholder, might provide a covenant not to compete with the business of the company.

Under §162(k),[3] a corporation may not deduct any amount paid or incurred in connection with the redemption of its stock except for those items specified in §162(k)(2). This provision was enacted in response to

3. Originally enacted by the Tax Reform Act of 1986 as §162(*l*).

Five Star Manufacturing Co. v. Commissioner, 355 F.2d 224 (5th Cir. 1966), in which the corporation was permitted to deduct the full amount distributed in redemption of 50 percent of its outstanding stock on the theory that elimination of the shareholder-director whose stock was redeemed was essential for the corporation's survival. The decision in *Five Star Manufacturing* certainly seems wrong — in measuring a corporation's profit or loss, amounts paid in redemption of stock should be irrelevant — but the legislative response may be overbroad.

The legislative history of §162(k) provides that the phrase "in connection with" should be construed broadly to include legal, accounting, brokerage, transfer agent, appraisal, and similar fees incurred in connection with the redemption. After INDOPCO, Inc. v. Commissioner, 112 S. Ct. 1039 (1992), might some part of the president's or comptroller's salary fall within the ambit of §162(k)?

The legislative history of §162(k) further provides that §162(k) should apply to amounts paid by the corporation for standstill agreements, whether lasting for a specified or indefinite time. Such amounts, often called "greenmail," might increase the value of the corporation's outstanding stock. If so, should the corporation be entitled to capitalize the greenmail, recovering it when the company is sold or liquidated? While §162(k) does not speak to this issue, courts are unlikely to allow recovery of redemption premiums falling within §162(k) at *any* time. For an intriguing analysis of greenmail, see Macey and McChesney, A Theoretical Analysis of Greenmail, 95 Yale L.J. 13 (1985).

How should a redemption premium be treated under §162(k) if the corporation receives not only shares but also a noncompetition agreement from the tendering shareholder? In the absence of §162(k), an amount paid for a noncompetition agreement is amortized over 15 years, see §197, unless the covenant is not related to the acquisition of a business, see §197(d)(1)(E). If, though, the redemption and noncompetition agreement are parts of a single effort to eliminate an unhappy or uncooperative shareholder-employee, might not a court hold that the entire payment received by the departing shareholder-employee was made "in connection with" the redemption? In other contexts, courts have been willing to interpret the phrase "in connection with" surprisingly broadly. See Alves v. Commissioner, 79 T.C. 864 (1982), aff'd, 734 F.2d 478 (9th Cir. 1984). Note that §162(k) cannot apply if there is no redemption, so the tax treatment of payments for standstill agreements and similar arrangements not connected to a redemption is left open by §162(k).

A corporation might also pay less than full value for redeemed stock. Why might a tendering shareholder accept less than fair market value? The effect of receiving less than full value for redeemed shares is an increase in value of all postredemption outstanding shares, so a shareholder who accepts less than full value for redeemed shares transfers some of her stock value to the other shareholders. To determine how such a transfer should be taxed, we must understand why such a transfer might be made. The following case concerns the most extreme situation, namely, a contribution of stock to the corporation by one shareholder without any return distribution.

Commissioner v. Fink
483 U.S. 89 (1987)

Justice POWELL delivered the opinion of the Court.

The question in this case is whether a dominant shareholder who voluntarily surrenders a portion of his shares to the corporation, but retains control, may immediately deduct from taxable income his basis in the surrendered shares.

Respondents Peter and Karla Fink were the principal shareholders of Travco Corporation, a Michigan manufacturer of motor homes. Travco had one class of common stock outstanding and no preferred stock. Mr. Fink owned 52.2 percent, and Mrs. Fink 20.3 percent, of the outstanding shares. Travco urgently needed new capital as a result of financial difficulties it encountered in the mid-1970s. The Finks voluntarily surrendered some of their shares to Travco in an effort to "increase the attractiveness of the corporation to outside investors." Mr. Fink surrendered 116,146 shares in December 1976; Mrs. Fink surrendered 80,000 shares in January 1977. As a result, the Finks' combined percentage ownership of Travco was reduced from 72.5 percent to 68.5 percent. The Finks received no consideration for the surrendered shares, and no other shareholder surrendered any stock. The effort to attract new investors was unsuccessful, and the corporation eventually was liquidated.

On their 1976 and 1977 joint federal income tax returns, the Finks claimed ordinary loss deductions totaling $389,040, the full amount of their adjusted basis in the surrendered shares. The Commissioner of Internal Revenue disallowed the deductions. He concluded that the stock surrendered was a contribution to the corporation's capital. Accordingly, the Commissioner determined that the surrender resulted in no immediate tax consequences, and that the Finks' basis in the surrendered shares should be added to the basis of their remaining shares of Travco stock. . . .

It is settled that a shareholder's voluntary contribution to the capital of the corporation has no immediate tax consequences. §263; [Treas. Regs.] §1.263(a)-2(f) (1986). Instead, the shareholder is entitled to increase the basis of his shares by the amount of his basis in the property transferred to the corporation. See §1016(a)(1). When the shareholder later disposes of his shares, his contribution is reflected as a smaller taxable gain or a larger deductible loss. This rule applies not only to transfers of cash or tangible property, but also to a shareholder's forgiveness of a debt owed to him by the corporation. [Treas. Regs.] §1.61-12(a) (1986). Such transfers are treated as contributions to capital even if the other shareholders make proportionately smaller contributions, or no contribution at all. See, e.g., Sackstein v. Commissioner, 14 T.C. 566, 569 (1950). The rules governing contributions to capital reflect the general principle that a shareholder may not claim an immediate loss for outlays made to benefit the corporation. Deputy v. du Pont, 308 U.S. 488 (1940); Eskimo Pie Corp. v. Commissioner, 4 T.C. 669, 676 (1945), aff'd, 153 F.2d 301 (C.A.3 1946). We must decide whether this principle also applies to a controlling shareholder's non pro rata surrender of portion of his shares. The Finks concede that a pro rata stock surrender, that by definition does not change the percentage ownership of any shareholder, is not a taxable event. Cf. Eisner v. Macomber, 252 U.S. 189 (1920) (pro rata stock dividend does not produce taxable income).

The Finks contend that they sustained an immediate loss upon surrendering some of their shares to the corporation. By parting with the shares, they gave up an ownership interest entitling them to future dividends, future capital appreciation, assets in the event of liquidation, and voting rights.[7] Therefore, the Finks contend, they are entitled to an immediate deduction. See §§165(a) and (c)(2). In addition, the Finks argue that any non pro rata stock transaction "give[s] rise to immediate tax results." For example, a non pro rata stock dividend produces income because it increases the recipient's proportionate ownership of the corporation. Koshland v. Helvering, 298 U.S. 441, 445 (1936). By analogy, the Finks argue that a non pro rata surrender of shares should be recognized as an immediate loss because it reduces the surrendering shareholder's proportionate ownership.

Finally, the Finks contend that their stock surrenders were not contributions to the corporation's capital. They note that a typical contribution to capital, unlike a non pro rata stock surrender, has no effect on the contributing shareholder's proportionate interest in the corporation. Moreover, the Finks argue, a contribution of cash or other property increases the net worth of the corporation. For example, a shareholder's forgiveness of a debt owed to him by the corporation decreases the corporation's liabilities. In contrast, when a shareholder surrenders shares of the corporation's own stock, the corporation's net worth is unchanged. This is because the corporation cannot itself exercise the right to vote, receive dividends, or receive a share of assets in the event of liquidation. . . .

A shareholder who surrenders a portion of his shares to the corporation has parted with an asset, but that alone does not entitle him to an immediate deduction. Indeed, if the shareholder owns less than 100 per-

---

7. As a practical matter, however, the Finks did not give up a great deal. Their percentage interest in the corporation declined by only four percent. Because the Finks retained a majority interest, this reduction in their voting power was inconsequential. Moreover, Travco, like many corporations in financial difficulties, was not paying dividends.

cent of the corporation's shares, any non pro rata contribution to the corporation's capital will reduce the net worth of the contributing shareholder.[10] A shareholder who surrenders stock thus is similar to one who forgives or surrenders a debt owed to him by the corporation; the latter gives up interest, principal, and also potential voting power in the event of insolvency or bankruptcy. But, as stated above, such forgiveness of corporate debt is treated as a contribution to capital rather than a current deduction. . . . The Finks' voluntary surrender of shares, like a shareholder's voluntary forgiveness of debt owed by the corporation, closely resembles an investment or contribution to capital. See B. Bittker & J. Eustice, Federal Income Taxation of Corporations and Shareholders §3.14, p. 3-59 (4th ed. 1979) ("If the contribution is voluntary, it does not produce gain or loss to the shareholder"). We find the similarity convincing in this case.

The fact that a stock surrender is not recorded as a contribution to capital on the corporation's balance sheet does not compel a different result. Shareholders who forgive a debt owed by the corporation or pay a corporate expense also are denied an immediate deduction, even though neither of these transactions is a contribution to capital in the accounting sense.[11] Nor are we persuaded by the fact that a stock surrender, unlike a typical contribution to capital, reduces the shareholder's proportionate interest in the corporation. This Court has never held that every change in a shareholder's percentage ownership has immediate tax consequences. Of course, a shareholder's receipt of property from the corporation generally is a taxable event. See §§301, 316. In contrast, a shareholder's transfer of property to the corporation usually has no immediate tax consequences.

The Finks concede that the purpose of their stock surrender was to protect or increase the value of their investment in the corporation. . . . They hoped to encourage new investors to provide needed capital and in the long run recover the value of the surrendered shares through increased dividends or appreciation in the value of their remaining shares. If the surrender had achieved its purpose, the Finks would not have suffered an economic loss. . . . In this case, as in many cases involving closely-held corporations whose shares are not traded on an open market, there is no reliable method of determining whether the surrender will result in a loss until the shareholder disposes of his remaining shares. Thus, the Finks'

10. For example, assume that a shareholder holding an 80 percent interest in a corporation with a total liquidation value of $100,000 makes a non pro rata contribution to the corporation's capital of $20,000 in cash. Assume further that the shareholder has no other assets. Prior to the contribution, the shareholder's net worth was $100,000 ($20,000 plus 80 percent of $100,000). If the corporation were immediately liquidated following the contribution, the shareholder would receive only $96,000 (80 percent of $120,000). Of course such a non pro rata contribution is rare in practice. Typically a shareholder will simply purchase additional shares.

11. It is true that a corporation's stock is not considered an asset of the corporation. A corporation's own shares nevertheless may be as valuable to the corporation as other property contributed by shareholders, as treasury shares may be resold. This is evidenced by the fact that corporations often purchase their own shares on the open market.

stock surrender does not meet the requirement that an immediately deductible loss must be "actually sustained during the taxable year." [Treas. Regs.] §1.165-1(b) (1986).

Finally, treating stock surrenders as ordinary losses might encourage shareholders in failing corporations to convert potential capital losses to ordinary losses by voluntarily surrendering their shares before the corporation fails. In this way shareholders might avoid the consequences of §165(g)(1), that provides for capital loss treatment of stock that becomes worthless. Similarly, shareholders may be encouraged to transfer corporate stock rather than other property to the corporation in order to realize a current loss. . . .[14]

We therefore hold that a dominant shareholder who voluntarily surrenders a portion of his shares to the corporation, but retains control, does not sustain an immediate loss deductible from taxable income. Rather, the surrendering shareholder must reallocate his basis in the surrendered shares to the shares he retains.[15] The shareholder's loss, if any, will be recognized when he disposes of his remaining shares. . . . We conclude only that a controlling shareholder's voluntary surrender of shares, like contributions of other forms of property to the corporation, is not an appropriate occasion for the recognition of gain or loss.

In this case we use the term "control" to mean ownership of more than half of a corporation's voting shares. We recognize, of course, that in larger corporations — especially those whose shares are listed on a national exchange — a person or entity may exercise control in fact while owning less than a majority of the voting shares. See Securities Exchange Act of 1934, §13(d), 48 Stat. 894, 15 U.S.C. §78m(d) (requiring persons to report acquisition of more than 5 percent of a registered equity security).

For the reasons we have stated, the judgment of the Court of Appeals for the Sixth Circuit is reversed.

---

14. Our holding today also draws support from two other sections of the Code. First, §83 provides that, if a shareholder makes a "bargain sale" of stock to a corporate officer or employee as compensation, the "bargain" element of the sale must be treated as a contribution to the corporation's capital. . . . Second, if a shareholder's stock is redeemed — that is, surrendered to the corporation in return for cash or other property — the shareholder is not entitled to an immediate deduction unless the redemption results in a substantial reduction in the shareholder's ownership percentage. §§302(a), (b), (d); [Regs.] §1.302-2(c) (1986). Because the Finks' surrenders resulted in only a slight reduction in their ownership percentage, they would not have been entitled to an immediate loss if they had received consideration for the surrendered shares. §302(b). Although the Finks did not receive a direct payment of cash or other property, they hoped to be compensated by an increase in the value of their remaining shares.

15. The Finks remained the controlling shareholders after their surrender. We therefore have no occasion to decide in this case whether a surrender that causes the shareholder to lose control of the corporation is immediately deductible. In related contexts, the Code distinguishes between minimal reductions in a shareholder's ownership percentage and loss of corporate control. See §302(b)(2) (providing "exchange" rather than dividend treatment for a "substantially disproportionate redemption of stock" that brings the shareholder's ownership percentage below 50 percent); §302(b)(3) (providing similar treatment when the redemption terminates the shareholder's interest in the corporation).

It is so ordered.

Justice BLACKMUN concurs in the result.

Justice WHITE, concurring.

Although I join the Court's opinion, I suggest that there is little substance in the reservation in footnote 15 of the question whether a surrender of stock that causes the stockholder to lose control of the corporation is immediately deductible as an ordinary loss. Of course, this case does not involve a loss of control; but as I understand the rationale of the Court's opinion, it would also apply to a surrender that results in loss of control. At least I do not find in the opinion any principled ground for distinguishing a loss-of-control case from this one.

Justice SCALIA, concurring in the judgment.

I do not believe that the Finks' surrender of their shares was, or even closely resembles, a shareholder contribution to corporate capital. Since, however, its purpose was to make the corporation a more valuable investment by giving it a more attractive capital structure, I think that it was, no less than a contribution to capital, an "amount paid out . . . for . . . betterments made to increase the value of . . . property," §263(a)(1), and thus not entitled to treatment as a current deduction.

[Dissenting opinion of Justice Stevens omitted.]

NOTE

1. *Stock surrenders and capital contributions.* The taxpayers in *Fink* argued that their non-pro rata stock surrenders were not capital contributions because nothing of value was added to the corporation's capital. Despite the remarks in footnote 11, surely it is the case that a corporation does not increase its wealth by the reacquisition of some of its shares. Were it otherwise, corporations could increase their wealth at will by coordinating pro rata stock surrenders. Moreover, because there is no significant difference between treasury stock and authorized but unissued stock — both can be sold to outside investors — the Court's comments in footnote 11 suggest authorizing additional stock as a fast way to corporate success. The Court's statement that reacquisition of corporate shares must increase corporate wealth or else corporations would not buy their own shares on the open market is a non sequitur: Many transactions between corporations and their shareholders do not increase corporate capital (e.g., the declaration of dividends) but nevertheless are done for sound business reasons. If a corporation believes its shares are undervalued on the open market, it may purchase (redeem) some of its outstanding stock. This purchase shifts wealth from the selling shareholders to those who continue to hold

stock of the corporation. Of course, no wealth — to the corporation or anyone else — is created by this activity.

2. *Stock surrenders and deductible losses.* While it is true that the corporation gains nothing by reason of a stock surrender, it is equally true that the surrendering shareholder loses something. In *Fink,* the surrender of 80,000 shares resulted in the diminution of the Fink's ownership from 72.5 percent to 68.5 percent. If the corporation were worth $1 million, that would be a dollar loss of $40,000. If the Finks lost value and the corporation did not gain it, where did it go?

To the other shareholders, of course. A non-pro rata stock surrender simultaneously reduces the percentage ownership of the surrendering shareholder and increases the value of all outstanding shares. If the surrendering shareholder continues to hold stock in the corporation, some of the value of the surrendered shares will reappear in the form of an increase in value of the remaining shares held by the surrendering shareholder.

Consider the case of X Corp.'s having two shareholders, A and B. A owns 75 shares of X with adjusted basis and fair market value of $100 per share, while B owns the remaining 25 shares of X with the same adjusted basis and fair market value. If A surrenders 50 of her shares, and still assuming that some loss deduction is appropriate, should A be entitled to a loss of $5,000? Note that the stock surrender reduced A's ownership of a corporation worth $10,000 from 75 percent to 50 percent, for an economic loss of $2,500. That value is thus transferred to B, while the remaining value of the surrendered shares (also $2,500) remains with A in the form of an increase in value of her remaining shares.

Should §302 apply in *Fink*? A stock surrender is just a redemption for $0; if §302 applies to the transaction, a loss will be allowed only if the shareholder qualifies under §302(a) via §302(b). Does this approach adequately respond to the Supreme Court's concerns articulated in *Fink*? Does it permit too great a loss deduction in some cases? Do you think §302 was intended to apply to stock surrenders?

Suppose a corporation redeems 10 shares for $80 when each share is worth $10. Should this be treated as a redemption of eight shares for full value and a surrender of two shares for no consideration? If so, the redemption portion of the transaction would be tested under §302(b), while the basis of the two surrendered shares would be capitalized under *Fink.*

D. REDEMPTIONS BY RELATED CORPORATIONS — §304

A "redemption" under §317(b) is the sale of corporate stock back to the issuing corporation. A similar transaction, though not falling within the definition of §317(b), is the sale of stock to a corporation *related* to the issuing corporation. For example, suppose individual *I* owns all the stock of *P* Corp., which in turn owns all the stock of *S* Corp. If *I* causes *P* to repurchase any of its stock, the transaction will be a "redemption" under §317(b), and, unless §302(b)(4) applies, the entire amount distributed will be taxed under the distribution rules of §301. If *I* instead sells some of his *P* stock to *S*, the transaction does not fall within the definition of a "redemption" even though the effect of the transaction is little different than a redemption of the stock by *P*.

In Rodman Wanamaker Trust v. Commissioner, 11 T.C. 365 (1948), aff'd, 178 F.2d 10 (3d Cir. 1949), the Tax Court held that such a sale of *P* stock to *S* does indeed qualify for exchange treatment because the redemption rules (now incorporated in §302) do not apply. In response, Congress added §115(g)(2) to the 1939 Code in order to close the loophole opened by *Rodman Wanamaker Trust,* and the substance of §115(g)(2) became the basis for current §304.

Section 304 addresses two related situations: (1) the sale of stock of one corporation to another corporation controlled by the taxpayer (i.e., the use of a brother-sister corporate pair), see §304(a)(1), and (2) the sale of parent stock to a subsidiary corporation as present in *Rodman Wanamaker Trust,* see §304(a)(2). In each case, §304(a) provides that the sale is subject to the redemption rules of §302 and, if the taxpayer fails to qualify for exchange treatment under §302(b), that the nominal sale will be recharacterized as a distribution subject to the rules of §301.

Rev. Rul. 71-563

1971-2 C.B. 175

Advice has been requested regarding the Federal income tax treatment of the transaction described below.

A, an individual, owns 100 shares of corporation *X* which is all the outstanding stock of *X. B,* the son of *A,* owns all the outstanding stock of Corporation *Y. A* sold 25 shares of stock of *X* to *Y* for cash. The purchase price of the *X* stock was its fair market value. The earnings and profits of *Y* exceeded the amount of cash paid by *Y* to *A* for the *X* stock.

Section 304(a)(1) of the Internal Revenue Code of 1954 provides that for purposes of section 302 and section 303 of the Code, if one or more persons are in control of each of two corporations and in return for property, one of the corporations acquires stock in the other corporation from the person so in control, then such property shall be treated as a distribution in redemption of the stock of the corporation acquiring such stock. In any such case, the stock so acquired shall be treated as having been transferred by the person from whom acquired, and having been received by the corporation acquiring it, as a contribution to the capital of such corporation. . . .

Section 304(c)(1) of the Code provides that for purposes of section

304 of the Code control means the ownership of stock possessing at least 50 percent of the total combined voting power of all classes of stock entitled to vote, or at least 50 percent of the total value of shares of all classes of stock.

Section 304(c)(3) of the Code makes section 318(a) of the Code (relating to the constructive ownership of stock) applicable to section 304 of the Code, with certain modifications not here relevant, for the purposes of determining control under section 304(c)(1) of the Code. Section 318(a)(1)(A) of the Code provides, in pertinent part, that an individual is considered as owning the stock owned, directly or indirectly, by his children.

Section 318(a)(2)(C) of the Code provides, in pertinent part, that if 50 percent or more in value of the stock in a corporation is owned, directly or indirectly, by any person, such person is considered as owning the stock owned, directly or indirectly, by such corporation, in that proportion which the value of the stock which such person so owns bears to the value of all the stock in such corporation.

A actually owned 100 percent of the stock of *X* before the transaction and by the application of section 318(a)(1)(A) of the Code *A* is considered to have owned all of the stock of *Y* before the transaction. Accordingly, since *Y* acquired the stock of *X* for cash from a person (*A*) in control of both the issuing corporation (*X*) and the acquiring corporation (*Y*), the transaction is considered to be an acquisition of stock by a related corporation within the meaning of section 304(a)(1) of the Code and thus a redemption of the stock of *Y,* the acquiring corporation. See, in this connection, Coyle v. United States, 415 F.2d 488 (4th Cir. 1968).

Under section 1.304-2(a) of the Income Tax Regulations, the amount received by *A* is treated as a distribution of property under section 302(d) of the Code unless the distribution is to be treated as received in exchange for stock pursuant to section 302(a) or section 303 of the Code. Section 303 of the Code (relating to distributions in redemption of stock to pay death taxes) is not applicable in the instant case. Section 302(a) of the Code is applicable if the requirements of section 302(b) of the Code are satisfied.

Section 304(b)(1) of the Code provides that the applicability of section 302(b) of the Code is determined by reference to the stock of the issuing corporation, *X*. Through the application of section 318(a)(2)(C) of the Code, *B* owns the 25 shares of the stock of *X* held by *Y*. The ownership by *B* of the 25 shares of the stock of *X* is attributed to *A* by reason of application of section 318(a)(1)(A) of the Code. Therefore, after the transaction *A* still owns 100 percent of *X* and there is no complete termination of *A*'s interest in the stock of *X* within the meaning of section 302(b)(3) of the Code nor is there a substantially disproportionate redemption within the meaning of section 302(b)(2) of the Code.

The "not essentially equivalent to a dividend" test of section

302(b)(1) of the Code cannot be met since there has been no meaningful reduction in A's proportionate interest in the stock of X as a result of the transaction. In determining the existence of a meaningful reduction, the constructive ownership rules of section 318 of the Code are applied (see United States v. Davis, 397 U.S. 301 (1970)).

The inapplicability of section 303 and section 302(a) of the Code results in the amount received by A being treated, pursuant to section 302(d) of the Code, as a distribution to which section 301 of the Code applies. Accordingly, the distribution is treated as a dividend to A from Y under section 301(c)(1) and section 316 of the Code.

Section 1.304-2(a) of the regulations provides that with respect to transactions to which section 304(a)(1) of the Code applies, the stock received by the acquiring corporation shall be treated as a contribution to the capital of such corporation and that section 362(a) of the Code is applicable in determining the basis of such stock. Section 1.304-2(a) of the regulations further provides that the transferor's basis for his stock in the acquiring corporation shall be increased by the basis of the stock surrendered by him.

Accordingly, the basis of the X stock in the hands of Y is the same as the basis of the X stock in the hands of A. Furthermore, since A owns no stock in Y directly after the transaction, the basis of the X stock surrendered is added to the basis of the 75 shares of X stock which A owns after the transaction.

NOTE

1. *"Control" under §304(c)*. Note that a person "controls" a corporation within the meaning of §304(c) if he owns at least 50 percent of the total voting power in the corporation *or* at least 50 percent of the total value of all shares of all classes of stock. Furthermore, the attribution rules of §318 apply in determining such control. See §304(c)(3). Note that, by virtue of §304(c)(3)(B), the reach of the attribution rules is broadened in the context of §304.

Suppose X Corp. has two classes of stock outstanding. Individual T owns all the shares of one class and none of the shares of the other class. The X Corp. stock owned by T gives T 40 percent of the vote but 60 percent of the fair market value of X Corp. If T sells some of the X stock to a corporation T controls, can §304 apply to the sale?

Section 304 will apply only if T controls both corporations, and control for purposes of §304(a) is defined in §304(c) to require "at least 50 percent of the total combined voting power of all classes of stock entitled to vote, or at least 50 percent of the total value of all classes of shares." T quite plainly fails the 50 percent vote test, but does T satisfy the 50 percent value test? If this test is applied separately to each class of stock, T fails the test because T owns none of one of the two classes; if the value test is applied to the aggregate of all outstanding classes, T satisfies it. Note that although Congress specified that all classes of stock are "combined" for determining the vote test, no similar specification appears in the value test. Nevertheless, in Rev. Rul. 89-57, 1989-1 C.B. 90, the Service held that the §304(c)(1) value test is applied to the aggregate value of stock held. Accordingly, T is deemed to be in control of X Corp.

If a taxpayer sells stock of one corporation to a second corporation for stock of the second plus other property, it may be that the taxpayer did not control the purchasing corporation before the transaction but does control it afterward. Does §304 apply to such a transaction? Yes. §304(c)(2). Note, though, that §304 applies only to the "other property" received by the taxpayer, not to the stock of the purchasing corporation she receives. Why? Because §304(a) applies only to the exchange of stock for "property," and "property" does not include stock of the distributing (i.e., acquiring) corporation. §317(a).

Aficionados of the §318 attribution rules will observe that application of §318 to §304 is troublesome. Consider a taxpayer who owns 100 percent of the outstanding stock of two corporations, Brother and Sister. If this taxpayer sells some Brother stock to Sister, it is clear that §304 will apply. But is §304(a)(1) or (a)(2) applicable? While §304(a)(1) seems the obvious candidate, application of §318 causes the taxpayer's stock in Sister to be attributed to Brother (and vice versa), thereby making Brother and Sister into a parent-subsidiary pair (with either (or both?) as the parent (or subsidiary)). By its terms, §304(a)(1) defers to §304(a)(2). Thus, this sale of Brother stock to Sister seems to be taxed under §304(a)(2). Does it matter whether §304(a)(1) or (a)(2) applies? See Notes 2 and 4 infra.

Neither the courts nor the Service has been inclined to rearrange a brother-sister §304 transaction when the taxpayer's actual stock ownership placed him within the confines of §304(a)(1). See, e.g., Coyle v. United States, 415 F.2d 488 (4th Cir. 1968); Rev. Rul. 71-563 above. It appears safe to assume that the attribution rules of §318(a) will not be applied to remove a transaction from §304(a)(1) and place it into §304(a)(2). See also Broadview Lumber v. United States, 561 F.2d 698 (7th Cir. 1977).

2. *Application of §302(b) to a §304 transaction.* Sales of stock described in §304(a) are subject to the redemption rules of §§302 and 303. Assuming the inapplicability of §303 (discussed at pages 213-214 supra), the sale will qualify for exchange treatment under §§1001 et seq. only if one of the tests in §302(b) is met. Otherwise, the proceeds received by the selling shareholder will be taxed according to the distribution rules of §301.

Pursuant to §304(b)(1), the tests of §302(b) are applied to the change (if any) in the shareholder's interest in the "issuing corporation" (i.e., the corporation whose shares are nominally being sold). Do not forget that the attribution rules of §318(a) are applicable to determinations under §302, even those triggered by §304. See Treas. Regs. §1.304-2(a).

Consider a taxpayer, *T*, who owns 60 of the 100 outstanding shares of Brother Corp. and 60 of the 100 outstanding shares of Sister Corp. How will *T* be taxed if she sells 20 shares of Brother stock (with basis of $10 per share) to Sister for $15 per share?

T actually owned 60 percent of the outstanding stock of Brother prior to the sale. After the sale, *T* actually owned 40 shares and constructively owned 12 more through her ownership of Sister. See §318(a)(2)(C). Thus, *T*'s ownership of Brother dropped from 60 percent to 52 percent, so *T* cannot qualify under §302(b)(2) or (3) (*T* neither has gone below 80 percent of her former percentage ownership of Brother nor owns less than 50 percent of Brother after the redemption, thereby failing to qualify under §302(b)(2) on two grounds). Assuming arguendo the inapplicability of §302(b)(1) and (4), *T* will have received a distribution in the amount of $300 taxable under §301.

If *T* had sold 40 shares instead of 20, she would have qualified for exchange treatment under §302(a). A sale of 40 shares would bring *T*'s postsale actual and constructive ownership down to 44 percent (20 percent actual and 24 percent constructive ownership), thereby qualifying her under §302(b)(2). As a consequence, *T* would have taxable gain of $200, that being the difference between her amount realized ($600) and her basis in the shares sold ($400).

The application of §304 to a sale of parent stock to its subsidiary corporation is similar, although the application of §318's attribution rules to the transaction is problematic. Consider the case of taxpayer *T* owning 60 of the 100 outstanding shares of Parent Corp., which in turn owns 100 percent of the stock of Sub Corp. How will *T* be taxed if he sells 30 shares of Parent to Sub?

Section 304(b)(1) requires that the tests of §302(b) be applied to *T*'s interest in Parent. His presale ownership of Parent was 60 percent. His postsale *actual* ownership was 30 shares. Can the shares sold to Sub be imputed back to *T*? The Service might seek to form a chain of attribution from Sub to Parent to *T*, but that would require attributing stock of Parent to itself. Treas. Regs. §1.318-1(b)(1) provides that "[a] corporation shall not be considered to own its own stock by reason of section 318(a)(3)(C) [attribution to corporations]." See D. Kahn, Basic Corporate Taxation §2.26(b) (3d ed. 1981).

Assuming that the Parent stock owned by Sub cannot be attributed to *T* through Parent, does that make *T*'s postsale ownership of Parent only 30 percent? Under Treas. Regs. §1.304-3(a), the transaction is treated "as though the parent corporation had redeemed its own stock." Might not the Service argue that T should be treated as owning 30 of the 70 outstanding shares of Parent? If so, T would still qualify for exchange treatment under §302(b)(2).

How should §302(b)(4) (applicable to redemptions in partial liquidation) be applied in the context of §304? While §302(b)(4) surely applies to determinations under §§302 and 304, neither section specifies which corporation (the issuing corporation or the acquiring corporation) must engage in a partial liquidation. One court has held that the *acquiring* corporation must pass the test of §302(b)(4) if the shareholder is to obtain exchange treatment. See Blaschka v. United States, 393 F.2d 983 (Cl. Ct. 1968).

Suppose F and F's son, S, own all the stock of X Corp. and Y Corp. X Corp. redeems all of F's stock, and F waives the family attribution rules under §302(c)(2) in reporting the transaction as an exchange under §302(b)(3). Two years later, F sells his Y Corp. stock to X Corp. in a transaction governed by §304. Under §304(a)(1), X Corp. is treated as redeeming F's X Corp. stock. Does this constructive redemption mean that F will be deemed to have acquired X Corp. stock in violation of §302(c)(2)(A)(iii)? The Service has ruled that the application of §304 does not cause F to run afoul of §302(c)(2)(A)(iii). Rev. Rul. 88-55, 1988-2 C.B. 45.

3. *Dividend income in a §304 transaction.* If a taxpayer subject to the rules of §304 has a sale recharacterized as a distribution pursuant to §302(d), then the amount of that distribution constituting a dividend will be determined by reference to the earnings and profits of both the issuing and the acquiring corporations. §304(b)(2). What is the function of the parenthetical in §304(b)(2)? Recall §312.

4. *Basis consequences of a §304 transaction.* If a taxpayer qualifies for exchange treatment in a §304 transaction, her basis in the redeemed shares will be used to offset the sale proceeds. Further, the acquiring corporation presumably will take a cost basis in those shares. But what happens if the taxpayer fails to qualify for exchange treatment and instead is subject to the distribution rules of §301?

In the case of a brother-sister §304 transaction, §304(a)(1) provides that "the stock so acquired shall be treated as having been transferred . . . as a contribution to the capital of [the acquiring] corporation." Accordingly, the taxpayer's basis in her stock of the acquiring corporation will be increased. See Treas. Regs. §1.304-2(a). What happens if the taxpayer has no *actual* ownership of stock of the acquiring corporation? Rev. Rul. 71-563, above. One possibility would be to transfer the basis to the person whose stock was attributed to the taxpayer under §318. An alternate possibility is to increase the taxpayer's basis in any remaining shares of the issuing corporation. Which do you prefer? See Coyle v. United States, 415 F.2d 488 (4th Cir. 1968).

And what of the acquiring corporation? It now owns stock of the issuing corporation, and since it is treated as having received that stock as a contribution to its capital, it carries over the shareholder's basis. See §362(a)(2).

Once again, the basis consequences attending a parent-subsidiary §304 transaction are more complex than the brother-sister situation. Of course, if the shareholder qualifies for exchange treatment under §302(a), then the shareholder recovers his basis as an offset against the amount realized and the acquiring corporation takes a cost basis. But if the transaction is subject to the distribution rules of §301, what happens to the shareholder's basis in the stock transferred?

In Broadview Lumber Co. v. United States, 561 F.2d 698 (7th Cir. 1977), the Service argued that the transaction should be treated as a contribution to the capital of the subsidiary (acquiring) corporation by the taxpayer. The court observed, however, that Congress specifically limited such treatment to brother-sister transactions. The court then held that the subsidiary corporation takes the stock with a cost basis. What does this imply as to the shareholder's basis consequences? Compare Rev. Rul. 70-496, 1970-2 C.B. 74, in which the Service ruled that a corporate taxpayer having no actual ownership of the acquiring corporation after a §304(a)(1) transaction simply loses its basis in the transferred shares.

5. *The relationship between §304 and §351.* If a taxpayer transfers stock of one corporation to a second corporation in exchange for stock of the acquiring corporation plus boot, it may be that both §351 and §304 apply to the transaction. These sections, however, have differing boot rules. Under §351, boot qualifies for exchange treatment and is taxable, if at all, only to the extent of gain on the transaction. Boot in a §304 exchange may be taxed as a dividend regardless of the amount of gain, if any, on the exchange. Because of the more favorable taxation of boot under §351, taxpayers have argued that §351 should override §304 when both are applicable. See, e.g., Haserot v. Commissioner, 46 T.C. 864 (1966), aff'd sub nom. Commissioner v. Stickney, 399 F.2d 828 (6th Cir. 1968).

Congress responded to this situation by providing that §304 overrides §351 (except with respect to certain acquisition indebtedness). See §304(b)(3). Once again, if the taxpayer receives only stock of the acquiring corporation without any boot, then §351 will be the exclusive taxing provision because stock of the acquiring corporation is not "property" for purposes of §304. See §317(a). Compare Rev. Rul. 78-422, 1978-2 C.B. 129, in which an individual transferred encumbered stock of one controlled corporation to another controlled corporation in exchange for stock of the acquiring corporation. Held, receipt of stock in the acquiring corporation is a §351 transaction but assumption by the acquiring corporation of the transferor's debt is like cash and therefore taxable under §304.

Citizens Bank & Trust Co. v. Commissioner _____
580 F.2d 442 (Cl. Ct. 1978)

Before Davis, Kunzig, and Bennett, Judges.

OPINION

PER CURIAM. [T]he court agrees with the trial judge's recommended decision. . . .

OPINION OF TRIAL JUDGE

MILLER, Trial Judge. . . .
Plaintiff, John D. MacArthur (John), has at all pertinent times been the sole shareholder, chairman of the board of directors and chief executive officer of Bankers Life and Casualty Company (Bankers), an insurance company. Telfer MacArthur (Telfer), plaintiff's brother, was experienced in the printing and publishing business and was president of Pioneer Publishing Company (Pioneer).

In its operations Bankers required a considerable amount of printed materials, such as applications, medical forms, advertising circulars, and policies. Up to 1950 it printed some of such materials itself, in the basement of its home office, and purchased others from various printing companies, including companies owned and operated by Telfer. During 1950, Telfer and plaintiff agreed to form a corporation, Brookshore Company, which they would jointly own and which would supply Bankers' printing needs at standard going rates. Telfer agreed to manage, staff and supervise Brookshore, and John agreed to furnish most of its capital and to have Bankers purchase its printing needs from it. Each was entitled to one-half of the outstanding stock. This agreement was effectuated in 1951.

In 1957, after Telfer had suffered a heart attack, he proposed to John that they enter into a mutual buy-out agreement. This agreement, executed June 29, 1957, acknowledged that they equally owned 2,235 of the outstanding 2,455 shares of Brookshore, and also all of the shares of Mackley Realty Company (Mackley), which they contributed to Brookshore. They agreed that upon the death of either, his estate was to sell his interest in Brookshore to the survivor and the survivor agreed to purchase such interest from the estate, at a stated price which increases with the passage of time prior to the date of death, with a maximum of $200,000 in the event death occurred after January 10, 1960.

Telfer died January 29, 1960. On February 10, 1960, John wrote to Telfer's widow, Elizabeth —

As you undoubtedly know, Telfer insisted that I buy his half of Brookshore in the event of his death. I have every intention of keeping faith with him. When you make your final selection of a lawyer and qualify as executrix, let somebody in my office know and I will arrange to make the payment.

Thereafter, in February and March 1960, John requested Wayne R. Cook, an attorney employed by Bankers, to negotiate with Elizabeth and her attorneys in connection with fulfilling the terms and conditions of the 1957 agreement.

While never expressly repudiating its rights and obligations under the 1957 agreement, the representatives of the estate were not receptive to the $200,000 offer. Their reasons included the following:

(a) They believed that one-half of Brookshore, including its subsidiary, Mackley, was worth a great deal more than $200,000.

(b) They wanted additional indemnity agreements from John against various liabilities which the estate might incur, and they did not want to deal with Bankers because of the belief that an insurance company could not properly enter into an indemnity agreement, and

(c) They also wanted John to purchase from the estate for additional consideration Telfer's stock interest in Pioneer.

On March 24, 1960, an agreement was entered into between Elizabeth, individually and as executrix under Telfer's will, and John. Elizabeth was to deliver all of the shares of Brookshore to John or upon his written direction. In return, John was to pay concurrently to Elizabeth $200,000 and to release, indemnify and hold harmless Elizabeth and Telfer's estate against any loss arising out of any claims by himself, by the various corporations, and by Telfer's former wife. In addition, Elizabeth agreed forthwith to deliver to John or upon his written direction the remaining shares of Pioneer, which the estate owned, in exchange for an additional $175,000. The agreement was also approved by representatives of Bankers, Brookshore and Mackley to indicate their approval of the releases.

On the same day, pursuant to the agreement, Bankers issued a check in the sum of $375,000 to a bank and the latter in turn issued a cashier's check in the same amount payable to the estate of Telfer. Wayne Cook, on behalf of Bankers, delivered the check to Elizabeth's attorneys, and she deposited it in the estate's account. In return, Elizabeth's attorneys delivered the Brookshore, Mackley and Pioneer shares to Bankers.

It is stipulated that $200,000 of the $375,000 was for the Brookshore and Mackley shares and that the fair-market-value of such shares was at least $244,000.

The Commissioner of Internal Revenue determined that because the $200,000 payment satisfied John's obligation in the same amount and because Bankers had earnings and profits in excess of $200,000, Bankers' payment in that amount constituted a dividend to John. This is also defendant's primary position in this case.

In support of its position defendant relies on two cases, Sullivan v. United States, 363 F.2d 724 (8th Cir. 1966), cert. denied, 387 U.S. 905 (1967) and Wall v. United States, 164 F.2d 462 (4th Cir. 1947).

In *Sullivan* the taxpayer was the majority stockholder in a corporation in which there was only one other stockholder, Nelson. Sullivan had unconditionally agreed that upon Nelson's termination of his employment he would repurchase the stock from Nelson at book value. When Nelson did leave, instead of repurchasing the stock himself, Sullivan caused the corporation to do so. In agreeing with the Government that Sullivan had received a dividend in the amount of the corporation's payment to Nelson, the court concisely stated its rationale (363 F.2d at 729):

> After the transaction was completed, the relevant facts were essentially as follows: (1) Sullivan's personal obligation had been discharged (2) Sullivan owned all of the outstanding shares of stock of the corporation (3) the corporation's assets were decreased by the amount paid to Nelson for his stock (4) Nelson's stock was held by the corporation as treasury stock. It is true that in terms of the financial worth of Sullivan's interest in the corporation, it was the same after the transaction as it was before. The transaction still resulted in an economic benefit to Sullivan, however, because he was relieved of his personal obligation to purchase Nelson's stock.

(Footnotes omitted.)

In *Wall*, plaintiff was one of two equal shareholders. Plaintiff purchased the shares of the other shareholder for a cash down payment plus promissory notes payable in 10 successive years, with the stock to be held by trustees as security for the notes but otherwise for the benefit of plaintiff. After only a single year, the corporation assumed payment of the annual liability on the notes. Plaintiff transferred to the corporation his equity in the stock held by the trustees and the corporation entered such stock on its books as treasury stock. The court upheld the Government's position that the annual payments represented dividend income to plaintiff because (at 464) —

> [t]he transaction is regarded as the same as if the money had been paid to the taxpayer and transmitted by him to the creditor; and so if a corporation, instead of paying a dividend to a stockholder, pays a debt for him out of its surplus, it is the same for tax purposes as if the corporation pays a dividend to a stockholder, and the stockholder then utilizes it to pay his debt.

Neither of these decisions is authority for the defendant's position herein. They do support the idea that a corporation's satisfaction of its stockholder's debt gives him an economic benefit; but defendant ignores the fact that a payment to or for the benefit of a stockholder is not the only element of dividend. A dividend also necessitates a distribution of corporate earnings and profits. I.R.C. §316. Therefore, an exchange of assets of equal value which does not reduce corporate net worth cannot be a distribution of earnings and profits and hence is not a dividend.

This was made clear in Palmer v. Commissioner of Internal Revenue, 302 U.S. 63, 69-70 (1937), wherein the Court stated:

> While a sale of corporate assets to stockholders is, in a literal sense, a distribution of its property, such a transaction does not necessarily fall within the statutory definition of a dividend. For a sale to stockholders may not result in any diminution of its net worth and in that case cannot result in any distribution of its profits.
>
> [T]he bare fact that a transaction, on its face a sale, has resulted in a distribution of some of the corporate assets to stockholders, gives rise to no inference that the distribution is a dividend within the meaning of §[316]. To transfer it from one category to the other, it is at least necessary to make some showing that the transaction is in purpose or effect used as an implement for the distribution of corporate earnings to stockholders.

While the issue in *Palmer* was whether or not a sale of corporate property to stockholders resulted in a dividend to them, the principles underlying the decision are equally applicable to an exchange of property arising out of a purchase by a corporation. Both the courts and the Commissioner of Internal Revenue have ruled that a corporate payment of money or property to a stockholder to acquire corporate assets at a fair price does not reduce earnings and profits and is not a dividend.

For the same reasons, a corporation's assumption and payment of its stockholder's obligation to purchase from a third person an asset of equal or greater value cannot be deemed a dividend to the stockholder if the corporation acquires the asset. Just such a case was presented in Easson v. Commissioner of Internal Revenue, 294 F.2d 653 (9th Cir. 1961). There the taxpayer owned real property which was encumbered by a mortgage with respect to which the taxpayer was personally liable on the underlying notes. He transferred the property subject to the mortgage to a corporation in exchange for all its stock, but remained personally liable on the notes. The Commissioner contended that when the corporation made payments on the mortgage notes the taxpayer in effect received dividend income because such payments discharged taxpayer's legal obligation. The court rejected that contention with the following explanation (at 661):

> While the corporation may incidentally have benefited taxpayer by reducing the mortgage, it is clear that the corporation did not thereby distribute any assets. The corporation owned the apartment subject to the mortgage and as the mortgage decreased its equity in the apartment house increased. Thus when it took money out of cash and applied that amount to the mortgage,

its net worth remained constant. Its total assets were unchanged because the credit to the cash account was offset by a corresponding debit to the fixed assets account.

And see also Stout v. Commissioner of Internal Revenue, 273 F.2d 345 (4th Cir. 1959).

Sullivan and *Wall* are distinguishable from the other cases discussed by the fact that the corporations there received no property in exchange for paying their stockholders' obligations. Because they received only their own stock, their net worth was reduced and they had to deplete their earnings and profits to make the payments. In substance, the transactions were stock redemptions in favor of the plaintiffs which were essentially equivalent to dividends and hence taxable as such. (See I.R.C. §302(b).) In *Sullivan,* as the extract from the opinion previously quoted shows, the court stated that it was a relevant fact that corporation's assets were decreased by its payment. In *Wall,* the taxpayer argued that because the shares acquired by virtue of the payments were kept in the corporate treasury they remained assets, but the court responded that irrespective of whether or not they were kept in the treasury (164 F.2d at 465), "As a practical matter, such shares are redeemed in the sense that they no longer constitute any liability of the corporation but represent nothing more than an opportunity to acquire new assets by a reissuance."

Since in return for the $200,000 payment to Telfer's estate Bankers received shares of Brookshore which had an agreed fair-market-value of at least $244,000, it is concluded that Bankers did not distribute any of its earnings and profits by virtue of having satisfied plaintiff's obligation to make such a purchase. Furthermore, the very fact that the purchase was such a bargain makes it difficult to understand how Bankers benefited plaintiff at all by taking over his opportunity to make the purchase. Indeed, the undisputed testimony was that Telfer's estate, the sellers, maintained in the negotiations that the $200,000 plaintiff offered was less than the fair value of their Brookshore shares and sought to avoid their agreement to sell them to plaintiff at such price. Thus it can hardly be said that plaintiff was benefited by being relieved of an "obligation," "liability" or "debt" in the onerous sense which those terms ordinarily connote.

Defendant argues alternatively that the $200,000 payment to Telfer's estate was a dividend pursuant to I.R.C. §304. . . .

Plaintiff and defendant agree that subsection 304(a)(1) is designed to prevent a stockholder who controls two corporations from drawing off accumulated corporate earnings through the device of selling part of his stock in one corporation to the other. Plaintiff had controlling interests in both corporations. Defendant contends that the 1960 transaction was the constructive equivalent of plaintiff obtaining the remaining 50 percent of Brookshore shares from Telfer's estate and then selling them to Bankers in return for Bankers assuming and paying plaintiff's obligation for the purchase price.

To apply section 304 in this manner would be to distort rather than to further the statutory purpose. The entire focus of the section is on closing a loophole. Sales proceeds received by a stockholder from a controlled corporation should be treated as dividend income rather than return of capital or capital gain if what the corporation acquires is nothing more than the stock of another corporation the same stockholder controls; for, under such circumstances, the sale is only a transfer from one pocket to another.

An obvious prerequisite for invoking subsection 304(a)(1) is that the stockholder must have received the sales proceeds. Here, however, when the transaction was completed the $200,000 sales proceeds were received by a third person, Telfer's estate, and not by plaintiff. The superseding of plaintiff's obligation to buy the stock at less than fair market value was not an assumption of a liability nor a benefit to plaintiff. It was a mere incident to Banker's payment and the estate's receipt of the purchase price.

Another prerequisite for application of the statute is that the stockholder must have owned the stock before the transfer; or else the corporation cannot have acquired it from him, but must have acquired it from a third person. Here, however, plaintiff did not own the additional 50 percent stock interest in Brookshore which was the subject of the acquisition by Bankers. Telfer's estate owned the shares and would not convey them to anyone until it received at least $200,000 in cash for them. Since it was Bankers and not plaintiff which paid the $200,000, there is no basis for imputing to plaintiff acquisition of the shares for himself or ownership at any time. Thus, Bankers necessarily acquired them from a third person and not from plaintiff.

It is concluded, therefore, that plaintiff is entitled to judgment. . . .

NOTE

Courts analysis of 304 is wrong

1. *The constructive dividend under §301.* The court was correct, was it not, when it distinguished *Sullivan* by noting that the corporation did not redeem its own shares but rather purchased the shares of another corporation? A corporation's satisfaction of its shareholder's liability should not be a dividend (more accurately, a distribution subject to the rules of §301) if the shareholder transfers valuable property to the corporation in exchange, except to the extent that the shareholder's liability exceeds the fair market value of the transferred property. Since Bankers received for its $200,000 payment stock of Brookshore worth at least $244,000, there should be no constructive dividend under §301. Focusing on the language of §301, was the distribution in *Citizens Bank* made with respect to the taxpayer's stock or made in exchange for the Banker's stock that the corporation acquired?

2. *The dividend under §304.* Was the court correct when it wrote that "[a]n obvious prerequisite for invoking subsection 304(a)(1) is that the

stockholder must have received the sales proceeds"? The effect of Bankers's $200,000 payment was to relieve the taxpayer from an obligation of the same amount; satisfaction of a taxpayer's liability has long been recognized as constructive receipt. Old Colony Trust Co. v. Commissioner, 279 U.S. 716 (1929). While it is true that the corporation received fair value for its payment, that value was in the form of stock of a corporation controlled by the taxpayer. Is not the exchange of stock of a controlled corporation for money or property, *or for the payment of an obligation,* precisely the situation addressed by §304?

E.   PROBLEMS

1.   *X* Corp. has a net value of $1 million and earnings and profits of $800,000. Of the 1,000 outstanding shares of *X*, 500 are owned by Father with a basis of $600 per share, and 500 are owned by Son with a basis of $700 per share. Father would like to transfer the value of his interest to Son, and he contemplates the following four transactions: (a) Have the corporation redeem Father's stock and then give the proceeds to Son; (b) have the corporation redeem the stock from Father's estate after Father's death and devise the proceeds to Son; (c) give Father's stock to Son and then cause the corporation to redeem the stock gifted to Son; (d) devise the stock to Son and have the corporation redeem it after Father's death.

   a.   What are the tax consequences to Father and Son of each of these transactions?
   b.   Suppose Father wants to pass the value of his stock on to Mother, his wife. Reconsider the tax consequences of each of the four transactions, assuming that Mother, rather than Son, will receive the value of Father's stock and that Mother, rather than Son, is a beneficiary of the estate.

2.   *X* Corp. is owned by two unrelated individuals, *P* and *Q. P* owns 60 shares with a basis of $60 per share, and *Q* owns 40 shares with a basis of $70 per share. *X* has earnings and profits of $2,000, and the fair market value of each share is $100. What tax consequences does each of the following transactions have for *P, Q,* and *X*?

   a.   *P* sells 10 shares to *Q* for $1,000.
   b.   *P* sells 10 shares to *X* Corp. for $1,000.
   c.   *P* sells 21 shares to *X* Corp. for $2,100.
   d.   *P* sells 50 shares to *X* Corp. for $5,000.
   e.   Suppose in (d) that —
       i.   *P* is *Q*'s sister.
       ii.   *P* is *Q*'s mother.
       iii. *P* and *Q* are each 50 percent partners in the *PQ* Partnership.
       iv.   *Q* is a corporation, and *P* owns 50 percent of the stock of *Q*.

3. Consider whether T qualifies for exchange treatment under §302(b)(4) on each of the following distributions.

a. X Corp. has operated a steel mill for many years. Because business has declined, X Corp. shuts down one of its furnaces, lays off 25 percent of its employees, and reduces production to 60 percent of its former capacity. X sells approximately 40 percent of its inventory as well as small machinery used with the closed furnace. The sale proceeds, as well as approximately 40 percent of X's working capital, is distributed to T and to the other X shareholders pro rata. Is it relevant whether T is an individual or a corporation? Must the shareholders turn in a portion of their shares?

b. Y Corp. has operated a log mill and a lumber yard for 10 years. The fair market value of the log mill is $250,000. The entire output of the log mill is sent to the lumber yard, although that output accounts for only 25 percent of the lumber yard's inventory. Y sells the log mill and distributes the proceeds to T, its 60 percent shareholder, in redemption of stock worth $200,000. Would it make a difference if Y had operated the lumber yard for only four years? If it had acquired the lumber yard four years ago?

c. Z Corp. has operated an ice cream parlor for 15 years. Seven years ago a small food menu was added, and the seating capacity was expanded. The food operation now accounts for more than half of Z's gross receipts and profits. Z Corp. distributes the ice cream equipment, ice cream trademark, and associated goodwill to T, its major shareholder in complete redemption of all of T's stock. T will continue to run the ice cream business at a new location.

4. Reconsider Problem 1(b), but assume that Father's estate consists of the X Corp. stock as well as cash of $800,000 and that the federal estate tax imposed on Father's estate is $400,000. What are the tax consequences if Father's estate consisted of only the X Corp. stock and $2 million of stock in a variety of other corporations? Assume Father's estate incurs no expenses described in §§2053 or 2054.

5. A owns all the outstanding X Corp. stock — 100 shares with an aggregate basis of $40,000. The stock has a $100,000 fair market value. P wants to purchase A's stock but has only $50,000. Assuming ample earnings and profits for X Corp., describe the tax consequences of each of the following situations:

a. X Corp. distributes $50,000 to A, who then sells her stock to P for $50,000.

b. A sells her stock to P for $100,000 (payable half in cash, half with a note). P then causes X Corp. to distribute $50,000 to her, using the cash to pay off the note. Would it matter if X Corp. redeemed some of P's stock?

c. A sells 50 shares to P for $50,000, and then X Corp. redeems A's remaining 50 shares for $50,000. What happens if the redemption precedes the sale?

     d.   If *A* were a corporation, how would *A* Corp. want to structure this transaction?

    6.   Individual *G* owns all 1,000 shares of *M* Corp. with an adjusted basis of $10 per share. *M* Corp. has net value of $1 million and substantial earnings and profits. *G* gives 10 shares of his *M* stock to his favorite charity, and those shares are redeemed shortly thereafter for $10,000.

     a.   What are the tax consequences to *G* of this series of transactions, and how does this compare with his having the stock redeemed before making the gift? Recall that a taxpayer is entitled to a deduction under §170 for the fair market value of intangible property given to a charity.

     b.   Suppose *G* retains for his life the income from the gifted stock (or from investments bought with the redemption proceeds). How would your answers change? How should the Commissioner attack such a transaction? See Grove v. Commissioner, 490 F.2d 241 (2d Cir. 1973), especially footnote 9.

    7.   *X* Corp. has 120 shares of stock outstanding, 40 owned by *B*, 40 by *C*, and 40 by *D*, with each shareholder having an adjusted basis of $40 per share. *B* and *C* have agreed that upon *C*'s demise, *B* will purchase *C*'s shares for their then current fair market value. Subsequent to the signing of this agreement but prior to *C*'s death, *C* purchases the 40 shares owned by *D* for $100 per share. Upon *C*'s death, *C*'s estate tenders all 80 shares to *B* for their current value of $125 per share. *B* desires to purchase only 40 of those shares, although the estate argues that the agreement between *B* and *C* should be understood to require a purchase of all the shares *C* owned at death. To settle their differences, *B* agrees to purchase 40 of the shares owned by *C*'s estate and *X* Corp. agrees to redeem the other 40 shares. What are the tax consequences of these transactions to *B*, *C* and *X* Corp., assuming *B* is an individual? How does the analysis change if *B* is a corporation? What steps could *B* take to increase the likelihood that a court would uphold a form of the transaction advantageous to *B*?

    8.   *B* owns 10 of the 100 outstanding shares of *X* Corp. with adjusted basis of $50 per share and fair market value of $550 per share. While attending the *X* Corp.'s annual meeting, *B* slips and falls. *B* agrees not to sue *X* Corp. in exchange for a payment of $15,000. As part of that agreement, *B* agrees to sell all his stock back to *X* Corp. for $50 per share. What are the tax consequences of these transactions to *B* and to *X* Corp.? What is the result if *B* agreed to sell his shares not to *X* Corp. but to individual *C*, an individual owning 45 of the outstanding shares of *X* Corp.?

    9.   Individual *T* owns all 10 outstanding shares of *X* Corp. with adjusted basis of $100 per share and fair market value of $75 per share. Unrelated individual *U* agrees to perform some accounting work for *X* Corp. in exchange for two shares of *X* Corp. from *T*. Assume the accounting work is worth $150. What are the tax consequences to *X* Corp., *T,* and *U* of the

transfer of stock from *T* to *U*? Is it relevant whether *X* Corp. is authorized to issue more than 10 shares? How would your answers change if the transfer of stock from *T* to *U* was not for accounting services but instead for a covenant from *U* not to compete with *X* Corp. for a period of three years?

10. *F* sells 70 shares of *X* Corp. stock to *Y* Corp. for $100 per share. Prior to the sale, *F* owned all 100 outstanding shares of *X* Corp., with a basis of $25 per share. *X* Corp. and *Y* Corp. individually have current and accumulated earnings and profits of $5,000. What are the tax consequences of the sale assuming the following situations?

a. *F* is the sole shareholder of *Y* Corp.

b. *F* owns 50 percent of the stock of *Y* Corp.

c. *F* owns no stock of *Y* Corp., but his son is the sole shareholder of *Y* Corp.

d. *F* is the sole shareholder of *Y* Corp.; *Y* Corp. has no current earnings and profits and has a $10,000 deficit accumulated earnings and profits account.

e. Reconsider your answers to (a) and (b) by assuming that *F* receives only $5,000 in cash and $2,000 in the form of *Y* Corp. stock.

6

Distributions of Stock

A. HISTORY

Suppose *X* Corp., with substantial earnings and profits, declares a dividend payable in its own shares. Should *X* Corp. shareholders be taxed on their receipt of the stock dividend? If the stock dividend consists of common stock distributed pro rata to holders of *X* Corp. common stock, the stock dividend has no real effect on the value of shareholders' interests in the corporation: They have more pieces of paper representing their interests in the corporation, but the aggregate value of their stock has not changed.

Now suppose each shareholder of *X* Corp. is allowed to elect a cash dividend or an equivalent stock dividend. Should shareholders electing to receive stock in lieu of cash be taxed as if they received cash that they then reinvested in *X* Corp. stock? Under general accounting principles, have the shareholders constructively received the cash they could have elected to receive? Does Treas. Regs. §1.4512(b) answer this question?

Congress and the courts have struggled with the taxation of stock dividends, with the Supreme Court early holding that not all stock dividends can be taxed under the sixteenth amendment. Of stock dividends that can be taxed, Congress has repeatedly tried to determine which are appropriate for taxation and which are not. The federal income tax treatment of distributions by a corporation of its own stock (and of rights to acquire its own stock) has evolved slowly. The important developments are summarized below.

1. 1913-1916

The Revenue Act of 1913 said nothing about stock dividends. Despite this omission, the Treasury sought to tax stock dividends under the catchall language of §22(a) of pre-1954 law, now §61(a). The Treasury position was upheld in Towne v. Eisner, 242 F. 702 (S.D.N.Y. 1917), but this decision was reversed by the Supreme Court, 245 U.S. 418 (1918), on the ground that a stock dividend is not "income" as that term was used in the revenue statute. The Court also said that "it is not necessarily true that income means the same thing in the Constitution and the [Revenue] Act." This suggested that the Court was not passing on the constitutionality of an explicit provision taxing stock dividends.

2. *1916-1921*

The Revenue Act of 1916 taxed all stock dividends (if covered by post-1915 earnings and profits). In Eisner v. Macomber, 252 U.S. 189 (1920), this provision was held unconstitutional as applied to a distribution of common stock on common stock by a corporation having no other class of stock outstanding. Recall the example of *X* Corp. above. A common on common stock dividend does not increase the wealth of the distributees. Does that distinguish a pro rata stock dividend from a dividend of cash or other property? No — while a pro rata cash dividend gives each shareholder some money, it simultaneously reduces the value of each shareholder's stock pro tanto. Does this suggest that stock dividends should be subject to the distribution rules of §301? Does it suggest that distributions of cash or other property ought not be taxable?

Justice Pitney's majority opinion in *Macomber* focused on the lack of any wealth transfer from the corporation to its shareholders as a consequence of the stock dividend. "Income," according to Justice Pitney, was "a gain, a profit, something of exchangeable value, proceeding from the property, severed from the capital . . . received or drawn by the recipient (the taxpayer), for his separate use, benefit and disposal." Thus, because "the stockholder has received nothing out of the company's assets for his separate use and benefit, . . . he has received nothing that answers the definition of income within the meaning of the Sixteenth Amendment."

The government argued alternatively that even if the stock dividend was not taxable in its own right, a tax on stock dividends is constitutional as a tax on the shareholder's proportionate share of undistributed corporate profits. Justice Pitney rejected this argument on two separate grounds.

> That Congress has power to tax shareholders upon their property interests in the stock of corporations is beyond question, and that such interests might be valued in view of the condition of the company, including its accumulated and undivided profits, is equally clear. But that this would be taxation of property because of ownership, and hence would require apportionment under the provisions of the Constitution, is settled beyond peradventure by previous decisions of this court.

The Government relies upon Collector v. Hubbard (1870), 12 Wall. 1, 17. . . . Insofar as this seems to uphold the right of Congress to tax without apportionment a stockholder's interest in accumulated earnings prior to dividend declared, it must be regarded as overruled by Pollock v. Farmers' Loan & Trust Co., 158 U.S. 601, 627, 628, 637. . . . [T]he government nevertheless contends that the Sixteenth Amendment removed this obstacle, so that now the *Hubbard* case is authority for the power of Congress to levy a tax on the shareholder's share in the accumulated profits of the corporation even before division by the declaration of a dividend of any kind. Manifestly this argument must be rejected, since the Amendment applies to income only, and what is called the stockholder's share in the accumulated profits of the company is capital, not income.

Justice Pitney, by holding that Congress lacks power under the sixteenth amendment to tax undistributed corporate earnings, seemingly constitutionalized the realization doctrine. Annual taxation of the unrealized appreciation in all capital assets would be an administrative nightmare, and Congress has never, in general, sought to do so. But does that mean that Congress cannot, under any circumstances, tax "unrealized" appreciation? We know, for example, that partnership income is taxable to the individual partners whether that income is distributed to them or not. Is the difference between a partnership and a corporation so great as to be of constitutional moment? Since *Macomber* the Supreme Court has not indicated that the realization doctrine is a constitutional necessity. See Surrey, The Supreme Court and the Federal Income Tax: Some Implications of Recent Decisions, 35 Ill. L. Rev. 779, 782 (1941). See also J. Sneed, The Configurations of Gross Income 125 (1967), suggesting that this aspect of *Macomber* be "consigned to the junk yard of judicial history."

Justice Pitney offered a second ground for rejecting the government's argument that "the new [stock] certificates measure the extent to which the gains accumulated by the corporation have made [the taxpayer] the richer." He observed that "it would depend upon how long [the taxpayer] had held the stock whether the stock dividend indicated the extent to which [the taxpayer] had been enriched by the operations of the company; unless he had held it throughout such operations the measure would not hold true." Consider, for example, a shareholder who purchases his stock one day before a stock dividend. Such a shareholder holds his shares with a basis equal to fair market value. If Congress should tax his stock dividend, what exactly is being taxed?

Justice Holmes dissented from *Macomber* in a short opinion, concluding with the following sentence: "The known purpose of [the Sixteenth] Amendment was to get rid of nice questions as to what might be direct taxes, and I cannot doubt that most people not lawyers would suppose when they voted for it that they put a question like the present to rest." Is Justice Holmes's dissent short on analysis or long on constitutional vision? When a case of constitutional dimension comes before the Supreme

Court, what role should the justices play? Technicians? Interpreters? Policy makers? How well is the Supreme Court able to comprehend and respond to technical tax questions of nonconstitutional import? See Wolfman, The Supreme Court in the *Lyons* Den: A Failure of Judicial Process, 66 Cornell L. Rev. 1075 (1981).

Justice Brandeis wrote a lengthy dissent to *Macomber*, focusing on the financial community's perception that stock dividends and cash dividends coupled with an option to purchase additional shares at a discount are equivalent. Justice Brandeis recognized that *any* dividend, whether in cash, property, or additional stock, decreases the value of all common stock in an amount precisely equal to the fair market value of whatever is distributed by the corporation. If one considers a shareholder's total wealth, then no pro rata dividend enriches her. Accordingly, if a distribution of cash can be taxed, why not all other corporate distributions?

3. 1921-1936

In response to *Macomber*, Congress provided in the Revenue Act of 1921 that "a stock dividend shall not be subject to tax," and this provision was carried forward until the enactment of the Revenue Act of 1936.

During this period, the Treasury regulations required the adjusted basis of the old stock to be allocated between the old shares and the dividend shares in proportion to their fair market values at the time of distribution. In Koshland v. Helvering, 298 U.S. 441 (1936), this regulation was held invalid as to a taxpayer who had received a dividend of common stock on nonvoting preferred shares. No such distribution was made on the common stock. The Supreme Court reasoned that the dividend shares, unlike those in *Macomber*, gave "the stockholder an interest different from that which his former stockholdings represented." Therefore, said the Court, the shares were constitutionally taxable when received. The Court then held that the failure of Congress to tax the dividend shares did not authorize the Treasury to allocate to the dividend shares part of the basis of the original shares. Consequently the old nonvoting shares retained their full basis for determining gain or loss on their disposition.

What are the consequences if a stock dividend is declared in which each shareholder receives one share of common stock for every share of common stock already owned? No rearrangement of interests in the corporation is worked, but each shareholder doubles her number of shares. A subsequent sale of the old stock would, were all the basis to remain in the old shares, allow each shareholder to reduce her interest in the corporation by half while using her entire stock basis to offset the sale proceeds.

Not long after deciding *Koshland*, the Court held in Helvering v. Gowran, 302 U.S. 238 (1937), that under the 1921-1936 statutes the basis of dividend shares was zero since they cost the stockholder nothing and were not taxed as income when received. Congress in 1939 enacted the predecessor of §307(a) of the 1954 Code, adopting the basis rules applied under the invalidated Treasury regulation. At the same time, Congress provided that the holding period of nontaxable shares includes the period during which the original shares were held. This provision is now §1223(5).

4. 1936-1954

In response to the *Koshland* holding that some stock dividends were constitutionally subject to tax, Congress provided in §115(f)(1) of the Revenue Act of 1936 that

> [a] distribution made by a corporation to its shareholders in its stock or in rights to acquire its stock shall not be treated as a dividend to the extent that it does not constitute income to the shareholder within the meaning of the Sixteenth Amendment to the Constitution.

In Helvering v. Griffiths, 318 U.S. 371 (1943), a majority of the Supreme Court held that this language was not intended by Congress to invite it to reconsider *Macomber*; the minority, on the other hand, saw such an invitation, accepted it, and expressed the view that *Macomber* should be overruled.

Just what stock dividends could be taxed under §115(f)(1) of the 1939 Code, as construed by the majority, was veiled in obscurity. In Strassburger v. Commissioner, 318 U.S. 604 (1943), the Supreme Court held (by a 5 to 3 vote) that a distribution of a newly created issue of nonvoting cumulative preferred stock by a corporation that had only common stock outstanding was not taxable. All the common stock was owned by a single stockholder, the taxpayer. The Court said:

> While the petitioner . . . received a dividend in preferred stock, the distribution brought about no change whatever in his interest in the corporation. Both before and after the event he owned exactly the same interest in the net value of the corporation as before. At both times he owned it all and retained all the incidents of ownership he had enjoyed before.

318 U.S. at 607.

5. 1954-1969

The 1954 Code retained the sweeping rule of the 1921-1936 period that distributions by a corporation of its own stock or of rights to acquire its own stock are not taxable to the shareholders, with two exceptions. If a corporation made optional distributions (under which the shareholder could take either cash or other property, or stock), the shareholder was taxed as if he took the cash or other property even if he chose stock. Distributions in discharge of preference dividends (e.g., dividends on preferred stock that, if not paid in one year, must be paid in a subsequent year before dividends on the common stock may be paid) for the current or preceding taxable year were made taxable under the second exception. These rules were relatively simple to understand and apply. The world of stock dividends became a complex one in 1969.

6. Tax Reform Act of 1969

Section 305 was extensively modified by the Tax Reform Act of 1969 to enlarge the category of taxable stock dividends. The pre-1969 rules were in general maintained, see §305(b)(1) and (b)(4), but new rules were added that taxed stock dividends having the effect of increasing the proportionate interests in the corporation of some shareholders while giving other shareholders cash or property, see §305(b)(2). Stock dividends that gave common stock to some holders of common stock and preferred stock to other holders of common stock also were taxable under the new law. §305(b)(3). Section 305(b)(5) backstops §305(b)(3) and (4) by making distributions of convertible preferred stock taxable. In addition, Congress authorized the promulgation of regulations to subject certain transactions having the effect of a stock dividend to taxation under the rules in §305(b). See §305(c).

B.   DISTRIBUTIONS OF STOCK AND STOCK RIGHTS UNDER §305

1.   The General Rule of Nontaxability under §305(a)

Subject to the exceptions contained in §305(b), §305(a) continues the *Macomber* rule that stock dividends are nontaxable on receipt. Furthermore, Congress has extended this rule to include the distribution of stock rights. §305(d)(1). Note, though, that the nonrecognition rule of §305(a) applies only to the distribution of a corporation's own stock (or rights to its stock) *made with respect to a shareholder's stock*. Distributions of stock as compensation to an employee or to pay off a debt of the corporation, for example, are not covered by §305, nor are distributions of stock by one corporation of stock in a second corporation. Such distributions, whether of stock or otherwise, will be taxed to the recipients under other provisions of the Code, usually §61. Cf. §83.

Stock dividends received tax free pursuant to §305(a) may be subject to substantial tax disabilities on disposition. Dividend stock (other than common stock received with respect to common stock) will be subject to the rules of §306 if it is received tax free under §305(a). See §306(c)(1)(A). These rules, discussed at pages 303-324 infra, may tax at ordinary rates the entire amount realized for the stock on disposition. In some cases it may be that taxation under §306 is harsher than would be immediate taxation on receipt under §305(b).

If a shareholder receives stock tax free under §305(a), then the basis in that stock is determined under §307(a). Section 307(a) requires an allocation of the old stock basis to both the old and new shares. This allocation is made in proportion to the relative fair market values of each share. Treas. Regs. §1.307-1(a). Thus, if the underlying rationale for tax-free receipt of dividend stock is that the taxpayer's interest has undergone a change in form but not in substance, see the discussion of *Macomber*, above, then the rule of §307(a) simply continues the identification of the old and new shares: The shareholder's old basis is allocated (without increase or decrease) to all shares constituting the new form of the old holding. How should the shareholder determine the holding period of the dividend stock? See §1223(5) (tacking).

What effect should a distribution by a corporation of its own stock have on the corporation's earnings and profits if the distributed stock is received tax free by the shareholders under §305(a)? See §312(d)(1)(B).

2. Exceptions to the General Rule: §305(b) and (c)

a. Actual Distributions

Section 305(b) contains a number of exceptions to the nonrecognition rule of §305(a). Section 305(b)(1) continues the pre-1969 rule that a distribution payable, at the election of any shareholder, in stock or property will be taxable regardless of the shareholder's choice. If she elects to receive property, the distribution rules of §301 apply directly. If she elects to receive stock, the same distribution rules apply by virtue of §305(b)(1). In these circumstances, Congress has taken the view that the shareholders electing to receive stock should be taxed as if they received cash that was then recontributed to the corporation in exchange for additional stock.

Section 305(b)(2) taxes the receipt of dividend stock if the effect of the stock dividend is to increase the proportionate corporate interests of some shareholders while giving other shareholders cash or property. If a shareholder's right to future dividends is increased, then he has an increase in the earnings and profits of the corporation within the meaning of

§305(b)(2)(B). Similarly, if a shareholder's right to participate in the corporation's eventual liquidating distribution is increased, he has had an increase in his share of corporate assets. Because most preferred stock has a preference as to dividends and a limitation on liquidation, distributions *of* or *on* preferred stock often will cause a change in relative shareholder interests in the earnings and profits as well as in the assets of the corporation. The examples in Treas. Regs. §1.305-3(e) help clarify the potential scope of §305(b)(2). In particular, be certain that you understand why the distribution described in example 1 is subject to §305(b)(2) while the distribution described in example 2 is not.

A stock dividend cannot be taxable under §305(b)(2) unless shareholders not receiving the stock dividend receive cash or other property as part of the same transaction. This "companion distribution" requirement is easily satisfied because, under Treas. Regs. §1.305-3(b)(3), "there is no requirement that the shareholders receiving cash or property acquire the cash or property by way of a [formal] corporate distribution with respect to their shares, so long as they receive such cash or property in their capacity as shareholders." Distributions of stock and cash or property separated by more than three years, however, will be presumed unrelated for determinations under §305(b)(2). Treas. Regs. §1.305-3(b)(4). Why might Congress have limited taxation under §305(b)(2) to those disproportionate stock dividends having companion distributions? In what way are such stock dividends similar to those taxable under §305(b)(1)?

Section 305(b)(3) taxes stock dividends when some shareholders of common stock receive common stock while others receive preferred stock. Such distributions often will have the disproportionate effect described in §305(b)(2). Why will they not fall within that subsection? Recall the definition of "property" in §317(a), applicable to §§301-318.

Section 305(b)(4) applies to distributions of stock or stock rights made with respect to preferred stock (in common parlance, stock dividends "on" preferred stock). What is the reason for taxing such dividends? Should preferred on preferred stock dividends be tax free under the reasoning of *Macomber*? Recall *Strassburger* and *Koshland,* discussed at pages 282-283 supra.

The second clause in §305(b)(4) excludes from the rule of §305(b)(4) certain changes to the conversion ratio of preferred stock. The conversion ratio of convertible preferred stock is most often changed when a stock dividend is declared by the corporation on its common stock since if the conversion ratio is not adjusted, the holders of the convertible preferred stock will have had their conversion rights diluted. Since a change in conversion ratio involves no actual distribution of stock or of stock rights, this final clause is misplaced. To be sure, changes in the conversion ratio of preferred stock can have the effect of a stock dividend, so such changes should, in appropriate circumstances, be treated as the equivalent of actual stock dividends. The taxation of constructive stock dividends, however, is addressed generally in §305(c), and the second clause in §305(b)(4) more appropriately belongs in that subsection. Section 305(c) is discussed at pages 296-303 infra.

Section 305(b)(5) taxes the distribution of convertible preferred stock. Suppose a corporation distributes preferred stock that is convertible into common stock. If some (but not all) of this stock is converted, the effect of the distribution is a disproportionate distribution of common and preferred stock. Since disproportionate distributions of common and preferred stock are taxable under §305(b)(3), distributions of convertible preferred stock must also be taxable unless it is shown that the distribution will not have the effect described in §305(b)(2). Why does §305(b)(5) reference §305(b)(2) rather than §305(b)(3)?

Frontier Savings Association v. Commissioner
87 T.C. 665 (1986), aff'd sub nom. Colonial Sav. Assn. v. Commissioner, 854 F.2d 1001 (7th Cir. 1988), acq., 1990-1 C.B. 1

[handwritten: Not equivalent to an opt. to get cash or stock]

SWIFT, Judge. . . .

Frontier Savings has been a member and stockholder of the Federal Home Loan Bank of Chicago (the "Chicago Bank") at all times since the organization of the Chicago Bank. . . .

The Federal Home Loan Bank system was designed primarily as a reserve credit facility for savings and loan associations and other home mortgage credit institutions. Savings and loan associations (such as Frontier Savings) and mutual savings banks that are members or stockholders in the district banks (hereinafter referred to as "members" or "member banks") are required by Federal law to maintain a certain capital stock ownership in the respective district banks of which they are members. The stock ownership requirements are determined at the end of each calendar year and are calculated with reference to each member bank's net home mortgage loans outstanding and total borrowings of each member from the district bank.

Each member bank generally must maintain a capital stock ownership interest in the district bank in an amount equal to at least one percent of the total outstanding balance of its home mortgage loans and at least equal to one-twelfth of total outstanding borrowings of the member bank from the district bank, as of December 31 of each year. Each share of stock in the district banks is valued by statute at its $100 par value. See 12 U.S.C. sec. 1426(b) and (c) (1978).

Based upon the above year-end calculations, member banks that are required to purchase additional stock of district banks must do so by January 31 of the following year at the par value of $100 per share. Member banks that own stock in district banks in excess of the required number of shares ("excess shares") may request that excess shares be redeemed by the district banks. . . .

At a meeting held on November 20, 1978, the board of directors of the Chicago Bank adopted a resolution to pay a 6.58-percent dividend to its stockholders of record as of December 31, 1978. Subject to the approval of the Federal Home Loan Bank Board, the resolution stated that the dividend would be paid in the form of shares of stock in the Chicago Bank. On December 22, 1978, the Director of the Office of District Banks, Federal Home Loan Bank Board, wrote a letter to the President of the Chicago Bank approving the stock dividend.

On December 22, 1978, the Chicago Bank mailed a bulletin to its member banks, informing them that a 6.58-percent stock dividend would be paid, with fractional shares to be paid in cash. The explanation made in the bulletin for paying a stock dividend, rather than a cash dividend, was as follows:

> (1)   Providing a stock rather than a cash dividend may enable your association to defer the payment of income taxes on the value of the stock dividend. You may wish to consult your tax adviser for the proper handling of a stock dividend.
>
> (2)   A stock dividend can be applied toward satisfying the stock investment requirement for members that experienced a growth in assets during 1978 or that will be required to purchase additional stock due to increased borrowings from the Bank.

The bulletin also explained that most member banks would be required to increase their stock holdings in the Chicago Bank due to that year's general increase in outstanding home mortgage loans. . . .

Enclosed with the December 22, 1978, bulletin mailed by the Chicago Bank to its member banks describing the 1978 stock dividend was a form entitled "Calculation of Bank Stock Requirement as of December 31, 1978." Using that form, each member bank could calculate the number of shares of stock it was required, under 12 U.S.C. sec. 1426(c) (1978), to own in the Chicago Bank as of December 31, 1978. If a member bank was required to purchase additional shares of stock, it could submit the form (reflecting the number of shares to be purchased) along with a check in payment therefor to the Chicago Bank. If the member bank held more shares than it legally was required to own, it could use the form to request the redemption of any excess shares. Although the Chicago Bank had no legal obligation to redeem excess shares, in prior years it routinely had done so.

On January 16, 1979, Frontier Savings completed the form calculating the number of shares of common stock in the Chicago Bank it was required to own based on its December 31, 1978, outstanding balance for home mortgage loans. That calculation indicated that Frontier Savings was required to purchase 678 additional shares of common stock in the Chicago Bank (after taking into account the shares received as part of the common stock dividend on December 29, 1978). Frontier Savings, therefore, sent a check in the amount of $67,800 to the Chicago Bank and 678 shares were credited to its stock account at the Chicago Bank. A new stock certificate was issued reflecting the ownership by Frontier Savings of a total of 10,332 shares of common stock in the Chicago Bank. During 1979, none of the shares of common stock in the Chicago Bank owned by Frontier Savings were redeemed or otherwise transferred.

Exclusive of the December 29, 1978, stock dividend received, on December 31, 1978, 195 of the 497 member banks owned sufficient shares of common stock in the Chicago Bank to meet their stock ownership requirements, and 302 member banks did not own sufficient shares to meet their stock ownership requirements. After receipt of the 1978 stock dividend, 69 member banks requested that the Chicago Bank redeem all or some of their excess shares. All such redemption requests were agreed to by the Chicago Bank and the following number of shares of common stock were redeemed by the Chicago Bank from its member banks in the months indicated:

Time Period	Shares Redeemed
December 1978	1,240
January 1979	62,575
February 1979	8,249
Remainder of 1979	22,256

During December of 1978 and 1979, 45 member banks redeemed a number of shares of stock in the Chicago Bank that was equal to or that exceeded the number of shares they received as their portion of the 1978 stock dividend. [A similar stock dividend and redemption occurred in late 1979 and early 1980.]

None of the shares of stock in the Chicago Bank received by Frontier Savings with respect to the 1978 and 1979 stock dividends were redeemed by the Chicago Bank or otherwise disposed of by Frontier Savings prior to 1982. In January of 1982, the Chicago Bank, at the request of Frontier Savings, redeemed 3,584 shares of its stock owned by Frontier Savings.

OPINION

The receipt of common stock dividends generally is not taxable to stockholders. Sec. 305(a). Where, however, dividends from a corporation are payable, at the election of the stockholders, in stock or property (such as cash), the receipt of dividends will be taxable to the stockholders under the provisions of section 301. Sec. 305(b)(1). In that circumstance the receipt of stock dividends will be taxable under sections 305(b)(1) and 301 regardless of whether the stockholders exercise their election to receive the dividends in cash or other property. Sec. 1.305-2(a), Income Tax Regs.

Respondent argues that by redeeming all of the common stock it was requested to redeem from its member banks in 1979 and 1980 (and apparently doing so in years before 1979), the Chicago Bank established such a policy and practice of redeeming excess stock upon request of the member banks that the member banks should be regarded as having had an "election" to receive the 1978 and 1979 stock dividends in cash. Respondent therefore argues that the stock dividends in question do not qualify for exemption from taxability under section 305(a) and should be taxable to the member banks under sections 305(b)(1) and 301. For the reasons explained below, we disagree. . . .

Congress vested in the district banks and in the Federal Home Loan Bank Board discretionary authority to redeem excess shares of common stock held by member banks. Our careful examination of the record herein satisfies us that the manner in which stock dividends were paid and redeemed in 1978 and 1979 by the Chicago Bank was consistent with that grant of discretionary authority and did not vest in the member banks the unilateral right to elect or to require the Chicago Bank to redeem excess shares upon request.

Respondent concedes that the Chicago Bank did not completely abdicate its discretionary authority to redeem its stock but respondent argues that authority was exercised so consistently in favor of redemption that member banks, as a practical matter, had the option or election to have excess shares redeemed at any time. Respondent contends that the option arose "from the circumstances of the distribution" citing section 1.305-2(a)(4), Income Tax Regs. As indicated, we have carefully examined the circumstances of the stock dividends in question and conclude that the member banks, including Frontier Savings, did not have the option or election to have the Chicago Bank redeem excess shares of common stock in the Chicago Bank.

In addition to the factors explained above, we think it significant that the stock dividends of the Chicago Bank were declared and distributed in late December of 1978 and 1979. Member banks, however, normally would not be able to determine until early in the following year (after actual distribution of the stock dividends) whether they would be able even to request a redemption of some of their common stock in the Chicago Bank. In other words, on the day of distribution of the stock dividends, member banks could not know (other than through estimates and projections) whether they would be required to retain the stock dividends they received as part of their required investments in the district bank or whether the stock dividends would qualify as excess shares, in which case redemption thereof, if requested, might occur depending on the decision of the Chicago Bank. . . .

We recognize that the issuance by the Chicago Bank in 1978 and 1979 of stock dividends instead of or in addition to cash dividends was motivated in part by tax considerations. We cannot conclude, however, on the facts before us that the stock dividends were a mere subterfuge for cash distributions or that the Chicago Bank had relinquished its discretionary authority to decline to grant stock redemption requests.

Respondent refers to Rev. Rul. 76-258, 1976-2 C.B. 95. Revenue Rulings are, of course, not binding on this Court. Estate of Lang v. Commissioner, 64 T.C. 404, 406-407 (1975), affd. 613 F.2d 770 (9th Cir. 1980). Respondent's litigating position herein is reflected in Rev. Rul. 83-68, 1983-1 C.B. 75. For the reasons explained above and under the facts of this case, we reject the conclusion reached therein that a history or practice of redemptions by the Chicago Bank makes the stock dividends received by petitioner herein taxable under sections 305(b)(1) and 301. . . .

Decisions will be entered under Rule 155.

Reviewed by the Court.

Sterrett, Goffe, Chabot, Nims, Parker, Whitaker, Korner, Shields, Hamblen, Cohen, Clapp, Jacobs, and Parr, JJ., agree with the majority opinion.

Simpson, J., dissents.

Gerber, Wright, and Williams, JJ., did not participate in the consideration of this case.

HAMBLEN, J., concurring.

I concur in the conclusion of the majority based upon the limited factual circumstances involved. If a discretionary act of the Board of Directors of a shareholder corporation to redeem stock dividends becomes a routine matter, it might, in my opinion, develop into an "option" that arises after the distribution or a distribution pursuant to a "plan." See secs. 1.305-2(a) and 1.305-3(b), Income Tax Regs. In such a situation, it seems the redemptions might be periodic rather than isolated. The broad rules of section 305 could invoke different considerations under other circumstances.

Sterrett, Cohen, and Jacobs, JJ., agree with this concurring opinion.

Rev. Rul. 78-375
1978-2 C.B. 130

Advice has been requested as to the treatment for federal income tax purposes of a "dividend reinvestment plan" where the shareholder may not only elect to receive stock of greater fair market value than the cash dividend such shareholder might have received instead, but also the shareholder may, through the plan, purchase additional stock from the corporation at a discount price which is less than the fair market value of the stock.

X is a corporation engaged in commercial banking whose shares of common stock are widely held and are regularly traded in the over-the-counter market. In order to raise additional equity capital for corporate expansion and to provide holders of X's common stock with a simple and convenient way of investing their cash dividends and optional payments in additional shares of X common stock without payment of any brokerage commission, X established an automatic dividend reinvestment plan. An independent agent will administer the plan and will receive the stock from X in the manner described below on behalf of a participating shareholder.

The plan provides the following:

(1)   Shareholders can elect to have all their cash dividends (less a quarterly service charge of $3x$ dollars that is paid to an independent agent of the shareholder) otherwise payable on common stock registered in the name of the shareholder automatically reinvested in shares of X common stock. The service charge is paid to the agent for administering the plan and maintaining the stock certificates for the shareholders. The shareholders who elect to participate in the plan acquire X stock at a price equal to 95 percent of the fair market value of such stock on the dividend payment date. The shareholder's option to receive a dividend in additional common stock in lieu of a cash dividend is not transferable apart from a transfer of the common shares themselves.

(2)   A shareholder who participates in the dividend reinvestment aspect of the plan as described in paragraph (1) above, in addition, has the option to invest additional amounts to purchase shares of X common stock at a price equal to 95 percent of the fair market value of such stock on the dividend payment date. Optional investments by a shareholder in any quarterly dividend period must be at least $4x$ dollars and cannot exceed $100x$ dollars. The shareholder's right to invest additional amounts under the plan is not transferable apart from a transfer of the common shares themselves.

There is no requirement to participate in the plan and shareholders who do not participate receive their cash dividend payments in full. Certain shareholders have chosen not to participate; therefore, they receive their regular quarterly cash dividend. While the plan continues in effect, a participant's dividends will continue to be invested without further notice to X.

Prior to the dividend payment date no cash dividend is available to either X's participating or nonparticipating shareholders. On the dividend payment date the participant receives written notification that X is acting to effectuate the participant's option to receive stock on that date. The crediting on the plan account and notification to the participant of the exact number of shares acquired (including fractional shares) takes place shortly after the dividend payment date.

A participant may withdraw from the plan at any time, upon written request. Upon withdrawal, certificates for whole shares credited to the participant's account under the plan will be issued and a cash payment based upon the market value of the participant's fractional share interest will be paid by X, through the participant's agent, to the participant. As an alternative, the shareholder may request that all or part of the whole shares credited to its account in the plan be sold for the shareholder's account. The sale will be made by an independent agent acting on behalf of such participant and the proceeds of the sale (less any brokerage commission and transfer tax) will be forwarded to the participant. With regard to the whole shares, X will neither purchase any shares of a participant nor pay any expense attributable to the sale of such stock. Upon a request for sale of a participant's shares, a cash payment equal to the market value of the participant's fractional share interest will be paid by X, through the participant's agent, to the participant. The purpose of the payment of cash is to save X the trouble, expense, and inconvenience of issuing and transferring fractional shares and is not designed to give any particular group of shareholders an increased interest in the assets or earnings and profits of X. . . .

In the present case, the distributions made by X while the plan is in effect are properly treated as payable either in X's stock or in cash at the election of X's common shareholders within the meaning of section 305(b)(1) of the Code. . . .

The optional investment aspect of the present case results in an increase in the proportionate interests of the shareholders making the purchase at a 5 percent discount, and this event increases their proportionate interests in the assets or earnings and profits of X within the meaning of section 305(b)(2)(B) of the Code. Furthermore, the fact that X shareholders who do not participate in the plan receive cash dividends constitutes a receipt of property by those shareholders within the meaning of section 305(b)(2)(A).

Accordingly, under the circumstances described above, it is held as follows:

(a) A shareholder of X who participates in the dividend reinvestment aspect of the plan will be treated as having received a distribution to which section 301 of the Code applies by reason of the application of section 305(b)(1). Pursuant to section 1.305-1(b) of the regulations, the amount of the distribution to a participating shareholder (including participating corporate shareholders) will be the fair market value of the X stock received on the date of the distribution (sections 1.301-1(b) and (d)), plus, pursuant to section 301, 3x dollars, the service charge subtracted from the amount of the shareholder's distribution.

(b) The basis of the shares credited to the account of a participating shareholder pursuant to the dividend reinvestment aspect of the plan will equal the amount of the dividend distribution, as provided in section 301(c) of the Code, measured by the fair market value of the X common stock as of the date of the distribution both as to noncorporate and corporate shareholders, pursuant to section 301(d). Section 1.301-1(h)(1) and (2)(i) of the regulations. The quarterly service charge paid by a participant who is an individual for the production of income or for the management, conservation, or maintenance of property held for the production of income, is deductible in the year paid by such participant under section 212, provided the individual itemizes deductions. . . . The quarterly service charge, which is paid in carrying on a trade or business by a participant who is an individual, is deductible in the year paid by such participant under section 162. A participant who is a corporation may deduct the service charge under section 162.

(c) A shareholder of X who participates in the optional payment aspect of the plan will be treated as having received a distribution to which section 301 of the Code applies by reason of the application of section 305(b)(2). Pursuant to section 1.305-3(a) of the regulations, the amount of the distribution to a participating shareholder will be the difference between the fair market value on the dividend payment date of the shares purchased with the optional payment and the amount of the optional payment. Section 1.305-3(b)(2).

(d) The basis to the shareholder who participates in the optional payment aspect of the plan is the excess of fair market value of the shares purchased with the optional payment over the optional payment (provided that this deemed distribution is taxable as a dividend under section 301(c)(1) of the Code) . . . plus the amount of the optional payment, pursuant to section 1012.

(e) A participant in the plan will not realize any taxable income upon receipt of certificates for whole shares that were credited to the participant's account pursuant to the plan. . . . Any cash received by an X shareholder in lieu of a fractional share interest will be treated as a redemption of that fractional share interest, subject to the provisions and limitations of section 302 of the Code. . . .

(f) A participant will recognize gain or loss pursuant to section 1001 of the Code when shares are sold or exchanged on behalf of the participant upon the participant's withdrawal from the plan, or when the participant sells the shares after its withdrawal from the plan. In accordance with section 1001, the amount of such gain or loss will be the difference between the amount that the participant receives for the whole shares and the participant's tax basis. Any cash received by the participants, who withdraw from the plan, in lieu of their fractional share interests will be treated as a redemption of that fractional share interest, subject to the provisions and limitations of section 302. . . .

NOTE

1.   *The shareholder's election under §305(b)(1).* What is the effect of the parenthetical expression in §305(b)(1)? See Treas. Regs. §1.305-2(a). Suppose a corporation issues two classes of common stock, class A and class B. The corporation's charter provides that dividends cannot be declared on one class without an equal dividend declaration on the other. Dividends on the class A stock will always be paid in cash, while dividends on the

class B stock will always be paid in additional shares of class B. Has a shareholder, by choosing to purchase shares of class B rather than class A, "elected" to receive stock dividends in lieu of property so that §305(b)(1) will apply to all stock dividends he will receive? This issue, a thorny one under pre-1969 law, was settled by the 1969 act (and the regulations promulgated thereunder) in favor of taxation. See Treas. Regs. §1.305-2(a)(4).

In *Frontier,* the corporation annually declared a stock dividend and then habitually agreed to redeem shares as requested by its stockholders. The Tax Court did not find the requisite shareholder election in such circumstances, although Judge Hamblen added in the concurring opinion that such a routine could run afoul of §305 if the redemptions were "periodic rather than isolated." Yet §305(b)(1) nowhere limits its application to periodic stock dividends. Judge Hamblen apparently was focusing on the taxation of certain redemptions as constructive stock dividends pursuant to §305(c). See discussion of §305(c) at pages 296-303 infra. Even in the absence of a provision such as §305(c), might not a corporation's habitual practice of declaring a stock dividend, if always followed by an optional redemption, fall within the ambit of §305(b)(1)? Was the transaction in *Frontier* more legitimate because of the statutory obligation of the corporation's shareholders to purchase additional stock as their assets and outstanding loans increased? Is it relevant, under §305(b)(1), whether the corporation and shareholders had no tax avoidance motives for the transaction giving rise to an effective election by the shareholders to receive stock or property?

2.   *Amount constituting dividend.* Distributions of stock falling within one of the provisions of §305(b) will be subject to the property distribution rules of §301. To noncorporate and corporate shareholders alike, the "amount" of the distribution under §301(b) is the fair market value of the dividend stock. See Treas. Regs. §1.305-2(b) (example 2). Of that amount, the recipient shareholder will have a dividend to the extent of her pro rata share of the distributing corporation's earnings and profits. §§301(c)(1), 316(a). The excess amount of the distribution, if any, will be applied against the shareholder's old stock basis to the extent thereof, §301(c)(2), with any amount in excess of basis treated as though received "in exchange" for the old stock, §301(c)(3). See pages 119-120 supra.

The rules of §305 generally apply to distributions of stock rights. See §305(d)(1). As indicated by Rev. Rul. 78-375 above, the fair market value of an immediately exercisable right to buy stock equals the difference between the current fair market value of the corporation's stock and the amount the holder of the right must pay to acquire the stock. If a stock right cannot be exercised for a specified time, e.g., three or five years, how should the right be valued? Cf. §83. If stock rights are received tax free under §305(a), then the shareholder must allocate a basis to them under §307. Note the special rule for stock rights received tax free that are worth less than 15 percent of the shareholder's old stock: Such rights have a zero basis unless the shareholder elects to allocate some of her old stock basis to them. §307(b).

3. *The companion distribution requirement of §305(b)(2)(A).* A stock dividend increasing the proportionate share of the recipient shareholder's interest in the assets or earnings and profits of the corporation will not fall within §305(b)(2) unless some other shareholder receives a distribution of property. §305(b)(2)(A). Why should taxation of the dividend stock to the recipient shareholder turn on the existence of a companion distribution of property to another shareholder?

Is it likely that a stock dividend will be made to one shareholder (or to one group of shareholders) while the remaining shareholders receive nothing of value? Might the other shareholder agree to a non-pro rata stock dividend if he will receive, as part of the deal, an increase in his salary as a corporate employee? See Treas. Regs. §1.305-3(b)(3) (companion distribution must be to a shareholder "in his capacity as a shareholder"). Would such a salary increase meet the companion distribution requirement of §305(b)(2)(A)? Recall that in Treas. Regs. §1.305-3(b)(4) stock and property distributions separated by more than 36 months are presumed unrelated.

4. *The definition of preferred stock.* Subsections (3), (4), and (5) of §305 refer to "preferred" stock. The Code does not define "preferred stock," although Treas. Regs. §1.305-5(a) provides, in the context of §305(b)(4), that

> [t]he term "preferred stock" generally refers to stock which, in relation to other classes of stock outstanding enjoys certain limited rights and privileges (generally associated with specified dividend and liquidation priorities) but does not participate in corporate growth to any significant extent. The distinguishing feature of "preferred stock" for the purposes of section 305(b)(4) is not its privileged position as such, but that such privileged position is limited and that such stock does not participate in corporate growth to any significant extent.

Does this definition of "preferred stock" comport with the underlying rationale of §305? Note in particular that nonvoting stock need not be "preferred" stock under this definition.

b. Constructive Distributions

Section 305(c) authorizes the promulgation of regulations subjecting certain transactions that have the effect of a stock dividend to the rules of §305(b). The Treasury Department responded in 1973 with Treas. Regs. §1.305-7. Under that regulation, "a change in conversion ratio, a change in redemption price, a difference between redemption price and issue price, a redemption which is treated as a distribution to which §301 applies, or any transaction (including a recapitalization) having a similar effect on the interest of any shareholder" may be treated as a constructive distribution of stock taxable under §305.

Suppose a corporation has two classes of stock outstanding, common and convertible preferred. If a common stock dividend is declared on the common stock, then the value of the convertibility feature of the preferred will be reduced unless some provision is made to increase its conversion ratio. For example, if each share of the preferred is convertible into one share of common, and if a one-for-one common stock dividend is declared on the common, then the conversion ratio of the preferred stock must be adjusted so that each share of preferred stock can be converted into two shares of common stock. Such a change in conversion ratio to account for stock dividends is called an "antidilution" provision. Treas. Regs. §1.305-7 has special rules for antidilution provisions. Because of the wording of §305(b)(4), some of the antidilution rules also appear in Treas. Regs. §1.305-3(d). (Recapitalizations are also addressed in Treas. Regs. §1.305-3, but consideration of recapitalizations is deferred until pages 539-546 infra.)

Rev. Rul. 78-60
1978-1 C.B. 81

Advice has been requested whether under section 302(a) of the Internal Revenue Code of 1954 the stock redemptions described below qualified for exchange treatment, and whether under section 305(b)(2) and (c) the shareholders who experienced increases in their proportionate interests in the redeeming corporation as a result of the stock redemptions will be treated as having received distributions of property to which section 301 applies.

Corporation Z has only one class of stock outstanding. The Z common stock is held by 24 shareholders, all of whom are descendants, or spouses of descendants, of the founder of Z.

In 1975, when Z had 6,000 shares of common stock outstanding, the board of directors of Z adopted a plan of annual redemption to provide a means for its shareholders to sell their stock. The plan provides that Z will annually redeem up to 40 shares to its outstanding stock at a price established annually by the Z board of directors. Each shareholder of Z is entitled to cause Z to redeem two-thirds of one percent of the shareholder's stock each year. If some shareholders choose not to participate fully in the plan during any year, the other shareholders can cause Z to redeem more than two-thirds of one percent of their stock, up to the maximum of 40 shares.

Pursuant to the plan of annual redemption, Z redeemed 40 shares of its stock in 1976. Eight shareholders participated in the redemptions. [No shareholder owned as much as 13 percent of the corporation's stock before or after the redemption. After the redemption, each shareholder actually and constructively owned at least 97 percent of his preredemption holding.]

Issue 1 . . .

None of the redemptions here qualified under section 302(b)(3) of the Code because all of the shareholders who participated in the redemptions continue to own stock of Z. Moreover, none of the redemptions qualified under section 302(b)(2) because none of the shareholders who participated in the redemptions experienced a reduction in interest of more than 20 percent, as section 302(b)(2)(C) requires. Therefore, the first question is whether the redemptions were "not essentially equivalent to a dividend" within the meaning of section 302(b)(1). . . .

In United States v. Davis, 397 U.S. 301 (1970), the Supreme Court of the United States said that for a redemption to qualify as not essentially equivalent to a dividend under section 302(b)(1) of the Code, the redemption must result in a meaningful reduction of the shareholder's proportionate interest in the corporation. The Court held that the business purpose of the redemption is irrelevant to this determination and that the ownership attribution rules of section 318(a) apply. Several of the shareholders of Z experienced reductions in their proportionate interests in Z (taking into account constructive stock ownership under section 318 of the Code) as a result of the 1976 redemptions. If their reductions were "meaningful," they are entitled to exchange treatment for their redemptions under section 302(a). Whether the reductions in proportionate interests were "meaningful" depends on the facts and circumstances.

In this case, an important fact is that the 1976 redemptions were not isolated occurrences but were undertaken pursuant to an ongoing plan for Z to redeem 40 shares of its stock each year. None of the reductions in proportionate interest experienced by Z shareholders as a result of the 1976 redemptions was "meaningful" because the reductions were small and each shareholder has the power to recover the lost interest by electing not to participate in the redemption plan in later years.

Accordingly, none of the 1976 redemptions qualified for exchange treatment under section 302(a) of the Code. All of the redemptions are to be treated as distributions of property to which section 301 applies.

Issue 2

Section 305(b)(2) of the Code provides that section 301 will apply to a distribution by a corporation of its stock if the distribution, or a series of distributions that includes the distribution, has the result of the receipt of property by some shareholders, and increases in the proportionate interests of other shareholders in the assets or earnings and profits of the corporation. . . .

Section 1.305-7(a) of the Income Tax Regulations provides that a redemption treated as a section 301 distribution will generally be treated as a distribution to which sections 305(b)(2) and 301 of the Code apply if the proportionate interest of any shareholder in the earnings and profits or assets of the corporation deemed to have made the stock distribution is increased by the redemption, and the distribution has the result described in section 305(b)(2). The distribution is to be deemed made to any shareholder whose interest in the earnings and profits or assets of the distributing corporation is increased by the redemption.

Section 1.305-3(b)(3) of the regulations provides that [a] distribution of property incident to an isolated redemption will not cause section 305(b)(2) to apply even though the redemption distribution is treated as a section 301 distribution.

Section 305 of the Code does not make the constructive stock ownership rules of section 318(a) applicable to its provisions.

The 16 shareholders of Z who did not tender any stock for redemption in 1976 experienced increases in their proportionate interests of the earnings and profits and assets of Z (without taking into account constructive stock ownership under section 318 of the Code) as a result of the redemptions. Shareholders B and X, who surrendered small amounts of their stock for redemption in 1976, also experienced increases in their proportionate interests. The 1976 redemptions were not isolated but were undertaken pursuant to an ongoing plan of annual stock redemptions. Finally, the 1976 redemptions are to be treated as distributions of property to which section 301 of the Code applies.

Accordingly, B, X and the 16 shareholders of Z who did not participate in the 1976 redemptions are deemed to have received stock distributions to which sections 305(b)(2) and 301 of the Code apply. See examples (8) and (9) of section 1.305-3(e) of the regulations for a method of computing the amounts of the deemed distributions.

Rev. Rul. 83-42
1983-1 C.B. 76

ISSUE

Is the distribution of common stock on convertible preferred stock, as described below, treated as the distribution of property to which section 301 of the Internal Revenue Code applies by reason of section 305(b)(4)?

X is a corporation that has both common and convertible preferred stock outstanding. The convertible preferred stock had been issued earlier in connection with the acquisition of an unrelated corporation. The convertible preferred stock is convertible into common stock according to a certain conversion ratio. The terms of the convertible preferred stock do not provide for anti-dilution protection by means of an increase in the conversion ratio made solely to take account of a stock dividend or stock split with respect to the stock into which such convertible stock is convertible.

On June 1, 1981, X distributed a 10 percent common stock dividend to the holders of its common stock. In addition, X distributed shares of its common stock to holders of its convertible preferred stock in order to offset the dilution of the holder's conversion rights. Dilution of the conversion rights of the holders of convertible preferred would have occurred but for the distribution of common stock to them because of the lack of a full adjustment in the conversion ratio of the preferred stock to reflect the stock dividend on the common stock.

LAW AND ANALYSIS

Section 305(a) of the Code provides generally that gross income does not include the amount of any distribution of the stock of a corporation made by such corporation to its shareholders with respect to its stock, except as otherwise provided in section 305(b) or (c).

Section 305(b)(4) of the Code provides that section 305(a) will not apply to a distribution by a corporation of its stock, and the distribution will be treated as a distribution of property to which section 301 applies, if the distribution is with respect to preferred stock, other than an increase in the conversion ratio of convertible preferred stock made solely to take account of a stock dividend or stock split with respect to the stock into which such convertible stock is convertible.

Section 1.305-5(a) of the regulations states, in part, that under section 305(b)(4), a distribution by a corporation of its stock made with respect to its preferred stock is treated as a distribution of property to which section 301 applies unless the distribution is made with respect to convertible preferred stock to take into account a stock dividend, stock split, or any similar event which would otherwise result in the dilution of the conversion right.

The exception contained in section 305(b)(4) of the Code would permit X to adjust the conversion ratio of its preferred stock to eliminate the dilution which resulted from the 10 percent common stock dividend on June 1, but it will not permit an actual distribution of stock to the holders of preferred stock, even if undertaken for the same anti-dilution purposes. The "distribution" referred to in section 1.305-5(a) of the regulations is only the deemed distribution which is considered to result when the conversion ratio is adjusted for the purpose described in section 305(b)(4). All other distributions on preferred stock are taxable, as expressly provided by section 305(b)(4).

HOLDING

The distribution of X common stock to holders of its convertible preferred stock is a distribution to which section 301 of the Code applies by reason of section 305(b)(4).

NOTE

1. *Redemptions treated as stock dividends to nonredeemed shareholders.* The effect of any non-pro rata redemption of common stock is to increase the proportionate interests of the nonredeemed shareholders while giving the redeemed shareholders cash or other property. This effect, described in §305(b)(2), causes redemptions to be ideal candidates for constructive stock dividend treatment under §305(c). Two substantial limitations, however, are imposed on the Commissioner's ability to treat a redemption to one shareholder as a stock dividend to others.

First, Congress in §305(c) granted authority to tax redemptions as constructive stock dividends only when the redemptions are taxed to the redeemed shareholder under §301 (e.g., when the redemption fails to qualify for exchange treatment under §302(a) for want of qualification under §302(b)(1)-(4)). Even though redemptions taxed as exchanges may have the effect of increasing the nonredeemed shareholders' corporate interests, such redemptions are not described in §305(c). Indeed, under §302(b)(1)-(3), only those redemptions causing the most significant change in the proportionate interests of the shareholders can qualify for exchange treatment. Yet §305(c) cannot apply to such redemptions.

Second, even redemptions taxed as distributions under §301 will not cause the nonredeemed shareholders difficulty under §305(c) so long as the redemption is "an isolated redemption and is not a part of a periodic redemption plan." Treas. Regs. §1.305-3(e) (example 10). The statute makes no special distinction for "isolated" redemptions. Why has the Treasury Department so limited application of §305(c)? If a corporation distributes cash to shareholder A and stock to shareholder B, then shareholder B will be taxed pursuant to §305(b)(2). If the same result is accomplished by redeeming a part of the stock of shareholder A, why should the taxation be different if the transaction is "isolated"?

In Rev. Rul. 77-19, 1977-1 C.B. 83, a corporation redeemed shares in 20 isolated transactions during the three prior years from deceased and retiring shareholders. It also redeemed the interests of minority shareholders. The Service ruled that the corporation was not engaged in a periodic redemption plan under §305(c) so as to trigger taxable constructive dividends to the continuing shareholders. Cf. Rev. Rul. 78-60, page 297 supra, in which the Service ruled that periodic small redemptions of stock pursuant to an ongoing plan of annual redemptions were taxable as dividends to the redeeming shareholders and as taxable distributions under §305(b)(2) and (c) to the continuing shareholders whose proportionate interests were increased thereby. See Dietzsch v. United States, 498 F.2d 1344 (Cl. Ct. 1974), in which an auto dealer, contractually obligated to use cash distributions from his corporation to purchase the stock of a co-shareholder in a program leading to eventual acquisition by the dealer of the entire ownership of the corporation, was held taxable on the distributions as a dividend. The court refused to view the various steps as an integrated transaction constituting a complete redemption of the co-shareholder and culminating in a tax-free stock dividend.

Some redemptions will not be subject to §305(c) because they are part of a transaction akin to a security arrangement. For example, in Rev. Rul. 78-115, 1978-1 C.B. 85, a corporation engaged in mandatory, periodic redemptions of nonparticipating, nonvoting stock that had been issued as partial consideration for a prior stock acquisition by the corporation. The Service ruled that such redemptions would not give rise to income to the nonredeemed shareholders under §305(c) because the redeemed stock was created solely to facilitate the prior acquisition when other forms of financing were unavailable. See also Treas. Regs. §1.305-3(e) (example 14).

Note that when §305(c) does apply to a redemption, it does not automatically trigger the recognition of income to any shareholder: Transactions described in §305(c) are recharacterized by that section as distributions increasing the proportionate interests of one or more shareholders in their corporation. The tax consequences of such a deemed distribution must be determined under §305(a) and (b)(2).

2. *Adjustment in conversion ratio.* As made clear in Rev. Rul. 83-42, above, the only antidilution provision excluded from taxation under §305(b)(4) and (c) is an increase or decrease in the conversion ratio of convertible preferred stock to account for stock distributions on, or stock splits of, the stock into which the preferred may be converted. What are the consequences if the conversion ratio of convertible preferred stock is adjusted to account for cash dividends paid on the common or on the preferred stock? See Treas. Regs. §1.305-3(e) (example 7). To what possible abuse does this example speak? What is the result if the preferred shareholders exercise their conversion rights shortly after a cash dividend paid on the common? Compare §305(b)(2).

Rev. Rul. 84-141, 1984-2 C.B. 80, discusses the consequences of a right given to holders of cumulative preferred stock to have dividend arrearages paid in common stock if cash dividends are unpaid for two consecutive quarters. The Service ruled that the holders of such cumulative preferred stock are subject to taxation under §305(c) and (b)(2) on the passage of two quarters in which the corporation fails to pay cash dividends. Since the holders of the preferred stock have an unqualified right to receive common stock in lieu of accrued dividends at that time, the Service ruled that they are taxable on the fair market value of the common stock they can elect to receive regardless of whether they elect to accept it.

C. TAINTING OF STOCK UNDER §306

While the taxation rules of §305(b) and (c) may seem all-inclusive, they are not: Many stock dividends will be tax free under the general rule of §305(a). In particular, a pro rata distribution of preferred stock to all holders of common stock is tax free. To reinforce comprehension of the last section, see if you can parse through the Code to arrive at this result.

How should the sale or redemption of shares received tax free as a stock dividend be taxed? Suppose a corporation has substantial earnings and profits that its sole shareholder would like to remove from corporate solution in the form of cash. A dividend could be declared, but that would produce ordinary income to the shareholder without any recovery of basis. In the absence of a partial liquidation, capital gain treatment on a redemption will be unavailable under §302(b)(1) under *Davis.* But suppose the shareholder follows a three-step plan: (1) declare a stock dividend on her common shares of nonvoting preferred stock redeemable for par at the corporation's option or at a fixed time in the near future; (2) sell this newly created preferred stock to someone outside for par; and (3) cause the corporation to redeem this preferred stock shortly after the sale. If the preferred stock pays a sufficiently high (and guaranteed) dividend rate until redemption, the shareholder should not have great difficulty in selling it. On that sale, the shareholder will claim capital gains under §1202(a). The purchaser will claim exchange treatment on the redemption pursuant to the complete termination safe harbor of §302(b)(3), and, because the purchaser will have a basis in the preferred stock equal to par, there will be no taxable gain on the redemption under §302(a). As an additional wrinkle, if the shareholder seeks a deduction rather than a capital gain, she might contribute the preferred stock to a charity rather than sell it to a third party.

How should this type of end-run around §§301 and 302 be addressed? Should the courts or Congress respond?

Chamberlin v. Commissioner ——————————————————————
207 F.2d 462 (6th Cir. 1953)

Before Simons, Chief Judge, and McAllister and Miller, Circuit Judges.

MILLER, Circuit Judge.

Petitioner C. P. Chamberlin seeks a review of an income tax deficiency determined by the Respondent for the calendar year 1946, and sustained by the Tax Court. . . .

The Metal Moulding Corporation, hereinafter referred to as the Corporation, is a Michigan corporation engaged in the business of manufacturing metal mouldings and bright work trim used in the manufacture of automobiles. . . . From 1940 until December 20, 1946, the issued and outstanding common stock totaled 1,002½ shares, of which Chamberlin and his wife together owned 83.8%. . . .

The business of the Corporation prospered, and after paying substantial cash dividends over a period of years, its balance sheet at the end of the first six months in 1946 reflected total assets of $2,488,836.53 and included in current assets $722,404.56 cash and $549,950 United States Government Bonds and notes.

On December 16, 1946, the Corporation's authorized capital stock was increased from $150,000 to $650,000, represented by 6,500 shares of $100 par value common stock. On December 20, 1946, a stock dividend was declared and distributed of five shares of common for each share of common outstanding, and the Corporation's accounts were adjusted by transferring $501,250 from earned surplus to capital account.

On December 26, 1946, the articles of incorporation were amended so as to authorize, in addition to the 6,500 shares of common stock, 8,020 shares of 4½% cumulative $100 par value preferred stock. On December 28, 1946, a stock dividend was declared of 1⅓ shares of the newly authorized preferred stock for each share of common stock outstanding, to be issued pro rata to the holders of common stock as of December 27, 1946, and the Company's accounts were adjusted by transferring $802,000 from earned surplus to capital account. The preferred stock was issued to the stockholders on the same day. Prior to the declaration of the preferred stock dividend, the Corporation at all times had only one class of stock outstanding.

On December 30, 1946, as the result of prior negotiations . . . all of the holders of the preferred stock, except the estate of Edward W. Smith, deceased, which owned 20 shares, signed a "Purchase Agreement," with The Northwestern Mutual Life Insurance Company and The Lincoln National Life Insurance Company, which instrument was also endorsed by the Corporation for the purpose of making certain representations, warranties and agreements. Under the "Purchase Agreement" 4,000 shares of the preferred stock was sold to each of the two insurance companies at a cash price of $100 per share plus accrued dividends from November 1st, 1946 to date of delivery. . . .

In the latter part of 1945, the Corporation's attorney and Chamberlin discussed with an investment firm in Chicago the possibility of selling an issue of preferred stock similar to the stock subsequently issued. The Corporation had such a large accumulated earned surplus it was fearful of being subjected to the surtax provided for by [§531], but at the same time Chamberlin, the majority stockholder, was not willing to have the Corporation distribute any substantial portion of its earned surplus as ordinary dividends because his individual income was taxable at high surtax rates. It was proposed that the issuance of a stock dividend to the stockholders and the sale of it by the stockholders would enable the stockholders to obtain accumulated earnings of the Corporation in the form of capital gains rather than as taxable dividends. . . .

The preferred stock contained the following provisions among others: The holders were entitled to cumulative cash dividends at the rate of $4.50 per annum payable quarterly beginning November 1, 1946; the stock was subject to redemption on any quarterly dividend date in whole or in part at par plus specified premiums and accrued dividends; it was subject to mandatory retirement in amounts not exceeding 2,000 shares on May 1, 1948 and 1,000 on May 1st on each succeeding year, depending upon the Corporation's net earnings for the preceding year, until fully retired on May 1, 1954. . . .

The Tax Court held that the issue of whether the stock dividend constituted income to the stockholders should be determined from a consideration of all the facts and circumstances surrounding the issuance of the dividend and not by a consideration limited to the characteristics of the stock declared as a dividend; that each case involving a stock dividend must be decided upon its own facts and circumstances as establishing whether the receipt of a particular kind of stock dividend was in fact taxable; that such a decision did not rest upon matters of form or nomenclature attending a stock dividend distribution but rather upon the real substance of the transaction involved; . . . but that considering the real substance of the transaction it was of the opinion that the stock dividend was not in good faith for any bona fide corporate business purpose, and that the attending circumstances and conditions under which it was issued made it the equivalent of a cash dividend distribution out of available earnings, thus constituting ordinary taxable income in the amount of the value of the preferred shares received. The Court also said that the real purpose of the issuance of the preferred shares was concurrently to place them in the hands of others not then stockholders of the Corporation, thereby substantially altering the common stockholders' pre-existing proportionate interests in the Corporation's net assets and thereby creating an entirely new relationship amongst all the stockholders and the Corporation. . . .

In our opinion, the declaration and distribution of the preferred stock dividend, considered by itself, falls clearly within the principles established in Towne v. Eisner, [245 U.S. 418 (1918)], and Eisner v. Macomber, [252 U.S. 189 (1920)], and is controlled by the ruling in the *Strassburger* case. Accordingly, as a preliminary matter, we do not agree with the Tax Court's statement that the stock dividend is taxable because as a result of the dividend and immediate sale thereafter it substantially altered the common stockholders' pre-existing proportional interests in the Corporation's net assets. The sale to the insurance companies of course resulted in such a change, but the legal effect of the dividend with respect to rights in the corporate assets is determined at the time of its distribution, not by what the stockholders do with it after its receipt. . . .

But respondent contends that the sale of the stock following immediately upon its receipt resulted in the stockholder acquiring cash instead of stock, thus making it a taxable dividend under Secs. 22(a) and 115(a), [1939] Internal Revenue Code. There are two answers to this contention.

A non-taxable stock dividend does not become a taxable cash dividend upon its sale by the recipient. . . . In none of the Supreme Court cases referred to above, dealing with the taxability of stock dividends, was the length of the holding period considered as a factor. Obviously, if the non-taxability of a stock dividend rests solely upon the principle that it does not alter the pre-existing proportionate interest of any stockholder or increase the intrinsic value of his holdings, the disposition of the stock dividend by the stockholder thereafter is not a factor in the determination.

The foregoing conclusion is supported by [§1223(5)], which provides that for the purpose of determining whether a non-taxable stock dividend which has been sold is a long-term capital gain there shall be included in the holding period the period for which the taxpayer held the stock in the distributing corporation prior to the receipt of the stock dividend. This necessarily recognizes that a stock dividend will often be sold before the expiration of six months after its receipt, and makes no distinction between a stock dividend held one day or for any other period less than six months. . . .

The other answer to the contention is that although the stockholder *acquired* money in the final analysis, he did not *receive* either money or property *from* the corporation. . . . The money he received was received from the insurance companies. It was not a "distribution" by the corporation declaring the dividend, as required by [§115(a), 1939 Code; and §316(a), 1954 Code].

We come then to what in our opinion is the dominant and decisive issue in the case, namely, whether the stock dividend, which, by reason of its redemption feature, enabled the Corporation to ultimately distribute its earnings to its stockholders on a taxable basis materially lower than would have been the case by declaring and paying the usual cash dividend, was a bona fide one, one in substance as well as in form. . . .

It seems clear that it was an issue of stock in substance as well as in form. According to its terms, and in the absence of a finding that it was immediately or shortly thereafter redeemed at a premium, we assume that a large portion of it has remained outstanding over a period of years with some of it still unredeemed after nearly seven years. It has been in the hands of the investing public, free of any control by the corporation over its owners, whose enforceable rights with respect to operations of the corporation would not be waived or neglected. Substantial sums have been paid in dividends. The insurance companies bought it in the regular course of their business and have held it as approved investments. For the Court to now tell them that they have been holding a sham issue of stock would be most startling and disturbing news. . . .

If the transaction lacks the good faith necessary to avoid the assessment it must be because of the redemption feature of the stock, which, in the final analysis, is what ultimately permitted the distribution of the corporate earnings and is the key factor in the overall transaction. Redemption features are well known and often used in corporate financing. If the one in question was a reasonable one, not violative of the general principles of bona fide corporate financing, and acceptable to experienced bona fide investors familiar with investment fundamentals and the opportunities afforded by the investment market we fail to see how a court can properly classify the issue, by reason of the redemption feature, as lacking in good faith or as not being what it purports to be. . . .

Each case necessarily depends upon its own facts. The facts in this case show tax avoidance, and it is so conceded by petitioner. But they also show a series of legal transactions, no one of which is fictitious or so lacking in substance as to be anything different from what it purports to be. Unless we are to adopt the broad policy of holding taxable any series of transactions, the purpose and result of which is the avoidance of taxes which would otherwise accrue if handled in a different way, regardless of the legality and realities of the component parts, the tax assessed by the Commissioner was successfully avoided in the present case. We do not construe the controlling decisions as having adopted that view. . . .

Fireoved v. United States
462 F.2d 1281 (3d Cir. 1972)

Before Adams, Rosen, and Hunter, Circuit Judges.

ADAMS, Circuit Judge.

This appeal calls into question the application of section 306 . . . and the "first in-first out rule" to a redemption of preferred stock in a corporation by plaintiff, one of its principal shareholders. In particular we are asked to decide whether the transaction here had "as one of its principal purposes the avoidance of federal income tax," whether a prior sale of a portion of the underlying common stock immunized a like proportion of the section 306 stock from treatment as a noncapital asset and whether another block of the redeemed stock should be considered to represent stock not subject to section 306.

I. FACTUAL BACKGROUND

On November 24, 1948, Fireoved and Company, Inc. was incorporated for the purpose of printing and selling business forms. At their first meeting, the incorporators elected Eugene Fireoved, his wife, Marie, the plaintiffs, and a nephew, Robert L. Fireoved, as directors of the corporation. Subsequently, the directors elected Eugene Fireoved as president and treasurer and Marie Fireoved as secretary. . . . On December 31, 1948, in consideration for $100 cash, the corporation issued Eugene Fireoved 100 shares of common stock; for $500 cash, it issued him five shares of preferred stock; and in payment for automotive equipment and furniture and fixtures, valued at $6,000, it issued him an additional 60 shares of preferred stock.

In 1954, when Mr. Fireoved learned that his nephew, Robert, was planning to leave the business, he began discussions with Karl Edelmayer and Kenneth Craver concerning the possibility of combining his business with their partnership, Girard Business Forms, that had been printing and selling business forms for some time prior to 1954. Messrs. Fireoved, Edelmayer and Craver agreed that voting control of the new enterprise should be divided equally among the three of them. Because Mr. Fireoved's contribution to capital would be approximately $60,000 whereas the partnership could contribute only $30,000, it was decided that preferred stock should be issued to Mr. Fireoved to compensate for the disparity. In furtherance of this plan . . . the following corporate changes were accomplished: the name of the company was changed to Girard Business Forms; the authorized common stock was increased from 100 to 300 shares and the authorized preferred stock was increased to 1000 shares; Mr. Fireoved exchanged his 100 shares of common and 65 shares of preferred stock for equal amounts of the new stock; an agreement of purchase was authorized by which the company would buy all the assets of the Edelmayer-Craver partnership in return for 200 shares of common and 298 shares of preferred stock; and Mr. Fireoved was issued 535 shares of the new preferred stock as a dividend[6] on his 100 shares of common stock, thereby bringing his total holding of preferred stock to 600 shares to indicate his $60,000 capital contribution compared to the $29,800 contributed by the former partnership.

As the business progressed, Mr. Edelmayer demanded more control

---

6. At the time Mr. Fireoved received his stock dividend, the company had accumulated earnings and profits of $52,993.06.

of the company. In response, Mr. Fireoved and Mr. Craver each sold 24 shares of common stock in the corporation to him on February 28, 1958.

On April 30, 1959, the company redeemed 451 of Mr. Fireoved's 600 shares of preferred stock at $105 per share, resulting in net proceeds to him of $47,355.[7] The gain from this transaction was reported by Mr. and Mrs. Fireoved . . . as a long term capital gain. Subsequently, the Commissioner . . . assessed a deficiency against the Fireoveds of $15,337.13 based on the Commissioner's view that the proceeds from the redemption of the 451 shares of preferred stock should have been reported as ordinary income and the tax paid at that rate based on section 306. . . .

II. BACKGROUND OF SECTION 306

Because we are the first court of appeals asked to decide questions of law pursuant to section 306, it is appropriate that we first examine the circumstances that led to the inclusion in 1954 of this section in the code.

Generally, a taxpayer will benefit monetarily if he is able to report income as a long term capital gain rather than as ordinary income. Under normal circumstances a cash dividend from a corporation constitutes ordinary income to the shareholder receiving such money. Therefore, it would be to the advantage of a shareholder if a method could be devised by which the money could be distributed to him, that would otherwise be paid out as cash dividends, in a form that would permit the shareholder to report such income as a long term capital gain.

A temporarily successful plan for converting ordinary income to long term capital gain is described by the facts of Chamberlin v. C.I.R., 207 F.2d 462 (6th Cir. 1953). There a close corporation had assets of $2.5 million, approximately half of which were in the form of cash and government securities. To have distributed the cash not required in the operation of the business to the shareholders as a dividend would have subjected them to taxation at ordinary income rates. The corporation therefore amended its charter to authorize 8,020 shares of preferred stock to be issued to the shareholders as a dividend on their common stock. The accounts of the corporation were adjusted by transferring $802,000 from earned surplus to the capital account. While these corporate changes were taking place, negotiations occurred between the shareholders and two insurance companies for the purchase of the newly issued preferred stock. In addition, the corporation constructed a timetable for retirement of the preferred stock, which proved satisfactory to the purchasing companies. When the transaction was completed, the selling shareholders reported the gain they realized from the sale of the preferred stock to the insurance companies as a long term gain from the disposition of a capital asset. The Commissioner

7. In 1959, the company had accumulated earnings and profits of $48,235.

contended that the gain should have been reported as ordinary income and accordingly assessed a deficiency against the selling shareholders. The tax court agreed with the Commissioner. On review, the Sixth Circuit reversed, holding for the taxpayer thus giving the approval of a federal court to what has been termed "a preferred stock bail-out."

The legislative reaction to the *Chamberlin* decision was almost immediate, resulting in the addition of section 306 to the 1954 code, in order to prevent shareholders from obtaining the tax advantage of such bail-outs when such shareholders retain their ownership interests in the company. . . .

For tax purposes, Congress created a new type of stock known as section 306 stock. When a corporation having accumulated or retained earnings and profits issues a stock dividend which is not otherwise subject to taxation at the time of issuance (other than common on common), the stock received is section 306 stock. The effect of owning such stock is that on its redemption, if the corporation has sufficient retained earnings at that time, the gain* is taxed at ordinary income rates while any loss resulting may not be recognized for federal tax purposes. Section 306(b) sets forth several exceptions to the general rule which serve to remove the section 306 taint from stock disposed of under those circumstances.

Based on the history of section 306 and its plain meaning evidenced by the provisions, it is not disputed that the 535 shares of preferred stock issued to Mr. Fireoved as a stock dividend in 1954 were section 306 stock. Additionally, it is clear that in 1959, when the company redeemed 451 shares of Mr. Fireoved's preferred stock, the general provisions of section 306 — aside from the exceptions — would require that any amount realized by Mr. Fireoved be taxed at ordinary income rates rather than long term capital gain rates, because the company had earnings at that time of $48,235 — more than the $47,355 required to redeem the stock at $105 per share.

Thus, the questions to be decided on this appeal are (1) whether certain of the exceptions to section 306 apply to permit the Fireoveds' reporting their gain as a long term capital gain, and (2) whether 65 of the 451 shares redeemed are not section 306 stock because of the first in-first out rule of Treasury Regulation §1.1012-1(c).

III. WAS THE DISTRIBUTION OF THE STOCK DIVIDEND "IN PURSUANCE OF A PLAN HAVING AS ONE OF ITS PRINCIPAL PURPOSES AVOIDANCE OF FEDERAL INCOME TAX"?

Mr. Fireoved asserts that the entire transaction should fall within the exception established by section 306(b)(4)(A). . . .

As a threshold point on this issue, the government maintains that

---

* "Gain" or "amount realized"? — EDS.

because Mr. Fireoved never attempted to obtain a ruling from the "Secretary or his delegate" the redemption should be covered by section 306(a), and the district court should not have reached the question whether the exception applied to Mr. Fireoved. Mr. Fireoved urges that the district court had the power to consider the matter de novo, even without a request by the taxpayer to the secretary or his delegate. Because the ultimate result we reach would not be altered by whichever of these two courses we choose, we do not resolve this potentially complex procedural problem.

The district court, based on the assumption that it had the power to decide the question, found that although one of the purposes involved in the issuance of the preferred stock dividend may have been business related, another principal purpose was the avoidance of Federal income tax.

Mr. Fireoved's analysis of the facts presented in the stipulations would reach the conclusion that the *sole* purpose of the stock dividend was business related. He relies heavily on that portion of the stipulation which describes why the decision was made to combine his business with the Edelmayer-Craver partnership: "the partnership could provide the additional manpower which the expected departure of Robert L. Fireoved from the corporation would require. Additionally, the partnership needed additional working capital which the corporation had and could provide." Based primarily on the latter sentence, Mr. Fireoved asserts that the district court had no choice but to find that the transaction was business related and that it therefore had no avoidance incentive.

In making this argument, however, Mr. Fireoved overlooks the plain import of the language of section 306(b)(4). Whether the section requires the decision to be made by the secretary or the district court, it is clear that "one of [the] principal purposes" of the stock dividend was for "the avoidance of Federal income tax." The stipulation demonstrates no more than that the reorganized company required more capital than could be supplied by the partnership alone. The stipulation is completely in harmony with the following fact situation: after the partnership was combined with the corporation, the business required the $30,000 contributed by the partnership and all of the $60,000 Mr. Fireoved had in the corporation. Mr. Fireoved decided to take the stock dividend rather than to distribute the cash to himself as a dividend, and then to make a loan to the corporation of the necessary money because if he took the cash, he would subject himself to taxation at ordinary income rates. Therefore "one of the principal purposes" of the stock dividend would be for "the avoidance of federal income tax."

In a situation such as the one presented in this case, where the facts necessary to determine the motives for the issuance of a stock dividend are peculiarly within the control of the taxpayer, it is reasonable to require the taxpayer to come forward with the facts that would relieve him of his liability. Here the stipulation was equivocal in determining the purpose of the dividend and is quite compatible with the thought that "one of the

principal purposes" was motivated by "tax avoidance." We hold then that
the district court did not err in refusing to apply the exception created by
section 306(b)(4)(A).[11]

**IV. Did the Prior Sale by Mr. Fireoved of 24% of His
Underlying Common Stock Immunize Such Portion
of the Section 306 Stock He Redeemed in 1959?**

The district court construed section 306(b)(4)(B) to mean that any time
a taxpayer in Mr. Fireoved's position sells any portion of his underlying
common stock and later sells or redeems his section 306 stock, an equivalent proportion of the section 306 stock redeemed will not be subject to
the provisions of section 306(a). The government has appealed from this
portion of the district court's order and urges that we reverse it, based on
the history and purpose of section 306 and the particular facts here.

The stipulations indicate that, "on February 28, 1958, Fireoved and
Craver each sold 24 shares of common stock in the corporation to Edelmayer," and that appropriate stock certificates were issued. From this fact,
Mr. Fireoved reasons that his sale of 24 of his 100 shares of common stock
was undertaken solely for the business purpose of satisfying Mr. Edelmayer's desire for more control of the corporation, and therefore he should
be given the benefit of section 306(b)(4)(B). In addition, Mr. Fireoved
contends that the disposition of his section 306 stock was related to a
business purpose because he used part of the proceeds to pay off a $20,000
loan that the company had made to him.

Mr. Fireoved has the same burden here of showing a lack of a tax
avoidance purpose that he had in section III supra. It is clear from the
limited facts set forth in the stipulations that he has not established that
the disposition of 24% of the 535 shares of the section 306 preferred stock
he owned "was not in pursuance of a plan having as one of its principal
purposes the avoidance of federal income tax."[12] More important, how-

---

11. It is important to note that apparently both Mr. Fireoved, in prosecuting this action
for a refund, and the government, in its defense, assumed that if the distribution and redemption of the preferred stock were not controlled by §306(a), the gain would be subject to
taxation as a long term capital gain. This is not necessarily the case at all. Whether or not
§306 governs the transaction, it nonetheless involves a redemption of stock by a corporation
to which §302 could apply. Under the tests set out in §302(b) — the relevant one of which
appears to be §302(b)(1) — Mr. Fireoved, who had the burden of proof, may well have been
unable to show that the redemption was not "essentially equivalent to a dividend." . . . We
hold, however, that it is now too late for the government to raise this issue.

12. Consistent with Mr. Fireoved's sale of 24 shares of common stock in 1958 could have
been his knowledge that one year later he would be selling his section 306 stock and a desire
on his part to avoid taxation at ordinary income rates. As noted later in the opinion, the sale
of just 24 shares was enough so that he retained effective control — in the form of veto
power — over the corporation. Moreover, the fact that Mr. Fireoved needed $20,000 of the

ever, is that an examination of the relevant legislative history indicates that Congress did not intend to give capital gains treatment to a portion of the preferred stock redeemed on the facts presented here.

It is apparent from the reaction evinced by Congress to the *Chamberlin* case, supra, that by enacting section 306 Congress was particularly concerned with the tax advantages available to persons who controlled corporations and who could, without sacrificing their control, convert ordinary income to long term capital gains by the device of the preferred stock bailout. The illustration given in the Senate Report which accompanied section 306(b)(4)(B) is helpful in determining the sort of transactions meant to be exempted by section 306(a):

> Thus if a shareholder received a distribution of 100 shares of section 306 stock on his holdings of 100 shares of voting common stock in a corporation and sells his voting common stock before he disposes of his section 306 stock, the subsequent disposition of his section 306 stock would not ordinarily be considered a tax avoidance disposition *since he has previously parted with the stock which allows him to participate in the ownership of the business.* However, variations of the above example may give rise to tax avoidance possibilities which are not within the exception of subparagraph (b). Thus if a corporation has only one class of common stock outstanding and it issues stock under circumstances that characterize it as section 306 stock, a subsequent issue of a different class of common having greater voting rights than the original common will not permit a simultaneous disposition of the section 306 stock together with the original common to escape the rules of subsection (a) of section 306.

S. Rep. No. 1622, 83d Cong., 2d Sess., 1954 U.S.C.C.A. News, pp. 4621, 4881 (emphasis added).

Thus, it is reasonable to assume that Congress realized the general lack of a tax avoidance purpose when a person sells *all* of his control in a corporation and then either simultaneously or subsequently disposes of his section 306 stock. However, when only a portion of the underlying common stock is sold, and the taxpayer retains essentially all the control he had previously, it would be unrealistic to conclude that Congress meant to give that taxpayer the advantage of section 306(b)(4)(B) when he ultimately sells his section 306 stock. Cf. United States v. Davis, 397 U.S. 301 (1970).

Shortly after Mr. Fireoved's corporation had been combined with the

---

proceeds to pay off a loan to the corporation would not meet his burden. The proceeds of the redemption totaled $47,355. Thus, although $20,000 of the redemption may not have been to avoid taxes, we can ascribe no purpose other than tax avoidance to the receipt of the additional $27,355. Therefore, since one of the principal purposes of the redemption of 451 shares of preferred stock was "the avoidance of Federal income tax," Mr. Fireoved may not take advantage of §306(b)(4)(B) for any part of the redemption.

Edelmayer-Craver partnership, significant changes to the by-laws were made. The by-laws provided that corporate action could be taken only with the unanimous consent of all the directors. In addition, the by-laws provided that they could be amended either by a vote of 76% of the outstanding common shares or a unanimous vote of the directors. When the businesses were combined in late 1954, each of the directors held $\frac{1}{3}$ of the voting stock, thereby necessitating a unanimous vote for amendment to the by-laws. After Messrs. Fireoved and Craver each sold 24 shares of common stock to Mr. Edelmayer, Mr. Fireoved held $25\frac{1}{3}\%$ of the common (voting) stock, Mr. Craver $25\frac{1}{3}\%$ and Mr. Edelmayer $49\frac{1}{3}\%$. It is crucial to note that the by-laws provided for a unanimous vote for corporate action, and after the common stock transfer, the by-laws were capable of amendment only by a unanimous vote because no two shareholders could vote more than $74\frac{2}{3}\%$ of the common stock and 76% of the common stock was necessary for amendment. Thus, although Mr. Fireoved did sell a portion of his voting stock prior to his disposition of the section 306 stock, he retained as much control in the corporation following the sale of his common stock as he had prior to the sale. Under these circumstances it is not consonant with the history of the legislation to conclude that Congress intended such a sale of underlying common stock to exempt the proceeds of the disposition of section 306 stock from treatment as ordinary income. Accordingly, the district court erred when it held that any of the preferred shares Mr. Fireoved redeemed were not subject to section 306(a) by virtue of section 306(b)(4)(B).

V. DOES THE RULE OF FIRST IN-FIRST OUT MEAN THAT 65 OF THE 451 REDEEMED SHARES WERE THOSE WHICH MR. FIREOVED ACQUIRED WHEN HE INCORPORATED HIS BUSINESS IN 1948 AND THUS SHOULD NOT BE TREATED AS SECTION 306 STOCK?

The district court held that 65 of 451 shares of preferred stock that Mr. Fireoved redeemed in 1959 represented the original shares issued to him in 1948 and were not, therefore, section 306 stock, and that the proceeds from their sales should be treated as a long term capital gain. The court reached this conclusion by applying Treas. Reg. §1.1012-1(c). This regulation provides that when an individual acquires shares of the same class of stock in the same corporation on different dates and for different prices, sells a portion of those shares, and cannot adequately identify which lots were sold, for the purpose of determining the basis and the holding period, the first shares acquired are deemed to be the first shares sold.

Both the district court and Mr. Fireoved reason that the 65 preferred shares he received in 1948 were the first such shares owned by him. In 1954, when the corporation was recapitalized, Mr. Fireoved surrendered his certificate for 65 shares, received a 535 share stock dividend and was issued a certificate representing 600 shares of preferred stock. When he disposed of 451 shares in 1959, it was impossible to identify which shares of the 600 share certificate were being sold. By applying the convenient tool of section 1.1012-1(c), one might conclude that the 65 original shares were sold first because they were received first.

Superficially, this analysis appears to be correct. However, it overlooks the existence of section 1223(5) of the code and the regulations issued pursuant thereto. This section governs the transaction in question because section 307 required Mr. Fireoved to allocate his investment in the underlying common stock between the stock and the preferred stock issued as a dividend. Section 1223(5) is then clear in that it will apply to all situations in which an allocation of basis has occurred pursuant to section 307. These provisions broadly state that the holding period for stock received as a stock dividend is equal to the period for which the underlying stock was held. Applying this test we discover that the preferred stock dividend of 535 shares was issued with respect to the original 100 shares of common received by Mr. Fireoved. Therefore, the holding period for the 535 shares dividend relates back to the date on which the underlying common was issued. Coincidentally, the original 65 shares of preferred stock were issued on the same date as the common. Because the constructive date of issuance for all of the 600 shares of preferred stock owned by Mr. Fireoved is identical, neither the 65 shares nor the 535 shares are first in, but rather are in at the same time.

Since it is impossible adequately to identify which shares were sold when Mr. Fireoved redeemed 451 shares of preferred stock, we hold that a pro rata portion of the 65 shares were redeemed in 1959. In other words, the percentage of the 600 shares of preferred which were not section 306 stock may be represented by the fraction 65/600. That percentage of the 451 shares redeemed in 1959, therefore, would not be section 306 stock. . . .

Rev. Rul. 81-91
1981-1 C.B. 123

ISSUE

Is the class B stock described below "section 306 stock" within the meaning of section 306(c) of the Internal Revenue Code?

FACTS

A corporation has outstanding a single class of common stock held by 10 individuals, each of whom owned 20 shares. For valid business reasons the corporation entered into a plan of recapitalization under which each outstanding share of common stock was surrendered to the corporation in exchange for one share of new class A stock plus one share of new class B stock of the corporation.

The recapitalization was a reorganization defined in section 368(a)(1)(E) of the Code and the exchanges were nontaxable under section 354(a)(1).

Each share of the class A and class B stock had a par value of $10x$ dollars. The class B shares were entitled to an annual cumulative dividend of 6 percent of par value payable before any dividend was payable on the class A shares, and a prior right to repayment up to par value in the event of liquidation. After the satisfaction of the class B stock's preferences, each share of class A and class B stock shared equally as to dividends and on liquidation. Each class of shares carried equal voting rights and neither class was by its terms redeemable.

LAW AND ANALYSIS

Section 306(c)(1)(B) of the Code provides, in part and in effect, that "section 306 stock" is any stock, except common stock, that is received by a shareholder pursuant to a plan of reorganization under section 368 with respect to the receipt of which gain or loss to the shareholder was to any extent not recognized by reason of section 354, but only to the extent that the effect of the transaction is substantially the same as the receipt of a stock dividend.

The term "common stock" as used in section 306 of the Code is not defined in that section or the related regulations. In determining whether newly issued stock is "common stock" for purposes of section 306, the "preferred stock bailout" abuse Congress sought to prevent by enactment of that section provides guidance. . . . A bailout occurs if shareholders, through section 306 stock or some other device, withdraw a corporation's earnings and profits at the more favorable tax rates for capital gains. The potential for a preferred stock bailout exists if the shareholders receive a pro rata distribution of two classes of stock in a recapitalization when the corporation has earnings and profits, and the stock of one class, because of its terms, can be disposed of without a surrender by the shareholders of significant interests in corporate growth. Thus, stock is other than "common stock" for purposes of section 306 not because of its preferred position as such, but because the preferred position is limited and the stock does not participate in corporate growth to any significant extent.

The class B stock enjoys voting rights on an equal basis with the class A stock, the only other class of stock outstanding. After satisfaction of its preference to dividends and as to assets in the event of liquidation, the class B stock shares equally with the class A stock. These rights in the class

B stock to participate in corporate growth are significant. Thus, a sale of the class B stock cannot occur without a loss of voting control and interest in the unrestricted growth of the corporation. Therefore, the bailout abuse that Congress sought to prevent by the enactment of section 306 cannot be effected through a sale of the class B stock.

HOLDING

The class B stock is "common stock" and is, therefore, excepted from the definition of section 306 stock under section 306(c)(1)(B) of the Code. . . .

Rev. Rul. 76-387
1976-2 C.B. 96

Advice has been requested whether, under the circumstances set forth below, the class A nonvoting common stock is "common stock" for purposes of section 306(c)(1)(B) of the Internal Revenue Code of 1954.

Corporation X had outstanding class A nonvoting common stock, class B voting common stock, and nonvoting preferred stock. The preferred stock was limited and preferred as to dividends, had no dividends in arrears, had a fixed liquidation preference, and was "section 306 stock" within the meaning of section 306(c) of the Code. Neither the class A nor the class B stock was limited or preferred with respect to dividends or distributions in liquidation and neither had a preference over the other in any respect. The only difference between the two classes of common stock was that the class B stock had voting rights while the class A stock did not. Neither the class A stock nor the class B stock was by its terms redeemable.

X desired to simplify its corporate structure by eliminating the preferred stock. Pursuant to a plan of recapitalization, the holders of the preferred stock exchanged such stock solely for shares of class A stock of equal value. The transaction qualified as a reorganization (recapitalization) under section 368(a)(1)(E) of the Code and no gain or loss was recognized to the exchanging shareholders pursuant to section 354. There was no intent to redeem the class A stock when the exchange was made.

Section 306(c)(1)(B) of the Code provides, in part, that "section 306 stock" is any stock, except common stock, that is received by a shareholder in exchange for other "section 306 stock" in pursuance of a plan of reorganization under section 368 with respect to the receipt of which gain or loss to the shareholder was to any extent not recognized. Therefore, if the class A stock in the instant case is "common stock," it is not "section 306 stock" within the meaning of section 306(c)(1)(B). Neither the Code nor the Income Tax Regulations define "common stock" for purposes of section 306.

In determining whether newly issued stock is "common stock" for purposes of section 306 of the Code, the bailout abuse Congress sought to preclude by enactment of that section provides guidance. . . . A bailout occurs if the stockholders can dispose of their stock in question without a loss of voting control and interest in the unrestricted equitable growth of the corporation.

While the class A nonvoting common stock in the instant case can be disposed of without a loss of voting control in *X,* it cannot be disposed of without the shareholder parting irretrievably with an interest in the unrestricted equitable growth of *X* represented by such stock.

Accordingly, the class A nonvoting common stock in the instant case is "common stock" for purposes of section 306(c)(1)(B) of the Code. . . .

NOTE

1. *The legislative response to the "preferred stock" bailout.* Section 306 is aimed squarely at the *Chamberlin* type of preferred stock "bailout" — that is, the conversion of potential dividend income into capital gain without diluting the shareholder's equity or control (other than by the restrictions imposed on the shareholder by the holders of the preferred shares). Note that §306 stock includes more than just preferred stock received tax free as a stock dividend. It includes, for example, preferred stock that is received tax free in a reorganization if the receipt of such stock "was substantially the same as the receipt of a stock dividend." §306(c)(1)(B)(ii). The §306 taint does not, however, attach to stock received in a taxable distribution. §301(c)(1)(A).

Under §306, the price of tax-free receipt of stock is, in general, ordinary income on disposition. In *Chamberlin* the preferred stock was worth $100 per share when issued, and the amount of the distribution was fully covered by earnings and profits. Had §306 been applicable to the sale of that stock, the first $100 per share received by the taxpayers for the preferred stock would have been fully includible in their gross incomes. Only the excess, if any, could qualify for sale or exchange treatment.

Query whether §306 would have been necessary had the reasoning of the Tax Court in *Chamberlin* been followed and the various steps viewed as an integrated transaction. Note also that the Tax Reform Act of 1969 substantially reduced the scope of §306 by enlarging the class of stock dividends subject to taxation at the time of distribution under §305. The pro rata distribution of preferred stock to the common shareholders, however, remains tax free, and such stock dividends generally give rise to §306 stock. See Rev. Proc. 77-37, 1977-2 C.B. 568, on the requirements for issuing ruling letters concerning whether convertible preferred stock is §306 stock.

2.   *Definition of "§306 stock."* The definition of "§306 stock" is in §306(c). Section 306(c)(1)(A) is the anti-*Chamberlin* rule, for it imposes a §306 taint on preferred stock received tax free under §305(a).

Preferred stock received tax free in a reorganization (or in a §355 divisive distribution) will also be §306 stock if it is received tax free and if the transaction substantially has the effect of a stock dividend. §306(c)(1)(B). Discussion of reorganizations is deferred until page 411, but it is important to note at this point that the net of §306 extends to the reorganization area. When preferred stock of an acquired corporation that is not "§306 stock" is exchanged for preferred stock of the acquiring corporation of equal value and with substantially similar terms, the preferred stock of the acquiring corporation is not "§306 stock" within the meaning of §306(c)(1)(B). Rev. Rul. 88-100, 1988-2 C.B. 46.

Under §306(c)(1)(C), a §306 taint is not removed by transferring §306 stock in a carryover basis transaction. For example, §306 stock received as a gift or in a §351 transaction is §306 stock. Stock received from a decedent, however, will not be §306 stock because of the fair market value basis rule of §1014. What is the effect of gifting §306 stock to a tax-exempt charity? See Rev. Rul. 76-396, 1976-2 C.B. 55 (§170(e) limits the deduction to the fair market value of the stock less the ordinary income component).

Section 306(c)(2) provides a long-standing rule that no §306 taint will attach to stock received in a distribution in which, had money been distributed instead of stock, no amount would have been includible in income. Thus, tax-free stock dividends cannot produce §306 stock if, at the time of the stock dividend, the corporation had no current or accumulated earnings and profits. This rule recognizes that it is the preferred stock bailout to which §306 speaks: If cash could have been "bailed out" without dividend treatment, then stock distributed in lieu of cash will work no end-run around the §301 distribution rules.

Section 306(c)(3) prevents an abuse of the §306(c)(2) rule. Suppose a taxpayer transfers stock of one controlled corporation (*X* Corp.) to a second controlled corporation (*Y* Corp.) in exchange for preferred stock of *Y* in a transaction qualifying under §351. Because *Y* stock is not "property" for purposes of §304, see §317(a), this transaction is excluded from the definition of §304. If the stock so received is subsequently sold or redeemed the effect of the acquisition and disposition could be to bail out earnings and profits of the corporations.

Such stock-for-stock exchanges are addressed by §306(c)(3). Stock (other than common stock) received in such an exchange will be §306 stock if, had cash been distributed in lieu of the stock, the shareholder would have received dividend treatment under §304. Thus, positive earnings and profits of either controlled corporation will cause noncommon stock received in such an exchange to be characterized as §306 stock.

Note that common stock distributed on common stock is not §306 stock. §306(c)(1)(A). Why not? What is common stock? According to Rev.

Rul. 81-91, page 315 supra, and Rev. Rul. 76-387, page 317 supra, common stock for purposes of §306 is any stock that participates without substantial restrictions in the future growth of the corporation. Does this definition of "common" stock adequately respond to the preferred stock bailout abuse? Is it consistent with the statutory language employed by Congress? Should it be consistent with the definition of "common" stock for purposes of §305? See Treas. Regs. §1.305-5(a), discussed in Note 4, page 296 supra.

Will a bailout using common stock necessarily succeed? The Commissioner will, in such circumstances, be forced to relitigate *Chamberlin*. See Rosenberg v. Commissioner, 36 T.C. 716 (1961) (recharacterizing sale of stock by shareholders as sale of stock by corporation followed by distribution of proceeds to old shareholders). The taxpayer will, however, have a new argument: By enacting the detailed rules of §306, Congress may have preempted the field. Should such a legislative preemption argument be accepted in this context?

3. *Disposition of §306 stock.* Section 306(a) provides one rule for disposition of §306 stock by redemption and another rule for all other dispositions (such as sales and exchanges). The redemption rule is simple: A shareholder redeeming §306 stock is subject to the distribution rules of §301 with respect to the amount realized (*not* gain) on the redemption. §306(a)(2). Thus, if the corporation has sufficient earnings and profits at the time of the redemption, the entire amount received by the shareholder can be fully includible at ordinary rates as a dividend.

If §306 stock is disposed of in a transaction other than a redemption, the rule is more complex. Under §306(a)(1), the amount realized in exchange for the §306 stock is treated as ordinary income, but only to the extent of the stock's ratable share of the corporation's earnings as of the time of the distribution of the §306 stock.

For example, suppose X Corp. has 100 shares of common stock outstanding, equally divided between A and B. Assume that these shares are worth $40 per share, that A's basis in each share is $20, and that X Corp. has earnings and profits of $1,500. What are the tax consequences to A if X Corp. declares a stock dividend payable as one share of $100 preferred stock for each five shares of common stock outstanding?

No gain is recognized on the stock dividend by virtue of §305(a). Under §307(a), A must allocate some of his basis in the common stock to the newly received preferred stock. That allocation is made in proportion to the relative fair market values of the common and preferred stock. Treas. Regs. §1.307-1(a).

Prior to the stock dividend, X Corp. had 100 shares of common stock outstanding with aggregate fair market value of $4,000. After the distribution, an additional 20 shares of $100 par value preferred stock are also outstanding. Assuming that the preferred stock is worth par, then the aggregate value of the outstanding preferred is $2,000, which leaves only

$2,000 in value for the common. Accordingly, one consequence of the stock dividend is to reduce the value of X Corp.'s common stock from $40 to $20 per share.

A now has $1,000 in common stock (50 shares at $20 per share) and $1,000 in value in preferred stock (10 shares at $100 per share), so he must allocate basis equally between the common and preferred stock. Since the total to be allocated is $1,000, A takes a basis of $10 per share in the common stock and $50 per share in the preferred stock. Is the preferred stock tainted under §306? Yes. See §306(c)(1)(A).

Suppose A sells his 10 shares of preferred stock for $105 per share. How will he be taxed? Absent §306, A would have a capital gain on each share of $105 minus $50, or $55. Under §306(a)(1), we must compute the difference between (1) A's amount realized on the sale and (2) the amount that would have been a dividend had cash been distributed in lieu of the preferred stock.

The fair market value of the preferred stock was $2,000. If cash of $2,000 had been distributed in lieu of the preferred stock, there would have been a dividend to A and B of $1,500, the amount of X Corp.'s earnings and profits. Since 20 shares of preferred stock were distributed, each share's "ratable share" (see §306(a)(1)(A)(ii)) of the dividend would have been $75.

Under §306(a)(1)(A), A will recognize $75 of the $105 amount realized per share as ordinary income. No further gain is recognized by A because the remaining $30 per share of amount realized is less than his basis in the stock. See §306(a)(1)(B). No loss can be recognized, §306(a)(1)(C), so A may add the unrecovered basis in the preferred stock (viz., $20 per share) to his basis in the common stock. See Treas. Regs. §1.306-1(b)(2) (example 2).

The rules for the redemption of §306 stock differ from those applicable to dispositions of §306 other than in redemption. When §306 stock is redeemed, the earnings and profits of the corporation at the time of redemption are relevant. See §§306(a)(2), 301(c)(1). For other types of dispositions, earnings and profits of the corporation at the time of the issuance of the §306 stock are important. See §306(a)(1)(A)(ii). The corporation's earnings and profits at time of issuance can be important even if the §306 stock is redeemed, for the absence of such earnings and profits can remove the stock from §306 ab initio. See §306(c)(2).

4. *Exceptions to the §306 rules.* The draconian rules just described are modified by the exceptions of §306(b). If the shareholder disposes of her entire stock interest (determined by applying the constructive ownership rules of §318) under circumstances set out in §306(b)(1), she can avoid the automatic ordinary income treatment. A redemption of §306 stock in partial or complete liquidation will also relieve the shareholder of §306 disabilities. §306(b)(2)(B).

An exchange of §306 stock in a nontaxable transaction (such as a tax-free reorganization or a §1036 exchange) is not a taxable disposition subject to the rules §306(a). See §306(b)(3). The stock received on the exchange ordinarily will be §306 stock unless it is common stock issued in a reorganization. See §306(c)(1)(B) and (C). A conversion of §306 stock into common stock will eliminate the §306 taint if the detailed rules of §306(e) are met. Those rules generally remove the taint from §306 stock if it is converted into common stock not further convertible into other stock or property.

Section 306(b)(4) describes two circumstances in which the disposition of §306 stock will not be subject to the rules of §306(a). Section 306(b)(4)(A) absolves a shareholder who establishes to the satisfaction of the Secretary of the Treasury (or the Secretary's delegate) that the distribution as well as the redemption or other disposition did not have, as one of its principal purposes, the avoidance of federal income taxes. If the taxpayer sells (or otherwise disposes of) the non-§306 stock at the same time as, or prior to, disposing of the §306 stock, then the taxpayer need convince the Secretary of the Treasury only that the disposition of the §306 stock did not have tax avoidance as one of its principal purposes. §306(b)(4)(B).

In a series of prior revenue rulings, the Service had ruled that §306 stock is not disposed of in pursuance of a tax avoidance plan whenever the stock is widely held. In Rev. Rul. 89-63, 1989-1 C.B. 90, the Service ruled that a shareholder may encounter liability under §306(a) upon disposition of stock of even a widely held corporation unless the shareholder can establish the absence of a tax avoidance motive.

The court in *Fireoved* was able to avoid a difficult procedural question raised by §306(b)(4): May a taxpayer litigate his qualification for §306(b)(4) characterization, or is an appeal to the Secretary of the Treasury his only avenue of relief under that section? The language of §306(b)(4) supports the latter reading, although the courts traditionally have sought to impose *some* judicial review on every exercise of administrative discretion. See, e.g., Crowell v. Benson, 285 U.S. 22 (1932); Johnson v. Robinson, 415 U.S. 361 (1974). See generally P. Bator, D. Meltzer, P. Mishkin & D. Shapiro, Hart and Wechsler's The Federal Courts and the Federal System 366-387 (3d ed. 1988). When Congress has deliberately granted broad discretion to an administrative agent, the scope of judicial review is appropriately narrow. Surely a taxpayer would have the right to challenge an administrative adverse determination under §306(b)(4) as arbitrary, capricious, or the result of bias or prejudice. But the taxpayer in *Fireoved* sought a favorable judicial determination under §306(b)(4) despite having failed to seek an administrative ruling under that section. Given the clear statement of administrative discretion in §306(b)(4), should not such a failure on the part of the taxpayer have foreclosed judicial review of the issue?

If a taxpayer disposes of §306 stock in a transaction that qualifies as a complete termination of interest under §306(b)(1), then he automatically avoids the harsh rules of §306(a). To so qualify, though, the taxpayer must terminate his interest in the corporation actually and constructively. See §306(b)(1)(A)(iii) and §§306(b)(1)(B), 302(c)(1). If a taxpayer reduces to zero his actual interest in the corporation but continues to have a constructive interest in the corporation, then he may seek an administrative ruling under §306(b)(4)(B). See Rev. Rul. 77-455, 1977-2 C.B. 93, in which a father owned a majority of the corporation's common stock and all the corporation's preferred stock subject to a §306 taint. The father sold some of his common and preferred stock to his son, who already held part of the common, and some to an unrelated party. The balance of the father's stock was redeemed by the corporation. The Service ruled that §306(b)(1) did not apply (because of the rules of constructive ownership) but that §306(b)(4) did apply because the father terminated his actual interest in the corporation.

In Pescosolido v. Commissioner, 91 T.C. 52 (1988), a graduate of Deerfield Academy and Harvard College gave 1,500 shares of appreciated §306 stock to the two institutions and deducted the fair market value of the stock. The IRS, pursuant to §170(e)(1)(A), limited the deduction to the taxpayer's basis in the stock because the stock would not have produced long-term capital gain if sold. Relying on §306(b)(4), the taxpayer argued that the stock would not have produced "tainted" ordinary income if sold because there was no tax avoidance on the distribution or disposition. The Tax Court ruled for the IRS, concluding that the taxpayer was aware that the consequences of the charitable contribution deduction would be the avoidance of ordinary income on the bailout of corporate earnings.

In *Fireoved*, the taxpayer sold a part of his non-§306 stock prior to the disposition of his §306 stock. His prior sale of common stock did not, however, reduce his voting interest in the corporation below that amount necessary to give him a veto over corporate decisions. The court held that under these circumstances the disposition of some of the voting common did not remove the §306 taint from even a proportionate share of the §306 stock. See Rev. Rul. 75-247, 1975-1 C.B. 104, following *Fireoved* in interpreting §306(b)(4)(B).

5. *A comparison of §305 and §306.* The success of the preferred stock bailout in *Chamberlin* turned on two key facts: (1) that the distribution of the preferred stock dividend was tax free on receipt and (2) that the sale of the dividend stock produced capital gain. This abuse could have been prevented either by taxing the stock dividend or by tainting the dividend stock. Which method should Congress have adopted? Do you agree with the congressional decision to employ both methods, sometimes taxing the stock dividend under §305(b) and other times tainting the dividend stock under §306? If, as a general rule, a tax liability should be imposed only

when funds are available to pay the tax, is taxation of stock dividends ever appropriate?

D. PROBLEMS

1. In the following, assume X Corp. has ample earnings and profits. Determine the tax consequences to M and N in the following situations:

    a. X Corp. has two classes of stock outstanding. M holds 100 shares of common stock, and N holds 100 shares of noncon-vertible preferred stock. X distributes:

        i. Common on common, but common shareholders can elect to receive cash instead of stock. Does it matter if all shareholders elect to receive stock?

        ii. Preferred on common and cash on preferred. Does it matter if the cash is distributed 18 months before or after the stock dividend?

        iii. Common on preferred and preferred on common.

    b. X Corp. has two classes of stock outstanding. M owns 100 shares of class A common, and N owns 100 shares of class B common. The class A and B shares participate ratably in both current and liquidating distributions. X distributes:

        i. Cash on the class A common and class B common on the class B common. How would your answer change if each class of stock were entitled to 50 percent of current and liquidating distributions?

        ii. Cash in redemption of one-quarter (25 shares) of the class B common.

        iii. Class A common on the class A common and preferred stock on the class B common.

    c. X Corp. has two classes of stock outstanding. M owns 100 shares of common, and N owns 100 shares of nonconvertible preferred. X distributes cash on the preferred and common on common. Would your answer change if the preferred stock were convertible into common stock?

2. X Corp. has 100 shares of stock outstanding, 80 owned by B and 20 by C. B and D, an unrelated party, form Y Corp., with B contributing his X stock to Y in exchange for 80 shares of Y common and 800 shares of Y $10 par-value preferred. D contributes $2,000 in cash for 20 shares of Y common and 200 shares of Y $10 par-value preferred. If the fair market value of the X stock is $100 per share and X has earnings and profits of $5,000, how much of the Y common and preferred stock is §306 stock in the hands of B and D? How does your answer change if B receives only 50 percent of the stock of Y Corp.?

3. *A* and *B* organize *X* Corp. in 1985, each contributing $10,000 in cash in return for 100 shares of common stock. In July 1986, *X* declared a dividend payable in preferred stock: one share of preferred stock for each share of common stock. At the date of distribution, the preferred stock had a fair market value of $200 per share. Immediately prior to the distribution, the common stock was worth $500 per share. On January 1, 1986, *X* had accumulated earnings and profits of $15,000, and *X* had $5,000 in current earnings and profits for 1986. On January 1, 1990, *X* had accumulated earnings and profits of $45,000, and *X* had $5,000 current earnings and profits for 1990. Determine the tax consequences of each of the following situations:

   a. In February 1990, *A* sold all her preferred stock to *P* for $11,000, and in January 1991 she sold her common stock to *Q* for $40,000.
   b. In February 1990, *X* redeemed all of *A*'s preferred stock for $11,000.
   c. In (b) above, *X* also redeemed 50 shares of *A*'s common stock for $20,000.
   d. In (c) above, assume there was neither accumulated nor current earnings and profits for 1986. How would your answer change if there had been $1 of current earnings and profits?

7

Liquidations

When a corporation is formed, a shareholder, in the absence of boot, ordinarily recognizes no gain or loss. §351. The price of this nonrecognition is the carryover of the shareholder's basis in the assets transferred to the corporation. §362(a). One might expect a similar statutory structure governing liquidations — that when the corporation is liquidated, no gain or loss would be recognized, but the shareholders would succeed to the corporation's basis in the assets distributed.

Alas, life is not so simple. A complete liquidation is ordinarily a recognition event for both the distributing corporation and the shareholders. The distributing corporation generally recognizes gain or loss on the distribution of its assets as if those assets were sold to the shareholders, and each shareholder generally recognizes gain or loss on the difference between the fair market value of the property received on the distribution and the shareholder's stock basis.

One reason for the nonrecognition pattern on incorporation and the recognition pattern on liquidation may be that there is a continuity of investment in moving a business from unincorporated to incorporated solution, but the same continuity of investment is ordinarily absent when the taxpayer liquidates the business. Often, the business has come to a halt, and the liquidated assets will either be sold for use in another business or used for personal purposes. A liquidation also represents the last opportunity to tax the shareholders on any earnings and profits accumulated by the corporation. Consequently, since 1924 Congress has provided that most often a liquidation will be a taxable event to shareholders. In many but not all respects a liquidation will be treated as if the shareholders sold the corporation's stock back to the corporation and the corporation sold the assets distributed to the shareholders. Note that the liquidation rules apply even if the shareholders continue the business after liquidation.

This chapter focuses on two common liquidation patterns. The first pattern, governed primarily by §§336 and 331, is embodied in the general rule summarized above (and discussed further at Section A infra). For example, suppose X Corp. has assets with an aggregate basis of $100 and a fair market value of $500. The sole shareholder, A, has a basis in the stock of $200. On liquidation X Corp. recognizes gain of $400 under §336. The gain recognized by A equals the difference between the fair market value of the property received and the basis of the surrendered stock, or in this example $300. A's basis in the assets received is the fair market value of those assets in accordance with §334(a). Note now (although it is discussed in more detail below) that historically a liquidating corporation recognized no gain or loss on a liquidation. The Tax Reform Act of 1986 repealed this application of the *General Utilities* doctrine in the liquidating context.

The second pattern involves the liquidation of a subsidiary by a parent corporation (see Section B infra). The subsidiary's assets remain in corporate solution, but the corporate structure has been simplified. Recognizing the continuity here that may be lacking when individuals receive corporate assets, Congress permits both the distributing corporation and the parent corporation to postpone recognition of gain. To illustrate, assume that A in the example above is a corporation rather than an individual. On liquidation there would be no gain to the liquidating corporation under §337. The liquidation is also a nonrecognition transaction for A, the parent corporation, pursuant to §332. The price for nonrecognition is the carryover of X Corp.'s basis in the assets under §334(b). A Corp. will take a $100 basis in the assets received on liquidation. Note that this pattern of taxation is available only if a parent corporation controls the subsidiary within the meaning of §332(b).

The two liquidation patterns outlined above do not operate in a vacuum. Events before, during, and after a liquidation must be considered in evaluating the tax consequences of the liquidation itself. Historically, statutory responses to events preceding or following a liquidation were found in former §337 and §338. Former §337 addressed the liquidating corporation's sale of assets prior to a liquidation (see page 337 infra). Be sure not to confuse former §337 with current §337. As explained below, the two provisions are unrelated. Section 338, in part, deals with the purchase of stock by a corporate shareholder, in some cases, prior to liquidation (see Section B infra).

What is a "liquidation"? That term is not defined in the Code, although the regulations offer some explanation. See Treas. Regs. §1.332-2(c). A liquidation is not necessarily synonymous with turning assets into cash; a distribution in kind is also within the "liquidation" concept. See Rev. Rul. 63-107, 1963-1 C.B. 71. A series of distributions in cancellation of a corporation's outstanding stock can also qualify as a liquidation. Treas. Regs. §1.332-2(c). It is not necessary that a liquidating corporation dissolve under state law. Moreover, a formal plan of liquidation need not be adopted. See, e.g., Kennemer v. Commissioner, 96 F.2d 177 (5th Cir. 1938). Nevertheless, failure to observe the corporate formalities of adopting a plan of liquidation may tempt the IRS: The early distributions may be treated as dividends rather than liquidating distributions. See, e.g., Estate of Maguire v. Commissioner, 50 T.C. 130 (1968).

Within what time frame must a liquidating distribution be effected to constitute a "complete liquidation"? What corporate activities will be inconsistent with a state of liquidation? Although there is no formal requirement, the longer the process and the more active the liquidating corporation, the more likely the Service will treat the distributions as dividends to the extent of earnings and profits. See Cleveland v. Commissioner, 335 F.2d 473 (3d Cir. 1964) (conduct of business by corporation after distributions rendered them dividends). But see Estate of Fearon v. Commissioner, 16 T.C. 385 (1951) (liquidating distribution more than 23 years after plan adopted respected; court found corporation had tried to dispose of assets). Regardless of the liquidation pattern, tax lawyers often use the three-year period set forth in §332 as a guide for the liquidation time frame.

A.   SECTION 331 LIQUIDATIONS

1.   *Treatment of Shareholders*

a.   Exchange Treatment under §331

Section 331(a)(1) provides that on a complete liquidation of a corporation, a shareholder's stock is treated as though it had been exchanged for the amount received by the shareholder from the liquidating corporation. If the stock is a capital asset in the hands of the stockholder, the liquidation will result in a capital gain or loss. The stockholder realizes and recognizes capital gain or loss on the difference between the adjusted basis of the stock surrendered and the value of what is received. See §1001. Thus, the earnings and profits account, so critical to the tax status of the distributions of a going concern, becomes irrelevant when the distribution is in complete liquidation. The analogy for §331(a)(1) is a sale by the stockholder of the shares to a third party. Is this analogy valid? Consistent with the recognition of gain or loss, §334(a) provides that the basis of property received in complete liquidation is its fair market value at the time of the distribution.

b. Treatment of Liabilities

The fair market value of property received in a liquidation is reduced by the liability to which the property is subject or that the shareholder assumes. See Rev. Rul. 59-228, 1959-2 C.B. 59. For example, suppose X Corp. holds two assets: depreciable real property with a basis of $4,000 and a fair market value of $11,000, and inventory with a basis of $2,000 and a fair market value of $5,000. The real property is subject to a $7,000 mortgage. T, the sole shareholder, has a basis in her X Corp. stock of $3,000. If X Corp. liquidates, T would recognize a $6,000 gain, and her basis in the land and inventory would be $11,000 and $5,000, respectively. §334(a). What would be T's gain or loss on a sale of these assets at fair market value? Does T's taxable gain or loss correspond to her economic gain?

Suppose a liquidating corporation distributes assets with a fair market value of $10,000 subject to a disputed liability for patent infringement. What is the amount distributed? If the liability cannot be valued, it will not be taken into account in valuing the distributed assets. Suppose two years later the shareholder pays the liability, which turns out to be $3,000. What is the nature of the deduction? See Arrowsmith v. Commissioner, 344 U.S. 6 (1952).

c. Contingent Assets

In some cases, the assets distributed may themselves be difficult to value even though there are no disputed liabilities. For example, if X Corp.'s only asset is a contingent contract right that is not valued on liquidation, the gain to the shareholders will remain "open" on the authority of Burnet v. Logan, 283 U.S. 404 (1931), until the contracts can be valued. In Rev. Rul. 58-402, 1958-2 C.B. 15, the Service announced that it "will continue to require valuation of contracts and claims to receive indefinite amounts of income, such as those acquired with respect to stock in liquidation of a corporation, except in rare and extraordinary cases." See also Treas. Regs. §1.1001-1(a). In Commissioner v. Carter, 170 F.2d 911 (2d Cir. 1948), a shareholder on liquidation received oil brokerage contracts that the parties stipulated had no ascertainable fair market value. In a later year, the shareholder collected commissions of $35,000 under the contracts. Is the gain ordinary or capital? The Second Circuit permitted the taxpayer capital gains treatment. Compare Waring v. Commissioner, 412 F.2d 800 (3d Cir. 1969), where a patent royalty contract was valued on liquidation. Consequently, future payments to shareholder in excess of the §334(a) basis were treated as ordinary income in the absence of a sale or exchange. See also Likins-Foster Honolulu Corp. v. Commissioner, 840 F.2d 642 (9th Cir. 1988) (Commissioner applied the open transaction doctrine to the liquidating corporation's claim for condemnation proceeds).

Code §453(j)(2) and Treas. Regs. §15A.453-1(d)(2)(iii) now attempt to curtail sharply the use of the open transaction doctrine. Can a taxpayer elect out of §453 and the above regulation? §453(d).

d. Installment Notes

If a liquidating corporation distributes installment notes in a §331 liquidation, the liquidating corporation must recognize the difference between the adjusted basis and the fair market value of the notes. §453B. Under some circumstances, the shareholders do not have to treat the distributed notes as part of the amount realized. §453(h). Instead, the former shareholders can treat payments on the notes as payments for the stock, thereby producing capital gain (or loss). This treatment for shareholders applies only if the sale or exchange that resulted in the installment obligation occurred during a 12-month period beginning on the date a plan of liquidating was adopted. Furthermore, the liquidation must take place within the same period. Installment obligations for the sale of inventory are accorded this treatment only if there is a bulk sale to one purchaser in one transaction. Installment sale reporting is not available if the stock of the liquidating corporation is publicly traded. §453(k)(2).

If §453(h) does not apply, then a shareholder of a liquidating corporation must treat the fair market value of any installment note distributed as an amount realized on the exchange of stock in the liquidating corporation.

e. Allocation of Stock Basis to Liquidating Distributions

If a shareholder acquires stock on different dates or at different prices, gain or loss is determined separately for each block. Treas. Regs. §1.331-1(e). In Rev. Rul. 68-348, 1968-2 C.B. 141, the Service sets forth several rules for calculating gain or loss when the liquidating distributions are made over more than one year. This ruling allows the shareholder to recover basis before reporting gain. For example, if A holds stock with a basis of $5,000 and receives $4,000 in year 1 and $4,000 in year 2 as a liquidating distribution, the $3,000 gain will be recognized by A in year 2. The same principle applies for losses. Suppose A's basis is $10,000. Assuming that the year 2 distribution is the last, A's $2,000 loss deduction will be deferred until year 2. Note that while §267(a)(1) generally disallows loss deductions on the sale or exchange of property between a shareholder and a corporation in which the shareholder owns directly or indirectly more than 50 percent of the stock, shareholder losses incurred on the complete liquidation of a corporation are exempted.

2. Treatment of Liquidating Corporation

a. Recognition of Gain or Loss at the Corporate Level

Recall that in a nonliquidating distribution, there is a shareholder-level tax if the corporation has earnings and profits and a corporate-level tax if the property distributed has a fair market value that exceeds the property's adjusted basis. See page 135 supra. Similarly, in a liquidating distribution, there are likely to be both corporate-level and shareholder-level tax consequences. For the shareholder-level tax consequences, see page 329 supra.

At the corporate level, §336(a) provides that on a liquidation gain or loss shall be recognized to the liquidating corporation as if the property were sold to the distributee at fair market value. The effect of §336(a) is to ensure a corporate-level tax even on preincorporation appreciation. Suppose B forms X Corp. by contributing property with a basis of $1,000 and fair market value of $9,000 in exchange for all the X Corp. stock in a transaction that qualifies under §351. On the exchange, X Corp. takes a basis of $1,000 in the property under §362(a), and B takes a $1,000 basis in the stock under §358. If X Corp. liquidates, the distributing corporation will recognize an $8,000 gain under §336(a), and B will recognize an $8,000 gain under §§331 and 1001. B will take a $9,000 basis in the property distributed under §334(a).

Why should §336 require a corporate-level tax on this preincorporation appreciation? Could Congress have written §336(a) in a manner that would exclude preincorporation appreciation? Congress did so in the case of preincorporation losses, as is discussed below.

If the property had a fair market value of $1,000 when B formed X Corp. and then increased in value to $9,000 prior to the liquidation, there is a stronger argument for a double tax on the liquidation — stronger in the sense that to the extent our corporate taxation system is a double tax system, it is not unreasonable to treat a corporation's built-in gains (and losses) in the same manner as recognized gains (or losses) if those built-in gains (or losses) arose during the corporation's existence.

When §336(a) treats the property as if it were sold to the shareholders, are the provisions generally associated with a sale invoked as well? For example, §1239 provides that in the case of a sale between certain related parties, any gain recognized shall be treated as ordinary if the property would be depreciable in the hands of the transferee. Section 1239(b) and (c)(1)(A) treat a corporation and a 50 percent (by value) shareholder as related. Suppose, for example, that *X* Corp. makes a liquidating distribution of an apartment building to *B*, its sole shareholder. The building has a basis of $100,000 and a fair market value of $500,000 and is not subject to depreciation recapture because *X* Corp. used the straight line method for depreciation. Assume the building is a capital asset in *X* Corp.'s hands. When *X* Corp. distributes the property, is the $400,000 gain that *X* Corp. must recognize a capital gain or ordinary income? There appears to be no language precluding the application of §1239.

Section 336 does not apply to all liquidating distributions. For example, a liquidation in the context of a reorganization is not governed by §336. §336(c). Suppose *X* Corp. transfers all its assets to *Y* Corp. and then liquidates in a transaction described in §368(a). If *X* Corp. distributes the appreciated Y Corp. stock as part of the reorganization, *X* Corp. does not recognize gain under §336(a). §361.

b. Treatment of Liabilities

Section 336(b) provides that if the property distributed in a complete liquidation is encumbered by a liability, the amount realized is not less than the amount of the liability. In effect, §336(b) codifies the result in Tufts v. Commissioner, 461 U.S. 300 (1983). Accordingly, if *X* Corp. owns property with a basis of $100,000 and a fair market value of $400,000, which is subject to a $600,000 liability. A distribution of that property will trigger a $500,000 corporate-level gain, which will be capital or ordinary depending on the nature of the property distributed. What will the amount realized be for purposes of evaluating the tax consequences to the shareholders?

c. Treatment of Corporate-level Losses

Unlike §311(b), which deals with nonliquidating distributions, §336(a) permits a distributing corporation to recognize losses if the adjusted basis of a distributed asset exceeds its fair market value. Why should a distributing corporation be treated differently in a liquidating distribution than in a nonliquidating distribution? In a liquidating distribution, the distributing corporation distributes all its property — any "gain" property as well as any "loss" property. In a nonliquidating distribution, however, the distributing corporation can "cherry pick" the assets to be distributed. It may choose to distribute "loss" property to recognize a loss for tax purposes while seeking refuge in the realization doctrine with respect to its undistributed and therefore unrealized "gain" property.

Even in a liquidating distribution, Congress has been concerned that taxpayers would take advantage of the loss allowance by artificially creating corporate-level losses. Suppose *B* owns all the stock of *X* Corp., whose assets have a basis of $70,000 and a fair market value of $100,000. Assume *B*'s stock basis is also $70,000. *B* also holds a piece of property with a basis of $130,000 and a fair market value of $50,000. If *X* Corp. liquidates, it will recognize a $30,000 gain under §336(a), and *B* will recognize a $30,000 gain under §331. Suppose instead that *B* exchanges the loss property for additional *X* Corp. stock in a transaction that qualifies under §351. (A contribution to capital will achieve the same results.) *B*'s basis in the *X* Corp. stock under §358 increases from $70,000 to $200,000, and *X* Corp.'s total basis in the assets increases to $200,000 under §362.

Now when *X* Corp. liquidates, it is treated as if it sold the property to its shareholder for $150,000, its fair market value. Accordingly, *X* Corp. would recognize a $50,000 loss under §336, and *B* would recognize a $50,000 loss under §331. Those losses will allow both *X* Corp. and *B* to offset other taxable income. Note that *B*'s basis in the loss property after the liquidation is $50,000, its fair market value under §334(a). But *B* will gladly surrender a higher basis in exchange for a double loss deduction — once by *X* Corp. and once by *B*.

Section 336 addresses this and other perceived abuses through two rules governing the treatment of losses. Under §336(d)(1), the liquidating corporation cannot recognize a loss on a distribution to a "related person" if the distribution is not pro rata or if the property distributed is "disquali-fied property." A "related person" is defined by reference to §267. Why didn't Congress simply provide that a liquidating distribution will be treated as if the liquidating corporation had sold the property to its share-holders at fair market value and then let §267 apply whenever it is trig-gered? Instead, Congress has enacted a different loss prevention rule in §336.

If the distributee is a related person, a liquidating corporation cannot recognize a loss unless the loss property is distributed pro rata. Suppose *X* Corp. has property with a basis of $100,000 and a fair market value of $60,000 and $20,000 in cash. *A* owns 75 percent of the *X* Corp. stock; *B* owns the remaining 25 percent. Under §336(d)(1)(A)(i), if *X* Corp. distrib-utes the loss property to *A* and the cash to *B*, *X* Corp. cannot recognize the loss. If, however, *X* Corp. distributes 75 percent of the loss property and 75 percent of the cash to *A* and the remainder to *B*, then *X* Corp. will be able to deduct the $40,000 loss on the property. Following the liquida-tion, *A* could buy *B*'s $15,000 interest in the property with the $15,000 of cash that was distributed to *A*. *B* would not be taxable on the sale because *B* would hold the $15,000 interest with a fair market value basis following the liquidation. §334(a). Because *A* and *B* can end up with a non-pro rata distribution, what is the purpose of the provision?

Even if there is a pro rata distribution to a related party, the liquidating corporation cannot recognize a loss if the distributed property is "disqualified property." That term is defined in §336(d)(1)(B) to mean property that is acquired by the liquidating corporation during the five-year period preceding liquidation if the property was acquired through a §351 transaction or as a contribution to capital. This "antistuffing" provision addresses the problem noted above, in which a shareholder with an unrealized loss transfers the property to a corporation (i.e., stuffs the corporation with loss property) just prior to liquidation in order to turn the unrealized loss into a double recognized loss — once at the corporate level and once at the shareholder level.

Notice that even if the property declines in value while held by the liquidating corporation, no loss will be permitted. Suppose *B* owns all the stock of *X* Corp. In year 4, *B* contributes to *X* Corp. additional property with a basis of $30,000 and a fair market value of $50,000. In year 7, *B* decides to liquidate *X* Corp. At the time of the liquidating distribution, the property still with a basis of $30,000 now has a fair market value of $10,000. Section 336(d)(1)(B) appears to preclude *X* Corp. from recognizing a loss under §336(a). Perhaps future regulations will soften the provisions in obvious nonabuse cases.

Section 336(d)(1)(B) also applies if the basis of property is determined by reference to the basis of property acquired in the described transaction. Thus, if a liquidating corporation acquires property in a §351 transaction three years prior to a liquidation, it cannot avoid the impact of §336(d)(1)(B) by exchanging the acquired property for like-kind property under §1031 prior to liquidation because the basis of property acquired in a §1031 transaction is determined in part from the basis of the property exchanged. §1031(d).

The second rule applying to liquidating distributions of loss property under §336 does not focus on the relationship between a liquidating corporation and its shareholders. They need not be related parties within the meaning of §267. This rule too is aimed at shareholders attempting to turn unrealized losses into double deductions — once at the corporate level and once at the shareholder level on the distribution. This rule, however, is triggered by and operates in a slightly different manner than the rule governing liquidating distributions to related persons. It might apply, for example, if each of four unrelated shareholders owns 25 percent of the stock of a corporation, although nothing in the language prevents the rule from operating even when there are related persons within the meaning of §267.

The rule is triggered by a distribution, sale, or exchange of property acquired in a §351 transaction (or as a contribution to capital) if the acquisition "was part of a plan a principal purpose of which was to recognize loss by the liquidating corporation with respect to such property in connection with the liquidation." §336(d)(2)(B). This rule applies to sales and exchanges as well as to distributions. Property acquired by the liquidating corporation "after the date two years before the date a corporation adopts a plan of liquidation" is presumed to be part of a loss recognition plan. Accordingly, a contribution of loss property after a corporation adopts a plan of liquidation will not generate a corporation-level loss on liquidation. Note that the two-year rule of §336(d)(2)(B) is measured by the date of adoption of a plan of liquidation, while the five-year rule of §336(d)(1)(B) is based on the date of distribution. Why didn't Congress use the same reference point in both provisions?

Suppose the §351 transfer occurs one year before a plan of liquidation is adopted but has no tax avoidance motive. The Secretary is given authority to promulgate regulations that will exempt nonabuse transfers occurring within the two-year period. The legislative history suggests that contributions of property to be used in the corporation's trade or business or contributions of property during the first two years of a corporation's existence may present such a nonabuse situation. Suppose the §351 exchange occurs more than two years before a plan of liquidation is adopted but has a loss recognition motive. The conference report states that "[the provision disallowing a loss] will apply only in the most rare and unusual cases under such circumstances." H.R. Rep. No. 841, 99th Cong., 2d Sess. (1986).

If the second rule applies, the liquidating corporation is not denied the entire loss deduction relating to offending property. Instead, for purposes of determining loss, the basis of the property is decreased by the excess of the basis of the asset on the date of contribution over its fair market value at that time. §336(d)(2)(A). Suppose that one year prior to adoption of a plan of liquidation, X Corp. acquires, in a §351 transaction, property that has a basis of $50,000 and a fair market value of $30,000. The property continues to decline in value, and on the date of the liquidating distribution it has a fair market value of $15,000. X Corp. will be able to recognize a loss of $15,000 — the decline that occurred while X Corp. held the property. Why doesn't §336 or §311 adopt a similar rule for preincorporation gain property, thereby limiting recognition to gain that occurred while the property was held by the corporation?

Suppose X Corp. acquires loss property in a §351 transaction. Within two years of the acquisition, X Corp. sells the property at a loss. Three years after the acquisition, X Corp. adopts a plan of liquidation and liquidates. Can X Corp. recognize the loss on the sale of the property?

d. Costs of a Liquidation

Thus far we have focused on the liquidating corporation's gain or loss resulting from the property distributed. How does the liquidating corporation treat the costs of liquidation? The costs associated with preparing and carrying out a plan of liquidation are deductible by the corporation as ordinary and necessary business expenses. See Connery v. United States, 460 F.2d 1130 (3d Cir. 1972); for the treatment of similar expenses in a reorganization context, see page 474 infra.

3. The Court Holding Co. Doctrine and Former §337

Commissioner v. Court Holding Co. ————————————
324 U.S. 331 (1945)

Mr. Justice BLACK delivered the opinion of the Court.

An apartment house, which was the sole asset of the respondent corporation, was transferred in the form of a liquidating dividend to the corporation's two shareholders. They in turn formally conveyed it to a purchaser who had originally negotiated for the purchase from the corporation. The question is whether the Circuit Court of Appeals properly reversed the Tax Court's conclusion that the corporation was taxable under [§61] for the gain which accrued from the sale. . . .

The respondent corporation was organized in 1934 solely to buy and hold the apartment building which was the only property ever owned by it. All of its outstanding stock was owned by Minnie Miller and her husband. Between October 1, 1939 and February, 1940, while the corporation still had legal title to the property, negotiations for its sale took place. These negotiations were between the corporation and the lessees of the property, together with a sister and brother-in-law. An oral agreement was reached as to the terms and conditions of sale, and on February 22, 1940, the parties met to reduce the agreement to writing. The purchaser was then advised by the corporation's attorney that the sale could not be consummated because it would result in the imposition of a large income tax on the corporation. The next day, the corporation declared a "liquidating dividend," which involved complete liquidation of its assets, and surrender of all outstanding stock. Mrs. Miller and her husband surrendered their stock, and the building was deeded to them. A sale contract was then drawn, naming the Millers individually as vendors, and the lessees' sister as vendee, which embodied substantially the same terms and conditions previously agreed upon. One thousand dollars, which a month and a half earlier had been paid to the corporation by the lessees, was applied in part payment of the purchase price. Three days later, the property was conveyed to the lessees' sister.

The Tax Court concluded from these facts that, despite the declaration of a "liquidating dividend" followed by the transfers of legal title, the corporation had not abandoned the sales negotiations; that these were mere formalities designed "to make the transaction appear to be other than what it was," in order to avoid tax liability. The Circuit Court of

Appeals drawing different inferences from the record, held that the corporation had "called off the sale, and treated the stockholders" sale as unrelated to the prior negotiations.

There was evidence to support the findings of the Tax Court, and its findings must therefore be accepted by the courts. Dobson v. Commr., 320 U.S. 489. . . . On the basis of these findings, the Tax Court was justified in attributing the gain from the sale to respondent corporation. The incidence of taxation depends upon the substance of a transaction. The tax consequences which arise from gains from a sale of property are not finally to be determined solely by the means employed to transfer legal title. Rather, the transaction must be viewed as a whole, and each step, from the commencement of negotiations to the consummation of the sale, is relevant. A sale by one person cannot be transformed for tax purposes into a sale by another by using the latter as a conduit through which to pass title. To permit the true nature of a transaction to be disguised by mere formalisms, which exist solely to alter tax liabilities, would seriously impair the effective administration of the tax policies of Congress. . . .

The decision of the Circuit Court of Appeals is reversed, and that of the Tax Court affirmed.

It is so ordered.

Reversed.

NOTE

1. Court Holding Co. Consider the *Court Holding Co.* situation in which *X* Corp. owns a piece of undeveloped land with a basis of $60 and a fair market value of $100. The sole shareholder, *A*, owns stock with a basis of $30 and a fair market value of $100. If *X* Corp. liquidated, former §336 protected *X* Corp. from gain recognition while *A* recognized a $70 gain under §§61, 1001, and 331. Former §336 embodied the *General Utilities* rule in a liquidation context. *A* took a $100 basis in the property pursuant to §334(a). If *A* then sold the property for $100, no further gain was recognized. What happened if the sale was attributed to the corporation as was the case in *Court Holding Co.*?

Court Holding Co. was limited by United States v. Cumberland Public Service Co., 338 U.S. 451 (1950), in which the shareholders first attempted to sell the stock of their corporation. The buyer refused to buy the stock, perhaps because the buyer did not want to assume any undisclosed liabilities to which the corporation was subject. The shareholders then offered to and did sell the assets that they acquired by liquidating the corporation. The Court of Claims held that the sale was made by the shareholders rather than the corporation. The Supreme Court affirmed, stating that, as in *Court Holding Co.*, it relied on the factual finding made by the lower court. The distinction was a delicate one: In *Court Holding Co.* the decision to liquidate seemed to come at the last moment solely for tax avoidance purposes, while in *Cumberland* the plan for a liquidation came early enough for the lower court to find that a genuine liquidation had in fact taken place.

In 1954, in response to the confusion created by *General Utilities, Court Holding Co.*, and *Cumberland,* former §337 was enacted to eliminate the corporate-level tax, whether the sale of assets was made by the corporation before the liquidation or by the shareholders after the liquidation.

2.   *Purpose of former §337.* Before reading another line, note well that what is now §337 has nothing to do with former §337, the anti-*Court Holding Co.* provision. Recall the *Court Holding Co.* fact pattern, in which X Corp. held an asset with a basis of $60 and a fair market value of $100 and its sole shareholder, A, held stock with a basis of $30. If there was a sale of the asset and a liquidation so that A ended up with $100 in cash (ignoring taxes), prior to former §337 the ordering of those two events was crucial in determining whether there was one tax or two. Former §337 was enacted to reduce the effect of the formalities of the transaction. Whether the sale is deemed to be made by the corporation or the shareholder, only one tax resulted — the tax to A on the liquidation. See §331.

3.   *Repeal of the* General Utilities *doctrine and former §337.* When Congress decided to repeal the *General Utilities* doctrine, the need for the anti-*Court Holding Co.* provision of former §337 disappeared. Suppose X Corp. holds assets with a basis of $40,000 and a fair market value of $90,000. If purchaser P wants to buy the assets, the tax consequences to X Corp. and its shareholders on a liquidation followed by a sale are a tax at the corporate level under §336 and a tax on the shareholder level. §331. If X Corp. were to sell the assets and distribute the proceeds, logically there also should be a corporate-level and shareholder-level tax. The need for former §337 protection arose only because former §336 gave the liquidating corporation nonrecognition.

Whether both a corporate- and shareholder-level tax on liquidation is appropriate or not, certainly one of the benefits of the repeal of former §337 is the elimination of some of the contentious areas outlined in the previous Note. No longer does a specially drafted nonrecognition provision apply to a sale in connection with a liquidation. Such a sale will be governed by §1001, producing a gain or loss that will be recognized under §1001(c).

4.   Court Holding Co. *after the repeal of* General Utilities. With the repeal of the *General Utilities* doctrine under the Tax Reform Act of 1986, you might wonder what, if anything, is left of the *Court Holding Co.* doctrine. Now that a corporation is taxed whether it sells or distributes property, is there a need to recharacterize a purported distribution followed by a sale as a sale followed by a distribution, or vice versa?

First, the *Court Holding Co.* rule — that steps in an integrated transaction are stepped together — applies in a variety of tax-motivated transactions. For example, a *Court Holding Co.* analysis may be helpful in determining whether the control requirement is satisfied in §351 transactions in which a shareholder sells the stock received immediately after the transfer of receipt of the stock. See page 52 supra.

Second, even in the liquidation context, the *Court Holding Co.* doctrine endures. Suppose B owns all the X Corp. stock with a basis of $2,000 and a fair market value of $5,000. Among its assets, X Corp. owns and has owned for several years an asset with a basis of $5,000 and a fair market value of $1,000. P, an unrelated purchaser, wants to buy the asset and starts to negotiate with B for the sale. The original negotiations contemplate the liquidation of X Corp. followed by a sale of the asset by B. Prior to the liquidation, X Corp. sells the asset to P and then distributes the proceeds.

If the transaction is respected, X Corp. will recognize a $4,000 loss on the sale under §1001 because it is unlikely that §336(d)(2) will apply to property acquired by the liquidating corporation more than two years prior to the adoption of the plan of liquidation. B will recognize a $3,000 gain on the liquidation under §§331 and 1001. If the transaction is not respected, the Service might recharacterize the transaction as a liquidation followed by a sale. In that event, X Corp. would recognize no loss on the liquidating distribution if the property was acquired by X Corp. within the five-year period ending on the date of the distribution. §336(d)(1). B would still recognize a $3,000 gain under §§331 and 1001. B would take a $1,000 basis in the asset under §334(a) and would not recognize gain or loss on the sale to P.

Ordering the transactions as a liquidation followed by a sale deprives B (and B's wholly owned corporation) of a loss deduction. The *Court Holding Co.* doctrine will continue to function in this and other situations in which differing tax consequences hinge on which taxpayer sold assets.

The loss restriction rule in §336(d)(2) is intended to operate when the §351 transfer and the adoption of a plan of liquidation occur within a two-year period. §336(d)(2)(B)(ii). No statutory provision seems to prevent a full recognition of loss by a corporation that receives a §351 transfer of loss property and that then sells the property. A double loss will then be created if the corporation liquidates, so long as the liquidation takes place outside the two-year period.

To illustrate, suppose B owns all the X Corp. stock with a basis and fair market value of $6,000. X Corp. holds assets with a basis and fair market value of $6,000. Now suppose B contributes to X Corp. property with a basis of $8,000 and a fair market value of $2,000. If X Corp. sells the property almost immediately and then adopts a plan of liquidation more than two years after the §351 transfer, arguably X Corp. will recognize a loss of $6,000 on the sale and B will recognize a loss of $6,000 on the liquidation (B's basis having increased by the basis of the contributed property).

Is the Service bound by this result, given the fact that it recognized the general problem and Congress specifically enacted §336(d)(2) to deal with it? Or can the Service rely on judicial principles such as *Court Holding Co.* to deny the loss deduction or to treat *B* as if *B* had made the sale? What if *B* played no part in the negotiation of the sale? If no liquidation had taken place, could the Service have attributed the sale to *B*?

5. *A corporate triple tax?* The U.S. corporate tax system seeks to tax corporate earnings twice — once when earned by the corporation and once when distributed to individual shareholders. To reinforce this double taxation paradigm, Congress has enacted §243 to provide a dividends-received deduction for dividends received by a shareholder-corporation. See page 134 supra.

The repeal of the *General Utilities* doctrine creates the potential for a triple tax in a liquidation context. Suppose *B* owns all the stock of *X* Corp., a holding company whose sole asset is all the stock of *Y* Corp. *P,* an unrelated purchaser, seeks to acquire all of *Y* Corp.'s assets (all of which are appreciated). Suppose *P* buys the *Y* Corp. stock from *X* Corp., and then *B* and *P* liquidate their corporations. *X* Corp. has already recognized gain on the sale of the *Y* Corp. stock (single tax), and *B* will recognize gain on the liquidation under §§331 and 1001 (double tax). *P* will recognize no gain on the liquidation of *Y* Corp. because *P* took a cost basis in the *Y* Corp. stock purchased from *X* Corp. When *P* liquidates *Y* Corp., the liquidating corporation will recognize gain (triple tax).

The triple tax could have been avoided if *Y* Corp. had sold its assets directly to *P,* followed by a liquidation of *X* Corp. and *Y* Corp. On the sale, *Y* Corp. would recognize gain (single tax). When *Y* Corp. liquidates into its parent *X* Corp., no gain is recognized. See the discussion of §§337 and 332 at page 342 infra. *B* recognizes gain on the liquidation of *X* Corp. (double tax).

In both examples above, *P* ends up with the assets having a fair market value basis and *B* ends up with cash. The triple tax possibility puts a premium on form and would undoubtedly precipitate *Court Holding Co.* arguments about who sold what. In §336(e), Congress has authorized the Treasury to promulgate regulations that will treat the sale of *Y* Corp. stock by *X* Corp. as if the *Y* Corp. assets were sold instead. In the example above, *X* Corp.'s gain on the sale would be the difference between the amount realized for the *Y* Corp. stock and the adjusted basis of the *Y* Corp. assets (single tax). The *Y* Corp. assets would then take a fair market value regardless of whether *P* liquidated *Y* Corp. No gain would be recognized on the sale of the *Y* Corp. stock itself, but *B* would recognize gain on the liquidation of *X* Corp. (double tax). This treatment, which reduces the triple tax to a double tax, is available if a corporation meets the substantial ownership tests under §1504(a)(2) (80 percent voting control and 80 percent of total value of outstanding stock). See page 570 infra.

6. *Growth of S corporations.* The repeal of the *General Utilities* doctrine has upped the ante for operating in corporate form — at least in corporate form under subchapter C. Subchapter S, discussed in Chapter 16, offers

qualifying taxpayers the advantages of corporate form with only a single shareholder level of taxation. Generally, there is no corporate-level taxation for an S corporation. This difference in treatment, combined with the repeal of the *General Utilities* rule, heightens the attraction of subchapter S status for a corporation contemplating a liquidation.

Suppose *X* Corp. with appreciated assets is planning to sell its assets and then liquidate. The sale will result in a corporate-level gain, and, assuming the *X* Corp. stock is appreciated, the liquidation will produce a shareholder-level gain under §§331 and 1001. Suppose instead that immediately prior to the sale and liquidation, *X* Corp. elects to be taxed under subchapter S. In the absence of a remedial provision, *X* Corp. would recognize no gain on the sale. The shareholders would recognize gain but, as a result, would recognize correspondingly less gain on the liquidation. The effect of the S election would be avoidance of a corporate-level tax.

Section 1374, discussed further in Chapter 16, now imposes a corporate-level tax equal to the highest rate under §11 (or §1201 if applicable) on any net gain (built-in gain) arising prior to the conversion from a C corporation to an S corporation that is recognized by the corporation through sale or distribution within 10 years after the date on which the S election took place. Any gain will be presumed to be a built-in gain unless the taxpayer can establish that the appreciation accrued after the conversion.

B. SUBSIDIARY LIQUIDATIONS AND RELATED PROVISIONS

1. Section 332 Liquidations

Section 332 provides in substance that no gain or loss shall be recognized on the liquidation of a subsidiary corporation. This provision, enacted in an earlier form in 1935, was proposed by the Treasury as a measure to encourage the simplification of elaborate corporate structures. In the absence of such a nonrecognition provision, a parent corporation could eliminate subsidiary corporations only by paying a capital gains tax under §331, assuming appreciation in the value of the subsidiary's stock. Furthermore, if a subsidiary distributed appreciated assets in the liquidation, it would have to recognize gain as well. §336.

Note that §332 by its terms is not optional; moreover, it provides for the nonrecognition of both gain and loss. While the technical requirements of §332 allow taxpayers often to avoid its nonelective nature when they so desire, the *Associated Wholesale Grocers* case that follows shows that the ability to manipulate §332 is not unrestrained.

Section 332's basis provision, §334(b), does not follow the usual practice of giving the property received on a tax-free exchange the same basis as the property given up — here, the stock of the subsidiary. For an example of the general rule, see §358, which applies to an exchanging shareholder in a §351 transaction. Instead, §334(b) ordinarily requires the transferee (the parent corporation) to take over the basis of the transferor — its subsidiary — in the distributed assets. Does this unusual principle seek to treat the parent as though it had operated the business, ab initio, without the intervening subsidiary's corporate veil? Note that the basis rule of §334 is consistent with the carryover basis applied to transferees in §351 transactions and in certain mergers, in which the transferee is considered the successor to the transferor.

Taken together, the nonrecognition principle of §332 and the carryover basis rule of §334(b) in effect remove from tax consideration any gain or loss unrecognized by the parent. Consider the following two situations:

	A	B
Parent's stock basis	$10,000	$10,000
Subsidiary's asset basis	3,000	17,000
Fair market value of subsidiary's assets	8,000	13,000

In situation A the parent has an unrecognized $2,000 loss in the stock of its subsidiary; if the parent liquidates within §332, no loss will be recognized on the liquidation, and the parent will hold the subsidiary's assets with a basis of $3,000, thereby producing a gain if the parent should then sell the assets. Conversely, in situation B the parent has a potential $3,000 gain in the subsidiary's stock. If the parent liquidates, no gain will be recognized, and the parent will take a $17,000 basis in the subsidiary's assets, which will produce a $4,000 loss if the parent sells on liquidation.

Associated Wholesale Grocers, Inc. v. United States _____
927 F.2d 1517 (10th Cir. 1991)

BRORBY, Circuit Judge. . . .
The material facts are not in dispute. In 1976, Super Market Developers, Inc. ("Super Market Developers") made a tender offer for all of the outstanding stock of Weston Investment Co. ("Weston"), a publicly traded holding company which owned a number of corporate supermarkets. Super Market Developers acquired approximately 99.97 percent of the total outstanding shares of Weston by 1980. The management of Super Market Developer's parent corporation, Associated Wholesale Grocers, Inc. ("Associated Grocers"), subsequently decided it was not in their best interests to own and operate grocery stores through subsidiary corporations. . . .

One of Weston's subsidiaries was Weston Market, Inc. ("Weston Market"), a grocery managed by Thomas Elder. In 1980, Mr. Elder expressed to taxpayer his interest in buying Weston Market. Taxpayer advised Mr. Elder that it was not interested in a transaction solely involving the stock or operating assets of Weston Market, but that it would be willing to continue discussions.

The parties eventually structured a disposition of Weston's stock which, taxpayer hoped, would enable it both to cash out Weston's minority shareholders without paying a premium and to recognize a substantial loss in the value of Weston's assets[1] when it sold Weston Market. The transaction took the form of two agreements between Super Market Developers and Elder Food Mart, Inc. ("Elder, Inc."), a corporation organized by Mr. Elder to facilitate the purchase of Weston Market. Both agreements were signed on December 11, 1980, and consummated on December 23, 1980.

Under the "Agreement and Plan of Merger," Weston was merged into Elder, Inc., with Elder, Inc. as the surviving corporation. Elder, Inc. exchanged $300,000 in cash and a non-interest bearing demand promissory note, with a face value of $9,049,703, for the Weston stock. The minority shareholders were entitled to receive $28.50 per share, or more, depending on their pro rata share of the cash and note exchanged for Weston stock.

Under the "Agreement and Plan of Reorganization," which took effect "immediately following the time of effectiveness of the merger," Super Market Developers bought back all the assets acquired by Elder, Inc. under the merger agreement except for the stock of Weston Market. In exchange for those assets, Super Market Developers paid "an amount equal to the principal amount of the promissory note . . . plus an amount equal to the cash received by the [minority] shareholders."

Taxpayer treated the transaction as a taxable sale of Weston's assets and declared a tax loss under I.R.C. §1001(a). Because the transaction brought Super Market Developers $2,353,258 less than its cost basis in the stock of Weston, the taxpayer reported that amount as a long-term capital loss in its 1980 consolidated federal income tax return and sought to carry back portions of the loss to each of the three prior years. The IRS denied the loss, concluding the transaction was not a sale but rather a complete liquidation of taxpayer's subsidiary, Weston. As such, the IRS concluded, recognition of the loss was barred by I.R.C. §332. The IRS assessed a deficiency which the taxpayer paid.

Upon the IRS's denial of taxpayer's claim for refund, taxpayer filed suit in the United States District Court for the District of Kansas. The district court applied the step transaction doctrine in holding that §332

1. Taxpayer was concerned by the difference between Super Market Developer's cost basis in the Weston stock — the amount it had paid for the stock, $11,727,716 — and the carryover basis representing the market value of Weston's assets, $9,374,458. Under I.R.C. §334, taxpayer would get the carryover basis for Weston's assets upon a complete liquidation of Weston.

bars the recognition of taxpayer's loss. *Grocers,* 720 F. Supp. at 890. The court granted summary judgment in favor of the government. Id. This appeal followed. . . .

ARGUMENTS ON APPEAL

The issue presented is whether, as a matter of law, the transaction of December 23, 1980 constitutes a taxable sale or other disposition of Weston's assets under I.R.C. §1001(a) or a non-taxable complete liquidation of Weston under I.R.C. §332.

Taxpayer argues the district court erred in accepting the government's characterization of the transaction as a non-taxable liquidation under §332, and in applying the step transaction doctrine to reach that conclusion. Taxpayer advances five reasons in support of its argument: (1) the transaction does not meet the enumerated requirements of §332; (2) case law rejects application of the step transaction doctrine in the §332 context; (3) this transaction was supported by business purposes which bar application of the step transaction doctrine; (4) even if it is applicable, the step transaction doctrine was improperly applied by the district court; and (5) application of the step transaction doctrine in this case will produce the harsh result of forever depriving taxpayer of the recognition of its tax loss. We now address those contentions.

I. INTERNAL REVENUE CODE §332

. . . The nonrecognition exception of §332 applies or, in other words, a distribution is considered to be in complete liquidation of a subsidiary, only if:

(1) the asset-receiving or "parent" corporation owns, on the date of the adoption of the plan of liquidation and continuously until the receipt of the assets upon liquidation, at least 80 percent of the total voting power and value of the subsidiary (§332(b)(1)); and

(2) the subsidiary distributes its property in complete cancellation or redemption of its stock (§332(b)(2), (3)); and

(3) the subsidiary transfers all of its property to the parent either:

    (a) within the taxable year (in which case the shareholders' adoption of the resolution authorizing the distribution of assets in complete cancellation or redemption of stock is considered an adoption of a plan of liquidation) (§332(b)(2)), or

    (b) in a series of distributions in accordance with a plan of liquidation under which all property is distributed within three years from the close of the year in which the first distribution is made. (§332(b)(3).)

See I.R.C. §332(b)(1)-(b)(3); 11 J. Mertens, The Law of Federal Income Taxation, §42.42 at 113-14 (1990); cf. Matter of Chrome Plate, Inc., 614 F.2d 990, 994 (5th Cir. 1980).

The significance of the statute in this dispute is apparent: if §332 applies, taxpayer cannot recognize its loss. If §332 is inapplicable, however, taxpayer is entitled to a substantial tax refund.

Taxpayer argues §332 is inapplicable for three reasons: the 80 percent ownership requirement was not continuously met; all of the assets of the subsidiary were not transferred to the parent; and taxpayer did not adopt a plan of liquidation. We will consider these arguments in turn.

II. 80% STOCK OWNERSHIP REQUIREMENT

The stock ownership requirement is found in §332(b)(1), which specifies an 80 percent voting and value requirement. That requirement is not specifically at issue here, as parties agree that taxpayer owned 99.97 percent of Weston's stock until the transactions occurred on December 23, 1980.

At issue is the continuity requirement of §332(b)(1) — whether taxpayer "has continued to be at all times until the receipt of the property" qualified under the 80 percent voting and value test. As explained by Treasury Regulation:

> The recipient corporation must have been the owner of the specified amount of such stock on the date of the adoption of the plan of liquidation and have continued so to be at all times until the receipt of the property. If the recipient corporation does not continue qualified with respect to the ownership of stock of the liquidating corporation and if the failure to continue qualified occurs at any time prior to the completion of the transfer of all the property, the provisions for the nonrecognition of gain or loss do not apply to any distribution received under the plan.

Treas. Reg. §1.332-2(a). The question, then, is whether taxpayer continued qualified with respect to the ownership of Weston stock until taxpayer received Weston's assets.

Section 332(b)(1) and Treas. Reg. §1.332-2(a) each direct our inquiry to two time periods: "the date of the adoption of the plan of liquidation" and "all times until the receipt of the property." We assume for the purposes of the first inquiry that the adoption of the "Agreement and Plan of Merger" by Weston shareholders on December 20, 1980 was an adoption of a plan of liquidation. Taxpayer undisputedly owned 99.97 percent of Weston's stock at that time.

The key dispute concerns the effect of the merger and reorganization transactions on December 23, 1980 — the date on which taxpayer received the property of its subsidiary. Taxpayer argues that because all of Weston's assets were transferred to Elder, Inc. and all of Weston's stock was cancelled under the merger, taxpayer's ownership of Weston stock was cut off before it received Weston's property. Therefore, taxpayer argues, because taxpayer owned no Weston stock when it subsequently received the property of its subsidiary under the reorganization, it did not continue qualified with respect to stock ownership under §332(b)(1).

The government urges this court to disregard Elder, Inc.'s transitory ownership of Weston by applying the step transaction doctrine in holding that the merger and reorganization "should be collapsed and viewed as a single transaction for tax purposes." The district court agreed and "view(ed) the execution of the two integrated agreements as one transaction which did not effect a bonafide sale of stock and conclude(d), as a matter of law, that Super Market Developers, at all relevant times, owned more than 80 percent of the outstanding shares of Weston. . . ." 720 F. Supp. at 890.

A. The Step Transaction Doctrine

"The step-transaction doctrine developed as part of the broader tax concept that substance should prevail over form." American Potash & Chem. Corp. v. United States, 399 F.2d 194, 207, 185 Ct. Cl. 161; see also Security Indus. Ins. Co. v. United States, 702 F.2d 1234, 1244 (5th Cir. 1983); Rosenberg, Tax Avoidance and Income Measurement, 87 Mich. L. Rev. 365, 400 (1988) [hereinafter Rosenberg]. Under the step transaction doctrine:

> interrelated yet formally distinct steps in an integrated transaction may not be considered independently of the overall transaction. By thus "linking together all interdependent steps with legal or business significance, rather than taking them in isolation," federal tax liability may be based "on a realistic view of the entire transaction."

Commissioner v. Clark, 489 U.S. 726, 738 (1989) (quoting 1 B. Bittker, Federal Taxation of Income, Estates and Gifts ¶4.3.5, p. 4-52 (1981)). . . .

Courts and commentators have identified several tests which are used with varying frequency in determining whether to apply the step transaction doctrine. Most sources identify three tests: see, e.g., Security Indus., 702 F.2d at 1244-45 (identifying the "end result," "interdependence," and "binding commitment" tests); McDonald's Restaurants of Illinois, Inc. v. Commissioner, 688 F.2d 520, 524-25 (7th Cir. 1982) (same); 11 J. Mertens, The Law of Federal Income Taxation, §§43.254-43.256 (1990) (same); Comments, Step Transactions, 24 U. Miami L. Rev. 60, 62-66 (1969) (identifying the "time," "intention," and "interdependency" tests). Others differ: see, e.g., King Enters., Inc. v. United States, 418 F.2d 511, 516 (Ct. Cl. 1969) (identifying "end result" and "interdependence" as the "two basic tests"); Schwartz, Liquidation-Reincorporation: A Sensible Approach Consistent with Congressional Policy, 38 U. Miami L. Rev. 231, 240 n.33

(1984) (same). The "end result" and "interdependence" tests are the most frequently applied. See *Security Indus.*, 702 F.2d at 1244, and Rosenberg, at 409, respectively.

Under the "end result" test, "purportedly separate transactions will be amalgamated into a single transaction when it appears that they were really component parts of a single transaction intended from the outset to be taken for the purpose of reaching the ultimate result." *King Enters.*, 418 F.2d at 516 (quoting Herwitz, Business Planning, 804 (1966)). The "end result" test, like the substance over form principle, is particularly pertinent to cases involving a series of transactions designed and executed as parts of a unitary plan to achieve an intended result. Such plans will be viewed as a whole regardless of whether the effect of so doing is imposition of or relief from taxation. The series of closely related steps in such a plan are merely the means by which to carry out the plan and will not be separated. . . .

The "interdependence test" requires an inquiry as to "whether on a reasonable interpretation of objective facts the steps were so interdependent that the legal relations created by one transaction would have been fruitless without a completion of the series." Paul & Zimet, "Step Transactions," Selected Studies in Federal Taxation 200, 254 (2d Series 1938), quoted in *King Enters.*, 418 F.2d at 516, and *Security Indus.*, 702 F.2d at 1244. The "interdependence test" focuses on the relationship between the steps, rather than on the "end result." *McDonald's Restaurants*, 688 F.2d at 524. Disregarding the tax effects of individual steps under this test is, therefore, "especially proper where . . . it is unlikely that any one step would have been undertaken except in contemplation of the other integrating acts. . . ." Kuper v. Commissioner, 533 F.2d 152, 156 (5th Cir. 1976).

We now consider taxpayer's claim that relevant case law bars the use of step transaction analysis in the context of §332. Taxpayer most heavily relies on Granite Trust Co. v. United States, 238 F.2d 670 (1st Cir. 1956), a taxpayer refund suit involving the liquidation of a corporate subsidiary. In *Granite Trust*, the First Circuit considered whether to allow the taxpayer to avoid the nonrecognition provisions of I.R.C. §112(b)(6) (1939), the predecessor to modern code section 332.

Taxpayer Granite Trust Company (Granite) expected to realize losses upon the liquidation of its wholly owned subsidiary, Building Corp. Granite therefore took two steps to avoid the nonrecognition provisions of §112(b)(6). First, Granite sold 20.5 percent of Building Corp.'s stock in order to circumvent the 80 percent ownership requirement of §112(b)(6). Id. at 672. Second, after adopting a liquidation plan, Granite sold twenty shares of stock and donated two shares to charity. Id. at 673. The dispositions were intended to circumvent the "second condition" of §112(b)(6), one which was not included in modern code section 332. See id. at 672 n.1, 675. That condition allowed recognition of gains or losses where the parent corporation, within a specified time period, disposed of stock in the subsidiary without making countervailing acquisitions. Id. at 675. The *Granite Trust* court ruled on the merits only as to the second step, and allowed taxpayer to recognize its loss. See id. at 675.

Because *Granite Trust*'s decision in favor of the taxpayer hinged on a provision which is no longer present in the Code, *Granite Trust* is not dispositive in this case. However, to the extent the *Granite Trust* court discussed provisions of §112(b)(6) which are still contained in modern §332, some of its reasoning is persuasive.

Granite prevailed over the government's arguments against its recognition of losses. First, the government advanced the "end-result" test in urging the court to ignore the intermediate steps in Granite Trust's liquidation of Building Corp. Id. at 674. The court rejected that argument, stating "the very terms of §112(b)(6) make it evident that it is not an 'end-result' provision, but rather one which prescribes specific conditions for the nonrecognition of realized gains or losses, conditions which, if not strictly met, make the section inapplicable." Id. at 675. The court found support in the legislative history of both §112(b)(6) (1939) and §332 (1954), and concluded "that taxpayers can, by taking appropriate steps, render the subsection applicable or inapplicable as they choose, rather than be at the mercy of the Commissioner on an 'end-result' theory." Id. at 676. The "interdependence test" was neither argued nor discussed.

Second, the government argued that there were in fact no valid sales made by the taxpayer, "that the sales of stock by [Granite Trust] should be ignored on the ground that they were not bona fide, and that the taxpayer therefore retained 'beneficial ownership.' " Id. at 677. . . .

The court ultimately concluded that because the facts "showed legal transactions not fictitious or so lacking in substance as to be anything different from what they purported to be," the sales must be given effect in the administration of §112(b)(6). Id. at 678. Therefore, the taxpayer was able to recognize the loss and claim a substantial tax refund.

In the present case, taxpayer asserts that *Granite Trust* and the legislative history discussed therein stand as a complete bar to any application of step transaction analysis in the context of §332. We disagree. As an initial matter, the First Circuit considered only the "end result" formulation of the step transaction doctrine. 238 F.2d at 675. As noted, the "interdependence test" was neither argued nor considered in *Granite Trust*.[7] The legislative history discussed in *Granite Trust* is equally silent as to the "interdependence test." Id. at 675-77. Taxpayer fails to appreciate the differences between, and the different functions performed by, the "interdependence" and "end result" tests. As the "interdependence" test ad-

---

7. Taxpayer argues that because the *Granite Trust* transactions "clearly" would have met the interdependence test had it been applied, the court's failure to use that test constitutes proof that it believed all forms of the step transaction doctrine to be inapplicable to §112(b)(6). We decline to indulge in such speculative reasoning.

dresses the relationship between, and therefore the integrity of, intermediate steps in a complex transaction, its application is not precluded by *Granite Trust*'s conclusion that a narrow focus on a transaction's "end result" is inappropriate in the context of §112(b)(6).

Furthermore, although the First Circuit concluded from the legislative history that "taxpayers can, by taking appropriate steps, render the subsection applicable or inapplicable as they choose," id. at 676, we think taxpayer misinterprets that conclusion. The nonrecognition mandated by §332 is not optional at the election of taxpayers within the reach of that section. . . . Steps taken by the taxpayer . . . are not immunized from "the question . . . whether the transaction under scrutiny is in fact what it appears to be in form." Chisholm v. Commissioner, 79 F.2d 14, 15 (2d Cir. 1935). . . .

Appellant also relies on Commissioner v. Day & Zimmermann, Inc., 151 F.2d 517 (3rd Cir. 1945), another case where a taxpayer was able to recognize a loss despite §112(b)(6). Yet the Third Circuit did not address the step transaction doctrine in *Day & Zimmerman*. The court took pains to verify the bona fides of the questioned transaction, and emphasized "there was no understanding of any kind between [the stock purchaser] and Day & Zimmerman by which the latter retained any sort of interest in the securities or proceeds therefrom. . . ." 151 F.2d at 519. After a detailed analysis of the motivations of the actors, the court concluded, "the facts before us so manifestly point to the legitimacy of the . . . purchase of stock that they offer no alternative but to accept that view of the transaction." Id.

Granite Trust discussed the significance of *Day & Zimmermann* in terms which indicate the preferred mode of analysis:

> The significant thing in the case is its ultimate rationale that the purported sales of stock to the treasurer were in fact sales, notwithstanding the tax motive which prompted the corporation to enter into the transaction; from which it would seem to be irrelevant how the transfer was arranged, or whether or not it occurred at a public auction or exchange, so long as the beneficial as well as legal title was intended to pass and did pass.

238 F.2d at 676 (emphasis added). Thus *Day & Zimmermann* reaffirms the necessity of determining whether the substance of a transaction matches its form. . . .

B. Business Purpose

. . . The law is unclear as to the relationship between the step transaction doctrine and the business purpose requirement. Our survey of the relevant cases suggests that no firm line delineates the boundary between the two. Most cases applying the step transaction doctrine, far from identifying business purpose as an element whose absence is prerequisite to that application, do not even include discussion of business purpose as a related issue. In some cases, the existence of a business purpose is considered one factor in determining whether form and substance coincide. In others, the lack of business purpose is accepted as reason to apply the step transaction doctrine. We have found no case holding that the existence of a business purpose precludes the application of the step transaction doctrine.

We therefore reject the contention that a valid business purpose bars application of step transaction analysis in this context. "A legitimate business goal does not grant [a] taxpayer carte blanche to subvert Congressionally mandated tax patterns." *Kuper,* 533 F.2d at 158. Moreover, we share the government's skepticism as to the alleged significance of taxpayer's claimed business purpose — that of cashing-out certain minority shareholders who collectively owned no more than 0.03 percent of Super Market Developer's stock. Having thus rejected taxpayer's arguments against the applicability of step transaction analysis, we now apply it to the disputed transaction.

C. Step Transaction Analysis Applied

. . . We are mindful of "the central purpose of the step transaction doctrine: ensuring that the tax consequences of a particular transaction turn on substance rather than form." *Security Indus.,* 702 F.2d at 1245. Under the "interdependence test" we focus primarily on the relationship between the steps, *McDonald's Restaurants,* 688 F.2d at 524, and in so doing inquire whether " 'the steps were so interdependent that the legal relations created by one transaction would have been fruitless without a completion of the series.' " *Security Indus.,* 702 F.2d at 1244 (quoting Paul & Zimet, "Step Transactions," in Selected Studies in Federal Taxation 200, 254 (2d Cir. 1938)). We find sufficient evidence of interdependence in the merger and reorganization agreements to answer that question conclusively.

The "Termination" clause included in the merger agreement is itself a strong indication of interdependence. That clause states:

> *Termination.* If the Agreement and Plan of Reorganization dated as of December 11, 1980, which has been entered into between the Surviving Corporation [Elder Food Mart, Inc.] and Weston Investments, Inc., . . . a Missouri corporation, is terminated prior to the Merger Date, then this Agreement of Merger shall simultaneously terminate without further action by the parties hereto.

Under the express terms of the merger agreement, the legal relations it created were entirely contingent on the continuing force of the reorganization agreement. Thus, the merger agreement would bear no fruit unless the two-step series could be completed.

The "Purchase and Sale" clause contained in plan of reorganization is another manifestation of the relationship between the two steps. It provides:

> The Buyer [Super Market Developers] agrees to purchase from the Seller [Elder, Inc.] and the Seller agrees to sell to the Buyer all of the assets of every kind and description acquired by the Seller pursuant to the Agreement of Merger, except for the shares of common stock of Weston. As part of the consideration to the Seller for the purchase described in this paragraph, the Buyer agrees to assume and discharge all of the obligations and liabilities of the Seller which were formerly the obligations and liabilities of the Merging Corporation [Weston] and which became the obligations and liabilities of the Seller pursuant to the Agreement of Merger.

So interdependent were the two steps that the parties who drafted the agreement setting forth the second step did not think it necessary to separately list the assets (valued at over nine million dollars) which were bought and sold, or the obligations and liabilities which were assumed and discharged therein — they simply referenced the first agreement "attached hereto."

We also consider the timing of the steps in assessing their interdependence. Again, that matter was squarely addressed by the parties to the transactions. Under the terms of the reorganization agreement:

> The merger shall become effective at, and the Merger Date shall mean, *for the purpose of this Agreement and the Agreement of Merger,* the close of business on the date when the Agreement of Merger is filed with the Secretary of State of the State of Missouri in accordance with Missouri law. The closing of the transactions provided for herein shall take place on the date (the "Closing Date") which is the same day as the Merger Date *immediately following* the time of effectiveness of the merger.

(Emphasis supplied). This provision is remarkable for at least two reasons. First, it allows virtually no time to pass between the effectiveness of the two steps which taxpayer vociferously argues are separate transactions. Second, the plan of reorganization actually sets forth the time at which the merger (supposedly a separate transaction controlled by a second agreement) will become effective. . . .

D. Substance Over Form

In giving effect to the substance of the overall transaction, we ignore acts taken in intermediate steps which the taxpayer has itself undone with subsequent steps. We also treat as significant the existence of an understanding between the parties that an interest in the assets transferred would be retained by the taxpayer. See *Granite Trust,* 238 F.2d at 677; *Day,* 151 F.2d at 519. The transaction of December 23, 1980 involved two steps —

the "merger" of Weston into Elder, Inc. and the "reorganization" of Super Market Developers and Elder, Inc. Under the first step, Elder, Inc. paid taxpayer $300,000 cash and a promissory note for all of Weston's assets. The shares of minority shareholders were also converted to cash. Under the second step, taxpayer "immediately" bought back the same assets except for Weston Market, paying "an amount equal to the principal amount of the promissory note . . . plus an amount equal to the cash received by the [minority] shareholders." Excepting the exchange of Weston Market for $300,000, all acts were undone: taxpayer got back the other assets; Elder, Inc. got the value of the note back; and taxpayer fully reimbursed Elder, Inc. for cashing out the minority shareholders.

The transparent form of the transaction fails to obscure its obvious substance: Elder, Inc. bought Weston Market for $300,000 cash, and Weston was liquidated. In light of this transactional substance, we reject taxpayer's claim to have disposed of Weston's stock before Weston's assets were distributed. Accordingly, taxpayer did continue qualified with respect to Weston stock ownership in the meaning of §332.

III. ASSET DISTRIBUTION AND LIQUIDATION PLAN

Taxpayer also argues the requirements of §332 were not met because all of Weston's assets were not transferred to Super Market Developers, and because the shareholders of Weston adopted a plan of merger, rather than a plan of liquidation. This argument is, of course, premised on the transactional form which we have rejected in favor of substance. . . .

Taxpayer argues, however, that because some but not all of Weston's assets were distributed to Super Market Developers, there was no transfer of all the property under the statute. Taxpayer further argues "Elder, Inc. kept the Weston Market subsidiary stock and, unlike a liquidation of Weston, [Super Market Developers] and the other individual shareholders of Weston did not receive stock of all of the subsidiaries owned by Weston." Taxpayer cites no authority in support of its argument.

Given our holding that the step whereby Weston stock was briefly transferred to Elder, Inc. must be disregarded, this argument is rejected. First, there was a resolution authorizing the distribution of Weston's assets in complete cancellation or redemption of all its stock — the shareholders of Weston approved the Plan of Merger by majority vote on December 20, 1980. Under the transactions of December 23, 1980, Weston stock was cancelled or redeemed and its shareholders — both Super Market Developers and the minority shareholders — received payment in distribution of Weston's assets. Second, Elder, Inc. did not "keep" the stock of Weston Market, as taxpayer suggests, because when the form of the transaction is ignored, the substance of the transaction is that Elder, Inc. did not buy Weston stock — it bought Weston Market. . . .

Finally, taxpayer's objection to the alleged "harshness" of the nonrecognition of its tax loss is insufficient to sustain its claim. We must apply the tax effects of the tax code to transactional substance, not form.

CONCLUSION

As the substance of the disputed transaction met the requirements of I.R.C. §332, no gain or loss shall be recognized. The district court's Order of September 19, 1989 granting summary judgment in favor of the government and denying taxpayer's motion for summary judgment is hereby affirmed.

NOTE

1. *80 percent stock ownership.* Section 332(b)(1) requires (through §1504(a)(2)) that the parent own stock (a) that possesses at least 80 percent of the total voting power of the stock of the subsidiary and (b) that has a value equal to at least 80 percent of the total value of the stock of the subsidiary, except nonvoting stock limited and preferred as to dividends. See §1504(a)(4). The stock must be held continuously from the date of adoption of a plan of liquidation until the final liquidation. Section 332 references §1504(a)(2), a definitional section pertaining to consolidated returns. See page 570 infra. The cross-reference is an attempt to ensure that the liquidation of a subsidiary not filing a consolidated return with its parent is treated the same as the liquidation of a subsidiary that does file a consolidated return.

If a parent lacks the necessary 80 percent control, can it come within the ambit of §332 by acquiring stock immediately before the liquidation? Compare Rev. Rul. 75-521, 1975-2 C.B. 120 (purchase from other individual shareholders just prior to plan of liquidation upheld), with Rev. Rul. 70-106, 1970-1 C.B. 70 (redemption of minority shareholder in order to boost parent over 80 percent mark failed where redemption was part of the liquidation plan). See also George L. Riggs, Inc. v. Commissioner, 64 T.C. 474 (1975) (acquisition of stock to qualify under §332 permitted). Suppose *S*, an individual, owns all the stock of *X* Corp. and *Y* Corp., each of which in turn owns 50 percent of *Z* Corp. If *Z* Corp. is liquidated, can *X* and *Y* rely on §332? Consider the applicability of §318.

If a parent can acquire stock to avail itself of §332, can it dispose of stock to avoid §332? Suppose a parent corporation has a basis of $10,000 in the stock of its wholly owned subsidiary, which owns a single asset with a basis of $12,000 and a fair market value of $8,000. Can the parent sell 21 percent of the subsidiary's stock to an unrelated purchaser in order to recognize the loss on the subsequent liquidation? In Commissioner v. Day & Zimmermann, Inc., 151 F.2d 517 (3d Cir. 1945), a parent sold enough stock in its subsidiary to reduce its ownership below the 80 percent standard. The shares were sold at a public auction to the parent's treasurer, who paid a fair market value price with his own funds. Even though the parent's sole purpose was to avoid §332, the court upheld the transaction. See also Granite Trust Co. v. United States, 238 F.2d 670 (1st Cir. 1956) (contribution of two shares worth $130 to charity allowed parent successfully to avoid §332 even though charity surrendered the shares in liquidation four days after receipt); Priv. Ltr. Rul. 9049001 (taxpayer, free to structure liquidation under either §331 or §332, chose §331 to step up the basis of the assets received).

Associated Wholesale Grocers sharply reminds taxpayers, however, that the ability to manipulate §332 is not without limitation. Did the court convince you that the earlier decisions in *Granite Trust* and *Day & Zimmermann* were distinguishable, or should the court simply have refused to follow those decisions? Is it significant that in those earlier cases there really was a disposition by the taxpayer, while in *Associated Wholesale Grocers* there was only a transitory disposition followed by an immediate repurchase?

Could the taxpayer have structured the transaction differently so that it would have been successful? Why didn't Super Market Developers first buy out the minority shareholders in Weston and then sell enough stock in Weston to Elder, Inc., to allow Elder, Inc., to receive the Weston Market stock on a liquidation of Weston while all the other assets were distributed to Super Market Developers? Would the sale of Weston stock to Elder, Inc., have been enough to bring Super Market Developers below the 80 percent ownership threshold for purposes of §332? The court determined that the Weston Market stock had a value of $300,000 and that Super Market Developers sold the Weston assets for $9,349,703 and purchased back all the assets of Weston (except Weston Market) for $9,049,703.

For a checklist of information to be submitted to the IRS in connection with a request for a ruling on the liquidation of a controlled subsidiary, see Rev. Rul. 90-52, 1990-2 C.B. 626.

2. *Timing of distribution.* For §332 to apply, the liquidation must take place within one of two prescribed time periods. Under §332(b)(2), a shareholder's resolution authorizing a distribution but not specifying a time period will qualify if the distribution is completed "within the taxable year." Under §332(b)(3), if the plan of liquidation provides for the transfer of all the subsidiary's property within three years of the close of the year during which the first distribution is made, §332 will apply (if the distributions are, in fact, made). Could the taxpayer in *Associated Wholesale Grocers* have avoided the application of §332 by spreading out the liquidating distributions?

In Cherry-Burrell Corp. v. United States, 367 F.2d 669 (8th Cir. 1966), the court liberally permitted the liquidation to qualify under §332, even though the liquidation was not completed within the time period, since the delay was involuntary. What is the effect of a taxpayer's deliberate effort to avoid the timing requirements? In Service Co. v. Commissioner, 165 F.2d 75 (8th Cir. 1948), the court held that a parent could not intentionally avoid §332 through noncompliance with the recordkeeping requirements of Treas. Regs. §1.332-6. But suppose the parent spreads the subsidiary's distributions out over more than four years. Might the Service try to argue that there was constructive receipt by the parent?

In Priv. Ltr. Rul. 9215016, the IRS ruled that the distribution of property by a subsidiary to its parent corporation under a plan of liquidation qualified under §332 even though the subsidiary retained its corporate charter, state insurance licenses, and sufficient assets to meet the minimum capital requirements of the state. The parent corporation's intention was to sell the charter and the insurance licenses to an unrelated party. The IRS ruled that the parent must complete the sale or dissolution of the subsidiary within twelve months of the final liquidating distribution.

3. *Basis, holding period, and carryovers.* As noted above, the parent's basis in the assets received on liquidation is the subsidiary's basis. §334(b). If a distributing subsidiary recognizes gain on a distribution to a parent corporation in a §332 liquidation (e.g., a distribution to a foreign parent corporation, see §367(e)(2)), a corresponding increase in the distributee's basis occurs under §334(b).

Because a parent corporation normally takes the subsidiary's stock basis in a §332 liquidation, the Code provides that the parent inherits the holding periods for the assets of the subsidiary. See §1223(2). In addition, the parent normally acquires the subsidiary's tax attributes under §381(a), including loss carryovers and earnings and profits account. But see §269(b), discussed at page 568 infra, which can deny the parent a loss carryover under some tax avoidance circumstances.

4. *Minority shareholders.* Since §332 applies only to parent corporations, minority shareholders must look to other provisions — typically, §§331(a) and 1001 — to determine their gain or loss on liquidation.

5. *Treatment of liquidating subsidiary.* Section 332(a) provides tax consequences only to the shareholder-parent on liquidation of a subsidiary. What are the tax consequences to the liquidating subsidiary? Current §337 (not to be confused with former §337) provides that no gain or loss shall be recognized to the liquidating corporation on the distribution to an 80 percent distributee in a §332 liquidation.

In situations in which the parent corporation is not taxable on its income, the nonrecognition rule will not apply. This follows from the fact that in these situations nonrecognition would be tantamount to permanent exclusion. For example, if the parent corporation is tax exempt, the liquidating subsidiary must recognize gain or loss in accordance with §336. §337(b)(2)(A).

There is an exception to this exception when the property distributed will be used in an unrelated trade or business of the tax-exempt organization because the parent would be taxed on gains in connection with such unrelated activities. §§337(b)(2)(B), 511, and 512. If the property ceases to be used in an unrelated trade or business, the tax-exempt organization will be taxed at that time on the lesser of the built-in gain at the time of liquidation or the difference between fair market value and adjusted basis at the time of cessation. Similarly, if the parent-corporation is a foreign corporation beyond the reach of U.S. federal taxation, a liquidating corporation may be taxed in accordance with §336. §367(e)(2).

Suppose the stock of *Y* Corp. is 80 percent owned by *X* Corp. and 20 percent by *B*, an individual. If *Y* Corp. liquidates, it recognizes no gain or loss on the property distributed to *X* Corp. But §337 does not apply to a liquidating distribution made to individual shareholders. Strangely enough, §336(a) does not apply in its entirety to the liquidating corporation with respect to the property distributed to minority shareholders. Instead, §336(d)(3) denies any loss to the liquidating corporation on such distributions. Presumably, Congress was concerned that a liquidating corporation would distribute gain property to a corporate parent, thereby avoiding gain under §337 while recognizing a loss on the distribution of loss property to the minority shareholders. But note that §336(d)(3) applies even if the liquidating distribution is pro rata to both the corporate parent and the minority shareholders. Apparently, Congress opted to treat a liquidating distribution to minority shareholders as if it were a nonliquidating distribution under principles similar to those in §311. This is not an unreasonable position since the premise of a §332 nontaxable liquidation is the simplification of a corporate structure in which the former activities of the subsidiary are carried on by the parent corporation and the minority shareholders, in effect, have their stock redeemed.

Section 337(b) contains another provision affecting the treatment of the liquidating subsidiary. Ordinarily, if a taxpayer transfers appreciated property in satisfaction of a debt, gain must be recognized. See, e.g., United States v. Davis, 370 U.S. 65 (1962). But if the transfer occurs in the context of a §332 liquidation, it might be very difficult to distinguish a taxable transfer from a subsidiary to a parent-creditor to satisfy the outstanding indebtedness from a nontaxable transfer in exchange for stock. Accordingly, §337(b) provides for nonrecognition of gain or loss on a distribution of property to a parent-creditor to satisfy an indebtedness. Section 334(b)(2) provides that the parent takes the subsidiary's basis in the assets. Compare §1041 in an unrelated context involving transfers between spouses.

6. *Overlap with reorganization provisions.* For a discussion of the relationship of subsidiary liquidations to reorganizations, see page 437 infra.

C.   THE TAXATION OF A LIQUIDATING CORPORATION AND CORPORATE TAKEOVER ACTIVITY

Prior to the repeal of the *General Utilities* doctrine, a liquidating corporation
did not ordinarily recognize a gain on the distribution of appreciated
property. See page 135 supra. The congressional decision to repeal the
doctrine was motivated in part by a concern that nonrecognition at the
corporate level created distortions that artificially encouraged corporate
acquisitions and liquidations. A major concern was that the absence of a
corporate-level tax under some circumstances might foster acquisitions for
tax rather than business reasons. For example, suppose *X* Corp. was a
publicly traded corporation with appreciated assets. As the *X* Corp. stock
is bought and sold, a shareholder-level tax will be levied on the appreciation under §1001. The current shareholders may actually hold stock with
very little unrealized gain if the stock has been heavily traded.

The ability of a purchaser *Y* Corp. under prior law to step up the basis
of the *X* Corp. assets with no corporate-level tax following a stock purchase
allowed *Y* Corp. to offer more for the stock of *X* Corp. than would be
offered in the absence of this tax treatment. The step-up in basis might
lead to larger depreciation deductions or less gain if the assets were sold.
Alternatively, the current shareholders of *X* Corp. had tax incentives to
liquidate the corporation and sell the assets since the liquidation would
not trigger a corporate-level gain and the shareholders would step up the
basis of the assets received so that little or no gain was recognized on the
postliquidation sale.

With the repeal of the *General Utilities* principle, *Y* Corp. cannot obtain
a step up in the bases of the *X* Corp. assets unless *X* Corp. recognizes a
corporate-level gain. Consequently, *Y* Corp. does not have a tax incentive
to purchase *X* Corp. Similarly, if the shareholders liquidate *X* Corp., it
must recognize a corporate-level gain in order for the shareholders to
obtain a step up in the bases of the assets. Consequently, the repeal perhaps
has removed one tax distortion that may have made corporations more
attractive as takeover targets or may have encouraged liquidations that
would not have taken place but for tax reasons.

In a tax system in which distortions abound, it is difficult to say that the
repeal of the *General Utilities* rule has removed tax incentives for inefficient
acquisitions or liquidations. Other provisions of the Code may create dis-

tortions that deter efficient acquisitions or liquidations. For example, limitations on the deductibility of interest used to finance stock or asset acquisitions may lead to a suboptimal level of acquisition activity. See §279. Maybe the *General Utilities* doctrine operated as a perfect counterbalance. Maybe not.

When it repealed the *General Utilities* doctrine, Congress did recognize that some relief from the two-tier tax on corporate earnings was appropriate to remove this major distortion. Indeed, the original proposal to repeal the *General Utilities* rule was coupled with a dividends-paid deduction. While the repeal has become law, however, there has been no relief from the corporate double taxation distortion. See generally Chapter 8.

D.   PROBLEMS

1.   Determine the tax consequences in the following situations.
a.   *X* Corp. is owned by unrelated individuals, *A* and *B,* who hold 80 percent and 20 percent, respectively, of the outstanding *X* Corp. stock. *A*'s stock has a basis of $300,000 and a fair market value of $800,000. *B*'s stock has a basis of $600,000 and a fair market value of $200,000. *X* Corp. holds two assets. Asset 1 has a basis of $200,000 and a fair market value of $500,000. Asset 2 has a basis of $800,000 and a fair market value of $500,000. Both assets were transferred to *X* Corp. in a §351 transaction two years ago. At that time asset 2 had a basis of $800,000 and a fair market value of $900,000. *X* Corp. has accumulated earnings and profits of $100,000, but no current earnings and profits. What are the tax consequences if *X* Corp. liquidates, distributing the assets pro rata?
b.   In (a), suppose asset 2 had a basis of $800,000 and a fair market value of $700,000 at the time of the §351 transfer.
c.   In (b), suppose the §351 transfer took place six years before the liquidation.
d.   In (c), suppose *X* Corp. distributes all of asset 2 and a $300,000 interest in asset 1 to *A* and the remaining $200,000 interest in asset 1 to *B.*
e.   In (a), suppose *A* and *B* are planning to sell the assets after liquidation. Does it matter whether *X* Corp. makes the sale and then distributes $1 million in cash or *A* and *B* make the sale following liquidation? In (b), would it matter?
f.   If *A* is a corporation, how does your answer to (a) change?
2.   Individuals *A* and *B* own all the stock of *X* Corp., which runs a factory that produces thermostatic devices. *X* Corp. also owns all the stock of *Y* Corp., which runs two businesses as separate unincorporated divisions.

Division 1 produces and sells electricity from solar heating; division 2 produces air conditioners. The primary asset of division 1 is undeveloped land on which the solar panels are situated. The primary asset of division 2 is a factory that produces air conditioners. P Corp., owned by individuals C and D, wants to acquire the assets of division 2. A and B would like to liquidate Y Corp. and operate both the thermostatic device business and solar panel business as unincorporated divisions of X Corp.

X Corp.'s basis in the Y Corp. stock is $650,000. The division 1 assets of Y Corp. have a combined basis of $700,000 and a fair market value of $400,000. The assets of division 2 have a combined basis of $60,000 and a fair market value of approximately $100,000. Consider the tax consequences of the following alternative methods of satisfying the goals of the parties.

  a. X Corp. liquidates Y Corp. and then sells the division 2 assets to P Corp.
  b. Y Corp. distributes the division 1 assets to X Corp. and sells the division 2 assets to P Corp. Y Corp. then liquidates.
  c. Y Corp. sells all its assets to P Corp. for approximately $500,000. P Corp. pays cash for the division 2 assets and issues a note for $400,000 for the division 1 assets. The note bears interest at the market rate and is due in 10 years. X Corp. then liquidates Y Corp. Sometime after P Corp.'s acquisition and the liquidation, X Corp. purchases the division 1 assets from P Corp. for $400,000, payable by a note.
  d. Y Corp. sells the division 1 assets to X Corp. for $400,000 and sells the division 2 assets to P Corp. Y Corp. then liquidates.
  e. X Corp. sells to P Corp. stock in Y Corp. equal to the fair market value of the division 2 assets held by Y Corp. X Corp. and P Corp. then liquidate Y Corp., with the division 1 assets distributed to X Corp. and the division 2 assets distributed to P Corp.
  f. Y Corp. adopts a plan of liquidation, sells the division 2 assets to P Corp. for cash, and then distributes the division 1 assets and the cash, completing the liquidation in 18 months.

8

Integration of the Corporate and Individual Income Taxes

A. THE INCIDENCE AND EFFECTS OF THE CORPORATE TAX

While corporations are the nominal payors of the corporate income tax, in substance that tax is paid by individuals. We know this must be true because corporations are fictional entities, and when we speak of a "corporation" we really are using that term as a convenient shorthand for a collection of contracts and legal relationships among shareholders, debt-holders, employees, suppliers, and customers. Accordingly, when a tax is levied on a corporation, the burden of that levy is shared by these groups of individuals, with some bearing a greater and others a lesser share of that burden.

No theory tells us precisely how the corporate tax is shared among the various possible groups of individuals. On one hand, it might be the case that the wages paid to employees and the costs paid to suppliers would be the same even if there were no corporate tax. If so, then the corporate tax is borne only by the stockholders and bondholders as well as by the corporation's consumers. On the other hand, the incidence of the corporate tax might lie on the employees alone or, possibly, on the shareholders and customers. Ultimately this is an empirical question, and unfortunately it is a very complex one. Accordingly, economists can estimate the incidence of the corporate tax only if they make significantly simplifying assumptions.[1] The true incidence of the corporate tax remains to this day a mystery.

1. See, e.g., Klein, The Incidence of the Corporation Income Tax: A Lawyer's View of a Problem in Economics, 1965 Wis. L. Rev. 576.

If we do not know who bears the burden of the corporate tax, why do we have one? After all, the revenue collected by the corporate tax could be replaced with some alternate levy such as an increased estate and gift tax or individual income tax, the incidence of which may be easier to determine. Presumably the burden of taxation in this country should be fair, and while different people may have different notions of fairness in this context, so long as we do not know who bears the corporate tax we cannot with confidence assert that its burden is imposed in accordance with *anyone's* concept of fairness.

A cynic might suggest that we have a corporate tax precisely because its incidence is unknown. Raising taxes is difficult for politicians: While most of us may not mind taxes imposed on other people, few of us willingly accept higher taxes imposed on ourselves. Indeed, because most tax increases are imposed on a well-defined group of individuals while the benefits of those tax revenues are spread among the entire electorate, it is easier for opponents of a tax to band together and lobby against an increase than it is for proponents to lobby in favor.

The incidence of the corporate tax is uncertain, so the possible return to voters who choose to fight it may be slight. Accordingly, the financial incentive to lobby against the corporate tax is diminished. Indeed, so long as voters perceive the corporate tax as imposed only on people other than themselves, it offers politicians the opportunity to raise funds seemingly without taking those funds from anyone.

Even without knowing the precise incidence of the corporate tax, we can make some observations. So long as the corporate tax is paid, it is borne by someone; so long as it is borne by someone, the tax system discourages investment in the corporate form. In addition, because of the way in which the corporate tax is implemented, it may encourage some forms of corporate behavior over others. The following excerpt from a recent Treasury Department report identifies possible distortions in economic behavior caused by imposition of the corporate tax. Latent within this discussion is the assumption that the corporate tax is borne exclusively by corporate shareholders. This assumption undoubtedly is false to some extent, but it also likely true to a great extent. As you read the excerpt you might seek to identify the extent to which its conclusions depend on knowledge of the incidence of the corporate tax.

Integration of the Individual and Corporate Tax Systems: Taxing Business Income Once 3-11 _____

Treasury Department Report 1992

The classical corporate income tax system distorts three economic and financial decisions: (1) whether to invest in noncorporate rather than corporate form, (2) whether to finance investments with debt rather than equity, and (3) whether to retain rather than distribute earnings. Apart from corporate and investor level tax considerations, nontax benefits and costs also influence those decisions. To the extent that the classical tax system distorts the choice of organizational form, financial structure, and dividend policy, economic resources can be misallocated.

. . . In deciding whether to undertake an investment, firms require that the investment provide a sufficient after-tax return to compensate investors. The cost of capital is the pre-tax rate of return that is sufficient to cover operating expenses, taxes, economic depreciation, and the investor's required after-tax rate of return. Thus, the cost of capital depends in part on the return firms must pay to suppliers of debt or equity capital to attract funds. The cost of capital also depends in part on such factors as tax rates, the investment's economic depreciation rate, the capital cost recovery deductions allowed on the investment, the inflation rate, and the source of financing for the investment. Because a higher cost of capital makes certain investments unprofitable, corporate and individual income taxes reduce investment incentives by raising the cost of capital. . . .

ORGANIZATIONAL FORM

A simple example illustrates the effect of the current corporate tax system on investment decisions. Suppose that an investor requires an after-tax rate of return of 8 percent and the investor's effective tax rate is 20 percent. An equity investment in a noncorporate enterprise must earn a return high enough to pay tax at the investor's rate (20 percent) and still yield the required 8 percent after-tax return.[11] The noncorporate investment must therefore earn a 10 percent pre-tax rate of return (net of depreciation) in order to cover the investor's income taxes and meet the required return $(0.10 \times (1 - 0.20) = 0.08)$. However, if the corporate tax rate is 34 percent and the corporation distributes all of its income, the cost of capital of an equity financed investment in the corporate sector in the above example is 15.2 percent. This 15.2 percent pre-tax return yields an 8 percent return after paying both the corporate tax and the investor level tax on dividends $(0.152 \times (1 - 0.34) \times (1 - 0.20) = 0.08)$. Since fewer investments can earn the higher required return (15.2 percent as opposed to 10 percent), the corporate tax discourages investment in the corporate sector by raising the cost of capital.

More complex calculations support this result. For example, a Con-

---

11. This simple example abstracts from other factors affecting the cost of capital, including: (i) differences between tax and economic depreciation; (ii) differences in tax rates among investors; and (iii) inflation.

gressional Research Service report estimates, under realistic assumptions, the total effective Federal income tax rate on corporate equity (taking into account both corporate level and shareholder level taxes) to be 48 percent, compared to 28 percent for noncorporate equity. Therefore, some corporations fail to undertake investments that would be profitable if the tax burden on corporate and noncorporate investments were the same. . . .

International comparisons add perspective on the effect of the corporate tax on the U.S. corporate sector. One measure is the ratio of corporate investment to investment in housing, which provides a comparison of resource allocation in different economies. . . . Throughout the period [1976-1989], the United States has had a lower ratio [of corporate gross fixed investment relative to private residential housing investment] than the United Kingdom. Although the U.S. ratio exceeded that for Japan and Australia until the early 1980s, corporate investment relative to housing has tended upwards over the whole period for Japan and Australia while the ratio for the United States has remained fairly stable, except for the 2 years following the Economic Recovery Tax Act of 1981 [when the ratio dropped significantly]. Indeed, for the last 4 years for which data are available, the United States has had essentially the lowest corporate investment per dollar of housing investment of any of the four nations. . . .

Another useful international comparison is the spread between the pre-tax return on corporate investment and the cost of funds in the United States and other countries. This spread, or corporate "tax wedge," generally depends upon the type of asset acquired, the corporate tax rate, the capital recovery allowances, the rate of inflation, and various other country specific factors. Table 1.1 presents a listing of preliminary [Organisation for Economic Co-operation and Development] calculations of the 1991 corporate tax wedge based on a standard mix of assets and sources of funding for a manufacturer located in several OECD member countries. According to these data, the corporate tax wedge in the United States is

Table 1.1

Corporate Tax Wedge for New Investments in Manufacturing 1991

Country	Corporate Tax Wedge
Canada	1.2
France	0.4
Germany	0.6
Japan	1.4
United Kingdom	0.9
United States	0.9

higher than in France or Germany, is approximately the same as in the
U.K., and is lower than in Canada and Japan.

CORPORATE CAPITAL STRUCTURE

Corporations have three alternatives for financing new investments: (1)
issuing new equity, (2) using retained earnings, or (3) issuing debt. There
can be important nontax benefits and costs of alternative corporate financing arrangements, and the tax system should avoid prejudicing financial
decisions.

The current classical corporate tax system discriminates against equity
financing of new corporate investment. . . . Because of the two levels of
taxation of corporate profits, the cost of equity capital generally exceeds
the cost of debt capital. The Congressional Research Service estimates,
under realistic assumptions, the total effective Federal income tax rate on
corporate debt to be 20 percent, compared with 48 percent for corporate
equity. Moreover, the total effective tax rate for debt financed corporate
than for equity financed corporate investment encourages the use of debt
by corporations, assuming nontax factors that affect financing decisions
do not change.

If a corporation borrows from an individual to finance an investment,
the corporation deducts the interest payments from its taxable income
and is therefore not taxed on the investment's pre-tax return to the extent
of the interest payments, although the lender is taxable on the interest at
the individual tax rate. Consequently, to the extent that corporations finance investment with debt, current law does not distort the choice between investment in the corporate and noncorporate sectors. Using the
assumptions in the numerical example set forth under "Organizational
Form," above, for a 100 percent debt financed corporate investment, the
cost of capital is 10 percent ($0.10 \times (1 - 0.2) = 0.08$, the required rate
of return). This cost is well below the 15.2 percent cost of capital for equity
financed investments for corporations that distribute income as dividends,
and is the same as the cost of capital for a noncorporate investment.

Historical data show U.S. corporate debt to be at relatively high levels
by postwar standards, with some, but not all, measures growing at an unusually rapid pace in the 1980s. Because there is no single, universally agreed-
upon measure of debt, the discussion below considers trends based on
alternative measures.

One group of debt measures focuses on corporate balance sheets: the
ratio of debt to total assets. The debt to asset ratio can be computed using
either book value (the par value of debt and the historical cost of assets
as reported for financial accounting purposes) or market value. . . . This
ratio grew from 43 percent in 1948 to 61 percent in 1989. Although the

ratio generally increased over the postwar period, it declined sharply beginning in 1975 and continued through the mid 1980s. Following that decrease, the ratio began to rise again and by 1989 had reached a postwar high of 61 percent. In 1989, this book-value debt to asset ratio was
more than 17 percentage points higher than in 1980, but only 10 percentage points higher than the pre-1980s peak of 51 percent reached in
1973.

. . . Like the book-value measure, the market-value ratio indicates that
corporate debt has generally increased since 1961. . . .

A second measure of leverage focuses on the importance of debt in
corporations' sources of additional funds rather than corporations' total
outstanding debt. . . . Over the entire postwar period, equity finance was
dominant. For nonfinancial corporations, retained earnings and new equity issues accounted for roughly 78 percent of funds raised. Debt provided
the balance, divided about equally between private issues (bank loans and
private placements) and public issues (bonds). Relative financing patterns
changed during the 1980s. While corporations continue to rely heavily on
retained earnings, they have sharply adjusted the composition of external
finance. Most notably, corporations have undertaken substantial repurchases of equity, financed mainly with debt. . . . The increase in nonfinancial corporate debt during the 1980s was largely matched by a
reduction in outstanding equity. [N]onfinancial corporations relied significantly more on internal funds (retained earnings) during the 1980s
than was the case for the postwar period as a whole.

Recent evidence suggests that share repurchases have contributed to
the increase in corporate debt. Rather than simply replacing dividends,
repurchases have been financed primarily by debt, which results in higher
interests costs. Increased share repurchases, therefore, accounts for part
of the recent increases in net interest payments, and may be viewed as one
method that firms have used to reduce their corporate tax liabilities. [B]y
1990, over one quarter of the interest payments of nonfinancial corporations was attributable to increased share repurchases. . . .

Debt finance may have nontax benefits. Analysts most sanguine about
high levels of corporate debt and debt-service burdens typically maintain
that the discipline of debt is desirable because it gives lenders indirect
means to monitor the activities of managers. This need for supervision
owes to the separation between ownership and management that is characteristic of the traditional corporate structure.

A disadvantage of higher debt levels is that they can increase nontax
costs of debt, including costs associated with financial distress. Even when
corporations avoid formal bankruptcy proceedings, they incur costs when
they cannot meet their interest obligations or when debt covenants restrict
operating flexibility. The costs include extra demands on executives' time,
supply disruptions, declines in customers' confidence, and, frequently,
significant legal fees. Corporations therefore must evaluate the tax and

nontax benefits of additional debt relative to these costs. Tax-induced distortions in capital structure can entail significant efficiency costs.

CORPORATE DIVIDEND DISTRIBUTIONS

The current system of corporate taxation also may distort a corporation's choice between distributing or retaining earnings and, if amounts are distributed, whether they are paid in the form of a nondividend distribution, such as a share repurchase. Differences in effective tax rates on dividends and retained earnings are significant.

Assessing the efficiency costs of such tax differentials requires an analysis of motives for corporate dividend distributions in the presence of relatively high taxes on such dividends compared to capital gains. This Report assumes that corporate dividends offer special nontax benefits to shareholders that offset their tax disadvantage,[26] and, accordingly, that corporations set dividend payments so that the incremental nontax benefit of dividends paid equals their incremental tax cost. Under this assumption, the amount of dividends paid out is expected to decrease as the tax burden on dividends relative to capital gains increases; empirical studies are consistent with this prediction. Investor level taxes on dividends also raise the cost of capital (and thereby reduce investment) to the extent that corporations pay out earnings as dividends. Thus, under the assumption used in this Report, dividend taxes reduce the payout ratio and real investment incentives.

The growth in share repurchases in the last decade supports this view of the linkage between the corporate tax and corporate dividends. Share repurchases provide a means of distributing corporate earnings with, in many cases, more favorable shareholder level tax treatment than dividend distributions. While a shareholder pays tax on the full amount of a dividend at ordinary income rates, the shareholder generally pays tax on the proceeds of a share repurchase only to the extent they exceed share basis and, in some cases, at a preferential capital gains rate. Share repurchases increased substantially from 1970 to 1990, growing from 1.2 billion (or 5.4

26. This assumption is controversial, since not all economic models of the effects of taxation on dividend payments maintain that nontax benefits are associated with dividend payments. There are two leading explanations why corporations continue to pay dividends in spite of the greater investor level tax burden on dividends than on capital gains attributable to retained earnings or share repurchases: the "traditional view" and the "new view." The "traditional view" asserts that dividends offer nontax benefits to shareholders that offset their tax [dis]advantage. Accordingly, dividend taxes distort payout decisions and raise the cost of capital. The "new view" assumes that dividend payments offer no nontax advantages to shareholders and that corporations have no alternative to dividends for distributing funds to shareholders. Under this assumption, dividend taxes reduce the value of the firm, but do not affect firms' dividend or investment decisions. This Report adopts the framework suggested by the "traditional view." . . .

of dividends) to 47.9 billion (or 34 percent of dividends), and peaking in 1989 at 65.8 billion (or 47 percent of dividends).

NOTE

1. *Market response to the corporate tax.* One might expect that the imposition of a corporate tax would drive the corporate form out of existence. That is, because the corporate tax can be avoided by operating a business in noncorporate form, all businesses would avoid the corporate tax by a simple change in organization. We see, though, that the corporation thrives. How can this be so?

Even though use of the corporate form increases the income taxes levied on a business enterprise, the corporate form may nonetheless be the most efficient choice. First, it is a *familiar* form of organization, and familiarity in this context may allow the organization to raise capital more cheaply than otherwise. For example, one alternative to the corporation is a Massachusetts Business Trust. Because this form of business organization is uncommon outside of the northeast United States, such a trust may need to educate potential investors before they would be willing to provide funds to the enterprise. This education (in the form of advertising, additional solicitation materials, or whatever) represents an additional cost of capital, a cost of capital that use of the more familiar corporate form would have avoided.

Use of the corporate form can offer other benefits. Many state laws offer benefits to corporations unavailable to other business organizations. See, e.g., Commissioner v. Bollinger, page 652 infra, in which state law provides corporations more complete access to capital markets than it does to other potential borrowers. Perhaps most important, corporations offer limited liability for their investors, centralized management, continuity of life for the enterprise without regard to the circumstances (such as death or bankruptcy) of investors, and easy transferability of investment interests (i.e., shares). Any form of business organization offering these advantages will be taxed as a corporation even if it is not formally incorporated. See Larson v. Commissioner, 66 T.C. 159 (1976).

2. *Relief from the corporate tax.* Not all corporations are subject to the corporate tax. Certain corporations, called "S corporations," pay no tax but instead pass their items of income and deduction through to their shareholders for inclusion on the shareholders' individuals returns. For these corporations there is no corporate tax (except to the extent they have income attributable to a prior taxable year when they were not S corporations, see §§1374-1375). Not all corporations are eligible for S status. S corporations may not have more than 35 shareholders nor may they have a corporate shareholder or a foreign shareholder. §1361(b)(1) In addition, S corporations may not have more than one class of stock

outstanding. §1361(b)(1)(D). These and other restrictions limit the feasibility of S corporations in many circumstances. S corporations are discussed further in Chapter 15.

A new form of business organization is the limited liability company. Limited liability companies are much like corporations in that they offer limited liability to their owners just as corporations offer limited liability to their shareholders. In addition, limited liability companies can have centralized management, as do corporations. In essence, a limited liability company is a corporation chartered under a state law that dispenses with the purely formal step of "incorporation." Thus, the state act authorizing the existence of a limited liability company avoids the terms "incorporation," using instead something like "organization" or "formation." While a limited liability company must file papers equivalent to articles of incorporation, because they are called "articles of organization" or something similar, the company is not in a technical sense a corporation. See page 646 infra.

Under current law, an unincorporated entity will be taxed as a corporation if it possesses three or more of the following characteristics: (1) continuity of life, (2) centralized management, (3) limited liability, and (4) transferability of interests. See Treas. Regs. §301.7701-2(a)(1). If a limited liability company lacks two or more of these corporate characteristics, it will be taxed as a partnership rather than as a corporation, and a partnership, like an S corporation, is not subject to tax but instead passes its items of income and deduction through to its owners for inclusion on their individual returns. See page 683 infra.

Even in the absence of formal relief from the corporate tax, the burden of the tax is lessened to the extent a corporation can make deductible interest payments.

B. METHODS OF INTEGRATION

Is there a simple way to eliminate the double tax burden imposed on profits earned in corporate form? One might think that simple elimination of the corporate tax would be the ideal solution, but in fact the problem is considerably more difficult. Indeed, if the corporate tax were repealed, corporate investments would offer a significant tax advantage over noncorporate investments.

In general, the exchange of one investment for another is a taxable transaction. To be sure, exceptions are made for certain like-kind property, see §1031, and for involuntary conversions, see §1034, but for the most part a taxpayer cannot roll one investment into another without the recognition of gain or loss. If, though, the corporate tax were repealed, investments made through corporations could be exchanged for other investments without the imposition of tax so long as the rollover was done by the corporation and not by the shareholder.

For example, suppose individual B creates X Corp. by contributing $10,000. X Corp. then purchases rental property, and assuming the corporate tax has been repealed, that rental income goes untaxed until distributed by X Corp. Thus, X Corp. might invest its rents in some new investment (say, a bond fund) and no tax will yet be due. Had B purchased the real estate directly, the rents would have been taxable upon receipt as would the bond interest.

To continue this example, X Corp. might eventually sell its rental property at a gain, and if the corporate tax is repealed, no tax on that gain will be due. X Corp. could, for example, take the sale proceeds and invest in some unrelated enterprise, all without the imposition of any tax. Of course, taxes will be imposed on B when X Corp. eventually makes distributions, but until that time B enjoys a deferral opportunity as compared with noncorporate investments. Of course, if B should die while holding the X Corp. stock, the liquidation of X Corp. into B's estate may escape taxation. See §§1014, 336, and 331.

If we are to make the income tax neutral with respect to the form that an investment takes, simply repealing the corporate income tax will not work. Instead, we need to find some way to integrate the corporate and individual income taxes so that income is taxed once, and only once, and at the proper time, whether earned within or without the corporate structure.

Complete integration of the individual and corporate income taxes is achieved when the taxable events of the corporation are reported directly by the corporation's shareholders are they arise. Taxation of S corporations, discussed more completely in Chapter 16, as well as of partnerships, governed by subchapter K, is an example of such direct reporting. See generally H. Abrams, Federal Income Taxation of Partnerships and Other Pass-Thru Entities (1993). Implementing a system of complete integration, however, is administratively difficult if the number of investors is large and their relationship to the investment complex, as is the case when a corporation has multiple classes of stock outstanding.[2] Two leading scholars have described the debate concerning integration of the corporate and individual income taxes as a clash between idealists and pragmatists.[3]

In considering ways in which the corporate and individual income taxes can be integrated, it is important to keep in mind that appreciation in corporate assets can be realized either by a corporate sale of the assets or by a shareholder sale of stock. To ensure that corporate investments do

2. See, e.g., Sunley, Corporate Integration: An Economic Perspective, 47 Tax L. Rev. 621, 625 (1992).

3. Break and Pechman, Relationship Between the Corporation and Individual Income Taxes, 28 Natl. Tax J. 341, 341 (1975); see also Yin, Corporate Tax Integration and the Search for the Pragmatic Ideal, 47 Tax L. Rev. 431 (1992).

not offer deferral opportunities, presumably we should tax such appreciation at the earlier of its realization at the corporate and shareholder levels.
To avoid the imposition of a corporate double tax, however, we must not
tax that realization a second time when recognized at the other level. In
the partnership context, these two concerns are addressed by the optional
basis adjustment in §743(b). In any proposal to fully integrate the corporate and individual income taxes, some similar mechanism must be included.

The following excerpt offers two possible means of partial integration,
that is, of integrating the corporate and individual income taxes with respect to distributed funds only. Under both proposals, undistributed corporate earnings would be subject to a corporate-level tax much as they are
today. For a discussion of the relative merits of full versus partial integration, see C. McLure, Must Corporate Income Be Taxed Twice 2-12 (1979).

Reporter's Study of Corporate Tax Integration 50-57 _____
American Law Institute (Federal Income Tax Project 1993)

There are three basic methods of accomplishing the results of integration
with respect to distributed corporate earnings: shareholder credit, dividend deduction, and split rates.

A. SHAREHOLDER CREDIT INTEGRATION

Under the most common form of integration abroad, shareholders would
treat dividend payments just as wage earners now treat wage payments
subject to withholding. Cash dividends received would be increased (or
"grossed up") by the amount of federal income tax paid by the corporations on the earnings distributed as dividends, just as cash wages are increased by amounts withheld. An eligible shareholder would compute the
tax at his regular rate on the gross dividend, and a tax credit would be
available for the amount of the gross-up, just as a credit is now available
for withholding on wages. Complete implementation of this system would
result in the corporate tax becoming simply a withholding tax on individual
income earned through corporate entities.

Consider a corporation that receives $100 in taxable income and pays
$30 in corporate taxes (assuming a 30 percent corporate tax rate). Table
4 indicates how distributions of $70 and $20 of after-tax corporate income
would be treated by shareholders whose tax rates were 20 percent or 40
percent. The grossed-up dividend is equal to the cash dividend (i.e., the
dividend net of corporate taxes) divided by $1 \times c$, where c equals the
corporate tax rate. Equivalently, the gross dividend equals the net dividend
multiplied by $1/(1 \times c)$, which equals 1.429 when the corporate tax rate

Table 4

Shareholder Credit Integration

		Distribution of $70		Distribution of $20	
	Shareholder tax rate	40%	20%	40%	20%
(1)	Cash distribution	$70	$70	$20	$20
(2)	Grossed-up dividend	100[a]	100[a]	29[b]	29[b]
(3)	Gross shareholder tax	40	20	12	6
(4)	Shareholder tax credit [(2)-(1)]	30	30	9	9
(5)	Net shareholder tax [(3)-(4)]	10	(10)	3	(3)
(6)	Net shareholder cash	60	80	17	23

a. $1.429 \times \$70 = \$100$.
b. $1.429 \times \$20 = \$29$.

is 30 percent. If all corporations were taxed at the same rate, a single gross-up rate could be used by all shareholders for all dividends for all corporations. Having included the gross dividend in income, the shareholder applies his personal tax rate (p) and reduces the resulting tax by the shareholder credit attributable to corporate tax payments. The credit is always the cash dividend times c, which would be .429 if c were 30 percent. Once again, if all corporations paid tax at the same rate, shareholder credits on all dividends could be determined by applying the same rate. As a result of the gross-up and credit, distributed after-tax corporate earnings are taxed to shareholders at a rate of $(p \times c)/(1 \times c)$, eliminating the separate burden of the corporate tax.

The results shown in Table 4 accomplish the goals of integration by applying the shareholder tax rate, and only the shareholder tax rate, to distributed corporate income. With a $70 distribution after corporate taxes, each shareholder is in the position he would be in if he had earned $100 on individual account; with a $20 cash distribution each shareholder is treated as though $29 of income had been earned on individual account. Achieving those results for the 20 percent taxpayer in our example would require that the credit could be used against taxes generated by other income or, if there were no other such taxes, that the credit be refundable. "Shareholder credit integration" along these lines is often referred to abroad as "imputation" because the corporate tax rate is imputed to the shareholder through the gross-up and credit. . . .

As these examples indicate, the shareholder credit leaves the additional cash flow from integration in the hands of shareholders if the corporation does not adjust its dividend payments in response to the shareholder credit. The credit mechanism is therefore sometimes said to be a superior form of integration because the benefits of integration can be denied foreign and tax-exempt shareholders by making the credit nonrefundable to such shareholders.

B. DIVIDEND DEDUCTION

Integration could also be accomplished by permitting a corporate deduction for amounts paid as dividends, just as a deduction is now permitted for amounts paid as interest. The immediate effect of the deduction would be to increase the corporation's cash flow, although some of that benefit might be passed on to its shareholders in the form of increased dividends. In the example illustrated in Table 4, equivalent results would be achieved under a dividend deduction if the cash distribution were increased by 42.0 percent, from $70 to $100 and from $20 to $29.

As the dividend deduction method initially results in more cash at the corporate level, it is sometimes advocated as a superior form of integration on the ground that one of the purposes of integration is to provide additional incentives for corporate capital formation. On the other hand, one of the method's defects is sometimes said to be its automatic extension of the benefits of integration to tax-exempt and foreign shareholders, as compared with the possibility of denying imputation credits to such investors under shareholder credit integration. Finally, a dividend deduction would be simpler from the perspective of shareholders, because dividends would not be subject to a withholding mechanism, as they would be under imputation.

C. SPLIT RATES

An alternative method of integration is to levy a corporate tax on distributed earnings at a rate below that applied to retained earnings. Complete integration with respect to distributed corporate earnings would require a tax rate of zero on distributions and would be indistinguishable from a full dividend deduction. Less-than-complete integration would involve a tax rate on distributed earnings greater than zero but lower than the rate for retained earnings, making it indistinguishable from a partial deduction for dividends. . . .

D. EQUIVALENCE OF INTEGRATION METHODS

The differences in cash flow under the shareholder credit and dividend deduction methods depend on the assumption that there will be no change in the amount of cash dividends paid by corporations in response to integration. To the extent cash dividends were reduced under the shareholder credit or increased under the dividend deduction, precisely the same results could obtain under either alternative. A choice between the two methods thus depends, in part, on the effect of imperfections in the capital markets and on whether those imperfections suggest that it would be better to have the initial increase in cash flow at the shareholder or the corporate level.

If, for enforcement purposes, a withholding tax on dividends were desirable under the dividend deduction method, that withholding tax would serve the same function as an equivalent rate corporate tax under the shareholder credit. The two integration methods would then be equivalent not only in their ultimate effect assuming perfect capital markets, but also in their immediate result. Under the dividend deduction the shareholder would include in income not only the cash dividends received, but also the withholding tax collected by the corporation, which is precisely the same process as that involved in grossing up the dividend under the shareholder credit. Likewise, the corporate tax on distributed earnings plus the withholding tax on distributed earnings under the dividend deduction would equal the corporate tax due under the shareholder credit. Table 5

Table 5

Equivalence of Shareholder Credit and Dividend Deduction (with Withholding) Methods of Integration

	Dividend Deduction	Shareholder Credit
Corporate taxable income (before dividend deduction)	$100	$100
Cash distribution	25	25
Corporate tax		
On taxable income (after dividend deduction)	19[a]	30
Withholding on distribution	11[b]	0
Total	30	30
Retained corporate earnings (after taxes and dividends)	45	45
Taxable dividend to shareholder	36[c]	36[d]
Gross shareholder tax	14	14
Shareholder credit (or withholding)	11	11
Net shareholder tax due	3	3
Net shareholder cash	22	22

a. 30% corporate tax rate applied to taxable income of $100 reduced by gross dividend of $36 (including $11 withholding tax).
b. 30% of gross distribution of $36.
c. $25 cash dividend plus $11 withholding.
d. $25 × 1.429 = $36.

illustrates this equivalence when the corporate tax rate is 30 percent, the withholding rate is 30 percent, and a cash distribution of $25 is made to a 40 percent taxpayer by a corporation that has $100 in taxable income.

Although the substantive results are the same under the two methods, the difference in labels might cause different legal, regulatory, or accounting consequences. For instance, the amount of the "dividend" paid for various purposes might differ. Under the dividend deduction, the dividend is arguably $36 in Table 5 because that is the amount deducted, and from which $11 is withheld, if the shareholder receives $25 in cash. Under the shareholder credit, the dividend paid by the corporation is arguably the cash distribution of $25, which gives rise to a credit of $11 on the grossed-up amount. Because part of the tax is characterized as "withholding" under the dividend deduction, the dividend appears to be the gross amount before withholding; under the shareholder credit, the dividend appears to be the cash distribution, net of corporate taxes. An $11 portion of the tax paid by the corporation might therefore be subject to different treatment by regulatory authorities or under tax treaties because it could be characterized as withholding (and therefore paid on behalf of shareholders) under the dividend deduction, but as a corporate tax under the shareholder credit mechanism.

There may also be differences in public perceptions regarding the two methods of distribution-related integration. One possibility is illustrated by the case of Jacques Chaban-Delmas, who as Prime Minister of France was attacked in the press for paying no personal income taxes for several years in the late 1960s, when no net taxes were due because of offsetting imputation credits. The possibility that high income individuals might appear not to be paying taxes would be less likely under a dividend deduction system, but it would be easier to argue that a corporation paid no or little taxes due to the deduction. . . .

NOTE

1. *The Treasury's proposal.* As the Reporter's study indicates, the shareholder credit method and the dividend deduction method of partially integrating the corporate and individual income taxes are functionally equivalent. And as that study also points out, most of the world currently employs the shareholder credit method of integration. It therefore came as a surprise to many when the Treasury recommended (in a portion of the report not excerpted above) that the United States adopt the dividend deduction method of integration. The reason underlying this recommendation was the Treasury's belief that the shareholder credit method is significantly more complex to implement than the dividend deduction method. This belief seems unusually parochial in light of the substantial international experience to the contrary. Further, adopting a method of integration at odds with what most of the world does presents additional

difficulties when a corporation earns profits in one country and then distributes those profits to a shareholder residing in a different country. See generally van Raad, Approaches to Internationally Integrated Taxation of Distributed Corporate Income, 47 Tax L. Rev. 613 (1992).

2.   *The role of subchapter S in an integrated tax world.* Professor Martin Ginsburg recently suggested that the provisions for S corporations should continue even if Congress adopts a shareholder credit or dividend deduction method of partial integration. Ginsburg, Maintaining Subchapter S in an Integrated Tax World, 47 Tax L. Rev. 665 (1992). The justification for this proposal is best said in Professor Ginsberg's words:

> Someone once suggested that the one thing that makes subchapter S look really good is subchapter K, the awesomely complex partnership tax provisions. The notion, to which I am much persuaded, is that subchapter S — setting aside the foolish complexity attracted when the S corporation has a subchapter C history — reflects a sensible and successful balance under which the investor surrenders flexibility, precision, and any claim for deduction in excess of her investment, and in exchange is absolved from ever having to master or to be mastered by anything like the partnership provisions' miserable contributed property rules or, worse, the "hot asset" distribution rules.
>
> I suggest that if subchapter K qualifies as an historic justification for subchapter S, general intergation under any Treasury or ALI [American Law Institute] prototype will qualify as a modern, new justification for subchapter S. The familiar K-S trade off, flexibility and precision for simplicity, and more particularly the way the Code expresses that tradeoff, appears exceedingly attactive when integration is center stage.

47 Tax L. Rev. at 670.

For a contrasting reply to Professor Ginsberg, see Schenk, Complete Integration in a Partial Integration World, 47 Tax L. Rev. 697 (1992).

C. PROBLEMS

1.   *X* Corp. intends to make a $100,000 investment in a new enterprise. *X* Corp. can raise the funds for this investment by issuing preferred stock or bonds. Assume the investment will yield 12 percent annually for five years and then will be returned to *X* Corp. Assuming the preferred stock can be sold if it offers a 10 percent annual return while bonds must pay 11 percent annual interest to be marketable, which should *X* Corp. issue? Assume *X* Corp. is in the 33.3 percent tax bracket.

2.   If the corporate and individual income taxes were partially integrated, what effect would you expect to see on interest rates?

III

ACQUISITION OF A CORPORATE BUSINESS: TAXABLE AND TAX FREE

9

Taxable Acquisitions

Suppose *X* Corp. holds assets with a basis of $300,000 and a fair market value of $900,000 as well as $204,000 in cash. *B*, an individual, owns all the *X* Corp. stock with a basis of $400,000. *P*, an unrelated purchaser, wants to acquire *X* Corp. and is willing to pay fair market value. Among the acquisition choices available are the following:

1. an asset purchase in which either
    a. *X* Corp. sells its assets to *P* and then liquidates, or
    b. *X* Corp. liquidates and *B* sells the former *X* Corp. assets to *P*;
2. a stock purchase in which *P* buys the stock of *X* Corp. from *B* and either
    a. liquidates *X* Corp., or
    b. continues to operate *X* Corp. as a corporation.

These options are not the only ones for *P* and *B*. The nontaxable reorganization provisions discussed in Chapter 10 may allow *B* to exchange the *X* Corp. stock for stock in *P*, if *P* is a corporation, or stock in a corporation set up by *P* to consummate the acquisition. Alternatively, *X* may be able to merge into *P* or a subsidiary of *P* in a nontaxable reorganization. The advantage of a nontaxable reorganization is, not surprisingly, that it is nontaxable. If a reorganization can be nontaxable, why would taxpayers ever structure a taxable acquisition? The answer lies in the stringent requirements, imposed by the Code, that a transaction must meet to qualify as a nontaxable reorganization. Often taxpayers cannot or choose not to meet the requirements. For example, if *B* insists on receiving cash from *P* rather than stock of *P* if *P* is a corporation or stock of a corporation set up by *P*, the transaction will be treated as a taxable acquisition.

A. ASSET PURCHASE

1. Overall Tax Treatment

In the example above, if P acquires the assets from X Corp. for $900,000, X Corp. must recognize gain on the sale of $600,000. If X Corp. is taxable at a 34 percent rate, the tax is $204,000, which is paid by X Corp. with its cash. If X Corp. then liquidates, B is taxable under §§331 and 1001 on $500,000. If B is taxable on the gain at a 36 percent rate, B pays tax of $180,000 and ends up with $720,000. P's basis in the assets purchased is $900,000. §1012. If P is a corporation and X merges into P in accordance with the state merger laws in a transaction in which B receives cash, for tax purposes the transaction is treated as a sale of the X assets followed by a liquidation of X. See West Shore Fuel, Inc. v. United States, 598 F.2d 1236 (2d Cir. 1979). For a discussion of tax-free mergers, see page 438 infra.

Suppose X Corp. sells the assets to P using the installment method of reporting. §453. Generally, when a corporation makes a liquidating distribution of an installment note, the corporation must recognize any remaining deferred gain in income. §453B. The shareholders must treat the fair market value of the note as an amount realized with respect to the stock. The shareholders take a basis in the notes equal to their fair market value. Rev. Rul. 66-280, 1966-2 C.B. 304. Any subsequent collection on the notes in excess of their bases is ordinary income.

An important exception is made to the shareholder recognition requirement when shareholders receive installment obligations arising from a sale or exchange of corporate assets after the adoption of a plan of liquidation if the liquidation is completed within 12 months of the adoption. §453(h). In this circumstance, shareholders recognize gain on the installment notes as they are paid. If the installment obligation arises from the sale of inventory, installment reporting is available to shareholders only if substantially all the inventory is sold in bulk to a single purchaser. Also, if depreciable property is sold to a party related to a shareholder (e.g., a relative or a corporation more than 50 percent owned by the shareholder), installment reporting is not available.

If, instead of selling its assets to P or merging into P, X Corp. first liquidates and then B sells the former X Corp. assets to P, the tax consequences are the same. On the liquidation, X Corp. recognizes a gain of $600,000 under §336, which it pays with the available cash.[1] B is taxed on the difference between the $900,000 fair market value of the X Corp. assets and B's $400,000 stock basis. After paying taxes of $140,000, which B has in a bank account, B ends up with the former X Corp. assets with a fair market value and basis of $900,000. §301(d). When B sells those assets to

---

1. Alternatively, X Corp. could liquidate, distributing its assets (including cash) subject to the corporate tax liability.

P, B recognizes no further gain and *P* takes a cost basis of $900,000 in the assets. §1012.

Notice that in both taxable acquisition patterns there are two levels of taxation — corporate-level taxation of *X* Corp. and shareholder-level taxation of *B*. In exchange for these two levels of taxation, *P* acquires the *X* Corp. assets with a stepped-up cost basis. As explained in Section B, it is possible for *P* to acquire *X* Corp. through a stock purchase with only a shareholder-level tax, but if there is no corporate-level tax, *P* does not take a stepped-up basis in the corporate assets.

2. Allocation of Purchase Price

Both the seller and the buyer have an interest in the allocation of the purchase price to the various assets sold. For the seller (whether it is *X* Corp. or *B*), gain or loss and the character of that gain or loss (i.e., capital or ordinary) is determined asset by asset. For the buyer, *P*, the allocation of the $900,000 purchase price determines how much basis is allocated to inventory, depreciable assets, and nondepreciable assets.

Historically, the parties to a sale often had adverse interests in allocating the purchase price among assets. Sellers wanted to allocate as much of the purchase price as possible to assets yielding tax-favored capital gain, such as land and goodwill. In contrast, buyers benefited from allocating as much as possible to inventory, depreciable property (e.g., buildings, equipment), and amortizable intangibles (e.g., covenant not to compete) to decrease the amount of ordinary income that the seller would have to recognize in the future. Because of these adverse interests, the Service typically respected negotiated purchase agreements that specifically allocated the purchase price to each asset sold. A buyer and seller were bound by the agreement unless mistake, undue influence, fraud, or distress were shown. See, e.g., Commissioner v. Danielson, 378 F.2d 771 (3d Cir. 1967).

Agreements often contain no specific allocation of purchase price. In these situations the seller and buyer historically have taken inconsistent positions whipsawing the government. For example, a buyer often allocated a portion of the purchase price to a covenant not to compete, which was amortizable over the life of the covenant (but produced ordinary income to the seller), while the seller wanted to allocate a portion of the purchase price to goodwill, which resulted in capital gain to the seller (but was not amortizable by the buyer). Also, if little or no differential existed between the rate of tax on capital gain and ordinary income, a seller often did not care about the allocation of purchase price and, along with the buyer, "ganged up" on the Service.

Code §1060 now requires a specific method of allocation that must be followed by both seller and buyer in the case of "any applicable asset acquisition." An "applicable asset acquisition" is any transfer (direct or indirect) of assets that constitute a trade or business and with respect to which the transferee's basis in the purchased assets is determined wholly by the consideration paid for the assets (i.e., cost basis). §1060(c).

The regulations under §1060 divide all assets into four classes. Class I comprises cash, bank deposits, and similar assets. Class II covers certificates of deposits, U.S. government securities, and readily marketable stock or securities. Class III includes all other assets except goodwill and going concern value, which make up class IV. The purchase price paid is allocated first to class I assets based on aggregate fair market value, then to class II assets, and so on. Within each class, the price is allocated to each asset according to fair market value. Any premium paid by the purchaser above the fair market value of the "hard" assets (e.g., tangible assets and specific intangibles such as patents and trademarks) is allocated to goodwill (and going concern value) rather than allocated proportionately to the "hard" assets.

Some allocation disputes under §1060 may be lessened by the enactment of §197, which generally requires 15-year straight-line amortization for all purchased intangibles. This provision is more favorable than prior law with respect to previously unamortizable intangibles such as goodwill. It is less favorable, however, for intangibles that were previously amortizable over shorter periods of time, such as covenants not to compete. The assets covered by §197 include the following: goodwill and going concern value; workforce in place; customer lists and other customer-based intangibles; favorable contracts with suppliers and other supplier-based intangibles; business books and records and any other information base; patents, copyrights, formulas, processes, know-how, designs, and similar items; computer software; franchises, trademarks, and trade names; licenses, permits, and other governmental rights; and covenants not to compete.

Some assets are specifically excluded from §197. These include the following: off-the-shelf intangibles (e.g., computer software sold in stores); interests in tangible property leases (e.g., a lease premium); interests in debt obligations; certain intangibles requiring contingent payments (e.g., payments for a franchise based on productivity); financial interests; interests in land; and fees for professional services (e.g., *INDOPCO*-type expenses). Some intangibles are covered by §197 only when there is a related acquisition of the assets or in some cases the stock of a business, including patents or copyrights and covenants not to compete.

Even though both goodwill and a covenant not to compete are amortizable over 15 years under §197, there may be incentives for buyers and sellers of assets to allocate purchase price to goodwill rather than a covenant not to compete. First, the sale of goodwill produces capital gain taxed at a maximum 28 percent rate; payments for a covenant not to compete may be taxed at a 39.6 percent rate if the seller is in the highest tax bracket. Second, for financial reporting purposes, goodwill is amortizable over 40 years, while a covenant not to compete is amortizable over the life of the agreement. Consequently, allocation to goodwill produces higher earnings for financial purposes.

B. STOCK PURCHASE

1. Individual Purchaser

Suppose that, instead of purchasing the assets of X Corp. either from X Corp. or from B after X Corp. liquidates, P purchases the X Corp. stock from B for $900,000.[2] On the sale, B recognizes gain of $500,000, pays tax of $180,000, and ends up with $720,000 of cash. Notice that P has acquired X Corp., and, compared with the asset purchases described above, there has been only a shareholder-level tax rather than both a shareholder-level and corporate-level tax. But also notice that P has acquired (indirectly through X Corp.) assets (other than the cash) that still have a $300,000 basis. In an asset purchase, P acquires the X Corp. assets with a basis of $900,000.

If P, an individual, wants to step up the basis of the X Corp. assets to $900,000, P can do so, but only if a corporate-level tax is paid. If, after buying B's X Corp. stock, P liquidates X Corp., under §336 X Corp. recognizes a $600,000 gain on the liquidation and a tax liability of $204,000, which is paid with X Corp.'s cash. P has no gain on the liquidation under §§331 and 1001 because P's basis in the X Corp. stock is $900,000, which is equal to the fair market value of the distributed assets. P's basis in those assets is $900,000. §334(a).

Obtaining a higher basis in X Corp.'s assets may benefit P. If the assets are depreciable, the depreciation deductions will be larger. Even if the assets are not depreciable, P will have less gain or a larger loss deduction if the assets are sold. But what price will P pay to acquire a stepped-up basis? P can acquire a stepped up basis in the X Corp. assets only if X Corp. recognizes a corporate-level gain on the liquidation. Normally, a taxpayer is not willing to trade immediate taxation for future tax benefits (e.g., larger depreciation deductions). If, however, X Corp. has a net operating loss carryover that is about to expire, a liquidation might provide a higher asset basis at no immediate tax cost. Also, if X Corp.'s assets have bases that exceed fair market value, liquidation may allow X Corp. an immediate

2. Although X Corp. has assets worth $1,104,000, if P anticipates that X Corp. will soon either sell its assets or liquidate (thereby recognizing a gain), P would be unwilling to pay more for the X Corp. stock than for the purchase of the assets directly. If P does not anticipate selling the X Corp. assets, P may be willing to pay up to $1,104,000 for X Corp. The actual purchase price is a function of the demand for B's stock.

loss that *P* may gladly trade for a lower fair market value basis in the assets upon liquidation.

2. Corporate Purchaser: §338

If *P* is a corporation (*P* Corp.) and does not intend to liquidate *X* Corp. after purchasing the *X* Corp. stock from *B*, the tax consequences are the same as if *P* were an individual. If *P* is an individual, however, *P* has a choice of recognizing a corporate-level gain and obtaining a stepped-up basis in the *X* Corp. assets through liquidation or holding the *X* Corp. assets in corporate solution with a basis of $300,000. When *P* is a corporation, if *P* Corp. liquidates *X* Corp., *X* Corp. does not recognize a corporate-level gain and *P* Corp. does not obtain the *X* Corp. assets with a stepped-up basis. §§337, 3332, 334(b). See page 342 supra. *P* Corp. can obtain a stepped-up basis in the *X* Corp. assets by purchasing them directly, but can *P* Corp. obtain a stepped-up basis if it purchases *B*'s *X* Corp. stock?

In §338 Congress has provided *P* Corp. with a means of obtaining a stepped-up basis in the *X* Corp. assets if *P* Corp. purchases *B*'s *X* Corp. stock; thus, from a tax standpoint, *P* Corp. is more likely to be indifferent whether it acquires *X* Corp. through an asset or stock purchase. For *P* Corp. to obtain a stepped-up basis, *X* Corp. must recognize the $600,000 gain inherent in its assets.

Before looking at the specifics of §338, it may be helpful to outline the provision. It applies when a corporation purchases within a 12-month period at least 80 percent of the voting stock and at least 80 percent of all other stock (not including nonvoting, preferred stock, limited as to dividends) of a target corporation and makes a timely election. If applicable, §338 deems the target corporation, *X* Corp. in the example above, to have sold all its assets. And who is the deemed purchaser? The purchaser in this deemed sale is also the target corporation, *X* Corp. In other words, *X* Corp. sells the assets to itself. The effect of this circular fiction is recognition of gain to the target corporation combined with a cost basis in the target's assets. In the example above, *X* Corp. would recognize a $600,000 gain and would take a $900,000 basis in the assets.

The application of §338 does not require *P* Corp. to liquidate *X* Corp. to secure a cost basis in *X* Corp.'s assets. If *P* Corp. does decide to liquidate following a §338 election, §§332 and 334 will apply, and *P* Corp. takes *X* Corp.'s $900,000 asset basis. To summarize, §338 represents Congress's effort to render the form of an acquisition (stock or asset) irrelevant to an acquiring corporation.

Note that §338 is unavailable (because it is unnecessary) if *P* is an individual. If *P* purchases *B*'s stock for $900,000, *P* could then liquidate *X* Corp. under §§331 and 336, with *X* Corp. recognizing a $600,000 gain (i.e., a $204,000 tax liability) and *P* receiving a $900,000 basis in *X* Corp. assets under §334(a). The election under §338 is necessary only when §§332 and 337 would otherwise prevent *P* Corp. from taking a fair market value basis in a subsidiary's basis. There does not appear to be a good reason, however, why §338 is not available to an individual who purchases stock of a corporation. The availability of §338 would mean that an individual purchaser would not have to liquidate a corporation in order to step up (or step down) the basis of corporate assets so long as the corporation was willing to recognize gain or loss on the deemed §338 sale.

Section 338 had greater importance prior to the repeal of the *General Utilities* doctrine, when it was possible under §338 to obtain a fair market value basis without any corporate-level recognition of gain. Under current law, *P* Corp. gets a stepped-up basis in the factory only if *X* Corp. recognizes a $600,000 gain. Generally, *P* Corp. will not make a §338 election to recognize gain now in order to obtain a stepped-up basis that may increase tax benefits in the future.

As mentioned above, in some situations a §338 election may still be made. Suppose in the example above that *X* Corp. has a net operating loss (NOL) of $600,000 or more from previous years. If *P* Corp. elects under §338, *X* Corp.'s $600,000 gain will be offset by the net operating loss and *X* Corp. will take a $900,000 basis in the factory on its deemed purchase. The $900,000 basis, rather than a $300,000 basis, may allow larger depreciation deductions, thereby decreasing *X* Corp.'s taxable income (or it may decrease gain or increase deductible loss on a sale of the assets). But even if *X* Corp. has an NOL from previous years, a §338 election may not be advisable: Often *P* Corp. may be able to use *X* Corp.'s NOL after *P* Corp. liquidates its subsidiary, or perhaps *X* Corp. can use its own NOL against future earnings. See §§381 and 382 at page 549 infra. If *X* Corp.'s NOL is about to expire, however, a §338 election may provide a tax benefit.

NOTE

1. *Qualified stock purchases.* The 80 percent requirements of §338 discussed above must be satisfied by a "qualified stock purchase." "Purchase," as defined in §338(h)(3), in general includes all acquisitions other than those in which the purchasing corporation carries over the transferor's basis. For example, acquisitions by gift or in a §351 transaction do not qualify. In addition, a "purchase" does not include an acquisition from a related party. §338(h)(3)(A)(iii). The 80 percent ownership must be acquired within a twelve-month acquisition period that begins with the date of the first acquisition by purchase. See §338(h)(1).

2. *Election.* Under §338(g)(1), an acquiring corporation can elect to treat the purchase of stock as a purchase of assets any time before the

fifteenth day of the ninth month following the month in which the requisite 80 percent control is acquired. The election is irrevocable. See §338(g)(3).

3. *Operation of §338*. The deemed sale by the target corporation to itself, set forth in §338(a)(1), will trigger recognition. In determining gain, the sale is deemed to take place at fair market value. Section 338(c)(1) provides an additional exception to the general nonrecognition rule of §338(a)(1). If the purchasing corporation does not purchase all the stock of the target (but acquires the requisite 80 percent), §338 will still apply.

Return to our example fact pattern, in which X Corp. holds assets with a basis of $300,000 and a fair market value of $900,000. If P Corp. acquires all the stock of X Corp. for $900,000 and makes the election, a $600,000 gain is recognized, and X Corp.'s basis in the factory becomes $900,000. Suppose P Corp. purchases 80 percent of the X Corp. stock for $720,000. If the election is made, X Corp. will still get a $900,000 basis because it will still recognize a $600,000 gain.

Turning from the deemed sale to the deemed purchase, we find even more complexity. The rules contained in §338(a)(2) and (b) determine the basis that the target has in its assets on the deemed purchase. The rules are set up to deal with two phenomena: First, a purchasing corporation may not purchase all the target's stock, yet a full step-up in basis is allowed; second, the purchasing corporation may have "nonrecently purchased stock" as defined in §338(b)(6), which is stock not acquired by purchase within the acquisition period and is treated separately from "recently purchased stock" as defined in §338(b)(6).

Section 338(b) uses a gross-up basis rule to determine the cost basis of the target's assets on the deemed purchase. The assets of the target are treated as purchased for an amount equal to the grossed-up basis of recently purchased stock plus the basis of nonrecently purchased stock. In our example, we can ignore the nonrecently purchased stock component because all the stock held by P Corp. was acquired by purchase within the acquisition period. If P Corp. acquires all the X Corp. stock for $900,000, §338(b)(1)(A) and (b)(4) provide that the basis of the X Corp. assets is $900,000 (P Corp.'s basis in the X Corp. stock) × 100 percent/100 percent, or $900,000, the same basis as if P Corp. had purchased the assets directly. If P Corp. acquires 80 percent of the X Corp. stock for $720,000, the new basis of the X Corp. assets is equal to $720,000 (P Corp.'s basis in the X Corp. stock) × 100 percent/80 percent, or $900,000. Note that the new basis of the X Corp. assets is the same whether P Corp. purchases 80 or 100 percent because in either case X Corp. will recognize a $600,000 gain.

The complexity worsens when nonrecently purchased stock is introduced since it must be excluded from the gross-up calculation. Suppose in our example that P Corp. acquires 80 percent of X Corp. stock for $720,000 during the acquisition period and that P Corp. held an additional

8 percent of the *X* Corp. stock (acquired before the qualified purchase date) with a basis of $20,000 and a fair market value of $72,000 on the acquisition date. The remaining 12 percent of the stock continues to be held by *B*. If *P* Corp. elects §338 after purchasing 80 percent of the *Y* Corp. stock, *X* Corp.'s basis in its assets will equal $720,000 (purchase price of the stock) × 92 percent/80 percent, or $828,000, plus the $20,000 basis of the nonrecently purchased stock, or a total basis of $848,000. Notice that the basis in the target's assets reflects the fact that $52,000 of appreciation has not been recognized on the nonrecently purchased *X* Corp. stock.

In the previous example, however, *P* Corp. can elect to fully step up the basis of the target's assets to $900,000 by recognizing gain on the nonrecently purchased stock (i.e., the 8 percent holding). In the example, the gain would be the difference between the $20,000 basis and the $72,000 deemed sales price under §338(b)(3) ($828,000 × 8 percent/92 percent). The effect of this election is to increase the §338(b)(1)(B) amount to $72,000, which, when added to the $828,000 grossed-up basis, provides a full $900,000 basis. The cost of this additional corporate-level step-up in asset basis is recognition of what otherwise could eventually be shareholder-level gain.

4. *Adjustments for liabilities.* Suppose in our example that *X* Corp.'s assets have a fair market value of $900,000 but are subject to a liability of $200,000. Further assume that *P* Corp. purchases all the *X* Corp. stock for $700,000 (i.e., the net value of *X* Corp.). Section 338(b)(2) and the regulations promulgated thereunder clarify that if *P* Corp. makes a §338 election, *X* Corp. still recognizes a gain of $600,000 and then takes a $900,000 basis in the assets it is deemed to sell to itself. Treas. Regs. §1.338(b)-1T(c)(1). Any tax liability resulting from the deemed sale by *X* Corp. is treated as a liability that increases *X* Corp.'s basis on its deemed purchase. Treas. Regs. §1.338(b)-1T(f)(1). In effect, the tax liability inherent in *X* Corp.'s appreciated asset probably reduced the cash *P* Corp. was willing to pay for the *X* Corp. stock in the same manner as would a mortgage on the factory.

5. *Allocation of basis.* In the example above, if *X* Corp. holds only one asset, the allocation of basis on a deemed §338 sale by *X* Corp. to itself is not a problem. If *X* Corp. holds more than one asset (including intangible assets such as goodwill), allocation of basis is necessary. In general, the regulations promulgated under §338(b)(5) require a residual method of allocation in which the basis determined under §338 is allocated to specified assets to the extent of their fair market values, with any balance allocated to goodwill and going concern value. This is the same method of allocation mandated by §1060 on asset sales. See page 382 supra.

Specifically, the target corporation (e.g., *X* Corp.) first reduces its basis by the amount of any cash and cash equivalents received (referred to as class I assets). Treas. Regs. §1.338(b)-2T(b)(1). Remaining basis then is allocated to liquid assets such as certificates of deposit, U.S. government securities, and other marketable stock or securities (referred to as class II assets) to the extent of their fair market values. Treas. Regs. §1.338(b)-2T(b)(2). Basis still remaining after allocation to class II is allocated to class III, which consists of all other tangible and intangible assets, excluding goodwill and going concern, to the extent of their fair market values. Finally, any remaining basis is allocated to goodwill and going concern value (class IV assets). If there is insufficient basis for any asset class, the available basis is allocated to each asset within the class in proportion to the fair market value of the assets. Treas. Regs. §1.338(b)-2T(c)(1).

Suppose *P* Corp. purchases the stock of *X* Corp. from its shareholder, *B*. The stock has a basis of $300,000 and a fair market value of $700,000. *P* Corp. pays $1 million in exchange for the stock and *B*'s covenant not to compete for five years. Under §197, *P* Corp. must amortize the amount paid for the covenant not to compete over the statutory 15-year period rather than the five-year period of the covenant itself. Note that because the *X* Corp. assets carry over their bases when *P* Corp. purchases the *X* Corp. stock from *B*, §197 does not permit *X* Corp. to amortize any amount allocated to goodwill even though *X* Corp.'s assets may be stepped up for accounting purposes. If *P* Corp. makes a §338 election, §197 will apply to *X* Corp.'s deemed sale to itself. Any amount of the purchase price allocated to goodwill or other intangibles will be amortizable over a 15-year period.

6. *Consistency requirements and deemed elections.* Sections 338(e) and (f) present purchasing corporations with an all-or-nothing choice regarding §338. If a §338 election is made, it applies not only to the target corporation but also to any "target affiliates" (§338(g)(6)) whose stock is purchased during the "consistency" period. §338(f). The consistency period basically is a three-year period that includes a year before the acquisition period, the 12-month acquisition period itself, and a one-year period following the acquisition period. §338(h)(4). Moreover, if a purchasing corporation does not make a §338 election, it will be deemed to have made an election if during the consistency period it acquires any asset of the target or an affiliate. §338(e). This deemed election prevents a purchasing corporation from stepping up the basis of desired assets by purchasing them directly while preserving the basis of other assets (and perhaps avoiding gain) by not electing §338.

In some situations the §338 deemed election can produce unwanted results. For example, suppose Target Corp. holds two assets: undeveloped land with a basis of $100,000 and a fair market value of $600,000, and a building with a basis of $300,000 and fair market value of $700,000. Target Corp. is owned by Parent Corp., which has a stock basis of $200,000 in the Target Corp. stock. Purchase Corp. wants to acquire Target Corp. and to step up the basis of the building (to increase the depreciation deductions) but not that of the undeveloped land. Suppose Purchase Corp. buys the building for $700,000 directly from Target Corp.; six months later, after the $700,000 has been distributed to Target Corp.'s shareholders or paid as compensation to Target's employees, Purchase Corp. buys the stock of Target Corp. from Parent Corp. for $600,000. Under §338(e), Purchase Corp. will be deemed to have made a §338 election and therefore Target Corp. will be deemed to have sold the land to itself, causing the recognition of a $500,000 gain.

Fortunately, the Service has provided purchasers with a means of protecting themselves against an inadvertent and unwanted §338 election. If the purchasing corporation files a "protective carryover [basis] election" in a timely fashion, there is no deemed §338 election should the purchaser later purchase the stock of the target corporation. The price for avoiding the deemed election under §338(e) is that the purchaser must take a carryover basis in the assets purchased directly from the target corporation. That is, so long as the purchaser agrees not to try selectively to step up the basis of some assets and not others, there is no deemed §338 election. In the example above, if Purchase Corp. agrees to take a $300,000 basis in the purchased building, Target Corp. is not deemed to have sold the land to itself when Purchase Corp. buys the stock of Target Corp.

7. *Acquisition of a subsidiary from a consolidated group.* An election that is available under §338 overlaps somewhat with §336(e). If, in the example above, Parent Corp. sells the stock of Target Corp. to Purchase Corp. for $1,300,000, there is a potential $1,100,000 gain. If Purchase Corp. elects to have §338 apply, Target Corp. would recognize a $900,000 gain on the deemed sale of both assets to itself. If, instead, Purchase Corp. bought the assets from Target Corp. directly, Target Corp. would recognize a $900,000 gain. There would be no further gain under §§332 and 337 if Parent Corp. then liquidated Target Corp. In other words, the parties can avoid the $1,300,000 gain to Parent Corp. if the assets are purchased directly.

If §338(h)(10) is elected, Parent Corp. does not recognize gain on the sale of stock. Instead, only Target Corp. will recognize gain ($900,000) on the deemed asset sale. For §338(h)(10) to apply, Parent Corp. and Target Corp. must file a consolidated return, the purchaser of stock must be a corporation, and both Purchase Corp. and the consolidated group must make the election. See generally Bartlett, The Joint Election under Section 338(h)(10), 42 Tax Law. 235 (1989).

Even if §338 is not elected or the §338(h)(10) election is not made because some of the requirements of that subsection are not met, Parent Corp. can in some cases rely on §336(e) to report a single gain of $900,000. If an individual, rather than Purchase Corp., buys the Target Corp. stock, §336(e) may cause the seller to recognize a $900,000 gain instead of a $1,300,000 gain. See generally Schler, Sales of Assets after Tax Reform: Section 1060, Section 338(h)(10), and More, 43 Tax L. Rev. 605 (1988).

C. BOOTSTRAP ACQUISITIONS

For a discussion of the tax consequences of bootstrap acquisitions in connection with a sale of a business, see page 396 infra.

D. EXPENSES IN CONNECTION WITH AN ACQUISITION

INDOPCO, Inc. v. Commissioner
112 S. Ct. 1039 (1992)

Justice BLACKMUN delivered the opinion of the court.

In this case we must decide whether certain professional expenses incurred by a target corporation in the course of a friendly takeover are deductible by that corporation as "ordinary and necessary" business expenses under section 162(a) of the federal Internal Revenue Code.

I

. . . Petitioner INDOPCO, Inc., formerly named National Starch and Chemical Corporation and hereinafter referred to as National Starch, is a Delaware corporation that manufactures and sells adhesives, starches, and specialty chemical products. In October 1977, representatives of Unilever United States, Inc., also a Delaware corporation (Unilever), expressed interest in acquiring National Starch, which was one of its suppliers, through a friendly transaction. National Starch at the time had outstanding over 6,563,000 common shares held by approximately 3700 shareholders. The stock was listed on the New York Stock Exchange. Frank and Anna Greenwall were the corporation's largest shareholders and owned approximately 14.5% of the common. The Greenwalls, getting along in years and concerned about their estate plans, indicated that they would transfer their shares to Unilever only if a transaction tax-free for them could be arranged.

Lawyers representing both sides devised a "reverse subsidiary cash merger" that they felt would satisfy the Greenwalls' concerns. Two new entities would be created — National Starch and Chemical Holding Corp. (Holding), a subsidiary of Unilever, and NSC Merger, Inc., a subsidiary of Holding that would have only a transitory existence. In an exchange specifically designed to be tax-free under section 351, Holding would exchange one share of its nonvoting preferred stock for each share of National Starch common that it received from National Starch shareholders. Any National Starch common that was not so exchanged would be converted into cash in a merger of NSC Merger, Inc., into National Starch.

In November 1977, National Starch's directors were formally advised of Unilever's interest and the proposed transaction. At that time, Debevoise, Plimpton, Lyons & Gates, National Starch's counsel, told the directors that under Delaware law they had a fiduciary duty to ensure that the proposed transaction would be fair to the shareholders. National Starch thereupon engaged the investment banking firm of Morgan Stanley & Co., Inc., to evaluate its shares, to render a fairness opinion, and generally to assist in the event of the emergence of a hostile tender offer.

Although Unilever originally had suggested a price between $65 and $70 per share, negotiations resulted in a final offer of $73.50 per share, a figure Morgan Stanley found to be fair. Following approval by National Starch's board and the issuance of a favorable private ruling from the Internal Revenue Service that the transaction would be tax-free under section 351 for those National Starch shareholders who exchanged their stock for Holding preferred, the transaction was consummated in August 1978.[2]

Morgan Stanley charged National Starch a fee of $2,200,000, along with $7,586 for out-of-pocket expenses and $18,000 for legal fees. The Debevoise firm charged National Starch $490,000, along with $15,069 for out-of-pocket expenses. National Starch also incurred expenses aggregating $150,962 for miscellaneous items — such as accounting, printing, proxy solicitation, and Securities and Exchange Commission fees — in connection with the transaction. No issue is raised as to the propriety or reasonableness of these charges.

On its federal income tax return for its short taxable year ended August 15, 1978, National Starch claimed a deduction for the $2,225,586 paid to Morgan Stanley, but did not deduct the $505,069 paid to Debevoise or the other expenses. Upon audit, the Commissioner of Internal Revenue disallowed the claimed deduction and issued a notice of deficiency. Petitioner sought redetermination in the United States Tax Court, asserting, however, not only the right to deduct the investment banking fees and expenses but, as well, the legal and miscellaneous expenses incurred.

The Tax Court, in an unreviewed decision, ruled that the expenditures were capital in nature and therefore not deductible under section 162(a) in the 1978 return as "ordinary and necessary expenses." National Starch and Chemical Corp. v. Commissioner, 93 T.C. 67 (1989). The court based its holding primarily on the long-term benefits that accrued to National Starch from the Unilever acquisition. Id., at 75. The United States Court of Appeals for the Third Circuit affirmed, upholding the Tax Court's findings that "both Unilever's enormous resources and the possibility of synergy arising from the transaction served the long-term betterment of National Starch." National Starch and Chemical Corp. v. Commissioner,

---

2. Approximately 21% of National Starch common was exchanged for Holding preferred. The remaining 79% was exchanged for cash.

918 F.2d 426, 432-433 (1990). In so doing, the Court of Appeals rejected National Starch's contention that, because the disputed expenses did not "create or enhance . . . a separate and distinct additional asset," see Commissioner v. Lincoln Savings & Loan Assn., 403 U.S. 345, 354 (1971), they could not be capitalized and therefore were deductible under section 162(a). 918 F.2d, at 428-431. We granted certiorari to resolve a perceived conflict on the issue among the Courts of Appeals.[3]

II

Section 162(a) of the Internal Revenue Code allows the deduction of "all the ordinary and necessary expenses paid or incurred during the taxable year in carrying on any trade or business." In contrast, section 263 of the Code allows no deduction for a capital expenditure — an "amount paid out for new buildings or for permanent improvements or betterments made to increase the value of any property or estate." The primary effect of characterizing a payment as either a business expense or a capital expenditure concerns the timing of the taxpayer's cost recovery: While business expenses are currently deductible, a capital expenditure usually is amortized and depreciated over the life of the relevant asset, or, where no specific asset or useful life can be ascertained, is deducted upon dissolution of the enterprise. Through provisions such as these, the Code endeavors to match expenses with the revenues of the taxable period to which they are properly attributable, thereby resulting in a more accurate calculation of net income for tax purposes. See, e.g., Commissioner v. Idaho Power Co., 418 U.S. 1, 16 (1974).

In exploring the relationship between deductions and capital expenditures, this Court has noted the "familiar rule" that "an income tax deduction is a matter of legislative grace and that the burden of clearly showing the right to the claimed deduction is on the taxpayer." Interstate Transit Lines v. Commissioner, 319 U.S. 590, 593 (1943); Deputy v. Du Pont, 308 U.S. 488, 493 (1940); New Colonial Ice Co. v. Helvering, 292 U.S. 435, 440 (1934). The notion that deductions are exceptions to the norm of capitalization finds support in various aspects of the Code. Deductions are specifically enumerated and thus are subject to disallowance in favor of

3. Compare the Third Circuit's opinion, 918 F.2d, at 430, with NCNB Corp. v. United States, 684 F.2d 285, 293-294 (C.A.4 1982) (bank expenditures for expansion-related planning reports, feasibility studies, and regulatory applications did not "create or enhance separate and identifiable assets," and therefore were ordinary and necessary expenses under section 162(a)), and Briarcliff Candy Corp. v. Commissioner, 475 F.2d 775, 782 (C.A.2 1973) (suggesting that *Lincoln Savings* "brought about a radical shift in emphasis," making capitalization dependent on whether the expenditure creates or enhances a separate and distinct additional asset). See also Central Texas Savings & Loan Assn. v. United States, 731 F.2d 1181, 1184 (C.A.5 1984) (inquiring whether establishment of new branches "creates a separate and distinct additional asset" so that capitalization is the proper tax treatment).

capitalization. See sections 161 and 261. Nondeductible capital expenditures, by contrast, are not exhaustively enumerated in the Code; rather than providing a "complete list of nondeductible expenditures," *Lincoln Savings,* 403 U.S., at 358, section 263 serves as a general means of distinguishing capital expenditures from current expenses. See Commissioner v. Idaho Power Co., 418 U.S., at 16. For these reasons, deductions are strictly construed and allowed only "as there is a clear provision therefor." New Colonial Ice Co. v. Helvering, 292 U.S., at 440; Deputy v. Du Pont, 308 U.S., at 493.

The Court also has examined the interrelationship between the Code's business expense and capital expenditure provisions. In so doing, it has had occasion to parse section 162(a) and explore certain of its requirements. For example, in *Lincoln Savings,* we determined that, to qualify for deduction under section 162(a), "an item must (1) be 'paid or incurred during the taxable year,' (2) be for 'carrying on any trade or business,' (3) be an 'expense,' (4) be a 'necessary' expense, and (5) be an 'ordinary' expense." 403 U.S., at 352. See also Commissioner v. Tellier, 383 U.S. 687, 689 (1966) (the term "necessary" imposes "only the minimal requirement that the expense be 'appropriate and helpful' for 'the development of the taxpayer's business,'" quoting Welch v. Helvering, 290 U.S. 111, 113 (1933)); Deputy v. Du Pont, 308 U.S. 488, 495 (1940) (to qualify as "ordinary," the expense must relate to a transaction "of common or frequent occurrence in the type of business involved"). The Court has recognized, however, that the "decisive distinctions" between current expenses and capital expenditures "are those of degree and not of kind," Welch v. Helvering, 290 U.S., at 114, and that because each case "turns on its special facts," Deputy v. Du Pont, 308 U.S., at 496, the cases sometimes appear difficult to harmonize. See Welch v. Helvering, 290 U.S., at 116.

National Starch contends that the decision in *Lincoln Savings* changed these familiar backdrops and announced an exclusive test for identifying capital expenditures, a test in which "creation or enhancement of an asset" is a prerequisite to capitalization, and deductibility under section 162(a) is the rule rather than the exception. We do not agree, for we conclude that National Starch has overread *Lincoln Savings.*

In *Lincoln Savings,* we were asked to decide whether certain premiums, required by federal statute to be paid by a savings and loan association to the Federal Savings and Loan Insurance Corporation (FSLIC), were ordinary and necessary expenses under section 162(a), as Lincoln Savings argued and the Court of Appeals had held, or capital expenditures under section 263, as the Commissioner contended. We found that the "additional" premiums, the purpose of which was to provide FSLIC with a secondary reserve fund in which each insured institution retained a pro rata interest recoverable in certain situations, "serve to create or enhance for Lincoln what is essentially a separate and distinct additional asset." 403

U.S., at 354. "As an inevitable consequence," we concluded, "the payment is capital in nature and not an expense, let alone an ordinary expense, deductible under section 162(a)." Ibid.

Lincoln Savings stands for the simple proposition that a taxpayer's expenditure that "serves to create or enhance . . . a separate and distinct" asset should be capitalized under section 263. It by no means follows, however, that *only* expenditures that create or enhance separate and distinct assets are to be capitalized under section 263. We had no occasion in *Lincoln Savings* to consider the tax treatment of expenditures that, unlike the additional premiums at issue there, did not create or enhance a specific asset, and thus the case cannot be read to preclude capitalization in other circumstances. In short, *Lincoln Savings* holds that the creation of a separate and distinct asset well may be a sufficient but not a necessary condition to classification as a capital expenditure. See General Bancshares Corp. v. Commissioner, 326 F.2d 712, 716 (C.A.8) (although expenditures may not "result in the acquisition or increase of a corporate asset, . . . these expenditures are not, because of that fact, deductible as ordinary and necessary business expenses"), cert. denied, 379 U.S. 832 (1964).

Nor does our statement in *Lincoln Savings,* 405 U.S., at 354, that "the presence of an ensuing benefit that may have some future aspect is not controlling" prohibit reliance on future benefit as a means of distinguishing an ordinary business expense from a capital expenditure. Although the mere presence of an incidental future benefit — "*some* future aspect" — may not warrant capitalization, a taxpayer's realization of benefits beyond the year in which the expenditure is incurred is undeniably important in determining whether the appropriate tax treatment is immediate deduction or capitalization. See United States v. Mississippi Chemical Corp., 405 U.S. 298, 310 (1972) (expense that "is of value in more than one taxable year" is a nondeductible capital expenditure); Central Texas Savings & Loan Assn. v. United States, 731 F.2d 1181, 1183 (C.A.5 1984) ("While the period of the benefits may not be controlling in all cases, it nonetheless remains a prominent, if not predominant, characteristic of a capital item."). Indeed, the text of the Code's capitalization provision, section 263(a)(1), which refers to "permanent improvements or betterments," itself envisions an inquiry into the duration and extent of the benefits realized by the taxpayer.

III

In applying the foregoing principles to the specific expenditures at issue in this case, we conclude that National Starch has not demonstrated that the investment banking, legal, and other costs it incurred in connection with Unilever's acquisition of its shares are deductible as ordinary and necessary business expenses under section 162(a).

Although petitioner attempts to dismiss the benefits that accrued to National Starch from the Unilever acquisition as "entirely speculative" or "merely incidental," the Tax Court's and the Court of Appeals' findings that the transaction produced significant benefits to National Starch that extended beyond the tax year in question are amply supported by the record. For example, in commenting on the merger with Unilever, National Starch's 1978 "Progress Report" observed that the company would "benefit greatly from the availability of Unilever's enormous resources, especially in the area of basic technology." App. 43. See also id., at 46 (Unilever "provides new opportunities and resources"). Morgan Stanley's report to the National Starch board concerning the fairness to shareholders of a possible business combination with Unilever noted that National Starch management "feels that some synergy may exist with the Unilever organization given a) the nature of the Unilever chemical, paper, plastics and packaging operations . . . and b) the strong consumer products orientation of Unilever United States, Inc." Id., at 77-78.

In addition to these anticipated resource-related benefits, National Starch obtained benefits through its transformation from a publicly held, freestanding corporation into a wholly owned subsidiary of Unilever. The Court of Appeals noted that National Starch management viewed the transaction as "swapping approximately 3500 shareholders for one." 918 F.2d, at 427; see also App. 223. Following Unilever's acquisition of National Starch's outstanding shares, National Starch was no longer subject to what even it terms the "substantial" shareholder-relations expenses a publicly traded corporation incurs, including reporting and disclosure obligations, proxy battles, and derivative suits. The acquisition also allowed National Starch, in the interests of administrative convenience and simplicity, to eliminate previously authorized but unissued shares of preferred and to reduce the total number of authorized shares of common from 8,000,000 to 1,000. See 93 T.C., at 74.

Courts long have recognized that expenses such as these, " 'incurred for the purpose of changing the corporate structure for the benefit of future operations are not ordinary and necessary business expenses.' " General Bancshares Corp. v. Commissioner, 326 F.2d, at 715 (quoting Farmers Union Corp. v. Commissioner, 300 F.2d 197, 200 (C.A.9), cert. denied, 371 U.S. 861 (1962)). See also B. Bittker & J. Eustice, Federal Income Taxation of Corporations and Shareholders, pp. 5-33 to 5-36 (5th ed. 1987) (describing "well-established rule" that expenses incurred in reorganizing or restructuring corporate entity are not deductible under section 162(a)). Deductions for professional expenses thus have been disallowed in a wide variety of cases concerning changes in corporate structure.[7]

7. See, e.g., McCrory Corp. v. United States, 651 F.2d 828 (C.A.2 1981) (statutory merger under 26 U.S.C. section 368(a)(1)(A)); Bilar Tool & Die Corp. v. Commissioner, 530 F.2d 708 (C.A.6 1976) (division of corporation into two parts); E.I. du Pont de Nemours & Co. v. United States, 432 F.2d 1052 (C.A.3 1970) (creation of new subsidiary to hold assets of prior

Although support for these decisions can be found in the specific terms
of section 162(a), which require that deductible expenses be "ordinary
and necessary" and incurred "in carrying on any trade or business," courts
more frequently have characterized an expenditure as capital in nature
because "the purpose for which the expenditure is made has to do with
the corporation's operations and betterment, sometimes with a continuing
capital asset, for the duration of its existence or for the indefinite future
or for a time somewhat longer than the current taxable year." General
Bancshares Corp. v. Commissioner, 326 F.2d, at 715. The rationale behind
these decisions applies equally to the professional charges at issue in this
case.

IV

The expenses that National Starch incurred in Unilever's friendly takeover
do not qualify for deduction as "ordinary and necessary" business expenses
under section 162(a). The fact that the expenditures do not create or
enhance a separate and distinct additional asset is not controlling; the
acquisition-related expenses bear the indicia of capital expenditures and
are to be treated as such.

The judgment of the Court of Appeals is affirmed.

It is so ordered.

NOTE

1. *Form of the transaction.* This transaction was structured as a taxable
reverse subsidiary (or triangular) merger. In some cases, a reverse subsidiary merger can be tax free to the participants. See page 468 infra. If this
had been a tax-free reverse subsidiary merger, the shareholders of National
Starch would have exchanged their stock for stock in Holding while NSC
Merger merged into National Starch. The result would be that former
National Starch shareholders, along with Unilever, would own stock of
Holding, which in turn would own National Starch. Shareholders owning
79 percent of the National Starch stock, however, apparently wanted cash
rather than Holding stock. If the parties attempted a tax-free reverse subsidiary merger in which shareholders of 79 percent of the National Starch
stock received cash, all the shareholders would be taxable, including those
that exchanged 21 percent of the National Starch stock for Holding Stock.

To secure tax-free treatment for the 21 percent exchanging stock for

---

joint venture); General Bancshares Corp. v. Commissioner, 326 F.2d 712, 715 (C.A.8) (stock
dividends), cert. denied, 379 U.S. 832 (1964); Mills Estate, Inc. v. Commissioner, 206 F.2d
244 (C.A.2 1953) (recapitalization).

stock, the parties agreed to a two-step transaction. First, Unilever and those National Starch shareholders desiring a stock-for-stock exchange formed Holding, with Unilever receiving voting common stock in exchange for the cash it transferred and National Starch shareholders receiving nonvoting preferred stock in exchange for their National Starch stock. This transaction qualified under §351, thereby providing nonrecognition for those National Starch shareholders making the exchange. Then, the remaining National Starch shareholders received cash for their stock as NSC Merger, Inc. merged into National Stock. This part of the transaction is treated as a redemption of the shareholders of National Starch. Rev. Rul. 78-250, 1978-1 C.B. 83. These shareholders were taxable on the difference between their adjusted bases in the National Starch stock and the cash received. Before undertaking this two-step transaction, the parties requested and received a private letter ruling from the Service. See Priv. Ltr. Rul. 7839060.

2. *Other friendly takeovers.* The result in *INDOPCO* does not necessarily mean that all expenses in friendly takeovers must be capitalized. The *INDOPCO* decision identified two categories of long-term benefits justifying capitalization rather than deductibility of acquisition expenses: (a) benefits generated by the resources of the acquiring company and (b) benefits obtained by a target by being a wholly owned subsidiary instead of a publicly held corporation (e.g., avoiding extensive reporting on disclosure requirements).

Certain types of acquisitions may not give rise to these types of long-term benefits. For example, in a leveraged buyout (LBO) by senior management of the target or outside purchasers, the acquiring group may form a new corporation that borrows the funds necessary to make the acquisition. Typically, repayment is made by the target corporation. In this type of leveraged acquisition, the acquiring corporation often has no resources that provide long-term benefits to the target. Moreover, the acquiring corporation often exchanges publicly traded, high-yield debentures for the existing stock of the target corporation. If so, then the target corporation may realize no future savings from reduced reporting requirements. Accordingly, expenses incurred by a target in this type of leveraged transaction may not create the future benefits that resulted in capitalization treatment under *INDOPCO.*

Even if a takeover results in capitalization of expenses under *INDOPCO,* in some cases a target may be able to eliminate the impact of capitalization by making a §338 election. See page 384 supra. Under the election, the capitalized expenditures should either be added to the basis of the assets sold or reduce the deemed sales price.

3. *Hostile takeovers. INDOPCO* addressed the deductibility of expenses in connection with a friendly takeover. Does *INDOPCO* require capitalization of expenses incurred in resisting a hostile takeover? Presumably, the *INDOPCO* test should apply: Capitalization is required if long-term benefits are created. If the expenses are incurred primarily to protect rather than to

acquire property, deductibility may be appropriate. For example, expenses incurred by a corporation to defend itself in a proxy contest are deductible. See, e.g., Rev. Rul. 67-1, 1967-1 C.B. 28. But see Treas. Regs. §1.212-1(k) (expenses to defend title to property must be capitalized). In other cases, corporate expenditures to defend the corporation were deductible. See, e.g., Dolese v. United States, 605 F.2d 1146 (10th Cir. 1979) (corporate expenses incurred in a divorce proceeding).

Costs associated with specific defensive strategies, such as negotiating with a "white knight," countertender offers, poison pill plans, and corporate charter amendments, however, are generally nondeductible capital expenditures if the plans are implemented. If the plans are abandoned, a loss deduction should be permitted under §165(a). See Rev. Rul. 73-580, 1973-2 C.B. 86.

4. *Loan fees.* Most acquisitions are financed with debt. For the purchaser, the cost of obtaining debt financing (such as fees for negotiating the loan and drafting loan documents and commitment fees) are amortized over the term of the loan. Rev. Rul. 70-359, 1970-2 C.B. 103; Rev. Rul. 70-360, 1970-2 C.B. 103. If borrowed funds are used to redeem the target's stock in a reverse subsidiary merger like the transaction in *INDOPCO,* the Service may attempt to deny a deduction or even an amortization of the loan fees. The Service bases its position on §162(k), which denies a deduction for any amount (except interest) incurred by a corporation in connection with the redemption of its stock. But see United States v. Kroy (Europe) Ltd., 92-2 U.S.T.C. (CCH) ¶50,611 (D. Ariz. 1992) (rejecting the Service's broad view of §162(k)).

5. *Organizational expenses.* The costs of organizing a new corporation as part of an acquisition can be amortized over a period of 60 months from the month in which the corporation begins business. §248.

E. CORPORATE ACQUISITIONS AND THE USE OF DEBT

Joint Committee on Taxation, Federal Income Tax Aspects of Corporate Financial Structures _____
101st Cong., 1st Sess. (Jan. 18, 1989)

III. EXAMPLES OF TRANSACTIONS THAT INCREASE DEBT OR REDUCE EQUITY, AND TAX CONSEQUENCES

There are various transactions which can increase the debt of a corporation or reduce its equity. The discussion below describes broad categories of these transactions and uses examples to illustrate their tax consequences. The examples assume that no restrictions on interest deductions or other tax benefits stemming from interest expenses apply. In many cases, however, such limitations are applicable. . . .

Although there are significant tax reasons which may lead a corporation to engage in these transactions, such transactions may also be motivated by reasons apart from Federal income tax considerations. For example, such transactions may be undertaken to increase the value of a corporation's stock, to enhance earnings per share calculations, to concentrate common stock holdings, to create treasury stock, as a defensive maneuver to ward off a takeover, or for other reasons. . . .

C. ACQUISITIONS INCLUDING LEVERAGED BUYOUTS

The acquisition of one corporation by another corporation may be structured in many different ways. An acquiring corporation may acquire control of the "target" corporation or it may acquire a small interest in the stock of another corporation as an investment. The acquiring corporation may finance the acquisition with debt (either by a new borrowing of the necessary funds or by keeping an old borrowing outstanding), or with its own retained earnings, or with funds contributed as new equity capital by investors.

An acquisition of the control of a target company may be a hostile or friendly transaction. It may be structured as an acquisition of the stock of the target company or an acquisition of the assets of the target company. The target company may continue to operate as an independent company in the same manner as before it was acquired, or it may be absorbed into the acquiring company or other companies owned by the acquiring company, or it may cease operations entirely and its assets be divided and sold.

1. Stock Acquisitions out of Retained Earnings

A corporation may finance the acquisition of the stock of another corporation with internally generated funds (i.e., its retained earnings). The purchase of the stock has no tax consequences to the shareholders of the purchasing corporation. Likewise, there are no tax consequences to the acquired corporation as a result of the acquisition. The taxable shareholders of the acquired corporation recognize any gain or loss on the sale of their shares.

There are generally no immediate tax consequences to the purchasing corporation as a result of the transaction. However, the total amount of funds in corporate solution, the earnings of which are subject to a corporate-level tax, may be reduced by the amount spent for the acquisition to the extent that shares are acquired by the acquiring corporation from noncorporate shareholders. Moreover, no compensating additional corporate tax may arise when earnings of the acquired corporation are distributed to the acquiring corporation. This is because earnings of the target company which are distributed to the acquiring corporation as dividends will either be nontaxable under the consolidated return rules, or, if the corporations do not file a consolidated return, will be eligible for the dividends received deduction.

2. Debt-financed Stock Acquisitions Including Leveraged Buyouts

A corporation may finance the acquisition of another corporation's stock by borrowing. The acquiring corporation may borrow using its own assets as security for the loan or it may borrow using the assets of the target company as security for the loan. In either case, debt has been substituted for equity at the corporate level. When the debt is secured by the acquired corporation's assets, the transaction is more likely to be called a "leveraged buyout."

Description

A leveraged buyout refers to a particular type of debt-financed acquisition of a "target" corporation. The purchasers borrow most of the purchase price of the target company, using the assets of the target company as security for the loan. After the acquisition, the target corporation may be able to service the debt obligation out of its cash flow from operations or the purchaser may sell the assets of the target company and use the proceeds to retire the debt.

A leveraged buyout may occur in many different contexts and may be used by many different types of purchasers. The leveraged buyout, also sometimes called a bootstrap acquisition, has long been used to acquire private (i.e., closely held) corporations. More recently, leveraged buyouts have been used to acquire large public companies. A public company may be "taken private" through a leveraged buyout if the purchasers of the target public corporation are a relatively small group of investors. If the purchasers of the target corporation in a leveraged buyout include the current management of the target company, the transaction is sometimes called a "management buyout." A division or a subsidiary of a company also may be purchased through a leveraged buyout.

A leveraged buyout of a target company is usually accomplished by a debt-financed tender offer by the existing corporation for its outstanding publicly held stock, or, alternatively, by a tender offer for the target corporation's stock by a largely debt-financed shell corporation established for this purpose. The target corporation will repurchase its stock from its shareholders or the shell corporation will buy all the stock of the target corporation.[76] If a shell corporation is used, the target corporation

---

76. Shareholders of the target company typically receive a premium for their stock above the price at which the stock has been trading on the market.

and the shell corporation will typically merge immediately after the acquisition.

As mentioned above, most of the funds for a leveraged buyout transaction are borrowed, with the purchasers contributing only a small amount of their own funds as equity. Lenders for these transactions have been banks, investment banks, insurance companies, pension funds, and pools of investors. Debt terms reflect the degree of leverage and the loan security involved. Some of the debt incurred frequently is below investment grade, i.e., so-called "junk" bonds.

Tax Consequences

A leveraged buyout is generally a taxable transaction with respect to the shareholders of the target corporation.[77] Taxable shareholders selling their stock recognize gain or loss on the sale of their shares.[78] There are no immediate tax consequences of a leveraged buyout at the corporate level since generally neither the repurchase by the target corporation of its own shares nor the purchase of the target corporation's shares by a shell corporation followed by the merger of the target and shell corporation is a taxable transaction.

The primary tax consequences of a leveraged buyout to the target corporation arise from the fact that the equity of the corporation has been replaced by debt. Income of the target corporation once paid to investors as nondeductible dividends on stock is instead paid to creditors as tax-deductible interest on debt. As a result of the interest deductions generated by the borrowing in a leveraged buyout, the target corporation may have little, if any, taxable income in the years following a leveraged buyout and may claim loss carrybacks producing a refund of taxes paid prior to the acquisition. Because the target corporation pays little, if any, of its operating income as Federal income taxes, the portion of the target corporation's income that was once being paid to the Federal government as Federal income taxes may instead be redirected to increase investor returns. However, to the extent increased investor returns are paid to taxable shareholders or holders of debt, there may be an increase in investor-level Federal income taxes paid.

Example III-C

[Company M, with 99,000 shares of stock outstanding and no debt, has $1.5 million annual income. M's federal income tax is $510,000 ($1.5 million × .34), leaving $990,000 of after-tax income, or earnings of $10

---

77. Of course, there will be no tax imposed on those shareholders that are not subject to U.S. income tax on their income, i.e., certain foreign investors and tax-exempt investors such as pension funds.

78. Taxable shareholders will generally recognize gain (i.e., the excess of the amount received over their basis in the stock) because acquirors typically pay a substantial premium for stock in a leveraged buyout transaction.

per share. *M*'s stock trades at $80 per share (or 8 × earnings per share).] Company *M* is acquired in a leveraged buyout. The acquirors pay $120 per share of stock, or 50 percent more than the price at which the stock has been trading on the market, for a total price of $11.88 million. Taxable selling shareholders recognize gain or loss on the sale of their shares.

The acquirors put up $880,000 of their own funds and raise the remaining $11 million of the purchase price by issuing notes paying 12 percent interest to be secured by the assets of Company *M*. The annual income of Company *M* after the leveraged buyout is unchanged.

The distribution of the operating income of Company *M* before and after the leveraged buyout is as follows:

	Before	*After*
Company *M* shareholders	$990,000	$0
Bondholders	0	1,320,000
Acquirors	0	118,800
Corporate income taxes	510,000	61,200
Total operating income	1,500,000	1,500,000

The leveraged buyout has redistributed the income stream of Company *M*. [T]he acquirors of Company *M*, rather than all the shareholders (in the case of a distribution with respect to stock) or the continuing shareholders of Company *M* (in the case of a stock redemption) receive the profit of $118,800. Company *M* shareholders who before the transaction received $990,000 a year in dividends now receive no distributions. New bondholders receive interest of 12 percent on $11 million, or $1.32 million. This is one third more than the entire amount of Company *M*'s after-tax income before the leveraged buyout, even though the operating income of Company *M* is the same before and after the leveraged buyout.

The taxable income of Company *M* has, however, been reduced from $1.5 million to $180,000 ($1.5 million minus $1.32 million) because most of the income of the company is paid out to investors as interest rather than dividends. Federal income taxes are thereby reduced from $510,000 to $61,200. Acquirors make an after-tax profit of $118,800 (pre-tax profit of $180,000 reduced by Federal income tax of $61,200), a 13.4 percent return on their $880,000 equity investment. The income tax reduction of $448,800 exactly pays for the increased returns to investors (bondholders and the acquirors) as a result of the leveraged buyout. Depending on whether the increased investor returns are paid to taxable shareholders or holders of debt, there may be an increase in investor-level Federal income taxes paid.*

---

*The engine that drives this example is the assumption that the Company *M* stock initially sells for $80 per share and can be redeemed for $120 per share. Is this a realistic assumption? The example assumes that *M*'s pretax borrowing cost is 12 percent; presumably its rate of return on investment would be higher than 12 percent. Even assuming that the rate of return on investment is 12 percent, *M*'s assets should be worth $12,500,000 ($1,500,000/.12) to

Actual Transactions

Leveraged buyouts of public companies have greatly increased in recent years, and the amounts involved in such transactions have risen dramatically. The largest leveraged buyout transaction to date is the proposed acquisition of RJR Nabisco by the investment firm of Kohlberg Kravis Roberts & Co. ("KKR") for nearly $25 billion. It is expected that this acquisition will be completed by February 1989. Other large leveraged buyout transactions include the acquisition of Beatrice Companies by KKR for $6.25 billion in April 1986, and the management buyout of R.H. Macy & Co., Inc. for $3.5 billion in July 1986.

Newspaper reports indicate that out of the approximately $25 billion needed for the RJR Nabisco acquisition, more than $22.5 billion will be borrowed. Secured bank debt will account for approximately $17.5 billion of the borrowing, with most of the remainder being provided by investment banking firms. A pool of investors organized by KKR will put up $1.5 billion as an equity investment. It has been reported that KKR will contribute approximately $15 million of its own funds as equity. RJR Nabisco shareholders will be paid $109 for each share of common stock. This is almost twice the price at which the stock was trading immediately prior to the announcement of the possible sale of the company. It has been reported that due to increased interest deductions, RJR Nabisco could save up to $682 million annually in Federal and state income taxes and be able to seek the refund of additional amounts of taxes paid in prior years due to the carryback of net operating losses. Other reports have projected the annual savings at $370 million.

In the Beatrice transaction, each common shareholder received $50 per share ($40 in cash). This price of $50 per share was 45 percent higher than the market value of the stock one month prior to the announcement date of the first offer. Financing for the Beatrice leveraged buyout included $6.5 billion in debt and $1.35 billion in equity capital. Four billion dollars of the debt was lent by banks and $2.5 billion came from a new issue of high yield bonds. The equity came from two sources. Six hundred million came from a buyout fund organized by KKR and subscribed to by institu-

---

produce the assumed annual pretax profit of $1,500,000. Yet the market seems to value the corporation at only $7,920,000 (99,000 shares × $80 per share).

Why might the market value of *M* be so much below its asset value? There may be a host of reasons. Perhaps the expected cost of a corporate-level tax is one reason. Also, stock may be undervalued because of information failure in the marketplace, or perhaps the assets are not efficiently deployed and transactions costs prevent a more efficient deployment. In any case, the example not surprisingly shows that if you can borrow at 12 percent to purchase an investment (i.e., *M* stock) that provides a return of almost 19 percent ($1,500,000 income/ (99,000 shares × $80 per share)), it's a good deal.

Notice that in this example the government receives less in taxes when debt is used. The example assumes that the benefits of this tax reduction are shared by the shareholders and the debt holders. As noted at page 361 supra, however, the reduction in taxes might also inure to employees, suppliers, customers, etc. Regardless of who benefits from the tax reduction, tax liability is lowered through the use of debt. — Eds.

tional investors and $750 million came from converting existing common stock to a new issue of preferred stock.

In the Macy transaction, each common share of stock outstanding received $68 in cash. This price of $68 per share was 55 percent higher than the market value of the stock one month prior to the announcement date of the first offer. On completion of the Macy leveraged buyout, the management group held 20 percent of the new company stock and an additional 20 percent was held by General Electric Co.'s credit union. Financing for the Macy leveraged buyout totalled approximately $3.7 billion. Out of this amount, almost $3.2 billion was debt: $770 million was lent from banks, $1.625 billion came from new issues of high yield bonds, and $800 million came from notes secured by mortgages. The remaining $500 million of the financing consisted of $200 million of excess cash of Macy's and $300 million was equity capital contributed by the acquirors.

D.   ROLE OF OVERFUNDED PENSION PLANS AND ESOPS IN LEVERAGED BUYOUTS

1.   Overfunded Pension Plans

In the case of a leveraged buyout, the assets in the overfunded pension plan of the target company may represent a source of capital to help finance the acquisition. An overfunded pension plan represents a pool of assets that may make a company a target for a takeover. Conversely, this pool of assets may be used by the company to ward off a hostile takeover. In recent years, some companies with significantly overfunded pension plans have been acquired by other companies. After the acquisition, the acquiring company terminated the overfunded pension plan and used the excess assets partially to finance the takeover. An overfunded plan represents an attractive source of cash even if the value of the assets are included in the purchase price.

Another possibility is that a company will itself terminate an overfunded pension plan to assist its efforts to thwart a hostile takeover attempt.

Consider the following example:

Example III-D

Corporation K is a widely held public corporation. K maintains a qualified defined benefit pension plan for the exclusive benefit of its employees. The trust is currently overfunded by approximately $100 million on a termination basis. That is, if the trust is terminated, its assets would exceed the present value of the benefits accrued under the plan by K employees up to the date of plan termination. LBO Fund (L) wants to acquire K.

Under almost any form of acquisition, L, subject to some limitations, could cause K to terminate its pension plan. The termination would enable

L, directly or indirectly, to obtain the $100 million. It could be used to assist *L* in paying for the acquisition, for general corporate purposes, or for any other purpose. While the $100 million would be included in the gross income of *K* upon termination of the plan, any net operating losses and loss carryovers of *K* could be used to offset that income. A nondeductible 15-percent excise tax would also apply to the reversion.

If *K*'s current management wanted to prevent an acquisition, it might terminate the plan itself and make use of the proceeds. *K* might be a less attractive takeover candidate in that event, for it would not have $100 million in readily available cash as an inducement to a potential acquiror.

This utilization of excess pension assets is not peculiar to a leveraged buyout, but is potentially available in any takeover or merger transaction. In addition, any pool of liquid assets, not just excess pension assets, would be attractive to potential acquirors.

2. Employee Stock Ownership Plans (ESOPs)

A leveraged ESOP can be used by an employer as a technique of finance to obtain funds for working capital or plant expansion, or as a means of financing a leveraged buyout. Use of this financing technique can result in a lower cost of borrowing than would be available if conventional debt or equity financing were used. In a typical transaction, the employer enters into a contract with the ESOP to sell the ESOP a specified number of shares of its stock. The ESOP borrows the funds needed to purchase the shares from a bank or other lender and pays them to the employer in exchange for the stock. In subsequent years, the employer makes tax-deductible cash contributions to the ESOP in the amount necessary to amortize the loan principal and interest payments thereon.

A leveraged ESOP may be used not only to provide the company with working capital but also to finance an acquisition of the stock or assets of another corporation. In a typical case, a leveraged ESOP maintained by the acquiring corporation or its subsidiary borrows funds in an amount equal to the amount needed to acquire the target corporation. The proceeds of the loan are used to purchase employer securities from the employer. The employer (or the subsidiary) then uses the proceeds of the sale to purchase the stock or assets of the target company.

One variation of this leveraged-ESOP financing technique is for the employer to purchase target stock, either directly or through a subsidiary, using funds borrowed from a financial institution or other lender. Once the acquisition has been completed, the newly acquired subsidiary establishes a leveraged ESOP. The ESOP borrows money and purchases stock in the subsidiary from the subsidiary (or from the acquiring corporation). The acquiring corporation then uses the proceeds of this sale to pay off the original acquisition loan. The subsidiary makes annual, deductible contributions sufficient to amortize the ESOP loan and pay interest.

Recently, leveraged ESOPs have been used in some situations to thwart hostile corporate takeover attempts. Leveraged ESOPs have also been used to accomplish leveraged buyouts by persons desiring to take the company private.

The establishment of an employee stock ownership plan (ESOP) may reduce the costs of financing a leveraged buyout, as evidenced by the following example.

Example III-E

Partnership *R* purchases Target Company *X* for $3.0 billion, financed by $2.4 billion of debt and $600 million of equity capital. As part of the buyout agreement, *X* establishes an ESOP for its employees. *X* borrows $250 million from a commercial lender and secures the loan by mortgages and asset pledges. *X* then lends $250 million to the ESOP on substantially the same terms as the terms of *X*'s loan from the commercial lender. The ESOP uses the loan proceeds to purchase $250 million of *X*'s stock.

The ESOP pays off the loan with contributions made by *X* in subsequent years. Such contributions will equal the annual principal and interest payments required by the ESOP on the loan from *X*. As the ESOP makes such loan payments, *X* uses the payments to satisfy its repayment requirements to the commercial lender.

Under present law, the contributions of *X* to the ESOP, which equal the principal and interest payments on *X*'s loan to the ESOP, generally are deductible under the rules governing deductions for contributions to qualified pension plans. Consequently, if an ESOP is established by *X*, *X* may deduct both the principal and interest payments on its loan. This result can be illustrated by comparing the following 2 cases:

Case 1. — *X* borrows $250 million from lender *A*. Only the interest on *X*'s payments to *A* are deductible.

Case 2. — *X* establishes an ESOP, which borrows $250 million from lender *A* and uses the proceeds to purchase capital stock from *X*. *X*'s payments to the ESOP equal the principal and interest payments on the ESOP's loan from *A*. *X*'s payments are fully deductible.

In case 2, *X* has, in effect, borrowed $250 million from a lender and gets the benefit of a full deduction for its loan repayments. A further advantage of the use of an ESOP in the buyout of *X* is the special interest exclusion allowed under present law (sec. 133). The commercial lender who loans $250 million to *X* is entitled to exclude from gross income 50 percent of the interest it receives on the loan. Typically, this tax benefit is passed on partially to the borrower in the form of a reduced cost of borrowing (i.e., rest rate on the loan).

A potential disadvantage of the use of an ESOP in this case is that the employees of *X* will receive an equity interest in *X*. As the ESOP loan is repaid, the stock of *X* purchased by the ESOP will be allocated to the accounts of the ESOP participants. Thus, the ownership of the shares acquired through the ESOP ultimately will be transferred to the ESOP participants. The advantages of using the ESOP to finance a leveraged buyout or other transaction may not outweigh the disadvantage of transferring equity interests to employees.

Actual Transactions

Leveraged ESOPs have been used in a variety of corporate financing transactions. For example, the Procter and Gamble Company plans to add $1 billion (financed by debt) to its existing ESOP (thereby giving the ESOP a 20-percent interest in the company's common stock) in a transaction designed to provide substantial tax benefits and to offer a shield against a threat of hostile takeover. Similarly, the recent establishment of the J. C. Penney Company ESOP is widely viewed as an effort to deter a hostile takeover.

Leveraged ESOPs have also been used to accomplish leveraged buyouts by persons desiring to take a company private. The leveraged ESOP of Parsons Corporation accomplished such a result.

IV.   POLICY ISSUES . . .

C.   RISKS OF EXCESSIVE CORPORATE DEBT

1.   Implication of Excessive Debt for Financial Stability and Economic Growth

Overview

Increased corporate indebtedness potentially has significant implications for the financial health of investors and issuers of the debt as well as for the economy as a whole. Corporate issuers with increased indebtedness must devote larger proportions of earnings and cash flow to interest payments. If leverage ratios are high, and if sales decline or expenses increase, firms may be forced to sell assets, reduce wage costs, or reduce capital and research expenditures. If such actions are insufficient to restore liquidity, debt restructuring or bankruptcy can result. Furthermore, losses incurred by investors holding the corporate debt of troubled firms could adversely affect their own balance sheets. If bankruptcies and debt restructurings are greater than expected, the negative effects could extend beyond distressed lenders and borrowers and reduce employment, income and growth in the economy as a whole. However, increased corporate indebtedness and even increased risk are not necessarily adverse developments, and there is by no means consensus among experts about the significance of increased debt. Some consider it an impending crisis; others consider it to be just one more aspect of financial innovation; yet others consider it as ultimately improving economic efficiency.

NOTE

1. *Acquisition indebtedness.* In the late 1960s, Congress expressed concern over acquisition activity that involved the use of various types of debt instruments, often convertible into common stock of the acquiring corporation. To discourage the use of debt in such acquisitions, Congress enacted §279, which disallows an interest deduction to an acquiring corporation on specified "corporate acquisition indebtedness." Essentially, "corporate acquisition indebtedness" is a debt obligation issued by an acquiring corporation to acquire a specified amount of stock or assets (i.e., two-thirds of the value of the trade or business assets) of another corporation if the following conditions are met:

1. the obligation is subordinated to trade creditors or unsecured creditors;
2. the obligation is convertible into stock of the issuing corporation;
3. the ratio of debt to equity exceeds 2:1 or the projected earnings of the acquiring corporation (or in some cases the combined corporations) does not exceed three times the interest paid or incurred with respect to the obligation.

If an acquiring corporation can avoid any one of these requirements, then §279 does not apply. For example, if the debt is not subordinated to trade creditors, §279 does not apply. If all three requirements are satisfied, then §279 denies an interest deduction in excess of $5 million paid on such corporate acquisition indebtedness. Accordingly, at a 7 percent interest rate, a corporation could have more than $70 million of debt outstanding without triggering §279.

2. *High-yield discount obligations.* In the aftermath of the stock market plunge of 1987, Congress acted again to curb the perceived misuse of corporate debt to fund major acquisitions, although its actions have a narrow scope. An interest deduction may be denied to issuers of any "applicable high-yield discount obligation." This type of obligation typically has an issue price that is significantly lower than the redemption price. The spread between the issue price and the redemption price is original issue discount (OID). Normally, an issuer of an OID bond accrues and deducts (and the lender includes) the spread over the life of the bond even though payment is not made until maturity. §§1272-1273. A related instrument is

the "payment in kind" (PIK) bond, in which instrument payments are in the form of other debt or stock of the issuer rather than cash. Both the high-yield and PIK bonds are attractive to issuers in providing deductions before any cash outlay is required.

Section 163(e)(5) divides the OID amount on these bonds between an interest portion that is deductible only when paid and a disqualified portion for which no deduction is allowed but which may qualify for a dividends received deduction for a corporate lender. This approach is a compromise between treating the instrument as equity (i.e., periodic payments would not be deductible) and treating it as debt. An "applicable high-yield discount obligation" is defined as an instrument with: (a) a maturity date of more than five years, (b) a yield to maturity that is at least 5 percentage points more than a designated federal rate, and (c) "significant original issue discount." §163(i).

3. *Debt-financed net operating losses.* Another focus of Congress in 1989 was the use of tax refunds to finance leveraged buyouts. These tax refunds were generated by the acquiring corporation's current net operating losses (NOLs) being carried back for three taxable years, thereby enabling the acquiring corporation to obtain a tax refund for those years. §172. In debt-financed acquisitions, often the interest deductions generated the NOL that resulted in a tax refund. Congress determined that interest incurred in a takeover was not sufficient to justify an NOL carryback.

Section 172(h) limits the carryback of NOLs if the losses are created by interest deductions attributable to a "corporate equity reduction transaction" (CERT). A CERT is either a "major stock acquisition" or an "excess distribution." A "major stock acquisition" is a planned acquisition by a corporation of 50 percent or more of the voting power or value of stock in another corporation. §172(h)(3)(B). An "excess distribution" is an unusually large distribution relative to the distributing corporation's distribution history or net worth. §172(h)(3)(C).

If the CERT limitation applies, interest attributable to the CERT (which may occur as much as two years after the year in which the CERT occurs) cannot be carried back to a year before the CERT. A de minimis rule provides that the limitation applies only if the interest expense in question exceeds $1 million. §172(h)(2)(D).

4. *Integration.* The limited statutory provisions discussed above may have the effect of limiting the use of debt in acquisition activity in some specific cases, but even taken together the attempts are uneven and certainly are complicated. A more general and principled approach to the debt-equity problem may be the integration of corporate and individual income taxes. Under some integration proposals, the tax differences between debt and equity would be either eliminated or lessened, thereby substantially removing tax incentives for debt-financed acquisitions.

For a discussion of integration, See Chapter 8.

F. PROBLEMS

T Corp., a profitable corporation, has the following assets and liabilities:

Assets	Basis	FMV
Inventory	$ 50,000	$ 250,000
Equipment ($50,000 §1245 recapture)	100,000	150,000
Land	150,000	300,000
Building (no recapture)	200,000	400,000
	500,000	1,100,000
Liabilities		
Bank Loan		200,000

A owns 50 shares of *T* Corp. stock with a basis of $300,000; *B* owns 40 shares of *T* Corp. stock with a basis of $200,000; *C* owns 10 shares of *T* Corp. stock with a basis of $50,000.

The shareholders of *T* Corp. have decided to sell the business to *P*. Ignoring the quantitative effects of the tax consequences, outline the tax considerations in the following alternatives:

1. *P*, an individual, pays $1.2 million to *T* Corp. for all its assets and assumes *T* Corp.'s bank loan. *T* Corp. then liquidates.
2. In (1), suppose *P* issues a $1.2 million note (bearing appropriate interest).
3. In (1), suppose *P* pays $1 million to the shareholders to purchase their stock in *T* Corp., and *T* Corp. does not liquidate.
4. In (3), suppose *P* decides to liquidate *T* Corp.
5. In (4), suppose *P* is a corporation (*P* Corp.). Suppose further that *P* Corp. borrowed the funds used to purchase the taxpayer stock, thereby generating interest deductions in excess of the income of *P* Corp. and *T* Corp. combined.
6. In (5), suppose *T* Corp. has a $700,000 NOL that is about to expire.
7. Suppose *P* Corp. purchases the land and building from *T* Corp. for $700,000. One year later, *P* Corp. purchases the stock of *T* Corp. for $1 million.
8. Suppose *A*, *B*, and *C* own the stock of *H* Corp., the only asset of which is the *T* Corp. stock. *H* Corp. and *T* Corp. file a consolidated return. *H* Corp.'s basis in the *T* Corp. stock is $200,000. *T* Corp. sells its assets to *P* Corp. (which assumes *T* Corp.'s liability) for $1 million and then liquidates. *H* Corp. then liquidates.
9. In (8) suppose that prior to any asset sale, *T* Corp. liquidates, then *H* Corp. liquidates. *A*, *B*, and *C* then sell the former *T* Corp. assets to *P* Corp. for $1 million.
10. In (8) suppose that rather than an asset sale, *P* Corp. purchases the stock of *T* Corp. from *H* Corp. for $1 million.

10

Acquisitive Reorganizations

A. INTRODUCTION

In its broadest sense, a corporate reorganization can mean any re-arrangement of corporate activity, including the division of a single corporation into two or more entities, the combination of two or more corporations into a single entity, and the continuation of a corporation's business by new shareholders. Sales of corporate shares and sales of corporate assets are thus "reorganizations" in this broad sense.

Consider the following example of an acquisitive corporate reorganization. Acquiring Corp. seeks to obtain the business assets of Target Corp. To this end, Acquiring purchases the productive assets of Target, paying with cash, Acquiring stock and securities, or some combination. Target then distributes the consideration received from Acquiring, along with its remaining assets, if any, to its shareholders in exchange for their shares of Target.

In the absence of any special taxing provisions, this transaction will be taxable at both the corporate and shareholder levels. First, Target Corp. will recognize gain or loss on the assets it sells to Acquiring Corp. as well as on the assets it does not sell but instead distributes as part of its liquidating distribution. See §§1001, 336. Second, the Target shareholders will recognize gain or loss on the exchange of their shares for the distributed assets to the extent the adjusted basis in their shares differs from the fair market value of the assets they receive. §331.

One might question whether one or both levels of taxation is appropriate. For example, suppose the consideration used by Acquiring Corp. consisted exclusively of its own common stock so that, in the liquidating distribution of Target Corp., the Target shareholders exchanged their shares of Target for shares of Acquiring. While this exchange works a change in the form of the shareholders' investment, it may have little real impact on the substance of their investment: They continue to own stock of a corporation conducting the business formerly conducted by Target.

In section 368(a), Congress has defined a set of reorganization patterns by which taxation at one or both levels can be avoided. Congress has in many sections shown its willingness to allow businesses to undergo a change in form without the imposition of tax. Section 351, for example, permits the tax-free incorporation of assets, and §721 performs a similar role in the formation of partnerships. The reorganization provisions reflect a similar congressional attitude in the context of corporate combinations and divisions. In this chapter we will look only at the provisions associated with combining two or more corporations — that is, we will examine the acquisitive reorganization provisions.

As you will soon discover, these reorganization provisions are exceedingly complex. Much of this complexity is a result of the conflicting congressional desires to (1) permit a mere change in the form of a corporate enterprise to be effected without immediate taxation while (2) not allowing the sale of a business to escape taxation simply because the business is incorporated. Although Congress and the courts have sought to develop reasonable criteria that distinguish nontaxable corporate reorganizations from taxable sales of corporate enterprises, the current statutory and judicial framework often seems to exalt form (and early tax advice) over substance.

Section 368(a) merely defines what constitutes a reorganization; the tax consequences following from these definitions are found elsewhere. For shareholders, the cornerstone of reorganization taxation is §354(a)(1). To obtain nonrecognition under §354(a)(1), a shareholder must exchange "stock or securities" for "stock or securities," the exchange must be "in pursuance of a plan of reorganization," and both the transferred and the received stock and securities must be "in a corporation a party to a reorganization."

As you know, stock represents an equity interest in a corporation, and a security is a debt interest. But not all corporate debt interests qualify as "securities" under §354(a)(1), and Congress has failed to define this important term. Transactions that constitute "reorganizations" are defined with specificity in §368(a), and a "party" to a reorganization is defined in §368(b). Congressional attention to these issues has not, unfortunately, minimized litigation over such crucial definitions, and the resulting judicial gloss on the statutory provisions has proved substantial.

Before turning to the cases, it is worthwhile to explore the statutory terrain. The principal definition of a "reorganization" is in §368(a)(1), and the various different forms of reorganizations described in that subsection are usually referred to without the preface "§368(a)(1)." Thus, we have A reorganizations (statutory mergers and consolidations), B reorganizations, and all types down to G reorganizations. The acquisitive reorganizations include the types A through D (although not all Ds are acquisitive reorganizations, as we shall see), and they are discussed in this section.

The A reorganization is a "statutory merger or consolidation." In a merger, one corporation (usually called the "acquiring" or "surviving" corporation) acquires all the assets of another corporation (usually called the "target" corporation), and all outstanding target shares are canceled, with the former target shareholders receiving some form of consideration usually including some combination of cash, stock, and debt of the acquiring corporation, and stock and debt of companies related to the acquiring corporation. Thus, if Target Corp. merges into Acquiring Corp., Target will disappear and Acquiring will end up with the assets of Target.

In a consolidation, two corporations join together to form a new, third corporation. Thus, X Corp. and Y Corp. might consolidate into Z Corp., with Z owning the combined assets of X and Y. All stock of X and Y will be canceled, and the former X and Y shareholders will receive consideration usually including some combination of cash, stock, and debt of Z.

Note that an A reorganization is a *statutory* merger or consolidation. The requirement that a merger or consolidation be "statutory" means that the transaction must satisfy some state or federal merger or consolidation statute. Typically, such a statute requires consent by the shareholders of the corporations involved in the transaction and imposes various procedural requirements to ensure that all affected parties (often including workers) are adequately apprised of the event. The nontax aspects of state or federal merger statutes are irrelevant to the tax consequences of the transaction except that the parties must comply with relevant nontax law to fall within the ambit of §368(a)(1)(A). It is worth mentioning now that not all statutory mergers and consolidations qualify as A reorganizations: The courts have felt free to add additional requirements beyond those imposed by the language of §368(a)(1)(A).

The C reorganization is sometimes called the "de facto merger provision" because a C reorganization accomplishes the same effect as an A reorganization without necessarily satisfying any nontax state or federal merger statute. In a C reorganization, the acquiring corporation acquires "substantially all" the assets of the target corporation and then the target corporation liquidates, distributing any of its assets not transferred to the acquiring corporation as well as whatever consideration was paid by the acquiring corporation for the target's assets. If the acquiring corporation uses its own stock as payment, then the former target shareholders will become shareholders of the acquiring corporation. Depending on the relative values of the acquiring and target corporations, the former target shareholders may end up with an insignificant percentage ownership interest in the acquiring corporation (as when a conglomerate swallows up a Mom and Pop grocery store) or a much more substantial interest in the acquiring corporation (when the acquiring corporation and the target corporation are of approximately equal value).

A B reorganization is very different from the A and C reorganizations. In a B reorganization, the acquiring corporation obtains at least 80 percent of the stock of the target corporation so that the target corporation ends up as a subsidiary of the acquiring corporation. One interesting aspect of the B reorganization is that it involves no corporate-level tax, even in the absence of special taxing provisions, because the corporate assets do not change hands. Thus, the effect of qualifying a transaction as a B reorganization is to allow the former shareholders of the target corporation to avoid recognition of gain (and of loss, although that is no advantage) on the sale of their shares to the acquiring corporation.

Section 368(a)(2) contains several provisions expanding the basic reorganization definitions to allow the use of parent-subsidiary combinations in place of a single corporate enterprise. In addition, and for reasons understood only by reference to the history of the reorganization provisions, part of the definition of a C reorganization is found in §368(a)(2). Section 368(b) defines the term "party to a reorganization," and as provisions have been added to §368(a)(2) that expand the use of parent-subsidiary pairs, so too has §368(b) been amended to expand the concept of a party to the reorganization.

Recall that §368 is a *definitional* section: It contains no provision specifying the taxation of parties to a reorganization. In Chapter 2 you were introduced to §354, the basic shareholder-level taxing provision. Section 356 addresses the shareholder taxation of boot (and §357 specifies the circumstances in which the assumption of a liability is treated as nonqualifying property), while §361 plays both roles at the corporate level. The associated basis rules are in §358 (for shareholders) and §§361 to 362 (for the corporate parties to the reorganization). As with most nonrecognition provisions in the Code, the deferral of gain or loss results in the taxpayer's retaining the adjusted basis of the property given up for the new property.

Although the requirements of the various types of statutory reorganizations differ, and certain transactions may fall under more than one type, several theories and factors are common to all reorganizations. Tax-free treatment is based on a *continuity of proprietary interest* principle: The new corporate structure is deemed to be substantially a continuation of the old, and this is the reason that gain or loss, although realized, is not recognized.

Each of the following three cases introduces different aspects of the continuity of proprietary interest doctrine. In *Paulsen*, the question presented is whether the consideration received by the shareholders of the acquired company constitutes a "proprietary" interest in the continuing venture. In *Kass*, the issue changes from quality to quantity: How much of the consideration received by shareholders of the acquired company must represent a "proprietary" interest? Finally, in *McDonald's*, the court focuses on the temporal aspects of the continuity of interest doctrine.

Paulsen v. Commissioner
469 U.S. 131 (1985)

Justice REHNQUIST delivered the opinion of the Court.

Commerce Savings and Loan Association of Tacoma, Wash., merged into Citizens Federal Savings and Loan Association of Seattle in July 1976. Petitioners Harold and Marie Paulsen sought to treat their exchange of stock in Commerce for an interest in Citizens as a tax-free reorganization under [Code] §§354(a)(1) and 368(a)(1)(A). The Court of Appeals for the Ninth Circuit, disagreeing with the Court of Claims and other Courts of Appeals, reversed a decision of the Tax Court in favor of petitioners. 716 F.2d 563 (1983). We granted certiorari . . . to resolve these conflicting interpretations of an important provision of the Internal Revenue Code.

At the time of the merger, petitioners . . . held . . . 17,459 shares of "guaranty stock" in Commerce. In exchange for this stock petitioners received passbook savings accounts and time certificates of deposit in Citizens. [T]hey did not report the gain they realized on their 1976 federal income tax return because they considered the merger to be a tax-free reorganization.

Before it ceased to exist, Commerce was a state-chartered savings and loan association incorporated and operated under Washington State law. It was authorized to issue "guaranty stock," to offer various classes of savings accounts, and to make loans. Each stockholder, savings account holder, and borrower was a member of the association. Each share of stock and every $100, or fraction thereof, on deposit in a savings account carried with it one vote. Each borrower also had one vote.

The "guaranty stock" had all of the characteristics normally associated with common stock issued by a corporation. Under the bylaws, a certain amount of guaranty stock was required to be maintained as the fixed and nonwithdrawable capital of Commerce. In accordance with Wash. Rev. Code Ann. §33.48.080 (Supp. 1981), holders of guaranty stock, but no other members, had a proportionate proprietary interest in its assets and net earnings, subordinate to the claims of creditors. Dividends could not be declared or paid on the guaranty stock unless certain reserves had been accumulated and dividends had been declared and paid on withdrawable savings accounts.

Citizens is a federally chartered mutual savings and loan association under the jurisdiction of the Federal Home Loan Bank Board. 12 U.S.C. §1461 et seq. It offers savings accounts and makes loans, but has no capital stock. Its members are its depositors and borrowers. Each savings account holder has one vote for each $100, or fraction thereof, of the withdrawal value of his savings account up to a maximum of 400 votes. Each borrower has one vote.

Citizens is owned by its depositors. Twice each year its net earnings and any surplus are to be distributed to its savings account holders pro rata to the amounts on deposit. Its net assets would similarly be distributed if liquidation or dissolution should occur. It is obligated to pay written withdrawal requests within 30 days, and may redeem any of its accounts at any time by paying the holder the withdrawal value.

The merger was effected pursuant to a "Plan of Merger," under which Commerce's stockholders exchanged all their stock for passbook savings accounts and certificates of deposit in Citizens. The plan was designed to conform to the requirements of Wash. Rev. Code §33.40.010 (1983), which provides for mergers between business entities, and to qualify as a tax-free reorganization under the terms of §§354(a)(1) and 368(a)(1)(A). Under the plan, Commerce stockholders received for each share a $12 deposit in a Citizens passbook savings account, subject only to the restriction that such deposits could not be withdrawn for one year. They also had the alternative of receiving time certificates of deposit in Citizens with maturities ranging from 1 to 10 years at the same $12-per-share exchange rate. The plan further provided that former Commerce stockholders could borrow against their deposits resulting from the exchange at 1.5% above the passbook rate as opposed to a 2% differential for other depositors. Following the exchange, the merged entity continued to operate under the Citizens name. . . .

Section 368(a)(1)(A) defines a "reorganization" to include "a statutory merger or consolidation," and §§7701(a)(3), 7701(a)(7), and 7701(a)(8) further define the terms "corporation" to include "associations," "stock" to include "shares in an association," and "shareholder" to include a "member in an association." There is no dispute that at the time of the merger Commerce and Citizens qualified as associations, petitioners qualified as shareholders, Commerce's guaranty stock and Citizens' passbook accounts and certificates of deposit qualified as stock, and the merger qualified as a statutory merger within these provisions of the Code. Accordingly, under the literal terms of the Code the transaction would qualify as a tax-free "reorganization" exchange rather than a sale or exchange on which gain must be recognized and taxes paid.

Satisfying the literal terms of the reorganization provisions, however, is not sufficient to qualify for nonrecognition of gain or loss. The purpose of these provisions is "to free from the imposition of an income tax purely 'paper profits or losses' wherein there is no realization of gain or loss in the business sense but merely the recasting of the same interests in a different form." Southwest Natural Gas Co. v. Commissioner, 189 F.2d 332, 334 (C.A.5), cert. denied, 342 U.S. 860 (1951) (quoting Commissioner

v. Gilmore's Estate, 130 F.2d 791, 794 (C.A.3 1942)). See Treas. Reg. §1.368-1(b) (1984). In order to exclude sales structured to satisfy the literal terms of the reorganization provisions but not their purpose, this Court has construed the statute to also require that the taxpayer's ownership interest in the prior organization must continue in a meaningful fashion in the reorganized enterprise. Pinellas Ice & Cold Storage Co. v. Commissioner, 287 U.S. 462, 468-470 (1933). In that case we held that "the seller must acquire an interest in the affairs of the purchasing company more definite than that incident to ownership of its short-term purchase-money notes." Id., at 470. We soon added the requirement that "this interest must be definite and material; it must represent a substantial part of the value of the thing transferred." Helvering v. Minnesota Tea Co., 296 U.S. 378, 385 (1935). Compare LeTulle v. Scofield, 308 U.S. 415, 420-421 (1940) (no retained property interest where transferor received transferee's bonds), with John A. Nelson Co. v. Helvering, 296 U.S. 374, 377 (1935) (continuity of interest satisfied where nonvoting preferred stock received). Known as the "continuity-of-interest" doctrine, this requirement has been codified in Treas. Reg. §§1.368-1(b), 1.368-2(a).

The present case turns on whether petitioners' exchange of their guaranty stock in Commerce for their passbook savings accounts and certificates of deposit in Citizens satisfies this continuity-of-interest requirement. More generally, we must decide whether a merger of a stock savings and loan association into a mutual savings and loan association qualifies as a tax-free reorganization. . . .

Citizens is organized pursuant to Charter K (Rev.), 12 C.F.R. §544.1(b) (as of July 1, 1976), which provides for raising capital "by accepting payments on savings accounts representing share interests in the association." These shares are the association's only means of raising capital. Here they are divided into passbook accounts and certificates of deposit. In reality, these shares are hybrid instruments having both equity and debt characteristics. They combine in one instrument the separate characteristics of the guaranty stock and the savings accounts of stock associations like Commerce.

The Citizens shares have several equity characteristics. The most important is the fact that they are the only ownership instrument of the association. Each share carries in addition to its deposit value a part ownership interest in the bricks and mortar, the goodwill, and all the other assets of Citizens. Another equity characteristic is the right to vote on matters for which the association's management must obtain shareholder approval. The shareholders also receive dividends rather than interest on their accounts; the dividends are paid out of net earnings, and the shareholders have no legal right to have a dividend declared or to have a fixed return on their investment. The shareholders further have a right to a pro rata distribution of any remaining assets after a solvent dissolution.

These equity characteristics, however, are not as substantial as they appear on the surface. Unlike a stock association where the ownership of the assets is concentrated in the stockholders, the ownership interests here are spread over all of the depositors. The equity interest of each shareholder in relation to the total value of the share, therefore, is that much smaller than in a stock association. The right to vote is also not very significant. A shareholder is limited to 400 votes, thus any funds deposited in excess of $40,000 do not confer any additional votes. The vote is also diluted each time a loan is made, as each borrower is entitled to one vote. In addition the Commissioner asserts, and petitioners do not contest, that in practice, when depositors open their accounts, they usually sign proxies giving management their votes.

The fact that dividends rather than interest are paid is by no means controlling. Petitioners have not disputed the Commissioner's assertion that in practice Citizens pays a fixed, preannounced rate on all accounts. As the Court of Appeals observed, Citizens would not be able to compete with stock savings and loan associations and commercial banks if it did not follow this practice. Potential depositors are motivated only by the rate of return on their accounts and the security of their deposits. In this latter respect, the Citizens accounts are insured by the Federal Savings and Loan Insurance Corporation (FSLIC), up to $40,000 in 1976 and now up to $100,000. 12 U.S.C. §1728(a). The Code treats these dividends just like interest on bank accounts rather than like dividends on stock in a corporation. The dividends are deductible to Citizens, §591, and they do not qualify for dividend exclusion by the Citizens shareholders under §116.

The right to participate in the net proceeds of a solvent liquidation is also not a significant part of the value of the shares. Referring to the possibility of a solvent liquidation of a mutual savings association, this Court observed: "It stretches the imagination very far to attribute any real value to such a remote contingency, and when coupled with the fact that it represents nothing which the depositor can readily transfer, any theoretical value reduces almost to the vanishing point." Society for Savings v. Bowers, 349 U.S. 143, 150 (1955).

In contrast, there are substantial debt characteristics to the Citizens shares that predominate. Petitioners' passbook accounts and certificates of deposit are not subordinated to the claims of creditors, and their deposits are not considered permanent contributions to capital. Shareholders have a right on 30 days' notice to withdraw their deposits, which right Citizens is obligated to respect. While petitioners were unable to withdraw their funds for one year following the merger, this restriction can be viewed as akin to a delayed payment rather than a material alteration in the nature of the instruments received as payment. In this case petitioners were immediately able to borrow against their deposits at a more favorable rate than Citizens' depositors generally. As noted above, petitioners were also in effect guaranteed a fixed, preannounced rate of return on their deposits competitive with stock savings and loan associations and commercial banks.

In our view, the debt characteristics of Citizens' shares greatly outweigh the equity characteristics. The face value of petitioners' passbook accounts and certificates of deposit was $210,000. Petitioners have stipulated that they had a right to withdraw the face amount of the deposits in cash, on demand after one year or at stated intervals thereafter. Their investment was virtually risk free and the dividends received were equivalent to prevailing interest rates for savings accounts in other types of savings institutions. The debt value of the shares was the same as the face value, $210,000; because no one would pay more than this for the shares, the incremental value attributable to the equity features was, practically, zero. Accordingly, we hold that petitioners' passbook accounts and certificates of deposit were cash equivalents.

Petitioners have failed to satisfy the continuity-of-interest requirement to qualify for a tax-free reorganization. In exchange for their guaranty stock in Commerce, they received essentially cash with an insubstantial equity interest. Under *Minnesota Tea Co.*, their equity interest in Citizens would have to be "a substantial part of the value of the thing transferred." 296 U.S., at 385. Assuming an arms'-length transaction in which what petitioners gave up and what they received were of equivalent worth, their Commerce stock was worth $210,000 in withdrawable deposits and an unquantifiably small incremental equity interest. This retained equity interest in the reorganized enterprise, therefore, is not a "substantial" part of the value of the Commerce stock which was given up. We agree with the Commissioner that the equity interests attached to the Citizens shares are too insubstantial to satisfy *Minnesota Tea Co.* The Citizens shares are not significantly different from the notes that this Court found to be the mere "equivalent of cash" in *Pinellas Ice & Cold Storage Co.*, 287 U.S., at 468-469. The ownership interest of the Citizens shareholders is closer to that of the secured bondholders in LeTulle v. Scofield, 308 U.S., at 420-421, than to that of the preferred stockholders in John A. Nelson Co. v. Helvering, 296 U.S., at 377. The latter case involved a classic ownership instrument — preferred stock carrying voting rights only in the event of a dividend default — which we held to represent "a definite and substantial interest in the affairs of the purchasing corporation." Ibid.

Petitioners argue that the decision below erroneously turned on the relative change in the nature and extent of the equity interest, contrary to the holding in *Minnesota Tea Co.* that "the relationship of the taxpayer to the assets conveyed [could] substantially chang[e]," and only a "material part of the value of the transferred assets" need be retained as an equity interest. 296 U.S., at 386. In that case, taxpayers received voting trust certificates representing $540,000 of common stock and $425,000 cash; 56% of the value of the assets given up was retained as an equity interest in the transferee. In *John A. Nelson Co.*, supra, the taxpayer received consideration consisting of 38% preferred stock and 62% cash. Here, in contrast, the retained equity interest had almost no value. It did not amount to a "material part" of the value of the Commerce stock formerly held by petitioners. See Southwest Natural Gas Co. v. Commissioner, 189 F.2d, at 335 (insufficient continuity of interest where stock received represented less than 1% of the consideration).

Petitioners' real complaint seems to be our willingness to consider the equity and debt aspects of their shares separately. Clearly, if these interests were represented by separate pieces of paper — savings accounts on the one hand and equity instruments of some kind on the other — the value of the latter would be so small that we would not find a continuity of proprietary interest. In order not "to exalt artifice above reality and to deprive the statutory provision in question of all serious purpose," Gregory v. Helvering, 293 U.S. 465, 469-470 (1935), it is necessary in the present case to consider the debt and equity aspects of a single instrument separately. . . .

Petitioners also complain that the result reached by the court below is inconsistent with the Commissioner's position that a merger of one mutual savings and loan institution into another mutual association or into a stock association would still qualify as a tax-free reorganization. See Rev. Rul. 69-3, 1969-1 Cum. Bull. 103. If the continuity-of-interest test turns on the nature of the thing received, and not on the relative change in proprietary interest, argue petitioners, the interest received in the merger of two mutual associations is no different from the interest received in the instant case.

As already indicated, shares in a mutual association have a predominant cash-equivalent component and an insubstantial equity component. When two mutual associations merge, the shares received are essentially identical to the shares given up. As long as the cash value of the shares on each side of the exchange is the same, the equity interest represented by the shares received — though small — is equivalent to the equity interest represented by the shares given up. Therefore, to the extent that a mutual association share reflects an equity interest, the continuity-of-interest requirement, as defined in *Minnesota Tea Co.*, is satisfied in an exchange of this kind. The fact that identical cash deposits are also exchanged does not affect the equity aspect of the exchange. In the case of a merger of a mutual association into a stock association, the continuity-of-interest requirement is even more clearly satisfied because the equity position of the exchanging shareholders is not only equivalent before and after the exchange, but it is enhanced. . . .

The judgment of the Court of Appeals is affirmed.

Justice Powell took no part in the decision of the case.

[Dissenting opinion of Justice O'Connor, in which the Chief Justice joined, is omitted.]

Kass v. Commissioner _____

60 T.C. 218 (1973), aff'd without opinion, 491 F.2d 749
(3d Cir. 1974)

DAWSON, Judge. . . .

The only issue for decision is whether petitioner, a minority share-holder of an 84-percent-owned subsidiary, must recognize gain upon the receipt of the parent's stock pursuant to a statutory merger of the subsidiary into the parent. . . .

For a period greater than 6 months prior to 1965, petitioner had owned 2,000 shares of common stock of Atlantic City Racing Association (herein called ACRA). . . .

ACRA was a New Jersey corporation which was formed in 1943 and which was engaged in the business of operating a racetrack. Its total authorized and outstanding stock consisted of 506,000 shares of common stock. It has approximately 500 stockholders. Track Associates, Inc. (herein called TRACK), is a New Jersey corporation which was formed on November 19, 1965. The total authorized capital stock of TRACK consisted of 500,000 shares of common stock. Its original capitalization consisted of 202,577 shares. Over 50 percent of the original issue was acquired by the Levy family and 8 percent was acquired by the Casey family. The remaining stock went to 18 other individuals. The Levys and the Caseys were also minority shareholders (whether computed separately or as a group) in ACRA. Their purpose in forming TRACK was to gain control over ACRA's racetrack business. They wanted to do away with ACRA's cumbersome capital structure and institute a new corporate policy with regard to capital improvements and higher purses for the races. Control was to be gained by establishing TRACK and then by (1) having TRACK purchase at least 80 percent of the stock of ACRA and (2) subsequently merging ACRA into TRACK.

The Levys acquired 48,300 shares of TRACK stock (out of the total original capitalization of 202,577 shares) in exchange for stock of ACRA. The Caseys acquired 3,450 shares in exchange for their ACRA stock. Together the Levys and Caseys purchased an additional 70,823 shares of TRACK stock as part of the original capitalization.

On December 1, 1965, TRACK offered to purchase the stock of ACRA at $22 per share, subject to the condition that at least 405,000 shares (slightly more than 80 percent of ACRA's outstanding shares) be tendered. As a result of this tender offer, which terminated on February 11, 1966, 424,764 shares of ACRA stock were received and paid for by TRACK. A total of 29,486 shares of ACRA stock were not tendered.

The board of directors of TRACK approved a plan of liquidation providing for the liquidation of ACRA by way of merger into TRACK. . . . At a special meeting of the shareholders of ACRA held on March 8, 1966, the aforementioned plan of liquidation and joint agreement were adopted. A copy of the notice of the meeting was sent to the petitioner, and it notified petitioner of the rights of a dissenting stockholder under New Jersey corporate law.

The merger having taken place, the remaining shares of ACRA that were not sold pursuant to the tender offer or the dissenting shareholder provisions were exchanged for TRACK stock, 1 for 1. The petitioner exchanged 2,000 shares of ACRA stock, with a fair market value at the time of $22 per share, for 2,000 shares of TRACK stock. She did not report any capital gain in connection with this transaction.

Petitioner contends that the merger of ACRA into TRACK, although treated at least in part as a liquidation at the corporate level, is at her level, the shareholder level, (1) a true statutory merger and (2) a section 368(a)(1)(A) reorganization, occasioning no recognition of gain on the ensuing exchange. . . . Respondent, on the other hand, argues that the purchase of stock by TRACK and the liquidation of ACRA into TRACK, which took the form of a merger, must be viewed at all levels as an integrated transaction; that the statutory merger does not qualify as a reorganization because it fails the continuity-of-interest test; and that, as a consequence, petitioner falls outside of section 354(a)(1) and must recognize gain pursuant to section [1001]. . . .

Respondent does not take the position that a statutory merger, such as the one we have here, can never qualify for reorganization-nonrecognition status. . . . Rather, his position is simply that the merger in question fails to meet the time-honored continuity-of-interest test. We agree with this and so hold. . . .

Reorganization treatment is appropriate when the parent's stock ownership in the subsidiary was not acquired as a step in a plan to acquire assets of the subsidiary: the parent's stockholding can be counted as contributing to continuity-of-interest, so that since such holding represented more than 80 percent of the stock of the subsidiary, the continuity-of-interest test would be met. Reorganization treatment is inappropriate when the parent's stock ownership in the subsidiary was purchased as the first step in a plan to acquire the subsidiary's assets in conformance with the provisions of section 334(b)(2).* The parent's stockholding could not be counted towards continuity-of-interest, so . . . there would be a continuity-of-interest of less than 20 percent. (Less than 20-percent continuity would be significantly less continuity-of-interest than that allowed in John A. Nelson Co. v. Helvering, 296 U.S. 374 (1935).) In short, where the parent's stock interest is "old and cold," it may contribute to continuity-of-interest.

---

* Under old §334(b)(2), a corporation could purchase 80 percent or more of the stock of a target corporation with appreciated assets and then liquidate the target and obtain a step-up in asset basis without recognition of a corporate-level tax. That provision has been repealed, and old §338 was enacted in its place. One central feature of the former §334(b)(2) was that the step-up in basis could be obtained only by liquidating the target. — EDS.

Where the parent's interest is not "old and cold," the sale of shares by the majority of shareholders actually detracts from continuity-of-interest.

In petitioner's case, TRACK's stock in ACRA was acquired as part of an integrated plan to obtain control over ACRA's business. The plan called for, first, the purchase of stock and, second, the subsidiary-into-parent merger. Accordingly, continuity-of-interest must be measured by looking to all the pre-tender offer stockholders rather than to the parent (TRACK) and the nontendering stockholders only; and by that measure the merger fails and petitioner must recognize her gain. . . .

Faced with the general rule as to the applicability of the continuity-of-interest test, petitioner makes the following arguments, which we will deal with separately.

One, the continuity-of-interest doctrine should not be applied because TRACK was formed by a few stockholders in ACRA in order to purchase the business and, in the process, to acquire a stepped-up basis for as many of the assets as possible via section 334(b)(2). "In effect, the situation was the same as the sale of stock by some shareholders to other shareholders." The petitioner meets herself coming, so to speak, when making this argument. Confronted with the problem of how to characterize the second event in the present two-event transaction, she contends that the transaction was a true statutory merger in both form and substance, at least insofar as she, a minority shareholder, was concerned. Now, confronted with the continuity-of-interest problem, she would have us treat the transaction in a manner inconsistent with the characterization previously given to the transaction, that of a merger. Furthermore, the parties to these events (the selling shareholders of ACRA, the organizers of TRACK, and the nontendering, nondissenting shareholders such as the petitioner) chose the steps that were followed. To allow one of them in a separate proceeding to characterize the facts as being in substance something else would lay the groundwork for an enormous amount of "whipsawing" by and against both taxpayers and the Government.

Two, in applying the continuity-of-interest test, if it is applied, the purchase of stock by TRACK and the subsequent merger should not be viewed as steps in an integrated transaction because the choice of merger over liquidation as a second step had independent significance to the minority shareholders and either choice would have suited TRACK. By so arguing, the petitioner attempts in effect to avoid the step-transaction doctrine and thus to limit the application of the continuity-of-interest test. If the merger can be separated from the stock purchase, the continuity-of-interest test might be applicable only with regard to ACRA's shareholders at the time of the statutory merger, namely, the parent corporation, TRACK, and the minority shareholders, including petitioner. We note at least one flaw: The choice — liquidation or merger — did make a difference to TRACK. If it had liquidated ACRA, TRACK would not have received all of ACRA's assets. Some of the assets would have gone to the minority shareholders, and it would have had to have purchased them from these shareholders at an additional price. By choosing to merge ACRA into itself, it was able to avoid this and other problems.

Three, if the purchase and merger are to be viewed as parts of a single transaction for continuity and reorganization purposes, then the incorporation of TRACK should also be integrated into the transaction for section 351 purposes; thus the petitioner should be viewed as having participated in a tax-free section 351 transaction along with the Levys and Caseys. Briefly, the answer to this argument is that while the purchase and the merger were interdependent events, petitioner's exchange of ACRA stock for TRACK stock was not "mutually interdependent" with the incorporation transfers made by the Levys, Caseys, and 18 other individuals. American Bantam Car Co., 11 T.C. 397, 405-407 (1948), affirmed per curiam 117 F.2d 513 (C.A.3, 1949). . . .

Four, assuming that the continuity-of-interest test is applied, it is met where all 16 percent of the stockholders of ACRA exchanged their stock for a total of 35 percent of the stock of TRACK. The 16-percent figure (really 16.04 percent) is the sum of the percentage of ACRA stock transferred to TRACK at the time of TRACK's formation (10.22 percent) plus the percentage of ACRA stock exchanged for TRACK stock following the statutory merger (5.82 percent). Fortunately, we need not engage in a game of percentages since the continuity figure argued for by petitioner, 16 percent, is not "tantalizingly" high. . . .

Finally, we emphasize that the petitioner is not any worse off than her fellow shareholders who sold their stock. She could have also received money instead of stock had she chosen to sell or to dissent from the merger. The nonrecognition of a realized gain is always an important matter. We hold that petitioner is not entitled to such favorable treatment in this case.

Reviewed by the Court. . . .

McDonald's Restaurants of Illinois v. Commissioner _____
688 F.2d 520 (7th Cir. 1982)

Before Cummings, Chief Judge, Bauer, Circuit Judge, and Grant, Senior District Judge.

CUMMINGS, Chief Judge. . . .

The pertinent facts as found by the Tax Court and supplemented by the record are not in dispute. In June 1977, when they filed their petitions in the Tax Court to review the deficiency assessments, taxpayers were 27 wholly owned subsidiaries of McDonald's Corporation (McDonald's), the Delaware corporation that franchises and operates fast-food restaurants. . . .

On the opposite end of the transaction at issue here were Melvin

Garb, Harold Stern and Lewis Imerman (known collectively as the Garb-Stern group). The group had begun with a single McDonald's franchise in Saginaw, Michigan, in the late 1950's and expanded its holdings to include McDonald's restaurants elsewhere in Michigan and in Oklahoma, Wisconsin, Nevada and California. After 1968 relations between the Garb-Stern group and McDonald's deteriorated. In 1971 McDonald's considered buying some of the group's restaurants in Oklahoma, but abandoned the idea when it became clear that the acquisition could not be treated as a "pooling of interests" for accounting purposes unless all of the Garb-Stern group's restaurants were acquired simultaneously. In November 1972, however, negotiations resumed, McDonald's having decided that total acquisition was necessary to eliminate the Garb-Stern group's friction.

The sticking point in the negotiations was that the Garb-Stern group wanted cash for its operations, while McDonald's wanted to acquire the Garb-Stern group's holdings for stock, consistent with its earlier expressed preference for treating the transaction as a "pooling of interests" for accounting purposes. McDonald's proposed a plan to satisfy both sides: it would acquire the Garb-Stern companies for McDonald's common stock, but it would include the common stock in a planned June 1973 registration so that the Garb-Stern group could sell it promptly.[3]

Final agreement was not reached until March 1973. Negotiations then were hectic; for a variety of accounting and securities-law reasons, the acquisition had to be consummated not before and not after April 1, 1973. The final deal was substantially what had been proposed earlier. The Garb-Stern companies would be merged in stages into McDonald's, which would in turn transfer the restaurant assets to the 27 subsidiaries that are the taxpayers here. In return the Garb-Stern group would receive 361,235 shares of unregistered common stock. The agreement provided that the Garb-Stern group could participate in McDonald's planned June 1973 registration and underwriting or in any other registration and underwriting McDonald's might undertake within six years (Art. 7.4); the group also had a one-time right to demand registration in the event that McDonald's did not seek registration within the first year (Art. 7.5). The Garb-Stern group was not obligated by contract to sell its McDonald's stock but fully intended to do so.

After the April 1 closing, both parties proceeded on the assumption that the Garb-Stern group's shares would be included in the June 1973 "piggyback" registration. In mid-June a widely publicized negative report about McDonald's stock caused the price to drop from $60 to $52 a share

---

3. The stock the Garb-Stern group received was unregistered. It could not be sold until it was registered or until the Garb-Stern group met the conditions of S.E.C. Rule 144 (2-year holding period and limitation of shares sold within 6-month period thereafter). 76 T.C. at 982 and n.17. Sale rather than retention was attractive to the Garb-Stern group, because McDonald's stock had paid no cash dividends from 1968 to the time of this transaction. Id. at 985, n.18.

in two weeks, and McDonald's therefore decided to postpone the registration and sale of additional stock. The Garb-Stern group acquiesced, although it had made no effort to withdraw from the registration before McDonald's decided to cancel it.

Through the rest of the summer, the price of McDonald's stock staged a recovery. In late August McDonald's decided to proceed with the registration, and the Garb-Stern group asked to have its shares included. The registration was announced on September 17 and completed on October 3, 1973. The Garb-Stern group thereupon sold virtually all of the stock it had acquired in the transaction at a price of more than $71 per share.

In its financial statements McDonald's treated the transaction as a "pooling of interests." In its tax returns for 1973, however, it treated it as a purchase. Consistent with that characterization, McDonald's gave itself a stepped-up basis in the assets acquired from the Garb-Stern group to reflect their cost ($29,029,000, representing the value of the common stock transferred and a $1-2 million "nuisance premium" paid to eliminate the Garb-Stern group from the McDonald's organization). It allocated that basis among various Garb-Stern assets, then dropped the restaurant assets to the 27 taxpayer subsidiaries pursuant to Section 351 of the Internal Revenue Code governing transfers to corporations controlled by the transferor. The subsidiaries used the stepped-up basis allocable to them to compute depreciation and amortization deductions in their own 1973 tax returns.

It is those deductions by the subsidiary taxpayers that the Commissioner reduced. He ruled that the transfer of the Garb-Stern group's assets to McDonald's was not a taxable acquisition but a statutory merger or consolidation under Section 368(a)(1)(A) of the Code, and that under Section 362(b) McDonald's was required to assume the Garb-Stern group's basis in the assets acquired. In turn, the subsidiaries were required to compute depreciation and amortization deductions on this lower, carryover basis. . . .

The Code distinguishes between taxable acquisitions and nontaxable (or more accurately tax-deferrable) acquisitive reorganizations under Sections 368(a)(1)(A)-(C) and 354(a)(1) for the following common-sense reason: If acquired shareholders exchange stock in the acquired company for stock in the acquiring company, they have simply readjusted the form of their equity holdings. They have continued an investment rather than liquidating one, and the response of the tax system is to adjust their basis to reflect the transaction but postpone tax liability until they have more tangible gain or loss.

To ensure that the tax treatment of acquisitive reorganizations corresponds to the rationale that justifies it, the courts have engrafted a "continuity of interest" requirement onto the Code's provisions. That test examines the acquired shareholders' proprietary interest before and after the reorganization to see if "the acquired shareholders' investment remains sufficiently 'at risk' after the merger to justify the nonrecognition tax treatment," 76 T.C. at 997.

The taxpayers, the Commissioner, and the Tax Court all agree that the Garb-Stern group holdings were acquired by statutory merger. They also agree that the "continuity of interest" test is determinative of the tax treatment of the transaction of which the statutory merger was a part. But the taxpayers on the one hand, and the Commissioner and the Tax Court on the other, part company over how the test is to be applied, and what result it should have produced. In affirming the Commissioner, the Tax Court recognized that the Garb-Stern group had a settled and firm determination to sell their McDonald's shares at the first possible opportunity rather than continue as investors, 76 T.C. at 989. It nonetheless concluded that because the Garb-Stern group was not contractually bound to sell, the merger and the sale could be treated as entirely separate transactions and the continuity-of-interest test applied in the narrow time-frame of the April transaction only. Thus tested, the transaction was in Judge Hall's view a nontaxable reorganization, and the taxpayer subsidiaries were therefore saddled with the Garb-Stern group's basis in taking depreciation and amortization deductions. The taxpayers by contrast argue that the step-transaction doctrine should have been applied to treat the April merger and stock transfer and the October sale as one taxable transaction. . . .

THE STEP-TRANSACTION DOCTRINE

The step-transaction doctrine is a particular manifestation of the more general tax law principle that purely formal distinctions cannot obscure the substance of a transaction. See e.g., Redding v. Commissioner, 630 F.2d 1169, 1175 (7th Cir. 1980), certiorari denied, 450 U.S. 913. As our Court there noted:

> The commentators have attempted to synthesize from judicial decisions several tests to determine whether the step transaction doctrine is applicable to a particular set of circumstances. . . . Unfortunately, these tests are notably abstruse — even for such an abstruse field as tax law.

Nonetheless, under any of the tests devised — including the intermediate one nominally adopted by the Tax Court and the most restrictive one actually applied in its decision — the transactions here would be stepped together. For example, under the "end result test," "purportedly separate transactions will be amalgamated with a single transaction when it appears that they were really component parts of a single transaction intended from the outset to be taken for the purpose of reaching the ultimate result." Here there can be little doubt that all the steps were taken to cash out the Garb-Stern group, although McDonald's sought to do so in a way that would enable it to use certain accounting procedures. Admittedly, not every transaction would be as pellucid as this one, but here the history of the parties' relationships, the abortive attempt to buy some of the group's holdings, the final comprehensive deal, and the Garb-Stern group's determination to sell out even in the face of falling prices in the stock[12] all are consistent and probative.

A second test is the "interdependence" test, which focuses on whether "the steps are so interdependent that the legal relations created by one transaction would have been fruitless without a completion of the series." This is the test the Tax Court purported to apply, 76 T.C. at 997-999, although its version of the test is indistinguishable from yet another formulation, the "binding commitment" test. That is, the Tax Court would have found interdependence only if the Garb-Stern group had itself been legally bound to sell its stock. In fact, the "interdependence" test is more practical and less legalistic than that. It concentrates on the relationship between the steps, rather than on the "end result." . . . Here it would ask whether the merger would have taken place without the guarantees of saleability, and the answer is certainly no. The Garb-Stern group's insistence on this point is demonstrated both by its historic stance in these negotiations and by the hammered-out terms of the agreement. Although the Tax Court emphasized the permissive terms about "piggyback" registration, it glossed over the Garb-Stern group's one-time right to force registration — and hence sale — under the agreement. The very detail of the provisions about how McDonald's would ensure free transferability of the Garb-Stern group's McDonald's stock shows that they were the quid pro quo of the merger agreement.

Finally the "binding commitment" test most restricts the application of the step-transaction doctrine, and is the test the Tax Court actually applied, despite its statements otherwise. The "binding commitment" test forbids use of the step-transaction doctrine unless "if one transaction is to be characterized as a 'first step' there [is] a binding commitment to take the later steps." The Tax Court found the test unsatisfied because the Garb-Stern group was not legally obliged to sell its McDonald's stock. We think it misconceived the purpose of the test and misapplied it to the facts of this case.

In the first place, the "binding commitment" test is the most rigorous limitation on the step-transaction doctrine because it was formulated to deal with the characterization of a transaction that in fact spanned several tax years and could have remained "not only indeterminable but unfixed

---

12. As indicated by their participation in the proposed "piggyback" registration scheduled for June 1973. The decision to postpone registration because of adverse publicity and a fall in the price of McDonald's shares was entirely McDonald's. . . .

for an indefinite and unlimited period in the future, awaiting events that might or might not happen." . . . By contrast this transaction was complete in six months and fell entirely within a single tax year. . . .

In the second place, the Tax Court underestimated the extent to which the parties were bound to take the later steps. The registration and underwriting provisions in the parties' agreement did not just enhance saleability; they were essential to it. Unless and until McDonald's registered the stock, it was essentially untransferable. . . . Second, although McDonald's had the choice of when during the first year after the merger it would seek registration, if it did nothing the Garb-Stern group could make a legally enforceable demand for registration in either year two or year three. On the other hand, if McDonald's did register stock during the first year but the Garb-Stern group chose not to "piggyback," the group's demand registration rights would be lost. These limitations made it extremely likely that the sale would — as it did — take place promptly. They are enough to satisfy the spirit, if not the letter, of the "binding commitment" test.

Under any of the three applicable criteria, then, the merger and subsequent sale should have been stepped together. Substance over form is the key. . . . Had the Tax Court taken a pragmatic view of the actions of the Garb-Stern group, it would have found that they clearly failed to satisfy the continuity-of-interest requirement that has been engrafted onto the Code provisions governing nonrecognition treatment for acquisitive reorganizations.

STATUTORY MERGER PRECEDENTS

Quite apart from the proper application of the step-transaction doctrine, the available precedents dealing with statutory mergers and the effect of post-merger sales by acquired shareholders — though scanty — strongly support the taxpayers. No case supports the myopic position adopted below that although "the crux of the continuity-of-interest test lies in the continuation of the acquired shareholders' proprietary interest" (76 T.C. at 997), the test *"by itself does not require any length of postmerger retention"* (id.) (emphasis supplied).

The taxpayers rely on, and the Tax Court was unsuccessful in distinguishing, Heintz v. Commissioner, 25 T.C. 132 (1955). The *Heintz* case differs from this case only in focusing on the tax liability of the acquired shareholders rather than the acquiring corporation. The facts of the case, somewhat simplified, are as follows.

Heintz and Jack (taxpayers) formed a company (Jack & Heintz, Inc.) to manufacture arms and ammunition during World War II. At the war's end, they determined to sell it rather than try to reorganize its production for peacetime. The buyer was the Precision Corporation, which had been formed to acquire Jack & Heintz. On March 5, 1946, Precision acquired almost all the outstanding shares of Jack & Heintz from the taxpayers for $5 million cash and 50,000 preferred shares of Precision, with a par value of $50 each. On March 6 Precision merged its newly acquired subsidiary with itself. At the time the deal was being negotiated, two of the parties representing the buyer assured the taxpayers that the Precision shares they had received as part payment would be sold in a public offering planned for thirty days after the merger (25 T.C. at 135), but this promise was nowhere reflected in the thirty-five page written agreement covering the whole transaction (id. at 137). Owing to unforeseen delays, the contemplated registration and sale did not take place, but the buyers helped arrange a private sale at $30 per share in August 1946. In their 1946 returns, the taxpayers reported long-term capital gain computed on a figure arrived at by deducting from the sale proceeds ($5 million in cash + $2,500,000 worth of Precision stock) their $112,000 basis in the Jack & Heintz stock. They also reported short-term capital losses of $1 million on the August private sale of the Precision stock.

The Commissioner assessed deficiencies, using exactly the reasoning the Tax Court has adopted in McDonald's case. He treated the transaction as a statutory reorganization, which had no immediate tax consequences (except that the cash component of the price was ordinary income). He then gave the taxpayers a carryover basis of $112,000, rather than a cost basis, in the Precision stock. Finally he treated the August sale as producing sizable capital gains ($1,500,000 less $112,000) rather than capital losses. Although the Commissioner's position is sketchily presented in the Tax Court's opinion, his treatment must have involved a conviction that neither the promise to sell the Precision stock nor the actual sale changed the character of the reorganization. . . .

As in the present case, the taxpayers' wishes to sell were clear and the transaction was designed to accommodate them. As in the present case, the acquiring corporation's promise was to facilitate the sale, not to guarantee it. As in the present case, the acquiring corporation did not require a reciprocal commitment from the acquired shareholders — for all that appears, Heintz and Jack were free to retain their equity interest in Precision. As in the present case, these understandings of the parties were not reflected in the written agreement. There is no principled way to distinguish the two cases, and the Tax Court's efforts to do so here (76 T.C. at 1001) are unsuccessful. . . .

ADDITIONAL CONSIDERATIONS

[T]he Commissioner's treatment of the McDonald's transaction — as affirmed by the Tax Court — seems opportunistic. [T]he Garb-Stern group has already been fully taxed because of its relatively prompt disposition; the Internal Revenue Service has had all the benefits of sale treatment on that end of the transaction. . . . Now the Service seeks to saddle the taxpayers with the disadvantageously low basis that goes with the "reorganization" label. On the other hand, . . . if the Garb-Stern group's basis had been higher than the fair market price of the McDonald's shares exchanged, the Commissioner could, consistently with his prior positions, have refused reorganization status and forced the taxpayers to accept a lower, cost basis for depreciation and amortization purposes. This is heads-I-win, tails-you-lose law.

If . . . the treatment here represents a considered change in the Service's treatment of reorganizations, then the Commission's victory in the Tax Court was pyrrhic and he should welcome reversal. The Tax Court's decision was barely six months old before tax planners were publicizing the possibilities for manipulating it. . . . The key to all of them is the extraordinary rigidity of the "binding commitment" test and the ephemeral continuity of interest the Tax Court seems to require. The decisions appealed from are reversed, with instructions to enter fresh decisions in the taxpayers' favor.

NOTE

1. *Continuity of proprietary interest.* The focus of the controversy in *Paulsen* is the venerable "continuity of proprietary interest doctrine," a doctrine that goes back more than 50 years. In Pinellas Ice & Cold Storage Co. v. Commissioner, 287 U.S. 462 (1933), the seller corporations, in exchange for their assets, received cash plus well-secured promissory notes payable in less than four months. The Supreme Court, holding that the transaction constituted a taxable sale rather than a tax-free reorganization, wrote: "Certainly, we think that to be within the [definition of a reorganization] the seller must acquire an interest in the affairs of the purchasing company more definite than that incident to ownership of its short-term purchase-money notes." 287 U.S. at 470.

Two years later, in Helvering v. Minnesota Tea Co., 296 U.S. 378 (1935), the Court upheld the tax-free status of a transfer by a corporation of substantially all its assets for voting trust certificates (worth about $540,000) representing 18,000 shares of common stock of another corporation as well as about $425,000 in cash. The 18,000 shares represented about 7½ percent of the outstanding stock of the transferee, a publicly held corporation. This substantial reduction in the transferor's control over the transferred assets caused the Board of Tax Appeals to deny reorganization treatment to the transaction. In coming to the opposite conclusion, the Supreme Court restated the rule of *Pinellas* and then wrote:

True it is that the relationship of the taxpayer to the assets conveyed was substantially changed, but this is not inhibited by the statute. Also, a large

part of the consideration was cash. This, we think, is permissible so long
as the taxpayer received an interest in the affairs of the transferee which
represented a material part of the value of the transferred assets.

296 U.S. at 386.

Minnesota Tea left open the questions (1) what constitutes an "interest
in the affairs of the transferee" and (2) how much of such an interest is
a "material part" of the value transferred. The first of these two questions
was answered in large part by John A. Nelson & Co. v. Helvering, 296 U.S.
374 (1935), and LeTulle v. Scofield, 308 U.S. 415 (1940).

In *LeTulle,* all the assets of a corporation were conveyed for $50,000
in cash plus $750,000 in bonds of the transferee payable serially over 11
years. The Supreme Court characterized the transaction as a sale, holding
that "[w]here the consideration is wholly in the transferee's bonds, or part
cash and part such bonds, we think it cannot be said that the transferor
retains any proprietary interest in the enterprise." 308 U.S. at 420-421. In
John A. Nelson & Co., however, the Court upheld the reorganization treatment of a transfer by a corporation of substantially all its assets for
$2 million plus nonvoting preferred stock of the transferee worth about
$1.25 million. The preferred stock was redeemable as well as nonvoting,
but the Court held that the statute had no requirement of participation
by the transferor in the transferee's management.

The line of cases from *Pinellas* through *LeTulle* stands for the proposition that if a transaction is to qualify as a "reorganization," the transferor
must receive some stock (a "material part") of the transferee in the exchange. Does this rule make sense? Is the distinction between nonvoting
preferred stock and subordinated debt sufficiently important to warrant
so great an emphasis? Compare Roebling v. Commissioner, 143 F.2d 810
(3d Cir. 1944), involving a corporation whose assets had been leased to a
second corporation on a 900-year lease calling for annual rent of $480,000.
The lessor corporation was merged into the lessee, and the shareholders
of the lessor exchanged their stock for 100-year bonds of the lessee paying
in aggregate $480,000 per year of interest. The exchanging shareholders
argued that their relationship to the underlying assets was no more distant
under the 100-year bonds than it had been under the 900-year lease, but
the court, relying on *LeTulle* and related cases, held that no reorganization
occurred.

Is the Supreme Court's opinion in *Paulsen* consistent with *Roebling?* If
the continuity of proprietary interest doctrine speaks only to the form of
consideration *received* in the exchange, then how can it be that the Supreme
Court is willing to sanction the tax-free merger of a mutual savings and
loan into a mutual savings and loan while refusing the same tax treatment
to a stock savings and loan merging into a mutual savings and loan? For
a thoughtful criticism of the continuity of proprietary interest doctrine,
ending with the suggestion that the doctrine be eliminated, see Wolfman,

"Continuity of Interest" and the American Law Institute Study, 57 Taxes 840 (1979).

For ruling purposes, Rev. Proc. 77-37, 1977-2 C.B. 568, sets forth the IRS position on the continuity of interest requirement. According to the revenue procedure, a favorable ruling may be obtained if 50 percent of the value received in a merger (or consolidation) is in the form of an equity interest in the acquiring corporation. There is no requirement that each shareholder receive at least 50 percent equity or even that a substantial percentage of shareholders not receive only cash. See Rev. Rul. 66-224, 1966-2 C.B. 114, in which two 25 percent shareholders were cashed out while the other two 25 percent shareholders received stock of the acquiring corporation. Held, the continuity of proprietary interest requirement was satisfied. See also Reilly Oil Co. v. Commissioner, 189 F.2d 382 (5th Cir. 1951) (31 percent of transferor's shareholders elected to receive cash). Of course, shareholders receiving cash or other boot in the reorganization will recognize some of their gain, if any, on the transaction under §356.

While a shareholder receiving cash will be taxed even though the reorganization as a whole meets the continuity of proprietary interest test, if the transaction fails that test, all shareholders (including those receiving only stock) lose the benefit of tax-free treatment. How is it that Kass is taxed on the merger of ACRA into TRACK when she exchanged her stock of the transferee corporation for nothing but stock of the acquiring corporation? The court in *Kass* ended its opinion with the observation that Kass was "not any worse off than her fellow shareholders who sold their stock." While that observation is true, it fails to recognize the injustice that has been worked on Kass: The other shareholders were appropriately taxed to the extent that they cashed out, but Kass did nothing but continue her corporate investment in equity form and so should be entitled to nonrecognition on the exchange.

What does *McDonald's* add to the continuity of proprietary interest doctrine? To qualify a merger as a tax-free reorganization under §368(a)(1)(A), must a taxpayer be able to prove how many of the transferor's shareholders retained their acquiring corporation stock for a lengthy period? For how long? If the acquiring corporation is publicly held and traded over an exchange, is such a showing possible? Recall that it was the government in *McDonald's* that sought to characterize the transaction as a reorganization. Should that have influenced the court? Note that because the Garb-Stern group sold its McDonald's stock after the acquisition, the government would have collected its tax on the shareholders' gain even if the reorganization status had been maintained. All that really was at issue in *McDonald's* was McDonald's basis in the acquired, appreciated assets; to keep that basis low, the government argued for reorganization status and the carryover basis rule of §362(b).

In each of these cases, the issue before the court was whether a transaction meeting all the statutory requirements of a "reorganization" should nevertheless be taxed as a sale. Given the precision of the definitions in §368, should the courts ask for more? Treas. Regs. §1.368-1(b) states:

> In order to exclude transactions not intended to be included, the specifications of the reorganization provisions of the law are precise. Both the terms of the specifications and their underlying assumptions and purposes must be satisfied in order to entitle the taxpayer to the benefit of the exception from the general rule.

Try to identify these "underlying assumptions and purposes." Can they be articulated with sufficient clarity to guide a court through the maze of §368?

If the thrust of the continuity of proprietary interest doctrine is to distinguish sales from mere changes in form, how should the merger of a closely held corporation into a publicly held corporation be characterized? Is the transfer a sale in substance if the transferor gets stock of a national corporation representing a relatively minor, marketable interest in an enterprise whose financial stability is almost totally independent of the newly acquired assets? In any event, can transactions of this type be effectively differentiated for tax purposes from the combination of two enterprises of approximately equal size when the formerly independent proprietors have a substantial stake in their old assets?

2. *Continuity of business enterprise.* Since the rationale for tax-free treatment of a reorganization is that the transaction is best viewed as a mere change in form of the business enterprise, can a corporate acquisition be tax free if the acquiring corporation does not continue the historic business of the acquired corporation? The Service argued against tax-free treatment in such circumstances, although the courts regularly rejected the Service's position. See, e.g., Bentsen v. Phinney, 199 F. Supp. 363 (S.D. Tex. 1961), in which the court determined that the doctrine of business continuity requires only that the assets of the acquired corporation be used in *some* business after the transaction. In Rev. Rul. 63-29, 1963-1 C.B. 77, the Service acquiesced in the reasoning of cases like *Bentsen,* holding that the amalgamation of a toy company and a steel company into a single corporation could qualify as a reorganization. The regulations, however, perpetuate the business continuity doctrine, requiring that the acquiring corporation either continue the historic business of the acquired corporation or use a "significant portion" of the acquired corporation's assets in a business. Treas. Regs. §1.368-1(d).

Note that no similar restriction binds the use of the acquiring corporation's assets. Rev. Rul. 81-25, 1981 C.B. 65. In considering the business continuity doctrine, you should recognize that labeling one corporation as the "acquiring" corporation and another as the "acquired" corporation usually is a matter of indifference. For example, if *A* Corp. and *B* Corp. merge, the decision whether to make *A* Corp. or *B* Corp. the survivor often will turn on such factors as which corporation has more goodwill associated with its name or whether either corporation owns an asset (such as a favorable long-term lease) that is difficult to transfer. Should the business continuity doctrine focus only on the continued use of the *acquired corporation's* assets when the reorganization involves a minnow swallowing a shark?

What are the tax consequences if the acquired corporation sells its historic assets prior to and in anticipation of the reorganization? See Rev. Rul. 87-76, 1987-2 C.B. 84 (no continuity of business enterprise). In Rev. Rul. 88-25, 1988-1 C.B. 803, however, the Service ruled that if a corporation having two businesses sold one for cash and transferred its remaining assets (plus the cash) for voting stock of an unrelated corporation, the transaction would qualify as a C reorganization. The Service emphasized that, because the first business was sold to an unrelated party and the proceeds were transferred as part of the C reorganization, the transaction was not divisive in nature.

3. *Business purpose.* The doctrines of continuity of proprietary interest and continuity of business enterprise were developed by the courts to deny tax-free reorganization status to transactions that closely resembled sales. Similarly, the business purpose doctrine was developed early on to deny tax-free status to transactions that meet all the formal requirements of a "reorganization" but lack a valid business purpose for the machinations. For example, in 1928 Gregory owned all the outstanding shares of the United Mortgage Corporation (UMC Corp.), which in turn owned 1,000 appreciated shares of the Monitor Securities Corporation. Gregory sought to effect a sale of the Monitor shares at a tax cost of only a capital gain tax at the shareholder level.

Had UMC Corp. distributed the Monitor shares to Gregory as a simple dividend, she would have recognized ordinary income on the distribution because UMC Corp. had adequate earnings and profits. (UMC Corp. would have recognized no gain on the distribution because in 1928 the Code contained no provision similar to §311(b).) To avoid this ordinary income, Gregory adopted the following strategy.

First, Gregory had UMC Corp. form a new corporation, Averill Corp., by transferring the Monitor shares to Averill in exchange for all the Averill stock. The Averill stock was then immediately distributed to Gregory from UMC Corp. Finally, within one week, the newly formed Averill Corp. was liquidated and the Monitor shares were distributed to Gregory in complete liquidation of Averill.

The reorganization statute at the time provided that a "reorganization" included "a transfer by a corporation of all or a part of its assets to another corporation if immediately after the transferor or its stockholders or both are in control of the corporation to which the assets are transferred." Accordingly, the formation of Averill Corp. met the formal requirements of a "reorganization." In addition, the statute provided that a distribution "in pursuance of a plan of reorganization, to a shareholder in a corporation a party to a reorganization, [of] stock or securities in such corporation or in another corporation a party to the reorganization, without the surrender by such shareholder of stock or securities in such corporation, [results in] no gain to the distributee from the receipt of such stock or securities." Thus, Gregory received the stock of Averill without tax. The final step in the plan, the complete liquidation of Averill, was taxable to Gregory, but since she was taxed at capital gain rates on the property distributed in complete liquidation, she had obtained her goal of stepping up the basis in the Monitor shares to fair market value at the cost of a single, capital gain tax. Gregory was then able to sell the Monitor shares to a third party without realizing or recognizing further gain.

In one of the most famous opinions in the tax law, Gregory v. Helvering, 293 U.S. 465 (1935), the Supreme Court denied reorganization status to the transaction:

> [T]he facts speak for themselves and are susceptible of but one interpretation. The whole undertaking, though conducted according to the terms of the [statute], was in fact an elaborate and devious form of conveyance masquerading as a corporate reorganization, and nothing else. The rule which excludes from consideration the motive of tax avoidance is not pertinent to the situation, because the transaction upon its face lies outside the plain intent of the statute. To hold otherwise would be to exalt artifice above reality and to deprive the statutory provision in question of all serious purpose.

Judge Learned Hand, author of the circuit court opinion in the *Gregory* case also denying reorganization status to the transaction, shortly thereafter wrote of the case:

> In Gregory v. Helvering . . . , the incorporators adopted the usual form of creating corporations; but their intent, or purpose, was merely to draught the papers, in fact not to create corporations as the court understood that word. That was the purpose which defeated their exemption, not the accompanying purpose to escape taxation; that purpose was legally neutral. Had they really meant to conduct a business by means of the two reorganized companies, they would have escaped whatever other aim they may have had, whether to avoid taxes, or to regenerate the world.

Chisolm v. Commissioner, 79 F.2d 14, 15 (2d Cir. 1935).

Line drawing and analysis in this area are difficult. Compare Judge Hand's later comments:

> The doctrine of Gregory v. Helvering . . . means that in construing words of a tax statute which describes commercial or industrial transactions we are to understand them to refer to transactions entered upon for commercial or industrial purposes and not to include transactions entered upon for no other motive but to escape taxation.

Commissioner v. Transport Trading & Terminal Corp., 176 F.2d 570, 572 (2d Cir. 1949).

While *Gregory* involved a divisive corporate reorganization, the business purpose doctrine can play an important role in acquisitive reorganizations as well. For an example of the interplay among the business purpose doctrine, the divisive reorganization provisions, and the acquisitive reorganization provisions, see Helvering v. Elkhorn Coal Co., 95 F.2d 732 (4th Cir. 1937). In *Elkhorn* the taxpayer transferred some of its assets to a newly formed subsidiary, and the subsidiary's stock was then distributed to the taxpayer's shareholders, much as in *Gregory*. By itself, such a transaction qualified as a tax-free divisive D reorganization. Then, however, the taxpayer transferred its remaining assets to an unrelated corporation in exchange for voting stock of this company, a transaction that, standing on its own, would constitute an acquisitive C reorganization. Finally, the taxpayer completely liquidated, distributing the stock of the acquiring corporation. (At the time, the subsequent liquidation was not required as part of the C reorganization. Under current §368(a)(2)(G), the liquidation of the transferor corporation is mandatory.)

The statute then provided, as it does now, that a corporation must transfer "substantially all" its properties to qualify as a C reorganization. By spinning off part of its assets to a newly formed corporation immediately prior to the nominal C reorganization, the taxpayer effectively circumvented the "substantially all" requirement. Since the creation of the subsidiary had no purpose other than to qualify the transaction as a tax-free reorganization, the transaction as a whole lacked the proper "spirit." Accordingly, the taxpayer's transfer of its assets to the acquiring corporation in exchange for voting stock of the acquirer, as well as the subsequent complete liquidation, was held to be a taxable event.

B. DEFINITIONAL ISSUES

As *Kass* demonstrates, whether a corporate rearrangement qualifies as a statutory "reorganization" is determined on the basis of the transaction as a whole rather than taxpayer by taxpayer. It therefore makes sense to ask whether a particular transaction fits within one of the specific reorganization definitions before considering the tax consequences of the transaction to any party. If you can conclude that a statutory reorganization has occurred, then you must determine the parties' tax consequences by looking first to sections such as §354 that explicitly provide for the tax treatment of exchanges incident to a reorganization. If you conclude that a transaction does not fall within any of the reorganization provisions, then the tax consequences of the transaction will be determined by reference to Code provisions applicable independent of the reorganization provisions. Do not assume that a transaction failing to qualify as a reorganization is necessarily taxable in full. For example, a failed reorganization may be a nontaxable liquidation under §332 or, as is often the case, the failed reorganization may contain within it a transaction protected from immediate taxation by §351. As a last warning, be sure to consider *all* the reorganization provisions before labeling a transaction as failing to qualify for reorganization treatment, for failure to qualify under one provision does not preclude qualification under other provisions. See page 455 infra.

Section 368(a) provides the definitions for the seven types of tax-free reorganizations. Reorganizations falling under §368(a)(1)(A), (B), (C), and some under (D) are acquisitive reorganizations used to combine two or more enterprises. Each type of reorganization has somewhat different criteria, and the form will determine which type has been sought or effected. There is some overlap among the various types, and aside from §368(a)(2)(A) providing that a reorganization qualifying as both a C and a D be taxed as a D, the Code does not determine which type takes priority. No rule of priority is needed, though, since the applicable taxing provisions generally do not distinguish the various types of reorganizations.

The choice of the proper type of reorganization is often governed by important nontax factors. For example, because of contingent liabilities of the transferor corporation, the acquiring corporation may prefer a C to an A or B; preservation of certain rights or licenses of the acquired corporation may require using a B; state and federal securities law requirements may vary depending on the form chosen; shareholder approval of both the transferor and the acquiring corporation are usually required in an A — expensive and time-consuming procedures in the case of publicly held corporations — whereas only approval by shareholders of the transferor may be required in a B or C; appraisal rights for dissenters are more easily awarded in a B than in an A or C. As the various criteria for the different types of reorganizations are examined, keep in mind that the underlying purpose of the criteria in any reorganization should be to separate a nonrecognition change in form from a taxable sale or exchange.

1. The A Reorganization: Statutory Mergers and Consolidations

In an A merger, shareholders of the transferor(s) exchange their stock for stock or debt of the acquiring corporation. In addition, they may receive cash or other property in the exchange. The statutory definition of an A reorganization does not limit the type of consideration that may be used, and in this sense the A reorganization provides the greatest flexibility of all the reorganization forms. The judicially created continuity of proprietary interest doctrine does, however, apply to A reorganizations, so a statutory merger or consolidation will fail to qualify as a reorganization under

§368(a)(1) unless stock of the acquiring corporation constitutes a "material and substantial part" of the consideration.

2. The B Reorganization: Stock for Stock

In a B reorganization, the acquiring corporation acquires stock of the target corporation, thereby making the target a controlled (but not necessarily wholly owned) subsidiary of the acquiring corporation. In a B reorganization, the sole consideration that can be used by the acquiring corporation is its voting stock (or the voting stock of its parent). The voting stock may be common, preferred, or a combination of the two, but voting stock of the acquiring corporation cannot be combined with voting stock of the acquiring corporation's parent. See Treas. Regs. §1.368-2(c). Because of the statutory requirement limiting consideration in a B to voting stock, the continuity of proprietary interest doctrine is automatically satisfied.

The acquiring corporation must have control, as defined in §368(c) (that is, 80 percent of the total combined voting power plus at least 80 percent of the total number of shares of all other classes) of the target corporation after the exchange. Such control need not be obtained in one transaction. For example, if 30 percent is obtained in one transaction and 51 percent in a second transaction, the second exchange is a B reorganization; the first transaction, however, if independent of the second, is not a B. See Treas. Regs. §1.368-2(c). In addition to this "creeping acquisition" of control, an increase in ownership by a corporation that already has actual 80 percent control can qualify as a B reorganization.

The main obstacle to a B reorganization is that any boot will destroy the transaction. See, however, Rev. Rul. 77-271, 1977-2 C.B. 116, in which a taxpayer exchanged stock of the target company for voting stock of equal market value of the acquiring company and, as part of the agreement, entered into an employment contract in exchange for additional shares of the acquiring corporation. The transaction was treated as a valid stock-for-stock exchange qualifying as a valid B followed by a stock-for-employment contract taxed as compensation income. A contract for fair cash salary for services to be rendered also is not treated as boot.

Although the acquiring corporation in a B reorganization must use only voting stock as consideration for the stock of the target corporation, no similar limitation is placed on the acquiring corporation's ability to acquire nonstock interests in the target corporation (such as debt instruments and stock options). See Rev. Rul. 70-269, 1970-1 C.B. 82 (stock options); Rev. Rul. 70-41, 1970-1 C.B. 77 (debt securities); Rev. Rul. 69-91, 1969-1 C.B. 106 (convertible debentures). Such nonstock purchases, though, are not part of the B reorganization and therefore are taxable transactions. See, e.g., Rev. Rul. 70-41, supra; Fisher v. Commissioner, 62 T.C. 73 (1974).

Payment by the acquiring corporation of the target corporation's share of reorganization expenses (such as legal, accounting, appraisal, printing, and registration fees) is not treated as boot in a B reorganization. At the same time, similar expenses of the target shareholders may not be paid by the acquiring corporation without disqualifying the transaction as a B. Rev. Rul. 73-54, 1973-1 C.B. 187.

Chapman v. Commissioner _____
618 F.2d 856 (1st Cir. 1980)

Before Coffin, Chief Judge, Campbell and Bownes, Circuit Judges.

LEVIN H. CAMPBELL, Circuit Judge. . . .

We must decide whether the requirement of Section 368(a)(1)(B) that the acquisition of stock in one corporation by another be solely in exchange for voting stock of the acquiring corporation is met where, in related transactions, the acquiring corporation first acquires 8 percent of the acquiree's stock for cash and then acquires more than 80 percent of the acquiree in an exchange of stock for voting stock. The Tax Court agreed with the taxpayers that the latter exchange constituted a valid tax-free reorganization. Reeves v. Commissioner, 71 T.C. 727 (1979). . . .

The events giving rise to this dispute began in 1968, when the management of ITT, a large multinational corporation, became interested in acquiring Hartford [Fire Insurance Company] as part of a program of diversification. In October 1968, ITT executives approached Hartford about the possibility of merging the two corporations. This proposal was spurned by Hartford, which at the time was considering acquisitions of its own. In November 1968, ITT learned that approximately 1.3 million shares of Hartford, representing some 6 percent of Hartford's voting stock, were available for purchase from a mutual fund. After assuring Hartford's directors that ITT would not attempt to acquire Hartford against its will, ITT consummated the $63.7 million purchase from the mutual fund with Hartford's blessing. From November 13, 1968 to January 10, 1969, ITT also made a series of purchases on the open market totalling 458,000 shares which it acquired for approximately $24.4 million. A further purchase of 400 shares from an ITT subsidiary in March 1969 brought ITT's holdings to about 8 percent of Hartford's outstanding stock, all of which had been bought for cash.

In the midst of this flurry of stock-buying, ITT submitted a written proposal to the Hartford Board of Directors for the merger of Hartford into an ITT subsidiary. . . . Received by Hartford in December of 1968, the proposal was rejected in February of 1969. A counterproposal by Hartford's directors led to further negotiations, and on April 9, 1969 a provisional plan and agreement of merger was executed by the two corporations. . . .

Concluding that the entire transaction [did not constitute] a nontaxable reorganization, the Service assessed tax deficiencies against a number of former Hartford shareholders who had accepted the exchange offer. Appellees, along with other taxpayers, contested this action in the Tax Court, where the case was decided on appellees' motion for summary judgment. For purposes of this motion, the taxpayers conceded . . . that the initial cash purchases of Hartford stock had been made for the purpose of furthering ITT's efforts to acquire Hartford. . . .

I

The single issue raised on this appeal is whether "the acquisition" in this case complied with the requirement [of a B reorganization] that it be "solely for . . . voting stock." It is well settled that the "solely" requirement is mandatory; if any part of "the acquisition" includes a form of consideration other than voting stock, the transaction will not qualify as a (B) reorganization. See Helvering v. Southwest Consolidated Corp., 315 U.S. 194, 198 (1942) (" 'Solely' leaves no leeway. Voting stock plus some other consideration does not meet the statutory requirement"). The precise issue before us is thus how broadly to read the term "acquisition." The Internal Revenue Service argues that "the acquisition . . . of stock of another corporation" must be understood to encompass the 1968-69 cash purchases as well as the 1970 exchange offer. If the IRS is correct, "the acquisition" here fails as a (B) reorganization. The taxpayers, on the other hand, would limit "the acquisition" to the part of a sequential transaction of this nature which meets the requirements of subsection (B). They argue that the 1970 exchange of stock for stock was itself an "acquisition" by ITT of stock in Hartford solely in exchange for ITT's voting stock, such that after the exchange took place ITT controlled Hartford. Taxpayers contend that the earlier cash purchases of 8 percent, even if conceded to be part of the same acquisitive plan, are essentially irrelevant to the tax-free reorganization otherwise effected.

The Tax Court accepted the taxpayers' reading of the statute, effectively overruling its own prior decision in Howard v. Commissioner, 24 T.C. 792 (1955), rev'd on other grounds, 238 F.2d 943 (7th Cir. 1956). The plurality opinion stated its "narrow" holding as follows:

> We hold that where, as is the case herein, 80 percent or more of the stock of a corporation is acquired in one transaction, in exchange for which only voting stock is furnished as consideration, the "solely for voting stock" requirement of section 368(a)(1)(B) is satisfied.

. . . The plurality treated as "irrelevant" the 8 percent of Hartford's stock purchased for cash, although the opinion left somewhat ambiguous the question whether the 8 percent was irrelevant because of the 14-month time interval separating the transactions or because the statute was not concerned with transactions over and above those mathematically necessary to the acquiring corporation's attainment of control.

II

For reasons set forth extensively in section III of this opinion, we do not accept the position adopted by the Tax Court. . . . As explained below, we find a strong implication in the language of the statute, in the legislative history, in the regulations, and in the decisions of other courts that cash purchases which are concededly "parts of" a stock-for-stock exchange must be considered constituent elements of the "acquisition" for purposes of applying the "solely for . . . voting stock" requirement of Section 368(a)(1)(B). We believe the presence of nonstock consideration in such an acquisition, regardless of whether such consideration is necessary to the gaining of control, is inconsistent with treatment of the acquisition as a nontaxable reorganization. . . .

III

A . . .

We begin with the words of the statute itself. The reorganization definitions contained in Section 368(a)(1) are precise, technical, and comprehensive. They were intended to define the exclusive means by which nontaxable corporate reorganizations could be effected. See Treas. Reg. §1.368-1 (1960); 3 J. Mertens, The Law of Federal Income Taxation §20.86 at 364 (1972). In examining the language of the (B) provision, we discern two possible meanings. On the one hand, the statute could be read to say that a successful reorganization occurs whenever Corporation X exchanges its own voting stock for stock in Corporation Y, and, immediately after the transaction, Corporation X controls more than 80 percent of Y's stock. On this reading, purchases of shares for which any part of the consideration takes the form of "boot" should be ignored, since the definition is only concerned with transactions which meet the statutory requirements as to consideration and control. To take an example, if Corporation X bought 50 percent of the shares of Y, and then almost immediately exchanged part of its voting stock for the remaining 50 percent of Y's stock, the question would arise whether the second transaction was a (B) reorganization. Arguably, the statute can be read to support such a finding. In the second transaction, X exchanged only stock for stock (meeting the "solely" requirement), and after the transaction was completed X owned Y (meeting the "control" requirement).

The alternative reading of the statute — the one which we are persuaded to adopt — treats the (B) definition as prescriptive, rather than merely descriptive. We read the statute to mean that the entire transaction which constitutes "the acquisition" must not contain any nonstock consideration if the transaction is to qualify as a (B) reorganization. In the example given above, where X acquired 100 percent of Y's stock, half for cash and half for voting stock, we would interpret "the acquisition" as referring to the entire transaction, so that the "solely for . . . voting stock" requirement would not be met. We believe if Congress had intended the statute to be read as merely descriptive, this intent would have been more clearly spelled out in the statutory language.

We recognize that the Tax Court adopted neither of these two readings. For reasons to be discussed in connection with the legislative history which follows, the Tax Court purported to limit its holding to cases, such as this one, where more than 80 percent of the stock of Corporation Y passes to Corporation X in exchange solely for voting stock. The Tax Court presumably would assert that the 50/50 hypothetical posited above can be distinguished from this case, and that its holding implies no view as to the hypothetical. . . . In order to distinguish the 80 percent case from the 50 percent case, it is necessary to read "the acquisition" as referring to at least the amount of stock constituting "control" (80 percent) where related cash purchases are present. Yet the Tax Court recognized that "the acquisition" cannot always refer to the conveyance of an 80 percent bloc of stock in one transaction, since to do so would frustrate the intent of the 1954 amendments to permit so-called "creeping acquisitions."

The Tax Court's interpretation of the statute suffers from a more fundamental defect, as well. In order to justify the limitation of its holding to transactions involving 80 percent or more of the acquiree's stock, the Tax Court focused on the *passage* of control as the primary requirement of the (B) provision. This focus is misplaced. Under the present version of the statute, the *passage* of control is entirely irrelevant; the only material requirement is that the acquiring corporation have control immediately after the acquisition. As the statute explicitly states, it does not matter if the acquiring corporation already has control before the transaction begins, so long as such control exists at the completion of the reorganization. Whatever talismanic quality may have attached to the acquisition of control under previous versions of the Code, see Part III B infra, is altogether absent from the version we must apply to this case. In our view, the statute should be read to mean that the related transactions that constitute "the acquisition," whatever percentage of stock they may represent, must meet both the "solely for voting stock" and the "control immediately after" requirements of Section 368(a)(1)(B). Neither the reading given the statute by the Tax Court, nor that proposed as the first alternative above, adequately corresponds to the careful language Congress employed in this section of the Code.

B

The 1924 Code defined reorganization, in part, as "a merger or consolidation (including the acquisition by one corporation of at least a majority of the voting stock and at least a majority of the total number of shares of all other classes of stock of another corporation, or substantially all the properties of another corporation)." Pub. L. No. 68-176, c. 234, §203(h)(1), 43 Stat. 257. Although the statute did not specifically limit the consideration that could be given in exchange for stock or assets, courts eventually developed the so-called "continuity of interest" doctrine, which held that exchanges that did not include some quantum of stock as consideration were ineligible for reorganization treatment for lack of a continuing property interest on the part of the acquiree's shareholders. See, e.g., Cortland Specialty Co. v. Commissioner, 60 F.2d 937, 939-40 (2d Cir. 1932), cert. denied, 288 U.S. 599 (1933); Pinellas Ice Co. v. Commissioner, 287 U.S. 462, 470 (1933).

Despite this judicial development, sentiment was widespread in Congress that the reorganization provisions lent themselves to abuse, particularly in the form of so-called "disguised sales." . . . The Senate Finance Committee . . . propos[ed] to retain these provisions, but with "restrictions designed to prevent tax avoidance." S. Rep. No. 558, 73d Cong., 2d Sess. 15. . . . One of these restrictions was the requirement that the acquiring corporation obtain at least 80 percent, rather than a bare majority, of the stock of the acquiree. The second requirement was stated in the Senate Report as follows: "the acquisition, whether of stock or of substantially all the properties, must be in exchange solely for the voting stock of the acquiring corporation." Id. at 17. The Senate amendments were enacted as Section 112(g)(1) of the Revenue Act of 1934. . . .

Congress revised this definition in 1939 in response to the Supreme Court's decision in United States v. Hendler, 303 U.S. 564 (1938), which held that an acquiring corporation's assumption of the acquiree's liabilities in an asset-acquisition was equivalent to the receipt of "boot" by the acquiree. Since virtually all asset-acquisition reorganizations necessarily involve the assumption of the acquiree's liabilities, a literal application of the "solely for . . . voting stock" requirement would have effectively abolished this form of tax-free reorganization. In the Revenue Act of 1939, Congress separated the stock-acquisition and asset-acquisition provisions in order to exempt the assumption of liabilities in the latter category of cases from the "solely for . . . voting stock" requirement. . . .

The next major change in this provision occurred in 1954. In that year, the House Bill, H.R. 8300, would have drastically altered the corporate reorganization sections of the Tax Code, permitting, for example, both stock and "boot" as consideration in a corporate acquisition, with gain recognized only to the extent of the "boot." . . . The Senate Finance Committee, in order to preserve the familiar terminology and structure of the 1939 Code, proposed a new version of Section 112(g)(1), which would retain the "solely for . . . voting stock" requirement, but alter the existing control requirement to permit so-called "creeping acquisitions." Under the Senate Bill, it would no longer be necessary for the acquiring corporation to obtain 80 percent or more of the acquiree's stock in one "reorganization." The Senate's proposal permitted an acquisition to occur in stages; a bloc of shares representing less than 80 percent could be added to earlier acquisitions, regardless of the consideration given earlier, to meet the control requirement. The Report of the Senate Finance Committee gave this example of the operation of the creeping acquisition amendment:

> [C]orporation A purchased 30 percent of the common stock of corporation W (the only class of stock outstanding) for cash in 1939. On March 1, 1955, corporation A offers to exchange its own voting stock, for all the stock of corporation W tendered within 6 months from the date of the offer. Within the 6 months period corporation A acquires an additional 60 percent of the stock of W for its own voting stock. As a result of the 1955 transactions, corporation A will own 90 percent of all of corporation W's stock, No gain or loss is recognized with respect to the exchanges of the A stock for the W stock.

1954 Senate Report, supra, at 273. . . . See also Treas. Reg. §1.368-2(c) (1960).

At the same time the Senate was revising the (B) provision (while leaving intact the "solely for . . . voting stock" requirement), it was also rewriting the (C) provision to explicitly permit up to 20 percent of the consideration in an asset acquisition to take the form of money or other nonstock property. See . . . §368(a)(2)(B). The Senate revisions of subsections (B) and (C) were ultimately passed, and have remained largely unchanged since 1954. . . . Proposals for altering the (B) provision to allow "boot" as consideration have been made, but none has been enacted.

As this history shows, Congress has had conflicting aims in this complex and difficult area. On the one hand, the 1934 Act evidences a strong intention to limit the reorganization provisions to prevent forms of tax avoidance that had proliferated under the earlier revenue acts. This intention arguably has been carried forward in the current versions through retention of the "solely for . . . voting stock" requirement in (B), even while the (C) provision was being loosened. On the other hand, both the 1939 and 1954 revisions represented attempts to make the reorganization procedures more accessible and practical in both the (B) and (C) areas. In light of the conflicting purposes, we can discern no clear Congressional mandate in the present structure of the (B) provision, either in terms of the abuses sought to be remedied or the beneficial transactions sought to be facilitated. At best, we think Congress has drawn somewhat arbitrary lines separating those transactions that resemble mere changes in form of ownership and those that contain elements of a sale or purchase arrangement. In such circumstances we believe it is more appropriate to examine the specific rules and requirements Congress enacted, rather than some questionably delineated "purpose" or "policy," to determine whether a particular transaction qualifies for favorable tax treatment. . . .

C

Besides finding support for the IRS position both in the design of the statute and in the legislative history, we find support in the regulations adopted by the Treasury Department construing these statutory provisions. We of course give weight to the statutory construction contemporaneously developed by the agency entrusted by Congress with the task of applying these laws. The views of the Treasury on tax matters, while by no means definitive, undoubtedly reflect a familiarity with the intricacies of the tax code that surpasses our own. . . .

D

Finally, we turn to the body of case law that has developed concerning (B) reorganizations to determine how previous courts have dealt with this question. Of the seven prior cases in this area, all to a greater or lesser degree support the result we have reached, and none supports the result reached by the Tax Court. [A]fter carefully reviewing the precedents, we are satisfied that the decision of the Tax Court represents a sharp break with the previous judicial constructions of this statute, and a departure from the usual rule of stare decisis, which applies with special force in the tax field where uncertainty and variety are ordinarily to be avoided.

Of the seven precedents, the most significant would seem to be Howard v. Commissioner, 238 F.2d 943 (7th Cir. 1956), rev'g, 24 T.C. 792 (1955), which stands out as the one case prior to *Reeves* that specifically addressed the issue raised herein. In *Howard*, the Truax-Traer Coal Company acquired 80.19 percent of the outstanding stock of Binkley Coal Company solely in exchange for Truax-Traer voting stock. At the same time and as part of the same plan of acquisition, Truax-Traer purchased the other 19.81 percent of Binkley's stock for cash. The taxpayers, former shareholders of Binkley who had exchanged their shares solely for voting stock, sold some of the Truax-Traer stock they had received in August 1950, the same year as the exchange. The Commissioner, treating the exchange as a taxable event and not a reorganization, employed a new holding period, beginning with the effective date of the exchange, and treated the taxpayers' gain on their sale of the Truax-Traer stock as a short-term capital gain. The Tax Court sustained the Commissioner, concluding the exchange had not been made "solely for . . . voting stock," as required by the 1939 Act, even though the cash purchases were not essential to Truax-Traer's acquisition of control. 24 T.C. at 804.

The Seventh Circuit, after reviewing the legislative history of Section 112(g)(1)(B) of the 1939 Code, agreed with the Tax Court's conclusion that the presence of cash purchases prevented the transaction from meeting the "solely" requirement of the statute. . . . The principal linchpin of the Seventh Circuit's decision was Helvering v. Southwest Consolidated Corp., 315 U.S. 194 (1942), in which the Supreme Court denied tax-free treatment to an asset acquisition under the 1934 Act because a substantial amount of the consideration was given in the form of stock warrants and cash. The Court first noted that under the law existing before 1934, this transaction would have been a perfectly valid tax-free reorganization. The revised statute, . . . had made the continuity of interest test much stricter, however:

> Congress has provided that the assets of the transferor corporation must be acquired in exchange "solely" for "voting stock" of the transferee. "Solely" leaves no leeway. Voting stock plus some other consideration does not meet the statutory requirement.

315 U.S. at 198. The Seventh Circuit noted that in the 1934 Act the asset and stock acquisition reorganizations were dealt with in the same clause both in the statutory language and in the legislative history. It therefore seemed reasonable to the Seventh Circuit to conclude that the Supreme Court's "no leeway" rule for asset acquisitions applied with equal force to stock acquisitions.

Appellees argue that *Southwest Consolidated* is distinguishable from the present facts, and, implicitly, that it should not have been relied on by the *Howard* court. This argument rests, in our view, on a strained reading of *Southwest Consolidated*. The taxpayers point out that the nonstock consideration in that case amounted to 37 percent of the total consideration, by the Tax Court's reckoning. Further, they say that the stock and nonstock consideration could not be separated where one bundle of assets was exchanged for one bundle of consideration, so that *Southwest Consolidated* was essentially a mixed consideration case. We disagree. Had the Supreme Court chosen to decide the issue of whether "substantially all" the assets of one corporation were obtained solely for voting stock, it could have allocated the consideration on a proportional basis, much as the Tax Court did in making its calculations. The Supreme Court did not consider, however, whether the voting stock consideration was sufficient to cover "substantially all" the assets, so that Section 112(g)(1)(B) would be satisfied. The Court determined rather that the presence of *any* nonstock consideration in the acquisition negated the possibility of a valid tax-free reorganization. While the facts were such that the Court could have reached the same result on another rationale, this does not detract from the weight of its words. The Seventh Circuit was, in our opinion, justified in resting its holding by analogy on the decision in *Southwest Consolidated*. . . .

Besides questioning its lineage, the Tax Court plurality made three attempts to distinguish the *Howard* case or undercut its holding. First, the Tax Court argued that *Howard* was a case in which "some stockholders involved in the one exchange transaction . . . received cash." 71 T.C. at 737. The impact of this distinction is less than clear. There was no finding in *Howard* that any stockholder received both cash and stock for the same shares. In both *Howard* and this case, more than 80 percent of the shares were exchanged for stock only, and additional shares were purchased for cash. The only possible meaning of the Tax Court's statement is that it did not consider the 1968-69 cash purchases and the 1970 exchange offer part of "one exchange transaction." Yet the taxpayers' specific concession on motion for summary judgment was that the two events should be assumed to constitute "parts of the 1970 exchange offer reorganization." We do not see how *Howard* can be distinguished from the present case other than on a finding that the cash and stock transactions here were unrelated as a matter of law, a finding the Tax Court specifically declined to make. (As we are remanding this latter issue to the Tax Court, we take no position on it now.)

The Tax Court's second attack on *Howard* . . . is equally unpersuasive. The fact that one shareholder of Binkley (the acquiree) received voting stock for some of its shares and cash for other shares, so that the 80 percent necessary for control was not acquired from shareholders receiving only stock, was not relied on by the Seventh Circuit. Furthermore, the focus of the statute is on the consideration furnished in the exchange, not on the consideration received by a particular shareholder. . . . Indeed, in this case there is no proof that some of ITT's earlier market purchases were not made from shareholders of Hartford who later exchanged other shares for ITT's voting stock. . . .

Even were we doubtful as to the correctness of the result reached in *Howard* (and we are not), we would nonetheless be reluctant to see a rule of tax law which has stood virtually unchallenged by courts for 25 years discarded so unceremoniously. As the dissenting judges of the Tax Court noted, much tax planning must proceed on the basis of settled rules. Avoidance of risk and uncertainty are often the keys to a successful transaction. Transactions may have been structured on the basis of *Howard*, with cash intentionally introduced to prevent reorganization treatment. Where a long standing tax rule of this sort is not clearly contrary to Congressional intent or markedly inconsistent with some generally accepted understanding of correct doctrine, we think the proper body to make changes aimed at improving the law is Congress, and not the courts. The complex and delicate judgments as to proper tax policy, and the balancing of interests between corporations, their shareholders, and the public, required to formulate appropriate rules in this area are not the proper province of courts. . . .

Our reading of the statute is reinforced by another more recent circuit decision as well. In Mills v. Commissioner, 331 F.2d 321 (5th Cir. 1964), rev'g, 39 T.C. 393 (1962), the issue was whether cash payments for fractional shares in an exchange prevented a nontaxable reorganization. General Gas Corporation, the acquiror, offered the three taxpayers, sole stockholders in three small gas corporations, shares of General common stock in exchange for all of their stock. The number of General shares to be exchanged at a value of $14 per share was to be determined by measuring the net book value of the three small corporations. In the event the purchase price was not evenly divisible by 14, cash was to be paid in lieu of fractional shares. As a result, each taxpayer received 1,595 shares of General stock and $27.36 in cash. The Tax Court held this transaction invalid as a tax-free reorganization, declining to adopt a de minimis rule. 39 T.C. at 400. The Fifth Circuit agreed that cash could not form any part of the consideration in a (B) reorganization, but concluded in reversing the Tax Court that the fractional-share arrangement was merely a bookkeeping convenience and not an independent part of the consideration. 331 F.2d at 324-25.

Taxpayers, and the Tax Court, argued that *Mills* was distinguishable, despite its sweeping language, because each shareholder of the acquired corporations received both stock and cash in the exchange. We have discussed earlier our reasons for rejecting any rule premised on the consideration received by the acquiree's shareholders. If *Mills* were distinguishable at all, it would be only because the consideration for some of the shares in *Mills* consisted of both stock and cash. But even this distinction evaporates when one notes that the one share in each exchange for which a fractional share would have been necessary never constituted more than 20 percent of the stock of any one of the acquiree corporations (since each shareholder held at least six shares in each corporation). In every exchange it was theoretically possible to identify a bloc of more than 80 percent of the stock of the acquiree which was exchanged solely for the voting stock of the acquiring corporation. Thus, in the only case raising the issue now before us under the 1954 Code, the Tax Court accepted as a premise that no cash was permissible as consideration in a (B) reorganization, even where the facts showed that control had passed solely for voting stock.

IV

We have stated our ruling, and the reasons that support it. In conclusion, we would like to respond briefly to the arguments raised by the Tax Court, the District Court of Delaware, and the taxpayers in this case against the rule we have reaffirmed today. The principal argument, repeated again and again, concerns the supposed lack of policy behind the rule forbidding cash in a (B) reorganization where the control requirement is met solely for voting stock. It is true that the Service has not pointed to tax loopholes that would be opened were the rule to be relaxed as appellees request. We also recognize, as the Tax Court and others have highlighted, that the rule may produce results which some would view as anomalous. For example, if Corporation X acquires 80 percent of Corporation Y's stock solely for voting stock, and is content to leave the remaining 20 percent outstanding, no one would question that a valid (B) reorganization has taken place. If Corporation X then decides to purchase stock from the remaining shareholders, the *Howard* rule might result in loss of nontaxable treatment for the stock acquisition if the two transactions were found to be related. See 71 T.C. at 740-41. The Tax Court asserted that there is no conceivable Congressional policy that would justify such a result. Further, it argued, Congress could not have felt that prior cash purchases would forever ban a later successful (B) reorganization since the 1954 amendments, as the legislative history makes clear, specifically provided that prior cash purchases would not prevent a creeping acquisition.

While not without force, this line of argument does not in the end persuade us. First of all, as already discussed, the language of the statute, and the longstanding interpretation given it by the courts, are persuasive reasons for our holding even in the absence of any clear policy behind Congress' expression of its will. Furthermore, we perceive statutory anomalies of another sort which the Tax Court's rule would only magnify. It is clear from the regulations, for example, that a corporation which already owned as much as 80 percent of another's stock, acquired solely for cash, could in some circumstances acquire all or a part of the remainder solely for voting stock as a valid (B) reorganization. Why, then, could not as little as 10 percent of an acquisition constitute a (B) reorganization, if made solely for voting stock, even though the remaining transactions totaling more than 80 percent were made for nonstock consideration? If it is true that Congress did not view related cash transactions as tainting a stock-acquisition reorganization, why would it enact a "solely for . . . voting stock" requirement at all, except to the extent necessary to prevent mixed consideration of the sort employed in the "disguised sales" of the twenties?

Possibly, Congress' insertion of the "solely for . . . voting stock" requirement into the 1934 Act was, as one commentator has suggested, an overreaction to a problem which could have been dealt with through more precise and discriminating measures. But we do not think it appropriate for a court to tell Congress how to do its job in an area such as this. If a more refined statutory scheme would be appropriate, such changes should be sought from the body empowered to make them. While we adhere to the general practice of construing statutes so as to further their demonstrated policies, we have no license to rework whole statutory schemes in pursuit of policy goals which Congress has nowhere articulated. Appellees have not shown us any reason to believe that reaffirmation of the settled rule in this area will frustrate the Congressional purpose of making the (B) reorganization provision generally available to those who comply with the statutory requirements.

A second major argument, advanced primarily by the district court in Pierson [v. United States, 472 F. Supp. 957 (D. Del. 1979), rev'd sub nom. Heverly v. Commissioner, 621 F.2d 1227 (3d Cir. 1980)], is that the previous cases construing this statute are suspect because they did not give proper weight to the changes wrought by the 1954 amendments. In particular, the court argued the liberalization of the "boot" allowance in (C) reorganizations and the allowance of creeping (B) acquisitions showed that Congress had no intent or desire to forbid "boot" of up to 20 percent in a (B) reorganization. As we have discussed earlier, we draw the opposite conclusion from the legislative history. Liberalization of the (C) provision shows only that Congress, when it wished to do so, could grant explicit leeway in the reorganization rules. . . .

A third argument asserts that reliance on the literal language of the 1954 Code, and in particular a focus on the interpretation of "acquisition," is unjustified because the 1954 Code was not intended to alter the status of (B) reorganizations under the 1934 and 1939 Codes. According to this argument, the acquisition of at least 80 percent of the acquiree's stock solely for voting stock was allowed under the pre-1954 version, and must still be allowed even though the present statute refers only to "the acquisition . . . of stock" with no percentage specified. This argument assumes the answer to the question that is asked. As *Howard* and *Southwest Consolidated* illustrate, it has been the undeviating understanding of courts, until now, that the pre-1954 statutes did not allow cash or other "boot" in a (B) reorganization. It cannot be inferred that Congress left intact a rule which never existed by enacting language inconsistent with such a rule.

Finally, we see no merit at all in the suggestion that we should permit "boot" in a (B) reorganization simply because "boot" is permitted in some instances in (A) and (C) reorganizations. Congress has never indicated that these three distinct categories of transactions are to be interpreted in pari materia. In fact, striking differences in the treatment of the three subsections have been evident in the history of the reorganization statutes. We see no reason to believe a difference in the treatment of "boot" in these transactions is impermissible or irrational. . . .

The case will be remanded to the Tax Court for further proceedings consistent with this opinion. . . .

NOTE

1. *The* Chapman *decision.* Notice how the taxpayer in *Chapman* waged a double-barreled attack against the *Howard* adverse precedent. Not only did the taxpayer seek to distinguish *Howard,* but the case cited for support

by the *Howard* court (Helvering v. Southwest Consolidated Corp.) also was distinguished. By this technique, the taxpayer offered the court the opportunity to overrule or distinguish the adverse precedent of *Howard*.

The court stated that it could discern no clear policy argument supporting one side's interpretation over the other. In that light, was the court's decision to adopt a narrow construction of the statute a good one, particularly when a "corporate reorganization" (in the colloquial sense) was effected? The Tax Court seemingly has accepted the *Chapman* construction of §368(a)(1)(B). Clark v. Commissioner, 86 T.C. 138, 142 n.5 (1986).

In fact, the Service argued that there was a good policy reason for rejecting the taxpayer's argument in this case. A voting block of 10 percent to 15 percent of a publicly held corporation often produces effective control. By purchasing about 8 percent of Hartford's stock, ITT was able to force on the Hartford board of directors a merger that it had already rejected on almost the same terms. Counsel for the government argued on appeal that a proper interpretation of the statute should not permit such "gunboat diplomacy." Would such a policy argument have been a proper basis for the court's holding?

The effect of the circuit court's decision in *Chapman* was to remand the case to the Tax Court for trial on the merits. While petitions for certiorari in *Chapman* and a related case were pending, however, the case was settled with ITT's agreement to make a one-time payment of $18.5 million to the U.S. Treasury. Since ITT was not a party to the action, why did ITT agree to pay the settlement? What should the tax consequences of this settlement have been to the former Hartford shareholders? In fact, the settlement included the provisions that ITT would not deduct the settlement payment and that no tax deficiencies would be asserted against the former Hartford shareholders. These shareholders, though, were bound to carry over their Hartford stock basis into their ITT stock.

In Rev. Rul. 85-139, 1985-2 C.B. 123, the Service ruled that the solely-for-voting-stock requirement of a B reorganization is not met when the acquiring corporation exchanges its voting stock for 90 percent of the target corporation's stock and a wholly owned subsidiary of the acquiring corporation acquires 10 percent of the target's stock for cash. Is the emphasis placed by *Chapman* and Rev. Rul. 85-139 on the "transaction" justified? To what extent should motives matter?

In Rev. Rul. 69-294, 1969-1 C.B. 10, *X* Corp. owned all the outstanding stock of *Y* Corp. *Y* owned more than 80 percent of the outstanding stock of *Z* Corp. To obtain direct ownership of 100 percent of *Z*, *X* caused *Y* to liquidate and *X* immediately thereafter acquired the minority stock in *Z* for its own voting stock. The Service ruled that the latter exchange was taxable and did not qualify as a B reorganization since *X*, as part of a single unified transaction, had acquired all the stock of *Z* but not "solely for" *X* voting stock. The reasoning was that more than 80 percent of the *Z* stock was received in exchange for its *Y* stock.

Suppose a corporation adopts a "poison pill" antitakeover provision giving shareholders the right to purchase at a bargain price additional shares of the company (or of any acquiring company) if there is a hostile takeover. Can the corporation now participate as the acquiring corporation in a B reorganization, or will the poison pill attached to its stock constitute impermissible nonstock consideration? The Service has consistently ruled that the poison pill rights do not constitute nonstock consideration. See Priv. Ltr. Rul. 9125013; Priv. Ltr. Rul. 8925087; Priv. Ltr. Rul. 8808081.

2. *Contingent stock.* An acquiring corporation in a merger may, in addition to issuing shares of stock outright to the shareholders of the target company, promise to pay additional shares on the occurrence of certain contingencies. The type of contingencies may be, for example, the earnings performance of the target company over some specified future period or the trading value of its stock. The use of contingent stock allows the parties to exploit differing expectations of the future to strike a deal that otherwise would be unobtainable. See H. Raiffa, The Art and Science of Negotiation 91-107 (1982).

Contingent rights to acquire stock that are issued in connection with a reorganization have been treated as stock rather than boot. See Carlberg v. United States, 281 F.2d 507 (8th Cir. 1960); Hamrick v. Commissioner, 43 T.C. 21 (1964). Rev. Proc. 77-37, 1977-2 C.B. 568, provides guidelines for advanced rulings when contingent or escrowed stock is involved. The most important of these relates to the maximum number of shares whose receipt can be made contingent (50 percent of the total that can be issued) and the time during which the contingencies must be resolved (five years). See also Rev. Proc. 84-42, 1984-1 C.B. 521 (amplifying Rev. Proc. 77-37).

Section 483 creates interest income in the case of contingent stock deferred for more than one year after the exchange unless interest is provided for in the form of additional shares. Solomon v. Commissioner, 570 F.2d 28 (2d Cir. 1977); accord, Jeffers v. United States, 556 F.2d 986 (Cl. Ct. 1977); Catterall v. Commissioner, 68 T.C. 413 (1977), aff'd sub nom. Vorbleski v. Commissioner, 589 F.2d 123 (3d Cir. 1978). But in Rev. Rul. 70-120, 1970-1 C.B. 124, the Service ruled that deferred payments do not exist in a reorganization in which bonus stock is issued in each shareholder's name and then is placed in escrow if the shareholders can vote the shares and receive dividends even though they may later be divested of the bonus shares. The result is that interest income under §483 can be avoided if all the stock is issued initially even though some is in effect made contingent by being placed in an escrow. Why? Note that under the regulations, the interest portion imputed on contingent stock is not treated as boot and will not destroy the tax-free status of the reorganization. Treas. Regs. §§1.483-2(a)(2), 1.483-2(b)(3)(i), and 1.483-1(b)(6) (examples 7 and 8).

3. *Cash in lieu of fractional shares.* In Rev. Rul. 66-365, 1966-2 C.B. 116, the Service ruled that cash paid in lieu of issuing fractional shares will not

be regarded as boot consideration in an acquisitive reorganization. This favorable ruling is limited, however, to those cases in which the cash is not a separately bargained-for consideration. In what circumstances might cash in lieu of fractional shares be separately bargained for? See also Rev. Rul. 69-34, 1969-1 C.B. 105, and Rev. Rul. 74-36, 1974-1 C.B. 85, extending this rule to E and F reorganizations.

3.   The C Reorganization: Stock for Assets

In a C reorganization, the transferor corporation exchanges at least "substantially all" its assets for voting stock of the acquiring corporation. In most circumstances, the transferor corporation must liquidate as part of the plan of reorganization. §368(a)(2)(G). Accordingly, the C reorganization is practically indistinguishable from a statutory merger. As in a B reorganization (and in distinction to a statutory merger), however, Congress has limited the allowable consideration in a C reorganization to voting stock of the acquiring corporation or of the acquiring corporation's parent. §368(a)(1)(C) (parenthetical language).

In United States v. Hendler, 303 U.S. 564 (1938), the Supreme Court held that the assumption by the acquiring corporation of a liability of the transferor corporation constitutes boot consideration. Since most businesses encumber their assets, the practical effect of the *Hendler* decision was to eliminate the C reorganization as a viable possibility. Congress responded by adding to the definition of a C reorganization that the acquiring corporation's assumption of a liability (or taking property subject to a liability) will not cause the transaction to lose its reorganization status. See §368(a)(1)(C). A further anti-*Hendler* rule was enacted in §357, discussed at pages 24-36 supra in the context of §351 incorporations and at page 492 infra in the context of reorganizations.

The technical traps of the reorganization provisions are vividly illustrated by some problems that have arisen under §368(a)(1)(C)'s requirement that the acquiring corporation acquire "substantially all of the properties" of another corporation. In Bausch & Lomb Optical Co. v. Commissioner, 267 F.2d 75 (2d Cir. 1959), the acquiring corporation owned 79 percent of the transferor corporation. The parent issued its stock for all the assets of the subsidiary, and the subsidiary then liquidated. The parent received back 79 percent of the newly issued stock, and the minority shareholders of the subsidiary became shareholders of the parent. Should the acquisition have been taxed as a C reorganization?

The court held that the transaction did not qualify as a C reorganization. In the court's view, the parent acquired 79 percent of the subsidiary's assets in exchange for stock of the subsidiary as part of the liquidation: Only the remaining 21 percent was acquired for voting stock of the parent.

Therefore, the parent received less than "substantially all" the subsidiary's properties in exchange for its own stock.

NOTE

1. *"Substantially all" the properties.* Under Rev. Proc. 77-37, 1977-2 C.B. 568, for advance ruling purposes, the Service will consider the substantially-all requirement to be met by the transfer of at least 70 percent of gross assets and 90 percent of the net assets. For example, if *X* Corp. owns assets with aggregate fair market value of $1 million subject to liabilities of $200,000, the transfer by *X* of $720,000 or more of its assets for voting stock of the acquiring corporation will satisfy this test.

The judicial interpretation of the substantially-all requirement may be more relaxed than the Service's ruling guidelines. The transferor corporation in a substitutive D reorganization, discussed infra, must also transfer substantially all its assets in the reorganization. See §354(b)(1)(A). In that context, a transfer of all the operating assets of the transferor has been held to satisfy the substantially-all test even when the value of those assets, as a percentage of the net worth of the corporation, has been low. See Smothers v. United States, page 458 infra (15 percent); Armour, Inc. v. Commissioner, 43 T.C. 295 (1961) (51 percent).

2. *The boot relaxation rule of §368(a)(2)(B).* While the "solely for voting stock" requirement is absolute in a B reorganization, Congress has provided in a C reorganization that property other than stock may be used as consideration if at least 80 percent of the fair market value of the acquired corporation's assets are acquired for voting stock. §368(a)(2)(B). In determining whether 80 percent of all property is acquired for voting stock, any liabilities assumed by the acquiring corporation are treated as money or other property. Thus, if the value of the transferor's properties is $100,000 subject to liabilities of $15,000, the acquiring corporation would be limited to paying $5,000 in money or other property in addition to assuming the liabilities. If the liabilities were $21,000, the only consideration allowed in a C reorganization would be voting stock. Since most businesses have substantial liabilities, the boot possibilities for C reorganizations are limited, if not nonexistent.

Can a failed B reorganization be converted into a successful C reorganization by prompt liquidation of the acquired subsidiary? For example, suppose *A* Corp. acquires all the stock of *T* Corp. in exchange for its voting stock worth $1 million plus cash of $100,000. Because of the cash, the acquisition is not a B reorganization. But suppose *A* promptly liquidates *T* Corp. Can the transaction be viewed as an indirect asset acquisition qualifying as a C reorganization? See American Potash & Chemical Corp. v. United States, 399 F.2d 194 (Cl. Ct.), aff'd, 402 F.2d 1000 (Cl. Ct. 1968) (failed B reorganization followed by liquidation of subsidiary cannot qualify as a C reorganization); Rev. Rul. 67-274, 1967-2 C.B. 141 (B reorganization followed by liquidation of acquired corporation taxed as a C reorganization). Should ITT have attempted to convert its Hartford acquisition into a C reorganization?

3. *Contingent stock.* In Rev. Rul. 78-376, 1978-2 C.B. 149, *X* Corp. acquired substantially all the assets of *Y* Corp. in a C reorganization. *A,* the sole shareholder of *Y,* received shares of *X,* a portion of which were placed in escrow as security pending the resolution of a contingent liability of *Y.* When the amount of the liability was determined, the escrowed shares had doubled in value. The agreement provided that the number of shares to be returned to *X* would be based on the amount of the liability and the value of the escrowed stock on the date of return. The Service ruled that *A* recognized gain on return of the shares equal to the excess of the fair market value of the shares not returned (which was equal to the liability) over their adjusted basis. *A*'s basis in the remaining shares was increased by the amount of the claim satisfied. Cf. Rev. Rul. 76-42, 1976-1 C.B. 102, in which no gain was recognized on the return of escrowed shares because the number of shares returned was based on their initial negotiated value and, therefore, the shareholder could receive no benefit or detriment from any changes in the fair market value of the escrowed stock returned. Are these two rulings consistent even assuming the validity of the rationale of the latter?

While escrowed stock is not treated as boot, stock rights, options, and warrants are not considered to be stock or securities but "other property." See Treas. Regs. §1.354-1(e); Helvering v. Southwest Consolidated Corp., 315 U.S. 194 (1942) (warrants). Why should the use of escrowed stock be permissible in B and C reorganizations while stock rights, options, and warrants are not?

4. *The Nondivisive D Reorganization*

The D reorganization at first blush seems peculiar in that it contemplates a *transfer* of assets from one corporation to another rather than an *exchange* of assets for stock or some other valuable consideration. Note, though, that such a transfer will not qualify as a D reorganization unless the transferor corporation (or its shareholders) controls the transferee corporation. By virtue of §368(a)(2)(H), "control" for a D reorganization is defined in §304(c) — a 50 percent test — rather than in §368(c) — an 80 percent test — applicable to the other types of reorganization. Were there no more to it than this, a nondivisive D reorganization would be a transfer of assets between a (broadly defined) brother-sister or parent-subsidiary pair.

But there is more. A transfer of assets to a corporation controlled by the transferor (or its shareholders) will not qualify as a D reorganization unless the asset transfer is accompanied by a distribution of stock or securities described in §354, 355, or 356. The two basic forms of D reorganizations are (1) those qualifying by virtue of a §354 distribution and (2) those qualifying by virtue of a §355 distribution. (D reorganizations qualifying under §356 are simply one of the two basic forms in which the distribution includes some boot as well as stock and securities.) We will consider only the first form of the D reorganization here; the second form — a D reorganization qualifying under §355 — effects a divisive reorganization and is discussed infra.

A D reorganization qualifying with a §354 distribution must satisfy the requirements of §354(b)(1). That section requires that the transferor corporation transfer substantially all its assets and then liquidate. The transferor may, but need not, receive stock, securities, or other property in exchange for its assets; whatever it receives, plus all assets not transferred, must be distributed in a complete liquidation.

The D reorganization qualifying with a §354 distribution is often called a "substitutive" (or "acquisitive") D reorganization because the transferee corporation is controlled by the same shareholders who controlled the transferor, §368(a)(1)(D), and it ends up with at least substantially all the transferor's assets, §354(b)(1). The substantially-all requirement of the substitutive D, as well as the forced liquidation of the transferor corporation, should remind you of the C reorganization. Both C and D reorganizations include the following features: (1) an exchange of substantially all the assets of one corporation for stock of another corporation, and (2) the immediate liquidation of the transferor corporation. The difference between the two is that continuity of proprietary interest is ensured in a C reorganization by requiring that 80 percent of the stock received by the transferor corporation be voting stock in the acquiring corporation (or in its parent), while continuity in a D reorganization is ensured by requiring that the shareholders of the transferor corporation control the acquiring corporation immediately after the transaction. Note that some overlap between C and D reorganizations is contemplated, and when such overlap occurs, the transaction is treated as a type D. §368(a)(2)(A).

Usually it is the taxpayer who argues that a corporate rearrangement qualifies as an A, B, or C reorganization, but often it is the Commissioner who argues in favor of the substitutive D, and the Commissioner may sometimes catch a taxpayer off guard. See *Smothers*, below. Consider individual T, who owns all the stock of X Corp. X Corp. has accumulated substantial amounts of cash and other liquid assets, and T would like to remove those assets from corporate solution at capital gain rates. Assuming that X Corp. has substantial accumulated earnings and profits, T would not want to cause X Corp. to declare a dividend, for under §301 T would have ordinary income equal to the full fair market value of the dividend distribution. Because T is the sole shareholder of X Corp., a redemption of some of T's stock will not qualify for exchange treatment under

§302(b)(1)-(3), and liquid assets (other than the proceeds from the sale of assets used in a business no longer conducted) cannot qualify for partial liquidation treatment under §302(b)(4).

T could cause *X* Corp. to liquidate, making capital gain treatment available under §331(a). But if *T* wishes to continue using the operating assets of *X* Corp. in corporate form, the complete liquidation of *X* might be considered too high a price to pay. One technique for *T* to try is to cause *X* Corp. to create a new subsidiary, *Y* Corp., and transfer to that subsidiary all the *X* Corp. operating assets. Such a transfer would be tax free under §351, and if *X* Corp. then liquidated, *T* would have removed the liquid assets from corporate solution without recognizing any ordinary income. Indeed, *T* would have the added benefit that *Y* corp. would not be burdened by the prior earnings and profits account of *X*.

Unfortunately for *T*, the creation of *Y* and liquidation of *X* will be taxed as a nondivisive D reorganization. Assuming that the operating assets of *X* constitute substantially all its assets (a point to be examined in Note 2 infra), *X* has transferred substantially all its assets to a corporation (*Y*) controlled by it or its shareholders immediately after the transaction. The distribution requirement of §354(b)(1) is satisfied by the complete liquidation of *X*. Thus, *T* will be taxed under §§354 and 356 on *T*'s exchange of *X* stock for the *X* liquid assets accompanied by the new *Y* stock. Under §356(a)(2), *T* may recognize ordinary income on the exchange, limited only by the amount of gain realized by *T* and by *X*'s earnings and profits.

The substitutive D reorganization is also used by the Commissioner to attack liquidation-reincorporations. For example, were *T* to liquidate *X* Corp. and then reincorporate the operating assets, the Commissioner would argue that the effect of the liquidation-reincorporation was a substitutive D reorganization in which the liquid assets were distributed as boot. In such a case, however, the Commissioner faces the preliminary difficulty of identifying the requisite distribution of stock or securities by the transferor. What argument would you advise the Commissioner to make?

Smothers v. United States

642 F.2d 894 (5th Cir. 1981)

Before Wisdom, Garza and Reavley, Circuit Judges.
WISDOM, Circuit Judge. . . .

This dispute arises from the dissolution of one of [the Smothers'] wholly-owned business corporations. The taxpayers contend that the assets distributed to them by that corporation should be taxed at the capital gain rate applicable to liquidating distributions. The Internal Revenue Service (IRS) counters by characterizing the dissolution as part of a reorganization, thereby rendering the taxpayers' receipt of the distributed assets taxable at ordinary income rates. The district court viewed the transaction as a reorganization and ruled for the IRS. We affirm.

I

In 1956, [the Smothers] and an unrelated third party organized Texas Industrial Laundries of San Antonio, Inc. (TIL). The Smothers owned all of its outstanding stock from 1956 through the tax year in issue, 1969. TIL engaged in the business of renting industrial uniforms and other industrial cleaning equipment, such as wiping cloths, dust control devices, and continuous toweling. It owned its own laundry equipment as well.

Shortly after the incorporation of TIL, the taxpayers organized another corporation, Industrial Uniform Services, Inc. (IUS), specifically to oppose a particular competitor in the San Antonio industrial laundry market. The taxpayers owned all of the stock of IUS from the time of its organization until its dissolution. Unlike TIL, IUS did not own laundry equipment; it had to contract with an unrelated company to launder the uniforms it rented to customers. J. E. Smothers personally managed IUS, as well as TIL, but chose not to pay himself a salary from IUS in any of the years of its existence.

IUS evidently succeeded in drawing business away from competing firms, for TIL purchased its main competitor in 1965. IUS continued in business, however, until 1969. On the advice of their accountant, the taxpayers then decided to dissolve IUS and sell all of its non-liquid assets to TIL. On November 1, 1969, IUS adopted a plan of liquidation in compliance with I.R.C. §337, and on November 30, it sold the following assets to TIL for cash at their fair market value (stipulated to be the same as their book value):

Assets	Amount
Noncompetitive covenant	$ 3,894.60
Fixed assets	491.25
Rental property	18,000.00
Prepaid insurance	240.21
Water deposit	7.50
Total	$22,637.56[3]

The noncompetitive covenant constituted part of the consideration received by IUS from its purchase of a small competitor. The fixed assets consisted of incidental equipment (baskets, shelves, and a sewing machine), two depreciated delivery vehicles, and IUS's part interest in an airplane. The rental property was an old apartment building in Corpus Christi on land with business potential. These assets collectively represented about 15% of IUS's net value. The parties stipulated that none of these assets were necessary to carry out IUS's business.

___

3. The parties stipulated that the purchase price was $22,637.56, and the district court found that as a fact. The items listed add to $22,633.56, however. We ignore the discrepancy and accept the stipulation.

After this sale, IUS promptly distributed its remaining assets to its shareholders, the taxpayers, and then dissolved under Texas law:

Assets	Amount
Cash (received from TIL)	$ 22,637.56
Cash (of IUS)	2,003.05
Notes receivable	138,000.00
Accrued interest receivable	35.42
Claim against the State of Texas	889.67
Liabilities assumed	(14,403.35)
Total	$149,162.35

TIL hired all three of IUS's employees immediately after the dissolution, and TIL continued to serve most of IUS's customers.

In computing their federal income tax liability for 1969, the taxpayers treated this distribution by IUS as a distribution in complete liquidation within §331(a)(1). Accordingly, they reported the difference between the value of the assets they received in that distribution, $149,162.35, and the basis of their IUS stock, $1,000, as long-term capital gain. Upon audit, the IRS recharacterized the transaction between TIL and IUS as a reorganization within §368(a)(1)(D), and therefore treated the distribution to the taxpayers as equivalent to a dividend under §356(a)(2). Because IUS had sufficient earnings and profits to cover that distribution, the entire distribution was therefore taxable to the Smothers at ordinary income rates. The IRS timely assessed a $71,840.84 deficiency against the Smothers. They paid that amount and filed this suit for a refund.

The district court held that the transaction constituted a reorganization and rendered judgment for the IRS. . . .

II

Subchapter C of the Internal Revenue Code broadly contemplates that the retained earnings of a continuing business carried on in corporate form can be placed in the hands of its shareholders only after they pay a tax on those earnings at ordinary income rates. That general rule is, of course, primarily a consequence of §301, which taxes dividend distributions as ordinary income. The Code provides for capital gain treatment of corporate distributions in a few limited circumstances, but only when there is either a significant change in relative ownership of the corporation, as in certain redemption transactions, or when the shareholders no longer conduct the business themselves in corporate form, as in true liquidation transactions. The history of Subchapter C in large part has been the story of how Congress, the courts, and the IRS have been called upon to foil attempts by taxpayers to abuse these exceptional provisions. Ingenious taxpayers have repeatedly devised transactions which formally come within these provisions, yet which have the effect of permitting shareholders to withdraw profits at capital gain rates while carrying on a continuing business enterprise in corporate form without substantial change in ownership. This is just such a case.

The transaction in issue here is of the genus known as liquidation-reincorporation, or reincorporation. The common denominator of such transactions is their use of the liquidation provisions of the Code, which permit liquidating distributions to be received at capital gain rates, as a device through which the dividend provisions may be circumvented. Reincorporations come in two basic patterns. In one, the corporation is dissolved and its assets are distributed to its shareholders in liquidation. The shareholders then promptly reincorporate all the assets necessary to the operation of the business, while retaining accumulated cash or other surplus assets. The transaction in this case is of the alternate form. In it, the corporation transfers the assets necessary to its business to another corporation owned by the same shareholders in exchange for securities or, as here, for cash, and then liquidates. . . . If formal compliance with the liquidation provisions were the only necessity, both patterns would enable shareholders to withdraw profits from a continuing corporate business enterprise at capital gain rates by paper-shuffling. Unchecked, these reincorporation techniques would eviscerate the dividend provisions of the Code.

That result can be avoided by recharacterizing such transactions, in accordance with their true nature, as reorganizations. A reorganization is, in essence, a transaction between corporations that results merely in "a continuance of the proprietary interests in the continuing enterprise under modified corporate form" — a phrase that precisely describes the effect of a reincorporation. Lewis v. Commissioner, 1 Cir. 1949, 176 F.2d 646, 648. Congress specifically recognized that the throw-off of surplus assets to shareholders in the course of a reorganization can be equivalent to a dividend, and if so, should be taxed as such. §§356(a)(1)-(2). The reincorporation transactions described above result in a dividend payment to the shareholders in every meaningful financial sense. The assets retained by the shareholders therefore should be taxed as dividends as long as the transaction can be fitted within the technical requirements of one of the six classes of reorganizations recognized by §368(a)(1).

In general, reincorporation transactions are most easily assimilated into §368(a)(1)(D) ("D reorganization"), as the IRS attempted to do in this case. A transaction qualifies as a D reorganization only if it meets six statutory requirements:

(1) There must be a transfer by a corporation (§368(a)(1)(D));
(2) of substantially all of its assets (§354(b)(1)(A));
(3) to a corporation controlled by the shareholders of the transferor

corporation, or by the transferor corporation itself (§368(a)(1)(D));

(4) in exchange for stock or securities of the transferee corporation (§354(a)(1));

(5) followed by a distribution of the stock or securities of the transferee corporation to the transferor's shareholders (§354(b)(1)(B));

(6) pursuant to a plan of reorganization (§368(a)(1)(D)).

On this appeal, the taxpayers concede that the transaction in issue meets every technical prerequisite for characterization as a D reorganization, except for one. They argue that since the assets sold by IUS to TIL amounted to only 15% of IUS's net worth, TIL did not acquire "substantially all of the assets" of IUS within the meaning of §354(b)(1)(A).

We hold to the contrary. The words "substantially all assets" are not self-defining. What proportion of a corporation's assets is "substantially all" in this context, and less obviously, what "assets" are to be counted in making this determination, cannot be answered without reference to the structure of Subchapter C. To maintain the integrity of the dividend provisions of the Code, "substantially all assets" in this context must be interpreted as an inartistic way of expressing the concept of "transfer of a continuing business." [I]t is in a sense simply a limited codification of the general nonstatutory "continuity of business enterprise" requirement applicable to all reorganizations.

This interpretation finds support in the history of §368(a)(1)(D) and §354(b)(1)(A). The Internal Revenue Code of 1939 had no provision equivalent to the "substantially all assets" requirement, and courts almost uniformly approved attempts by the IRS to treat reincorporation transactions as reorganizations within the predecessor of §368(a)(1)(D) in the 1939 Code. The "substantially all assets" requirement of §354(b)(1)(A) and the amendment of §368(a)(1)(D) incorporating that requirement were added during the 1954 recodification as part of a package of amendments aimed at plugging a different loophole — the bail-out of corporate earnings and profits at capital gains rates through divisive reorganizations. There is no indication that Congress wished to relax the application of the reorganization provisions to reincorporation transactions. Indeed, the committee reports indicate the contrary. The Senate report accompanying the bill that contained the "substantially all assets" requirement of §354(b)(1)(A) and the parallel amendment to §368(a)(1)(D) stated that the purpose of those changes was only "to insure that the tax consequences of the distribution of stocks or securities to shareholders or security holders in connection with divisive reorganizations will be governed by the requirements of section 355." The report expressly noted that except with respect to divisive reorganizations, the reorganization provisions "are the same as under existing law and are stated in substantially the same form." Even more significantly, the original House version of the 1954 Code contained a provision specifically dealing with reincorporation transactions. That provision was dropped in conference because the conferees felt that such transactions "can appropriately be disposed of by judicial decision or by regulation within the framework of the other provisions of the bill." As the court said in Pridemark, Inc. v. Commissioner, 4 Cir. 1965, 345 F.2d 35, 40, this response shows that "the committee was aware of the problem and thought the present statutory scheme adequate to deal with it." By implication, this passage approved the IRS's use of the predecessor of §368(a)(1)(D) to meet the problem, and shows that the "substantially all assets" amendment was not thought to restrict its use.

Courts have almost unanimously so interpreted the "substantially all assets" language. Moreover, they have also interpreted the other technical conditions for a D reorganization in ways that accomplish the congressional intent to reach reincorporation transactions. For example, the literal language of §368(a)(1)(D) and §§354(a), 354(b)(1)(B) requires that the transferee corporation "exchange" some of its "stock or securities" for the assets of the transferor, and that those items be "distributed" to the shareholders of the transferor, before a D reorganization can be found. Yet both of those requirements have uniformly been ignored as "meaningless gestures" in the reincorporation context, in which the same shareholders own all the stock of both corporations. Smothers does not even challenge the applicability of that principle here.

Properly interpreted, therefore, the assets looked to when making the "substantially all assets" determination should be all the assets, and only the assets, necessary to operate the corporate business — whether or not those assets would appear on a corporate balance sheet constructed according to generally accepted accounting principles. Two errors in particular should be avoided. Inclusion of assets unnecessary to the operation of the business in the "substantially all assets" assessment would open the way for the shareholders of any enterprise to turn dividends into capital gain at will. For example, if we assume that "substantially all" means greater than 90%, then a corporation need only cease declaring dividends and accumulate surplus liquid assets until their value exceeds 10% of the total value of all corporate assets. The shareholders could then transfer the assets actively used in the business to a second corporation owned by them and liquidate the old corporation. Such a liquidating distribution would be a dividend in any meaningful sense, but an interpretation of "substantially all assets" that took surplus assets into account would permit the shareholders to treat it as capital gain. Indeed, such an interpretation would perversely treat a merely nominal distribution of retained earnings as a dividend, but would permit substantial distributions to be made at capital gain rates. Courts therefore have invariably ignored all surplus assets and have focused on the operating assets of the business — the tangible assets actively used in the business — when making the "substantially all assets" assessment.

Second, exclusion of assets not shown on a balance sheet constructed according to generally accepted accounting principles from the "substantially all assets" assessment would offer an unjustified windfall to the owners of service businesses conducted in corporate form. The most important assets of such a business may be its reputation and the availability of skilled management and trained employees, none of which show up on a standard balance sheet. Other courts have correctly recognized that in appropriate cases those intangible assets alone may constitute substantially all of the corporate assets. Otherwise, for example, a sole legal practitioner who owns nothing but a desk and chair could incorporate himself, accumulate earnings, and then set up a new corporation and liquidate the old at capital gain rates — as long as he is careful to buy a new desk and chair for the new corporation, rather than transferring the old.

When these principles are applied to this case, it is plain that "substantially all of the assets" of IUS were transferred to TIL, and that the transaction as a whole constituted a reorganization. TIL and IUS were both managed and wholly owned by Smothers. By the nature of its business, IUS was wholly a service enterprise; indeed, the parties stipulated that none of the tangible assets of IUS were necessary to the operation of its business. The extent to which those tangible assets were transferred to TIL is therefore entirely irrelevant. IUS's most important assets — its reputation, sales staff, and the managerial services of Smothers — were all transferred to TIL. TIL rehired all three of IUS's employees immediately after IUS's liquidation, and continued to serve IUS's old customers. The same business enterprise was conducted by the same people under the same ownership, and the only assets removed from corporate solution were accumulated liquid assets unnecessary to the operation of the business. To treat this transaction as other than a reorganization would deny economic reality; to permit Smothers to extract the retained earnings of IUS at capital gain rates would make a mockery of the dividend provisions of the Internal Revenue Code.

We do not perceive ordinary income treatment here to be particularly harsh, or a "tax trap for the unwary." It places the Smothers only in the position they would have been in if they had extracted the retained earnings of IUS as the Code contemplates they should have by periodically declaring dividends.

Affirmed.

GARZA, Circuit Judge, dissenting.

After carefully reading the majority's opinion, I find that I must respectfully dissent. Unlike my Brothers, who apparently feel that it is their duty to "plug loopholes," I would remain content in applying the tax law as it reads leaving the United States Congress to deal with the consequences of the tax law as it has been drafted. The only issue before this Court on appeal is whether or not IUS transferred "substantially all of its assets" to TIL. Instead of dealing with this straightforward question, the majority has made a case of evil against liquidation-reincorporation abuses and, in an attempt to remedy every such perceived abuse, they have relieved the Congress of its burden to change the law heretofore requiring that "substantially all" of a corporation's assets be transferred to now read that "only those assets necessary to operate the corporate business" be transferred in order to meet the "D reorganization" requirements. Essentially, the majority has changed the definition of "substantially all assets" to mean only "necessary operating assets." I believe if Congress had meant "necessary operating assets" it would have said so instead of specifically requiring that "substantially all" of the assets be transferred. In my mind "substantially all" plainly means *all* of the assets except for an *insubstantial* amount. Under such a definition, the sale of 15% of IUS's assets to TIL could hardly be defined as "substantially all" of IUS's assets.

However, even after having redefined "substantially all" to mean "necessary operating assets," the IUS liquidation still falls short of the "D reorganization" requirements because the stipulated facts are that absolutely none of the assets sold from IUS to TIL were necessary operating assets for either corporation. Faced with an absence of a proper factual setting, the majority goes on to define necessary operating assets as including a corporation's intangible assets. Now while a sale of intangible assets might be an appropriate consideration in determining whether or not "substantially all" assets of a corporation have been transferred, such a consideration simply has no bearing in this case. All of the assets transferred to TIL were depreciated tangible objects sold at book value after which IUS completely ceased all business operations. There simply was no other transfer of IUS's intangible assets as a continuing business.

The majority has placed great emphasis on the fact that three of IUS's route salesmen were subsequently employed by TIL and that Mr. Smothers' managerial services were available to TIL. Regardless of whether or not these facts enhanced TIL's business, the fact remains that neither the route salesmen or Mr. Smothers' services were *transferred* as assets from one corporation to another. After IUS ceased business its route salesmen were free to seek any employment they desired. Likewise, Mr. Smothers was never obligated to perform services for TIL. From these facts I cannot agree that there was a transfer of a continuing business. The majority imputes adverse tax consequences to IUS's stockholders simply because TIL offered new employment to the route salesmen who were unemployed upon cessation of IUS's business operations. The majority places future stockholders, in Mr. Smothers' position, of choosing between unfavorable tax consequences and helping secure future employment to loyal and deserving employees whom otherwise would be unemployed.

Although the Internal Revenue Service has never questioned the bona fides of IUS's liquidation, the majority has gone beyond the stipulated facts by characterizing the liquidation as a tax avoidance scam. I simply cannot agree. After starting from scratch, Mr. Smothers worked for over a dozen years refraining from drawing salary in order that IUS could pay its taxes, employees and other operating expenses and in order for IUS to become a successful self-sustaining business enterprise. Mr. Smothers was successful but, now that he no longer could devote his service to IUS, his years of labor are now labeled by the majority as a mere "paper shuffle." I do not share the majority's attitude.

The reasons for my position can be more easily understood by a simple review of the bottom-line facts. After IUS began showing a profit and started accumulating a cash surplus, instead of immediately investing in a building or in other equipment for its operations, it continued its operations as before. Now, if IUS had purchased real property or depreciable personal property for its operations (instead of leasing as it had been) and had sold these properties pursuant to its plan of liquidation, certainly no argument would be made that the money initially invested in those properties should have been declared by IUS as dividends. However, instead of investing its accumulations, IUS simply put them in its bank account as the tax laws allow and presumably faced any tax consequences posed by such an accumulation.

After IUS ceased operations, was liquidated, and its assets distributed to its stockholders in exchange for their stock, the I.R.S. issued a deficiency, not because IUS was reorganized within the meaning of . . . §368(a)(1)(D), but rather because the I.R.S. felt the accumulated earnings of IUS coupled with long-term capital gains rates applicable to the stock exchange provided an undesirable windfall to IUS's stockholders. In essence, the I.R.S. sought to expand the "D reorganization" provisions, lessen the availability of long-term capital gains treatment to corporate stockholders, and totally ignore the purpose of the tax upon improperly accumulated surplus as provided in . . . §531. The majority seeks to do equity for the I.R.S. position by "treating" the IUS liquidation as a "D reorganization." I do not believe the taxpayers or the tax laws are served by upholding an I.R.S. deficiency for the sole purpose of "plugging loopholes." The lesson to be learned from the majority's opinion is clear — future corporations faced with similar circumstances need only invest their otherwise accumulated surplus in some method other than savings. In the process of liquidation they need sell whatever assets exist to third parties unrelated to their stockholders and their stockholders should make no effort to find future employment for the corporation's employees.

It seems to me that in its attempt to "plug" a perceived "loophole," the majority is giving this Court's imprimatur to a variation of the same so-called "mockery" of the tax laws sought to be prevented by its opinion.

For these reasons, I respectfully dissent.

NOTE

1. *The control requirement.* A substitutive D reorganization requires, under §368(a)(2)(H), that shareholders of the transferor corporation

meet the §304(c) control test in the transferee corporation so that when more than 50 percent of the transferred stock is owned by others, the courts will not find a D reorganization. See, e.g., Gallagher v. Commissioner, 39 T.C. 144 (1962) (decided under prior 80 percent control test). The Service has argued for application of the §318 attribution rules in testing for control, but this position has been generally rejected. See, e.g., Breech v. United States, 439 F.2d 409 (9th Cir. 1971). Without relying on the attribution rules, however, the court in Stanton v. United States, 512 F.2d 13 (3d Cir. 1975), attributed a wife's 49 percent interest in a new corporation to her husband when she had not transferred any assets to the new corporation for its stock. The court viewed the wife's interest as first held by the husband and then transferred to her as a gift.

Should the continuity of proprietary interest doctrine be part of the gloss on substitutive D reorganizations, given that the transferor's assets will in all events be continued in corporate form controlled by proprietary owners of the transferor? From another perspective, should this doctrine apply not only to limit the entrance of new owners but also to prohibit the elimination of some of the old owners?

2. *Substantially all the assets.* The court in *Smothers* was willing to treat 15 percent of the transferor corporation's assets as "substantially all" because the 15 percent at issue included all the corporation's operating assets. To the same effect, see Moffatt v. Commissioner, 363 F.2d 262 (9th Cir. 1966) (64.52 percent); Armour, Inc. v. Commissioner, 43 T.C. 295 (1964) (51 percent). Are these courts, as Judge Garza argued in dissent in *Smothers,* giving insufficient deference to the words used by Congress in §354(b)(1)?

Liquidation of the transferor corporation was not required as part of a C reorganization until 1984. Until then, the C reorganization did not so closely resemble the nondivisive D reorganization. Given the current similarity of the C and nondivisive D reorganizations, should the interpretation of "substantially all" in §368(a)(1)(C) be informed by these judicial decisions explicating the terms of a substitutive D reorganization? If some but not all of the assets of *T* Corp. are transferred to *A* Corp. in exchange for voting stock of *A*, and *T* then liquidates, is the transaction more like a sale than a continuation of *T*'s business? If the shareholders of *T* lack control of *A* (so that the transaction is not a substitutive D), is the transfer of all the operating assets of *T* more like a sale than a reorganization? Recall Rev. Proc. 77-37, discussed at page 455 supra, in which "substantially all" means 70 percent of a corporation's gross assets and 90 percent of its net assets.

3. *The transfer requirement.* A service-intensive business may have few or no operating assets. Suppose such a business operating in corporate form is completely liquidated, followed by the formation of a corporation engaged in a similar business employing the same workers and servicing the same clients or customers. Can the Commissioner attack such an arrangement as a nondivisive D reorganization? Under the definition of a D

reorganization in §368(a)(1)(D), the transferor corporation must "transfer" substantially all its assets to the acquiring corporation. In the example posed above, have the employees or customers been "transferred" within the meaning of §368(a)(1)(D)?

It has been suggested that employees cannot be "transferred" in this sense. Warsaw Photographic Associates, Inc. v. Commissioner, 84 T.C. 21 (1985). But in Moffatt v. Commissioner, 363 F.2d 262 (9th Cir. 1966), it was held employees could be so "transferred." See also Simon v. Commissioner, 644 F.2d 339 (5th Cir. 1981), in which a nonassignable franchise right was "transferred" within the meaning of §368(a)(1)(D) when the franchise liquidated and the franchise reissued to a corporation controlled by shareholders of the liquidated corporation.

Note also the willingness of the court in *Smothers* to excuse the absence of a distribution. Should the ability to look through form be limited to the government? Compare Commissioner v. Danielson, 378 F.2d 771 (3d Cir. 1967).

5. Triangular Reorganizations

Before 1954, the acquiring corporation in a B or C reorganization could issue only its own stock as consideration for the stock or assets of the other corporation. See Groman v. Commissioner, 302 U.S. 82 (1937). In 1954, the definition of a C reorganization was amended — by adding the parenthetical phrase of §368(a)(1)(C) — to permit use of stock of the parent of the acquiring corporation. A similar statutory change subsequently was made to permit the use of the stock of a parent corporation in a B reorganization. A B or C reorganization using voting stock of the parent of the acquiring corporation is called a parenthetical B or C reorganization.

One reason for the widespread use of subsidiaries in the reorganization context is that state law may require the shareholders of the acquiring corporation as well as the shareholders of the transferor corporation to vote their approval of the reorganization. This is especially likely in the case of an A reorganization. If the acquiring corporation is publicly held, then the cost of obtaining shareholder consent might be prohibitive. By using a subsidiary as the nominal acquiring corporation, only the vote of the subsidiary's shareholders — usually the board of directors of the parent company — is needed.

While there is no parenthetical A reorganization, §368(a)(2)(D) plays that role. Under this provision, a statutory merger using stock of the acquiring corporation's parent will qualify as a reorganization so long as the transaction would have qualified as an A reorganization had stock of the acquiring corporation been used. Thus, because the continuity of proprietary interest doctrine restricts the consideration that may be used in an A reorganization, it applies to limit the allowable consideration in a

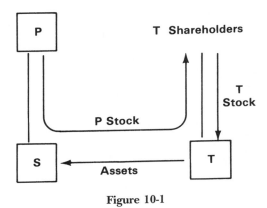

Figure 10-1

§368(a)(2)(D) reorganization. Note also that no stock of the subsidiary may be used. See Figure 10-1.

It may be that the acquisition can be structured more easily as a merger of the acquiring corporation into the target corporation. For example, the target corporation might be the lessee on a favorable long-term lease. In such a case, the acquiring corporation will cause a controlled subsidiary to merge into the target company. As part of the plan, shareholders of the target will exchange their target stock for stock of the acquiring corporation. Such a transaction constitutes a reorganization so long as the only consideration used is voting stock of the parent. §368(a)(2)(E). See Figure 10-2.

Reorganizations described in §368(a)(2)(D) are called "forward triangular (or subsidiary) mergers," while reorganizations described in §368(a)(2)(E) are called "reverse triangular (or subsidiary) mergers." One requirement imposed on both forms of triangular mergers is that

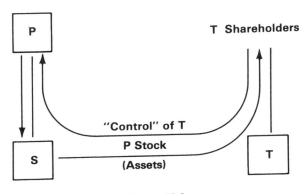

Figure 10-2

substantially all the properties be continued in the surviving company. An alternate route to similar results is afforded by §368(a)(2)(C), which permits a corporation to acquire stock or assets in exchange for its own stock and then to transfer the acquired stock or assets to a subsidiary.

C.   TAXATION

1.   *Overview*

Once it is determined that a reorganization has occurred, the tax consequences to all affected corporations and shareholders must be considered. The provisions applicable to the reorganizing corporations are §§357, 361, and 362, while the provisions applicable to their shareholders include §§354, 356, and 358. Other sections implicated by a tax-free reorganization include §§269, 381, and 382, discussed in Chapter 13.

In general, these rules provide that gain or loss is not recognized and that basis is continued unchanged. At the corporate level, this means that the acquiring corporation takes the acquired assets with a carryover basis and that no gain or loss is recognized by either corporation. At the shareholder level, the effect of a corporate reorganization usually is an exchange of stock of the transferor corporation for stock of the acquiring corporation. In the absence of boot, shareholders will not recognize gain or loss on such an exchange and will transfer their basis from the stock given up to the stock received.

Receipt of boot may, at the corporate or shareholder level, trigger the recognition of gain. The definition of a B reorganization precludes the use of boot, while A, C, and D reorganizations allow it. Do not confuse the notion of boot as used in the provisions taxing reorganizations — boot here meaning property other than that permitted to be received without the recognition of gain — with allowable consideration in the definitions of the various types of reorganizations in §368(a)(1). For example, if the acquiring corporation in a C reorganization uses its own securities as well as voting stock consideration to acquire all the assets of a corporation, the securities will constitute boot and will disqualify the reorganization if the total boot exceeds 20 percent of the total consideration. If the boot is less than 20 percent of the consideration, however, the transaction will qualify as a C reorganization. In this case, will distribution of the securities by the acquired company cause recognition to its shareholders? Not necessarily, for, at the shareholder level, securities of the acquiring corporation are not treated as boot unless a shareholder receives securities in excess of those given up. See §354(a)(2).

Do not forget the importance of §368(b)'s definition of the "parties" to a reorganization. At the corporate level, the reorganization provisions apply only to corporations that are parties to the reorganization. See §361(a). At the shareholder level, nonrecognition will apply only to exchanges of stock and securities of corporations that are, once again, parties to the reorganization.

The corporate parties to a reorganization are specified in §368(b). When the 1954 Code was enacted, §368(b) contained only the first sentence of the current provision. As Congress expanded the definition of a reorganization, it also expanded the definition of parties to a reorganization in §368(b).

In a statutory merger qualifying as an A reorganization, the parties to the reorganization are the two merging corporations. In a statutory consolidation, the parties are the consolidating corporations and the newly formed survivor. In the simple B and C reorganizations (in which stock of the acquiring corporation is used rather than stock of its parent), the parties are only the transferor corporation and the acquiring corporation. If a parenthetical B or C reorganization is effected, then the parties include the transferor corporation, the acquiring corporation, and the parent of the acquiring corporation.

In the case of forward triangular reorganizations under §368(a)(2)(D), the parties include both merging corporations and the acquiring corporation's parent. In the case of reverse triangular reorganizations under §368(a)(2)(E), the parties include both merging corporations and the transferor's parent. Lastly, when acquired assets are dropped down to a controlled subsidiary of the acquiring corporation pursuant to §368(a)(2)(C), the controlled subsidiary as well as the transferor and acquiring corporations are parties to the reorganization. In each case, then, the parties to a reorganization include those corporations *and only those corporations* playing a role in the definition of the reorganization.

2. *Corporate-level Taxation*

Five main issues arise in the corporate-level taxation of reorganizations: (1) recognition of gain or loss by the transferor corporation; (2) recognition of gain or loss by the acquiring corporation; (3) the basis of the assets acquired by the acquiring corporation; (4) the impact of the reorganization on net operating losses, earnings and profits accounts, and other tax attributes of corporations; and (5) the tax treatment of expenses incurred by the corporate parties incidental to the reorganization.

Turn first to the taxation of the transferor corporation. Recognition of gain and loss by the transferor corporation is governed by §361. Under §361(a), the transferor corporation recognizes no gain or loss on the exchange of its property for the stock and securities of another corporate party to the reorganization. Further, if the transferor corporation receives other property (boot) in addition to qualifying stock and securities, again no gain or loss is recognized so long as the boot is distributed as part of the reorganization. §361(b)(1)(A). Note that a distribution to a creditor *does* satisfy this requirement. §361(b)(3). Because the transferor corporation will almost always liquidate as part of the reorganization (see §368(a)(2)(G)(ii) for the possible exception), recognition by the transferor corporation is unlikely.

In some circumstances, however, assumption by the acquiring corporation of debts of the transferor corporation is treated as the transfer of money (i.e., as boot, see §357(b) (liability assumed or acquired for tax avoidance), §357(c)(1) (nondeductible liability in excess of basis)). Here the transferor corporation will recognize gain because there is no possibility of distributing the boot. Note that the transferor corporation will never recognize loss on the exchange. §361(b)(2).

Will the transferor corporation recognize gain or loss on its liquidating distribution pursuant to the reorganization? Loss will not be recognized, but gain might be. The transferor corporation's liquidating distribution might include three classes of property: (1) stock or securities of a corporate party acquired from the acquiring corporation, (2) property other than stock or securities (i.e., boot) from the acquiring corporation, and (3) property held by it and not transferred to the acquiring corporation as part of the reorganization.

As to class (1), such stock and securities constitute "qualified property" within the meaning of §361(c)(2)(B) and so will not trigger recognition on the distribution. §361(c). As to class (2), there is no gain to be recognized because the property should not be appreciated: The transferor corporation's basis in boot acquired from the acquiring corporation is fair market value under §358(a)(2). As to class (3), gain will be recognized to the extent the distributed property is appreciated. §361(c)(2)(A). Note that the usual rules applicable to complete liquidations do not apply in this context. §361(c)(4).

What of the acquiring corporation? Before examining the various types of reorganizations individually, recall that §1032 broadly provides that a corporation does not recognize gain or loss on the receipt of property in exchange for its own stock. Since this general provision can apply to exchanges pursuant to a plan of reorganization, it usually will protect the acquiring corporation from the recognition of all gain or loss on the issuance of its stock. Indeed, it has precisely this effect on the acquiring corporation in a nonparenthetical B reorganization.

The acquiring corporation in an A or C or substitutive D reorganization (or in a forward triangular reorganization) may use nonstock consideration. To the extent it does so, gain or loss can be recognized by the acquiring corporation. The use of its own securities ordinarily will not give rise to gain since the acquisition of property for debt is not a taxable event to the acquiring taxpayer. Cash boot also will avoid recognition of gain or loss to the acquiring corporation. The use of appreciated or loss property however, will cause the acquiring corporation to recognize gain or loss. See §1001.

Use of stock of the acquiring corporation's parent in a parenthetical B or C reorganization presents one of the few gaps in the reorganization provisions: No section specifically provides that the acquiring corporation does not recognize gain or loss on the exchange. In Rev. Rul. 57-278, 1957-1 C.B. 124, the Service ruled without discussion that the acquiring corporation does not recognize gain or loss in these circumstances, and that rule has been endorsed by Prop. Treas. Regs. §1.1032-2. Because the parenthetical B and C reorganizations closely resemble the nonparenthetical B and C reorganizations followed by a drop-down of assets under §368(a)(2)(C) — transactions fully protected by §1032 — nonrecognition of gain or loss to the acquiring corporation is appropriate in parenthetical B and C reorganizations.

So much for the recognition of gain or loss at the corporate level. In A, C, and substitutive D reorganizations, the acquiring corporation acquires assets of the transferor. The basis of those assets, determined under §362(b), will be carried over from the transferor corporation, increased by the amount of gain, if any, recognized to the transferor on the exchange. The same basis rule applies, by virtue of the last sentence of §362(b), to the stock of the target corporation acquired in a B reorganization. As to the applicability of §362(b) to a parenthetical B reorganization, see Treas. Regs. §§1.358-4, 1.362-1. The basis of the stock of the acquired subsidiary in the hands of the acquiring corporation in a reverse triangular reorganization has been a sore spot in the reorganization provisions for many years. Prop. Treas. Regs. §1.358-6(c)(2) addresses this issue.

Until 1984, the transferor corporation in a C reorganization was not required to liquidate as part of the reorganization. If it did not liquidate, its basis in the stock (and boot) received in the transaction was determined under §358. Now that the definition of a C includes the requirement that the transferor liquidate, see §368(a)(2)(G), that issue becomes moot. In some circumstances, however, the liquidation requirement can be waived, see §368(a)(2)(G)(ii), and then basis becomes important. In such cases the transferor corporation's basis is determined under §361(b)(2).

It may seem as though these reorganization provisions are exceedingly complex. They are. It may also seem as if you must constantly refer back and forth among the various taxing sections to determine the consequences of a reorganization to all the corporate parties. You must. The only way to become confident in your ability to parse through the complexity of the reorganization provisions is to practice. An example of the technique used to analyze the corporate-level tax effects of a reorganization follows. Remember that a similar exercise should be performed with respect to the shareholder-level tax effects.

X Corp. and *T* Corp. agree to the following plan. *T* will transfer most of its assets to *X* in exchange for (1) voting stock of *X* worth $80,000,

(2) securities of X worth $8,000, (3) real estate worth $5,000, and (4) the assumption by X of a $5,000 liability of T. The fair market value of the assets X will receive is $98,000, and X's adjusted basis in the real estate is $3,500. Immediately after the exchange, T will liquidate, distributing the stock and securities of X, the real estate, and its remaining assets (worth $2,000 and with adjusted basis of $1,000) to its shareholders in complete liquidation. Assume that T's basis in the transferred assets totals $60,000 and that T's shareholders do not own a significant amount of X stock before or after the transaction.

Is this transaction a reorganization? It would fall under §368(a)(1)(C) but for X's transfer of the securities and the real estate. The boot relaxation rule of §368(a)(2)(B) permits boot in a C reorganization, and because the amount of the stock is equal to or greater than 80 percent of the value of the acquired corporation (it is exactly 80 percent), this is in fact a C reorganization pursuant to §368(a)(1)(C), (a)(2)(B). Note that one additional dollar of boot in lieu of stock would have destroyed the reorganization.

How is T taxed? T has a *realized* gain of $38,000 (amount realized of $98,000 less adjusted basis of $60,000 in the assets transferred). None of that gain, however, will be recognized by virtue of §361(b)(1)(A). T will be taxed on $1,000 of gain on its liquidating distribution because it did not transfer all its appreciated property to X: distribution of the retained assets is taxable in full under §361(c)(2). Distribution of the stock and securities received on the exchange is protected from recognition by §361(c)(2)(B), while distribution of the acquired real estate is protected from recognition by the basis rule of §358(a)(2).

How is X taxed? Section 1032 protects X from the recognition of gain with respect to the T assets acquired for its stock. Further, since gain is not recognized to a taxpayer who purchases assets, X is also absolved from recognition with respect to the T assets acquired for X's securities or for the assumption of T's liability. As to the assets acquired for the real estate, X is subject to taxation under §1001(a). Thus, X recognizes a gain of $1,500 on the exchange.

What is X's basis in the assets acquired from T? Under §362(b), X takes a basis equal to T's basis in those assets ($60,000), increased by any gain recognized by the transferor corporation, namely T. Since T recognized no gain on the exchange, X's basis in the assets is $60,000.

Lastly, consider the tax treatment of any expenses incurred by the corporate parties to a reorganization. Such expenses might include attorney and accountant fees as well as printing costs of a prospectus and related documents. Similar expenses often are incurred in connection with an initial incorporation, and, by virtue of §248, they can be amortized over a period not less than 60 months. No similar provision, however, authorizes the amortization of reorganization expenses. See the discussion of *INDOPCO* at page 390 supra.

3.   Shareholder-level Taxation

Shareholder-level taxation of a reorganization is governed by §§354, 356, 358, and 1001(a). To some shareholders — notably the shareholders of the transferor corporation — the effect of a reorganization is an exchange of their shares in one corporation for stock and securities of another corporation, sometimes accompanied by other property, or "boot." Such an exchange is fully taxable under the general rule of §1001(a) governing dispositions of property unless some more particular provision, usually §354 or §356, applies. §1001(c). Other shareholders will not be parties to any exchange as a result of the reorganization. Shareholders of the acquiring corporation, for example, usually have no change in their stock and debt interests as a result of a reorganization. For such shareholders, no special taxing provision is needed since the absence of an exchange ensures that they will recognize no gain or loss as a consequence of the reorganization (unless §305(c) applies).

If, as part of a plan of reorganization, a shareholder exchanges stock and securities in one "party" to the reorganization for stock and securities of another "party" to the reorganization, no gain or loss is recognized on the exchange, §354(a), subject to an exception for the excess principal amount of securities received, §354(a)(2). This nonrecognition rule will fully cover, for example, shareholders of the transferor (i.e., nonsurviving) corporation in an A statutory merger if all they received in the reorganization was stock of the acquiring (i.e., surviving) corporation. Section 354(a) will also ensure nonrecognition for the shareholders of the target corporation in a B reorganization.

If a shareholder receives property in addition to stock and securities of a party to the reorganization (or if excess securities are received), then the boot rule of §356(a) is implicated. Under that section, gain (if any) on the exchange will be recognized, but only to the extent of the boot received.[1] Suppose, for example, that N Corp. merges into O Corp. in a statutory merger qualifying as an A reorganization. The terms of the merger provide that each shareholder of N will receive one share of O common stock, one share of O $10 par value preferred stock, and $5 in cash for each share of N surrendered.

If taxpayer T owns one share of N stock prior to the merger, how will T be taxed when exchanging that share for one share of O common, one share of O preferred, and cash of $5? To compute T's realized gain, we must know T's adjusted basis in the N share and the fair market value of the O shares. Assume that T bought the N share for $20, that the O common

---

1. If the boot includes corporate debt, then recognition of gain will be subject to the installment sale provisions. See §453(f)(6). In particular, if the gain is taxed under §356(a)(1) as capital gain rather than under §356(a)(2) as a dividend, recognition can be deferred until payment on the debt is received. The characterization of boot under §356(a)(1) and (2) is discussed at pages 478-491 infra.

is worth $40, and that the *O* preferred is worth $10. Given these values, *T* has realized a gain of $35 on the exchange.

T's exchange does not fall within the terms of §354(a) because of the receipt of the cash. The exchange is described, however, in §356(a). By the terms of that section, *T* will recognize gain on the exchange, but in an amount limited to the value of the boot. Thus, *T* will recognize a gain of $5 on the exchange. The character of that gain is discussed at pages 478-491 infra.

T's basis in the *O* common and preferred stock is determined under §358. Under the rule of §358(a), *T*'s combined basis in the two shares equals $20 − $0 (other property) − $5 (cash) − $0 (loss) + $5 (dividend or gain), or $20. That amount is allocated to the stock in proportion to fair market values, so that 40/50th's (80 percent, or $16) is allocated to the *O* common, and 10/50th's (20 percent, or $4) is allocated to the *O* preferred. See §358(b)(1); Treas. Regs. §1.358-1, -2. Note that if *T* had received noncash boot, it would be given a basis equal to fair market value. §358(a)(2).

Shareholders of the transferor corporation in a C reorganization will also fall within the ambit of §354 because, when the transferor corporation liquidates as part of the plan of reorganization, such shareholders will exchange their stock in the transferor for the assets it holds at liquidation, and those assets will include voting stock of the acquiring corporation. The same is true of shareholders of the transferor corporation in a substitutive *D* reorganization to the extent that they receive stock and securities of the acquiring corporation in the exchange.

NOTE

1. *Securities as qualifying property.* Section 354 provides for the tax-free receipt of stock *or securities* by a shareholder in connection with a reorganization. A security is a debt instrument, but not all debt instruments are "securities" for this purpose. If nonrecognition is granted on the theory that the taxpayer has changed an investment in form only, why shouldn't all debt be treated as boot? The answer seems to be that some corporate debt gives the holder as much or more of an interest in the future performance of the assets transferred as a stock interest. Debt obligations that qualify for nonrecognition treatment are referred to as "securities." The leading case on the definition of a security is Camp Wolters Enterprises v. Commissioner, 22 T.C. 737, 751 (1954), aff'd, 230 F.2d 555 (5th Cir. 1956), in which the Tax Court stated:

> The test as to whether notes are securities is not a mechanical determination of the time period of the note. Though time is an important factor, the controlling consideration is an overall evaluation of the nature of the debt,

degree of participation and continuing interest compared with similarity of the note to a cash payment.

Prior to the Installment Sales Revision Act of 1980, the distinction between a security and a note could be very significant. The receipt of a note was immediately taxable to the transferor whereas the receipt of a security was not. As indicated at page 37 supra, this distinction in tax treatment has been removed, although other differences in tax treatment remain.

The most important factor separating securities from nonqualifying debt is the length of maturity of the obligation. If taxpayer T transfers property to X Corp. in exchange for some stock and six-month notes, the notes will be treated as boot, falling on the cash end of the spectrum. If the mix were stock and 30-year debentures, full nonrecognition would be available. Between these extremes lies a bog. Notes with a five-year term or less rarely will qualify as securities, while obligations with a term of 10 years or more seem likely to qualify. In the following cases, obligations were classified as securities: Parkland Place Co. v. United States, 354 F.2d 916 (5th Cir. 1966) (10-year 6 percent interest-bearing note where no interest paid); Nye v. Commissioner, 50 T.C. 203 (1968) (10-year note); Camp Wolters Enterprises v. Commissioner, supra (five- and nine-year subordinated notes). Notes were not treated as securities in the following cases: Bradshaw v. United States, 683 F.2d 365 (5th Cir. 1982) (notes maturing annually for five years); Adams v. Commissioner, 58 T.C. 41 (1972) ($2^{1}/_{4}$-year note); Raich v. Commissioner, 46 T.C. 604 (1966) (demand note retired within four years).

As the court in *Camp Wolters* points out, the maturity date is not the only consideration. Consider D'Angelo Associates v. Commissioner, 70 T.C. 121 (1978), in which a demand note was held a security. No interest and only half of the principal of the note had been paid after 16 years. In addition, the corporation did not have sufficient liquid assets to retire the debt. Rental income was to provide funds for repayment. Finally, the note was subordinated to another liability encumbering the transferred assets. The open-ended maturity date of the note in combination with the other features gave the transferor "a continuing participation in the affairs of the debtor corporation." See also United States v. Mills, 399 F.2d 944 (5th Cir. 1968) (one-year unsecured notes where renewal expected; jury decision).

While securities do qualify under §354 for nonrecognition treatment when a taxpayer receives a combination of stock and securities, what happens if a taxpayer receives only securities in exchange for property? Historically, securities could be received tax free under §351 just as they still can be received under §354. The Service addressed the possibility of receiving only securities in that context. In *Rev. Rul. 73-472*, 1973-2 C.B. 114, four individuals transferred property to a new corporation; three received back stock, and the fourth individual, *D,* received securities in amounts equal to the value of the property transferred. The Service held that *D* would not qualify under §351:

> Although *D* is one of the transferors, the ownership of securities provides him with no proprietary interest in the corporation, but rather an interest only as a creditor. In LeTulle v. Scofield, 308 U.S. 415, 420 (1940) . . . , it was stated:
>
>> Where the consideration is wholly in the transferee's bonds, or part cash and part such bonds we think it cannot be said that the transferor retains any proprietary interest in the enterprise. On the contrary, he becomes a creditor of the transferee. . . .

Id. Consequently, the Service ruled that *D* would recognize gain or loss in accordance with §§1001 and 453.

2. *Securities as boot.* Although §354(a)(1) classifies the exchange of stock and securities for stock and securities as an event of nonrecognition, it is not the case that receipt of securities of a "party" to the reorganization always will be tax free. By virtue of the limitation in §354(a)(2), the nonrecognition rule of §354(a)(1) is unavailable to a taxpayer who receives securities as part of the exchange if the principal amount of the securities received is greater than the principal amount of securities surrendered.

If a taxpayer receives excess securities in a reorganization exchange, gain (if any) will be recognized under the boot rule of §356. Consistent with §354(a)(2), only the excess principal amount of the securities received will be treated as boot under §356. See §356(d). In one of the more bizarre rules of the Code, it is the fair market value of the excess principal amount, and not the excess principal amount itself, that is treated as boot.

Consider example 4 of Treas. Regs. §1.356-3(b). Pursuant to a plan of reorganization, *D* exchanges a security with principal amount of $1,000 for 100 shares of stock plus a security with principal amount of $1,200 and fair market value of $1,100. The excess principal amount of the security received is $200, and the fair market value of that amount is $200 × (1,100/1,200), or $183.33. Accordingly, *D* can recognize gain of up to $183.33 on the exchange.

3. *Characterization of gain.* Does a shareholder who receives boot as part of a reorganization recognize capital gain or ordinary income? Usually, the character of gain recognized on an exchange described by §356(a)(1) is determined by reference to the property given up. For example, if the stock and securities surrendered were all capital assets held longer than six months, any gain recognized would be long-term capital gain. This general rule, however, is limited by §356(a)(2).

Under §356(a)(2), if some gain must be recognized and the exchange has the effect of a distribution of a dividend, then the taxpayer must treat any gain recognized as dividend income, limited only by the taxpayer's ratable share of the earnings and profits of the corporation. This section poses two difficult questions: When does an exchange have the effect of a "distribution of a dividend"? In computing the earnings and profits limitation, which corporation's earnings and profits should be used?

Commissioner v. Clark
489 U.S. 726 (1989)

Justice STEVENS delivered the opinion of the Court.

Justice Scalia joins all but Part III of this opinion.

This is the third case in which the Government has asked us to decide that a shareholder's receipt of a cash payment in exchange for a portion of his stock was taxable as a dividend. In the two earlier cases, Commissioner v. Estate of Bedford, 325 U.S. 283 (1945), and United States v. Davis, 397 U.S. 301 (1970), we agreed with the Government largely because the transactions involved redemptions of stock by single corporations that did not "result in a meaningful reduction of the shareholder's proportionate interest in the corporation." Id., at 313. In the case we decide today, however, the taxpayer in an arm's length transaction exchanged his interest in the acquired corporation for less than one percent of the stock of the acquiring corporation and a substantial cash payment. The taxpayer held no interest in the acquiring corporation prior to the reorganization. Viewing the exchange as a whole, we conclude that the cash payment is not appropriately characterized as a dividend. We accordingly agree with the Tax Court and with the Court of Appeals that the taxpayer is entitled to capital gains treatment of the cash payment.

I

In determining tax liability under the Internal Revenue Code, gain resulting from the sale or exchange of property is generally treated as capital gain, whereas the receipt of cash dividends is treated as ordinary income. The Code, however, imposes no current tax on certain stock-for-stock exchanges. In particular, §354(a)(1) provides, subject to various limitations, for nonrecognition of gain resulting from the exchange of stock or securities solely for other stock or securities, provided that the exchange is pursuant to a plan of corporate reorganization and that the stock or securities are those of a party to the reorganization.

Under §356(a)(1) of the Code, if such a stock-for-stock exchange is accompanied by additional consideration in the form of a cash payment or other property — something that tax practitioners refer to as "boot" — "then the gain, if any, to the recipient shall be recognized, but in an amount not in excess of the sum of such money and the fair market value of such other property." That is, if the shareholder receives boot, he or she must recognize the gain on the exchange up to the value of the boot. Boot is accordingly generally treated as a gain from the sale or exchange of property and is recognized in the current tax-year.

Section 356(a)(2), which controls the decision in this case, creates an exception to that general rule. . . . Thus, if the "exchange . . . has the effect of the distribution of a dividend," the boot must be treated as a dividend and is therefore appropriately taxed as ordinary income to the extent that gain is realized. In contrast, if the exchange does not have "the effect of the distribution of a dividend," the boot must be treated as a payment in exchange for property and, insofar as gain is realized, accorded capital gains treatment. The question in this case is thus whether the exchange between the taxpayer and the acquiring corporation had "the effect of the distribution of a dividend" within the meaning of §356(a)(2).

The relevant facts are easily summarized. For approximately 15 years prior to April 1979, the taxpayer was the sole shareholder and president of Basin Surveys, Inc. (Basin), a company in which he had invested approximately $85,000. The corporation operated a successful business providing various technical services to the petroleum industry. In 1978, N.L. Industries, Inc. (NL), a publicly owned corporation engaged in the manufacture and supply of petroleum equipment and services, initiated negotiations with the taxpayer regarding the possible acquisition of Basin. On April 3, 1979, after months of negotiations, the taxpayer and NL entered into a contract.

The agreement provided for a "triangular merger," whereby Basin was merged into a wholly owned subsidiary of NL. In exchange for transferring all of the outstanding shares in Basin to NL's subsidiary, the taxpayer elected to receive 300,000 shares of NL common stock and cash boot of $3,250,000, passing up an alternative offer of 425,000 shares of NL common stock. The 300,000 shares of NL issued to the taxpayer amounted to approximately 0.92% of the outstanding common shares of NL. If the taxpayer had instead accepted the pure stock-for-stock offer, he would have held approximately 1.3% of the outstanding common shares. The Commissioner and the taxpayer agree that the merger at issue qualifies as a reorganization under §§368(a)(1)(A) and (a)(2)(D).

Respondents filed a joint federal income tax return for 1979. As required by §356(a)(1), they reported the cash boot as taxable gain. In calculating the tax owed, respondents characterized the payment as long-term capital gain. The Commissioner on audit disagreed with this characterization. In his view, the payment had "the effect of the distribution of a dividend" and was thus taxable as ordinary income up to $2,319,611, the amount of Basin's accumulated earnings and profits at the time of the merger. The Commissioner assessed a deficiency of $972,504.74.

Respondents petitioned for review in the Tax Court, which, in a reviewed decision, held in their favor. 86 T.C. 138 (1986). The court started from the premise that the question whether the boot payment had "the effect of the distribution of a dividend" turns on the choice between "two judicially articulated tests." Id., at 140. Under the test advocated by the Commissioner and given voice in Shimberg v. United States, 577 F.2d 283 (C.A.5 1978), cert. denied, 439 U.S. 1115 (1979), the boot payment is treated as though it were made in a hypothetical redemption by the acquired corporation (Basin) immediately prior to the reorganization. Under this test, the cash payment received by the taxpayer indisputably would have been treated as a dividend. The second test, urged by the taxpayer and finding support in Wright v. United States, 482 F.2d 600 (C.A.8 1973), proposes an alternative hypothetical redemption. Rather than concentrating on the taxpayer's pre-reorganization interest in the acquired corporation, this test requires that one imagine a pure stock-for-stock exchange, followed immediately by a post-reorganization redemption of a portion of the taxpayer's shares in the acquiring corporation (NL) in return for a payment in an amount equal to the boot. Under §302 of the Code, which defines when a redemption of stock should be treated as a distribution of dividend, NL's redemption of 125,000 shares of its stock from the taxpayer in exchange for the $3,250,000 boot payment would have been treated as capital gain.

The Tax Court rejected the pre-reorganization test favored by the Commissioner because it considered it improper "to view the cash payment as an isolated event totally separate from the reorganization." 86 T.C., at 151. Indeed, it suggested that this test requires that courts make the "determination of dividend equivalency fantasizing that the reorganization does not exist." Id., at 150 (footnote omitted). The court then acknowledged that a similar criticism could be made of the taxpayer's contention that the cash payment should be viewed as a post-reorganization redemption. It concluded, however, that since it was perfectly clear that the cash payment would not have taken place without the reorganization, it was better to treat the boot "as the equivalent of a redemption in the course of implementing the reorganization," than "as having occurred prior to and separate from the reorganization." Id., at 152 (emphasis in original).

The Court of Appeals for the Fourth Circuit affirmed. 828 F.2d 221 (1987). Like the Tax Court, it concluded that although "[s]ection 302 does not explicitly apply in the reorganization context," id., at 223, and although §302 differs from §356 in important respects, id., at 224, it nonetheless provides "the appropriate test for determining whether boot is ordinary income or a capital gain," id., at 223. Thus, as explicated in §302(b)(2), if the taxpayer relinquished more than 20% of his corporate control and retained less than 50% of the voting shares after the distribution, the boot would be treated as capital gain. However, as the Court of Appeals recognized, "[b]ecause §302 was designed to deal with a stock redemption by a single corporation, rather than a reorganization involving two companies, the section does not indicate which corporation (the taxpayer) lost interest in." Id., at 224. Thus, like the Tax Court, the Court of Appeals was left to consider whether the hypothetical redemption should be treated as a pre-reorganization distribution coming from the acquired corporation or as a post-reorganization distribution coming from the acquiring corporation. It concluded:

> Based on the language and legislative history of §356, the change-in-ownership principle of §302, and the need to review the reorganization as an integrated transaction, we conclude that the boot should be characterized as a post-reorganization stock redemption by N.L. that affected (the taxpayer's) interest in the new corporation. Because this redemption reduced (the taxpayer's) N.L. holdings by more than 20%, the boot should be taxed as a capital gain.

Id., at 224-225.

This decision by the Court of Appeals for the Fourth Circuit is in conflict with the decision of the Fifth Circuit in *Shimberg*, 577 F.2d 283 (1978), in two important respects. In *Shimberg*, the court concluded that it was inappropriate to apply stock redemption principles in reorganization cases "on a wholesale basis." Id., at 287; see also ibid, n. 13. In addition, the court adopted the pre-reorganization test, holding that "§356(a)(2) requires a determination of whether the distribution would have been taxed as a dividend if made prior to the reorganization or if no reorganization had occurred." Id., at 288.

To resolve this conflict on a question of importance to the administration of the federal tax laws, we granted certiorari. 485 U.S. 933 (1988).

II

We agree with the Tax Court and the Court of Appeals for the Fourth Circuit that the question under §356(a)(2) of whether an "exchange . . . has the effect of the distribution of a dividend" should be answered by examining the effect of the exchange as a whole. We think the language and history of the statute, as well as a common-sense understanding of the economic substance of the transaction at issue, support this approach.

The language of §356(a) strongly supports our understanding that the transaction should be treated as an integrated whole. Section 356(a)(2) asks whether "*an exchange* is described in paragraph (1)" that "has the effect of the distribution of a dividend." (Emphasis supplied.) The statute does not provide that boot shall be treated as a dividend if its payment has the effect of the distribution of a dividend. Rather, the inquiry turns on whether the "exchange" has that effect. Moreover, paragraph (1), in turn, looks to whether "the property received in *the exchange* consists not only of property permitted by section 354 or 355 to be received without the recognition of gain but also of other property or money." (Emphasis supplied.) Again, the statute plainly refers to one integrated transaction and, again, makes clear that we are to look to the character of the exchange as a whole and not simply its component parts. Finally, it is significant that §356 expressly limits the extent to which boot may be taxed to the amount of gain realized in the reorganization. This limitation suggests that Congress intended that boot not be treated in isolation from the overall reorganization. See Levin, Adess, & McGaffey, Boot Distributions in Corporate Reorganizations — Determination of Dividend Equivalency, 30 Tax Lawyer 287, 303 (1977).

Our reading of the statute as requiring that the transaction be treated as a unified whole is reinforced by the well-established "step-transaction" doctrine, a doctrine that the Government has applied in related contexts, see, e.g., Rev. Rul. 75-447, 1975-2 Cum. Bull. 113, and that we have expressly sanctioned, see Minnesota Tea Co. v. Helvering, 302 U.S. 609, 613 (1938); Commissioner v. Court Holding Co., 324 U.S. 331, 334 (1945). Under this doctrine, interrelated yet formally distinct steps in an integrated transaction may not be considered independently of the overall transaction. By thus "linking together all interdependent steps with legal or business significance, rather than taking them in isolation," federal tax liability may be based "on a realistic view of the entire transaction." 1 B. Bittker, Federal Taxation of Income, Estates and Gifts, ¶4.3.5, p. 4-52 (1981).

Viewing the exchange in this case as an integrated whole, we are unable to accept the Commissioner's pre-reorganization analogy. The analogy severs the payment of boot from the context of the reorganization. Indeed, only by straining to abstract the payment of boot from the context of the overall exchange, and thus imagining that Basin made a distribution to the taxpayer independently of NL's planned acquisition, can we reach the rather counterintuitive conclusion urged by the Commissioner — that the taxpayer suffered no meaningful reduction in his ownership interest as a result of the cash payment. We conclude that such a limited view of the transaction is plainly inconsistent with the statute's direction that we look to the effect of the entire exchange.

The pre-reorganization analogy is further flawed in that it adopts an overly expansive reading of §356(a)(2). As the Court of Appeals recognized, adoption of the pre-reorganization approach would "result in ordinary income treatment in most reorganizations because corporate boot is usually distributed pro rata to the shareholders of the target corporation." 828 F.2d, at 227; see also Golub, "Boot" in Reorganizations — The Dividend Equivalency Test of Section 356(a)(2), 58 Taxes 904, 911 (1980); Note, 20 Boston College L. Rev. 601, 612 (1979). Such a reading of the statute would not simply constitute a return to the widely criticized "automatic dividend rule" (at least as to cases involving a pro rata payment to the shareholders of the acquired corporation), but also would be contrary to our standard approach to construing such provisions. The requirement of §356(a)(2) that boot be treated as dividend in some circumstances is an exception from the general rule authorizing capital gains treatment for boot. In construing provisions such as §356, in which a general statement of policy is qualified by an exception, we usually read the exception narrowly in order to preserve the primary operation of the provision. See Phillips, Inc. v. Walling, 324 U.S. 490, 493 (1945) ("To extend an exemption to other than those plainly and unmistakably within its terms and spirit is to abuse the interpretative process and to frustrate the announced will of the people"). Given that Congress has enacted a general rule that treats boot as capital gain, we should not eviscerate that legislative judgment through an expansive reading of a somewhat ambiguous exception.

The post-reorganization approach adopted by the Tax Court and the Court of Appeals is, in our view, preferable to the Commissioner's approach. Most significantly, this approach does a far better job of treating the payment of boot as a component of the overall exchange. Unlike the pre-reorganization view, this approach acknowledges that there would have been no cash payment absent the exchange and also that, by accepting the cash payment, the taxpayer experienced a meaningful reduction in his potential ownership interest.

Once the post-reorganization approach is adopted, the result in this case is pellucidly clear. Section 302(a) of the Code provides that if a redemption fits within any one of the four categories set out in §302(b), the redemption "shall be treated as a distribution in part or full payment in exchange for the stock," and thus not regarded as a dividend. As the Tax Court and the Court of Appeals correctly determined, the hypothetical post-reorganization redemption by NL of a portion of the taxpayer's shares satisfies at least one of the subsections of §302(b). In particular, the safe harbor provisions of subsection (b)(2) provide that redemptions in which the taxpayer relinquishes more than 20% of his or her share of the corporation's voting stock and retains less than 50% of the voting of stock after the redemption, shall not be treated as distributions of a dividend. Here, we treat the transaction as though NL redeemed 125,000 shares of its common stock (i.e., the number of shares of NL common stock foregone in favor of the boot) in return for a cash payment to the taxpayer of $3,250,000 (i.e., the amount of the boot). As a result of this redemption, the taxpayer's interest in NL was reduced from 1.3% of the outstanding common stock to 0.9%. See 86 T.C., at 153. Thus, the taxpayer relinquished approximately 29% of his interest in NL and retained less than a 1% voting interest in the corporation after the transaction, easily satisfying the "substantially disproportionate" standards of §302(b)(2). We accordingly conclude that the boot payment did not have the effect of a dividend and that the payment was properly treated as capital gain.

III

The Commissioner objects to this "recasting [of] the merger transaction into a form different from that entered into by the parties," Brief for the

United States 11, and argues that the Court of Appeals' formal adherence to the principles embodied in §302 forced the court to stretch to "find a redemption to which to apply them, since the merger transaction entered into by the parties did not involve a redemption," id., at 28. There are a number of sufficient responses to this argument. We think it first worth emphasizing that the Commissioner overstates the extent to which the redemption is imagined. As the Court of Appeals for the Fifth Circuit noted in *Shimberg*, "[t]he theory behind tax-free corporate reorganizations is that the transaction is merely 'a continuance of the proprietary interests in the continuing enterprise under modified corporate form.' Lewis v. Commissioner of Internal Revenue, 176 F.2d 646, 648 (1 Cir. 1949); Treas. Reg. §1.368-1(b). See generally Cohen, Conglomerate Mergers and Taxation, 55 A.B.A.J. 40 (1969)." 577 F.2d, at 288. As a result, the boot-for-stock transaction can be viewed as a partial repurchase of stock by the continuing corporate enterprise — i.e., as a redemption. It is of course true that both the pre- and post-reorganization analogies are somewhat artificial in that they imagine that the redemption occurred outside the confines of the actual reorganization. However, if forced to choose between the two analogies, the post-reorganization view is the less artificial. Although both analogies "recast the merger transaction," the post-reorganization view recognizes that a reorganization has taken place, while the pre-reorganization approach recasts the transaction to the exclusion of the overall exchange.

Moreover, we doubt that abandoning the pre- and post-reorganization analogies and the principles of §302 in favor of a less artificial understanding of the transaction would lead to a result different from that reached by the Court of Appeals. Although the statute is admittedly ambiguous and the legislative history sparse, we are persuaded — even without relying on §302 — that Congress did not intend to except reorganizations such as that at issue here from the general rule allowing capital gains treatment for cash boot. The legislative history of §356(a)(2), although perhaps generally "not illuminating," Estate of Bedford, 325 U.S. at 290, suggests that Congress was primarily concerned with preventing corporations from "siphon[ing] off" accumulated earnings and profits at a capital gains rate through the ruse of a reorganization. See Golub, 58 Taxes, at 905. This purpose is not served by denying capital gains treatment in a case such as this in which the taxpayer entered into an arm's length transaction with a corporation in which he had no prior interest, exchanging his stock in the acquired corporation for less than a one percent interest in the acquiring corporation and a substantial cash boot.

Section 356(a)(2) finds its genesis in §203(d)(2) of the Revenue Act of 1924. See 43 Stat. 257. Although modified slightly over the years, the provisions are in relevant substance identical. The accompanying House Report asserts that §203(d)(2) was designed to "preven[t] evasion." H.R. Rep. No. 179, 68th Cong., 1st Sess. 15 (1924). Without further explication, both the House and Senate Reports simply rely on an example to explain, in the words of both Reports, "[t]he necessity for this provision." Ibid; S. Rep. No. 398, 68th Cong., 1st Sess., 16 (1924). Significantly, the example describes a situation in which there was no change in the stockholders' relative ownership interests, but merely the creation of a wholly owned subsidiary as a mechanism for making a cash distribution to the shareholders:

> Corporation A has capital stock of $100,000, and earnings and profits accumulated since March 1, 1913, of $50,000. If it distributes the $50,000 as a dividend to its stockholders, the amount distributed will be taxed at the full surtax rates.
>
> On the other hand, Corporation A may organize Corporation B, to which it transfers all its assets, the consideration for the transfer being the issuance by B of all its stock and $50,000 in cash to the stockholders of Corporation A in exchange for their stock in Corporation A. Under the existing law, the $50,000 distributed with the stock of Corporation B would be taxed, not as a dividend, but as a capital gain, subject only to the 12½ per cent rate. The effect of such a distribution is obviously the same as if the corporation had declared out as a dividend its $50,000 earnings and profits. If dividends are to be subject to the full surtax rates, then such an amount so distributed should also be subject to the surtax rates and not to the 12½ per cent rate on capital gain.

Id., at 16; H.R. Rep. No. 179, at 15. The "effect" of the transaction in this example is to transfer accumulated earnings and profits to the shareholders without altering their respective ownership interests in the continuing enterprise.

Of course, this example should not be understood as exhaustive of the proper applications of §356(a)(2). It is nonetheless noteworthy that neither the example, nor any other legislative source, evinces a congressional intent to tax boot accompanying a transaction that involves a bona fide exchange between unrelated parties in the context of a reorganization as though the payment was in fact a dividend. To the contrary, the purpose of avoiding tax evasion suggests that Congress did not intend to impose an ordinary income tax in such cases. Moreover, the legislative history of §302 supports this reading of §356(a)(2) as well. In explaining the "essentially equivalent to a dividend" language of §302(b)(1) — language that is certainly similar to the "has the effect . . . of a dividend" language of §356(a)(2) — the Senate Finance Committee made clear that the relevant inquiry is "whether or not the transaction by its nature may properly be characterized as a sale of stock. . . ." S. Rep. No. 1622, 83d Cong., 2d Sess., 234 (1954); cf. United States v. Davis, 397 U.S., at 311.

Examining the instant transaction in light of the purpose of §356(a)(2), the boot-for-stock exchange in this case "may properly be characterized as a sale of stock." Significantly, unlike traditional single corporation redemptions and unlike reorganizations involving commonly owned corporations, there is little risk that the reorganization at issue was used as a ruse to distribute a dividend. Rather, the transaction appears in all respects relevant to the narrow issue before us to have been comparable to an arm's length sale by the taxpayer to NL. This conclusion, moreover, is supported by the findings of the Tax Court. The court found that "[t]here is not the slightest evidence that the cash payment was a concealed distribution from BASIN." 86 T.C., at 155. As the Tax Court further noted, Basin lacked the funds to make such a distribution:

> Indeed, it is hard to conceive that such a possibility could even have been considered, for a distribution of that amount was not only far in excess of the accumulated earnings and profits ($2,319,611), but also of the total assets of BASIN ($2,758,069). In fact, only if one takes into account unrealized appreciation in the value of BASIN's assets, including good will and/or going-concern value, can one possibly arrive at $3,250,000. Such a distribution could only be considered as the equivalent of a complete liquidation of BASIN. . . .

Ibid. In this context, even without relying on §302 and the post-reorganization analogy, we conclude that the boot is better characterized as a part of the proceeds of a sale of stock than as a proxy for a dividend. As such, the payment qualifies for capital gains treatment.

The judgment of the Court of Appeals is accordingly affirmed.

Justice WHITE, dissenting.

The question in this case is whether the cash payment of $3,250,000. by N.L. Industries, Inc. (NL) to Donald Clark, which he received in the April 18, 1979, merger of Basin Surveys, Inc. (Basin), into N.L. Acquisition Corporation (NLAC), had the effect of a distribution of a dividend under §356(a)(2), to the extent of Basin's accumulated undistributed earnings and profits. Petitioner, the Commissioner of Internal Revenue (Commissioner) made this determination, taxing the sum as ordinary income, to find a 1979 tax deficiency of $972,504.74. The Court of Appeals disagreed, stating that because the cash payment resembles a hypothetical stock redemption from NL to Clark, the amount is taxable as capital gain. 828 F.2d 221 (C.A.4 1987). Because the majority today agrees with that characterization, in spite of Clark's explicit refusal of the stock-for-stock exchange imagined by the Court of Appeals and the majority today, and because the record demonstrates, instead, that the transaction before us involved a boot distribution that had "the effect of the distribution of a dividend" under §356(a)(2) — hence properly alerted the Commissioner to Clark's tax deficiency — I dissent.

The facts are stipulated. Basin, Clark, NL, and NLAC executed an

Agreement and Plan of Merger dated April 3, 1979, which provided that on April 18, 1979, Basin would merge with NLAC. The statutory merger, which occurred pursuant to §§368(a)(1)(A) and (a)(2)(D) of the Code, and therefore qualified for tax-free reorganization status under §354(a)(1), involved the following terms: Each outstanding share of NLAC stock remained outstanding; each outstanding share of Basin common stock was exchanged for $56,034.482 cash and 5,172.4137 shares of NL common stock; and each share of Basin common stock held by Basin was canceled. NLAC's name was amended to Basin Surveys, Inc. The Secretary of State of West Virginia certified that the merger complied with West Virginia law. Clark, the owner of all 58 outstanding shares of Basin, received $3,250,000. in cash and 300,000 shares of NL stock. He expressly refused NL's alternative of 425,000 shares of NL common stock without cash. See App. 56-59.

Congress enacted §354(a)(1) to grant favorable tax treatment to specific corporate transactions (reorganizations) that involve the exchange of stock or securities solely for other stock or securities. See Paulsen v. Commissioner, 469 U.S. 131, 136 (1985) (citing Treas. Reg. §1.368-1(b), and noting the distinctive feature of such reorganizations, namely continuity-of-interests). Clark's "triangular merger" of Basin into NL's subsidiary NLAC qualified as one such tax-free reorganization, pursuant to §368(a)(2)(D). Because the stock-for-stock exchange was supplemented with a cash payment, however, §356(a)(1) requires that "the gain, if any, to the recipient shall be recognized, but in an amount not in excess of the sum of such money and the fair market value of such other property." Because this provision permitted taxpayers to withdraw profits during corporate reorganizations without declaring a dividend, Congress enacted the present §356(a)(2), which states that when an exchange has "the effect of the distribution of a dividend," boot must be treated as a dividend, and taxed as ordinary income, to the extent of the distributee's "ratable share of the undistributed earnings and profits of the corporation. . . ." Ibid.; see also H.R. Rep. No. 179, 68th Cong., 1st Sess., 15 (1924) (illustration of §356(a)(2)'s purpose to frustrate evasion of dividend taxation through corporate reorganization distributions); S. Rep. No. 398, 68th Cong., 1st Sess., 16 (1924) (same).

Thus the question today is whether the cash payment to Clark had the effect of a distribution of a dividend. We supplied the straightforward answer in United States v. Davis, 397 U.S. 301, 306, 312, when we explained that a pro rata redemption of stock by a corporation is "essentially equivalent" to a dividend. A pro rata distribution of stock, with no alteration of basic shareholder relationships, is the hallmark of a dividend. This was precisely Clark's gain. As sole shareholder of Basin, Clark necessarily received a pro rata distribution of monies that exceeded Basin's undistributed earnings and profits of $2,319,611. Because the merger and cash obligation occurred simultaneously on April 18, 1979, and because the statutory merger approved here assumes that Clark's proprietary interests continue in the restructured NLAC, the exact source of the pro rata boot payment is immaterial, which truth Congress acknowledged by requiring only that an exchange have the effect of a dividend distribution.

To avoid this conclusion, the Court of Appeals — approved by the majority today — recast the transaction as though the relevant distribution involved a single corporation's (NL's) stock redemption, which dividend equivalency is determined according to §302 of the Code. Section 302 shields distributions from dividend taxation if the cash redemption is accompanied by sufficient loss of a shareholder's percentage interest in the corporation. The Court of Appeals hypothesized that Clark completed a pure stock-for-stock reorganization, receiving 425,000 NL shares, and thereafter redeemed 125,000 of these shares for his cash earnings of $3,250,000. The sum escapes dividend taxation because Clark's interest in NL theoretically declined from 1.3% to 0.92%, adequate to trigger §302(b)(2) protection. Transporting §302 from its purpose to frustrate shareholder sales of equity back to their own corporation, to §356(a)(2)'s reorganization context, however, is problematic. Neither the majority nor the Court of Appeals explains why §302 should obscure the core attribute of a dividend as a pro rata distribution to a corporation's shareholders; nor offers insight into the mechanics of valuing hypothetical stock transfers and equity reductions; nor answers the Commissioner's observations that the sole shareholder of an acquired corporation will always have a smaller interest in the continuing enterprise when cash payments combine with a stock exchange. Last, the majority and the Court of Appeals' recharacterization of market happenings describes the exact stock-for-stock exchange, without a cash supplement, that Clark refused when he agreed to the merger.

Because the parties chose to structure the exchange as a tax-free reorganization under §354(a)(1), and because the pro rata distribution to Clark of $3,250,000 during this reorganization had the effect of a dividend under §356(a)(2), I dissent.

NOTE

1.   *Who wins after* Clark? By treating the boot as distributed as part of the reorganization rather than as a redemption occurring prior to the reorganization, the Supreme Court in *Clark* made it easier for most taxpayers to avoid dividend treatment under §365(a)(2). But you should not assume that *Clark* represents a victory for all taxpayers, especially for those who own stock in the acquiring corporation as well as in the target corporation. Consider the following example.

T Corp. merges into *A* Corp. when each share of *T* Corp. stock and of *A* Corp. stock is worth $50. Assume that individuals *P, Q* and *R* own stock in *T* Corp. and *A* Corp. as follows:

	Number of Shares	
	T Corp.	*A Corp.*
P	60	0
Q	60	90
R	0	30
	120	120

The merger gives *P* $1,500 in cash and 30 shares of *A* Corp. stock, while *Q* receives $2,500 in cash and 10 shares of *Y* Corp. stock. Accordingly, after the merger *A* Corp. has 160 shares of stock outstanding, of which *P* owns 30, *Q* owns 100, and *R* owns 30.

Following the approach adopted by the Supreme Court in *Clark*, we treat the transaction as if *P* and *Q* received only stock in the reorganization and then some of that stock was redeemed. Because each share of *A* Corp. is worth $50, the $1,500 boot received by *P* corresponds to 30 shares of *A* Corp. and the $2,500 boot received by *Q* corresponds to 50 shares of *A* Corp. Accordingly, we treat the transaction as if *P* and *Q* each received 60 shares of *A* Corp. stock in the reorganization and then 30 of *P*'s shares and 50 of *Q* shares were redeemed.

Thus, *A* Corp. is treated as having 240 shares outstanding, 60 owned by *P*, 150 owned by *Q*, and 30 owned by *R*. The effect of the hypothetical redemption is to reduce *P*'s ownership of *A* Corp. from 25 percent (60 of 240 shares) to 18.75 percent (30 of 160 shares) and to leave *Q*'s ownership of *A* Corp. at 62.50 percent (from 150 of 240 shares to 100 of 160 shares). On this redemption, *P* will qualify for exchange treatment under §§302 (b)(2) and 302(a) while *Q* will receive dividend income (assuming adequate earnings and profits).

Under the approach articulated in *Shimberg* and rejected by the Supreme Court in *Clark*, the taxation of *P* and *Q* is reversed, with *P* having dividend income and *Q* enjoying capital gain. Under this approach, *P* and *Q* are treated as if they receive the boot in a redemption prior to the merger. As a result of this hypothetical redemption, *P*'s interest in *T* Corp. increases from 50 percent (60 of 120 shares) to 75 percent (30 of 40 shares) because each $50 received by the shareholders is treated as the redemption of one share of *T* Corp. stock. *Q*'s interest similarly decreases from 50 percent (60 of 120 shares) to 25 percent (10 of 40 shares). Accordingly, this hypothetical redemption results in dividend income to *P* and capital gain to *Q*. The observation by the Supreme Court in *Clark* that its rejection of the *Shimberg* approach is a pro-taxpayer result is thus not always true when shareholders of the target corporation also own stock in the acquiring corporation.

2. *Measuring earnings and profits.* Prior to the Supreme Court's deci-

sion in *Clark,* the Service ruled that it would not follow the *Wright* (now *Clark*) meaningful reduction test. Rev. Rul. 75-83, 1975-1 C.B. 112. The Service rejected *Wright* on the ground that the earnings and profits of the transferor corporation should be available as a source of dividend income once dividend equivalency is established under §356(a)(2). The Supreme Court in *Clark* did not have occasion to determine the proper measure of earnings and profits because in that case the distribution of boot did not have the effect of a dividend, but the Tax Court had the following to say on this issue: "There is no reason why the redemption cannot be considered as having been made by one corporation with the consequences to be measured by the earnings and profits of another corporation." Clark v. Commissioner, 86 T.C. 138 (1986), aff'd, 828 F.2d 221 (4th Cir. 1987), aff'd, 489 U.S. 726 (1989); see also American Manufacturing Co. v. Commissioner, 55 T.C. 204 (1970) (no combination allowed); Atlas Tool Co. v. Commissioner, 614 F.2d 860 (3d Cir. 1980) (same); Davant v. Commissioner, 366 F.2d 874 (5th Cir. 1966) (combination allowed); Rev. Rul. 70-274, 1970-1 C.B. 81 (same). Indeed, because the approach adopted by the Supreme Court in *Clark* treats the redemption as part of the full reorganization, it would seem appropriate to make the earnings and profits of *both* corporations available for dividend income. Compare the earnings and profits computation in §304(b)(2).

3. *Dividend income versus dividend gain.* Section 356(a)(2) has one structural aspect that is difficult to justify. While the receipt of boot will give rise to gain taxable at ordinary rates if the effect of the boot is dividend equivalency, it is still *gain,* rather than the amount of the boot, that is taxable under §356(a)(2). If the effect of the boot is the receipt of a dividend, why is the taxpayer allowed basis recovery before recognizing income? Indeed, if there is no gain on the exchange, then the taxpayer will not recognize any income under §356(a)(2) regardless of the amount of the boot or dividend equivalency.

D. THE STATUS OF CREDITORS IN CORPORATE REORGANIZATIONS

The materials in this chapter focus primarily on the consequences of a corporate reorganization to the shareholders of the corporation whose assets are transferred. Almost always, however, the corporation will have creditors. How are they affected by the reorganization? Do they recognize gain or loss if they surrender their claims and in exchange receive stock or securities of the reorganized corporation or other claims against it?

At the outset it should be noted that the creditors will not necessarily participate in the reorganization exchange. For example, in a B reorganization, the creditors of the acquired corporation may simply ride through the reorganization, preserving intact their claims against their respective debtors.

Alternatively, the acquiring corporation may assume the transferor corporation's liabilities or take the properties subject to those liabilities, still without any exchange by the creditors. Ordinarily, this will not constitute boot to the transferee. §357. Nor will creditors recognize gain or loss since their claims have not been paid, retired, or exchanged. Moreover, §368(a)(1)(C) states explicitly that the requirement that the acquisition be solely for the acquiring corporation's voting stock in a C reorganization is not breached by the corporation's assuming liabilities or taking property subject to liabilities.

Frequently, however, there will be an exchange. The creditors may surrender bonds, debentures, or notes of one corporation and receive stock or securities of another corporation. In general, the exchange will qualify under §354. One difficulty that may arise is that short-term notes (whether given up or received) may not qualify as "securities." See pages 476-478 supra.

There may be other problems as well. If in conjunction with a B reorganization (stock for stock) the acquiring corporation issues bonds in exchange for bonds of the acquired corporation, will the transaction fall outside of §368(a)(1)(B) on the ground that it is not "solely" for voting stock? If the stock-for-stock exchange qualifies, will the bondholders' exchange be "in pursuance of a plan of reorganization" under §354(a)(1)? See Rev. Rul. 70-41, 1970-1 C.B. 77 (exchange of debt of the acquired corporation for stock of the acquiring corporation incident to B reorganization is taxable). Similarly in a C reorganization, if the acquiring corporation issues its own evidences of indebtedness to creditors of the transferee corporation instead of merely assuming the liabilities, should the transaction lose its status as a reorganization?

E. REORGANIZATIONS OF INSOLVENT OR FINANCIALLY DISTRESSED CORPORATIONS

Under prior law, a transfer of all or part of a corporation's assets to another corporation pursuant to a court-approved plan under the Bankruptcy Act could qualify for tax-free treatment under separate rules applicable to "insolvency reorganizations." In the Bankruptcy Tax Act of 1980, Congress ended the separate regime for debtor corporations in a title 11 (bankruptcy) case by adding a new category of tax-free corporate reorganization under §368(a)(1): the G reorganization. Congress made this change to encourage and facilitate the rehabilitation of bankrupt debtor corporations. As a consequence, many prior law requirements for tax-free treatment were removed, parties were given additional flexibility in structuring the acquisition, and, most importantly, the acquiring corporation was permitted to succeed to the tax attributes of the acquired corporation (such as its net operating loss carryovers). S. Rep. No. 1035, 96th Cong., 2d Sess. 34-25 (1980).

As is often the case, change is not without its problems. While there are benefits to the G reorganization, qualifying transactions must also conform to certain statutory and judicial requirements imposed on all tax-free reorganizations. It is apparent that many of these regular tax reorganization requirements cannot be easily adapted and applied to the unique circumstances faced by a bankrupt corporation.

Difficulties aside, the G reorganization is the most flexible of the acquisitive tax-free reorganization provisions. It is a hybrid provision that borrows most of its characteristics from the other acquisitive reorganization provisions. It is similar to an A reorganization (a state law merger) in that it requires two corporations, and the only limit on the nature of consideration used by the acquiring corporation is the judicial continuity of proprietary interest doctrine discussed at the beginning of this chapter. State law merger requirements, however, need not be met. It is similar to a C reorganization in that it contemplates an acquisition of assets of one corporation by another corporation, but it does not require an exchange of assets solely (as relaxed by statute) for voting stock of the acquiring corporation. It is most like an acquisitive D reorganization, except that it does not require that the shareholders of the acquired corporation also be "in control" of the acquiring corporation.

A G reorganization is defined as (1) a transfer of assets (2) by one corporation to another corporation in a title 11 (bankruptcy) or similar case (3) followed by a distribution as described in §354, §355, or §356 of the consideration received in the transaction. Each of these three requirements is discussed below.

A G reorganization requires that a corporation transfer all or a part of its assets to another corporation, provided one of the corporations is in a bankruptcy (or similar) case and provided the transfer occurs pursuant to a plan of reorganization approved by the bankruptcy court. §368(a)(3)(B). Thus, the transfer of stock of the debtor corporation to its creditors in satisfaction of their claims will not qualify as a G reorganization (although such a transaction may have no adverse tax consequences). Similarly, out-of-court transactions, chapter 7 liquidating cases, and foreign reorganizations are ineligible.

For example, suppose Loss Corp. is hopelessly insolvent. Immediately prior to filing a bankruptcy petition, Loss Corp. agrees to transfer all its assets to Public Corp. in exchange for Public Corp. common stock; Loss Corp. will then distribute the stock received to its creditors in satisfaction of their claims. This acquisition will not qualify as a G reorganization because it did not occur within a title 11 or similar case. Accordingly, the transaction will be tax free only if it meets the standards of one of the other acquisitive reorganization provisions such as the A, C, or D.

As a second example, suppose Loss Corp. is in a chapter 11 bankruptcy case. Loss Corp.'s plan of reorganization provides for a transfer of cash and certain nonoperating assets to secured creditors and of all newly authorized common stock to its unsecured creditors. All previously authorized outstanding common stock is canceled. Loss Corp.'s plan will not qualify as a G reorganization because Loss Corp. has not transferred its assets to another corporation. Although not qualifying as a G reorganization, this transaction likely qualifies for tax-free treatment as an E recapitalization, a form of tax-free reorganization discussed in Chapter 12. See S. Rep. No. 1035, 96th Cong., 2d Sess. 36 (1980).

Distribution of stock or securities of the acquiring corporation in a transaction that qualifies under §354 raises some difficult obstacles. Section 354(b) requires that substantially all the assets of the acquired corporation be transferred to the acquiring corporation. In the context of the C reorganization, the Service requires (for advanced rulings) that at least 90 percent of the net assets and 70 percent of the gross assets be transferred in the reorganization. Rev. Proc. 77-37 (§3.01), 1977-2 C.B. 568. Congress has indicated that the substantially-all requirement be interpreted liberally in the context of the G reorganization in view of the underlying purpose of the provision to facilitate the rehabilitation of financially troubled corporations. Accordingly, substantially all the assets of the debtor corporation should be acquired even if the debtor sells assets to pay creditors or to rearrange its business affairs so as to obtain creditor approval of its plan of reorganization. S. Rep. No. 1035, 96th Cong., 2d Sess. 36-36 (1980). In private rulings, the Service has relaxed its definition of "substantially all" in the context of a G reorganization. See Priv. Ltr. Rul. 8726055; Priv. Ltr. Rul. 8521083.

In addition to the substantially-all requirement, §354(a) requires that stock or securities of the acquiring corporation be distributed to a holder of stock or securities of the acquired corporation. If holders of securities in the acquired corporation actually receive stock or securities (or if shareholders in the acquired corporation actually receive stock) in the acquiring corporation pursuant to the plan of reorganization, the transaction should qualify as a G reorganization even if the value of the stock or securities received represents a small percentage of the value of the total equity consideration given in the transaction. Thus, the threshold exchange requirement of §354(a) should be satisfied if one securityholder receives stock or securities (or if one shareholder receives stock) pursuant to the plan of reorganization. The threshold exchange requirement of §354(a) will not be satisfied, however, if (as is often true in the typical corporate bankruptcy) all the old stock of the debtor corporation is canceled (because there is no equity left) and the acquiring corporation's stock is distributed to short-term creditors whose debt instruments do not rise to the dignity of a tax security.

For example, suppose Loss Corp. is in a chapter 11 bankruptcy case. Loss Corp.'s plan of reorganization provides for the transfer of substantially all its assets to Public Corp. in exchange for Public Corp. common stock with fair market value of $450 and cash of $550. The plan calls for the transfer of cash and certain nonoperating assets to secured creditors and for the distribution of all the Public Corp. common stock to Loss Corp.'s unsecured creditors. One unsecured creditor holds a 10-year bond with a locomotive printed on the face of the certificate. Assume that a locomotive is clear evidence that the bond is a "security" for tax purposes. The old Loss Corp. common stock is canceled, and the shareholders receive nothing under the plan. Because substantially all the assets were acquired by Public Corp. in exchange for an amount of common stock that should satisfy the continuity of proprietary interest doctrine, and because at least one Loss Corp. securityholder received stock pursuant to the plan, the transaction should qualify as a tax-free G reorganization.

The transaction in this example would not qualify as a G reorganization if all of Loss Corp.'s unsecured creditors held only short-term debt. One possible way to avoid this technical trap in the statute is to convert the claims of the creditors into stock of the acquired debtor corporation before the G reorganization is consummated, relying on Helvering v. Alabama Asphaltic Limestone Co., 315 U.S. 179 (1942). In that case, the Supreme Court held that creditors of an insolvent corporation who received stock of a reorganized corporation had a "continuing interest" because, under the full priority rule of bankruptcy proceedings, they had "effective command over the disposition of the properties" of the old corporation.

In Neville Coke & Chemical Co. v. Commissioner, 148 F.2d 599 (3d Cir. 1945), however, the court held that noteholders of a reorganized corporation who exchanged their notes for debentures and common stock could not claim nonrecognition of their gain under what is now §354. The court relied on *Pinellas* and *LeTulle* as establishing that notes received on an exchange do not evidence a continuing interest in the enterprise and are not "securities." It then held that the notes are equally deficient if given up in the exchange. The debtor was in financial difficulties at the time of the exchange, but the court was unwilling to find that the creditors already owned the entire equity, and in fact the old stockholders did participate in the exchange. If, however, the creditors of a distressed corporation in reorganization received stock or securities evidencing a proprietary interest in the enterprise, is it not probable that the claims they gave up, whatever their form, already represented in economic reality a proprietary interest in the assets? For a forceful statement of this view, see Griswold, "Securities" and "Continuity of Interest," 58 Harv. L. Rev. 705 (1945).

In addition to the statutory requirements, a G reorganization must meet judicial requirements imposed on all tax-free corporate reorganizations. Principally, these include continuity of proprietary interest, continuity of business enterprise, and business purpose. These are discussed at pages 431-437 supra. Finally, if a transaction qualifies as both a G reorganization and a different reorganization under another provision (or under §332 or §351), the transaction is treated as qualifying only as a G reorganization. §368(a)(3)(C).

F. POLICY

Recall that the initial justification for the reorganization provisions was that a corporate rearrangement should be taxable if it resembles a sale but should be tax free if it more closely appears to be a mere change in form of the business enterprise. From that relatively simple notion has grown the complexity you have just discovered.

The simple fact is that most corporate acquisitions can be structured either as reorganizations or as taxable transactions. While not formally elective, reorganization status is practically a matter of choice. The detailed rules of the Code seeking to distinguish tax-free reorganizations from taxable sales have little effect beyond increasing the transaction and uncertainty costs to taxpayers contemplating acquisitive transactions.

Those corporate rearrangements qualifying as reorganizations under §368 are, in general, tax free at both the corporate and shareholder level. Nonqualifying transactions will be taxable at one or both levels, depending on the form selected by the parties. On one hand, a corporate acquisition structured as the sale of shares by the acquired corporation's shareholders will be taxed at the shareholder level only: Because the corporate assets are not formally transferred, no corporate-level tax is imposed. On the other hand, sale by the target of its assets will produce a corporate-level tax, but the shareholders of the target corporation will be safe from taxation until the sale proceeds are distributed.

At the corporate level, this distinction makes little sense. Any bulk transfer of corporate assets is a rearrangement of the business enterprise. Tax-free treatment of any such transaction, *however effected,* is an appropriate incident to the change in form of a business. So long as asset basis is preserved, no corporate-level tax will be avoided. If the corporate parties desire a step-up in basis and are willing to be taxed on the transaction as the price for that step-up, that result should also be acceptable to the Treasury. Section 338 has adopted this elective approach to rearrangements of corporate control effected by sale of the target corporation's stock. Should Congress permit the bulk sale of corporate assets to go untaxed with an accompanying carryover basis rule, the tax treatment of corporate reorganizations will become fully elective.

At the shareholder level, the appropriate taxation seems to turn on what each shareholder receives in the reorganization. That is, the exchange of stock and securities for stock and securities incident to a corporate acquisition ought to be tax free regardless of what other shareholders receive. Kass, for example, should have been entitled to nonrecognition even though most of her co-shareholders properly were taxed.

Accordingly, shareholder-level taxation should be independent of corporate-level taxation: Whether the corporate parties elect nonrecognition or taxable exchange is a matter of indifference to the shareholders. As a result, cases like *McDonald's*, page 424 supra, should not arise. Further, the taxation of each shareholder should be independent of the taxation of all other shareholders: In particular, the continuity of proprietary interest should be abolished. These basic reforms, along with several others, have been proposed by the American Law Institute. See ALI, Federal Income Tax Project: Subchapter C — Proposals on Corporate Acquisitions and Dispositions (1982). In turn, the ALI reforms largely have been embraced by the Senate Finance Committee. See Staff of the Senate Finance Committee, The Subchapter C Revision Act of 1985, 99th Cong., 1st Sess. (Comm. Print 1985).

G. PROBLEMS

1. Determine whether the following transactions are "reorganizations" within the meaning of §368.

   a. *X* Corp. has 100 shares outstanding, 40 owned by *A*, 40 by *B*, and 20 by *C*. The fair market value of *X* Corp. stock is $100 per share. *Y* Corp. is owned by 10 individuals. For every dollar of stock held by the *Y* shareholders, they each hold four dollars in 20-year notes of *Y*. *X* Corp. merges into *Y* Corp., with *A*, *B*, and *C* receiving two shares of *Y* stock (worth $100 per share) and an $800 20-year note of *Y* for every 10 shares of *X* stock tendered. What is the result if *A* and *B* receive only notes and *C* receives only stock? Could there be a "reorganization" as to *C* alone?

   b. *F* owns all the stock of *M* Corp., and *G* owns all the stock of *N* Corp. *M* Corp. is worth $1 million, and *N* Corp. is worth $100,000. *M* and *N* consolidate into newly formed *O* Corp., with *F* receiving 100 shares of class A common and *G* receiving 10 shares of class B common. Both classes have equal rights to dividends and on liquidation and both vote. The corporation, however, can redeem the class B shares at any time. What is the result if the class A shares can be redeemed at any time? If the class B shares can be redeemed for 80 percent of their fair market value?

   c. *L* Corp. has lost money in the computer business for several years, and *P* Corp. is a profitable publisher of children's books. What are the consequences if *L* merges into *P*, with the *L* shareholders receiving stock of *P*, assuming that most of the *L* assets will be sold and *P* Corp. will not enter the computer business? If the merger is structured such that *P* merges into *L*, once again assuming that the *L* assets will be sold and only publishing will continue? If *L* and *P* formally consolidate into new corporation *LP*?

d.   To ensure a ready source of newsprint, News Corp. purchases 85 percent of the stock of Paper Co. for cash. One year later, News Corp. acquires the remaining stock of Paper Co. in exchange for its own voting preferred stock. What is the result if News Corp. used voting stock of its parent corporation? Of its wholly owned subsidiary? Could News Corp. use its own nonvoting common stock? Can News Corp. pay the cost of registering the stock received by the shareholders of Paper Co.?

e.   *T* owns all 100 outstanding shares of *Z* Corp. The shares have an aggregate value of $100,000 and are subject to a mortgage of $15,000 incurred by *T* to remodel her home. Big Corp. acquires all the stock of *Z* by exchanging 85 shares of its $1,000 par value voting preferred for the *Z* shares and assumption of the outstanding debt. What is the result if it took the shares subject to the debt but *T* remained personally liable on it?

f.   Target Corp. owns assets with a fair market value of $200,000 subject to debts of $50,000. Acquiring Corp. exchanges its voting stock worth $150,000 for the Target assets subject to the debt, and Target promptly liquidates. What are the consequences if Acquiring Corp. paid Target Corp. $50,000 to discharge the debts as part of the acquisition? If Acquiring Corp. uses cash of $25,000 and takes the assets subject to $25,000 of debt? How do your answers change if the debt was only $30,000?

g.   Suppose in (f) that Acquiring Corp. exchanges voting stock of its Parent Corp. (rather than its own voting stock) for the Target Corp. assets and that after the exchange Acquiring Corp. transfers the assets acquired from Target Corp. to Holding Corp., a wholly owned subsidiary of Acquiring Corp. Assume Acquiring Corp. is a wholly owned subsidiary of Parent Corp.

h.   *P* Corp. owns operating assets worth $300,000 as well as investment real estate worth $700,000. *F* owns all the stock of *P* Corp. *P* transfers all its assets to *Q* Corp. in exchange for common stock of *Q* worth $800,000 and cash of $200,000. *P* then liquidates, distributing the *Q* stock and cash to *F*. Prior to the transaction, *Q* was wholly owned by individual *S*. After the transaction, *F* owns 40 percent of *Q* and *S* owns 60 percent. What is the result if *P* did not transfer the real estate, receiving in exchange for the operating assets stock of *Q* worth $300,000 and representing a 20 percent interest? Is it relevant whether *F* and *S* are father and son?

i.   Corner Grocery Corp. is acquired by the *BQ* National Chain in the following steps. *BQ* forms a wholly owned subsidiary Sub Corp. Corner Grocery then merges into Sub Corp., with the shareholders of Corner Grocery receiving their consideration half in the form of *BQ* voting preferred stock and half in debentures of *BQ*. What are the consequences if the debentures were debt of the subsidiary? If the stock had been nonvoting?

j. Suppose in (i) that Corner Grocery owns a favorable lease that cannot be transferred. Accordingly, the transaction is structured as follows. *BQ* forms Sub Corp. by contributing *BQ* preferred stock. Sub Corp. is then merged into Corner Grocery, with *BQ* receiving 1,000 shares of Corner Grocery voting stock in exchange for its shares of Sub Corp. At the same time, the former shareholders of Corner Grocery exchange all their common stock of Corner Grocery for the *BQ* preferred owned by Sub Corp. How does your answer change if the former owners of Corner Grocery also owned nonvoting preferred stock in Corner Grocery and those preferred share remain outstanding after the merger?

2. *T* Corp. has 1,000 shares of common stock outstanding, owned 60 percent by *A* and 40 percent by *B*. *A* and *B* each have a basis of $100 per share in their *T* Corp. stock. *T* owns a factory with fair market value of $800,000 and adjusted basis of $300,000, subject to a mortgage of $500,000. *T* also owns inventory with adjusted basis of $100,000 and fair market value of $200,000. *P* Corp., a widely held public corporation, wishes to acquire all the *T* Corp. assets in a tax-free reorganization. Discuss the tax consequences of each of the following.

a. *P* transfers $500,000 of its voting preferred stock to *T* in exchange for all the assets subject to the mortgage, followed by the complete liquidation of *T*.

b. *P* transfers $400,000 of its voting common stock to *T* Corp. in exchange for the factory subject to the mortgage as well as half the inventory. *T* then completely liquidates, distributing both the *P* stock and the remaining inventory to its shareholders pro rata.

c. *P* transfers $400,000 of its voting common stock and $100,000 of its long-term bonds to *T* in exchange for all its assets subject to the mortgage, followed by a complete liquidation of *T*.

d. How do your answers to (c) change if there had been no mortgage on the factory and *P* had transferred $900,000 of its voting stock as well as $100,000 of securities? If *P* had transferred voting stock worth $900,000 plus land with fair market value of $100,000 and adjusted basis of $50,000?

3. *X* Corp. has 100 shares outstanding, 50 owned by individual *A* and 50 by individual *B*. *Y* Corp. also has 100 shares outstanding, 80 owned by *B* and 20 by individual *C*. *X* Corp. has earnings and profits of $1,000, and *Y* Corp. has earnings and profits of $1,500. *A*'s basis in the *X* Corp. stock is $20 per share; *B*'s basis in the *X* Corp. stock is $10 per share; *B*'s basis in the *Y* Corp. stock is $10 per share; *C*'s basis in the *Y* Corp. stock is $30 per share. The shares of *X* and *Y* are worth $50 per share.

X Corp. merges into Y Corp. under applicable state law. As part of the merger, A receives $1,000 in cash and 30 shares of Y. B receives $1,500 in cash and 20 shares of Y. Accordingly, the ownership of Y Corp. after the merger is as follows: A owns 30 shares, B owns 100 shares, and C owns 20 shares.

What are the tax consequences to A and B of this merger? Assume that A, B, and C are unrelated to one another.

4.   L Corp. is involved in a bankruptcy proceeding. In 1995 and as part of the court-supervised plan of reorganization, Big Corp. transfers its preferred stock worth $50,000 to L Corp. in exchange for L's fully depreciated operating assets. L Corp. then liquidates, distributing the Big Corp. preferred stock and its nonoperating assets (short-term certificates of deposit with adjusted basis of $22,000 and fair market value of $25,000) to its sole debtholder, H, in complete satisfaction of L's $100,000 debt to H. The shareholders of L Corp. receive nothing, and their stock in L Corp. is canceled. What are the tax consequences of this transaction to Big Corp., to H, to L, and to the former shareholders of L?

11

Divisive Reorganizations

A. TAXATION UNDER §355

Coady v. Commissioner
33 T.C. 771 (1960), aff'd per curiam, 289 F.2d 490
(6th Cir. 1961)

TIETJENS, Judge: . . .

The issue for decision is whether the transfer by the Christopher Construction Company of a portion of its assets to E. P. Coady and Co. in exchange for all of the Coady Company's stock, and the subsequent distribution by the Christopher Company of such Coady stock to petitioner in exchange for his Christopher stock, constituted a distribution of stock qualifying for tax-free treatment on the shareholder level under the provisions of section 355 of the 1954 Internal Revenue Code.

All of the facts were stipulated, are so found, and are incorporated herein by this reference. . . .

Christopher Construction Co., an Ohio corporation, is now engaged, and for more than 5 years prior to November 15, 1954, was engaged, in the active conduct of a construction business primarily in and around Columbus, Ohio. In an average year the Christopher Company undertook approximately 6 construction contracts, no one of which lasted for more than 2 years. Its gross receipts varied between $1,500,000 and $2,000,000 per year.

At its central office, located at 16 East Broad Street in Columbus, the Christopher Company kept its books of account, paid its employees, prepared bids for its jobs, and, excepting minor amounts of tools and supplies, made its purchases. In addition, it maintained temporary field offices at each jobsite. It also maintained a central repair and storage depot for its equipment. Equipment in use on particular jobs was kept at the jobsite until work was terminated. Then, it would either be returned to the central depot or moved to another jobsite.

At all times material hereto, the stock of the Christopher Company was owned by M. Christopher and the petitioner. For a number of years, petitioner owned 35 per cent of that stock and Christopher owned 65 per cent. However, on April 19, 1954, petitioner purchased 15 per cent of the total stock from Christopher. From that date until November 15, 1954, each owned 50 per cent of the company's stock.

Sometime prior to November 15, 1954, differences arose between the petitioner and Christopher. As a result, they entered into an agreement for the division of the Christopher Company into two separate enterprises. Pursuant to that agreement, the Christopher Company, on November 15, 1954, organized E. P. Coady and Co., to which it transferred the following assets, approximating one-half the Christopher Company's total assets:

A contract for the construction of a sewage disposal plant at Columbus, Ohio, dated June 1, 1954.

A part of its equipment.

A part of its cash, and certain other items.

In consideration for the receipt of these assets, E. P. Coady and Co. transferred all of its stock to the Christopher Company. The Christopher Company retained the following assets, which were of the same type as those transferred to E. P. Coady and Co.:

A contract for a sewage treatment plant in Charleston, West Virginia.

A part of its equipment.

A part of its cash.

Immediately thereafter, the Christopher Company distributed to the petitioner all of the stock of E. P. Coady and Co. held by it in exchange for all of the stock of the Christopher Company held by petitioner. The fair market value of the stock of E. P. Coady and Co. received by petitioner was $140,000. His basis in the Christopher Company stock surrendered was $72,500.

Since the distribution, both E. P. Coady and Co. and the Christopher Company have been actively engaged in the construction business.

On their 1954 Federal income tax return, petitioner and his wife reported no gain or loss on the exchange of the Christopher Company stock for the stock of E. P. Coady and Co.

Respondent determined that petitioner realized a capital gain on that exchange in the amount of $67,500, 50 per cent of which was taxable in 1954.

Petitioner contends that the distribution to him of the E. P. Coady and Co. stock qualified for tax-free treatment under the provisions of section 355 of the 1954 Code, arguing that it was received pursuant to a distribution of a controlled corporation's stock within the meaning of that section.

Respondent on the other hand maintains petitioner's receipt of the Coady stock did not fall within those distributions favored by section 355, inasmuch as the 5-year active business requirements of 355(b) were not met. More particularly he argues that section 355 does not apply to the separation of a "single business"; and, inasmuch as the Christopher Company was engaged in only one trade or business (construction contracting), the gain realized by petitioner upon receipt of the Coady stock was taxable. As authority for his position respondent points to that portion of his regulations which expressly provides that section 355 does not apply to the division of a single business.[2]

Thus, the issue is narrowed to the question of whether the challenged portion of the regulations constitutes a valid construction of the statute, or whether it is unreasonable and plainly inconsistent therewith. Though this appears to be a case of first impression, the question has not gone without comment. . . .

Section 355 of the 1954 Code represents the latest of a series of legislative enactments designed to deal with the tax effect upon shareholders of various corporate separations. Where the 1939 Code contained three sections, 112(b)(3), 112(b)(11), and 112(g)(1)(D), which controlled the tax impact of these exchanges, present law groups the statutory requirements into two sections, 355 and 368(c). A careful reading of section 355, as well as the Finance Committee report which accompanied its enactment, reveals no language, express or implied, denying tax-free treatment at the shareholder level to a transaction, otherwise qualifying under section 355, on the grounds that it represents the division or separation of a "single" trade or business. . . .

The active business requirements of 355(b)(1) prohibit the tax-free separation of a corporation into active and inactive entities. Section 355(b)(1)(A) extends the provisions of §355(a) only to those divisive distributions where the distributing corporation and the controlled corporation are engaged immediately after the distribution in the active conduct of a trade or business. In the case of those distributions which involve liquidation of the transferor, 355(b)(1)(B) requires that immediately before the distribution the transferor have no assets other than stock or securities in the controlled corporations, and that immediately thereafter each of the controlled corporations is engaged in the active conduct of a trade or business. Neither 355(b)(1)(A) nor (B) concerns itself with the existence of a plurality of businesses per se; rather both speak in terms of a plurality of corporate entities engaged in the active conduct of a trade or business, a distinction we believe to be vital in light of provisions of 355(b)(2). . . .

Respondent maintains that a reading of 355(b)(2)(B) in conjunction

_____

2. This regulation has been repealed. — Eds.

with the requirement of 355(b)(1) that both "the distributing corporation, *and* the controlled corporation . . . , [be] engaged immediately after the distribution in the active conduct of a trade or business" (emphasis supplied) indicates Congress intended the provisions of the statute to apply only where, immediately after the distribution, there exist two separate and distinct businesses, one operated by the distributing corporation and one operated by the controlled corporation, both of which were actively conducted for the 5-year period immediately preceding the distribution. In our judgment the statute does not support this construction.

[T]he only reference to plurality appears in section 355(b)(1), and deals with corporate entities, not businesses. Recognizing the divisive nature of the transaction, subsection (b)(1) contemplates that where there was only one corporate entity prior to the various transfers, immediately subsequent thereto, there will be two or more *corporations*. In order to insure that a tax-free separation will involve the separation only of those assets attributable to the carrying on of an active trade or business, and further to prevent the tax-free division of an active corporation into active and inactive entities, subsection (b)(1) further provides that each of the surviving corporations must be engaged in the active conduct of a trade or business.

A careful reading of the definition of the active conduct of a trade or business contained in subsection (b)(2) indicates that its function is also to prevent the tax-free separation of *active* and *inactive* assets into *active* and *inactive* corporate entities. This is apparent from the use of the adjective "such," meaning beforementioned, to modify "trade or business" in subsection (b)(2)(B), thus providing that the trade or business, required by (b)(2)(B) to have had a 5-year active history prior to the distribution, is the same trade or business which (b)(2)(A) requires to be actively conducted immediately after the distribution. Nowhere in (b)(2) do we find, as respondent suggests we should, language denying the benefits of section 355 to the division of a single trade or business.

Nor can respondent derive support for his position by reading subsections (b)(1) and (b)(2) together, inasmuch as the plurality resulting therefrom is occasioned, not by any requirement that there be a multiplicity of businesses, but rather by the divisive nature of the transaction itself: i.e., one corporation becoming two or more corporations. Moreover, from the fact that the statute requires, immediately after the distribution, that the surviving corporations each be engaged in the conduct of a trade or business with an active 5-year history, we do not think it inevitably follows that each such trade or business necessarily must have been conducted on an individual basis throughout that 5-year period. As long as the trade or business which has been divided has been actively conducted for 5 years preceding the distribution, and the resulting businesses (each of which in this case, happens to be half of the original whole) are actively conducted after the division, we are of the opinion that the active business requirements of the statute have been complied with.

Respondent argues his construction of section 355 is confirmed by the report of the Senate Committee on Finance which accompanied the 1954 Internal Revenue Code. He refers us to that portion of the report which provides:

Present law contemplates that a tax-free separation shall involve only the separation of assets attributable to the carrying on of an active business. Under the House bill, it is immaterial whether the assets are those used in an active business but if investment assets, for example, are separated into a new corporation, any amount received in respect of such an inactive corporation, whether by a distribution from it or by a sale of its stock, would be treated as ordinary income for a period of 10 years from the date of its creation. Your committee returns to existing law in not permitting the tax free separation of an existing corporation into active and inactive entities. It is not believed that the business need for this kind of transaction is sufficiently great to permit a person in a position to afford a 10-year delay in receiving income to do so at capital gain rather than dividend rates. Your committee requires that *both* the business retained by the distributing company and the business of the corporation the stock of which is distributed must have been actively conducted for the 5 years preceding the distribution, a safeguard against avoidance not contained in existing law. [Emphasis supplied.]

He argues that use of the term "both," with reference to the business retained by the distributing corporation and that operated by the controlled corporation, indicates that Congress intended there be in operation and existence during the 5 years preceding the distribution two or more separate and distinct businesses. We do not agree.

A reading of the quoted section of the report in its entirety reveals that the committee was addressing itself to the nature and the use of the particular assets which were transferred (active v. inactive), rather than to any distinction between one or more businesses. This is obvious when the entire paragraph is considered in the light of its topic sentence. The committee notes that under present law only assets attributable to the carrying on of an active trade or business may be separated tax free. After acknowledging a departure from this requirement in the House bill, the committee disapproves of the position taken by the House, and indicates it is returning to existing law by not permitting the tax-free separation of a corporation into active and inactive entities, and strengthens this provision by requiring that both the business retained by the distributing corporation and that of the controlled corporation must have been actively conducted for 5 years preceding the distribution. The excerpt makes no mention of trades or businesses per se.

Respondent next argues the regulations upon which he relies are entitled to additional stature due to the fact that the Technical Amendments Act of 1958 (72 Stat. 160), which was intended to eliminate unintended benefits and hardships contained in the 1954 Code, was enacted subsequent to their promulgation, and, while making extensive changes in many sections of the statute, made no change in section 355. He relies upon the rule which attributes congressional approval to long-standing regulations under a section of the Internal Revenue Code where the section has been often amended without a revision of its administrative interpretation. See Lykes v. United States, 343 U.S. 118 (1952), rehearing denied 343 U.S. 937 (1952).

We note that the final regulations under subchapter C of the 1954 Code became effective on December 2, 1955, and that the Technical Amendments Act of 1958 was enacted on September 2, 1958. Further we note that section 355 has not been amended since its enactment in August of 1954. Thus, it is apparent that the challenged regulations have neither the longevity nor the congressional approval alluded to in Lykes v. United States, supra.

There being no language, either in the statute or committee report, which denies tax-free treatment under section 355 to a transaction solely on the grounds that it represents an attempt to divide a single trade or business, the Commissioner's regulations which impose such a restriction are invalid, and cannot be sustained. Commissioner v. Acker, 361 U.S. 87 (1959).

Finally, respondent argues that there is presently pending in Congress legislation (H.R. 4459) which would revise section 355(a)(1)(B) so as to permit a nontaxable distribution if either: (1) The active business requirements of 355(b) are met; or (2) it is established to the satisfaction of the Secretary or his delegate that the distribution is not made for the purpose of avoiding tax. As interpretative of this pending legislation, respondent directs our attention to a report dated December 11, 1958, of The Advisory Group on Subchapter C of the Internal Revenue Code of 1954, appointed by the House Subcommittee on Internal Revenue Taxation, wherein it is stated at page 65:

> It is further provided in section 355(a)(1)(B)(ii) of the proposed revision that even though the transaction does not otherwise qualify under section 355 because of failure to satisfy the active business requirements or the 20 percent distribution requirement, it will nevertheless qualify under section 355 if it is established to the satisfaction of the Secretary or his delegate that the distribution is not in pursuance of a plan having as one of its principal purposes the avoidance of Federal income tax. *For example, even if the controlled corporation and the distributing corporation are not engaged in separate businesses, the Secretary or his delegate might find that a division of a single business qualifies under section 355, particularly where after the division certain stockholders will own stock in only one of the corporations and the remaining stockholders will own only stock in the other corporation.* Permitting some latitude in administration of the section should serve to prevent a rigid interpretation of the requirements of clause (i). [Emphasis supplied.]

Relying on the italicized language, respondent argues that under the law as presently written, the division of a single trade or business does not qualify for tax-free treatment under section 355.

The short answer to this argument is that *pending* legislation in no way is binding on this Court. Until enacted, H.R. 4459 represents a course of action Congress may or may not take. Moreover, the cited report was not prepared by any congressional committee, but rather by an advisory group appointed to assist in a study of subchapter C of the 1954 Code. Quite possibly, the proposed revision of section 355 was occasioned by the restrictive nature of the Commissioner's regulations, rather than by any interpretation of the nature of existing law. In any event, respondent's reliance upon either the bill or the report as indicative of existing law is misplaced.

Inasmuch as the parties treat the distribution as otherwise qualifying under section 355 for tax-free treatment, and inasmuch as we have found that portion of the regulations denying application of section 355 to the division of a single business to be invalid, we conclude that petitioner properly treated the distribution to him of the stock of E. P. Coady and Co. as a nontaxable transaction.

No evidence having been introduced with respect to the addition to tax under section 294(d)(2) of the 1939 Code, it is sustained subject to our holding on the above issue.

Reviewed by the Court.

Decision will be entered under Rule 50.

Pierce, J., dissents.

[Dissents by Judges Harron and Atkins omitted.]

Rev. Rul. 59-400
1959-2 C.B. 114

Advice has been requested whether a distribution of stock by a corporation engaged in the hotel and real estate business qualifies under the nontaxable provisions of section 355 of the Internal Revenue Code of 1954.

M corporation was engaged in two businesses, operating a hotel and renting improved real estate (both commercial and residential). The hotel business was started upon organization in 1920 and has been actively conducted up to the present time. In 1934, *M* corporation also entered into the rental real estate business when it purchased property, constructed a garage and automobile agency facilities thereon and rented it to a dealer. In the intervening years, it acquired other rental properties which it has continued to operate. In 1954, the hotel had a fair market value of $550x$ dollars and a net book value of $350x$ dollars. The rental properties had a fair market value of $305x$ dollars and a net book value of $167x$ dollars.

During the five-year period commencing with 1954, the operation of the hotel business resulted in earnings, after taxes, of $240x$ dollars, and the operation of the real estate business resulted in earnings of approximately 75x dollars. In 1958, a new rental office building was built for 400x dollars, some 175x dollars thereof being provided by loans from banks. At the beginning of 1959, the hotel business was placed in a new corporation N, and the stock thereof distributed to the shareholders of M on a pro rata basis. N corporation received the hotel, plus certain receivables and other hotel business assets. M corporation retained the real estate liabilities and assets, which at that time had a net book value of 372x dollars and a fair market value of 705x dollars.

Section 355 of the Code states, in part, that in order for a distribution of stock to qualify under the nontaxable provisions of such section, each of the corporations involved must be engaged in a trade or business which has been actively conducted throughout the five-year period ending on the date of distribution, and that the transaction must not be used principally as a device to distribute the earnings and profits of either corporation.

The purpose behind the five-year limitation of section 355 is to prevent the corporate earnings of one business from being drawn off for such a period and put into a new business and thereby, through the creation of a marketable enterprise, convert what would normally have been dividends into capital assets that are readily saleable by the shareholders.

It is the position of the Internal Revenue Service that where a corporation which is devoted to one type of business also engages in the rental business, and substantial acquisitions of new rental property are made within the five-year period preceding the separation of these businesses, a "spin-off" transaction will not qualify under section 355 unless it can be shown that the property acquisitions were substantially financed out of the earnings of the rental business and not out of the earnings of the other business.

From the facts presented herein, it is readily apparent that there has been a very substantial increase in the rental properties subsequent to 1954, primarily as a result of the addition of the large office building in 1958. Further, it is also apparent that, viewing the transaction most favorably to the taxpayer, earnings properly attributable to the hotel business, in the amount of approximately 150x dollars, have been employed in increasing the real estate business. In view of this substantial financing out of the earnings of the hotel business, it is held that the distribution of the stock of N corporation to the shareholders of M corporation will not qualify as a nontaxable distribution under section 355 of the Code.

NOTE

1. *An introduction to §355.* To understand §355, you need to understand the abuse it is intended to forestall. Suppose X Corp. has been successful for many years so that it has substantial earnings and profits as

well as substantial cash and liquid assets. The shareholders of X Corp. would like to get some of its profits into their hands without recognizing dividend income. Of course, a shareholder could sell stock at capital gain rates or redemptions could be structured to obtain the same effect, but in either case the favorable capital gain treatment is obtained only at the cost of giving up some control of the corporation and its future profit-making capability.

Consider the following plan. X Corp. creates new Sub Co. in a §351 transaction, transferring its cash and liquid investments to Sub Co. in exchange for all of Sub Co.'s stock. The Sub Co. stock is then distributed by X Corp. to its shareholders, and, if that distribution were tax free to X Corp. and to its shareholders, Sub Co. could then liquidate; by this mechanism the cash and liquid assets of X Corp. would be removed from corporate solution as capital gain. Or, instead of liquidating Sub Co., the shareholders could sell their stock in Sub Co. to obtain capital gains, and the purchasers would have a cost basis in the Sub Co. stock so that its assets could be bailed out in the future without difficulty.

Note that the effect of placing the X Corp. assets in a separate corporation (Sub Co.) allows the X Corp. shareholders to part with their Sub Co. stock without relinquishing any control over the operating assets of X Corp. As we saw when we looked at redemptions,[1] and again at stock dividends,[2] a shareholder should be able to avoid dividend treatment only by reducing ownership of the ongoing profit-making ability of the corporation. If divisive reorganizations permitted the tax-free separation of operating assets from investment assets, earnings and profits could be bailed out with abandon.

To ensure that corporate divisions do not become bailouts, §355 imposes three distinct hurdles. First, the active trade or business requirement of §355(a)(1)(C) mandates that each of the corporations after the division be engaged in a long-standing active trade or business. Thus, the transaction cannot simply separate operating assets from investment assets. Second, the device limitation of §355(a)(1)(B) provides that the transaction cannot be used "principally as a device for the distribution of earnings and profits." This broadly worded provision allows the courts to police divisive transactions with an eye toward the underlying policy of §355; in addition, it has allowed Treasury to promulgate a business purpose test in the regulations. Third, the distribution requirement of §355(a)(1)(D) limits tax-free treatment to divisive transactions in which the corporations separate completely: With limited exceptions, the distributing corporation cannot retain any ownership of the corporation whose stock it is distributing. These three requirements are discussed in the Notes that follow.

In all §355 transactions, one corporation distributes stock and securi-

1. See page 215 supra.
2. See pages 315-318 supra.

ties of one or more other corporations, thereby converting a parent-subsidiary structure into a brother-sister structure. In the language of §355, the corporation distributing the stock and securities is called the "distributing" corporation, and the corporations whose stock and securities are distributed are called the "controlled" corporations. In a §355 transaction, there is only one distributing corporation and there can be one or more controlled corporations.

2. *The active trade or business requirement.* Section 355(a)(1)(C), by incorporating §355(b), requires that both the distributing corporation and the controlled corporation be engaged immediately after the transaction in the active conduct of trades or businesses that have been conducted for at least five years. As *Coady* illustrates, this requirement can be met by dividing one active trade or business into two, sometimes called a vertical division. See also Treas. Regs. §1.355-3(c) (example 4), expressly allowing a vertical division.

Note that while the businesses must have been conducted for five years prior to the transaction, they need not have been conducted by the distributing corporation or by the controlled corporation during that entire period. That is, the requirement can be met if one or both of the businesses were acquired during the five-year period. Both businesses must, however, have been actively conducted by *someone* during the preceding five years, and acquisition of the businesses by the distributing corporation or by the controlled corporation must not have occurred within the five-year period unless the acquisition was tax free, see §355(b)(2)(C).

For example, suppose *X* Corp. has actively engaged in the toy manufacturing business for more than five years. Three years ago it acquired a software distributing company, Sub Co., in a tax-free B reorganization; Sub Co. had been actively conducting the software distributing business for more than two years prior to the reorganization. The distribution by *X* Corp. of the Sub Co. stock will satisfy the active trade or business requirement of §§355(a)(1)(C) and 355(b), although if *X* Corp. had purchased the Sub Co. stock in a taxable transaction, the requirement of §355(b)(2)(C) would not be met.

Consider the following variation on this example. Once again, suppose *X* Corp. acquired the Sub Co. stock in a tax-free B reorganization, but now assume Sub Co. acquired the software distributing business one year before in a taxable transaction. Now, the distribution of Sub Co. stock by *X* Corp. will fail the active trade or business test by reason of §355(b)(2)(D). See also the example in Treas. Regs. §1.355-3(b)(4)(ii). The effect of §355(b)(2)(D) is to require that all transfers of the trades or businesses used by the taxpayer to satisfy the requirements of §355(a)(1)(C) occurring during the five-year testing period be by way of tax-free transactions, including §351 formations and §368(a)(1) reorganizations.

Note that the limitation of §355(b) applies to the acquisition of a *business,* not to the acquisition of particular *assets.* For example, suppose again that X Corp. has actively engaged in the business of manufacturing toys for more than five years. Suppose further that one year ago X Corp. purchased for cash in a fully taxable transaction all the assets of one of its competitors in the toy manufacturing business and that these assets were then used to form a wholly owned subsidiary, Sub Co., in a §351 transaction. X Corp. can distribute the stock of Sub Co. without violating the active trade or business requirement because both the distributing corporation (X Corp.) and the controlled corporation (Sub Co.) are actively conducting the toy manufacturing business immediately after the transaction and X Corp. had been actively conducting this business for more than five years. That is, §355(b) does not prohibit the distribution of a part of a business representing a recent expansion, even if the expansion was by purchase, so long as the expansion continues the historic business of the distributing company. See Treas. Regs. §1.355-3(c) (examples 7 and 8).

Let us consider one more variation on this theme. Suppose X Corp. does not acquire the assets of one of its competitors but instead acquires the stock of one of its competitors (Sub Co.). Now, the distribution of the Sub Co. stock will fail to satisfy §355(b) because of the language in §355(b)(2)(D). See also Nelson v. Commissioner, 61 T.C. 311 (1973); Boettger v. Commissioner, 51 T.C. 324 (1968). Thus, expansion by purchase of assets will not violate §355(b), although the functionally equivalent expansion by purchase of a company will. To the same effect, in Burke v. Commissioner, 42 T.C. 1021 (1965), it was held that establishing a new branch located in a different city was an extension of the same business and not a new business. In Lockwood's Estate v. Commissioner, 350 F.2d 712 (8th Cir. 1965), the court found that a business that spun off part of its activities by the establishment of a new manufacturing and sales corporation for the same products in a different state was merely the continuation of a single business and that the spun-off subsidiary could use the length of time its parent had been in business to qualify under the five-year test.

If the distributing corporation or the controlled corporation is liquidated, the effect of the §355 distribution and subsequent liquidation is the same as a partial liquidation. It should come as no surprise, then, that both divisive distributions and partial liquidations include an active trade or business requirement. Compare §355(b) with §302(e)(2). Unfortunately, the terms of these two provisions are not precisely the same — there is nothing like §355(b)(2)(D) in §302(e).

In a functional division, two different facets of one business are separated into two corporations. A valid functional division satisfies the technical tests of §355, provided that after the division both companies remain operating entities engaged in the active conduct of a business. If the division creates a passive corporation, the active business requirement is not met and the division will not be tax free under §355. In Rafferty v. Commissioner, 452 F.2d 767 (1st Cir. 1971), no active business was found when the spun-off corporation's activity after the division involved leasing back

real estate to its parent. The court found the economic activities were
an investment rather than an active trade or business. But cf. King v.
Commissioner, 458 F.2d 245 (6th Cir. 1972), finding an active business
when the corporation's only source of income was a long-term net lease
of realty to the parent; there the real property was fit only for a single use,
was needed in the business, and, therefore, was not suitable for a bailout.

Treas. Regs. §1.355-3(b)(2)(iii) states that whether a trade or business
is actively conducted is a question of fact but that generally the corporation
must perform active and substantial management and operational functions. See also Rev. Rul. 86-125, 1986-2 C.B. 57, in which the Service ruled
that the rental of an office building does not constitute an active trade or
business when the property is managed by an independent contractor
rather than by employees of the corporation.

Suppose a coal mine sells coal only to its owner, a steel mill, which in
turn sells steel only to its owner, a manufacturer of automobiles. May the
coal mine be spun off to the shareholders of the automobile manufacturer?
May the steel mill be spun off? While there was doubt under the old
regulations, the current regulations contain examples of such horizontal
divisions of an integrated business that meet the active conduct test. See
examples 10-12 of Treas. Regs. §1.355-3(c). In the vertical division, there
was the question as to whether the statute permitted a division of a single
business into two businesses, which has been answered affirmatively by
Coady. In a functional division (e.g., the company sells machinery and its
subsidiary services such machinery), there is first the question as to whether
after the division both entities are engaged in an active trade or business
as in *Rafferty* and *King.* Even if the answer is affirmative, the second question
is whether each business is properly "aged." In *Burke* and *Lockwood* the
spun-off business could tack on the parent's history to meet the aging
requirement while in *Boettger* it could not. The integrated business division
asks whether there can be an active conduct of a trade or business if there
are no outside customers. Cf. Groetzinger v. Commissioner, 480 U.S. 23
(1987) (full-time gambler betting on his own account was engaged in a
trader business for purposes of §§62(1) and 162).

Note that under Treas. Regs. §1.355-2(d)(2)(iv)(C), the division of
an integrated business may be considered a "device" for the distribution
of earnings and profits if one of the postseparation corporations engages
in a business that has as its principal function the service of the other
postseparation corporation, if this captive business can be sold without
adversely affecting the primary business. What is the rationale behind this
limitation?

3. *The device limitation: in general.* The "device" language of
§355(a)(1)(B) stems from congressional recognition that the existence of
the active conduct of a trade or business is not sufficient assurance that
the division of an existing corporation will not be used as a bailout. The
most active trade or business can be sold. In addition to objective tests,

Congress included the catchall subjective "device" test as another weapon against a division serving as a vehicle for a bailout. The Service considers several primary indicia in finding a device. Prearranged sales of the stock of either the distributing or controlled corporation have been viewed with suspicion, §355(a)(1)(B) and Treas. Regs. §1.355-2(d)(2)(iii). Treas. Regs. §1.355-2(d)(2)(iii)(B)-(D) states that a sale reasonably anticipated by the parties shall be considered as agreed on before the distribution and that, regardless of whether a sale is negotiated before the distribution, a postdistribution sale will be taken into evidence in determining a device.

Under §355(a)(2)(A), a corporate distribution may be tax free whether the distribution is or is not pro rata. Treas. Regs. §1.355-2(d)(2)(ii), however, suggests that a pro rata distribution presents the greatest potential for the withdrawal of earnings and profits and is more likely to be a device. Compare the policy behind §302. Another indicator of a device is the nature of the assets divided between the two corporations; Treas. Regs. §1.355-2(d)(2)(iv) states that the transfer or retention of cash or liquid assets (including securities and accounts receivable) not related to the reasonable needs of the business will be evidence of a device.

Did the transaction described in Rev. Rul. 59-400 above fail to qualify under §355 because it was a "device" for the distribution of earnings and profits? Note that no postdistribution sale was involved in the ruling. If the driving force behind §355 is that a taxpayer should be unable to obtain the earnings of a corporation as capital gains without relinquishing an interest in the ongoing profit-making capability of the corporation, then the division involved in Rev. Rul. 59-400 offered the potential of cashing out the earnings of both businesses by selling only one.

4. *The device limitation: business purpose.* In Commissioner v. Wilson, 353 F.2d 184 (9th Cir. 1965), the court was unable to discern a business or a nonbusiness motive for the division and refused to upset the Commissioner's determination that the corporate division was a "device" because of the absence of a discernible motive for the transaction. Had there been a finding of a tax avoidance motive, of course, the taxpayer would have been no better off. But what would be the outcome if the trial court had found that the motive behind the division was wholly nontax related? In Rafferty v. Commissioner, 452 F.2d 767 (1st Cir. 1971), a closely held corporation was divided to facilitate nontax estate planning. The court upheld the Commissioner's characterization of the transaction as a device on the theory that nontax personal motives of a taxpayer cannot protect a transaction that has a considerable potential for bailing out earnings and profits at capital gain rates.

Note that in *Wilson* the Court required a business purpose notwithstanding the arguably more specific device language of §355. Is the requirement of a business purpose redundant? Not if the device language is limited to facts that constitute evidence of a bailout, e.g., a prearranged sale. The business purpose requirement can preclude from §355 those divisions that have a potential bailout in the future and that are not explained by nontax reasons. The ambiguity of such divisions is resolved in the proposed regulations by assuming that their underlying purpose is a bailout. Is *Wilson* clear support for such an across-the-board approach? One might raise the question why putting oneself in the position for a future bailout should be allowed even with a valid purpose. But note that the business activities separated in *Wilson* could originally have been put into two corporations separately owned by the shareholders; these problems would never have arisen in such an arrangement. This is the perplexing question in the corporate division area mentioned at the outset. Regulations have explicitly incorporated the *Wilson* rule that the absence of a business purpose, even if there is no tax avoidance purpose, will be fatal to the reorganization. See Treas. Regs. §1.355-2(b)(1).

Examples of valid business purposes are now found in Treas. Regs. §1.355-2(b)(5) (examples 1, 2, 5, and 8). The relationship between a corporate business purpose and a "device" is now found in Treas. Regs. §1.355-2(d)(3)(ii). The regulations now impose a best-fit requirement: The transaction will fail §355 if the business purpose could be accomplished in a tax-free manner without involving the distribution of stock, unless the alternative transactions are impractical or unduly expensive. Treas. Regs. §1.355-2(b)(3).

The regulations provide that a valid corporate purpose is not the reduction of federal taxes even if that reduction would come about other than from a bailout or similar transaction to which §355 speaks. Treas. Regs. §1.355-2(b)(2). In particular, the regulations provide that a distribution made to facilitate an election under subchapter S is not protected by §355 for want of a valid business purpose. Treas. Regs. §1.355-2(d)(5) (example 6).

This aspect of the regulations should be subject to challenge. Note that the statute fails to include an explicit "business purpose" requirement. Accordingly, such a requirement can be defended only as an attempt to further the purpose of §355. Is there any suggestion that §355 was intended to limit the number of subchapter S elections? Surely the ghost of Gregory v. Helvering has reappeared once too often if the Treasury feels secure in promulgating regulations exorcising all divisive transactions motivated by any attempt to minimize federal taxes even without the dangers to which §355 speaks.

In Rev. Rul. 85-122, 1985-2 C.B. 118, the Service ruled that the business purpose requirement of §355 is met if an unprofitable ski resort is separated from a profitable golf and tennis resort to meet the recommendation of the securities underwriter advising the corporation on marketing of debentures of the golf and tennis resort. And in Rev. Rul. 85-127, 1985-2 C.B. 119, the Service ruled that the business purpose requirement is met when two active businesses are split apart to retain the services of a key employee of one of the two businesses.

5. *Shareholder versus corporate business purpose.* The regulations state that a transaction does not qualify under §355 if carried out for purposes not germane to the business of the corporations. Treas. Regs. §1.355-2(b)(2) states that when the business purpose serves the shareholder as well as the corporation, there may be no problem, but if the transaction is undertaken solely for the personal reasons of the shareholder, the distribution will not qualify under §355. Note Parshelsky's Estate v. Commissioner, 303 F.2d 14 (2d Cir. 1962), suggesting the business purpose could be a shareholder purpose rather than a corporate business purpose, but the Court in *Rafferty*, Note 2 supra, rejected the suggestion that a shareholder investment purpose was sufficient. This issue pervades the entire reorganization area.

In Rev. Rul. 88-34, 1988-1 C.B. 115, *X* Corp. owned all the stock of *Y* Corp. The president of *Y* Corp. had recently retired, and individual *A* was identified as a prospective new president. *A* insisted that he receive an equity interest in *Y* Corp. as part of his compensation without acquiring any interest in *X*. To facilitate the transfer of *Y* stock to *A*, *X* Corp. spun off *Y* by distributing the *Y* stock pro rata to the *X* shareholders. The Service ruled that the spin-off of *Y* Corp. satisfied the business purpose test of former Treas. Regs. §1.355-2(c) because "the distribution enables the subsidiary corporation [*Y* Corp.] to hire the key employee it believes is necessary to the continued success of the business." Without knowing more about *A*'s reasons for insisting on acquiring an interest in *Y* but not in *X*, has a shareholder purpose been transmuted into a corporate purpose? The current regulations take a more skeptical view of these transactions. See Treas. Regs. §1.355-2(b)(5) (example 8).

6. *The distribution requirement.* By virtue of §355(a)(1)(D), the distributing corporation must either distribute all the stock and securities that it holds in the controlled corporation or distribute an amount of stock constituting "control" (as defined by §368(c)) *and* must satisfy the Treasury that the retention of stock in the controlled corporation was not in pursuance of a tax avoidance plan. Why this emphasis on a complete, or nearly complete, separation of the two corporations?

Consider individual *T*, who owns all the outstanding stock of *X* Corp. *X* has actively conducted two distinct businesses for more than five years. *X* transfers one of its two businesses to newly formed *Y* Corp. in exchange for common and callable preferred stock of *Y*, and the *Y* common stock is then distributed to *T*. If this transaction qualified as a tax-free divisive D reorganization, *T* would be in a position to bail out earnings and profits of *Y* Corp. by selling the stock of *X*. To see this, observe that *X* Corp.'s assets include preferred stock of *Y* Corp., so a sale of *X* would include a sale of the *Y* preferred. A purchaser of *X* would pay *T* not only for the value of the *X* operating assets but also for the value of the *Y* preferred stock, and *T* would have only a capital gain on this sale. When the *Y* preferred stock is then redeemed, the bailout is complete. To avoid this type of transaction, Congress placed the "control" requirement in §355(a)(1)(D). Why doesn't §306 handle this abuse?

In Commissioner v. Gordon, 391 U.S. 83 (1968), the distribution of the requisite 80 percent control of the distributed corporation took place in two steps (occurring in 1961 and 1963), and the court held that §355 was not satisfied; the first distribution (of less than 80 percent) was independent in the sense that a further distribution, though contemplated, was not promised or required by the plan. Another issue in the case — whether a distribution of stock pursuant to the exercise of stock rights qualifies under §355 — was left unanswered by the court. On remand it was held that the stock rights did not constitute stock within §354(a), 424 F.2d 378 (2d Cir. 1970). Treas. Regs. §1.355-1(b) states that stock rights or stock warrants are not included in the term "stock or securities."

7. *The forms a divisive transaction can take.* Corporate divisions have generated a lexicon of colorful labels, namely, the "spin-off," the "split-off," and the "split-up." In a *spin-off*, the existing corporation, X, transfers some of its assets to Y Corp., newly organized for the purpose, in exchange for Y's stock, which X then distributes to its shareholders. In a *split-off*, X also transfers some of its assets to Y for Y's stock, but X distributes the Y stock in exchange for part of its own stock. In a *split-up*, X transfers part of its assets to Y Corp. and the rest to Z Corp., both newly organized for the purpose, and then completely liquidates, distributing the Y and Z stock in exchange for its own. The economic consequences to X's stockholders of all three methods are practically identical.

Both the split-off and the split-up can be useful when feuding shareholders seek to go their separate ways. For example, suppose X Corp. is owned equally by individuals A and B. If A and B often disagree on important corporate questions, they may decide to sever their business relationship by dividing their business between two companies. On one hand, if X Corp. transfers half of its assets to newly formed Y Corp., whose stock is distributed to B in exchange for his stock in X, then a split-off has been used to divide X. On the other hand, if X Corp. transfers half of its assets to Y Corp. and half to Z Corp. and then distributes the Y stock to A and the Z stock to B in complete liquidation, a split-up has been used to accomplish the same end.

With one exception, §355 treats all divisive reorganizations the same way. It is applicable both to distributions (spin-offs) and to exchanges (split-ups and split-offs). Moreover, the old corporation can distribute (a term that is defined to include exchanges) the stock and securities of a controlled corporation that it already owns or one created expressly to effect the corporate division. The requirements of §355 that are of particular interest are those in §355(a)(1)(B) and §355(b). Note that §354(b) prevents divisive reorganizations from avoiding the more restrictive provisions of §355 by qualifying under §354.

Not all corporate divisions will be "reorganizations" within the meaning of §368(a)(1). If the division is effected by transferring assets to a newly created subsidiary and then distributing the subsidiary's stock, the transaction is a D reorganization qualifying by virtue of a distribution described in §355. If the division is effected by distributing stock of an existing subsidiary without transferring assets as part of the plan, then §355 is applicable to the distribution of the subsidiary's stock without application of §368(a)(1)(D). While all forms of divisive rearrangements are referred to as "divisive reorganizations," the touchstone of such a transaction is not qualification under §368(a)(1)(D) but application of §355. The tax treatment of a §355 distribution, however, can turn on whether the transaction is a "reorganization" under §368(a)(1)(D).

8. *Taxation of divisive transactions.* Section 355(a)(1) permits a shareholder exchanging stock or securities for stock or securities in a divisive transaction to defer recognition of gain (and loss) realized on the exchange. It plays the same role with respect to divisive transactions as §354(a)(1) plays with respect to acquisitive reorganizations. And like §354, gain (but not loss) will be recognized by a shareholder receiving boot or excess securities. See §§356(a), 356(b), 355(a)(3).

Under some circumstances, boot in a divisive transaction will be taxed under the same rule governing boot in an acquisitive reorganization. In particular, dividend income is limited to the amount of gain realized on the transaction. See §356(a)(2). If the divisive transaction is structured as a *distribution* rather than as an *exchange,* however, the rule of §356(b) applies, subjecting not the gain but the value of the boot received to taxation as a dividend. In light of §355(a)(2) permitting pro rata exchanges in a divisive transaction, an astute taxpayer should always be able to avoid the harsh rule of §356(b).

How is the corporation taxed in a §355 transaction? One would expect that the distribution of stock and securities would be tax free and that gain (but not loss) would be recognized on the distribution of other property. If the divisive transaction happens to be a D reorganization (that is, if a newly formed subsidiary was created and spun off), current law produces these results under §361(b)(3) (nonrecognition on distribution of stock or securities) and §361(c) (recognition of gain but not loss on distribution of other property). If the transaction is not a "reorganization" because the controlled corporation is preexisting, the same taxation results from §355(c).

Suppose X Corp. has for many years owned 90 percent of the stock of Y Corp., which engages in an active trade or business. The remaining 10 percent of the Y Corp. stock was acquired by X one year ago in a taxable transaction. If X distributes all the Y stock to its shareholders, is the distribution tax free under §355? Under §355(a)(3)(B), stock acquired within five years of the distribution in a taxable transaction is treated as boot rather than as qualifying property.

Section 355 imposes no restriction on the type of stock or securities that can be distributed in a divisive reorganization. If debt securities are distributed, however, they will constitute boot under §356(d) to the extent their principal amount exceeds the principal amount of any securities that are surrendered; if preferred stock is distributed, it may be tainted by §306(c)(1)(B). See §356(e). See, e.g., Rev. Rul. 77-335, 1977-2 C.B. 95, where in a §355 spin-off by a parent of the subsidiary's common and preferred stock, the preferred was §306 stock. The ruling stated that §306 status is determined by reference to the earnings and profits of the distributing corporation — i.e., the parent. Section 355(a)(4) refers to §356 for the treatment of boot; §356(a) determines the amount of gain to be recognized and how it is to be taxed; §356(c) prohibits recognition of loss. See Rev. Rul. 74-516, 1974-2 C.B. 121, abandoning the automatic dividend rule in reorganization boot distributions and adopting instead a dividend equivalence test under the principles of §302(b)(1).

Suppose *P* Corp. owns 100 percent of the outstanding stock of Sub Corp., and assume the Sub Corp. stock constitutes 25 percent of the value of *P* Corp. Further, assume the Sub Corp. stock is worth $250,000 and *P* Corp.'s adjusted basis in the Sub Corp. stock equals $100,000. *T* Corp. would like to acquire Sub Corp. without the imposition of a corporate-level tax.

If a distribution by *P* Corp. of the Sub Corp. stock will qualify under §355, *P* and *T* can adopt the following plan. First, *T* Corp. will purchase 25 percent of the outstanding shares of *P* Corp. Second, after waiting a sufficient time to satisfy the continuity of interest requirement of Treas. Regs. §1.355-2(c), *P* Corp. will distribute its Sub Corp. stock to *T* in redemption of *T*'s stock of *P*. If §355 applied without limitation, *T* would acquire Sub Corp. from *P* without the imposition of a corporate-level tax, yet *T*'s basis in the Sub Corp. stock will equal its fair market value of $250,000 (because that is what *T* Corp. paid for the *P* Corp. stock it purchased, which was then redeemed). Prior to the transaction, the Sub Corp. stock had a basis of only $100,000 in the hands of *P* Corp. Thus, *T* Corp. has effectively purchased a corporate asset (the Sub Corp. stock) without the selling corporation (*P* Corp.) recognizing any gain.

Section 355(d) responds to this type of transaction not by disqualifying the transaction under §355 but instead by forcing the distributing corporation (here, *P* Corp.) to recognize gain on the distribution of the stock of the controlled corporation (here, Sub Corp.). Note that §355(d) will apply if, immediately after the transaction, a shareholder holds 50 percent or more of the distributing corporation *or* of the controlled corporation if that interest was acquired within five years and was acquired by "purchase," which is defined quite broadly in §355(d)(5).

What is the abuse to which §355(d) speaks? In general, one corporation cannot transfer an appreciated asset to a second corporation without the imposition of a corporate-level tax. To be sure, there are exceptions to this rule for tax-free reorganizations, as discussed in Chapter 10, and for affiliated corporations filing a consolidated return, as discussed in Chapter 13. Aside from these exceptional cases, the transfer of an asset from one corporation to another is a taxable event for the transferor corporation.

In the example above, the Sub Corp. stock initially held by *P* Corp. ended up in the hands of *T* Corp. Yet, were §355 to apply to the transaction, there would be no taxation to *P* Corp. Although application of §355 to this transaction would not permit any assets to be removed from corporate solution, the legislative history of §355(d) indicates that this type of transaction is inconsistent with the repeal of the *General Utilities* doctrine, discussed at pages 135-138 supra.

How should earnings and profits be allocated between the distributing and the controlled corporation? See §312(h). When the controlled corporation is newly formed, Treas. Regs. §1.312-10 provides that the earnings and profits "generally" should be made in proportion to the fair market value of the business or businesses retained by the distributing corporation as compared with the value of the business or businesses transferred to the controlled corporation.

9.   *Nonqualifying transactions.* If a spin-off does not qualify under §355, and if the fair market value of the distributed stock exceeds its adjusted basis, gain will be recognized by the distributing corporation. §311(b). In addition, the distribution falls under §301 and will be taxed as a dividend to the extent of the distributing corporation's earnings and profits. But suppose the nonqualifying distribution takes the form of a split-up. Such a transaction amounts to a complete liquidation of the distributing corporation and presumably will be taxed as any other corporate liquidation. Can a taxpayer argue that a *successful* split-up be taxed as a complete liquidation rather than as a §355 division, particularly if the distribution includes boot? See Telephone Answering Service Co. v. Commissioner, 63 T.C. 423 (1974), aff'd, 546 F.2d 423 (4th Cir. 1976), especially footnote 14. See also Rev. Rul. 84-71, 1984-1 C.B. 106, in which the Service ruled that §351 could apply to a transfer that was part of a larger acquisitive transaction failing to qualify for reorganization treatment.

10.   *Criss-cross transactions.* If *A* owns 50 percent of the stock of *X* Corp. and of *Y* Corp. and *B* owns the other 50 percent of *X* and *Y*, can they employ §355 to effect a rearrangement of their investments so that *A* will become the sole owner of *X* and *B* the sole owner of *Y*? What might be the mechanics of such a division? Treas. Regs. §1.355-4 holds such a transaction taxable, and the cases have generally integrated the various steps and found such a transaction taxable. See Portland Manufacturing Co. v. Commissioner, 56 T.C. 58 (1971), aff'd, 75-1 U.S.T.C. (CCH) ¶9449; Kuper v. Commissioner, 61 T.C. 624 (1974), aff'd, 533 F.2d 152 (5th Cir. 1976); Atlee v. Commissioner, 67 T.C. 395 (1976), following Portland. Contra, Badanes v. Commissioner, 39 T.C. 410 (1962), allowing such a division. Can §355 be used to accomplish an exchange under which *A*, owning all

the stock of *X* Corp., and *B*, owning all the stock of *Y* Corp., each succeed in becoming the sole owner of the other's corporation? Rev. Rul. 71-336, 1971-2 C.B. 299, prohibits a somewhat similar plan. But see Rev. Rul. 77-11, 1977-1 C.B. 93, for a successful way of dividing two 50 percent-owned brother-sister corporations of differing size, *X* and *Y*, owned equally by *A* and *B*, by a non-pro rata split-off. *X* Corp. transferred 1,850*x* dollars in assets representing half of its net worth to *Z*, a newly formed corporation, for 1,850 shares of *Z*'s voting common stock. *Y* Corp. transferred 350*x* dollars in assets representing half of its net worth to *Z* for 350 shares of *Z*'s voting common stock. Section 351 covered these exchanges. *X* then distributed all the *Z* stock to *B* in exchange for all of *B*'s stock in *X*. Since this is a controlling interest and since the other requirements of §355 were met, this exchange was tax free. *Y* then distributed all the *Z* stock to *B* in exchange for all of *B*'s stock in *Y*. A capital gains tax on *B*'s gain was payable on this exchange since *Y* could not distribute a controlling interest in *Z*. As a result, *A* owned all the stock of *X* and *Y* without tax, and *B* owned all the stock of *Z* at the cost of the capital gain incurred on the exchange with *Y* Corp.

Bhada v. Commissioner

89 T.C. 959 (1987), aff'd, 892 F.2d 39 (6th Cir. 1989)

NIMS, Judge: . . .

McDermott, Inc. (McDermott), was a Delaware corporation at all relevant times. From 1959 until December 10, 1982, McDermott was the parent corporation to a group of corporations hereinafter referred to as the McDermott Group. From 1959 until December 10, 1982, McDermott International, Inc. (International), was a wholly-owned subsidiary of McDermott and a controlled foreign corporation within the meaning of section 957.

Pursuant to a plan of reorganization adopted on October 28, 1982, by the boards of directors of McDermott and International, International made an offer to exchange cash and shares of its own stock (International Common) for shares of the common stock of McDermott (McDermott Common). . . .

Under the terms of the offer, International was to exchange one share of International Common plus $0.35 for each outstanding share of McDermott Common. The offer was conditioned upon the tendering of a minimum of 22 million shares of McDermott Common. International also retained the right to refuse to accept more than 30 million shares of McDermott Common.

On December 10, 1982, International accepted, pursuant to the terms of the Offer, all shares of McDermott Common tendered by each shareholder holding 99 or fewer of such shares and accepted a portion of all the shares of McDermott Common tendered by each shareholder holding 100 or more of such shares, as was determined on the terms concerning proration stated in the Prospectus. International acquired 30 million shares of McDermott Common for which it gave $10,500,000 and 30 million shares of International Common. As a result of the exchange, International held approximately 68 percent of the voting power in McDermott, and former holders of McDermott Common who participated in the exchange held approximately 90 percent of the voting power in International.

Petitioners participated in the December, 1982, transactions. In response to the Offer, petitioners Rohinton and Patricia Bhada tendered to International 26 shares of McDermott Common and received in return 26 shares of International Common and $9.10 in cash. . . . On December 10, 1982, the fair market value of one share of International Common was $19. . . .

Section 304(c) provides, in part, that control, for purposes of section 304, means ownership of stock possessing at least 50 percent of the total combined voting power of all classes of stock entitled to vote, or at least 50 percent of the total value of shares of all classes of stock.

If section 304(a)(2) applies to the December, 1982, transaction, the International Common and cash received by petitioners must be treated as a distribution in redemption of their stock in McDermott, and it will be necessary to apply section 302 to determine the character of the amounts received by petitioners in International Common and cash. The parties have agreed that the cash received by petitioners is property for purposes of section 304(a)(2) and that if section 304 does not apply to the International Common received by petitioners, the tax consequences of the receipt of that stock will then be governed by section 1001.[2]

Section 304 does not apply to the International Common received by petitioners unless this stock was "property" for purposes of section 304(a)(2). The term "property" is defined in section 317(a), which provides: "For purposes of this part, the term 'property' means money, securities, and any other property; except that such term does not include stock in the corporation making the distribution (or rights to acquire such stock)."

Respondent argues that the true nature of the transaction between International and petitioners was an exchange of International Common for McDermott Common rather than a distribution by International of its stock in exchange for McDermott Common. It is respondent's position

2. Section 351 does not apply in this case because of the failure to meet the 80 percent control requirement of section 351. Although the former McDermott shareholders owned 90 percent of the total voting power in International after the December, 1982, exchange, they did not own at least 80 percent of the total of all other classes of stock of International. McDermott at all relevant times owned all of the shares of a class of voting preferred stock of International. Respondent speculates that if section 304 does not apply to the December, 1982, transaction, the former shareholders of McDermott will suffer no adverse tax consequences and will in many cases recognize a loss for tax purposes.

that the term "distribution" in section 317(a) refers only to a distribution by a corporation with respect to its stock to its shareholders in their capacity as shareholders. Because International gave its stock to McDermott's shareholders and not to its own shareholders, respondent maintains that there was no distribution as defined in section 317(a). We disagree.

... Respondent finds support for his definition of the term "distribution" by asserting that the term "distribution" as it appears in every section in Part I of Subchapter C refers to a distribution by a corporation to its shareholders in relation to its stock. However, in section 304 itself Congress has used the term "distribution" in its generic sense. Section 304(b)(3)(A), provides, "Except as otherwise provided in this paragraph, subsection (a) (and not section 351 and not so much of sections 357 and 358 as relates to section 351) shall apply to any property received in a distribution described in subsection (a)."

At first glance, it is difficult to determine whether the term distribution in section 304(b)(3)(A) refers to the distribution of property by the acquiring corporation to shareholders of the parent corporation that triggers the application of section 304 or to the hypothetical redemption distribution by the parent to its own shareholders that follows when section 304(a)(2) applies. This ambiguity is resolved, however, by section 304(b)(3)(B), which provides in pertinent part:

> (B) Certain assumptions of liability, etc.—
>   (i)   In general. — In the case of an acquisition described in section 351, subsection (a) shall not apply to any liability —
>   (I)   assumed by the acquiring corporation, or
>   (II)   to which the stock is subject, if such liability was incurred by the transferor to acquire the stock. For purposes of the preceding sentence, the term "stock" means stock referred to in paragraph (1)(B) or (2)(A) of subsection (a).

Section 304(b)(3)(B) provides that in a transaction described in both sections 304(a) and 351, section 304(a) does not apply to certain liabilities assumed by the acquiring corporation or to which the stock is subject. The reference to the assumption of liabilities by the acquiring corporation indicates that section 304(b)(3)(B) refers to the actual transaction, i.e., the distribution of property by the acquiring corporation to shareholders of another corporation rather than the hypothetical redemption under section 304(a). Because section 304(b)(3)(B) refers to the actual transaction that triggers section 304, we can only conclude that section 304(b)(3)(A) also refers to the actual transactions when it uses the term distribution. Accordingly, the term distribution in section 317(a) does not exclusively refer to a distribution by a corporation to its shareholders with respect to its stock.

From this it follows that International "distributed" its own stock to petitioners in the December, 1982, exchange and that such stock is not to be deemed property. This is because the International Common was the stock of the corporation making the distribution, it was not property, and section 304 does not apply.[3]

Respondent contends, however, that section 304(b)(3)(B) refers to actual transactions but that section 304(b)(3)(A) refers to the hypothetical redemption that occurs when section 304 applies. Respondent reasons that section 304(b)(3)(B) concerns liabilities assumed (a much more difficult matter to express in terms of the hypothetical transaction), whereas the conflict between sections 304 and 351 does not arise until after the hypothetical redemption distribution comes into play. We decline to adopt respondent's reading of the statute. Neither section 304(b)(3)(B) nor section 304(b)(3)(A) applies unless there is a conflict between sections 304 and 351. Respondent's analysis assumes that there is no relationship between sections 304(b)(3)(B) and 304(b)(3)(A). The language of the statute does not support respondent's position nor does anything in the legislative history suggest such a contorted reading of the statute. . . .

Before section 304(b)(3) was enacted, it was possible for taxpayers to avoid the application of section 304 to property received in addition to stock in an exchange of stock for stock of a related corporation if they met the 80 percent control requirement of section 351.

To prevent such a circumvention of section 304, Congress enacted section 304(b)(3). The Conference Report explains:

> The conference agreement extends the anti-bailout rules of sections 304 and 306 of present law to the use of corporations, including holding companies, formed or availed of to avoid such rules. Such rules are made applicable to a transaction that, under present law, otherwise qualifies as a tax-free incorporation under section 351.
>
> Section 351 generally will not apply to transactions described in section 304. Thus, section 351, if otherwise applicable, will generally apply only to the extent such transaction consists of an exchange of stock for stock in the acquiring corporation. . . .

[H. Rept. 97-760 (Conf.), to accompany H.R. 4961 (Pub. L. 97248) (1982), 1982-2 C.B. 600, 635.]

Thus, it appears from the Conference Report that Congress was concerned only with the treatment of property received in a transaction that fell under the provisions of both sections 304 and 351. Congress must have assumed that section 304 would not apply to the stock of the acquiring corporation received by the shareholders of the related corporation because the stock of the acquiring corporation in a section 304(a) transaction is not property.

---

3. Because we hold for petitioners in this case, we need not address their other arguments.

Respondent maintains that section 304(b)(3) was directed only at brother-sister transactions described in section 304(a)(1) rather than parent-subsidiary transactions described in section 304(a)(2). Therefore, respondent explains, the stock of a sister corporation received in a 304(a)(1) transaction is not property for purposes of section 304, but the stock of the acquiring subsidiary corporation in a section 304(a)(2) transaction is property. We disagree. Section 304(b)(3) specifically mentions that it applies to both sections 304(a)(1) (brother-sister transactions) and 304(a)(2) (parent-subsidiary transactions). Section 304(b)(3)(B)(i). . . .

Our conclusion comports with the purpose of section 304(a)(2). Section 115(g)(2) of the Internal Revenue Code of 1939, from which section 304 is derived, was enacted in response to the decision in Rodman Wanamaker Trust v. Commissioner, 11 T.C. 365 (1948), affd. 178 F.2d 10 (3d Cir. 1949), in which the Court treated the cash received by the taxpayer from a subsidiary in return for shares of its parent's stock as proceeds of a sale rather than a dividend. . . .

In this case, the cash received by petitioners constitutes assets withdrawn from International in exchange for stock of its parent, McDermott, and the parties agree that section 304 applies to the cash. However, in receiving International Common in return for McDermott Common, petitioners did not withdraw assets from International or McDermott. The transaction resulted in a change in the ownership structure of the two corporations. Congress did not intend to prevent such a change in corporate ownership by enacting section 304. . . .

Finally, respondent maintains that if section 304 does not apply in this case, petitioners will be able to avoid the provisions of section 355. Respondent characterizes the transaction in this case as an indirect redemption by a parent corporation (McDermott) of its own stock in return for the stock of its subsidiary (International). Had McDermott distributed the International stock to its shareholders in this way, section 355 would have required dividend treatment of the stock International received by petitioners. We have already rejected respondent's argument that section 355 was meant to prevent indirect redemptions. Dunn Trust v. Commissioner, 86 T.C. 745 (1986). . . .

Moreover, the transaction in this case differs from the exchange envisioned by respondent.

Had McDermott redeemed its stock and issued 30 million shares of International to petitioners, the corporations would have split up. As a result of the redemption, petitioners would have held an equity interest in International and would have given up most of their interest in McDermott.

In this case, however, petitioners exchanged their McDermott stock with International for stock in International. After this transaction, International became the parent of McDermott, and petitioners became the owners of a direct equity interest in the operations of International and an indirect equity interest in the operations of McDermott.

A transaction in which a parent redeems its own stock by distributing the stock of a subsidiary divides the corporations, and assets are withdrawn from the parent. The redeeming shareholders can bail out corporate assets in such a transaction by selling off the stock of the subsidiary. The result can be equivalent to a distribution of a dividend. Accordingly, a division actually effected by such a transaction is generally tested for dividend equivalence under section 302.

The transaction in this case, however, was not divisive, and, therefore, the anti-bailout provisions of section 355 are not relevant. After the December, 1982, exchange, a holder of International Common could not dispose of his interest in International without disposing of his interest in McDermott at the same time. Thus, no bailout was possible in this case.

Respondent maintains, however, that a holding for petitioners in this case will permit other taxpayers to bail out assets from corporate solution. In support of his argument, respondent presents two hypothetical examples. Respondent's first example involves an exchange of stock as follows:

> Assume that P Corp. owns all the stock of its subsidiary, S Corp. S Corp. has no other class of stock. The value of P is ten times greater than the value of S. The P shareholders desire to cash in on the stock of S at capital gains rates. To this end, S Corp. offers to exchange newly created shares of itself (the same class of stock) representing 80% of the voting power in S Corp. to P's shareholders for shares of P on a value-for-value basis. The P shareholders participate in the exchange with the intent of later disposing of the stock of S at capital gains rates. A direct distribution would have been taxed under I.R.C. §§301 or 302. Respondent's position in this case would treat this indirect distribution in the above transaction just as a direct distribution would have been treated. Petitioners' position would undermine I.R.C. §355 by treating the transaction as a nontaxable exchange under I.R.C. §351 followed by a sale under I.R.C. §1001 at capital gains rates.

Respondent's second example involves the receipt of preferred stock of the subsidiary by shareholder of the parent, as follows:

> Suppose P corporation owns all the stock of S corporation and that P and S each have substantial earnings and profits. P's shareholders want to receive the economic benefit of these earnings but . . . want to avoid dividend treatment. To this end, they cause S to acquire from each of them 10% of their respective P shareholdings in exchange solely for nonvoting limited preferred stock of S. . . . Sometime after the exchange, the P shareholders sell all of their S preferred stock for cash to unrelated third parties. Absent the application of section 304(a)(2), the above example results in the follow-

ing tax consequences. The exchange of P stock for preferred stock will result in capital gain to the P shareholders. They will thus take a fair market value basis in the S preferred stock. Their subsequent sale of the preferred stock will result in no taxation to them assuming its value remains constant. . . . The S preferred stock will not be section 306 stock in the hands of the P shareholders since, even assuming arguendo that §306(c)(3) applies to parent-subsidiary transactions, the requirements of §306(C)(3) are not met in that the P stock/S preferred stock exchange was not a transaction described in §351. Since the S preferred stock is not section 306 stock, its sale by the P shareholders will not result in ordinary income to them under §306.

Respondent may have discovered a potential for bailout under the provisions of section 304.[12] However, the examples presented by respondent are not before us, and we decline to adopt an interpretation of section 304 in contravention of the language of that statute and its legislative history.

Moreover, it seems apparent that the bailout potential perceived by respondent in his examples can be achieved by a value-for-value exchange of stock or an exchange of common stock for preferred between brother and sister corporations, and respondent has conceded that section 304 does not apply to the stock of the acquiring corporation received in a brother-sister transaction described in section 304(a)(1).

To reflect the foregoing, an appropriate order will be issued.

NOTE

1. *Corporate divisions effected without §355.* Although Congress intended §355 to be the exclusive vehicle granting tax-preferred treatment to divisive transactions, taxpayers wishing to avoid the strict limitations of §355 have sought to fit their corporate divisions within the umbrella of less restrictive provisions. In *Bhada,* a stock-for-stock exchange turned the parent-subsidiary pair into a brother-sister pair (albeit with cross-ownership between the brother and sister) and so had the effect of a divisive reorganization. Had the Tax Court held that stock of the distributing corporation constituted "property" for the application of §304(a), the transaction might have been taxed as a distribution, just as a failed §355 transaction is taxed. Unfortunately, the court ruled that §304(a) does not cover the stock of the subsidiary corporation because such stock is stock of the distributing corporation within the meaning of §317(a). Thus, the transaction effected a tax-free divisive reorganization without having to satisfy the hur-

---

12. Bittker and Eustice recognize this potential for bailout as a weakness in section 304 as it is presently written. See Bittker & Eustice, Federal Income Taxation of Corporations and Shareholders, par. 9.32, pp. 9-53–9-54 (4th ed. 1979).

dles imposed by §355. The Tax Court, while acknowledging that its holding might create an end-run around §355, wrote: "[W]e decline to adopt an interpretation of section 304 in contravention of the language of the statute and its legislative history." 89 T.C. at 977.

Commissioner v. Morris Trust
367 F.2d 794 (4th Cir. 1966)

Before Haynsworth, Chief Judge, J. Spencer Bell, Circuit Judge, and Stanley, District Judge.

Haynsworth, Chief Judge.

Its nubility impaired by the existence of an insurance department it had operated for many years, a state bank divested itself of that business before merging with a national bank. The divestiture was in the form of a traditional "spin-off," but, because it was a preliminary step to the merger of the banks, the Commissioner treated their receipt of stock of the insurance company as ordinary income to the stockholders of the state bank. We agree with the Tax Court, that gain to the stockholders of the state bank was not recognizable under §355 of the 1954 Code.

In 1960, a merger agreement was negotiated by the directors of American Commercial Bank, a North Carolina corporation with its principal office in Charlotte, and Security National Bank of Greensboro, a national bank. [T]hough American was slightly larger than Security, it was found desirable to operate the merged institutions under Security's national charter, after changing the name to North Carolina National Bank. . . .

For many years, American had operated an insurance department. This was a substantial impediment to the accomplishment of the merger, for a national bank is prohibited from operating an insurance department except in towns having a population of not more than 5000 inhabitants. To avoid a violation of the national banking laws, therefore, and to accomplish the merger under Security's national charter, it was prerequisite that American rid itself of its insurance business.

The required step to make it nubile was accomplished by American's organization of a new corporation, American Commercial Agency, Inc., to which American transferred its insurance business assets in exchange for Agency's stock which was immediately distributed to American's stockholders. At the same time, American paid a cash dividend fully taxable to its stockholders. The merger of the two banks was then accomplished.

Though American's spin-off of its insurance business was a "D" reorganization, as defined in §368(a)(1), provided the distribution of Agency's stock qualified for nonrecognition of gain under §355, the Commissioner contends that the active business requirements of §355(b)(1)(A) were not met, since American's banking business was not continued in unaltered corporate form. He also finds an inherent incompatibility in substantially simultaneous divisive and amalgamating reorganizations.

Section 355(b)(1)(A) requires that both the distributing corporation and the controlled corporation be "engaged immediately after the distribution in the active conduct of a trade or business." There was literal compliance with that requirement, for the spin-off, including the distribution of Agency's stock to American's stockholders, preceded the merger. The Commissioner asks that we look at both steps together, contending that North Carolina National Bank was not the distributing corporation and that its subsequent conduct of American's banking business does not satisfy the requirement.

A brief look at an earlier history may clarify the problem. . . .

Nonrecognition of gain in "spin-offs" was introduced by the Revenue Act of 1924. Its §203(b)(3), as earlier Revenue Acts, provided for nonrecognition of gain at the corporate level when one corporate party to a reorganization exchanged property solely for stock or securities of another, but it added a provision in subsection (c) extending the nonrecognition of gain to a stockholder of a corporate party to a reorganization who received stock of another party without surrendering any of his old stock. Thus, with respect to the nonrecognition of gain, treatment previously extended to "split-offs" was extended to the economically indistinguishable "spin-off."

The only limitation upon those provisions extending nonrecognition to spin-offs was contained in §203(h) and (i) defining reorganizations. The definition required that immediately after the transfer, the transferor or its stockholders or both be in control of the corporation to which the assets had been transferred, and "control" was defined as being the ownership of not less than eighty percent of the voting stock and eighty percent of the total number of shares of all other classes of stock.

With no restriction other than the requirement of control of the transferee, these provisions were a fertile source of tax avoidance schemes. By spinning-off liquid assets or all productive assets, they provided the means by which ordinary distributions of earnings could be cast in the form of a reorganization within their literal language.

The renowned case of Gregory v. Helvering, 293 U.S. 465, brought the problem to the Supreme Court. The taxpayer there owned all of the stock of United Mortgage Corporation which, in turn, owned 1000 shares of Monitor Securities Corporation. She wished to sell the Monitor stock and possess herself of the proceeds. If the sale were effected by United Mortgage, gain would be recognized to it, and its subsequent distribution of the net proceeds of the sale would have been a dividend to the taxpayer, taxable as ordinary income. If the Monitor stock were distributed to the taxpayer before sale, its full value would have been taxable to her as ordinary income. In order materially to reduce that tax cost, United Mortgage spun-off the Monitor stock to a new corporation, Averill, the stock of which was distributed to the taxpayer. Averill was then liquidated, and the taxpayer sold the Monitor stock. She contended that she was taxable only on the proceeds of the sale, reduced by an allocated part of her cost basis of United Mortgage, and at capital gain rates.

The Supreme Court found the transaction quite foreign to the congressional purpose. It limited the statute's definition of a reorganization to a reorganization of a corporate business or businesses motivated by a business purpose. It was never intended that Averill engage in any business, and it had not. Its creation, the distribution of its stock and its liquidation, the court concluded, was only a masquerade for the distribution of an ordinary dividend, as, of course, it was. . . .

Underlying such judicially developed rules limiting the scope of the nonrecognition provisions of the Code, was an acceptance of a general congressional purpose to facilitate the reorganization of businesses, not to exalt economically meaningless formalisms and diversions through corporate structures hastily created and as hastily demolished. Continuation of a business in altered corporate form was to be encouraged, but immunization of taxable transactions through the interposition of shortlived, empty, corporate entities was never intended and ought not to be allowed.

While these judicial principles were evolving and before the Supreme Court declared itself in Gregory v. Helvering, an alarmed Congress withdrew nonrecognition of gain to a stockholder receiving securities in a spin-off. It did so by omitting from the Revenue Act of 1934, a provision comparable to §203(c) of the Revenue Act of 1924.

Nonrecognition of gain to the stockholder in spin-off situations, however, was again extended by §317(a) of the Revenue Act of 1951, amending the 1939 Code by adding §112(b)(11). This time, the judicially developed restrictions upon the application of the earlier statutes were partially codified. Nonrecognition of gain was extended "unless it appears that (A) any corporation which is a party to such reorganization was not intended to continue the active conduct of a trade or business after such reorganization, or (B) the corporation whose stock is distributed was used principally as a device for the distribution of earnings and profits to the shareholders of any corporation a party to the reorganization."

If this transaction were governed by the 1939 Code, as amended in 1951, the Commissioner would have had the support of a literal reading of the A limitation, for it was not intended that American, in its then corporate form, should continue the active conduct of the banking business. From the prior history, however, it would appear that the intention of the A limitation was to withhold the statute's benefits from schemes of the Gregory v. Helvering type. It effectively reached those situations in which one of the parties to the reorganization was left only with liquid assets not intended for use in the acquisition of an active business or in which the early demise of one of the parties was contemplated, particularly, if its only office was a conduit for the transmission of title. The B limitation was an additional precaution intended to encompass any other possible use of the device for the masquerading of a dividend distribution.

The 1954 Code was the product of a careful attempt to codify the judicial limiting principles in a more particularized form. The congressional particularization extended the principles in some areas, as in the requirement that a business, to be considered an active one, must have been conducted for a period of at least five years ending on the distribution date and must not have been acquired in a taxable transaction during the five-year period. In other areas, it relaxed and ameliorated them, as in its express sanction of non-pro rata distributions. While there are such particularized variations, the 1954 Code is a legislative reexpression of generally established principles developed in response to definite classes of abuses which had manifested themselves many years earlier. The perversions of the general congressional purpose and the principles the courts had developed to thwart them, as revealed in the earlier cases, are still an enlightening history with which an interpretation of the reorganization sections of the 1954 Code should be approached.

Section 355(b) requires that the distributing corporation be engaged in the active conduct of a trade or business "immediately after the distribution." This is in contrast to the provisions of the 1951 Act, which, as we have noted, required an intention that the parent, as well as the other corporate parties to the reorganization, continue the conduct of an active business. It is in marked contrast to §355(b)'s highly particularized requirements respecting the duration of the active business prior to the reorganization and the methods by which it was acquired. These contrasts suggest a literal reading of the post-reorganization requirement and a holding that the Congress intended to restrict it to the situation existing "immediately after the distribution."

Such a reading is quite consistent with the prior history. It quite adequately meets the problem posed by the Gregory v. Helvering situation in which, immediately after the distribution, one of the corporations held only liquid or investment assets. It sufficiently serves the requirements of permanence and of continuity, for as long as an active business is being conducted immediately after the distribution, there is no substantial opportunity for the stockholders to sever their interest in the business except through a separable, taxable transaction. If the corporation proceeds to withdraw assets from the conduct of the active business and to abandon it, the Commissioner has recourse to the back-up provisions of §355(a)(1)(B) and to the limitations of the underlying principles. At the same time, the limitation, so construed, will not inhibit continued stockholder conduct of the active business through altered corporate form and with further changes in corporate structure, the very thing the reorganization sections were intended to facilitate.

Applied, to this case, there is no violation of any of the underlying limiting principles. There was no empty formalism, no utilization of empty corporate structures, no attempt to recast a taxable transaction in nontaxable form and no withdrawal of liquid assets. There is no question but that American's insurance and banking businesses met all of the active business requirements of §355(b)(2). It was intended that both businesses be continued indefinitely, and each has been. American's merger with Security, in no sense, was a discontinuance of American's banking business, which opened the day after the merger with the same employees, the same depositors and customers. . . . There was a strong business purpose for both the spin-off and the merger, and tax avoidance by American's stockholders was neither a predominant nor a subordinate purpose. In short, though both of the transactions be viewed together, there were none of the evils or misuses which the limiting principles and the statutory limitations were designed to exclude.

We are thus led to the conclusion that this carefully drawn statute should not be read more broadly than it was written to deny nonrecognition of gain to reorganizations of real businesses of the type which Congress clearly intended to facilitate by according to them nonrecognition of present gain.

The Commissioner, indeed, concedes that American's stockholders would have realized no gain had American not been merged into Security after, but substantially contemporaneously with, Agency's spin-off. Insofar as it is contended that §355(b)(1)(A) requires the distributing corporation to continue the conduct of an active business, recognition of gain to American's stockholders on their receipt of Agency's stock would depend upon the economically irrelevant technicality of the identity of the surviving corporation in the merger. Had American been the survivor, it would in every literal and substantive sense have continued the conduct of its banking business.

Surely, the Congress which drafted these comprehensive provisions did not intend the incidence of taxation to turn upon so insubstantial a technicality. Its differentiation on the basis of the economic substance of transactions is too evident to permit such a conclusion.

This, too, the Commissioner seems to recognize, at least conditionally, for he says that gain to the stockholders would have been recognized even if American had been the surviving corporation. This would necessitate our reading into §355(b)(1)(A) an implicit requirement that the distributing corporation, without undergoing any reorganization whatever, whether or not it resulted in a change in its corporate identity, continue the conduct of its active business.

We cannot read this broader limitation into the statute for the same reasons we cannot read into it the narrower one of maintenance of the same corporation identity. The congressional limitation of the post-distribution active business requirement to the situation existing "immediately after the distribution" was deliberate. Consistent with the general statutory scheme, it is quite inconsistent with the Commissioner's contention.

The requirement of §368(a)(1)(D) that the transferor or its stockholders be in control of the spun-off corporation immediately after the transfer is of no assistance to the Commissioner. It is directed solely to control of the transferee, and was fully met here. It contains no requirement of continuing control of the transferor. Though a subsequent sale of the transferor's stock, under some circumstances, might form the basis of a contention that the transaction was the equivalent of a dividend within the meaning of §355(a)(1)(B) and the underlying principles, the control requirements imply no limitation upon subsequent reorganizations of the transferor.

There is no distinction in the statute between subsequent amalgamating reorganizations in which the stockholders of the spin-off transferor would own 80% or more of the relevant classes of stock of the reorganized transferor, and those in which they would not. The statute draws no line between major and minor amalgamations in prospect at the time of the spin-off. Nothing of the sort is suggested by the detailed control-active business requirements in the five-year predistribution period, for there the distinction is between taxable and non-taxable acquisitions, and a tax free exchange within the five-year period does not violate the active business-control requirement whether it was a major or a minor acquisition. Reorganizations in which no gain or loss is recognized, sanctioned by the statute's control provision when occurring in the five years preceding the spin-off, are not prohibited in the postdistribution period. . . .

Nor can we find elsewhere in the Code any support for the Commissioner's suggestion of incompatibility between substantially contemporaneous divisive and amalgamating reorganizations. The 1954 Code contains no inkling of it; nor does its immediate legislative history. The difficulties encountered under the 1924 Code and its successors, in dealing with formalistic distortions of taxable transactions into the spin-off shape, contain no implication of any such incompatibility. Section 317 of the Revenue Act of 1951 . . . did require an intention that the distributing corporation continue the conduct of its active business, but that transitory requirement is of slight relevance to an interpretation of the very different provisions of the 1954 Code and is devoid of any implication of incompatibility. If that provision, during the years it was in effect, would have resulted in recognition of gain in a spin-off if the distributing corporation later, but substantially simultaneously, was a party to a merger in which it lost its identity, a question we do not decide, it would not inhibit successive reorganizations if the merger preceded the spin-off.

The Congress intended to encourage six types of reorganizations. They are defined in 368 and designated by the letters "A" through "F." The "A" merger, the "B" exchange of stock for stock and the "C" exchange of stock for substantially all of the properties of another are all amalgamating reorganizations. The "D" reorganization is the divisive spin-off, while the "E" and "F" reorganizations, recapitalizations and reincorporations, are neither amalgamating nor divisive. All are sanctioned equally, however. Recognition of gain is withheld from each and succes-

sively so. Merger may follow merger, and an "A" reorganization by which
Y is merged into *X* corporation may proceed substantially simultaneously
with a "C" reorganization by which *X* acquires substantially all of the
properties of *Z* and with an "F" reorganization by which *X* is reincorpo-
rated in another state. The "D" reorganization has no lesser standing.
It is on the same plane as the others and, provided all of the "D" requirements are met, is as available as the others in successive reorganizations. . . .

A decision of the Sixth Circuit appears to be at odds with our conclusion. In Curtis [v. United States, 336 F.2d 714 (6th Cir. 1964)], it appears
that one corporation was merged into another after spinning-off a warehouse building which was an unwanted asset because the negotiators could
not agree upon its value. The Court of Appeals for the Sixth Circuit affirmed a District Court judgment holding that the value of the warehouse
company shares was taxable as ordinary income to the stockholders of the
first corporation.

A possible distinction may lie between the spin-off of an asset unwanted by the acquiring corporation in an "A" reorganization solely because of disagreement as to its value and the preliminary spin-off of an
active business which the acquiring corporation is prohibited by law from
operating. We cannot stand upon so nebulous a distinction, however. We
simply take a different view. The reliance in *Curtis* upon the Report of the
Senate Committee explaining §317 of the Revenue Act of 1951, quite
dissimilar to the 1954 Code, reinforces our appraisal of the relevant materials.

To the extent that our own decision in [Helvering v. Elkhorn Coal
Co., 95 F.2d 732 (4th Cir. 1937)] is relevant, it tends to support our conclusion, not to militate against it.

Elkhorn was one of the interesting cases which contributed to the
development of the judicial principles which served, as best they could, to
confine pretensive arrangements in the early days long before adopting of
the 1954 Code. Mill Creek Coal Company wanted to acquire for Mill Creek
stock one of the mining properties of Elkhorn. Had the bargain been
effectuated, directly, it would have been clearly a taxable transaction, for
Elkhorn had other mining properties. In an attempt to avoid the tax,
Elkhorn's other properties were spun-off to a new Elkhorn; old Elkhorn
conveyed its remaining properties to Mill Creek for stock and by successive
transactions, Elkhorn stockholders wound up owning stock in new Elkhorn
which owned all of old Elkhorn's mining properties, except the ones transferred to Mill Creek, and the Mill Creek stock received by old Elkhorn.
They were in precisely the same position as they would have been in if old
Elkhorn had transferred the Mill Creek properties to Mill Creek for stock.
It was an obviously transparent attempt to circumvent the requirement
that substantially all of the properties must be transferred to qualify for
nonrecognition in what would now be classified as a "C" reorganization.
The contention in *Elkhorn* was not that its stockholders realized gain

on the spin-off. The opinion denying a rehearing, particularly, suggests the absence of recognizable gain as a result of the spin-off. It approved the recognition of gain as a result of the subsequent "C" reorganization.

It is difficult now to envision any other result in *Elkhorn,* since the stockholders' purpose of formalistic transformation of a clearly taxable transaction into the form of a series of untaxable transactions was so blatant. Nothing of the sort is represented here. Interestingly, however, *Elkhorn* would question the recognition of gain in the merger exchange here, as to which the Commissioner wisely makes no contention under the 1954 Code, not recognition of gain at the earlier spin-off step. As to the first step, the *Elkhorn* opinion appears to oppose the Commissioner's present position.

For the reasons which we have canvassed, we think the Tax Court . . . correctly decided that American's stockholders realized no recognizable taxable gain upon their receipt in the "D" reorganization of the stock of Agency.

Affirmed.

NOTE

1.   Morris Trust *and* Elkhorn Coal. The court in *Morris Trust* argued that its decision was supported by its prior opinion in *Elkhorn Coal,* in which a divisive reorganization followed by a C reorganization was held taxable. In *Morris Trust,* a divisive reorganization followed by an A reorganization was held tax free. Since a C reorganization is nothing but a de facto merger (that is, a de facto A reorganization), can these two decisions be squared?

In *Elkhorn Coal* the Commissioner sought to tax the shareholders on the distribution made pursuant to the nominal C reorganization. In *Morris Trust,* however, he sought to recharacterize the initial divisive reorganization as a taxable transaction. Was that the Commissioner's fatal error in *Morris Trust?* Would the court in *Morris Trust* have sustained a challenge to the tax-free status of the merger of American into Security?

Congress has limited the C reorganization to acquisitions of "substantially all" the transferor corporation's assets. If a C reorganization could be preceded by a tax-free divisive D reorganization, the transferor could spin off any unwanted assets before transferring its remaining assets to the acquiring corporation, thereby circumventing the C reorganization's substantially-all requirement. *Elkhorn Coal* refused to permit the substantially-all limitation to be emasculated in this way. Would a contrary decision have been so bad? What abuse might the Commissioner fear?

2.   *The statutory symmetries of §355.* The court in *Morris Trust* recognized that if the spin-off had been followed by a merger of the insurance company rather than of the bank, the spin-off would have failed to satisfy the requirement in §368(a)(1)(D) that the shareholders be in control of the spun-off company immediately after the transaction. The court said, how-

ever, that there is no similar requirement that the shareholders control
the distributing corporation immediately after the transaction. Since a
divisive D reorganization involves splitting one corporation into two, it
would be peculiar for a control requirement to be imposed on the shareholders with respect to only one of the resulting corporations.

Section 368(a)(1)(D) requires that the shareholders control the spun-
off corporation immediately after the transaction. There is no explicit
requirement that they also control the distributing corporation for the
simple reason that the shareholders, *by definition,* already control it —
they are, after all, its shareholders. Simply put, a divisive reorganization
contemplates that the shareholders of the spin-off corporation be former
(and perhaps current) shareholders of the distributing corporation.

To be sure, the shareholders might sell or exchange their stock in the
distributing corporation immediately after the transaction, but if they do
so, the tax-free status of the transaction will be in jeopardy under the
"device" language of §355(a)(1)(B). Indeed, the same statutory provision
forbids the planned sale or exchange of the stock of either the distributing
corporation or of the spun-off corporation. Thus, to meet the express
requirement of a divisive D reorganization, former shareholders of the
distributing corporation must control both corporations after the transaction.

The effect of following a divisive reorganization with an acquisitive
reorganization is to introduce new shareholders into the transaction. If
these new shareholders acquire a sufficient interest in one of the corporations so as to cause the former shareholders to lose "control," the transaction fails to meet the condition imposed on divisive reorganizations under
§355(a)(1)(B). Yet, the Treasury has promulgated a regulation under §355
stating that a planned exchange will not run afoul of the "device" language
in §355(a)(1)(B) if the exchange is tax free under the reorganization
provisions. Treas. Reg. §1.355-2(d)(2)(iii)(D). What weight does this
proposed regulation give to the inner parenthetical in §355(a)(1)(B)?
Where does this proposed regulation leave *Elkhorn Coal?* Does a tax-free
exchange after a divisive reorganization present an opportunity for
abuse?

3. *Some concluding thoughts on §355.* The corporate division problem
is another example of some of the internal conflicts or strains of the
present system of taxing corporations and their shareholders. If *A* forms
two separate corporations and lets them grow independently, *A* is free to
deal separately with them. But, if *B* starts the same business activities in a
single corporation, it will be difficult for *B* to separate them later without
adverse tax consequences: A distribution from *B*'s corporation of one of
its businesses, even in corporate form, resembles a dividend. *B* will argue
that she should be allowed to achieve the same results as *A* so long as
she keeps the business activities in "corporate solution," but unless the
distribution passes the complicated tests of §355, it will not be tax free.

Confusion stems from the corporate system's allowing the retention of earnings without a direct tax on shareholders. If stock is sold, earnings to the extent reflected in the sale price are usually taxed at the shareholder level as capital gains. But if the earnings are distributed to the shareholder by an ongoing corporation, they are taxed as dividends. A tax-free division of a single corporation with retained earnings into two separate corporations gives the shareholder the potential to sell one at capital gains rates, the economic equivalent of a dividend distribution from the original corporation. Recall §302(b)(4) and the circumstances under which part of a business enterprise may be distributed at capital gains rates as a partial liquidation.

B. PROBLEMS

1.   For the past 15 years, X Corp. has engaged in the business of heavy construction. X Corp. transfers half of the company's heavy machinery and other operating assets along with one long-term contract to newly formed Y Corp. in exchange for all of Y Corp.'s stock, and this stock is promptly distributed pro rata to the shareholders of X Corp. Immediately after the transaction, both corporations actively conduct the business formerly conducted by X Corp. It is anticipated that Y Corp. will be liquidated within the taxable year.

   a.   Does the distribution of Y Corp. stock qualify as a tax-free divisive reorganization under §368(a)(1)(D) and §355?

   b.   Does the analysis change if it is X Corp. that will be liquidated and its assets distributed in the near future?

2.   A and B each own 50 percent of the stock of X Corp. A's basis in the X stock is $600, and B's stock basis is $1,400. X Corp. carries on (and has carried on for more than five years) two lines of business: (a) the manufacture and sale of computer games (Gameco division) and (b) the manufacture and sale of denim sleepwear (Denco division). The assets of each division have a value of $2,000 and adjusted basis of $800. No liabilities exist, and there are joint earnings and profits of $1,000.

   a.   On January 1, 1988, X transfers all the Gameco assets to newly formed Y Corp. in exchange for all of Y's stock. X also transfers all its Denco assets to newly formed Z Corp. in exchange for all of Z's stock. X then liquidates and distributes the Y and Z stock ratably to A and B. What are the tax consequences to A and B?

   b.   Suppose instead that X transferred the Gameco assets to Y Corp. and retained the Denco assets. Immediately thereafter, X distributes the Y stock to A in exchange for all of A's stock in X.

   c.   What are the results if X transfers the Gameco assets to Y and then distributes the Y stock equally to A and B?

   d.   How do your answers to (b) change if most of the assets of Gameco consist of appreciated securities traded on the New York stock exchange?

e. How do your answers to (b) change if Denco was purchased three years before with profits from Gameco? If X had purchased the stock of Holding Corp. three years before with profits from Gameco, Holding Corp.'s only asset then being stock of Denco, and, shortly after X's acquisition of the Holding Corp. stock, Holding Corp. liquidated under §332 so that X acquired the stock of Denco under §332?

3. Parent Corp. owns the entire outstanding stock of Sub-1 Corp., Sub-2 Corp., and Sub-3 Corp. X, Y, and Z each purchase one-third of the outstanding shares of Parent Corp. and Parent Corp. subsequently distributes the stock of Sub-1 to X, the stock of Sub-2 to Y, and the stock of Sub-3 to Z. What are the tax consequences of the distributions to Parent Corp., X, Y, and Z? How would your answers change if the distributions had been pro rata so that X, Y, and Z each ended up with a one-third interest in Sub-1, Sub-2, and Sub-3? Assume each corporation has actively conducted a trade or business for more than five years.

4. X Corp. purchases all the outstanding stock of Y Corp. for $200,000. Y Corp.'s assets include all the outstanding stock of Z Corp. with adjusted basis of $60,000 and fair market value of $100,000. Three years later, P Corp. acquires all the outstanding stock of Y Corp. from X Corp. in exchange for its own voting preferred stock in a transaction described in §368(a)(1)(B). How are P Corp. and Y Corp. taxed if Y Corp. distributes all its stock in Z Corp. one year after the P-X B reorganization, assuming the active business requirement of §355(c) is met?

5. X Corp., a successful corporation with substantial earnings and profits, has 100 shares of stock outstanding, wholly owned by individual B. B owns 50 of these shares with adjusted basis of $10 per share and the other 50 shares with adjusted basis of $1,000 per share. Assume each share of X Corp. is worth $1,000. X Corp. transfers cash of $50,000 to newly formed Y Corp. in exchange for 100 shares of Y Corp. stock. One year later, B transfers the 50 shares of X Corp. stock having adjusted basis of $1,000 per share to Y Corp. in exchange for 100 shares of Y Corp. common stock. What are the tax consequences of this exchange to individual B? How will B be taxed if her stock of Y Corp. is subsequently redeemed?

12

One-Party Reorganizations

A. RECAPITALIZATIONS

A recapitalization, in general, refers to a readjustment of the capital structure of a single, existing corporation. Because the term "recapitalization" is not defined in the Code, however, its scope is uncertain. Many types of conversions have been swept into its meaning by cases and rulings. As with other tax-free reorganizations, discussed in Chapters 10 and 11, the assumptions underlying nonrecognition are that the stock received in a recapitalization is a continuation of the old stock with a mere change in form and that gain or loss consequently should not be recognized, except as to boot received in the exchange.

The classic recapitalization occurs when a closely held family corporation has older owners close to retirement age who wish to transfer the opportunity for growth to younger managers, often their children. Typically, the recapitalization in such a case will involve an exchange of the older owners' common stock for preferred. This suits the estate planning needs of the retiring owners by keeping future equity appreciation out of their estates while retaining for them, in more secure form, their capital in the corporation. In addition, dividends on the preferred stock may provide the older owners with a stable retirement income. The recapitalization also suits the younger managers, who are eager to be rewarded for their efforts by the equity growth of the corporation but are unable to buy significant amounts of the old common stock. Risk of future loss also will be transferred to the new equityholders since the preferred stock has a preferred position over the common.

Another common type of recapitalization, filling a much different need and with a host of problems beyond the scope of this discussion, occurs with a financially distressed corporation. In such a case, the debtors and shareholders may together recapitalize the company's debt and equity structure, or they may contribute their debt and equity interests to a new corporation. See pages 492-496 infra.

If an exchange of stock for stock is treated as a tax-free recapitalization, then the substitute basis rules of §358 apply so that the basis of the stock received remains the same as the stock surrendered. In a recapitalization, the corporation usually retains all its tax attributes — e.g., no change in the basis of its assets, no effect on its earnings and profits. The corporation's tax existence, in other words, continues without interruption. No special provision for the carryover of tax attributes (such as a net operating loss) is needed, so the rules of §381 applicable to most reorganizations generally do not apply to recapitalizations.

Section 305(b) and (c) can make taxable certain disproportionate recapitalization exchanges when the effect of the transaction is a non-pro rata stock dividend. The Service does not, however, usually raise the §305(b) and (c) problems in the isolated recapitalization of a closely held corporation. See Rev. Rul. 75-93, 1975-1 C.B. 101, in which a disproportionate recapitalization exchange did not trigger §305(c) because it was not part of a plan to periodically increase equity interests. To the same effect, see Gen. Couns. Mem. 39088 (Dec. 7, 1983). See also Treas. Regs. §1.305-3(e) (examples 10, 11, and 12).

Recapitalizations can cover a variety of stock exchanges. For examples, see Treas. Regs. §1.368-2(e) as well as the following: common stock for preferred stock, Rev. Rul. 74-269, 1974-1 C.B. 87; and preferred stock for common stock, Rev. Rul. 77-238, 1977-2 C.B. 115. Recall from page 319 supra that an exchange of common stock for preferred stock may cause the preferred to be §306 stock under §306(c)(1)(B).

Recapitalizations also can include exchanges of bonds as well as of stock. The Service has ruled that convertible bonds may be exchanged for stock. See Rev. Rul. 72-265, 1972-1 C.B. 122. Bonds may be exchanged for bonds, and there is no original issue discount (see §1273) on a bond-for-bond and bond-for-stock recapitalization. See Rev. Rul. 77-415, 1977-2 C.B. 311. In Rev. Rul. 77-437, 1977-2 C.B. 28, the Service ruled that a debtor corporation recognized income from the cancellation of indebtedness on a bond exchange to the extent that the face value of the old bonds exceeded the face value of the new bonds.

A controversial problem in the recapitalization area has been the exchange of stock for bonds, as illustrated in *Bazley* below. It always has been clear that a distribution of its own debt securities by a corporation with earnings and profits is a taxable dividend. See page 142 supra. But the status of debt securities issued by a corporation in the course of a corporate recapitalization has been less clear. The 1939 Code provided (as does the "general rule" laid down in §354(a)(1) of the 1954 Code) that no gain or loss was to be recognized if stock or securities of a corporation that was a party to a "reorganization" were exchanged for stock and securities of the same corporation; the 1939 Code, like §368(a)(1)(E) of the current Code, defined a "reorganization" to include a recapitalization. Suppose, then, that a corporation "recapitalized" by calling in its outstanding common stock and issuing in exchange other common stock (with a different par value or some other alteration of rights) plus bonds, debentures, or notes. Should the transaction be a tax-free exchange of the old stock for the new stock and bonds or other debt instruments? Should it be treated as a taxable sale or exchange? As a dividend of the debt instruments? *Bazley* considers this problem. For the effect of §354(a)(2) enacted in 1954, see the Note following *Bazley*.

Bazley v. Commissioner
331 U.S. 737 (1947)

Mr. Justice FRANKFURTER delivered the opinion of the Court. . . .

[T]he Commissioner of Internal Revenue assessed an income tax deficiency against the taxpayer for the year 1939. Its validity depends on the legal significance of the recapitalization in that year of a family corporation in which the taxpayer and his wife owned all but one of the Company's one thousand shares. These had a par value of $100. Under the plan of reorganization the taxpayer, his wife, and the holder of the additional share were to turn in their old shares and receive in exchange for each old share five new shares of no par value, but of a stated value of $60, and new debenture bonds, having a total face value of $400,000, payable in ten years but callable at any time. Accordingly, the taxpayer received 3,990 shares of the new stock for the 798 shares of his old holding and debentures in the amount of $319,200. At the time of these transactions the earned surplus of the corporation was $855,783.82.

The Commissioner charged to the taxpayer as income the full value of the debentures. The Tax Court affirmed the Commissioner's determination, against the taxpayer's contention that as a "recapitalization" the transaction was a tax-free "reorganization" and that the debentures were "securities in a corporation a party to a reorganization," "exchanged solely for stock or securities in such corporation" "in pursuance of a plan of reorganization," and as such no gain is recognized for income tax purposes. [§§368(a)(1)(E) and 354(a)(1).*] The Tax Court found that the recapitalization had "no legitimate corporate business purpose" and was therefore not a "reorganization" within the statute. The distribution of debentures, it concluded, was a disguised dividend, taxable as earned income under [§§61(a) and 301]. 4 T.C. 897. The Circuit Court of Appeals

---

* Section 354(a)(2), which limits greatly the general rule of §354(a)(1), was not enacted until 1954. — EDS.

for the Third Circuit, sitting en banc, affirmed, two judges dissenting. 155 F.2d 237.

Unless a transaction is a reorganization contemplated by [§368(a)], any exchange of "stock or securities" in connection with such transaction, cannot be "in pursuance of the plan of reorganization" under [§354]. While [§368(a)] informs us that "reorganization" means, among other things, "a recapitalization," it does not inform us what "recapitalization" means. "Recapitalization" in connection with the income tax has been part of the revenue laws since 1921. . . . Congress has never defined it and the Treasury Regulations shed only limited light. Treas. Reg. [§1.368-1(b)]. One thing is certain. Congress did not incorporate some technical concept, whether that of accountants or of other specialists, into [§368(a)], assuming that there is agreement among specialists as to the meaning of recapitalization. And so, recapitalization as used in [§368(a)] must draw its meaning from its function in that section. It is one of the forms of reorganization which obtains the privileges afforded by [§368(a)]. Therefore, "recapitalization" must be construed with reference to the presuppositions and purpose of [§368(a)]. It was not the purpose of the reorganization provision to exempt from payment of a tax what as a practical matter is realized gain. Normally, a distribution by a corporation, whatever form it takes, is a definite and rather unambiguous event. It furnishes the proper occasion for the determination and taxation of gain. But there are circumstances where a formal distribution, directly or through exchange of securities, represents merely a new form of the previous participation in an enterprise, involving no change of substance in the rights and relations of the interested parties one to another or to the corporate assets. As to these, Congress has said that they are not to be deemed significant occasions for determining taxable gain. . . .

In a series of cases this Court has withheld the benefits of the reorganization provision in situations which might have satisfied provisions of the section treated as inert language, because they were not reorganizations of the kind with which [§354], in its purpose and particulars, concerns itself. See Pinellas Ice & Cold Storage Co. v. Commissioner, 287 U.S. 462; Gregory v. Helvering, 293 U.S. 465; Le Tulle v. Scofield, 308 U.S. 415. . . .

Since a recapitalization within the scope of [§368] is an aspect of reorganization, nothing can be a recapitalization for this purpose unless it partakes of those characteristics of a reorganization which underlie the purpose of Congress in postponing the tax liability.

No doubt there was a recapitalization of the Bazley corporation in the sense that the symbols that represented its capital were changed, so that the fiscal basis of its operations would appear very differently on its books. . . . What is controlling is that a new arrangement intrinsically partake of the elements of reorganization which underlie the Congressional exemption and not merely give the appearance of it to accomplish a distribution of earnings. . . .

What have we here? No doubt, if the Bazley corporation had issued the debentures to Bazley and his wife without any recapitalization, it would have made a taxable distribution. Instead, these debentures were issued as part of a family arrangement, the only additional ingredient being an unrelated modification of the capital account. The debentures were found to be worth at least their principal amount, and they were virtually cash because they were callable at the will of the corporation which in this case was the will of the taxpayer. One does not have to pursue the motives behind actions, even in the more ascertainable forms of purpose, to find, as did the Tax Court, that the whole arrangement took this form instead of an outright distribution of cash or debentures, because the latter would undoubtedly have been taxable income whereas what was done could, with a show of reason, claim the shelter of the immunity of a recapitalization-reorganization. . . .

A "reorganization" which is merely a vehicle, however elaborate or elegant, for conveying earnings from accumulations to the stockholders is not a reorganization under [§368]. This disposes of the case as a matter of law, since the facts as found by the Tax Court bring them within it. And even if this transaction were deemed a reorganization, the facts would equally sustain the imposition of the tax on the debentures under [§356(a)(1) and (2)]. Commissioner v. Estate of Bedford, 325 U.S. 283. . . .

Other claims raised have been considered but their rejection does not call for discussion.

Judgments affirmed.

Mr. Justice Douglas and Mr. Justice Burton dissent in both cases for the reasons stated in the joint dissent of Judges Maris and Goodrich in the court below. Bazley v. Commissioner, 3 Cir., 155 F.2d 237, 244.

NOTE

1. *The 1954 changes in §354.* While the 1954 Code continued the general nonrecognition rule for shareholder exchanges incident to reorganizations, it added §354(a)(2) limiting nonrecognition to cases in which the principal amount of securities (debt instruments) received does not exceed the principal amount of debt instruments surrendered. By virtue of §354(a)(2), in conjunction with §356(a) and (d), the debentures in *Bazley* would have been taxed as boot even if the transaction had been held a reorganization since no debt instruments were surrendered.

Does §354(a)(2) render *Bazley* obsolete? Securities constituting boot received in a reorganization may be taxed under the installment sale provisions. See §453(f)(6) (last sentence). If such taxation is available, then gain will be deferred until payment on the securities is received. See §453(c). But if under *Bazley* an exchange is held to be a distribution taxable under §301 rather than a recapitalization, installment sale treatment is unavailable and the securities will be taxable on receipt. Accordingly, *Bazley* is still important for its gloss on the definition of a "recapitalization." Note that installment sale treatment will never be available with respect to securities that are "readily tradable." §453(f)(4)-(5).

Securities received as boot in a reorganization will not qualify for installment sale treatment under §453(f)(6) if receipt of the securities has the effect of a dividend. See §356(a)(2). Recall *Clark,* page 479 supra, defining dividend equivalency. For a discussion of the relationship between the reorganizations provisions and the installment sale provisions, see Siegel, Installment Sales — Relationship to Section 385 Regulations, Section 337 Sales, and Other Concepts, 40 N.Y.U. Inst. Fed. Tax. ch. 46, at §46.06 (1982). See also Prop. Regs. §1.453-1(f)(2).

2.   *The effect of* Bedford. *Bedford,* cited by the Supreme Court in *Bazley,* involved these facts: Under a recapitalization plan, a shareholder exchanged 3,000 shares of cumulative preferred stock (par value $100) for 3,500 shares of cumulative preferred stock (par value $75), 1,500 shares of common stock (par value $1), and $45,240 of cash. The shareholder's gain (the difference between the adjusted basis of the shares given up and the value of the stock plus cash received) was $139,740. The corporation's earnings and profits were sufficient to cover the entire cash distribution. The government admitted that the transaction was a reorganization exchange, and the taxpayer admitted that the cash was property not permitted to be received tax free — i.e., boot. The only issue was whether under what is now §356(a)(1) and (2) the boot should be taxed as capital gain — like a sale of stock for cash — or as a dividend. The Court, conceding that the matter was not "wholly free from doubt," concluded that because the corporation had earnings and profits, the distribution of cash had "the effect of the distribution of a taxable dividend." The result of *Bedford* became generally known as the automatic dividend rule. That rule has now become discredited. See pages 479-491 supra.

3.   *The "dividend limited to gain" rule of §356.* In citing §356 and *Bedford* as an alternative route to the same result reached by the "no reorganization" route, the Court in *Bazley* may have overlooked the fact that §356(a) requires boot to be treated as a dividend only if, and to the extent that, the taxpayer realizes a gain on the exchange itself. For example, suppose individual *A* owns the 100 outstanding shares of *X* Corp. with adjusted basis and fair market value of $100 per share. What are the tax consequences under §§354 and 356 if *A* exchanges all the stock for 50 shares of newly issued common stock worth $40 per share plus securities with a fair market value of $8,000, assuming that the exchange constitutes a "recapitalization" within the meaning of §368(a)(1)(E)? Since there is no gain (within the meaning of §1001(a)) on the exchange, *A* recognizes no income under §356 despite the presence of boot.

Turning to *Bazley,* the value of the stock and securities received may well have exceeded the taxpayer's basis for the stock surrendered, but the Tax Court made no finding to this effect. Even if there had been such a finding, the amount of the taxpayer's gain might have been less than the value of the distributed securities. Under the Supreme Court's holding in *Bazley*, the taxpayer recognized the full value of the securities received as income without any offset for his basis in the stock turned in. Accordingly, even a taxpayer captured by the excess securities rule of §354(a)(2) may profit by arguing in favor of reorganization treatment for the exchange.

4. *Use of debt in a corporation's capital structure.* On incorporation, corporations often issue bonds or debentures to the incorporators, in addition to stock, so that the corporation can lay a foundation for the deduction of interest under §163. See pages 36-38 supra. Moreover, the bonds can be retired at the capital gain rate pursuant to §1271, whereas the redemption of stock would be open to the Pandora's box of §302. See pages 185-219 supra. In addition, an accumulation of surplus by the corporation to pay off the indebtedness, unlike an accumulation for the purpose of redeeming stock, may be permissible under §531, see pages 597-598 infra. *Bazley* and §354(a)(2) mean that a corporation that does not issue debt securities for these purposes to its shareholders at the time of incorporation will not find it easy to rectify its error in a tax-free manner later.

5. *Bankruptcy workouts and other debt restructurings.* When a corporation's financial health becomes impaired, the rights of creditors often are increased. For example, the failure of a corporation to make interest payments when due may entitle bondholders to take control of the company's board of directors. If the corporation's fortunes do not improve, the creditors may seek to restructure their interests in the enterprise; in the extreme case, the creditors may seek to oust the shareholders entirely.

Consider the situation in which a corporation replaces its outstanding debt with new debt having different terms. For example, short-term, low-interest notes might be replaced with long-term, higher-interest bonds. What are the tax consequences of such a debt swap?

Under Prop. Treas. Regs. §1.1001-3, "a significant modification of a debt instrument . . . is deemed to result in an exchange of the original instrument." Accordingly, gain or loss can be recognized by the debtholder. If, for example, the value of the debt received exceeds the holder's adjusted basis in the debt surrendered, gain will be recognized on the exchange. This might be the case when the corporation's distress has been reflected in the market price of its notes so that current holders of those notes may have paid significantly less than face value. What constitutes a "significant modification" is contained in Prop. Treas. Regs. §1.1001-3(e).

The transaction will also be taxable to the corporation, which raises the possibility of cancellation of indebtedness income to the corporation if it substitutes current low value debt for outstanding obligations initally issued for face value. Thus, if a corporation exchanges $1,100 face value bonds having a current fair market value of $800 for each $1,000 short-term note outstanding, the corporation will recognize $200 of cancellation of indebtedness income on each exchange. Unless the exchange occurs while the corporation is insolvent or in a bankruptcy proceeding, the cancellation of indebtedness income will be taxable immediately. See §§61(a)(12), 108(a). If the insolvency exception applies, it is limited to the extent of the debtor corporation's insolvency. §108(a)(3).

A corporation might also swap stock for debt. To the extent that the value of such stock is less than the issue price of the surrendered debt, once again the corporation will be faced with recognition of cancellation of indebtedness income except to the extent §108 applies. Further, if application of §108 to an insolvent or bankrupt corporation permits the corporation to exclude some or all of its cancellation of indebtedness income, the corporation will be forced to reduce its tax attributes (including its tax credits, NOL carryovers, and adjusted basis) as the tax "payment" for the exclusion. See §108(b).

B. REINCORPORATIONS

Suppose a corporation changes the state of its incorporation. Formally, the shareholders must relinquish their old shares in exchange for new ones. Should such an exchange be a taxable event? In a case that antedated special statutory treatment for corporate reorganizations, the Supreme Court held that the reincorporation of General Motors Corporation from New Jersey to Delaware (coupled with a transfer of $5 million from the corporation's earned surplus account to its capital account and minor changes in the terms of the corporation's preferred stock) was a taxable event to shareholders exchanging General Motors (New Jersey) common stock for General Motors (Delaware) common stock. Marr v. United States, 268 U.S. 536 (1925).

The definition of a "reorganization" now includes such reincorporations and other changes in the identity or form of one corporation. See §368(a)(1)(F). As with recapitalizations, the limitations applicable to the carryover of tax attributes in a reorganization are generally not applicable to reincorporations under §368(a)(1)(F). See, e.g., §381(b) and pages 550-551 infra. Until the Tax Equity and Fiscal Responsibility Act of 1982, F reorganizations were not expressly limited to mere changes in the form, identity, or place of incorporation of a *single* corporation, and case law had treated the amalgamation of multiple corporations as an F reorganization so long as there was a sufficiently high percentage of common ownership. See, e.g., Davant v. Commissioner, 366 F.2d 874 (5th Cir. 1966); Reef Corp. v. Commissioner, 368 F.2d 125 (5th Cir. 1966). The Conference Report accompanying TEFRA of 1982 included the following: "This limitation [added to §368(a)(1)(F)] does not preclude the use of more than one entity to consummate the transaction provided only one operating company is involved. The reincorporation of an operating company in a different State, for example, is an F reorganization that requires that more than one corporation be involved." H.R. Conf. Rep. No. 760, 97th Cong., 2d Sess. 541 (1982). Accordingly, regardless of the extent of common ownership or control, the amalgamation of two or more corporations cannot be an F reorganization. See pages 456-468 supra for application of the D reorganization in such circumstances.

C. PROBLEMS

1. *X* Corp. has 100 shares of common stock outstanding, 80 owned by *A* and 20 by *B*. The fair market value of the *X* Corp. stock is $100 per share, and *X* Corp. has substantial earnings and profits. *A*'s basis in the *X* Corp. stock is $20 per share, while *B*'s basis in the *X* Corp. stock is $40 per share. What are the tax consequences to *A*, *B*, and *X* Corp. of the following alternative transactions?

    a. As part of a single transaction, *A* exchanges all her *X* Corp. stock for 800 shares of newly issued, nonvoting preferred stock (worth $10 per share) and *B* exchanges all his *X* Corp. stock for 100 shares of newly issued common stock.

    b. As part of a single transaction, *A* exchanges her *X* Corp. stock for 20 shares of a new class of common stock and long-term bonds with face amount and fair market value of $6,000. *B* exchanges his *X* Corp. stock for 20 shares of the newly issued common stock. How would your answer change if *A*'s basis in the *X* Corp. stock were $100 per share?

    c. How would your answers to (b) change if *B* were *A*'s son?

2. *Y* Corp., doing poorly but not yet insolvent, acquires $1 million face value of its outstanding, long-term bonds in exchange for 800 shares of newly issued preferred stock with par value of $1,000 per share. What are the tax consequences of the exchange to *Y* Corp? How would your answer change if the exchange were made pursuant to a conversion privilege in the cancelled bonds?

3. *Z* Corp. has outstanding 20-year unsecured bonds with face value of $100,000 and fair market value of $70,000. What are the tax consequences to *Z* Corp. and to its bondholders if it exchanges these instruments for secured bonds bearing the same interest rate and maturity? What is the result if the new secured bonds have a face value and fair market value of $70,000?

13

Combining Tax Attributes: Net Operating Losses and Affiliated Corporations

A. CARRYOVER OF TAX ATTRIBUTES

In transactions covered by §§351, 355, and 368, the Code has specific provisions relating to the carryover of basis with respect to property transferred or stock exchanged. Thus, §358 provides, generally speaking, for a transfer of the adjusted basis of exchanging shareholders to the new stock or securities acquired by them. Similarly, §362 provides that property acquired by a corporation in connection with a §351 transaction or in connection with a reorganization shall, generally speaking, have the same basis as the property had in the hands of the transferor. See also §1223 relating to the holding period of property received in connection with such transactions.

Corporations have a great many more tax attributes than basis and holding periods of assets. Different corporations will employ different accounting methods, will have elected certain methods of depreciation with respect to property, will have positive or negative earnings and profits accounts, may or may not have foreign tax credits, and may or may not have unused investment tax credit carryovers or net operating loss carryovers. Consistent with the philosophy of the nonrecognition provisions such as §§351, 355, and the transactions to which §368 applies, these tax attributes should remain undisturbed after such transactions. One would also expect similar rules to apply in the case of those special mergers consisting of liquidations of controlled subsidiaries into their parents to which §§332, 337, and 334(b) apply.

Thus, if two corporations merge, one would expect that after the merger, in calculating whether distributions were made out of earnings and profits, one would look to the combined earnings and profits of the two corporations. Section 381 (providing for carryover of tax attributes in certain tax-free exchanges) and other provisions of the Code generally carry out such expected results.

It should be noted, however, that when a corporation's existence is terminated by a purchase of all its assets, the attributes of the former corporation are obliterated by the transaction. Similarly, when a corporation makes an election under §338 to be treated as if it sold its assets to itself, the former corporation's attributes are obliterated. See pages 384-389 supra for a discussion of §338. Thus, in certain cases a §338 election will involve a trade-off between a step-up in basis and the loss of carryover tax benefits. For example, if a corporation purchases stock of a subsidiary with appreciated assets and a large net operating loss, a §338 election may be inadvisable because although the purchaser would lose the step-up in basis for the subsidiary's assets, the NOL would be preserved if no election is made. At the same time, the gain that would be recognized if a §338 election is made can be offset by an NOL, thereby providing a step up in basis at no tax cost.

The foregoing simplified discussion has ignored the problems created over many decades by what some call the "traffic" in corporations having substantial net operating losses and corporations having other desirable tax attributes (for example, high-basis, low-value assets). Individuals having business deductions in excess of income can carry such losses back or forward as prescribed by §172 but cannot readily sell these tax benefits to others. When such net operating loss carryovers are lodged in a corporate entity, however, sale of the loss is no more difficult than the sale of the stock of the corporation — provided that the tax attributes are not reduced or eliminated by the transfer of the stock.

This "trafficking" in loss corporations has been resisted by the Treasury and the Congress for a number of decades, as described below.

1. Section 381

Section 381 provides for the carryover of tax attributes from a transferor corporation to an acquiring corporation in certain transactions. The transactions covered are (1) a liquidation of a controlled subsidiary and (2) A, C, or F tax-free reorganizations as well as certain nondivisive D reorganizations and G reorganizations involving bankruptcy. Note that in a §368(a)(1)(B) stock-for-stock reorganization, no need for the rules of §381 arises since the corporate existence of the acquired company continues even though an exchange occurs at the shareholder level. The same holds true for §368(a)(1)(E) recapitalizations. In other words, §381 deals, as its opening sentence states, with "the acquisition of assets of a corporation by another corporation." See Baicker v. Commissioner, 93 T.C. 316 (1989) (no carryovers in divisive reorganizations; not a §381 transaction).

The attributes inherited in a qualified transaction are subject to the operating rules of §381(b). It provides that the taxable year of the transferor shall close on the date of distribution or transfer, defined as the date when the distribution or transfer is completed or when substantially all the property has been transferred and the transferor ceases all activities other than liquidating activities. Treas. Regs. §1.381(b)-(1)(b). Section 381(b)(3) provides that the acquiring corporation may not carry back a postacquisition net operating loss or net capital loss to a preacquisition year of the transferor. Here the rules do not impinge on the carryover of the transferor's attributes to the transferee but instead block the transferee's use of its own losses — e.g., against income of a transferor corporation for a year prior to the merger. See also the discussion of CERTS at page 408 supra. Note that the rules of §381(b) do not apply to an F reorganization. See page 546 supra. Why is there no need to limit the carryback of postacquisition losses in an F reorganization? At one time, an F reorganization could involve the fusion of a parent and subsidiary. See page 546 supra. This led to a "loss-tracing requirement" set forth in Rev. Rul. 75-561, 1975-2 C.B. 129, intended to limit the carryback so that postreorganization losses generated by one business could not be used to offset prereorganization losses generated by another business. See National Tea Co. v. Commissioner, 793 F.2d 864 (7th Cir. 1986), approving the loss-tracing procedure.

Suppose Y Corp. with a wholly owned subsidiary, Sub Corp., acquires X Corp. in a forward triangular merger in which X Corp. merges into Sub Corp. and the former X Corp. shareholders receive Y Corp. stock. See page 468 supra. If Sub Corp. incurs a net operating loss after the acquisition, can that NOL be carried back, or does §381(b)(3) prevent the carryback? In Bercy Industries, Inc. v. Commissioner, 640 F.2d 1058 (9th Cir. 1981), the court permitted the carryback even though the reorganization was not a B, E, or F reorganization. See §381(b) and Treas. Regs. §1.381(a)-1(b)(3)(i). Notwithstanding what seems to be clear legislative language, the court had little difficulty reaching this result when Sub Corp. was merely a shell. Should a court reach the same result in a triangular merger if Sub Corp. is not a shell?

Section 381(c) lists numerous tax attributes of the transferor that carry over to the transferee. Of these the most prominent one that will be discussed in greater detail is the net operating loss carryover of §381(c)(1). Note that while loss carryovers are transferred to the acquiring company, they can be used only against future income of the transferee. Other important inherited attributes include the transferor's earnings and profits. §381(c)(2). Under §381(c)(2)(A) the earnings and profits or deficit in earnings and profits of the transferor carry over to the transferee, but under §381(c)(2)(B) an inherited deficit in earnings and profits may be applied only against the transferee's posttransfer earnings and profits and not against the transferee's accumulated earnings and profits.

Under §381(c)(4) the acquiring corporation must continue to use the transferor's accounting method if both corporations have been using the same method. If different methods were used, the regulations specify the appropriate method to be used. See Treas. Regs. §1.381(c)(4)-(1)(c) and (d). Specific accounting provisions are provided under §381(c)(5) for inventories, under §381(c)(6) for depreciation allowance computation, under §381(c)(8) for installment obligations, and under §381(c)(16) for assumed expense liabilities.

2.   Section 382

Suppose in year 1 of its existence, X Corp. operates at a $100 loss (i.e., deductions exceed income by $100). In year 2, X Corp. produces $100 of income. Overall, X Corp. has $0 of income, and its tax consequences should reflect that. Strict adherence to the annual accounting concept would prevent X Corp. from offsetting income in year 2 with the loss in year 1. In fact, X Corp. is permitted to carry forward the year 1 loss to offset the income earned in year 2. §172. Similarly, if X Corp. had earned $100 of income in year 1 and had suffered a $100 loss in year 2, the year 2 loss could be carried back to offset the year 1 income (i.e., X Corp. would file an amended return for year 1). Under §172(b), a corporation can generally carry a loss back three years and forward 15 years if necessary, using up the loss in the earliest years in which income is sufficient to absorb the loss.

Now suppose X Corp. has a $100 loss in year 1 and Y Corp. has $100 of income in year 1. If X Corp. merges into Y Corp. and the X Corp. shareholders receive Y Corp. stock, should Y Corp. be able to use the $100 loss to offset the $100 of income? After all, if X Corp. could carry its losses back and forward, why should it not be permitted to carry its losses sideways to offset Y Corp.'s income? This situation gives rise to the concern that the merger of X into Y Corp. is motivated solely by the presence of the net operating losses. For example, suppose X Corp.'s assets at the time of the merger are worth $0. Even so, Y Corp., if it pays taxes at a 35 percent rate, may be willing to exchange up to $35 of Y Corp. stock for the X Corp. stock in the merger if the use of the X Corp. net operating loss will save $35 in taxes that Y Corp. would otherwise pay on its $100 of income.

While it is by no means clear that such a tax-motivated purchase is inefficient, Congress has since 1954 wrestled with the perceived problem of "trafficking" in net operating losses. On one hand, the carryover provisions perform an averaging function that allows corporations to overcome the limits of our annual accounting system. On the other hand, when NOLs are used to offset totally unrelated income (such as the acquisition of a corporation solely to obtain its NOLs), perhaps no legitimate averaging function is performed.

Prior to the Tax Reform Act of 1986, former §382 limited the amount of NOLs that could be used by an acquiring corporation to offset postacqui-sition income. (Section 381(b)(3) prevents an acquiring corporation from using an acquired NOL to offset preacquisition income.) This total loss of some NOLs was harsh on transactions in which the former shareholders of the acquired corporation continued to control the acquiring corpora-tion. At the same time, discontinuities in the way former §382 worked presented opportunities for tax avoidance in certain transactions.

To address these concerns, current §382 adopts the following ap-proach: After a substantial ownership change, the earnings that can be offset by a net operating loss are limited, but the amount of the net op-erating loss that can be used by the acquiring corporation is not directly limited. The limitation-on-earnings approach is intended to approximate the results that would occur if a loss corporation's assets were combined with those of a profitable corporation in a partnership. In such a case, only the loss corporation's share of the partnership's income could be offset by the corporation's NOL carryforward See §704(c). Generally, the loss corporation's share of the partnership's income is limited to earnings generated by the assets contributed by the loss corporation. Section 382(f) prescribes an objective rate of return (the federal long-term tax-exempt rate) on the value of the corporation's net equity. The annual limitation, then, is the product of the prescribed rate and the value of the loss corpora-tion's equity immediately before a specified ownership change. §382(b).

For example, suppose X Corp., a calendar year taxpayer, has $1 million of net operating loss carryforwards. On January 1, 1994, all the stock of X Corp. is sold in a transaction that triggers §382. On that date, the value of X Corp.'s stock was $500,000 and the applicable rate of return was 10 percent. In 1994 (and for each year thereafter), X Corp. could offset $50,000 (10 percent × $500,000) of income with the NOL carryforward. The same limitation would apply if X Corp. were merged into another corporation so long as an ownership change occurred as defined in §382(g). To the extent that X Corp. does not earn enough in 1994 (or in subsequent years) to absorb the $50,000 amount, the excess loss is carried forward to 1994 and is added to the $50,000 NOL limitation allowed in that year. §382(b)(2). The following Notes consider the details of §382.

The §382 limitation, although somewhat artificially determined, ap-plies regardless of the actual performance of a loss company. For example, suppose all the stock of L Corp., a loss corporation, is sold by B to P in a transaction that triggers §382. After the acquisition, the amount of income that can be offset by the preacquisition NOLs is determined under §382 (i.e., the value of L Corp. multiplied by the federal long-term tax-exempt rate). This limitation applies even if L Corp. after the acquisition produces more income than the §382 limitation deems produced. Conversely, if L Corp. is merged into P Corp. in a transaction that triggers §382, P Corp. can offset income as determined under §382 even though the assets of the former L Corp. do not in fact produce that amount of income. Note that using the federal long-term tax-exempt rate as a proxy for the actual return on the assets may produce too large or too small a deduction. Once the §382 limitation is determined, however, it is used every year until the pre-change NOLs are used up.

NOTE

1. *Ownership changes.* New §382 applies if an "ownership change" occurs. §382(a), (j), (k)(3). An ownership change arises if the percentage of stock of the new loss corporation owned by one or more 5 percent shareholders has increased by more than 50 percentage points as a result of an "owner shift" or an "equity structure shift." §382(g), (i). Note that a series of unrelated transactions may be aggregated to constitute an "ownership change" but that all such transactions must have occurred during a single three-year testing period. §382(g), (i).

Notice that an ownership change occurs when there is a 50 percentage point change, not a 50 percent change. To illustrate, suppose A owns 20 percent of L Corp. If A acquires additional stock bringing A's ownership to 30 percent, no ownership change has occurred even though A has increased his ownership of L Corp. by 50 percent. For an ownership change to occur, A would have to increase ownership in L Corp. to 71 percent.

An owner shift includes any change in stock ownership by "5 percent shareholders" (those holding 5 percent or more in value of corporate stock during the testing period). For purposes of the 5 percent rule, all non-5 percent shareholders are aggregated as a single 5 percent shareholder. Owner shifts may occur in the following transactions: a purchase of stock from existing shareholders or the corporation; a §351 exchange; a redemption; exercise of stock conversion rights; or a combination of the foregoing.

For example, assume that the stock of L Corp. is publicly traded and that no shareholder owns 5 percent or more. No owner shift will occur so long as no person becomes a 5 percent shareholder. That is, random trading does not bring about an owner shift because the 5 percent shareholder (i.e., the aggregation of all of the non-5 percent shareholders) owns 100 percent before and after each trade. If, however, all the stock of widely held L Corp. is purchased by A, B, and C, none of whom were previous shareholders and each of whom acquires a one-third stock interest, a more than 50 percent owner shift occurs since their ownership has gone from 0 percent to 100 percent.

Similarly, if L Corp. — closely held by A, B, and C, each of whom is a one-third shareholder — makes a public offering so that 51 percent of the stock will be held by non-5 percent shareholders, a more than 50 percent owner shift will occur since all the stock owned by non-5 percent shareholders is treated as owned by one 5 percent shareholder, and that interest increases from 0 percent to 51 percent.

An "equity structure shift" includes any tax-free reorganization (other than a divisive D, an F, or a G reorganization). §382(g)(3). A more than 50 percent equity shift occurs if after the shift the percentage of stock held by one or more of the new loss corporation's 5 percent shareholders is at least 50 percentage points more than the percentage of the old loss corporation's stock held by them during the testing period. The old loss corporation is the corporation with NOLs before the reorganization; the new loss corporation is the corporation entitled to use the NOLs after the reorganization. §382(k).

To illustrate an equity structure shift, suppose *L* Corp., a loss corporation, is merged into *P* Corp. in a tax-free transaction with *P* Corp. surviving. No shareholder of either corporation is a 5 percent shareholder. In the merger, the former *L* shareholders receive 49 percent of the stock of *P*, and the remaining stock of *P* is owned by *P* shareholders unrelated to the *L* shareholders. There has been a more than 50 percent equity structure change of *L* because the *P* shareholders (all of whom are non-5 percent shareholders and therefore lumped together as a single 5 percent shareholder) have gone from 0 percent owners of *L* to 51 percent shareholders of the new loss corporation. Had the former *L* shareholders received at least 50 percent of the *P* stock, there would have been no triggering equity structure change.

You may recall that in the context of an owner shift, all less than 5 percent shareholders are treated as a single 5 percent shareholder so that the constant buying and selling of a publicly traded corporation's stock does not cause problems under §382. In a reorganization (i.e., an equity structure shift), however, there may be two groups of less than 5 percent shareholders that are separately treated — the shareholders of the acquired and acquiring corporations. Each of these groups is treated separately for purposes of testing an ownership change. §382(g)(4)(B). Otherwise all reorganizations involving publicly held corporations would escape §382. Accordingly in the previous example, an ownership change occurs when the less than 5 percent shareholders of the acquiring corporation become 51 percent owners of the new loss corporation.

The relevant testing period used for determining whether an ownership change has occurred spans the three years preceding any owner shift or equity structure shift. §382(i)(1). Therefore, a series of unrelated transactions occurring during the testing period together may constitute an ownership change. If an ownership change has occurred earlier, the testing period for determining whether a second ownership change has occurred begins the day after the first exchange has occurred. §382(i)(2). In measuring whether an ownership change has occurred during the testing period, it is necessary to measure the difference between a 5 percent shareholder's highest and lowest percentage ownership during that period. For example, suppose *X* Corp. has 200 shares of common stock owned by *A* (100 shares), *B* (50 shares), and *C* (50 shares). On January 2 of year 1, *A* sells 60 shares to *B*. On January 1 of year 3, *A* purchases *C*'s entire interest in *X* Corp.

Overall, *B*, a 5 percent shareholder, has increased his interest by 30 percentage points (from a 25 percent owner to a 55 percent owner). *A* has decreased her ownership percentage from 50 percent to 45 percent; *C* has decreased his ownership from 30 percent to 0 percent. At first glance it appears that the 5 percent shareholders together have increased their ownership by only 30 percentage points, not the more than 50 percentage points necessary to trigger §382. *A*'s percentage ownership from his lowest ownership during the testing period, however, has increased from 20 percent after the sale to *B* to 45 percent after the purchase from *C*. This increase of 25 percentage points when added to the 30 percentage point increase for *B* now triggers the restrictions under §382. See Treas. Regs. §1.382-2T(c)(4).

For both owner shifts and equity structure changes, a series of transactions during the testing period may trigger the operation of §382. For example, suppose the following events occur in 1994: *B*, an individual, purchases 40 percent of the stock of *L*. *L* then is merged into *P* — which is wholly owned by *B* — in a tax-free transaction. In exchange for their stock in *L*, the *L* shareholders (none of whom was a 5 percent shareholder, other than *B*) receive stock with a value representing 60 percent of the *P* stock (*B* receives 24 percent, the other shareholders 36 percent). The merger is treated as a more than 50 percent equity structure change since immediately after the merger, *B* owned 64 percent of the combined entity (40 percent by virtue of *B*'s ownership prior to the merger plus 24 percent received in the merger), which is more than 50 percentage points over 0 percent, the lowest percentage in *L* owned by *B* during the testing period.

2.   *Constructive ownership.* Suppose in case #1 that *B* owns all the stock of *L* Corp., a corporation with NOLs, and all the stock of *P* Corp. If *P* Corp. acquires all the *L* Corp. stock in a B reorganization, *P* Corp. has gone from a 0 percent shareholder in *L* Corp. to a 100 percent owner. Section 382 should not apply here, however, because there really has not been a change in ownership (i.e., *B* continues to own both corporations). Conversely, suppose in case #2 that *B* owns all the stock of *H* Corp., which in turn owns all the stock of *L* Corp. *P* Corp. is wholly owned by *C*, an individual who is unrelated to *B*. *B* sells the stock of *H* Corp. to *P*. Here, §382 should apply because of a change in ultimate ownership from *B* to *C* even though *H* Corp.'s direct ownership of *L* Corp. has remained at 100 percent.

Under §318(*l*)(3), the constructive ownership rules apply with modification in determining owner shifts and equity structure changes. Stock owned by entities (e.g., corporations, partnerships, trusts) are deemed owned by their shareholders or beneficiaries in proportion to their interests in the entity. It is only the stock of individuals that counts in determining ownership changes under §382. In case #1 above, because *B*, the ultimate beneficiary of *L* Corp.'s NOLs, remained a 100 percent shareholder of *L* Corp., §382 does not limit the carryover of *L* Corp.'s NOLs.

Similarly, suppose the stock of *X* Corp., a publicly traded corporation, is not owned by any 5 percent shareholders. If *X* Corp. distributes to its shareholders all the stock of its wholly owned subsidiary, *Y* Corp., no ownership change occurs. Through the attribution rules, the shareholders of *X* Corp. owned 100 percent of *Y* Corp. before the transaction and 100 percent after. In case #2, when *P* purchases the stock of *H* Corp., which owns *L* Corp., even though *H* Corp.'s direct ownership of *L* Corp. has not changed the ultimate beneficiary of *L* Corp.'s NOLs has changed. *C* has gone from a 0 percent owner of *L* Corp. to a 100 percent owner because *C* is deemed to own the *L* Corp. stock that *H* Corp. owns (i.e., *C* owns *P* Corp., which owns *H* Corp., which owns *L* Corp.).

3. *Preferred stock.* Certain preferred stock is not counted in determining ownership changes. §382(k)(6). Under this standard, the term "stock" does not include stock that is not entitled to vote, is limited and preferred as to dividends, does not participate in corporate growth to any significant extent, has redemption and liquidation rights that do not exceed the issue price (except for a reasonable redemption premium), and is not convertible. §1504(a)(4). Note that stock that may be labeled "common" stock may be treated as "preferred" stock, and stock labeled "preferred" stock may be treated as "common" stock for purposes of this rule. The Secretary has broad discretion in deciding what stock is counted in determining whether an ownership change has occurred. §382(k)(6).

The preferred stock provision is intended legislatively to reverse the result in Maxwell Hardware Co. v. Commissioner, 343 F.2d 713 (9th Cir. 1965). In that case a loss corporation's old shareholders retained common stock representing more than 50 percent of the corporation's value, thereby avoiding the application of former §382. New shareholders, however, received special preferred stock that carried with it 90 percent participation in earnings attributable to newly contributed property. Section 382 would apply in *Maxwell Hardware* because the new shareholders went from 0 percent to 100 percent participating stock ownership even though the stock they received was called preferred stock.

4. *Options.* For the purpose of determining whether an ownership change has occurred, the stock of a loss corporation that is subject to an option is treated as acquired by the option holder for purposes of testing whether *that holder* has undergone an ownership change. This may result in some options being considered as exercised while other options are ignored. For example, suppose *A* owns 100 shares (i.e., all the outstanding shares) of *X* Corp. *A* sells 40 shares to *B* and grants *B* an option to purchase the remaining 60 shares from *A*. At the same time, *A* has an option to purchase 100 new shares from *X* Corp. In testing whether *B* has triggered the §382 ownership test, only *B*'s option is assumed to have been exercised. Accordingly, *B* has gone from a 0 percent shareholder to a 100 percent shareholder, thereby triggering the limitation of §382. Treas. Reg. §1.382-2T(h)(4)(ii) (example 2). Note that if *A*'s option were also considered to

be exercised, *B*'s percentage increase would be only 50 percent, not the more than 50 percent amount necessary to trigger §382.

You may recall that the IRS took a similarly selective approach to option exercise in the redemption area in *Patterson Trust,* page 203 supra. There, the court struck down the IRS attempt based on the language of the statute. Is Treas. Regs. §1.382-2T(h)(4)(ii) (example 2) valid?

5. *Continuity of business.* Following an ownership change, a loss corporation's NOL carryforwards (including applicable built-in losses) are disallowed unless during the two-year period following the ownership change the new loss corporation either (1) continues the old loss corporation's historic business or (2) uses a significant portion of the old loss corporation's assets in a business. §382(c). This continuity requirement is the same requirement that must be satisfied to qualify as a tax-free reorganization under §368. Treas. Regs. §1.368-1(d). See page 434 supra. The purpose of the requirement is to try to distinguish acquisitions motivated by NOLs from acquisitions motivated by the acquired corporation's assets or business. An extreme example of tax-motivated behavior is the subject of Alprosa Watch Corp. v. Commissioner, 11 T.C. 240 (1948). In that case a shareholder purchased the stock of a loss corporation, sold the assets back to the original shareholders, and infused the corporation with a new business. The court, prior to any version of §382, allowed the use of NOLs to offset postacquisition income. How would this situation be treated under §382?

6. *Section 382 limitation.* For any taxable year after the change date (that is, the date of a triggering ownership change), the amount of a loss corporation's taxable income for any year that can be offset by a prechange loss cannot exceed the §382 limitation. §382(a). The §382 limitation is an amount equal to the value of the loss corporation before the exchange multiplied by the federal long-term tax-exempt rate in effect on the change date. §382(b), (f). Once the §382 limitation is computed, it stays in effect regardless of fluctuations in the federal long-term tax-exempt rate.

The value of the corporation is the value of its stock. Because the ability to use NOLs increases when the value of the loss corporation increases, there may be an incentive for the shareholders of a loss corporation to increase the value of that corporation by contributing cash or other property immediately prior to an ownership change for which the shareholders would receive additional compensation from the acquiring party. Congress has discouraged this technique through an "antistuffing" rule under which the value of any prechange capital contribution is disregarded in determining the value of a corporation. §382(*l*)(1). Generally, any contribution received within two years of an ownership change is covered by the antistuffing rule if it does not contribute to the corporation's trade or business.

Congress was also concerned that the value of a loss corporation might be inflated because of investment assets held by the loss corporation to generate income to be offset by the corporation's business NOLs. The general aim of §382 is to limit the use of acquired NOLs to offset a hypothetical level of income generated by the loss corporation's business assets. To the extent that a loss corporation's investment assets inflate the use of the NOLs, §382's purpose is circumvented. Section 382(l)(4) provides, however, that if at least one-third of a loss corporation's assets consist of nonbusiness assets, the value of the corporation for purposes of the §382 limitation does not include the nonbusiness assets (reduced by any attributable indebtedness). In applying this one-third test, stock of a 50 percent or more owned subsidiary will not be considered a nonbusiness asset. Instead, §382(l)(6) adopts a look-through rule that considers the appropriate percentage of the subsidiary's assets deemed to be owned by the parent.

Just as Congress did not want nonbusiness assets to inflate the usable NOLs, it also did not want business assets to inflate the usable NOLs if those assets were going to be removed from the corporation. For example, assets used to redeem stock of the loss corporation is not counted in determining the §382 limitation. In general, the value of an old loss corporation is determined immediately prior to an ownership change. §382(e)(1). The value of the old loss corporation equals the value of its stock (including preferred stock). If, however, a redemption or other corporate contraction contributes to an ownership change, the value of the corporation is determined immediately after the ownership change. §382(e)(2). This will result in a lower value because corporate assets were used in the redemption. The effect of this special valuation rule is to discourage "bootstrap" acquisitions in which the purchasers finance the acquisition of a loss corporation with the corporation's own assets.

If a corporation is insolvent, its value may be $0, effectively eliminating all NOLs after an ownership change. Section 382(l)(5) provides a special rule that does not limit the use of NOLs for corporations involved in bankruptcy or similar proceedings if at least 50 percent of the loss corporation's stock immediately after the change is owned by former shareholders and certain long-term creditors. If a second ownership change occurs within two years after the initial change, however, the §382 loss limitation is reduced to zero. Special provisions prevent a purchaser from acquiring a loss corporation's debt immediately before initiating a bankruptcy proceeding, exchanging the debt for stock without triggering the §382 limitation, and then using the NOLs immediately and without limitation.

If the §382 limitation amount exceeds taxable income, the excess carries over. §382(b)(2). For example, suppose the §382 limitation amount for L Corp. with $1 million in NOLs is $100,000 per year. In the first year after an ownership change, the new loss corporation produces $70,000 of income, all of which is offset by the NOL carryover. In the second year, the new loss corporation can use $130,000 of the NOLs to offset income produced. In some situations, even though §382 does not directly result in the permanent loss of NOLs, the §382 limitation, combined with the 15-year carryforward limitation in §172, does result in a loss of NOLs. In the example above, if *L* Corp. had $2 million of NOLs and the §382 limitation is $100,000 per year, the new loss corporation will not be able to use $500,000 of the NOLs to offset postownership change income.

Under §382, the federal long-term tax-exempt rate must be multiplied by the value of the loss corporation to determine whether NOLs are limited. By specifying that the long-term rate for federal obligations be used, Congress intended to provide a reasonable risk-free rate of return that a loss corporation could obtain in the absence of a change of ownership. Congress discounted the long-term *taxable* rate on federal obligations, however, by requiring the use of the long-term *tax-exempt* rate on federal obligations. This requirement was intended to take into account the fact that the purchase price of the loss corporation's stock reflects not only asset value but also the value of the NOLs themselves. Accordingly, Congress attempted to balance overvaluation of the worth of the loss corporation with undervaluation of the rate of return on the loss corporation's assets.

7.   *Built-in gains.* The purpose of §382 is to limit the use of a loss corporation's NOLs to the income deemed to be produced by the loss corporation. The income that can be offset by the NOLs is not only the expected future income from operations but also any inherent gain in a loss corporation's appreciated assets. Section 382(h)(1)(A) allows a loss corporation with an "unrealized net built-in gain" to increase its §382 limitation by the "recognized built-in gain" for any taxable year within the five-year recognition period. See I.R.S. Notice 90-27, 1990-1 C.B. 336 (recognition period extended for an installment sale). A "net unrealized built-in gain" is defined as the amount by which the value of a corporation's assets exceeds the aggregate bases immediately before the ownership shift. A "recognized built-in gain" is defined as any gain recognized on the disposition of an asset during the recognition period if the taxpayer establishes that the asset was held by the loss corporation before the change date and that the gain is allocable to the period before the change date. The recognized built-in gain cannot exceed the net unrealized built-in gain reduced by the recognized built-in gains for prior years in the recognition period.

8.   *Built-in losses.* The term "prechange loss" to which §382(a) applies includes NOL carryforwards arising prior to the change year, the allocable portion of a corporation's NOLs for the year in which the change occurs, and certain recognized built-in losses and deductions. §382(d), (h)(1)(B). The limitation on built-in losses and deductions reflects the fact that a corporation interested in purchasing a loss corporation with $1 million of NOLs might also be interested in purchasing a corporation with no NOLs but having an asset with a basis of $1.1 million and a fair market value of $100,000. The purpose of the restrictions on built-in losses is to curtail trafficking in a corporation with assets (having built-in losses) that can be sold to offset the acquiring corporation's income from other sources. Un-

der §382(h)(1)(B), if a loss corporation has a net unrealized built-in loss, any recognized built-in loss during the five-year recognition period is treated as a prechange loss and is therefore subject to the §382 limitation. Thus, if the ownership change occurs in 1993, and there is a net unrealized built-in loss, recognition of that loss in 1994 when the asset is sold will be subject to the §382 limitation along with prechange NOLs. A de minimis rule ignores a corporation's net unrealized built-in loss if it does not exceed the lesser of (a) 15 percent of the fair market value of the assets of the corporation or (b) $10 million. §382(h)(3)(B).

"Net unrealized built-in loss" is defined as the amount by which the aggregate adjusted bases of a corporation's assets exceeds the fair market value of the assets immediately before the ownership change. A "recognized built-in loss" is any loss recognized on the disposition of an asset during the five-year recognition period except to the extent the taxpayer can prove either that the asset was not held by the loss corporation immediately prior to the exchange or that the loss was allocable to a period after the change date. §382(h)(2)(B).

Depreciation or amortization deductions during the five-year recognition period are treated as recognized built-in losses to the extent attributable to the excess of adjusted basis over fair market value. §382(h)(2)(B). Also, amounts that accrue before the change date but are allowable as deductions after such date (such as deductions deferred under §267, §465, or §469) are treated as built-in losses. §382(h)(6).

9. *Anti-abuse rules.* Section 382 does not alter the continuing application of §269, see pages 563-569 infra, or the separate return limitation year (SRLY) rules under the consolidated return regulations. See pages 570-578 infra. Moreover, §382(m) authorizes the Secretary to prescribe regulations to prevent avoidance of §382 through the use of related persons, pass-through entities, or other intermediaries. See, e.g., Treas. Regs. §1.382-2T(k)(4).

3. Section 383

Section 383(a) authorizes the Secretary to promulgate regulations that will limit capital loss carryforwards under §1212 to the taxable income of the loss corporation not exceeding the §382 limitation. Any capital loss carryforward used in a postchange year will reduce the §382 limitation that is applied to prechange losses. Similar rules are adopted for excess credits (e.g., the alternative minimum tax credit under §53 or the foreign tax credit under §901) and passive activity losses.

4. Section 384

Section 382 does not inhibit a loss corporation from acquiring a profitable corporation if there is no ownership change with respect to the loss corporation. In this situation, there is no trafficking in losses; rather, the loss corporation seeks to improve its economic performance through the acquisition. Accordingly, suppose *L* Corp., a loss corporation owned by *B,* acquires *P* Corp., a profitable corporation owned by *C,* for cash, and assume *L* Corp. and *P* Corp. report tax liability on a consolidated return. The ability of *L* Corp. to use its preacquisition NOLs to offset *P* Corp.'s postacquisition income is not inhibited by §382. The same is true if *P* Corp. merged into *L* Corp. so long as no ownership change in *L* Corp. takes place.

But suppose *P* Corp. is a "burnt-out" tax shelter — an entity that has produced depreciation deductions for its owners and that now has a large built-in gain because the bases of its assets have been adjusted downward under §1016 while the property's fair market value has not decreased correspondingly. For example, assume that after generating depreciation deductions *P* Corp. has depreciable assets with an aggregate basis of $50,000 and a fair market value of $300,000, subject to a $250,000 mortgage liability. If *P* Corp. sells the assets, the taxes on the $250,000 gain exceed the $50,000 of cash that *P* Corp. can expect to receive on an arm's-length sale.

Suppose the stock of *P* Corp. is acquired by *L* Corp., and either they file a consolidated return or *P* Corp. merges into *L* Corp. In the absence of a remedial provision, *L* Corp.'s preexisting NOLs can be used to offset gain generated by the postacquisition sale of the acquired assets. *L* Corp. may be happy to pay $50,000 in cash to acquire the appreciated assets. *C,* the ultimate seller of the tax shelter, may be happy to receive any cash or other property for *C*'s interest in the burnt-out shelter. But Congress was unhappy with this technique of "laundering" the built-in gain from the sale of assets with preexisting NOLs.

Section 384 originated as an effort to deny the use of any preacquisition NOLs by a loss corporation to offset any built-in gains of an acquired corporation recognized during a five-year recognition period following an acquisition. But the provision was broadly drafted so that it also applies to a corporation with built-in gains that acquires a corporation with preacquisition NOLs. Even though §382 might permit the use of some NOLs by the acquiring corporation in this situation, §384 may apply to deny their use against recognized built-in gains of the acquiring corporation.

Section 384 applies if one corporation acquires control of another corporation and either corporation is a gain corporation (i.e., a corporation with net unrealized built-in gain at the time of acquisition). Control is defined as stock representing at least 80 percent of vote and value of the acquired corporation. §384(c)(5). Section 384 also applies to an asset acquisition if the acquisition qualifies as a tax-free A, C, or acquisitive D reorganization. If both the acquiring and the acquired corporations were part of the same control group under §1563 (using a 50 percent ownership test) during the previous five-year period (or the term of a corporation's existence, if shorter), §384 will not apply.

If §384 is applicable, the provision denies the use of any "preacquisition loss" of a loss corporation (but not of the gain corporation) to offset any "recognized built-in gain" of the gain corporation during the five-year recognition period. §384(a). In the examples above, L Corp.'s NOLs cannot be used to offset gain recognized on the sale of P Corp.'s appreciated assets. The term "preacquisition loss" includes NOLs and net unrealized built-in losses that are recognized during a five-year recognition period. §384(c)(3)(A). The term "recognized built-in gain" refers to any gain on the disposition of an asset during a five-year recognition period except to the extent that it can be established that the asset was not held by the gain corporation on the acquisition date. §384(c)(1)(A).

In some cases, §§382 and 384 overlap; in others, one or neither of the provisions applies. Suppose B owns all the stock of L Corp., a company with NOLs, and C owns all the stock of P Corp., a company with built-in gains. If L Corp. purchases all the stock of P Corp. and together they file a consolidated return, §382 will not prevent the use of L Corp.'s losses against P Corp.'s future income because there is no ownership change for L Corp. Section 384, however, will prevent the use of the NOLs to offset any built-in gains recognized by P Corp. during the five-year recognition period.

If, instead, L Corp. merges into P Corp. and C ends up with more than 50 percent of the surviving corporation, §382 will limit the use of L Corp.'s NOLs and §384 will also apply to limit any NOLs allowable under §382 that would otherwise be used to offset any of P Corp.'s recognized built-in gains. If P Corp. had no built-in gains prior to the merger, then only §382 would apply to limit the use of the NOLs. If, in the preceding example, L Corp. and P Corp. were both long-standing subsidiaries of H Corp., neither §382 nor §384 would apply to limit the use of the NOLs.

Suppose L Corp. and P Corp., which are unrelated, form a joint venture partnership, LP, which attempts to allocate income under the partnership agreement disproportionately to L Corp. As a technical matter, there has been no triggering event for purposes of §382 or §384. Nevertheless, Congress has given the Service authority to apply these loss limitation principles in abuse situations. §§382(m)(3), 384(f)(1).

5. Section 269

Enacted in 1943, §269 provides for the disallowance of tax benefits when tax avoidance is the principal purpose for the acquisition of control of a corporation or for transfers of property. Section 269, which can apply to either an asset acquisition or a stock acquisition, provides the Service with a powerful weapon because it is subjective in application: The provision can apply when the acquirer (or persons controlling the acquirer) possesses a "bad" state of mind. Under §269(a) the Service can disallow the deduction of an NOL carryover if the control of a corporation or corporate assets was acquired for the principal purpose of avoiding or evading federal income tax by securing a deduction. To invoke §269, there are two requirements: (1) an acquisition and (2) a tax avoidance motive. The presence of §§382-384 does not limit the application of §269. Treas. Regs. §1.269-7. So it is possible that NOLs that would be allowed under §382 may nevertheless be disallowed under §269.

On its face §269 seems to cover the acquisition by a profitable business of a loss corporation with an NOL carryover. But does the provision apply to an acquisition of a profitable business by a loss corporation?

Commissioner v. British Motor Car Distributors
278 F.2d 392 (9th Cir. 1960)

Before Pope, Hamlin and Merrill, Circuit Judges.

MERRILL, Circuit Judge.

The taxpayer corporation incurred losses while engaged in the business of selling home appliances. It disposed of all its assets and the corporate shares were then sold to new owners, who used the corporation to operate a previously going automobile business. The question here presented is whether the taxpayer is entitled to carry over the losses incurred in the old business, where it is clear that the principal purpose of the acquisition of the taxpayer by the new owners was to avoid taxes.* The Tax Court, five judges dissenting, ruled in the affirmative. . . .

British Motor Car Company was a partnership consisting of Kjell H. Qvale, who had an 85 per cent interest, and his wife, who had a 15 per cent interest. The partnership had existed from about May 1, 1948, and engaged, in San Francisco, in the business of importing, distributing and selling foreign automobiles and parts. On September 11, 1951, the partnership submitted an offer to counsel for the Empire Home Equipment Company, in which the former offered to buy the outstanding stock of the corporation from its then owners for $21,250.00, upon the conditions, inter alia, that the corporation would increase its authorized capital and change its name. The offer was accepted. On November 2, 1951, Empire changed its name to British Motor Car Distributors, Ltd. On November 30, 1951, the partnership acquired all the outstanding shares of stock and immediately thereafter transferred its net assets (exclusive of the acquired shares) to the corporation in exchange for an additional 15,923 shares of stock. It is not claimed that there was any business purpose in the acquisition.

In the tax years ending October 31, 1952, and October 31, 1953, the corporation operated profitably in the automobile business. In its income and excess profits tax returns for those years, it carried forward the net

---

* The tax years in question predate the enactment of §382. — EDS.

operating losses that it had sustained in the appliance business in its fiscal years ending in 1949, 1950 and 1951. . . .

The Tax Court, in its construction of [§269(a)], adhered to its view as expressed in T.V.D. Company, 27 T.C. 879, 886, following the dictum in Alprosa Watch Company, 11 T.C. 240, to the effect that "it is manifest from the unambiguous terms of [§269] that it applies only to an acquiring corporation." The court points out that here the corporation is seeking to make use of its own previous loss; that it is the corporation, and not its new stockholders, which is securing the benefit of the deduction. *Alprosa Watch* is quoted to the effect that [§269(a)] "would seem to prohibit the use of a deduction, credit or allowance only by the acquiring person or corporation and not their use by the corporation whose control was acquired."

We do not read the language of the section, "securing the benefit of a deduction," as applying only to the actual taking of such deduction by the taxpayer. We should be closing our eyes to the realities of the situation were we to refuse to recognize that the persons who have acquired the corporation did so to secure *for themselves* a very real tax benefit to be realized by them *through* the acquired corporation and which they could not otherwise have realized.

This is not, as the corporation protests, a disregard of its corporate entity. Since [§269(a)] is expressly concerned with the persons acquiring control of a corporation, we must recognize such persons as, themselves, having a significant existence or entity apart from the corporation they have acquired. To ignore such independent entity simply because such persons are also the stockholders of their acquisition is to ignore the clear demands of [§269(a)]. It is not the fact that they are stockholders which subjects them to scrutiny. Rather, it is the fact that they are the persons specified by the section: those who have acquired control of the corporation. They may not escape the scrutiny which the section demands by attempting to merge their identity with that of their acquisition.

Section [§269(a)] contemplates that it shall not be limited to corporate acquirers. While Clause (2) is specifically limited to corporate acquirers, Clause (1) deals with "persons" as acquirers. That Clause (1) is to include noncorporate acquirers could not be more clearly implied. Nor do we find any sound reason, if this device for tax avoidance is to be struck down, for doing the job only when the tax avoider is a corporation. Legislative history indicates that a much broader construction was intended.[3]

---

3. H.R. No. 871, 78th Congress, First Session (1944 Cum. Bull. 901, 938):

This section is designed to put an end promptly to any market for, or dealings in, interests in corporations or property which have as their objective the reduction through artifice of the income or excess profits tax liability.

The crux of the devices which have come to the attention of your committee has been some form of acquisition on or after the effective date of the Second Revenue

To limit the effect of [§269(a)] to cases in which the taxpayer is seeking to deduct as its own a loss incurred by another would seem to limit Clause (1) to corporate acquirers. Who but a corporation could claim as its own a loss which had been incurred by an acquired corporation? Certainly an individual could not do so. The construction here contended for by the taxpayer corporation would then clearly frustrate legislative purpose. . . .

The corporation contends, as stated by the Tax Court, that the benefit to the stockholders (as distinguished from that to the corporate taxpayer) is too tenuous to bring the section into play. Tenuous or not, it is the benefit which actuated these persons in acquiring this corporation and is thus the very benefit with which this section is concerned. It is not for the courts to judge whether the benefit to the acquiring persons is sufficiently direct or substantial to be worth acquiring. That judgment was made by the acquirers. The judicial problem is whether the securing of the benefit was the principal purpose of the acquisition. If it was, the allowance of the deduction is forbidden.

Judgment reversed. The deductions claimed by the taxpayer are disallowed and judgment is entered for the Commissioner.

NOTE

1.   *Acquisition requirement.* In *British Motor Car,* the stock of a floundering, inefficient corporation was sold, and the new owners changed the operation of the business to make it more efficient. Under these circumstances, should §269 come into play? Does the tax system create a disincentive for an inefficient business to become efficient, or does it simply remove tax benefits from consideration in a business decision, forcing the decision to rise or fall on its own merits?

It is now clear that §269 applies not only when NOL carryovers are acquired by a profitable business but also when the *benefits* of an NOL carryover are acquired by a loss corporation acquiring a profitable business.

Act of 1940, but the devices take many forms. Thus, the acquisition may be an acquisition of the shares of a corporation, or it may be an acquisition which follows by operation of law in the case of a corporation resulting from a statutory merger or consolidation. The person, or persons, making the acquisition likewise vary, as do the forms or methods of utilization under which tax avoidance is sought. Likewise, the tax benefits sought may be one or more of several deductions or credits, including the utilization of excess profits credits, carry-overs and carry-backs of losses or unused excess profits credits, and anticipated expense of other deductions. In the light of these considerations, the section has not confined itself to a description of any particular methods for carrying out such tax avoidance schemes but has included within its scope these devices in whatever form they may appear. For similar reasons, the scope of the terms used in the section is to be found in the objective of the section, namely, to prevent the tax liability from being reduced through the distortion or perversion effected through tax avoidance devices. . . .

See also Vulcan Materials Co. v. United States, 446 F.2d 690, 698 (5th Cir. 1971). How would *British Motor Car* be decided under §382? Notice that the partnership that owned 0 percent of British Motor Car Distributors before the transaction in question owns 100 percent afterwards. Note that even if §382 would apply to this situation today, §269 might also apply to deny the use of the NOLs permitted by §382. Treas. Regs. §1.269-7.

If you conclude that both §§382 and 269 would apply in *British Motor Car* because of the ownership change, can §269 ever apply in a situation where §382 does not? Suppose *L* Corp., a loss corporation, acquires *P* Corp., a profitable corporation. If *L* Corp. and *P* Corp. file a consolidated return, the Service may in some circumstances argue that §269 prevents the use of *L* Corp.'s NOLs to offset *P* Corp.'s postacquisition income. For example, if the former shareholders of *P* Corp. continue to exercise real control over *P* Corp.'s governance even though *L* Corp. has acquired enough control to permit consolidated reporting, §269 may apply. See, e.g., Briarcliff Candy Corp. v. Commissioner, 54 T.C.M. (CCH) 667 (1987).

The acquisition test under §269 is triggered by either of the following: (1) Any person or persons acquiring sufficient stock to hold at least 50 percent of either the total combined voting power or total value of all shares (§269(a)(1)) or (2) a corporation acquiring property of another corporation with a carryover basis (§269(a)(2)). Section 269(a)(2) is used primarily to disallow NOL carryovers resulting from a corporate reorganization with an improper purpose involving unrelated corporations. Generally, an acquisitive reorganization would activate the carryover basis rule of §362 and would, in the absence of §269, enable the acquiring corporation to carry over the acquired corporation's tax attributes under §381. If the transferor is controlled directly or indirectly by the acquirer or its shareholders immediately before the acquisition, §269 does not apply. §269(a)(2). Accordingly, a merger between commonly controlled corporations will not result in the loss of any NOL carryovers. See Rev. Rul. 66-214, 1966-2 C.B. 98.

For a discussion of the acquisition requirement, see Hermes Consolidated, Inc. v. United States, 14 Cl. Ct. 398 (1988) (acquisition structured to avoid 50 percent threshold was successful).

2. *Tax avoidance motive.* The term "evasion or avoidance of tax," though not defined, is not restricted to behavior that would precipitate criminal or civil fraud penalties. Treas. Regs. §1.269-1(b). Acquiring an NOL carryover that the acquirer would not otherwise enjoy will result in the avoidance of tax that would otherwise be paid on the profits of the acquirer. Note, however, that tax avoidance must be the "principal purpose" — the purpose that exceeds any other purpose in importance. Treas. Regs. §1.269-3(a). Determining the principal purpose is a question of fact. The regulations describe certain transactions that will ordinarily indicate the proscribed purpose. See, e.g., Treas. Regs. §1.269-3(b)(1), setting forth an example quite similar to the facts in *British Motor Car.*

Since tax reduction is often a motive behind an acquisition of a business with favorable tax attributes, what business purpose will suffice as a principal purpose of the acquisition? One typical business purpose for the acquisition of corporate control is the seller's insistence that the acquirer purchase stock rather than assets. See Glen Raven Mills v. Commissioner, 59 T.C. 1 (1972), a court-reviewed opinion in which the seller's insistence on a package deal in conjunction with some other factors was sufficient to constitute the principal purpose of the acquisition. What is the result if the *purchaser* insists on acquiring stock? For other business purposes, see American M.A.R.C., Inc. v. United States, 19 A.F.T.R.2d 929 (C.D. Cal. 1967) (a genuine belief that the acquired business could be turned around); Fairfield Communities Land Co. v. Commissioner, 47 T.C.M. (CCH) 1194 (1984) (acquisition of loss corporation to obtain cash and broaden the shareholder base); Clarksdale Rubber Co. v. Commissioner, 45 T.C. 234 (1965) (expansion of acquirer's business); Naeter Brothers Publishing Co. v. Commissioner, 42 T.C. 1 (1964) (combined operation favored by lenders).

Suppose an acquisition is 40 percent motivated by tax avoidance, 30 percent motivated by a desire for expansion, and 30 percent motivated by a desire to "go public" (which the acquisition would allow). Is tax avoidance the primary motive, or in making that determination, can a corporation combine all nontax motives? In U.S. Shelter Corp. v. United States, 13 Cl. Ct. 606 (1987), the court allowed the corporation to combine the nontax motives, concluding that §269 did not apply.

Authority is split with respect to whether §269 applies to losses incurred after an acquisition. Compare Borge v. Commissioner, 405 F.2d 673 (2d Cir. 1968) (§269 can apply to postacquisition losses), with Herculite Protective Fabrics Corp. v. Commissioner, 387 F.2d 475 (3d Cir. 1968) (postacquisition losses were true economic loss to acquirer and not subject to §269).

3. *Section 269(b).* Recall that pursuant to §§332 and 334(b) a parent liquidating a subsidiary generally recognizes no gain but inherits the subsidiary's basis in its assets. See pages 342-358 supra. Under §381(a)(1), a parent can succeed to the tax attributes of its liquidated subsidiary as well. If the parent has purchased the stock of a subsidiary, the parent can make an election under §338 to step up (or step down) the basis of the subsidiary's assets. See discussion at pages 384-389 supra. If the election is made, the sale destroys the subsidiary's tax attributes, including any NOL carryovers (although the NOLs can offset any gain on the deemed §338 sale). If no election is made and the subsidiary is liquidated, the parent might succeed to the subsidiary's tax attributes.

Under §269(b)(1), the Service can disallow any deduction or other tax attribute that otherwise would be acquired if (1) there is a qualified stock purchase, (2) a §338 election is not made, (3) the acquired corporation is liquidated pursuant to a plan adopted within two years of acquisition, and (4) the principal purpose of the liquidation is tax avoidance. The liquidation of a newly purchased subsidiary ordinarily indicates that the principal purpose of the liquidation is tax avoidance, in the absence of evidence to the contrary. H.R. Rep. No. 432 (pt. II), 98th Cong., 2d Sess. 1623 (1984).

4. *Relationship between §§269 and 382*. Section 382 is triggered by objective criteria, §269 by subjective tax avoidance purpose. Because of its breadth, §269 can apply to disallow an NOL carryover that would not be disallowed under §382. Treas. Regs. §1.269-7. Indeed, deliberate avoidance of §382(a) may indicate that use of the NOL carryovers was the principal purpose for the acquisition. Luke v. Commissioner, 351 F.2d 568 (7th Cir. 1965). Conversely, the application of §382 may suggest the absence of a tax avoidance purpose.

6. *The* Libson Shops *Doctrine*

Libson Shops v. Hoehler, 353 U.S. 382 (1954), involved the merger into a single corporation of 16 other corporations (each operating a separate retail store). Both the survivor and the 16 corporations were owned by the same shareholders in the same proportions. The surviving corporation sought to apply the premerger operating losses of three of the corporations to the postmerger income of the entire enterprise. The court held that the losses could be applied against the postmerger income of the businesses that had produced the losses but not against the income generated by the other stores. *Libson Shops* was decided under 1939 Code. The status of the case under the 1986 Code is not clear.

In Maxwell Hardware Co. v. Commissioner, 343 F.2d 713 (9th Cir. 1965), two new investors purchased some nonvoting preferred stock in an unsuccessful hardware store business. The corporation used the proceeds to purchase real estate from the new investors. Operated as a separate division, the real estate venture became profitable, and the corporation used the NOL carryover from the hardware operation to offset the profits. Sections 382 and 269 were unavailable to the Service because the preferred stock purchased by the investors did not meet the acquisition requirements of either provision. The Service relied on what it regarded as the overriding judicial principles of *Libson Shops* to deny the NOL carryover, but the Ninth Circuit in reversing the Tax Court determined that the judicial gloss of *Libson Shops* was not part of the 1954 Code. See also Frederick Steel Co. v. Commissioner, 375 F.2d 351 (6th Cir. 1967). Shortly after the decision in *Maxwell Hardware*, the Service announced its intention to apply the *Libson Shops* doctrine to deny NOL carryovers if a substantial shift in the benefits of the carryover has taken place. T.I.R. 773 (Oct. 13, 1965). The conference report accompanying the Tax Reform Act of 1986, however, states that the *Libson Shops* doctrine no longer applies when §382 applies.

Thus, if §382 permits but limits the use of an NOL, *Libson Shops* cannot preclude what §382 allows. How would *Libson Shops* be decided under §382? Does *Libson Shops* continue to have vitality for those acquisitions that fall outside §382? See B. Bittker and J. Eustice, Federal Income Taxation of Corporations and Shareholders ¶14.46 (6th ed. 1993).

B. AFFILIATED CORPORATIONS

In principle, every corporation reports its income and deductions separately from other corporations. Of course, the Service may seek exceptions to this principle if the corporate form is used to reallocate income. See pages 658-680 infra. The consolidated return provisions offer an opportunity for taxpayers to ignore this principle when several businesses are operated in several corporations rather than in only one. The use of multiple corporations might be the result of internal growth (i.e., new corporations formed via §351), purchase, or reorganization (i.e., a subsidiary acquisition through a B reorganization).

Why would individuals choose to operate a business or businesses through multiple corporations rather than through a single corporation? There may be a host of reasons — both nontax and tax motivated. Some of the nontax reasons for maintaining, acquiring, or forming multiple corporations include (1) minimizing potential tort liability (see Walkovszky v. Carlton, 18 N.Y.2d 414 (1966) (ownership of taxi fleet in many corporations, each owning only one or two cabs)); (2) regulatory restraints or benefits of combining businesses within a single corporation; (3) avoiding state law complications; (4) the existence of favorable, nonavailable contractual arrangements; (5) alleviation of labor problems; and (6) the existence of corporate goodwill.

Some of the tax advantages associated with multiple corporations include (1) the availability of differing accounting methods, table years, and other elections; (2) reallocation of income to avoid progressive tax rates; (3) the availability of multiple tax benefits, such as the accumulated earnings tax credit; (4) more favorable disposition of unwanted assets, e.g., through a tax-free spin-off (see pages 508-520 supra); and (5) greater flexibility with regard to earnings and profits and shareholder distributions. Many of these tax advantages have been limited. See Chapter 15.

Notwithstanding the tax advantages that sometimes attend multiple corporations, affiliated groups of corporations often find it desirable to file as though they constitute a single corporation. Under §§1501-1504, affiliated groups of corporations are given a privilege of making a single consolidated tax return that (roughly speaking) allows them to be treated as a single corporation for tax purposes. Only corporations controlled by a common parent corporation may make the election. Thus, if *B*, an individual, owns the stock of *X* Corp. and *Y* Corp., the two corporations may not file a consolidated return. If *B* owns the stock of *H* Corp., which owns the stock of *X* Corp. and *Y* Corp., then *X* Corp., *Y* Corp., and *H* Corp. can file a consolidated return.

Once the election is made for a taxable year, the corporations must continue to file on a consolidated basis unless the Commissioner consents to a termination or the common parent corporation is no longer in existence. Pursuant to a broad statutory grant (§1502), the Treasury has promulgated detailed regulations that often provide, for corporations filing consolidated returns, different rules than normally apply under the Code. These regulations constitute the "law" of consolidated returns. Under §1501, a group electing to file a consolidated return consents to these regulations.

NOTE

1.   *Eligibility for filing.* A consolidated return may be filed by an "affiliated group" of corporations. Under §1504, that term means certain "includible" corporations linked through specified stock ownership requirements. Most corporations are includible, with certain exceptions such as tax-exempt corporations, insurance companies, certain foreign corporations, regulated investment companies, and S corporations. But see United States Padding Corp. v. Commissioner, 865 F.2d 750 (6th Cir. 1989) (subsidiary formed to comply with foreign government practice and policy was an includible corporation). The stock ownership provision of §1504 requires one or more chains of includible corporations connected to a common parent such that (a) stock with at least 80 percent of the voting power of all classes of stock and at least 80 percent of the value of each includible corporation must be owned directly by one or more of the other includible corporations, and (b) the common parent must also meet the 80 percent tests with respect to at least one of the other includible corporations. Note that the direct ownership requirement rules out corporations owned by an individual or group of individuals or by a nonincludible corporation. If a consolidated return election is made by an affiliated group, all includible corporations in the group must file a consolidated return.

Under the stock ownership rules of §1504(a), "stock" does not include certain nonvoting preferred stock. §1504(a)(4). Accordingly, such stock is often used by members of an affiliated group to raise outside equity capital without destroying the right to file a consolidated return. Under §1504(a)(5), options are generally ignored in determining eligibility unless not treating the option as exercised would result in substantial federal tax savings and it is reasonably certain that the option will be exercised. Treas. Regs. §1.1504-4.

Even with a statutory definition of "affiliated group," some courts have denied the privilege of filing consolidated returns to a corporation that acquires another corporation solely to use its tax attributes on a consolidated return. For example, in Elko Realty Co. v. Commissioner, 29 T.C. 1012, aff'd per curiam, 260 F.2d 949 (3d Cir. 1958), a successful corporation acquired the stock of two other corporations that had been operating at a loss. Relying in part on the business purpose principle of Gregory v. Helvering, page 435 supra, the court denied the parent's right to file a consolidated return in the absence of a business purpose for the acquisition. See also R.P. Collins & Co. v. United States, 303 F.2d 142 (1st Cir. 1962) (§269 used to deny loss deductions on consolidated return). But see Zanesville Investment Co. v. Commissioner, 335 F.2d 507 (6th Cir. 1964) (consolidated returns permitted when postaffiliation losses of some members offset income from other members).

In light of the current regulations, first promulgated in 1966, that restrict the use of preaffiliation and some postaffiliation net operating losses regardless of acquisition purpose, is the approach of the court in *Elko Realty* appropriate? See Treas. Regs. §§1.1502-15, 1.1502-21, 1.1502-22. Even when these restrictions apply, the regulations do not deny consolidated return treatment as did the court in *Elko Realty*.

2. *Election to file a consolidated return and other accounting considerations.* A consolidated return may be filed only if all affiliated corporations consent. §1502. Once an election is made, the affiliated group must continue to file on a consolidated basis unless the Commissioner grants permission to discontinue for "good cause." Treas. Regs. §1.1502-75(a)(2). See Rev. Proc. 91-11, 1991-1 C.B. 470 (procedures for deconsolidation).

The taxable year for a consolidated return is based on the common parent's annual accounting period. In general, subsidiaries must adopt the parent's period. Treas. Regs. §1.1502-76(a)(1). But the subsidiaries are not required to adopt the accounting method of the common parent. Instead, each member of the group employs the method that would be used if it were filing a separate return. Treas. Regs. §1.1502-17(a).

Each member of an affiliated group is severally liable for the entire tax.

3. *Computation of a consolidated return: in general.* The basic concept underlying the treatment of a consolidated return is that the affiliated group is in effect a single taxable entity, notwithstanding the existence of multiple corporate forms. As such, the tax liability ought to be based on dealings with "outsiders" rather than dealings within the group. With this "single taxpayer" approach in mind, consider the basic computational features.

The tax liability of an affiliated group filing a consolidated return is based on "consolidated taxable income." To determine the consolidated taxable income, the separate taxable income (or loss) of each group member is determined separately (subject to special rules relating to intercompany transactions and distributions, accounting methods, etc.). Treas. Regs. §1.1502-12. These separate incomes are then combined. In addition, each member's capital gains and losses, charitable contributions, §1231 transactions, and net operating losses are aggregated for purposes of applying the various statutory limitations. Treas. Regs. §1.1502-11. The gross consolidated tax liability is then computed in accordance with §§11, 541, 531, 1201, etc., on the consolidated taxable income. Finally, any consolidated investment credit or foreign tax credit is subtracted. Treas. Regs. §1.1502-2.

4. *Computation of a consolidated return: intercompany transactions.* One of the most significant aspects of the consolidated return regulations is the treatment of intercompany transfers. The regulations distinguish (a) deferred intercompany transactions, in which the purchaser must capitalize the expense, from (b) all other intercompany transactions for which payments are currently deductible. With respect to the latter category, the regulations require the payor and the payee to deduct and include the amounts within the same taxable year. The net effect is a "wash" so far as the group's consolidated taxable income is concerned.

The regulations' treatment of deferred intercompany transactions is more complicated. These transactions include sales or exchanges of property and the performance of services for which payments must be capitalized. The regulations adopt a "suspense account" concept. By deferring the "selling" corporation's gain or loss until the occurrence of certain specified events, the regulations attempt to match the inclusion of gain or the reporting of loss by the selling corporation with appropriate depreciation deductions by the purchasing corporation. Treas. Regs. §1.1502-13T. Thus, gain or loss is reported by the selling corporation at the same rate at which the asset is depreciated. In the case of inventory, Treas. Regs. §1.1502-18 generally taxes the gain on intercompany sales of inventory to the selling corporation, but only when the purchasing corporation sells the property to an outsider.

Events that trigger the recognition of the deferred gain or loss include the sale of property by the purchasing corporation to an outsider; the departure of the selling or purchasing member from the affiliated group prior to sale to an outsider; in some cases, the filing of separate returns by affiliated group members; and worthlessness, collection, or redemption of debt instruments used to purchase the property. If the acquired property is sold by the purchasing member on the installment method under §453, deferred gain is reported by the selling member as collections are made by the purchasing member. If the selling member is a dealer, however, sale by the purchasing member to an outside purchaser on the installment method must be reported by the selling member immediately. The selling member cannot defer gain on the purchasing member's resale. Treas. Regs. §1.1302-13T(m).

5. *Computation of a consolidated return: intercompany distributions.* Con-

sistent with the theme that an affiliated group is a single taxable entity, dividend distributions between members of the group are eliminated from the computation of consolidated taxable income. Treas. Regs. §1.1502-14(a)(1). The "investment basis adjustment" rules generally require that the parent's basis in the common stock of a subsidiary be reduced by the amount of intercompany dividend distributions, Treas. Regs. §1.1502-32. This reduction will increase the parent's gain (or decrease its loss) on any eventual sale of the stock. The theory behind this downward adjustment in basis is similar to that underlying the treatment of S corporations. See Chapter 16. Because the parent's stock basis is adjusted upward when a subsidiary earns income, the distribution from that subsidiary must decrease the basis. In keeping with that theory, there is no basis adjustment for distributions from years before 1966 or from post-1966 years in which no consolidated return was filed since for both of these situations there was no previous upward basis adjustment.

Nondividend distributions under §301(c)(2) and (3) also reduce basis and are tax free to the distributee. Distributions of property are governed by rules similar to those in §§301 and 311, except that any gain recognized by the distributing corporation is governed by the intercompany transaction rules discussed in Note 4 supra. Treas. Regs. §1.1502-13.

Distributions in liquidation are treated under the normal liquidation rules, see Chapter 7; Treas. Regs. §1.1502-14.

6. *Investment basis accounts and excess loss accounts.* In accordance with the single taxable entity concept, the consolidated return regulations attempt to avoid a duplicate recognition of investment gain (or loss) by a parent corporation that is attributable to earnings (or losses) of a subsidiary that have already been accounted for on the consolidated return. The "investment basis adjustment" (IBA) provisions of Treas. Regs. §1.1502-32 require a parent to make annual adjustments to its basis in the stock of the subsidiaries. The result is a fluctuating stock basis. In general, basis is increased for the "adjusted taxable income" of the subsidiary and for the subsidiary's share of any consolidated net operating (or capital) losses that were able to be carried back to a prior year. Basis is decreased by any utilized losses attributable to the subsidiary and by most distributions under §301. The regulations specifically set forth whether the additions and subtractions from basis apply to common or preferred (if any) stock. For an example of the adjustments required by Treas. Regs. §1.1502-32 with respect to depreciation deductions, see Woods Investment Co. v. Commissioner, 85 T.C. 274 (1985).

Basis adjustments are made in other contexts as well. See, e.g., §301(c)(2), discussed at page 120 supra, and §1367, discussed at page 700 infra, but in these situations basis cannot be reduced below zero. The IBA rules do permit a negative basis for the parent's stock in the subsidiary. This negative basis is defined by Treas. Regs. §1.1502-32(e)(1) as an "excess loss account" (ELA). The account will create income in the hands of the parent upon the occurrence of certain specified events. Treas. Regs. §1.1502-19. For example, assume P has a stock basis of $30 in the stock of S, its subsidiary, and that P and S file a consolidated return. If S suffers a $50 loss that is fully used to offset some of the group's consolidated taxable income, the ELA account will be $20. If P later sells the S stock for $20, a $40 gain must be recognized — the $20 sales proceeds plus the $20 ELA. The tax returns reporting loss deductions of $50 and gain of $40 will correspond to the economic result to P of its investment in S — $30 paid for the stock less $20 received on the sale.

7. *Limitations on consolidated reporting.* Congress and the Treasury have perceived a danger in consolidated reporting when a loss corporation is acquired to apply its net operating loss deductions (or other favorable tax attributes) against income of profitable affiliated group members. The problem here is the same as that raised in a reorganization or purchase context under §§381 and 382. See pages 549-570 supra. Indeed, when applicable, those provisions govern the treatment of affiliated group members. Members of a consolidated group are treated as a single entity (i.e., as if the group's subsidiaries were unincorporated). Treas. Regs. §1.1502-91(a)(1). See generally Treas. Regs. §1.1502-91 to -99.

The regulations also describe the parent change method, focusing on ownership changes with respect to a loss group's common parent stock. Treas. Regs. §1.1502-92(b)(1). For example, suppose B owns all the stock of P Corp., which files a consolidated return with its 80 percent owned subsidiary, Subco. Individual C owns the other 20 percent of Subco. During year 1, the P Corp. group incurs a $200 consolidated NOL, attributable entirely to Subco. In year 2, B sells 60 percent of P Corp. to D, an unrelated individual. C retains the 20 percent minority interest in Subco. Because the consolidated group is treated as a separate entity for purposes of §382, the sale of stock from B to D triggers §382 (i.e., D's ownership in the P Corp. group has gone from 0 percent to 60 percent) even though D's ownership in Subco would not trigger §382 (i.e., after the purchase D owns 60 percent × 80 percent, or 48 percent of Subco). Under §382, the P Corp. group's use of Subco's NOL will be limited. See page 552 supra.

The regulations also provide for an antiabuse rule (i.e., the modified parent change method), which in some cases counts the acquisition of a subsidiary's stock by a shareholder of the parent in testing for a §382(g) change of ownership in the parent. Treas. Regs. §1.1502-93(b)(3). For example, suppose an existing shareholder of the parent owns 10 percent of the parent's stock. If that shareholder acquires an additional 35 percent of the parent's stock and 16 percent of the subsidiary's stock, an ownership change is triggered.

Special rules apply to new members entering or leaving a loss group. Treas. Regs. §§1.1502-94 (entering members), 1.1502-95 (departing members).

In calculating the §382 limitation, the value of the stock of each member of the loss group (other than stock owned directly or indirectly by another member) is multiplied by the federal long-term tax-exempt rate. For example, suppose *B* owns all the stock of *P* Corp., which owns 80 percent of the stock of *L* Corp. *C*, who is unrelated to *B*, owns the other 20 percent of the *L* Corp. stock. *P* Corp. and *L* Corp. file a consolidated return. *P* Corp.'s stock has a value of $1,000, and *L* Corp.'s stock has a value of $500. *L* Corp. has an NOL of $600 incurred while a member of the *P* Corp. group. *B* sells 100 percent of the *P* Corp. stock to *C*. The sale is an ownership change for the *P* Corp. group, triggering §382. The consolidated §382 limitation is the product of the long-term tax-exempt rate and $1,100, the sum of *P* Corp.'s $1,000 value and the $100 value of the *L* Corp. stock not owned by a member of the *P* Corp. group (i.e., *C*). If the long-term tax-exempt rate is 10 percent, then the *P* Corp. group can offset up to $110 of consolidated taxable income each year with *L* Corp.'s NOL.

Other rules under §382 generally apply in the consolidated group context to the entire group. For example, the ability to use an NOL is increased if a loss group has a net unrealized built-in gain that is recognized during the five-year recognition period. Treas. Regs. §1.1502-92(h). See page 560 supra. Also, the business continuity requirement of §382 is applied to the group as a whole. Treas. Regs. §1.1502-93(d).

While §382 does apply to consolidated groups, the regulations impose an additional limitation on the group's ability to use the NOLs of one member to offset consolidated taxable income. This limitation is known as the "separate return limitation year," or SRLY. Treas. Regs. §1.1502-1(f). Generally, preaffiliation losses cannot be utilized to offset postaffiliation consolidated taxable income, except to the extent that the new member of the group contributes to the consolidated income. Treas. Regs. §1.1502-21(c). A SRLY member's contribution to consolidated taxable income is determined on a cumulative basis over the period during which the SRLY member is a member of the consolidated group. Also, the SRLY limitation can be applied on a subgroup basis to SRLY members who were previously affiliated in another group and who continue to be affiliated in the new group. Similar rules exist for other tax attributes. See Treas. Regs. §1.1502-4(f) (foreign tax credit carryovers), §1.1502-22(c) (capital loss carryovers). The SRLY rule appears to duplicate the §382 limitation, but there are situations in which the SRLY rule applies while §382 does not.

For example, suppose *B*, an individual, and *P* Corp. each own 50 percent of *L* Corp. stock. *L* Corp. has NOLs. If *P* Corp. purchases an additional 30 percent of the *L* Corp. stock from *B*, no ownership change has occurred under §382 because no shareholder of *P* Corp. has increased ownership in *L* Corp. by more than 50 percentage points. But even though §382 does not limit the use of *L* Corp.'s losses by the *P* Corp. group if it files a consolidated return, the SRLY rule limits the use of *L* Corp.'s preconsolidation NOLs by the *P* Corp. group. Under Treas. Regs. §1.1502-

21(c), the deduction of the SRLY loss by the *P* Corp. group is limited to the taxable income of the member with the SRLY loss (i.e., *L* Corp.). When the acquired corporation with a SRLY loss is part of a group of related corporations, the taxable income of this SRLY subgroup can be offset by the SRLY loss. Treas. Regs. §1.1502-21(c)(2).

If a corporation with a SRLY loss is acquired in a transaction that triggers a §382 ownership change, then §382 applies separately to the new loss member rather than on a consolidated basis. Suppose in the example above that *P* Corp. initially owns no stock of *L* Corp. but then acquires 100 percent of *L* Corp., which has a SRLY loss. This acquisition of *L* Corp. triggers §382 because the shareholders of *P* Corp., which owned 0 percent of *L* Corp. prior to the acquisition, own 100 percent after the acquisition. Although §382 applies, because *L* Corp. has a SRLY loss §382 does not apply on a consolidated basis. Instead, the §382 limitation applies to *L* Corp. separately. This separate §382 application is in addition to, and not in lieu of, the SRLY limitation. Accordingly, if the §382 limitation would allow the consolidated group to deduct a portion of *L* Corp.'s NOL but in fact *L* Corp. produces no consolidated taxable income under the SRLY rule, then no deduction is permitted.

Suppose a profitable corporation acquires another corporation, not because it has any net operating losses but rather because it has a large debt that is about to become worthless. Or perhaps the corporation to be acquired has assets that it is about to sell at a loss. The consolidated return regulations discourage the acquisition of a corporation with such "built-in" losses when the purpose of the acquisition is the use of those losses to offset postaffiliation income attributable to other members of the consolidated group. Treas. Regs. §1.1502-15. The reach of these regulations can be significant. For example, normal operating expenses of a cash basis subsidiary that accrued in a preaffiliation year but were paid in a consolidated return year were held subject to the built-in deduction limitations. Rev. Rul. 79-279, 1979-2 C.B. 316.

The regulations define "built-in" deductions as those that are "economically accrued" by a corporation in a SRLY prior to acquisition but that are realized in a tax sense after the acquisition in a consolidated return year. These deductions are not disallowed by the regulations; instead, they are subject to the §382 and SRLY limitations on the carryover of preaffiliation losses. See §382(h). Some exceptions to these "built-in" loss limitations are made if the realization of the loss does not occur for at least five years or if the aggregate basis of the corporation's assets does not exceed the value of those assets by more than 15 percent. Finally, no restrictions are placed on the acquirer's own built-in deductions.

For the rules governing "outbound" transactions (i.e., those in which a corporation moves from a consolidated to a separate return), see generally Treas. Regs. §§1.1502-21(b), 1.1502-22(b).

8. *Advantages and disadvantages of consolidated reporting.* With the basic

framework of the consolidated return regulations in mind, consider the advantages and disadvantages of consolidated reporting. The advantages include (a) using losses of an affiliate to offset income from another affiliate, (b) making tax-free intercorporate distributions, and (c) deferring gain (or loss) on intercompany transactions (e.g., sales).

Among the disadvantages of filing a consolidated return are (a) being subject to consistency requirements for election and accounting periods (although Treas. Regs. §1.1502-17(a) permits separate accounting methods for each member in accordance with §446); (b) sharing a single graduated tax rate, accumulated earnings tax credit, and other special exemptions and credits; (c) being subject to a binding election; and (d) complying with complex consolidated return regulations.

C.   PROBLEMS

1.   B owns all the stock of L Corp., which has $2 million of NOL carryovers. P Corp. is a profitable business that earns approximately $300,000 a year. What effect does each of the following transactions have on the NOL carryovers?

    a.   B contributes sufficient cash to L Corp. to enable L Corp. to purchase the assets of P Corp.

    b.   L Corp. sells all its assets and uses the proceeds to purchase the assets of P Corp.

    c.   L Corp. acquires the stock of P Corp. for cash, P Corp. liquidates, and L Corp. continues to operate P Corp.'s profitable business.

2.   Discuss the application of §382 in the following situations.

    a.   L Corp., a corporation with NOL carryforwards, is closely held by four unrelated individuals, A, B, C, and D, each of whom owns 25 percent of the L Corp. stock. There is a public offering of L Corp.'s stock. No person who purchases stock in the offering acquires 5 percent or more, and neither A, B, C, nor D acquires any additional stock. As a result of the offering the new shareholders own stock representing 60 percent of the outstanding L Corp. stock. Consider the restrictions, if any, on L Corp.'s use of the NOL carryforwards.

    b.   Suppose in (a) that L Corp. is publicly held, with no shareholder owning more than 2 percent of the outstanding stock.

    c.   Suppose L Corp. is wholly owned by B. L Corp. merges into P Corp., a publicly held corporation in which no shareholder owns more than a 2 percent interest. After the merger, B owns 60 percent of P Corp. Two years later, P Corp. sells additional stock to C equal to 50 percent of the stock value.

3.   Determine the tax consequences in the following situations.

    a.   X Corp. is wholly owned by individual A, and its stock has a value of $3,000; *X* Corp. has NOL carryforwards of $10,000. *Y* Corp. is wholly owned by individual *B*, and its stock has a value of $9,000; *Y* Corp. has NOL carryforwards of $100. *Z* Corp. is owned by individual *C*, and its stock has a value of $18,000; *Z* Corp. has no NOL carryforwards. *X* Corp., *Y* Corp., and *Z* Corp. consolidate into *W* Corp. in a transaction that qualifies under §368(a)(1)(A). The applicable long-term tax-exempt rate on such date is 10 percent. As a result of the consolidation, *A* receives 10 percent of *W* stock, *B* receives 30 percent, and *C* receives 60 percent. *W*'s taxable income before any reduction for its NOLs is $1,400. Consider whether the NOLs can be used to offset *W*'s income.

b. Suppose in (a) that *X* Corp. holds an asset with a basis of $1,000 and a fair market value of $1,600 at the time of the consolidation. The asset is sold by *W* in year 1, thereby producing $600 of *W*'s $1,400 of taxable income.

c. Suppose in (a) that *X* Corp. holds an asset with a basis of $1,600 and a fair market value of $1,000 at the time of the consolidation. The asset is sold by *W*. Excluding this transaction and the use of any NOLs, *W* Corp. has taxable income of $2,000.

4. *L* Corp., a loss company with preacquisition losses, is wholly owned by *B*, and *P* Corp., a profitable corporation with built-in gains, is wholly-owned by *C*. Consider whether §382 or §384 or both apply in the subparts below and what tax consequences follow.

a. *L* Corp. purchases all the *P* Corp. stock for cash and does not elect §338.

b. Suppose in (a) that *L* Corp. elects §338.

c. *P* Corp. purchases all the *L* Corp. stock for cash and does not elect §338.

d. *L* Corp. merges into *P* Corp., and *B* ends up with 60 percent of the *P* Corp. stock.

e. Suppose in (d) that *B* ends up with 40 percent of the *P* Corp. stock.

f. Suppose *L* Corp. and *P* Corp. form *L-P*, a joint venture partnership. Under the *L-P* partnership agreement, much of the *L-P* income is allocated to *L* Corp.

5. Forco, a foreign corporation that cannot make use of U.S. tax benefits, is planning a new U.S. venture to be operated through *L* Corp. It is expected that *L* Corp. will generate tax losses in its first several years. To make use of the expected losses, Forco finds a U.S. partner, *P* Corp., a profitable U.S. corporation. Forco and *P* Corp. form *L* Corp., with Forco receiving preferred stock with a fair market value of $800,000 and *P* Corp. receiving common stock with a fair market value of $200,000. The preferred stock is preferred as to dividends and on liquidation, but it has an adjustable rate feature whereby the level of dividends is set by reference to certain yields of U.S. Treasury obligations. In addition, this preferred

stock is convertible into another class of preferred stock, identical in all respects to the outstanding preferred except that the adjustable rate feature references different U.S. Treasury obligations. Can *L* Corp. and *P* Corp. file a consolidated return allowing *P* Corp. to offset its profits with *L* Corp.'s losses? Consider §1504(a).

6.   *P* Corp. has three wholly owned subsidiaries having the following items of income and loss:

	X	Y	Z
Ordinary business income (loss)	$300	($80)	$ 40
§1231 gains (loss)	80	40	(40)
Capital gains (loss)	20	40	(100)
§170 contributions	60		

What is the group's consolidated taxable income?

7.   In Problem 6, what are the tax consequences of the following transactions?

   a.   *P* Corp. leases computer software from *X* Corp., paying an annual $300 royalty.

   b.   *P* Corp. pays interest of $60 to *Y* Corp. on an intercorporate loan.

   c.   In year 1, *P* Corp. sells land with a basis of $300 and a fair market value of $400 to *Z* Corp. *Z* Corp. resells the land in year 2 to an unrelated party for $650.

   d.   Suppose in (c) that *Z* Corp. sells the property on the installment method.

   e.   Suppose in (c) that the property sold to *Z* Corp. is depreciable property that *Z* Corp. uses in its trade or business. *Z* Corp. depreciates the property using a straight-line method over 10 years.

8.   Discuss the tax consequences of the following situations.

   a.   *P* Corp. owns all the stock of *X* Corp., with which it files a consolidated return. *P* Corp.'s basis in the *X* Corp. stock is $100. In year 1, *X* Corp. earns $30 and makes no distribution. In year 2, *X* Corp. earns $20 and makes a $50 distribution to *P* Corp.

   b.   Suppose in (a) that in year 1, *P* Corp. earns $200 and *X* Corp. has a net operating loss of $160. In year 2, *P* Corp. earns $100 and *X* Corp. suffers a $140 loss. *P* Corp. sells its *X* Corp. stock in year 3 for $80.

IV

MISCELLANEOUS CORPORATE TAX TOPICS

14

Penalty Provisions

The heart and soul of subchapter C is that distributed corporate earnings from operations should be taxed twice — once when the corporation earns them and again when they are distributed. Furthermore, it is Congress's intention that both taxes should be at ordinary income rates. The propriety or impropriety of these guiding principles has been explored in Chapter 8.

It is of course not true that Congress intended that all corporate earnings be taxed twice at ordinary income rates. For example, X Corp. might earn $10,000, which is taxed as ordinary income at corporate rates. Rather than distributing the earnings in the form of a dividend, X Corp. might accumulate the earnings, thereby increasing the value of the outstanding stock. Shareholder A might then sell stock, arrange for X Corp. to redeem stock under §302, or liquidate X Corp. under §331. All three of these possibilities would permit A to receive, directly or indirectly, the corporate earnings at capital gains rates. Notice that if any of these events is undertaken by A's estate, there may be no gain recognized. Moreover, so long as X Corp. makes no distribution, the cash that otherwise would have been paid in taxes by a dividend-receiving shareholder can continue to earn income, thereby providing shareholders with the benefits of deferral.

Aware that subchapter C contains the seeds of its own circumvention, Congress has enacted various penalty provisions to keep taxpayers on the straight and narrow. In this chapter we will consider three: the accumulated earnings tax (§§531-537), the personal holding company tax (§§541-547), and the collapsible corporations provision (§341). The first two are taxes levied on the corporation in addition to normal corporate taxes (e.g., §§11 and 55). The collapsible corporations provision exacts its penalty by turning what would otherwise be a shareholder's capital gains income into ordinary income.

A. ACCUMULATED EARNINGS TAX

What tax pressures are there on corporations and their shareholders to accumulate income? Historically corporate tax rates have been lower than individual tax rates. Prior to 1982, the maximum rate for individuals was 70 percent, while corporations were taxed at a 46 percent maximum rate. This differential led some individuals to incorporate their businesses so as to accumulate earnings at the corporate level for eventual distribution at a time when the individual was in a lower tax bracket. During the period of accumulation, the taxpayer might gain access to the earnings through loans. Even with the reduction of the top rate for individuals from 50 percent to 39.6 percent while the corporate rate is 35 percent, accumulation can be an attractive strategy. Once a corporation has earned and paid tax on income, the decision whether to distribute is only partially related to any differential between corporate and individual tax rates. The decision is also related to two factors — deferral and the capital gains/ordinary income differential. Accumulation allows the corporation to postpone payment of taxes that would be due on distribution, enabling it to invest the amount that would have been paid in taxes. For example, suppose a corporation has $1,000 available for distribution. Suppose further that the corporation will be taxed on income generated by the $1,000 at a 35 percent rate while an individual will be taxed at a 31 percent rate. The fact that the corporate rate is less than the individual rate does not necessarily mean that the corporation should distribute the $1,000. If there is a distribution, the $1,000 itself is taxable to the shareholders (albeit at a 31 percent rate), resulting in only $690 available to generate income.

Compounding the incentive to avoid a shareholder-level tax on corporate earnings available for distribution is the capital gains/ordinary income differential (when it exists). A shareholder has an incentive to capture corporate earnings through transactions that will produce capital gains — sale, redemption, or liquidation — rather than through a distribution. In the example above, if the corporation does not distribute the $1,000, the value of the corporation's stock increases by $1,000, which can be realized by the shareholders at a capital gains rate upon eventual disposition. There may be no tax on the sale of the shareholder's stock following the shareholder's death. §1014.

The accumulated earnings tax is a penalty tax imposed by Congress to discourage the use of a corporation to accumulate earnings in order to shelter individual shareholders from receiving dividends taxable at the shareholder level. The motive triggering the tax is the accumulation of earnings beyond the reasonable needs of the business — a question of fact turning on subjective intent. The base of the accumulated earnings tax in any taxable year is the corporation's "accumulated taxable income" for that year, a term that must be distinguished from "earnings and profits" either of the current year or accumulated from prior years. Section 535 defines "accumulated taxable income" as taxable income less (1) the dividends-paid deduction of §561 and (2) the unused portion, if any, of the one-time accumulated earnings credit ($250,000 for most corporations). §535(c). The credit generally allows accumulation of $250,000 with impunity. Certain adjustments are made to taxable income under §535(b) to account for the fact that taxable income does not necessarily reflect dividend-paying capacity. Accordingly, taxable income is reduced by income taxes paid. Taxable income also is reduced by nondeductible charitable contributions, capital losses, net capital gain, and the taxes attributable thereto. Ignored in the computation of accumulated taxable income are intercorporate dividends-received deductions, net operating losses, partially tax-exempt interest, and capital loss carryovers since they merely affect the computation of tax liability but do not absorb cash available for dividends. Section 531 imposes a 39.6 percent tax on accumulated taxable income.

The accumulated earnings tax is essentially focused on cash available for distribution. Only cash that is not needed or used for the reasonable needs of the business is considered available for distribution. It follows that if cash is made unavailable for distribution to shareholders because it is invested in other assets not needed in the business, these unnecessary assets may be counted as unreasonably accumulated and available for distribution. Treas. Regs. §1.537-2. For example, the IRS is likely to maintain that cash used to make loans to shareholders or their relatives or to purchase a portfolio of stocks or properties unrelated to the corporation's business is the equivalent of cash on hand that could have and should have been paid out to shareholders. But if a corporation's earnings are used to buy a new business, to expand the present business, to meet working capital needs, to retire stock of a minority shareholder, or to pay off business debt, the corporation may be able to avoid imposition of the accumulated earnings tax. A thinly capitalized business with debt borrowed from outside sources may not have difficulty with the §531 tax since the repayment of debt is a reasonable business need. It has been held, however, that the §531 penalty cannot be imposed on a corporation that could have easily borrowed funds but chose instead to forgo dividends and build up cash to meet its business needs. See, e.g., Myron's Enterprises v. United States, 548 F.2d 331, 335 n.6 (9th Cir. 1977).

Ivan Allen Co. v. United States
422 U.S. 617 (1975)

Mr. Justice BLACKMUN delivered the opinion of the Court. . . .

The issue here is whether, in determining the application of §533(a), listed and readily marketable securities owned by the corporation and purchased out of its earnings and profits, are to be taken into account at their cost to the corporation or at their net liquidation value, that is, fair market value less the expenses of, and taxes resulting from, their conversion into cash.

I

The pertinent facts are admitted by the pleadings or are stipulated:

The petitioner, Ivan Allen Company (the taxpayer), is a Georgia corporation incorporated in 1902 and actively engaged in the business of selling office furniture, equipment, and supplies in the metropolitan Atlanta area. It files its federal income tax returns on the accrual basis and for the fiscal year ended June 30.

For its fiscal years 1965 and 1966, the taxpayer paid in due course the federal corporation income taxes shown on its returns as filed. Taxable income so reported was $341,045.82 for 1965 and $629,512.19 for 1966. App. 59, 84. During fiscal 1965 the taxpayer paid dividends consisting of cash in the amount of $48,945.30 and 870 shares of Xerox Corporation common that had been carried on its books at a cost of $6,564.34. During fiscal 1966 the taxpayer paid cash dividends of $50,267.49; it also declared a 10% stock dividend. Id., at 56. The dividends paid were substantially less than taxable income less federal income taxes for those years.

Throughout fiscal 1965 and 1966, the taxpayer owned various listed and unlisted marketable securities. Prominent among these were listed shares of common stock and listed convertible debentures of Xerox Corporation that, in prior years, had been purchased out of earnings and profits. Specifically, on June 30, 1965, the corporation owned 11,140 shares of Xerox common, with a cost of $116,701 and a then fair market value of $1,573,525, and $30,600 Xerox convertible debentures, with a cost to it of $30,625 and a then fair market value of $48,424. On June 30, 1966, the corporation owned 10,090 shares of Xerox common, with a cost of $102,479 and a then fair market value of $2,479,617, and the same $30,600 convertible debentures, with their cost of $30,625 and a then fair market value of $69,768. Id., at 55.

According to its returns as filed, the taxpayer's undistributed earnings as of June 30, 1965, and June 30, 1966, were $2,200,184.77 and $2,360,146.52, respectively. Id., at 70, 91. The taxpayer points out that the marketable portfolio assets represented an investment, as measured by cost, of less than 7% of its undistributed earnings and of less than 5% of its total assets. Brief for Petitioner 4.

It is also apparent, however, that the Xerox debentures and common shares had proved to be an extraordinarily profitable investment, although, of course, because these securities continued to be retained, the gains thereon were unrealized for federal income tax purposes. The debentures had increased in fair market value more than 50% over cost by the end of June 1965, and more than 100% over cost one year later; the common shares had increased in fair market value more than 13 times their cost by June 30, 1965, and more than 24 times their cost by June 30, 1966.

Throughout fiscal 1965 and 1966 the taxpayer's two major shareholders, Ivan Allen, Sr., and Ivan Allen, Jr., respectively owned 31.20% and 45.46% of the taxpayer's outstanding voting stock. . . .

It is agreed that the taxpayer had reasonable business needs for operating capital amounting to $1,198,309 and $1,455,222 at the close of fiscal 1965 and fiscal 1966, respectively. Id., at 56. It is stipulated, in particular, that if the taxpayer's marketable securities are to be taken into account at *cost*, its net liquid assets (current assets less current liabilities), at the end of each of those taxable years, and fully available for use in its business, were then exactly equal to its reasonable business needs for operating capital, that is, the above-stated figures of $1,198,309 and $1,455,222. It would follow, accordingly, that the earnings and profits of the two taxable years had *not* been permitted to accumulate beyond the taxpayer's reasonable and reasonably anticipated business needs, within the meaning of §533(a), App. 57, and no accumulated earnings taxes were incurred. It is still further stipulated, however, that if the taxpayer's marketable securities are to be taken into account at *fair market value* (less the cost of converting them into cash), as to the ends of those fiscal years,[5] the taxpayer's net liquid assets would then be $2,235,029 and $3,152,009, respectively. Id., at 56. From this it would follow that the earnings and profits of the two taxable years *had* been permitted to accumulate beyond the taxpayer's reasonable and reasonably anticipated business needs. Then, if those accumulations had been for "the purpose of avoiding the income tax with respect to its shareholders," under §532(a), accumulated earnings taxes would be incurred.

The issue, therefore, is clear and precise: whether, for purposes of applying §533(a), the taxpayer's readily marketable securities should be taken into account at cost, as the taxpayer contends, or at net liquidation value, as the Government contends. . . .

II

Under our system of income taxation, corporate earnings are subject to tax at two levels. First, there is the tax imposed upon the income of the corporation. Second, when the corporation, by way of a dividend, distributes its earnings to its shareholders, the distribution is subject to the tax

---

5. It is stipulated that the cost of converting the taxpayer's marketable securities into cash would have been the sum of a maximum of 6% of the fair market value of the securities (payable as a brokerage commission) and a maximum of 25% of such amount of the fair market value as exceeds the sum of the brokerage commission and the cost of the securities (payable as capital gains taxes). App. 55.

imposed upon the income of the shareholders. Because of the disparity between the corporate tax rates and the higher gradations of the rates on individuals, a corporation may be utilized to reduce significantly its shareholders' overall tax liability by accumulating earnings beyond the reasonable needs of the business. Without some method to force the distribution of unneeded corporate earnings, a controlling shareholder would be able to postpone the full impact of income taxes on his share of the corporation's earnings in excess of its needs.

In order to foreclose this possibility of using the corporation as a means of avoiding the income tax on dividends to the shareholders, every Revenue Act since the adoption of the Sixteenth Amendment in 1913 has imposed a tax upon unnecessary accumulations of corporate earnings effected for the purpose of insulating shareholders. . . .

It is to be noted that the focus and impositions of the accumulated earnings tax are upon "accumulated taxable income," §531. This is defined in §535(a) to mean the corporation's "taxable income," as adjusted. The adjustments consist of the various items described in §535(b), including federal income tax, the deduction for dividends paid, defined in §561, and the accumulated earnings credit defined in §535(c). The adjustments prescribed by §§535(a) and (b) are designed generally to assure that a corporation's "accumulated taxable income" reflects more accurately than "taxable income" the amount actually available to the corporation for business purposes. This explains the deductions for dividends paid and for federal income taxes; neither of these enters into the computation of taxable income. Obviously, dividends paid and federal income taxes deplete corporate resources and must be recognized if the corporation's economic condition is to be properly perceived. Conversely, §535(b)(3) disallows, for example, the deduction, available to a corporation for income tax purposes under §243, on account of dividends received; dividends received are freely available for use in the corporation's business.

The purport of the accumulated earnings tax structure established by §§531-537, therefore, is to determine the corporation's true economic condition before its liability for tax upon "accumulated tax income" is determined. The tax, although a penalty and therefore to be strictly construed, Commissioner v. Acker, 361 U.S. 87, 91 (1959), is directed at economic reality.

It is important to emphasize that we are concerned here with a tax on "accumulated taxable income," §531, and that the tax attaches only when a corporation has permitted "earnings and profits to accumulate instead of being divided or distributed," §532(a). What is essential is that there be "income" and "earnings and profits." This at once eliminates, from the measure of the tax itself, any unrealized appreciation in the value of the taxpayer's portfolio securities over cost, for any such unrealized appreciation does not enter into the computation of the corporation's "income" and "earnings and profits."

The corporation's readily marketable portfolio securities and their unrealized appreciation, nonetheless, are of profound importance in making the entirely discrete determination whether the corporation has permitted what, concededly, are earnings and profits to accumulate beyond its reasonable business needs. If the securities, as here, are readily available as liquid assets, then the recognized earnings and profits that have been accumulated may well have been unnecessarily accumulated, so far as the reasonable needs of the business are concerned. On the other hand, if those portfolio securities are not liquid and are not readily available for the needs of the business, the accumulation of earnings and profits may be viewed in a different light. Upon this analysis, not only is such accumulation as has taken place important, but the liquidity otherwise available to the corporation is highly significant. In any event — and we repeat — the tax is directed at the accumulated taxable income and at earnings and profits. The tax itself is not directed at the unrealized appreciation of the liquid assets in the securities portfolio. The latter becomes important only in measuring reasonableness of accumulation of the earnings and profits that otherwise independently exist. What we look at, then, in order to determine its reasonableness or unreasonableness, in the light of the needs of the business, is any failure on the part of the corporation to distribute the earnings and profits it has.

Accumulation beyond the reasonable needs of the business, by the language of §533(a), is "determinative of the purpose" to avoid tax with respect to shareholders unless the corporation proves the contrary by a preponderance of the evidence. The burden of proof, thus, is on the taxpayer. A rebuttable presumption is statutorily imposed. To be sure, we deal here, in a sense, with a state of mind. But it has been said that the statute, without the support of the presumption, would "be practically unenforceable. . . ." United Business Corp. v. Commissioner, 62 F.2d 754, 755 (C.A.2), cert. denied, 290 U.S. 635 (1933). What is required, then, is a comparison of accumulated earnings and profits with "the reasonable needs of the business." Business *needs* are critical. And need, plainly, to use mathematical terminology, is a function of a corporation's liquidity, that is, the amount of idle current assets at its disposal. The question, therefore, is not how much capital of all sorts, but how much in the way of quick or liquid assets, it is reasonable to keep on hand for the business. United Block Co. v. Helvering, 123 F.2d 704, 705 (C.A.2 1941), cert. denied, 315 U.S. 812 (1942); Smoot Sand & Gravel Corp. v. Commissioner, 274 F.2d 495, 501 (C.A.4), cert. denied, 362 U.S. 976 (1960) (liquid assets provide "a strong indication" of the purpose of the accumulation); Electric Regulator Corp. v. Commissioner, 336 F.2d 339, 344 (C.A.2 1964). . . .[9]

The taxpayer itself recognizes, and accepts, the liquidity concept as a basic factor, for it "has agreed that the full amount of its realized earnings invested in its liquid assets — their cost — should be taken into account

9. In this case we are concerned only with readily marketable securities. We express no view with respect to items of a different kind, such as inventory or accounts receivable.

in determining the applicability of Section 533(a)." Brief for Petitioner 15. It concedes that if this were not so, "the tax could be avoided by any form of investment of earnings and profits." Reply Brief for Petitioner 5. But the taxpayer would stop at the point of cost and, when it does so, is compelled to compare earnings and profits — not the amount of readily available liquid assets, net — with reasonable business needs.

We disagree with the taxpayer and conclude that cost is not the stopping point; that the application of the accumulated earnings tax, in a given case, may well depend on whether the corporation has available readily marketable portfolio securities; and that the proper measure of those securities, for purposes of the tax, is their net realizable value. Cost of the marketable securities on the assets side of the corporation's balance sheet would appear to be largely an irrelevant gauge of the taxpayer's true financial condition. Certainly, a lender would not evaluate a potential borrower's marketable securities at cost. Realistic financial condition is the focus of the lender's inquiry. It also must be the focus of the Commissioner's inquiry in determining the applicability of the accumulated earnings tax.[11] This taxpayer's securities, being liquid and readily marketable, clearly were available for the business needs of the corporation, and their fair market value, net, was such that, according to the stipulation, the taxpayer's undistributed earnings and profits for the two fiscal years in question were permitted to accumulate beyond the reasonable and reasonably anticipated needs of the business.

III

Bearing directly upon the issue before us is Helvering v. National Grocery Co., 304 U.S. 282 (1938). There the fact situation was the reverse of the present case inasmuch as that taxpayer corporation had unrealized losses in the value of marketable securities it was continuing to hold. After the Court upheld the accumulated earnings tax against constitutional attack, id., at 286-290, it observed: "Depreciation in any of the assets is evidence to be considered by the Commissioner and the Board (of Tax Appeals) in determining the issue of fact whether the accumulation of profits was in excess of the reasonable needs of the business." Id., at 291. . . .

The precedent of *National Grocery* has been applied in accumulated earnings tax cases, with courts taking into account the fair market value of liquid, appreciated securities. Battelstein Investment Co. v. United States, 442 F.2d 87, 89 (C.A.5 1971); Cheyenne Newspapers, Inc. v. Com-

---

11. We see little force in any observation that our emphasis on liquid assets means that a corporate taxpayer may avoid the accumulated earnings tax by merely investing in nonliquid assets. If such a step, in a given case, amounted to willful evasion of the accumulated earnings tax, it would be subject to criminal penalties. See, e.g., §7201 of the 1954 Code 26 U.S.C. §7201.

missioner, 494 F.2d 429, 434-435 (C.A.10 1974). . . . American Trading & Production Corp. v. United States, 362 F. Supp. 801 (Md. 1972), aff'd without published opinion, 474 F.2d 1341 (C.A.4 1973), which the taxpayer continues to assert is in conflict with the present case, deserves mention. The taxpayer there had accumulated earnings and profits of something less than $10 million. Its anticipated business needs were about $12 million. But it owned stocks, primarily oil shares, having a total cost of $5,593,319 and an aggregate current market value in excess of $100 million. The District Court excluded these stocks in making its determination whether earnings had accumulated in excess of reasonable business needs. It did so on several grounds: that the shares constituted "original capital," a term the court used in the sense that the stocks "were properly held and retained as an integral part of its business and were utilized . . . as a base for borrowings for the needs of other parts of (the taxpayer's) business," 362 F. Supp., at 810; that the statute was not intended to require the conversion of assets of that kind into cash in order to meet business needs, even though that capital "has explosively increased in value," id., 362 F. Supp., at 808; and that "there was substantial evidence" that the stocks "were not readily salable," id., 362 F. Supp., at 809.

Whatever may be the merit or demerit of the other grounds asserted by the District Court in *American Trading* — and we express no view thereon — we are satisfied that the court's determination as to the absence of ready salability, under all the circumstances, provides a sufficient point of distinction of that case from this one, so that it provides meager, if any, contrary precedent of substance to our conclusion here.

IV

The arguments advanced by the taxpayer do not persuade us:

1. The taxpayer, of course, quite correctly insists that unrealized appreciation of portfolio securities does not enter into the determination of "earnings and profits," within the meaning of §533(a). As noted above, we agree. The Government does not contend otherwise. It does not follow, however, that unrealized appreciation is never to be taken into account for purposes of the accumulated earnings tax.

As has been pointed out, the tax is imposed only upon accumulated taxable income, and this is defined to mean taxable income as adjusted by factors that have been described. The question is not whether unrealized appreciation enters into the determination of earnings and profits, which it does not, but whether the accumulated taxable income, in the determination of which earnings and profits have entered, justifiably may be retained rather than distributed as dividends. The tax focuses, therefore, on current income and its retention or distribution. If the corporation has freely available liquid assets in excess of its reasonable business needs, then accumulation of taxable income may be unreasonable and the tax may attach. Utilizable availability of the portfolio assets is measured realistically only at net realizable value. The fact that this value is not included in earnings and profits does not foreclose its being considered in determining whether the corporation is subject to the accumulated earnings tax.

2.   We see nothing in the "realization of income" concept of Eisner v. Macomber, 252 U.S. 189 (1920), that has significance for the issue presently under consideration. . . . We note again, however, that the accumulated earnings tax is not on unrealized appreciation of the portfolio securities. It rests upon, and only upon, the corporation's current taxable income adjusted to constitute "accumulated taxable income."

3.   The taxpayer also argues that the effect of the Court of Appeals decision is to force the taxpayer to convert its appreciated assets in order to meet its business needs. It suggests that management should be entitled to finance business needs without resorting to unrealized appreciation. The argument, plainly, goes too far. On the taxpayer's own theory that marketable securities may be taken into account at their cost, a situation easily may be imagined where some conversion into cash becomes necessary, if the corporation is to avoid the accumulated earnings tax. . . .

We might add that the existence of the Code's provisions for the accumulated earnings tax, of course, will affect management's decision. So, too, does the very existence of the corporate income tax itself. In this respect, the one is no more offensive than the other. Astute management in these tax-conscious days is not that helpless, and shrinkage, upon liquidation, of one-fourth of the appreciation hardly equates with loss. Such business decision as is necessitated was expressly intended by the Congress. All that is required is the disgorging, at the most, of the taxable year's "accumulated taxable income."

4.   It is no answer to suggest that our decision here may conflict with standard accounting practice. The Court has not hesitated to apply congressional policy underlying a revenue statute even when it does conflict with an established accounting practice. See, e.g., Schlude v. Commissioner, 372 U.S. 128 (1963); American Automobile Ass'n v. United States, 367 U.S. 687, 692-694 (1961). It is of some interest that the taxpayer itself, for the tax years under consideration, reflected the market value as well as the cost of its marketable securities on its balance sheets. App. 112, 118. This appears to be in line with presently accepted practice. See R. Kester, Advanced Accounting 117-118, 122-124 (4th ed. 1946).

The judgment of the Court of Appeals is affirmed.

[Justice Powell's dissenting opinion is omitted.]

NOTE

1.   *Unreasonable accumulations.* Section 532(a) imposes the accumulated earnings tax on corporations that accumulate to avoid taxes. Section

533 presumes that accumulation "beyond the reasonable needs of the business" reflects the improper tax avoidance motive. What constitutes the "reasonable needs of the business" is discussed in the Notes that follow. But even if we know the reasonable needs of the business, to determine whether an accumulation is improper we need to know more than the earnings and profits account. When a corporation accumulates income in a year under scrutiny, it is not enough to compare reasonable business needs with earnings and profits to determine whether current accumulation is appropriate. The earnings and profits account may be misleadingly large or small.

In *Ivan Allen,* earnings and profits were not sufficient to meet reasonable business needs if the Xerox stock was valued at cost. Valuation at fair market value, however, meant that current earnings were available for distribution. Should the result in *Ivan Allen* have been different if the appreciated property were timberland instead of stock? Contrast *Ivan Allen* with Electric Regulator Corp. v. Commissioner, 336 F.2d 339 (2d Cir. 1964), in which earnings and profits at first glance seemed ample to meet business needs, but closer analysis revealed that prior earnings and profits had been reinvested in the corporation and that current accumulations were necessary to meet business needs. Indeed, as the court in *Electric Regulator* pointed out, had the corporation made the dividend distributions the IRS required, corporate assets would have been insufficient to meet reasonable business needs. In addition to focusing on accumulation of earnings and profits, it is equally important to consider what assets are on hand to meet the reasonable business needs.

2. *Burden of proof: presumptions.* Under §532, a corporation is subject to the accumulated earnings tax if it is "formed or availed of for the purpose of avoiding the income tax with respect to its shareholders . . . by permitting earnings and profits to accumulate instead of being divided or distributed." What is the relationship between this provision and the statutory presumptions — if that is what they are — of §533(a) (unreasonable accumulation shall be "determinative of the purpose to avoid the income tax with respect to shareholders" unless the corporation proves to the contrary by a preponderance of evidence) and §533(b) (if corporation is a mere holding company or investment company, this fact shall be "prima facie evidence of the purpose to avoid the income tax")?

Section 534 allows the taxpayer to shift the burden of proof to the government in Tax Court proceedings. Before mailing a notice of deficiency, the government may send a notification informing the taxpayer that the proposed notice of deficiency includes an amount imposed under §531. See Myco Industries v. Commissioner, 98 T.C. 270 (1992) (Commissioner's notice was not adequate to shift burden of proof to taxpayer because the notice failed to state the years for which the tax was asserted). The taxpayer may then submit a statement setting forth the grounds on which it will rely to prove it has not been accumulating unreasonably. The Tax Court will rule in advance on the sufficiency of the taxpayer's §534(c) statement (Rule 142 of Rules of Practice). If the statement is sufficient or if the notification has not been sent by the government, the burden is on the Service. Why is this procedure limited to Tax Court proceedings? For a §534(c) statement held insufficient because of vagueness, see Rutter v. Commissioner, 81 T.C. 937 (1983).

The purpose behind the notification procedure of §534 presumably is to encourage administrative resolution of accumulated earnings tax issues. We know that the burden of proof will be on the Commissioner for failure to notify the taxpayer of an impending deficiency notice based on §531. Where should the burden be placed if the Commissioner sends notification but then asserts a deficiency before the taxpayer has replied to the notification? See Manson Western Corp. v. Commissioner, 76 T.C. 1161 (1981).

In United States v. Donruss Co., 393 U.S. 297 (1969), the government argued that to rebut the presumption of §533(a) the taxpayer must establish by a preponderance of the evidence that tax avoidance was not "one of the purposes" for accumulating earnings beyond the reasonable needs of the business. In contrast, the taxpayer argued that the presumption could be rebutted by showing that tax avoidance was not the "dominant, controlling, or impelling" reason for the accumulation. The Court accepted the government's interpretation, saying that the taxpayer's interpretation "would exacerbate the problems that Congress was trying to avoid" by the statutory emphasis on the reasonableness of the accumulation rather than on the "vagaries of corporate motive." The taxpayer's construction "would allow taxpayers to escape the tax when it is proved that at least one other motive was equal to tax avoidance. We doubt that such a determination can be made with any accuracy, and it is certainly one which will depend almost exclusively on the interested testimony of corporate management." 393 U.S. at 308.

Will a finding of a shareholder deadlock be sufficient to rebut the §533 presumption of an improper purpose? In Atlantic Properties v. Commissioner, 519 F.2d 1233 (1st Cir. 1975), four of the five shareholders representing 75 percent of the vote wanted a dividend distribution, while one shareholder representing the other 25 percent wanted to accumulate. The corporate by-laws required an 80 percent vote for dividend distribution. The court found the corporation subject to the accumulated earnings tax. The same result was reached in Hedberg-Freidheim Contracting Co. v. Commissioner, 251 F.2d 839 (8th Cir. 1958), in which two shareholders were deadlocked. Cf. Casey v. Commissioner, 267 F.2d 26 (2d Cir. 1959), in which two shareholders were deadlocked but an unreasonable accumulation was not found.

3. *Reasonable needs of the business: anticipated needs.* Section 537(a)(1), providing that the term "reasonable needs of the business" includes the "reasonably anticipated needs of the business," was enacted in 1954. The Senate Report on the 1954 Code (page 318) says of §537:

It is intended that this provision will make clear that there is no requirement that the accumulated earnings be invested immediately in the business so long as there is an indication that future needs of the business require such accumulation. In any case where there exists a definite plan for the investment of earnings and profits, such corporation need not necessarily consummate these plans in a relatively short period after the close of the taxable year. However, where the future needs of the business are uncertain or vague, or the plans for the future use of the accumulations are indefinite, the amendment does not prevent application of the accumulated earnings tax.

The Senate Report also states (pages 69-70):

If the retention of earnings is justified as of the close of the taxable year, subsequent events should not be used for the purpose of showing that the retention was unreasonable in such year. However, subsequent events may be considered to determine whether the corporation actually intended to consummate the plans for which the earnings were accumulated.

For cases in which §537(a)(1) has been construed, see Motor Fuel Carriers v. United States, 559 F.2d 1348 (5th Cir. 1977) (reversing Tax Court finding that plans too indefinite though later consummated); Cheyenne Newspapers v. Commissioner, 494 F.2d 429 (10th Cir. 1974) (accumulations prohibited for contingencies that were unreasonable); Bahan Textile Machinery Co. v. United States, 453 F.2d 1100 (4th Cir. 1972) (plans too vague and loans to shareholder's relatives indicate prohibited purpose); Sterling Distributors v. United States, 313 F.2d 803 (5th Cir. 1963) (plans sufficiently definite even though later abandoned); Vulcan Steam Forging Co. v. Commissioner, 35 T.C.M. (CCH) 110 (1976) (possible relocation of business justified accumulations for three years, but not for fourth year when relocation plans were abandoned). See also Myron's Enterprises v. United States, 548 F.2d 331 (9th Cir. 1977), in which taxpayer-lessee had made offers for six years to purchase property from lessor and had, during the six years, accumulated funds for the purchase and remodeling. The court of appeals found the plans were sufficiently definite and reversed the district court, which had held that reasonable needs must be reduced by the amount the sole shareholder would have been willing to lend the corporation.

In this era of high damage awards, can a corporation claim that accumulation is necessary to protect against liability? Treas. Regs. §1.537-1(f) sets forth a list of factors for determining whether an accumulation for anticipated product liability losses is reasonable. Some of the factors include (1) previous product liability experience, (2) the extent of commercial product liability insurance, (3) the income tax consequences of the taxpayer's product liability losses, and (4) the taxpayer's future potential liability in light of reasonable expansion plans.

4. *Reasonable needs of the business: working capital needs.* The cases of

Bardahl Manufacturing Corp. v. Commissioner, 24 T.C.M. (CCH) 1030 (1965), and Bardahl International Corp. v. Commissioner, 25 T.C.M. (CCH) 935 (1966), created a statistical formula for determining the reasonably anticipated working capital needs of a business for an operating cycle. The operating cycle is the period of time required to convert cash into inventory, inventory into accounts receivable, and accounts receivable into cash. For example, if three months elapse from the purchase of the inventory to the receipt of payment in cash for the goods manufactured and sold, then the working capital needs are 25 percent of total annual operating costs and costs of goods sold. The length of the cycle depends on the type of business involved. In addition to the amount of working capital so determined, *Bardahl I* recognized the need for funds to pay for such items as the cost of plant expansion, the stockpiling of raw materials, and notes and other liabilities payable in one year (including accrued income taxes). The *Bardahl* formula is now relied on as a guide to determine permissible accumulations, but it is not always rigidly applied, Thompson Engineering Co. v. Commissioner, 80 T.C. 672 (1983) (*Bardahl* formula inappropriate to measure business needs of mechanical contractor without routine operating cycle), rev'd, 751 F.2d 191 (6th Cir. 1985) (Tax Court impermissibly substituted its judgment for that of taxpayer). In Delaware Trucking Co. v. Commissioner, 32 T.C.M. (CCH) 105 (1973), the court found as reasonable the working capital needs for one cycle plus an additional 75 percent of that amount for anticipated increased labor costs and other costs resulting from inflation. See also Hughes, Inc. v. Commissioner, 90 T.C. 1 (1988) (working capital less than business needs; no accumulated earnings tax liability).

5. *Reasonable business needs: diversification.* What is "the" business, as this term is used in §533(a)? The regulations state that a corporation's business "is not merely that which it has previously carried on but includes, in general, any line of business which it may undertake." Treas. Regs. §1.537-3(a). Does this mean that a small grocery store may aspire to become a department store or a nationwide chain of stores — or to monopolize the manufacture and sale of widgets? The regulations under the 1939 Code, Treas. Regs. 118, §39.102-3(a), included the sentence just quoted but went on to warn that "a radical change of business when a considerable surplus has been accumulated may afford evidence of a purpose to avoid the surtax." This sentence was dropped in 1959. In defining "reasonable needs," the regulations speak favorably of an accumulation "to acquire a business enterprise through purchasing stock or assets" but disapprove of "investments in properties or securities which are unrelated to the activities of the business of the taxpayer corporation." Treas. Regs. §§1.537-2(b)(2), 1.537-2(c)(4).

If the business needs of another corporation can be taken into account, must the relationship between the corporations be that of parent-subsidiary, or will a brother-sister affiliation be sufficient? See Treas. Regs.

§1.537-2(c)(3); Latchis Theaters v. Commissioner, 214 F.2d 834 (1st Cir. 1954) (accumulations to aid brother-sister corporation not sufficient reason). But compare Inland Terminals v. United States, 477 F.2d 836 (4th Cir. 1973), in which a subsidiary's accumulations to meet the business needs of its parent corporation were held to qualify as reasonable accumulations.

In Chaney & Hope, Inc. v. Commissioner, 80 T.C. 263 (1983), an individual, Mr. Hope, owned all the stock of brother-sister corporations. One corporation was engaged in the construction business; the other held large amounts of liquid assets. The brother-sister corporations were established for a variety of nontax business reasons. Both corporations agreed to indemnify the Travelers Indemnity Co., the company furnishing the bonding required on construction projects. Travelers insisted that both corporations sign the indemnity agreement. The court determined that the accumulations by one corporation to help the other corporation were unreasonable.

In *Chaney & Hope,* the court conceded that the total amount accumulated by the brother-sister corporations was reasonable in light of the bonding requirements. Why then should the taxpayer lose merely because of the nature of the corporate structure when if Mr. Hope had operated with one corporation the accumulation would have been reasonable? Note also that if the corporations had been parent-subsidiary, the accumulation would have been reasonable. Treas. Regs. §1.537-3(b). Through the attribution rules isn't every brother-sister relationship a parent-subsidiary relationship as well? See page 264 supra. Do the attribution rules apply to §531? In Hughes, Inc. v. Commissioner, 90 T.C. 1 (1988), the court held that a corporation is not liable for the accumulated earnings tax when earnings were accumulated to purchase the stock of an affiliated corporation, the taxpayer's primary customer, as part of a strategy to prevent a takeover of the purchased corporation.

6. *Reasonable business needs: payment of corporate debts.* In Helvering v. Chicago Stock Yards Co., 318 U.S. 693 (1943), involving a one-person corporation that was accumulating earnings for the purpose, among others, of paying off certain obligations of its subsidiaries, the Court suggested that the taxpayer's stockholder, had the taxpayer's surplus been distributed to him, could have equally well paid off the obligations in question. Does this suggest that despite a corporation's capital requirements, the §531 tax may be imposed if the earnings could have been distributed to the stockholders and reinvested by them in the corporation? What would this do to the reasonable business needs test in §535(c)? In Smoot Sand & Gravel Corp. v. Commissioner, 241 F.2d 197 (4th Cir. 1957), this suggestion was rejected on a showing that a distribution would have been subject to a tax rate of 89 percent in the shareholder's hands.

If at the time of organization the corporation issues both common stock and notes or bonds to its organizers, is accumulation for the retirement of the debt at or before maturity a reasonable need of the business? Note the reference in Treas. Regs. §1.537-2(b)(3) to a "sinking fund for the purpose of retiring bonds issued by the corporation." In *Chicago Stock Yards Co.*, there is a suggestion that the existence of long-term obligations might not be a satisfactory excuse for the accumulation of surplus if the obligations might be readily refinanced at the due date. Despite this suggestion, the payment of corporate debts is often regarded as a reasonable need of the business without regard to the possibility of refinancing the obligations. See, e.g., Gazette Telegraph Co. v. Commissioner, 19 T.C. 692 (1953), involving a corporation that on organization (a) issued common stock of a par value of $250,000 and 10-year promissory notes of a face amount of $250,000 to its organizers and (b) borrowed $400,000 from a bank, to acquire assets of a net value of about $900,000. Within about four years, both the notes and the bank loan were paid off. The court found that the notes were bona fide, that the capitalization was not too thin, and that the future intended repayment of the obligations was a reasonable need of the business that justified the accumulation of earnings.

7. *Reasonable needs of the business: redemptions.* In general, redemption of common or preferred stock will not be regarded as a proper reason for accumulating surplus. See Pelton Steel Casting Co. v. United States, 251 F.2d 278 (7th Cir. 1958) (accumulation to redeem majority interest shareholder not for reasonable needs of the business). Special circumstances, however, might justify an accumulation for the purpose of reducing shareholders' interests. See Gazette Publishing Co. v. Self, 103 F. Supp. 779 (E.D. Ark. 1952) (elimination of potentially disruptive minority stock interest); Mountain State Steel Foundries v. Commissioner, 284 F.2d 737 (4th Cir. 1960) (accumulation to redeem stock may be a reasonable business need). More recently, in Technalysis Corp. v. Commissioner, 101 T.C. No. 27 (1993), the court ruled that a corporation with accumulated earnings beyond its reasonable business needs was not subject to §531 when the accumulation was made to redeem shares at some future time in accordance with a general redemption plan.

See §537(a)(2) and (3) and §537(b) permitting accumulations to redeem stock under §303 (redemption to pay death taxes, etc., discussed at page 213 supra) and under the "excess business holdings" provisions applicable to tax-exempt private foundations.

Suppose *X* Corp. with accumulated earnings and profits earns $500,000 in year 5. That year *X* Corp. redeems all the stock of shareholder *A*. Assume the redemption reduces the current earnings and profits account to zero. See §312(n)(7). Prior to year 5, the accumulated earnings and profits were not deemed unreasonable. Can *X* Corp. face accumulated earnings tax liability for its year 5 activities if no earnings and profits accumulated in year 5? Recall that the base of the accumulated earnings tax is accumulated taxable income, §535, not earnings and profits for the year.

Even if the taxpayer manages to get rid of its earnings and profits for the year in question, apparently there may still be accumulated earnings tax liability. In GPD, Inc. v. Commissioner, 508 F.2d 1076 (6th Cir. 1974), the sole shareholder followed a pattern, over a period of years, of donating some of his shares of the corporation's stock to charity and later causing the corporation to redeem the stock from the charity. The redemptions in the tax year in question eliminated the corporation's current earnings and profits. The Tax Court held the accumulated earnings tax to be improper for the year. The circuit court reversed and assessed §531 liability. The court reasoned that normally, if there is no surplus cash on hand at the end of a year, there will be no accumulated earnings tax liability. Here, there was none, but there had been cash generated during that year that was found to be used for a nonbusiness purpose, i.e., the redemption of shares from the charity. Because there was accumulated taxable income for the year, the liability was imposed. A distribution of a dividend to shareholders reduces accumulated taxable income (and earnings and profits), §535(a), but a non-pro rata redemption as in GPD, Inc. does not reduce accumulated taxable income. See §§535(a), 561, and 562. For a case following GPD, Inc., see Lamark Shipping Agency, Inc. v. Commissioner, 81 T.C.M. (CCH) 284 (1981). Notwithstanding the circuit court's reasoning in GPD, Inc., it does seem odd to proclaim liability for accumulating income when the corporation has not accumulated any income for the year in question. See Doernberg, The Accumulated Earnings Tax: The Relationship between Earnings and Profits and Accumulated Taxable Income in a Redemption Transaction, 34 Fla. L. Rev. 715 (1982). Also, should accumulation for charitable purposes be treated as an impermissible purpose under the statute?

8. *The minimum accumulated earnings credit.* By virtue of §535(c)(2), a corporation may accumulate up to $250,000 of earnings and profits (overall, not annually) without being subject to the accumulated earnings tax. Of course, accumulation in excess of $250,000 is permitted if the taxpayer can show the accumulation is necessary to meet the reasonable needs of the business. Only the $250,000 minimum credit, however, is allowed to a corporation that is a "mere holding or investment company," §535(c)(3). Section 535(c)(1) does not allow these companies to accumulate based on the reasonable needs of the business. See Rev. Rul. 77-368, 1977-2 C.B. 201 (need for liquidity cannot be considered for investment or holding company).

When the Economic Recovery Tax Act of 1981 increased the minimum credit from $150,000 to $250,000, the $150,000 credit was retained for corporations whose "principal function . . . is the performance of services in the field of health, law, engineering, architecture, accounting, actuarial science, performing arts, or consulting." Why do these corporations receive a smaller credit than a mere investment corporation that has no business whatsoever?

To discourage the multiplication of corporate entities as a means of multiplying the allowable credit, §1551 was amended to apply to the accumulated earnings credit as well as to limit the use of the lower corporate rates. Moreover, if an affiliated group of corporations claims the 100 percent deduction for intracorporate dividends, the group is entitled to only one $250,000 minimum accumulated earnings credit. §243(b).

9. *Publicly held corporations and the accumulated earnings tax.* How likely is it that §531 will be applied to a publicly held corporation? See Trico Products Corp. v. Commissioner, 137 F.2d 424 (2d Cir. 1943), and Trico Products Corp. v. McGowan, 169 F.2d 343 (2d Cir. 1948), in which, although there were more than 2,000 stockholders, six stockholders owned about two-thirds of the total shares. After the taxpayer paid a total of about $3.2 million in §531 surtaxes and interest, a minority stockholder brought a stockholder's derivative action against the directors for subjecting the corporation to the §531 penalty. The action was settled by a payment of about $2.5 million by the defendants to the corporation. See Mahler v. Trico Products Corp., 296 N.Y. 902, 72 N.E. 622 (1947).

See Golconda Mining Corp. v. Commissioner, 507 F.2d 594 (9th Cir. 1974), in which it was held that the accumulated earnings tax could not be applied to a publicly held company unless a small group of shareholders controlled at least 50 percent of its stock. The position of the IRS is that, in an appropriate case, there is no legal impediment in applying §531 to a publicly held corporation. See Rev. Rul. 75-305, 1975-2 C.B. 228. Apparently, Congress agreed with the IRS. In 1984 Congress enacted §532(c), which states that the accumulated earnings tax may be imposed on a corporation without regard to the number of shareholders. The Conference Report (at page 829) indicates, however, that it may be difficult to establish the requisite tax avoidance motive in the case of a widely held operating company in which no individual or group has legal or effective control.

In Techanalysis Corp. v. Commissioner, 101 T.C. No. 27 (1993), the court in dicta commented that widely held corporations can be subject to the accumulated earnings tax if the proscribed purposes exist. Technalysis itself had approximately 1,500 shareholders, and approximately 30 percent of the stock was held by the five members of the board of directors.

B. PERSONAL HOLDING COMPANY TAX

The personal holding company tax is another weapon that the Commissioner has, along with the accumulated earnings tax, to curtail the practice of accumulating profits in a corporation to avoid individual tax rates. The tax was enacted in 1934 to reach passive investment income and personal services earnings that are allowed to accumulate in a corporation. The personal holding company tax is a mechanical one, and tax avoidance motives are irrelevant or statutorily presumed. It therefore is possible to stumble unwittingly into being a personal holding company.

Two tests are applied to determine if income is personal holding company income: the stock ownership test and the income test. The tax generally applies to closely held corporations since, under the stock ownership test, more than 50 percent of the value of the stock must be owned directly or indirectly by five or fewer individuals. To make the ownership determination, the attribution rules of §544 apply. Under the income test at least 60 percent of "adjusted ordinary gross income" must be personal holding company income under §543(a), a term discussed in the Notes following the principal cases.

The rate of tax imposed on undistributed personal holding company income is 39.6 percent. Because the purpose of the tax is not to raise revenue but to encourage dividend distributions from personal holding companies, relief is available under the dividends-paid deduction and the deficiency dividend provisions. See Note 4 following the principal cases. The cases that follow illustrate the difficulties in determining what constitutes personal holding company income.

Thomas P. Byrnes, Inc. v. Commissioner —————————
73 T.C. 416 (1979)

NIMS, Judge. . . .

FINDINGS OF FACT . . .

Thomas P. Byrnes (Byrnes) has been petitioner's president [and controlling shareholder] since its inception. As a result of his experience with the Fram Corp. and the Detroit Gasket Manufacturing Co. Byrnes had acquired knowledge regarding the application and use of oil filters and gaskets, particularly in the automotive industry. In 1956, Byrnes became employed by the Goshen Rubber Co. (Goshen) as one of its sales representatives.

Goshen manufactures precision automobile filter gaskets. Due to his prior sales experience, Byrnes' expertise was especially well suited to Goshen's needs. By the time of the commencement of his relationship with Goshen, Byrnes had developed contacts in the filter industry in addition to having obtained a detailed and technical knowledge of precision automobile filter gaskets. Consequently, he has assisted Goshen in engineering many of its filter gaskets. He has also been one of Goshen's largest sales producers.

Byrnes sold Goshen's products as a sole proprietor between 1956 and April 16, 1963, the date of petitioner's incorporation. Byrnes by then had decided to conduct his sales business in corporate form in order to limit any potential product liability resulting from the sale of Goshen's products and to improve his tax situation, especially by way of a better pension plan. During the 3 years in issue, petitioner's only employees have been Byrnes and a secretary. . . .

On April 14, 1972, petitioner and Goshen executed a . . . written contract. Like the previous agreement between petitioner and Goshen, nowhere was Byrnes individually named or described. This contract stated, in pertinent part:

Termination Policy

3.   In the event GRC any time hereafter shall determine that Representative is either unwilling or incapable of making satisfactory presentation and explanation of the technical features of Company's products, to customers and prospective customers, or, is unwilling or unable technically to reasonably assist such customers in the adaptation of GRC products to the intended use thereof by customer, or, in the event GRC shall determine that Representative has been disloyal in any respect, specifically including the furnishing directly or indirectly of "know how" and technical information to competitors of GRC, has been dishonest or has committed a crime involving moral turpitude, or, for any other reason adjudged by Company to be detrimental to the best interests of Company, in any of such events, GRC shall have the absolute right to forthwith terminate the within Agreement. In such event, Representative's termination pay will be limited to and based upon commissions accrued to the date of such termination, including shipments made on the date of such termination and none thereafter. . . .

Miscellaneous

2.   Representative shall not hire or in any manner engage the services of additional sales personnel to call on GRC customers in the territory assigned to Representative without first discussing it with the Sales Manager or Vice President in charge of sales of GRC. . . .

. . . Petitioner and Goshen entered into revised contracts on October 30, 1975, and on March 1, 1976. These contracts were similar to the 1972 contract although they did not contain paragraph number 2 under the "Miscellaneous" heading quoted above. The following paragraphs are from both of these contracts:

Relationship Created

1.   The Representative is not an employee of the principal for any purpose whatsoever but is an independent Sales Representative. The Company is interested only in the results obtained by the Representative who shall have sole control of the manner and means of performing under the Contract. However, the Company in unusual situations shall have the right to request Representative to collect accounts, investigate consumer complaints, attend

sales meetings, periodically report to GRC, conform to any policy of selling effort, follow prescribed itineraries, keep records of business transactions and make adjustments. . . .

Any new salesman may be required to visit GRC affiliated plants at the direction of GRC for instruction and to satisfactorily pass such oral or written examination in these areas prior to being qualified to represent GRC in the sales area. . . .

OPINION

The issue for our decision is whether the sales commissions petitioner received for the sale of Goshen's products represented personal holding company income within the meaning of section 543(a)(7). The parties have stipulated that the stock ownership requirement of section 542(a)(2) is satisfied.

It is respondent's position that Goshen had the right to designate the individual(s) who would perform the services required by the sales representation contracts and, in effect, designated Byrnes. Petitioner maintains that Goshen had no such right and did not designate Byrnes.

At the outset, we should make note of what we are not required to decide in this case. We are not required to decide whether Byrnes retained such control over the commission income received by petitioner as to cause such income to be taxable to Byrnes under section 61, and not to petitioner. Cf. Foglesong v. Commissioner, T.C. Memo. 1976-294.* Unlike the situation in *Foglesong*, Byrnes, individually, is not a party to this proceeding. Thus, lacking an essential actor in the drama before us, we must make do with what we have, and for reasons stated below, we hold for petitioner.

Respondent contends that Goshen, in effect, possessed a veto power over petitioner's ability to hire either additional sales personnel or a replacement for Byrnes. According to respondent, this veto power amounted to a right to designate under section 543(a)(7) and was manifested by: . . . the clause in the 1972 contract requiring prior discussion; and the clauses in the 1975 and 1976 contracts that empowered Goshen to require new sales personnel to visit one of its plants to undergo instruction and testing. . . .

The 1972 contract is the most important one in terms of our decision since it covers most of the period in question. In this contract, petitioner was no longer required to obtain Goshen's written permission in order to hire a new employee. A prior discussion with the sales manager or vice president of sales was all that was required. This language does not give Goshen the right to designate the individual(s) who would perform under

---

* The memorandum decision in *Foglesong* was only the first phase of a protracted litigation. The decision was reversed in Foglesong v. Commissioner, 621 F.2d 865 (7th Cir. 1980). See the discussion of the Foglesong v. Commissioner litigation at page 678 infra. — EDS.

the contract. Joseph Lantz, Goshen's senior vice president and former vice president in charge of sales and marketing, testified that these discussions were generally informal and often held long after the new employee had been selling Goshen products, so that several topics might be considered at the same meeting. Lantz testified:

> all of our representatives, they are commission salesmen. They pay all their own expenses. We don't help with their expenses, their entertainment or anything. And, as such, they are independent operators according to our legal people. So they have a right to hire and fire who they choose. All we wanted to do is be certain that the customers are serviced properly so we can maintain our position in the industry. So when we discussed it with him, it's up to him to do the investigation for new personnel.
>
> If you look at the caliber of our representatives, you'll find that we had extreme confidence in their judgment and it wasn't necessary for me to pass on any new applicant.

The testing requirement in the 1975 and 1976 contracts likewise does not confer on Goshen the right to designate who will perform. These clauses merely allow Goshen to insure that those who sell its products are technically qualified to do so.

Respondent also argues that each of these contracts designates Byrnes as the individual who would perform the services. Granted that Byrnes was the driving force behind petitioner's operations, nowhere in any of the agreements is he designated, either by name or description, as the individual who would perform under the contract. Only petitioner was bound to perform after its incorporation.

The cases cited by both parties support this analysis. In General Management Corp. v. Commissioner, 46 B.T.A. 738 (1942), aff'd, 135 F.2d 882 (7th Cir. 1943), cert. denied 320 U.S. 757 (1943), a contract between petitioner and another corporation expressly named a 50-percent shareholder of the petitioner as the specific individual to perform comptroller services for the other corporation. There was also a clause providing for termination of the contract if the individual died and the corporation receiving the services could not find a satisfactory replacement. On these essential facts, the Board had no difficulty in finding personal holding company income.

In Allen Machinery Corp. v. Commissioner, 31 T.C. 441 (1958), the contract that was held to generate personal service income was made directly with an individual and was subsequently assigned to the taxpayer-corporation. There, it was evident that the third-party corporation was looking to the individual, personally, for performance: in the event of an assignment, the contract provided for cancellation if the individual ceased to control or furnish advice to the assignee corporation. Again, the individual in question was specifically named in the contract.

In Able Metal Products, Inc. v. Commissioner, 32 T.C. 1149 (1959), another case holding that the contract resulted in personal holding company income, the shareholders were specifically designated by name and were required to personally supervise the services which the corporation would render. Further, the third-party corporation could terminate the contract if the individuals terminated their interests in or employment with the corporation.

The contract in Kurt Frings Agency, Inc. v. Commissioner, 42 T.C. 472 (1964), aff'd per curiam, 351 F.2d 951 (9th Cir. 1965), involved an individual who represented various clients in the entertainment field as their manager. The Court held that amounts received pursuant to the contract resulted in personal holding company income since the manager was specifically designated by name in the contracts as the individual specified to perform the required services.

It is apparent from the above cases that petitioner's contracts with Goshen did not produce personal holding company income within the meaning of section 543(a)(7). There is no specific naming of Byrnes individually as the one who was obligated to perform under the various sales representation agreements. Byrnes' failure to supervise the work petitioner had contracted to perform would not, in and of itself, provide the basis for a breach of contract action as would have been the case in *Kurt Frings*. Likewise, there is no clause expressly requiring Byrnes' continued employment with, or interest in, petitioner similar to the one in *Able*. If, for example, Byrnes had sold his interest to his son, Goshen would not thereby have possessed the right to terminate the contract simply because Byrnes was no longer rendering his services on behalf of the petitioner.

Respondent's attempts to distinguish S. O. Claggett v. Commissioner, 44 T.C. 503 (1965), and Foglesong v. Commissioner, supra, two cases finding an absence of personal holding company income, are without merit. In *Claggett*, an individual and a corporation formed a partnership. The individual subsequently formed a corporation which was substituted as partner under the partnership agreement. The Commissioner argued that the partnership agreement constituted a personal service contract under section 543(a)(7), and that the individual, Sam Claggett, was personally obligated to perform services for the original corporate partner by reason of the prior agreement. Contrary to respondent's interpretation of *Claggett*, the Court did not hold that the partnership agreement failed to constitute a personal service contract under section 543(a)(7). That issue was left open. Rather, the Court based its decision on the lack of designation since there was no contractual provision "specifying by name or description that Sam would be the person to perform the services."

Foglesong involved a situation similar to the instant case: the contract obligated a closely held corporation to perform services under a sales representation contract. The Court held that contract did not beget personal holding company income. Since the contract was with the corporation, it, and not the individual shareholder, was the party obligated to perform.

Respondent has insisted that we adopt a finding similar to the one expressed in Rev. Rul. 75-67, 1975-1 C.B. 169, namely that a taxpayer, by agreeing to perform services that are so unique (via a specific individual) as to preclude substitution, has effectuated the individual's designation. We cannot accept this characterization of Byrnes' services. Byrnes did play an important role in Goshen's sales operations, and his services were indeed valuable. It cannot, however, be said that his services were so valuable and unique as to be irreplaceable.

Respondent has maintained that the contracts before us clearly demonstrate the intent of the parties that Byrnes would personally act as petitioner's sales representative in this technical field. We fail to perceive such intent. The most reliable evidence of this intent surely would have been a specific designation of Byrnes in the contract. Although the parties anticipated that he would be rendering his services on petitioner's behalf, there simply was no contractual obligation for him to do so. The mere expectation that Byrnes would be the individual to carry on the expected activities on behalf of Goshen, without specific designation thereof, is insufficient to transform the amounts received into personal holding company income.

We hold that the commissions received were not personal holding income under section 543(a)(7). As a result, petitioner is not subject to personal holding company tax under section 541.

Decision will be entered for the petitioner.

Kenyatta Corp. v. Commissioner _____
86 T.C. 171 (1986), aff'd, 812 F.2d 577 (9th Cir. 1987)

FEATHERSTON, Judge: . . .

FINDINGS OF FACT

BACKGROUND

. . . Petitioner was incorporated under the laws of the State of Washington on July 9, 1973. However, no organizational meeting was held for petitioner, and no stock certificates were ever issued. Each year from its inception through the close of its 1978 fiscal year, petitioner's president was William F. Russell (hereinafter Russell).

Russell, a former professional basketball player, has long been a well known and highly regarded sports personality. Since 1969, following his retirement from professional basketball, Russell has been employed, first by Felton Productions and later by petitioner, to provide a variety of his own personal services. These services included hosting radio talk shows, making personal appearances, lecturing on college campuses, sportscasting, writing newspaper columns, coaching and managing a professional basketball team, speaking on radio and television programs, and performing services for various advertising and promotional efforts. . . .

OPINION

The only issue to be decided is whether petitioner was a personal holding company within the meaning of section 542(a) during 1978 and is, therefore, subject to the personal holding company tax. A corporation is a personal holding company if it meets a stock ownership test and a "tainted income" test which are specified in section 542(a). . . .

STOCK OWNERSHIP TEST

The stock ownership test prescribed by section 542(a)(2) is satisfied if, at any time during the last half of the taxable year, more than 50 percent in value of the corporation's outstanding stock is owned, directly or indirectly, by or for not more than five individuals. Petitioner argues that because no stock certificates were issued, the corporation does not meet the requirements of the stock ownership test. However, the issuance of stock certificates is not determinative of stock ownership for purposes of section 542(a)(2). Section 1.542-3(b), Income Tax Regs.; Collateral Equities Trust v. Commissioner, 39 B.T.A. 834, 839-840 (1939). Furthermore, Covey, the attorney responsible for organizing petitioner, testified that Russell was intended to be the majority stockholder in the corporation and that the majority of the equity in petitioner belonged to Russell in "some unfocused way."

More important, petitioner's articles of incorporation show that it had only one class of stock, and its 1978 tax return designated Russell as holder of 100 percent of petitioner's voting stock. This sworn statement of voting stock ownership is an admission to which we give substantial weight. Waring v. Commissioner, 412 F.2d 800, 801 (3d Cir. 1969), affg. per curiam a Memorandum Opinion of this Court; Times Tribune Co. v. Commissioner, 20 T.C. 449, 452 (1953). Finally, nothing in the record establishes that anyone other than Russell owned any of petitioner's outstanding stock at any time during its 1978 fiscal year.

In light of petitioner's admission under oath and its failure to carry its burden of proving that someone other than Russell owned the majority of petitioner's outstanding stock, we find that at least 50 percent of the value of petitioner's outstanding stock was owned by not more than five individuals within the meaning of section 542(a)(2).

TAINTED INCOME TEST

The tainted income test provided by section 542(a)(1) is met if at least 60 percent of the corporation's "adjusted ordinary gross income" for the taxable year constitutes "personal holding company income." Section 543(a), which defines personal holding company income, provides in pertinent part:

> (a)   General Rule. — For purposes of this subtitle, the term "personal holding company income" means the portion of the adjusted ordinary gross income which consists of: . . .
>
>> (7)   Personal service contracts. —
>>
>> (A)   Amounts received under a contract under which the corporation is to furnish personal services; if some person other than the corporation has the right to designate (by name or by description) the individual who is to perform the services, or if the individual who is to perform the services is designated (by name or by description) in the contract; and
>>
>> (B)   amounts received from the sale or other disposition of such a contract.
>
> This paragraph shall apply with respect to amounts received for services under a particular contract only if at some time during the taxable year 25 percent or more in value of the outstanding stock of the corporation is owned, directly or indirectly, by or for the individual who has performed, is to perform, or may be designated (by name or by description) as the one to perform, such services.

Petitioner contends, first, that petitioner's income did not arise from personal service contracts within the meaning of section 543(a)(7), and, alternatively, to the extent petitioner had income from personal service contracts which would constitute personal holding company income, such income did not equal 60 percent or more of its adjusted ordinary gross income.

Determination of whether a contract is a personal service contract again requires examination of the contract under two statutory tests. The flush language of section 543(a)(7) requires that the designated person (herein Russell) own at least 25 percent of the corporation's stock at some time during the taxable year (stock ownership test). We have found as a fact that Russell owned at least 50 percent in value of petitioner's stock; therefore, this test is met.

The stock ownership test having been met, we turn now to the language of section 543(a)(7)(A), which requires that the individual who is to perform the services be designated, by name or description, in the contract or that such individual can be so designated by some person other than the corporation (designation test). We will examine each contract separately to determine whether it meets this requirement.

1.   Seattle SuperSonics

During 1977, Russell was employed by FNI, then owner of the Sonics, as coach and general manager of the professional basketball team. Russell's employment was covered under two separate contracts, a coaching agreement between FNI and Russell himself, and a public relations agreement between FNI and petitioner. The public relations agreement obligated petitioner to provide Russell's services in connection with certain public relations activities for the Sonics, including a series of pre-game radio programs. The public relations agreement . . . designates Russell by name as the individual who was to perform the services and states its purpose in naming Russell. Because the public relations agreement designates Russell by name as the individual to perform the services, the contract meets the designation test under section 543(a)(7). General Management Corp. v. Commissioner, 46 B.T.A. 738, 747 (1942), affd. 135 F.2d 882 (7th Cir. 1943); Kurt Frings Agency, Inc. v. Commissioner, 42 T.C. 472, 478-479 (1964), affd. per curiam 351 F.2d 951 (9th Cir. 1965).

Petitioner's argument with respect to the public relations agreement is based entirely on attacking the validity of the document itself. Petitioner does not contend that the document, which was signed by or on behalf of both parties, is completely false but that the document upon which our findings are based is an interim draft which does not represent the "final agreement" of the parties.

Petitioner contends that Russell was not designated by name or description in the final agreement between the parties because other sports personalities were substituted for Russell when he was unavailable for or unwilling to make certain personal appearances. While we have found as a fact that petitioner made such substitutions, that fact does not prove petitioner's point. First, it is not clear from the record that the substitutions for Russell were made with respect to appearances covered by petitioner's agreement with FNI. The testimony of both Russell and Dias indicate that petitioner was in the business of providing talent for speaking engagements and public appearances, which may or may not have been associated with the Sonics or FNI. Second, the public relations agreement, as we read it, does not preclude such substitutions.

Finally, if the public relations agreement admitted in evidence is not the final agreement between the parties, as petitioner contends, petitioner has not met its burden of proving that the final agreement between petitioner and FNI by its terms did not designate Russell as the individual who was to perform the services. Rule 142(a).

2.   KIRO-TV

The issue with respect to Russell's employment with KIRO-TV is not whether the contract designated Russell by name or description, but whether the contract for Russell's services was between KIRO-TV and Russell or between KIRO-TV and petitioner. If the agreement was made with Russell personally, the income therefrom would be properly taxable to Russell and would not qualify as petitioner's personal holding company income. Sec. 543(a), (b). We think the weight of evidence shows that the contract for Russell's services was between KIRO-TV and Russell personally.

First, we note that the contract governing Russell's employment with KIRO-TV was not produced at trial. However, the program director for KIRO-TV at that time testified that the contract was with Russell personally, that he had no knowledge of petitioner at the time his station contracted with Russell, and that he was never asked to pay petitioner in connection with Russell's services. Rather, payments for Russell's services were by checks made payable to him personally. Based on the foregoing, we find that the agreement with KIRO-TV for Russell's services was made with him personally; and, therefore, the payments from KIRO-TV do not constitute personal holding company income to petitioner.

3. ABC Sports

In 1977, petitioner contracted with ABC Sports to provide Russell's services as commentator, host, co-host, expert analyst, interviewer, and the like in connection with television sports and news programs. During its 1978 fiscal year, petitioner received payments totaling $53,145.05 pursuant to its agreement with ABC Sports. Petitioner admits that the contract with ABC Sports specifically designated Russell as the person who was to perform the services and that the income from their agreement is "tainted income."

4. Seattle Times

In September 1977, petitioner agreed to furnish Russell's services in providing material for a weekly column to appear in the Seattle Times. With respect to petitioner's agreement with the Seattle Times, petitioner relies on section 1.543-1(b)(8)(ii), Income Tax Regs., in arguing that the services of other individuals were "important and essential" to the contract; and, therefore, the amounts attributable to their services should not be included in personal holding company income. We disagree.

The Regulation was interpreted by this Court in Kurt Frings Agency, Inc. v. Commissioner, 42 T.C. 472 (1964), affd. per curiam 351 F.2d 951 (9th Cir. 1965). The taxpayer in that case was a corporation engaged in the business of representing various clients in the entertainment field as their manager. Each contract executed between the taxpayer and the various artists designated "Kurt Frings," the sole stockholder, as the individual required to personally supervise the artists' business. The taxpayer also employed a number of subagents who represented and negotiated contracts for some of the artists under contract. The taxpayer argued that the services performed by its subagents were "important and essential" within the meaning of section 1.543-1(b)(8)(ii), Income Tax Regs., and, therefore, an allocation must be made to determine the income attributable to the services performed by Kurt Frings. The taxpayer relied on the following language from the Regulation:

> [T]he contract, is addition to requiring the performance of services by a 25-percent stockholder who is designated . . . requires the performance of services by other persons which are important and essential. . . .

This Court found that the controlling word in the Regulation is "requires" and that the word must be given its ordinary and common meaning. Because the contracts designated Kurt Frings and required no other persons to perform the services, the Court held that the contract was a personal service contract within the meaning of section 543(a)(7).

Nowhere in the Seattle Times contract are the services of anyone other than Russell required; rather, the agreement specifies that Russell will perform all terms and conditions under the contract. In addition, petitioner produced no evidence to indicate that the Seattle Times knew of or even contemplated the use of "ghost writers" for the columns. Based on the record in the instant case and in keeping with our earlier interpretation of the Regulation, we find that the Seattle Times contract did not require the services of others which were important and essential.

5. Cole & Weber

In 1977, petitioner received $15,000 from Cole & Weber, an advertising and public relations firm, as a talent fee for Russell's services in connection with a series of television commercials for a local dairy company. The commercials featured Russell and Jack Patera, then coach of the Seattle Seahawks, and depicted Russell as Patera's "shape up" coach encouraging him to become physically fit through exercise and dieting. No contract between Cole & Weber and Petitioner for Russell's talent was produced at trial. Payment for Russell's services was made by check payable to petitioner, and Covey included the payment in his bank deposits and disbursements list referred to in our findings. Cole & Weber billed the dairy company for "Talent — Bill Russell" in the amount of $15,000.

Petitioner's primary contention is that Russell's talent was not unique and petitioner could have substituted the services of other individuals to appear in the commercials. However, we think the evidence clearly demonstrates that Russell's talents were unique and substitution would not have been possible. The entire campaign involved Russell, who only months before coached the Sonics, "coaching" Patera, then coach of the Seahawks, to lose weight. The advertisement would not have been as clever or as amusing had someone other than Russell acted as Patera's "shape up" coach. Newspaper advertisements promoting the television commercials featured pictures of both coaches, one stating: "It takes all Bill Russell's skill to get Jack Patera to stick to his diet and exercise," and a Seattle

Times column concerning the campaign was entitled "Getting in Shape with Two Coaches."

In any event, petitioner has not sustained its burden of proof on this issue. Because Russell performed the services for Cole & Weber, petitioner must show that Russell was not designated, by name or description, in the contract and that petitioner had the right to designate, by name or description, the person to perform the services. Sec. 543(a)(7)(A); Rule 142(a). Petitioner failed to produce the agreement governing the advertising campaign or to present evidence to support its position.

PERSONAL HOLDING COMPANY INCOME COMPUTATION

Pursuant to our foregoing analysis of the five agreements under which petitioner received income during its 1978 fiscal year, we have found that the following amounts were derived from personal service contracts and, therefore, constitute personal holding company income to petitioner:

Contract	Personal Holding Company Income
Seattle Supersonics	$20,833.30
ABC Sports	53,145.05
Seattle Times	4,750.00
Cole & Weber	15,000.00
Total	$93,728.35

A corporation is not a personal holding Company, within the meaning of section 542(a), unless at least 60 percent of its adjusted ordinary gross income for the taxable year is personal holding income. According to its tax return, petitioner's adjusted ordinary gross income for its 1978 fiscal year is $138,895. Because petitioner's personal holding company income of $93,728.35 exceeds 60 percent ($83,337) of petitioner's adjusted ordinary gross income, petitioner is a personal holding company subject to the personal holding company tax imposed by section 541. . . .

NOTE

1. *Sixty percent of adjusted gross income test.* Since 1964 the income test has required that at least 60 percent of the corporation's adjusted ordinary gross income for the taxable year be personal holding company income. Before 1964, the comparable requirement was 80 percent. To compute adjusted ordinary gross income, ordinary gross income is first defined by excluding from gross income the gains from the sale or other disposition of capital assets and §1231(b) assets. §543(b)(1). Then adjustments to ordinary gross income are made by subtracting depreciation, taxes, interest, and rent from rental income and mineral royalties. §543(b)(2). These

adjustments are intended to determine whether the rental activities substantially contribute to the corporation's net income or constitute high
gross/low net income activities, engaged in to minimize the importance
of the corporation's other personal holding company income. Under
§543(b)(2)(C) interest on condemnation awards, judgments, and tax refunds and interest earned by certain dealers in U.S. securities is also excluded. The following items are included in adjusted ordinary gross
income: dividends, interest, royalties including special rules for mineral,
oil, and gas royalties and copyright royalties, produced film rents, rental
payments from a 25 percent or more shareholder, personal service contract
payments, and income from trusts and estates.

Under §542(b), corporations filing consolidated returns are on a consolidated basis eliminating intragroup dividends and interest. Interest that
is includible in adjusted ordinary gross income includes imputed interest
under §483 and probably original issue discount, Treas. Regs. §§1.1232-
3A(a) and 1.279-2(b)(2).

2. *Personal holding company income.* Section 543(a) is the product of
congressional efforts to distinguish the "tainted" personal holding company income from income that offers a "legitimate" reason to operate in
corporate form.

Why does the taxpayer win in *Byrnes* and lose in *Kenyatta*? Isn't it as
clear in *Byrnes* as it is in *Kenyatta* that anyone contracting with the personal
service corporation was really contracting for the services of the corporation's shareholder? Do these cases exalt form over substance? In RAS of
Sand River, Inc. v. Commissioner, 935 F.2d 270 (6th Cir. 1991), the taxpayer was wholly owned by a single individual. Although a written contract
between the taxpayer and its customer for engineering services did not
designate a particular person to perform the work or give the customer
the right to designate who would perform the services, the court found
that an oral agreement with the customer required the sole shareholder
to perform the engineering services. The court was not influenced by the
fact that the shareholder's services were not unique or irreplaceable.

Other categories of personal holding company income pose difficult
interpretation problems as well. In Allied Industrial Cartage Co. v. Commissioner, 647 F.2d 713 (6th Cir. 1981), an individual owned all the stock in
two corporations — one of which leased trucks and real estate to the
other corporation. The Service argued that the rental income was personal
holding company income under §543(a)(6). The court held that the use
of the rental property could not be attributed to the individual because a
business nexus existed for the corporate arrangement and no personal
benefit accrued to the shareholder. See also Silverman & Sons Realty Trust
v. Commissioner, 620 F.2d 314 (1st Cir. 1980).

In *Allied Industrial Cartage,* the contours of §543(a)(6) were at issue.
That provision is aimed at rents paid by shareholders to a corporation for
the use of an incorporated yacht, country home, or similar property. Can

a shareholder avoid §543(a)(6) by arranging for a controlled corporation to rent the property? See the discussion of disguised dividends at page 142 supra.

Section 543(a)(2) treats certain other rental payments as personal holding company income. To distinguish an active rental business from passive rental receipts, the provision invokes a special formula. The adjusted income from rents is included as personal holding company income unless the rents amount to 50 percent or more of adjusted ordinary gross income (an "active" rental business) and the dividends paid at least equal the amount by which nonrent personal holding company income for the year exceeds 10 percent of its ordinary gross income. (Who dreams up these formulas?) If a taxpayer fails the numerical tests, can it still argue that the rental business is "active" by demonstrating a high level of services rendered in connection with the rental activities? See Eller v. Commissioner, 77 T.C. 934 (1981) (income from operation of commercial shopping center and mobile home park was personal holding company income despite level of services in which §543(a)(2) tests were not met; exhaustive review of the area).

Copyright royalties are considered personal holding company income under §543(a)(4). See Irving Berlin Music Corp. v. United States, 487 F.2d 540 (Cl. Ct. 1973), in which licensing receipts were found to be royalties for use of copyright property, subject to tax as personal holding company income, and not compensation for services. Cf. Rev. Rul. 75-202, 1975-1 C.B. 170, in which a transfer of the exclusive right to a copyright, subject to a contingent reversion, was held a sale and therefore did not give rise to personal holding company income.

Other categories of personal holding company income include dividends, interest, royalties (other than royalties from minerals, oil, gas, or copyrights), and annuities (§543(a)(1)); mineral, oil, and gas royalties (§543(a)(3)); produced film rents (§543(a)(5)); and income from trusts and estates (§543(a)(8)).

It is not always easy to distinguish royalties from other payments. In Dothan Coca-Cola Bottling Co. v. United States, 745 F.2d 1400 (11th Cir. 1984), the court held that amounts paid to the taxpayer by subbottlers constituted rent for the use of tangible real and personal property rather than royalties for the use of the taxpayer's franchise. The payments were 20 cents per gallon of Coke syrup sold by the taxpayer to the subbottlers. While adjusted income from rents can constitute personal holding company income, the Service conceded that the rents did not meet the personal holding company income requirements of §543(a)(2).

An area of recent interest concerns whether income received by a computer software company from licensing arrangements is personal holding company income. Prior to the Tax Reform Act of 1986, all royalties were considered personal holding company income regardless of the taxpayer's level of involvement in the activity. See Priv. Ltr. Rul. 8450025. The

Tax Reform Act of 1986 amended §543(a)(1) to except certain software royalties if the corporation receiving the royalties (1) is actively engaged in the business of developing computer software, (2) derives at least 50 percent of its gross income from such software, (3) incurs substantial trade or business expenses, and (4) distributes most of its passive income other than the royalties. See §543(a)(1) and (d).

3. *Stock ownership test.* Recall that in addition to the personal holding company income requirement, there is also a stock requirement — that at any time during the last half of the taxable year, more than 50 percent in value of the corporation's outstanding stock is owned, directly or indirectly, by or for not more than five individuals. §543(a)(2). Some trusts and tax-exempt organizations are considered "individuals" under §543(a)(2), presumably because they are susceptible to domination by the other corporate shareholders. Note that if fewer than 10 shareholders own a corporation, the stock ownership test is automatically satisfied.

The "directly or indirectly" language of §543(a)(2) is a dead giveaway that attribution rules apply. Section 544 provides the applicable rules that differ in some respects from §318. For example, there is attribution between siblings and no 50 percent threshold for attribution from corporations.

4. *Dividends-paid deduction; deficiency dividend procedure.* Under §545, the base for the tax is the corporation's taxable income with certain adjustments. The adjustments include decreasing taxable income by the amount of taxes paid, net capital gains reported, and the dividends-paid deduction described in §561. That provision incorporates the dividends-paid deduction (the sum of dividends paid during the taxable year and within two and one-half months of the last day of the taxable year to a limited extent), consent dividends determined under §565, and the dividend carryover of §564. Dividends paid in property will qualify for a reduction under Treas. Regs. §1.562-1(a) to the extent of the property's adjusted basis at the time of distribution. This regulation was upheld in Fulman v. United States, 434 U.S. 528 (1978). Are *Fulman* and the regulation still sound law in light of the changes in §311 brought about by the Tax Reform Act of 1986? If a corporation's taxable income is increased on the distribution of appreciated property, shouldn't the dividends-paid deduction be an amount equal to the adjusted basis plus any gain recognized to the corporation on the distribution? See §312(b). Otherwise the distribution of appreciated property may actually increase a corporation's personal holding company tax liability.

After the corporation's liability for personal holding company tax has been determined, it may mitigate or eliminate tax liability under the deficiency dividend procedure of §547, but the liability for interest and penalties is not eliminated by this procedure. Section 547 permits the corporation to make a dividend distribution to shareholders on which the shareholders are taxed currently, and the corporation may use this distribution to reduce its already determined past personal holding company liability.

5. *Foreign personal holding companies.* Foreign personal holding companies are dealt with by §§551-558. Because the corporation itself is thought to be beyond U.S. jurisdiction, each U.S. stockholder is taxed directly on his proportionate share of the corporation's undistributed income. Taxing the stockholder on undistributed income was held constitutional in Eder v. Commissioner, 138 F.2d 27 (2d Cir. 1943), despite the fact that the undistributed income was "blocked" and could not have been transferred to the United States. In 1962 this technique was used to tax some U.S. shareholders of so-called controlled foreign corporations on some of the corporation's undistributed income. §§951 et seq.

6. *Regulated investment companies, mutual funds, and real estate investment trusts.* Certain regulated investment companies (including mutual funds) may elect under subchapter M (§§851-855) to be subject to corporate taxation on only their undistributed income. These corporations, which must distribute currently at least 90 percent of their income, are treated as conduits through which the income from investments passes to their stockholders, and their long-term capital gains retain that character on distribution to the stockholders.

Sections 856-858 provide that certain real estate investment trusts (REITS) that distribute a specified percentage of current income shall be treated as corporations, with the important exception that distributed income is to be taxed to the beneficiaries rather than to the trust. The conduit concept is patterned on the treatment of regulated investment companies. The rules relating to and the treatments of investment companies and REITS differ in important ways from those corporations electing subchapter S, discussed in Chapter 16.

C. COLLAPSIBLE CORPORATIONS

To make sense of §341, the collapsible corporation provision, it is necessary to recall the tax laws existing prior to the Tax Reform Act of 1986. Recall, specifically, that under former §336, a liquidating corporation normally did not recognize gain on a liquidating distribution. Add to that the fact that there existed a substantial capital gains/ordinary income differential. Those two factors paved the way for a perceived misuse of corporate form to turn ordinary income into capital gains.

Suppose a film producer formed a corporation, exchanging $50,000 for all the corporate stock. The film was produced by the corporation and had a fair market value of $550,000. The exhibition profit would be taxed as ordinary income to the corporation, which is in the trade or business of producing motion pictures. The shareholder would have ordinary income on the distribution of proceeds. Suppose instead that the producer liquidates the corporation. Under §§331 and 334(a), the producer would recognize a $500,000 capital gain and take a $550,000 basis in the film. Under former §336, there was no gain to the liquidating corporation. By amortizing the basis in the film against the expected rentals, the producer could avoid any ordinary income recognition. Note that if this series of transactions were respected for tax purposes, the producer would have avoided ordinary income at the corporate level and again at the shareholder level, reporting only a single capital gain.

It was this conversion of ordinary income to capital gain that led to enactment of the collapsible corporation provision in 1958. The term "collapsible corporation" refers to a corporation used to convert ordinary income into capital gains, which having served this purpose is collapsed, i.e., liquidated.

Prior to the enactment of §341, use of collapsible corporations appealed to builders as well as motion picture producers. Suppose a builder formed a corporation with $50,000, and the corporation built a house with a fair market value of $250,000. Sale of the house by the corporation (or by an unincorporated builder) would produce ordinary income. Liquidation converted ordinary income into capital gains (§331) and provided a fair market value basis (§334) that offset the proceeds from the sale of the house by the builder following liquidation. Again under former §336, there was no gain to the liquidating corporation. As an alternative route to capital gains treatment, the builder would sell the stock to a purchaser who would then cause the corporation to liquidate. The builder would recognize a capital gain on the sale of the stock, while the purchaser would take a cost basis in the stock under §1012 that would result in no gain on an immediate liquidation. The purchaser of stock would take a fair market value basis in the house on liquidation under §334 and would recognize no income on an immediate sale of the house.

Section 341 requires that a shareholder's gain on the liquidation or sale of stock in a collapsible corporation be reported as ordinary income.

Ironically, the passage of the Tax Reform Act of 1986 eliminated any need for the complex collapsible corporation provisions, although the provision still stands. The repeal of the *General Utilities* doctrine removes the tax avoidance potential. Now an individual cannot remove appreciated assets from a corporation without paying a corporate-level tax under either §311 (nonliquidating distribution) or §336 (liquidating distribution). In both examples above, the liquidating corporation would recognize gain on the distribution of property to its shareholders.

It is true that the taxpayer can still avoid that gain by selling the stock. The new purchaser, however, will then own a corporation that must recognize that gain, and presumably the purchase price will reflect that fact. With the repeal of the *General Utilities* rule it is impossible for a shareholder to obtain a step-up in basis of distributed property without a corporate-level tax.

Finally, as noted at page 631 infra, §341(f) arms a taxpayer with the power to completely bypass §341 in many circumstances. To sum up, §341 makes little sense after the repeal of the *General Utilities* doctrine. Moreover, since it often can be bypassed, the provision serves only as a trap for the unwary. Nevertheless, because the tax laws have been known to change from time to time, it is appropriate to consider some of the intricacies of §341.

The case below predates the repeal of the *General Utilities* principle but is nevertheless instructive in illustrating the long reach of §341.

King v. United States _____
641 F.2d 253 (5th Cir. 1981)

LEWIS R. MORGAN, Circuit Judge. . . .

Plaintiffs, Rolland L. King and his wife, Arlene P. King, brought this action in the federal district court seeking a refund for taxes they claim were overpaid for the years 1968, 1969 and 1970. Although taxes had been paid on the income in question at the capital gains rate, the Commissioner of Internal Revenue determined on audit that the income was not entitled to long-term capital gains treatment and issued a deficiency notice. Plaintiffs paid the deficiency, but simultaneously filed for a refund for overpayment. . . .

The taxpayer King and his partner Smith formed King & Smith, Inc. in 1954 to develop a residential area east of Sarasota known as Forest Lakes. During its first year the corporation bought an option to purchase 1200 acres east of Sarasota at $2,000 per acre (hereinafter referred to as the Minute Maid option). King & Smith, Inc. ceased developing property by the end of 1955 because the individuals King and Smith had formed another corporation, South Gate Development Company, Inc. (hereinafter referred to as South Gate Development), in March of 1955 to continue the real estate development projects. By March of 1956 the land subject to the Minute Maid option held by King & Smith, Inc. had greatly increased in value primarily because of the success of the real estate developments of the corporation. At this time the taxpayer and his partner Smith sold all of their stock in King & Smith, Inc. to one D. H. Burk for approximately $1,673,000.00, with most of the purchase price payable over time as the remainder of the Minute Maid option was exercised. A part of the option had been exercised, with some of the land having been sold to South Gate Development. In 1955, because of a requirement that residential developments have a central water supply, King and Smith formed a utility corporation, South Gate Water & Sewer Company, Inc. (hereinafter referred to as South Gate Water), to supply water to the areas developed by South Gate Development. King and Smith each owned 50 percent of the stock in the utility corporation, which obtained a water franchise from the county and constructed a central water plant. South Gate Development constructed the water lines that were to carry water from the South Gate Water plant to the individual lots. After completion, these lines were conveyed by South Gate Development to South Gate Water without payment of consideration. In 1959 South Gate Development ceased developing property and in May of the same year, King and Smith sold all of their stock in South Gate Water to General Water Works Corp., an unrelated corporation engaged in the operation of several utility systems. Part of the purchase price was paid at closing and the remainder was paid over a period of time based upon the number of new customers connected to the system.

In 1958 Sarasota County instituted a requirement that all residential developments must be serviced by a central sewer system. King and Smith incorporated the Greater Sarasota Sewer Company to satisfy this requirement for their real estate developments, with each owning 50 percent of the stock in the corporation. The corporation obtained a sewer franchise from Sarasota County covering parts of the South Gate subdivision and other areas of Sarasota and built a plant and central disposal system. South Gate Development constructed several sewage collection systems, lift stations and other appurtenances in the area of its development within the Greater Sarasota Sewer Co. franchise. These systems were connected to the plant and central disposal system of Greater Sarasota Sewer Co. and after completion were conveyed to the sewer company without consideration. In 1965 King and Smith sold all of their stock in Greater Sarasota Sewer Co. to Florida Cities Water Company (hereinafter referred to as Florida Cities), a subsidiary of a company which operates several private utility systems. Part of the payment was made at closing and the remainder was scheduled to be paid semiannually based on the number of connections made to the system.

The taxpayer King, along with three other parties, formed in 1960 Gulf Gate Utilities, Inc. (hereinafter referred to as Gulf Gate Utilities) in which King was a 45 percent stockholder. The corporation obtained from Sarasota County both a water and sewer franchise covering an area of land south of the city known as the Gulf Gate area. Gulf Gate Utilities built a central water and sewage plant to which sewage collection and water distribution lines built by real estate developers were connected. The R. L. King Company and the First Development Corporation, two corporations in which King was a 50 and 25 percent stockholder respectively, built sewage and water lines and connected these to the central plants of Gulf Gate Utilities. After completion these development companies conveyed the lines and appurtenances to Gulf Gate Utilities without charge. In December of 1965 the stockholders of Gulf Gate Utilities sold the stock in the corporation to Florida Cities, using a method of payment similar to the payment plan for the Greater Sarasota Sewer Co. stock.

In mid-December of 1965 both Greater Sarasota Sewer Co. and Gulf Gate Utilities filed consents with the Internal Revenue Service under section 341(f) of the Internal Revenue Code to have subsection 2 of that provision apply to the assets of the corporation. These consents, if effective, would prevent the gain from the sale of stock from being treated as ordinary income under section 341. In the years 1968, 1969 and 1970, the taxpayer reported the income from the sale of stock of all three utility companies and King & Smith, Inc. as capital gain. . . .

I

[The Court's discussion of burden of proof is omitted.]

II

The principle substantive matter on appeal to this court concerns the application of the collapsible corporation provision of Section 341 of the Internal Revenue Code of 1954 to the sale of certain corporate stocks by the taxpayer.[7] The primary purpose behind the provisions of section 341 is to prevent the taxpayer from converting what would otherwise be ordinary income into capital gain by liquidating or selling the stock of a corporation before realization of substantial income. See generally B. Bittker & J. Eustice, Federal Income Taxation of Corporations and Shareholders para. 12.04 (4th Ed. 1979). The device utilized by the taxpayer for such purposes is referred to as a collapsible corporation, as described in section 341(b)(1) of the Code. . . .

Based on [§341(b)], the taxpayer first argues that the utility corporations in question were formed principally for the operation of the utility franchises, not for the construction of property. Although this stated purpose is a reasonable one and the one most likely found in the corporations' articles of incorporation, the court is not bound to accept the self-serving statements of the taxpayer as to intent. The purpose of a corporation is determined from the function of the corporation, not the underlying motives of the taxpayer. See Braunstein v. Commissioner, 374 U.S. 65 (1963).

---

7. This discussion of collapsibility applies only to the South Gate Water and Greater Sarasota Sewer utility corporations because the district court found the consent filed under §341(f) effective as to Gulf Gate Utilities, Inc. Although a consent was also filed as to Greater Sarasota Sewer, the court applied the five year limitation rule under §341(f)(5) to find that the consent was effective to the sale of stock of only one of the corporations. Except for the effective consent of Gulf Gate Utilities, Inc., the discussion that follows would apply to that utility corporation as well.

In a case such as this one where the only live testimony is that of the taxpayer, the court may look to the activities that took place and from those activities draw the inference that the corporation was formed for the construction of property. See Payne v. Commissioner, 268 F.2d 617, 621 (5th Cir. 1959). This judicial finding is subject to the clearly erroneous standard on review, and we find that in this case the determination was not clearly erroneous. Furthermore, the language of section 341 provides that a corporation *availed of* for the construction of property may also be deemed collapsible. Although the ultimate purpose of the utility corporations may have been to provide utility services, the corporations were at least availed of for the construction of the utility systems.

Taxpayer further suggests that the construction of the utility system was incidental to the purpose of the corporation and consumed only a brief period of time when considered in light of the entire length of the franchise grant. Apparently this claim is based on the word "principally"[11] as used in section 341(b)(1) and on the definition of collapsible corporation as explicated by Treasury Regulation section 1.341-5(b)(3). The Regulation provides that the construction of property must be substantial in relation to the other activities of the corporation. First, the taxpayer misreads the provision as a restriction or qualification for finding a corporation collapsible. Subsection (a) of the Regulation clearly provides that the Regulation only describes situations that will usually result in the finding that collapsibility is or is not appropriate. Furthermore, the specific provision cited by the taxpayer requires that "*[a]t the time of the manufacture, construction, production, or purchase* . . . such activity was substantial in relation to the other activities of the corporation." Treas. Regs. §1.341-5(b)(3) (1955) (emphasis added). The Regulation is not requiring substantial activity during the length of time the corporation may exist, i.e., the length of the franchise grant, but simply indicates that the activity must be substantial during the time of construction. During the time of the only actual construction by the utility corporations, the construction was the primary, if not only, activity of the corporation. During construction of the entire water and sewer systems, construction was still a significant enough activity of the corporation to constitute substantial activity. Therefore, the provisions of the Regulations do not affect the decision of the court below.

In addition to our technical examination under the Regulation, we find in agreement with the lower court that the construction of the water and sewer systems was not incidental, but rather was crucial, to the operation of the utility franchises. Without the construction of the utilities' water and sewer systems, the purposes of the utility corporations could not be

---

11. At one time commentators speculated that the word "principally" should modify the phrase "with a view to." However, several courts have now held that "principally" must be read to modify the phrase "manufacture, construction, or production of property." Farber v. Commissioner, 312 F.2d 729 (2d Cir.), cert. denied, 374 U.S. 828 (1963). . . .

accomplished. The district court did not err in finding that for the purposes of section 341 treatment, the corporations in question were formed,
or at least availed of, principally for the construction of property.

Taxpayer further argues that the limited activity of the utility corporations toward the building of the utility systems was not sufficient to constitute "construction" by the corporation. The taxpayer suggests that the
corporation primarily only purchased and installed equipment for the
central plants, with the bulk of the construction on the utility systems'
water lines and sewer connections being done by private developers. The
taxpayer's argument, however, must fail. The courts have held that minimal
acts constitute sufficient activity to satisfy the requirement of construction
or production of property. See, e.g., Farber v. Commissioner, 312 F.2d 729
(2d Cir.), cert. denied, 374 U.S. 828 (1963) (payments of fees for zoning
permits and payment for utility connections held to be sufficient for a
finding of collapsibility); Abbott v. Commissioner, 258 F.2d 537 (3d Cir.
1958) (contract for sale of land with agreement to install streets, sewers
and utilities sufficient for a finding of collapsibility). Furthermore, the
provision of section 341(b)(2)(A) permits a finding of collapsibility if the
corporation "engaged in the manufacture, construction, or production of
property *to any extent.*" (emphasis added). The construction activity of the
corporations that consisted of constructing the central water and sewer
plants of the utility systems was sufficient to satisfy the requirement of
construction under section 341(b).

Recent cases have held that the development of intangible property
is included in the concept of production or construction of property. Estate
of C. A. Diecks, 65 T.C. 117 (1975) (development of cable vision system
and related franchise in production of property within the meaning of
§341(b)(1)); Computer Sciences Corp., 63 T.C. 327 (1974) (development
of a computer program for preparation of income tax return was production of property within the meaning of §341(b)(1)). We hold in this case
that in addition to the construction of the system, the development of the
utility system franchises was production of intangible property within the
meaning of §341(b)(1).

The final definition challenge by the taxpayer is based on the controversial phrase of section 341(b)(1) requiring that the construction of property, etc. occur "with a view to" the sale or exchange of stock before the
realization of substantial income along with the realization of gain by the
taxpayer. The requisite view must exist prior to completion of the construction or production of property by the corporation. See Treas. Reg. §1.341-
2(a)(3); Payne v. Commissioner, supra, 268 F.2d 617. The taxpayer argues
that the construction of property by the corporation, i.e., the construction
of the central water and sewer plants, was completed prior to the time that
the view to sell the stock existed. However, the finding made by the lower
court and affirmed by this court is that the construction by the corporation
was the construction of the entire water system. The completion dates of

the central plants are not controlling because construction on substantial parts of the water system continued as additional water and sewer lines were constructed and connected to the main system. At least one court has held that the laying of lines, in that case cable lines, and the connecting of new customers was continuous activity that constituted construction.[15] We agree with that reasoning, particularly in light of our opinion that the purpose of the utility corporations was construction of utility systems. It is irrelevant that private developers actually constructed the lines, connected them to the system, and then transferred them to the utility corporations. Such arrangements are common among real estate developers where utility systems are required. Nevertheless, the construction by the private developer is deemed construction by the utility corporation for purposes of section 341 because the utility corporation had as its purpose and function the construction of a utility system. This court will not permit a technical arrangement involving construction to defeat the finding of collapsibility. Where corporations were formed or availed of principally for the construction of utility systems, the construction of the systems continued during construction of the entire system whether carried out by the utility corporations or by private developers.[16]

Taxpayer has emphatically argued to this court that a utility corporation has never been held to be a collapsible corporation and could not be because of the positions previously argued. We have disposed of the technical arguments made under section 341(b)(1). Concerning taxpayer's final appeal, the Code section in question sets no limitation on the kinds of corporations subject to its provisions. Although section 341 (formerly section 117(m)) was originally designed to control tax abuses in the movie and construction industries, any corporation which satisfies the definitional requirements may be collapsible. The Tax Court in Estate of C. A. Diecks, supra, 65 T.C. 117, held that a cable vision corporation operating under a franchise grant was collapsible. The factual similarity between the two kinds of corporations is obvious. Both the utility and the cable services involve franchises that provide from a centralized network services to individual homes. The cable and utility networks providing the service are operated and maintained by the corporations. Although many utility corporations may not satisfy the statutory requirements, the special circumstances of this case permit a finding that the corporations were collapsible. Therefore, despite taxpayer's argument that a utility corporation has never been held to be collapsible, we find in agreement with the lower court that the corporations in question satisfied the basic statutory requirements and were indeed collapsible corporations.

15. Estate of C. A. Diecks, supra, 65 T.C. at 123.
16. In this case the record reveals that the private development companies transferring the lines and appurtenances to the utility corporations were for the most part corporations in which taxpayer held a controlling interest. Although not of particular legal significance in the case, this fact indicates the "close ties" between the developer and the utility corporations.

III

Having concluded that the corporations were collapsible under section 341(b), we must consider the taxpayer's arguments concerning exceptions and limitations to the basic definitional requirements. Under section 341(d)(2) taxpayer cites the limitation requiring that at least 70 percent of the gain on the sale of stock must be attributable to the constructed property in order for the corporation to be deemed collapsible. The tax-payer argues that the gain was primarily attributable to the franchises, the customer lists and connecting lines. Although some of the gain was most likely attributable to these assets of the corporation, Treasury Regulation Section 1.341-4(c)(3) provides that gain may be "attributable to" the constructed property even when the gain is represented by appreciation in other property. In the present case little or no gain would have accrued without the construction of the central water system. Because the gain attributable to the franchises, customer lists, and connecting lines was the result of the construction of the central water system, the gain on these assets was attributable to the property actually constructed by the utility corporations. Furthermore, construction may be attributed to a corporation other than the one that actually performed the construction. See Jack Farber, 36 T.C. 1142, aff'd, 312 F.2d 729 (2d Cir. 1963). Thus, even if the gain was attributed to the property constructed by the private developers, and this construction was not deemed construction by the corporation, the gain would still be attributed to the "constructed property" for the purpose of section 341(d)(2). . . .

In a final argument urging exemption from section 341 treatment, taxpayer suggests that the exception of section 341(e) is applicable. The provisions of section 341(e) were enacted primarily to provide exceptions in situations where property held by corporations, if held by individuals, would have afforded capital gain treatment on its sale. The assets of a corporation are considered at both a corporate and shareholder level to determine whether a significant increase in value has occurred of assets which would produce ordinary income upon sale. If the net unrealized appreciation in the "tainted" assets, i.e., or ordinary income assets in the hands of the corporation or certain shareholders, is more than 15 percent [of the net worth of the corporation], the corporation is not entitled to relief under section 341(e).

Crucial to the application of section 341(e) to a corporation is the definition of "subsection (e) assets," as described in section 341(e)(5)(A) of the statute. Taxpayer in this case bases his argument under section 341(e) on the ground that the utility corporations owned no subsection (e), i.e., ordinary income, assets, and therefore had zero unrealized appreciation in subsection (e) assets. However, taxpayer erroneously bases his position that the corporations had no subsection (e) assets on the assumption that "[t]hese assets as they relate to utility-type corporations have to be inventory, stock in trade or property held primarily for sale to customers in the ordinary course of business." Under section 341(e)(5)(A)(iii), property used in the trade or business[23] is a subsection (e) asset if its sale would produce ordinary income in the hands of a more than 20 percent shareholder. The water and sewer systems were such property because they were property used in the trade or business that in the hands of the taxpayer would have produced ordinary income upon sale. The district judge found that the taxpayer was in the business of developing real estate. That finding is not clearly erroneous; in fact, everything in the record regarding taxpayer's business transactions and corporate involvements supports that finding. Because local ordinances required developers to provide utility services to real estate developments, the business of developing real estate was broad enough to include the development of utility systems. Thus, the gain from the sale of the utility property would have been ordinary income in the hands of the taxpayer. The utility systems owned by South Gate Water and Greater Sarasota Sewer were subsection (e) assets under the definition of section 341(e)(5)(A)(iii). The taxpayer had the burden of proof to show that the statutory requirements of section 341(e) were met. Failing to show that the net unrealized appreciation in the utility systems was not less than 15 percent of the corporation's net worth, the taxpayer cannot claim the sanctuary of section 341(e).

As the district court found, the statutory requirements of collapsible corporations were satisfied as to the South Gate Water and Greater Sarasota Sewer corporations, and none of the limitations or exceptions applied to prevent collapsible treatment. The district court was not clearly erroneous in its findings of fact and correctly concluded that these corporations were collapsible. We now turn to the question of collapsibility concerning the King & Smith, Inc. corporation.

IV

[The court ruled that King & Smith, Inc. was a collapsible corporation because it "purchased" property — the option — with a view to the sale of stock by its shareholders before the realization of a substantial part of the taxable income to be derived from the property. The purchased option constituted a "section 341 asset" as defined by §341(b)(3). Specifically, the option was found to be property held for sale to customers within the meaning of §341(b)(3)(B). Since all the other requirements under §341 were met, taxpayer's sale of stock resulted in ordinary income.]

---

23. Property used in the trade or business is defined in §341(e) by reference to §1231(b) of the Code. The provisions of §1231(b) refer to depreciable property used in the trade or business which would not be included in the inventory of the taxpayer and is not held by the taxpayer primarily for sale to customers in the ordinary course of business. The utility systems in the present case are such property.

Having concluded that the corporations in the case were collapsible and that the income from the trust account was ordinary income, the decision of the lower court is affirmed.

NOTE

1. *Definition of "collapsible corporation."* A "collapsible corporation," as the term is defined by §341(b)(1), must be formed or availed of:

a. principally for the manufacture, construction, or production of property, for the purchase of certain categories of property (primarily property held for sale to customers in the ordinary course of its trade or business), or for the holding of stock in another corporation so formed or availed;

b. with a view to (1) a sale or exchange of its stock, or a distribution to its shareholders, before it has realized two-thirds of the taxable income to be derived from the manufactured or purchased property, and (2) a realization by the shareholders of gain attributable to the property.

Requirement (a) is satisfied by many corporations, especially since the concept of "manufacture, construction, or production of property" is defined very expansively. In *King,* note that corporations other than the purported collapsible corporations had a substantial role in the construction activities. Moreover, construction was only a part of the activities in which the corporations engaged. See also Treas. Regs. §1.341-2(a)(5); Farber v. Commissioner, 312 F.2d 729 (2d Cir. 1963) (predevelopment activity of filing applications for building permits and paying fees and deposits constituted construction); Manassas Airport Industrial Park v. Commissioner, 66 T.C. 566 (1976), aff'd per curiam, 557 F.2d 1113 (4th Cir. 1977) (postliquidation obligation to build access road found to be evidence of uncompleted construction); cf. Rev. Rul. 77-306, 1977-2 C.B. 103 (lessor's lease of additional land to lessee and continuing right to approve changes to building not construction modifying Rev. Rul. 69-378, 1969-2 C.B. 49, which reached the opposite result because there lessor also participated in the financing by subordinating its mortgage and participated in success of venture by receiving a percentage of gross rentals collected). See also Rev. Rul. 72-422, 1972-2 C.B. 211, stating that the dollar amount expended is irrelevant in determining whether taxpayer has engaged in construction under §341.

Query: Can a personal service firm be considered a collapsible corporation on the ground that it was formed or availed of for the "production of property" or goodwill? Were the intangible franchises considered property in *King?* See also Computer Sciences Corp. v. Commissioner, 63 T.C. 327 (1974) (proprietary computer program and interview forms held to be produced property); F.T.S. Associates v. Commissioner, 58 T.C. 207 (1972) (marketing rights to secret process is produced property).

Much litigation concerning the definition of "collapsible corporation" has turned on whether requirement (b) was satisfied, i.e., whether
the shareholders had the requisite "view" at the proper time. What reason
for the corporations was offered by the taxpayer in *King*?

With the repeal of the *General Utilities* doctrine, all appreciated corporate assets will eventually produce gain at the corporate level. How then
can there be a requisite view to avoid tax on the appreciation? It is true
that a shareholder can dispose of stock before that corporate-level gain is
recognized, but won't the amount paid for the stock reflect the impending
tax? Suppose you could buy stock of two corporations that were identical
except that one corporation held appreciated assets that would result in a
corporate-level tax on sale or distribution while the other held appreciated
assets that would yield no corporate-level tax. Would you pay the same
amount for the stock of each corporation?

The regulations speak of a "view" that exists before the manufacture,
construction, production, or purchase of property is completed and are
willing to overlook a subsequently conceived "view," at least in ordinary
circumstances. Treas. Regs. §1.341-2(a)(3). This approach has led to a few
shareholder victories. See Jacobson v. Commissioner, 281 F.2d 703 (3d
Cir. 1960) (sale not contemplated until after construction was completed;
held, not collapsible); Temkin v. Commissioner, 35 T.C. 906 (1961) (sale
attributable to ill health of a principal shareholder, arising after construction was completed; held, not collapsible); *F.T.S. Associates,* supra (following *Temkin,* decision to sell after operations ceased and taxpayer insolvent);
Computer Sciences Corp., supra (view to sell formulated after production of
computer program reduced to commercial value). See Crowe v. Commissioner, 62 T.C. 121 (1974), in which the prohibited view was not found to
exist; the taxpayer had no freedom of choice in the sale of stock because
of a unilateral option held and exercised by the other shareholder to
buy him out in the event of a disagreement. Presumably the purchasing
shareholder in *Crowe* cannot liquidate without addressing the potential
collapsibility problem.

When §341 was first enacted, commentators engaged in a lively debate
over the reference of the adverb "principally" in §341(b)(1). In Weil v.
Commissioner, 252 F.2d 805 (2d Cir. 1958), the court said that "principally" modifies only "manufacture, construction," etc. and that the "view"
need not be "the principal corporate objective." See *King,* page 621 supra,
at footnote 11. Although the *Weil* decision has gained a large measure of
support, no court has as yet worked out the implications of the statement
in the regulations that the "view" requirement is satisfied even if a sale,
liquidation, etc., is no more than "a recognized possibility." Treas. Regs.
§1.341-2(a)(2).

Because a finding of the prohibited view is a factual one, taxpayers
must always consider the possibility that the Service will argue for collapsibility whenever a corporation's shareholder sells its stock or causes it to
liquidate.

Under Rev. Proc. 86-3, 1986-1 C.B. 416, the Service will issue rulings that a corporation has not been formed or availed of with a view to the action stated in §341(b) when the enterprise has been in existence for at least 20 years with substantially the same owners and has been conducting substantially the same trade or business.

2. *Realization of two-thirds of taxable income.* Prior to the Deficit Reduction Act of 1984, §341(b) imposed a "substantial part" test in lieu of the "two-thirds" requirement. The former language led to some confusion and ultimately a restrictive view of §341's applicability. Under the former language, it was not clear whether a corporation was collapsible if it had realized a substantial part of the income to be derived from the collapsible property before the liquidation or sale, even though a substantial amount remained to be realized thereafter. A major exception to a finding of collapsibility was provided in Rev. Rul. 72-48, 1972-1 C.B. 102, in which the IRS announced that a realization of one-third of the taxable income took an asset outside the reach of §341. In keeping with the ruling the Service substituted an acquiescence for its prior nonacquiescence in Commissioner v. Kelley, 293 F.2d 904 (5th Cir. 1961), in which a corporation that realized 33 percent of potential income was held noncollapsible.

Under the current language, it is now clear that to avoid §341 a corporation must realize at least two-thirds, rather than one-third, of the potential income. Unquestionably this legislative change has broadened the reach of §341 to many unsuspecting corporations and their shareholders.

3. *The operative effects of §341.* If a corporation is collapsible, the shareholders (subject to certain exceptions) must report as ordinary income any gain from a sale or exchange of the stock, a distribution in partial or complete liquidation, or a nondividend distribution under §301(c)(3)(A) that would otherwise be reported as long-term capital gain. Although §341(a) does not explicitly mention gain on a redemption of shares, it must be assumed that redemptions are covered. Indeed, a redemption qualifying under §302(b) is characterized as an "exchange," thereby falling within the purview of §341(a).

As a result of the Tax Reform Act of 1986, §341 transforms short-term capital gain into ordinary income. Consider the outcome when a shareholder has capital losses that normally can be offset against short-term capital gain realized on a sale or liquidation of a collapsible corporation. Note that §341 has no impact if the shareholder incurs a loss on the transaction.

4. *Minority shareholders.* In determining whether the forbidden view exists, the regulations look to "those persons in a position to determine the policies of the corporation, whether by reason of their owning a majority of the voting stock of the corporation or not," Treas. Regs. §1.341-2(a)(2). Since the punitive rules of §341(a) apply to all shareholders of a collapsible corporation, a minority shareholder cannot escape by showing that she did not share in the forbidden view. But if she is the only shareholder who

sells her stock, the corporation may not be collapsible because the dominant shareholders did not intend to sell *their* shares before a substantial part of the income was realized by the corporation. See Goodwin v. United States, 320 F.2d 356 (Cl. Ct. 1963), holding the collapsible provision inapplicable when the stock of a minority shareholder is redeemed and the majority shareholders continue to run the corporation.

Regardless of his view, however, a person who owns (directly and constructively) no more than 5 percent of the collapsible corporation's stock may be able to avail himself of the exception of §341(d)(1).

5. *The limitations of §341(d).* By virtue of §341(d), §341 does not apply to gain realized more than three years after the construction, etc., is completed or to gain recognized during a taxable year unless more than 70 percent of it was attributable to the collapsible property or, if certain conditions are satisfied, to persons owning not more than 5 percent of the corporation's stock. The three-year rule is difficult to satisfy in view of the broad meaning given to "manufacture, construction, or production," and the 5 percent rule is limited in its usefulness because of the constructive ownership rules of §341(d) (last sentence). Why didn't the corporations in *King* satisfy the three-year rule? The 70 percent rule may be significant if the corporation holds both collapsible and noncollapsible property; if enough of the gain is attributable to the latter category, the gain attributable to the collapsible property slips through unscathed by §341. When the corporation's principal or only asset is real estate on which it has constructed a building, however, shareholders have not been very successful in establishing that 30 percent or more of their gain was of the noncollapsible variety. See, e.g., Farber v. Commissioner, 312 F.2d 729 (2d Cir. 1963), and cases cited therein.

The Deficit Reduction Act of 1984 made it more difficult to qualify under the 70 percent exception by referring to the two-thirds requirement of §341(b)(1)(A). Under prior law, it was possible for a corporation with more than one project to avoid collapsible status if the corporation had realized gain on one of the projects. Now, it is more likely that a shareholder will be unable to qualify under §341(d)(2). For example, suppose a corporation has completed one of two projects for sale to customers (§1221), and the sole shareholder liquidates, realizing a $100,000 gain, $40,000 attributable to the completed project and $60,000 attributable to the uncompleted project. Under prior law, the shareholder would qualify for the 70 percent exception since only 60 percent of the gain was attributable to collapsible assets. Now, §341(d)(2) and (b)(1) combine to force ordinary income treatment for the entire gain since the corporation has not realized two-thirds of the ordinary income; therefore, all the gain was attributable to collapsible assets.

6. *Distributions of "excess" mortgage proceeds by collapsible corporation.* Much of the §341 litigation has concerned corporations that constructed apartment houses or other buildings under the Federal Housing Act and

were able to borrow, on federally insured mortgages, more than the cost of construction. This excess of the mortgage loan over the corporation's cost might be attributable to construction economies, to inflation in the value of previously acquired land, to overly generous appraisals by the federal authorities, or to the uncompensated personal efforts of the shareholders.

Before 1954, it was common for such excess mortgage proceeds to be distributed to shareholders before the corporation had any earnings and profits (so the distribution would not be a taxable dividend). In Commissioner v. Gross, 236 F.2d 612 (2d Cir. 1956), the court held that such a distribution was to be applied against the shareholder's basis for his stock and that any excess over his basis was capital gain under §301(c)(3)(A). This result was changed by the enactment in 1954 of what is now §312(i), under which a distribution creates earnings and profits if the corporation's assets are subject to a loan that was made, guaranteed, or insured by the United States and that exceeds the adjusted basis of the mortgaged property. A distribution in these circumstances, therefore, will be a taxable dividend to the shareholders.

Section 312(i) does not make §341 unnecessary as to such construction companies, however, because §312(i) does not apply if the shareholders benefited from the excess mortgage money by selling their stock rather than by causing the corporation to distribute the funds to them. See also Zorn v. Commissioner, 35 T.C.M. (CCH) 1048 (1976), in which excess mortgage proceeds obtained from a private lender and distributed to shareholders led to a factual finding of the prohibited view and therefore collapsibility.

7. *The amnesty of §341(e).* In Braunstein v. Commissioner, 374 U.S. 65 (1963), the Supreme Court refused to grant judicial relief to a corporation that held rental property that would have been a capital asset in the shareholder's hands, despite the absence of a tax avoidance motive. Section 341(e), inapplicable to the taxable year before the Supreme Court in *Braunstein* (1950), was enacted in 1958 in recognition of the fact that §341 not only prevents some taxpayers from transmuting potential ordinary income into capital gain but also forces others to report as ordinary income a gain that would have been taxed as capital gain if realized without the intervention of a corporation. But §341(e) accomplishes its intended purpose in remarkably labyrinthine fashion, and its involutions are not easily summarized.[1]

Roughly speaking, its underlying theory is that the collapsible corpora-

---

1. As an aside, it is interesting to note that the taxpayer's attorney in *Braunstein*, who unsuccessfully argued against the literal language of §341 and in favor of the spirit of the provision, also argued for the taxpayer in *Chamberlin*, page 304 supra. There, he scored a stunning victory by arguing that the preferred stock bailout was not addressed by any language in the Code and was, therefore, not subject to recharacterization, despite the fact that the transaction violated the spirit of the dividend provisions.

tion provisions should not be applied if the net unrealized appreciation in the corporation's "subsection (e) assets" (property that would produce ordinary income if sold by the corporation or by its principal shareholders) amounts to less than 15 percent of the corporation's net worth, defined in §341(e)(7). As the *Braunstein* opinion indicates, in determining whether property constitutes a "subsection (e) asset," §341(e) looks not only to the corporation's trade or business but also to the trade or business of the corporation's principal shareholders (those owning, directly or constructively, more than 20 percent — sometimes 5 percent — of the stock); sometimes §341(e) takes account of a hypothetical trade or business that is imputed to a shareholder because of the activities of other corporations in which the shareholder owned stock, directly or constructively, in the past. See Diecks v. Commissioner, 65 T.C. 117 (1975), in which no taint was found to exist for a 20 percent shareholder since his other businesses were unrelated; furthermore, because the corporation had no appreciated §341(e) assets, a stock sale qualified for §341(e). Under §341(e)(12) and Treas. Regs. §1.341-6(b)(2)(iii), in determining whether gain from the sale or exchange of property will be considered as ordinary income, recapture amounts, e.g., under §1245, are disregarded. See Rev. Rul. 78-285, 1978-2 C.B. 137, in which a shareholder does not exceed the 20 percent ownership limitation when the sale of his stock to an unrelated buyer reduces his ownership to less than 20 percent prior to the corporation's adoption of plan of liquidation; with respect to that shareholder, the corporation is not considered to be collapsible. Cf. Granite Trust Co. v. United States, 238 F.2d 670 (1st Cir. 1956), for a similar result on a parent-subsidiary liquidation.

Because two of the principal shareholders in *Braunstein* had been engaged in the real estate construction business for many years, directly or through other corporations (36 T.C. 22, 23 (1961)), they might not have qualified for relief under §341(e) even if it had been in force in 1950. If they had been investors in real estate, with no interests in other corporations, however, and if the buildings were held by the corporation for rental purposes, then §341(e)(1) would have applied, the buildings would not be "subsection (e) assets," and hence none of the corporation's net worth would have been attributable to unrealized appreciation in such assets — with the result that the corporation (regardless of the shareholders' "view") would not be collapsible.

8. *Consents under §341(f).* Another escape hatch for the shareholders of a collapsible corporation was provided by the enactment in 1964 of §341(f), under which the shareholders can sell their stock on the normal capital gain basis, provided the corporation agrees to recognize gain (if any) on its "subsection (f) assets" (primarily real estate and noncapital assets) when, as, and if it disposes of them in a transaction that would otherwise qualify for nonrecognition of gain. Such a consent ensures that all the unrealized gain on most collapsible property (and more) will be

recognized at the corporate level regardless of the mode employed by the corporation to dispose of the property (e.g., on a distribution in liquidation). An exception is also provided for certain transfers (e.g., in corporate reorganizations, §351 transfers, and §332 liquidations of a subsidiary), provided the transferee files a similar consent.

Consider the §341(f) election in light of the Tax Reform Act of 1986. With the repeal of the *General Utilities* doctrine, every corporation, regardless of a §341(f) election, will recognize gain on the sale or distribution of all appreciated assets. (A §341 election would cause recognition on an involuntary conversion, but that is a small exception.) Accordingly, there is virtually no cost in making a §341(f) election because the corporation is electing treatment that would happen anyway under §§1001, 311, and 336. By making the election, a corporation at no cost will enable its shareholders to avoid recharacterization under §341(a). Is it malpractice for a corporation not to make a §341(f) election?

D. PROBLEMS

1.   Does an individual shareholder ever have an incentive to accumulate income in a corporation if the shareholder's marginal tax rate is lower than the corporate marginal tax rate?

2.   In view of the repeal of the *General Utilities* rule by the Tax Reform Act of 1986, is there any justification for maintaining §341? Does §341(f) render §341 totally impotent? Consider §341(f)(5).

15

The Corporation as a Separate Taxable Entity

A. DEFINITION OF A CORPORATION

1. Morrissey v. Commissioner

In Morrissey v. Commissioner, 296 U.S. 344 (1935), the petitioners set up a trust to develop some tracts of land and to construct and operate a golf course. The trustees were authorized to buy, sell, lease, and operate the land owned by the trust; to construct and operate the golf course and club house; to make loans and investments; and to manage the property as if they were the owners. The trustees had no power to bind the beneficiaries. Beneficial interests in the trust were evidenced by transferable certificates. The trust was to continue for 25 years and was not terminated by the death of a trustee or beneficiary. During the years before the court, the trust developed the land, sold some of the lots, and constructed a golf course and club house, which were transferred to a corporation in exchange for its stock. The trustees leased and operated the golf facilities from the corporation for a period of time, but later their activities were confined to the collection of installments on the lots that were sold, the receipt of dividends from the incorporated golf facilities, and distributions to beneficiaries.

The Supreme Court held that the corporate income tax was properly imposed on the trust, which was deemed an "association" for tax purposes. See §7701(a)(3), which defines "corporation" to include "association." The characteristics necessary to tax a business enterprise as an association were set forth by the Court as follows: (a) associates, (b) an objective to carry on a trade or business, (c) continuity of life of the enterprise,

633

(d) centralized management representing the owners, (e) limited liability for the owners, and (f) free transferability of ownership interests.

2. Professional Corporations

The Service was successful in arguing for association status in *Morrissey*. Subsequent to the *Morrissey* decision, however, certain taxpayers sought the sanctuary of association status for tax purposes even though such classification carried with it the possibility of a corporate-level tax. Doctors and other professionals practicing in unincorporated associations or partnerships wanted association status to take advantage of qualified pension and profit-sharing plans, then only available to corporate employees. Since most states prohibited the incorporation of professionals, many professionals formed associations adhering to the *Morrissey* characteristics. In this setting, the Service found itself arguing against association status. In Kintner v. United States, 216 F.2d 418 (9th Cir. 1954), the Ninth Circuit ruled that a professional medical service association was a corporation for federal tax purposes even though a state law prohibited the practice of medicine by corporations. For a good review of the history of professional corporations, see Richland Medical Association v. Commissioner, 953 F.2d 639 (4th Cir. 1992).

3. The Association Regulations

In 1960 the Service reacted to defeats in *Kintner* and other cases by enacting Treas. Regs. §301.7701-2, which codify the basic characteristics of an association described in *Morrissey*. These regulations set forth two prerequisites to association status: (1) an objective to carry on business for profit and (2) associates, although associates may be ignored in the one-person corporation or sole proprietorship situation. In lieu of an uncertain weighing of the various *Morrissey* factors, the regulations further provide a mechanical numbers test. An unincorporated organization shall not be classified as an association unless such organization has three of four listed corporate characteristics: continuity of life, centralization of management, limited liability, and free transferability of ownership interests. These characteristics are defined in a manner stacked against corporate classification.

In light of the strict federal regulations, professionals lobbied state legislatures to enact professional corporation statutes permitting operation in corporate form. The Service's reaction to this turn of events was to issue specific regulations in 1965 intended to ignore the professional corporation statutes for federal tax purposes. The 1965 regulations were struck down as arbitrary, legislative in nature, and discriminatory by all courts that considered them. See, e.g., Kurzner v. United States, 413 F.2d 97 (5th Cir. 1969); O'Neill v. United States, 410 F.2d 888 (6th Cir. 1969); United States v. Empey, 406 F.2d 157 (10th Cir. 1969). When the solicitor general decided not to apply for certiorari in *Kurzner,* the IRS announced that it would no longer contest this issue. See Rev. Rul. 70-101, 1970-1 C.B. 278, listing the state statutes that will be recognized as conferring corporate status on professional service organizations. Subsequent rulings have added state statutes as they are enacted to the list set out in Rev. Rul. 70-101. In 1977, the 1965 regulations were revoked.

Despite recognition as a corporation, the personal service corporation and its shareholder-employees may be subject to a reallocation of income under principles developed in cases such as Lucas v. Earl. See Sargent v. Commissioner, 93 T.C. 572 (1989). See also page 658 infra.

4. Is a Limited Partnership an Association?

While the Service was still waging war to make federal corporate status unavailable for professionals, it found itself fighting to impose corporate status on certain noncorporate enterprises — limited partnerships. Reliance on the restrictive association regulations allowed limited partnerships operating much like corporations easily to escape that classification. These limited partnerships were used to market "tax shelters" to individual investors who might not otherwise be able to make such investments on their own. The partnership form was ideal since it allowed limited partners to take their pro rata shares of partnership losses or credits, which could then be used to offset income from other sources and thereby shelter income. Often the losses in the early years of a partnership exceeded a partner's actual cash investment in the partnership.[1] Faced with these proliferating "tax shelter" cases, the Service argued that a limited partnership should be taxed as a corporation under some circumstances, in which case the entity's losses would not pass through to the partners but could be used only by the entity.

The *Larson* decision that follows marks a watershed in the classification battle.

---

1. The ability of a partner to take loss deductions stems in part from the *Crane* doctrine, which allows purchase indebtedness to be included in basis, thereby increasing depreciation deductions. See Crane v. Commissioner, 331 U.S. 1 (1949). While there may be a day of reckoning for the partner who receives large loss deductions in the early years, there has been no shortage of genius in finding ways to postpone or avoid that day or at least make it less painful by qualifying for capital gains treatment on any recapture.

Larson v. Commissioner _____
66 T.C. 159 (1976)

TANNENWALD, Judge. . . .

OPINION

Petitioners owned limited partnership interests in Mai-kai and Somis, two real estate ventures organized under the California Uniform Limited Partnership Act, Cal. Corp. Code secs. 15501 et seq. (West Supp. 1976) (hereinafter referred to as CULPA). The partnerships incurred losses during the years in issue, and petitioners deducted their distributive shares of such losses on their individual shares of such losses on their individual tax returns. Respondent disallowed those deductions on the ground that the partnerships were associations taxable as corporations, as defined in section 7701(a)(3), and not partnerships as defined in section 7701(a)(2). Petitioners allege that the partnerships fail all of the tests of corporate resemblance established by respondent's Regulations (Regs. §301.7701-2); respondent contends that all those tests are satisfied. Both sides agree that the Regulations apply and are controlling, and our opinion and decision are consequently framed in that contest; the validity of respondent's Regulations is not before us. In our previous (now withdrawn) opinion dated October 21, 1975, we concluded that respondent should prevail. Upon reconsideration, we have come to the opposite conclusion and hold for petitioners.

The starting point of the Regulations' definition of an "association" is the principle applied in Morrissey v. Commissioner, 296 U.S. 344 (1935), that the term includes entities which resemble corporations although they are not formally organized as such. *Morrissey* identified several characteristics of the corporate form which the Regulations adopt as a test of corporate resemblance. For the purpose of comparing corporations with partnerships, the significant characteristics are: continuity of life; centralization of management; limited liability; and free transferability of interests. Other corporate or noncorporate characteristics may also be considered if appropriate in a particular case. An organization will be taxed as a corporation if, taking all relevant characteristics into account, it more nearly resembles a corporation than some other entity. Regs. §301.7701-2(a)(1). This will be true only if it possesses more corporate than noncorporate characteristics.

The Regulations discuss each major corporate characteristic separately, and each apparently bears equal weight in the final balancing. This apparently mechanical approach may perhaps be explained as an attempt to impart a degree of certainty to a subject otherwise fraught with imponderables. In most instances, the Regulations also make separate provision for the classification of limited partnerships. Petitioners rely heavily on those provisions, while respondent seeks to distinguish them or to minimize their importance.

1. CONTINUITY OF LIFE . . .

A corporation possesses a greater degree of continuity of life than a partnership, since its existence is not dependent upon events personally affecting its separate members. Because of their more intimate legal and financial ties, partners are given a continuing right to choose their associates which is denied to corporate shareholders. A material alteration in the makeup of the partnership, as through the death or incapacity of a partner, either dissolves the partnership relation by operation of law or permits dissolution by order of court. Uniform Partnership Act, secs. 31 and 32 (hereinafter referred to as UPA). Partners are then free to withdraw their shares from the business, though they may agree to form a new partnership to continue it. A partner is also given the right to dissolve the partnership and withdraw his capital (either specific property or the value of his interest) at will at any time (UPA sec. 31(2)), although he may be unable to cause the winding up of the business and may be answerable in damages to other partners if his act breaches an agreement among them (UPA secs. 37 and 38(2)). The significant differences between a corporation and a partnership as regards continuity of life, then, is that a partner can always opt out of continued participation in and exposure to the risks of the enterprise. A corporate shareholder's investment is locked in unless liquidation is voted or he can find a purchaser to buy him out.

In a partnership subject to the Uniform Limited Partnership Act (hereinafter referred to as ULPA), this right of withdrawal is modified. A limited partner can withdraw his interest on dissolution (ULPA sec. 16), but he can neither dissolve the partnership at will (ULPA sec. 10) nor force dissolution at the retirement, death, or insanity of a general partner if the remaining general partners agree to continue the business in accordance with a right granted in the partnership certificate (ULPA sec. 20). CULPA section 15520 further provides that a new general partner can be elected to continue the business without causing dissolution, if the certificate permits.

The sole general partner in the limited partnerships involved herein was a corporation, whose business was the promotion and management of real estate ventures. As a practical matter, it is unlikely that either Mai-Kai or Somis would have been dissolved midstream and the partners afforded an opportunity to withdraw their investments. Petitioners argue that the partnerships nevertheless lacked continuity of life because they could be dissolved either at will by, or on the bankruptcy of, the general partner. We turn first to the effect of bankruptcy of GHL.

California Uniform Partnership Act section 15031(5) (West Supp. 1976) (hereinafter referred to as CUPA) provides that a partnership is dissolved on the bankruptcy of a partner. CUPA section 15006(2) makes that act applicable to limited partnerships unless inconsistent with statutes relating to them. CULPA nowhere provides for dissolution or nondissolution in the event of bankruptcy. Section 15520, which merely covers dissolution and countervailing action by the remaining partners under certain circumstances, does not provide for such event. CUPA section 15031(5) therefore applies. Since the bankruptcy of GHL would bring about dissolution by operation of law, each limited partner would be entitled to demand the return of his contribution (CULPA sec. 15516). Somis and Mai-Kai simply do not satisfy the Regulations' test of continuity, which requires that the "bankruptcy . . . of *any member* will not cause a dissolution of the organization." (Emphasis supplied.)[11]

The fact that under the agreements involved herein a new general partner might be chosen to continue the business does not affect this conclusion. Respondent seizes upon this aspect of the agreements to argue that the limited partners could anticipate the bankruptcy of GHL and elect a new general partner. But this element does not detract from the hard fact that if GHL became bankrupt while it was the general partner of Somis and Mai-Kai, there would at best be a hiatus between the event of bankruptcy and the entry of a new general partner so that, from a legal point of view, the old partnerships would have been dissolved. Moreover, at least in the case of Mai-Kai, a vote of 100 percent of the limited partners was required to elect a new general partner. Glensder Textile Co., 46 B.T.A. 176 (1942), held that such contingent continuity of life did not resemble that of a corporation. Respondent's Regulations incorporate this conclusion.

We hold that the partnerships involved herein do not satisfy the "continuity of life" test as set forth in respondent's Regulations. We recognize that our application of respondent's existing Regulations to the event of bankruptcy results in a situation where it is unlikely that a limited partnership will ever satisfy the "continuity of life" requirement of those Regulations. But the fact that the Regulations are so clearly keyed to "dissolution" (a term encompassing the legal relationships between the partners) rather than "termination of the business" (a phrase capable of more pragmatic interpretation encompassing the life of the business enterprise) leaves us with no viable alternative. In this connection, we note that respondent is not without power to alter the impact of our application of his existing Regulations. See Morrissey v. Commissioner.

---

11. In light of our conclusion that GHL has not been shown to have had a substantial interest in the partnerships, it may be argued that it was not a "member" for the purpose of the Regulations. Such an argument, however, we find to be structurally incompatible with the Regulations, which consider the substantiality of a partner's interest in the partnership only in connection with centralization of management and transferability of interests. Cf. Regs. §301.7701-2(d)(2) (fourth sentence).

In view of our conclusion as to the effect of GHL's bankruptcy, we find it unnecessary to deal with the contentions of the parties as to whether, under California law, GHL had the legal power to dissolve both Mai-Kai and Somis so as to counteract the "continuity of life" elements contained in the rights of the limited partners under the partnership agreements and certificates. . . .

2. CENTRALIZED MANAGEMENT

In the corporate form, management is centralized in the officers and directors; the involvement of shareholders as such in ordinary operations is limited to choosing these representatives. In a general partnership, authority is decentralized and any partner has the power to make binding decisions in the ordinary course (UPA sec. 9). In a limited partnership, however, this authority exists only in the general partners (ULPA secs. 9 and 10), and a limited partner who takes part in the control of the business loses his limited liability status (ULPA sec. 7). From a practical standpoint, it is clear that the management of both Mai-Kai and Somis was centralized in GHL. The sole general partner was empowered by law as well as by the partnership agreements to administer the partnership affairs. However, respondent's Regulations specify that —

> In addition, limited partnerships subject to a statute corresponding to the Uniform Limited Partnership Act, generally do not have centralized management, but centralized management ordinarily does exist in such a limited partnership if substantially all the interests in the partnership are owned by the limited partners.

[Regs. §301.7701-2(c)(4).] In other words, even though there may be centralized administration by a general partner, the "centralization of management" test will not be met if the general partner has a meaningful proprietary interest. See Zuckman v. United States, 524 F.2d 729 (Ct. Cl. 1975). In specifying this additional condition, respondent has adopted the theory of *Glensder Textile Co.*, supra, that managing partners with such interests in the business are not "analogous to directors of a corporation" because they act in their own interests "and not *merely* in a representative capacity for a body of persons having a limited investment and a limited liability." (46 B.T.A. at 185; emphasis added.) It is thus necessary to look to the proprietary interest of GHL in order to determine whether the additional condition imposed by respondent's Regulations has been met.

Unlike the taxpayers in Zuckman v. United States, supra, petitioners herein have failed to show that the limited partners did not own all or substantially all the interests in the partnerships involved herein within the meaning of the Regulations. GHL's interests in Mai-Kai and Somis were subordinated to those of the limited partners. Petitioners have not attempted to demonstrate that GHL's capital interests had any present value during the years in issue, and it is clear that, because of the subordinate provisions, it had no present right to income during those years. Petitioners would have us look to the anticipated return on the partnership properties in future years to determine that GHL had a substantial proprietary stake in the business independent of its management role. They have not, however, proved by competent evidence that such a return could in fact be expected, relying instead on unsupported projections; nor have they shown that any such future profit would be reflected in the present value of GHL's interest. Although there was testimony that GHL expected profits from the subordinated interests when the limited partnerships were liquidated, we are not convinced that the possibility of such income at an indefinite future date had value during the years at issue. GHL reported gross income of $906,930.89 from fiscal 1969 to fiscal 1974, out of which only $118 represented a partnership distribution (from a partnership not involved herein).

Furthermore, the limited partners in Somis and Mai-Kai possessed the right to remove GHL as the general partner. Thus, GHL's right to participate in future growth and profits was wholly contingent on satisfactory performance of its management role,[17] and not at all analogous to the independent proprietary interest of a typical general partner. In *Glensder Textile Co.*, supra, our conclusion that centralization of management was lacking rested not only on the fact that management retained a proprietary interest but also on the fact that the limited partners could not "remove the general partners and control them as agents, as stockholders may control directors." 46 B.T.A. at 185.

Petitioners argue that such power of removal and control could be given to limited partners under the ULPA, that CULPA (which makes specific reference to such power) is a statute corresponding to ULPA, and that accordingly respondent's Regulation requires a decision in their favor on this issue. In our opinion, the Regulation was not intended to provide a blanket exemption from association status for ULPA limited partnerships, regardless of the extent to which the partners by agreement deviate from the statutory scheme. It states only that a limited partnership in an ULPA jurisdiction generally will lack centralized management. We have repeatedly held that an organization is to be classified by reference to the rights and duties created by agreement as well as those existing under State law. *Bush #1*, 48 T.C. at 228; Western Construction Co., 14 T.C. 453, 467 (1950), aff'd. per curiam 191 F.2d 401 (9th Cir. 1951); Glensder Textile Co., 46 B.T.A. at 183. The effect of such organic laws as ULPA (and CULPA) is to provide a rule which governs in the absence of contrary agreement.

17. On removal, GHL would have been entitled to receive the cash value of its interest, both by statute (CUBA sec. 15038(1)) and, in the case of Somis, by agreement. To the extent of that value, GHL would have a vested present proprietary interest to protect. The petitioners had the burden of showing that such value existed and that it was substantial; they have done neither. . . .

Where the theme is obscured by the variations, it is the latter which set the tone of the composition. Neither ULPA nor CULPA requires that the limited partners be given the right to remove the general partner; in fact, ULPA does not even mention such a possibility. By reserving that right, the limited partners in Mai-Kai and Somis took themselves out of the basic framework of ULPA and hence out of the shelter of the Regulation, which is based on *Glensder.*

We conclude that Somis and Mai-kai had centralized management within the meaning of respondent's Regulations.

3. LIMITED LIABILITY

Unless some member is personally liable for debts of, and claims against, an entity, Regs. §301.7701-2(d)(1) states that the entity possesses the corporate characteristic of limited liability. The Regulation provides that "in the case of a limited partnership subject to a statute corresponding to the Uniform Limited Partnership Act, personal liability exists with respect to each general partner, except as provided in subparagraph (2) of this paragraph." The first sentence of subparagraph (2) establishes a conjunctive test, under which a general partner is considered not to have personal liability only "when he has no substantial assets (other than his interest in the partnership) which could be reached by a creditor of the organization *and* when he is merely a 'dummy' acting as the agent of the limited partners." In other words, personal liability exists if the general partner *either* has substantial assets *or* is not a dummy for the limited partners. We do not agree with respondent's assertion, made for the first time in connection with the motion for reconsideration, that the Regulation should be read disjunctively. Although the purpose of subparagraph (2) was ostensibly to delineate the conditions under which personal liability of a general partner *does not exist,* practically, all the remaining material in the subparagraph outlines the conditions under which such personal liability does exist. In several examples, personal liability is said to exist, either because the general partner has substantial assets or because he is not a dummy for the limited partners. See Zuckman v. United States, supra. In no instance is there a suggestion that both conditions established by the first sentence of subparagraph (2) need not be satisfied. . . .

While it may be doubtful that GHL could be considered to have had substantial assets during the years in issue, we find it unnecessary to resolve this question since it is clear that GHL was not a dummy for the limited partners of Somis and Mai-Kai. Respondent contends that GHL fell within the "dummy" concept because it was subject to removal by the limited partners, and thus was subject to their ultimate control. While it is true that a mere "dummy" would be totally under the control of the limited partners, it does not follow that the presence of some control by virtue of the power to remove necessarily makes the general partner a "dummy." It seems clear that the limited partners' rights to remove the general partner were designed to give the limited partners a measure of control over their investment without involving them in the "control of the business"; the rights were not designed to render GHL a mere dummy or to empower the limited partners "to direct that business actively through the general partners." Glensder Textile Co., 46 B.T.A. at 183. Moreover, the record indicates that the limited partners did not use GHL as a screen to conceal their own active involvement in the conduct of the business; far from being a rubber stamp, GHL was the moving force in these enterprises. With a minor exception, the persons controlling GHL were independent of and unrelated to the limited partners.

In view of the foregoing, we conclude that personal liability existed with respect to GHL, and the partnerships lack the corporate characteristic of limited liability.

4. Transferability of Interests

A stockholder's rights and interest in a corporate venture are, absent consensual restrictions, freely transferable by the owner without reference to the wishes of other members. A partner, on the other hand, can unilaterally transfer only his interest in partnership "profits and surplus," and cannot confer on the assignee the other attributes of membership without the consent of all partners (UPA secs. 18(g), 26, and 27). Respondent's Regulations recognize and rely upon this distinction.

The Regulations state that if substantially all interests are freely transferable, the corporate characteristic of free transferability of interests is present. Since we have concluded, for the purposes of this case, that the limited partners should be considered as owning substantially all the interests in Mai-Kai and Somis, we turn our attention to the question whether their interests were so transferable.

A transferee of a limited partnership interest may become a substituted limited partner with the consent of all members or under a right given in the certificate. CULPA sec. 15519. The partnership certificates of Mai-Kai and Somis are silent in this regard. However, when the provisions of the agreements relating to transferability and the power of an assignee to obtain a judicial amendment of the partnership certificate (see CULPA secs. 15502(1)(a)X and 15525) are taken into account, it would appear that the agreements rather than the certificates should be considered the controlling documents herein. Indeed, petitioners do not seek to draw any solace from the certificates, positing their arguments as to lack of transferability on the agreements themselves.

Both partnership agreements permit the assignment of a limited partner's income interest with the consent of the general partner, which may not unreasonably be withheld. Petitioners have not suggested any ground on which consent could be withheld. The requirement of consent, circumscribed by a standard of reasonableness, is not such a restriction on transfer as is typical of partnership agreements; nor is it the sort referred to by the Regulations. In our opinion, the limited partners' income rights were freely transferable. See Outlaw v. United States, 494 F.2d 1376, 1384 (Ct. Cl. 1974).

Petitioners also argue that transferability is limited by the requirement that, in the event of a proposed assignment, a limited partner's capital interest first be offered to other members under certain circumstances. While an assignment for less than fair market value could be prevented in this manner, there was no requirement that such an offer be made if an interest was to be sold to a third party at fair market value. Thus, there was no "effort on the part of the parties to select their business associates," as is characteristic of the usual partnership arrangement. J. A. Riggs Tractor Co., 6 T.C. 889, 898 (1946). We think that these interests possessed considerably more than the "modified" form of free transferability referred to in subparagraph (2) of the Regulation.

In sum, an assignee for fair consideration of a limited partner's interest in Somis or Mai-Kai could acquire all of the rights of a substituted limited partner within the framework of the agreement and governing State law, without discretionary consent of any other member. Any restrictions or conditions on such a transfer were procedural rather than substantive. The right of assignment more closely resembles that attending corporate shares than that typically associated with partnership interests. Mai-Kai and Somis therefore possessed the corporate characteristic of free transferability of interests.

5. OTHER CHARACTERISTICS

Both parties have identified other characteristics of Mai-Kai and Somis which they allege are relevant to the determination whether those entities more closely resemble partnerships or corporations. Some of these are within the ambit of the major characteristics already discussed. Petitioners point to the fact that, unlike a corporate board of directors, GHL as manager lacked the discretionary right to retain or distribute profits according to the needs of the business. This argument is in reality directed to the issue of centralized management. The same is true of respondent's analogy between the limited partners' voting rights and those of corporate shareholders. To be sure the partnership interests were not represented by certificates but this factor conceivably is more properly subsumed in the transferability issue. See Morrissey v. Commissioner, 296 U.S. at 360. Moreover, those interests were divided into units or shares and were promoted and marketed in a manner similar to corporate securities — an additional "characteristic" which we have not ignored (see Outlaw v. United States, supra), but which we do not deem of critical significance under the circumstances herein. Similarly, we do not assign any particular additional importance to the facts that the partnerships have not observed corporate formalities and procedures (Morrissey v. Commissioner, supra; Giant Auto, Parts, Ltd., 13 T.C. 307 (1949)) or that, unlike general partners, limited partners were not required personally to sign the partnership certificates. Finally, respondent argues that the limited partnerships resemble corporations because they provide a means of pooling investments while limiting the liability of the participants. Cf. Helvering v. Combs, 296 U.S. 365 (1935). As it relates to the facts of this case, this point is subsumed in our earlier discussion. To the extent that it presages an attempt to classify *all* limited partnerships as corporations, it is in irreconcilable conflict with respondent's own Regulations.

6. CONCLUSION

The Regulations provide that an entity will be taxed as a corporation if it more closely resembles a corporation than any other form of organization. They further state that such a resemblance does not exist unless the entity possesses more corporate than noncorporate characteristics. If every characteristic bears equal weight, then Mai-Kai and Somis are partnerships for tax purposes. We have found that they possess only two of the four major corporate characteristics and that none of the other characteristics cited by the parties upsets the balance.[22] On the other hand, if the overall corporate resemblance test, espoused by *Morrissey* and adhered to by the Regulations, permits us to weigh each factor according to the degree of corporate similarity it provides, we would be inclined to find that these entities were taxable as corporations. Each possessed a degree of centralized management indistinguishable from that of a pure corporation; the other major factors lie somewhere on the continuum between corporate and partnership resemblance. Were not the Regulations' thumb upon the scales, it appears to us that the practical continuity and limited liability of both entities would decisively tip the balance in respondent's favor. However, we can find no warrant for such refined balancing in the Regulations or in cases which have considered them. See Zuckman v. United States, 524 F.2d 729 (Ct. Cl. 1975); Outlaw v. United States, supra; Kurzner v. United States, 413 F.2d 97, 105 (5th Cir. 1969) ("four equally weighted procrustean criteria"); Regs. §§301.7701-2(a)(3) and 301.7701-3(b)(2). Cf. Estate of Smith v. Commissioner, 313 F.2d 724, 736 (8th Cir. 1963) ("substantially

---

22. Indeed, considering the importance of predictability in applying respondent's Regulations, we would not be inclined to give such lesser characteristics controlling weight unless their materiality was unmistakable, a situation which does not obtain in this case.

greater noncorporate characteristics both in number *and in importance*").
Only in connection with free transferability of interests do the Regulations
recognize a modified and less significant form of a particular characteristic.[23]

Our task herein is to apply the provisions of respondent's Regulations
as we find them and not as we think they might or ought to have been
written. See and compare David F. Bolger, 59 T.C. 760, 771 (1973). On
this basis, petitioners must prevail.

Decisions will be entered under Rule 155.

Reviewed by the Court.

Fay and Hall, JJ., did not participate in the consideration and disposition of this case.

[Two concurring and five dissenting opinions omitted.]

NOTE

In the absence of congressional guidance, courts have faced a difficult
task in determining the tax treatment of limited partnerships. Compare
Zuckman v. United States, 524 F.2d 729 (Cl. Ct. 1975), holding a limited
partnership not an association, with Larson v. Commissioner, 65 T.C. No.
10 (1975) (*Larson I*), holding a fairly typical California limited partnership
an association. Even though the *Larson I* opinion was withdrawn for reconsideration within a month after its issuance, it created a near panic among
some real estate groups. *Larson II,* the opinion reproduced above, came
as a relief to many taxpayers. In an apparent response to *Larson II,* the
Treasury in 1977 proposed and in the ensuing clamor immediately thereafter withdrew new regulations that would have classified most limited partnerships as associations. Several days after withdrawal, then-Secretary
William Simon announced that regulations would not be reproposed. In
April 1979 the Treasury agreed to follow *Larson II.*

The *Zuckman* and *Larson* opinions reflect a judicial policy of unwillingness to become involved in the recharacterization battle, when the taxpayers manage to satisfy the existing regulations on a technical or literal level.
Such an approach is close to saying that "form is form," i.e., if a state
adopts the UPA or the ULPA and the partnership agreement adheres to
either act, the partnership form will be acknowledged for tax purposes.
The result is that taxpayers and their counsel will usually be able to arrange
the transaction to get the desired results, i.e., association or partnership
status. Since Congress has given little policy guidance about why corporations are taxed in one manner and partnerships are taxed in another, it

---

23. Even if we had found that the interests of the limited partners in Somis and Mai-
Kai possessed only such modified form of free transferability, petitioners would still prevail,
since the balance would be two characteristics favoring partnership status and something less
than two characteristics favoring corporate status.

may be reasonable for courts to follow the *Larson/Zuckman* approach. This leaves it to Congress to tell the courts how and where to draw the lines differently if it disagrees.

5. Limited Liability Companies

Rev. Rul. 93-6
1993-3 I.R.B. 8

ISSUE

Is *M,* a Colorado limited liability company, classified for federal tax purposes as an association or as a partnership?

FACTS

M is organized as a limited liability company pursuant to the provisions of the Colorado Limited Liability Act (Act), Colo. Rev. Stat. secs. 7-80-101 through 7-80-913 (1990). *M* is authorized under its articles of organization to engage in any and all business and activity permitted by the laws of the State of Colorado. *M* has five members, each of whom is elected as a manager of *M.*

Section 7-80-401(1) of the Act provides that management of the limited liability company's business and affair is vested in a manager or managers. Section 7-80-402 provides that managers shall be elected at each annual meeting. All managers must be elected annually unless the articles provide for staggered two or three year terms.

Section 7-80-705 of the Act provides that members and managers are not liable under a judgment, decree, or order of a court, or in any other manner, for a debt, obligation, or liability of the limited liability company.

Section 7-80-702(1) of the Act provides that the interest of each member in a limited liability company constitutes the personal property of the member and may be transferred or assigned as provided in the operating agreement. However, if all of the other members of the limited liability company other than the member proposing to dispose of the member's interest do not approve of the proposed transfer or assignment by unanimous written consent, the transferee of the member's interest has no right to participate in the management of the business and affairs of the limited liability company or to become a member. The transferee is only entitled to receive the share of profits or other compensation by way of income and the return of contributions, to which that member otherwise would be entitled.

Section 7-80-801 of the Act provides that a limited liability company organized under the Act is dissolved upon the occurrence of any of the following events: (1) when the period fixed for the duration of the company expires; (2) by the unanimous written agreement of all the members; or (3) upon the death, retirement, resignation, expulsion, bankruptcy, or dissolution of a member or the occurrence of any other event that terminates the continued membership of a member in the limited liability company, unless there are at least two remaining members and the business of the limited liability company is continued by the consent of all the remaining members under a right to do so stated in the articles of organization within 90 days after the termination. Under *M*'s articles of organization, upon the withdrawal of a member, the consent of all the remaining members must be obtained to continue the business of *M*.

LAW AND ANALYSIS

Section 7701(a)(2) of the Internal Revenue Code provides that the term "partnership" includes a syndicate, group, pool, joint venture, or other unincorporated organization, through or by means of which any business, financial operation, or venture is carried on, and which is not a trust or estate or a corporation.

Section 301.7701-1(b) of the Procedure and Administration Regulations states that the Code prescribes certain categories, or classes, into which various organizations fall for purposes of taxation. These categories, or classes, include associations (which are taxable as corporations), partnerships, and trusts. The tests, or standards, that are to be applied in determining the classification in which an organization belongs are set forth in sections 301.7701-2 through 301.7701-4.

Section 301.7701-2(a)(1) of the Regulations sets forth the following major characteristics of a corporation: (1) associates, (2) an objective to carry on business and divide the gains therefrom, (3) continuity of life, (4) centralization of management, (5) liability for corporate debts limited to corporate property, and (6) free transferability of interests. Whether a particular organization is to be classified as an association must be determined by taking into account the presence or absence of each of these corporate characteristics.

Section 301.7701-2(a)(2) of the Regulations provides that an organization that has associates and an objective to carry on business and divide the gains therefrom is not classified as a trust, but rather as a partnership or association taxable as a corporation. It further provides that characteristics common to partnerships and corporations are not material in attempting to distinguish between an association and a partnership. Since associates and an objective to carry on business and divide the gains therefrom are generally common to corporations and partnerships, the determination of whether an organization that has these characteristics is to be treated for tax purposes as a partnership or as an association depends on whether there exists centralization of management, continuity of life, free transferability of interests, and limited liability.

Section 301.7701-2(a)(3) of the Regulations provides that if an unincorporated organization possesses more corporate characteristics than noncorporate characteristics, it constitutes an association taxable as a corporation.

In interpreting section 301.7701-2 of the Regulations, the Tax Court, in Larson v. Commissioner, 66 T.C. 159 (1976), acq., 1979-1 C.B. 1, concluded that equal weight must be given to each of the four corporate characteristics of continuity of life, centralization of management, limited liability, and free transferability of interests.

In the present situation, M has associates and an objective to carry on business and divide the gains therefrom. Therefore, M must be classified as either an association or a partnership. M is classified as a partnership for federal tax purposes unless the organization has a preponderance of the remaining corporate characteristics of continuity of life, centralization of management, limited liability, and free transferability of interests.

Section 301.7701-2(b)(1) of the Regulations provides that if the death, insanity, bankruptcy, retirement, resignation, or expulsion of any member will cause a dissolution of the organization, continuity of life does not exist. Section 301.7701-2(b)(2) provides that an agreement by which an organization is established may provide that the business will be continued by the remaining members in the event of the death or withdrawal of any member, but the agreement does not establish continuity of life if under local law the death or withdrawal of any member causes a dissolution of the organization.

Under the Act, unless there are at least two remaining members of M and the business of M is continued by the consent of all the remaining members, M is dissolved upon the death, retirement, resignation, expulsion, bankruptcy, dissolution of a member or occurrence of any other event that terminates the continued membership of a member of the company. If a member of M ceases to be a member of M for any reason, the continuity of M is not assured because all remaining members must agree to continue the business. Consequently, M lacks the corporate characteristic of continuity of life.

Section 301.7701-2(c)(1) of the Regulations provides that an organization has the corporate characteristic of centralized management if any person (or any group of persons that does not include all the members) has continuing exclusive authority to make the management decisions necessary to the conduct of the business for which the organization was formed.

Section 301.7701-2(c)(2) of the Regulations provides that the persons who have this authority may, or may not, be members of the organization and may hold office as a result of a selection by the members from time to time, or may be self-perpetuating in office. Centralized management can be accomplished by election to office, by proxy appointment, or by any other means which has the effect of concentrating in a management group continuing exclusive authority to make management decisions.

Section 301.7701-2(c)(4) of the Regulations provides that there is no centralization of continuing exclusive authority to make management decisions, unless the managers have sole authority to make the decisions. For example, in the case of a corporation or a trust, the concentration of management powers in a board of directors or trustees effectively prevents a stockholder or a trust beneficiary, simply because that person is a stockholder or beneficiary, from binding the corporation or the trust.

Under the Act, the management of a limited liability company is vested in managers elected by the company's members. The elected managers may or may not be members of the company, and may or may not include all members of the company. Members, by sole virtue of being members, do not possess managerial authority. Although all of M's members are elected managers of M, M nevertheless possesses centralized management, because, as provided by the Act, authority to make management decisions rests solely with the five members in their capacity as managers rather than as members.

Section 301.7701-2(d)(1) of the Regulations provides that an organization has the corporate characteristic of limited liability if under local law there is no member who is personally liable for the debts of, or claims against, the organization. Personal liability means that a creditor of an organization may seek personal satisfaction from a member of the organization to the extent that the assets of the organization are insufficient to satisfy the creditor's claims.

Under the Act, the members of M are not liable for M's debts, obligations, or liabilities. Consequently, M possesses the corporate characteristic of limited liability.

Section 301.7701-2(e)(1) of the Regulations provides that an organization has the corporate characteristic of free transferability of interests if each of the members or those members owning substantially all of the interests in the organization have the power, without the consent of other members, to substitute for themselves in the same organization a person who is not a member of the organization. For this power of substitution to exist in the corporate sense, the member must be able, without the consent of other members, to confer upon the member's substitute all the attributes of the member's interest in the organization. The characteristic of free transferability does not exist if each member can, without the consent of other members, assign only the right to share in the profits but cannot assign the right to participate in the management of the organization.

Under the Act, a member of M can assign or transfer that member's interest to another who is not a member of the organization. However, the assignee or transferee does not become a substitute member and does not acquire all the attributes of the member's interest in *M* unless all the remaining members approve the assignment or transfer. Therefore, *M* lacks the corporate characteristic of free transferability of interests.

M has associates and an objective to carry on business and divide the gains therefrom. In addition, *M* possesses the corporate characteristics of centralized management and limited liability. *M* does not, however, possess the corporate characteristics of continuity of life and free transferability of interests.

HOLDING

M has associates and an objective to carry on business and divide the gains therefrom but lacks a preponderance of the four remaining corporate characteristics. Accordingly, M is classified as a partnership for federal tax purposes.

NOTE

A limited liability company (LLC) is a hybrid entity combining the corporate benefit of limited liability for the owners and the partnership's tax advantage of pass-through treatment for income tax purposes. Although Wyoming pioneered the LLC in 1977, the LLC did not generate significant interest until 1988, when the IRS issued Rev. Rul. 88-76, 1988-2 CB 360, which classified an LLC formed under Wyoming law as a partnership for federal income tax purposes. Rev. Rul. 93-6, above, is typical of the IRS rulings that have followed the original 1988 ruling. Interest in the LLC heightened with increased certainty that an LLC could avoid the entity-level tax imposed on C corporations. More than 35 states now allow the formation of LLCs; only eight states recognized LLCs in 1991.

To form an LLC, articles of organization (not incorporation) must be filed with the appropriate state authority. An LLC is owned by "members" rather than by shareholders or partners. In most cases, an LLC must have at least two members. This requirement is consistent with the LLC's classification for income tax purposes as a partnership. A corporation, partnership, LLC, trust, estate, or other entity, as well as individuals, may be members. Contributions to an LLC in exchange for a membership interest may be made in the form of cash, property, the use of property, services, or any other valuable consideration. In some states, contributions may also be made in the form of a promissory note or other binding obligation.

Generally, an LLC is not required to have an operating agreement. Some states, however, require the adoption of an operating agreement and specify certain mandatory provisions. In the absence of an operating agreement, an LLC is governed by its articles and state law. Provisions with respect to an LLC's affairs generally may be included in an operating agreement to the extent that they are not inconsistent with state law or the LLC's articles. Typically, LLC statutes often rely on "default rules," or statutory provisions that apply unless an LLC's articles or operating agreement specifies otherwise. Default rules allow an LLC to be customized to suit the needs of its members.

Members of an LLC are usually permitted under state law to customize both distribution of cash and property and allocation of profits and losses to the members through the operating agreement or the articles. In the absence of any financial provisions in the operating agreement or in the articles, distributions are generally made and profits and losses are allocated on a proportional basis in accordance with the members' respective contributions. In most states, unless otherwise provided in the articles or operating agreement, a member has the right to withdraw on six months' notice. A withdrawing member is entitled to fair value of the membership interest.

One of the major advantages of an LLC is that it provides limited liability to all its members and managers. The typical state act provides that an individual or entity does not have any personal obligation for the liabilities of an LLC solely by reason of being a member, manager, or other agent of the LLC. Some states permit a member to waive limited liability. The ability to insulate an LLC member from personal liability as a member, regardless of management activities, is one of the primary distinctions between an LLC and a limited partnership. For example, under the Revised Uniform Limited Partnership Act (RULPA), a limited partner who participates in the partnership's management can become personally liable for partnership obligations.

Unless an operating agreement or the articles provide to the contrary, a membership interest is assignable in whole or in part. The assignment of a membership interest enables the assignee only to receive, to the extent assigned, the distributions from the LLC to which the assignor would otherwise be entitled. For the assignee to participate in the management and affairs of the LLC and to exercise other membership rights, in most states the remaining members must unanimously consent to the assignee's admission as a member. Although a state's act may not prohibit an agreement — outside of the operating agreement — that allows an assignee to become a member on the direction of fewer than all the members, such an agreement may cause an LLC to be classified as a corporation for federal income tax purposes.

B. DUMMY CORPORATIONS

We have seen that in some situations the Service will attempt to treat a noncorporate enterprise as a corporation. See, e.g., Larson v. Commissioner, pages 636-645 supra. What happens if a corporation attempts to ignore its own corporate status? Can a taxpayer that has chosen to operate in corporate form under applicable state law ignore that form for federal tax purposes? With corporate tax rates higher than individual rates, the issue is a significant one.

Commissioner v. Bollinger
485 U.S. 340 (1988)

Justice SCALIA delivered the opinion of the Court.

Petitioner the Commissioner of Internal Revenue challenges a decision by the United States Court of Appeals for the Sixth Circuit holding that a corporation which held record title to real property as agent for the corporation's shareholders was not the owner of the property for purposes of federal income taxation. 807 F.2d 65 (1986). We granted certiorari . . . to resolve a conflict in the courts of appeals over the tax treatment of corporations purporting to be agents for their shareholders. . . .

I

Respondent Jesse C. Bollinger, Jr., developed, either individually or in partnership with some or all of the other respondents, eight apartment complexes in Lexington, Kentucky. (For convenience we will refer to all the ventures as "partnerships.") Bollinger initiated development of the first apartment complex, Creekside North Apartments, in 1968. The Massachusetts Mutual Life Insurance Company agreed to provide permanent financing by lending $1,075,000 to "the corporate nominee of Jesse C. Bollinger, Jr." at an annual interest rate of eight percent, secured by a mortgage on the property and a personal guaranty from Bollinger. The loan commitment was structured in this fashion because Kentucky's usury law at the time limited the annual interest rate for noncorporate borrowers to seven percent. Ky. Rev. Stat. §§360.010, 360.025 (1972). Lenders willing to provide money only at higher rates required the nominal debtor and record title holder of mortgaged property to be a corporate nominee of the true owner and borrower. On October 14, 1968, Bollinger incorporated Creekside, Inc., under the laws of Kentucky; he was the only stockholder. The next day, Bollinger and Creekside, Inc., entered into a written agreement which provided that the corporation would hold title to the apartment complex as Bollinger's agent for the sole purpose of securing financing, and would convey, assign, or encumber the property and disburse the proceeds thereof only as directed by Bollinger; that Creekside, Inc., had no obligation to maintain the property or assume any liability by reason of the execution of promissory notes or otherwise; and that Bollinger would indemnify and hold the corporation harmless from any liability it might sustain as his agent and nominee.

Having secured the commitment for permanent financing, Bollinger, acting through Creekside, Inc., borrowed the construction funds for the apartment complex from Citizens Fidelity Bank and Trust Company. Creekside, Inc., executed all necessary loan documents including the promissory note and mortgage, and transferred all loan proceeds to Bollinger's individual construction account. Bollinger acted as general contractor for the construction, hired the necessary employees, and paid the expenses out of the construction account. When construction was completed, Bollinger obtained, again through Creekside, Inc., permanent financing from Massachusetts Mutual Life in accordance with the earlier loan commitment. These loan proceeds were used to pay off the Citizens Fidelity construction loan. Bollinger hired a resident manager to rent the apartments, execute leases with tenants, collect and deposit the rents, and maintain operating records. The manager deposited all rental receipts into, and paid all operating expenses from, an operating account, which was first opened in the name of Creekside, Inc., but was later changed to "Creekside Apartments, a partnership." The operation of Creekside North Apartments generated losses for the taxable years 1969, 1971, 1972, 1973, and 1974, and ordinary income for the years 1970, 1975, 1976, and 1977. Throughout, the income and losses were reported by Bollinger on his individual income tax returns.

Following a substantially identical pattern, seven other apartment complexes were developed by respondents through seven separate partnerships. For each venture, a partnership executed a nominee agreement with Creekside, Inc., to obtain financing. (For one of the ventures, a different Kentucky corporation, Cloisters, Inc., in which Bollinger had a 50 percent interest, acted as the borrower and titleholder. For convenience, we will refer to both Creekside and Cloisters as "the corporation.") The corporation transferred the construction loan proceeds to the partnership's construction account, and the partnership hired a construction supervisor who oversaw construction. Upon completion of construction, each partnership actively managed its apartment complex, depositing all rental receipts into, and paying all expenses from, a separate partnership account for each apartment complex. The corporation had no assets, liabilities, employees, or bank accounts. In every case, the lenders regarded the partnership as the owner of the apartments and were aware that the corporation was acting as agent of the partnership in holding record title. The partnerships reported the income and losses generated by the apartment complexes on their partnership tax returns, and respondents reported their distributive share of the partnership income and losses on their individual tax returns.

The Commissioner of Internal Revenue disallowed the losses reported by respondents, on the ground that the standards set out in National Carbide Corp. v. Commissioner, 336 U.S. 422 (1949), were not met. The

Commissioner contended that *National Carbide* required a corporation to have an arm's-length relationship with its shareholders before it could be recognized as their agent. Although not all respondents were shareholders of the corporation, the Commissioner took the position that the funds the partnerships disbursed to pay expenses should be deemed contributions to the corporation's capital, thereby making all respondents constructive stockholders. Since, in the Commissioner's view, the corporation rather than its shareholders owned the real estate, any losses sustained by the ventures were attributable to the corporation and not respondents. Respondents sought a redetermination in the United States Tax Court. The Tax Court held that the corporations were the agents of the partnerships and should be disregarded for tax purposes. Bollinger v. Commissioner, 48 T.C.M. 1443 (1984), ¶84,560 P-H Memo T.C. On appeal, the United States Court of Appeals for the Sixth Circuit affirmed. 807 F.2d 65 (1986). We granted the Commissioner's petition for certiorari.

II

For federal income tax purposes, gain or loss from the sale or use of property is attributable to the owner of the property. See Helvering v. Horst, 311 U.S. 112, 116-117 (1940); Blair v. Commissioner, 300 U.S. 5, 12 (1937); see also Commissioner v. Sunnen, 333 U.S. 591, 604 (1948). The problem we face here is that two different taxpayers can plausibly be regarded as the owner. Neither the Internal Revenue Code nor the Regulations promulgated by the Secretary of the Treasury provide significant guidance as to which should be selected. It is common ground between the parties, however, that if a corporation holds title to property as agent for a partnership, then for tax purposes the partnership and not the corporation is the owner. Given agreement on that premise, one would suppose that there would be agreement upon the conclusion as well. For each of respondents' apartment complexes, an agency agreement expressly provided that the corporation would "hold such property as nominee and agent for" the partnership, App. to Pet. for Cert. 21a, n.4, and that the partnership would have sole control of and responsibility for the apartment complex. The partnership in each instance was identified as the principal and owner of the property during financing, construction, and operation. The lenders, contractors, managers, employees, and tenants — all who had contact with the development — knew that the corporation was merely the agent of the partnership, if they knew of the existence of the corporation at all. In each instance the relationship between the corporation and the partnership was, in both form and substance, an agency with the partnership as principal.

The Commissioner contends, however, that the normal indicia of agency cannot suffice for tax purposes when, as here, the alleged principals are the controlling shareholders of the alleged agent corporation. That, it asserts, would undermine the principle of Moline Properties v. Commissioner, 319 U.S. 436 (1943), which held that a corporation is a separate taxable entity even if it has only one shareholder who exercises total control over its affairs. Obviously, *Moline*'s separate-entity principle would be significantly compromised if shareholders of closely held corporations could, by clothing the corporation with some attributes of agency with respect to particular assets, leave themselves free at the end of the tax year to make a claim — perhaps even a good-faith claim — of either agent or owner status, depending upon which choice turns out to minimize their tax liability. The Commissioner does not have the resources to audit and litigate the many cases in which agency status could be thought debatable. Hence, the Commissioner argues, in this shareholder context he can reasonably demand that the taxpayer meet a prophylactically clear test of agency.

We agree with that principle, but the question remains whether the test the Commissioner proposes is appropriate. The parties have debated at length the significance of our opinion in National Carbide Corp. v. Commissioner, supra. In that case, three corporations that were wholly owned subsidiaries of another corporation agreed to operate their production plants as "agents" for the parent, transferring to it all profits except for a nominal sum. The subsidiaries reported as gross income only this sum, but the Commissioner concluded that they should be taxed on the entirety of the profits because they were not really agents. We agreed, reasoning first, that the mere fact of the parent's control over the subsidiaries did not establish the existence of an agency, since such control is typical of all shareholder-corporation relationships, id., at 429-434; and second, that the agreements to pay the parent all profits above a nominal amount were not determinative since income must be taxed to those who actually earn it without regard to anticipatory assignment, id., at 435-436. We acknowledged, however, that there was such a thing as "a true corporate agent . . . of an owner-principal," id., at 437, and proceeded to set forth four indicia and two requirements of such status, the sum of which has become known in the lore of federal income tax law as the "six *National Carbide* factors":

[1] Whether the corporation operates in the name and for the account of the principal, [2] binds the principal by its actions, [3] transmits money received to the principal, and [4] whether receipt of income is attributable to the services of employees of the principal and to assets belonging to the principal are some of the relevant considerations in determining whether a true agency exists. [5] If the corporation is a true agent, its relations with its principal must not be dependent upon the fact that it is owned by the principal, if such is the case. [6] Its business purpose must be the carrying on of the normal duties of an agent.

Id., at 47 (footnotes omitted).

We readily discerned that these factors led to a conclusion of non-agency in *National Carbide* itself. There each subsidiary had represented to its customers that it (not the parent) was the company manufacturing and selling its products; each had sought to shield the parent from service of legal process; and the operations had used thousands of the subsidiaries' employees and nearly $20 million worth of property and equipment listed as assets on the subsidiaries' books. Id., at 425, 434, 438, and n.21.

The Commissioner contends that the last two *National Carbide* factors are not satisfied in the present case. To take the last first: The Commissioner argues that here the corporation's business purpose with respect to the property at issue was not "the carrying on of the normal duties of an agent," since it was acting not as the agent but rather as the owner of the property for purposes of Kentucky's usury laws. We do not agree. It assuredly was not acting as the owner in fact, since respondents represented themselves as the principals to all parties concerned with the loans. Indeed, it was the lenders themselves who required the use of a corporate nominee. Nor does it make any sense to adopt a contrary-to-fact legal presumption that the corporation was the principal, imposing a federal tax sanction for the apparent evasion of Kentucky's usury law. To begin with, the Commissioner has not established that these transactions were an evasion. Respondents assert without contradiction that use of agency arrangements in order to permit higher interest was common practice, and it is by no means clear that the practice violated the spirit of the Kentucky law, much less its letter. It might well be thought that the borrower does not generally require usury protection in a transaction sophisticated enough to employ a corporate agent — assuredly not the normal modus operandi of the loan shark. That the statute positively envisioned corporate nominees is suggested by a provision which forbids charging the higher corporate interest rates "to a corporation, the principal asset of which shall be the ownership of a one (1) or two (2) family or (2) family dwelling," Ky. Rev. Stat. §360.025(2) (1987) — which would seem to prevent use of the nominee device for ordinary home-mortgage loans. In any event, even if the transaction did run afoul of the usury law, Kentucky, like most States, regards only the lender as the usurer, and the borrower as the victim. See Ky. Rev. Stat. §360.020 (1987) (lender liable to borrower for civil penalty), section 360.990 (lender guilty of misdemeanor). Since the Kentucky statute imposed no penalties upon the borrower for allowing himself to be victimized, nor treated him as in pari delictu, but to the contrary enabled him to pay back the principal without any interest, and to sue for double the amount of interest already paid (plus attorney's fees), see Ky. Rev. Stat. section 360.020 (1972), the United States would hardly be vindicating Kentucky law by depriving the usury victim of tax advantages he would otherwise enjoy. In sum, we see no basis in either fact or policy for holding that the corporation was the principal because of the nature of its participation in the loans.

Of more general importance is the Commissioner's contention that the arrangements here violate the fifth *National Carbide* factor — that the corporate agent's "relations with its principal must not be dependent upon the fact that it is owned by the principal." The Commissioner asserts that this cannot be satisfied unless the corporate agent and its shareholder principal have an "arm's-length relationship" that includes the payment of a fee for agency services. The meaning of *National Carbide*'s fifth factor is, at the risk of understatement, not entirely clear. Ultimately, the relations between a corporate agent and its owner-principal are always dependent upon the fact of ownership, in that the owner can cause the relations to be altered or terminated at any time. Plainly that is not what was meant, since on that interpretation all subsidiary-parent agencies would be invalid for tax purposes, a position which the *National Carbide* opinion specifically disavowed. We think the fifth *National Carbide* factor — so much more abstract than the others — was no more and no less than a generalized statement of the concern, expressed earlier in our own discussion, that the separate-entity doctrine of *Moline* not be subverted.

In any case, we decline to parse the text of *National Carbide* as though that were itself the governing statute. As noted earlier, it is uncontested that the law attributes tax consequences of property held by a genuine agent to the principal; and we agree that it is reasonable for the Commissioner to demand unequivocal evidence of genuineness in the corporation-shareholder context, in order to prevent evasion of *Moline*. We see no basis, however, for holding that unequivocal evidence can only consist of the rigid requirements (arm's-length dealing plus agency fee) that the Commissioner suggests. Neither of those is demanded by the law of agency, which permits agents to be unpaid family members, friends, or associates. See Restatement (Second) of Agency §§16, 21, 22 (1958). It seems to us that the genuineness of the agency relationship is adequately assured, and tax-avoiding manipulation adequately avoided, when the fact that the corporation is acting as agent for its shareholders with respect to a particular asset is set forth in a written agreement at the time the asset is acquired, the corporation functions as agent and not principal with respect to the asset for all purposes, and the corporation is held out as the agent and not principal in all dealings with third parties relating to the asset. Since these requirements were met here, the judgment of the Court of Appeals is affirmed.

Justice Kennedy took no part in the consideration or decision of this case.

NOTE

Justice Scalia's opinion is refreshing in its unwillingness to submerge the Court in an abstract test or a game of words involving the fifth *National*

Carbide factor. Instead, the opinion finds a genuine principal-agent relationship in the existence of a written agreement when the property was acquired, in the fact that the corporation functioned as an agent for all purposes, and in the fact that the corporation held itself out as an agent in all third-party dealings.

Why wasn't the Court bothered by the argument that the decision was furthering evasion of state usury laws? Did Kentucky mean to prohibit the type of arrangements made by the taxpayers, or did the law have a more limited purpose?

Bollinger has established a certain symmetry in the tax laws. We know from *Larson* that the Service will argue that an organization should be taxed like a corporation if it has certain corporate attributes even if it is nominally a partnership or other type of entity. After *Bollinger,* a taxpayer can argue that what is nominally a corporation does not function as a corporation and therefore should be ignored for tax purposes.

Not all cases involving the agency issue concern corporations formed for the purpose of circumventing state usury limitations. See, e.g., Elot H. Raffety Farms v. United States, 511 F.2d 1234 (8th Cir. 1975) (the court of appeals recognized a corporation even though it was used only to avoid a foreign law requirement prohibiting conduct of a business by aliens). In Interstate Transit Lines v. Commissioner, 319 U.S. 590 (1943), a parent corporation was denied a deduction under §162(a) for a payment to its wholly owned subsidiary to defray the subsidiary's operating deficit for the taxable year, despite the fact that by contract it was entitled to the subsidiary's profits and was obliged to reimburse the subsidiary for its losses. The Court held that the subsidiary's operating deficit was not an expense of the parent's business. The case was complicated by the fact that the subsidiary was organized to engage in operations (intrastate transportation in California) that were forbidden to the parent because it was a foreign corporation. The Court was not called on to decide whether the parent's payments should be treated as an additional investment in the subsidiary.

C. REALLOCATION OF INCOME AND RELATED ISSUES

With corporate tax rates lower than the top individual tax rates, individuals have incentives to allocate income to corporations they control. Moreover, historically corporations have offered pension incentives to owner-employees not available to individual entrepreneurs. For example, prior to 1982 the pension opportunities available to employees of corporations far exceeded those available to the self-employed. In response to this disparity, professionals such as doctors and lawyers created wholly owned professional service corporations for which they would work. These corporations would be in the business of hiring out their sole employee (the doctor or lawyer) to his prior employer. The income that the corporation received was paid to its sole employee partly in cash and partly in the form of a lucrative pension plan. Thus, the professional service corporation often was used solely to obtain greater pension benefits.

Personal service corporations also offer income-splitting opportunities. For example, an architect might work exclusively for her professional service corporation for a salary far less than the fees received by the corporation for her services. Since the corporation will deduct the architect's salary under §162 as an ordinary and necessary business expense, the corporation's taxable income will be only that proportion of its receipts that it retains. The architect's taxable income, on the other hand, will equal her salary. By dividing receipts between herself and her corporation, no income goes untaxed, but the architect's compensation is taxed between two taxpayers, thereby taking advantage of the progressive rates of the income tax to reduce the total tax liability.

The allocation of income phenomenon is not restricted to shareholders trying to shift income to controlled corporations; it is a dominant issue for intercorporate allocations as well. In many cases U.S. corporations subject to U.S. taxation have an incentive to shift income to a related foreign corporation that may not be subject to U.S. taxation and is often subject to little foreign taxation. For example, suppose a U.S. corporation with a foreign subsidiary in a low tax jurisdiction manufactures thermostats at a cost of $100 that it sells to the subsidiary, which resells the thermostats to unrelated purchasers in the subsidiary's jurisdiction at a price of $500. If the U.S. parent charges the subsidiary $140 for the thermostats, it will have $40 subject to U.S. taxation. The $360 gain the subsidiary realizes on the resale is typically not subject to U.S. taxation. Often the Service in this type of situation will attempt to reallocate some of the subsidiary's income to the U.S. parent. The following case is typical.

Bausch & Lomb, Inc. v. Commissioner
933 F.2d 1084 (2d Cir. 1991), aff'g 92 T.C. 525 (1989)

OPINION

MAHONEY, Circuit Judge

BACKGROUND

. . . In 1978, B & L was a major participant in the soft contact lens industry, controlling upwards of 50.6 per cent of the United States market. Between 1978 and 1980, B & L prepared long range forecasts that predicted increasing demand for soft contact lenses in international markets, particularly in Europe. In 1978, B & L began to investigate the possibility of an overseas manufacturing facility to complement its existing plant in Rochester, New York. Responding to various incentives offered by the Industrial Development Authority of the Republic of Ireland ("IDA"), including a tax holiday on all export profits through 1990, B & L determined to establish a manufacturing facility in Waterford, Ireland. The Tax Court:

> found as fact that [B & L] had sound business reasons for the establishment of B & L Ireland. [B & L] had reason to believe that manufacturing capacity at its Rochester facility was inadequate to meet expected increases in soft contact lens demand. [B & L] determined that it was prudent to establish additional manufacturing capacity overseas in order to minimize regulatory delays, establish an alternative supply source to the Rochester facility, and to have a facility capable of more efficiently servicing the increasingly important European markets. Ireland was determined to be the location at which these objectives could be realized most cost effectively due to the incentives offered by the Republic of Ireland to induce the location of manufacturing facilities within the Republic. Since a non-Irish company could not receive [IDA-sponsored] financing, there were sound business reasons for incorporating an Irish manufacturing facility rather than merely operating the facility as a division of B & L.

. . . Accordingly, B & L Ireland was incorporated on February 1, 1980, and B & L, B & L Ireland, and the IDA entered into an agreement on or about February 10, 1981 that specified the incentives to be provided for the venture by the IDA and the reciprocal commitments undertaken by B & L and B & L Ireland. B & L Ireland agreed, inter alia, not to enter into any royalty commitments, except that B & L Ireland could pay royalties to B & L or any subsidiaries in an amount not to exceed five percent of B & L Ireland's annual net sales.

Among the reasons for B & L's success was its manufacturing expertise. In the early 1960s, a Czechoslovakian chemist developed the "spin cast" method of manufacturing soft contact lenses, a process that uses centrifugal force by injecting a mixture into a spinning mold. As a result of a number of licensing agreements and lawsuits, B & L obtained nonexclusive rights to use the patents secured on the first spin cast machines. B & L acquired two spin cast machines from the inventor and, between 1966 and 1981, made several significant process modifications that increased the yield of usable lenses to a commercially acceptable level. Through 1982, B & L was the only manufacturer in the United States using the cost effective spin cast method. Thus, B & L was able to produce lenses at a cost of $1.50 each, which was far below its competitors' costs. During 1981 and 1982, for example, a competitor of B & L had per unit costs of over $4.00 using a cast molding process, and over $6.00 using a lathing process.

In January 1981, B & L granted B & L Ireland a non-exclusive license to manufacture lenses using B & L's spin cast technology. In addition, the

license agreement entitled B & L Ireland to any improvements resulting
from B & L's ongoing research and development in the manufacture of
contact lenses, and permitted B & L Ireland to sell soft contact lenses
anywhere under B & L's trademarks. In exchange, B & L was to receive a
royalty of five percent of the subsidiary's net contact lens sales. The agreement was terminable upon the written notice of either party.

B & L Ireland began manufacturing lenses in March 1981. It performed all processing, packaging, inspecting and labeling at its Waterford
facility, with the exception of some insignificant expiration date labeling
on a limited number of lenses done in Rochester in 1981. Thus, when
lenses left Ireland, they were ready for sale to optical practitioners and
chains. B & L Ireland's unit sales were 1,116,000 and 3,694,000 lenses for
the years 1981 and 1982, respectively. B & L was under no contractual
obligation to purchase any lenses from B & L Ireland, but sixty-one percent
of B & L Ireland's total sales in 1981 and fifty-six percent in 1982 were to
B & L for resale in the United States. The balance of B & L Ireland's sales
were to overseas affiliates of B & L. Throughout that two year period, the
intercompany transfer price was $7.50 per lens. The purchasers also paid
the duty and freight charges, which in the case of B & L were $0.62 per
lens.

The Commissioner's proposed deficiency sought to "reflect an arm's
length consideration for the use of [B & L's] intangible assets by B & L
Ireland" by limiting B & L Ireland to "a net profit before taxes of 20
percent of sales." The notice of deficiency, invoking section 482, accordingly reallocated from B & L Ireland to B & L taxable income in the
amounts of $2,778,000 and $19,793,750 for the years 1980 and 1981, respectively, with an offsetting elimination of the royalty income that B & L
Ireland had reported for those years, resulting in a net reallocation of
$2,359,331 for 1981 and $18,425,750 for 1982. In response to B & L's
petition to the Tax Court for redetermination of the deficiencies, the
Commissioner further contended that the reallocation was necessary "because of the lack of arms-length pricing between" B & L and its subsidiary.

The Tax Court was presented with nearly 200 pages of stipulated facts,
and conducted an eight day trial. At the outset of its opinion, the court
determined that the transfer price that B & L paid to B & L Ireland for
lenses and the royalty rate that B & L Ireland paid to B & L for use of
its manufacturing technology and related intangibles had independent
significance, and thus should be examined separately. 92 T.C. at 584. First,
the court upheld the $7.50 per lens transfer price as adequately supported
by comparable price data. Id. at 589-93. The court was also of the view
that its determination could be sustained under the alternative resale price
method. Id. at 593-94. Second, the court rejected the royalty rates suggested by each side and, drawing upon the expert testimony presented by
the parties as well as other evidence in the record, concluded that realloca-

tion should be based upon a royalty rate equal to twenty percent of B & L Ireland's net sales. 92 T.C. at 611.

This appeal followed.

DISCUSSION

. . . We next address the merits of the appeal. In doing so, we will follow the approach of the Tax Court, addressing seriatim: (1) whether the transfer price that B & L paid to B & L Ireland for lenses and the royalty rate that B & L Ireland paid to B & L for use of its manufacturing technology and related intangibles had independent significance and thus should be examined separately; and if so, whether the Tax Court committed clear error in valuing (2) the transfer price for the lenses and (3) the royalty rate for the intangibles. Preliminarily, however, we summarize the applicable Regulations, which are "binding on the Commissioner." United States Steel Corp. v. Commissioner, 617 F.2d 942, 947 (2d Cir. 1980); see Lansons, Inc. v. Commissioner, 622 F.2d 774, 776-77 (5th Cir. 1980).

A. The Regulatory Background

The Commissioner has adopted Regulations implementing section 482 that are pivotal to the decision of this case. First, as to the transfer price for lenses, Treas. Reg. §1.482-2(e)(1) provides that in the event of a transfer of tangible property between commonly controlled entities at other than an arm's length price . . . , the district director may make appropriate allocations between the seller and the buyer to reflect an arm's length price for such sale or disposition. An arm's length price is the price that an unrelated party would have paid under the same circumstances for the property involved in the controlled sale. Since unrelated parties normally sell products at a profit, an arm's length price normally involves a profit to the seller. Id. Treas. Reg. §1.482-2(d)(1) and (2), which deals with transfers of intangible property between commonly controlled entities, provides an essentially identical rule applicable to the royalty paid by B & L Ireland for the use of B & L's intangibles.

Section 1.482-2(e) goes on to specify particular methods to deal with the transfers of tangible property, to wit:

1) The comparable uncontrolled price method relies upon the price prevailing in comparable sales between entities that are not members of the same control group. §1.482-2(e)(2).
2) The resale price method starts with the price which the buyer in the controlled sale is anticipated to charge upon resale to an entity outside the control group; that resale price is then reduced by the profit markup of a comparable uncontrolled buyer/reseller. §1.482-2(e)(3).

3) The cost plus method adds to the cost of producing the subject property a markup equal to the profit percentage of a comparable uncontrolled seller. §1.482-2(e)(4).

These methods must be applied sequentially. That is, "if there are comparable uncontrolled sales . . . , the comparable uncontrolled price method must be utilized because it is the method likely to result in the most accurate estimate of an arm's-length price. . . ." §1.482-2(e)(1)(ii). "If there are no comparable uncontrolled sales, then the resale price method must be utilized if the standards for its application are met. . . ." Id. If not, either the resale price method or cost-plus method may be used, "depending upon which method is more feasible and is likely to result in a more accurate estimate of an arm's-length price." Id. If the standards for applying one of the three methods are met, that method must be utilized "unless the taxpayer can establish that, considering all the facts and circumstances, some [other] method of pricing . . . is clearly more appropriate." §1.482-2(e)(1)(iii). If however, none of the three methods can reasonably be applied in a given case, "some appropriate method of pricing other than those described . . . , or variations on such methods, can be used." Id.

The general theory of the cited Regulations, as well as the others promulgated by the Commissioner to implement section 482, is to treat each of the individual members of a commonly controlled group as a separate entity, transactions between which are taxable events to be conformed to the economic realities that would obtain between independent economic entities conducting the identical transactions at arm's-length. See Commissioner v. First Sec. Bank, 405 U.S. 394, 400 & n.10 (1972) (quoting Treas. Reg. §1.482-1(b)(1) (1971)); Note, Multinational Corporations and Income Allocation Under Section 482 of the Internal Revenue Code, 89 Harv. L. Rev. 1202, 1205, 1209 (1976) ("Note"). This contrasts with the alternative theoretical model, the unitary entity theory, which considers all commonly controlled entities as "parts of the same unitary business," with the result that "intercompany transactions cannot produce a real economic profit or loss and must therefore be eliminated from tax consideration." Note at 1206.

We now turn to the issues addressed by the Tax Court.

B. Independent Significance of Transfer Price and Royalty Rate

The Tax Court framed this issue in the following terms:

As a preliminary matter, we must first address [the Commissioner's] contention that it is inappropriate to analyze the transfer price and royalty rate used by B & L separately, on the theory that B & L and B & L Ireland would have constructed their relationship in a different manner had they been conducting their affairs at arm's length. [The Commissioner] argues that B & L would never have agreed to license its spin cast technology which allowed it to produce soft contact lenses for approximately $1.50 per lens and then purchase lenses from the licensee for $7.50 per lens. [The Commissioner] argues that B & L would have been unwilling to pay an independent third party much more than its costs would have been had it chosen to produce the contact lenses itself. [The Commissioner] is indifferent as to whether the royalty is increased or the transfer price is decreased as long as the result is that B & L Ireland receives only its costs of production and a reasonable mark up. In essence, [the Commissioner] argues that B & L Ireland was little more than a contract manufacturer the sale of whose total production was assured and who thus was not entitled to the return normally associated with an enterprise which bears the risk as to the volume of its product it will be able to sell and at what price.

92 T.C. at 583.

The Commissioner's position is not without force. It failed, however, to persuade the Tax Court, which concluded that B & L was not committed to purchase the entire output of B & L Ireland, and that B & L Ireland accordingly should not be considered a contract manufacturer entitled only to a modest markup on its manufacturing costs. 92 T.C. at 584; see also *Eli Lilly & Co.*, 856 F.2d at 863-64 & n.9 (rejecting Commissioner's "contract manufacturer" contention); G.D. Searle & Co. v. Commissioner, 88 T.C. 252, 373 (1987) (same). The Tax Court further noted that B & L Ireland was not guaranteed a continuing $7.50 resale price, and that the price declined to $6.50 in 1983 as a result of market pressures. 92 T.C. at 584. It is undoubtedly true, as the Commissioner contends, that B & L was in a general sense committed to the success of B & L Ireland. We nonetheless find no clear error in the Tax Court's conclusion that:

> The most that can be said is that B & L Ireland had certain expectations as to the volume and price of lenses it could anticipate selling to B & L or its affiliates. However, such expectations are no different than those which any supplier has with regard to the business of a major customer and do not constitute a guarantee which effectively insulated B & L Ireland from market risks.

Id.; accord, Sundstrand Corp. v. Commissioner, 96 T.C. No. 12, slip op. at 187 (Feb. 19, 1991).

Furthermore, the structure of the Commission's Regulations argues against the "contract manufacturer" thesis advanced by the Commissioner. The allowance of a markup of production costs, as the contract manufacturer theory postulates and as the Commissioner's notice of deficiency in this case explicitly provided, is simply an application of the cost-plus method provided in the Commissioner's Regulations. See Treas. Reg. §1.482-2(e)(4). Those Regulations explicitly provide, however, that the comparable uncontrolled price method is to be utilized, in preference to the cost-plus method, if the conditions for application of the former method are satisfied. See Treas. Reg. §1.482-2(e)(1)(ii). Since, as will hereinafter appear, we find those conditions to be fulfilled in this case, we are accordingly constrained by section 1.482-2(e)(1)(ii) to reject the Commissioner's contention that B & L Ireland should be treated as a contract manufacturer.

We therefore proceed to independent consideration of the Tax Court's treatment of the transfer price paid by B & L for the lenses manufactured by B & L Ireland, and the royalty rate paid by B & L Ireland to B & L for the use of B & L's intangibles.

C. Transfer Price for Lenses

The Commissioner contends that the Tax Court erred in finding that the standards for the comparable uncontrolled price method were met. That method must be applied if, but only if, comparable uncontrolled sales are available. Treas. Reg. §1.482-2(e)(1)(ii). The Commissioner focuses on the meaning of the term "comparable," on which the Regulations elaborate as follows:

> Uncontrolled sales are considered comparable to controlled sales if the physical property and circumstances involved in the uncontrolled sales are identical to the physical property and circumstances involved in the controlled sales, or if such properties and circumstances are so nearly identical that any differences either have no effect on price, or such differences can be reflected by a reasonable number of adjustments to the price of uncontrolled sales. For this purpose, differences can be reflected by adjusting prices only where such differences have a definite and reasonably ascertainable effect on price.

Id. §1.482-2(e)(2)(ii).

The Tax Court premised its ruling upon numerous sales by four different lens manufacturers to unrelated lens distributors. All comparable sales prices were reduced by $0.62, an adjustment that compensated for B & L's unique practice of paying the duty and freight charges on its lens purchases. After this adjustment, all these sales were at a price that exceeded the $7.50 transfer price paid by B & L, with one exception. One manufacturer, the Amsco/Lombart division of the American Sterilization Company, transacted some sales (less than half) that, when adjusted, indicated a transfer price less than $7.50, but the Tax Court gave these sales little weight because, unlike the uniform price charged by B & L Ireland, they set different prices for standard and thin lenses. All other adjusted comparable sales, including Amsco/Lombart single price sales, indicated a transfer price above $7.50, with many exceeding $10.00.

The Tax Court's conclusion that these sales were comparable was premised on findings of fact that B & L functioned as a distributor with respect to the lenses it purchased from B & L Ireland, and that the soft contact lenses at issue were generally considered a fungible commodity. The Commissioner disputes the former finding. He contends that in addition to its distribution functions, B & L "supplied the know-how necessary to manufacture the lenses, the Bausch & Lomb and Soflens trademarks, the FDA approval required for sales on the United States market, the fruits of its ongoing research and development, and ready-made foreign and domestic markets."

We find this argument unconvincing. As was implicit in our prior determination that the transfer price for lenses and royalty rate for intangibles should be accorded independent consideration, the provision of know-how, trademarks, FDA approval, and ongoing research and development is properly taken into account hereinafter with respect to the royalty to be imputed to B & L Ireland on an arm's length basis for the transfer of these intangibles. Further, the provision of ready made markets is entirely consistent with the role of a distributor.

The position urged by the Commissioner would preclude comparability precisely because the relationship between B & L and B & L Ireland was different from that between independent buyers and sellers operating at arms length. This, however, will always be the case when transactions between commonly controlled entities are compared to transactions between independent entities.

We addressed a similar contention by the Commissioner in United States Steel Corp. v. Commissioner, 617 F.2d 942 (2d Cir. 1980). The Commissioner there argued that identically priced shipping services supplied to competitors of United States Steel by its subsidiary were not comparable to the services supplied by the subsidiary to United States Steel because of the special parent/subsidiary relationship that existed between them. We responded that the Commissioner's approach might "recognize economic reality; but . . . [would] also . . . engraft a crippling degree of economic sophistication onto a broadly drawn statute, which — if 'comparable' is taken to mean 'identical,' . . . — would allow the taxpayer no safe harbor from the Commissioner's virtually unrestricted discretion to reallocate." Id. at 951.

Similarly, the position urged by the Commissioner herein amounts to reading so broadly the requirement in Treas. Reg. §1.482-2(e)(ii) that the "circumstances involved" in comparable uncontrolled sales and controlled sales under section 482 review be "identical," or "nearly identical," as to threaten effective nullification of the comparable uncontrolled price method. That method is postulated in the Commissioner's Regulations, however, as the method of choice for testing transfers of tangible property between commonly controlled entities. We therefore decline to adopt the suggested interpretation of section 1.482-2(e)(ii).

D. The Royalty Rate for B & L's Intangibles

The relevant Regulation provides two methods for determining an arm's-length price for the transfer or use of intangible property. If the transferor has made similar transfers to unrelated parties, "the amount of the consideration for such transfers shall generally be the best indication of an arm's-length consideration." §1.482-2(d)(2)(ii). In the absence of an adequately similar transaction, the arm's length consideration may be determined with reference to a lengthy list of applicable factors. §1.482-2(d)(2)(iii).

The 1981 licensing agreement provided that B & L Ireland would pay royalties to B & L in the amount of five percent of B & L Ireland's total sales. Conceding that this royalty was unreasonably low, B & L presented expert opinions at trial that an arm's length consideration would have been five percent of the average price realized by B & L and its subsidiaries upon the sale of the lenses to unrelated third parties ("ARP"). The Commissioner's experts calculated a much higher rate, between twenty-seven and thirty-three percent of ARP.

The Tax Court rejected the positions presented by both parties' experts. Concluding that there were no sufficiently similar transactions upon which to base an arm's length rate, the court focused on two of the factors listed in the applicable Regulation: the "prospective profits to be realized . . . by the transferee through its use . . . of the property," and the "capital investment and starting up expenses required of the transferee." §1.482-2(d)(2)(iii)(g) and (h). The court relied primarily upon a proposal made by B & L to the IDA in early 1980, related internal B & L projections, and especially a Special Expenditure Application ("SEA") submitted to B & L management on October 15, 1980 with respect to the Waterford facility as the best indications of (1) the profits that an independent entrepreneur would anticipate from the use of spin cast technology, and (2) the capital investment required to generate those profits.

The Tax Court made two adjustments to the SEA projections in order to reflect the approach of a "prudent investor" in the circumstances. First, the court reduced the projected output at the Waterford facility during the years 1986 through 1989 to account for anticipated "erosion in the demand for both standard and thin lens sales as prolonged wear lenses made of new materials became available." Second, the court made reductions in projected transfer prices for 1983 and beyond on the basis that lower cost competitors would enter the market and drive down prices.

Reasoning that the purpose of a licensing agreement is to divide the profits attributable to use of the licensed intangibles, the Tax Court then reached the following determination:

> Using our best judgment, we find that at arm's length B & L Ireland would have been willing to invest in the lens production facility even if required to share approximately 50 percent of the profits therefrom with B & L as consideration for use of its intangibles. . . . This equates to a royalty rate of 20 percent of [B & L Ireland's] net sales.

92 T.C. at 611; cf. *G.D. Searle & Co.*, 88 T.C. at 376 (royalty rate determined on basis of court's "best judgment based on a consideration of the entire record before [it]"); Ciba-Geigy Corp. v. Commissioner, 85 T.C. 172, 236 (1985) (same).

In response to this analysis, the Commissioner contends that the SEA projections did not correspond to the actual experience of the parties because: (1) the Waterford facility ended up with greater manufacturing capacity than the projections had assumed; and (2) a decision was made in late 1981 for that facility to maximize lens production by producing for the United States market, whereas the SEA projections assumed production primarily or exclusively for foreign markets. Since the license agreement between B & L and B & L Ireland was terminable at will, the Commissioner contends, B & L would have scrapped the agreement, if dealing at arm's length with an independent party, and insisted upon the negotiation of new terms.

We are not persuaded. Considerable deference to the Tax Court's evaluation of trial evidence, and especially expert testimony, is appropriate in appellate review of this sort of complex factual determination. See *Eli Lilly & Co.*, 856 F.2d at 872. Here, as in R.T. French Co. v. Commissioner, 60 T.C. 836 (1973), another case involving section 482 reallocation of royalties paid to a foreign affiliate, the Tax Court was entitled to conclude that "what later transpired in no way detracted from the reasonableness of the agreement when it was made." Id. at 852.

It is true that in *R.T. French Co.* the agreement had a fixed term, see id., whereas here the agreement between the parties was terminable at will. We regard this as too thin a foundation, however, for the Commissioner's argument that B & L would surely have terminated the agreement and negotiated new terms if dealing with an independent licensee, at least in the absence of a fuller record as to the manufacturing alternatives available to B & L at the time it was decided to increase lens production at B & L Ireland. Cf. *Sunstrand Corp.*, slip op. at 169 (rejecting ready availability of alternative source of manufacture in view of specialized manufacturing know-how required to produce complex avionic device). Accordingly, we perceive no basis to reject the Tax Court's carefully considered determination as clearly erroneous.

CONCLUSION

The decision of the Tax Court is affirmed.

1. Section 482 in General

Section 482 authorizes the IRS to allocate gross income, deductions, and credits among related taxpayers to the extent necessary to prevent evasion of taxes or to reflect clearly the income of related taxpayers. The regulations implementing §482 are based on the principle that transactions between related parties should be evaluated on an "arm's length" basis — that is, how unrelated parties would structure the transaction.

Section 482 can apply whenever two taxpayers are "owned or controlled directly or indirectly by the same interests." In determining control, the IRS focuses on the realities of the situation rather than on whether there is formal legal control. Treas. Reg. §1.482-1(b)(3). Section 482 can apply to domestic and foreign corporations, but because of the steep graduation in §11 there is little to be gained by assigning income to a related U.S. corporation. In the international context, §482 is often applied to allocate income from a foreign subsidiary to a U.S. parent. The provision also applies, however, in the converse situation to allocate income from a foreign parent to a U.S. subsidiary or between commonly owned corporations, one foreign and one domestic.

The arm's-length character of a transaction between related parties (i.e., a controlled transaction) is best tested by comparing the results of the transaction in question with the results of unrelated taxpayers engaged in comparable transactions under comparable circumstances (i.e., uncontrolled transactions). The use of comparables is important in all the arm's-length methods described below. For two transactions to be considered comparable, an uncontrolled transaction need not be identical. When necessary, a reasonable number of adjustments may be made to account for material differences between a controlled and an uncontrolled transaction.

Comparability of two transactions can be established by looking at the following factors: functions, risks, contractual terms, economic conditions, and property or services. Treas. Regs. §1.482-1T(c). For two transactions to be comparable, the parties normally should perform the same functions (e.g., research and development, product design, assembly, marketing, warranty administration, transportation, and warehousing) with respect to the transactions. Also, the risks borne by the parties to each transaction should be similar. In comparing prices, the contractual terms (e.g., quantity, duration, warranty) of the transactions should be comparable. For purposes of comparison, the economic conditions surrounding the two transactions (e.g., market alternatives for buyers and sellers, geographic markets, market size, and composition) should be similar. Finally, the nature of the property or services transferred should be comparable in both transactions.

The reallocation principles of §482 are best understood in the context of specific types of transactions. What follows is a summary of the principles that can apply to some of the more basic transactions addressed by the temporary regulations. In any situation involving §482, the result is heavily dependent on the facts. Taxpayers receive little guidance from the decided cases. Newly proposed temporary regulations attempt to provide more certainty in reallocating income, but uncertainty still abounds. This uncertainty has made reallocation of income one of the most pervasive tax problems faced by multinational corporations.

a. Sales

When Parentco, a U.S. corporation, sells goods to Subco, a foreign subsidiary, which then resells the goods to unrelated purchasers, the gain that must be recognized by Parentco on the sale to Subco for U.S. tax purposes is determined in accordance with the arm's-length price that an unrelated purchaser would have paid under the same circumstances. The same is true if Parentco is a foreign parent corporation that sells goods to Subco, its wholly owned U.S. subsidiary, which resells to unrelated purchasers in the United States or if the foreign and U.S. corporations have a common parent corporation. The temporary regulations detail the following pricing methods: the comparable uncontrolled price method, the resale price method, the cost plus method, and the comparable profits method. Treas. Regs. §1.482-3T. Under some circumstances other methods are also permitted.

In a world with perfect information available at no cost, all methods would generate the identical allocation between parent and subsidiary corporation. A comparable transaction involving unrelated parties transacting at an arm's-length price is the best method of allocation. If that information is not available, working backward from the ultimate price charged by Subco to an unrelated purchaser may produce an arm's-length price for the sale from Parentco to Subco (i.e., the resale price method). If that information is not available, perhaps an arm's-length price can be determined by working forward from the actual manufacturing cost incurred by Parentco (i.e., cost plus method).

Under the "best method rule" of the temporary regulations, the arm's-length price for a particular transaction should be determined using the method that provides the most accurate measure of an arm's-length result — hardly a shocking rule. Treas. Regs. §1.482-1T(b)(2)(iii). Use of the resale price method is generally appropriate when a manufacturer sells products to a controlled distributor that, without further processing or the use of significant intangibles, resells the products in uncontrolled transactions. Use of the cost plus method ordinarily is appropriate when a manu-facturer sells products to a controlled taxpayer that resells after further processing or the use of significant intangibles. The comparable uncon-trolled price method, if data are available, usually provides the most accu-rate measure of an arm's-length price.

Comparable uncontrolled price method. Under the comparable uncon-trolled price method, the price for tax purposes deemed paid by Subco to Parentco is determined on the basis of "uncontrolled sales" made by Parentco to unrelated buyers. Treas. Regs. §1.482-3T(b). An uncontrolled sale might include a sale made by Parentco to an unrelated purchaser if, like Subco, the purchaser is not an end-user. Also, comparable sales of the same product between two unrelated parties would provide information. In determining comparability, differences in the product or the circum-stances surrounding the sale (e.g., volume discounts, whether the pur-chaser is a wholesaler or retail customer) are taken into account. For unique products or products in which the seller has a virtual monopoly, there may not be comparable uncontrolled prices.

Resale price method. If the comparable uncontrolled price method is unavailable (e.g., lack of comparables), the temporary regulations then permit use of the resale price method, particularly when the related pur-chaser does not add significant value to the product (e.g., if the purchaser is a distributor) or does not use significant intangibles. Treas. Regs. §1.482-3T(c). The resale price method is intended to measure the value of the distribution function performed by a related purchaser. Starting with the applicable resale price charged to unrelated purchasers, the resale price method determines an appropriate gross profit that is subtracted to deter-mine the deemed transfer price on the sale between the related corpora-tions. An appropriate gross profit is determined by multiplying the applicable resale price by an appropriate gross profit margin, which is essentially profit as a percentage of gross sales in uncontrolled transactions.

Cost plus method. The cost plus method is most appropriate when there are no comparable unrelated sales and the related purchaser does more than mere distribution (e.g., the subsidiary adds substantial value to the product) or uses significant intangibles. Treas. Regs. §1.482-3T(d). Under this method, the costs of the company selling to the related party are determined and an appropriate gross profit markup is applied to deter-mine the deemed sales price paid by the related party. Treas. Regs. §1.482-3T(d).

Comparable profits method. The comparable profits method is based on the principle that similarly situated taxpayers will tend to earn similar returns over a reasonable period of time. The comparable profits method determines arm's-length consideration for a controlled transfer of property by referring to objective measures of profitability (profit-level indicators) derived from uncontrolled taxpayers that engage in similar activities with other uncontrolled taxpayers. An arm's-length range of constructive operating profits is determined by applying the profit-level indicators to the tested party. A controlled transaction will be considered arm's length if the tested party's actual operating profits are within the arm's-length range of the constructive operating profits. The tested party can be either party to a controlled transaction — generally the one that provides the simplest, and therefore the most easily compared, operations. In the case of the license of an intangible, the licensee will normally be the tested party.

Profit-level indicators are financial ratios that measure the relationships among profits, costs incurred, and resources employed. For example, the rate of return on capital employed is the ratio of operating profit to operating assets. This measure may provide an acceptable profit-level indicator if the tested party has substantial fixed assets or working capital. The temporary regulations also provide a number of financial ratios, such as the ratio of operating profit to sales and the ratio of gross profit to operating expenses, that may serve as profit-level indicators. For a comparable uncontrolled company that has gross profits of $140 and operating expenses of $100, for example, the ratio of gross profits to operating expenses is 1.4. If the tested party has operating expenses of $50, then one point in the arm's-length range of constructive operating profits is $70.

In an example taken from the temporary regulations, the comparable profit method is used to determine the transfer price for an intercompany sale of goods. Treas. Regs. §1.482-5T(g). Foreign Parent (FP) manufactures consumer products. A U.S. subsidiary (USS) purchases these products for distribution in the United States. Similar products are produced by other companies but none of them is sold to uncontrolled taxpayers. Because no comparable uncontrolled transactions exist and because there is insufficient data for use of either the cost plus or resale price methods, the comparable profits method is used by the IRS to verify the price paid by USS to FP for the tangible property purchased in 1994.

USS is selected as the tested party because of the availability of reliable data. USS has the following financial profile:

	1992	1993	1994	Average
Operating assets	$310,000	$310,000	$310,000	$310,000
Sales	500,000	560,000	500,000	520,000
Cost of goods sold	393,000	412,400	400,000	401,800
Purchases from FP	350,000	365,000	350,000	355,000
Other	43,000	47,400	50,000	46,800
Operating expenses	80,000	110,000	106,600	98,200
Operating profit	27,000	37,600	(4,600)	20,000

To test the transfer price paid by USS to FP for the consumer products, the IRS would identify comparable parties to USS (i.e., wholesale distributors in the same industry segment that perform similar functions and assume similar risks). Because working capital plays a significant role in generating operating profit, the IRS might choose the rate of return on capital as a profit-level indicator. Calculating the average ratio of operating profits to operating assets for each of the uncontrolled distributors and multiplying that ratio by the average operating assets of USS for the three-year testing period leads to the following constructive operating profits (COP) for USS:

Unrelated Distributor	OP/OA	USS COP
A	8.0%	$24,800
B	23.3	72,230
C	16.9	52,390
D	8.0	24,800
E	11.5	35,650
F	6.3	19,530
G	5.3	16,430
H	2.7	8,370
I	8.5	26,350
J	7.5	23,250

If the IRS determines that the products sold by the distributors are not similar enough to allow the use of all the constructive operating profits, top and bottom constructive operating profits will be lopped off and the "interquartile" range (i.e., the 25th to the 75th percentile) of results will be used. In this example, the interquartile range is $19,530 to $35,650. Because USS's reported average operating income of $20,000 falls within this range, the 1994 transfer pricing used by USS will be accepted by the IRS even though there is an operating loss for 1994. If USS's average operating income for the three-year period were $0, the IRS would determine a transfer price that increases USS's operating profit to the median of the arm's-length range (i.e., $24,800) for 1994.

Other methods. All the methods just described and those described below relating to transactions other than sales depend in part on the availability of comparable transactions. Comparables are often difficult to locate, whether in the context of sales, services, or rentals of tangible property or licenses of intangible property. Moreover, product sales often are interrelated to the licensing of intangibles (e.g., manufacturing patents) used to produce the products. The difficulty in determining arm's-length prices for interrelated items has led to the development of alternative income allocation approaches used for determining the price of intercompany sales of inventory as well as royalty rates on intercompany licenses. Treas. Regs. §1.482-3T(e). An appropriate method might include an allocation of overall profit based on an acceptable rate of return on invested capital or on a comparison of rates of return to operating costs.

In E. I. DuPont de Nemours & Co. v. United States, 608 F.2d 445 (Ct. Cl. 1979), the U.S. parent company used a Swiss subsidiary, DISA, as a European distributor. DuPont structured its prices so that DISA would capture 75 percent of the combined profits even though DISA performed virtually no special services. Relying on the resale price method, DuPont contended that 21 similar companies selling similar products experienced average markups of between 19.5 percent and 38 percent, comparing favorably with DISA's 26 percent gross profit margin. The court rejected DuPont's position because the record did not establish sufficient similarities of the 21 distributors to DISA.

Instead, the court relied on two methods presented by the IRS in allocating income. Under the first method, the ratio of gross income to total operating costs (sometimes referred to as the "Berry ratio," in honor of its founder) of DISA was substantially greater than a broad sampling of firms that were functionally similar to DISA. After the proposed §482 allocation, the ratios were more in line. The second method focused on the rate of return on capital of 1,133 companies that did not necessarily have functional similarities to DISA but instead reflected a comprehensive selection of industry as a whole. DISA's rate was the highest of the sampling. Even with the §482 adjustment, DISA's ratio was higher than 96 percent of the companies.

b. Services

When one corporation performs services for or on behalf of a related corporation, the corporation purchasing the services is deemed to pay an arm's-length price to the corporation performing the services. The arm's-length price is deemed to equal the direct and indirect costs incurred in connection with the services performed; the regulations do not generally require the allocation of a profit for services performed between related parties if the services are incidental to the business function of the corporation. Treas. Regs. §1.482-2A(b)(2).

c. Rentals of Tangible Property

When a taxpayer leases tangible property (e.g., machinery, equipment, real estate) to a related taxpayer, the regulations deem the user to have paid an arm's-length rental if the lease does not so provide. Treas. Regs. §1.482-2A(c). An arm's-length rental is the amount that would have been charged on a transaction between unrelated parties. If the owner of a lease makes the property available to a related entity through a sublease, the arm's-length price is an amount equal to the owner's deductions (i.e., rent, maintenance, utilities, etc.). There is no deemed profit in the sublease situation.

d. Licenses of Intangible Property

Payments to a related party for a license or transfer of an intangible may be reallocated by the IRS if the payments are not deemed to be at arm's length. Intangible property for purposes of §482 is defined as including any patent, invention, formula, process design, pattern, know-how, copyright, trademark, franchise, license, or contract. §936(h)(3)(B). Three methods for determining an arm's-length price for the transfer of an intangible are available: the comparable uncontrolled transaction (CUT) method, the comparable profits method (CPM), and the "other" method. Treas. Regs. §1.482-4T(a). Generally, the comparable uncontrolled transaction method likely is the best method for determining an arm's-length price.

The comparable uncontrolled transaction method. Under the comparable uncontrolled transaction method, the arm's-length consideration for a controlled transfer of intangible property (i.e., transactions between related parties) is equal to the consideration charged in a comparable uncontrolled transaction (i.e., transactions between unrelated parties). Treas. Regs. §1.482-4T(c). An uncontrolled transaction is considered comparable to a controlled transaction if the intangibles to be compared are in the same class of intangibles, relate to the same type of products within the same general industry, and have substantially the same profit potential (i.e., net present value). The temporary regulations identify six classes of intangibles. Treas. Regs. §1.482-4T(b). For example, patents, inventions, formulas, processes, designs, patterns, and know-how are in the same class; trademarks, trade names, and brand names are in the same class. These rules are intended to ensure that the circumstances surrounding the controlled and uncontrolled transactions are comparable.

The comparable profit method. Under this method, no adjustment is made to the operating income of a taxpayer if the income falls within the arm's-length range of results, which is a range of operating incomes for similar taxpayers. If the operating income does not fall within the arm's-length range, adjustments may be made in a taxpayer's transfer price to place the taxpayer within the arm's-length range.

Periodic adjustments. Payments to a related party for a license or transfer of an intangible must be "commensurate with the income" attributable to the intangible. §482 (second sentence). The practical effect of the "commensurate with" language is that royalty arrangements between related parties can be periodically adjusted by the IRS to reflect changing market conditions. For example, royalty payments deemed received by a U.S. corporation from intangible property licensed to its foreign subsidiary might be adjusted periodically to reflect how the property actually performs in the hands of the licensee. If five or 10 years after the original license the intangible becomes extremely valuable, that increase in value (i.e., increased sublicensing royalties or increased sales of property incorporating the intangible) may be taxable to the licensor even if the royalty rates at the time of the original license were reasonable under the facts known at that time. This provision represents an extraordinary view of what an arm's-length transaction is — substituting an ex post determination for an ex ante determination. The fact that a royalty agreement at the time it was concluded provided for arm's-length payments does not guarantee that an adjustment will not be made in a subsequent year. Treas. Regs. §1.482-4T(e)(2).

e. Loans

Like other transactions between related parties, a loan from one corporation to a related corporation must be made at arm's length; otherwise, the IRS may reallocate interest income between the parties. If U.S. Co. makes a loan to Subco, its foreign subsidiary, and charges inadequate interest, U.S. Co. has effectively transferred the earning of interest beyond U.S. tax jurisdiction. Conversely if Subco lends money to U.S. Co. and charges an artificially high interest rate, the interest deduction otherwise available to U.S. Co. diverts income to Subco. To prevent this assignment of income, the IRS generally imposes an arm's-length interest rate.

2. The Interplay of §482 and Foreign Law

The purpose of §482 is to force taxpayers for tax purposes to deal at arm's length with related parties. Suppose, however, that related parties are prohibited from setting an arm's-length price because of a foreign government law or regulation. For U.S. tax purposes, should §482 apply notwithstanding the impossibility of paying an arm's-length price?

In Procter & Gamble Co. v. Commissioner, 961 F.2d 1255 (6th Cir. 1992), Procter and Gamble (hereinafter P&G) owned all the stock of Procter and Gamble A.G. (hereinafter AG), a Swiss corporation engaged in marketing P&G's products in countries where P&G did not have a marketing subsidiary. AG licensed and paid royalties to P&G for the use of P&G's patents, trademarks, tradenames, knowledge, and assistance. AG, in turn, sublicensed the patents, etc., to its subsidiaries throughout Europe and the Middle East. The income earned by AG from its sublicensing activities was taxable directly to P&G under the controlled foreign corporation provisions (§§951-959). AG organized a Spanish subsidiary, Gamble Espana, S.A. (hereinafter Espana) to manufacture and sell its consumer and industrial products in Spain. The Tax Court found that during the years in question, Spain prohibited the payment of royalties from Espana to AG.

Notwithstanding the Spanish prohibition against royalty payments to a parent corporation, the IRS determined that a royalty equal to 2 percent of Espana's net sales should be allocated to AG (and therefore be taxable to P&G). The IRS reasoned that no taxpayer would give away the right to use property in an arm's-length transaction. The only reason AG was willing to forgo a royalty payment from Espana was that, as a parent corporation, AG would reap the benefit of Espana's use of the royalty property in the form of increased stock value. A nonshareholder-licensor would not agree to license the use of its property unless it received royalty payments in exchange; otherwise, the income produced by the transferred property would inure to the benefit of the licensee's shareholders. Indeed, Spanish law recognized this fact by permitting the payment of royalties to unrelated licensors. Accordingly, there can be little doubt that it was the relationship of AG to Espana that gave rise to the uncompensated use of P&G's property.

Although the relationship of AG to Espana made the transaction possible, it was the existence of Spanish law that made the royalty payment impossible. Relying on the Supreme Court holding in Commissioner v. First Security Bank of Utah, 405 U.S. 394 (1972) (income shifted from a bank to a captive insurance company could not be allocated under §482 because receipt of insurance commissions by the bank would have violated U.S. banking laws), the Tax Court in *Procter & Gamble* ruled that the Service could not allocate income between related corporations when the purported misallocation was caused by foreign law. As a result of the Tax Court's decision, Procter & Gamble did not have to report royalty income deemed received by AG. See Exxon Corp. v. Commissioner, 66 T.C.M. (CCH) 1707 (1993).

A danger arises in allowing foreign law to impede the application of §482. It is not difficult to imagine that some taxpayers may actually encourage (and be willing to pay for) foreign governments to prevent certain arm's-length payments between related taxpayers so as to lower U.S. taxes. Should the United States allow foreign law to govern what is taxable in the United States when under the arm's-length principle of §482 the United States considers income to be subject to U.S. taxation?

3. Income Shifting and the Assignment of Income Doctrine

Historically, the use of personal service corporations, discussed at page 634 supra, was motivated in part by the opportunities to lower income by dividing profits between a corporation and owner-employees. In Rubin v. Commissioner, 429 F.2d 650 (2d Cir. 1970), the Tax Court's application of the assignment of income doctrine to a taxpayer and his personal service corporation was reversed. Despite this reversal, the Tax Court continued to sustain assignment of income challenges to personal service corporations. The Tax Court was reversed again in Foglesong v. Commissioner, 621 F.2d 865 (7th Cir. 1980) (*Foglesong I*) (a chemical engineer owned 98 percent of a personal services corporation), and it finally conceded in Keller v. Commissioner, 77 T.C. 1014 (1981), that the assignment of income doctrine cannot be used to reallocate income away from a corporation to its employee-shareholder so long as the corporation is a viable entity. In *Keller* and in *Foglesong I,* the Tax Court observed that since §482 could apply to a taxpayer who worked as an employee for his controlled corporation, application of the assignment of income doctrine would be redundant.

In *Foglesong I* the circuit court gave the following explanation for why the assignment of income doctrine could not be used to reattribute income reported by Foglesong's corporation to Foglesong.

> Personal service corporation tax cases reveal a tension between "the principle of a graduated income tax . . . and the policy of recognizing the corporation as a taxable entity distinct from its shareholders in all but extreme cases." Rubin v. Commissioner, 429 F.2d 650, 652 (2d Cir. 1970). The impact of the graduated income tax is eroded when income is split artificially among several entities or over several tax years. The assignment of income doctrine under Section 61 (as formulated by Lucas v. Earl) seeks to recognize "economic reality" by cumulating income diffused among several recipients through "artificial" legal arrangements. The attribution of income to its "true earner" is simply a species of recognizing "substance" over "form."
>
> But, if the issue is one of attributing the income of a corporation to its sole stockholder-employee who "really" earned it, we encounter the important legal policy of the law favoring recognition of the corporation as a legal person and economic actor. . . .
>
> Under the circumstances of this case, we think it inappropriate to attempt to weigh "business purpose" against "tax avoidance motives" in a determination whether the assignment of income doctrine of Lucas v. Earl should apply, in effect, to substantially disregard the corporate form. [T]o apply Lucas v. Earl in this fashion under the circumstances present here is effectively (and more realistically) to nullify the determination that the Corporation is a viable, taxable entity and not a sham. . . .

Do you agree with the majority in *Foglesong I* that application of the assignment of income doctrine would have been tantamount to disregard of the corporate entity? Recall that Foglesong was not the sole shareholder of the corporation. If the corporation had been held a sham, would all the income have been includible by Foglesong? In his dissenting opinion in *Keller,* Judge Wilbur wrote, 77 T.C. at 1042: "Mere existence — either of Mrs. Earl or petitioner's corporation — does not carry automatic immunity from the assignment of income doctrine." If Foglesong had signed the same employment documents with his sister rather than with the corporation, could the assignment of income doctrine have been applied? Suppose his sister owned a large chemical engineering firm?

In Sargent v. Commissioner, 93 T.C. 572 (1989), the court ruled that hockey players were employees of their hockey teams notwithstanding the fact that they had formed personal service corporations that contracted with the teams. *Keller* was distinguished on the ground that there was no issue as to who was the employer.

Foglesong I held out the promise that §482 could apply to allocate income between a personal services corporation and an employee-owner. But in Foglesong v. Commissioner, 691 F.2d 848 (7th Cir. 1982) (*Foglesong II*), the court ruled that §482 did not apply where an owner-employee worked exclusively for the corporation because the owner-employee under these circumstances did not operate a separate trade or business to which income could be allocated under §482. But see Haag v. Commissioner, 855 F.2d 855 (8th Cir. 1988) (rejecting *Foglesong II* and allocating much of the income of a corporation performing medical services to the owner-employee doctor). See also Rev. Rul. 88-38, 1988-1 C.B. 246 (IRS will not follow *Foglesong* on the separate business issue).

4. Denial of Tax Benefits under §269A

Although Congress in 1982 substantially equalized the pension benefits available to employees and the self-employed, thereby removing a major incentive to form a personal services corporation, it also enacted §269A. That section resembles §482 by providing for income and deduction reallocations rather than tax benefit denial. But it is triggered by forming or acquiring control of a corporation with a principal purpose of avoiding tax or obtaining benefits otherwise unobtainable. The Conference Committee wrote of §269A: "The conferees intend that the provisions [of §269A] overturn the results reached in cases like Keller v. Commissioner, 77 T.C. 1014 (1981), where the corporation served no meaningful purpose other than to secure tax benefits which would not otherwise be available." H.R. Rep. No. 760, 97th Cong., 2d Sess. (1986).

Suppose a husband, *H,* and wife, *W,* simultaneously graduate from law school. They form *WH* Corp., for which each works and in which each is a 50 percent shareholder. The corporation then hires out its two employees to two separate law firms for $50,000 per year. The corporation pays H and W only $35,000 each and retains (and pays taxes on) $30,000. Will this device reduce H and W's overall tax liability? Can the Commissioner wage a successful challenge to the scheme under §269A?

Regulations under §269A provide a safe harbor from reallocation. An owner-employee first is considered to have borne the taxes incurred by a personal services corporation proportionate to the owner's stock ownership. That tax liability is then compared with the owner-employee's liability if the compensation paid to the corporation had been paid directly to the owner-employee. If by this comparison the incorporation reduced the owner-employee's taxes by 10 percent or less and by no more than $2,500, then §269A does not apply. Treas. Regs. §1.269A-1.

5.   The "Graduated Bracket Amount" and §1561(a)

For some corporations, the corporate income tax rates are progressive. See page 81 supra. Just as individual taxpayers might seek to assign income to family members in lower tax brackets, so too might affiliated corporations seek to divide profits among several related entities so as to take advantage of the graduated corporate rates available to low-profit corporations. In §1561(a), Congress has provided that the "component members" of a "control group" must share a single run through the corporate progressive rates. A "control group" consists of a parent and its controlled subsidiary, §1563(a)(1); a brother-sister pair, §1563(a)(2); or three or more corporations, each of which is a member of a parent-subsidiary group or a brother-sister group and one of which is a common parent corporation, §1563(a)(3). The "component members" of controlled groups are defined in §1563(b). See §1561. Suppose A owns 40 percent and B owns 60 percent of the stock of X Corp. A owns all the stock of Y Corp. Are X Corp. and Y Corp. a brother-sister controlled group, or must there be a commonality of control? See United States v. Vogel Fertilizer Co., 455 U.S. 16 (1982).

D.   PROBLEMS

1.   Tax Loss Associates is a real estate limited partnership organized under the Uniform Limited Partnership Act as enacted by California. See Larson v. Commissioner, page 636 supra. The partnership consists of a single general partner — Tax Aid Corp. — and 300 limited partners. Tax Aid Corp. has a minor capital interest in the partnership but expects to benefit from future partnership growth. While Tax Aid Corp.'s interest in

the partnership is small, the corporation is well capitalized. Tax Aid Corp. has a contractual arrangement with the limited partners whereby they are required to purchase insurance for the general partner, covering any liability for debts of, and claims against, the partnership for which Tax Aid Corp. is personally liable. If you are consulted by a potential limited partner about the likelihood of a loss pass-through from the partnership to investors, what advice would you give? Would other information be helpful?

2.   State *X* has a limited liability company act similar to that described in Rev. Rul. 93-6, page 646 supra. Under the act, a limited liability company can be set up by a single member. Suppose *B* establishes a wholly owned LLC. How will the profits of the LLC be taxed?

3.   Management Corp. is in the business of managing real estate investments made by limited partnerships in which it serves as the general partner. The limited partnerships are organized by Management Corp., which is compensated for both its management and organizational services. For a variety of reasons, banks making mortgage loans to the partnerships generally prefer that title to the property be held by a corporation. Management Corp. performs that function for the partnerships, which in turn compensate the corporation for its role. When Management Corp. performs this function, it represents to everyone it deals with that it is serving as an agent for the partnership. What else do you need to know to determine whether the corporation or the partnership is entitled to any deductions arising from the real estate activities?

4.   USCO, a large U.S. oil company doing business in Saudi Arabia, is prohibited under Saudi law from selling any oil for more than $12 a barrel. The prohibition does not extend to resale by any purchaser from USCO. USCO's costs of exploration are $9 a barrel. USCO sells the oil at $12 a barrel to Subco, a wholly owned subsidiary located in Finland, a low tax jurisdiction. Subco then resells the oil to independent purchasers at a price of $20 a barrel. Can the IRS reallocate any of Subco's profits to USCO? Consider Commissioner v. First Security Bank of Utah, 405 U.S. 394 (1972). Should *First Security* apply in an international context?

5.   Rock Star earns between $500,000 and $1 million in royalties and salary under a contract with Recording Co. To defer recognition of most of this income until after Rock Star's greatness fades, Rock Star agrees to work exclusively for Deferral Corp., a wholly owned corporation of Rock Star's tax lawyer. Assume Deferral Corp. is located in the Cayman Islands, and its income is not subject to any U.S. or foreign income taxation. Deferral Corp. agrees to pay Rock Star annual compensation of $750,000 in the form of a lifetime, $75,000 per year annuity. Thus, after one year, Rock Star will receive $75,000 for life, after two years, Rock Star will receive $150,000 for life, etc. The contract between Rock Star and Deferral Corp. can be canceled at the beginning of each year by either party.

a.   How should Rock Star and Deferral Corp. be taxed if Deferral Corp. enters into a new contract with Recording Co. after the old

contract expires, obligating Rock Star to record and perform for
Recording Co. on the same terms as before?

b. Suppose Recording Co. refuses to sign with anyone other than
Rock Star. Rock Star accordingly signs with Recording Co. and
then assigns all his rights and obligations under the Recording
Co. contract to Deferral Corp. in exchange for the lifetime annuity.
How should Rock Star and Deferral Corp. be taxed?

16

S Corporations and Their Shareholders

Before analyzing the operation of subchapter S in detail, it is helpful to illustrate briefly how the provisions work. Suppose *A* forms a corporation, *S* Corp., by contributing $10,000 in exchange for all of *S* Corp.'s stock. *S* Corp. is engaged in the business of economic consulting and forecasting through an employee, *E*. Assume *A* is an investor and does no consulting. Assume further that the election for *S* Corp. to be treated as an "S corporation," see §1361, is appropriately and timely made. Regardless of whether a corporation elects to be treated as an S corporation, §§351 et seq. govern the tax consequences on formation of the corporation. See Chapter 3. In accordance with §358, *A* will take a $10,000 basis in the *S* Corp. stock.

Suppose that in year 1 *S* Corp. earns $28,000 from its consulting services but incurs $11,000 of deductible expenses for wages paid to *E*. If *S* Corp. were a C corporation, governed exclusively by the provisions of subchapter C, it would report gross income of $28,000 and taxable income of $17,000. *A* would have no tax consequences until a distribution was made. As an S corporation, however, *S* Corp. pays no taxes. Instead, the items of gain and deduction flow through to the shareholders. *A* has $17,000 to be included in income. While *A* has $17,000 in income for tax purposes, in fact the $17,000 is in the corporate treasury. It is as though *A* received a $17,000 distribution, included it for tax purposes, then contributed it back to the corporation. The deemed contribution increases *A*'s stock basis from $10,000 to $27,000.

Suppose that in year 2 *S* Corp. earns nothing but makes a $17,000 distribution to *A*. If *S* Corp. were governed by subchapter C, *A* would have a $17,000 dividend since the accumulated earnings and profits (ignoring taxes paid) from year 1 were $17,000. This is the double tax imposed by subchapter C: The corporation is taxed when it earns income, and the shareholder is taxed when that income is distributed. Under subchapter

S, A was taxed in year 1, when the income was earned, but there will be no further tax in year 2, when that previously taxed income is distributed. The distribution in year 2 is a return of A's investment and will reduce A's basis from $27,000 to $10,000.

In year 3, S Corp. suffers a $3,000 operating loss. The deduction for that loss will be taken by A, who holds stock with a fair market value of $7,000. If the basis of A's stock were not reduced to reflect the fact that a loss deduction was taken, A could sell the stock and reap another $3,000 loss deduction. To prevent this double counting, A is required to reduce stock basis by the amount of the loss.

Not only do gains and losses flow through to shareholders, but the character of the gains and losses flow through as well. For example, capital gains (or losses) realized and recognized by S Corp. on a sale pass through to shareholders as capital gains (or losses); tax-free interest received retains its tax-exempt quality.

A natural tension exists between the provisions of subchapter S (single tax) and those of subchapter C (double tax). For example, a C corporation that has already been taxed on earnings at corporate rates not exceeding 34 percent would love to elect the subchapter S provisions so as to make a nontaxable distribution of those earnings to its shareholders, who would reduce their stock bases rather than recognize income. In drafting and redrafting subchapter S, Congress has sought to shore up the operating provisions with other sections guarding against opportunistic use of subchapter S.

After examining the eligibility requirements for subchapter S election, this chapter will focus on how the election is made and what causes termination of an election. Next, the treatment of S corporation shareholders and the S corporation itself are considered. Finally, the relationship between subchapter S and other provisions, including subchapter C, is explored.

One important point that should be made at the outset is that S corporations are subject to the provisions of both subchapter C and subchapter S to the extent they do not conflict. §1371(a)(1). Of course, to the extent a provision in subchapter S is inconsistent with a provision in subchapter C, the provision in subchapter S controls. Id.

A. ELIGIBILITY AND ELECTION

Kean v. Commissioner
469 F.2d 1183 (9th Cir. 1972)

BYRNE, JR., District Judge:

Appellants, petitioners in the Tax Court, were shareholders in Ocean Shores Bowl, Inc., hereinafter referred to as Bowl, a Washington corporation. They appeal from a judgment of the Tax Court, 51 T.C. 337, invalidating Bowl's election under Subchapter S, . . . and disallowing petitioners' deductions on their personal tax returns of their pro rata shares of Bowl's 1962 and 1963 net operating losses.

Bowl was formed on March 20, 1962 and had only one class of stock issued and outstanding. On October 30, 1962 Bowl filed a timely election to be taxed as a small business corporation pursuant to [§1362] of the Internal Revenue Code of 1954. Consents to such election were contemporaneously filed by all of the shareholders of record and their wives. As a result of the election, Bowl's net operating losses of $15,316 for the short taxable year 1962 and $56,638.28 for 1963 were deducted in pro rata shares by petitioners on their 1962 and 1963 personal income tax returns.

Some Bowl debentures and 125 shares of Bowl stock were held in the name of petitioner, William MacPherson. He and his brother, petitioner Murdock MacPherson, were engaged in the real estate business in a company called MacPhersons, Inc. Each brother owned 45% of the stock of MacPhersons, Inc. with the remaining 10% being held by their mother. William and Murdock MacPherson had many joint investments which were conducted without any written agreement. Whoever initiated the investment would normally be responsible for its management. Neither held a power of attorney for the other. The books and records of MacPhersons, Inc. were maintained by its employee, Donald Minkler.

On their 1962 joint income tax return William MacPherson and his wife deducted the net operating loss of Bowl accruing to the 125 shares in William's name. In 1963 William MacPherson and his wife deducted one half of the net operating loss for that year attributed to said shares while Murdock MacPherson and his wife deducted the other one half on their joint return. In 1964 the William MacPhersons and the Murdock MacPhersons each reported the sale of one half of the 125 shares of Bowl stock and one half of the Bowl debentures. All of these returns were prepared by Donald Minkler.

A 1965 Internal Revenue Service audit disclosed that the 125 shares of Bowl stock and Bowl debentures, issued to William MacPherson in 1962, were purchased with a MacPhersons, Inc. check. The cost of the purchase was charged on the books of MacPhersons, Inc. equally against the drawing accounts of William and Murdock. Murdock MacPherson has never been repaid by William MacPherson for the amounts taken out of his drawing account to pay for the stock and debentures.

Murdock MacPherson was not a shareholder of record of Bowl. Neither he nor his wife were mentioned in the Subchapter S election filed with the Internal Revenue Service in October, 1962; nor did they file a consent to the election. None of the other shareholders knew that Murdock MacPherson was involved in any way with Bowl until the 1965 audit.

The Tax Court held that Bowl's Subchapter S election was invalid because Murdock MacPherson, as a beneficial owner of Bowl stock, was a shareholder within the meaning of [§1362] and had not consented to the corporation's election. Based on this finding, the court disallowed petitioners' deduction of their pro rata shares of the corporation's net operating losses.

Subchapter S of the Internal Revenue Code of 1954 allows a small business corporation, as defined by [§1361], to elect to be exempt from corporate income taxes with the consequence that its shareholders are taxed directly on the corporation's earnings or may deduct the corporation's losses. Section [1362(a)(2)] provides that the corporation's election is "valid only if all persons who are shareholders . . . consent to such election."

Petitioners contend that since Murdock MacPherson was not a shareholder of record and was not able to exercise any rights as a shareholder under Washington law, he was not a "shareholder" under [§1362]. We disagree. The question of who is a shareholder as the term is used in Subchapter S must be determined by federal rather than state law. . . . Treasury Regulation §1.1371-1(d)(1), implementing Subchapter S, states that "Ordinarily, the persons who would have to include in gross income dividends distributed with respect to the stock of the corporation are considered to be shareholders of the corporation."*

Petitioners challenge the validity of this regulation on the ground that it has no statutory basis and is in conflict with the legislative history. They rely on a portion of the report of the Senate Finance Committee discussing Subchapter S which stated:

> An election may be made to supply the tax treatment provided by this new subchapter only if all of the shareholders consent to this election. For this purpose the shareholders are those of record as of the first day of the taxable year in question, or if the election is made after that time, shareholders of record when the election is made.

S. Rep. No. 1900, 85th Cong., 2nd Sess., p. 87.

The Tax Court in Alfred N. Hoffman, 47 T.C. 218, 235 (1966), aff'd sub nom. Hoffman v. Commissioner of Internal Revenue, 391 F.2d 930 (5th Cir. 1968), in considering the contention that a shareholder of record rather than the beneficial owner of the stock must consent to the Subchapter S election, discussed the report of the Senate Finance Committee as follows:

> While this use of the words "of record" furnishes some support for petitioner's position, it is entirely inconsistent with the basic congressional purpose to tax the undistributed corporate income only to the persons who are accountable for dividends paid by the corporation, and those persons are the real

* This regulation has been withdrawn and more specific guidance is now provided. See Treas. Regs. §1.1362-6(b)(2). — Eds.

owners of the stock whether or not they are the shareholders "of record." In the circumstances, we must rely upon the all pervasive legislative purpose and not upon the foregoing fragmentary phrase in the committee report.

Subchapter S allows shareholders of a small business corporation to elect alternative tax consequences resulting from stock ownership. Without a Subchapter S election the corporation is liable for corporate taxes, the shareholders cannot deduct corporate losses, and only distributed dividends are subject to the personal income tax. If the election is made, the corporation is exempt from corporate taxes and the shareholders may deduct corporate net operating losses but must pay personal income tax on all corporate income whether distributed or not. The desirability of a Subchapter S election depends upon the individual tax considerations of each shareholder. The final determination of whether there is to be an election should be made by those who would suffer the tax consequences of it. . . .

A treasury regulation which supplies the definition that Congress omitted must be sustained unless unreasonable and obviously inconsistent with the statute. Bingler v. Johnson, 394 U.S. 741, 89 S. Ct. 1439, 22 L. Ed. 2d 695 (1969); Commissioner of Internal Revenue v. South Texas Lumber Co., 333 U.S. 496. Treasury Regulation §1.1371-1(d)(1) is consistent with the basic purpose of Subchapter S and reasonably implements the legislative mandate.

We conclude, as did the Tax Court, that William and Murdock MacPherson jointly invested in the 125 shares of Bowl stock issued to William MacPherson. Murdock MacPherson was the beneficial owner of one half of that stock in William MacPherson's name and must be considered a "shareholder" for the purpose of [§1362]. Murdock MacPherson's failure to file a consent invalidates Bowl's Subchapter S election. Therefore, petitioners were not entitled to deduct their pro rata shares of Bowl's net operating loss for 1962 and 1963. . . .

Finally, petitioners contend that the District Director abused the discretion reposed in him by Treas. Reg. §1.1372-3(c)* and that the Tax Court erred in refusing to review the exercise of the District Director's discretion.

After the judgment of the Tax Court finding that Bowl's Subchapter S election was invalid due to Murdock MacPherson's failure to consent, petitioners requested of the District Director an extension of time, pursuant to Treas. Reg. §1.1372-3(c), in which to file consents. All the petitioners offered to file new consents for the years 1962 and 1963.

The District Director denied the request. Petitioners then filed a motion in the Tax Court for retrial, further trial or reconsideration, seeking

---

* Treas. Regs. §1.1372-3(c) is now reissued as Treas. Regs. §1.1362-6(b)(3)(iii). — EDS.

a review of the discretion exercised by the District Director. The Tax Court denied the motion.

The District Director advised petitioners that he was rejecting the request for an extension because the Tax Court had "issued an opinion in these cases . . . and because we do not feel the circumstances of this matter meet the requirements of Regs. §1.1372-3(c)."

The fact that the Tax Court had issued an opinion invalidating Bowl's Subchapter S election was not a basis for refusing to allow petitioners an extension of time to file consents. At the time the opinion was filed, no request had been made to the District Director and nothing in the opinion precluded him from granting a subsequent request for extension.

Additionally, there is no valid basis for the District Director's determination that the requirements of Treas. Reg. §1.1372-3(c) had not been met. Under the regulation the failure to file a consent will not invalidate the Subchapter S election and an extension of time to file new consents should be granted if it is shown to the satisfaction of the District Director that: (1) there was reasonable cause for the failure to file such consent, and (2) the government interest will not be jeopardized by treating the Subchapter S election as valid. There was reasonable cause for Murdock MacPherson's failure to file a timely consent. Murdock MacPherson was not a shareholder of record. He believed that whatever ownership interest he had in the shares did not necessitate his consent to Bowl's election. When the Internal Revenue Service disagreed with this position, the petitioners sought a judicial determination. Until the Tax Court issued its opinion, Murdock MacPherson did not know that his consent was required to consummate Bowl's election under [§1362]. Furthermore, there is nothing to indicate that any government interest is jeopardized by now validating the Subchapter S election.

At the time of the Subchapter S election, petitioners, other than possibly the MacPhersons, did not know or have reason to suspect that Murdock MacPherson had any ownership interest in Bowl's stock. The District Director's failure to exercise his discretion so as to allow petitioners to file their consents deprives eight taxpayers of deductions taken in good faith ten years earlier and saddles each taxpayer with a substantial liability for back taxes. It is apparent that Treas. Reg. §1.1372-3(c) was promulgated to prevent the harsh result reached in cases of this kind.

The District Director abused his discretion by arbitrarily refusing to allow petitioners an extension of time in which to file their consent to Bowl's Subchapter S election. Mensik v. C.I.R., 328 F.2d 147 (7th Cir. 1964); Bookwalter v. Mayer, 345 F.2d 476 (8th Cir. 1965).

We affirm the opinion of the Tax Court, except with regard to its refusal to review the exercise of the District Director's discretion, and order the District Director to grant petitioners an extension of time to file the consents pursuant to Treas. Reg. §1.1372-3(c).

Rev. Rul. 86-110

1986-2 C.B. 150

ISSUE

If a corporation's election to be an S corporation is automatically terminated because the corporation inadvertently had one or more ineligible shareholders for a limited period of time before discovery and correction, is the corporation treated as continuing to be an S corporation under section 1362(f) of the Internal Revenue Code during the period when it had one or more ineligible shareholders?

FACTS

X corporation is an electing small business corporation. A, the majority shareholder of X, on advice of counsel, transferred shares of X stock to two irrevocable trusts for the benefit of A's minor children. Neither trust was an eligible shareholder under section 1361(c)(2) or section 1361(d)(3) of the Code because neither trust was treated by sections 671 through 679 as entirely owned by an individual that is a citizen or resident of the United States and because each trust had more than one income beneficiary. Thus, under section 1362(d)(2), the transfer of stock to the trusts resulted in an automatic termination of the S corporation election.

It was not A's desire or expectation to terminate the election when the transfer of the stock was made to the trusts. A acted on the advice of counsel that such transfers would not jeopardize the Subchapter S election, and A would not have made the transfers but for this advice. X and its shareholders continued to file returns and report income in a manner consistent with their belief that the election was still in effect.

Within a reasonable period of time after discovery of the termination, A took steps to correct the problem so that X once more qualified as a small business corporation. In addition X, and each shareholder of X, agreed to make any adjustments required by the Service with respect to such period as the Service might specify.

LAW AND ANALYSIS

Section 1361(a) of the Code provides that the term "S corporation" means, with respect to any tax year, a small business corporation for which an election under section 1362(a) is in effect.

Section 1361(b)(1) of the Code defines a "small business corporation" as a domestic corporation that is not an ineligible corporation and does not (A) have more than 35 shareholders, (B) have as a shareholder, a person (other than an estate and other than a trust described in section 1361(c)(2)) that is not an individual, (C) have a nonresident alien as a shareholder, and (D) have more than one class of stock.

Section 1361(c)(2) of the Code provides that four types of domestic trusts may be shareholders of an S corporation: a trust that is treated as owned by an individual who is a citizen or resident of the United States; a trust that was treated as owned by an individual who was a citizen or resident of the United States immediately before the death of the deemed owner and that continues in existence after such death, but only for the 60-day period (or 2-year period if the entire corpus of the trust is includible in the gross estate of the deemed owner) beginning on the day of the deemed owner's death; a trust with respect to stock transferred to it pursuant to the terms of a will, but only for the 60-day period beginning on the day on which such stock is transferred to it; and a trust created primarily to exercise the voting power of stock transferred to it.

Section 1361(d) of the Code provides that a qualified subchapter S trust can be treated as a trust described in section 1361(c)(2) if a beneficiary of the trust makes an election for such treatment. A qualified subchapter S trust is a trust the terms of which require that (i) during the life of the current income beneficiary, there shall be only one income beneficiary of the trust; (ii) any corpus distributed during the life of the current income beneficiary may be distributed only to such beneficiary; (iii) the income interest of the current income beneficiary in the trust shall terminate on the life of the current income beneficiary, the trust shall distribute all of its assets to such beneficiary. In addition, all the income of the trust must be distributed (or required to be distributed) currently to one individual who is a citizen or resident of the United States.

Section 1362(d)(2) of the Code provides that an election under section 1362(a) will be terminated whenever (at any time on or after the first day of the first taxable year for which the corporation is an S corporation) the corporation ceases to be a small business corporation.

Section 1362(f) of the Code provides that if (1) an election by any corporation is terminated under section 1362(d)(2) or (3) of the Code, (2) the Secretary determines that the termination was inadvertent, (3) no later than a reasonable period of time after discovery of the terminating event, steps are taken so that the corporation is once more a small business corporation, and (4) the corporation, and each person who was a shareholder during the period specified under section 1362(f), agree to make such adjustments (consistent with the treatment of the corporation as an S corporation) as may be required by the Secretary with respect to that period, then, notwithstanding the terminating event, such corporation will be treated as continuing to be an S corporation during the period specified by the Secretary.

S. Rep. No. 97-640, 97th Cong., 2d Sess. 12 (1982), 1982-2 C.B. 718, 723, discusses section 1362(f) of the Code. It states in part:

> If the Internal Revenue Service determines that a corporation's subchapter S election is inadvertently terminated, the Service can waive the effect of the terminating event for any period if the corporation timely corrects the event and if the corporation and the shareholders agree to be treated as if the election has been in effect for such period.

Under the facts presented, since A transferred stock to trusts that are ineligible shareholders under section 1361(b)(1) of the Code, X ceased to be a small business corporation, thereby terminating its S corporation election. However, the termination was inadvertent. A acted on advice of counsel and would not have made the transfers but for this advice. Further, A took the necessary steps to correct the problem within a reasonable time after discovery of the termination and X and its shareholders agreed to make such adjustments as may be required by the Secretary.

HOLDING

The S corporation is treated as continuing to be an S corporation under section 1362(f) of the Code for the period specified by the Service during which it had one or more ineligible shareholders.

NOTE

1. *Small business corporation.* An S corporation is defined as a "small business corporation" for which an election is in effect. §1361(a)(1). All other corporations are referred to as C corporations. A "small business corporation" is a domestic corporation that does not have (1) more than 35 shareholders, (2) any shareholders who are not individuals (or estates or certain kinds of trusts), (3) any nonresident shareholders, and (4) more than one class of stock. §1361(b)(1). Note that these requirements do not separate small from large business corporations in terms of business size but only in terms of number of shareholders.

Even if the requirements in §1361(a)(1) are satisfied, certain corporations are ineligible for S corporation status. If a corporation is a member of an affiliated group of corporations as defined in §1504, an election is not available. For example, a corporation owning 80 percent or more of the stock of another corporation cannot elect S corporation status, although there is an exception if the controlled subsidiary corporation is inactive. See §1361(c)(6). Other ineligible corporations include insurance companies, financial institutions, and certain domestic corporations that avail themselves of preferential treatment on foreign income.

2. *Number and nature of shareholders.* When subchapter S was enacted, the number of permitted shareholders was 10. Gradually the permitted number has increased to the current level of 35. §1361(b)(1)(A). In raising the number to 35, Congress noted that the number corresponds to the private placement exemption under the federal securities law. Unfortunately, Congress gave no indication why that is a meaningful correspondence. Husband and wife (and their estates) are treated as one shareholder so that in theory 70 people — 35 couples — could form an S corporation even if each shareholder holds stock in his or her own name.

Aside from individuals and their estates, certain trusts may also be shareholders, including grantor trusts in which the grantor is treated as owner or in which under §678 a person who is not the grantor may vest the trust income or corpus in himself; voting trusts; and certain trusts acquiring stock from an estate (but only for a 60-day period). §1361(c)(2). Section 1361(d) also makes a "qualified subchapter S trust" an eligible shareholder. A qualified subchapter S trust is one that distributes all its income to a single beneficiary who makes a timely election to be treated as the owner of the trust under §678. The trust must also contain terms that clearly channel the trust benefits to the income beneficiary. §1361(d)(3).

The availability of certain trusts as eligible shareholders offers estate tax planning opportunities. A taxpayer can remove from her estate appreciated S corporation stock (or S corporation stock that the taxpayer anticipates will appreciate) by setting up an appropriate grantor trust. For example, suppose *T* creates an irrevocable, nonreversionary trust for the benefit of *C,* her child, in which an independent trustee (but not an adverse party) has the power to add beneficiaries. *T* transfers S corporation stock to the trust. Section 674 renders *T* the owner of the trust with all the income, deductions, and credits attributable to her under §671. The stock, however, will not be includible in her estate for estate tax purposes.

3. *One-class-of-stock requirement.* Items of S corporation income, loss, deduction, and credit are passed through to its shareholders in proportion to relative stock ownership. §1366(a). The conventional reason offered for the one-class-of-stock requirement is the preservation of simplicity in the allocation of corporate income and deductions: Were there multiple classes of stock, allocation of corporate income among all shareholders would require some method of allocation among the classes as well as among shares within each class. In the partnership area, entity-level tax items can be allocated among the partners almost without limitation, subject only to the "substantial economic effect" requirement that those partners allocated taxable income ultimately receive pro tanto distributions while those partners allocated deductions receive pro tanto less. See §704(b).

Why shouldn't the subchapter S provisions accommodate special allocations through differing equity interests (e.g., common and preferred stock), perhaps by allocating corporate tax items among classes of outstanding shares by reference to the relative values of those shares? The inability to make special allocations is a significant difference between subchapter S and the partnership provisions. Note, though, that for closely held corporations whose shares are not traded publicly, allocating corporate tax items among its shareholders based on relative values of stock ownership would pose significant valuation difficulties.

Although it might seem as if determining whether a corporation has more than one class of stock cannot be controversial, the infinite ways in which corporate investment can be fashioned belies that assessment. A corporation having two classes of stock identical in all respects other than voting rights does not violate the one-class-of-stock limitation, for example, because the statute specifically provides that differences in voting rights are ignored. §1361(c)(4). As a more complex example, suppose a family-owned corporation sells stock outside the family only to employees, and suppose these employees are required to sell their shares back to the corporation upon termination of their employment. If the corporation retains the right to fire its employees at will, the corporation effectively can deny distribution and liquidation rights to the shares of the employees by terminating the employees' employment status. Does this make the employees' shares sufficiently inferior as to constitute a second class of stock?

This question and a host of others are answered by Treas. Regs. §1.1361-1(*l*). Under that regulation, a corporation is not treated as having more than one class of stock if "all outstanding shares of stock [of the corporation] confer identical rights to distribution and liquidation proceeds." Treas. Regs. §1.1361-1(*l*)(2)(i). Further, "[t]he determination of whether all outstanding shares of stock confer identical rights to distribution and liquidation proceeds is made based on the corporate charter, . . . applicable state law, and binding agreements relating to distribution and liquidation proceeds." Id. The various corporate documents determining the shareholders' rights are called the "governing instruments," and the regulations specifically provide that these governing instruments do *not* include buy-sell agreements, agreements restricting the transferability of shares, and similar arrangements unless (1) a principal purpose of the agreement is to circumvent the one class of stock requirement and (2) the agreement establishes a price that, at the time the agreement is entered into, is significantly above or below the fair market value of the stock. Treas. Regs. §1.1361-1(*l*)(2)(iii)(A).

Thus, the buy-sell agreement triggered by termination of employment in the family corporation example above would not cause the employees' shares to constitute a second class of stock unless the buy-sell agreement was entered into to circumvent the one-class-of-stock requirement and the sale price was set significantly above or below fair market value. The regulations provide that a sale price set at book value or between book value and fair market value will not be considered significantly above or below fair market value. Treas. Regs. §1.1361-1 (*l*) (2) (iii) (A). Indeed, there would not be two classes of stock in this example even if the sale price was set significantly above or below fair market value because the regulations provide that "[b]ona fide agreements to redeem or purchase stock at the time of death, divorce, disability, or termination of employment are disregarded." Treas. Regs. §1.1361-1 (*l*) (2) (iii) (B).

As you know from your study of subchapter C, the Commissioner is free to assert that corporate investments nominally classified as debt should be reclassified as equity. If such a reclassification argument prevailed in the case of an S corporation, the effect seemingly would be to create a second class of stock that would then terminate the corporation's subchapter S election. Section 1361(c)(5) creates a safe harbor for "straight debt," and debt that meets the requirements of this section will not be considered a second class of stock even if it could be reclassified as equity under general debt-equity principles. "Straight debt" is a written, unconditional promise to pay on demand or on a specified date a sum certain of money if the interest rate and dates are not contingent on profits or the borrower's discretion, if the debt is not convertible into stock, and if the creditor would be a permitted subchapter S shareholder.

Suppose an S corporation issues debt that does not meet the safe harbor requirements. Does the debt issuance automatically spoil the subchapter S election? The safe harbor is not exclusive; taxpayers may still prevail with nonstraight debt. For example, the current regulations provide that debt held in proportion to stock will not be considered a second class of stock. Treas. Regs. §1.1371-1 (*l*) (4) (ii) (B) (2). More generally, a corporate instrument not nominally classified as equity (such as debt, call options, and other financial instruments) will not violate the one-class-of-stock requirement unless (1) the instrument is reclassified as equity under general principles of tax law and (2) a principal purpose of issuing the instrument is to circumvent the rights to distribution or liquidation conferred on the corporation's outstanding shares by the governing instruments or to circumvent the limitations on eligible shareholders. Treas. Regs. §1.1361-1 (*l*) (4) (ii) (A). While these rules should allow most corporations to issue debt without running afoul of the one-class-of-stock limitation, the ability of the Commissioner to challenge financial instruments based in part on the principal purpose underlying the issuance of the instruments means that few corporate planners can give complete assurance that a corporation's subchapter S election is inviolate. For a trenchant criticism of the proposed regulations upon which the current regulations are based, see generally Ginsburg and Levin, The New Subchapter S One

Class of Stock Proposed Regulations: Much Better, But Still Not Awfully Good, 53 Tax Notes 81 (Oct. 7, 1991).

4. *Election.* A qualifying small business corporation does not automatically attain S corporation status. Section 1362(a) requires that the corporation elect and that all shareholders must consent to the application of the subchapter S rules. For an election to be valid in year 2, the election can be made at any time during year 1 or at any time on or before the fifteenth day of the third month of year 2. §1362(b). Any subsequent election is treated as an election for year 3. Moreover, an election during the first 2½ months of year 2 will be treated as effective for year 3 if at any point during the first 2½ months the corporation was not a "small business corporation" or some shareholder did not consent (e.g., a shareholder who sold before the election was made). Once elected, subchapter S status remains in effect until termination. §1362(c).

When subchapter S was rewritten, the regulation at issue in *Kean* was not repromulgated. Should that be taken as evidence that only shareholders of record need consent to §1362 election? Probably not: Treas. Regs. §1.1362-6(b)(2) makes clear that the beneficial owner of shares often must consent to the election.

5. *Termination by revocation.* Subchapter S status can be terminated in three ways: (1) revocation, (2) failure to satisfy the small business corporation requirements, or (3) receipt of excessive passive income. Termination by revocation requires consent by holders of a majority of the outstanding stock (voting and nonvoting). §1362(d). Note that this does not require consent by a majority of the outstanding shareholders. If, for example, one individual owns 51 percent of the corporation's outstanding stock, that shareholder can elect termination without the consent (or over the objection) of all other shareholders.

If the revocation is filed by the corporation on or before the fifteenth day of the third month of a taxable year, normally it is effective as of the first day of that year. A later filing is effective on the first day of the next taxable year. Section 1362(d)(1)(D) permits the corporation to specify a prospective date for revocation. For example, a calendar year corporation that files a revocation on June 8, 1986, can specify any date on or after June 8. If the revocation occurs during a taxable year, §1362(e) divides the transitional year into two short years, with subchapter S governing the first and subchapter C the second.

6. *Termination by ceasing to be a small business corporation.* If an S corporation ceases to be a small business corporation within the meaning of §1361(b), subchapter S status terminates immediately. Thus, if there are more than 35 shareholders, or stock is transferred to an ineligible shareholder, or a second class of stock is issued, subchapter S status ends.

Under prior law, a new shareholder could terminate the election by failing to consent during the first 60 days. The 1982 act eliminated this method of termination. Nevertheless, in the absence of a shareholder agreement, a new shareholder (or old ones) can still wield great power over subchapter S status. For example, a new shareholder could terminate the election by transferring some shares to a corporation or to some other ineligible shareholder.

7. *Termination by excess passive investment income.* Section 1363(d) applies when a corporation has passive investment income equal to more than 25 percent of its gross receipts for each of three consecutive years. In addition, the corporation must have accumulated earnings and profits at the end of each of the three years in question. §1363(d)(3). This second requirement ensures that a termination forced by excess passive investment income can apply only to an S corporation that was a C corporation for one or more prior years. Further, even if an S corporation was a C corporation in one or more prior years, it still will not be subject to termination because of excess passive investment income unless it had positive earnings and profits when it changed to an S corporation and it has failed to distribute those subchapter C earnings and profits during its S corporation existence. The problems incident to a transition from C corporation to S corporation status can be complex and are considered below. See pages 718-721, 722-723 infra. Note, though, that if a corporation should run afoul of §1368(d), termination takes effect only at the beginning of the next taxable year.

"Passive investment income" is defined as gross receipts derived from royalties, rents, dividends, interest, annuities, and gains from the sale or exchange of stock or securities. Often corporations will try to characterize rental or royalty payments as service income to escape passive investment income penalties. See, e.g., Rev. Rul. 81-197, 1981-2 C.B. 166 (amounts paid for airplane with a pilot and supplies not considered rent). Calculation of the passive income threshold will be considered in connection with the special tax on excess passive income at page 719 infra.

8. *Treatment of the termination year.* For any termination that is effective during the year, a corporation will have both an S short year and a C short year. §1362(e). The terminating corporation can either prorate its income for the full year between the two short years or, with the consent of all the shareholders (including all former shareholders holding stock in the termination year and all shareholders holding stock on the first day of the C short year), elect to actually close its S corporation books at the end of the S short year. Because the corporate rates under §11 are graduated, the income for the C short year is annualized, the tax is computed, and the portion of the tax that the C short year bears to the whole year is payable. §1362(e)(5).

For example, suppose a nonresident alien purchases stock in *S* Corp. on March 15, so the *S* short year ending on March 14 comprises one-fifth of the year. If *S* Corp. has $100,000 of taxable income for the year or $50,000 of taxable income as of March 14, it can prorate the $100,000 or choose to close its books and treat $50,000 of income as earned in the last four-fifths of the year. If proration results, the full $22,250 tax on $100,000 must be multiplied by 292/365, or four-fifths, to figure the $17,800 tax for the C short year. If S Corp. closes its books on March 14, the $50,000 of income for the C short year must be annualized by multiplying $50,000 by 365/292, or five-fourths, which results in $62,500 of annual income. The §11 tax on $62,500 is $10,625, which then must be multiplied by 292/365, or four-fifths, to determine the $8,500 tax attributable to the C short year. Note that special provisions apply to these allocation rules if significant changes in stock ownership occur during the termination year. See §1362(e)(6).

9. *Election after termination.* Section 1363(g) requires that a corporation wait five years before reelecting subchapter S status following termination unless the IRS consents to earlier election. The IRS has consented when the taxpayer inadvertently exceeded the passive income requirements. See, e.g., Priv. Ltr. Rul. 8327056 (decline in real estate market lowered active income); Priv. Ltr. Rul. 8207048 (loss of casino license lowered active income). Reelection has also been permitted when significant ownership changes occurred after termination. See, e.g., Priv. Ltr. Rul. 8207055 (current shareholder owned no stock in termination year); Priv. Ltr. Rul. 8326097 (complete change of stock ownership). When these factors are absent, the Service is likely to deny reelection. See, e.g., Priv. Ltr. Rul. 8310015 (receipt of passive income within corporation's control); Priv. Ltr. Rul. 8336014 (revocation with no change in stock ownership).

Section 1362(f) offers additional relief for inadvertent terminations. If the IRS determines that a termination was inadvertent, the termination may be treated as though it never occurred if the corporation moves quickly to correct the defect and agrees to any adjustments required by the IRS. The legislative history indicates that the inadvertent termination rule should apply when no tax avoidance would result from continued subchapter S treatment. For example, suppose a corporation, in good faith, mistakenly determined that it had no earnings and profits and, as a result, violated the excess passive income requirement (excess passive income for three years with earnings and profits in each of those years). See §1362(d)(3). If the shareholders agree to treat the earnings as distributed, including them in income, the IRS might waive termination. The legislative history suggests a similar result if the one class of stock requirement is inadvertently breached but no tax avoidance resulted.

In Rev. Rul. 86-110, page 689 supra, the Service held that §1362(f) was applicable when the taxpayer relied on the advice of his lawyer. Contrast this largesse on the part of the Service with the Service's view in failure to file or negligence cases under §§6651 and 6653 that reliance on counsel is not a defense. See, e.g., Kroll v. United States, 547 F.2d 39 (7th Cir. 1977). Perhaps §1363(f) is a congressional admission that the provisions of subchapter S are so complicated that there can be no negligence. See, e.g., Lucas v. Hamm, 56 Cal. 2d 583 (1981) (no negligence when lawyer misinterpreted the rule against perpetuities because of its complexity).

B. TREATMENT OF S CORPORATION SHAREHOLDERS

In general, an S corporation is not a taxpayer. §1363(a).[1] Rather, an S corporation computes its taxable income and then passes that income through to its owners. Those owners are its shareholders, and each shareholder reports a proportion of the corporation's income based on the shareholder's relative ownership of the corporation's outstanding shares. §1366(a). For example, if shareholder Q owns 20 of the 100 outstanding shares of S Corp.'s outstanding stock, then Q reports 20 percent of S Corp.'s taxable income or loss. If a shareholder's percentage of stock ownership changes during the year, the corporation's income is allocated ratably to each day of the year and then passed through to each shareholder in proportion to the shareholder's ownership interest on each day. §1377(a).

The tax effect of some corporate-level items may depend on the shareholder's individual tax circumstances. For example, because capital losses can offset only capital gains (plus up to $3,000 of ordinary income, see §1211(b)), the ability of an S corporation shareholder to deduct excess corporate capital losses will turn on whether the shareholder has additional capital gains. Whenever an item of corporate-level income, loss, deduction, or credit may depend on noncorporate circumstances of the shareholders, the item keeps its character as it passes through to the shareholders. §1366(b). Capital gains, capital losses, and charitable contributions accordingly retain their character as they pass through to S corporation shareholders. Items whose characterization will not affect the computation of a shareholder's tax liability are called "nonseparately computed income and loss" items. See §1366(a)(1)(B).

As items of corporate income pass through to S corporation shareholders, the shareholders adjust their stock basis upward. §1367(a)(1). Similarly, as corporate deductions pass through shareholders adjust their stock basis downward. §1367(a)(2). These rules ensure that corporate-level items of income and deduction taxed to the shareholders when recognized at the corporate level will not be taxed to the shareholders a second time upon disposition of their shares.

For example, suppose individual *I* creates S Corp., an electing S corporation, by contributing cash of $1,000 in exchange for 100 shares of S

---

1. An S corporation having C corporation earnings and profits can be a taxpayer. See pages 718-721 infra.

Corp. stock. This transaction is tax free to *I* and to *S* Corp., and *I* takes a basis in the stock of $1,000. If the corporation purchases a corporate bond paying interest of 10% per year, it will earn $100 during the year. This income will be passed through and taxed to *I,* and *I* will increase her stock basis to $1,100.

The corporation now has assets worth $1,100, consisting of a bond worth $1,000 and cash of $100. If *I* sells all her shares in *S* Corp., she should receive $1,100 for them. Because of the basis adjustment under §1367(a)(1), *I* will not recognize gain on this sale.

Suppose that *I* does not sell her shares of *S* Corp. but instead *S* Corp. distributes its $100 of earnings to *I* as a dividend. Because the earnings were already taxed to *I,* they should not be taxed a second time upon distribution, and that is indeed the rule. Under §1368(b)(1), *I* receives the distribution tax free and then, under §1367(a)(2)(A), *I* reduces her stock basis downward by the $100 received in the distribution. Thus, the effect of the distribution is to reduce the value of the corporation to $1,000 and to return *I*'s stock basis to $1,000 as well. If *I* then sells her stock of *S* Corp., she will receive $1,000 for it and again will recognize no gain or loss.

Reconsider this example but assume that the corporation purchases a state bond rather than a corporate bond. Now, the $100 interest received is tax exempt so that *I* has no taxable income from the corporation's activity during its first year. Should *I* be entitled to adjust her basis upward for tax-exempt income as she adjusted it for taxable income? The answer is yes, see §1367(a)(1)(A) incorporating §1366(a)(1)(A) by reference, and this rule ensures that tax-exempt income received by the corporation does not become taxable to the shareholder upon disposition of her shares. That is, if *I* could not adjust her stock basis up to $1,100, she would recognize a gain of $100 if she sold her *S* Corp. shares for their current fair market value of $1,100. The basis adjustment in §1367(a)(1)(A) for tax-exempt income ensures that the income remains tax free to the shareholder not only when recognized by the corporation but also when recognized implicitly by the shareholder on disposition of her shares. As you might expect, passed through corporate deductions and nondeductible, noncapitalizable expenses (such as illegal bribes and kickbacks) reduce a shareholder's basis in her S corporation stock. See §1367(a)(2)(B)-(E).

As mentioned previously, if a shareholder's percentage of stock ownership changes during the year, the corporation's items of income and deduction are allocated ratably to each day of the year and then are passed through to each shareholder in proportion to the shareholder's ownership interest on each day. §1377(a). These items of income and deduction are passed through to the shareholders on the last day of the corporation's taxable year. §1366(a)(1). Under §1378, an S corporation is not free to choose its taxable year but instead must take the calendar year as its taxable year unless it can demonstrate a business purpose for some other taxable year. Because almost all S corporation shareholders are individuals using the calendar year as their taxable years, the rule of §1378 ensures that most shareholders will share a common taxable year with their small business corporations. Note that shareholders will obtain some deferral to the extent their taxable years do not coincide with that of their S corporation, with the greatest deferral enjoyed by a shareholder whose taxable year ends immediately before that of the corporation.

NOTE

1. *Distributions in excess of basis.* As discussed above, distributions from an S corporation to its shareholder are tax free and adjust stock basis downward by the amount of the distribution. But suppose the amount of the distribution exceeds the shareholder's stock basis. Is stock basis reduced below zero, leaving the shareholder with a negative adjusted basis in his shares?

A shareholder cannot reduce stock basis below zero. See the parenthetical in §1367(a)(2). Instead, the distribution is taxable as capital gain to the shareholder to the extent the amount of the distribution exceeds his stock basis. §1368(b)(2). This gain merely offsets what would otherwise be the shareholder's negative stock basis so that a distribution producing gain under §1368(b)(2) always leaves the shareholder's stock basis at zero.

For example, suppose an S corporation distributes $120 to one of its shareholders having an adjusted basis in her stock of $100. This distribution will produce gain of $20 to the distributee and he will reduce his stock basis to $0. The gain will be long- or short-term depending on the shareholder's holding period of her S corporation stock.

If a shareholder owns multiple shares with different adjusted bases, determining the appropriate basis adjustment becomes more complex. Consider the following example. Individual Z owns two of the 10 outstanding shares of S Corp. stock, one with an adjusted basis of $100 and the other with an adjusted basis of $150. If S Corp. makes a distribution to Z of cash or property worth $80, the distribution is tax free to Z, §1368(b)(1), and Z reduces his stock basis by the amount of the distribution, §1366(a)(2)(A). This reduction is made pro rata share-by-share so that Z's post-distribution shares' bases become $60 and $110. Treas. Regs. §1.1367-1(c)(3).

Now change this example by assuming that the amount of the distribution was $220 rather than $80. Once again Z receives the distribution tax free under §1368(b)(1), and Z reduces his aggregate stock basis from $250 to $30. This adjustment is made pro rata share-by-share so that each share receives a downward adjustment of $110. Because no share can take a negative basis, however, Z reduces his basis in the share having a predistribution basis of $100 down to $0, and the additional $10 of negative adjustment that could not be absorbed by that share is allocated to the other share. Thus, Z ends up owning one share with adjusted basis of $0 and a second share with adjusted basis of $30. See Treas. Regs. §1.1367-1(g)(example 2).

2. *Distributions of property.* As you know, a nonliquidating corporate distribution of property can trigger recognition of gain but not of loss to the distributing corporation. §311(a)(1), (b)(1). When an S corporation distributes appreciated property, the corporate gain is passed through to the shareholders like any other gain. While this passed-thru gain will be includible on the shareholders' individual returns, it also will increase their stock bases. Further, the distribution will allow the shareholders to receive a greater portion of the distribution tax-free because the basis increase is taken into account *prior to* determining the tax consequences of the distribution to the distributee-shareholder. §1368(d)(1); see also Treas. Regs. §1.1368-3 (example 1).

For example, suppose individual B owns 50 percent of the outstanding stock of S Corp. with an adjusted basis of $10,000 in those shares. If the corporation distributes property to B having a fair market value of $15,000 and an adjusted basis to the corporation of $11,000, the corporation will recognize a gain of $4,000 on the distribution. Of this $4,000 gain, half will be includible to B because B owns half of the corporation's outstanding stock. In addition, if the corporation recognizes no other items of income or deduction during the year, B will recognize a gain on the distribution of $3,000 because the $15,000 amount of the distribution exceeds B's year-end adjusted stock basis by that amount: B's year-end adjusted stock basis equals its value at the beginning of the year, or $10,000, plus B's share of any pass through income or less any pass through loss, here $2,000 of gain.

Note what is implicit in this example: The tax consequences of a distribution to the shareholder-distributee cannot be determined until the close of the S corporation's taxable year because corporate-level recognition of income and loss during *any part* of the year will have an impact. For example, if the corporation should lose money or otherwise incur net deductions after the distribution, the distributee may recognize more income on the distribution than expected because the passed-through deductions will decrease the distributee's stock basis. Similarly, corporate income recognized after the distribution may reduce the distributee's gain on the distribution. Note that in each case the postdistribution passed-through deductions or income may but need not change the tax consequences of the distribution to the distributee: It might be the case that the distributee's stock basis can absorb the amount of the distribution with or without taking into account the distributee's share of corporate-level income and deduction.

3. *Distributions by S corporations having subchapter C earnings and profits.* When an existing S corporation having subchapter C earnings and profits makes a distribution to a shareholder with respect to her stock, the distribu-

tion plausibly might be taxed under subchapter C's scheme (dividend income to the extent of earnings and profits, then recovery of basis, then gain) or under subchapter S's scheme (recovery of basis, then gain). If the S corporation has no subchapter C earnings and profits (because it was never a C corporation, it had no earnings and profits when it elected S corporation status, or because it distributed all its earnings and profits in prior years), taxation under subchapter C is not relevant. But if there are positive earnings and profits from a prior C existence, §1368(c) provides a three-tiered analysis. First, distributions that do not exceed the "accumulated adjustments account" are treated as a return of capital to the extent of the taxpayer's stock basis. The calculation of the accumulated adjustments account will be considered in more detail at Note 4 infra. For now it is sufficient to think of the accumulated adjustments account as the net income produced by the S corporation less previous distributions. An S corporation, then, is treated as distributing its post-S election earnings before distributing the earnings and profits it accumulated during its subchapter C existence.

If the distribution exceeds the accumulated adjustments account, it will be treated as a dividend to the extent of the accumulated earnings and profits of the corporation. §1368(c)(2). This treatment corresponds to the treatment of a C corporation under §301(c)(1). Finally, if the distribution exceeds the corporation's accumulated earnings and profits, any excess is treated in the same manner as provided in §301(c)(2) and (3) — first, as a return of capital (reducing stock basis), and then most likely as a capital gain.

Suppose S Corp. had previously been a C corporation and had $15,000 of accumulated earnings and profits at the time of the subchapter S election. A, the sole shareholder, has a stock basis of $8,000. In year 1 S Corp. earns $6,000 of net income, which is reported by A on A's return and which increases the stock basis from $8,000 to $14,000. §§1366, 1367. In year 2 S Corp. earns an additional $2,000 (which is passed through to A and raises the stock basis to $16,000) and makes a $25,000 distribution. The first $8,000 of distribution is deemed to be a return of the post-S election net income (the accumulated adjustments account). §1368(c)(1). The distribution reduces the basis of A's S stock from $16,000 to $8,000. §1367(a)(2)(A). The next $15,000 of distribution is deemed the disgorging of the accumulated earnings and profits and will be treated as a dividend by A under §301. The final $2,000 distributed will be treated as a return of capital, reducing A's basis from $8,000 to $6,000.

If the distributions during the year exceed the accumulated adjustments account, the account is allocated among the distributions pro rata rather than on a first-come, first-served basis. §1368(c).

If an S corporation terminates its election, what happens to the accumulated adjustments account? After all, the accumulated adjustments account consists of net income that has already been taxed to the shareholders. Will the income be subject to another tax when there is a post-S termination distribution? Section 1371(e) provides the corporation with an opportunity to distribute the previously taxed income. Any cash distribution made during the "posttermination transition period" will reduce a shareholder's stock basis to the extent of the accumulated adjustments account. In general the posttermination transition period is one year. Note that the grace period is available only for cash distributions. Property distributions will be taxed in accordance with the usual subchapter C rules. If the accumulated adjustments account is not exhausted by the end of the period, it is lost forever, and subsequent distributions will be taxed in accordance with §301(a) and (c). Shareholders of an S corporation may elect unanimously not to reduce basis during the posttermination transition period even if the accumulated adjustments account is not zero. The effect of such an election is to allow corporations to treat distributions as dividends in an effort to avoid liability under either the accumulated earnings tax or the personal holding company tax. The same election is available to S corporation shareholders with respect to any distributions made by an S corporation during its existence. See §1368(e)(3).

4. *Accumulated adjustments account.* Recall that the accumulated adjustments account is important for corporations that have subchapter C accumulated earnings and profits. The account serves as a means of determining whether distributions consist of already taxed subchapter S income, which will not again be taxed at the shareholder level, or subchapter C earnings and profits, which will produce dividends. §1368(c). On the first day of an S corporation's first taxable year, the accumulated adjustments account is zero. Subsequently, it is adjusted up and down in the same manner as stock basis is adjusted. §1368(e)(1)(A).

The accumulated adjustments account is increased by income items of the corporation, including all separately stated and nonseparately stated items. Tax-exempt income does not increase the account. If S Corp., with accumulated earnings and profits, earns $20,000 of gross operating income in postelection year 1, the account will be $20,000, reflecting the fact that the $20,000 of income will pass through to the shareholders. A distribution of $20,000 is merely a return of income that has already been taxed. What happens if in year 1 S Corp. earns $20,000 of tax-exempt income, which it distributes? The earning of the tax-exempt income does not result in income for the shareholders. §1366(a)(1)(A). What about the distribution? Since tax-exempt income is excluded from the accumulated adjustments account, the $20,000 distribution in year 1 will be taxed as a dividend to the extent of the corporation's earnings and profits. §1368(c)(2).

Just as the accumulated adjustments account increases by items of income, it decreases by all loss and deduction items. In the example above, if S Corp. spent $8,000 in producing the $20,000 of operating income, the accumulated adjustments account would be $12,000, representing the amount on which the shareholder was taxed and which is available for tax-free distribution. If S Corp. incurred $23,000 of deductions, the $3,000 loss for the year would produce a negative accumulated adjustments account. The account would have to be restored to a positive figure before tax-free distributions could be made. §1368(c)(1). In addition to losses and deductions, nondeductible expenses also decrease the account (with the exception of expenses incurred in producing tax-exempt income). For example, suppose X Corp. paid an illegal bribe of $8,000 to help earn the $20,000 of operating income. While §162(c) prevents a deduction for the bribe, the payment reduces the amount available for distribution stemming from S corporation operation. Consequently, the accumulated adjustments account is also reduced from $20,000 to $12,000. Distributions beyond that amount are deemed to come from the accumulated earnings and profits.

Not only corporate expenses but also corporate distributions reduce the accumulated adjustments account to the extent the distributions come from the account or represent a nontaxable return of capital. If S Corp. earns $20,000 of net income in year 1 and distributes $20,000 in year 2, the account is reduced from $20,000 to zero to begin year 3.

The decrease in the accumulated adjustments account as a result of a redemption parallels the decrease in the earnings and profits account for a subchapter C corporation. See §§1368(e)(1)(B) and 312(n)(7) and discussion at pages 219-221 supra.

5.   *Pass-through deductions in excess of basis.* To ensure that corporate deductions reduce shareholder taxes once, and only once, passed-through deductions must reduce shareholder basis. §1367(a)(2)(B). As a consequence, deductions in excess of basis cannot be claimed by the shareholder but must be deferred until there is stock basis to absorb them. See §1366(d). For determining this basis limitation, though, we use the shareholder's *debt basis* as well as his equity basis. Debt basis in this context means the shareholder's basis, if any, in loans he has made to the corporation. That is, debt basis refers to basis enjoyed by the shareholder not in his capacity as shareholder but rather in his capacity as lender. Of course, if the shareholder has made no loans to the corporation, the shareholder's debt basis will be zero.

Each shareholder who is also a creditor of an S corporation has two bases — debt as well as equity — in his corporate investment, and the statute specifies how pass-through income and deductions affects each. Under §1367(b)(2), pass-through losses reduce debt basis only after equity basis is fully exhausted, and subsequent pass-through income will increase debt basis before equity basis until the debt basis has been fully restored.

For example, suppose individual Q forms S Corp. by contributing $10,000 in exchange for 100 shares of S Corp. stock. In addition, suppose Q lends $40,000 to S Corp., and assume the loan is respected for tax purposes (that is, the loan is not recharacterized as equity). If the corporation distributes $15,000 to Q, Q must report $5,000 of income because the amount of the distribution exceeds Q's stock basis by that amount and debt basis cannot absorb distributions, only pass-through deductions. Of course, Q in this example must reduce her stock basis to $0.

Assume S Corp. invests its remaining cash of $35,000 in some productive activity, and assume further that this activity produces a deductible loss of $5,000 in the following year. Although Q's stock basis is zero, this $5,000 may pass through to Q because it can be absorbed by Q's debt basis. That is, Q will report the $5,000 loss on her individual return and will reduce her debt basis to $35,000.

If S Corp. recognizes $10,000 of income the following year, that income will pass through to Q and will increase Q's basis. Because debt basis is restored before equity basis, the first $5,000 of pass-through income increases Q's debt basis from its current value of $35,000 back to its initial value of $40,000. §1367(b)(2)(B). The remaining $5,000 of basis increase is applied to Q's stock basis, increasing its basis from zero to $5,000. Any future pass-through of income will increase Q's stock basis *only*, unless Q's debt basis subsequently is reduced: Debt basis can never be increased under §1367(b)(2)(B) beyond its initial value.

To the extent a shareholder uses some of her debt basis to absorb pass-through deductions, that basis is unavailable to offset sale proceeds from disposition of the note or to offset repayment on the loan. For example, reconsider the situation above, in which Q's stock basis is reduced to zero and Q's debt basis is reduced to $35,000 by reason of a $15,000 corporate distribution and $10,000 of pass-through deduction. If the corporation now repays the $40,000 loan in full, Q must recognize $5,000 of income. To be sure, receipt of loan principal generally is not taxable, but when debt basis has been used to absorb pass-through loss, it is unavailable to offset repayment proceeds. Thus, the ability of an S corporation shareholder to use debt basis to absorb pass-through deduction does not result in a doubling of the shareholder's debt basis but only in a shifting of basis away from the obligation itself.

Suppose S Corp. is formed by A, who contributes $10,000 in exchange for all the S Corp. stock and lends $5,000 to the corporation as well. In year 1, if S Corp. has operating losses of $18,000, only $15,000 will pass through to A. The excess that is disallowed as a deduction will be treated as incurred in the following year if there is sufficient basis to absorb the loss. §1366(d)(2). Otherwise the loss is carried forward again. This represents a significant change from prior law, which provided that unused losses and deductions disappeared for tax purposes.

If the S corporation election is terminated, the unused losses and deductions are carried over into the posttermination transition period — essentially the first year after termination. To the extent that a shareholder's stock basis is insufficient to absorb all the unused losses or deductions, they are irretrievably lost.

6. *Dispositions of shares not in redemption.* The sale or exchange of stock in an S corporation is taxed just like the sale or exchange of stock in a

C corporation. That is, gain or loss is recognized on each share based on the excess of the amount realized over the shareholder's adjusted basis in the stock. See §1001. Disposition of stock in an S corporation, however, is more complex than disposition of stock in a C corporation because (1) the disposition affects the pass-through of corporate-level tax items, (2) the disposition can affect the taxation of distributions made to the selling shareholder, and (3) distributions, as well as pass-through of corporate-level items of income and deduction, affect stock basis so that a shareholder who sells stock of an S corporation cannot determine the amount of gain or loss on the sale until the close of the corporation's taxable year.

Disposition of shares in an S corporation will affect taxation of the corporate-level items because such items are passed through in proportion to relative stock ownership on a day-by-day basis. §1377(a)(1). For example, suppose individual *A* owns 50 of the 100 outstanding shares of *S* Corp., an S corporation using the calendar year as its taxable year. Halfway through the year, *A* sells 25 of those shares to individual *B*. If the corporation has net taxable income for the year of $2,000, *A* must report $750 on his individual return: $500 for six months ownership of 50 percent of *S* Corp. and $250 for six months ownership of 25 percent of S Corp.

Suppose *A* had sold all 50 of his shares in *S* Corp. Now, *A* reports only $500 of *S* Corp.'s income, that being half the income for half the year. Note that because the corporation's income is allocated pro rata to each day of the year, see §1377(a)(1), it does not matter *when* during the year that S Corp. earned the income. Thus, *A* reports the same $500 whether S Corp. earned $1,000 in each half year or if *S* Corp. lost $1,000 in the first six months and then earned $3,000 in the last six months.

A shareholder who sells her entire interest in an S corporation during the middle of the corporation's taxable year might prefer that her share of the corporation's tax items not depend on corporate activities occurring after she terminates her interest in the enterprise. If all shareholders agree, they may elect to treat the corporation's taxable year as ending on the date of sale, with a new taxable year beginning on the following day. §1377(a)(2). If such an election is filed, the selling shareholder will be taxable on her share of corporate activities occurring only on or prior to the day she terminates her interest in the S corporation. Similarly, the purchasing shareholder will be taxable on her share of corporate activities occurring after the sale.

Disposition of some or all of a shareholder's stock in an S corporation also affects the taxation of distributions made to the selling shareholder prior to the sale of the stock. Recall that distributions of cash or property are tax free to the distributee-shareholder to the extent that the amount of the distribution does not exceed the distributee-shareholder's stock basis. §1368(b)(1). Recall also that it is the shareholder's stock basis as of the close of the corporation's taxable year that is used in this comparison;

the shareholder's stock basis is adjusted for pass-through items of income and deduction.

If a shareholder sells some or all of his shares during the taxable year, §1367(a) adjustments to the basis of the transferred shares for pass-through items of income and deduction are effective *immediately prior* to the stock transfer. Treas. Regs. §1.1367-1(d)(1). Because §1367(a) adjustments include the downward basis adjustments for distributions, see §1367(a)(2)(A), this regulation presumably applies to these downward adjustments as well. To understand what this means, assume individual A owns 40 of the 100 outstanding shares of S Corp., an S corporation using the calendar year as its taxable year. As of January 1, A owns these 40 shares with an adjusted basis of $10 per share. On June 31, A sells 15 of his 40 shares to individual C for $15 per share. During the entire calendar year, S Corp. earns $200.

To compute A's gain on the sale of the 15 shares, we must know A's adjusted basis in those shares. We begin with A's adjusted basis of $10 per share as of the beginning of the calendar year. We then increase that adjusted basis for A's share of the corporation's income. Treating June 31 as the midpoint of the year, $100 of the corporation's gain is allocated to the period from January 1 through June 31 and the remaining $100 is allocated to July 1 through December 31. Accordingly, each of the 100 outstanding shares is allocated $1 for the first half of the year, so that A's stock basis as of June 31 is increased to $11 per share. Thus, the sale of 15 shares for $15 per share yields a taxable gain of $4 per share, or $60 total gain. In addition, A must report $65 of pass-through income for the year.

Add to this example the additional fact that A received a distribution of $80 sometime during the first half of the year. Now, we must adjust the basis of the transferred shares not only for the pass-through income allocable to the pretransfer period but also for the distribution. The tax effect of the $80 distribution is to reduce A's stock basis by $80 total, or $2 per share. Accordingly, A's adjusted basis in the shares as of the date of sale is now $9,[2] producing a taxable gain of $6 per share or $90 total. Individual A still reports pass-through income of $65 on his individual return.

7. *Distributions in redemption of shares.* No special rules govern the redemption of shares by an S corporation, so subchapter C's provisions control. As you may recall, noncorporate shareholders of a C corporation generally prefer that a redemption be taxed as an exchange so that the amount distributed will be treated first as a recovery of basis and second as taxable gain. In contrast, corporate shareholders of a C corporation generally prefer that a redemption be taxed as a dividend so that it will qualify for the dividends-received deduction of §243.

---

2. This $9 per share adjusted basis is computed as follows: initial basis of $10 plus pass-through income of $1 less distribution of $2 equals $9.

You might think that shareholders of an S corporation lacking subchapter C earnings and profits would be indifferent to the choice of exchange or dividend treatment of a redemption. After all, exchange treatment yields recovery of basis followed by capital gain, and distribution treatment under §1368(b) seems to produce the same result. Nonetheless, there is a difference between exchange treatment and taxation under §1368(b), and this difference causes taxation under §1368(b) to be slightly more favorable than exchange treatment.

If a redemption is taxed as an exchange, the shareholder will not recognize income except to the extent that the amount of the distribution exceeds the shareholder's adjusted basis in the shares being redeemed. If, though, the redemption is taxed not as an exchange but rather under §1368(b)(1), the distributee recognizes no gain except to the extent that the amount of the distribution exceeds the shareholder's basis in *all* her stock of the corporation. Thus, taxation as a distribution makes more stock basis available than does taxation as an exchange. If the shares have declined in value, however, exchange treatment might be preferred: Loss can be recognized on a redemption taxed as an exchange although no loss is recognized under §1368(b)(1).

Liquidating distributions made by an S corporation are taxed under the same provisions applicable to C corporations, notably §331 to the shareholders and §336 to the corporation.

8. *Family corporations.* To prevent family-owned S corporations from allocating S corporation income to low-bracket family members through non-pro rata distributions, §1366(e) authorizes the IRS to make any necessary adjustments. For example, suppose a high-bracket shareholder performs services for the corporation at no salary in an attempt to divert some of the corporate income to his children, who are shareholders. Or suppose the parent makes a no-interest loan to the corporation. In both situations, reallocation of the corporate pass-through items is appropriate to reflect the value of the services or the capital, respectively.

Can a *shareholder* invoke §1366(e) to allocate a non-pro rata distribution to family members who received less than their proportional distribution? In Johnson v. Commissioner, 720 F.2d 963 (7th Cir. 1983), the taxpayer-parent who received a disproportionately large distribution tried to reallocate to his low-bracket children. Using the powerful legal maxim "the taxpayer, having made his bed must lie in it," the court rejected the taxpayer's affirmative use of the predecessor to §1366(e).

Estate of Leavitt v. Commissioner
875 F.2d 420 (4th Cir. 1989)

MURNAGHAN, Circuit Judge:
The appellants, Anthony D. and Marjorie F. Cuzzocrea and the Estate of Daniel Leavitt, Deceased, et al., appeal the Tax Court's decision holding

them liable for tax deficiencies for the tax years 1979, 1980 and 1981. Finding the appellants' arguments unpersuasive, we affirm the Tax Court.

I

As shareholders of VAFLA Corporation, a subchapter S corporation during the years at issue, the appellants claimed deductions under [§1366] of the Internal Revenue Code of 1954 to reflect the corporation's operating losses during the three years in question. The Commissioner disallowed deductions above the $10,000 bases each appellant had from their original investments.

The appellants contend, however, that the adjusted bases in their stock should be increased to reflect a $300,000 loan which VAFLA obtained from the Bank of Virginia ("Bank") on September 12, 1979, after the appellants, along with five other shareholders ("Shareholders-Guarantors"), had signed guarantee agreements whereby each agreed to be jointly and severally liable for all indebtedness of the corporation to the Bank. At the time of the loan, VAFLA's liability exceeded its assets, it could not meet its cash flow requirements and it had virtually no assets to use as collateral. The appellants assert that the Bank would not have lent the $300,000 without their personal guarantees.

VAFLA's financial statements and tax returns indicated that the bank loan was a loan from the Shareholders-Guarantors. Despite the representation to that effect, VAFLA made all of the loan payments, principal and interest, to the Bank. The appellants made no such payments. In addition, neither VAFLA nor the Shareholders-Guarantors treated the corporate payments on the loan as constructive income taxable to the Shareholders-Guarantors.

The appellants present the question whether the $300,000 bank loan is really, despite its form as a borrowing from the Bank, a capital contribution from the appellants to VAFLA. They contend that if the bank loan is characterized as equity, they are entitled to add a pro rata share of the $300,000 bank loan to their adjusted bases, thereby increasing the size of their operating loss deductions. Implicit in the appellants' characterization of the bank loan as equity in VAFLA is a determination that the Bank lent the $300,000 to the Shareholders-Guarantors who then contributed the funds to the corporation. The appellants' approach fails to realize that the $300,000 transaction, regardless of whether it is equity or debt, would permit them to adjust the bases in their stock if, indeed, the appellants, and not the Bank, had advanced VAFLA the money. The more precise question, which the appellants fail initially to ask, is whether the guaranteed loan from the Bank to VAFLA is an economic outlay of any kind by the Shareholders-Guarantors. To decide this question, we must determine whether the transaction involving the $300,000 was a loan from the Bank to VAFLA or was it instead a loan to the Shareholders-Guarantors who then gave it to VAFLA, as either a loan or a capital contribution.

Finding no economic outlay, we need not address the question, which is extensively addressed in the briefs, of whether the characterization of the $300,000 was debt or equity.

II

To increase the basis in the stock of a subchapter S corporation, there must be an economic outlay on the part of the shareholder. See Brown v. Commissioner, 706 F.2d 755, 756 (6th Cir. 1983), affg. T.C. Memo 1981-608 (1981) ("In similar cases, the courts have consistently required some economic outlay by the guarantor in order to convert a mere loan guarantee into an investment."); Blum v. Commissioner, 59 T.C. 436, 440 (1972) (bank expected repayment of its loan from the corporation and not the taxpayers, i.e., no economic outlay from taxpayers).[8] A guarantee, in and of itself, cannot fulfill that requirement. The guarantee is merely a promise to pay in the future if certain unfortunate events should occur. At the present time, the appellants have experienced no such call as guarantors, have engaged in no economic outlay, and have suffered no cost.

The situation would be different if VAFLA had defaulted on the loan payments and the Shareholders-Guarantors had made actual disbursements on the corporate indebtedness. Those payments would represent corporate indebtedness to the shareholders which would increase their bases for the purpose of deducting net operating losses under §1374(c)(2)(B). *Brown*, 706 F.2d at 757. See also Raynor v. Commissioner, 50 T.C. 762, 770-71 (1968) ("No form of indirect borrowing, be it guaranty, surety, accommodation, comaking or otherwise, gives rise to indebtedness from the corporation to the shareholders until and unless the shareholders pay part or all of the obligation.").

The appellants accuse the Tax Court of not recognizing the critical distinction between [§1366(d)(1)(A)] (adjusted basis in stock) and [§1366(d)(1)(B)] (adjusted basis in indebtedness of corporation to shareholder). They argue that the "loan" is not really a loan, but is a capital contribution (equity). Therefore, they conclude, [§1366(d)(1)(A)] applies and [§1366(d)(1)(B)] is irrelevant. However, the appellants once again fail to distinguish between the initial question of economic outlay and the secondary issue of debt or equity. Only if the first question had an affirmative answer, would the second arise.

The majority opinion of the Tax Court, focusing on the first issue of

---

8. Even the Eleventh Circuit case on which the appellants heavily rely applies this first step. See Selfe v. United States, 778 F.2d 769, 772 (11th Cir. 1985) ("We agree with *Brown* inasmuch as that court reaffirms that economic outlay is required before a stockholder in a Subchapter S corporation may increase her basis.").

economic outlay, determined that a guarantee, in and of itself, is not an event for which basis can be adjusted. It distinguished the situation presented to it from one where the guarantee is triggered and actual payments are made. In the latter scenario, the first question of economic outlay is answered affirmatively (and the second issue is apparent on its face, i.e., the payments represent indebtedness from the corporation to the shareholder as opposed to capital contribution from the shareholder to the corporation). To the contrary is the situation presented here. The Tax Court, far from confusing the issue by discussing irrelevant matters, was comprehensively explaining why the transaction before it could not represent any kind of economic outlay by the appellants.

The Tax Court correctly determined that the appellants' guarantees, unaccompanied by further acts, in and of themselves, have not constituted contributions of cash or other property which might increase the bases of the appellants' stock in the corporation.

The appellants, while they do not disagree with the Tax Court that the guarantees, standing alone, cannot adjust their bases in the stock, nevertheless argue that the "loan" to VAFLA was in its "true sense" a loan to the Shareholders-Guarantors who then theoretically advanced the $300,000 to the corporation as a capital contribution. The Tax Court declined the invitation to treat a loan and its uncalled-on security, the guarantee, as identical and to adopt the appellants' view of the "substance" of the transaction over the "form" of the transaction they took. The Tax Court did not err in doing so.

Generally, taxpayers are liable for the tax consequences of the transaction they actually execute and may not reap the benefit of recasting the transaction into another one substantially different in economic effect that they might have made. They are bound by the "form" of their transaction and may not argue that the "substance" of their transaction triggers different tax consequences. Don E. Williams Co. v. Commissioner, 429 U.S. 569, 579-80 (1977); Commissioner v. National Alfalfa Dehydrating & Milling Co., 417 U.S. 134, 149 (1974).[10] In the situation of guaranteed corporate debt, where the form of the transaction may not be so clear, courts have permitted the taxpayer to argue that the substance of the transaction was

---

10. On the other hand, the Commissioner is not so bound and may recharacterize the nature of the transaction according to its substance while overlooking the form selected by the taxpayer. Higgins v. Smith, 308 U.S. 473, 477 (1940). In doing so, the Commissioner usually applies debt-equity principles to determine the true nature of the transaction. As the *Selfe* court noted:

> This principle is particularly evident where characterization of capital as debt or equity will have different tax consequences. Thus in *Plantation Patterns* the court held that interest payments by a corporation on debentures were constructive stockholder dividends and could not be deducted by the corporation as interest payments. There, the former Fifth Circuit recharacterized debt as equity at the insistence of the Commissioner.

Selfe, 778 F.2d at 773.

in actuality a loan to the shareholder. See *Blum*, 59 T.C. at 440. However, the burden is on the taxpayer and it has been a difficult one to meet. That is especially so where, as here, the transaction is cast in sufficiently ambiguous terms to permit an argument either way depending on which is subsequently advantageous from a tax point of view.

It is important to note that those cases did not involve the question posed here of whether an economic outlay existed because it clearly did. Actual payments were made. The only question was what was the nature of the payments, debt or equity.

In the case before us, the Tax Court found that the "form" and "substance" of the transaction was a loan from the Bank to VAFLA and not to the appellants:

> The Bank of Virginia loaned the money to the corporation and not to petitioners. The proceeds of the loan were to be used in the operation of the corporation's business. Petitioners submitted no evidence that they were free to dispose of the proceeds of the loan as they wished. Nor were the payments on the loan reported as constructive dividends on the corporation's Federal income tax returns or on the petitioners' Federal income tax returns during the years in issue. Accordingly, we find that the transaction was in fact a loan by the bank to the corporation guaranteed by the shareholders.

Whether the $300,000 was lent to the corporation or to the Shareholders/Guarantors is a factual issue which should not be disturbed unless clearly erroneous. Finding no error, we affirm.

It must be borne in mind that we do not merely encounter naive taxpayers caught in a complex trap for the unwary. They sought to claim deductions because the corporation lost money. If, however, VAFLA had been profitable, they would be arguing that the loan was in reality from the Bank to the corporation, and not to them, for that would then lessen their taxes.* Under that description of the transaction, the loan repayments made by VAFLA would not be on the appellants' behalf, and, consequently, would not be taxed as constructive income to them. See Old Colony Trust Co. v. Commissioner, 279 U.S. 716 (1929) (payment by a corporation of a personal expense or debt of a shareholder is considered as the receipt of a taxable benefit). It came down in effect to an ambiguity as to which way the appellants would jump, an effort to play both ends against the middle, until it should be determined whether VAFLA was a profitable or money-losing proposition. At that point, the appellants attempted to treat the transaction as cloaked in the guise having the more beneficial tax consequences for them.

Finally, the appellants complain that the Tax Court erred by failing

---

* Is the court correct in this assertion? — EDS.

to apply debt-equity principles[11] to determine the "form" of the loan. We believe that the Tax Court correctly refused to apply debt-equity principles here, a methodology which is only relevant, if at all,[12] to resolution of the second inquiry — what is the nature of the economic outlay. Of course, the second inquiry cannot be reached unless the first question concerning whether an economic outlay exists is answered affirmatively. Here it is not.

The appellants, in effect, attempt to collapse a two-step analysis into a one-step inquiry which would eliminate the initial determination of economic outlay by first concluding that the proceeds were a capital contribution (equity). Obviously, a capital contribution is an economic outlay so the basis in the stock would be adjusted accordingly. But such an approach simply ignores the factual determination by the Tax Court that the Bank lent the $300,000 to the corporation and not to the Shareholders-Guarantors.

The appellants rely on Blum v. Commissioner, 59 T.C. 436 (1972), and Selfe v. United States, 778 F.2d 769 (11th Cir. 1985), to support their position. However, the appellants have misread those cases. In *Blum,* the Tax Court declined to apply debt-equity principles to determine whether the taxpayer's guarantee of a loan from a bank to a corporation was an indirect capital contribution. The Tax Court held that the taxpayer had failed to carry his burden of proving that the transaction was in "substance" a loan from the bank to the shareholder rather than a loan to the corporation. The *Blum* court found dispositive the fact that "the bank expected repayment of its loan from the corporation and not the petitioner." *Blum,* 59 T.C. at 440.

---

11. . . . The appellants correctly state that the First, Fifth and Ninth Circuits have all applied traditional debt-equity principles in determining whether a shareholder's guarantee of a corporate debt was in substance a capital contribution. See Casco Bank & Trust Co. v. United States, 544 F.2d 528 (1st Cir. 1976), cert. denied, 430 U.S. 907 (1977); Plantation Patterns v. Commissioner, 462 F.2d 712 (5th Cir. 1971), cert. denied, 409 U.S. 1076 (1972); Murphy Logging Co. v. United States, 378 F.2d 222 (9th Cir. 1967). What the appellants fail to point out, however, is that those cases each involved activated guarantees, i.e., actual advances or payments on defaults. Therefore, the issue in those cases was not whether the taxpayer had made an "investment" — an economic outlay — in the corporation. The investment was admitted. The issue in those cases asked what was the nature of the investment — equity or debt. None of those cases involved the disallowance of deductions claimed by a shareholder pursuant to §1374 for his or her share of an electing corporation's operating losses where there had simply been no economic outlay by the shareholder under the guarantee.

12. In a [§1366] subchapter S corporation case, the inquiry whether or not the economic outlay, assuming there is one, is debt or equity appears not to matter since the economic outlay, regardless of its characterization as debt or equity, will increase the adjusted basis. . . . There are no different tax consequences from the point of view of the taxpayer on the narrow issue of what amount of net operating losses may be deducted. Therefore, application of debt-equity principles in a case such as this one appears to be a red herring. However, we do not reach that issue because the Tax Court's factual finding that the appellants have shown no economic outlay on their part is not clearly erroneous.

With regard to *Selfe,* the Tax Court stated:

> the Eleventh Circuit applied a debt-equity analysis and held that a shareholder's guarantee of a loan made to a subchapter S corporation may be treated for tax purposes as an equity investment in the corporation where the lender looks to the shareholder as the primary obligor. We respectfully disagree with the Eleventh Circuit and hold that a shareholder's guarantee of a loan to a subchapter S corporation may not be treated as an equity investment in the corporation absent an economic outlay by the shareholder.

The Tax Court then distinguished *Plantation Patterns,* 462 F.2d 712 (5th Cir. 1972), relied on by *Selfe,* because that case involved a C corporation, reasoning that the application of debt-equity principles to subchapter S corporations would defeat Congress' intent to limit a shareholder's pass-through deduction to the amount he or she has actually invested in the corporation. The Tax Court also distinguished In re Lane, 742 F.2d 1311 (11th Cir. 1984), relied on by the *Selfe* court, on the basis that the shareholder had actually paid the amounts he had guaranteed, i.e., there was an economic outlay. In *Lane,* which involved a subchapter S corporation, the issue was "whether advances made by a shareholder to a corporation constitute debt or equity. . . ." Id. at 1313. If the advances were debt, then Lane could deduct them as bad debts. On the other hand, if the advances were capital, no bad debt deduction would be permitted. Thus, the issue of adjusted basis for purposes of flow-through deductions from net operating losses of the corporation was not at issue. There was no question of whether there had been an economic outlay.

Although *Selfe* does refer to debt-equity principles, the specific issue before it was whether any material facts existed making summary judgment inappropriate. The Eleventh Circuit said:

> At issue here, however, is not whether the taxpayer's contribution was either a loan to or an equity investment in Jane Simon, Inc. The issue is whether the taxpayer's guarantee of the corporate loan was in itself a contribution to the corporation [as opposed to a loan from the bank] sufficient to increase the taxpayer's basis in the corporation.

The *Selfe* court found that there was evidence that the bank primarily looked to the taxpayer and not the corporation for repayment of the loan. Therefore, it remanded for "a determination of whether or not the bank primarily looked to Jane Selfe [taxpayer] for repayment [the first inquiry] and for the court to apply the factors set out in In re Lane and I.R.C. section 385 to determine if the taxpayer's guarantee amounted to either an equity investment in or shareholder loan to Jane Simon, Inc. [the second inquiry]." Id. at 775. The implications are that there is still a two-step analysis and that the debt-equity principles apply only to the determination of the characterization of the economic outlay, once one is found.

Granted, that conclusion is clouded by the next and final statement of the *Selfe* court: "In short, we remand for the district court to apply *Plantation Patterns* and determine if the bank loan to Jane Simon, Inc. was in reality a loan to the taxpayer." Id. To the degree that the *Selfe* court agreed with *Brown* that an economic outlay is required before a shareholder may increase her basis in a subchapter S corporation, *Selfe* does not contradict current law or our resolution of the case before us. Furthermore, to the extent that the *Selfe* court remanded because material facts existed by which the taxpayer could show that the bank actually lent the money to her rather than the corporation, we are still able to agree. It is because of the *Selfe* court's suggestion that debt-equity principles must be applied to resolve the question of whether the bank actually lent the money to the taxpayer/shareholder or the corporation, that we must part company with the Eleventh Circuit for the reasons stated above.

In conclusion, the Tax Court correctly focused on the initial inquiry of whether an economic outlay existed. Finding none, the issue of whether debt-equity principles ought to apply to determine the nature of the economic outlay was not before the Tax Court. The Tax Court is affirmed.

NOTE

1. *Shareholder guarantee of corporate debt.* The *Leavitt* court recognized that the issue before it was a difficult one. A guarantor of corporate debt is liable on the debt in the sense that such a guarantor will be called upon to pay the debt if the corporation is unable to do so. Thus, if the corporation cannot repay the loan, the guarantor will be poorer by the amount of the debt. In this sense, such a guarantor is in the same economic position as a shareholder who makes a loan to the same corporation: If the corporation is unable to pay the debt, the lending shareholder will suffer the loss of repayment without an ability to pass on that loss. The statute explicitly gives debt basis to such a shareholder-lender, and because a shareholder-guarantor is in a virtually identical economic position, the shareholder's claim to debt basis for the guarantee is strong.

There *are*, however, differences between a guarantor and a lender that go unstated by the taxpayer's argument. As we have discussed, a shareholder-lender has basis in the debt, basis that can be shifted by operation of §1366(d) into the shareholder's stock. A shareholder-guarantor, though, has no such basis. Accordingly, there is no basis to shift into equity basis for the guarantor.

Suppose a shareholder-guarantor is given debt basis for the guarantee, and suppose further that this debt basis is then used by the shareholder to absorb passed-through corporate loss under §1366(d). If the corporation then repays the debt (by making full payment to the lender, not to the shareholder-guarantor), it must be the case that the guarantor recognizes income. That is, we are forced to treat extinguishment of the guarantee as income to the extent that the shareholder receives and uses debt basis under §1366(d). While this certainly could be done, we usually do not think of debtor repayment as a taxable event to a guarantor.[3]

As we have seen, there is little economic difference between a shareholder-lender and a shareholder-guarantor. The court in *Leavitt* nonetheless held that a shareholder-guarantor is unable to exploit the debt basis advantage of §1366(d) explicitly made available to shareholder-lenders. The court distinguished lenders from guarantors by observing that lenders make an actual outlay corresponding to their economic risk of loss while guarantors, although bearing the same risk of loss, make no such outlay.

What do you think of the *Leavitt* court's distinction between lenders and guarantors? Suppose an S corporation shareholder borrows funds from an unrelated bank for use in the corporation's business. The bank may insist that the shareholder pledge her stock as partial security for the loan, and the loan proceeds might be payable directly to the corporation. In such circumstances, has there been an "actual outlay" by the shareholder sufficient to satisfy the *Leavitt* court? Has the loan been made to the shareholder or to the corporation, and should the shareholder's tax consequences turn on such hairline distinctions if other alternatives are available?

Tax law rarely turns on physical outlay, although it often turns on economic reality. To be sure, for cash basis taxpayers actual cash flow is crucial in determining the timing of income and deduction. But cash basis accounting is an anomaly, a concession to simplify accounting for individuals and small businesses. Usually, tax consequences are independent of cash flow. For example, a taxpayer's basis in purchased property is "cost" under §1012, and cost includes not only actual outlays but also promises to make outlays in the future; that is, purchase money debt goes into basis. If tax consequences should follow economic reality unless Congress explicitly directs otherwise, how should *Leavitt* have come out?

The Eleventh Circuit in *Selfe* accepted the argument that a loan from a third party to an S corporation should be treated as made to a shareholder-guarantor *if* the third-party lender looks primarily to the shareholder-guarantor for repayment. On this theory, a court should seek to determine whether the loan, nominally made to the corporation, would not have been made but for the guarantee by one or more shareholders. Yet, what if the loan would have been made without the guarantee but not on the same terms? For example, what if the effect of a guarantee is to allow the corporation to borrow at a lower interest rate? So long as the corporation has any assets whatsoever, the lender can look to some extent to the corpo-

---

3. If a guarantor is called upon to make good on her guarantee and she then receives payment from the debt, such payment will be taxable to the extent the guarantor deducted the initial payment. Use of the guarantee to absorb passed-through corporate loss would thus play the same role as did the deduction arising from payments made by the guarantor.

ration for repayment. Presumably a lender who makes a loan to a corporation and then obtains a shareholder guarantee can and will look to both
the corporation and the guarantor for repayment, and it is unrealistic to
focus on one to the exclusion of the other. Note that the Fourth Circuit
in *Leavitt* explicitly disagreed with the *Selfe* analysis. So far, the Fifth and
Sixth Circuits as well as the Tax Court have agreed with the *Leavitt* court
that shareholder guarantees of corporate debt do not give rise to shareholder debt basis for purposes of §1366(d).

So who has the better of the argument? Section 1366(d) allows a
shareholder of an S corporation to deduct pass-through losses to the extent
of the shareholder's equity and debt basis. This provision makes no mention of shareholder guarantees. But, as discussed above,[4] a shareholder
guarantee of corporate third-party debt is in many ways the equivalent of
a direct loan from the shareholder-guarantor. So should the guarantee
contribute to the shareholder's debt basis for purposes of §1366(d)?

The premise of §1366(d) seems to be that a shareholder of an S
corporation should be permitted to deduct her share of pass-through losses
to the extent of the shareholder's investment in the corporation. By explicitly including both equity and debt investment in §1366(d), Congress has
taken the welcome if unusual step of recognizing that equity and debt are
but two bands in a single spectrum. That is, investing in corporate equity
and investing in corporate debt both reflect a shareholder's decision to
seek profit from the corporation's business activity, with the difference
between equity and debt largely being a greater or lesser risk of nonpay-
ment and a greater or lesser possible profit.

From this perspective, a shareholder guarantee of corporate debt is
similar to both equity and debt investments in that the guarantee represents a shareholder decision to place capital at risk in the venture. The
guarantee is unusual in that it offers no opportunity for profit: Unless the
shareholder-guarantor is compensated for the guarantee, the best that
the shareholder-guarantor can hope for is that the guarantee will prove
unnecessary. Of course, such uncompensated guarantees usually are not
made out of disinterested generosity but instead are made to improve the
prospects of the shareholder's equity (and debt, if any) investment in the
corporation.

Economically, then, a shareholder guarantee of an S corporation's
third-party debt is an additional investment of the shareholder in the corporate activity made to maintain or improve the shareholder's existing
investment. Whether an investment is made with the shareholder's own
funds, directly borrowed funds, or implicitly borrowed funds (i.e., by guaranteeing third-party debt) should be substantively irrelevant. By including
both debt and equity investments within its embrace, §1366(d) represents
a triumph of substance over form. The *Leavitt* court, unfortunately, empha-

---

4. See page 715 supra.

sized just the reverse, and so the decision seems wrong. *Leavitt* has been followed in Harris v. United States, 902 F.2d 439 (5th Cir. 1990); Goatcher v. United States, 944 F.2d 747 (10th Cir. 1991); and Uri v. Commissioner, 949 F.2d 371 (10th Cir. 1991).

C.   TREATMENT OF THE S CORPORATION

While it is generally accurate to state that subchapter S eliminates the corporate-level tax, there are some notable exceptions. These exceptions mark a distinction between subchapter S corporations and partnerships for which there is no entity-level tax.

1.   *Excess Net Passive Income*

Excessive passive income can terminate an S corporation election, but only under extreme situations. See discussion at page 696 supra. In less extreme situations, a corporate-level tax can be imposed on excess net passive income. The reason for special provisions dealing with passive income is to discourage the use and benefits of corporate form for passive investment as opposed to productive activity. Note, though, that §1375 applies only to a corporation that has subchapter C earnings and profits. More accurately, then, the focus of the provision is on previously productive C corporations that elect subchapter S to eliminate corporate-level taxes while providing investment income to shareholders.

The trigger for §1375 is "passive investment income." §1375(a)(2), (b)(3), and §1362(d)(3)(D). The term includes gross receipts derived from royalties, rents, dividends, interest (except interest arising from inventory sales), annuities, and gains from the sale or exchange of stock or securities. Litigation abounds over the rent category. Treas. Regs. §1.1362-2(c)(5)(ii)(B) adopts a threshold rule for situations in which the lessor provides services along with the use of property. If the services are significant or costs incurred are substantial, none of the payments constitutes rent; otherwise, the rents are all included in income. For rental property, the supplying of maid services is deemed significant while the furnishing of heat and light, the cleaning of public entrances, and the collection of garbage are not significant. Compare Priv. Ltr. Rul. 8343094 (fees for parking were not rent when corporation's employees directed people to parking spaces, operated food concessions, provided maintenance and security) with Crouch v. United States, 692 F.2d 97 (10th Cir. 1982) (owner of apartment complex received rent even though corporation provided swimming pool, recreation room, laundry room, redecoration of apartments every three years, utility hookups, and custodian for day-to-day repairs).

The tax on passive income is triggered if a corporation with subchapter C accumulated earnings and profits has passive investment income that constitutes more than 25 percent of the S corporation's gross receipts. Under prior law, corporations would avoid the passive income restrictions by churning capital assets (not including stock or securities) to generate gross receipts. To take an extreme example, suppose S Corp., which has a passive income problem, buys an asset for $50,000 and sells it for $50,000 and repeats the process. Each sale generates $50,000 of gross receipts. Now §1362(d)(3)(C) includes only the net income from capital gains transactions.

If the threshold tests are met, the tax is 35 percent of "excess net passive income." "Net passive income" is passive investment income reduced by the deductions directly connected with the production of that income. "Excess net passive income" is that portion of net passive investment income as the excess of passive income over 25 percent of gross receipts bears to the passive investment income for the year.

For example, assume S Corp., with accumulated earnings and profits, has gross receipts for the year totaling $100,000, of which $75,000 is passive investment income. S Corp. incurred $15,000 of expenses in producing the passive income, so it has net passive income of $60,000. Since the $75,000 of passive income exceeds 25 percent of gross receipts — $25,000 — there is a 35 percent tax on the excess net passive income. That excess is determined by multiplying the $60,000 net passive income by a fraction whose numerator is the $50,000 excess of gross passive income over 25 percent of gross receipts and whose denominator is the $75,000 gross passive income for the year. Excess net passive income is $40,000 and 35 percent of that figure leaves a corporate tax of $14,000.

Suppose in the example above that S Corp. had gross receipts of $100,000 but taxable income of $10,000 because of depreciation and other business deductions. To tax S Corp. on $40,000 of excess net passive income when it has only $10,000 of taxable income would be harsh indeed. Section 1375(b)(1)(B) limits the excess net passive income that is taxable to an amount not in excess of the corporation's taxable income.

2. Built-in Gains

Under §1374 a corporate-level tax is imposed on any net gain that was unrealized at the time of conversion to an S corporation and is subsequently recognized within a 10-year recognition period beginning on the date of conversion. §1374(a), (d)(3). The gain under §1374 will be taxed at the maximum corporate rate applicable to the income. Thus, if the gain stems from the sale or exchange of a capital asset held for more than one year, then the alternative rate on capital gain income under §1201 will apply; otherwise, the top rate under §11 will apply. §1374(b). Currently, both the top corporate rate and the alternative rate on capital gains are 35 percent.

If there is a tax computed under §1374, the S corporation shareholders will reduce the pass-through of the recognized built-in gain by the proportionate share of the tax. §1366(f)(2). Furthermore, in determining the amount of the tax, the corporation will be allowed to use unexpired net operating losses, capital loss carryovers, and other tax attributes that arose while it was a C corporation, notwithstanding §1371(b)(1). §1374(b)(2). If gain is recognized under §1374, no adjustment is made to the stock basis of the shareholders. See §1367.

By definition, §1374 does not apply to any corporation that has been an S corporation since its inception. §1374(c)(1). Moreover, it does not apply to a C corporation converted into an S corporation if at the time of the conversion there was no "net unrealized built-in gain." §1374(c)(2). A net unrealized built-in gain exists if at the time of subchapter S election the fair market value of the assets exceeds the aggregate adjusted bases of the assets. §1374(d)(1). Under this definition, a corporation's "net realized built-in gain" is set once the corporation converts to S corporation status and need not be recomputed year by year.

When §1374 applies, it reaches a "net recognized built-in gain," defined as any gain recognized during the 10-year recognition period. §1374(a), (d)(2). If, however, the corporation can establish that the gain arose from an asset that was not held by the corporation when the corporation converted to an S corporation or that the gain arose after the conversion, then those gains will not be subject to §1374. In addition, the built-in gains recognized in any taxable year are reduced by the built-in recognized losses for that year, such losses being defined in §1374(d)(4) to include recognized losses on the disposition of property to the extent of the loss (if any) in the property at the time of conversion. Note that the net recognized built-in gains for any taxable year cannot exceed the corporation's total net unrealized built-in gain as of the time of conversion to S corporation status less all net built-in gains recognized already. §1374(c)(2). In addition, a corporation's net recognized built-in gain cannot exceed the corporation's taxable income for the year (as defined in §1375(b)(1)(B)). §1374(d)(2)(A). Any recognized net built-in gain not taxed because it exceeds the corporation's taxable income for the year is carried forward as recognized built-in gain to the corporation's next taxable year. §1374(d)(2)(B).

From these definitions, built-in losses play two roles in the operation of §1374. First, they implicitly reduce the corporation's net unrealized built-in gain under §1374(d)(1) and thereby limit the total reach of §1374. Second, such losses reduce the impact of §1374 in any year in which they are recognized so long as built-in gains are also recognized in the same year.

Consider the following example. Suppose *X* Corp., an S corporation, held assets with aggregate fair market value of $80,000 and aggregate adjusted basis of $30,000 at the time its S election became effective. Under §1374(d)(1), the corporation's net unrealized built-in gain equals $80,000 less $30,000, or $50,000. Suppose that among the assets is one with a basis of $10,000 and a fair market value of $6,000. If shortly after the S election *X* Corp. sells this asset at a $4,000 loss and another asset with a built-in gain of $13,000, the §1374 tax will be imposed on the $9,000 net figure. But, because the amount of net gain taxed under §1374 is limited to the corporation's taxable income for the year, if the corporation has a loss from operations for the taxable year of $5,000 so that the corporation's taxable income for the year is only $4,000, §1374 will tax only $4,000 of the net recognized built-in gain and the remaining $5,000 will be carried forward to the next year.

3. Distributions of Appreciated Property

Both liquidating and nonliquidating distributions by an S corporation are taxable events for the S corporation and its shareholders in accordance with the provisions governing those transactions by C corporations. §1371(a). Under §453B(h), an S corporation can avoid recognition of gain on certain installment obligations distributed in complete liquidation if the shareholders step into the corporation's shoes with respect to reporting the amount and character of any gain collected on the notes. In general, an S corporation is treated as having sold distributed property to its shareholders, thereby triggering recognition of gain in a nonliquidating distribution or gain or loss in a liquidating distribution. See §311 (nonliquidating distribution), §366 (liquidating distribution). In some cases, the deemed sale can trigger a corporate-level tax under §1374 as well.

4. Corporate Elections

Section 1363(c)(1) mandates that the S corporation make most elections that affect the computation of items received from the corporation. For example, deciding the method of depreciation, whether to take a reduced investment tax credit, and whether to postpone the recognition of discharge of indebtedness income under §108 are all made at the corporate level. The §163(d) limitation on interest deductions for investment indebtedness, however, must be made at the shareholder level. See §1363(c)(2).

5. Computation of Corporate Taxable Income

The computation of taxable income for an S corporation is very similar to computation for a partnership. See §§1363(b) and 702(a)(2). This means that the computation is similar to an individual's computation except that certain deductions, such as personal exemptions and charitable contributions, are not allowed since the shareholders will account for those individually. The corporation must report its income on a calendar year basis unless there is a business reason for adopting a different accounting period. §1378.

D.   RELATIONSHIP OF SUBCHAPTER S TO OTHER PROVISIONS

We have already observed congressional awareness of the potential misuse of subchapter S by subchapter C corporations. Section 1374, for example, imposes a corporate-level tax on certain built-in gains, and §1368(c) governs distributions to corporations with accumulated earnings and profits. In this section, the interplay between subchapters S and C will be explored further, along with other provisions affected by or affecting the operation of subchapter S.

1.   Coordination with Subchapter C

Unless inconsistent with the subchapter S provisions, subchapter C governs the treatment of S corporations. Obviously, taxation of the income earned and distributed by an S corporation is governed by subchapter S. The formation of an S corporation under §351, redemptions, and liquidations are governed by subchapter C. §1371(a)(1). If an S corporation is a shareholder in another corporation, the S corporation-shareholder will be treated as an individual. §1371(a)(2). Among other consequences, there will be no §243 dividends-received deduction, the amount distributed will be the fair market value of any property, and §332 will be unavailable on a liquidation of an S corporation's subsidiary.

   In general, no adjustments will be made to an S corporation's earnings and profits account during its existence as an S corporation. Adjustments will be made, however, for transactions governed by subchapter C, including redemptions or dividends to S corporations with accumulated earnings and profits under §1368(c)(2). §1371(c).

2.   Carryovers between C Year and S Year

Life would be sweet if a C corporation with a net operating loss could make an S election, pass through the losses to the shareholders to the extent of their basis, and then terminate the S election. Section 1371(b) prevents carryovers and carrybacks from years in which a corporation was not an S corporation to any year during which an S election is in effect. The provision does not toll the applicable carryover period, but if the S election is terminated in time, the corporation can use the carryover.

There is reciprocal treatment for carryovers from an S year. Carryovers or carrybacks incurred while an S corporation cannot be used by a C corporation at the corporate level following termination. However, losses and deductions not used by an S corporation prior to termination can be used by the shareholders during the "post-termination transition period" — essentially the year following termination. To the extent a shareholder's basis is insufficient to absorb all the unused losses or deductions, they are irretrievably lost. See §§1366(d)(3), 1377(b).

3. Coordination with Worthless Stock and Bad Debt Provisions

Suppose that a poorly performing S corporation finally is plunged into bankruptcy, rendering the shareholders' stock worthless. Do the shareholders get the worthless stock deduction under §165(g) before accounting for the corporate income and loss items? Section 1367(b)(3) allows the shareholders to account for the corporate items before taking the §165(g) deduction. This ordering permits taxpayers to take ordinary deductions for operating losses rather than the restricted long-term capital losses that result under §165(g). See §1211.

There is a parallel treatment of bad debts. If a shareholder's stock basis has been reduced to zero under §1367 because of the pass-through of operating losses, the shareholder is entitled next to offset the basis of any corporate debt and claim the resulting loss deduction before taking a bad debt deduction under §166(d). See §§1367(b)(3) and 1366(d).

4. Fringe Benefits

With regard to fringe benefits, the subchapter S vehicle has some advantages over a partnership. For shareholder-employees holding 2 percent or less of the outstanding S corporation stock, the following excludible benefits are available to employees, while still qualifying as deductible business expenses for the corporation: $5,000 paid by reason of the employee's death under §101(b); amounts paid to or for certain accident and health plans under §§105 and 106; up to $50,000 of group term life insurance on the employee's life under §79; and meals or lodging furnished for the convenience of the employer in accordance with §119.

Shareholder-employees holding more than a 2 percent stock interest will be treated in the same manner as partner-employees in a partnership. There will be no deduction for the corporation and no exclusion for the shareholder-employees.

5. Attribution Rules

Under §1372(b), the 2 percent threshold discussed above must be computed with reference to the attribution rules. See §318. In a family corporation, it may not be possible to take advantage of corporate fringe benefits.

For purposes of the attribution rules, a subchapter S corporation is treated as a partnership. Attribution to and from the S corporation will be made in proportion to a shareholder's stock interest. For C corporations, attribution is allowed only when a shareholder owns 50 percent or more of the corporate stock. The more expansive application of the attribution rules to S corporations and their shareholders means, for example, that it may be more difficult for an S corporation or its shareholders to meet the safe harbor requirements of §302(b)(2) on a redemption.

6. Loss Limitation Provisions

Consistent with the treatment of partnerships, the passive loss limitations under §469 apply at the shareholder level. See discussion at page 86 supra. The same principles apply to the at-risk rules under §465(a)(1).

7. Coordination with Administrative Provisions

All administrative and judicial proceedings for the assessment and collection of tax deficiencies or for refunds related to an S corporation must be conducted at the corporate level in a unified proceeding rather than at the shareholder level. §§6241-6245. Shareholders of an S corporation must file their returns in a manner consistent with the corporate return, unless the Service is notified of any inconsistency.

8. Is an S Corporation a Partnership?

Despite the use of the term "small business corporation" in subchapter S, the size of the corporation's income, assets, net worth, or other financial characteristics plays no part in determining its eligibility under subchapter S; the only restriction of this type is that it may not have more than the permitted number of shareholders. More important than labels, however, is the fact that an electing corporation remains a corporation — not only as a matter of state law but also for many federal income tax purposes. This point cannot be overemphasized because it is often erroneously said that subchapter S permits corporations to be treated as partnerships. In fact, there are many differences between a partnership and an electing small business corporation. Even when the election is in effect, corporate redemptions, liquidations, reorganizations, and many other transactions are governed by the tax law applicable to corporations rather than by the law of partnerships; if the election is terminated, the corporate income tax will once again become fully applicable. Recognizing these facts, some commentators have sought to sum up such corporation with a label — "pseudo-corporation," "conduit-corporation," and "hybrid corporation," to say nothing of more barbarous coinages like "corpnership" and "pseudo-type corporation." The more neutral terms "electing corporation" or "S corporation" or "tax-option corporation" seem preferable because they serve as a constant reminder that the corporation does not cease to be a corporation by electing to come under subchapter S. See Eustice, Subchapter S Corporations and Partnerships: A Search for the Pass Through Paradigm (Some Preliminary Proposals), 39 Tax L. Rev. 345 (1984).

E.   PROBLEMS

1.   On January 1, 1995, 35 individuals form a corporation to engage in a manufacturing business. Respond to the following:
   a.   Should they elect subchapter S?
   b.   How do they make the election?
   c.   Can the shareholders elect a corporate fiscal year ending on January 31? Why might they want to?
   d.   Do you recommend any shareholder restrictions if an election is made?
2.   Determine whether a corporation has more than one class of stock outstanding in the following situations.
   a.   The corporation issues two classes of stock identical in every way except that one class carries 10 votes per share while the other carries one vote per share.
   b.   All shareholder-employees are required to sell their shares back to the corporation upon termination of employment at $10 per share.
   c.   All married couples who purchase stock must provide with purchase a buy-sell agreement (upon any terms they desire) automatically effective on divorce or separation. Why might the other shareholders want to be certain that all of a married couple's shares end up with one or the other on divorce or separation?
   d.   Any employee fired with or without cause must sell his shares back to the corporation at cost.
   e.   Holders of the corporation's long-term debt are entitled to exchange that debt for nonvoting preferred stock if the corporation misses two consecutive interest payments.

f.   A nonresident alien employee is given a bonus in the form of 10 shares of "phantom stock" whereby the employee is paid additional compensation each time a dividend is declared by the corporation on its stock; the shareholder will receive upon termination of employment a lump-sum payment equal to the increase (if any) in 10 shares of the corporation's outstanding stock between the time the phantom stock was issued and the time of termination of the employee's employment.

g.   One of the 35 shareholders is a trust formed by *T*. Under the terms of the trust instrument, the income in the discretion of an independent trustee is distributable to *D*, *T*'s daughter. At the end of nine years, the corpus and any accumulated income are distributed to *H*, *T*'s spouse.

3.   *X* Corp. has been an S corporation since it was formed in 1995. As of January 1, 1998, the 100 outstanding shares of *X* Corp. have been owned 10 shares each by 10 different individuals. On March 15, 1998, one of these 10 individuals sells her stock to a nonresident alien. As of March 14, 1998, the corporation has earned $50,000 in income and had $20,000 in deductions. As of December 31, 1998, the corporation has $200,000 of income and $60,000 of deductions for the year. How do the parties account for income and deductions? Assume there have been no dispositions of stock in *X* Corp. other than the transfer of 10 shares to the nonresident alien.

4.   Individuals *B*, *C*, and *D* form *X* Corp., an S corporation. *B* contributes real estate with adjusted basis of $600 and fair market value of $1,000 in exchange for 100 shares of *X* Corp. stock. *C* contributes inventory with an adjusted basis of $2,000 and fair market value of $1,000 in exchange for 100 shares of *X* Corp. *D* contributes cash of $100 and services worth $900 in exchange for 100 shares of *X* Corp. What are the tax consequences of the formation to *B*, *C*, *D*, and *X* Corp., and what are the tax consequences to all the parties if the real estate and inventory are sold by the corporation during its first taxable year?

5.   In Problem 4, what is the result if the corporation, in addition to selling its assets, makes a distribution of $20 per share halfway into its first taxable year? How does your answer change if shareholder *B* sells 35 of her shares to shareholder *C* and 35 of her shares to shareholder *D* one-quarter of the way into the year? How does it change if the sale from *B* to *C* and *D* took place three-quarters into the year? Assume in each case that the sale price is $11 per share.

6.   *Y* Corp. has always been an S corporation. As of January 1, 1994, individual *J* owns all 100 outstanding shares of *Y* Corp., half with an adjusted basis of $2 per share and half with an adjusted basis of $18 per share. On March 1, 1994, *Y* Corp. distributes Blackacre to *J*. At the time of the distribution, *Y* Corp. has an adjusted basis in Blackacre of $5,000 and Blackacre is worth $17,000. What are the tax consequences of this distribution, assuming:

a.   *Y* Corp. has taxable income of $3,000 for the year?

b.   *Y* Corp. has a net loss of $2,000 for the year?

c.   *Y* Corp. has taxable income of $3,000 for the year, and *Y* Corp. redeems the 50 high-basis shares owned by *J* for $15 per share on July 1, 1994?

d.   How does your answer to (a) change if the corporation had an adjusted basis in Blackacre of $20,000?

7.   Individual *K* forms *Z* Corp., an S corporation, by contributing cash of $10,000 in exchange for 100 shares of *Z* Corp. stock. In addition, *K* contributes $10,000 in exchange for a long-term bond paying an appropriate rate of interest. During its first taxable year, *Z* Corp. borrows $75,000 from the bank. For the entire year, *Z* Corp. recognizes a taxable loss $12,000. Also during that year, *Z* Corp. distributes $20,000 to *K* with respect to his stock. What are the tax consequences of the distribution to *K*? How would your answer change if *K* had guaranteed repayment of the loan from the bank? Could *K* improve his tax position without substantially altering his economic position? Could *K* improve his tax position by contributing his note to the corporation?

8.   Will the tax benefit rule allow a shareholder of an S corporation avoid equity basis reduction under §1367(a)(2)(B)-(D) as well as debt basis reduction under §1367(b)(2) if the shareholder has no taxable income against which the pass-through of corporate-level deductions can apply?

9.   *X* Corp., a C corporation using the calendar year as its taxable year, elects S corporation status effective January 1, 1997. As of that day, the corporation has earnings and profits of $8,000. During 1997, the corporation recognizes net taxable income of $6,000 and net tax-exempt income of $4,000. Also during that year, the corporation distributes $10,000 to each of its two shareholders at the rate of $2,500 per calendar quarter per shareholder (distributed February 14, May 15, August 15, and November 15). As of January 1, 1997, shareholder *B* owns 50 shares with an adjusted basis of $20 per share, and shareholder *C* owns 50 shares with an adjusted basis of $100 per share. What are the tax consequences of these distributions to each shareholder?

10.   *Y* Corp., a C corporation using the calendar year as its taxable year, owns four capital assets with adjusted bases and fair market values as of January 1, 1997, as follows:

Asset	Adjusted Basis	Fair Market Value
Asset 1	$5,000	$8,000
Asset 2	5,000	3,000
Asset 3	5,000	7,000
Asset 4	5,000	9,000

Y Corp. elects S corporation status effective January 1, 1997. During 1997, *Y* Corp. sells assets 1 and 2 for $6,000 and $3,000, respectively. During 1998, *Y* Corp. sells asset 3 for $2,000. During 1999, *Y* Corp. sells asset 4 for $20,000. Compute the corporation's tax under §1374 for 1997-1999. How would your answer change if the adjusted basis of asset 2 as of January 1, 1997, had been $9,000?

    11.   *M* Corp. is an S corporation having $100 in C corporation earnings and profits. In 1995, *M* Corp. has taxable gross receipts of $100,000, of which $50,000 is royalty income. The corporation also has deductions of $10,000 for the year, all of which are allocable to the royalty income. Compute *M* Corp.'s tax liability under §1375 as well as its taxable income for the year. How might the shareholders of *M* Corp. avoid §1375?

Table of Cases

729

Table of Revenue Rulings and Procedures and Other Miscellaneous IRS Pronouncements

Index